Marilyn Wood's
WONDERFUL
WEEKENDS

by Marilyn Wood

A FROMMER BOOK
Published by Prentice Hall Press
New York

Copyright © 1984, 1987
by Marilyn Wood

All rights reserved
including the right of reproduction
in whole or in part in any form

Published by Prentice Hall Press
A Division of Simon & Schuster, Inc.
Gulf + Western Building
One Gulf + Western Plaza
New York, New York 10023

Library of Congress Cataloging in Publication Data

Wood, Marilyn, 1948-
Marilyn Wood's Wonderful weekends.

"A Frommer book."
Includes index.
1. Middle Atlantic States—Description and travel—
Guide-books. 2. New England—Description and travel—
1981-   —Guide-books. 3. New York Region—
Description and travel—Guide-books. I. Title. II.
Title: Wonderful weekends.
F106.W795 1987   917.4'0443   87-6991
ISBN 0-671-62864-X

Manufactured in the United States of America

Contents

Each chapter below contains descriptions of the following: Getting There • Special Events & Festivals • Attractions • Inns • Hotels • Bed-and-Breakfast Places • Breakfast/Brunch Places • Saturday Luncheon Choices • Romantic Dining • Evening Entertainment • Activities

The Activities sections include the following, wherever applicable: Antiquing • Beaches • Bicycling • Birdwatching • Boating • Camping • Canoeing • Fishing • Fruit Picking • Golf • Hiking • Horseback Riding • Ice Skating • Picnicking • Shopping • Skiing • State Parks • Swimming • Tennis • Tubing • Windsurfing

---

MASSACHUSETTS

NEW JERSEY

MAPS

Acknowledgments

I could not have completed this second edition without the help of many dedicated people who work long and hard for the various state and local tourist organizations and who gave me so much help and always added to the pleasure of an already-delightful assignment. Among them were: in Connecticut, Barnett Laschever, Chuck Norwood, Cyndi Miller, Constance Carlson, Suzanne Besser, Laura M. Bradley, Janet Serra, Margaret Gagnon, Dave Iavonne, Elaine Noh, Bettie Perreault, Jane Snaider, and Vivian Stanley; in Delaware, Daniel Bockover and Cheryl Snuffer; in Massachusetts, Bill Wilson and Sue Carrion; in New Hampshire, Jay Dinkle; in New York, Steve Apesos, Marylou Bartolotta, Sheryl Woods, Michele Vennard, and Betsy Boyd; in Pennsylvania, Maria di Battista, Melissa Rosenberry, Cheryl Slavinsky, and Joan Toner; in Philadelphia, Samuel B. Rogers and Andi Coyle; in Rhode Island, David C. Petrillo; in Vermont, Polly Rollins, Mike Williams, Arne Hammerlund, and Louise Hughes. A big thank you to you all!

I'd also like to thank Frank Schwartz, Steve Murphy, and Paul Pasmantier for making this second edition possible, along with the editorial staff at Prentice Hall Press—Travel. And finally, heartfelt thanks to Gloria McDarrah for her blue penciling, Fred Bidgood for his suggestions and, as always, meticulous copyediting; to Amy Herzberg and Kathleen Driscoll for their swift typing; and to Marge Steuer for her support, encouragement, and incredible patience.

Eight Important Topics

PRICES AND HOURS: Although the author made every effort to obtain correct and current prices and hours for various establishments and attractions, these can change swiftly and dramatically. Changes in ownership, changes in policy, and inflation can all affect this information. For future prices, add about 10% to 15% to the given rates per year.

RESERVATIONS: These are a must on weekends. For accommodations they should be made well in advance, in some cases as much as three months ahead of time and in exceptional circumstances as much as a year in advance (at Saratoga, for example, during the racing meet). Dinner reservations, especially for Friday and Saturday night, should also be made ahead of time.

MINIMUM STAYS: Most places demand minimum stays on weekends and often during their high season. This information has not always been included, so always check ahead.

WEEKEND PACKAGES: As promotions, these are created and discontinued constantly. If the particular package mentioned doesn't exist, don't be surprised —the management will most likely be offering another very similar promotional package.

DEPOSITS: These are often nonrefundable since they are the innkeeper's only defense against those folks who don't show up, especially when the weather is inclement. Always clarify this when you book.

TAXES: These have not been included in the quoted rates. Percentages vary from state to state.

A NOTE ON THE DINING LISTINGS: Since this book is designed for people who are taking weekend breaks, where possible the restaurants are listed under headings that reflect this fact. That is, "Dinner Only" means that the restaurants listed under this heading are not open for lunch on Saturday or Sunday. It does not mean that they don't serve lunch at all—they may well do so on weekdays but they are not open for lunch to weekenders.

DROP A LINE: Have you discovered a delightful inn, a great B & B, a fantastic restaurant, or a unique attraction that you feel should be featured in this book? Or have you been dissatisfied with any particular establishment mentioned in these pages? Or do you have any suggestions for the book in general? Then please do drop me a line and I'll respond to and follow up on your comments. Just write to Marilyn Wood, Prentice Hall Press, Gulf + Western Building, 15th floor, One Gulf + Western Plaza, New York, NY 10023.

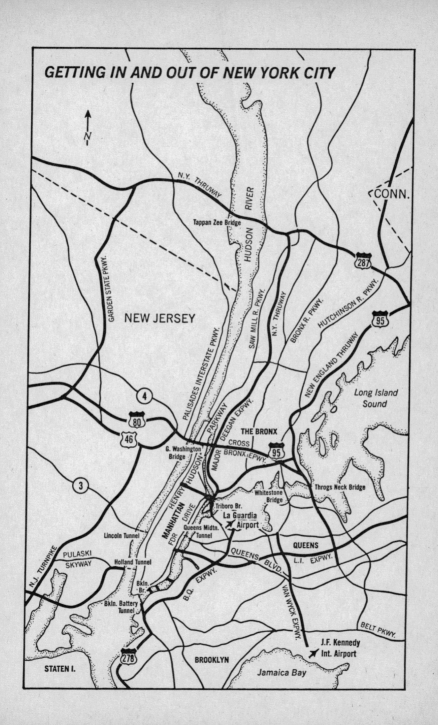

GETTING IN AND OUT OF NEW YORK CITY

N

CONN.

N.Y. THRUWAY

HUDSON RIVER

Tappan Zee Bridge

287

GARDEN STATE PKWY.

NEW JERSEY

PALISADES INTERSTATE PKWY.

SAW MILL R. PKWY.

N.Y. THRUWAY

BRONX R. PKWY.

HUTCHINSON R. PKWY.

NEW ENGLAND THRUWAY

95

Long Island Sound

4

80

46

PARKWAY

MAJOR DEEGAN EXPWY.

THE BRONX

CROSS

G. Washington Bridge

BRONX EXPWY.

95

3

HENRY HUDSON

Whitestone Bridge

Throgs Neck Bridge

Triboro Br.

La Guardia Airport

MANHATTAN

FDR DRIVE

Lincoln Tunnel

Queens Midtn. Tunnel

QUEENS

N.J. TURNPIKE

PULASKI SKYWAY

Holland Tunnel

QUEENS BLVD.

L.I. EXPWY.

Bkln. Br.

B.Q. EXPWY.

VAN WYCK EXPWY.

Bkln. Battery Tunnel

BELT PKWY.

278

J.F. Kennedy Int. Airport

STATEN I.

BROOKLYN

Jamaica Bay

INTRODUCTION

By Thursday most of us harried city or suburban dwellers are looking forward to the weekend, eagerly anticipating a break from our busy work routine and the chance to get away from the tarmac, to relax, calm our jangled nerves, and rediscover who we really are. And that is what this book is all about: two- or three-day breaks among the lakes, or the mountains, or the forests, or down along the shore, or even in another exciting but refreshingly new metropolis—and all within two to four hours' driving time of the city of New York.

So often we forget that the city is surrounded by many alluring, yet serene hideaways and head off either for far-flung destinations or else to a summer house to which we retreat every weekend for three or four months or more, rain or shine, to meet the same faces and the same vistas. Why not take a risk and explore what's around you in your own backyard, meet new faces and new friends, and explore new places every weekend? In short, why not come weekending?

There are country markets and fairs, horse shows, music, theater, apple and oyster festivals, flower shows, antique car markets, horse races, and a myriad of other festive celebrations and events to attend. There are all kinds of unique museums and art galleries to visit; historic homes filled with the drama and personalities of those that have lived there; whole villages that seem to exist as tranquilly today as they did 200 years ago; fascinating communities of Shakers, mystics, and Amish to discover; artists' and writers' studios to view; ostentatious and lavish mansions by the sea where outrageous events were staged; fantastic buildings created by personalities like Frederic E. Church and Henry Chapman Mercer; and whole areas of countryside, shore, and mountain to explore by gliding, hiking, camping, fishing, skiing, sailing, swimming, or doing whatever you relish and enjoy. Or you can simply opt for a rocking chair, a cocktail, and a broad veranda overlooking a verdant garden or vista.

And while you're enjoying all this, you can stay in 17th-century riverside inns; old sea captains' homes; luxurious hotels that once welcomed Paganini; Italianate, Greek Revival, and castle-like mansions that once belonged to robber barons; bracketed and gingerbread Victorian fantasies with turrets and lacy trimmings; farms where you'll be wakened by the crowing of the cockerel; old mills; and even a caboose surrounded by quiet fields. Your choices are endless, and so, too, are the delights of the table—juicy, sweet lobsters from New England's waters, continental cuisine served in elegant hotel dining rooms or old-world taverns, pizza with clam sauce in New Haven or cheesesteaks in Philadelphia, hearty farm meals, and picnics savored at music festivals or by the ocean.

To arrange your weekend though, in a way that suits your particular needs and quirks of personality, requires a certain amount of planning. When you only have two days, you need to know where you want to stay, and you can't waste precious moments in trekking to a well-regarded restaurant at Saturday noon only to find that it's closed or in circling around looking for a perfect picnicking spot.

This guide has been researched and written to forestall such problems and to deliver you, the weekender, from any such headaches, leaving you free to concentrate on roaming and fully enjoying your weekend your way. It is designed to help you step-by-step in the planning process. Each destination opens with a section that includes details about getting there by car or public transportation, estimated driving times, and a list of any ultra-special seasonal events that you may want to plan your weekend around (or plan to avoid, depending on your attitude toward crowds). Getting out of the city on a Friday afternoon or evening can be a real hassle and you may well want to choose public transportation over driving. If you do decide to rent a car, book well in advance. Unfortunately, detailed road maps are really beyond the scope of this book, but can be had from the Automobile Association of America, if you're a member (tel. 734-9232).

After these opening sections, there follows a brief general introduction to the history and highlights of the place, and then a detailed description of what your weekend is really all about: what to see, what to do, and what to explore. Inevitably, it's a very personal choice. For example, when it comes to museums, you may feel like Louis Kahn, who commented (although he designed several), "I get tired immediately upon entering a museum," or conversely like Thomas Hoving, who described a museum as a "place for people to battle against the blows of technology and the misery of life." You may regard the ocean in the words of Wallace Stevens as "dirty, wobbly, and wet," or you may relish sailing on it as much as Sir Francis Chichester obviously did. You may relegate sports and those that practice them to the "Toy Department," or you may very much enjoy the challenge of rigorous exercise. Therefore I have described the many choices available to you and offered some guidance about how to organize your two or three days and what I consider the real highlights of each destination. You, of course, will pursue your own interests, whether they're architecture, historic houses, antiques, graveyards, gardens, art galleries, museums, theater, birdwatching, or more active pursuits from windsurfing to skiing, swimming, golf, horseback riding, and so on. These last I have covered in an activities section at the end of each chapter (except in certain cases where it made more sense to place them at the end of each section in the chapter). In this section I have located public sports facilities wherever possible, but make no claims to their quality and standards of service.

The problem of accommodations is tackled next, and while we're on the subject I cannot urge you strongly enough to make reservations, in peak summer and fall seasons as much as five or six months in advance, *especially on weekends.* I have selected what I consider especially appealing accommodations—an Italian palazzo, a working Mennonite farm, a converted grist mill—including a great number of inns and bed-and-breakfast places wherever they exist, grand and sometimes funky downtown hotels which often offer very alluring weekend packages, and on rare occasions, your typical motel chain for those who desire that kind of accommodation or where there simply is no other alternative. In each case, I have endeavored to convey the atmosphere and type of lodging and treatment that a visitor can expect to receive. Rates are included, but I urge you always to check before you leave, because undoubtedly prices will have changed by the time this book reaches your hands. And do keep in mind that many inns have two- or sometimes three-night minimums on weekends and also that weekend packages are offered on a space-available basis. Although this does not pretend to be a camper's guide, I have included some camping ideas, usually state parks and other wilderness areas. Commercial campgrounds and trailer parks are not listed here.

Next, the problem of meals. I know an Englishwoman who built a very successful restaurant around the honest, nutritious breakfast that she served, and which is so difficult to find unless you know where to go—freshly squeezed juices, farm eggs, fine Canadian bacon and good spicy sausage, homemade breads and muffins. Unless your hotel provides breakfast, you, too, will have to search for a breakfast or brunch spot, unless you're willing to settle for the easily found Howard Johnson's, McDonald's, or Denny's. Wherever I can, I've tried to help you out, although it has not always been easy and in some cases I've given up. Similarly, Saturday lunch can prove very elusive—many restaurants close for lunch on Saturday—and so I have tried to find the best of those that are available. Often though, on a balmy Saturday you'll want to take a picnic somewhere overlooking the ocean or a river. Sadly, I have discovered that unlike in France or England, where you can pull into a field and stretch out among the poppies with a fine bottle of wine, some garlic sausage, and a baguette, it's a little harder and more formal in the United States. So I've tried to direct you to state parks and other idyllic settings for your leisurely meal *en plein air* and also, wherever possible, to the suppliers of your picnic fare.

For dinner I have described a selection of restaurants serving a diversity of cuisines for you to choose from. In each destination I have also included unique local favorites, like Louis' Lunch, Sally's, or Pepes in New Haven, Groff's farm in Mount Joy, famous hoagie or cheesesteak places in Philadelphia and Atlantic City, a beloved lobster-in-the-rough establishment on the Connecticut shoreline. In all cases I have relied on a mixture of my own judgment and experience as well as local recommendations. Hours and prices are all included to help your planning.

And finally, although many of the country destinations that appear in this book lack any rousing nightlife (which is precisely why you've chosen to go there), I have tried to include some nightlife options, if only a quiet, cozy convivial bar.

So let's weekend. T. H. White wrote, "The Victorians had not been anxious to go away for the weekend. The Edwardians, on the contrary, were nomadic." Let's be positively nomadic. And one final thing—if you feel like it, you can always rewrap this volume in a brown paper cover and rename it "Midweek Breaks" if your working routine affords you such blissful luxury.

Either way, happy traveling!

CONNECTICUT

HARTFORD

DISTANCE IN MILES: 113
ESTIMATED DRIVING TIME: 2½ hours

DRIVING: FDR Drive to the New England Thruway (I-95), to I-91.
BUS: Trailways (tel. 212/730-7460) goes to Hartford. So do Greyhound (tel. 212/635-0800, or toll free 800/528-6055) and Bonanza (tel. 212/564-8484 for schedules, 635-0800 for tickets).
TRAIN: Amtrak services Hartford. You *may* have to change in New Haven. For information, call 212/736-6288.

Special Events to Plan Your Trip Around
JUNE: Rose Festival
JULY: River Festival—music, boat races, fireworks (July 4).
SEPTEMBER/OCTOBER: Berlin Fair (about ten miles south of Wethersfield) has all kinds of arts, crafts, bakery, needlework, photo, livestock and other exhibits along with such country events as horse and oxen draws, frog jumps, naildriving contests and corn husking bees (usually last weekend in September).

 For info on fairs write to the Connecticut Department of Economic Development, 210 Washington Street, Hartford, CT 06106 and request the pamphlet compiled by the Association of Connecticut Fairs.

 Chrysanthemum Festival, Bristol (last week of September and first in October).

OCTOBER: Apple Harvest in Southington, about 14 miles from Hartford

—parade, arts, crafts, and apple-related fare (early October). Contact Southington Chamber of Commerce (tel. 628-8036).

DECEMBER: Festival of Lights when Constitution Plaza is ablaze with 250,000 Christmas lights (from the day after Thanksgiving to New Year's Day).

For further information about these events and Connecticut in general, call or write Travel Office, Department of Economic Development, 210 Washington Street, Hartford, CT 06106 (tel. 203/566-3385; toll free from Maine through Virginia 800/243-1685, or in Connecticut 800/842-7492).

For specific information about Hartford, contact the Greater Hartford Convention & Visitors Bureau, One Civic Center Plaza, Hartford, CT 06103 (tel. 203/728-6789). About Farmington, Farmington Valley/West Hartford Visitors Bureau, Box 1550, Old Avon Village, 41 E. Main St. (Rte. 44) Avon, CT 06001 (tel. 203/674-1035).

The New England Vacation Center, 630 Fifth Avenue, Concourse Shop 2, New York, NY 10020 (tel. 212/307-5780) also provides information.

State capital and world-famous insurance center, Hartford may not be your idea of a dream weekend destination, but you may well be pleasantly surprised, for the city and its environs do offer a lot to the visitor.

For me the most thrilling experience is a visit to Mark Twain's bulky, convoluted mansion and the smaller, simpler-looking home of Harriet Beecher Stowe that stands only a hundred yards away from Twain's. They were two of the many notable residents of Nook Farm, a brilliant intellectual community that thrived here in the mid- to late-1800s. Just around the corner in West Hartford, you can also visit the home of the indefatigable compiler of the American Dictionary, Noah Webster. Downtown Hartford possesses the first public art museum established in the United States, the very fine Wadsworth Atheneum, and some first-rate architecture, including buildings by Henry Hobson Richardson, and, of course, Charles Bulfinch's first commission, the Old State House, where the Hartford Convention met in 1814–1815 to discuss the possible secession of New England from the Union. You can also seek out the plaque that commemorates the Hartford Charter Oak, in which the Connecticut charter was safely hidden from Sir Edmund Andros, James II's governor-general of New England who had demanded its surrender. At the center of the city there's also a 41-acre park, complete with a nostalgic, working carousel, which is the site of many fun events.

And right outside Hartford there are several side trips. At the Hill-Stead Museum in the lovely village of Farmington, you can view a collection of Manet and other impressionist artists, hanging in an antique-furnished home. From here it's only 15 minutes to historic Simsbury. Only a ten-minute drive south of the city lies the historic village of Wethersfield, or else you can visit the old prison in East Granby and nearby New England Air Museum for a look at aviation history. In short, plenty to keep you amused during a two-day weekend.

A Suggested Itinerary

Spend Saturday exploring downtown Hartford—the Old State House, Travelers Tower, Wadsworth Atheneum, Bushnell Park, and the Museum of Connecticut History (which, by the way, closes at 1 P.M. on Saturday and remains closed for the rest of the weekend). If there are only one or two spots you want to visit, you might just take the morning and then head out to Nook Farm to visit Mark Twain's and Harriet Beecher Stowe's houses, and if you have time, Noah Webster's home. Or you can choose to devote Sunday to these attractions. Sunday can also be spent exploring the environs—the Hill-Stead Museum, Wethersfield (although it's much better to go Saturday), the old prison at Granby, or historic Simsbury.

Getting Around

If you don't have a car, you can ride **Connecticut Transit** for a basic fare of 75¢. For information, call 203/525-9181.

HARTFORD ATTRACTIONS

The Convention and Visitors Bureau has developed a walking tour, and you can pick up the brochure at the Visitors Information Center in the Old State House. HOURS: Daily, Monday to Saturday from 10 A.M. to 5 P.M. and on Sunday from noon to 5 P.M. Highlights en route include:

The Old State House

Charles Bulfinch's first commission, at 800 Main St. (tel. 203/522-6766), in the center of Hartford is beautiful in its simplicity and rich in the historical events that it has witnessed: the Hartford Convention to discuss the possibility of New England's secession from the Union; an 1868 visit by Charles Dickens, who complimented the conduct of the court; and in 1839 the dramatic first trial of the *Amistad* prisoners, slaves who had mutinied and seized the vessel on which they were being transported from the Spanish West Indies. It also served as the state capitol from 1796 to 1878. Today it functions as an arts and cultural center, but you can still tour the graceful symmetrical rooms that served variously as the court, senate, and house chambers and also view Gilbert Stuart's only full-length portrait of General Washington. Check out the fine crafts shop downstairs. HOURS: Monday to Saturday from 10 A.M. to 5 P.M., on Sunday from noon to 5 P.M.
    Walking south along Prospect Street you'll come to:

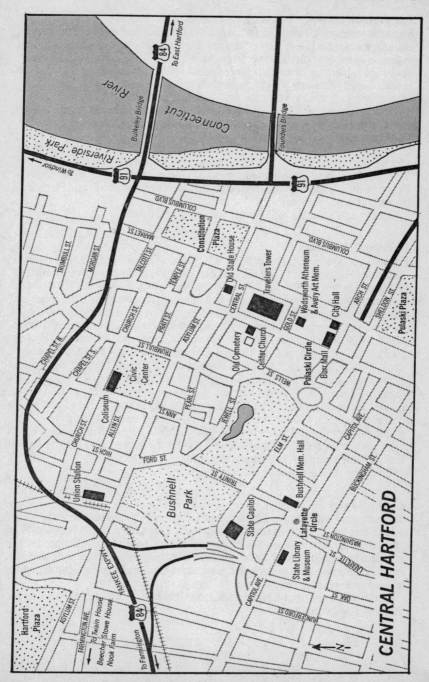

CENTRAL HARTFORD

The Traveler's Tower

From the tower at 700 Main St. (tel. 203/277-2431), 527 feet above the street, you can enjoy a real bird's-eye view of the city. Strangely enough, a peregrine falcon makes its home here on the tower from November to March each year. This particular bird, member of an endangered species, first showed up in 1982 and has returned each year since. Folks who work in the building call him Phineas. Elevator and stairs are used to reach the top. You must call for an appointment.

This is also the home office of the Travelers Insurance Companies, whose first customer had his life insured for $5,000 for a trip from the post office to his home. Total premium: 2¢. The tower occupies the site of the old Sanford Tavern, where Sir Edmund Andros demanded the charter and from which the charter was taken and squirreled away in an oak tree. The original oak succumbed to a storm in 1856, but its grandchild supposedly stands on the grounds of the Center Church. From the top of the tower you can look down upon Constitution Plaza, Hartford's triumph of urban renewal.

Continue south along Main Street and you'll come to:

Wadsworth Atheneum

Located at 600 Main St. (tel. 203/247-9111), across the street from Carl André's very controversial *Stone Field* (36 boulders, seemingly thrown down haphazardly, commissioned in 1975 for $87,000), the Wadsworth is a delight. It's a perfect size for the museum-goer, housed in five buildings around a sculpture court and filled with a very fine selection of art—Monets, Renoirs, a couple of Boudins, a group of interesting American primitives, including a quite lovely polychromed-wood statue of a child with lamb by Asa Ames, a roomful of large 19th-century Hudson River landscapes by Thomas Cole and Frederic Church, plus several works by Henry Tanner. Modern art by Sol Lewitt, Duane Hanson, and Joseph Cornell occupies the upstairs galleries. Other highlights are collections of Colt firearms, Greek and Roman bronzes, period costumes, silver, and furniture. HOURS: Tuesday to Sunday from 11 A.M. to 5 P.M. ADMISSION: $3 for adults; free to children under 13, and for everyone from 11 A.M. to 1 P.M. on Saturday.

On your way out, don't miss Alexander Calder's *Stegosaurus,* tucked (if you can use such a word of this massive sculpture) away between the Atheneum and the adjacent Municipal Building in Burr Mall.

From the Atheneum cross Main Street to:

Center Church

Its first pastor was Thomas Hooker, who left Cambridge, Massachusetts, in 1635 –1636 and walked to Newtown or, as we call it, Hartford. He is believed to be buried under or near a corner of the present church, which has stood since 1807. It contains several Louis Tiffany windows, but it is only open from noon to 3 P.M. daily. Take some time to explore the adjacent Ancient Burying Ground, where the gravestones date back to 1640.

From the burial ground and church, take Gold Street west, down the hill, crossing Jewell Street into:

Bushnell Park

Here in this 41-acre park shaded by some 500 trees you can rest a while, but children and antique or art lovers, do see the **carousel** with its 48 hand-carved, brilliantly painted horses and ornate lovers' chariots, complete with calliope, and automatic drums and cymbals. Built in 1914, it was brought here from Canton, Ohio, and operates daily in summer (weekends only in spring and fall). For only 25¢ you can recapture part of your childhood and try to grab at the brass ring. Note also the **Civil War Soldiers Memorial** that arches over Trinity Street. The architect loved his work so much that he and his wife are buried in the East Tower.

Exit the park via Trinity Street south to Capitol Avenue. On the corner, pop into **Bushnell Memorial Hall** for a look at the art deco interior, and then proceed up Capitol Avenue (going west) past the equestrian statue of Lafayette with a turtle placed near the horse's left rear hoof, supposedly the sculptor's wry comment on the ten-year delay that preceded his payment!

Museum of Connecticut History and the State Capitol

On the south side of Capitol Avenue, diagonally across from Bushnell Hall, you'll find the State Library, Supreme Court, and the **Baldwin Museum of Connecticut History** at 231 Capitol Ave. (tel. 203/566-3056), where the original Royal Charter and the Colt firearms collection are displayed along with documents, portraits, and artifacts relating to Connecticut history. HOURS: Monday to Friday from 9 A.M. to 4:45 P.M., on Saturday from 9 A.M. to 1 P.M. ADMISSION: Free.

And finally, head toward Richard Upjohn's **State Capitol,** the most impressive building in Hartford, easily identified by its shimmering golden dome, topped by a spire. A tour will acquaint you with its many eclectic details, murals, statues, and furnishings, all reflecting the history of the state, but only if you visit during the week (every 30 minutes from 9:30 A.M. to 2:30 P.M. in summer, every 1¼ hours from 9:15 A.M. at other seasons).

Some Special Highlights for Architectural Buffs

Besides the highlights already mentioned above, you'll most likely want to see Henry Hobson Richardson's 1877 Cheney Building, now called simply the **Richardson.** Restaurants and specialty shops occupy the lower floors; luxury apartments the upper floors. It's on Main Street north of the Old State House.

Constitution Plaza, undertaken in the late '50s and early '60s, east of the Old State House, was one of the first urban-renewal projects to combine shopping, office space, and parking facilities. On the plaza is an unusual fountain designed not to splash, no matter how hard the wind blows, and the only two-sided elliptical building in the country, the home of Phoenix Mutual Life.

The Butler-McCook Homestead

The oldest home in Hartford, at 396 Main St. (tel. 203/522-1806), remained in a single family until the 20th century and its interior reflects a full range of stylistic changes from 1782 to the turn of this century. HOURS: May 15 to October 15, Tuesday to Thursday and on Sunday from noon to 4 P.M. ADMISSION: $2 for adults, 50¢ for children.

Contact the **Antiquarian and Landmarks Society,** 394 Main St. (tel. 203/247-8996), for details about other houses—the Nathan Hale Homestead in Coventry, or the Victorian Italianate Isham-Terry house in Hartford.

AREA ATTRACTIONS

Nook Farm

An important cultural-intellectual community, Nook Farm, 77 Forest St., off Farmington Ave., was settled in the last half of the 19th century by interrelated families and friends. Among them were such celebrities as Isabella Beecher Hooker, women's rights leader; Charles Dudley Warner, author and editor of the *Hartford Courant;* William Gillette, the playwright and actor famous for his portrayal of Sherlock Holmes; and most famous of all, Mark Twain and Harriet Beecher Stowe.

Painted his favorite turkey red, Twain's house is large, grand, and rather ungainly compared to the smaller Beecher house across the way. Once inside, you'll discover more quirks incorporated into the house by the ornery eccentric humorist. For example, the telephone, which he despised and abhorred, is located in a closet, and the etched windows in the top-floor study where he wrote *Tom Sawyer, Huckleberry Finn,* and several other volumes, depict the items that Twain considered most important in life—smoking, drinking, and billiards. In the bedroom he placed the pillows at the foot of his bed so that he could gaze at the ornate, carved Venetian headboard, for which he had paid a princely sum. Twain lived here with his wife, three daughters, and 11 cats from 1874 to 1881, when his debts (he had lost $750,000 in two capital investment ventures) forced him to sell the house and flee to Europe on a lecture tour. A visit to the house is particularly rewarding because it reflects Twain's whimsical personality, and because you're able to enter the rooms instead of having to peer in from outside.

The Beecher house, built in 1871, is far more ordinary in many ways. Harriet moved here in 1873 and stayed until her death in 1896. The house still has many pieces of Mrs. Stowe's furniture, paintings by her, and also the kitchen designed to her specifications as outlined in *The American Woman's Home,* which she co-authored with her sister. They were first to recommend that plants be hung in windows instead of curtains! Whereas Twain's house contains a specific writing room, albeit filled with a full-size billiard table, the Beecher house has no such room, only a tiny desk, where she supposedly wrote many of her 33 (yes, that's right) books. One gets the impression that she probably wrote on the run, wherever and whenever she could grab the time between her daily tasks. For information call 203/525-9317. HOURS: June 1 to August 31, Tuesday to Sunday from 10 A.M. to 4:30 P.M.; September 1 to May 31, Tuesday to Saturday from 9:30 A.M. to 4 P.M., and on Sunday from 1 to 4 P.M. Closed Monday and major holidays. ADMISSION: $3.75 for adults, $1.50 for children under 16 for the Twain house; $3 for adults and $1.25 for children under 16 for the Stowe house; $6 for adults, $2.75 for children for both houses. DIRECTIONS: Take Exit 46 off I-84.

From Nook Farm you can take Farmington Avenue west to West Hartford's Main Street, turning left down Main Street to the:

Noah Webster House/Historical Society of West Hartford

At 227 S. Main St. (tel. 203/521-5362), you can view the 18th-century farmhouse and birthplace of the author of *Blue Backed Speller* (1783) and *American Dictionary* (1828). The home and museum contain period furnishings, Webster memorabilia, and varied changing exhibits. HOURS: Monday to Thursday from 10 A.M. to 4 P.M. and on Sunday from 1 to 4 P.M. ADMISSION: $2 for adults, $1 for children 6 to 15.

By the way, if you're interested in other Hartford literary landmarks, *New Yorker* editor Brendan Gill grew up in a rambling turn-of-the-century home at 735 Prospect St., while Wallace Stevens lived a few blocks away at 118 Westerly Terrace. In West Hartford, Sinclair Lewis resided briefly at 27 Belknap Rd.

Science Museum of Connecticut

Here in West Hartford, you'll also find the Science Museum, 950 Trout Brook Dr. (tel. 203/236-2961), with a small aquarium, mini-zoo, planetarium, and lots of "hands-on" activity that the kids'll love. HOURS: Monday to Saturday from 10 A.M. to 5 P.M., on Sunday from 1 to 5 P.M. Closed on major holidays. ADMISSION: $3.50 for adults, $2 for children under 12. Get back onto Farmington Avenue and it will take you to Farmington's attractions.

Hill-Stead Museum, Farmington

Located at 671 Farmington Ave. (tel. 203/677-9064), this was once the home of self-made millionaire and steel magnate Alfred Pope, a pioneer collector of impressionist art. After his death his daughter, Theodate Pope, preserved his collection in its original setting at the family home, which she had helped design for him at the tender age of 16. She became the wife of John Wallace Riddle, former ambassador to Russia and Argentina, and one of the first women in this country to become an architect. A number of notable personages visited her at Hill-Stead. Painter Mary Cassatt loved to walk through these rooms; Henry James described the house in *The American Scene* as "apparently conceived—and with great felicity—on the lines of a magnificent Mount Vernon"; Isadora Duncan danced in the gardens; and poet John Masefield contemplated the surrounding pastoral meadows. The Monets, Degas, Whistlers, and Manets are hung as if the house were still occupied, in rooms filled with collections of netsuke, majolica, Bari bronzes, Chinese porcelain, clocks, rugs, and fine antiques, an American bull's-eye mirror here, a Chippendale secretary there. HOURS: Wednesday to Sunday from 2 to 5 P.M. By guided tour only. Closed major holidays, and mid-January to mid-February. ADMISSION: $2.50.

Other Farmington Attractions

Other Farmington sights include the **Stanley Whitman House,** 37 High St. (tel. 203/677-9222), built around 1715 and perhaps most interesting for its kitchen and typical Connecticut colonial herb garden. HOURS: May to October, Tuesday to Sunday from 1 to 4 P.M.; in March, April, November, and December, on Sunday from 1 to 4 P.M. ADMISSION: $2 for adults, $1 for children.

And while you're in Farmington, drive past the **stately homes** that line Main Street (many built before 1835), noticing also the unmarked but renowned **Miss Porter's School,** one of the oldest and finest boarding schools for girls in the country, founded in 1844 when tuition was $200 for 42 weeks of instruction and board. Jackie Onassis was one of the school's more famous pupils.

Only a 20-minute drive south of Farmington, the **New Britain Museum of Art,** 56 Lexington St. (tel. 203/229-0257), has a fine collection of American art including works by Gilbert Stuart, William Jennys, Frederic Church, Albert Bierstadt, John Singer Sargent, Childe Hassam, and Charles Burchfield. They are displayed in a fine old residence. More modern works can be found in the new wing. HOURS: Tuesday to Sunday from 1 to 5 P.M. ADMISSION: Free.

Massacoh Plantation in Historic Simsbury

After Mystic, Massacoh Plantation, 800 Hopmeadow St. in Simsbury (tel. 203/658-2500), is the largest historical complex in Connecticut, representing three centuries of Farmington Valley history from 1670 when Simsbury was first settled by about 12 families from Windsor. The Phelps House (1771) is the cornerstone. It has been decorated the way it would have been in 1827 to 1849 when it operated as the Canal Hotel, a stop on the 24-hour route from Northampton, Massachusetts, to New Haven, Connecticut. The house remained in the Phelps family until 1962, and consequently its history is known and the house itself has been well preserved. Inside among the more intriguing features are the original canvas ceiling, witches' crosses on each side of the fireplace in the tavern, and the coffin door (so called because it was wide enough to get a coffin through, and the door that all inhabitants went through last). In the kitchen you'll learn how those early cooks determined the temperature of the beehive ovens, and see the cooking utensils and staples they used—horsehair sifters, stick whisks, and sugar cones. Upstairs the splendid ballroom was used for special family and other social occasions. Don't miss viewing the very rare Higley copper, minted in 1737, which states "Value Me as You Please" on it. This coin was first struck in 1737 by Dr. Samuel Higley.

Also on the grounds stands a replica of a 1683 meetinghouse, an ice house, a white barn filled with old sleighs and carriages, including an authentic tin peddler's cart that was used until 1925, a schoolhouse originally built in 1740 and refurbished in 1825, and the fuse building from the local Ensign Bickford Company which houses original fuse and primer cord equipment. There's also McDaniels Art Gallery.

HOURS: May to October, Tuesday to Sunday from 1 to 4 P.M.; in winter only the Phelps House is open Tuesday to Friday. ADMISSION: $3 for adults, $1.50 for children.

On the way out to Simsbury you'll be able to view in the distance the **Heublein Tower** (tel. 203/677-0662) standing atop the mountain ridge 1,000 feet above the Farmington River in Talcott Mountain State Park. This 165-foot-high folly was built in 1914 as a summer home for Gilbert Heublein. It can be visited to enjoy the panoramic views from late April to Labor Day on weekends only. Access is from Route 185.

New England Air Museum

Only ten miles north of Hartford off I-91 on Rte. 75, this museum at the Bradley Airport, Windsor Locks (tel. 203/623-3305), will give you a telescoped view of aviation history. Here are over 80 aircraft, ranging from romantic biplanes and box-like steel kites strung together with straps, to World War II fighters like the spunky little "Spitfire" and modern jets and helicopters (Igor Sikorsky emigrated from Kiev to Connecticut), all of them meticulously restored. Movies are shown daily. The museum even has parts of a gas balloon used by a Malcolm Forbes of the 1880s—Silas Brookes. HOURS: 10 A.M. to 5 P.M. daily except major winter holidays. ADMISSION: $4.50 for adults, $2 for children 6 to 11.

Historic Prison and Copper Mine in East Granby

Just off Rte. 20 west of the airport lies Old Newgate Prison and copper mine (tel. 203/653-3563) in East Granby, where you can tour the dungeon-like chambers of this first chartered copper mine, which became Connecticut's first state prison and housed British sympathizers during the American Revolution. HOURS: Mid-May to October 31, Wednesday to Sunday from 10 A.M. to 4 P.M. ADMISSION: $1.75 for adults, 75¢ for children.

Old Wethersfield

About eight miles south of Hartford, Old Wethersfield, the onion-raising capital of the colonies in the 18th century, is now a fascinating historic district where over 150 pre-1850 structures have been preserved. Barns, warehouses, and carriage houses have been transformed into shops selling everything from crafts and antiques to toys and gardening supplies. For information call 563-5727. HOURS: Tuesday to Saturday from 10 A.M. to 5 P.M.

If shopping is not your favorite pastime, two historic sites are worth visiting. The **Buttolph Williams House** (1692), at Broad and Marsh Streets (tel. 203/529-0460), shelters an outstanding collection of pewter, Delft, fabrics, and furniture, and displays a fine 17th-century kitchen filled with wooden plates and salvers, wrought-iron utensils, and a rare semicircular settle.

The **Webb-Deane-Stevens Museum,** 211 Main St. (tel. 203/529-0612), consists of three 18th-century homes that were used for Washington's conference with Rochambeau to plot the strategy that led to the defeat of the British at Yorktown. Each of the houses reflects the individual lifestyle of its owner: merchant, diplomat, and tradesman. The decorative arts collections span the period from 1640 to 1840. HOURS: Tuesday to Saturday from 10 A.M. to 4 P.M. and on Sunday from 1 to 4 P.M., May 15 to October 15 only. ADMISSION: $1.50 per house or $4 for all three, 50¢ per house for children.

For more information on other local historic houses, call the Wethersfield Historical Society at 529-7656.

A Family Excursion to Lake Compounce

Lake Compounce, America's oldest amusement park, re-opened its doors in 1986 after a multi-million dollar renovation turned it into **Hershey Lake Compounce**, Lake Avenue (I-84, Exit 31), Bristol (tel. 203/582-6333). It has retained its Victorian charm. The carousel still spins to the calliope's song, but now there's more: a thrilling Wildcat roller coaster, a mountain flume and other water rides. Performers of all sorts entertain on the main stage. Turn-of-the-century shops, arcades, and dining places also draw the crowds to this attractively located amusement park where the lake still sparkles at the foot of the mountain. Open in summer only. Call for schedule and admissions.

HARTFORD LODGING

Sad to say, Hartford has no really outstanding accommodations, but all the hotels do offer attractive weekend packages.

The Summit, 5 Constitution Plaza, Hartford, CT 06103 (tel. 203/278-2000), for example, at the time of my research, was offering three packages: the Summit Send-Off, a two-day/one-night package that included room, champagne welcome, transportation to and from the airport, taxes and gratuities, and parking, priced at $65 per night double occupancy; the Lovers Getaway, either a three-day/two-night or two-day/one-night package that adds a love tub bath basket, dinner in Gabriel's, an evening at the Rendezvous Room, and breakfast, for only $75 a night; and a more luxurious package priced at $95 per night.

The hotel is well situated downtown, and the three restaurants and two lounges make it an appealing choice. In the Rendezvous Room such greats as Margaret Whiting, Julius LaRosa, Billy Eckstine, Johnny Ray, and Buddy Greco have all appeared in the last year, and you're bound to enjoy a good show and romantic dancing in this cabaret on weekends.

The **Parkview Hilton,** One Hilton Plaza, Hartford, CT 06103 (tel. 203/249-5611). Here, the Terrace on the Park restaurant is a favorite Hartford spot, featuring a lavish buffet brunch on Sunday from 11 A.M. to 3 P.M. ($12.95), as well as dinner Monday to Saturday. Health club available. RATES: A one-night weekend package including room, dinner, and breakfast sells for $120.

The **Sheraton-Hartford,** 315 Trumbull St. (at the Civic Center Plaza), Hartford, CT 06103 (tel. 203/728-5151), a lively, very well located accommodation, offers an indoor pool, restaurant—the Stage Cafe for continental and New England favorites that range in price from $12 to $20. The Hartford Trading Company, for nightly entertainment and video lounge, completes the facilities. RATES: $93 to $120 single, $108 to $135 double. Weekend packages are available.

For budget accommodations, try the **Ramada Inn—Capitol Hill,** 440 Asylum St., Hartford, CT 06103 (tel. 203/246-6591), right next door to the Amtrak station and only four blocks from the Old State House. RATES: $68 double; weekend packages too.

There are three other possibilities on the outskirts. **Susse Chalet Inn,** 185 Brainard Rd., Hartford, CT 06114 (tel. 203/525-9306), has an outdoor pool. RATES: $37 single, $41 double. The **Imperial Inn** is at 927 Main St., Hartford, CT 06103 (tel. 203/289-7781). RATES: $40 double. And the **Holiday Inn** is at 50 Morgan St., Hartford, CT 06120 (tel. 203/549-2400). RATES: $71 to $87 double; also weekend packages.

A more interesting choice would be to contact the local bed-and-breakfast organization, **Nutmeg Bed and Breakfast,** 222 Girard Ave., Hartford, CT 06105 (tel. 203/236-6698), which will guide you to B&B's throughout the state. Send $2.50 for a directory. RATES: $35 to $75 double.

HARTFORD DINING

Breakfast/Brunch Choices
For these, look under the sections headed "Lunch and Dinner Choices" or "Dinner Only" for The Brownstone (tel. 203/525-1171), Au Musée (tel. 203/549-1319), and Avon Old Farms Inn (tel. 203/677-2818); and under "Area Dining and Lodgings" for the Standish House (tel. 203/721-1113) in Wethersfield, Apricots (tel. 203/673-5903) and the Reading Room (tel. 203/677-7997) in Farmington, and the Simsbury House (tel. 203/658-7658) in Simsbury.

Luncheon Choices
For light casual fare, there are many choices in the modern Civic Center, where the Promenade houses a collection of bright, cafeteria-style fast-food outlets, all sharing common dining areas. Among them are **Shelley's Deli** (tel. 203/278-1510), great for well-stuffed sandwiches around the clock; **George's** (tel. 203/527-3900), offering omelets and quiches as well as crêpes from 11 A.M. to 9 P.M. daily; **Buon Apetito** (tel. 203/522-4635), for pizza and hoagie lovers; and the **Noisy Oyster Seafood Bar & Grill** (tel. 203/728-5868), for fresh clams, oysters, and assorted chowders.

Lunch and Dinner Choices
For a serene unique setting, **Au Musée,** 600 Main St. (tel. 203/724-4848), is indeed at the Wadsworth Atheneum. The interior has a minimalist black-and-gray look accented by one or two large Chinese urns and other porcelain pieces, but in summer the restaurant moves outside into the courtyard.

The menu is small and select. At lunch, items range from $6.75 to $12.50. Among the selections, try the shrimp terrine with fish, vegetables, and tarragon tomato sauce or baked French goat cheese with mixed salad greens served with garlic croutons. Omelets and croque monsieur, along with more substantial dishes like blackened redfish or lamb braised with black and green olives, garlic, tomatoes, wine, and herbs, complete the menu. Save room for the tempting desserts—my favorite is lemon mousse in raspberry purée. Dinner, at $28 prix fixe, features four or so dishes—for example, roast duck with almond and liqueur sauce, tournedos with tomato béarnaise sauce, blackened redfish, or filet of sole with a salmon mousse filling, poached and served with saffron leek sauce. Appetizers like mussels cooked with cream and curry, smoked trout, and smoked salmon might begin the meal.

LUNCH: Tuesday to Saturday from 11:30 A.M. to 2 P.M. DINNER: Friday and Saturday only, from 5:30 to 9:30 P.M. BRUNCH: Sunday from 11:30 A.M. to 2:30 P.M.

Gaetano's, 1 Civic Center Plaza (tel. 203/249-8624), offers fine northern Italian cuisine in a sleek, modern environment of Breuer-style chairs covered in a crushed velvet, complemented by salmon-pink tablecloths. Seating arrangements vary from etched-glass enclosed booths to special octagonal gazebo-like enclosures for parties of eight or more.

Dinner dishes, priced from $13.25 to $16.50, include tenderloin tips and filet of sole stuffed with crabmeat, along with the more Italian-style saltimbocca and veal pavari with pimentoes, artichokes, mushrooms, and tomatoes. Pastas are also available, including capellini Angelica and pesto with capers, onions, and pepperoncini. The filet mignon Gaetano is stuffed with prosciutto, cheese, and sautéed in cognac and mustard sauce. Rack of lamb, veal Madeira, and baked scrod on a bed of shredded zucchini are additional choices.

LUNCH: Monday to Saturday from 11:30 A.M. to 2:30 P.M. DINNER: 5:30 to 10:30 P.M.

Frank's City Place, 185 Asylum St., City Place (tel. 203/527-9291), is a veteran, having served Hartford since 1944. Popular with politicos in particular, the restaurant proudly displays photos of those among the famous who have eaten here, from the late Ella Grasso to Pope John Paul II. The atmosphere is modern and unpretentious—cane-seated Breuer chairs, salmon-pink napkins. The menu is traditional, featuring about 20 items like broiled chicken, broiled scrod with lemon butter, veal Marsala or française, filet mignon, and prime rib. Desserts are primarily Italian—tortoni, canolli, spumoni. Prices range from $15 to $21.

LUNCH: Daily from 11:30 A.M. to 3 P.M. DINNER: Daily from 4 to 10:30 P.M. BRUNCH: Sunday from 11:30 A.M. to 2:30 P.M.

For typical Mexican food and drinks, **Margaritaville,** 1 Civic Center Plaza (tel. 203/724-3331), packs a lively crowd into its warren-like space filled with alcoves, stucco, tiles, and Mexican artifacts.

LUNCH: Monday to Saturday from 11:30 A.M. to 3 P.M. DINNER: Daily from 4:30 to 10 P.M.

So, too, does **Chuck's Steakhouse,** in the Hartford Civic Center (tel. 203/241-9100). A book-lined corridor leads to a restaurant filled with bamboo chairs and tables spread with rust-colored tablecloths. Steaks are priced from $12. The bar is low lit and comfortable.

LUNCH: Monday to Saturday from 11:30 A.M. to 3 P.M. DINNER: Sunday to Thursday from 4:30 to 10 P.M., on Friday and Saturday until 11 P.M.

Once a typical cozy Italian bistro, **Carbone's,** 588 Franklin Ave. (tel. 203/249-9646) has recently been redecorated in a plush rather nondescript style featuring upholstered beige booths and classical Italian prints. A non-smoking area sports modern wicker Breuers. The food is well prepared and there's plenty of it. The menu offers a full range of pastas, seafood, and meat dishes, priced from $9.25 to $16. Among the pastas are paglie e fieno in a gorgonzola sauce, which you can follow with such items as beef filets in cognac and mustard, chicken inglese (marinated with lemon, olive oil, and sherry, and broiled with mustard sauce) or veal zingarelli (sautéed with spinach, veal sausage, artichokes, and mushrooms, and baked with Italian sharp cheese).

LUNCH: Monday to Saturday from 11:30 A.M. to 2:30 P.M. DINNER: 5 to 10 P.M. daily.

Ficara, 438 Franklin St. (tel. 203/549-3238), also right in the center of Hartford's Little Italy, comes highly recommended. The pasta is made on the premises, and each dish is cooked to order and served in this homey room with its blue tablecloths and simple chairs. The chef's name is Sebby and several dishes on the menu carry his name—like chicken Sebby, for example, which is a boneless breast topped with layers of prosciutto, peppers, and provolone cheese, baked in butter and sherry wine sauce; or shrimp Sebby, which is similar but substitutes eggplant for peppers and adds a little lemon to the sauce. Other dishes include classics like veal française, sorrentino, or pizzaiola. To start, the stuffed mushrooms with clams, shrimp, wine, breadcrumbs, a little cheese, and seasoning are perfect; or try the hot appetizers—a plate of stuffed clams, fried shrimp, clams casino, fried calamari, and stuffed mushrooms. Pasta lovers will relish the pasta romana with mushrooms, peas, prosciutto, and cream, or the fettuccine Alfredo. Cheesecake, baba au rhum, and spumoni appear on the dessert list. Entrees run $11 to $18; pasta, $7 to $10.

LUNCH: Monday to Saturday from 11:30 A.M. to 2 P.M. DINNER: Monday to Saturday from 5 to 10 P.M. You'll need reservations, and please note that the restaurant plans a move so check the address and telephone number.

Trucs, 735 Wethersfield Ave. (tel. 203/249-2818), is famous and recommended by *Gourmet* for the best Oriental cuisine in Hartford. Among the favorite entrees are bo huc lac, or shaking beef, which is actually cubes of filet mignon marinated in a special sauce then sautéed in garlic and served with vinaigrette sauce on a bed of watercress. Or try vit quay, lacquered duck marinated in five spices and garlic sauce, and roasted with crisp skin and served with orange; or the equally popular barh xeo ("happy pancake"), a rice-batter pancake stuffed with shrimp, pork, chicken, fresh mushrooms, onions, and bean sprouts, served in Vietnamese sauce. Several appetizers are worth noting: ha noi soup, containing sliced beef and rice sticks, or special shrimp rolls (kha gro Truc dac biet), a triangular roll stuffed with crabmeat, pork, and vegetable around a large shrimp and then wrapped in crisp rice paper and served with sauce. America inspires the desserts, which range from lemon, chocolate, or apricot mousse, to a very special binh chocolate that spreads almond paste between cake and mousse (chocolate mousse cake).

The atmosphere is pleasing. The front part of the restaurant is given over to a tiled solarium while the rear offers a long light-oak bar and comfortable bamboo chairs set with tables covered with forest-green tablecloths and glass.

LUNCH: Tuesday to Saturday from 11 A.M. to 2 P.M. DINNER: Tuesday to Saturday from 5 to 11 P.M., on Sunday and Monday from 4 to 9:30 P.M.

Dinner Only

Panache, 357 Main St. (tel. 203/724-0810), was on everyone's lips as the number-one Hartford restaurant when I was last visiting. The decor alone makes a vivid impression—brilliant-purple foyer, curvaceous dividing walls that set off the bar area, and Botticelli-red and ocean mist (a kind of green/turquoise) dining room walls that set off the black upholstered Breuer chairs and Erté prints. Huge fresh flower arrangements, large potted palms, and jet-black bar add extra drama.

The menu also lives up to the restaurant's name. Among the appetizers, try the fresh foie gras and truffles sautéed with sweet butter, madeira, and cream. A different selection of pâtés and mousses is made daily. The main courses start at $18 for roast baby chicken with tarragon mustard and white wine, rising to $32 for a roast saddle of venison with a sour-cherry cognac sauce. At lunch there's always a vegetarian dish, a pasta creation, quiche, and other dishes like shrimp Szechuan or crab cakes.

LUNCH: Tuesday to Friday from noon to 2 P.M. DINNER: Monday to Thursday from 5:30 to 9 P.M., on Friday and Saturday until 10 P.M.; closed Sunday.

The Brownstone, at the corner of Trumbull and Asylum Streets (tel. 203/525-1171), is located in an 1860–1865 building originally constructed for the Charter Oak Bank, and the old beams, brick floors, stained glass, and brass accents attest to that era. Luncheon always features a special chef's inspiration, a fish and pasta of the day, plus the full menu of sandwiches, soups, and fish and meat entrees from $4 to $8. Steaks and seafood predominate on the dinner menu—swordfish steak au poivre, shrimp New Orleans, steak with sautéed onions, sesame chicken —priced from $12 to $18 for a 12-ounce sirloin. Brunch features some unusual items: crab imperial, huevos rancheros, plus the more common eggs Benedict and similar, for $11.

LUNCH: Monday to Friday from 11:30 A.M. to 3 P.M. DINNER: Monday to Thursday from 5 to 10 P.M., on Friday and Saturday until 11 P.M. BRUNCH: Sunday from 11 A.M. to 3 P.M.

L'Americain, 2 Hartford Square (tel. 203/522-6500), is currently gaining a reputation as the finest dining establishment in Hartford and was recently mentioned in *Vogue* as a "worthy sidetrip." Housed in an old red-brick building, the two dining rooms are traditionally furnished with Queen Anne chairs and fine napery.

Start with one of the more unusual appetizers, a marinated salad of wild mushrooms, fresh herb noodles, and nasturtium leaves, or a warm goat cheese and Westphalian ham braised with escarole and lavender. Main courses offer a delicious roast duckling with mint and fresh peach sauce, or, in season, a sliced breast of pheasant on a corn crêpe served with a whisky game sauce and roasted peppers, all priced from $14 to $25. A similar luncheon menu comes at roughly half the price, $5 to $8.50. A little difficult to find . . . just off Columbus Boulevard.

LUNCH: Monday to Friday from 11:30 A.M. to 2 P.M. DINNER: Monday to Saturday from 6 to 9:30 P.M.

Spencers, 10 Capitol Ave. (tel. 203/247-0400), offers two bars, an outdoor terrace, and a downstairs formal dining room in a landmark building. A professional, sophisticated crowd gathers here for predinner cocktails. The menus change seasonally. The food could most aptly be described as nouvelle—spiced ham in Brie with walnuts and Kahlúa, shrimp Clemenceau with vermouth and artichoke, roulades of sole and asparagus with a champagne shrimp sauce, and rack of lamb au poivre with Dijon chardonnay cream sauce. To start there's a selection of appetizers (oysters, etc.) and soups; desserts change daily. On Sunday a $15 brunch, including a drink, offers a full menu from steak and eggs to chicken Rochambeau.

LUNCH: Monday to Friday from 11:30 A.M. to 2 P.M. DINNER: Daily from 5:30 to 11 P.M. BRUNCH: Sunday from 11 A.M. to 3 P.M.

Capitol Fish House, 391 Main St. (tel. 203/724-3370), specializes in fresh seafood, everything from mahi mahi with herb butter to blackened redfish, from broiled shad (in season) to halibut in cucumber or béarnaise sauce. According to the management the fish is delivered twice a day, before lunch and before dinner. There are 12 to 15 daily specials. One of the more unusual dishes is the cioppino —lobster, shrimps, clams, scallops, mussels, and white fish simmered in tomatoes, garlic, and dry wine, and served over linguine. If you opt for oysters as a starter it's comforting to know they're only served when they're at their best. Other delicious appetizers? Iced mussels à la Bombay, steeped in a curry-pepper sauce, and sea scallops wrapped in bacon with water chestnuts. Prices for main courses run from $9.50 to $17.

A long oak bar with oak booths takes up the front part of the space while in the back there are two slightly more formal rooms where tables sport beige tablecloths, hurricane lamps, and two carnations (or similar), plus plants and exposed brick.

LUNCH: Monday to Friday from 11:30 A.M. to 2:30 P.M. DINNER: Monday to Thursday from 5 to 10 P.M., on Friday and Saturday to 10:30 P.M.; closed Sunday.

AREA DINING AND LODGING

Avon—Lunch or Dinner

Chef/owner Jonathan of **Park Place,** 3 Canal Court, Avon Park North (tel. 203/ 677-6318), is a New Zealander who also spent considerable time in Singapore, Hong Kong, and elsewhere in the Orient, so many of his dishes have Oriental accents. Brunch at Jonathan's is original, very different from the usual all-you-can-eat buffet routines. Start with homemade garlic sausage or a seafood chowder. Follow with shrimp Hunan, a mixture of shrimp with baby corn, miniature pati pans squash, tomatoes, and mushrooms in a brown Hunan sauce. At dinner he creates such entrees as lamb with a mango chutney sauce, or veal with lobster and wild mushrooms. Prices run $18 to $20.

Prettily housed in a converted carriage barn when I visited, Jonathan told me he would be moving soon but he had no definite location, so look him up in the phone book—it's worth it!

LUNCH: Tuesday to Saturday from 11:30 A.M. to 2 P.M. DINNER: Tuesday to Sunday from 6 to 9:30 P.M. BRUNCH: Sunday from noon to 3 P.M. Closed Monday.

Avon Old Farms Inn, Avon (tel. 203/677-2818). The Forge Room at this old 1757 inn is especially inviting, particularly in winter when a blazing fire casts a warm glow over the stone floors and the blacksmith's tools that adorn the walls. The tables have been artfully arranged, leaving the actual horse stalls intact. You can also opt to dine in the two small rooms off the entrance that are the inn's oldest, or else in the two other large, modern, and, to me, less appealing sections.

Come in July or August on Friday night and you can partake of their clambake; otherwise choose from a primarily American menu—a roast rib of beef au jus served with a popover, shrimp filled with a walnut stuffing, and their own veal sentino (medallions of veal broiled with asparagus, mushrooms, and a mild imported Danish cheese), chosen by Craig Claiborne and Pierre Franey for inclusion in their *Veal Cookery*. Prices range from $9 to $17 with a special prix fixe available at $13.50. The brunch also draws crowds for a huge $15 buffet spread.

LUNCH: Tuesday to Saturday from noon to 2:30 P.M. DINNER: Tuesday to Thursday from 5:30 to 9:30 P.M., on Friday until 10 P.M., on Saturday until 10:30 P.M., and on Sunday until 8:30 P.M. BRUNCH: Sunday from 11 A.M. to 3:30 P.M.

Wethersfield—Lunch or Dinner

Standish House, 222 Main St., Wethersfield (tel. 203/721-1113), is a fitting restaurant. Located in a 1787 house built originally for a wealthy merchant family, it has experienced several incarnations, first as a home and subsequently as a hotel (from 1840), bank, and headquarters for the board of education. The various dining rooms are conservatively decorated in late colonial style with Chippendale or Queen Anne chairs, chintz or stenciled wallpapers, brass chandeliers, swag curtains, Oriental rugs and carpet on the wideboard floors.

The menu changes seasonally. The food is highly recommended. At dinner, start with a mussel soup provençal with aioli or a galantin of duck with a Cumberland sauce. Main courses run from $13.75 for chicken breast braised in zinfandel to $19.75 for New York pepper steak cooked in balsamic vinegar and shallots. Fish lovers might try the swordfish rémoulade. Dessert choices include a strawberry shortcake, chocolate cake Palmer (chocolate cake layered with rum crème anglaise) and a Kahlúa sundae (vanilla ice cream with maple syrup and Kahlúa).

At lunchtime you can enjoy such interesting dishes as crabcakes with lemon butter, veal marengo, avocado and spinach salad with apples and mustard seed mayonnaise, priced from $5.25 to $8.25.

Brunch items are also stimulating—mixed grill with fried eggs, French pancakes with fruit filling, or omelet with cream cheese and salmon, from $8.50 to $12.

LUNCH: Tuesday to Saturday from noon to 2 P.M. DINNER: Tuesday to Saturday from 6 to 9 P.M., on Sunday from 5 to 8 P.M. BRUNCH: Sunday from noon to 2:30 P.M.

Farmington—Lunch or Dinner

The **Reading Room,** Mill Lane, Farmington (tel. 203/677-7997), is a simple old country place overlooking the Farmington River. Through the six-over-six windows you'll likely see mallards taking off and landing on the surface of the water. Originally built in 1650 for Stephen Hart, it became the property of Roger Hooker in 1759 and later, in 1917, of playwright Winchell Smith, who allowed D. W. Griffith to film the climax of *Way Down East* here.

Daily specials supplement the limited menu of roast duck with Cumberland sauce, sole homard (served with lobster, mushroom, and spinach), and rack of lamb, priced from $13 to $20, including salad and vegetable. In summer the lawn is used as dining space. On Sunday the champagne brunch menu lists items from $6.75 to $12, including lobster and asparagus omelet with cheese, eggs Florentine or Benedict, crabmeat rarebit, etc.

LUNCH: Monday to Saturday from 11:30 A.M. to 2:30 P.M. DINNER: Monday to Saturday from 5:30 to 10 P.M. BRUNCH: Sunday from 11 A.M. to 3 P.M.

Apricots, 1593 Farmington Ave., Farmington (tel. 203/673-5903). Crowds gather downstairs in the pub with piano entertainment. Upstairs there are two dining rooms, one having a river view from the paned windows. The menu changes weekly, but just to give you some idea of what to expect, here are some recent offerings: rack of lamb with either a mustard hollandaise or sauce provençal, grilled swordfish with orange and green onion in a walnut butter sauce, wood-smoked duckling with green peppercorn sauce and cranberry chutney, and sautéed shrimp, cucumbers, and tomatoes in a rosemary, basil, and white wine butter. Among the appetizers the same menu offers poached shrimp with a champagne chive beurre blanc, pâté with a Cumberland sauce, and escargots en vol au vent with garlic cream. Prices for entrees run from $14.50 to $22.50. A lighter pub menu is also available. Brunch, at $12, includes traditional egg dishes along with items like fish or pasta du jour and seafood crêpe plus a buffet of breads and desserts.

LUNCH: Monday to Saturday from 11:30 A.M. to 2:30 P.M. DINNER: Monday to Saturday from 6 to 10 P.M., on Sunday from 5:30 to 9 P.M. BRUNCH: Sunday from 11:30 A.M. to 3 P.M.

Simsbury—Lodging and Dining

Simsbury House, 731 Hopmeadow St. (Rte. 10), Simsbury, CT 06070 (tel. 203/658-7658), is a restored red-brick Georgian home, built in 1820 by Elisha Phelps, son of Noah Phelps, American patriot. From the gracious entrance with leaded windows, a scrolled staircase leads to the 34 prettily decorated rooms, most with antique reproductions and color schemes derived from the colonial period —Wedgwood blue and cranberry. Bedspreads are French chintz, lamps are porcelain, and in some rooms a Federal-style clubfooted desk serves as a bedside table. Two leather or pastel-colored upholstered wing chairs are comfortable. For storage, the large armoire and chest of drawers with brass handles serve well. Bathrooms are tiled, towels fluffy, and the amenities include shampoo, body lotion, emery boards, hair conditioner, sewing kit, etc. Rooms have telephones and air conditioners. Some rooms have balconies; some also have four-poster beds without canopies, and some are tucked away under the sloping ceilings of the roof. RATES: $100 to $135 double.

On the ground floor, the parlor with its Federal-style fireplace is inviting —comfortable sofa, wing chairs, and collection of newspapers and magazines. A small service-only bar is furnished with Chippendale chairs and card tables.

The dining room downstairs is gaining a reputation for its food. Besides the regular menu, which changes seasonally, daily specials might offer venison in a red wine and truffle sauce, tuna with a pommery mustard butter, or halibut with basil and tomatoes, served in a lobster and cream sauce. Other choices? Filet of sole baked with fresh herbs, mussels, and vermouth or sweet butter; grilled Cornish hen with California white zinfandel sauce; sirloin grilled and served with a shallot and red wine sauce; and duckling studded with peppercorns and served with port wine sauce and cranberry relish. The Kahlúa crème brûlée and phyllo with strawberries and raspberry sauce make a perfect ending to a first-class meal. Brunch consists of classic egg dishes.

LUNCH: 11:30 A.M. to 2:30 P.M. DINNER: Weekdays from 5 to 9 P.M., weekends until 10 P.M. BRUNCH: Sunday from 11 A.M. to 3 P.M.

Additional Simsbury Dining

A sawmill and gristmill dating from 1680, **Hop Brook,** 77 West St. (tel. 203/651-0267), is now a triplex restaurant reached by a rust-colored footbridge. The bottom level houses a copper-hooded square bar with Windsor-style bar stools, a huge stone fireplace, and historic local photos, all tucked under massive beams. The other levels are dining rooms, furnished with antiqued tabletops, Windsor chairs, and copper and plant accents. In summer there's a deck; year round you can look out over the smooth mill pond.

The food is typically American with a dash of nouvelle—for example, lobster pie and a Hop Brook pot of steamers, shrimp, lobster, and fresh fish. There's always a roast on the menu. Grilled steaks and fish include blackened redfish, along with blackened shrimp, chicken, and filet mignon. Prices run from $9 to $22. Appetizers include Cajun shrimp, chowder, New Orleans gumbo, and raw bar.

LUNCH: Monday to Saturday from 11:30 A.M. to 2:30 P.M. DINNER: Sunday to Thursday from 5 to 10 P.M., on Friday and Saturday until 11 P.M. BRUNCH: Sunday from 11 A.M. to 3 P.M.

The **Chart House,** 4 Hartford Ave. (tel. 203/658-1118), located in a pleasant clapboard house bordered by pretty flower gardens, offers a series of small dining rooms as well as an enclosed sun porch set with white wicker furniture and splashes of greenery. The food is traditional American—seafood and steak from $10 to $22.

DINNER: Monday to Thursday from 5:30 to 10 P.M., on Friday and Saturday until 11 P.M., on Sunday from 4 to 9 P.M.

EVENING ENTERTAINMENT

First, for current events check the *Hartford Courant* listings.

The Performing Arts

Theater (comedies, dramas) can be found at the **Hartford Stage,** 50 Church St. (tel. 203/527-5151).

The **Hartford Ballet** (tel. 203/525-9396), the **Hartford Symphony** (tel. 203/246-8742), and the **Connecticut Opera** all perform at Bushnell Memorial Hall, 166 Capitol Ave. (tel. 203/527-0713), which also hosts Broadway musicals and shows.

The **Civic Center** (tel. 203/727-8080) presents concerts, ice shows, and other similar popular events.

Spectator Sports

From October to May the **Hartford Whalers** (tel. 203/728-3366) are home at the Civic Center. For tickets to games, call toll free 800/WHALERS.

Hartford Jai-Alai, 89 Weston St. (tel. 203/525-8611), operates from early January to the end of August, evenings Tuesday through Saturday, with Sunday matinees at 1 P.M.

Dancing/Bars

Dining and dancing can be found at the Esplanade at the **Hilton** (tel. 203/249-5611). Other popular spots for drinking and live entertainment include **36 Lewis Street** (tel. 203/247-2300), providing an assortment of musical entertainment from New Wave to rhythm and blues and top-40s, and **Russian Lady Café,** 191 Ann St. (tel. 203/525-3003), filled with artifacts rescued from buildings doomed to demolition (even the statue that adorns the exterior was rescued from the old Rossia Insurance building). Live rock bands perform. Hours are 4 P.M. to 2 A.M., on Sunday from 6 P.M.

For cocktails, there's **Brown Thomson & Co.,** 942 Main St. (tel. 203/525-1600), and several places already listed in the restaurant section—the **Brownstone** at Trumbull and Asylum Streets (tel. 203/525-1171) and **Spencers,** 10 Capitol Ave. (tel. 203/247-0400).

HARTFORD ACTIVITIES

ANTIQUING: The greatest selection of antiques stores can be found in nearby Coventry and west of Hartford in Farmington, along Rte. 44 in Avon, Canton, and farther west.

CANOEING: On the Farmington River. Contact Mainstream Outfitters, Rte. 44, Canton, CT 06019 (tel. 203/693-8780). Canton is about 13 miles from Hartford, just beyond Avon.

FRUIT PICKING: Plenty of picking around South Glastonbury. *South Glastonbury:* Bell Town Orchards, 475 Matson Hill Rd. (tel. 203/633-2789), apples and blueberries; Louis C. Ethier, 517 Woodland St. (tel. 203/633-1575), strawberries and blueberries; Rose's Berry Farm, Matson Hill Road (tel. 203/633-7467), strawberries and blueberries. In *Avon* there's Woodford's Pickin Patch, Nod Rd. (tel. 203/677-9552), strawberries, tomatoes, squash, peppers, beans, and pumpkins. For full information contact Marketing Division of the Department of Agriculture, 165 Capitol Ave., Hartford, CT 06106.

GOLF: *Avon:* Bel Compo Golf Club, Rte. 44 (tel. 203/678-1358). *Farmington:* Tunxis Plantation Country Club, Town Farm Road (tel. 203/677-1367); Westwoods Golf Course, Rte. 177 (tel. 203/677-9192). *Hartford:* Keney Park Golf Club, Enfield St. (tel. 203/722-6548); Goodwin Park Golf Club, Maple Ave. (tel. 203/722-6561), with 27 holes. *Simsbury:* Simsbury Farms Golf Club, Old Farms Rd. (tel. 203/658-6246).

HORSEBACK RIDING: *Avon:* McGrane's Stables, Lovely St. (tel. 203/673-3486); River Farms, Waterville Rd. (tel. 203/678-9817). *Farmington:* Farmington Valley Polo Club, Town Farm Rd. (tel. 203/677-8427). *Simsbury:* Folly Farm Stables, 69 Hartford Rd. (tel. 203/658-9943).

ICE SKATING: On the pond in Elizabeth Park, Prospect Avenue and Asylum Street.

PICNICKING: The city's own Elizabeth Park and Rose Garden, at Prospect Avenue and Asylum Street, makes a lovely setting for a picnic among the 900 varieties of roses that bloom there through the summer long. Or else head for the banks of the Connecticut River, by taking the first exit east of Hartford on I-91. Pick up supplies downtown at the Civic Center in **Gordon's Produce** (tel. 203/525-8290); **John Williams's Pastry Shop** (tel. 203/278-4143), which is open from 9 A.M. to 6 P.M. on Saturday, noon to 5 P.M. on Sunday; or at any of the other food vendors on the ground floor.

TENNIS: Public courts are available at Elizabeth Park and at various public high schools. Call the Convention and Visitors Bureau for details (tel. 203/728-6789).

TUBING: For year round information call 203/739-0791, or in summer 203/693-6465.

THE LITCHFIELD HILLS, NORWALK, & THE DANBURY-RIDGEFIELD AREA

DISTANCE IN MILES: Norwalk, 45; Westport, 47; Danbury, 66; Woodbury or Litchfield, 99; Sharon, 111; Winsted, 117
ESTIMATED DRIVING TIMES: 1 hour to Westport, 2¼ hours to Litchfield, 2¾ hours to Winsted

DRIVING: Take the Henry Hudson Parkway north to the Sawmill River Parkway, to Rte. 684 north to Brewster, and then get on I-84 east to Danbury (Exit 7). Take Rte. 7 north to New Milford, and then Rte. 202 east to Litchfield.

For the Salisbury area, take the Taconic to Rte. 44 all the way into Salisbury; or take I-684 to Rte. 22 north to Rte. 44.

For Winsted, take I-84 to the Waterbury exit, and pick up Rte. 8 north.
BUS: Greyhound (tel. 212/635-0800, or toll free 800/528-6055) travels to Litchfield, Norwalk, Fairfield, and Ridgefield.

Bonanza (tel. 212/635-0800 for tickets or 564-8484 for schedules) travels to New Milford/Kent, Southbury, Winsted, Ridgefield, Danbury, and Waterbury.
TRAIN: Closest destinations by train are: Brewster, Danbury, and Waterbury East (via Metro-North's Harlem line), and South Norwalk, Westport, Southport, and Fairfield (via Metro-North's New Haven line). Call 212/532-4900.

Special Events to Plan Your Trip Around

MAY: Dogwood Festival, Greenfield Hill, Fairfield (usually the first and second weekends in May).

Sports car racing at Lime Rock begins on Memorial Day weekend and continues on major holidays throughout the summer (tel. 203/435-2572).

JUNE: Winsted Laurel Festival with parade, water skiing exhibition, and other entertainments. Contact the Mayor's office (tel. 203/379-2713).

JUNE TO MID-SEPTEMBER: Falls Village Music Mountain Chamber concerts with the Manhattan String Quartet and others (tel. 203/496-1222 for information and reservations).

JULY: Round Hill Scottish Games, Norwalk (July 4).

Open House tour, Litchfield (usually the Saturday after July 4).

Yale at Norfolk with the Tokyo String Quartet (tel. 203/436-3690 for information, 203/542-5537 for the box office), at the Ellen Battell Stoeckel Estate.

Sharon Audubon Festival—lectures and nature walks led by top authorities (late July).

AUGUST: SONO Arts Celebration, Washington & South Main Sts., usually the first weekend. Art of Northeast USA at the Silvermine Guild Center for the Arts, 1037 Silvermine Rd., Norwalk (tel. 203/466-5617).

SEPTEMBER: Goshen County Fair (usually Labor Day weekend).

Norwalk Oyster Festival—arts, crafts, boat parade, fireworks, and folk dancing, and of course, oysters (usually the weekend after Labor Day). Contact the Norwalk Seaport Association, 81 Washington St., South Norwalk, CT 06854 (tel. 203/838-9444).

Charles Ives Musical Fair at Danbury (tel. 203/748-7022), featuring all kinds of music that Ives loved to incorporate into his own compositions—hymns, ragtime, songs, and marches performed at various locations around the westside campus of Connecticut State University, plus Main Street events and all kinds of entertainments from jugglers to magicians, and puppeteers (usually the last weekend in September).

Chrysanthemum Festival, Bristol (last week of September, first of October). Contact the Bristol Chamber of Commerce, 55 N. Main St., Bristol, CT 06010 (tel. 203/589-4111).

OCTOBER: Riverton Fair (usually the second weekend in October).

Salisbury Antiques Fair and Fall Festival (usually the second weekend in October). Contact the Salisbury Town Hall (tel. 203/435-9009).

For further information about these events and Connecticut in general, call or write the Travel Office, Department of Economic Development, 210 Washington St., Hartford, CT 06106 (tel. 203/566-3385, or toll free 800/243-1685 from Maine through Virginia, 800/842-7492 in Connecticut).

For specific information about: the Litchfield area, contact the Litchfield Hills Travel Council, P.O. Box 1776, New Preston, CT 06777 (tel. 203/868-2214); Danbury, Bethel, and Ridgefield, contact the Housatonic Valley Travel Commission, 72 West St. (P.O. Box 406), Danbury, CT 06810 (tel. 203/743-0546).

Norwalk, write or call Yankee Heritage District, 35 South Main St., Norwalk, CT 06854 (tel. 203/854-7810).

The New England Vacation Center, 630 Fifth Ave., Concourse Shop 2, New York, NY 10020 (tel. 212/307-5780), also provides information.

A weekend spent exploring Litchfield and the northwest corner of Connecticut, or the so-called Litchfield Hills, will take you along roads bordered by hedgerows dotted with colorful roadside wildflowers, past old russet sagging barns, through forest and field over rolling hills to the classic New England town of Litchfield and the lesser-known but picturesque hamlets of Cornwall, Sharon, and Salisbury, all perfect in their quiet unassuming way, hence their appeal to the recent influx of wealthy residents—Henry Kissinger, Tom Brokaw, Oscar de la Renta, Philip Roth, and Vladimir Horowitz. In Salisbury you're only four miles from the Massachusetts border, 12 miles from the southern Berkshire town of South Egremont, and well within striking distance of Tanglewood and Lenox. The prime reason, though, for visiting this pretty part of Connecticut is to unwind in the countryside, by cycling along back roads, stopping at roadside inns, enjoying historic villages where gracious houses stand under stately old trees surrounded by perfectly manicured green velvet lawns, browsing in the many antique stores, seeking out craft and country fairs, hiking through the forests, boating on the lakes, canoeing and fishing the rivers, and generally refreshing and resuscitating the tarnished urban spirit.

From Salisbury you can travel east to Norfolk, with a detour south to Falls Village, center for canoeing the Housatonic River, or to Lime Rock, the auto racing track. From Norfolk it's only ten miles or so to Riverton, home of the Hitchcock chair factory, and Winsted, site of a spring mountain laurel festival. Another ten miles brings you to Torrington, which is only a stone's throw from Litchfield. The Southbury-Woodbury area also makes for a particularly fine antiquing weekend.

Another weekend can be enjoyed exploring the revitalized Historic District of South Norwalk and afterward driving north to Wilton, Cannons Crossing, and into Ridgefield and the nearby towns of Bethel and Danbury. Each has something to offer the visitor, as you'll discover farther on.

The Litchfield Hills

LITCHFIELD

LITCHFIELD ATTRACTIONS

Graceful tree-lined streets, 18th-century residences, and the much-photographed Congregational church at the east end of the village green make Litchfield a fine example of a late 18th-century New England town. Begin your explorations by picking up a map at the historical society on the corner of South Street and the Green, or at the information booth on the west end of the Green (summers only).

Spend some time at the **Litchfield Historical Society, Library, and Museum,** P.O. Box 385, Litchfield, CT 06759 (tel. 203/567-5862), viewing the permanent display of portraits by Ralph Earl, including one of Mariann Wolcott, whose brother, Oliver, was a town luminary and a signer of the Declaration of Independence. A lady of great determination, if her portrait is anything to go by, she undoubtedly helped mold the bullets cast from the statue of George III that had been dragged from New York to her very own back yard during the Revolution. HOURS: April through November, Tuesday to Saturday from 11 A.M. to 5 P.M. ADMISSION: Free.

Note: Once a year Litchfield's **historic homes** are opened to the public, usually during the second weekend in July. Confirm the dates with the historical society or the Litchfield Hills Travel Council.

From the society, a walk down South Street will bring you to the **Samuel Seymour House** (third house down on the right), now the Episcopal Rectory, but once John C. Calhoun's lodging place while he attended **Tapping Reeve's Law School** (tel. 203/567-5862), located in the two buildings next door.

Tapping Reeve was a graduate of Princeton, who moved to Litchfield in 1773, bringing his frail wife, Sally, sister of Aaron Burr, who became Reeve's first law student. On the tour of the house you can see the parlor that Reeve used initially as a classroom and several rooms filled with the usual period antiques. What is most interesting is the wonderfully detailed inventory of his 1824 estate, which lists, among other things, "60 pounds of butter (not good) @ 10¢—$6; 160 pounds of ham and shoulders @ 6¢ a pound—$9.60," and "dwelling house and homestead . . . $3,600."

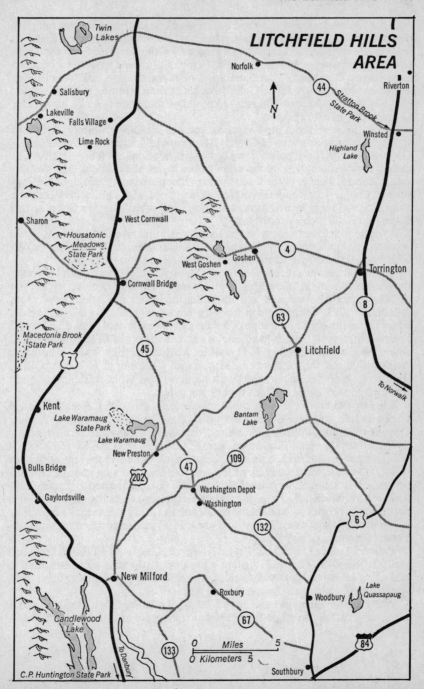

LITCHFIELD HILLS
AREA

N

Twin Lakes

Salisbury

Lakeville
Falls Village

Lime Rock

Sharon

Housatonic Meadows State Park

West Cornwall

West Goshen Goshen

Cornwall Bridge

Macedonia Brook State Park

7

45

Kent

Lake Waramaug State Park

Lake Waramaug

New Preston

202

Bulls Bridge

47

109

Gaylordsville

Washington Depot
Washington

132

New Milford

Roxbury

67

Candlewood Lake

133

C.P. Huntington State Park

To Danbury

Norfolk

44

Stratton Brook State Park

Riverton

Winsted

Highland Lake

4

Torrington

8

63

Litchfield

To Norwalk

Bantam Lake

6

Woodbury

Lake Quassapaug

84

Southbury

Miles
0   5
Kilometers
0   5

In the law school building next door, to which he later moved, you can view portraits of the many famous men who emerged from this first law school, including two vice-presidents, Aaron Burr and John C. Calhoun; three Supreme Court justices; six cabinet members; the artist George Catlin; and well over a hundred congressmen. The school's curriculum and rules and the personal lives of Judge Reeve and his partner, Judge Gould, also make for interesting reading. HOURS: Mid-May to mid-October, Thursday to Monday from noon to 4 P.M. ADMISSION: $1 for adults, free for children.

Across the street from the law school you can see **Oliver Wolcott's house,** to which the equestrian statue of George III was dragged all the way from Bowling Green after it had been pulled down by New York's Sons of Liberty. Here it was melted down into bullets by the redoubtable ladies of Litchfield. Mr. Wolcott was, of course, a signer of the Declaration of Independence, member of the Continental Congress, and governor of Connecticut from 1796. During his lifetime he entertained George Washington, Lafayette, and Alexander Hamilton at this house that is still in the Wolcott family.

If you continue south to where the road divides and take the right fork, you'll come to another famous son's house, that of **Ethan Allen,** the Revolutionary War hero who captured Fort Ticonderoga with his Green Mountain Boys.

Heading in the other direction up North Street from the Green will bring you to the **home of Benjamin Talmadge** (1775), George Washington's aide, past the site of **Miss Pierce's School,** the first institution of higher education for women, founded in 1792. Young women from the school continued to take their daily walks under the elms to the tune of a flute and flageolet until 1855. Just beyond Prospect Street, on the left-hand side, is also the site of the **Beecher homestead,** where Henry Ward Beecher and his sister, Harriet Beecher Stowe, were born. Ahead of you, in the middle of the fork, stands the house of Alexander Catlin, uncle to the more famous George, and a member of the Wolcott, Talmadge group that formed the Litchfield China trading company.

You can also browse through the shops clustered along West Street facing the Green and along **Cobble Court** at South and East Streets behind Crutch & MacDonald's pharmacy. Within a few miles of the village are several interesting spots.

The **White Memorial Foundation,** west of Litchfield on Rte. 202 (tel. 203/567-0857), established in 1913, is a lovely place to stroll, whatever the season. Within this 4,000-acre wildlife sanctuary there are 35 miles of hiking and riding trails, several picnic areas, and a museum (tel. 203/567-0015) dedicated to conservation and ecology, which includes various exhibits of interest to children and adults like a working beehive, fish, and stuffed birds (open Tuesday to Saturday from 9 A.M. to 5 P.M., on Sunday from 11 A.M. to 5 P.M.). Field trips are offered on Saturday. Perfect for cross-country skiing.

Two miles east of Litchfield, **Haight Vineyard,** Chestnut Hill Road, Litchfield (tel. 203/567-4045), off Rte. 118, offers walks through the vineyards, fermentation and aging areas, and the usual tastings. HOURS: Monday to Saturday from 10:30 A.M. to 5 P.M., on Sunday from noon to 5 P.M.

White Flower Farm, just south of Litchfield, is a 200-acre retail and mail-order plant nursery that you might enjoy, either for shopping or just viewing the colorful displays in the eight-acre garden and the greenhouse which is especially beautiful in July when the begonias bloom.

Lourdes Shrine, off Rte. 118, has a grotto and is a quiet place for contemplation.

LITCHFIELD LODGING AND DINING

Litchfield itself has no truly special places to stay, except for the **Tollgate Hill Inn,** P.O. Box 39, Litchfield, CT 06759 (tel. 203/567-4545), which is actually three miles north of the village Green. Innkeeper Fritz Zivic and his wife, Anne, have meticulously restored this fine 225-year-old colonial, retaining those small details —like the original iron latches and hinges, and the salmon milk-paint in the bar —that give a place a special feel.

They have furnished their ten guest rooms (two with TV) with locally made reproductions of antique cherry candlestands, Shaker tables, quilt stands, and a butler's bar, and added extra-special elements like goose-down comforters and choice Hinson wallpapers. The two front rooms have fireplaces and four-poster canopy beds. There's also one large room that has cable TV, a tape deck, fireplace, and a library bar/fridge tucked away in an old schoolhouse on the property, and another two-room suite available with TV and a VHS. Each room is different, and is known by its predominating color: peach, red, green, brown, lavender, and blue. Overnight guests can enjoy breakfast—freshly squeezed fruit juice, croissants, banana or blueberry bread with sweet butter—in their rooms, served on fine china arranged on a wicker tray.

The dining rooms consist of a small formal room with an arched corner cupboard and Oriental carpet, a low-ceilinged tavern room, and a very large "Ballroom" overlooked by a real fiddlers loft. Each will have a welcoming fire in winter. The seasonal menus offer dishes that are primarily American with a touch of European—shellfish pie (shrimp, scallops, lobster, and crab in a cream sauce), fresh fish, roast beef, thick veal chop, game dishes, and always a pasta of the day, for prices ranging from $14 to $19. Lunch features several interesting sandwiches —cottage cheese and watercress, and a béarnaise burger.

RATES: $90 to $130. LUNCH: Noon to 3 P.M. daily. DINNER: 5:30 to 9:30 P.M. weekdays, until 10:30 P.M. on weekends. BRUNCH: Saturday and Sunday from noon to 3 P.M. Closed Tuesday November through May. Closed also the first two weeks of March.

Litchfield Dining

The best dining is to be found at the Tollgate Hill Inn and the restaurants around Lake Waramaug, most notably the Hopkins and Boulders Inns which follow.

In Litchfield itself, **Anthony's Place and Tavern on the Green,** West Street (tel. 203/567-5016), is an appealing luncheon spot where you can enjoy a good-sized fresh salad, a large dish of eggplant parmigiana, and a glass of wine for under $7 in a simple country-style dining room. Sandwiches, burgers, salads, and Italian specialties are also available. Dinner prices range from $7 to $13.

LUNCH: 11:30 A.M. to 4:30 P.M. daily. DINNER: 5 to 10 P.M. daily.

Right opposite the Green, the **Litchfield Food Company,** West Street (tel. 203/ 567-0448), prepares spectacular box lunches and picnics. The hamper might include smoked salmon with capers, chicken breast stuffed with cheese and herbs, artichoke hearts in vinaigrette, a baguette, chocolate mousse balls rolled in hazelnuts, fresh seasonal fruit, and catawba sparkling grape juice. A box lunch for one costs $8.50. Picnics for two can be purchased for $24, $26, or $28. You can also buy sandwiches, soups, and salads.

HOURS: Monday to Saturday from 9:30 A.M. to 5:30 P.M.

AREA LODGING AND DINING

At Nearby Lake Waramaug

Choice accommodations lie about 15 minutes' drive west of Litchfield around Lake Waramaug, a summer resort area originally settled in the 1890s. Each one of the four accommodations here will appeal to a different type of personality.

The largest is a mini-resort-like property, the **Inn at Lake Waramaug,** New Preston, CT 06777 (tel. 203/868-0563, or toll free 800/LAKE INN), run by the delightful and extremely hospitable John and Karen Koiter. To describe it as a resort probably gives the wrong impression, for it has more of the atmosphere of an old country inn. Set on a hill overlooking the lake, with acres of spacious lawns shaded by grand sugar maples, the core of the main building was built as a colonial home around 1795, and it's here that people gather round the fire in the parlor for long conversations that go on into the night, or curl up privately with one of the many books available to guests. In the large dining room, with a lovely porch for outside morning or evening dining, fires blaze at night or on chilly mornings. The resort label stems from the many facilities available—indoor swimming pool, table tennis, billiard and game room, clay tennis court, rental bicycles, and a full complement of lakeside facilities, including rental canoes and sailboats, free rowboats, and a showboat steamer that plies the lake afternoons during the summer. Winter activities include ice skating on the lake, cross-country skiing, horsedrawn sleigh rides, sledding, and tobogganing.

Breakfast is served inside or out on the terrace with a view of the lake and the lovely trees and shrubs on the property. Cereal, fresh fruits of all sorts, and breads are spread out, while main dishes are all cooked to order. Lunch is taken lakeside (in the summer) if you wish, and dinner is served in the dining room with a special candlelight buffet on Saturday. Filet mignon, lobster, fish, and veal are the specialties, priced from $11 to $17.25.

There are five rooms in the original inn, each with private bath and queen-size canopy beds (no telephones). The other 18 accommodations are in motel-style buildings, where rooms are tastefully decorated, several featuring queen-size canopy beds and working fireplaces. Rooms 30 through 35 offer prime views of the lake. All are air-conditioned.

RATES (including breakfast and dinner): $86 per person, double occupancy, for rooms in the main inn, $96 for rooms with canopy bed and fireplace, $86 for rooms with picture windows onto lake; a standard room is $76. *Note:* On holiday weekends a three-night minimum stay is required; two-night minimum on weekends at other times. LUNCH: From 11:30 A.M. DINNER: 5:30 to 8:30 P.M.

The **Boulders Inn,** Rte. 45, New Preston, CT 06777 (tel. 203/868-7918), is smaller and seems quieter, but also offers a private beach for swimming, canoes, Sunfish, bicycles, and a tennis court. As the name suggests, the main 1895 building is of fieldstone and shingles and shelters five pleasant Victorian rooms, all with private bath, several with sunny window seats overlooking the lake, and all furnished with marble-top tables, down comforters, and oak chests. The comfortable living room furnished with sofas, wing chairs, and well-stocked bookcases gives lake views. Nine contemporary cottages, each with a porch, fireplace, and picture window facing the lake, are also available, nicely tucked away on the wooded hillside for ample privacy.

The inn's stone-walled dining room has a good reputation for serving such delights as boned duck breast maçonnaise (served with a red wine and shallot sauce) or chicken paprikash, seasoned and served with sour cream sauce flavored with onion, green pepper, and sherry, and accented with sweet paprika. A full breakfast of eggs, pancakes, or omelets is served, and also afternoon tea. From Memorial Day to Labor Day three meals are served daily; September and October, dinner is served five nights only, and a Sunday brunch is also served. Thereafter meals are served less frequently, only three or four nights a week.

Guests must take breakfast and dinner during the summer, and whenever meals are being served MAP rates apply. LUNCH: Noon to 2 P.M. daily in summer. DINNER: 6 to 8:30 P.M. daily in summer. RATES (including breakfast and dinner, double occupancy): $54 per person during the summer and also on winter weekends. In winter MAP rates are reduced on Wednesday and Thursday to $44 per person; Sunday to Tuesday in winter the dining room is closed and then room-only rates are $48 in the inn, $56 in the cottages. Open year round.

The **Hopkins Inn,** New Preston, CT 06777 (tel. 203/868-7295), is known primarily for serving the best food in the area. When you dine here under the spreading chestnut tree, on a terrace overlooking the lake, watching the sun go down and the sky fill with stars, waited upon by young women dressed in colorful dirndls, you will swear you're dining by the Danube. The Swiss and many Austrian favorites on the continental menu will only help to confirm the impression —backhendl with lingonberries, wienerschnitzel, and some fantastic Austrian desserts. Figure $25 per person for dinner.

The lemon-yellow house, built in 1847 as a summer home, possesses nine rooms, available April through November. None contains a TV or telephone; the furnishings are adequate in their homey old-fashioned way. If you're lucky, you'll be given a room with a brass bed or an Eastlake-style sofa.

The back tavern room is remarkable for its folk-painted bar and huge, rough-hewn beams.

RATES: $49 per night double with private bath and lake view, $44 double with private bath only, $42 with lake view and shared bath. An apartment also rents for $60.

The dining room is open April to December. BREAKFAST: 8:30 to 9:30 A.M. daily, May to October. LUNCH: Tuesday to Saturday from noon to 2 P.M., May to October. Mid-afternoon snacks Tuesday to Saturday, June through August. DIN-

NER: Tuesday to Thursday from 6 to 9 P.M., until 10 P.M. on Friday, on Saturday from 5:30 to 10 P.M., on Sunday from 12:30 to 8:30 P.M. Only dinner is served in April, November, and December. Make sure you have dining reservations, especially on Friday and Saturday.

Note: The **Hopkins Winery** (tel. 203/868-7954) is diagonally across from the inn, and worth a browse and tasting. Open weekends year round from 11 A.M. to 5 P.M.; May 1 to January 1, daily from 11 A.M. to 5 P.M.

The Birches Inn, West Shore Road, New Preston, CT 06777 (tel. 203/868-0229). On the more remote, west side of the lake, owners Heinz and Christa Holl have created a distinctly Austrian atmosphere, serving such specialties as sauerbraten, wienerschnitzel, and fresh Austrian pastries including an extra-special apfelstrudel. A wood fire in the stone fireplace warms the congenial piano bar in winter.

Accommodations consist of ten plain, paneled, rather old-fashioned rooms, all but one offering a view of the lake, plus a cottage—literally on the water—with a balcony and three guest rooms with private bath, that is probably the nicest accommodation. Canoes, rowboats, and bicycles are available for rent. On weekends meals are obligatory.

RATES (including breakfast and dinner): $65 per person double, $70 in the cottage, $60 and $70 respectively for room only during the week without meals. The inn is closed Tuesday.

New Preston Dining

Le Bon Coin, Rte. 202, New Preston (tel. 203/868-7763), is a typical French restaurant located in a small house in quite an isolated spot. The decor is simple —country paneling, lace curtains, and paintings of typical French scenes—but the food is good and there's always a variety of enticing specials.

Start with smoked salmon and caviar or venison pâté. Choose from among steak au poivre, filet of sea bass with almonds and grapes, paillarde of beef, veal with lemon sauce, halibut béarnaise, duck bigarade, or other classic Gallic-inspired dishes. Crêpes suzette or crème caramel make a perfect conclusion to the meal. Prices run from $12 to $19.

LUNCH: Monday and Thursday to Saturday from noon to 2 P.M. DINNER: Monday and Wednesday to Friday from 6 to 9 P.M., on Saturday to 10 P.M., on Sunday from 5 to 9 P.M.

NORTH TO SALISBURY—KENT, CORNWALL BRIDGE, LAKEVILLE, AND SALISBURY

AREA ATTRACTIONS

From Lake Waramaug take Rte. 45 north to Rte. 7. To go to the center of Kent, take Rte. 7 south, passing **Kent Falls State Park,** well-known for its 200-foot water cascade that is especially lovely in spring, and the **Sloane Stanley Museum** (tel. 203/927-3849), which has an extensive collection of early American tools all amassed by the late artist and writer Eric Sloane to commemorate "the early American's ingenuity, craftsmanship and reverence for wood." Lathes, chisels, scythes, and axes are all displayed to emphasize their many and versatile uses. Sloane's cluttered studio has also been faithfully re-created and some of his paintings are also on view in a special gallery.

HOURS: Late-May to October 31, Wednesday to Sunday from 10 A.M. to 4:30 P.M. ADMISSION: $1.50.

In Kent Center there are many fine antique shops, boutiques, and several art galleries. For example, **Kent Antiques Center** is located in Kent Station Square on Main Street (tel. 203/927-3313). **Paris–New York–Kent Gallery,** also in Kent Station Square (tel. 203/927-3357), has a solid reputation as a fine art gallery.

If you like, you can continue south on Rte. 7 to Bull's Bridge, stopping en route at the **Bull's Bridge Glass Works and Gallery** (tel. 203/927-3448), located in three barns. You'll also pass **Bull's Bridge,** which dates back to the Revolution and is one of two covered bridges in the state open to automobile traffic.

Head back to Kent and follow Rte. 7 north for about ten miles, passing **Cornwall Bridge Pottery** (tel. 203/672-6545), renowned for stoneware, and the village of Cornwall Bridge to the junction of Rte. 128 in West Cornwall. West Cornwall is well known for its fine craftsmen, but best known for its **covered bridge,** which was built in 1837 of native oak. The covered bridge is located on Rte. 128 (off Rte. 7 north, five miles north of Cornwall Bridge). West Cornwall has two excellent craft stores worth browsing: **Cornwall Bridge Pottery Store** (tel. 203/672-6545), and **Ian Ingersoll Cabinetmakers** (tel. 203/672-6334), which specializes in reproduction furniture in the Shaker tradition.

From West Cornwall, return south on Rte. 7 to Cornwall Bridge and take Rte. 4 to Rte. 41 into Sharon. In this charming old town noted for its large, gracious homes, stop in at **Andres,** where flowers, plants, natural foods, spices, and take-out sandwiches are all sold. There's always an eye-catching display of flowers outside.

From Sharon, pick up Rte. 41 north through Lakeville, home of **Hotchkiss School,** to Salisbury. This picturesque village is the site of a busy flea market in late September and also of a large antiques fair in the fall when the foliage is at its peak.

LODGING AND DINING IN KENT

Flanders Arms, Kent, CT 06757 (tel. 203/927-3040), is a beautiful, large, Federal-style, gray-clapboard home that was an inn in the '20s and '30s. Mark de Vos now operates this large rambling home, which comfortably housed his children until recently, as a bed-and-breakfast.

There are four rooms—two with private baths, two sharing—all tastefully decorated in Laura Ashley chintz, country style. Pine hutches, rockers, or similar usually stand on wide board floors against strong colors like forest green, terracotta, or Wedgwood blue. Old iron latches, embroidery anglaise on the beds, and heavy wooden shutters add a definite period feel. A continental breakfast is served in a bright room on marble-top tables. Other rooms are not open to guests. The gardens, trees, and lawn are extensive.

RATES: $60 to $70.

Owner Dolph Traymon's piano artistry alone makes the **Fife 'n' Drum,** Rte. 7, Kent (tel. 203/927-3509), worth a trip. Dolph, a Juilliard graduate who used to play for Peggy Lee and Frank Sinatra, plays here nightly. Some would say the very popular tap room is also worth a trip. The food rates too.

A mixture of barn siding, bricks, and country scenes, the dining room is actually quite formal and a few of the dishes are flambéed tableside. Duckling with a brandied sauce, steak au poivre, and chateaubriand are classic favorites, along with veal and fish dishes. The roast chicken with herbs is simple but tasty; fettuccine Alfredo and other pastas are available. Prices run $11 to $18.

Luncheon changes daily. Brunch also changes weekly, and along with the eggs Benedict will also offer roast leg of lamb, chicken au poivre, or similar.

LUNCH: Monday to Saturday from 11:30 A.M. to 3 P.M. DINNER: Monday to Thursday from 5 to 9:30 P.M., on Friday and Saturday until 10 P.M., and on Sunday from 3 to 9 P.M. BRUNCH: Sunday from 11:30 A.M. to 3 P.M.

For nine years Ernie and Penny Schnitzler have been welcoming folks to their country restaurant, the **Milk Pail,** Rte. 7, Kent (tel. 203/927-3136). Beamed ceiling, a few farm implements, a cozy fireside in winter, and a summer patio with a clear view across cow-dotted fields to Mount Algo make for pleasant dining anytime of year. The menu changes daily but certain items will probably appear: chicken Cordon Bleu, crab-stuffed shrimp or sole, mustard chicken, filet mignon, all priced from $10.25 to $16.50, including soup or salad, baked potato or curried rice, and vegetable. Sunday brunch features fish, beef, and chicken, as well as egg dishes and sandwiches. A popular pianist entertains on Friday and Saturday.

LUNCH: Tuesday to Saturday from 11:30 A.M. to 2:30 P.M., on Sunday from 3 to 4 P.M. DINNER: Tuesday to Saturday from 5 to 9:30 P.M., on Sunday from 4 to 8 P.M. BRUNCH: Sunday from noon to 3 P.M.

DINING IN BULL'S BRIDGE AND GAYLORDSVILLE

Named after Jacob and Mary Bull, who established the first inn here during the American Revolution, **Bull's Bridge Inn,** on Rte. 7 between Kent and Bull's Bridge (tel. 203/927-3263), is a local favorite. Folks gather at the bar separating the two simple dining rooms. There's a small patio with an awning for summer dining. The menu offers typical continental/American dishes like pan-fried trout with lemon butter, beef brochette, filet mignon, veal saltimbocca Victor with prosciutto and mozzarella sautéed with mushrooms, and duckling bigarade. Prices range from $10 to $13. Bull's Bridge is also known locally for its Sunday brunch.

LUNCH: Tuesday to Saturday from 11:30 A.M. to 2 P.M. DINNER: Tuesday to Saturday from 6 to 9 P.M., on Friday and Saturday to 10 P.M., and on Sunday from 5 to 9 P.M. BRUNCH: Sunday from noon to 3 P.M.

Fox & Fox, Rte. 7, Gaylordsville (tel. 203/354-6025), is a pretty restaurant located in a converted barn with a river view. Light oak, pale-pink tablecloths, and candlelight make the room positively glow at night. Summer daytime dining is pleasant too, on a patio decorated with flowers and a colored awning, overlooking the Housatonic. Favorite dishes include Cajun-style barbecued shrimp; sweetbreads sautéed with mushrooms, green olives, and cream; Indian lamb steak, marinated in a curry and served with chutney; red wine vinegar chicken; and saltimbocca à la romano. Luscious desserts range from chocolate éclairs, pecan pie, and Linzer torte to a refreshing frozen lemon soufflé.

LUNCH: Monday to Friday from noon to 2:30 P.M. DINNER: Monday from 6 to 9 P.M., on Friday and Saturday to 10 P.M., and on Sunday from 5 to 8 P.M. Closed Tuesday, Wednesday, and Thursday.

LODGING AND DINING IN CORNWALL BRIDGE AND WEST CORNWALL

The **Cornwall Inn,** Rte. 7, Cornwall Bridge (tel. 203/672-6884), is well known to the locals for its excellent food. A roadside hostelry, it offers a really warm, homey welcome in two rooms. The cooking is plain and fine—steak, duckling, prime rib, stuffed sole and shrimp, fettuccine with clam sauce, from $10.

By the time this book is published the inn will also have five guest rooms, which the owner assured me would be very attractive with wide plank floors and country antique furnishings. You may want to check for yourself.

LUNCH: Wednesday to Saturday from 11:30 A.M. to 3 P.M. DINNER: 5:30 to 9 P.M. Tuesday to Saturday, noon to 8 P.M. on Sunday. BRUNCH: Sunday from 11:30 A.M. to 3 P.M.

Fresh Fields, in West Cornwall (tel. 203/672-6601), has a serene location overlooking a fast-flowing brook. In summer the deck is the preferred dining area. Other times, diners sit on burgundy or dusty-pink banquettes at butcher-block tables in a light, modern ambience. The menu changes daily but here are some items that might be available: grilled tuna with lime and cilantro marinade, grilled loin of pork with mustard barbecue sauce, barbecued roast duck with a red wine and currant sauce, New York strip steak with ancho chili butter and jalapeño. Most dishes are cooked on the mesquite grill. Prices range from $10 to $15. Appetizers might include gefilte fish with fresh horseradish, a Créole gumbo, crab shrimp, ham and andouille sausage, and chilled asparagus with lemon soy vinaigrette. Desserts change frequently too, but are extravagant, like the mile-high ice cream pie consisting of three layers of ice cream on a chocolate cookie crust topped with meringue and hot fudge. Lemon and orange tart, white-chocolate mousse with raspberry sauce, or fresh strawberry shortcake are other tempting possibilities. Lunch offers soups, salads, sandwiches, and hot dishes. Upstairs there's a bar with ficus and a sky-like mural.

A pretty pricey brunch is served on Sunday which includes an appetizer sampler (smoked salmon and trout pâté, cheese, and fruit), fresh orange juice, salad, and a variety of main courses. Among the possible choices are cheese blintzes, eggs scrambled with vegetables and venison sausage, grilled swordfish with cilantro butter, barbecued roast duck, and more. A dessert like apple and pear crisp will close the filling meal. Prices run $10 to $22, depending on the main-course choice.

LUNCH: 11:30 A.M. to 2:30 P.M. daily in July and August, Wednesday to Sunday at other times. DINNER: 5:30 to 9 P.M. daily in July and August (Wednesday to Sunday otherwise), on Friday and Saturday until 10 P.M., on Sunday from 5 to 9 P.M. BRUNCH: Sunday from noon to 2:30 P.M.

LODGING AND DINING ACROSS THE BORDER IN DOVER PLAINS, N.Y.

The **Old Drovers Inn,** on East Duncan Road, three miles south of Dover Plains off Rte. 22 (tel. 914/832-9311), is loaded with atmosphere. The stairs leading to the three rooms creak, and so do the floors. Ceilings are low. Upstairs, the library offers guests three walls of shelved books for pleasure reading in the comfy chairs placed in front of the wood-molded fireplace. Two other sitting rooms are also available, both with fireplaces—one more formally furnished in Empire style with a striking bull's-eye mirror. The three guest rooms are variously furnished. One has a sleigh bed; another contains cannonball beds, wing chairs for fireside dozing, candlestand tables, and blue-green wainscoting. The suite has two beds, a fireplace, coved ceiling, desk, wing chairs, and an antique shaving mirror, among its comfortable surroundings.

The bar and dining room has extremely low-beamed ceilings; pewter and china adorn the back room with its attractive old booths; copper pans, scoops, and strainers grace the brick fireplace. Tables are set with candles and golden cloths. The bill of fare is written on a blackboard, and although it changes daily it's likely to offer the following for dinner: browned turkey hash with mustard sauce, broiled double-cut rack of lamb chops, salmon filet sautéed with a basil sauce, veal chop with morrels. Appetizers might include grilled goat cheese wrapped in grape leaves, vegetable terrine with tomato vinaigrette, chicken-and-corn or cheddar cheese soup, an Old Drovers specialty. Prices run $17 to $26.50. Luncheon fare is similar but priced from $11.75 to $18.75. The outdoor dining patio is lovely in summer.

RATES: $115 to $130 double. LUNCH: Monday, Thursday, and Friday from noon to 2:30 P.M. DINNER: Monday, by reservation only (last booking at 7 P.M.); on Thursday from 5:30 to 8:30 P.M., on Friday until 9:30 P.M., on Saturday from noon to 9 P.M., and on Sunday from 1 to 8:30 P.M.; closed Tuesday and Wednesday.

A VERY SPECIAL NEW YORK RETREAT IN AMENIA

For a truly inspirational weekend retreat, **Troutbeck,** Leedsville Road, Amenia, NY 12501 (tel. 914/373-9681, 373-8580, 373-8581, or 373-9772), is exceptional. Acres of flower- and shrub-filled gardens spread around this lovely ivy-covered Tudoresque country house, which once belonged to Myron B. Benton, a poet-naturalist friend of John Burroughs, Emerson, and Thoreau, and was also a gathering place for the literati and liberals in the 1920s. A little brook courses through the gardens (you'll cross a small humpbacked stone bridge to reach the slate-roofed portico) and along its banks daffodils, crimson, gold, and purple tulips, and blue grape hyacinth blossom in spring. Lilacs and apple blossom add their fragrant scent and colors. Wooden seats dot the lawns—ideal perches for quiet contemplation. Beyond the gardens are over 400 wooded acres.

During the week the property is used for conferences, but on weekends it's open to anyone. Thirty-one accommodations are in the main house or in nearby buildings.

The house is filled with gorgeous authentic antiques. The entrance-parlor floors are covered with Oriental runners and rugs; Chinese porcelain lamps harmonize with a white porcelain elephant, while burgundy upholstered French chairs, Queen Anne chairs, and a carved sideboard all blend perfectly together. Beamed ceilings, leaded windows, and fresh-flower bouquets underline the very English atmosphere. For quiet conversation there's a luxuriously comfortable sitting room with grand piano and a small bar with a handsome fireplace.

Of the 30 rooms, 26 have private bath. All have queen-size beds with electric blankets and are decorated differently with antique reproductions. Some are furnished in Early American; in the Troutbeck rooms the style is European. Some have fireplaces, canopy beds, and porches. Twelve are in the main house, 18 in the farmhouse.

The dining room overlooks the pond. The menu changes weekly but a Saturday menu might begin with your choice of broccoli-apple soup, mussels steamed in tomatoes, wine, olives, garlic, and herbs, or sautéed shitaake mushrooms with ginger and watercress, followed by a choice of salad and entree. The entrees might consist of six or so dishes—sautéed salmon with vermouth and shrimp sauce, calves' liver with sherry vinegar and caramelized onions, boneless chicken breast with couscous and garlic sauce, shell steak with pinot noir and herbs, or leg of lamb marinated in baked yogurt and coriander and served with Indian condiments. Among the desserts there might be a Sachertorte, pear kuchen, or banana rum torte. There's an open bar and wine is served during meals.

For your pleasure there are also tennis courts, indoor and outdoor pools, 13,000 books, and also videotapes.

RATES: For a weekend, from Friday at 5 P.M. through Sunday at 2 P.M., including all meals and all spirits, you'll pay $500 to $725 *per couple.* For one night only the charge is $250 to $400 per couple, including three meals.

LAKEVILLE LODGING AND DINING

Although the exterior of the **Interlaken Inn,** Rte. 112, Lakeville, CT 06039 (tel. 203/435-9878), seems to scream "modern convention complex," the rooms will win you over with their plush comforts, especially those eight duplex town-house suites at the back of the property, which have a full kitchen, living room with fireplace, a sleeping loft containing two double beds, two bathrooms, and a deck shaded by pines and other trees for privacy. Sunnyside's ten old-world rooms have brass beds and antiques, while the 55 deluxe rooms have a pleasant contemporary look. An additional six rooms are located in a fine old English Tudor-style house. These are furnished with Queen Anne reproductions.

The grounds are beautifully kept. You can lounge by the outdoor heated pool or on the shore of Lake Wononscopumic, where canoes, paddle boats, and rowboats are available. Two tennis courts, pitch-and-putt course, game room, and sauna complete the facilities. The Vineyard serves food in a contemporary atmosphere—fresh seafood, rack of lamb, veal with morels, medallions of beef sautéed with a port and ginger sauce, and salmon filet sautéed with saffron, white wine, and cucumbers. Terrines, pâtés, and soups are among the appetizers. And for dessert, save room for chocolate decadence, a rich chocolate mousse cake layered with raspberry confit and chocolate cream and served with a raspberry sauce, or the laken torte—a walnut and maple cake soaked in rum and served with crème Chantilly. Entree prices range from $10 to $17. The Circuit Lounge, overlooking the pool and cocktail lounge, doubles as a luncheon spot. It's filled with "auto art," for sale to Lime Rock visitors. Tuesday to Saturday night bands entertain here; at Sunday brunch there's usually a folk singer or two, and at dinner a soft guitarist-vocalist.

There's also a deck for summer cocktails, lunch, Saturday dinner, and Sunday brunch. Brunch is buffet style, offering prime rib, ham, smoked salmon, salads, canapés, and much more, for $13 per person.

RATES: Deluxe rooms and Sunnyside, $98 double on weekends, $84 weekdays; town-house suites, $175 double. Rates are reduced in winter. Located west of Rte. 41 on Rte. 112. BREAKFAST: 8 to 10:30 A.M. daily. LUNCH: Noon to 2:30 P.M. daily. DINNER: Monday to Thursday from 6 to 9 P.M., until 10 P.M. on Friday and Saturday, and on Sunday from 4 to 9 P.M. BRUNCH: Sunday from 11:30 A.M. to 2:30 P.M.

Yesterday's Yankee, Lakeville, CT 06068 (tel. 203/435-9539), displays much of Dick Alexander's handiwork—the settle table and the kitchen corner cupboard, for example. Dick restores and makes furniture, and his workshop is out back in the big old barn, where you can watch him at work.

The house, built in 1744, retains the keeping room with the original hearth with brick oven, a kettle hanging there even today. Guests can enjoy the familiar comforts of the parlor, reading or relaxing on the Windsor rocker and wing chairs in front of the fireplace. There are plenty of books to read.

Three rooms are available. Their doors are low and still possess the old iron latches. The sloping eaves make the rooms interesting. They are pleasantly furnished with antique-style towel racks, candlestand tables, rockers, and fluffy comforters and lace anglaise pillows on the beds. All share a bathroom. The Alexanders' request no smoking in the rooms.

In the beamed sunlit kitchen a breakfast of juice and fruit compote, followed by shirred eggs or omelets or Grand Marnier french toast, is prepared. The outside deck set with potted plants is pleasant.

RATES: $55 to $60.

Lakeville Dining

Chez Riette at Miner's Cottage, Rtes. 44 and 41, Lakeville (tel. 203/435-2889). Don't let the location in front of a motel, albeit an attractively landscaped one, deter you from trying this excellent restaurant, where ex-New Yorkers Tony and Riette Molendijk serve some top-notch cuisine created by their son, Albert. A typical luncheon menu might offer a classic poulet grand-mère with onions, mushrooms, and bacon; an unusual dish of artichoke hearts stuffed with crabmeat and served with a light curry sauce; or more commonly a variety of croissants stuffed with different fillings. At dinner there are always three or four specialties to follow the venison pâté with a Cumberland sauce or the smoked trout with horseradish sauce. The poached salmon with mushroom tarragon sauce or the rack of lamb choron served with a smooth tomato hollandaise are prime choices. In addition to the printed menu there are also daily specials like roast duckling with Cumberland sauce, red snapper with lemon butter, or twin tournedos of beef flamed in bourbon. Some special appetizers are also offered: for example, chicken liver mousse with orange sauce or a seafood pâté. Prices run $14 to $18.

The brunch menu gives you a choice of champagne, mimosa, or juice, followed by a selection of about eight entrees—omelets (cheese and herb; spinach, tomato, and mushroom; garlic sausage and mushroom; etc.), egg dishes, chicken crêpes, or artichokes with crabmeat in a light curry sauce. The entree prices run $5.50 to $9.50.

Dine either in the 1844 clapboard cottage's small, pretty dining room with flattering pink tablecloths or under the red-and-white-striped awning in summer.

LUNCH: Wednesday to Saturday from noon to 2:30 P.M. DINNER: Wednesday and Thursday from 6 to 9 P.M., on Friday and Saturday until 10 P.M., on Sunday from 5 to 8 P.M. BRUNCH: Sunday from noon to 3 P.M. Closed Monday and Tuesday.

The **Holley Place Restaurant,** Holley Street (tel. 203/435-2727), is located in an 1866 building, once the home of the oldest pocketknife factory in the United States (founded in 1844).

The owner's interest in history is also expressed by the remarkable collection of local historic photographs that hang in the large high-ceilinged beamed tavern room, furnished with Windsor chairs and slate-top tables. Among them is one showing a group mourning President McKinley's assassination, another precisely what the bitter blizzard of 1888 was like. The smaller, more formal restaurant, lit by a skylight, is decorated in soft peach and blue hues; the china is Villeroy & Boch. The food, served by aproned waitresses, is the same in both rooms, and tends to light cuisine: grilled calves' liver, fresh fish, sautéed chicken. Prices range from $10 to $17. Hamburgers and such items as beef salad with horseradish and poached bass with cucumber salad make up the lunch menu.

DINNER: Monday, Wednesday, and Thursday from 6 to 9 P.M., on Friday and Saturday until 10 P.M., on Sunday from 4 to 8 P.M. BRUNCH: Sunday from 11:30 A.M. to 2 P.M. Closed Tuesday.

The **Woodland Restaurant,** Rte. 41 (tel. 203/435-0578), is a light and airy plant-filled restaurant. Here, in one of the six large booths you can dine at lunchtime on a Woodlands specialty of a muffin with mushrooms, onions, and tomatoes, and more substantially at dinner on such items as breast of chicken sesame, stuffed filet of sole, scampi, sirloin, and daily specials. Most dishes range from $8 to $13.

LUNCH: Tuesday to Saturday from 11:30 A.M. to 2:30 P.M. DINNER: Tuesday to Thursday from 5:30 to 9 P.M., on Friday and Saturday to 10 P.M., and on Sunday to 8:30 P.M. BRUNCH: Sunday from noon to 3 P.M. Closed Monday and also for two weeks in February.

SALISBURY LODGING AND DINING

The **Ragamont Inn,** Main Street, Salisbury, CT 06068 (tel. 203/435-2372), has offered solace and sustenance to the passing traveler for the last 180 years, and today people are still sitting out happily dining under the striped green-and-white awning shielded from the main street by a hedge, or else cozily ensconced in the dining room with wide plank floors warmed by a blazing fire.

All 12 rooms in the inn are different and very fairly priced—a suite with a fireplace and low-beamed ceiling renting for only $72. Room 6 is particularly attractive, thanks to the cast-iron stove, pine floor, shield-back chairs, and old desk that give it character.

The dining room is known for its many Swiss-inspired dishes of chef-owner Rolf Schenkel—sauerbraten, wienerschnitzel, jaegerschnitzel (with white wine and mushrooms), along with fine fresh scrod, salmon, swordfish, and other seafood. Entrees range from $11 to $17. The Linzer torte and peach custard pie are dessert favorites, while at brunch there are raclette and beef burgundy to add some interest to the usual eggs Benedict and waffles menu (most dishes around $8).

RATES: $54 to $72, May 1 to November 1. LUNCH: Tuesday to Sunday from noon to 2 P.M. DINNER: Tuesday to Thursday and Sunday from 6 to 9 P.M., on Friday and Saturday to 10 P.M. BRUNCH: Sunday from 11:30 A.M. to 2 P.M. Closed Monday.

Under Mountain Inn, Rte. 41, Salisbury, CT 06068 (tel. 203/435-0242), is located five miles out of Salisbury in a secluded 1732 white clapboard farmhouse. Here Peter and Marged Higginson offer seven rooms, all with private bath, providing a serene home away from home. The downstairs parlors are exceedingly comfortable. Among the early American furnishings you'll find an antique Welsh cupboard that Marged's grandfather made. The guest rooms are also comfortable and will most likely contain a comfortable large bed, a couple of Williamsburg blue wing chairs, and a fine chest-on-chest placed on wide-plank floors. Early American wallpapers add character too.

In the three small, intimate dining rooms with fireplaces a variety of seafood, game (in season), roast goose, and steak-and-kidney pie are served, and for British expatriates, believe it or not, bangers and mash. Marged will also provide a "proper" cup of tea out of a pot with tea cozy. For dessert there's authentic sherry trifle and a selection of home-baked pies. The Union Jack flies outside, *and the Manchester Guardian* is available, along with a number of books about Britain.

RATES: $80 per person, MAP; midweek, room only is available for $98.50. On those days when the restaurant is closed Marged will prepare an early (6 P.M.) prix-fixe dinner for approximately $15 to $19. DINNER: July through October, on Thursday, Sunday, and Monday from 6 to 8:30 P.M., on Friday and Saturday to 9:30 P.M. (closed Tuesday and Wednesday); from November through June the dining room is open to the public only on Friday and Saturday.

At the 200-year-old **White Hart Inn,** On the Green, Salisbury, CT 06068 (tel. 203/435-2511), the tavern with a double fireplace is a popular spot, and a modern-looking bar-lounge has recently been added. The rooms contain white-painted furniture and all the modern conveniences (air conditioning, phone, and TV).

RATES: $58 to $120 double on weekends, $44 to $100 weekdays. LUNCH: Monday to Saturday from noon to 2:30 P.M.; a Sunday buffet is served from noon to 2 P.M. DINNER: Monday to Thursday from 6 to 9 P.M., on Friday and Saturday to 9:30 P.M.; Sunday dinner is a buffet, from 5 to 8 P.M.

Salisbury Dining

The best dining is at the **Ragamont Inn** (see "Salisbury Lodging and Dining," above).

At **La Villa,** in the Marketplace, Academy Street (tel. 203/435-9655), you'll find simple dining on plain cedar tables with blackboard choices ranging from veal francese, shrimp provençale, and chicken tarragon, all under $10. DINNER: 5:30 to 8:30 P.M. weekdays, until 9:30 P.M. on weekends. Dinner is the only meal served.

EAST TO NORFOLK, RIVERTON, AND WINSTED

AREA ATTRACTIONS

From Salisbury, you can take Rte. 44 all the way to Norfolk, which in mid-June and July hosts the **Yale Chamber Music concerts** (tel. 203/542-5537), featuring the Tokyo String Quartet, at the Ellen Battell Stoeckel Estate.

To get a sense of this quintessential New England village take a walk around the **Green** noting the Eldridge Fountain, designed by Stanford White; the tall-steepled Church of Christ (circa 1814), which is next to the White House (home of the Yale Summer School of Music and Art); the Richardsonian-style library (circa 1888); and the Historical Society Museum, which features a small collection of Connecticut clocks and other local historical artifacts.

Norfolk also has some offbeat attractions. For example, pay a visit to **harpsichord maker** Bill Dudash's studio on Maple Avenue (tel. 203/542-5753), purchase some plants at **Hillside Gardens,** Litchfield Road, Norfolk (tel. 203/542-5345), and view the gardens of Mary Ann and Frederick McGourty, who are well known in horticultural circles. The **Horse and Carriage Livery,** (tel. 203/542-6085), is another interesting stop, and fun if you want to sign up for a horse-drawn ride in winter or summer.

Norfolk also has three state parks for hiking and picnicking: **Haystack Mountain** (from Norfolk, follow Rte. 44 west and take Rte. 272 North for one mile to the entrance), **Campbell Falls State Park** (located another six miles along Rte. 272), and **Dennis Hill State Park** (Rte. 272 South). Haystack and Dennis Hill both have stone monuments at their summits affording grand views.

Back on Rte. 44, you can either proceed into Winsted, the self-proclaimed mountain laurel capital, and then double back on Rte. 20 to Riverton, or you can drive directly to Riverton by cutting off on one of the back roads.

Riverton was once called Hitchcocksville after the famous **Hitchcock chairs,** still manufactured in the original factory where Lambert Hitchcock made his first chair (in 1826) on the bank of the Farmington River, down the street from the Old Riverton Inn. The factory store (tel. 203/379-4826) is open Monday to Saturday from 10 A.M. to 5 P.M., on Sunday from noon to 5 P.M.

The **Hitchcock Museum** (tel. 203/379-1003), housed in an old church, displays original furniture stenciled by Hitchcock and his contemporaries. HOURS: June through October 11, Tuesday to Saturday from 11 A.M. to 4 P.M. and on Sunday from 1 to 4 P.M.; in April and May, on Saturday only, from 11 A.M. to 4 P.M.

The **Seth Thomas Clock Outlet** (tel. 203/379-1077) sells clocks made by America's oldest clockmaker. HOURS: Tuesday through Saturday from 10 A.M. to 5 P.M., on Sunday from 11 A.M. to 5 P.M.

Nearby, **People's State Forest,** Rte. 44, Barkhamsted, is a must during fall, as is the area around Winsted in spring when this town throws a big **Mountain Laurel Festival.** Best place to view the blossoms is at Indian Lookout, off Rte. 4 in Torrington, halfway to Litchfield.

NORFOLK LODGING AND DINING

The **Mountain View Inn,** Rte. 272, Norfolk, CT 06058 (tel. 203/542-5595), offers a Victorian change of pace. An Eastlake sofa and chairs, a handsome sideboard, and grandfather clock furnish the parlor. The oak staircase leads to 11 rooms, six with private bath, all furnished differently, some with brass, others with wicker, and still others with heavier Victorian pieces. Owner Doris Feldman serves a continental breakfast of fruit breads and fresh fruit, while the dinner menu features such classic dishes as steak au poivre, duckling with brandied cherry sauce, and a fish of the day, priced from $10 to $15.50. Guests can relax on the porch overlooking a corner of the five-acre grounds and walk to the chamber music concerts at the Yale Summer School. There's swimming in nearby Toby Lake-Pond.

RATES: Midweek, $70 double in a room with shared bath; on weekends, $85 double for a room with private bath. DINNER: Thursday to Saturday from 6 to 9 P.M. and on Sunday from 1 to 6 P.M.

Dick and Joy Pygman and their daughter, April, are the enthusiastic owners/innkeepers at the **Blackberry River Inn,** Rte. 44, Norfolk, CT 06058 (tel. 203/542-5100). They have upgraded the 16 rooms (three with fireplaces), furnishing them with chintz and maple pieces in a country style. Double fireplaces warm the public areas in the lounge-parlor where people *may* be jumping to the old joanna. A blackboard menu lists the restaurant's four or five seasonal dishes—perhaps native Norfolk lamb chops or leg of lamb; tournedos with shiitake mushrooms; linguine Portuguese with scallops, mussels, shrimp, and clams cooked in a red or white wine sauce with spicy seasoning; duck with blackberry sauce; salmon; and more. There's always a vegetarian dish too. Prices range from $15 to $19, including salad and vegetables. During the Yale Music Festival a chamber group usually entertains.

There are 17 acres to enjoy, particularly in winter on cross-country skis. An outdoor pool and a tennis court complete the facilities. Closed March.

RATES: $90 for rooms with fireplace, $100 to $125 for suites. DINNER: Friday from 6 to 9 P.M., on Saturday until 9:30 P.M., and on Sunday from 5 to 8 P.M.

Manor House, the Inn at Norfolk, Maple Avenue (P.O. Box 701), Norfolk, CT 06058 (tel. 203/542-5690), is indeed as grand as it sounds. A late Victorian home with tall Elizabethan chimneys and lattice windows, it was built in 1898 by Charles Spofford, an architect who helped design, of all things, the London subway. He was the son of Ainsworth Rand Spofford, a publisher in Cincinnati who served in Abe Lincoln's administration. Charles was friendly with Louis Tiffany, who gave the windows that adorn the library and the living room as a housewarming gift. Fine architectural details can be found throughout the house—a classical stucco frieze in the living room depicting Day being led by Night across the Sky, an Italianate green tile fireplace in the dining room, cherry-paneled staircase, and geometric patterns everywhere.

Mannequins dressed in antique costumes are scattered about, reflecting the inspiration of Diane Tremblay, who runs the place along with husband, Henry. Both love catering to guests, providing information about the area, and preparing breakfast, which is served in quite a formal dining room at a large table surrounded by shield-back chairs. A large sideboard and silver service add to the gracious atmosphere. Orange waffles, blueberry pancakes, scrambled eggs with chives, and poached eggs with lemon butter and cheese sauce might be some of the breakfast choices. Homemade breads will accompany these. So will honey from the beehives on the property, or perhaps raspberries, also from their own raspberry canes.

Eight rooms, two with fireplaces, are available, all different. The Spofford Room is large with carved-wood fireplace and a variety of furnishings—rocker, chest of drawers, dressing table, and cane-backed sofa. Lace curtains adorn the windows; a dusty-pink comforter covers the bed which has a handsome headboard created from a mantel shelf. In the bathroom, the sink is marble. The Lincoln Room also has a fireplace; a sleigh bed with pretty floral comforter and Madame Récamier sofa are two of the more characterful pieces. La Chambre is a small but charming room furnished with brass bed and lilac wing chairs.

As a bonus, lucky guests may be treated to chamber concerts given in the splendid sunken living room where there's a grand piano. Three concerts are given each year; seating is limited to 50. Additional guest amenities include games (board games, Trivial Pursuit, etc.) available in a light and airy conservatory-style room; and chairs and tables for outdoor relaxing.

RATES: $60 to $85 double, $45 to $70 single.

Deanne Raymond has created luxurious surroundings at **Greenwoods Gate,** Greenwoods Road East, Norfolk, CT 06058 (tel. 203/542-5439), in her 1797 center-hall colonial home. The parlor is richly furnished with Oriental carpeting, pale-lemon wing chairs, drop-leaf cherry table, needlepointed French-style chair, and grand piano. Focal point of the room is the fireplace. The breakfast room contains a round table and, among other fine objects, a breakfront and Deanne's teapot collection. A fireplace also. The coziest room is undoubtedly the wood-paneled country-style kitchen decorated with wicker baskets, and a cookie-cutter collection. Here Deanne prepares breakfasts of fresh juice and fruit compote, featuring such dishes as cream cheese and strawberry omelets, Grand Marnier french toast, or an open-face frittata with spinach, onions, and feta cheese. A deck off the kitchen furnished with white wicker makes an ideal breakfast spot.

All the rooms have fresh flowers, starched, ironed sheets on the beds, and perfumes and other amenities in the bathrooms. Otherwise, they're all different. The E. J. Truscott Suite, off the kitchen, is very romantic: Belgian lace pillows and coverlet grace the brass-iron bed, while an Empire chest, porcelain lamps, marble bedside table, and a dollhouse filled with charming miniatures are all set against pretty blue wallpaper. The Lucy Phelps Room is small but prettily turned out in a rose color. The most spectacular and most private accommodation is the Lewis Thompson Suite. Here you'll find a Jacuzzi bathroom and always a split of champagne. A small foyer leads into a bilevel pink-and-blue room, the lower half serving as a sitting room. Upstairs the cherry bed sits under a brilliant stained-glass window. It's like being in your own dollhouse.

RATES: $100 to $120 double, $150 for the Thompson Suite, $50 for Lucy Phelps Room.

RIVERTON LODGING AND DINING

The **Old Riverton Inn,** Rte. 20 (P.O. Box 6), Riverton, CT 06065 (tel. 203/379-8678), has been quenching the thirsty and hungry and soothing the tired since 1796—the uneven floors and small doorways testify to its age. Right on Rte. 20, the plain but homey rooms are all different. Room 3, for instance, has a candlewick bedspread, chest, chair, and an adjustable wooden floor lamp, while the bathroom has a clawfoot tub-shower. Another room contains wicker chairs and a spinning wheel.

Wooden tables and placemats in the low-beamed dining room provide a traditional setting for the fare—good seafood and steaks, plus such specialties as veal française (with mushrooms and wine) and chicken marengo, from $11 to $17.

RATES (including breakfast): $50 to $56 double, $60 to $62 twin, $78 queen-size. LUNCH: Tuesday to Sunday from noon to 2:30 P.M. DINNER: Tuesday to Friday from 5 to 8:30 P.M., to 9 P.M. on Saturday, and from noon to 8 P.M. on Sunday. Closed Monday.

SOUTHBURY, WOODBURY, WASHINGTON, AND ROXBURY

AREA ATTRACTIONS

Let's start our tour in Southbury at the junction of Rte. 6 and I-84. Follow Rte. 6 east, passing Southbury Plaza. Take your first left at the set of lights to Heritage Village, a condominium complex that also shelters the **"Bazaar,"** containing 25 specialty shops, two art galleries, three restaurants, and a resort—all under one roof.

Retrace your route and continue on Rte. 6 east toward Woodbury along the **"Grand Army Highway of the Republic,"** so called because of its rich history as a major thoroughfare, used by George Washington, Lafayette, and Rochambeau during the Revolutionary War. For an optional side trip you can take Rte. 64 east off Rte. 6 to the **Whittemore Sanctuary,** especially recommended for birdwatchers, and to **Lake Quassapaug** in Middlebury, a large natural lake open to the public for swimming and boating. A family amusement park, **Quassy,** is also located on the shoreline.

Going back on Rte. 6 East, you'll come to Woodbury, dubbed the antiques capital of Connecticut, if not of the nation! There are close to 40 really fine **specialist antique shops** to browse and shop—featuring everything from early American furniture and paintings to country French, to 18th-century English, to Oriental and Navajo rugs, to art deco. Write for the "Woodbury Antique Buyer's Guide," obtainable from the Litchfield Hills Tourist Commission.

The two most historic points of interest in Woodbury are the **Herd House** and the **Glebe House,** which are located within 1,500 yards of each other on Hollow Road (off Rte. 6 in the center of Woodbury). The Herd House is in fact two houses that have been joined together (one circa 1680, the other circa 1720). It is furnished with period furniture and features a well-stocked herb garden. The Glebe House, also on Hollow Road (tel. 203/263-2855), dates from the 1700s and was owned by the town's first Episcopal priest, John Rutgers Marshall, who managed to survive the turmoil and oppression suffered by many New England Anglicans who were often presumed to be Loyalists—whether or not they were in fact. Weeks after American Independence was secured, a group of clergy met secretly at Glebe House to elect Samuel Seabury the first American bishop of the Episcopal church, an action which effectively assumed both the separation of church and state and thereby helped establish religious tolerance in the new nation. Today the house is furnished with period furniture and displays documents tracing the development of the Episcopal church. HOURS: Saturday through Wednesday from 1 to 4 P.M. (by appointment only, December through March).

From Woodbury, continue on Rte. 6 north to the junction of Rte. 61, taking it to **Bethlehem.** Best time to visit is at Christmas when a special festival is held featuring holiday arts and crafts, hayrides, festive music, a mini-festival of lights, and, of course, a post office where thousands of letters get the "Bethlehem" Christmas stamp. In August a horse show is also held at the Bethlehem Fairgrounds followed by a country fair in September.

At the junction of Rtes. 61 and 132, take 132 west and travel through pastoral bucolic scenery. At the junction of Rtes. 132 and 47, take 47 north to Washington, a picturesque town much of whose charm derives from its setting on top of a hill. The heart of town lies, of course, on the Green around the Congregational church, built on the site of the original 1742 meetinghouse. Facing the Green are lovely 18th-century residences and a small post office housed in a colonial white-clapboard building that it shares with the country drugstore. The **Museum of the Gunn Memorial Library** is located on the Green and exhibits collections of 18th- and 19th-century furniture, china, dolls, and dollhouses in this 1781 colonial house.

Farther along Rte. 47 lies Washington Depot, with an assortment of stores.

The **Hickory Stick Bookshop** (tel. 203/868-0525) is worth stopping at for new and secondhand books. It's a civilized place that even provides wing chairs for really leisurely browsing.

Retrace your steps along Rte. 47 to the junction with 199 and turn right. Follow 199 for about 1¼ miles and turn right at the sign for the **American Indian Archeological Institute,** in Washington (tel. 203/868-0518), which traces local Indian history through displays of their artifacts. Cases contain exhibits taken from a local paleo-Indian site—bone harpoons, adzes and net sinkers, semi-lunar knives, and soapstone vessels. Artifacts from the so-called Woodland period include luminescent turtle-shell bowls, copper and shell beads, and hand-thrown decorated pots. Kaolin pipes, beaded moccasins, and metal axes represent a later contact period, from 1550 to 1700. Probably the most interesting display, particularly for children, is the reconstruction of a longhouse made by Onondaga Indians and filled with everyday utensils and artifacts. A display case in the same room exhibits several beautiful objects, including a pillbox made of birchbark and moose hair, a rattle of elm and basswood bark, and a pair of cornshuck slippers. The immense, 12,000-year-old mastodon skeleton found at the Pope Estate in Farmington in 1913 will also impress the kids. It stood 9 feet tall at the shoulder, had a 13-foot-long tail, and weighed ten tons. You can also walk a 20-minute trail along which trees and plants are marked, tracing the evolution of the natural habitat from 12,000 years ago to today, and view a simulated archeological site, and also a woodland encampment. HOURS: Monday through Saturday from 10 A.M. to 4:30 P.M., on Sunday from 1 to 4:30 P.M.; closed major holidays. ADMISSION: $2 for adults, $1 for children 6 to 18.

Continue on Rte. 199 into the quiet, scenic village of Roxbury, which celebrates **Old Roxbury Days** the last weekend in July with a fiddlin' contest, chicken barbecue, antique car display, arts, crafts, and more. From Roxbury, Rte. 317 leads to Rte. 67, which takes you back to Rte. 6 and into Southbury.

A SOUTHBURY RESORT

The **Harrison Inn,** Heritage Village, on the Village Green, Southbury, CT 06488 (tel. 203/264-8200), makes an ideal base for exploring the Woodbury/Washington/Roxbury area of the Litchfield Hills. It's not a small personal inn; rather, it's a large accommodation with full facilities, including a large game room equipped with pool tables, dartboards, table tennis, and gaming tables; a bar that throbs on weekend nights; and rooms containing stereo/tapedeck radio and a full supply of audio cassettes from Beethoven to Boy George for rent. Yet it still has a rustic feel. Rooms look past silver birches over a green golf course to wooded hills beyond.

Accommodations affect a country style—beds have knotty-pine bedboards, walls are paneled barn-board style, and brass lamps and country chests with iron handles underline the rustic. Upholstered chairs and a desk add comfort, prints of waving grasses and knotty tree boughs accent the natural look. TV, telephone, and bathrooms with shampoo and special soaps are additional conveniences. So, too, are the double sinks.

The Timber restaurant is a large high-ceilinged room. Service, when I was there, was a little erratic but the hostess/maître d's humor could save any situation. The prime rib is excellent and the rest of the primarily American menu is also fine.

Besides the already-mentioned facilities there's an outdoor swimming pool, golf course, two tennis courts, cross-country ski trails, saunas, and whirlpool. And a health club equipped with Universal machines. For shopping, the Heritage Village Bazaar is right next door. Bicycles are also available, and trout fishing too. All this is only 1½ hours from Manhattan! The management is also building an indoor pool.

RATES: $85 to $105 single, $98 to $125 double. Reasonably priced weekend packages are offered throughout the year.

WOODBURY LODGING AND DINING

The **Curtis House,** Main Street (U.S. 6), Woodbury, CT 06798 (tel. 203/263-2101), claims to be the state's oldest inn, first operated by Anthony Stoddard in 1754. The venerable Federal clapboard building with black shutters and 12-on-12 windows is crowned by tall brick chimneys. An elegant portico surmounted by a balcony leads into the center hall. Past the grandfather clock, a creaking staircase leads to the 14 rooms (eight with private bath and canopy bed, six sharing baths). Four additional air-conditioned rooms are located in the carriage house. In Room 22 you'll find canopy beds with white canopies and coverlets, standing on painted floorboards. A chest of drawers, a side chair, and a metal closet complete the furnishings. Other rooms are similar. Some rooms have TV; none has a phone.

The public rooms on the ground floor have great character. Ceilings and door frames are low, floors uneven, and furnishings comfortably old. The ticking of the wall clock adds to the homey feel of the place. In the parlor you can curl up in the wing chairs or on the sofas and watch TV or read the magazines that are scattered on a table for guests' reading pleasure. The dining room, decorated in colonial cranberry, has a similar air. The fare is typically New England—roast stuffed turkey, broiled bluefish, roast leg of lamb (on weekends only), priced from $11 to $16.75.

RATES: $30 to $55, single or double, with bath; $20 to $25 without. LUNCH: Monday to Saturday from noon to 2 P.M. DINNER: Monday to Saturday from 5 to 9 P.M., on Sunday from noon to 8 P.M. Closed Christmas Day.

Young chef Steven Kopf presides at **The Bistro,** 107 Main St. North, Woodbury (tel. 203/263-0466), which is gaining a reputation for good food. It's an unpretentious place with chintz banquettes and one or two hanging plants. Filet mignon au poivre, an individual beef Wellington, and seafood bistro, a combination of shrimp, scallops, mussels, and clams in a cream sauce served over linguine are on the small menu which is supplemented by such daily specials as poulet champagne or Norwegian salmon. Desserts always include a chocolate specialty of the day, as well as appetizing hazelnut torte or fruit tarts. Prices run from $12.50 to $15.50 and are prix fixe, including soup, salad, dessert, and coffee.

Sunday brunch offers egg dishes as well as such items as chicken gratin, seafood crêpe, fish of the day—the $10 price includes a drink choice, soup du jour, bread and preserves, dessert, and coffee or tea.

LUNCH: Monday to Saturday from noon to 2:30 P.M. DINNER: Monday to Saturday from 6 to 9 P.M., on Sunday from 5 to 8 P.M. BRUNCH: Sunday from noon to 2:30 P.M. Reservations recommended.

Portofino, 10 Sherman Hill Rd., Woodbury (tel. 203/263-2371), has won several *Connecticut* magazine awards. On Rte. 6, it's tucked away with all the other similar-looking shops. Inside, gleaming brass rails separate floor levels, everything sparkles, and drop lights shine on white cloths. The specialty is northern Italian cuisine—shrimp Fra Diavolo, chicken marsala, and various pasta dishes, at average prices of $12 to $13.

LUNCH: Wednesday through Monday from 11:30 A.M. to 2 P.M. DINNER: Monday, Wednesday, and Thursday from 5 to 9:30 P.M., on Friday and Saturday to 10 P.M., and on Sunday to 8 P.M. Closed Tuesday.

A Breakfast Choice

Phillips, in the Middle Quarter shopping complex, in Woodbury, is famous for muffins, chicken pies, and good breakfasts. You'll probably have to join the line, unless you're willing to sit at the counter instead of in the booths.

WASHINGTON AND WASHINGTON DEPOT LODGING AND DINING

Such a pretty town as Washington warrants an old-fashioned comfortable inn, and the recently reopened **Mayflower Inn,** Rte. 47, Washington, CT 06793 (tel. 203/868-0515), could well prove worthy. Cross the bridge by the pond inhabited by two swans and take the winding tree-lined drive that leads to the house on the crest of the hill. The owners, Peter and Michelle Korzilius, had only recently arrived from California and were busy renovating and getting the place shipshape when I visited. Certainly there's a lot to be done, but they have already made great progress. The public areas are extremely comfortable and prettily decorated. In the parlor, wing chairs, upholstered in a large floral print fabric, stand in front of the carved-wood fireplace along with several sofas. Antique candlestands, tables, a grand piano, and such decorative items as an egret decoy give an intimate homey feel to the room.

There are 23 rooms available: eight in the main house, the rest in other buildings on the property. Some rooms have been nicely decorated. Room 101, for instance, has wall-to-wall carpeting, chintz wallpaper, Wedgwood blue quilt on the bed, wing chairs, chest of drawers, and a desk. Room 102 possesses an exceptionally large balcony and a four-poster bed among its furnishings. Rooms on the upper floors share bathrooms and are presentable, although their redecoration is planned and needed. Let me know if they are.

The bar room is made cozy by its cherry paneling and book-filled shelves. The Mayflower Room was indeed built to the specifications of that ship's dining room. Placemats with Audubon botanical and ornithological prints are laid on polished wood tables. Lunch is served here. There's also a large sunny main dining room. In summer the front porch also doubles as a dining area. The menus are seasonal, featuring continental cuisine like frogs' legs provençale, duckling with caraway seeds and braised red cabbage, chicken braised in red wine sauce with mushrooms and onions, or filet mignon béarnaise. Prices range from $11 to $17. Chocolate torte, lemon mousse, and crème caramel are a few choice desserts.

At brunch ($11), salads and desserts are arranged buffet style, while main dishes—Dutch apple pancakes, beef bourguignon, roast or fish of the day, plus egg dishes—are cooked to order.

RATES: $40 to $60 double. LUNCH: Tuesday to Saturday from noon to 3 P.M. DINNER: Tuesday to Sunday from 6 to 9 P.M. BRUNCH: Sunday from noon to 3 P.M.

For casual dining, **Jonathan's**, Rte. 47, Washington Depot (tel. 203/868-0509), offers a deck with an awning overlooking a chuckling brook and a dining room of light oak, bentwood chairs, and stained glass. Menus change weekly and feature continental/American dishes like Hawaiian chicken, jambalaya, beer-batter shrimp, grilled steaks and seafood, roast duckling, Cajun blackened prime rib. Prices run $10 to $13. Brunch is more interesting than most: besides eggs Benedict or steak and eggs, you can choose among beef Stroganoff and two seafood items.

LUNCH: Monday and Wednesday to Saturday from 11:30 A.M. to 2:30 P.M. DINNER: Monday, Wednesday, and Thursday from 5 to 9:30 P.M., on Friday and Saturday until 10 P.M., on Sunday from 4 to 9 P.M. BRUNCH: Sunday from 11:30 A.M. to 2:30 P.M.

LITCHFIELD HILLS ACTIVITIES

ANTIQUING: Stores abound in Kent, Litchfield, New Preston, Salisbury, and Woodbury (which has the greatest number of all). If you cross the border into Massachusetts on Rtes. 7 and 7A around Sheffield and Ashley Falls, you'll discover another good hunting ground.

CAMPING: White Memorial Foundation, on Rte. 202 west of Litchfield (tel. 203/567-0089), has several camping areas, open mid-May to October, the most popular being at Point Folly, a peninsula extending into Bantam Lake, and convenient for swimming, and fishing.

Lake Waramaug State Park, New Preston, CT 06777 (tel. 203/868-0220), also has 88 sites, open from mid-May to October 1.

Macedonia Brook State Park, Kent, CT 06757 (tel. 203/927-4100), offers 84 sites near a brook in the Appalachian Trail area.

Housatonic Meadows State Park, Cornwall Bridge, CT 06754 (tel. 203/672-6772), has 104 sites near the river.

Hemlock Hill Resort Campground, Hemlock Hill Rd. (P.O. Box 828), Litchfield, CT 06759 (tel. 203/567-0920), offers 100 wooded sites, two outdoor pools, and other facilities.

CANOEING: Riverrunning Ltd., Main Street, Falls Village, CT 06031 (tel. 203/824-5579).

North American Whitewater Expeditions, Inc., 167 Todd St., Hamden, CT 06518 (tel. 203/248-8924).

Clarke Outdoors, Rte. 7, West Cornwall, CT 06796 (tel. 203/672-6365), has canoes and kayaks for rent and provides shuttle service. Approximate charge per day is $26, plus.

COUNTRY FAIRS: Send for the address of the Association of Connecticut Fairs by writing to the State Department of Tourism. The association will send their list of these fun-filled celebrations with their contests, auctions, entertainments, and demonstrations.

FISHING: *Barkhamsted:* West Hill Pond, off Rte. 44. *Cornwall:* Housatonic Meadows State Park, Rte. 7, Cornwall Bridge. *Litchfield:* Lake Waramaug State Park, Rte. 45. Mount Tom State Park, Rte. 202. *Salisbury:* East Twin Lake, off Rte. 44. *Sharon:* Mudge Pond, off Rte. 4.

FRUIT PICKING: *Cornwall:* Harriet L. Clark, Litchfield Rte. 1. (tel. 203/672-6248), for raspberries. *Sharon:* Ellsworth Hill Farm and Orchard, Rte. 4 (tel. 203/364-0249), for apples and strawberries. *Washington Depot:* Hallock Orchards, Calhoun St. (tel. 203/868-2244), for apples. *Watertown:* Panilaitis Farm, Bunker Hill Rd. (tel. 203/274-0021), for sweet corn, tomatoes, and snap beans.

GOLF: *Litchfield:* Stonybrook Golf Club, Milton Road (tel. 203/567-9977), with nine holes.

HIKING: *Cornwall:* Mohawk Mountain, from Rte. 4. *Kent:* Kent Falls State Park, Rte. 7. *Litchfield:* White Memorial Foundation, Rte. 202; Mount Tom State Park, a few miles west of Bantam on Rte. 202. *Norfolk:* Haystack Mountain State Park on Rte. 272 north and Dennis Hill State Park on Rte. 272 south are both spectacular. *Salisbury:* Bear Mountain, from Rte. 41.

For detailed hiking trail information, write to the Connecticut Forest and Park Association, P.O. Box 389, East Hartford, CT 06108.

HORSEBACK RIDING: *Bantam:* Sunny Ray Farm, Rte. 202 (tel. 203/567-0522). *Litchfield:* Lee's Riding Stable, Inc., East Litchfield Road, Rte. 118 (tel. 203/567-0785).

ICE SKATING: On Lake Waramaug or at Mount Tom State Park.

MOUNTAIN LAUREL VIEWING: From mid to late June at Indian Lookout, Torrington.

PICNICKING: You can always dine on the Green in Litchfield. More secluded spots are to be found at the White Memorial Foundation, Lake Waramaug State Park, Kent Falls State Park, or Mount Tom. Pick up supplies at the

Litchfield Food Company, a gourmet take-out just off the Green, or at **Uncommon Strudel,** Litchfield Commons, Rte. 202.

SKIING: *Cornwall:* Mohawk Mountain, Cornwall, CT 06753 (tel. 203/672-6100), off Rte. 4, has a vertical rise of 640 feet, five lifts, and a 90% snowmaking capacity.

Cross-country skiing can be enjoyed at: *Kent:* Macedonia Brook State Park, off Rte. 341. *Litchfield:* White Memorial Foundation and Mount Tom State Park, on Rte. 202 just west of Bantam. *New Preston:* Around Lake Waramaug. *Woodbury:* Woodbury Ski & Racquet Area, Rte. 47 (tel. 203/263-2203), has 60 miles of trails.

Wilderness Shop, Rte. 202, Sports Village, Litchfield (tel. 203/567-5905), rents skis. Also at The Sports Scene Rte. 7, Kent (tel. 203/927-3852).

STATE PARKS: *Barkhamsted:* People's State Forest, Rte. 44, has hiking trails, picnicking, fishing, and cross-country skiing. *Cornwall:* Mohawk Mountain State Park, off Rte. 4, Cornwall-Goshen-Litchfield, offers picnicking and downhill and cross-country skiing. *Cornwall Bridge:* Housatonic Meadows State Park, on Rte. 7 one mile north of town, has camping, fishing, picnicking, and hiking on the Appalachian Trail available. *Kent:* Kent Falls State Park, Rte. 7, is picturesque for picnicking; Macedonia Brook State Park, off Rte. 341, has excellent hiking, fishing, picnicking, and cross-country skiing. *Norfolk:* Haystack Mountain State Park, on Rte. 272 north, and Dennis Hill State Park, on 272 south, have hiking and picnicking. *Washington:* Mount Tom State Park, Rte. 202, Morris-Washington-Litchfield, offers hiking, stocked fishing, swimming, picnicking, and cross-country skiing; Lake Waramaug, on Rte. 475, five miles north of New Preston, has swimming, camping, fishing, and picnicking facilities. For info, write: Dept. of Environmental Protection, Office of State Parks and Recreation, State Office Bldg., 165 Capitol Ave., Hartford, CT 06106 (tel. 203/566-2304).

SWIMMING: *Kent:* Macedonia Brook State Park, off Rte. 341. *Litchfield-Bantam:* Mount Tom State Park, off Rte. 202. *New Preston:* Lake Waramaug State Park.

From Norwalk to Ridgefield

Only about half an hour's drive from New Preston lies the Ridgefield-Danbury area, which you can also use as a base (there are three inns) to explore Litchfield to the north, Candlewood Lake, Bethel, and adjacent areas. From

Ridgefield it's only a short drive to the coastal towns of Westport and Norwalk, where we begin.

AREA ATTRACTIONS

Norwalk
Not exactly on everyone's "A" list for a weekend retreat, Norwalk actually surprises. There's plenty to see and do—a fantastic mansion, the famous oyster festival, a fast-developing street in South Norwalk lined with art galleries, antique stores, and chic restaurants, and a maritime center in the making in the very near future. Once a thriving industrial center, the city has a concentration of wonderful 19th-century buildings, many of which are located in the Historic District along Washington Street. Many of these Italianate-style buildings were constructed between 1870 and 1920 and feature cast iron trim, delicately detailed façades, and corbeled brick work. Today many of them have been refurbished and now house galleries and other eye-catching stores and restaurants.

The harbor, too, is poised for a maritime renaissance. Once a major schooner and steamboat port, it also became a major oystering center. Between 1885 and 1910 the industry was at its height. Later, oystering declined because of harbor pollution and a major hurricane that damaged the beds. Recently though it has been revived and it's now a $3 to $4 million industry and the excuse for one of Norwalk's largest festivals. The whole waterfront now is also being developed and linked to the Historic District. The linchpin of all this will be the $22 million Maritime Center, scheduled to open this year, featuring an aquarium, IMAX film theater, museum focusing on Long Island Sound's maritime history, and a waterfront park complete with a water amphitheater.

The Lockwood Mathews Mansion Museum, 295 West Ave. (tel. 203/838-1434), is Norwalk's well-kept secret. This magnificent French Renaissance Revival mansion, still in the process of being restored, was built in 1863 for LeGrand Lockwood of Lockwood and Co., a banking and brokerage firm that had invested very successfully in railroads. Between 1864 and 1868 LeGrand spent $1.5 million to construct this home, but he only lived in it for four years because in 1869, when the gold market was manipulated, he was forced to mortgage it. He died shortly thereafter. The Mathews family purchased the mansion and lived in it for the next 60 years, which probably accounts for the minimal number of changes that have been made to the structure over the years. From the outside it doesn't look very splendid, but the interiors are magnificent. Much of the work was completed by European stonecutters and woodcarvers, who were hired at $1 and 50¢ per day respectively. Today their skills would be priceless. From the entrance portico, three-inch-thick mahogany doors lead into the central hallway, supported by smooth gray-and-white marble pillars. The library has a coffered ceiling, and the floors are inlaid with eight different woods; it's lit by a chandelier with a fringe. The coffered ceiling in the music room is embellished with paintings of musical instruments. Bird's-eye maple doors and a marble fireplace surmounted with delicate etched-glass panels add even more luxury. The drawing room contains the only furniture original to the house—a circular ottoman and a carved Victorian sofa, its medallions matching those that crown the door frames. In the tiny turreted game room a Waterford chandelier lights the painted walls and ceiling, which are being restored to their former luster. The dining room has incredible carving on view and a richly decorated gold-leaf ceiling.

From the rotunda, 42 feet high and topped by a skylight, a grand staircase with carved inlaid bannisters leads to the bedrooms, two of which are used for semipermanent special exhibitions. When I was there they were occupied by a display of musical boxes of all sorts, including a musical clock picture, a grand piano player piano, and a domed musical tableau with flitting bird, clock, and waterfall. The Italian marble bathrooms, English ceramic bowls and bath enclosed in solid oak with etched-glass, are also worth noting. The tour of this exquisite testimony to fine craftsmanship lasts about an hour.

HOURS: March to mid-December, Tuesday to Friday from 11 A.M. to 3 P.M., on Sunday from 1 to 4 P.M.; closed Saturday and major holidays. ADMISSION: $3 for adults.

At **Stew Leonard's,** 100 Westport Ave. (tel. 203/847-7213), a sign on the oven boasts that 1,080 dinner rolls, 480 filled croissants, 450 hard rolls, 450 butter croissants, 360 grinders, and 120 Italian loafs can all be baked on one rack! A few paces away in the dairy processing plant, cartons of milk are filled and move around like massed soldiers on a conveyor belt—ten million quarts of milk sold in a year. In the juice plant, 151 million oranges are used to produce 29 million quarts of juice.

Stew Leonard has built a rip-roaring business because his store serves the customer in the full sense. First, it's fun. Life-size musical puppets perform country music in the canned-goods area; a human dairy cow trots down the aisles greeting customers; outside, the little farm—complete with water mill, real live crowing cocks and geese—attracts the kids. And then there are those personal touches: a suggestion box, a whole wall of photographs of happy customers pictured proudly carrying their Stew Leonard shopping bags all over the world from Spain to Alaska, and a photo gallery of "neighbors and customers"—Senator Weicker, Phil Donahue, Marlo Thomas, Bette Davis, and Henry Kissinger among them. Photographs of all the managers and personnel also smile down from the walls. Fish, meat, lobsters, caramel corn—the foods are all here in this emporium where Rule 1, boldly displayed at the entrance, states: "Customer is always right!" It's followed by Rule 2: "If the customer is ever wrong, reread Rule 1."

You may not have planned to do any food shopping on the weekend, but this is a veritable attraction in itself and one that New York City supermarkets might take note of. HOURS: 7 A.M. to 11 P.M. daily.

South Norwalk's Washington Street

Galleries, antique shops, striking restaurants, and boutiques line this long street that leads down to the beaches and seems to have blossomed in anticipation of the new maritime center which will open in the near future and which, as a mini Mystic, is expected to draw thousands of visitors.

Starting at the junction of Washington and North Main, here are several stores of note: **Images,** at no. 68a (tel. 203/852-7114), is a sculpture gallery; **Primo** sells up-to-the-minute lighting fixtures; and **Faïence** offers really pretty household accessories, china, gifts, and soaps. **Designers Loft,** at no. 122, is shared by two or three artists, including a jeweler, a batik screen specialist, and a woman who creates spectacular handmade fringed and ornate lampshades that sell for hundreds of dollars. **Festivities** specializes in gourmet items, porcini, cèpes, all kinds of oils and vinegars, coffees, and teas. You can also obtain salads, and sandwiches, along with such dishes as veal with basil sauce and sit and eat at one of the four tables. **Precious** has fine jewelry. **Sassafras** features folk art. Modern art creations are displayed at **John Cusano,** another gallery.

On the opposite side of the street starting at the river end, doll fanciers will love the collection of dollhouses and furniture at **Molly Brody Miniatures.** One of my all-time favorite stores on the street is **Artisan's Choice** at no. 133 (tel. 203/853-2193), specializing in fine antique and modern arts from Burma, Thailand, and elsewhere in Southeast Asia. Just up the street, at no. 127 **Brookfield-Sono Crafts Center** (tel. 203/853-6155) contains a retail store, several artisans' studios, and also offers classes (which may even be going on as you wander through). **Washington Street Bookstore** stocks new and old books. **Darien Junction** ice cream will satisfy those dairy/sugar cravings.

Silvermine, Wilton, Cannon Crossing, Ridgefield, and Danbury
In nearby New Canaan, you can call at the **Silvermine Guild Center for the Arts,** 1037 Silvermine Rd. (tel. 203/966-5617 or 966-5618), a complex of galleries and studios well known for the annual New England Exhibit and the biennial National Print Show. Founded in 1922 by the Silvermine Guild of Artists. HOURS: Daily, except Monday, from 12:30 to 5 P.M.

From Norwalk, Rte. 7 will deliver you swiftly to the community of Wilton.

Wilton Heritage Museum, Wilton Historical Society, 249 Danbury Rd., Wilton (tel. 203/762-7257), is housed in a handsome 1756 central-chimneyed colonial and offers the opportunity to view a series of authentically furnished and decorated period rooms: an early-18th-century kitchen; a later-period parlor in which the beams have been boxed in and which contains a treasured Ralph Earl portrait and a cupboard of Norwalk redware (once common cookware, but now more treasured than fine European china because of its rarity); and an 1835 early Empire formal dining room with canvas painted floor cloth. Upstairs, the 1825–1829 late Federal bedroom contains a fluted pencil four-poster and some exquisite samplers, silhouettes, and "mourning pictures," while the Doll and Toy Room charms with such figures as a penny wooden doll and an apple doll. The museum also has quite an extensive costume collection and examples are displayed on mannequins. Two rooms on the ground floor are used for temporary exhibitions (when I visited, a textile display of patterns and designs, showing the processes by which they were made). A nice time to visit is at Christmas season when the house is decorated for a Victorian Christmas and candlelight tours are given. HOURS: Tuesday to Thursday, and Sunday from 1 to 4 P.M.

Cannon Crossing, Cannondale Railroad Station, Wilton (tel. 203/762-2875), reminds me for some reason of *Brigadoon*. It's a small village of sorts, dreamed of and assembled here by actress June Havoc. In fact she rescued it and restored it, investing her life's savings from stage, screen, and TV appearances. Years ago June's husband found a derelict mill here and they used to come by together and picnic. Nine years ago she bought the 8½ acres on both sides of the river, restored the mill, and set about saving other local landmarks. Now there are 11 stores open. Part of the still-functioning station operates as the Depot, run by Benedictines who sell capes from Guatemala, crafts and fabrics from Turkey, China, and other less rich nations, along with religious and philosophical books and tapes. June moved the schoolhouse here and it now serves as a delightful restaurant, the Old Schoolhouse Café. Here you can sit on the flagstone patio under the sycamore and maple, listening to the flowing river while you sample an omelet, salad niçoise, broccoli-ham quiche, pasta salad, or similar offerings at prices from $5.75 to $7.25 (open from 11 A.M. to 5 P.M.; closed Monday). Other shops are located in the Cow Barn and the Keeping Barn, including Penny Ha'Penny, which specializes in English foodstuffs—jams, jellies, Heinz salad creams, crackers, sweets —as well as gifts and crafts. Green Willow Antiques operates out of the original farmhouse. Other stores worth exploring vend quilts, pillows, and other country items; the tinsmith Jim sells his hand-wrought items styled after early American patterns; a florist assembles her very own beautifully fetching flower arrangements.

As I said, there is a *Brigadoon* quality about the place. HOURS: Year round, Tuesday through Sunday from 11 A.M. to 5 P.M.

Continue north on Rte. 7 to the junction of Rte. 102, turn left, and follow the signs into Ridgefield.

Here, begin at the **Keeler Tavern Museum** (1733), 132 Main St. (tel. 203/438-5485). From 1772 when this old building became an inn, it was a regular stop on the stagecoach run between New York and Boston. It was also a Revolutionary meeting place, no doubt the reason why the British lobbed a cannonball— which is lodged there to this day—at it in 1777 during the Battle of Ridgefield. For over 130 years it remained in the Keeler family, until 1907 when architect Cass Gilbert purchased the property as his summer home, adding some interior embellishments. Tour the tap room, ladies parlor, dining rooms, and sleeping rooms and a most well-equipped kitchen. The gardens also provide a peaceful oasis. HOURS: Wednesday, Saturday, Sunday, and holiday Mondays from 1 to 4 P.M.; closed January. ADMISSION: $2 for adults, $1 for children under 12.

The **Aldrich Museum,** 258 Main St. (tel. 203/438-4519), housed in a 1783 building, displays changing shows of contemporary artists and offers a quiet sculpture garden for contemplation. HOURS: May to December, Wednesday to Friday from 2 to 4 P.M., on Saturday and Sunday from 1 to 5 P.M.; January to April, on Friday from 2 to 4 P.M., on Saturday and Sunday, from 1 to 5 P.M. ADMISSION: $1.

From Ridgefield, take Rte. 35 north to join Rte. 7, which will take you into Danbury. Here, every year in the town of his birth, the **Charles Ives Festival** is held in a serene meadow/forest setting. Behind the pagoda-style bandshell extending out over a pond, the weeping willows drop to the water's edge. Local lore claims that there's one native frog that croaks in time with the music. Picnics are a must.

The **Scott Fanton Museum,** 43 Main St., Danbury (tel. 203/743-5200), features textiles, woodworking tools, and Revolutionary War memorabilia, and also includes the Dodd Hat shop which interprets the history of the hat-making industry. The museum also maintains Charles Ives's birthplace, which contains many of his original furnishings including his piano.

From Danbury it's just a hop to **Candlewood Lake,** an attractive summer romping ground great for picnicking, boating, swimming, and fishing. Or, just east of Danbury lies **Bethel,** a town with attractive 18th-century homes standing along South Main Street. Note the 1750 House, the Opera House, and Dicksons. The town is conveniently located for exploring **Putnam Memorial State Park,** a haven for picnicking, cross-country skiing, and hiking.

If you prefer the shore to wandering the backroads of southwestern Connecticut, then it's only a short hop from Norwalk into Westport. Beach access is a problem because a sticker is required. You'll either have to stay at the Inn at Longshore or else head for Sherwood Island State Park (tel. 203/226-6983), which tends to become very crowded after Memorial Day.

NORWALK AREA LODGING AND DINING

The most appealing place to stay is the **Silvermine Tavern,** Silvermine and Perry Avenues, Norwalk, CT 06850 (tel. 203/847-4558). There are six rooms in the lovely old inn, which overlooks the mill pond, and four over the country store across the street. Rooms are simple and unremarkable with white candlewick spreads, pine knob beds, lace curtains, a desk, two chairs, and a dresser, all homey style. The public areas are furnished far more lavishly with antiques and there are two parlors with fireplaces, one with a TV. The tavern is a pleasant quaffing spot: old farm implements and folk art on the walls, and a female figure beside the bar testifying to the not-so-long-ago state law that banned women from coming within a foot or so of the bar. The dining patio, overlooking the swans on the mill pond, features a standard colonial meal of seafood, roast beef, steak, and chicken, with prices ranging from $9.50 to $24 for a full shore dinner consisting of a two-pound lobster, New England chowder, mussels in wine, soft-shell crab, and potato and vegetable.

RATES: $70 to $76 double. *Note:* A 20-dish buffet brunch is served on Sunday from 11 A.M. to 2:30 P.M. Lunch and dinner daily, except Tuesday.

Norwalk Dining

Pasta Nostra, 116 Washington St. (tel. 203/854-9700), has a most striking look—black-and-white mosaic tile floor, track lighting, a combination of banquettes, bentwood chairs, and oak tables. The name surely derives from the dramatic (to say the least) modern religious paintings that are displayed on the walls.

The aromas here, though, are very appetizing. Among the special hors d'oeuvres are delicious stuffed peppers, olivata and caprino (ground black olives spread on olive oil toast served with goat cheese rolled in herbs). The pastas are all made on the premises. Try agnolotti Max (which comes with a pesto and tomato sauce), or the smoked salmon in cream over angel hair, or cultivated mushrooms and porcini cooked with onions, wine, and cognac, tossed with devil's hair pasta. In all, there are a dozen. Cannoli, almond macaroons, and cheesecakes round out the menu. Pasta dishes run about $11.

LUNCH: Tuesday to Saturday from 11:45 A.M. to 2:45 P.M. DINNER: Friday from 6 to 9 P.M., on Saturday until 10 P.M. Closed Sunday and Monday.

Donovan's, 138 Washington St. (tel. 203/838-3430), was here long before the street became (newly) fashionable, having been established in 1889. It's a simple beer-and-hamburger joint with blue gingham tablecloths, prize fighter portraits looking down at the wooden tables and booths.

LUNCH: 11:30 A.M. to 3:30 P.M. daily. DINNER: 6 to 11 P.M. daily.

At the corner of Washington and South Main, **Jasper's Oyster Bar and Restaurant,** 2–4 S. Main St. (tel. 203/852-1716), a bright, high-ceilinged space, attracts a good crowd. Rose tablecloths, topped with glass, make for a pretty dining room. The menu features a selection of seafood as well as dishes for "fish frowners," priced from $11.25.

LUNCH: 11:30 A.M. to 3 P.M. daily. DINNER: Monday to Saturday from 5 to 10:30 P.M., on Sunday from 3 P.M.

Water Street Restaurant, 50 Water St. (tel. 203/854-9630), serves American/continental food with a dash of Cajun flavoring. The atmosphere is casual: posters, plants, and brick walls sums it up. The action is at the square bar upfront. Most of the dishes have a spicy flair—Cajun seafood gumbo (a hearty stew filled with oysters, crabmeat, shrimp, and smoked sausage in a spicy roux with tomatoes, green peppers, and scallions), baked fish Santa Fe (baked in a coating of cumin, coriander, and chili powder), roast chicken with salsa, or less spicy choices like a plain 12-ounce sirloin grilled over charcoal. Prices run from $9.50 to $12.

LUNCH: Monday to Friday from 11:30 A.M. to 3 P.M. DINNER: Monday to Thursday from 5:30 to 9:30 P.M., on Friday and Saturday from 6 to 11 P.M., on Sunday from 5 to 9 P.M.

Meson Galicia, 250 Westport Ave. (tel. 203/846-0223), also known as Rte. 1, has earned a reputation locally for fine food. It's an attractive bilevel restaurant: the upper tier consists of a gallery of booths fashioned from church pews and delightfully separated by lace curtain dividers, the lower being a skylit dining room with Windsor chairs. It serves authentic Spanish food to the accompaniment of Spanish background music. Besides the daily specials—halibut in green sauce, roast chicken with Tío Pepe sherry sauce—the menu features dishes like duckling with olives, baked salmon with shrimp and scallops in green sauce, or paella, priced from $13.75 to $18.50. For starters, the seafood emphasis is also clear —Mediterranean seafood soup, mussels with saffron and wine sauce, gambas a la plancha (six grilled shrimp in savory lobster-and-garlic sauce). Desserts are a chocoholic's delight, and the fruit tarts are also spectacular.

The adjacent bar accented with stained glass and decorated with jai alai "gloves" serves tapas—octopus, chorizos, calamares, shrimp, etc., for $4.50 and up.

LUNCH: Monday to Friday from noon to 3 P.M. DINNER: Monday to Thursday from 5:30 to 10 P.M., on Friday and Saturday from 5:30 to 11 P.M., on Sunday from 5 to 10 P.M.

A traditional local favorite, the **Lighthouse Restaurant,** 2 Wilton Ave. (tel. 203/846-3266), thrives especially on weekends when happy diners feast on a variety of seafood—swordfish, sautéed crabmeat, poached salmon, cioppino, broiled fish, Alaskan king crab legs, and broiled or deep-fried scallops, priced from $11 to $24.

Among the appetizers you'll find oysters casino or Rockefeller, scungilli salad, or clams from the raw bar, as well as stuffed mushrooms and a shell macaroni stuffed with crab, shrimp, and scallops in a cheese sauce with wine. Italian specialties are available too—veal parmesan, francese, etc.—for non-fish eaters. The atmosphere is typical fish restaurant: fish tanks in which brilliantly colored tropical fish glide around, porthole-like stained-glass windows, and plain wooden booths.

LUNCH: Monday to Friday from noon to 3 P.M. DINNER: Sunday to Thursday from 5:30 to 10 P.M., on Friday and Saturday until 11 P.M.

Trimmed lawns and flowering borders suggest that the **Silver Star,** 210 Connecticut Ave. (tel. 203/852-0023), is no ordinary diner. And indeed it's not. It's 750 square feet of space complete with large semicircular bar with lots of chrome and Mylar and a hefty dash of extra pizzazz. It's also the best place around here to obtain a breakfast—36 omelets to choose from alone! And you'll be dining in a formal dining room off tables set with tablecloths under glass, seated on cushy Breuer-style chairs. Or you can choose the more typical diner quarters.

The dinner menu is extensive, featuring seafood, chicken, beef, and veal dishes —everything from shrimp teriyaki to liver anglaise and veal marsala, with prices ranging from $8 to $19. And furthermore, if you can't find anywhere else open, the Silver Star's lights will be blazing and the folks noshing.

HOURS: Sunday to Thursday from 6 A.M. to 3 P.M., on Friday and Saturday open 24 hours.

South and East Norwalk
South Norwalk also has two restaurants right down on the Norwalk riverfront.

The outdoor dining deck at **Sono Seaport,** 100 Water St. (tel. 203/854-9483), is the most popular. Fresh fish and shellfish are the specialty, priced from $5.50 to $14.75.

HOURS: 11 A.M. to 10 P.M. daily.

The Pier (tel. 203/838-8200) also overlooks the water, but offers inside dining only and is a summer-only spot from May to September.

In East Norwalk, just a few blocks away, **Skipper's,** Beach Road, Cove Marina (tel. 203/838-2211), also offers waterfront dining year round. Lobsters from the tank and fresh seafood are the specialties, along with steak, chops, and chicken.

HOURS: 11:30 A.M. to 10 P.M. Daily except Monday.

RIDGEFIELD AREA LODGING AND DINING
The Elms, 500 Main St., Ridgefield, CT 06877 (tel. 203/438-2541), has been thriv-

ing as an inn since 1799, so a traveler can expect the comforts of a room like number 42 with a large inviting four-poster canopy bed, or number 32 with a similar four-poster, French needlepointed chairs, an oak dresser, and a rocker. There are 4 rooms in the main house and another 16 in the annex, all beautifully contemporary in style with a smattering of antiques. TV, telephone, and climate control included.

Meals are exquisitely served, either in the colonial-style low-beamed tavern or in a series of small intimate dining rooms. The luncheon menu includes an expertly prepared steak tartare, really first class; dinner often brings game—venison, pheasant, and partridge—along with the more usual, although finely prepared, rack of lamb, roast duckling, filet of sole, and veal. Complete dinners begin at $23. À la carte entrees range from $11.75 to $21.

RATES: $89 to $115 double (with continental breakfast). LUNCH: Noon to 2:30 P.M. Thursday to Tuesday. DINNER: Thursday to Saturday and Monday and Tuesday from 6 to 9:30 P.M., on Sunday from 5 to 8:30 P.M. BRUNCH: Sunday. Closed Wednesday.

The other hostelry in Ridgefield, the **West Lane Inn,** 22 West Lane, Ridgefield, CT 06877 (tel. 203/438-7323), occupies a handsome two-story mansion set back on a broad lawn and framed by a stand of majestic old maples. The front porch is set into a center semicircular bay that adds infinite interest to the façade and also to the interior spaces. Inside, a gracious staircase crowned at the top with a rare spindlework screen leads to 14 unusually large rooms, some with fireplace, two queen-size beds, chintz-covered wing chairs, a bamboo desk and bed headboard. All the rooms have private bath, color TV, radio, and phone.

RATES: $105 double, $150 with fireplace (including breakfast).

Adjacent to the inn but under separate management is the **Inn at Ridgefield** (tel. 203/438-8282), serving classic French fare (steak au poivre, duck à l'orange) in elegant surroundings at $31 prix fixe. Closed Monday. Lunch and dinner; brunch on Sunday from noon to 3 P.M.

Stonehenge, Rte. 7, Ridgefield, CT 06877 (tel. 203/438-6511), is really the most appealing inn in the area, for it is out of town, surrounded by trees, with a rambling English-style garden in front and a pond charmingly inhabited by ducks, swans, and Canadian geese in the back.

Off the entrance in the parlor are fine antiques, books, and some very special Mathew Brady portraits, each explicated by a text about the subject's life.

There are 13 rooms, 3 in the main inn and 10 in the cottages on the property, furnished with bed, marble-top bedside tables, and a large dresser, plus the modern conveniences of telephone, TV, and air conditioning.

The dining room overlooking the pond offers first-class cuisine including such à la carte specialties as a whole roast suckling pig (requiring five days' notice), duckling with orange or pepper sauce, buffalo and pheasant (in season), or a $37 prix fixe. Salmon tablecloths and old prints make for a romantic setting in the outer porch dining room, while the pine-paneled Druid piano bar-parlor, warmed by a fire in winter, makes for a cozy dining nook.

RATES (including continental breakfast): $100 to $140 double. LUNCH: Wednesday to Monday from noon to 2 P.M. DINNER: 6 to 9 P.M. Monday to Saturday, on

Sunday from noon to 7:30 P.M. BRUNCH: Sunday from noon to 2:30 P.M. Closed Tuesday.

At the **Coq Hardi,** Big Shop Lane (tel. 203/431-3060), the food looks as appetizing as it tastes. For example, at a recent meal the goose-breast appetizer arrived looking like a delicate rose—petals created from carrot strips and slices of goose breast, and arranged around an artichoke heart. And it was delicious. My dining partner's chicken mousse, however, was less successful. For the main course, the carré d'agneau was juicily pink and served with a refreshing orange-mint sauce, potatoes, and cauliflower. Other entrees might include calamari with pasta, breast of duck with a port wine sauce, shallots, and apples, or a vegetarian plate. Prices run $18 to $26. The desserts are worth waiting for, especially —at least for my taste—the fresh raspberries with cream served in a pastry case.

The setting in a converted old barn is warm and intimate, and the ambience enhanced by a classical music background. Tables are set with pink tablecloths and elegant place settings. Four or so ceramic cockerels add a splash of fantasy life. Some of the tables are placed in an outer veranda-like area whose windows are covered with lace curtains.

LUNCH: Tuesday to Friday from noon to 2 P.M. DINNER: Tuesday to Saturday from 6 to 9 P.M., on Sunday from 5:30 to 8:30 P.M. BRUNCH: Sunday from noon to 2 P.M.

DANBURY AND BETHEL LODGING AND DINING

In the same family for the past three generations, **Best Western Stony Hill Inn,** U.S. 6, Bethel, CT 06801 (tel. 203/743-5533), is probably Danbury's nicest accommodation. Rooms in the motel-style units are absolutely spotless—even the telephone mouthpieces are turned over to show that they've been cleaned and sanitized. Furniture is modern, consisting of a table, two chairs, dresser, bed, and color TV. The property is set well back from the road behind a well-treed grassy slope and pond with resident swans. An outdoor fenced-in pool and play area with swings and slide will keep the kids happy. In the main building people gather for cocktails in a comfortable room with a large fireplace. The dining room looks out onto the pond. While you're here, see the wooden replica of Washington Crossing the Delaware, one of the few artifacts that was saved from the famous, now-mourned Danbury Fair.

RATES: $62 for two beds, $56 for one bed.

Tuxedo Junction, 2 Ives St., Danbury (tel. 203/748-2561), is a good-time nostalgic kind of place. People elbow each other at the long bar alongside scenes from Marilyn Monroe's classics, the Little Rascals, Honeymooners, and other old popular favorites. On the other side of the room the murals were painted by local Jack Barrows, caricaturing everyone from Elvis Presley to W. C. Fields. Entertainment is provided on Sunday, Monday, and Tuesday. In summer, dine outside under the colorful awning. A $7 brunch offers steak and eggs, quiche Lorraine, and other egg dishes.

HOURS: 11:30 A.M. to 11 P.M. daily.

Bethel Dining

San Miguel, 8 P. T. Barnum Square (tel. 203/748-2396), is popular for a full variety of Mexican cuisine—burritos, enchiladas, chimichangas, chile rellenos—and daily specials like paella. Prices range from $8 to $12.50.

DINNER: Tuesday to Thursday from 5 to 9 P.M., on Friday and Saturday to 10 P.M., on Sunday until 9 P.M.

Everyday's, 178 Greenwood Ave. (tel. 203/797-1390), is a great local favorite for breakfast. It's always jammed with people seated at the festive tables set with floral tablecloths under glass. Grape-vine wreaths, country landscapes, and photographs of locals add interest to the small interior. Egg dishes, pancakes, and similar available from $1.35 to $4.

HOURS: Monday to Saturday from 7 A.M. to 3 P.M., on Sunday to 2 P.M.

WESTPORT LODGING AND DINING

The **Inn at Long Shore,** 260 Compo Rd. South, Westport, CT 06880 (tel. 203/226-3316), occupies a prime location overlooking Long Island Sound. There are 14 rooms; the restaurant takes full advantage of the view and provides reasonable fare; but the biggest attractions are the golf course, eight clay tennis courts, pool and beach facilities.

The restaurant, J. B. Tipton's, offers a selection of dishes like rack of lamb, sirloin steak, catch of the day, baked scrod, bouillabaisse, pastas, and blackened pork tenderloin.

RATES: $135 double. LUNCH: In summer, 11:30 A.M. to 2:30 P.M. daily. DINNER: In summer, Sunday to Thursday from 5:30 to 9 P.M., on Friday and Saturday until 10:30 P.M. BRUNCH: Sunday from 11:30 A.M. to 2:30 P.M. Closed Monday in winter.

The town is filled with restaurants, many concentrating more on their pretty locations than on their food, unfortunately. Here's a brief rundown:

Le Chambord, 1572 Post Rd. East (tel. 203/255-2654), is considered the top restaurant.

Right on Main Street, **Chez Pierre** (tel. 203/227-5295) produces coq au vin, duck à l'orange, rack of lamb, chateaubriand, and veal marsala, at prices starting at $17. LUNCH: Monday to Saturday from noon to 2 P.M. DINNER: Monday to Saturday from 6 to 9 P.M., on Friday and Saturday until 10 P.M. Closed Monday.

Several Chinese and Japanese restaurants can be found along Rte. 1 (Boston Post Road) going east.

DINING IN WESTON

Cobbs Mill Inn, on Rte. 57 north in Weston (tel. 203/227-7221), offers pretty dining on a terrace under the falls at the former grist mill. Veal Cordon Bleu, filet mignon béarnaise, wienerschnitzel, venison, duck, and chicken, at prices from $16, are the order of the day.

DINNER: Monday to Saturday from 4 P.M., on Sunday from noon.

RIDGEFIELD AREA ACTIVITIES

ANTIQUING: There are about half a dozen shops in Bethel; in Ridgefield, the

Black Pond Antiques Center, 605 Ethan Allen Hwy., has another half dozen or so; Southport is another great center, where there are a number clustered along Pequot Avenue.

BOATING: At Candlewood Lake boats can be rented.

FISHING: Candlewood Lake (Squantz Cove), New Fairfield, off Rte. 39 (tel. 203/797-4165), and at Lattins Cove, Danbury, off Rte. 7, north of I-84.

FRUIT PICKING: Blue Jay Orchard in Bethel (tel. 203/748-0119) has apples, peaches, pears, and strawberries.

GOLF: *Danbury:* Richter Park Golf Course, Aunt Hack Rd. (tel. 203/792-2552). *Fairfield:* H. Smith Richardson Golf Club, Hoydens Lane (tel. 203/255-5016). *New Milford:* Candlewood Valley Country Club, Rte. 7 (tel. 203/354-9359). *Norwalk:* Oak Hills Park, Fillow St. (tel. 203/866-7932). *Ridgefield:* Ridgefield Golf Club, Ridgebury Rd. (tel. 203/748-7008).

HIKING: Putnam Memorial State Park.

SKIING: Cross-country skiing available in Putnam Memorial State Park.

NEW HAVEN

DISTANCE IN MILES: 74
ESTIMATED DRIVING TIME: 1½ hours

DRIVING: FDR Drive to the New England Thruway (I-95).
BUS: Trailways (tel. 212/730-7460) goes to New Haven. So do Greyhound (tel. 212/635-0800, or toll free 800/528-6055) and Bonanza (tel. 212/635-0800 for tickets or 564-8484 for schedules).
TRAIN: Amtrak travels to New Haven. For information call 212/736-6288.

Special Events to Plan Your Trip Around
JUNE: National Trolley Festival and Craft Fair (usually the fourth weekend). Contact Branford Trolley Museum (tel. 203/467-6927).
St. Andrew's Festival, patron saint of Amalfi (usually the fourth weekend).
JULY: Guilford Handcrafts on the Green (usually the third weekend). For info, contact the Guilford Handcrafts Center (tel. 203/435-5947).
New Haven Jazz Festival on the Green (tel. 203/787-8956), which has featured such greats as Count Basie, Lionel Hampton, and the Duke Ellington Orchestra (every weekend).
SEPTEMBER: The New Haven Bed Race, when decorated beds take to the streets, and the Odyssey Greek Festival, filled with music, food, and entertainment (both usually the weekend after Labor Day). Call 203/795-1347 for details.
OCTOBER OR NOVEMBER: "The Game," when Yale takes on its arch-rival, Harvard, and thousands fill the lots surrounding the Bowl, setting up tail-

gate picnics, parties, gourmet spreads, and cocktails in a thoroughly festive atmosphere.

For further information about these events and Connecticut in general, call or write the Travel Office, Department of Economic Development, 210 Washington St., Hartford, CT 06106 (tel. 203/566-3385, or toll free 800/243-1685 from Maine through Virginia, 800/842-7492 in Connecticut).

For specific information about New Haven, contact the New Haven Convention & Visitors Bureau, 900 Chapel St., New Haven, CT 06510 (tel. 203/787-8367).

The New England Vacation Center, 630 Fifth Ave., Concourse Shop 2, New York, NY 10020 (tel. 212/307-5780), also provides information.

Today, for the umpteenth time in its history, the city of New Haven seems poised for yet another cultural renaissance. In a city that already has two of the finest regional theaters in the nation, two more have been lovingly restored to their former magnificence, and around them a whole entertainment area is being developed. Throughout the city whole neighborhoods have been spruced up; buildings have been reclaimed and transformed into restaurants offering all types of cuisine and entertainment; Wooster Square has been returned to its original role as a quiet, gracious city enclave; State Street is fast building a reputation as an antique lover's delight; and all this activity is taking place against the backdrop of the Gothic spires and towers of Yale University, with its many fine museums and art galleries as additional attractions.

For any weekend visitor New Haven offers a heady blend of the old and new, plenty of exciting theater, music, art galleries, and museums, and all the life and exuberance associated with a university campus and a town that is once again on the rise.

Settled in 1637–1638 by a group of Puritans led by Theophilus Eaton and John Davenport, New Haven was the major town of a separate theocratic colony that included Milford, Guilford, Stamford, Branford, and Southold on Long Island. The early years were hard. Harassed by the Dutch and Swedes, many merchants left and a weakened colony was reluctantly incorporated into Connecticut in 1665, and New Haven became joint capital with Hartford from 1701 to 1875.

The early 18th century brought better times. The Collegiate Institute School was moved here and its name changed to Yale in 1717; trade flourished at least until the Embargo of 1812, which ruined the city once again. In the mid-19th century the city rose again, manufacturing thrived, and New Haven contributed many industrial firsts to the nation and indeed the world: the first commercial telephone exchange in 1879; the first rubber footwear plant; and the first corkscrew and the first lollipop. Many of the developers of these processes lie buried in Grove Street Cemetery and their contributions are on display in the various historical society collections.

Those in search of more recent history will want to seek out the house where Meryl Streep stayed while attending the Yale School of Drama, or the abode of Doonesbury's creator Garry Trudeau, or more darkly, the hotel where John Hinckley stayed while stalking Jodie Foster.

A Suggested Itinerary

Spend one day exploring downtown New Haven, starting at the Visitors Information Center. See the Green, the Yale Center for British Art, Yale Art Gallery, the old university campus and Beinecke Library, and wind up at the Grove Street Cemetery to make a souvenir grave rubbing before dinner and the theater.

The next day can either be spent antiquing along State Street and exploring the Wooster Square area, or visiting the Yale Music Collection, the Peabody, and the Historical Society. Or you can explore the shoreline, either aboard the *Liberty Belle* or by visiting Fort Nathan Hale and/or Lighthouse Point. Or you can take I-95 out to East Haven–Branford to view and ride the trolleys that have been restored at the museum there, with a stop on the way back at Teletrack for an evening's racing. Your choices are really quite varied!

NEW HAVEN ATTRACTIONS

Any tour of New Haven should begin at the **New Haven Visitors & Convention Bureau,** 900 Chapel St., New Haven, CT 06510 (tel. 203/787-8367), facing the Green.

The Green

The 16-acre Green has been the focal point of New Haven community life since 1638 and is still owned and operated by a small group of descendants of the original settlers. Today it's the site for many special summer events and Sunday-evening summer concerts. Here, a little over a century ago, American football was born under the tutelage of Yale's innovative rugby coach, Walter Camp, and a much later sport was invented, Frisbee throwing, inspired by Yalies hurling their pie plates through the air across the Green.

Three famous old churches stand on the Green—at the Elm Street end the United Congregation Church (1812–1815), the Gothic Revival Trinity Church designed by Ithiel Town, and the First Congregational (or Center Church), copied from London's St. Martin in the Fields. If you have time to visit only one, then see the Center Church and go down to the crypt, containing 120 graves and stones preserved when the church was built over the town's burying ground. Many historically important figures, including Benedict Arnold's first wife and James Pierpont, one of Yale's founding fathers, were buried here. HOURS: 9 A.M. to noon and 1 to 4:30 P.M. weekdays, on Saturday from 9 A.M. to noon.

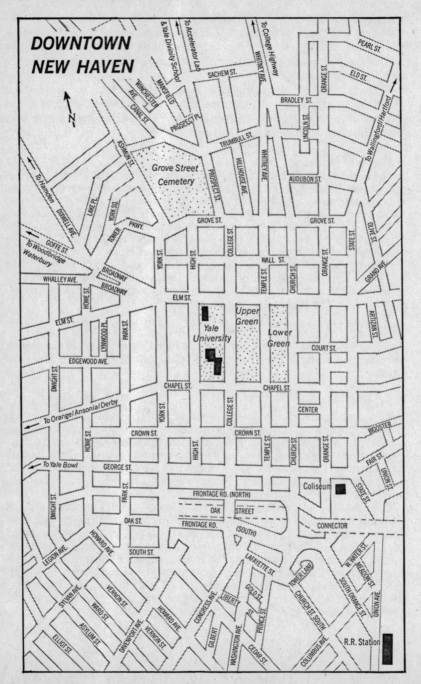

DOWNTOWN NEW HAVEN

Yale University and the Beinecke Library

For any first-time visitor, obviously Yale University will be the number-one attraction. For information and tours (1:30 P.M. weekends, 10:30 A.M. and 2 P.M. weekdays), go to Phelps Gate, 344 College St., between Chapel and Elm, opposite the Green (tel. 203/436-8330).

The 1¼- to 1¾-hour tours will show you the exterior of Connecticut Hall (1750) and Vanderbilt Hall, a dorm for women in which the Vanderbilt Suite can be occupied by *any* Vanderbilt who attends Yale. The tour is often amusing—at Branford College, much of what looks old is fake, deliberately designed so as to attract students by its supposed venerability. Depending on which college your guide resides at, you will see inside one of the 12 colleges—dining rooms, library, lounges, etc. The gym, the largest in the world, also houses a suspended swimming pool and several cruise tanks and batting cages. Sterling Library contains four million volumes in a church-like Gothic building. Guides will initiate you into the mysteries of Mory's, the "Whiffenpoof Song," and other historical Yale lore.

If you prefer to tour on your own, then be sure to see the Old Campus and Connecticut Hall, home to Nathan Hale, Eli Whitney, and Noah Webster; Battell Chapel; Harkness Tower (1920), famed for its 54-bell carillon (played at 8 A.M., 6 P.M., and 10 P.M. daily), and Wrexham Tower, both in the Branford College Quadrangle; the Sterling Memorial Library; Woolsey Hall; and the Beinecke Library (at Wall and High Streets), where you can view one of the rare Gutenberg Bibles, Audubon's *The Birds of America,* and changing displays drawn from the library's vast collection of letters and manuscripts, including those of Mark Twain, Jack London, and Ernest Hemingway, to name only a few. Inside the windowless building light streams through 1½-inch-thick translucent marble panels that take on brilliantly changing hues during the passage of the day. HOURS: Saturday from 8:30 A.M. to 12:15 P.M. and 1:30 to 5 P.M., on Sunday from 2 to 5 P.M.

Yale Center for British Art

This sleek, steel-clad center at 1080 Chapel St. at the corner of High (tel. 203/432-2800), was the last major commission of the late Louis I. Kahn, who designed the building specifically to attract rather than intimidate visitors, and as a result it's the only museum in the nation with storefronts on the ground level. The interior lighting is also innovative: the skylights are placed so that the sun's rays hit no painting directly. It houses the largest collection of British art outside England and its principal resource is the collection of British paintings, sculpture, and rare books given to Yale University by Paul Mellon. The collection surveys the development of British art, life, and thought from the Elizabethan period to the present day with special emphasis on works from the period between the birth of Hogarth (1697) and the death of Turner (1851), considered by many to be the "golden age" of English art. HOURS: Tuesday to Saturday from 10 A.M. to 5 P.M., on Sunday from 2 to 5 P.M.; closed Monday and major holidays. ADMISSION: Free.

Yale Art Gallery

This gallery, at 1111 Chapel St. (tel. 203/432-0600), possesses a lovely sculpture garden and combines the old and the new in its two buildings, one of Gothic Italian palazzo design built in 1928 and the other Yale's first modern commission by Louis Kahn, who designed the space with movable walls that really allows for great flexibility and creativity when museum shows are set up. It was founded in 1832 by John Trumbull, who laid down certain terms, the most peculiar being that his paintings should "never be alienated" from New Haven, that he and his wife were to be buried under the paintings, and that if these conditions were ever violated, the paintings and presumably their bodies were to go to Harvard—even stranger when you consider he was a Harvard man to begin with.

The highlights are many. In the ancient collection the findings at Dura-Europos, and the Assyrian reliefs; van Goghs, Gauguins, and Manets are found on the second floor, and early Renaissance and European on the third floor. The most renowned is probably the Garvan Collection of Decorative Arts, which combines painting, furniture, and decorative arts, including an outstanding silver collection. HOURS: Tuesday to Saturday from 10 A.M. to 5 P.M., on Sunday from 2 to 5 P.M. ADMISSION: Free.

Having explored the major downtown sights, you can pop out to some other attractions, two associated with the university:

Peabody Museum
The Peabody Museum is at 170 Whitney Ave. (tel. 203/432-5050). Rudolph Zallinzer's massive mural depicting part of the North American continent as it appeared 350 to 70 million years ago makes an evocative backdrop for the life-size prehistoric monsters in the Great Hall. Other galleries offer a 500-million-year journey through the natural history of our planet. HOURS: Monday to Saturday from 9 A.M. to 4:45 P.M., on Sunday from 1 to 4:45 P.M. ADMISSION: $1 for adults, 50¢ for children.

New Haven Colony Historical Society
This museum at 114 Whitney Ave. (tel. 203/562-4183), contains fine exhibits of antique dolls, toys, pewter, ceramics, glass, silver, furniture, paintings, and photographs—all relating New Haven's 300 years of history. Among the items are, interestingly enough, Eli Whitney's cotton gin and Benedict Arnold's druggist sign that hung over his shop on Chapel Street. HOURS: Tuesday to Friday from 10 A.M. to 5 P.M., on Saturday and Sunday from 2 to 5 P.M. ADMISSION: Free.

The society also operates the **Pardee-Morris House** (1780), New Haven's oldest residence. Rebuilt shortly after it was burned during the British invasion of New Haven in 1779, the Pardee-Morris House now houses an extensive collection of 17th- to early-19th-century furniture and decorative arts. Operated by the New Haven Colony Historical Society (tel. 203/562-4183 or 467-0764) the house is located five miles south of New Haven off I-95. HOURS: Saturday and Sunday from 11:30 A.M. to 4 P.M. in June and August, and by appointment. ADMISSION: Donation.

Yale's Collection of Musical Instruments
At 15 Hillhouse Ave. (tel. 203/436-4935), the avenue that Dickens described as the most beautiful in America, this collection contains 800 exquisite antique musical instruments dating from the 16th to the 19th century. Demonstrations are given. HOURS: Only when the university is in session, Monday to Wednesday from 1 to 4 P.M., on Sunday from 2 to 5 P.M.

Teletrack
If all this museum watching doesn't appeal to you, then you can always buzz over to Teletrack, 600 Long Wharf Dr. (tel. 203/789-1943 or 789-1637). Place your bets and experience all the thrill of the track at this unique facility where harness racing from Roosevelt and Yonkers, and horse racing from Belmont, Aqueduct, and Saratoga, and even Britain's Grand National, is shown live on a large 24- to 32-foot screen. Down in the huge auditorium, people will be yelling out urging their horses on. You can enjoy a pleasant lunch or dinner here at the Clubhouse Balcony and Restaurant, offering a great view of the screen. HOURS: Monday, Wednesday, Thursday, Friday, and Saturday from noon, and Monday to Saturday evenings from 7 P.M. For dinner reservations, call 203/624-3749. ADMISSION: $4.20 to the Clubhouse level, $2.40 to the auditorium.

Wooster Square and State Street
Close by you can explore Wooster Square, the heart of the old Italian neighborhood, once, strange to say, a resort area, now a quiet haven of magnificent restored old homes set around a garden with a statue of Columbus in the middle. Wooster Street, of course, is the place in New Haven to go for authentic Italian cuisine.

A few blocks north and west of here lies State Street, where you can easily spend an afternoon browsing in the many antique stores, vintage clothing emporiums, and craft-oriented shops that line the street, especially between Humphry and East Streets. A fun part of town with plenty of restaurants to pop into for a break.

City Parks
Ascend to **East Rock Park,** East Park Road (take the I-91 Willow Street exit; tel. 203/787-8142), for an aerial view of the city, harbor, and Long Island Sound. An ideal hiking and picnicking spot. For entrance, take Orange Street to Farnam Drive.

In **West Rock Park** at the other end of the city in Westville, you can hike along the trails and also discover the Judge's Cave, where three regicides who condemned Charles I were sheltered from British authorities. The bountiful mountain laurel makes this lovely in springtime. West Rock Nature Center (tel. 203/787-8016) on Wintergreen Avenue offers 40 acres of woodland with trails and a small zoo. Take Whalley Avenue to Blake Street; turn right, then left, onto Springside Avenue, and left on Wintergreen.

Edgewood Park (bounded by Chapel Street on the south, Boulevard on the east, Yale Avenue on the west, and Edgewood and Whalley Avenues on the north) is filled in summer with cyclists, kids feeding the ducks at the pond or cavorting in the playgrounds, people playing soccer, throwing Frisbees, or just snoozing in the sun. Another good place for a picnic.

Some Offbeat Attractions
Marvelous Egyptian Revival gates designed by Henry Austin lead to the **Grove Street Cemetery,** 227 Grove St., established in 1796 and the final resting place for such redoubtable figures as Noah Webster, Eli Whitney, Charles Goodyear, Roger Sherman (signer of the Declaration of Independence and of the Constitution), Theophilus Eaton (city founder), and other famous men and women associated with New Haven's and the nation's history. Bring ink, rice paper, a slab of glass, and a roller, and make a souvenir grave rubbing. HOURS: Gates close at 4 P.M.

Mythical Yale destinations include **Graffiti Alley,** by the Yale Co-op on Broadway, and Morse College to see Claes Oldenburg's phallic *Lipstick,* which the college saw fit to accept after it was rejected for its originally commissioned location, the Beinecke Plaza.

When you visit the **Center for British Art,** don't miss the Art and Architecture Building, a huge concrete hulk at the corner of York and Chapel Streets, which has been both damned and lauded since Paul Rudolph designed it in 1961. Try to find the entrance. Another architectural attraction is the **Ingalls Rink** on Prospect and Sachem, affectionately dubbed "The Whale" because of its shape, and designed by Eero Saarinen of TWA terminal fame at Kennedy Airport.

Exploring the Shoreline
The M/V *Liberty Belle,* docked at Long Wharf Pier, offers cruises of Long Island Sound, New Haven Harbor, and Branford Harbor sailing several times daily, May through October. Cruise lengths vary from a 30-minute lunch break to a 2½-hour cruise of the harbor and sound. Moonlight cruises with dancing to live bands are also offered. Call 203/562-4163 for details, or write to P.O. Box 2054, New Haven, CT 06521. Prices range from $2 to $10.

Lighthouse Point Park recreational area (tel. 203/787-8005) is the place to go for picnicking, swimming, windsurfing, and sail- or fishing-boat rentals. Kids will love the old-fashioned carousel. To get there, take I-95 to Exit 50; turn right at the second light onto Townsend Avenue, and follow it down to Lighthouse Road. Open Memorial Day to Labor Day. Parking charge.

At **Fort Nathan Hale** (tel. 203/787-8790), where the first of several forts was built in 1657, you can see breastworks, bunkers, gun emplacements, and a Civil War–era drawbridge that literally rolls back. Imagine yourself as one of the 19 soldiers who valiantly defended the position against British warships, until those courageous 19 ran out of ammunition on July 5, 1779. To get there, take I-95 north to Exit 50, and turn right on to Woodward Avenue.

Shoreline Trolley Museum
Rattan seats and amusing old ads are just part of the excitement of riding in an open trolley car, vintage 1911, three miles down the line at the Shoreline Trolley

Museum, 17 River St., East Haven (tel. 203/467-6927). Afterward, take some time to view some of the 108 trolleys in the barns, each an example of beautiful coachwork and artistry with polished woods, stained-glass windows, and wrought-iron work. Oldest example here is an 1880 horse car from Toronto. HOURS: April and November, Sunday only; May and September, weekends only; Memorial Day to Labor Day, daily. ADMISSION: $3.50 for adults, $1.75 for children 2 to 11. Take I-95 north to Exit 51, and turn right at Hemingway Avenue.

Cruising the Thimble Islands and Visiting Guilford

During the summer, cruises of the 24 Thimble Islands, where 'tis rumored Captain Kidd hid some treasure in the 1600s, are available aboard the *Sea Mist* (tel. 203/481-4841). During the summer (from May through Columbus Day) morning breakfast cruises are offered every Sunday. Aboard the *Volsunga III* (tel. 203/481-3345, 488-9978 after Memorial Day), pilot Captain Crab, an alias for Capt. Dwight Carter, a longtime resident of the islands, imparts the island's myths and mysteries to you along the way.

Today the islands are occupied by about 100 residents, including such celebrities as Robert Redford, Garry Trudeau, and Frank Converse. Both boats leave from Stony Creek Dock (Exit 56 off I-95). En route from the cruise, drive the scenic Rte. 146 between Stony Creek and Guilford, taking a detour right down to the sound at Mulberry Point. In Guilford, of course, there are plenty of historic gracious homes set around the Green, famous for its great summer craft fair.

If you do go to Guilford, then stop for tea at the **Apple Doll House Tea Room,** Rte. 77, just off Exit 58 on I-95 (tel. 203/453-2933), a small and cozy place where tables are clustered around a fieldstone fireplace. Quiches, sandwiches, homemade soups, salads, and desserts are all available at reasonable prices. Whatever your purchase, you'll be contributing to SARAH, the Shoreline Association for the Retarded and Handicapped.

Also in Guilford, the **Century House,** 2455 Boston Post Rd. (tel. 203/453-2216), has a warm, romantic air—the large fieldstone fireplace, weathered beams, and paneling help to create this atmosphere. It has recently been taken over by new management and was about to reopen as we went to press. It promises continental cuisine, seafood, and steaks, priced from $9.

LUNCH: Noon to 2 P.M. daily. DINNER: 6 to 10 P.M. on weekdays, until 11 P.M. on weekends. BRUNCH: Sunday from noon to 2 P.M.

NEW HAVEN LODGING

It's surprising that a university town of New Haven's stature possesses no really spectacular lodgings. The **Colony Inn,** 1157 Chapel St., New Haven, CT 06511 (tel. 203/776-1234), is the city's deluxe hotel, offering a degree of elegance in its 85 rooms decorated in a country French style with Oriental accents and well appointed with telephone, color TV, radio, and climate control. Bathrooms also contain those little niceties—shoeshine, soap, and shampoo, etc. The Encore Greenhouse Restaurant, a solarium-type room with streetside view festooned with Victorian-style lamps and potted and hanging ferns, functions as a full-service restaurant offering such dinner entrees as veal Bercy, filet mignon, and pasta dishes. On Sunday an $11 brunch buffet is served. On weekends people dance from 9:30 A.M. on. A cocktail lounge completes the facilities.

RATES: $68 to $73 single, $78 to $83 double.

The largest property is the **Park Plaza,** 155 Temple St., New Haven, CT 06510 (tel. 203/772-1700), offering 300 rooms furnished in typical contemporary style with all the modern comforts of color TV, telephone, and air conditioning. Its greatest drawing card, the Top of the Park restaurant, provides a bird's-eye view of the Green and the university at breakfast, lunch, or dinner. Two lounges and an outdoor pool complete the facilities. RATES: $80 double. A Weekend at the Park package includes accommodation and continental breakfast or champagne brunch buffet at the Top of the Park on Sunday (depending on the night), $90 for double occupancy.

At **Howard Johnson's Motor Lodge—Long Wharf,** 400 Sargent Dr., New Haven, CT 06511 (tel. 203/562-1111), rooms have all been recently renovated. Facilities include an outdoor pool.

RATES: $72 double.

Other choices include the **Holiday Inn,** 30 Whalley Ave., New Haven, CT 06511 (tel. 203/777-6221), with 150 rooms and an outdoor pool.

New Haven has only one downtown hostelry with any real character, somewhat similar to the Chelsea in New York but not nearly as funky, the **Hotel Duncan,** 1151 Chapel St., New Haven, CT 06511 (tel. 203/787-1273), which many a visiting celebrity—Christopher Walken, Henry and Jane Fonda, Rita Moreno, George Hearn, Carroll Baker, and Athol Fugard, to name only a few—has chosen to call home. At the back of the somewhat plain lobby, furnished with vinyl chairs standing on a linoleum floor, the elevator, still manned by an operator, will take you to your room. Most likely it will be a large high-ceilinged chamber, filled with eclectic and somewhat faded furniture, heated by cast-iron radiators, and still appointed with a nonworking 1920s radio hanging on the wall. Private bath, color TV, and phone are in most rooms.

RATES: $35 single, $50 double.

About three miles out on Whalley Avenue just beyond Westville, the **New Haven Inn and Conference Center,** 100 Pond Lily Ave., New Haven, CT 06525 (tel. 203/387-6651), is a pleasant place to stay. The lobby is filled with antique reproductions. Fully tiled burgundy bathrooms also contain built-in hairdryers, soap, and shampoo, and the 125 rooms themselves are attractively decorated in light pastels with bamboo furnishings. All have remote-control color TVs, clock radios, towels, Touch-tone phones. Other facilities include a health club and indoor pool.

RATES: $55 single, $65 to $69 double.

Bed-and-Breakfast

One other choice is to contact Jack Argenio of **Bed and Breakfast Ltd.,** P.O. Box 216, New Haven, CT 06513 (tel. 203/469-3260). Call anytime in summer; the rest of the year, between 4 and 9 P.M. weekdays or anytime on weekends. Jack's organization has over 125 statewide listings, many of which are in New Haven.

RATES: Prices range from $35 to $60 a night.

NEW HAVEN DINING

Legendary New Haven Favorites
Mention New Haven and several traditional favorites leap to mind. First, there's **Louis' Lunch,** 261-263 Crown St. (tel. 203/562-5507), home of the first hamburger, created supposedly for a man in a hurry by owner Louis Lassen in 1900. Don't ask for ketchup or mustard. Louis' grandson remains faithful to his grandfather's original concept and would never dream of allowing you to mar a hamburger that way. Forget it. Toast, onion, and tomato—that's it. The hamburgers served here, cooked on vertical grills, are so mythically memorable that when Louis' was threatened with demolition, Yalies and patrons from all over the world sent bricks to help in the reconstruction of their beloved hamburger joint. Check out the walls—the bricks are all here! Unfortunately, Louis' doesn't open on weekends, but you still should know about this one!
HOURS: Monday to Friday from 9 A.M. to 4:30 P.M.

Or you can stop at another legendary culinary landmark, **Pepes,** 157 Wooster St. (tel. 203/865-5762), home since 1925 of the first American pizza. A family operation where Aunt Rachel, sister of original owner Frank, still works four or five hours a day preparing pies for the authentic Italian coal-fired brick ovens, which turn out a very special product. Try their famous clam pizza with white sauce.
HOURS: Monday, Wednesday, and Thursday from 4 to 11 P.M., on Friday and Saturday from 11:30 A.M. to midnight, on Sunday from 2:30 to 11 P.M.; closed Tuesday.

Some pizza lovers, though, choose another culinary landmark on Wooster Street, **Sally's,** at no. 237, because they prefer, they say, the thinner-crusted pizza.
HOURS: Tuesday to Thursday, Saturday, and Sunday from 4:30 to 11:30 P.M., on Friday from noon to 1 A.M.; closed Monday.

After some slices of pizza, trot down to **Libby's** (tel. 203/772-0380), for pastries —napoleons, cannoli, éclairs, rhum baba—and gelato and cappuccino. Italian colors and white wrought-iron chairs and tables provide the informal atmosphere.
HOURS: Tuesday, Wednesday, Thursday, and Sunday from 10:30 A.M. to 10 P.M., on Friday and Saturday to midnight.

Breakfast/Brunch
At **Atticus Bookstore-Café,** 1082 Chapel St. (tel. 203/776-4040), you can sit surrounded by books on display, even peruse a few while you're waiting for the very special croissants (chocolate, almond, or plain butter) and cup of choice tea or coffee. Linger as long as you like. This is also a good place later in the day to sample some yummy homemade desserts, including some real Viennese pastries, or any of the sandwiches, pâté, and salads, mostly under $5.
HOURS: Monday to Thursday from 8 A.M. to midnight, on Friday and Saturday until 1 A.M., on Sunday from 10 A.M. to 8 P.M.

Nothing but a bagel will satisfy your breakfast appetite? Head for **New York**

Bagels, 172 York St. (tel. 203/773-3089). Nine varieties are offered along with kosher and nonkosher sandwiches in a light and airy setting.

HOURS: 7 A.M. to 7 P.M. (on Monday until 5 P.M.).

For more formal brunches, head for the **Chart House,** 100 S. Water St. (tel. 203/787-3466), **500 Blake Street,** off Whalley Avenue in Westville (tel. 203/387-0500), or the **Elm City Diner,** 1228 Chapel St. (tel. 203/776-5050).

Lunch Choices

Success has turned what used to be a tiny hole-in-the-wall restaurant, **Claire's Corner Copia,** 1000 Chapel St. (tel. 203/562-3888), into a popular restaurant seating 60. Stop in for a breakfast of homemade muffins, scones, quiches, frittata, granola, and cappuccino and yogurt shakes. At lunch, choose a croissant sandwich, pita-bread sandwiches, soups, and a whole spectrum of meatless Mexican foods like quesadillas, burritos, tostadas, tacos, guacamole, and eggplant Veracruz. Evenings the menu is supplemented by additional Italian, Indian, French, and American dishes. Prices range from $2 to $6. No written menu here—just the blackboards.

HOURS: Sunday to Thursday from 8 A.M. to 10 P.M., on Friday and Saturday until 11 P.M.

Middle Eastern fare—baba ghannouj and hummus—can also be found at **Mamoun's Falafel Restaurant** at 85 Howe St. Under $5 a plate.

HOURS: 11 A.M. to 3 A.M. daily.

Lunch or Dinner Choices

Annie's Firehouse Restaurant, 19 Edwards St. (tel. 203/865-4200), occupies a refurbished old firehouse, complete with exposed pipes and brick walls, and furnishings that include a box office booth from the Alvin Booth Theater in New York, which doubles as a cashier's desk. Great soups, home-baked breads, salads, and sandwiches are priced in the $5 to $10 range. At dinner more ambitious dishes are featured—sea scallops in a sherry cream sauce, herbed lamb chops, Sasha's Dijon chicken. The selections reflect the season. Prices range from $9.25 to $15.50. Beer and wine only.

LUNCH: Monday to Saturday from 11:30 A.M. to 3 P.M. DINNER: Monday to Thursday from 5:30 to 9:30 P.M., on Friday and Saturday until 10 P.M., and on Sunday from 5 to 9 P.M. BRUNCH: Sunday from 11 A.M. to 2:30 P.M.

Another traditional Yale favorite, the **Old Heidelberg,** 1151 Chapel St. (tel. 203/777-3639), is the oldest restaurant in New Haven, established in 1757. Generations of Yalies have carved their names on the tabletops while waiting for steaks, seafood, continental, and American fare. Prices run from $5.50 for sandwiches to $17.50 for pescadora, a fragrant mixture of lobster, shrimp, mussels, clams, calamari, scallops, and fish of the day, served over linguini.

Jellybeans were free here even before Ronald Reagan walked onto a larger stage set. Long Wharf or other theater celebrities staying at the Hotel Duncan (above the restaurant) often stop in for some postshow relaxation.

HOURS: Monday to Thursday from 11:30 A.M. to 1 A.M., on Friday and Saturday until 2 A.M., and on Sunday from 4 to 11 P.M.

A more modern spot with a traditional flavor is **Gentree Ltd.**, 194 York St. (tel. 203/562-3800), formerly a men's clothing store that turned out many a Yale man in fine fashion. Owners Henry Milone and Houston Striggow have retained the handsome interior paneling and even managed to carve a booth out of what was previously a clothes rack. Specialties include nachos, really delicious barbecued chicken and ribs, a variety of unique grilled fish dishes prepared in a marinade, prime rib, plus salads and sandwiches, all at reasonable prices.

HOURS: 11:30 A.M. to 1 A.M. weekdays, until 2 A.M. on weekends. BRUNCH: Sunday from 10:30 A.M. to 3 P.M.

For Chinese food, New Havenites swear by **Blessings,** 45 Howe St. (tel. 203/624-3557), where, although the surroundings are familiar—Formica tables and placemats and a minimum of decor—the food is surprising. For example, among the specials you'll find a purple-leaf soup made with seaweed, eggs, and chicken stock, and such unusual appetizers as broiled scallops with Chinese sausage. Classic dishes like Peking duck and Hsiang-Su duck are served along with Szechuan and Cantonese dishes on a menu that lists over 100 dishes. During the week a luncheon buffet is served. On weekends you'll have to choose from the menu. Prices at dinner range from $6.25 to $8.50 (except for the Peking duck). Lunch prices are less.

LUNCH: Monday to Saturday from 11:30 A.M. to 2:30 P.M. DINNER: Monday to Saturday from 5 to 9 P.M. Closed Sunday.

Leons, 321 Washington Ave. (tel. 203/777-5366), is another all-time favorite that has been here for years serving excellent and unusual Italian dishes. The portions are enough for two, and the prices reasonable. At lunchtime the menu features a whole array of pastas, seafood, cioppino, scampi oreganata, lobster Fra Diavalo, and veal dishes—pizzaiola, marsala, parmigiana, and cacciatore—all under $9. Reckon on $15 to $21 at dinner. It's really a great place to go.

LUNCH: Tuesday to Friday from noon to 2:30 P.M. DINNER: Tuesday to Saturday from 5 to 10 P.M., on Sunday from noon to 8 P.M.

For Japanese cuisine, seek out **Hatsune,** 93 Whitney Ave. (tel. 203/776-3216), in the basement at the corner of the building. Two rooms with simple wood screens for decor and a separate lounge area make up the restaurant. A la carte dishes—tonkatsu, sukiyaki, tempura, negimaki—are all priced from $9 to $17. Try the bento, an assortment of sushi and sashimi, tempura, and hatsune fish, served in a delicate, decorated lacquer box for $18.75.

LUNCH: Monday to Saturday from 11:45 A.M. to 2:30 P.M. DINNER: 5 to 10 P.M. daily. BRUNCH: Sunday from 1 P.M.

Fitzwilly's, 338 Elm St. (tel. 203/624-9438), is another traditional New Haven favorite. Here in this old firehouse where every corner and crevice is filled with plants, daily specials like linguini with white clam sauce, Boston scrod, or clam chowder are always available, and there's even a dessert special. The full menu is served all day, and features an array of American favorites including steak, seafood, sandwiches, salads, and other dishes too numerous to mention. Prices range from $5 to $12. On weekends you're likely to find the place jammed with students and other folks so you may have to wait for a table.

HOURS: 11:30 A.M. to midnight daily.

Ross Proctor, owner of the **Elm City Diner,** 1228 Chapel St. at Howe (tel. 203/

776-5050), is a passionate preservationist who rescues diners and fills them with people, entertainment, and offbeat food and cocktails (at least as far as the regular diner goes).

This one's a beauty. It was placed on site in 1955 and is a late '40s-style modern-era diner with monarch ceiling. At night it's spectacular: the bar lights up, spotlights shimmer, and myriad reflections flash from mirrors, chrome, and stainless steel that abounds throughout. The piano jazz/standards accompaniment (Thursday, Friday, and Saturday from 9:30 P.M. on) adds style. It seats 60 or so. At dinner burgers and salads are supplemented by a raft of entrees like linguini puttanesca (anchovies, capers, tomatoes, olives, and basil), shrimp Créole, barbecued chicken and ribs, and even Mexican pizza. Prices run from $9 to $13. Similar fare is available at lunch, with many of the dishes inspired by Mexican cuisine. Try the "firefighter," for example: two fried eggs, chili, guacamole, salsa, grated cheese on a corn tortilla. Portions are enough for two.

LUNCH: Monday to Saturday from 11 A.M. to 5 P.M. DINNER: Monday to Thursday from 5 P.M. to 12:30 A.M., on Friday and Saturday until 1:30 A.M., and on Sunday until 12:30 A.M. BRUNCH: Sunday from 11 A.M. to 5 P.M.

For a quick convenient lunch, **Chapel Square Mall** hosts a variety of counters that share common seating areas. **Oriental Express** offers Chinese dishes; **Mercato** tempts with stuffed shells and meatball sandwiches and similar; moussaka and stuffed peppers are available at the **Gourmet Greek,** while **Galleria** has a formal dining area and full menu featuring such items as braciole and steak pizzaiola. **Frying Fish** operates a raw bar and also makes crab and lobster rolls and other fish sandwiches; **Atticus Bookstore** has another branch here. Pizza, subs, hot dogs, potatoes with fillings, deli, ice cream, yogurt sundaes, and cookies can all be found here. The best tables overlook the Green.

HOURS: Regular shopping hours only, and not on Sunday.

Dinner Only

Casa Marra Ristorante, 321 East St. (tel. 203/777-5148), is located in an old factory building that has been transformed into a series of dining areas set around a courtyard open to the sky. Dine on finely seasoned Italian specialties—veal perugina with chicken livers, braccioletta (thin sirloin seasoned with parmesan and garlic, and served in tomato sauce with mushrooms), a full selection of pasta like paglie fieno (green noodles with salmon cream sauce), and fish dishes, priced from $8 to $20.

LUNCH: Noon to 3 P.M. on weekdays. DINNER: Monday to Friday from 5 to 10 P.M., on Saturday until 2 A.M. Closed Sunday.

Head for **Basels,** 993 State St. (tel. 203/624-9361), for spicy moussaka and far more tasty Greek specialties—chicken micrasiatiko (chicken breast simmered in wine sauce with mushrooms, scallions, and chopped walnuts), baked lamb in tomato sauce, or veal in a crock with kasseri (a marvelous cheese-flavored dish). On Friday and Saturday nights the evening will be made even more memorable by the stirring Greek bouzouki music and dancing that starts around 9 P.M.

LUNCH: Monday to Friday from 11:30 A.M. to 2 P.M. DINNER: Tuesday to Thursday from 5 to 9 P.M., on Friday and Saturday until 2 A.M. Closed Sunday.

Enthusiasm, flair, and love of cooking inform **Christopher Martin's,** 860 State St. (tel. 203/776-8835). Martin is the chef; Christopher, the maître d'/business expert. The room is simple and tasteful. The food is well prepared and dishes are accompanied by a bowl of fresh cooked vegetables—potatoes and squash, for example. There's always a selection of specials: shad with grapes and zinfandel sauce, for example, or rack of lamb (five pieces), served with a different sauce of the day. Dishes are often named after waitresses or kitchen helpers, like the veal Giorgio made with cranberries. Prices range from $9.50 or thereabouts for such items as chicken Santa Cruz (breast of chicken, avocado, and tomato with a light wine sauce), scallops Dijon, or baby back ribs, to slightly more expensive dishes like stuffed loin of pork (chestnut stuffing laced with glace viande), or filet mignon au poivre vert. Top price is $14.25. Several pasta dishes appear including an unusual one with walnut sauce made with butter, garlic, cream cheese, and walnuts. Appetizers are fairly traditional—oysters Rockefeller, shrimp cocktail—except for the Brie en croûte and baked chanterelles. When it comes to desserts Martin caters to the current chocolate obsession. There are several that are heavy chocolate, as well as almond amaretto cake, and "Mounds" (originally made for his mother, who happens to love Mounds). The wine list is carefully selected and extremely reasonably priced—a Georges Duboeuf Beaujolais Villages for $9. Jazz is planned on weekends.

LUNCH: Monday to Friday from 11:30 A.M. to 3 P.M. DINNER: Monday to Friday from 5 to 10 P.M., on Saturday and Sunday until 10:30 P.M. BRUNCH: Sunday during the winter only.

At **Audubon Café,** 60 Audubon St. (tel. 203/785-0277), neon lights and a profusion of greenery make a visually striking scene at night. The menu offers a popular American mix of salads, soups, and burgers for lunch, and fresh fish—scampi Pernod, scallops mornay—steaks, and teriyaki dishes at night. Prices run $7 to $13.

LUNCH: Monday to Saturday from 11:30 A.M. to 5 P.M. DINNER: Monday to Thursday from 5 to 11 P.M., on Friday and Saturday until midnight, on Sunday until 10 P.M. BRUNCH: Sunday from 11:30 A.M. to 3 P.M.

People rave about **Delmonaco's,** 232 Wooster St. (tel. 203/865-1109), for its beautiful Neapolitan garden-like setting, where the light streams through a stained-glass skylight onto stucco walls, rich brown carpeting, and hanging plants. The southern Italian specialties are also wonderful, from the soups and salads (escarole and bean soup; insalata napoletana with lettuce, chicory, black olives, oil, and lemon) to the main seafood and meat dishes—13 veal creations cooked in classic Italian ways, and plenty of beef steaks either cooked simply or with continental-style sauces, plus, of course, pasta and chicken entrees. Prices range from $15 to $19.

LUNCH: Monday through Friday from 11:30 A.M. to 2:30 P.M. DINNER: Monday through Saturday from 5 to 11 P.M., on Sunday from 1 to 10 P.M. Closed Tuesday.

Even a bona fide Italian who prefers not to sample Italian restaurant fare will willingly go to **Tony and Lucille's,** 127 Wooster St. (tel. 203/787-1620), for the sauces really are as good as home-cooked ones and the calzones are super-special. Pizza is also available. Everything on the menu is under $10, and served in simple surroundings at tables covered with red gingham tablecloths.

LUNCH: Monday to Friday from noon to 3 P.M. DINNER: Monday to Friday from 5 to 10 P.M., on Saturday and Sunday from 4 P.M.

Claudio's, 937 State St. (tel. 203/777-5490), is a bright, highly attractive restaurant that is fast becoming a New Haven favorite. If you can get past the cabinet displaying all kinds of desserts and Italian specialties, you'll discover a dining room filled with tables covered in pale-blue cloths; the light oak Windsor chairs are set on crisp Italian tile floors. Fresh flowers add color to each table. Entrees, priced from $13, are typically Italian—steak pizzaiola, saltimbocca a la romana. Pastas are also available. On the other side of the entrance there's also an area where light lunches are served.

LUNCH: Monday to Friday from 11:30 A.M. to 2 P.M. DINNER: Monday to Thursday from 5:30 to 8:30 P.M., on Friday and Saturday until 9:30 P.M. Closed Sunday.

Tucked away down an alley off State Street, **La Casa d'Orso,** 588 East St. (tel. 203/777-3436), makes its own pasta and pastries, which are beguilingly displayed: among them, row upon row of chocolate cannolis complete with chocolate case as well as chocolate cream. In the striking burgundy-and-jade room you can feast on a variety of pasta, chicken, pork, veal, and seafood dishes—fettuccine Alfredo, lasagne, manicotti, pasta with clam sauce, shrimp Florentine, chicken marsala, veal with mushrooms and peppers.

LUNCH: Tuesday to Friday from 11:30 A.M. to 2:30 P.M. DINNER: Monday to Thursday from 5 to 9 P.M., on Friday and Saturday from 5 to 10 P.M., and on Sunday from 4 to 8 P.M.

Azteccas, 14 Mechanic St. (tel. 203/624-2454), isn't your average Mexican restaurant—it attempts to add a dash of authenticity. Appetizers include ceviche, scallops marinated in lime juice with tomatoes, chilis and avocado slices, and a hearty thick black-bean soup. Chimichanga (a tortilla filled with beef, chicken, or vegetable topped with guacamole, salsa, and sour cream) and pescado en cilantro (fish broiled and covered with green tomato and coriander sauce) are two of the specialties priced from $9.50. Enchiladas (verde or poblanas), tostadas, and other, more typical Mexican dishes are also available.

The decor is far from being typically Mexican—unless rose-colored napkins and salmon-pink tablecloths are the latest Mexicana theme.

LUNCH: Monday to Friday from 11:30 A.M. to 2:30 P.M. DINNER: Monday to Thursday from 5 to 9 P.M., on Friday and Saturday until 10 P.M. Closed Sunday.

Lunch, 245 Crown St. (tel. 203/782-0038 or 782-0040), is a serene gray and sparsely decorated storefront whose windows are now filled with upholstered and cushioned window seats. Wrought-iron chairs and tables stand on tiled floors. The food has a Middle Eastern flavor: hummus and taboulleh are among the appetizers. Armenian pizza (lah magoon) with ground lamb and beef, and boereg (three cheese-filled pastries) are unusual menu items. For the more traditional-minded, try baked Brie with baguette or turkey and Brie with lettuce, tomato and Dijon. Prices are under $5, some under $3.

LUNCH: Monday to Saturday from 11 A.M. to 4 P.M. *Note:* Hours tend to be erratic, so check.

The mesquite grill is much used at the **Rusty Scupper,** 501 Long Wharf Dr. (tel. 203/777-5711), a bilevel restaurant whose large-pane windows look across New

Haven Harbor to City Point. The menu is extensive—mesquite-grilled mako, bluefish, trout, and rack of lamb, along with Cajun blackened redfish, baked haddock, prime rib, lobster tail, and other classic American favorites. Prices run from $10 for shrimp tempura to $18 for lobster tail. Start with clams casino, oysters Rockefeller, smoked trout, or the stuffed mushrooms, which are indeed filled with crabmeat. Desserts are typical: cheesecake, walnut fudge pie, apple pie, etc.

LUNCH: Monday to Friday from 11:30 A.M. to 2 P.M., on Sunday from 11 A.M. to 3 P.M. DINNER: Monday to Thursday from 5 to 10 P.M., on Friday and Saturday until 11 P.M., on Sunday from 5 to 10 P.M.

Hidden away on the waterfront in City Point, a now-gentrifying neighborhood, **Chart House,** 100 S. Water St. (tel. 203/787-3466), is favored for brunch and cocktails and dining by the water. Upstairs the cocktail lounge offers a bar menu of spiced shrimp, shrimp cocktail, oysters casino and Rockefeller.

Both the restaurant and bar probably grant the best view over the harbor insofar as it includes fewer storage tanks than most. Naugahyde couches set under a peaked cedar ceiling provide comfortable places for drinking and chatting. Focal point of the dining room is a double chimney in the center of the room. Laminated navigational charts serve as tabletops for plates of steak and lobster, Hawaiian chicken, fresh fish, teriyaki kebabs—a simple, limited menu printed on a paddle board. Prices are $10 to $20.75. At brunch, eggs Benedict and similar typical dishes are served with either a glass of champagne or orange juice, muffins, and fruit salad.

DINNER: Monday to Thursday from 5 to 10 P.M., until 11 P.M. on Friday and Saturday. BRUNCH: Sunday from 11 A.M. to 3 P.M.

EVENING ENTERTAINMENT

First, check the *New Haven Advocate* for listings. Be sure also to check the bulletin boards in front of the Yale Post Office at Elm and High Streets. There's always something going on—good, bad, or indifferent—around the university.

The Performing Arts

Theater flourishes in New Haven. The **Long Wharf,** 222 Sargent Dr. (tel. 203/787-4282), under the leadership of Arvin Brown, has been producing original and classical drama for years. *American Buffalo* and *Streamers* are just two examples of recent plays that opened in New Haven and moved successfully to Broadway. The season runs from October to late June. Take Exit 46 off I-95.

The **Yale Repertory Theater** is the professional theater adjunct of the Yale School for Drama. Meryl Streep gave many performances here. More recently, the Rep has built an international reputation as a crucible for the development of new plays, including those by Athol Fugard and August Wilson. Located at 1120 Chapel St. (tel. 203/432-1234 for the box office), in the former Calvary Baptist Church.

Two more recent additions to the theater scene are the Palace Performing Arts Center and the recently reopened 1,700-seat **Shubert Performing Arts Center,** 257 College St. (tel. 203/562-5666), which over the years since it first opened in

1914 saw so many famous openings—*The Desert Song, My Fair Lady, Oklahoma!, West Side Story.* It has been restored to its former glory, with its gilt pillars, "cupcake" box seats, and ornate plasterwork, and now hosts Broadway shows like *Cats* and the recent revival of *Arsenic and Old Lace,* as well as recitals by opera singers, a seasonal presentation of *The Nutcracker,* and performances by a variety of major artists. Tickets cost $10 to $40, depending on the show.

The 2,000-seat **Palace Performing Arts Center,** 254 College St. (tel. 203/624-8497), formerly the Sherman Theater, reopened in early 1984 and presents concert series, musical events, film festivals, etc.

Also check into **Yale Drama,** 222 York St. (tel. 203/865-4300).

The **New Haven Symphony** performs at Woolsey Hall, corner of College and Grove Streets. Call 776-1444 for their schedule. Also, find out what's happening at the **Yale Music School** (tel. 203/436-1971), or at **Trinity Church** on the Green. Groups to look for include the Yale Concert Band, Yale Glee Club, Yale Jazz Ensemble, the Bach Society, New Haven Civic Orchestra, and the Community Choir.

Spectator Sports

Yale offers football, fencing, polo, hockey, swimming, wrestling, crew, tennis, and golf. Write to **Yale Sports Information,** 402A Yale Station, New Haven, CT 06520 (tel. 203/436-0100).

Veteran's Memorial Coliseum, 275 S. Orange St. (tel. 203/772-4330), also hosts sports events.

Teletrack (tel. 203/789-1943) offers simulcasts of horse and harness racing as well as special programs like the New Haven Symphony Sunday Pops Concerts. HOURS: Noon to 9 P.M.

Jai alai is played in nearby Milford at 311 Old Gate Lane (tel. toll free 800/243-9660). HOURS: May through November, Monday to Friday from 7 P.M., on Saturday from 11:45 A.M. and 7 P.M. Take Exit 40 off I-95.

Bars/Dancing/Jazz/Cabaret

Jazz can often be heard at **Sprague Hall,** 435 College St. (tel. 203/436-1971), at Wall Street. Other likely spots include the **Foundry Café,** 104 Audubon St. (tel. 203/776-5144), which features daily jazz and is famous for Friday summer lunchtime bag-it-with-Bach sessions in the courtyard; and the **Elm City Diner,** 1226 Chapel St. (tel. 203/776-5050), one of the few places open on Sunday evenings. This 1950s diner has been converted into a slick '30s-decor diner with a little jazz on the side. On July weekends the Green hosts the **New Haven Jazz Festival.**

Sports fiends hang out in **Kavanaghs,** 1166 Chapel St. (tel. 203/624-0520), surrounded by memorabilia and photographs of such heroes as Babe Ruth up at bat or of moments like Dan McGill scoring against Princeton.

Funky describes the **Old Barge,** at 289 S. Front St. (tel. 203/776-7972), where a mixed crowd of white-collar, blue-collar, and any other kind of collar join in sing-alongs or dance to the honky-tonk aboard this creaky 130-year-old river barge.

Go east on Grand Avenue. Turn left on South Front Street. Snacks available. HOURS: Until 1 A.M. daily.

500 Blake Street (tel. 203/387-0500) is a popular spot for Italian-American food (it's really great) that also offers a comfy piano bar and a rathskeller featuring occasional vocal or instrumental accompaniment to the piano from Thursday to Saturday night.

A likely dancing spot? **Bumpers,** 71 Whitney Ave. (tel. 203/777-1738).

NEW HAVEN ACTIVITIES

ANTIQUING: Shops abound along State Street, which I have already mentioned. Several stores are also located in the 800-block of Whalley Avenue.

BICYCLING: Rentals available in Edgewood Park.

FISHING: Aboard the *Blue Fin,* Smith Bros. Boat Yard at the end of Howard Avenue (tel. 203/624-5895).

FRUIT PICKING: *Guilford:* Bishop's Orchards, 1355 Boston Post Rd. (tel. 203/453-2338), apples, strawberries, and raspberries. *Hamden:* Paradise Nurseries, 63 Newcastle Dr. (tel. 203/288-4779), tomatoes, peppers, and eggplant. *New Haven:* Onofrio Market, Inc., 440 Lombard St. (tel. 203/865-9027), strawberries and peppers.

GOLF: *Branford:* Twin Lakes, Twin Lakes Road (tel. 203/488-8778). *Fair Haven:* Alling Memorial Golf Course, 35 Eastern St. (tel. 203/787-8013). Call ahead on Thursday for Saturday, or on Friday for Sunday. *Hamden:* Laurel View Country Club, West Shepard Ave. (tel. 203/281-0670); Meadowbrook Country Club, Dixwell Avenue (tel. 203/281-4847).

HIKING: Try West Rock Park, at Blake Street and Springside Avenue.

HORSEBACK RIDING: *Branford:* Hickory Hills Stables, 94 Mill Plain Rd. (tel. 203/481-2178). *Hamden:* Blue Valley Stable, Old Lane Road (tel. 203/248-1462).

ICE SKATING: Coogan Pavilion, Edgewood Park, (tel. 203/787-8001); Salperto, Woodward Avenue (tel. 203/787-8006).

PICNICKING: Several parks make picnicking easy. Head for East Rock or West Rock Park or Lighthouse Point, picking up supplies along the way at À **la Carte,** 50 Whitney Ave. (tel. 203/865-1525), which will assemble a feast of cheeses and gourmet foods to go.

Edgewood Park is also a lovely woodland oasis closed to traffic during the summer.

SAILBOAT RENTAL: Sail New Haven, 2 Lighthouse Point Rd. (tel. 203/469-6754).

SWIMMING: Either at Lighthouse Point Park ($1 per car) or at Morse Park Beach at 2nd and Beach Avenue in West Haven ($2 per car).

TENNIS: Courts exist at the bottom of East Rock Park (tel. 203/787-6086) and are free. The New Haven Racquet Club, Old Amity Road, off Rte. 63, Bethany (tel. 203/393-0550), charges anywhere from $8 to $15 an hour plus a small guest fee.

ESSEX & THE CONNECTICUT RIVER VALLEY

DISTANCES IN MILES: Middletown, 101; Essex, 110; Old Saybrook, 113
ESTIMATED DRIVING TIME: about 2½ hours

DRIVING: Take I-95 north to Rte. 9 going to Essex. For Middletown, take the Merritt Parkway to I-91 and then pick up Rte. 66 east.
BUS: Greyhound (tel. 212/635-0800, or toll free 800/528-6055) and Trailways (tel. 212/730-7460) travel to Middletown.
TRAIN: Amtrak travels to Old Saybrook. For information call 212/736-6288.

Special Events to Plan Your Trip Around
MAY: Essex Shad Festival.
JULY: Niantic Lions Lobster Festival in East Lyme—seafood, arts and crafts (July 4).

The Deep River Muster of Fife and Drum. Contact Deep River Town Hall (tel. 203/526-5783)—usually the third weekend in July.
SEPTEMBER: The Durham Fair, the largest in the state—call 203/349-3625 (usually the last weekend in September).
OCTOBER: Head of the Connecticut Regatta, Middletown (usually Columbus Day weekend).
NOVEMBER/DECEMBER: Wesleyan Potters Exhibit and Sale, Middletown.
DECEMBER: Torchlight Parade, muster, and carol sing, Old Saybrook (usually the second Saturday in December).

For further information about these events and Connecticut in general, call or write the Travel Office, Department of Economic Development,

210 Washington St., Hartford, CT 06106 (tel. 203/566-3385, or toll free 800/243-1685 from Maine through Virginia, 800/842-7492 in Connecticut).

For specific information about the area (except Essex and Old Lyme), contact the Connecticut Valley Tidewater Commission, 70 College St., Middletown, CT 06457 (tel. 203/347-6924).

The New England Vacation Center, 630 Fifth Ave., Concourse Shop 2, New York, NY 10020 (tel. 212/307-5780), also provides information.

Today you can stand at the lower reaches of the Connecticut River and survey a scene that has changed little since Adrian Block first sailed up the river in 1614, for here the banks of the river have remained largely unscarred by industrial mills and manufacturing plants. The towns you'll encounter—Old Lyme, Hadlyme, and East Haddam on the east bank and Old Saybrook, Essex, Deep River, Chester, Haddam, and Middletown on the west bank—are all, except perhaps Middletown, entrancing, quiet old towns that have managed to retain their 18th- and 19th-century serenity undisturbed by the heavy industry that marred so many other New England river towns.

No wonder the Indians called this river the Quinnehtukqut or "long tidal river" —its waters, abundant with salmon and shad, flowing 400 miles from the Québec –New Hampshire border all the way south to Long Island Sound. At one time salmon was so plentiful that it was given to the servants, while shad was reserved for the animals. Although the Dutch discovered the river, it was John Winthrop, Jr., who came from the Massachusetts Bay Colony south to found another colony at the behest of certain English Puritans and Cromwellian followers. This colony flourished largely because of the gifts of the river and the trade that the waterway encouraged. Ivoryton, for example, was so named because it was the final destination for shiploads and cartloads of ivory brought from the East to this small town, where the Pratt Read factory continues to this day to turn out piano and organ keys, albeit no longer ivory ones. Neighboring Essex grew into a major shipbuilding town where the first American navy boat, the 24-gun *Oliver Cromwell,* was constructed during the American Revolution, a fact that the British never forgot. They took vengeance during the War of 1812, when they bribed a local youth to help them navigate the treacherous sandbars at the narrow neck of the river and then proceeded to shell the town and to destroy 28 ships, or $160,000 worth of American shipping. Today anchored in that same harbor are all shapes and sizes of yachts and pleasure craft. Their bronzed crews, sporting Topsiders and crewnecks, can be found winding down after a day's sail over a pint of ale or a drink in the old tap room at the area's finest hostelry, the Griswold Inn.

Farther upriver, East Haddam was also a great shipbuilding town that turned out many of the great schooners that sailed downriver to the four corners of the world. One of the shipbuilders, William Goodspeed, was also a hotel owner and theater lover who wanted to attract people to the area. So he built his very own Goodspeed Theater, a six-story gingerbread extravaganza in East Haddam where he located the theater on the top floor and his offices and a general store below. For years people traveling upriver stopped to attend a show. Sometimes whole Broadway shows were transported here to Goodspeed's theater, which thrived from 1876 until the 1920s, when river travel was eclipsed by the railroad and, more important, by the automobile. Goodspeed's opera house became a state garage and warehouse. Threatened with demolition in the '50s, it was narrowly rescued from the wrecker's ball by a dedicated group of people. Now audiences can enjoy wonderful evenings of entertainment in this Victorian gem of an auditorium, currently dedicated to preserving the legacy of American musical theater.

Close by, on the southernmost hill of the so-called Seven Hills, William Gillette was so moved by the beauty of the wooded bluffs and the river that one evening, on a return journey from Long Island, he cancelled his plans for a summer mansion at Greenport and built his idiosyncratic castle right here instead.

During the late 19th century it was a common sight to see a huge side-wheeler churning up the river from New York to Hartford on a 140-mile journey that, with luck, might take 18 hours. Such steamer passenger service continued up until 1931, when it finally succumbed to the motor car and the railroad, which had already come to the valley in 1871. Today you can take a nostalgic ride aboard one of the old-style locomotives that used to steam alongside the river. As the age of sail and steam gave way to the motor car, the river towns returned to a slumber and continued that way unmarred by any industrial development. Lacking any waterfalls and therefore waterpower, they avoided the destiny that had created such industrial towns as Holyoke and Springfield. Instead they seemed to remain in an earlier era, when the tall masts of schooners and the smokestacks of steamers jammed the river, and when life flowed at a gentler pace—as it still does today —making the whole area a wonderfully refreshing, magical place to retreat for a weekend. Ramble through these pristine old towns, and browse in antique stores; wander down narrow streets lined with rambling colonial homes, and stop in at warm and comfortable country inns. Experience the nostalgic joy of climbing aboard the big steam locomotive that runs from Essex to Chester, or cruise the river aboard all kinds of vessels passing the same wooded bluffs and seeing the same beauty that inspired William Gillette to build his castle here. Canoe, swim, fish, go fruit picking, cross-country ski, skate on the lakes, enjoy an evening at the Goodspeed, stop in at art galleries and craft shops, and just revel in the countryside, shoreline, and riverbanks that Childe Hassam loved to paint. You'll return totally rejuvenated, if you return at all.

A Suggested Itinerary

The best way to explore the whole area is to drive a loop pretty much as follows:

Take Rte. 9 south from Middletown, and turn onto Rte. 9A along the river to Chester. At Chester turn east on Rte. 148, and take the old ferry to Hadlyme and Gillette Castle. Continue east on Rte. 148 and then 82, and then turn south on 156 to Old Lyme. Cross the river by bridge on I-95 south, and take Rte. 154 looping around to Saybrook Point, Fenwick, and back to Rte. 1, which will take you to Westbrook and out to Clinton and Hammonasset State Park. From here take 153 via Ivoryton to Essex. From Essex, follow Rte. 9 north to 82, and cross the bridge into East Haddam. Continue on 82 to the junction of 151, which will lead you through Moodus and eventually link up to Rte. 66. Cross the bridge at Portland, and you're back in Middletown. You can, of course, choose to start and finish your loop anywhere, depending on where you decide to overnight. To make things simple, I have tried to follow this particular itinerary, because logic demands it, not because it reflects my personal preferences. Those should be very clear anyway.

MIDDLETOWN–CHESTER–DEEP RIVER

AREA ATTRACTIONS

Home to **Wesleyan University,** a lovely campus in itself, **Middletown** offers cultural events—concerts, theater, and art shows, many staged at the university's Center for the Arts. Call 203/347-9411, ext. 2807, for a schedule. **Wesleyan Potters Craft Center,** 350 S. Main St. (tel. 203/347-5925), is also here. Best time to visit is during their annual sale from Thanksgiving through mid-December, when all kinds of crafts are on display. Wander around the old campus, and make sure to note what's going on at **Harbor Park,** a riverside park that's the location for many special events, including the culmination of the **Head of Connecticut Regatta** on Columbus Day weekend.

To the west of Middletown, lies the small town of **Durham,** an old farming community that has changed little since the 19th century, and where you can recapture the era at the annual **Durham Fair,** the largest and one of the most popular in the state.

Southwest of Middletown, **Middlefield** offers **Powder Ridge Skiing Area** (tel. toll free 800/243-3377, 800/622-3321 in Connecticut) and **Lyman Orchards,** at the junction of Rtes. 147 and 157 (tel. 203/349-9337), a real treat at appleblossom time or at harvest in the fall. The orchard's 25,000 trees are spread over 300 acres (60% apples), and you can pick your own apples, strawberries, raspberries, pumpkins, and peaches. The farm, owned by the Lyman family since 1741, possesses a fascinating history and occupies some of the most scenic land in the valley. The farm store, Greenfield's, has all kinds of goodies: raw honey; home-baked pies, breads, and cookies that come out of the ovens right there on the premises; varieties of squash and melon that I had never seen—in other words a mass of farm-fresh produce all at very good prices. Events are also often scheduled during the summer and fall weekends. The store is open from 8 A.M. to 6 P.M. daily. The golf course here, also a part of the farm and quite spectacularly designed by Robert Trent Jones, has eight water holes on the front nine.

From Middletown you can head south for **Chester,** a small, pretty village worth strolling around and browsing in its antique, book, and craft stores, before heading for the ferry (in operation since 1769), which will take you across the river to Hadlyme and Gillette Castle. (It only operates from April through November.)

A MIDDLETOWN-CROMWELL LODGING

In Cromwell, just west of Middletown, you can find modern accommodations plus an array of facilities at the **Treadway Cromwell Hotel,** Rte. 72, 100 Berlin Rd., Cromwell, CT 06416 (tel. 203/635-2000). A domed indoor pool surrounded by tropical plants, a lush garden dining room, multilevel lounge with skylit bar and dancing, plus two outdoor lighted tennis courts keep the place hopping. The 169 rooms, some with cathedral ceilings, some of them located across the road in the so-called Knights Inn, are all very nicely furnished and fully appointed with color TV, phone, and climate control.

RATES: $110 double. WEEKEND PACKAGE: $59 double.

MIDDLETOWN LODGING AND DINING

Town Farms Inn, River Road, Middletown, CT 06457 (tel. 203/347-7438), is located in a red-brick mansard-roofed building fronted by flowering borders displaying lilies, petunias, and other seasonal flowers. The famous River Room, with its river views, intriguing murals, and chandeliers fashioned in Europe from Connecticut glass, is now a pleasant place for cocktails and light supper. The flagstone terrace outside provides a spectacular summer drinking spot. There are three dining rooms. The warm cranberry-colored Indian Room, furnished with portraits of Indians, one or two examples of basketwork, ships' models, and warmed by a wood fire blazing in the Delft-tiled hearth, is a favorite. The study has a collection of local historic photographs and a number of books, while a third room features a fireplace with a fine balustered mantel. Dinner classics include poached salmon with a raspberry butter sauce; breast of duck, sliced and served with blueberry cassis sauce; veal medallions sautéed with leeks and red peppers, flamed with brandy, and finished with cream; shrimp and scallops baked in curry cream, topped with puff pastry, and garnished with chutney; or a 14-ounce sirloin steak garnished with boursin cheese and stuffed tomato. Prices range from $13 to $20. Salads and light dishes are offered at lunch. The Sunday buffet jazz brunch at $11.95 has become an institution, while on Sunday night dinner from the regular menu is offered.

Behind the restaurant and linked by a covered entrance portico are 48 rooms, which were under construction when I visited. I'm sure they'll be very similar to those I saw at the Inn at Chester, which is under the same ownership—furnished with stylish antique reproductions.

RATES: $80 double. LUNCH: Noon to 2 P.M. daily. DINNER: Monday to Thursday from 6 to 9 P.M., on Friday and Saturday to 10 P.M., on Sunday from 5 to 9 P.M. BRUNCH: Sunday from 11:30 A.M. to 2 P.M.

Harbor Park, 80 Harbor Dr. (tel. 203/347-9999) is designed to make you feel as though you're aboard ship, with its sailcloth-canvas partitions attached to the

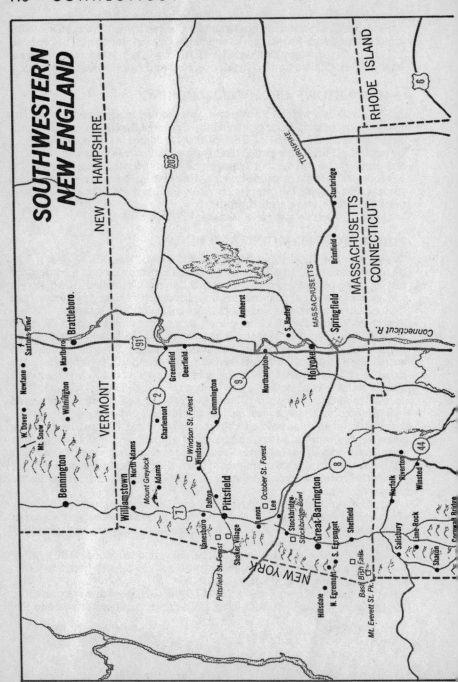

SOUTHWESTERN
NEW ENGLAND

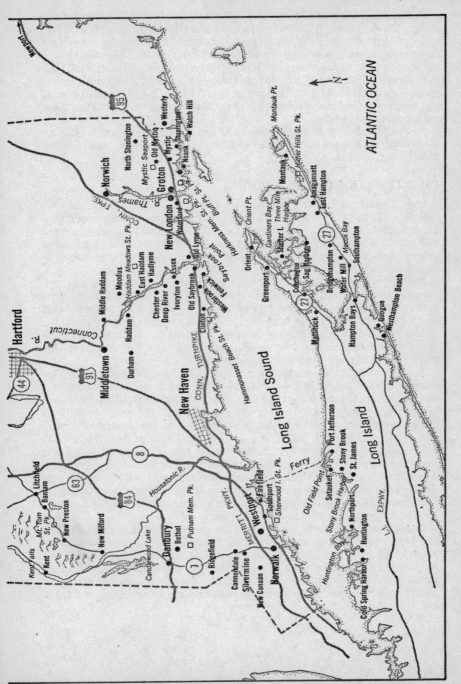

staircase railings and neon-lighted mast at the center of the multilevel restaurant-lounge. On the ground floor is a large lounge that gives astounding views of the river, as do the two dining levels above. Specialties include a lobster pot—their version of a clambake consisting of a 1½-pound lobster, a pound each of steamers and mussels, and an ear of corn served in a pewter pot, plus steaks, chicken teriyaki, fresh seafood—scrod, broiled sole, paupiettes of sole with shrimp mousse, scampi primavera—and more. The prices, from $10 to $19, include salad, bread, and vegetable. On Sunday there's a 25-item buffet brunch as well as made-to-order omelets and waffles.

LUNCH: Monday to Saturday from 11:30 A.M. to 3 P.M. DINNER: Sunday to Thursday from 5 to 9 P.M., on Friday and Saturday to 11 P.M. BRUNCH: Sunday from 11 A.M. to 3 P.M.

CHESTER LODGING AND DINING

A truly idyllic retreat surrounded by state forests, the **Inn at Chester,** 318 W. Main St., Chester, CT 06412 (tel. 203/526-4961), bears the very personal stamp of David Joslow and his wife, who enlarged their old colonial farmhouse and created a 48-room inn with a very fine dining room and a number of other facilities. In the process, the old and the new have been harmoniously combined to create a hospitable old-world air.

The very spacious rooms are decorated elegantly with antique reproductions: the most formal have Chippendale-style chest and desk; the less formal rooms have specially made antique country pieces—hoop-back Windsor chairs, club foot tables, and porcelain or brass lamps. In all the rooms (except three in the main house) the TV is tucked away discreetly in a cabinet; telephone and air conditioning complete the appointments. Extra touches include fresh flowers and the services of a masseuse if you wish, on the premises.

The old barn that was moved here makes a delightful restaurant setting for some superb cuisine, which has been thoroughly "discovered." When I visited, I was faced with a choice among appetizers of an oyster with braised leeks and caviar, a smoked seafood trilogy, terrine with pistachios, and the house specialty—a luscious mushroom strudel consisting of various mushrooms blended with cream and white wine. Entrees, priced from $16 to $23.50, include rack of lamb with brown sauce, roast duckling with cranberry sauce, John B. tenderloin stuffed with herbs and wrapped in bacon, salmon with lime sauce, and sea scallops braised in vermouth. Soups (try the black bean, accompanied by chopped egg, onions, and California sherry), omelets, liver, chicken, salads, and burgers compose the luncheon menu; breakfast brings a refreshing fruit compote, homemade granola, a variety of fresh fruits, and assorted egg dishes.

Guests may retire downstairs either to the exercise room or the billiard room and library (some wonderful volumes, too) warmed by a fire on winter nights. From spring to early fall the grounds resemble an English garden redolent with the scent of lilac and the color of roses, hollyhocks, and many other flowering plants and shrubs. For outdoor exercise there's a tennis court and 1½ miles of nature trails in the woods. Nearby Cedar Lake is good for swimming or ice skating.

RATES: $85 double. BREAKFAST: Monday to Friday from 6:30 to 9:30 A.M., on Saturday and Sunday from 8 to 10 A.M. LUNCH: Monday to Saturday from noon to 2:30 P.M. DINNER: Monday to Saturday from 5 to 9 P.M., on Sunday until 8 P.M. BRUNCH: Sunday from noon to 2:30 P.M.

Chester Dining

As close as you'll get to a French country bistro, the **Restaurant du Village**, 59 Main St. (tel. 203/526-5301), is always gaily bedecked with plants and flowers placed in window boxes and along the small alley that leads to the entrance. Inside, you'll find two small rooms: one a cozy lounge-dining area with a terracotta bar; the other, a small, intimate dining room made a little more formal by the gilt-framed paintings that grace the walls. The menu changes frequently, but the cuisine is always imaginative. At the time of my visit, appetizers included several terrines, especially a duck terrine with orange rind and a core of duck filet, and a trout mousse served hot with a crayfish sauce. There were about eight main dishes to choose from, among them a veal chop sautéed with chive and watercress sauce, and rib eye of beef with green peppercorn whisky and tarragon sauce, a filet of salmon sautéed and served with a sorrel cream sauce, swordfish steak sautéed with a basil cream sauce, sautéed breast of duck with fresh peaches and blueberries, and a sautéed filet of beef with a Pommery mustard sauce. Prices range from $18 to $22.50. Game is often featured. Desserts also change, but if you're lucky, you'll be treated to a piquant roulade au citron (a sponge cake coated with lemon curd and rolled, served with a puree of raspberry) or a luscious rich chocolate cream. DINNER: Tuesday to Sunday 5:30 to 10 p.m. from Memorial Day through Labor Day. Closed Tuesday the rest of the year. Usually open weekends only January through March.

A covered bridge over the Pattaconk Creek leads to the **Chart House**, Rte. 9, Exit 6 (tel. 203/526-9898), located in a restored brush factory, which now offers cozy dining and a pleasant lounge with oak furnishings and plush sofas. The emphasis is on steaks and prime rib, although there's a chicken teriyaki on the menu as well.

DINNER: Monday to Saturday from 5:30 P.M., on Sunday from 4 to 9 P.M.

In Chester proper, next door to the Restaurant du Village, for a casual lunch or dinner head for the **Pattaconk Inn** (tel. 203/526-9285), a restaurant-tavern where you can get daily specials along with fish and chips, London broil, or sirloin marinated in burgundy and dark beer, and a variety of burgers, priced under $8. Eat in the bar, in the atrium room out back, or out on the patio. At lunch, sandwiches are all under $5.

LUNCH: Daily. DINNER: Tuesday to Sunday.

Fiddler's Seafood, 4 Water St. (tel. 203/526-3210), is a plain and simple restaurant room decked out in Wedgwood blue and furnished with bentwood chairs set at tables spread with white tablecloths. Nautical lithographs decorate the walls. A variety of fish is offered, depending on availability—swordfish, baked or stuffed sole, clams, shrimp casino, lobster, and bouillabaisse. Prices range from $10 to $15.

LUNCH: Tuesday to Saturday from 11:30 A.M. to 2 P.M. DINNER: Tuesday to

Thursday from 5:30 to 9 P.M., on Friday and Saturday until 10 P.M., on Sunday from 4 to 9 P.M. Closed Monday.

For light food in a modern pubby atmosphere, try the **Stage Door,** North Main Street (tel. 203/526-2532). Sandwiches, burgers, pastas, soups, and salads are available either in the dining room at wood tables while you are seated on upholstered burgundy-colored banquettes or in the bar lit by splashy green-glass lanterns—a wee touch of the Irish.

LUNCH: Tuesday to Saturday from 11:30 A.M. to 2:30 P.M. DINNER: Tuesday to Thursday from 5:30 to 8:30 P.M., on Friday and Saturday until 9:30 P.M., on Sunday from 3 to 8 P.M.

DEEP RIVER LODGING

An obvious love of life and an incredible amount of energy are reflected in **Riverwind,** Main Street, Deep River, CT 06417 (tel. 203/526-2014), both of which belong to Barbara Barlow, proud owner of this engaging bed-and-breakfast. Barbara hails from Smithfield, Virginia, where she taught learning-disabled children for many years. Her current life evolved from her part-time work as a restoration specialist. When she was asked to restore a house in Connecticut, she fell in love with the area, opened an antique store, and then set about renovating this 1850 beige clapboard house. And a wonderful job she has done too, filling it with curious personal collectibles and furnishings. As her father was a hog farmer, Barbara has a definite fondness for pigs, so all kinds of references appear throughout —tiny wooden toys, weathervanes, and other "pig" art, not to mention the Smithfield hams hanging in the kitchen. Bird's nests also appear frequently tucked away in different places.

In the parlor and breakfast room across the hall antiques abound—decoys, a sleigh, a collection of arrowheads that Barbara personally unearthed from Virginia soil, a basket filled with large cones, an old quilt draped over a wooden field rake and tacked above the fireplace, a blanket chest that serves as a coffee table. Breakfast is served at a harvest table in front of the fire in winter.

The four rooms are up the stairs (each step prettified by dried flower arrangements). Each room is different but all feature colorful old quilts and floor stenciling. The Smithfield Room's centerpiece is a maple rope bed (converted, of course!), supplemented by a sidetable and a maple chest with a mirror above. Personal accents include a miniature doll's chest that belonged to her grandmother, and the *Oxford Book of English Verse* tucked into the night table. In Zelda's green room, with its high carved oak bed and rope rug, the bathroom is most entertaining (check out the 1862 wall plaque). This room also contains an old Virginia hotel washstand and Barbara's grandmother's oak hall tree. The Havlow Room is named after her family farm and features pine furnishings and charming cornhusk dolls representing the travelers on the Yellow Brick Road.

For guests' leisure there's a game room with board games, and a porch furnished with wicker. For breakfast you can expect—what else?—Smithfield ham and pig-shaped biscuits, coffee cake, fruit compote, and fresh fruit. In the back yard there are hibachis for guests' use; feel free to pour yourself a welcome glass of sherry from the decanter in the living room.

RATES: $70 to $85.

Barbara is also planning to open another four rooms, some with sitting rooms, which should be ready by the time this book appears in bookstores.

Selden House, 20 Read St., Deep River, CT 06417 (tel. 203/526-9195), is a gray clapboard Victorian on four beautiful acres. Originally built in 1890 for a Mr. Selden, a well-known local shipbuilder, the house features fine oak doors and staircase, stained-glass accents, and rounded windows. Linda Wiergna, a hospital administrator, and her husband, Bob, a research chemist, have lovingly restored the building and offer seven rooms, three with private bath. The favorites are undoubtedly nos. 1 and 5. One is extraordinarily spacious even though it accommodates a lot of furniture—high-backed carved Victorian bed, drop-leaf table, dresser, armchair. Small items add charm: a Japanese-style ceramic jar, a parasol on the wood mantel (yes, the fireplace works), a pitcher and wash basin on the dresser. Room 5 is a very bright and sunny room with a skylight from which you can see the river in the distance. Third-floor rooms have sloping ceilings and knee walls. No two are furnished in the same way. Pine or oak dressers, pineapple posters, high Victorian bed and even a 19th-century Danish sleigh bed are examples of the diverse furnishings. A potpourri (lavender, rose, etc.) scents each room.

The ground-floor parlor is comfortably Victorian with Oriental accents. A Chinese screen converted into a cabinet houses a stereo from which classical music usually emanates. A Victorian sofa and carved armchairs stand in front of the fireplace. A second parlor will have been turned into a library with floor-to-ceiling bookcases by the time you read this. There's also an enclosed porch where you can sit on wicker chairs surveying the firs, yews, maples, and other trees that stand quietly on the grounds.

RATES: $55 to $85.

HADLYME AND GILLETTE CASTLE

Just off Rte. 82 rise the towers of **Gillette Castle,** where actor William Gillette and his 15 cats lived from 1919 to 1937 in this 24-room Rhenish fantasy. Constructed out of granite and hand-hewn timbers, the house will amaze you with the eccentric mechanical devices invented by Gillette himself—huge cantilevered wooden locks on the massive entrance doors, wooden light switches, a dining table and desks that slide on metal runners, a cocktail cabinet rigged with several locks, and mirrors placed strategically to view who was into the liquor or who was at the front door, so that he could decide whether or not he was home. On the terrace, overlooking the river and the grounds, he entertained his friends—most notably with his outdoor railroad that cascaded down from Grand Central along the river's bluffs across a fragile bridge strung between two massive outcroppings of rock. He was greatly amused; they were more greatly frightened.

In the upstairs rooms, among Gillette's personal memorabilia are photographs depicting this stunningly handsome man as he appeared in *Dream Maker, Secret Service,* and *Private Secretary,* and in his most famous role as Sherlock Holmes. Fascinating to peruse are his scrapbooks, theater reviews, letters, personal notes that he wrote to neighboring children, anecdotes, watercolors and oils, and an incredible number of cutesy cat artifacts. The whole place is capped by a magnificent view from the tower, which you can climb only if you visit off-season.

So attached was he to his idiosyncratic creation that in his will he stated that "this 122-acre property should not pass to any blithering saphead who has no conception of where he is or with what surrounded." After his death it became a state park in 1943. HOURS: Memorial Day to Columbus Day, 11 A.M. to 5 P.M. daily. ADMISSION: $1 for adults, free for under-12s.

OLD LYME

AREA ATTRACTIONS

Miss Florence was the mentor, patron, and friend of many of America's great turn-of-the-century painters—Childe Hassam, Henry Ward Ranger, Willard Metcalf, Charles Ebert, Guy and Carleton Wiggins—who painted the surrounding landscapes when they spent their summers boarding at her Georgian mansion in Old Lyme between 1900 and 1915. Her home is now appropriately the **Florence Griswold Museum,** at 96 Lyme St. (tel. 203/434-5542). When they were unable to come up with the rent, these artists would paint the door panels and overmantels of the house with Connecticut scenes as a way of repaying their unbusinesslike landlady. Today these treasured examples of the American impressionist movement are on view on the lower floor of the house. HOURS: June to October, Tuesday to Saturday from 10 A.M. to 5 P.M., on Sunday from 1 to 5 P.M.; November to May, Wednesday to Sunday from 1 to 5 P.M. ADMISSION: $1 for adults, 50¢ for children.

Across the street these same artists built a museum-gallery for their summer exhibits. It's still a prestigious summer gallery today and the home of the **Lyme Art Association,** 70 Lyme St., which sponsors several shows a year. HOURS: May to mid-October, Tuesday to Saturday from noon to 5 P.M., on Sunday from 1 to 5 P.M. ADMISSION: Donation.

Elizabeth Tashjian is an attraction in herself (indeed she's been on the "Tonight Show" and several other personality-oriented shows) at her very own **Nut Museum,** 303 Ferry Rd. (tel. 203/434-7636). In her 19th-century mansion, so nutty is she about nuts, she has gathered all kinds of paintings, sculptures, nutcrackers, and "nutty" artifacts. HOURS: Wednesday and weekends from 2 to 5 P.M. May to November. ADMISSION: $2 and one nut of any variety.

OLD LYME LODGING AND DINING

Canopy beds, lace curtains, and colorful quilts add charm and elegance to most of the rooms at the **Bee and Thistle Inn,** 100 Lyme St., Old Lyme, CT 06371 (tel. 203/434-1667), an attractive 1756 residence set back from the road on 5½ acres of tree-shaded gardens along the Lieutenant River.

The 11 rooms, 9 with private bath, include a twin with pine furnishings and Oriental rugs, and a large two-room family suite—one room containing a double, a single, and a couch-bed; the other, a single—renting for only $68 a night. Fires light up the parlors in winter, making the wing chairs and comfy sofas all the more inviting.

Breakfast, lunch, and dinner are served either by the fireside in the pretty dining room or on the two adjacent terracotta-tile terraces. Freshly squeezed juices, fresh fruits, omelets or strawberry crêpes, and kippers, accompanied by homemade muffins, make for a satisfying breakfast delivered to your room, or served on the sun porches or in front of the fire. Soups, sandwiches, and fish and meat entree selections compose the luncheon menu. Dinner brings fresh seafood (halibut baked in white wine, lemon, and butter, and served with a crabmeat compound butter; or New England shore dinner in a pot, which is a half lobster with a mélange of seafood, chicken, and vegetables), game (breast of pheasant sautéed with shallots and lingonberries and cream, for example), and classic veal, beef, and lamb dishes, like lamb noisettes sautéed with garlic and zinfandel served on red Swiss chard, or pork tenderloin served over a mushroom duxelle and finished with a rosemary port brown sauce. Prices run from $15 to $18.

The grounds run down to the Lieutenant River, where you can sit peacefully in the garden watching the river flow.

RATES: $56 to $92 double. BREAKFAST: 8:30 to 10 A.M. daily. LUNCH: Daily, except Tuesday and Sunday, from 11:30 A.M. to 2 P.M. DINNER: Daily, except Tuesday, from 6 to 10 P.M. BRUNCH: Sunday from 11 A.M. to 2 P.M.

Across the street, a different ambience prevails at the **Old Lyme Inn,** Lyme Street, Old Lyme, CT 06371 (tel. 203/434-2600), an impressive 1850s farmhouse-mansion with a tree-shaded lawn and a bannistered porch. Large tapestries cover the walls of the high-ceilinged Empire-style dining room, which is handsomely decorated in royal blue. Polished silver and fine stemware are placed on white tablecloths along with a single salmon-colored rose. Well known for its cuisine, the restaurant was twice awarded three stars by the *New York Times.* Just some of the tempting dishes available are lobster in a brandy and cream sauce, fresh pheasant stuffed with mushrooms and herbs and served with a game sauce garnished with seedless grapes, and medallions of lamb served with wild rice and a bleu-cheese cream sauce. Prices range from $16 to $23. To start there are half a dozen seafood, shellfish, and meat dishes to choose from, as well as a couple of soups. If the raspberry cheesecake japonaise is on the menu, order it: layers of meringue and chocolate topped with fresh strawberries—who could possibly resist?

If you arrive early you can wait for a table in the handsome Victorian bar before going into the chestnut-paneled dining room. In the front hall, by the way, note the paintings and stenciling done by Gigi Horr-Liverant depicting local scenes, as well as the many paintings and watercolors found throughout, all collected by innkeeper Diana Atwood who carries on the local tradition in her appreciation of art and artists.

The antique curly-maple staircase leads to 13 rooms, each furnished differently with ornate mirrors, old chests, and cannonball or canopy beds covered with candlewick spreads. All accommodations have private bath, air conditioning, radios, and phones, and you'll also find some extra little touches, like witch hazel made in nearby Essex, and mints on your pillow.

RATES (including continental breakfast): $95 to $125 double. Open year round Tuesday to Sunday, except Christmas and the first two weeks of January. LUNCH:

Tuesday to Saturday from noon to 2 P.M. DINNER: Tuesday to Saturday from 6 to 9 P.M., on Sunday from noon to 9 P.M.

OLD SAYBROOK

AREA ATTRACTIONS

From Old Lyme drive down to Old Saybrook and then head out along Rte. 154 to **Saybrook Point,** marked by two lighthouses—the inner one more photographed than the outer. Loop around from Saybrook Point across South Cove past the select community of **Fenwick,** which counts Katharine Hepburn among its residents, and through **Westbrook,** a typical beachfront community with shingled homes (here Frankie's serves dependable shore dinners; Bill's Seafood accepts the bathing-suit crowd), all the way out to **Hammonasset State Park.** By the way, if you can see across the Sound to Long Island as you go, they say it's going to rain within 72 hours.

Saybrook Cruises

Saybrook Point Cruises depart for 1½-hour trips to Essex Harbor, or two-hour trips around the Sound. From mid-June to Labor Day, boats leave from a pier near the Dock Restaurant at Saybrook Point. There's also a one-hour sunset cruise. Prices go from $4 to $8. For information, contact Deep River Navigation Company, River Street (P.O. Box 312), Deep River, CT 06417 (tel. 203/526-4954).

OLD SAYBROOK LODGING

A fieldstone mansion, the **Castle Inn** at Cornfield Point, Hartlands Drive, Old Saybrook, CT 06475 (tel. 203/388-4681), is blessed with a spectacular location atop the cliffs overlooking Long Island Sound with a distant view of Saybrook Point. It was built around 1906 as a summer cottage for Hartford Insurance's George Watson Beach, and the interior has retained such lavish decorative features as the stained-glass panels that grace the entrance and the doors leading into the dining room. Sadly, although the 21 rooms are large and many have inviting window seats and glorious views, the furnishings tend to faded Scandinavian modern. Room 119 with its wicker furnishings is an exception. No telephone or TVs here. An outdoor pool and access to a private beach are distinct pluses. Also, occasionally on Friday and Saturday evenings there's dining and dancing and live entertainment Friday through Sunday in the cocktail lounge.

　RATES: (including a continental breakfast): $65 to $85 double. LUNCH: Monday to Saturday from noon to 2:30 P.M. DINNER: Monday to Friday from 5 to 9:30 P.M., until 10:30 P.M. on Saturday, on Sunday from 3 to 9 P.M. BRUNCH: Sunday buffet from 11:30 A.M. to 3 P.M.

　To get there, take I-95 to Exit 67. Bear right. Go to the third light, and turn left onto Main Street. Go two more lights, and turn right onto Maple Avenue. Go to the stop sign, and bear left, taking the first right onto Hartland Drive.

　The **Sandpiper Motor Inn,** 1750 Boston Post Rd. (U.S. 1), Old Saybrook, CT

06475 (tel. 203/399-7973), is a modern accommodation with fully equipped rooms (Touch-tone phone, color TV) decked out in pastel tones, dusky-rose carpeting, floral quilts, and light-oak furnishings. There's a fenced-in outdoor pool.

RATES: $64 to $78, the higher price for rooms with couch and wet bar. Prices are reduced in winter.

OLD SAYBROOK DINING

The Dock at Saybrook Point (tel. 203/388-4665) takes full advantage of the water view and the vista across the mouth of the Connecticut River to Great Island. Watch the barges and other craft slipping by or the anchored yachts bobbing at dockside while you dine on some exceptionally well-prepared seafood —haddock, swordfish, scampi, scallops, bluefish, sole, and lobster—cooked in a variety of ways, along with the usual steak, veal parmigiana, and chicken for the unconvinced or uninitiated fish diner. Prices run $9 to $20. Lobsters are one of the prime attractions and you'll find the place bursting on weekend nights with sometimes as much as a two-hour wait in store. Repair to the bar (follow the marvelous scent of the popcorn) and wait, listening to the entertainment—a piano-and-drums combo the night I stopped by. In winter a fire in the fieldstone fireplace will warm your very cockles. Start with a sampler of the chowders or some choice morsels from the raw bar and then move on to the seafood. If the halibut special in dill sauce is available, I highly recommend it.

On Sunday a Dixieland brunch is served from 11 A.M. to 2 P.M. buffet style, although the omelets and waffles are cooked to order. The nightly entertainment varies from jazz to pianist/vocalist.

LUNCH: Monday to Saturday from 11:30 A.M. to 4 P.M. DINNER: Monday to Thursday from 4 to 9 P.M., until 10 P.M. on weekends. BRUNCH: Sunday from 11 A.M. to 2 P.M.

A '50s drive-in on Rte. 1, **Johnny Ads** (tel. 203/388-4032) is famous for its foot-long hot dogs enjoyed by the bathing-suit crowd. Some of the local dignitaries also enjoy them too, as did the late Governor Grasso who popped in when she summered in East Lyme.

At the large modern waterfront complex, the **Marina Restaurant,** Ferry Point, Old Saybrook (tel. 203/388-1441), houses a variety of facilities, all of them relatively casual as befits a shoreline eatery. The Boaters Bar offers a raw bar and snack menu. Upstairs the restaurant serves steaks and seafood, priced from $7 to $14. In summer the patio is a favorite gathering place. Occasionally there might be some jazz or similar entertainment.

LUNCH: 11:30 A.M. to 2 P.M. daily. DINNER: 6 to 10 P.M. daily. BRUNCH: Sunday from 11:30 A.M. to 2 P.M. These hours are tentative, so please check.

For casual dining, try the popular **Saybrook Fish House,** 99 Essex Rd. (tel. 203/388-4836), where among the nautical regalia of nets and lanterns you can obtain a variety of fresh fish broiled in white wine and butter sauce and a wide choice of shellfish, from shrimp, lobster, and scampi to scungili and little necks. No reservations are taken and the wait on Saturday nights could be long (maximum of about two hours). There are always some appetizers at the bar if you're really famished. Complete dinners are priced from $10 to $17.

LUNCH: Monday to Friday from noon to 2:30 P.M. DINNER: Monday to Friday from 5 to 8:30 P.M., on Saturday from 4 to 10 P.M., and on Sunday from 2 to 9 P.M.

For a change of cuisine, there's also **Luigi's**, 670 Boston Post Rd. (tel. 203/388-9190), another informal spot that offers pizza and sandwiches along with more substantial fare like scampi, mussels marinara, veal parmigiana, spaghetti with clam sauce, and one or two steaks.

HOURS: Tuesday to Thursday and Sunday from 11 A.M. to 9 P.M., on Friday and Saturday from noon to 10 P.M. Closed usually for two weeks in January.

Hear the whistlestopping trains come and go at **O'Brannigans** (tel. 203/388-6611), a restaurant installed at the Old Saybrook railroad station. The dining room incorporates a bar with a balcony, porch-like dining area sporting green tables, bentwood chairs, and some additional real-live greenery. The food, with a dash of Irish, is typical—burgers, sandwiches, fish of the day, etc.—at reasonable prices (from $10 at dinner). There's entertainment on Friday and Saturday night —folk singers when I visited.

LUNCH: Monday to Thursday from 11:30 A.M. to 3:30 P.M., on Friday and Saturday until 4 P.M. DINNER: Monday to Thursday from 4 to 10 P.M., on Friday and Saturday to 11 P.M., and on Sunday to 9:30 P.M. BRUNCH: Sunday from 10:30 A.M. to 2:30 P.M.

WESTBROOK LODGING AND DINING

Arlene and Ed Amatrudo fell in love with their **Captain Stannard House,** 138 S. Main St., Westbrook, CT 06498 (tel. 203/399-7565). It's quite understandable, for the house is a beauty with its peaked gables, central cupola, and fan window over the entrance. The original building dates back to about 1860, when it was built by sea captain Stannard, who owned and commanded several ships that sailed mostly to the Orient. He also owned the legendary *Savannah,* which was used in the Mexican War. The house has served various purposes during its lifetime, from dance studio and upholstery shop to boys' school and rooming house. On the ground floor Ed and Arlene operate an antique shop filled with antique jewelry and other mostly small collectibles. A breakfast of orange juice, cereals, home-made fruit-and-nut breads, coffee, and herb teas is served here in the middle of these treasures, or you can request that it be delivered to your door on a wicker tray.

All the rooms have air conditioning and private bath, plus nice touches like fresh flowers, fruit basket, plants, clock radio, and books and magazines, as well as liquid soap and air freshener in the bathrooms. The rooms all differ. Captain's Quarters has a four-poster whose net canopy has a pretty pale-blue lacy trim. Walls have stenciled borders; a chair and rocker offer comfortable seating. There's also a suite consisting of a bedroom furnished with cannonball-style bed, dresser, and table, with an adjacent sitting room completely furnished with comfortable couch/bed, TV, rocker, wicker table and armchair, and a drinks cart equipped with glasses.

Ed and Arlene have traveled a lot during their previous careers and so are very mindful of business travelers' needs also. There's an office with a phone available and they will fulfill any special requests that you might have. Downstairs there's a fridge for your use. Beach passes are available for the local strand, which is only eight minutes' walk away. In summer guests can use the bicycles, play croquet or horseshoes, or simply relax on the very large lawn.

RATES: (including continental breakfast of homemade muffins, juice, and coffee): $65 to $75 double, $135 for the suite.

Interested in local color, lots of people, and food at reasonable prices? Then a table at **Bill's Seafood,** Boston Post Road (Rte. 1), in Westbrook (tel. 203/399-7224), will suit you just fine. Sit out there on the deck and watch the craft maneuver under the bridge into the marina, while you feast on crab and lobster rolls, clams, fish, or whatever else is scrawled on the blackboard. Inside, the dining room is strictly Formica-top tables in a bar room. Real seafarers flock here.

HOURS: Sunday to Thursday from 11:30 A.M. to 9 P.M., on Friday and Saturday until 10 P.M.

A BEACHFRONT LODGING IN MADISON

The **Madison Beach Hotel,** 94 W. Wharf Rd., Madison, CT 06443 (tel. 203/245-1404), is a real seaside place, with a certain Victorian flavor. From the parking lot, climb the few steps into the gray weathered balconied building and there are the dunes and the Sound spread before you, dotted with rocky outcroppings and a brilliant windsurfer's sail. Turn back into the lobby and sink into a cushioned wicker rocker or step out on to the veranda and really breathe the shore air.

The 32 rooms with private bath, heat, and air conditioning have all been recently renovated. Second- and third-floor rooms have balconies; they are simply furnished with hardy seaside furniture. All have TV and telephone. Bathrooms feature pine floors. These are simple seaside accommodations.

The Wharf Dining room is attached to the hotel and shares the same marvelous view of the Sound on two sides. Fresh flowers grace the bar. Pink napkins and tablecloths, rattan furniture, and silk flower arrangements give a tropical air to the room. Dinner menu prices range from $11 for deep-fried clams to $16 for king crab legs. There's always a chicken and veal du jour, along with filet mignon and prime rib. Salads, sandwiches, and burgers, make up the luncheon menu. Upstairs, the Crow's Nest sports nautical rigging and decor, a central bar from which to view the ocean scene or, even better, from an outside balcony table. Before you leave, check out the guest register dating from 1920—you might recognize some of the names.

RATES: mid-May to the end of September, $75 to $95 single, $85 to $120 double; off-season, $60 to $80 single and $70 to $105 double. Open from May to mid-November.

ESSEX

ESSEX ATTRACTIONS

The town of Essex itself is an attraction, with its quiet tree-lined streets bordered by fine old **colonial houses,** many of them shipbuilders' and sea captains' homes that have survived from the days when Essex was a great shipbuilding town. Take some time to walk the streets, browse in the stores, pop into the Griswold, and explore the harbor area at the foot of Main Street where the old (1878) **steamboat dock** has been restored. It now houses the River Museum (tel. 203/767-8269) displaying models, tools, paintings, and instruments, all relating to the river's history and that era when a 230-ton side-wheeler was a common sight en route from Hartford to New York. The museum also includes a replica of the first United States submarine, the 1775 *Turtle.* HOURS: April to December, Tuesday to Sunday from 10 to 5 P.M.; otherwise, weekends only, from 1 to 4 P.M. ADMISSION: $1.50 for adults, 50¢ for children.

The **Valley Railroad** came to the valley in 1871, and today you can take a nostalgic trip courtesy of the Valley Railroad, Railroad Avenue (tel. 203/767-0103), aboard an old steam locomotive from Essex to Chester. The trip can be combined with a cruise up the river, past Gillette Castle and the Goodspeed Opera House, so you can hear the lore and tales of the river and even picnic aboard.

At the station people cluster along the platform, anticipating the roar of the train coming down the tracks, smoke hissing and billowing and whistle blasting its arrival. At the station the engineer stokes the roaring orange-red fire in the firebox before slowly pulling out at the "All Aboard" signal. You can either ride in the 1915 passenger cars or in the 1927 Pullman parlor car (which has luxurious brocade blinds) on plush ruby-red swivel armchairs, while you listen to the old radio's background music from the '20s and '30s. The train trip to Chester uses three tons of coal and 3,000 gallons of water on its rhythmic journey past the tidal wetlands, where wild rice and bull reeds sway, and along the riverbank to Chester and back to Deep River. Here those taking the riverboat cruise debark. The whole trip (rail and river combined) takes about 2½ hours. Although it's beautiful at any time of the year, summer and fall are particularly spectacular; so, too, is December, when Santa Claus boards the train on weekends. Different schedules prevail in spring, summer, and fall, and there's a special Santa schedule. ADMISSION: Train only, $7 for adults, $3 for children; train and cruise, $10 and $5 respectively; $2 extra for the parlor car.

ESSEX LODGING

Affectionately known as "the Gris," the **Griswold Inn,** Main Street, Essex, CT 06426 (tel. 203/767-0991), is the kind of place that inspires genuine love and loyalty from visitors and residents alike. In this lovely old 1776 inn the food is good and fairly priced, and the atmosphere is extremely congenial and unpretentious. People enjoy themselves here, and you're quite likely to engage the people at the next table in conversation—it would not automatically be frowned on. The tavern is always festive, as is the crowd that frequents it—a mixture of locals and sailors and yachting crew in summer. An old popcorn dispenser stands and dispenses in the corner, a cast-iron stove warms the place, while a small Christmas tree sparkles year round. There's entertainment every night, and impromptu dancing. Friday night's banjo entertainment is especially popular and so, too, is Monday's sea chanteys. The series of dining rooms located behind and off the tavern present a museum-quality display of Currier and Ives shipping prints, many related to the days when Essex turned out the fastest clippers on the ocean. This large dining room is, in fact, a covered bridge. Fires blaze in each dining room in the winter.

A traditional treat is the Gris's Sunday Hunt Breakfast, when you can help yourself to unlimited servings of eggs, bacon, ham, sausage, grits, fried potatoes, kippers, chicken, lamb kidneys, creamed chipped beef, smelts, and whatever other dishes are offered that particular day. It's served from 11:30 A.M. to 2:30 P.M. and costs a modest $9. At dinner the menu offers a goodly number of fish dishes and traditional items like Yankee pot roast or prime rib, all priced from $10 to $15. Save some room for the mud slide pie for dessert.

Accommodations are found up the creaky stairs, along the low, uneven corridors, where the rooms are quaint and old-fashioned, with exposed beams, hooked rugs on the floors, old armoires, and perhaps a marble-top vanity or similar in the corner. All have private bathrooms and air conditioning. Some even have water views. House guests help themselves to fresh fruit and toasted muffins served with fine jams and marmalades in the library in the morning.

RATES (including continental breakfast): $68 double. In summer you'll need to reserve several months in advance, especially on weekends.

ESSEX DINING

See the accommodations section for the description of the Griswold.

Tumbledown's Café, Main Street (tel. 203/767-0233). The word "café" doesn't conjure the right image to me, for Tumbledown's is more of a cozy, casual, convivial bar-restaurant with a distinctly nautical flavor. In the Sail Loft bar oars stretch from one end of the ceiling to the other; the dining room sports an upturned scull, ships' lanterns and models, and even a rack of navigational charts. Pretty floral tablecloths cover the tables. Famous for barbecue items, fried clams, beef, chicken fingers, chili, and a steamed vegetable dish. Try the nachos or buffalo wings to start. Other dishes are priced from $9 to $12 (top price is for sirloin).

HOURS: Daily for lunch and dinner.

Oliver's Taverne, Plains Road (tel. 203/767-2633), offers good-value burgers and sandwiches, all under $6. Good place for luncheon, it's also a popular nighttime spot. Great for beer lovers, since it stocks beers from all over the world.

HOURS: Lunch and dinner daily.

The Gull, Pratt Street (tel. 203/767-0916), at the docks in Essex, is bright and informal and offers two dining choices. Upstairs the full menu is served, featuring such items as caviar egg or smoked salmon with frozen vodka for appetizers and poached bluefish, bouillabaisse, and a selection of meat dishes as entrees, priced from $10 to $18. Downstairs, the Laughing Gull serves lighter fare—quiches, cabbage rolls, and sandwiches.

LUNCH: 11:30 A.M. to 2:30 P.M. weekdays, until 3 P.M. on weekends. DINNER: Tuesday through Sunday from 5:30 to 9 P.M.

IVORYTON

IVORYTON LODGING AND DINING

It's not exactly a *House Beautiful* inn, but the **Ivoryton Inn,** Main Street, Ivoryton, CT 06442 (tel. 203-767-0422), a sage-gray clapboard building that began operating in 1790, offers good value. Prices are some of the lowest in the area for the 27 homey rooms with beige carpeting, chintz wallpaper, and ruffled coverlets. The owners are planning to redo the rooms, even adding some stenciling. An exceptional value is a $65 unit consisting of a large double and a connecting room with twins—ideal for families. They share a bathroom.

Breakfast is served in a comfortable dining room where tables, spread with white tablecloths, are set on polished wood floors. Dinner is served Friday and Saturday only, and specials are written on a blackboard. Choices might include pasta with pesto Alfredo, flounder meunière, or chicken Cordon Bleu.

RATES: $45 to $75.

The **Copper Beech Inn**, Main Street, Ivoryton, CT 06442 (tel. 203/767-0330), was recently voted the most popular restaurant in the state for the ninth consecutive year. Formal dinner with silver service is served in three lovely dining rooms each furnished in a different period style. The wood paneling, collections of American cut glass, and other fine accents provide an elegant atmosphere. To the rear of the inn, a real greenhouse has been transformed into a cocktail area comfortably set with wicker chairs and small tables. The menu usually contains about 18 items, such as poached filet of salmon with shrimp, served with a sauce of white wine, butter, shallots, lemon, and saffron; roast pheasant stuffed with wild rice, served with a sauce of pheasant stock, red wine, brandy, and wild mushrooms; sautéed veal sweetbreads in a sauce of white wine, lemon, and capers; as well as beef Wellington, served with a sauce made with madeira and truffles. Prices range from $20 for roast duckling with a sauce of peaches, duck stock, and champagne, to $25.50 for chateaubriand bouquetière. Favorite appetizers are clams topped with crabmeat and roasted with Pernod, garlic butter, and a hazelnut dressing; sautéed shrimp in a sauce of brandy, cream, diced tomato, and fresh tarragon; and wild mushrooms wrapped in puff pastry with a sauce of cream, Swiss and Romano cheeses, and white wine. If you're really feeling flush, then there's always beluga caviar and pâté de foie gras, poached and served with an aspic with madeira wine, shallots, and truffles.

Connecticut magazine readers have singled out the inn's desserts as the best in the state. Among them there's an individual trifle made with vanilla sponge cake soaked in sherry, layered with custard and fresh fruit, and topped with whipped cream and slivered almonds; chocolate crêpes filled with chocolate mousse and served with vanilla custard sauce; or fresh berries marinated in Grand Marnier, covered with whipped cream, and topped with a crust of caramelized brown sugar; along with profiteroles, and Sachertorte.

If you wish to dine here, you'll need to reserve a month in advance for a weekend, two weeks for a weekday.

There are also 13 accommodations, 9 of them in a restored carriage house, all with private bath and air conditioning, and elegant decor. Carriage house rooms have Jacuzzi tubs, TVs, and French doors leading onto decks.

RATES: $80 to $135 double per night. DINNER: Tuesday through Saturday from 6 to 9 P.M., on Sunday from 1 to 9 P.M.

CENTERBROOK DINING

In neighboring Centerbrook, the **Fine Bouche,** Main Street (tel. 203/767-1277), has a reputation for being "brilliant but inconsistent." Under the control of young French-inspired chef Steven Wilkinson, the restaurant turns out fine classic French cuisine priced à la carte from $14.50 to $19.50. Or you can opt for the $32.50 prix fixe. On my last visit, sadly the terrine of duck with orange and Grand Marnier and the lobster with avocado and sliced tomatoes in a basil vinaigrette were both unavailable. I began with the hors d'oeuvres variés—a plate of small servings of smoked salmon, cucumber sprinkled with caviar, Brie, potatoes, and cucumber in a dill sauce. A smooth, flavorsome lobster bisque followed. After a salad the selle d'agneau followed, cooked in a delicious brown sauce with herbs and accompanied by fresh green beans, puréed beets, and potatoes lyonnaises. My dining partner's meal began with prosciutto and melon, proceeded with tuna mingled with tomatoes, herbs, garlic, and Niçoise olives—a meal in itself —followed by filet mignon with a béarnaise sauce. It was an excellent meal but not outstandingly memorable in the way that some meals can be.

During the day people stop by the Fine Bouche pâtisserie for desserts like Sachertorte or blueberry cheesecake. But the pièce de résistance, for which Wilkinson is famous, is a marjolaine, an almond-hazelnut meringue layered with crème fraiche.

The ambience varies from room to room. The front porch room is airy and Oriental in flavor, having been furnished with rattan chairs. In the two other rooms, chintz wallpapers, Federal-style fireplace, and chair rails impart a more formal colonial atmosphere.

LUNCH: Tuesday to Saturday from 11:30 A.M. to 2 P.M. DINNER: Tuesday to Saturday from 6 to 9 P.M.

Pelicans, 30 Main St. (tel. 203/767-0155), is a fun place and one of the few in the area that stays open late. On Friday and Saturday night there's entertainment in the upstairs bar. The dining rooms are modern (nicest room in my opinion has a fieldstone fireplace); in summer the deck is a good choice. They sport pelican art and artifacts.

Entrees run from $9.50 for breast of chicken to $15 for filet mignon with herb butter. There's also a selection of pastas (julienne of capicolla—artichoke hearts, tomatoes, and garlic served over fettuccine), gourmet pizzas (leeks, bacon, and shiitake, or eggplant, pesto, and mozzarella), and a children's menu. At luncheon, soups, salads, sandwiches, and such items as crabmeat broil, chicken burrito, and curried shrimp salad are available, most under $5.

LUNCH: 11:30 A.M. to 2:30 P.M. daily. DINNER: Monday to Thursday from 5:30 to 9 P.M., on Friday and Saturday until 10 P.M., on Sunday from 4 to 9 P.M. BRUNCH: Sunday from noon to 3 P.M.

KILLINGWORTH LODGING AND DINING

When I visited the **Killingworth Inn,** 249 Rte. 81 (at the junction of Rte. 80), Killingworth, CT 06417 (tel. 203/663-1103), it was preparing to open. Innkeeper Diane Dennen proudly showed me the interior of this handsome 1789 clapboard building, shepherding me through the old speakeasy lined with rough-hewn timbers, up the staircase past walls painted with garlands and flowers in 1945 by a local artist, and into the summer dining room that has an exquisite tongue-and-groove ceiling.

There will be five rooms available, sharing two baths. Each will sport chintz wallpapers, brass beds, and other antique finds that Diane intends to amass. Top-floor rooms are tucked under the eaves.

RATES: $55 to $65.

Just down the road from the Killingworth Inn, the **Country Squire**, Rte. 80, Killingworth (tel. 203/663-2820), is a charming country restaurant located in a white clapboard house. Here you can sit out on the patio at tables topped with yellow and white umbrellas and look out over the pretty grounds that also happen to contain several buildings housing 20 antiques dealers.

Inside the 1794 home is a series of dining rooms, a small formal colonial-style room, and a large barn-like space with rafters, paneling, and a copper-hooded fireplace—an obvious addition. Country placemats and high-backed settles all reinforce the country/rustic air.

The menu is brief and simple, offering catch of the day, sirloin, lamb chops, game hen, baked scallops, surf and turf, prime rib, and duck with cranberry chutney. Entrees at dinner run from $12 to $19; Sunday brunch is $9.95; items on the lunch menu are in the $4 to $8 range.

LUNCH: Monday to Saturday from 11:30 A.M. to 2:30 P.M. DINNER: Tuesday to Saturday from 5 to 9 P.M., on Sunday from noon to 8 P.M. BRUNCH: Sunday from 11:30 A.M. to 2:30 P.M.

HADDAM, EAST HADDAM, AND MOODUS

AREA ATTRACTIONS

East Haddam is the home of the **Goodspeed Opera House,** a gorgeously intricate Victorian structure. Built in 1876 by wealthy entrepreneur and shipbuilder William Goodspeed, it thrived as a theater until the 1920s when traffic and life passed it by. The theater, set atop the six-floor building, has been beautifully restored and dedicated to the preservation of the American musical. You can take a behind-the-scenes tour of the opera house on Monday from July 13 to October 12 (except for September 28 and October 5). HOURS: Tours are given between 1 and 3 P.M. ADMISSION: $1 for adults, 50¢ for children under 12. Around it a small village of antique, craft (especially good), and gift stores has grown up.

Just across the river you can see the **cruise boats** that sail daily from Haddam down the river and across the Sound to the ports of Sag Harbor and Greenport, where you have three hours to explore before the return journey. Evening music excursions are also given aboard the *Yankee Clipper*—Dixieland and Oldies but Goodies. For more information, contact New England Steamboat Lines, Marine Park, Haddam, CT 06438 (tel. 203/345-4507). Usually from end of June through Labor Day.

East of East Haddam lies Moodus, where craft lovers will want to visit **Down on the Farm,** Banner Road, off Rte. 149 (tel. 203/873-9905), a craft center housed in a former chicken farm. Here in summer you can watch glassblowing, woodworking, and other skills being performed. The store features high-quality glass, ceramics, quilts, silkscreened items, candles, and jewelry. HOURS: July 1 to mid-January, Tuesday to Sunday from 11 A.M. to 5 P.M.; Thursday to Sunday otherwise.

Along the way, just outside East Haddam on Rte. 82, you may want to stop at the **Christmas Shoppe** (tel. 203/873-9352), where 'tis the season year round. HOURS: Memorial Day to December 24, 10 A.M. to 5 P.M. daily.

EAST HADDAM LODGING

At night the 1826 Victorian mansion, the **Inn at Goodspeed's Landing—Gelston House,** East Haddam CT 06423 (tel. 203/873-1411), right across from the Goodspeed Opera House, takes on a particular romance with its riverside setting, luminous interior, and summer garden strung with twinkling lights. The pink tablecloths and napkins and low lights in the dining room make it positively romantic, and especially when it's filled with pre-theater diners the atmosphere is charged with a certain anticipation.

A meal might begin with seafood strudel (scallops, crab, and mussels encased in a flaky pastry), almond Brie (warm Brie enveloped in toasted almond), or mushrooms stuffed with crabmeat, cheese, and herbs and baked in a sherry butter. Among the main courses, choices run to chicken dijonnaise, veal Oscar, cioppino, roast duck with an apricot sauce, and roast rib of beef, priced from $11 to $19. Brunch features typical omelets and egg dishes, plus six or so special items like lamb strudel (morsels of fresh lamb and fresh vegetable wrapped in filo dough and served with lamb sauce) and crabmeat Devonshire (English muffins topped with crabmeat and mushrooms in a sherried cream sauce with Munster cheese). If you have to wait for a table, there's an elegant mirrored bar lit by gilt sconces and emerald-green Waterford crystal chandeliers.

Upstairs are six rooms: three doubles and three suites. They are extremely large accommodations, some with river views through floor-to-ceiling Palladian-style windows (Room 21, for instance). Drop-leaf side tables, colored engravings of landscapes hanging above a sleigh bed, an Empire-style table nestled against two period side chairs, a secretary complete with a set of Kipling and other books, ceramic table lamps, and beige wall-to-wall carpeting bestow a special quality upon the rooms. Touch-tone phones (including one in the bathroom) and Gilchrist & Soames soaps, talc, shoeshine, and shampoo in all of the bathrooms also add to one's sense of well-being.

RATES: $80, single or double; $160 for suites. LUNCH: Monday to Friday from 11:30 A.M. to 2:30 P.M., on Saturday from noon to 4 P.M., and on Sunday from 11 A.M. to 2 P.M. DINNER: Monday from 5:30 to 9 P.M., Tuesday to Thursday from 5 to 9 P.M., on Friday and Saturday until 10 P.M., and on Sunday from 3 to 8 P.M. These are summer hours; please check for winter equivalents.

At the **Stonecroft Inn,** 17 Main St., Goodspeed Landing, East Haddam, CT 06423 (tel. 203/873-1754), owner Paul Higgins considers his new career an extension of his love of entertaining. Recently retired from Boston banking, Paul enjoys meeting his many diverse guests, cooking, tending his herb garden, and conversing. In his 1832 home, close to the Opera House, built originally by and for a blacksmith, he offers five rooms, all with private bath. The two front rooms on the first and second floors have four-posters and fireplaces; the other three are tastefully furnished with antique side tables, chest, broken scroll mirror, Oriental runners, elegant side chairs, and comfortable beds. Throughout the house you'll find Oriental accents—vases, plates—and Ansel Adams reproductions. The parlor is cozy and small with a classic wood Federal mantel and fireplace; comfortable antiques abound.

Breakfast is taken in the kitchen (made warm in winter by a blazing fire) at a refectory-style table. An aproned Paul whips up a full breakfast of French toast with sausage, blueberry muffins, and fresh-squeezed juice or something similar. Weather permitting, breakfast can be enjoyed on the porch overlooking the herb garden, tubs of geraniums, and the lush red maple that shimmers on the lawn.

RATES: $75 to $90.

Only a few hundred yards from the Goodspeed Opera House, the **Bishopsgate Inn,** Goodspeed Landing, East Haddam, CT 06423 (tel. 203/873-1754), is run by Molly and Dan Swartz, who have created a cozy but elegant atmosphere with a certain theatrical flavor. Both are transplanted New Yorkers and both have long associations with the theater, Dan as director of the Brooklyn Center at Brooklyn College and Molly as a buyer for several costume houses. There are six rooms in this 1818 home, four with private bath and fireplaces, furnished with Empire-style and pine country pieces, and Molly is planning to add more antiques as they go along. The suite features a huge bathroom with a double sink and sauna. A continental breakfast of home-baked items like apple-crisp bread is served in the country kitchen.

RATES: $75 to $95 double.

Tudor fantasy and a romantic formal candlelit breakfast make **Whispering Winds Inn,** 93 River Rd., East Haddam, CT 06423 (tel. 203/526-3055), a special bed-and-breakfast. Lou Hayn is an enthusiastic host who has created some dramatic breakfast dishes, including baked puffed pancakes served with hot apples and sausage. Accompaniments will include home-baked goods— blueberry and other fruit muffins, banana- or strawberry-nut bread, freshly squeezed orange juice, and fresh fruit. On your arrival you'll be offered sherry or tea.

The house is very secluded, and from the front there's a glorious view over the trees down to the Connecticut River. Fresh flowers from the 2½-acre gardens add color throughout the house. Anne, his wife, a schoolteacher, is a collector of clocks, which are found throughout the house—from grandmother type to banjo style. The public rooms are furnished comfortably and encourage conviviality. The main parlor has a fieldstone fireplace, grand piano, and comfortable seating arrangements. There's also a bar and recreation room, and most popular of all a den with cathedral ceiling which is warmed by a fire in the winter. Note the brilliant stained-glass window in the room's gallery.

The two accommodations are homey and have those personal touches like bookcases filled with books, fresh flowers, and even a shell collection gathered by Lou and Anne's daughter. One room is on the ground floor and has contempo-

rary furnishings; the upstairs room is warm and inviting and has a river view.
RATES: $65.

A MOODUS RESORT

In the quiet countryside just east of East Haddam there are several resorts, if that's your style. The most famous is **Frank Davis,** Moodus, CT 06469 (tel. 203/873-8681), a 56-acre resort set on 500 acres and run by very special host Frank Davis for the last 21 years. Frank meets and greets his guests, and attends to every little detail of running the resort—an enormous task. His wife, Dot, assists him, along with 300 or so employees. A workaholic, Frank even operates a bakery that churns out 17 million éclairs during the winter when the resort is closed.

This will not be everyone's idea of a weekend retreat. In season there's round-the-clock entertainment. There's a large outdoor pool, miniature golf, scuba lessons, art lessons, movies, tennis courts, an exercise room, sauna, whirlpool, canoes, and many other facilities designed to keep the whole family occupied. As Frank puts it, the resort "provides a vacation for people who don't know how to vacation." And you'll be roused at 7:30 A.M. (Sunday included) by a band made up of enthusiastic drummers, trumpeters, and cymbal clashers—all your fellow guests, believe it or not!

The 211 rooms are located in fairly modern two-floor motel units, in older cabins back in the woods, or in even older cabins at the river's edge. Down on the Salmon River, a tributary of the Connecticut River, besides the boats and canoes for use by guests you'll find a quiet oasis (Frank owns both sides of the river, which helps keep it that way) where an early-morning breakfast is served every Tuesday as the sun rises behind the trees. There's no bar, but set-ups are provided for those interested, and wine or champagne is served at special events or celebrations.
RATES: $54 to $75 American Plan, daily.

EVENING ENTERTAINMENT

Theater

The **Goodspeed Opera House,** East Haddam (tel. 203/873-8668), is dedicated to preserving the works of America's musical greats—Irving Berlin, Jerome Kern, Cole Porter. It's also the birthplace of such recent Broadway successes as *Annie* and *Man of la Mancha.* Tickets: $15 to $24. The season runs from mid-April to early December.

The **Ivoryton Playhouse,** Main Street, Ivoryton (tel. 203/767-8348), offers summer stock and community-oriented events.

The **National Theater of the Deaf** also gives performances during the summer either outside or inside depending on the weather at The Meeting House, Goose Hill Rd., Chester (tel. 203/526-4971).

Evening Cruises

Dixieland and Oldies but Goodies are part of the entertainment aboard the *Yankee Clipper,* which travels up the river from the last week of June through Labor

Day. For information, contact New England Steamboat Lines, Marine Park, Haddam, CT 06438 (tel. 203/345-4507).

One-hour sunset cruises also leave from Saybrook Point. Contact Deep River Navigation Company, River Street, Deep River, CT 06417 (tel. 203/526-4954).

Other Entertainments—Bars

The **Griswold Inn**, Main Street, Essex (tel. 203/767-0991), always has some good musical entertainment on hand: Dixieland, sea chanteys, banjo, etc., and people dance on Friday and Saturday nights. **Oliver's Taverne** is a popular drinking spot, and so, too, is the **Marina.** For quieter entertainment, just take a stroll around Essex or Chester or down by the water by the light of the moon or the setting sun.

AREA ACTIVITIES

ANTIQUING: There are four or five interesting stores for browsing in Essex, and one or two in Chester, including a store that specializes in making lamps of all kinds patterned after the old designs. Other shops are dotted around the whole area.

BICYCLING: Rentals available at Sew n' So in Essex (tel. 203/767-8188).

BOATING: Offshore rentals at the dock in Essex (tel. 203/767-0743).

CAMPING: The area possesses several choice camping spots, including some special camping reserved for canoeists where the only access is by canoe —making for a genuine camping experience. These campsites are available by reservation only between May 1 through September 30. Write to: Donald Grant, Manager, Gillette Castle State Park, East Haddam, CT 06423 (tel. 203/526-2336), at least three weeks in advance of your chosen dates. Such camping exists at Hurd State Park, East Hampton; Gillette Castle State Park, Hadlyme; and Selden Neck State Park, Lyme.

Camping with shore access can be found at either Hammonasset State Park, P.O. Box 271, Madison, CT 06443 (tel. 203/245-2785), where 538 sites are available near the two-mile sandy beach; or at Rocky Neck State Park, P.O. Box 676, Niantic, CT 06357 (tel. 203/739-5471), with 169 sites.

For wilderness camping try Devil's Hopyard State Park, East Haddam, CT 06423 (tel. 203/873-8566), so called because, the story goes, the Devil lived there, presumably brewing beer if you want to be literal about it.

For detailed information on state parks, call 203/566-2304.

CANOEING: For canoe tours, write to David Harraden, 65 Black Point Rd., Niantic, CT 06357 (tel. 203/739-0791). Down River Canoes, P.O. Box 283, Haddam, CT 06438 (tel. 203/345-8355), also offers one- and three-day weekend trips on the Connecticut River. Instruction given and rentals available.

FISHING: Bashan Lake, off Rte. 82 in East Haddam; Moodus Reservoir, with access two miles east of Moodus and one mile southeast of Rte. 149.

FRUIT PICKING: *Cromwell:* Shakus Berry Farm, 149 Berlin Rd. (tel. 203/635-0709), strawberries. *East Haddam:* Founders School Farm, River Rd. (tel. 203/873-8658), sweet corn, squash, beans, pumpkins. *Middlefield:* Lyman Orchards, junction of Rtes. 147 and 157 (tel. 203/349-1566), apples, raspberries, sweet corn, tomatoes, squash, pumpkins.

GOLF: Lyman Meadow Golf Club, Rte. 157 (tel. 203/349-8055); Tournament Players Club, Golf Club Rd., Cromwell (tel. 203/635-2211); Cedar Ridge Golf Course, Drabik Rd., East Lyme (tel. 203/739-7395), 18 holes, par 54.

HIKING: Plenty of state parks in the area possess trails—Hurd, Gillette Castle, Selden Neck, Chatfield Hollow. For detailed information, write to the Connecticut Forest and Park Association, P.O. Box 389, East Hartford, CT 06108 (tel. 203/346-2372).

HORSEBACK RIDING: Cricklewood Farm, off Rte. 82 between Salem and Colchester (tel. 203/859-2124), offers lessons only; Cave Hill Stables, Moodus (tel. 203/873-8476, or 873-8347 in summer).

PICNICKING: The river affords plenty of picnicking opportunities. At Hurd State Park you'll have to climb down to the river. Pick up supplies in Middletown or East Haddam. Farther south, Gillette State Park makes a beautiful setting for a picnic. Pick up supplies in Chester and take the ferry across the river to the Park. Haddam Meadows State Park also offers picnicking beside the river in a largely unwooded area that is filled with goldenrod and all kinds of wildflowers. Stop in East Haddam for supplies.

For shore picnics, head for Rocky Neck and Hammonnasset State Parks. Pick up supplies in Old Lyme and Clinton respectively.

SAILING: Sail Away Sailing School and Offshore Rentals at Essex's Steamboat Dock (tel. 203/767-0743).

SKIING: Downhill at Powder Ridge, Middlefield, CT 06455 (tel. 203/349-3454), off Rte. 147, provides five slopes, four chair lifts, and 21 trails.

STATE PARKS: For information, contact the Department of Environmental Protection, State Parks and Recreation, 165 Capitol Ave., Hartford, CT 06106 (tel. 203/566-2304).

SWIMMING: Shore swimming at Rocky Neck State Park, East Lyme (tel. 203/739-5471), with a boardwalk, etc. $4 weekend parking; also at Harvey's

Beach, Old Saybrook; in Chester at Cedar Lake; Some of the resorts in Moodus open their facilities for the day for a moderate fee: for example, Frank Davis (tel. 203/873-8681).

TENNIS: Check with the local chamber of commerce for high school locations.

MYSTIC & THE CONNECTICUT SHORELINE

DISTANCES IN MILES: New London, 121; Mystic, 130; Norwich, 138; Westerly, Rhode Island, 147
ESTIMATED DRIVING TIMES: 2¾ to 3½ hours

DRIVING: Take the FDR Drive to the New England Thruway (I-95).
BUS: Greyhound (tel. 212/635-0800, or toll free 800/528-6055) travels to New London, Groton, Mystic, and Norwich.
TRAIN: Amtrak travels to New London, Mystic, and Westerly. For information, call 212/736-6288.

Special Events to Plan Your Trip Around

MAY: Sea Music Festival at the Mystic Seaport (usually in mid-May).
JUNE: Rose/Arts Festival in Norwich, featuring entertainment, arts, crafts, and the Big Rose parade (usually in early June).

Yale-Harvard Regatta, New London (usually the second Saturday in June). Contact Southeastern Connecticut, Tourism District, 8 Mill St., New London, CT 06320 (tel. 203/444-2206).

Windjammer Weekend at Mystic Seaport, when schooners and sail-training vessels gather before the race to Newport (mid-June).

JULY: Blessing of the Fleet in Stonington Harbor—mass, procession, and blessing in the Portuguese tradition (usually the second Sunday in July).

Mystic Outdoor Art Festival (early August).

Antique and Classic Boat Rendezvous at the Mystic Seaport, complete with flotilla (usually in late July).

Coast Guard Day, New London and Mystic Seaport (usually the last Saturday in July).

DECEMBER: Lantern Light Tours at Mystic Seaport.

For further information about these events and Connecticut in general, call or write the Travel Office, Department of Economic Development, 210 Washington St., Hartford, CT 06106 (tel. 203/566-3385), or toll free 800/243-1685 from Maine through Virginia, 800/842-7492 in Connecticut.

The New England Vacation Center, 630 Fifth Ave., Concourse Shop 2, New York NY 10020 (tel. 212/307-5780), also provides information.

For specific information about the area, contact the Southeastern Connecticut Tourism District, Ye Olde Towne Mill, 8 Mill St., New London, CT 06320 (tel. 203/444-2206); Mystic Chamber of Commerce, 2 Roosevelt Ave., Mystic, CT 06355 (tel. 203/536-8559); Mystic & Shoreline Visitor Information Center, Olde Mistick Village, CT 06355 (tel. 203/536-1641); Norwich Chamber of Commerce, 35 Main St., Norwich CT 06360 (tel. 203/887-1647).

If you've ever felt the call of the sea or the desire for puttering around in boats, then you'll be strongly attracted to Mystic and the Connecticut shoreline, which puts you in direct touch with the sea and the lives of seafarers who went out from these whaling and shipbuilding towns to risk their lives on the oceans of the world.

In Mystic, obviously, you'll want to see the two prime attractions, the seaport and the aquarium, plus the life on the river that cuts through downtown Mystic. You can even choose to spend one or both days of your weekend sailing out of Mystic harbor aboard a replica of the old tall-masted schooners that used to sail from here around the world. Across the harbor, in Stonington, an unspoiled old whaling town that still maintains a fishing fleet, the streets are lined with clapboard sea captain's homes, many now owned by celebrities. Stonington is also the place to go for some fine romantic dining. North of Mystic and Stonington, you can take trips along the backroads to a cider mill, a vineyard, or the historic Denison Homestead, where you can wander along the trails in the scenic nature reserve. At Groton, the first nuclear submarine, the *Nautilus,* can be toured, and so, too, can the old World War II submarine, the U.S.S. *Croaker,* a sober reminder of how far and how fast technology has come since the 1940s. Various boat trips also leave from here, including interesting oceanographic expeditions. Across the other side of the Thames River's mouth, New London has some surprises. If you drove through you'd think it was just another rather ugly industrial town, but in fact it possesses one of the East Coast's finest arboretums, a fine small museum, a special dollhouse and doll museum, the impressive Coast Guard Academy, and the summer home of one of America's greatest playwrights, Eugene O'Neill. Only 30 minutes up the Thames River from New London lies Norwich, an old town that has a fascinating art and sculpture museum, the Slater Memorial, a very lovely recently restored lodging place with full spa treatments, and an Indian museum nearby.

Besides all these attractions, the area affords wonderful opportunities for fishing, sailing, windsurfing, hiking, swimming, and exploring a coastline dotted with state parks like Harkness and Bluff Point, and lined with fine beaches from New London's Ocean Beach, complete with boardwalk and amusement park, to the more rugged and natural beaches of Rhode Island.

A Suggested Itinerary

For the first-time visitor, you'll want to spend the first half day at the seaport, the second half at the aquarium, and the next day exploring New London and Groton's attractions. For those familiar with the seaport, you may want to skip it altogether and explore the coastline—Harkness State Park and New London–Groton—on the first day and then drive east to Stonington, Misquamicut, and Watch Hill on the next day. Or you can strike inland and wander along the backroads to Norwich.

MYSTIC-STONINGTON

AREA ATTRACTIONS

Mystic Seaport

On Rte. 27 (tel. 203/572-0711), there's always something happening at this 17-acre replica of a 19th-century seafaring village, the largest marine museum in the United States, built appropriately enough on the site of the George Greenman and Company shipyard, which constructed such vessels as the *David Crockett,* whose average speed on 25 voyages around Cape Horn to San Francisco was never equalled.

For today's seafarers, the coal-fired steamboat *Sabino* (1908) chugs out from the dock every hour, daily from May to mid-October, for a 30-minute trip down the Mystic River; at Christmas time lantern-light tours and caroling add to the holiday festivities of a 19th-century town; sea chantey and other music festivals are put on in the summer; and as you stroll through the village you'll hear the clanking and the hammering of the many craftsmen and artisans still demonstrating and practicing nautical trades—barrel making, sailmaking, figurehead carving, and ship smithing. In the stores alongside them you can view the products that would have been on sale and have whatever you wish explained to you. In the clockmaker's store, for instance, you may even learn how to work an astrolabe.

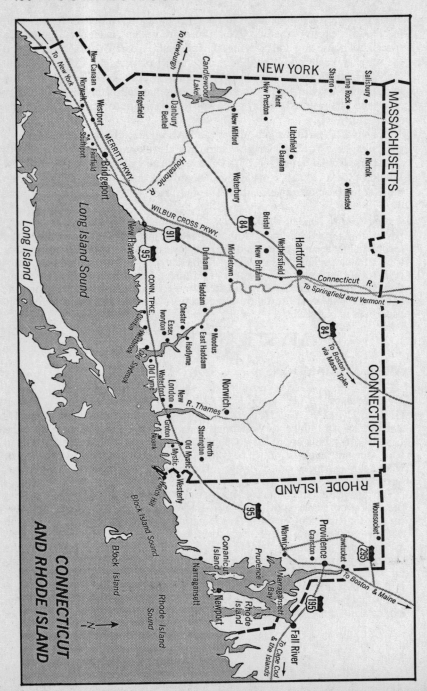

CONNECTICUT AND RHODE ISLAND

Hearth-cooking demonstrations go on in Buckingham House, while the many special demonstrations of seafaring skills range from sail setting and furling aboard the square-rigged *Joseph Conrad* (1882) to whaleboat rowing.

By the way, the whaling film is extremely informative and will give you some idea of how hair-raising a "Nantucket sleigh ride" can be, and just how short-lived but vital the whale industry was in the mid-1800s. Another informative show (a small fee is charged), given at the Planetarium, concerns celestial navigation.

To get a fix on the context of it all, you may want to begin in the Stillman building, which has an exhibit relating New England's fishing and shipping history. Don't miss the beautiful and moving (when you think under what emotional and physical conditions this art was practiced) scrimshaw that is displayed on the upper floor, or the dramatic, and sometimes alarming or even amusing, figureheads in the Wendell Building across the way.

Although the museum actually owns about 300 craft—smacks, sloops, sandbaggers, even something called a New Haven sharpie—there are three main boats to go aboard: the last survivor of America's once-vast fleet of wooden whaleships, the *Charles W. Morgan,* whose 37 voyages between 1841 and 1921 yielded 54,483 barrels of oil and 152,934 pounds of whalebone; the 1921 *L. A. Dunton,* a fishing schooner that went regularly to the Grand Banks and whose lower deck and hold give you a very good idea of the arduous task a fisherman faced living in such cramped quarters for so long at sea; and the square-rigged *Joseph Conrad* (1882).

Although the museum suggests that you spend at least four hours here, you could very easily spend a day, dreaming deep about the myths and mysteries of the sea and those that sail upon her. In summer you'll find many crowds, so get there early; nicest time to visit (as usual) is in the spring or fall when everything seems less frantic. Fast food is available at the Galley; full-service meals at the Seamen's Inne, whose tavern section is the coziest and most appealing, but where only good luck and timing will ensure a seat. HOURS: The 40 or so exhibit buildings and ships are open from 9 A.M. to 5 P.M.; the grounds stay open until 7 P.M. (to 8 P.M. between Memorial and Labor Day); exhibits are open from 9 A.M. to 4 P.M. November to April. ADMISSION: In summer, $9 for adults, $4.50 for children; $7 and $3.50 respectively in winter.

Mystic Marinelife Aquarium

At the Aquarium, Coogan Boulevard, Exit 90 off I-95 (tel. 203/536-9631), do attend one of the hourly training sessions given in the Marine Theater, where the natural talents of dolphins, sea lions, and whales never cease to amaze and delight audiences. Dolphins leap 20 feet in the air, performing triple spirals, even "walking on their tails" and sweeping through the water, propelled by the 8½ horsepower in their tails to reach speeds of 50 and 60 miles an hour. You'll also view the white Beluga whale kissing and cavorting with his trainer and sea lions goofing around, tossing and balancing balls, talking back and waving their farewell. Also, don't miss Seal Island, where all kinds of sea lions, gray seals, and fur seals can be viewed in their natural habitats. If you talk to their enthusiastic keepers, who know each one by name, you'll learn that there is quite a social hierarchy. For example, they'll point out the old seal leaning against the wall and snoozing, who is really too old to care or do anything except struggle ashore at feeding time —which she prefers to attend last because she wants "no hassle." Feeding time is always fun, and each creature, by the way, has its own finicky habits—this one wants only tails, another only heads, and so on. Cute. Back inside you can view sand tiger sharks close enough to examine their sharp teeth (by the way, if they lose one, they replace it immediately), a giant 25-pound Pacific octopus, seahorses, peculiar fish that burrow in the sand, a blue lobster, and exhibits dealing with particular habitats—over 6,000 species of fish and marine mammals in all. HOURS: From 9 A.M. daily. ADMISSION: $6 for adults, $3 for children 5 to 17.

Cruising from Mystic

Recapture the aura of the days when Mystic was filled with whaleships and schooners lying cheek by jowl against smacks and packet sloops by cruising aboard either the *Mystic Whaler* or the *Mystic Clipper,* both windjammer schooners that sail on regular one-, two-, three-, or five-day voyages on Long Island and Block Island Sounds, calling at Sag Harbor, Block Island, Newport, and other ports. They leave from Whaler's Wharf, Mystic. For information, contact Out O'Mystic Schooner Cruises at 7 Holmes St., Mystic, CT 06355 (tel. 203/536-4218). Prices about $60 for a one-day sail (including breakfast and lunch) on weekends.

Another much older schooner, built in 1888, the *Charlotte Ann* has been rebuilt and offers half-day or full-day sails, leaving from Steamboat Wharf in downtown Mystic from June to the end of August. Contact Voyager Cruises, Steamboat Wharf, Mystic, CT 06355 (tel. 203/536-0416). The same company also operates the *Voyager,* which sails on two- or three-day trips to Block Island, Newport, and Sag Harbor.

Downtown Mystic, Old Mystic, and Environs

After your visit to the seaport, take a walk down Gravel and High Streets, past the many **historic houses** that have been outlined in the Mystic Chamber of Commerce's walking tour. Each one has a tale attached. For example, at 27 Gravel St., seances were conducted by Matilda Appleman, who also sheltered slaves traveling the Underground Railroad.

You may also want to explore downtown Mystic at the river's mouth, where the bascule **drawbridge** joins the two municipalities of Stonington and Groton. Actually, there's no such political entity as Mystic. This downtown area was developed when shipbuilding became big business in the mid to late 1800s. Drop in and browse the crafts, fashion, book, gift, and antique stores here, including **Factory Square.**

Up the river, Old Mystic slumbers quietly along with its post office, general store, and a few residences. You may want to visit the so-called **Olde Mistick Village** (tel. 203/536-4941), which is in fact at the junction of I-95 on Rte. 27, a quaint shopping complex designed to look like a New England village of around 1720, whose shops are usually open from 10 A.M. to 5:30 P.M. Monday to Thursday and

Saturday, until 9 P.M. on Friday. The **Memory Lane Doll and Toy Museum,** Olde Mistick Village (tel. 203/536-3450), displays 1,500 dolls from all over the world dating from the 1800s to the present. The oldest is made of hand-carved wood with glass eyes and is over 250 years old. Among the more venerable are a 200-year-old Queen Anne and a glass-eyed china Queen Elizabeth I. Others are German, French, Oriental, and made variously of bisque, china, and all kinds of other materials. Many of them are classics from Greiner, Chase, Simon-Halbig, Heubach, Jumeau, etc. Besides the dolls there are also fun items like a Schoenhut Circus with an incredible assortment of animals, cars, trains, farmhouses, and more. HOURS: Monday to Saturday from 10 A.M. to 6 P.M., on Sunday from noon to 6 P.M. ADMISSION: 50¢ for adults, 25¢ for children.

From here you can drive out to **Clyde's Cider Mill** (bring your own containers) on North Stonington Road, Old Mystic (tel. 203/536-3354), which operates during fall. Or drive east to visit **Clark Vineyards,** on Taugwonk Road (tel. 203/535-0235), one of the few wineries that have located in this area. HOURS: Tours are given Tuesday, Thursday, and Saturday from 10 A.M. to 5 P.M.; in January and February by appointment.

Looping back toward Stonington, you can stop at the **Denison Homestead and Nature Center,** Pequotsepos Road, Mystic. Since 1722 the homestead (tel. 203/536-9248) belonged to five generations of Denisons, one of Connecticut's first families, and it is interesting because each room has been furnished to reflect the five different periods. Trails criss-cross the 125-acre sanctuary (tel. 203/536-1216). HOURS: The home is open from May 15 to October 15, Tuesday to Sunday from 1 to 5 P.M.; closed Monday. ADMISSION: $1.75 for adults, 50¢ for children.

Stonington Village/Watch Hill

In the dining section I'll describe two restaurants where you might want to dine, but before you do, take some time to discover this old whaling village, where Stephen Vincent Benet and James MacNeill Whistler both had residences, where Edgar Allan Poe loved to visit, and where today many a celebrity chooses to hide away. Narrow streets lined with old sea captains' homes and Victorian residences cluster on a peninsula running between Stonington Harbor on one side and the Pawcatuck River and Fisher's Island Sound on the other. Stroll down Water Street to the **Stonington Light** (1840), which now houses a collection of whaling and fishing artifacts, toys, Stonington firearms, and stoneware (tel. 203/535-1440). HOURS: May to October, Tuesday to Sunday from 11 A.M. to 4:30 P.M. ADMISSION: $1 for adults, 50¢ for children under 12.

From Stonington, it's only a short drive to **Watch Hill,** a quiet gracious shore enclave that possesses a number of rambling Victorian shore hotels like the Ocean House, which have seen better days. The town is not too crowded, and while you're here stroll down to the carousel, stop at the Book & Tackle Shop stacked with piles of old and new books and a good selection of historic postcards, have an ice cream across the street or a cup of coffee and a snack, walk to the Watch Hill Lighthouse, or just sit out on the Harbour House's deck and watch the scene.

MYSTIC LODGING

Until recently the **Inn at Mystic**, Rte. 1, Mystic, CT 06355 (tel. 203/536-9604), was called the Mystic Motor Inn, and indeed it still does look very much like a classy motor inn. The reason for the new name is the addition of the "Inn and Gatehouse" an imposing Colonial Revival mansion with a classical pediment supported by Corinthian columns that stands on a hill at the back of the property. The mansion's ground-floor formal dining room and parlor, with their exquisite 17th-century pine paneling and carved mantel decorated with Delft tiles, are open to guests and used for weddings and parties, while upstairs the ten guest rooms are lavishly furnished with canopy beds, antique sofas, and porcelain lamps. Four rooms even have whirlpool baths that you can stand in and still look out over the harbor.

Besides the new inn, the place has some other outstanding attributes. First, the view of the harbor; second, 13 acres of landscaped grounds that slope down to the river; and third, some very comfortable rooms, many of which are prettily furnished with antique reproductions of Federal-style mirrors and desks, brass lamps, and full- or half-canopy beds. TVs are tucked away in cabinets. The East Wing rooms, which were built in 1978, are even more luxurious, with their fireplaces, wing chairs, handsome highboys, bathrooms with Jacuzzi tubs, bidets, and sliding doors that lead to a balcony.

The Flood Tide Restaurant has a good reputation. Here in a pretty country dining room such classics as beef Wellington, chateaubriand, rack of lamb, and whole roast chicken are all nicely presented. There's even a vegetable fiesta—an assortment of sautéed vegetables served on a silver platter. The mixed grill (lamb chops, beef tenderloin, smoked sausage, liver, and pork) adds a dash of English flavor. A tasty array of appetizers includes smoked fisherman's platter (smoked salmon, smoked trout, and smoked bluefish served with Pommery sauce) and crêpes filled with venison ragoût (a stew of venison and chanterelles) flavored with juniper. Prices run $10 to $20. Other dishes include roast duckling with peach glaze, broiled filet mignon wrapped in bacon and served with mushroom caps and sauce Foyot, veal Zurich, and several other seafood and veal dishes. Special dessert treats are the bananas Foster and the chocolate fondue, although there are plenty of other delectable choices. The restaurant is open year round, and so is the wine bar and piano lounge.

Additional facilities include a heated outdoor swimming pool, tennis courts, and canoes and sailboats for rent.

RATES: In the motor inn, $85 to $95 in summer and $60 to $80 in winter; in the inn and gatehouse, $100 to $140 in summer and $85 to $130 in winter. Special packages are available during winter and spring months, usually including two nights' accommodations, and sometimes dinner. BREAKFAST: Buffet style, 7:30 to 10:30 A.M. daily. LUNCH: Monday to Friday from 11:30 A.M. to 2:30 P.M. DINNER: Sunday to Thursday from 5:30 to 9:30 P.M., on Friday and Saturday until 10 P.M. BRUNCH: Sunday from 11 A.M. to 3 P.M.

Clean and nicely kept rooms can be found at the **Whalers Inn,** 20 E. Main St., Mystic, CT 06355 (tel. 203/536-1506), just 100 yards or less from the river bridge. In the older section of this 40-room establishment designed around a motor court, the rooms tend to be small, with one double bed; all the rooms are clean and basic. Downstairs the Binnacle restaurant serves breakfast, and burger and sandwich fare throughout the day. For those traveling by train, the Inn is only four blocks from the railroad station. RATES: $32 to $38 single, $38 to $75 double.

A **Mystic Hilton,** Coogan Blvd., Mystic, CT 06355 (tel. 203/572-0731) was about to open when I visited and will have 187 rooms, an indoor-outdoor pool, restaurant, and lounge.

Other Mystic accommodations run to the typical modern chains like **Days Inn,** Rte. 27 (P.O. Box 88), Mystic, CT 06355 (tel. 203/572-0574); **Howard Johnson's,** Rte. 27, Mystic, CT 06355 (tel. 203/536-2654); and the **Ramada Inn,** Rte. 27 (P.O. Box 427), Mystic, CT 06355 (tel. 203/536-4281).

RATES: Summer rates for doubles run $62, $75, and $75 respectively.

A Bed-and-Breakfast in Old Mystic

In Old Mystic, two miles from the coast, Ruth Keyes and Verne Sasek have lovingly restored an 18th-century colonial farmhouse, the Crary Homestead, transforming it into a delightfully secluded retreat—the **Red Brook Inn,** 10 Welles Rd. (P.O. Box 237), Old Mystic, CT 06372 (tel. 203/572-0349).

The three accommodations, all with air conditioning, are furnished with period pieces—canopy beds, antique rockers, cherry side tables, early American chests, and in the West Room, an unusual so-called Mammy bench rocker, an ingenious early timesaver. Some of the rooms have fireplaces, two share bathrooms. Downstairs in the parlor guests can gather around the fire for a game of chess or backgammon, while admiring Ruth's glass collection that includes many whale-oil lamps. The keeping room, however, is her real pride and joy, containing a wide colonial hearth, with all the necessary equipment for hearthside cooking that Ruth in fact practices. Here your breakfast will be served on fine china, and most likely will offer apple, zucchini, or banana-nut bread; fresh peaches, grapefruit, or other seasonal fruit; muffins; walnut waffles or blueberry pancakes; and some unusual corn sticks. The 7½ acres of grounds provide adequate seclusion and make an ideal picnicking area or place for a game of croquet. RATES: $80 to $130 double. Special winter packages, including two nights' accommodation, a Friday-night fireside colonial dinner home-cooked over an open hearth, two breakfasts, and snacks at various times, cost $300 and up per couple.

On the same property and also owned by the same couple, the **Historic Haley's Tavern** (ca. 1790) was brought from two miles away and reassembled here. Originally built in the 1740s by a man named Smith, it was bought by Elijah Haley and operated as a stagecoach inn. It's full of atmosphere: the doors are low, the floors creak, the original hinges and latches have survived, and the windows are either 12-over-12 or 12-over-8. It's also notable for the museum-quality paneled rooms and original tap room.

Each of the rooms is individually decorated with period antiques. Ross Haley's large suite contains a handsome pencil four-poster with netted canopy, stoneware lamps, wing chairs, chest, couch, blanket chest, and small rush-seated ladder-back. Oriental throw rugs cover the floor and there's a working fireplace. On the solid-walnut cannonball bed in the Henry Haley Room is spread a States quilt depicting all the state flowers. It was crafted in Michigan. Two rockers are placed beside the fireplace. In the Mary Virginia Room, also with fireplace and chimney cupboard above, there's another canopy bed, made in Stonington around 1820, sporting a crocheted canopy. Each room is finished off with decorative antiques —mirrors, silhouettes, early American paintings, etc.

On the first floor there's a small, comfortable parlor furnished with interesting antiques including an early glass collection. The warmest, probably most atmospheric room is the kitchen with its large open hearth, early American tables, and a breakfront filled with pewter. A full breakfast consisting of such items as broccoli quiche or walnut waffles with home-baked muffins and freshly squeezed juice is served here or outside on the flagstone patio. All in all, it's a secluded country retreat surrounded by 60 wooded acres.

RATES: $80 to $130 (the first for the Jenny Lind Room and the last for the Ross Haley Room).

Note: Both of these homes make up the Red Brook Inn. In winter from November through March Ruth prepares colonial dinners for guests much as the 18th-century house dwellers would have, over an open hearth. Cornish hens or other roasts turn on the spit; various kettles containing the season's vegetables simmer above the fire, and out of the bake oven come fresh loaves and fruit pies—a memorable evening meal for all.

MYSTIC DINING

Breakfasts/Lunches

The croissants at **Rolling in Dough,** 22 Holmes St. (tel. 203/536-6698), are renowned. Other fare includes broccoli melt, meatball croissant, tuna melt, quiches, and salads, priced around $4 or $5. **BeeBees,** West Main Street (tel. 203/536-4577), is another favorite breakfast spot. **Twin Sisters Deli,** 4 Pearl St. (tel. 203/536-1244), is good for sandwiches and other luncheon fare.

Picnics and Other Food to Go

Grossman's fish and cheese market is open daily: Monday to Wednesday from 8:30 A.M. to 7 P.M., on Thursday, Friday, Saturday, and Sunday from 10 A.M. to 6 P.M. **The Market,** 375 Noank Rd. in West Mystic, is a deli/bakery that makes picnics to go.

Lunch and Dinner

The **Captain Daniel Packer Inne,** 32 Water St. (tel. 203/536-3555), has a very attractive ambience, especially in the downstairs low-beamed tavern which is made even cozier by the fire. The upstairs dining room is traditional—Windsor chairs, and polished wood tables with placemats, lit by hurricane lamps. The food is also traditional. Start with little necks, escargots, or stuffed mushrooms before moving on to stuffed shrimp, chicken bordelaise, or veal or duck à la bigarade, from $9 to $14. At lunch, burgers and sandwiches, quiche, and such dishes as baked stuffed sole are available—from $4 to $8.

LUNCH: Monday to Saturday from 11:30 A.M. to 3 P.M. DINNER: Monday to

Thursday from 5 to 10 P.M., on Friday and Saturday until 10:30 P.M., on Sunday from 4 to 10 P.M. BRUNCH: Sunday from 11 A.M. to 2:30 P.M.

The Landing, 73 Steamboat Wharf (tel. 203/572-0549), offers riverfront dining on mainly fish—scrod broiled in lemon butter, blackened redfish, jambalaya, Louisiana seafood gumbo—supplemented by some meat items. Favored appetizers are the Louisiana spicy boiled shrimp and the coconut beer-batter chicken fingers. Prices run $9 to $16.

HOURS: 11 A.M. to 9 P.M. daily.

In Olde Misticke Village, the well-liked **Steak Loft** (tel. 203/536-2661), set in a pretty, barn-like building decorated with plenty of farm gadgets, purveys (surprise) steaks—sirloin, teriyaki, tenderloin—from $10 to $17. Seafood and chicken are also on the menu.

The **Mystic River Tavern,** Holmes Street (tel. 203/536-2674), occupies a great vantage point from which to view the life of the river and the boats passing under the rare bascule bridge right in downtown Mystic. The menu offers an assortment of steaks and seafood, including steak teriyaki, shrimp kebabs, fish and chips, and stuffed sole. Prices range from $10 to $14. At lunch, burgers and sandwiches are the primary fare. The upstairs tavern features entertainment and on Friday the banjo nights are jumping. LUNCH: Monday to Saturday from 11:30 A.M. to 3 P.M. DINNER: Monday to Friday from 5 to 9 P.M., until 10 P.M. on Saturday, and from noon to 9 P.M. on Sunday.

Dinner Only

J. P. Daniels, Rte. 184, Old Mystic (tel. 203/572-9564), is a favorite romantic dining spot housed in a comfortably rustic historic old barn whose raftered ceiling is high enough to hang a sleigh and a carriage from it.

The place is warmly lit at night. Among the appetizers you might choose stuffed mushrooms, little necks, cannelloni, or an antipasto salad consisting of peppers, olives, pimentos, salami, and provolone cheese on greens.

The entree selections include veal marsala, Oscar, or française, filet mignon au poivre, and steak J. P. Daniels—sirloin rubbed with garlic, oregano, and shallots, grilled, and served on a bed of peppers and onions. Stuffed boneless duckling with seasoned fruit stuffing enhanced in Curaçao, and poulet Dijon flavored with tarragon and rosemary are also prime temptations. So, too, is the excellent bouillabaisse. Prices run $10 to $16. Desserts are classics like peach Melba and chocolate mousse.

LUNCH: Monday to Friday from 11:30 A.M. to 2 P.M. DINNER: Monday to Thursday from 5 to 9:30 P.M., on Friday and Saturday until 10 P.M.

STONINGTON LODGING

Just east of Mystic lies this charming unspoiled old whaling town. Here there are a couple of accommodations.

At **Lasbury's Guesthouse,** 24 Orchard St., Stonington, CT 06378 (tel. 203/535-2681), the owners rent out three rooms: one with private bath, and two in a separate cottage sharing a bath.

RATES: $55 midweek, $60 on weekends, and $65 on holidays.

The **Farnan House,** 10 McGrath Court, Stonington, CT 06378 (tel. 203/535-0634), also offers rooms in another nice old Stonington house.

RATES (including continental breakfast): $50 to $55 double.

STONINGTON DINING

From Mystic, you may well prefer, as many locals do, to pop over to Stonington, where you have two fine choices for dining. For romantic dining there's **Harbor View,** Cannon Square (tel. 203/535-2720), where the front tap room is always, in summer at least, filled to the rafters with seafaring and other convivial sorts, all crammed into the small atmospheric bar (in which you can also obtain a fine lunch or dinner). Behind, in the low-lit dining room patrons are entertained by a harpist, and dine looking out over the harbor on such dishes as bouillabaisse, poached sole with shrimp and mushrooms, mussels, rack of lamb, and assorted veal dishes, priced from $14 to $18. Ham, shrimp cocktail, turkey, vegetables, potato au gratin, fettuccine, crab Benedict, fruits, and pastries make up the big Sunday buffet brunch spread.

LUNCH AND DINNER: 11:30 A.M. to 10 P.M. daily. BRUNCH: Sunday from 11 A.M. to 4 P.M.

Just up the street, **Noah's,** 115 Water St. (tel. 203/535-3925), is unpretentious and comfortable, yet still pretty at night. It's frequented by a local crowd that enjoys the moderately priced limited menu which always features a pasta of the day and such fresh seafood as a cod Portuguese or a broiled flounder. Prices begin at $7, rising to $11.50 for filet mignon.

BREAKFAST: Tuesday to Sunday from 7 to 11 A.M. LUNCH: Tuesday to Saturday from 11:30 A.M. to 2:30 P.M., on Sunday from 12:15 to 2:30 P.M. DINNER: Tuesday to Thursday and Sunday from 6 to 9 P.M., on Friday and Saturday until 9:30 P.M. Closed Monday.

Behind Harborview, right down at the water's edge, **Skipper's Dock** (tel. 203/535-2000) offers a plain setting for steamed lobster, fish (broiled, grilled with herb butter, pan-fried with clam butter, or poached with Roquefort sauce and served on a bed of spinach), and a clambake consisting of fish chowder, a one-pound lobster, mussels, steamers, sausage, a chicken quarter, and corn on the cob. Prices run $9 to $16.

HOURS: In summer, daily from 11:30 A.M. to 10 P.M.; in fall and off-season, Wednesday to Sunday from 11:30 A.M. to 9 P.M. Closed in January, February, and March.

NOANK LODGING

The exterior of the **Palmer Inn,** 25 Church St., Noank, CT 06340 (tel. 203/572-9000), is very impressive with its semicircular 30-foot-high columned portico, and so, too, is the interior of this 16-room mansion built in 1907 for a member of the famous Palmer shipbuilding family. With its high ceilings supported by wood columns among other architectural details, I especially like the sunrise-sunset fan stained-glass windows that change colors during the day.

Don and Patty Cornish have restored it, furnishing the six rooms (one with fireplace) in a Victorian manner. Two share a bathroom and third-floor rooms are tucked interestingly under the eaves. One room possesses a king-size wicker bed, couch, chair, and side table, all of wicker. A favorite room is the dusky-rose master suite (with fireplace), where the walls are covered in French turn-of-the-century–design wallpapers, the windows have lace curtains, and the furnishings are oak. The satin eider adds a luxurious touch. One room has access to the semicircular balcony above the portico, offering a view past the church steeple to the water. In the brass room stands a brass bed and oak dresser, among the furnishings; the bathroom retains the old clawfoot tub and pedestal sink. The oak suite contains Eastlake oak pieces and has a little balcony and stained-glass windows. All four rooms have Crabtree and Evelyn soap, shampoo, shoe polish, and other niceties.

The guests gather in the large parlor around the fireplace or at the table at breakfast. In the smaller parlor, a comfortable sofa, wing chairs, and board games are the attractions.

At breakfast you'll find fresh fruits, home-baked items, and entertaining conversation, helped along by Patty, an ex-clinical psychologist who thrives on meeting and chatting with guests and seems to have hotelkeeping in her blood. She'll even show you, on those long winter nights, how to make a pomander.

RATES: $75 to $115 double.

NOANK DINING

For summer luncheon or an early-evening dinner, you can't beat **Abbot's Lobster in the Rough,** 117 Pearl St. (tel. 203/536-7719), at the western tip of Mystic harbor in Noank, also formerly a whaling town, but a far less opulent one than Stonington on the opposite side of the harbor. Stonington residents were ship captains and ship owners; Noank's were whalers, plain and simple.

Here, at the water's edge the view only adds to the succulent flavor of the lobster. Wait while your order of lobster, crab or lobster roll ($5 to $7), mussels, clams, or steamers is cooked in the large steamers behind the counter, and then take it outside to the colorful picnic tables where you can observe the river craft and the gulls circling overhead, breathe the salty air, and listen to the halyards clinking against the masts and summoning you to the sea. Prices are very reasonable—$9 for a 1⅛-pound lobster served with cole slaw, drawn butter, and chips; $25 for a two- to three-pounder. Other items are priced from $3. A seafood dinner of clam chowder, shrimp cocktail, mussels and/or steamers, and steamed lobster goes for only $16. Before you leave, tour the holding facility, where they keep up to 22,000 pounds of these delicious crustaceans. Bring your own wine and beer.

To get there, take Rte. 1 to Rte. 215 into Noank and turn down Pearl Street.

HOURS: Noon to 9 P.M. daily from May to September, shorter hours in September and early October; closed at other times.

At the **Sea Horse Restaurant,** Marsh Road (tel. 203/536-1670), a simple local tavern-style spot, you can obtain really fresh fish at reasonable prices—broiled flounder; fisherman's platter of fried clams, shrimp, scallops, and fish; and surf and turf—from $7.50 to $12. At luncheon there's fish and chips and sandwiches for under $5.

HOURS: 11 A.M. to 9 P.M. weekdays, until 10 P.M. on weekends.

The Fisherman, 937 Groton Long Point Rd. (tel. 203/536-1717), also serves good fresh seafood even in winter, when a fire warms the hearth and a pianist entertains. Here, a wide choice of fresh seafood—scrod, sole amandine, swordfish, stuffed shrimp—is supplemented by steaks, chicken française, beef Wellington, and on weekends only, prime rib. Prices begin at $9.50.

LUNCH: From 11:30 A.M. daily except Monday. DINNER: From 5 P.M. daily except Monday.

SHELTER HARBOR, R.I., LODGING

From Mystic-Stonington, if you take Rte. 1 or the more scenic Rte. 1A, which rejoins Rte. 1 beyond Westerly, you will reach Shelter Harbor, a tiny community originally laid out as a musician's retreat, where the streets are named after composers like Bach and Verdi.

You can stay at the **Shelter Harbor Inn**, Rte. 1, Westerly, RI 02891 (tel. 401/322-8883), a restored 18th-century farmhouse, whose sunporch-bar has become a popular gathering place on weekend nights. The two small parlors offer the comforts of leather armchairs, braided rug, stove, and plenty of reading material.

In the dining room, where floral wallpaper, pine cabinets, and wainscoting impart a country air, the staple menu of seafood, beef, veal, lamb, and chicken is supplemented by daily specials—a cold buttermilk shrimp soup with chives or smoked bluefish with a horseradish sauce, for example. Entrees run $10 to $14. Breakfast (8 to 10 A.M.) offers omelets, blueberry-gingerbread pancakes, granola, and other items. Besides the usual egg dishes, brunch includes broiled scrod with herb butter and other fish dishes, hazelnut chicken with orange-thyme cream, and other favorites. Champagne and muffins are also served. Prices range from $6 to $9.

There are ten guest rooms in the house, three with fireplaces, each comfortably furnished, and ten recently decorated rooms in the barn. In the brand-new Coach House there are four additional rooms with fireplaces. Some of the rooms have private decks, and all have access to a third-floor deck with panoramic views and a hot tub.

While you're here, try your hand at paddle tennis on the two lighted courts. The inn also has access to a two-mile stretch of beach a short drive away in Weekapaug.

RATES (including breakfast): $70 to $84 double from Memorial Day to October 31, $66 to $84 from November 1 to Memorial Day. LUNCH: 11:30 A.M. to 2:30 P.M. daily. DINNER: Monday to Saturday from 5 to 9 P.M., on Sunday from 4 P.M. BRUNCH: Sunday from 11 A.M. to 3 P.M.

GROTON–NEW LONDON

GROTON ATTRACTIONS

Shipbuilding continues to this day in Groton, where the nation's largest submarine producer, the General Dynamics Corporation, is located. Here the six-story-high Trident submarines are being built, each costing $1½ billion and taking from four to five years to construct.

The highlight of any visit, especially for men and boys, is a tour of the brand-new $7.9-million **Nautilus Memorial Museum,** off Rte. 12 at the Naval Submarine Base (tel. 203/449-3174 or 449-3290); take Exit 86 off I-95. The displays in the museum building relate the history of submarine development, from the legend of Alexander the Great's descending in a glass barrel, as depicted in a medieval manuscript, to Sir Edmund Halley's 1690 "diving tub," and one version that might have worked—William Bourne's boat described in *Inventions and Devices* (1578) consisting of a flexible inner hull of leather acting as one wall of a ballast tank against a rigid wooden outer hull. On one wall there's a 50-foot-long scale model of a fleet boat showing everything detailed to one inch. The Nautilus Room traces the history of the subs bearing the name, from the first launched in 1954 that sent out the message "under nuclear power." Video stations show films of loading missiles, a day in the life of a submariner, etc. In earlier models, like the U.S.S. *Gate,* the men can be seen running around in shorts because of the heat (this was before air conditioning). En route to the boat a whole wall of models shows all classes of submarines ever built, from the *Holland* to the *Nautilus,* clearly depicting a steady process of streamlining. You can also use the periscopes to sight trucks speeding along I-95.

The tour of the "boat" itself is most fascinating. Only 60 people are allowed aboard at one time, so get there early or be prepared to wait, often on a windy footbridge/gangplank. The *Nautilus* was the first nuclear-powered submarine. It broke records by cruising deeper (400 feet), faster (20 knots), and for longer periods (287 hours covering 4,039 miles in one stretch) than any other. It carries 111 sailors and officers in highly confined quarters where every space-saving device is used—fold-away sinks, narrow bunks that double as storage boxes. While on board you'll carry an electronic wand that activates commentaries about each area—navigation center, radar room, sonar room, attack center, radio room, and the 10-foot by 2½-foot-wide galley. The 1950s pinups were donated by the original crew!

HOURS: Mid-April to September 30, Wednesday to Monday from 9 A.M. to 5 P.M.; October 15 to March 31, Wednesday to Monday from 9 A.M. to 3:30 P.M. Closed Tuesday, the first week in January, the first two weeks in April and October, and major holidays. ADMISSION: Free.

Nearby, a visit to the U.S.S. *Croaker,* 359 Thames St. (tel. 203/448-1616), provides further insights into the lives of the men who operated the early boats (a term reserved only for submarines in the navy). Engine room temperatures surged to 125° in the cramped quarters shared by the 68 enlisted men and officers during dives that lasted anywhere from 28 to 35 hours—when the oxygen gets rather thin. Built in 1943, it cost $3 million (compare that with today's Trident). HOURS: April 15 to October 15, daily from 9 A.M. to 5 P.M., until 3 P.M. at other times.

From the *Croaker,* head back up the hill to the earthworks of **Fort Griswold,** Monument Street (tel. 203/445-1729), which was attacked by a British force led by Benedict Arnold on September 6, 1781. When the American officer surrendered and handed over his sword, it was turned against him and he fell to his death. A massacre followed. Today the park provides glorious views of the Thames River and Fisher's Island. HOURS: Memorial Day to Labor Day from 9 A.M. to 5 P.M. daily, 9 A.M. to 3 P.M. weekends only at other times.

Cruises from Groton

Project Oceanography, Avery Point, Groton, sponsors enormously interesting 2½-hour trips led by expert guides aboard an Enviro-Lab. You'll learn how to use oceanographic instruments, pull in a trawl net filled with fish, and how lobsters are caught. For information, call 203/448-1616 in season, 203/445-9007 at other times. The boat departs from the Submarine Memorial Dock. ADMISSION: $9 for adults, $7 for children.

For fantasy you can voyage Bogart and Hepburn style aboard either the *River Queen,* a replica of her African counterpart, or the *River Queen II,* both of which travel past the U.S.S. *Nautilus* and the submarine base, up to the Coast Guard Academy, and back past the U.S.S. *Croaker.* For information, call 203/445-8111. The price is $5.

At sunset a Dixieland band goes with you for a two-hour cruise. The cost is $12, and the cruise sails from the Thames Harbour Inn, 193 Thames St., Groton. Call 203/445-8111 for more information.

NEW LONDON ATTRACTIONS

The **Coast Guard Academy,** Mohegan Avenue and Rte. 32 (tel. 203/444-8270), has made its home here since 1910. Today at the visitor's pavilion you can view a slide program that will introduce you to cadet life, and also visit the museum to see the nautical models, paintings, and memorabilia. Dress parades are held in spring and fall (usually on Friday; call for dates), and you can also go aboard the 295-foot square-rigged training barque the *Eagle* on Sunday in spring and fall from 1 to 4 P.M.

On this cutter cadets receive undersail training handling more than 20,000 square feet of sail, over 20 miles of rigging. More than 200 lines must be coordinated during a major ship maneuver and the cadets must learn the name and function of each line.

HOURS: The visitor's pavilion is open May to October daily from 10 A.M. to 5 P.M.; the rest of the year from 9 A.M. to 4 P.M. weekdays.

Two other attractions are almost next door to each other. The **Connecticut Arboretum,** Williams Street (tel. 203/447-1911), on the Connecticut College campus, is one of the East's finest small (415 acres) preserves with many miles of hiking trails. The **Lyman Allyn Museum,** 625 Williams St. (tel. 203/443-2545), is a richly rewarding small museum. The period furniture collection on the ground floor is especially well diagrammed and described so that, in effect, any visitor can trace the hallmarks of each period from Jacobean through Queen Anne, Chippendale, Hepplewhite, and Empire to early Victorian. The glass collection includes Tiffany, art glass, art nouveau, and Stiegel. China and clocks are also on display, along with a rare and lovely collection of English silver pocket nutmeg graters.

Downstairs will have special appeal to children, for it contains an outstanding collection of dollhouses, doll furniture, toys, and dolls. Among them are French bisque heads, wood-peg-jointed dolls, all-wood American dolls, auto peripatetikos (walking dolls), china and wax and pâpier-maché heads.

Upstairs a series of small galleries display Greek terracottas; Egyptian, Roman, ancient Near Eastern, pre-Columbian, African, Indian, and Japanese art and artifacts; and 19th-century impressionist paintings. The Chinese galleries are especially strong.

HOURS: Tuesday to Saturday from 1 to 5 P.M., on Sunday from 2 to 5 P.M. ADMISSION: Free.

New London was a great whaling port, second only to New Bedford in its heyday. To get a sense of its history, pick up a map at the New London Chamber of Commerce, 1 Whale Oil Row, and walk around. Explore Huntington Street, Captain's Walk, and Whale Oil Row, stopping at no. 3, **The Tale of the Whale Museum** (tel. 203/422-8191). Inside, view a fully equipped whaleboat, scrimshaw, whale-oil lamps, charts, and other navigational aids. HOURS: Tuesday to Sunday from 1 to 5 P.M.; closed Monday.

From the museum turn left and walk two blocks, turning left onto Washington Street and then take the first right onto Starr Street—a whole street lined with 21 restored 19th-century homes once belonging to whaling folk.

Take a left onto O'Neill Drive and right onto Pearl Street to view the **New London Custom House** (1833) on Bank Street. It was customary for the Customs officer to climb up into the attic and onto the roof to scan the harbor and check that no whaling ships had avoided paying duty. Inside, maritime artifacts are displayed.

HOURS: Monday to Friday from 8 A.M. to 4:30 P.M.

Shaw's Mansion is also open, named after Nathaniel Shaw who was appointed naval agent for the colonies by the Continental Congress. HOURS: Tuesday to Saturday from 1 to 4 P.M.

Eugene O'Neill spent much of his boyhood in New London at **Monte Cristo,** at 325 Pequot Ave., New London (tel. 203/443-0051), a gray-and-white frame house in which the family summered from 1884 to 1921. It was named after the play that paid his father $50,000 a year. When the family summered here the area was a popular summer resort on the Thames. From here, O'Neill went to sea, returning in 1924 to work as a cub reporter on the *New London Telegraph*. This was the setting for *Long Day's Journey into Night* and the comedy *Ah, Wilderness!*, and no doubt its oceanside setting inspired this young lad to sail the seas and write about the life he experienced there.

For O'Neill fans, and for anyone who empathizes with the tragedy of the O'Neill family, this house has tremendous emotional impact, especially the eerie Long Day's Journey into Night Room containing the playwright's desk, the table from the original Broadway production, James O'Neill's rum jug, and in which you can observe the small changes that O'Neill slipped into his stage setting.

The 15-minute introductory film is one of the best of its kind that I've ever seen, professionally filmed and dramatically portraying the family: dashing matinee idol father James, whose good looks and golden voice made him one of the most promising actors in the U.S. but who sacrificed his talent for money; mother Mary Ellen Quinlan from Indiana, whose morphine addiction began when she sought relief from the pain of childbirth and who gave up her dream of becoming a concert pianist when she married James Tyrone; brother Jamie, who died of alcoholism; and Eugene, born in a Broadway hotel in October 1888, whose life was dogged by a secret shame and a need to escape from reality.

Unfortunately, you cannot visit on weekends. HOURS: Monday to Friday from 1 to 4 P.M.; by appointment at other times. ADMISSION: $2.

Nearby, the **Eugene O'Neill Theater Center,** 305 Great Neck Rd., Waterford (tel. 203/443-5378), has been established on grounds that sweep down to the Sound. This is a must for any theater lover, especially during the summer Playwrights' Conference from early July to early August when a dozen or so plays selected from nearly 2,000 are developed in staged readings. Two recent Broadway hits were both developed here—*Agnes of God* and *Nine.* Later in the summer a similar opera-musical theater conference is held. At other times you may catch a workshop in session, as I did when students were practicing their fencing for those swashbuckling period roles.

GROTON LODGING

Best Western's **Olympic Inn,** 360 Rte. 12, Groton, CT 06340 (tel. 203/445-8000), has 104 pretty rooms furnished with desk, sofa, dressers, and modern amenities. Exercise room, saunas, lounge, and restaurant complete the facilities. The place is sparkling new.

RATES: $60 to $70 in winter, $70 to $90 in summer.

Going west from Mystic, tracing the coastline will bring you to Groton Long Point, where the houses cluster along the shore. The only accommodation to be found among the many residences is the **Shore Inn,** 54 E. Shore Rd., Groton Long Point, CT 06340 (tel. 203/536-1180), facing out across the Sound to Fisher's Island. The seven accommodations are pleasant.

RATES (with continental breakfast): $42 to $48.50 in high season (higher price is for room with private bath), less before Memorial Day.

NEW LONDON LODGING AND DINING

A grand fountain plays in front of the entrance to the **Lighthouse Inn,** 6 Guthrie Pl., New London, CT 06320 (tel. 203/443-8411), a rambling old resort hotel that was undergoing renovation when I stopped by. The ground-floor public rooms filled with Eastlake and other Victoriana are elegant with their 15-foot-high ceilings. Swag drapes cover the windows and the cocktail lounge with a fireplace even has a chintz ceiling. The dining room looks out onto the Sound.

The house was built in 1902 as a summer residence for the Guthries of Pittsburgh. The 27 rooms in the main building, all with private bath, have been spectacularly renovated. Some of them are huge, especially those that have bay windows. Each room has been decorated with different fine chintz wallpaper and cream swag drapes. One room retains Mr. Guthrie's built-in shirt-and-sock closet complete with stepladder. The third-floor rooms, with sloping ceilings, are particularly appealing. There are 24 more accommodations, located in the carriage house and other buildings on the estate. Some have canopy beds. Tennis courts and a swimming pool are planned.

On Saturday there's dining and dancing to a four-piece orchestra. The dining room offers typical continental/American cuisine—scrod with lemon butter, filet mignon with béarnaise, veal marsala, and chicken à la Ritz, breaded with almonds sautéed in butter and served in orange cream sauce.

RATES: $95 to $175 double. The lower price is for smaller nonwaterfront rooms and carriage-house rooms; the higher, for a waterfront suite with whirlpool bath.

Queen Anne, 265 Williams St., New London, CT 06320 (tel. 203/447-2600), is a downtown bed-and-breakfast set in an intricately decorated Victorian with witches cap tower and an ornate frieze on its peaked gable. Two parlors, both with fireplace, are comfortably furnished for guests' use, and in summer the rockers on the porch are favorite lounging places.

The eight rooms, all with private bath and air conditioning, are variously and quite beautifully furnished. The ground-floor Garden Room is particularly charming with a canopy bed sporting a pink eiderdown and made even more comfortable by a velvet Eastlake couch and rocking chair. The Captain's Room has a working oak fireplace and a brass bed among its comforts. There's also a lovely bridal suite featuring a private balcony and fireplace, and furnished with a brass canopy bed and deep-blue swag drapes. Breakfast brings a full complement of eggs, breads, and fruit.

RATES: $50 to $100, including breakfast and afternoon tea.

At the waterfront, which is being fully redeveloped à la South Street Seaport, a new Radisson hotel is scheduled to open in the fall of 1987.

Thames Landing Oyster House, 2 Captain's Walk (tel. 203/442-3158), possesses a worthy seafaring history and atmosphere. Try one of the bisques—clam, mussel, lobster, crab—each is delicious. Oysters, cherrystones, fresh fishes, and a petite bouillabaisse ($7.50) all appear on the menu. A separate bar is a popular gathering spot.

HOURS: Sunday to Thursday from 11 A.M. to 9 P.M., until midnight on Friday and Saturday.

At the old 1790 **Bulkeley House,** 111 Bank St. (tel. 203/443-9599), a colonial atmosphere in the lunch/bar area is created by the beams, wide-board floors, and the old Federal-style mantel painted a sage green. In the back the Icehouse pub is decorated with nautical ensigns and regalia, including a rowboat hung from the ceiling. Shaker-style sconces, corner cupboards, decoys, and low beamed ceilings continue the theme in the more formal upstairs dining room.

The fare fits the ambience—potted chicken (steamed chicken pieces and vegetables in a light cream sauce, served in a crock), grilled lamb chops, steak-and-kidney pie, steaks, beefeater scallops sautéed with mushrooms and parsley, and deglazed with gin in cream sauce. Prices run $10 to $14. Appetizer choices include several chowders, escargots with garlic butter, and baked Brie served with sherried almonds and French bread. Soups, sandwiches, and fish and meat dishes make up the lunch menu; brunch offers traditional eggs and omelets plus a tavern sampler (kielbasa, venison sausage, bangers, and pork loin, along with other English favorites).

LUNCH: 11:30 A.M. to 3 P.M. daily. DINNER: Monday to Thursday from 5 to 9 P.M., until 10 P.M. on weekends, on Sunday from 4 to 9 P.M. BRUNCH: Saturday and Sunday from 11 A.M. to 3 P.M.

NORWICH

From Groton and New London, the River Thames flows northward to Norwich, about a 30-minute drive away.

NORWICH ATTRACTIONS

The outstanding discovery in Norwich (for me at least) was the **Slater Memorial Museum,** Norwich Free Academy, 108 Crescent St. (tel. 203/887-2506). First, Stephen Earle's Romanesque building is a magnificent treasure in itself; second, the main galleries, filled with plaster casts of famous Greek and Renaissance sculptures, are amazing for their beauty, their number, and their rarity, for they would be impossible to secure today; and third, the other collections are also very fine. There are wonderful temple carvings in the Oriental collection; exquisite ceramics, baskets, beadwork, and masks among the Indian artifacts; some choice American primitives and some entrancing watercolors by George Henry Clements (1854–1935) in the art collections. And these are just the highlights. HOURS: June to August, Tuesday to Sunday from 1 to 4 P.M.; at other times of the year, Monday to Friday from 9 A.M. to 4 P.M. and Saturday and Sunday from 1 to 4 P.M. Closed holidays. ADMISSION: Free.

Representative of the time when Norwich was the 12th-largest city in the colonies, the **Leffingwell Inn,** 348 Washington St. (tel. 203/889-9440), is a fine example of a 1675 colonial residence that opened as a public house in 1701 and served as an important stage stop between Boston and New London. The rooms are full of interest, and the commentary always lively. HOURS: In summer, Tuesday to Saturday from 10 A.M. to noon and 2 to 4 P.M., on Sunday from 2 to 4 P.M. (closed Monday); in winter, weekends only, by appointment, from 2 to 4 P.M. ADMISSION: $3 for adults, $1 for children.

While you're in Norwich, take a drive around the village and explore the **Norwichtown Historic District,** an area around the Green where over 50 pre-1800 homes are concentrated, one of them the home of signer of the Declaration of Independence Samuel Huntington. Visit also **Yantic Falls,** off Sachem Street, off Rte. 2, known locally as Indian Leap because of the legend that during the last great battle between the Narragansetts and Mohegans in 1643, one band of Narragansetts were forced to plunge into the falls and were killed. The **Indian Burial Grounds** on Sachem Street are the resting place of Uncas, Mohegan chief who gave the land for settlement.

Another highlight is the 350-acre **Mohegan Park,** Mohegan Avenue, off Rtes. 2 and 32, which offers swimming and picnicking, a zoo (tel. 203/887-1891), and a beautiful rose garden where 2,500 bushes bloom from May to November. Best time to visit is late June.

Downtown Norwich also possesses many historic buildings of architectural interest. Pick up the Norwich Chamber of Commerce's series of walking tours (tel. 203/889-9440) and explore.

A Nearby Indian Museum

A visit to the **Tantaquidgeon Indian Museum,** Rte. 32, Uncasville (tel. 203/848-9145), is a unique experience. It's a very personal collection begun in 1931 by the late John Tantaquidgeon and his son, Harold, direct descendants of Uncas, chief of the Mohegan Nation. It's housed in a stone building behind the home of Harold and Gladys Tantaquidgeon.

Eighty-six-year-old Gladys will relate the history of the local Indians; the artifacts also tell their own story. Photographs capture all the Mohegan descendants of Occum, who were born in 1723 in a wigwam. He attended school locally and traveled to England soliciting funds, greatly impressing the Earl of Dartmouth, whose donations helped found Dartmouth College. Among the artifacts are roach or crest-type headdresses of deer hair, food bowls made only of sugar maple or applewood, sculptures by Ralph Sturges, a birchbark Penobscot canoe, corncob dolls, snowshoes, warclubs fashioned from roots, birch buckets, exquisitely crafted straw baskets (including Makawisaug, tiny baskets that were used to put out a little cornbread or meat for the Little People in the forest), stone axes (including one whose blade took seven hours to fashion), and wampum beads made from clam and conch shells. There are also models showing the Green Corn Festival (last celebrated here in 1938), when brush arbors are built and thanks given for the corn harvest and also depicting village scenes in which inhabitants are spearfishing, deer hunting, gathering corn, tanning skins, etc.

Another room, devoted to Plains and West Coast Indians, is filled with Navajo, Seminole, Hopi, and Tlingit artifacts, including a dramatic wolf Kachina doll and a majestic Cree headdress.

HOURS: May through October, Tuesday to Sunday from 10 A.M. to 4 P.M. ADMISSION: Donation requested.

NORWICH LODGING

The **Norwich Inn,** Rte. 32, Norwich, CT 06360 (tel. 203/886-2401, or toll free 800/892-5692), is a particularly appealing accommodation, one of several East Coast enterprises owned by West Coast real estate magnate Edward Safdie, who has restored this old landmark to its former elegance, with a dash of tropical and plantation-style largesse. Built in 1929, the inn originally drew such celebrities as George Bernard Shaw, Charles Laughton, and Frank Sinatra before it fell into decay. Now the place exudes elegance and romance, especially at night when a faint breeze stirs the potted palms and ferns, and floodlights around the central courtyard pool cast dancing shadows on the walls of the gallery that leads into the dining room. The 75 guest rooms are all designed in warm shades of cinnamon, sand, and Nantucket blue, and have such added touches as ruffled curtains, pretty linens, botanical prints, dried-flower wreaths, quaint step stools for the four-poster beds, and ceiling fans. Chintz-covered armchairs and sofas, country-print wallpapers, pine armoires, and brass fittings and old tubs in the bathrooms all create a comfortable country air. They also contain TVs, Touch-tone telephones, and Gilchrist & Soames soaps and toiletries in the bathrooms.

In summer you can sip a frosty mint julep in the peach-colored sun room or on a snowy evening relax by the fire in the Prince of Wales bar. For dining you have a choice of the outdoor deck overlooking the lovely Norwich golf course, or the elegant Grill that presents among the appetizers (although the menu changes daily) cold stuffed loin of rabbit in a savory tomato sauce or a smoked salmon mousse. Main dishes might include roast Cornish game hen in a honey-mustard glaze, broiled swordfish in lemon sauce, salmon with dill, and sirloin steak. The herbs come from the inn's own garden. Prices run $12.50 to $16.50. Classic desserts include strawberry shortcake and crème caramel.

The spa opened in late 1986. Drawing on his success with such renowned spas as the Sonoma Mission Inn and Spa in California, the California Terrace and Spa in Monte Carlo, Monaco, and the Greenhouse in Arlington, Texas, Edward F. Safdie planned a spectacular facility here. Designed around a central indoor pool, the spa will feature glass-enclosed exercise rooms, soundproof treatment rooms for massage, hydrotherapy, loofah scrubs, and deep-cleansing facials. The treatment is carefully designed to each individual's needs and goals for a revitalization of both mind and body. Five-day, weekend, and one-day Revitalizer programs will be offered. Among the spa facilities are rowing machines, a cross-country ski machine, fitness bicycles, weight-training equipment, mini-trampoline, and free weights, along with fitness classes that range from aerobics to yoga, stress management, and weight training. Body treatments—massage, cellulite massage, herbal wrap, and hydrotherapy—and beauty treatments are also offered. In addition, golf and tennis are available.

RATES: $75 to $110 double in winter and spring, $85 to $120 double in summer and fall. A standard five-day spa package (room, three meals per day, and full spa treatments) costs from $850 per person double; weekend spa packages start at $290 per person.

Less expensive accommodations can be found at the **Sheraton Norwich,** One Sheraton Plaza, Norwich, CT 06360 (tel. 203/889-5201), which also offers such extras as an indoor pool and tennis court. RATES: Various packages are available, including the Catch Twenty, which provides two nights' accommodation plus $20 of Sheraton play money to spend around the hotel, all for $100 per couple.

The **Norwich Motel,** 181 W. Town St., Norwich, CT 06360 (tel. 203/889-2671), offers above-average motel accommodations with a nice outdoor pool. RATES: $42 to $45 double.

NORWICH DINING

Besides the Norwich Inn, Norwich also possesses an interesting historic place for luncheon or dinner, **Chelsea Landing,** Water Street (tel. 203/889-9932), located in a building that has been standing since 1761 and was variously a distillery, a hotel, and a grocery store. It's a cozy and simple place, with gingham tablecloths on the tables. The seafood is invariably good, and is supplemented by a menu that features Yankee pot roast, sandwiches, and omelets, all at incredibly low prices —$5.25 tops at lunch, from $7 to $14 at dinner.

LUNCH: Monday to Friday from 11:30 A.M. to 2:30 P.M. DINNER: Sunday to Thursday from 5:30 to 9 P.M., until 10 P.M. on Friday and Saturday.

AREA ACTIVITIES

ANTIQUING: Several stores are worth visiting in Stonington; also one or two in downtown Mystic.

BALLOONING: Mystic River Balloon Ride, 17 Carriage Dr., Stonington (tel. 203/535-0283).

BEACHES: Ocean Beach, Ocean Ave., New London (tel. 203/447-3031), offers a pleasant sandy beach complete with boardwalk, concessions, and an amusement park that features a fun triple water slide and an outdoor pool. This is New London's most crowded playground.

Most people head east toward the beach at Watch Hill, R.I., if they prefer quiet and dignity, or to Misquamicut, the honky-tonk of Rhode Island beaches that appeals to the younger crowd.

Harkness State Park and Bluff Point State Park both possess quieter ways to enjoy the shoreline.

BICYCLING: Rentals are available in Mystic at Bicycle World, 75 W. Main St. (tel. 203/536-4819), and at Mystic Valley Bicycling, 26 William St. (tel. 203/536-4767).

BOATING: Shaffer's Boat Livery, Mason's Island Road, Mystic (tel. 203/536-8713), has cruising boats for rent. Spicer's Marinas in Noank (tel. 203/536-4978) and in Groton (tel. 203/445-9729) also rent sailing and other craft.

FISHING: *Groton:* The largest party-fishing boat, the *Hel-Cat II,* sails from the Hel-Cat dock, 181 Thames St. (tel. 203/535-2066 or 445-5991), charging about $30 per person per day for regular fishing trips. *Mystic:* Boats can be rented from Shaffer's Boat Livery, Mason's Island Rd. (tel. 203/536-8713). *New London:* The party boat *Captain Bob II* sails from New London's City Dock (tel. 203/442-1777). *Waterford:* Try Captain John's Sport Fishing Center, 15 1st St. (tel. 203/443-7259), or Mijoy, 12 River St. (tel. 203/443-0663), whose boats sail year round from the Noank Shipyard in Noank or Marster's Dock in New London; prices start at $22.

Several lakes in North Stonington also offer good fishing: try Billings Lake (north from Rte. 2 on Cossaduck Road) or Wyassup Lake (off Rte. 2 about four miles north of North Stonington).

FRUIT PICKING: *East Lyme:* Scott's Orchards, Boston Post Rd. (tel. 203/739-2529), for apples and strawberries; The Yankee Farmer, 441 Old Post Rd. (tel. 203/

739-5209), for apples, strawberries, and tomatoes. *Norwich:* Malerba Brothers, 634 New London Turnpike (tel. 203/887-2913), for strawberries; Irving Deutsch, 116 Gifford St. (tel. 203/889-1213), for strawberries.

GOLF: *Groton:* Shennecossett Municipal, Plant St. (tel. 203/445-0262); Trumble Golf Course, High Rock Rd. (tel. 203/445-7991). *Norwich:* Norwich Municipal, 685 New London Turnpike (tel. 203/889-6973). *Stonington:* Pequot Golf Club, Wheeler Rd. (tel. 203/535-1898); Elmridge-Pawcatuck Golf Club (tel. 203/599-2248).

HIKING: Ideal spots for walking are the Connecticut Arboretum, Williams St., New London (tel. 203/447-1911); Bluff Point State Park, in Groton; and also the coastline from Watch Hill out to Napatree Point.

HORSEBACK RIDING: Applewood Farm, Ledyard (tel. 203/536-2022); Wintechog Ranch, North Stonington (tel. 203/535-3171); Whispering Pines Riding, 221 Butlertown Rd., Waterford (tel. 203/442-6235), at $7.50 per hour.

PICNICKING: For shore picnicking, my first choice would be Harkness State Park, where you can spread your feast out and dine looking across the Sound before going down to explore the beach (no swimming). Take Rte. 1 out of New London to Rte. 213. There's an adjacent special facility for the disabled with wooden ramps that run out onto and along the beach. Rocky Neck State Park is similar. Fort Griswold makes an ideal spot overlooking the Thames River and Fisher's Island. Or you might head for Bluff Point and Coastal Reserve, Groton, a 100-acre nature reserve. In Norwich, Mohegan Park is the place.

STATE PARKS: *Groton:* Bluff Point Coastal Reserve, Depot Road, for great hiking, fishing and picnicking; Haley Farms State Park, Rte. 215, Brook Street, has nature trails, hiking, and biking paths. *Waterford:* Harkness Memorial State Park, Rte. 213, has picnicking and fishing plus a shoreline for walking (no bathing). For general info, call 203/443-5725.

SWIMMING: See "Beaches."

TENNIS: *East Lyme:* Lyme Racquet Club, 22 Colton St. (tel. 203/739-6281). *Mystic:* For local high school courts, call the Mystic Visitor Information Bureau (tel. 203/535-4721). The Inn at Mystic also has a court. *Waterford:* Waterford Racquet Club, 6 Fargo Rd. (tel. 203/442-9466). *Westerly, R.I.:* Pond View Racquet Club, Shore Road (tel. 401/322-9842).

WINDSURFING: Windsurfing of Mystic, 13 W. Main St. (tel. 203/536-7121), charges $20 an hour for lessons, $10 an hour for board rental.

MASSACHUSETTS

THE CENTRAL BERKSHIRES & PIONEER VALLEY

DISTANCE IN MILES: Egremont, 120; Great Barrington, 125; Springfield, 153; Pittsfield, 168; Williamstown, 176; Deerfield, 178
ESTIMATED DRIVING TIMES: Egremont, 2½ hours; Deerfield and Williamstown, 3½ hours

DRIVING: For the southern Berkshires (Great Barrington, Lenox, Lee, the Egremonts), take the Taconic Parkway to Rte. 23 (Hillsdale Exit) to Great Barrington and then Rte. 7 north for Stockbridge, Lenox, and Lee. Pick up Rte. 20 to Pittsfield and then Rte. 2 for Williamstown. For Williamstown, you can also take the New York State Thruway (I-87) to Albany, picking up I-787 to Troy to Rte. 2 east.

For Deerfield, take I-95 north to I-91 north to Exit 24. Historic Deerfield is just off Rtes. 5 and 10.

BUS: Greyhound (telephone: 212/635-0800, or toll free 800/528-6055) travels to Lenox, Lee, as well as Pittsfield. Closest stop to Deerfield is Greenfield, from which Deerfield is a five-mile taxi ride. Bonanza (telephone: 212/635-0800 for tickets or 564-8484 for schedules) goes to Great Barrington, Stockbridge, Lee, Lenox, as well as Pittsfield, Williamstown, and North Adams. Peter Pan Bus Lines (tel. 212/564-8484) services Amherst, Northampton, Holyoke, and Springfield.

TRAIN: Amtrak stops at Springfield. Call 212/736-6288.

Special Events to Plan Your Trip Around

SUMMER FESTIVALS: End of June through Labor Day—Jacob's Pillow Dance Festival (tel. 413/243-0745); Williamstown Theatre Festival (tel. 413/458-8145); Berkshire Theatre Festival (tel. 413/298-5576 after June 1); Tanglewood (tel. 413/637-1666), or write to Boston Symphony Orchestra, Symphony Hall, Boston, MA 02115 (tel. 617/266-1492).

JUNE: American Craft Enterprises Fair Craftfair in West Springfield (formerly held in Rhinebeck, NY).

JULY: Aston Magna Festival, Great Barrington (tel. 413/528-3595), features 17th- and 18th-century works performed on original instruments at various locations on weekends.

AUGUST/SEPTEMBER: South Mountain Chamber Concerts, South Mountain, Box 23, Pittsfield, MA 01201 (tel. 413/442-2106).

SEPTEMBER: Josh Billings Race combines a 26-mile cycle trip from Great Barrington to the Stockbridge Bowl, two laps by canoe around the lake, and a 6½ mile run to Tanglewood (usually mid-September).

The Big E, a 12-day fair held at the Eastern States Exposition Grounds, West Springfield (usually the weekend after Labor Day). For info call 413/737-2443.

OCTOBER: Harvest festival at the Berkshire Garden Center in Stockbridge.

For further information about these events and Massachusetts in general, call or write the Massachusetts Division of Tourism, 100 Cambridge St., Boston, MA 02202 (tel. 617/727-3201).

For specific information about the area, contact the Berkshire Visitors Bureau, Berkshire Common Plaza Level, Dept. MA, Pittsfield, MA 01201 (tel. 413/443-9186); or the Stockbridge Chamber of Commerce, Stockbridge, MA 01262; or the Lenox Chamber of Commerce, P.O. Box 646, Lenox, MA 01240.

For Deerfield area information, contact the Pioneer Valley Convention & Visitors Bureau, 56 Dwight St., Springfield, MA 01103 (tel. 413/787-1548); or the Mohawk Trail Association P.O. Box 7, Dept. MA, North Adams, MA 01347 (tel. 413/664-6256).

For specific information about each town, contact the following: Amherst Chamber of Commerce, 11 Spring St., Amherst, MA 01002 (tel. 413/253-9666); Greater Northampton Chamber of Commerce, 62 State Street, Northampton, MA 01060 (tel. 413/584-1900); South Hadley Chamber of Commerce, 362 N. Main St., South Hadley, MA 01075 (tel. 413/532-2864); or the Worcester County Convention and Visitors Bureau,

350 Mechanics Tower, Worcester, MA 01608 (tel. 617/753-2920), for the Sturbridge area.

It would require many weekends to "do" the Berkshires, because the events and attractions are so many and so varied. First, of course, there are all the outstanding cultural events—Tanglewood, the Williamstown Theatre Festival, South Mountain chamber music concerts, Jacob's Pillow Dance Festival—that bring people flocking to this scenic area of lakes and wooded hills. There's the history that yields all kinds of attractions, some of a literary or artistic kind like the homes of Herman Melville, Edith Wharton, Nathaniel Hawthorne, William Cullen Bryant, Daniel Chester French, and Norman Rockwell, and others of a more worldly kind, like the sumptuous mansions that line the streets and dot the countryside around Lenox and Stockbridge, namely Blantyre, Bellefontaine, Wheatleigh, and Naumkeag. And last but far from least is the landscape—Mounts Greylock, Everett, and Monument—and the forests that surround them, granting all kinds of opportunities for hiking, skiing, blueberrying, birdwatching, picnicking, and just plain basking in the beauty of it all. In short, it's a very rich area to mine for weekends or longer stays.

The first settlers of the Berkshires were the Mahkeenac Indians, who, driven by the Iroquois from the Hudson Valley, found the lush streams, lakes, and wooded hills around Stockbridge and Great Barrington abundant hunting and fishing grounds. As the pioneers moved west from the Massachusetts Bay Colony, they, too, moved into the area, establishing thriving farming and trading communities —the first at Sheffield in 1733 and the second at Stockbridge in 1735. Some of the settlers attempted to convert the Indians to Christianity, as did the Rev. John Sergeant, whose Mission House can still be seen today in Stockbridge. During the Revolutionary War, Berkshire County supported the patriots' cause, and indeed, as early as 1774 the townsfolk of Great Barrington showed their resistance by refusing to allow royal judges to sit in court. The domestic turmoil of the Revolution was also experienced here when Daniel Shay led his famous farmers rebellion against the Articles of Confederation in 1787, an event recalled today by a marker on Rte. 23 in South Egremont, where he supposedly surrendered to Col. John Ashley of Sheffield. Soon after the Revolution the Shakers arrived. This community of pacifist celibates who dedicated their lives to hard work established their City of Peace in 1790 at Hancock, and it is a fascinating place to visit today.

Less simple folk soon followed, turning the area into a playground for the wealthy. First to arrive was Boston financier Samuel Gray Ward, who persuaded his friends, the Higginsons, to join him. Such figures as Nathaniel Hawthorne,

Herman Melville, Oliver Wendell Holmes, Henry Wadsworth Longfellow, and James Russell Lowell came soon after, but these early comers were people of modest means compared to the wealthy that followed. Largely attracted by the stories written by these authors about the Berkshires, they built ever more lavish and ostentatious mansions and mock palaces in their efforts to imitate the European aristocracy. These people represented the great fortunes that had been made from steel, milling, railroads, and other industries in the 19th century, and they looked for places to vacation and display their wealth. Those who enjoyed the ocean summered at such resorts as Newport, Cape May, and Bar Harbor, while those who preferred the mountains discovered the Berkshires and Saratoga Springs. Edith Wharton, tired of Newport and marriage, built her $40,000 mansion here in 1901 and used to drive the dusty roads in her large automobile, with her frequent visitor, Henry James, often at her side. Harley Proctor of Proctor & Gamble also built a cottage in Lenox, and other industrialists like George Westinghouse, the Vanderbilts, and Andrew Carnegie established great estates in the area. From about 1880 to 1900 the Berkshires experienced their heyday. Thereafter their popularity declined with the advent, among other things, of the automobile and later of the airplane, both of which afforded increased mobility to all. The mansions stood empty and useless, and most of them were sold off and converted into schools, camps, and guesthouses. Bellefontaine, for example, which had been copied from Louis XV's Petit Trianon and reputedly cost $1 million to build in 1899, sold for a mere $70,000 in 1946.

Despite the wealthy influx, the Berkshires always retained their image as an artistic creative colony. Nathaniel Hawthorne wrote his *Tanglewood Tales* looking out over Lake Mahkeenac (the Stockbridge Bowl). In 1850 he met Herman Melville at a Monument Mountain picnic, and they visited each other often. Melville even dedicated *Moby-Dick* to him. William Cullen Bryant, editor of the *New York Post,* Oliver Wendell Holmes, Henry Wadsworth Longfellow, and James Russell Lowell are just a few of the writers associated with the Berkshires. The artist Daniel Chester French built his Chesterwood in 1898, and much later Norman Rockwell, chronicler of America's small-town life, came to the Berkshires. The artistic tradition of the area was further entrenched with the establishment of major cultural events like the Berkshire Music Festival, founded in 1936 when Sergei Koussevitsky conducted the first concert at Tanglewood; the Jacobs Pillow Dance Festival, established by Ted Shawn five years later; and the Berkshire Theatre Festival, which had already been stirring audiences for many years and helped to establish the careers of such legendary figures as James Cagney, Ethel Barrymore, and Katharine Hepburn. These summer events still draw enormous crowds, but no matter what time of year you choose to visit the Berkshires, they will always delight. In winter they present the idyllic winter scenes captured in Norman Rockwell's famous seasonal illustration of Stockbridge. There's skiing at Catamount, Jiminy Peak, Brodie, Berkshire East, and Butternut, cross-country skiing everywhere, skating on the lakes, and sledding, as well as hot toddies and blazing fires in quaint old-fashioned inns to help recover from outside exertions. Whether you come to ski or nod by the fireside in winter, to wander amid the mountain laurel in spring, to view the fantastic palette of the trees in fall, or to spread out your blanket and picnic under the stars at Tanglewood to the sounds of Beethoven or Mozart, you'll experience a deep thrill and contentment that will leave you wanting to return time and time again.

Suggested Itineraries Through the Berkshires

You'll probably want to visit several times during the summer, once to attend one or more of the cultural events, again to visit all the attractions clustered around Stockbridge or farther north in Hancock and Williamstown, and still again to experience the mountains and lakes by hiking, fishing, or canoeing. Therefore I have not arranged this chapter around a single typical weekend, but rather have tried to outline all the possibilities that each town and area offers. It's up to you to choose. To guide you a little, though, here are a few suggested drives through the Berkshires that will help you in planning your explorations.

The Central Berkshires:

1. From Pittsfield, drive along Rte. 20 (about five miles) to Hancock Shaker Village, and from there down to Tanglewood, via Rte. 41, and West Stockbridge. On Rte. 183, directly across from the Tanglewood entrance, a country road leads to the Pleasant Valley Wildlife Sanctuary. From here head east and pick up Rte. 7 into Lenox, before heading south again on 7 to the Mount, Edith Wharton's mansion. Return to Rte. 20 and take it south to Lee, en route to the Jacob's Pillow Dance Festival set off the road. Take Rte. 20 to Rte. 8, which will lead you, via Washington and Hinsdale, into Dalton for a tour of the Crane Museum (weekdays only), and then wind up at Arrowhead just south of Pittsfield.

2. From Pittsfield, go northeast along Rte. 8 to Adams, birthplace of Susan B. Anthony. Pick up Rte. 116 to Savoy going through town. Just outside, take a right on River Road, which will lead you to Windsor Jambs in the Windsor State Forest and eventually into Cummington, where a detour along Rte. 9 will bring you to William Cullen Bryant's birthplace. Backtrack along Rte. 9 past Notchview into Dalton and finally Pittsfield.

The Southern Berkshires:

1. Starting from Great Barrington, proceed east along Rte. 23 through Monterey before turning north to Tyringham, past sculptor Sir Henry Hudson Kitson's fantasy gingerbread house. From there loop round along Rte. 102, through South Lee into Stockbridge, to explore all of that village's highlights.

2. Starting in Sheffield, take Rte. 7 north to Great Barrington, stopping at Searles Castle and dropping into the Albert Schweitzer Center, if it interests you. From here, get onto Rte. 23 to South Egremont. En route you can turn off at the junction of Rte. 41 to explore Mount Everett and BashBish Falls. Then double back to South Egremont and take 41 south to Sheffield, turning right off Rte. 7 at

the Bushnell-Sage Library in Ashley Falls, from which you can reach Bartholomew's Cobble and the Ashley House.

Northern Berkshires:
1. Drive from Williamstown along the Mohawk Trail all the way to Whitcomb Summit, where you can choose either to continue along the trail to Shelburne Falls, turn back, or else turn into the Savoy Mountain State Forest, visiting Tannery Falls and following a new loop back into North Adams for the return to Williamstown.
2. Devote a good part or a whole day to exploring Mount Greylock's slopes from Lanesborough.

The Berkshires

LENOX

LENOX ATTRACTIONS

Today, you can stay in many of the old mansions that were once the summer retreats for such industrial magnates as Harley Proctor, George Westinghouse, and Andrew Carnegie, who were drawn to the Berkshires' unspoiled beauty, and the tidy farms and streets of Lenox in particular.

Besides these wonderful mansions, the main attraction for visitors is, of course, the Berkshire Music Festival of Tanglewood, just outside Lenox, overlooking the lovely Stockbridge Bowl, which inspired Nathaniel Hawthorne to write his *Tanglewood Tales*. Although the festival may have lost some of its earlier musical seriousness and serenity, it still attracts dedicated listeners to its shaded lawns and large music shed, and is still a very pleasant way to spend some of your time in the Berkshires. (For detailed information, see "Cultural Events in the Berkshires," below.)

A walk around the village past the rambling old clapboard houses is always a pleasure. On your way, at the corner of Walker and Main Streets you'll pass the old **Curtis Hotel,** a noted 19th-century stage stop that welcomed such illustrious guests as Chester Alan Arthur, Franklin Delano Roosevelt, Dwight Eisenhower, Jenny Lind, and Sergei Koussevitzky. Today it has been remodeled into a home for the retired.

From here be sure to walk to the top of the hill on Main Street to see the **"Church on the Hill,"** a very fine New England Congregational church erected in 1805.

At the junction of Rtes. 7 and 7A, you can tour **The Mount** (tel. 413/637-1899), an impressive mansion with a dramatic widow's walk, octagonal tower, and ter-

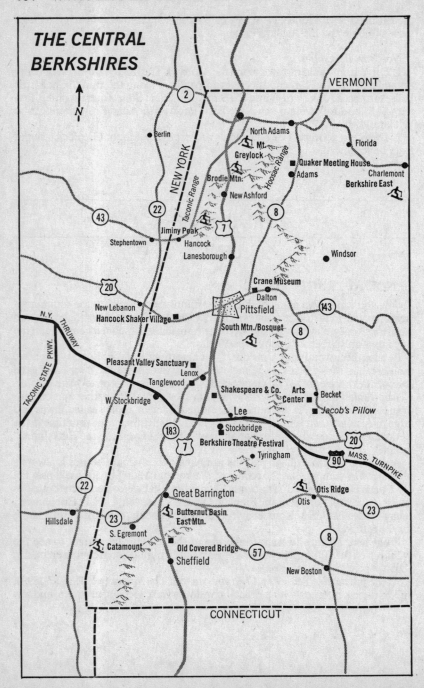

THE CENTRAL
BERKSHIRES

N

VERMONT

Berlin

North Adams

Mt.
Greylock

Florida

Brodie Mtn.

Quaker Meeting House

Adams

Charlemont

Berkshire East

New Ashford

NEW YORK

Taconic Range

Hoosac Range

43

22

7

8

Jiminy Peak

Stephentown

Hancock

Lanesborough

Windsor

20

Crane Museum

New Lebanon

Dalton

Hancock Shaker Village

Pittsfield

143

N.Y. THRUWAY

South Mtn./Bosquet

8

Pleasant Valley Sanctuary

Lenox

TACONIC STATE PKWY.

Tanglewood

Shakespeare & Co.

Arts
Center

Becket

W. Stockbridge

Jacob's Pillow

Lee

183

Stockbridge

7

Berkshire Theatre Festival

20

Tyringham

90

MASS. TURNPIKE

22

Otis Ridge

Great Barrington

Otis

23

23

Hillsdale

Butternut Basin
East Mtn.

S. Egremont

Catamount

Old Covered Bridge

57

8

Sheffield

New Boston

CONNECTICUT

race with balustrade and Greek urns. Here Edith Wharton lived while she wrote her novel *Ethan Frome* (1911), which is set in the Berkshire countryside. Tours are given on weekends until 3:30 P.M.; later Shakespeare takes over the grounds.

For a change of pace, the **Pleasant Valley Wildlife Sanctuary**, West Mountain Road (tel. 413/637-0320), maintained by the Audubon Society, offers miles of nature trails. It's located just off Rte. 7 north of Lenox.

LENOX LODGING

Although there are plenty of wonderful accommodations within a 30-minute drive of Tanglewood, which I'll describe later, Lenox is the closest place to stay, and the village is full of notable hostelries. You'll have to book well in advance, pay ahead, and probably stay a minimum of two or three nights.

The true connoisseur stays house-party style at **Blantyre**, East Street, Lenox, MA 01240 (tel. 413/637-3556 after May 1, 413/298-3806 off-season), built in 1902 for Robert Paterson, the president of W. J. Sloane, director of a Manhattan Bank, and a friend of Carnegie. Costing $135,000 ($300,000 with furnishings), it was the most expensive and lavish villa in the Berkshires (The Mount cost only $40,000). It was modeled after his wife's Scottish ancestral home.

In its heyday, when the summer set walked to and from each other's houses attended by maids with lanterns, it was the scene of tea parties, games, charades, and formal balls and dinners. Thereafter it experienced a checkered but nevertheless fascinating history. In 1925 it, along with 250 acres, was sold to a Howard Cole for a mere $25,000; it served briefly as a country club before being bought by D. W. Griffith, who dreamed of turning it into an East Coast studio, but died before he could do so. Various owners tried to make something of it until finally Senator and Mrs. Fitzpatrick, the inspiration behind the Red Lion in Stockbridge, bought it and created this luxurious accommodation.

So magnificent, and veritably museum quality, are the furnishings, that the proprietors have had to close the house to uninvited visitors because too many were coming to gawk at the splendor. In the main hall, lit by shimmering chandeliers, Elizabethan and Jacobean pieces and Oriental vases are arrayed before the ornately carved fireplace. The similarly furnished music room also features a priceless Coromandel screen and a grand piano. There are four rooms and four suites in the main house and 14 additional, beautifully appointed rooms in the carriage house, located by the open-air swimming pool.

The suites are spectacular. The Cranwell has a dramatic four-poster and various furnishings, all beautiful genuine antiques—ormolu mirrors, inlaid tables, porcelain lamps, couches and chairs covered with fine fabrics. The ceilings are at least 14 feet high, with elegant moldings. A pink fireplace, gilt-framed portraits, pencil poster with dusky-rose eider, a silver brush set on a mahogany desk, and even a bathroom with crystal light fixtures and a marble sink are just a few of the highlights of the Laurel Suite. All bathrooms contain shampoo, conditioner, lotions, bath salts, and Crabtree & Evelyn soaps.

Note that there are only 23 rooms, and so you may well not be able to secure a room unless you reserve at least one year ahead. Please don't harass the staff —this is simply a fact which is beyond their control.

In the paneled dining room hung with rich tapestries guests sit at a long Tudor refectory table bearing a lace tablecloth and impressive table settings of crystal and fine china. At $65 per person, the six-course dinner is probably the best bargain in Lenox for distinguished, made-to-your-order cuisine. For breakfast the conservatory makes a beautifully bright setting.

Other facilities include the aforementioned swimming pool and four tennis courts.

RATES: Suites run from $300. A large double with a fireplace is $250; minus the fireplace, $200. Carriage house accommodations are $200 to $225. A two-day minimum stay is required in July, August, and October.

Overlooking a lake, **Wheatleigh,** West Hawthorne Street (P.O. Box 824), Lenox, MA 01240 (tel. 413/637-0610), the magnificent former home of the Countess de Heredia, has 22 acres of lawn and gardens. Modeled after a 16th-century Italian palazzo, it was built on the site of the Gideon Smith tavern, a Tory who was hanged for his folly. The gravel driveway ends in a circular courtyard with a central stone fountain standing in front of the intricately worked wrought-iron grille and elegant portico. Inside, the most striking features of the great entry hall are the huge white marble fireplace, sculpted with cupids and flowers, and the grand staircase, also of marble.

Upstairs are 11 very spacious rooms and four smaller accommodations, each possessing its own flavor and mood. They all have extremely high ceilings, marble fireplaces, and large, old-fashioned bathrooms. Some have canopy beds; the rooms in the rear have lovely views of the lake. The house also has a unique tower accommodation that stands alone—a duplex that Leonard Bernstein always chose to stay at when he was conducting at Tanglewood.

The restaurant at Wheatleigh is also a gem and has been compared to many of the great restaurants in New York City. The menu is a $49 prix fixe. Just as an example, here's the menu that was offered on Thanksgiving last year: appetizers included Malpeque oysters gratinéed with spinach and foie gras; a warm salad of scallops, mâche, celery root, and orange; ravioli of winter squash with lobster sauce; carpaccio of venison with truffle oil; grilled cèpes; and baby sweet corn and Minnesota wild rice soup. Among the entrees were roast turkey with chestnut and sage stuffing, maple-glazed Vermont ham with pomegranate sauce, filets of halibut braised in hard cider and cream, and tenderloin of beef with wild mushroom sauce, all served with gingered yams, brussel sprouts with shallots, and sherry and other accompaniments. For dessert there was pumpkin flan with cinnamon Chantilly, warm rhum babas with marinated fruits, tarte Tartin with crème fraiche, and gâteau Clichy, a delicious blending of chocolate, apricot preserve, and chestnut crème. Breakfast offers an interesting array of egg dishes, including poached eggs with crabmeat and mornay sauce served on an English muffin. The pretty blue/rose decor is distinctly English—linen tablecloths, Chippendale-style chairs, and English ceramic wall plaques dating from the 1830s.

On the 22-acre grounds landscaped by Frederick Law Olmsted are a serene rock garden, a pool surrounded by fragrant pine and conifers, and a tennis court. In winter the grounds are good for cross-country skiing.

RATES: $145 to $275 June through October, $95 to $225 off-season. BREAKFAST: 8 to 10:30 A.M. daily. DINNER: Tuesday to Sunday from 6 to 9 P.M.

The beautiful residence now known as the **Gateways Inn,** 71 Walker St., Lenox, MA 01240 (tel. 413/637-2532), was once Harley Proctor's mansion. Wrought-iron gates mark the entrance to the drive that leads to the classical white-columned portico; a balustrade runs along the top of the front façade. Inside, a sweeping staircase leads to nine large elegant accommodations, three with fireplaces, all furnished differently with large Victorian pieces, most often of mahogany. All rooms have private bath, many featuring old-fashioned pedestal sinks.

Owner Gerhard Schmid represents the United States at the culinary Olympics, and the Gateways is known for excellent cuisine, albeit served in rather plain surroundings. A $22.50 prix fixe will include a salad and your choice from such entrees as a delicately flavored rack of lamb, veal sweetbreads, or medallions of veal Lucullus (with chanterelles and white asparagus in a hollandaise sauce). The restaurant is especially noted for its desserts: apfelstrudel, luscious Black Forest torte, and strawberries Gateways—fresh strawberries with kirschwasser, whipped cream, and Melba sauce, all blended together into one super taste treat.

RATES (including continental breakfast): July through October, $70 to $75 Monday to Wednesday, $105 to $110 Thursday to Sunday: November through June, $55 to $65 in midweek, $80 to $90 on weekends. Three-night minimum on weekends July through October. DINNER: In winter, Monday to Saturday from 5 to 9 P.M.; daily in summer.

Note: If you stay at the Gateways, you can use the pool, bicycles, and tennis court at the Haus Andreas, nearby in Lee, under the same management.

Idyllically situated across from the west entrance to Tanglewood, the **Apple Tree Inn,** 224 West St. (P.O. Box 699), Lenox, MA 01240 (tel. 413/637-1477), does in fact stand on 22 acres in the midst of a fragrant apple orchard, bordering the 750-acre Pleasant Valley bird sanctuary. The rooms in the 100-year-old house with dormers and classical portico offer spectacular views over the Stockbridge Bowl and daisy-dappled fields to the hills beyond. There are 11 rooms and two suites in the main house. Room 4 has eyelet lace pillowcases on the bed, attractive Schumacher flower-and-bird wallpaper, ruffled curtains, and an inviting window seat, along with an armchair and a braided rug. Room 2, or the Blue Room, affords a large pineapple bed with step stool, two armchairs, a small ormolu mirror placed over a chest, and lace curtained French doors that lead to a private terrace with a magnificent view. Room 1 is decorated in forest green. The brass bed sports an apple-green and pink eider and frilly linens; the floors have a rag rug; pine furnishings and two chairs and a table are planted firmly in the bay. Room 3 is where Leontyne Price chooses to stay in a pretty country room of celery and pink hue. A brass bed, marble-top side tables, fireplace, and dresser complete the decor. Rooms 5 and 6 have skylights while the suite (no. 8) has books and records as well as a fireplace, TV, and other amenities. Third-floor rooms come in odd, interesting shapes. Brass beds, quilts, wing chairs, and braided rope rugs continue the country theme. A newer guest lodge has 20 rooms which are motel style but still pleasant, clean, and tasteful, and some people prefer them because they're closer to the pool. All of the accommodations are air-conditioned and have private bath.

The pool is spectacularly located. An arbor walk under climbing roses and clematis leads to it and it's surrounded by flagstones and flower borders of roses, poppies, tulips, stocks, and other flowers. From here there's a marvelous view over the valley to distant hills. There's also a clay tennis court for tennis enthusiasts, plus cross-country ski trails and miles of hiking.

For guests' comfort there's a parlor decorated with plush couches and armchairs, small chess and backgammon tables, and a piano where you might be lucky enough to find one of the featured Tanglewood artists "rehearsing."

There are two dining rooms. The former billiard room with a large brick fireplace, oak beams and paneling, and known as the Tavern, serves late-night snacks in summer and full meals in winter. The circular Gazebo is lighter in ambience, furnished in dusky rose with white bentwood chairs. The tented ceiling is strung with tiny lights. In summer you can dine to the symphonic melodies wafted here by the evening breezes from Tanglewood. There's also a deck for outdoor dining brightened by colored umbrellas and also by rambling roses and window boxes filled with pansies. The food is continental/American—veal marsala, poached halibut with a tomato-basil butter, steak with sautéed mushrooms, chicken Colombo (breast of chicken with leek and fresh citrus filling served with cream mint sauce). Several pasta dishes are also available, like paglie e fieno, a white and green fettuccine with mushroom-ham-cream sauce. Desserts include profiteroles, pie of the day, and seasonal fruits. Brunch varies. In summer there's likely to be cheese blintzes, smoked salmon, salads, and eggs Sardou or Florentine. Dinner prices range from $9 to $18. You can always retire here after the concert for a late-night snack and nightcap.

RATES: Summer (June 26 to October 9) weekends, $90 for a double with shared bath in the main house, $135 to $200 for a double with private bath, and $230 to $250 for a suite; or $110 to $120 for guest-lodge rooms. Spring weekends, $80 for a double with shared bath in the main house, $110 to $150 for a double with private bath, and $175 to $190 for a suite; or $75 to $90 for guest-lodge rooms. Winter weekends, $65 for a double with shared bath in the main house, $80 to $140 for a double with private bath, and $145 to $175 for a suite; or $50 to $65 for guest-lodge rooms. For fall weekends there's about a 20% discount on summer rates. Weekday rates are about 25% less than the weekend rates listed above.

The **Birchwood Inn,** 7 Hubbard St., Lenox, MA 01240 (tel. 413/637-2600), is a really tastefully decorated and impeccably run newcomer to the Lenox scene. Set halfway up the hill, across from the "Church on the Hill," it was originally built in the late 1700s for the Dana family. Later it became a veteran's home before Paul and Gail MacDonald rescued it and turned it into a stunning inn. All 11 rooms (six with private bath) are individually and very distinctively decorated, with antique reproductions and beautiful wallpapers. Four rooms have four-poster canopy beds. Downstairs, the sunken living room is especially charming with its inviting window seats, gilt mirrors, and bookcases filled with interesting volumes; a smaller den makes a cozy stopping place for late-night conversation before retiring.

Additional accommodations consisting of one-bedroom efficiency apartments are located in the carriage house.

RATES (including continental breakfast): $70 to $120 in midweek, $80 to $150 on weekends, with rooms sharing a bath from $50 to $70.

Across the street from the Birchwood Inn, **Whistler's Inn**, 5 Greenwood St., Lenox, MA 01240 (tel. 413/637-0975), is named after the second owner of the house, Whistler's nephew. There's a charming air about this French/English Tudor mansion built in 1820 with its mansard roof and lattice windows, approached via a lovely lych gate. On the ground floor the music room has a grand piano and a marvelous library complete with comfortable wing chairs and a marble fireplace to read beside; the formal dining room has a large table and Chippendale chairs seating eight. Upstairs, there are 11 rooms, all with private bath. Six rooms have dormer windows and sloping ceilings, and painted chests among the furnishings: there are two doubles with brass beds and three others with cannonball or pineapple bedsteads. The two master bedrooms, which have fireplaces and couches, are particularly welcoming. On sunny days you can take a light breakfast of muffins and coffee or tea out on the back veranda overlooking the seven acres of grounds.

RATES: June 16 to October 31, $60 to $120 in midweek, $70 to $160 on weekends; November 1 to June 15, $50 to $105 in midweek, $55 to $130 on weekends.

Peggy and Richard Houdek, who migrated from California where he was an arts administrator and music critic and she was managing editor of *Performing Arts* magazine, naturally sought a culturally rich area in which to relocate as innkeepers. They found an 1804 landmark building, **Walker House**, 74 Walker St., Lenox, MA 01240 (tel. 413/637-1271), only minutes from Tanglewood. Being music lovers, they have decorated all eight of the spacious rooms (all with private bath, five with working fireplaces) in honor of a particular composer. In the somber-colored ground-floor Beethoven room, which has a fireplace, are portraits and a bust of the genius himself; upstairs there's a lighter, sunnier Chopin room, a brilliant-blue Tchaikovsky room, a summery green-and-white Verdi room, and three other rooms named after Handel, Puccini, and Mozart, and an intimate room honoring Debussy. Downstairs, there's a large comfortable parlor with a grand piano, a cozy hearth, plenty of fine reading material, and some atrociously healthy plants. Similarly healthy-looking specimens share the long wide veranda with comfortable wicker furniture. Breakfast conversation flows easily at the tables, and fast friendships are made, solemn promises delivered, and cards and addresses exchanged over a morning repast of fresh juice or baked fruit, Peggy's home-baked muffins, and plenty of piping-hot, freshly ground coffee. And then, of course, the special delight of a stay here is the sound of glorious classical music that usually fills the house throughout the day. There are also two acres of wooded grounds to explore and complimentary bicycles for guests.

RATES: In July and August, $90 to $125 on weekends, $65 to $80 in midweek (Monday to Wednesday); for most of June and September, $70 to $90 on weekends, $50 to $70 in midweek; in October, $85 to $110 on weekends, $65 to $100 in midweek; from November to approximately June 24, $70 to $90 on weekends, $50 to $70 in midweek.

Seven Hills, Country Inn and Resort, 100 Plunkett St., Lenox, MA 01240 (tel. 413/637-0060), is a lavish, gracious resort that has much to recommend it. The public rooms are extravagantly furnished; the 27 acres include two tennis courts, a pool, and very well-kept landscaped gardens. Personnel are selected from the major music schools—Juilliard, Mannes, Manhattan, and Peabody—and when they're not waiting tables they perform. The nightclub is most elegant with its softly lit mauve-pink tented ceiling and low plush sofas, and features a variety of Broadway and jazz artists on weekends, like Natalie Lamb and Ed Linderman. On Monday, Tuesday, and Wednesday local artists perform.

The whole place is built on a grand scale. The so-called living room is more like a baronial hall, with floor-to-ceiling gilt mirrors, intricately carved and needle-pointed Charles II chairs, a central double fireplace of carved wood on one side and wedding cake stucco on the other, ornamented with cherubs and gryphons. Other features include another grand piano, handsome large carved sideboards, and dragon-decorated chairs. Window seats look out over the wide balustered flagstone terrace set with tables and marble benches. The balustrade supports a series of sculpted lions. Gravel paths lead between carved pillars and vine arbors down to the pool. The gardens are filled with peonies, shrubs, and trees.

In the Music Room every Wednesday and Sunday the waitresses and waiters perform, and although the management doesn't like to publicize particular names, many famous artists have performed here. Folk and square dancing is also enjoyed once a week during the summer.

The 55 rooms are varied and located in either the main building or in motel-style units. A carved paneled staircase decorated with two compelling landscapes leads to what, to me, are the nicest rooms. Room 1 has a fireplace, large mahogany chest, Williamsburg cane eagle chair, side chair, and dresser, all set on a slate-blue carpet against similarly colored paper, ball fringe curtains, and eyelet lace linens. Room 3 also has a fireplace and a small balcony. Room 9 possesses a burled maple bed and marble-top dresser coupled with bold floral-and-bird wallpaper. It, too, has a fireplace.

A light supper menu is served in the Nightspot, where there's a $5 cover charge. Owner Howard Green and his wife, Phyllis, plan to open a 24-seat restaurant and to offer a $40 prix-fixe menu. When I visited, the carved walnut Italian chairs, the Oriental-style Van Luit wallpaper, and the bronze and porcelain chandelier had all been ordered and the chef was already preparing succulent dishes. For additional entertainment there's a library with TV and a small lounge with an upright piano and a wood fireplace.

Seven Hills is definitely an experience. It's a chance to taste the opulent way of life that used to exist in the Berkshires but with a refreshing lack of excessive pretense.

RATES: $90 to $100 per person, MAP, in summer; room only (with breakfast), $80 double in spring and fall.

Cliffwood Inn, 25 Cliffwood St., Lenox, MA 01240 (tel. 413/637-3330), occupies a large mansion filled with the eclectic objets d'art collected by Hector Bellini and Don Thompson. Fantastic paintings worth looking at abound throughout; the huge living room is filled with objects from all over the world—ginger jars and Oriental figurines on one table, French and Italian pieces on another, an embroidered Chinese tablecloth on yet another. Floor-to-ceiling mirrors and a marble fireplace whose mantel supports tall candlesticks add to the grand atmosphere.

French doors lead to a wide back porch where begonias hang and rockers overlook the garden. The oval dining room is furnished with Charles II–style chairs, ornate gilt-framed Italian medallions hang behind the sideboard, and a marble fireplace completes the scene. Dinner is served to guests on Friday and Saturday nights. Although the menu changes, a meal might begin with salmon sausage with fresh tomatoes followed by a choice of Cornish game hens or veal with prosciutto and cheese, and finish with brandy peaches in a raspberry sauce. The price is $30, including complimentary wine. Hector and Don will also prepare picnics for Tanglewood.

An impressive semicircular drive leads to the oval portico supported by classical Ionic columns. The detailing of this building—carved shell and urn moldings above the windows, some of which are oval—is quite fine and certainly worthy to be the summer home of the American ambassador to France, for whom it was built around 1900. In the entry hall 18th-century marble French tables support majolica and other exquisite porcelain. To the right there's a favorite little corner anchored by a fireplace with window seats.

There are eight rooms, most with private bath, and each is decorated differently. Room 7, on the third floor, has a midnight-blue and peach coverlet on the bed and matching ruffles and curtains, as well as a pale-blue rug, gilt-framed oil paintings, and a fireplace among its attractions. Room 1 has a fireplace and a small sitting area. Room 8's bathroom has an old-fashioned tub and marble corner sink. The bed is carved oak, the sidetable marble-topped; a wardrobe, chest, and chair complete the furnishings.

RATES: May 24 (approximately) to September 10, $50 to $100 in midweek, $60 to $125 on weekends (the lower price for shared bath, the higher for a suite); September 10 to May 24, $40 to $70 in midweek, $50 to $90 on weekends.

Under Ledge, 76 Cliffwood St., Lenox, MA 01240 (tel. 413/637-0236), is a large, lovely old (1896) home set back from the street on the knoll of a hill on four acres. Here Marcie Lanoue raised a large family, and two of her children, Thomas and Cheryl, still assist her today in the running of this bed-and-breakfast.

A handsome oak staircase whose walls are covered with ormolu mirrors leads to the rooms. All rooms are air-conditioned, have roughly 12-foot-high ceilings, and are proportionately large. Room 4 has a private balcony from which you can watch the sun gilding the treetops in evening. Inside, the fireplace is surmounted by a mirror that reflects the candlesticks standing on the mantel. A cushioned white-wicker rocker, sofa, armoire, mahogany chest topped with shaving mirror, and iron-and-brass bed complete the room furnishings. Books and oval wood-framed portraits bestow character. A separate hallway furnished with a desk within the suite leads to the private bathroom and spacious closets.

The other rooms are similarly large. Room 6 features a brass bed, a marble-top sidetable and dresser, oak rocker and table, and love seat covered in brown/orange floral fabric that matches the curtains. On the fireplace mantel stand brass candlesticks and horse figurines. A beige/brown carpet completes the decor. Celery and rose are the predominant colors in Room 3. Top-floor rooms, like no. 11, have interesting under-eaves shapes and share baths.

In the bay window of the living room stands a grand piano; other entertainments consist of games, books, magazines, and conversation. Breakfast is taken in a bright semicircular sun room. Muffins, fresh fruit, coffee, and tea will help start the day. The wicker chairs on the flower-brightened porch are also inviting.

RATES: $50 (for shared bath) to $120 (for large rooms) in July, August, and October; less off-season.

The **Village Inn,** 16 Church St., Lenox, MA 01240 (tel. 413/637-0020), is the one place where you can stop for a formal English Devonshire cream tea, complete with tiny crustless tea sandwiches and homemade scones and preserves, accompanied by a pot of fine tea of your choice. It is served in the dining room from 3:30 to 5 P.M. At this friendly, comfortable place, run by Clifford Rudisill and Ray Wilson, the public areas are, in my opinion, more charming than the rooms. The reception desk, which doubles as a small bar, faces the small parlor where comfortable armchairs near the hearth are ideal for sipping a glass of sherry and chatting or for a good read. Across the hall in the larger parlor there's a TV and a grand piano, and plenty of antique furnishings to loll comfortably in. The 27 rooms are eclectically furnished in a homey, old-fashioned way. Some have canopy beds. The Harvest Dining Room has an excellent reputation for value. Menu selections might include leg of lamb with rosemary, sage, and thyme; breast of chicken with creamed Dijon sauce; and filet mignon with bordelaise, priced from $8.75 to $13.50. There's also a downstairs tavern for after-concert snacks.

RATES: November to June, $65 to $95; July to October, $75 to $120. Year round, except October, there's a 20% discount on Monday, Tuesday, and Wednesday. Two-night minimum on weekends. DINNER: 6 to 10 P.M. weekends only; breakfast and tea served daily.

At the **Candlelight Inn,** just around the corner at 53 Walker St., Lenox, MA 01240 (tel. 413/637-1555), handsome breakfronts, copper kitchenware, chintz curtains, and a beamed ceiling all contribute to the French Provincial air of this candlelit dining room, warmed by a fire in winter. Here, ample portions of classic continental fare are served—shrimp moutard, scampi, chateaubriand, cioppino, steak au poivre, and many varieties of fresh seafood, for example, all priced from $13 to $19. Upstairs, six rooms, all with private bath, are available.

RATES: $55 to $100 a night, depending on the season. In July and August a three-night minimum is required on weekends.

LUNCH: 11:30 A.M. to 2:30 P.M. daily. DINNER: Monday to Saturday from 5 to 10 P.M., from 4 P.M. on Sunday. BRUNCH: Sunday from 11:30 A.M. to 3 P.M.

Approached by a half-mile pine- and spruce-lined drive, the 230-acre former Vanderbilt estate has been converted into a time-sharing resort, **Foxhollow Inn,** Rte. 7, Lenox, MA 01240 (tel. 413/637-2000), where you may stay if there's space available. The accommodations are located in the manor house and in guest cottages scattered around the property. Facilities include a swimming pool, riding stables, sailboats on Laurel Lake, tennis courts, a cross-country skiing center, and skating on the ponds. The restaurant is open to the public; the Hunts End lounge has entertainment on weekends; there's a lovely garden court for cocktails, and also theater entertainment (in summer only).

RATES: $100 to $145 double, depending on the type of room—standard, deluxe, or a suite. There's a 25% reduction Monday through Wednesday. Three-day minimum on weekends. WINTER WEEKEND PACKAGES: $200 to $305 per person, including two nights' accommodation, one dinner, and two breakfasts. DINNER: 6 to 10 P.M. daily.

If you prefer modern accommodations with all the razzmatazz of televisions, phones, bars, and lounges, then there are plenty around, like the **Berkshire Quality Inn**, 390 Pittsfield/Lenox Rd. (Rte. 7), Lenox, MA 01240 (tel. 413/637-1100), which has an indoor-outdoor pool (temporarily closed) and tennis courts; or the **Susse Chalet**, Rtes. 7 and 20, Lenox, MA 01240 (tel. 413/637-3560), which also has a pool.

RATES: $34.75 double in winter, $46.75 double in summer.

The **Yankee Motor Lodge**, Rtes. 7 and 20, Lenox, MA 01240 (tel. 413/499-3700), has made some gesture toward achieving a New England atmosphere by installing fireplaces in some of its 60 rooms. Pool also.

RATES: $106.50 to $118.50 ($138.50 for a room with a fireplace) in season, $61.50 to $72.50 ($88.50 for a fireplace) at other times.

Tanglewood operates an **accommodations hotline** providing rooms in local homes. Call the festival number: 413/637-1940.

LENOX DINING

Besides the outstanding restaurants at the Gateways, Wheatleigh, and other inns already mentioned, there's also another fine dining room plus several more casual lunch and dinner places.

Paolo's Auberge, 306 Pittsfield/Lenox Rd. (tel. 413/637-2711), at the junction of Rtes. 7 and 7A, was a great success when I visited the area. Located in a 1725 home, the restaurant consists of four dining rooms, each with a different atmosphere. Downstairs rooms tend to colonial early American flavor with beamed ceilings, Windsor chairs, Federal-style mantels; the upstairs room is considerably lighter—more art deco and decorated in blue with white bentwood chairs. The so-called country room is primarily used for overflow customers. The menu is certainly very tempting. Chicken rouladen filled with cheese, oven-roasted pheasant hunter style, shrimp in curry sauce with grilled banana, or beef medallions with green peppercorn sauce all compete for attention. Interestingly, the chef always offers a vegetarian dish. Prices run $17.50 to $23.

Start with the delicate lobster bisque, salmon quenelles in lobster sauce, or delicious ravioli stuffed with crabmeat and served with sage butter. A four course Sunday brunch is served—soup, salad, main course, and dessert for $14.50. By reservation only.

DINNER: 6 to 9 P.M. daily. BRUNCH: Sunday from 11:30 A.M. to 2 P.M.

The Restaurant, 15 Franklin St. (tel. 413/637-9894), is a comfortable, casual California-style place that sports a miscellaneous collection of postcards, banknotes, business cards, and buttons covering one entire wall in the front. Here you can tuck into oversize portions of good honest dishes—poached salmon béarnaise, vegetable curry, tournedos of beef, fettuccine, plus some flavorful homemade soups, salads, and burgers. There's a great selection of beers. Prices range from $6 to $18.

LUNCH: Thursday to Tuesday from noon to 2:30 P.M. DINNER: Thursday to Tuesday from 6 to 10 P.M. (until 9 P.M. on Sunday). BRUNCH: Sunday from 11 A.M. to 2 P.M. Closed Wednesday and usually the month of November.

The **Church Street Café,** 69 Church St. (tel. 413/637-2745), is a local favorite for soups, salads, burgers, and pasta dishes, all priced under $6 and served in a pleasant light-wood and plants atmosphere. For dinner there's always a fresh fish and pasta of the day, along with such items as charcoal-grilled pork medallion with apples, or soy and sesame grilled duck. Prices range from $10 to $15.

HOURS: 11:30 A.M. to midnight daily in summer; closed Sunday in winter.

Just across the street, the **Café Lucia,** 90 Church St. (tel. 413/637-2640), is a fine lunch choice, serving soups, sandwiches, and salads, including caponata, an eggplant-and-tomato salad garnished with hard-boiled eggs, black olives, tomato, basil, and mozzarella. Egg dishes like zucchini frittata (made from eggs, cheese with mushrooms, and zucchini), pâté plate, and chilled mussels in white wine complete the selections. There's a pleasant outdoor patio under an awning.

LUNCH: Daily in summer. DINNER: In summer, 5:30 to 9 P.M. daily; in winter, Tuesday to Thursday from 5:30 to 9 P.M., on Friday and Saturday until 9:30 P.M.; closed Sunday and Monday.

Cheesecake Charlie's, 83 Church St. (tel. 413/637-9729), serves breakfast from 8 to 11 A.M. but the prime attraction is the 13 flavors of cheesecake plus daily specials. There's even a cheesecake ice cream!

Picnic Suppliers

Obviously you'd expect to find many picnic suppliers in Lenox for all those bountiful Tanglewood spreads. Here are some of them:

Crosby's, 62 Church St. (tel. 413/637-3396), offers gourmet food to go from 10 A.M. to 6 P.M. (until 8 P.M. on Friday and Saturday). Special desserts can be found at **Suchele Bakers,** 31 Housatonic St. (tel. 413/637-0939), open Wednesday to Saturday from 9 A.M. to 5 P.M., until 1 P.M. on Sunday. For less spectacular but constantly available fare, head for the **Price Chopper,** on the Pittsfield/Lenox Road (tel. 413/443-5449), is open 24 hours, except on Sunday. **A Moveable Feast,** behind 100 Main St. (tel. 413/637-1785), offers gourmet items along the lines of gazpacho and vichyssoise, chicken with grapes and walnuts and tarragon (salade de poulet à la Debussy), and boeuf à la Brahms (marinated steak on a bed of rice with ginger and scallions).

LEE

Although Lee has lived largely in the shadow of Lenox, and achieved a reputation for being lively and more modern, but careless of its beauty, recently the town has shown greater interest in preserving its past, as you'll see from the descriptions of accommodations that follow. Still, the main attraction is the superb Jacob's Pillow dance festival just east of Lee in Becket.

From Lee's Sullivan Station a vintage steam engine also takes passengers on a jaunt through the hills from Lee to Great Barrington. Operated by the Berkshire

Scenic Railway Museum, Sullivan Station, Railroad St. (tel. 413/243-2872). HOURS: May to October weekends and holidays.

LEE-SOUTH LEE LODGING AND DINING

Under the same management as the Gateways in Lenox, the **Haus Andreas,** Stockbridge Rd. (R.R. 1, Box 605B), Lee, MA 01238 (tel. 413/243-3298), is a 200-year-old mansion with a pastoral view. Originally built by a Revolutionary War soldier, it was modernized by George Westinghouse, Jr., and was briefly, in 1942, the residence of Queen Wilhelmina of the Netherlands, her daughter, Princess Juliana, and her granddaughters, Beatrix (now the queen) and Irene. The public areas include a large drawing room with a baby grand piano, a good reading area with a fireplace, and a TV room. Although all of the seven rooms (three with fireplace) are furnished differently, you might find an intricately carved mahogany bedstead or a marble-top chest. It's a lovely, quiet place (no TVs or phones in the rooms), and it has a pool, bicycles for guest use, and a tennis court. RATES (including continental breakfast): In summer, $65 to $95 in midweek, $85 to $155 on weekends; in winter, $50 to $85 in midweek, $60 to $110 on weekends (the lower prices are for rooms with shared bath). In July and August a minimum stay of four nights is required; in June, September, and October, a two-night minimum.

The **Federal House Inn,** Rte. 102, South Lee, MA 01260 (tel. 413/243-1824). The decor and antique furnishings in the public areas of this classically proportioned restored Federal house lead you to expect more of the ten accommodations upstairs. They're pleasant enough to be sure, with chintz wallpapers, white candlewick spreads, and plank floors, but they're not as distinguished as one might have hoped. Most share bathrooms; two have private bath. The dining rooms, however, have been a smash hit on the Tanglewood dining scene. Two elegant rooms, each with only about seven tables, are the setting for some classic continental cuisine—oysters, clams, or escargots for starters; followed by such possibilities as chicken tarragon, steak au poivre, rack of lamb, and escalope of veal with a champagne sauce. Prices run from $14.50 to $22.50. Brunch features such main courses as leg of lamb, swordfish, and calves' liver, as well as egg dishes, from $7 to $11. RATES: $90 on weekends, $70 in midweek. DINNER: Wednesday to Sunday from 6 to 9 P.M. (until 10 P.M. on weekends). BRUNCH: Sunday from noon to 2:30 P.M.

If you stay at the **Historic Merrell Tavern Inn,** Main Street (Rte. 102), South Lee, MA 01260 (tel. 413/243-1794), just down the street, you'll be overnighting in a truly historic hostelry that has an authentic circular colonial bar, complete with grille work, which has survived intact since its installation in 1817. Now listed in the National Register of Historic Places, this brick Federal building (1794) with double balcony was bought in 1980 by Faith and Charles Reynolds, two ex-teachers who have carefully restored it according to architectural and historical records. It looks as much like a stagecoach stop as it ever did, from the small entry hall featuring a tall case clock, Federal mirror, and candlesticks, to the parlor-bar (now used for breakfast) with fireplace, pewter, and appropriate period furniture. The original iron latches have been retained throughout the house. Upstairs the nine rooms, all with private bath, have been handsomely decorated with period furnishings and canopy beds.

RATES (including full breakfast): mid June to October 31, $210 to $250 for a two-night weekend, $70 per night midweek; November 1 to mid-June, $115 to $130 ($180 with a fireplace) for a two-night weekend, $60 ($75 with fireplace) per night midweek. During September and October a fireplace room is $90 per night weekdays.

Note: Swimming is available at Benedict Pond in Beartown Mountain State Park, only ten minutes' drive away.

The **Morgan House**, Main Street, Lee, MA 01238 (tel. 413/243-0181), is not a typically well-seasoned New England inn for the well-heeled traveler. Located on the main street of Lee, its 11 far-from-elegant rooms are extremely spare and simple. Built in 1826 as a private residence, it was converted into a stagecoach inn in 1853 and received such renowned visitors as Ulysses Grant and George Bernard Shaw, whose carefully preserved signatures can be seen on the wall by the reception desk. The tavern bar is frequented by locals, and the low-ceilinged tavern dining room serves pork chops, chicken breast, and other honest beef, steak, and seafood dishes from $8 to $15 in a warm unpretentious atmosphere of polished wood tables and paneling. It's a convenient popular lunch spot. Prices and quality are hard to beat for such dishes as calves' liver, sautéed scallops, baked stuffed shrimp, plus sandwiches and salads priced from $7 to $9.50. There are always even lower-priced daily specials—pork sausage with mash, scrod au gratin, beef carbonade, all under $7. The old photographs of the place and its denizens make for fascinating historical viewing.

RATES: In season, $45 to $55 in midweek, $70 to $90 on weekends; off-season, $35 to $45 in midweek, $45 to $55 on weekends. LUNCH: Monday to Saturday from 11:30 A.M. to 2:30 P.M. DINNER: Monday to Thursday from 5 to 9 P.M., on Friday and Saturday until 10 P.M., on Sunday from noon to 9 P.M.

The **Kingsleigh**, 32 Park St., Lee, MA 01238 (tel. 413/243-3317), is right on the main road in Lee. One small room in this 1840 house is an antique shop, and furnishings and artifacts in rooms throughout the house are indeed for sale. Just ask ex–New Yorkers/owners Linda and Arthur Segal for the price (they're numbered).

Four rooms are prettily and thoughtfully decorated (two with private bath). The bathrooms are equipped with lavender water and nightlight, and there are plants in many rooms. Room 2, a large front room, has an oak double bed and a dresser on which stand candlesticks. Ruffled white curtains contrast with the blue-and-pink chintz wallpaper. Wallpapers are all different, my favorite being a floral-bird combination. Room 3 reveals some idiosyncratic touches—a hat hanging on closet pegs, flowers that were painted on the wall by Linda, and a doll.

Breakfast varies from day to day. It might be bacon and eggs, walnut pancakes, or bagel, lox, and cream cheese. You can enjoy it in the terracotta dining room at a marble-top table, in the country kitchen at a casual bar, or even outside at the tables with umbrellas.

RATES: May 1 through October, $45 to $65 on weekdays, $65 to $85 on weekends; November through March, $40 to $55 on weekdays, $55 to $75 on weekends.

The **Inn at Lee,** 51 Park St., Lee, MA 01238 (tel. 413/243-0321), occupies an interesting Victorian house. The beamed rooms, carved cherry woodwork, and stained glass (particularly in the bar) evoke an old country atmosphere. The three dining rooms include the gold room, where owner Mary Ann McGrath hangs her cardinal collection. Breakfast is served here.

Upstairs, the rooms are eclectically and highly personally furnished. Dramatic bird-of-paradise wallpaper covers the walls of the staircase leading to the seven rooms (two sharing baths, three in the carriage house). Original features of the house add extra flavor—for instance, a painted carpet in the little sitting room at the top of the stairs. Colors of the rooms are strong. Chinese red provides the background for a painted blue/red chest, oak dresser, trunk, and bed with bright country quilt. There's also a cozy little room with peacock-blue coverlet.

Cocktails are served on the porch. The menu is simple, offering such popular items as veal Oscar and piccata, chicken Cordon Bleu, stuffed Cornish game hen, stuffed shrimp, and a roast duck and roast pork of the day. Prices run $10 to $15.

RATES: June through Labor Day and fall foliage season, $75 to $85 double with private bath on weekends, $50 to $60 in midweek; $65 double with shared bath on weekends, $40 in midweek; less in other months.

LUNCH: 11:30 A.M. to 3 P.M. daily in summer. DINNER: 5 to 9 P.M. daily in summer. Closed Tuesday in winter.

The **Black Swan Inn,** on Laurel Lake, Rte. 20W, Lee, MA 01238 (tel. 413/243-2700), is a modern accommodation with a fine situation on Laurel Lake. All 40 rooms have private bath, air conditioning, Touch-tone phone, TV, chest, two armchairs, and table, plus celery-and-rose quilts on the beds. Lakeside rooms have decks. Plans are afoot for an additional 13 rooms with Jacuzzi tubs and gas operated fireplaces. A pool abuts the lake for sunning. An exercise room, steamroom, sauna, game room, and boats complete the facilities. There's a lounge with central fireplace and a chintz country dining room. At breakfast you can obtain bagels as well as French toast and similar items. Dining room specialties are Hungarian, prepared by innkeeper George Kish, a native of Budapest. Everything from wienerschnitzel and Hungarian goulash to stuffed cabbage and chicken paprikás, priced from $10 to $13.

RATES: $90 to $125 in summer, $50 to $65 in shoulder season, $45 to $55 in winter.

The **Oak n' Spruce,** South Lee, MA 01260 (tel. 413/243-3500), is a comfortable unpretentious resort where the rooms are simple and the public areas homey. The facilities, though, include tennis courts, horseback riding, outdoor and indoor swimming pools, a nine-hole par-3 golf course across the road, easy downhill skiing, and a fitness center.

RATES: May 25 to June 24 (MAP, double occupancy), $68.50 per person in midweek, $85 per person on weekends; June 25 to September 2 (MAP, double occupancy), $80 per person in midweek, $100 per person on weekends; September 3 to October 28 (MAP, double occupancy), $68.50 per person in midweek, $92.50 per person on weekends; October 29 to December 18 (MAP, double occupancy), $68.50 per person in midweek, $80 per person on weekends; December 18 to May 26 (room only), $50 in midweek, $60 on weekends (add $30 for MAP).

Celebrity seekers should know about **Joe's Diner** in Lee (tel. 413/243-9756), one of the few places that stays open late and serves good solid food that is well appreciated by the performers at local theater and musical centers. You can fortify yourself with a full pork dinner here for a mere $5.

Sullivan Station, (tel. 413/243-2082), housed in a converted railway station, is a good Saturday luncheon spot and also convenient at the beginning or end of the scenic ride that leaves from here. Various "railroad" sandwiches are offered, like the RR Express, a six-ounce open steak sandwich served with potato; and the Whistlestop, hot sausage served on a Vienna roll with sautéed peppers and onions. Fancier dinner items include baked scrod mozzarella, broiled lamb chop, and char-broiled sirloin, priced from $9 to $13.

HOURS: 11:30 A.M. to 9:30 P.M. daily in summer, Wednesday to Sunday until May 1. BRUNCH: Sunday from 11 A.M. to 3 P.M. year round.

BED-AND-BREAKFAST IN NEARBY BECKET

Canterbury Farm, Fred Snow Rd., Becket, MA 01223 (tel. 413/623-8765), is really secluded, located on a dirt road off Rte. 8 about 1½ miles south of Becket. It's popular with ski tourists. The three upstairs rooms share bath without shower and are decorated in plain country style with colorful quilts, braided rugs, and country dressers on wide-board floors. One ground-floor room has a private bath with full bath and shower. It's a genuine old 1780 farmhouse with sloping door frames and a lived-in look, run by a young couple with a baby. Breakfast of eggs and muffins is served. There are seven miles of ski trails to traverse; skis are available for rent and lessons are also given.

RATES: $40.

STOCKBRIDGE

STOCKBRIDGE ATTRACTIONS

A prime attraction for many is the old **Old Corner House** (tel. 413/298-3822) on Main Street, where you can see Norman Rockwell's famous pictures that captured the essence of a way of life in an earlier, more innocent America. Born in New York City in 1894, Rockwell moved to Stockbridge in 1953, and he remained here, working in his studio over Nejaime's Market, until he died in 1978. He is buried in Stockbridge cemetery. In his life he painted 4,000 pictures, many of them covers for the *Saturday Evening Post* and *McCall's,* but only 50 of them are shown here each year and then on a rotating basis. You may well see his first *Saturday Evening Post* cover (it appeared in 1916) of the schoolboy pushing a baby carriage, or one of my favorites, a family seen heading off for a day trip or vacation, children hanging out the window in their excitement, grandma sitting under her hat like a solemn stooge, and the same family returning, children downcast and grandma still stolid, stern, and unmoved. HOURS: 10 A.M. to 5 P.M. daily except Tuesday; closed for two weeks in January. ADMISSION: $3 for adults, 50¢ for children.

Along Main Street, stop in at the **Mission House,** (tel. 413/298-3239), built in 1739 and home of the Rev. John Sergeant, first missionary to the Stockbridge Indians. The house has a fine collection of furnishings, and the garden is also interesting, displaying plants only from that period. HOURS: Memorial Day to Columbus Day, Tuesday to Saturday from 10 A.M. to 4:30 P.M., on Sunday and holidays from 11 A.M. to 3:30 P.M. only. ADMISSION: $3 for adults, $1 for children under 16.

Across the street from the Red Lion, **St. Paul's Episcopal Church** has some famous associations—McKim was the architect; the baptistery was created by Auguste St. Gaudens; one of the nave windows is by Tiffany, and the chancel window by LaFarge.

Farther along Main Street you'll come to the **Children's Chimes,** erected on the site of the original mission church by David Dudley Field, as a memorial to his grandchildren. They are played every evening at sunset from "apple blossom time until frost."

The modest cottage where Hawthorne wrote *Tanglewood Tales* can also be seen on Hawthorne Street near Tanglewood. Of the view (still unchanged) across the Stockbridge Bowl, he wrote: "I cannot write in the presence of that view."

The marvelous house on Prospect Hill, **Naumkeag** (tel. 413/298-3239) was designed by Stanford White in 1886 for Joseph H. Choate, President Wilson's ambassador to the Court of St. James. The 26 sumptuous rooms and the formal gardens with fountains and Chinese pagodas give a good insight into the opulent lifestyle of the time. HOURS: Daily, except Monday, from late June until Labor Day; weekends only to Columbus Day. ADMISSION: $4.50 for both the house and the garden, $3 for the house only, $2.50 for the garden only, and $1 for children under 16.

A must in Stockbridge is a visit to the **Berkshire Garden Center,** Rtes. 102 and 183 (tel. 413/298-3926), a glorious place in any season. From spring to early fall the spectacular 15 acres of flowering shrubs display primrose, delphiniums, clematis, roses of all hues, brilliant azaleas, and rhododendrons, a variety of annuals and perennials, and (in spring) apple blossom and dogwood. In the herb garden, every fragrant plant is labeled. The gift shop has some interesting items. HOURS: Mid-May to early October, from 10 A.M. to 5 P.M. ADMISSION: $3 for adults, 50¢ for children 6 to 12.

Daniel Chester French referred to his summer home, **Chesterwood,** off Rte. 183 (tel. 413/298-3579), as heaven, and certainly the view of Monument Mountain, both from the house and from his radiant 23-foot-high studio, does warrant such a description. The skylit studio, where he worked from 1898 to 1931, is most remarkable for the floor-to-ceiling double doors through which he rolled his sculptures on a small railroad trestle out into the daylight to examine them. One can also imagine his taking a break to entertain guests in the adjoining reception area furnished with fireplace, library, and piano at the front of the studio, which has sketches, plaster casts, and bronze models of his sculpture, including the seated Lincoln and the Minute Man statue at Concord North Bridge. From the house and studio, you can wander through the gardens. In the barn there are sketches and working models of many of his other famous works—*Brooklyn* and *Manhattan,* formerly at the entrance to the Manhattan Bridge, and *Alma Mater* at Columbia University, for example.

Chesterwood is about two miles west of Stockbridge. Take Rte. 102 west to Rte. 183; turn left and drive for about a mile and follow the signs. HOURS: May 1 to October 31, 10 A.M. to 5 P.M. daily. ADMISSION: $4 for adults, $1 for children 6 to 18.

STOCKBRIDGE LODGING AND DINING

The large country inn, the **Red Lion,** Main Street, Stockbridge, MA 01262 (tel. 413/298-5545), whose porch faces the main street, has become a symbol of hospitality in Stockbridge and the Berkshires. Many vacationers come expressly to visit the Red Lion, flocking into the front parlor where the fires blaze, and overflowing into the snug tavern or downstairs into the larger Victorian pub, known as the "Lion's Den," with nightly entertainment. The original structure, which served as a small tavern on the Albany–Hartford–Boston stage route in 1773, was destroyed by fire in 1896. A string of celebrities has bedded down here, among them Presidents McKinley, Teddy Roosevelt, Coolidge, and FDR, and also William Cullen Bryant and Henry Wadsworth Longfellow.

Today there are air-conditioned accommodations for 175 guests in rooms that are individually decorated, some nostalgically with wicker beds. In summer the courtyard, colorfully decorated with flowers, makes a lovely dining spot. A swimming pool completes the facilities.

The dining room specializes in New England favorites—scrod, prime rib, and chicken pot pie—ranging from $9 to $19. Two remarkable features of the Red Lion are the friendly personnel and the quality of the food, which are sustained even when 1,800 people are served per day (200 at breakfast, 500 at lunch, and 1,100 at night). At a recent meal the swordfish was moist and served with delicious roasted potatoes and peas, and garnished with lemon neatly covered with cheesecloth; my dining partner's prime rib was juicy and certainly prime. Celery, carrots, squash, and onion in vinegar dressing preceded dinner, along with hot rolls. Salads, too, were fine.

Crystal chandeliers, large ornate gilt mirrors, willow-pattern china, damask tablecloths, and a posy of fresh flowers on each table set the elegant tone. Teapots lining the lintel of the partition add interest. At the Red Lion you'll be living amid the charm of Staffordshire china, colonial pewter, and 18th-century furniture.

RATES: November 1 to May 22, $60 double or $72 twin with private bath in midweek, $70 double or $85 twin on weekends; May 23 to October 31, $75 double or $90 twin with private bath in midweek, $100 double or $120 twin on weekends; year round, rooms with nearby shared bath cost $44 to $65. In July and August a minimum two-night stay is required on weekends. BREAKFAST: Monday to Friday from 7:30 to 10 A.M., on Saturday from 8 to 10 A.M. LUNCH: Monday to Saturday from noon to 2:30 P.M. DINNER: Monday to Thursday from 6 to 9 P.M., on Friday and Saturday to 9:30 P.M., on Sunday from noon to 9 P.M. Jacket and tie for men required at dinner; no jeans permitted.

A discreet wooden sign hangs out front of the **Inn at Stockbridge,** Rte. 7 (P.O. Box 2033), Stockbridge, MA 01262 (tel. 413/298-3337). Step onto the classical portico and into the plushly furnished parlor-hall graced with a grand piano, and comfortable wing chairs set around the hearth. The library-sitting room offers an extensive collection of fine books (all catalogued, by the way). Although the seven rooms (five with private bath) are not as lavishly decorated with antiques, they are all very pretty. The three small rooms that share a bath are furnished in a pleasant sophisticated country style.

Hosts Donald and Lee Weitz also serve a full breakfast on fine china and Wedgwood. Lee, a professionally trained home economist, turns out some extraordinary fare—fresh fruit cup, cheese-and-ham soufflé, cinnamon coffee cake, and a very special brew. Sunday breakfasts are extra-special, consisting of a mimosa followed by eggs Benedict and banana bread.

At the back of the house, the garden's lilacs and other flowering shrubs provide a welcome retreat. So does the pool.

RATES: May 28 to October 31, on weekends, $125 to $160 double with private bath, $85 with shared bath; in midweek, $105 to $140 with private bath, $75 with shared bath. Off-season, $65 to $105. In July and August there's a three-night minimum on weekends.

Set on a quiet back road not far from Stockbridge, the **Williamsville Inn,** Rte. 41, West Stockbridge, MA 01266 (tel. 413/274-6580), has all the pleasures of an English country inn. It has the physical makings of a delightful accommodation, a small and cozy 1797 farmhouse with wide-plank floors, fireplaces throughout the public areas, comfortable wing chairs, and antiques. There are 15 rooms, two with fireplaces, some with four-posters, country furniture, and private bathrooms. There's also a pool and tennis court.

The three dining rooms serve French cuisine—bouillabaisse, veal with morels, filet of beef, and duckling with poached pear and sweet red wine, for example. Entrees range from $18 to $21. For dessert, try the chocolate mousse cake, Williamsville mocha, or the varied parfaits.

RATES: $85 to $95 in July and August, $80 to $90 in September and October, $74 to $100 from November to May (the higher price is for the rooms with a fireplace). Suites are more expensive. A three-day minimum is required on holiday weekends, a two-day minimum on all other weekends. DINNER: Monday to Thursday from 6 to 9 P.M., on Friday from 5:30 to 9 P.M., on Saturday and Sunday from 5 to 9 P.M. during the summer.

Picnicking Supplies in Stockbridge

Stockbridge choices include **Nejaime's Market,** on Main Street (tel. 413/298-4246), which displays unusual Middle Eastern delights—tabouli, hummus, baba ghannouj, spinach pies, and barbecued foods. HOURS: 7:30 A.M. to 6 P.M. daily.

The **Elegant Picnic,** also on Main Street (tel. 413/298-4010 or 298-4059), lives up to its name by providing smoked pheasant, lamb, shrimp, and fabulous desserts. HOURS: 9 A.M. to 9 P.M. daily.

WEST STOCKBRIDGE

West Stockbridge has been touted as the "new" au courant place in the Berkshires, but unless you like wandering around artificially old shops and boutiques, there's really little else here, except for one restaurant that has a deeply moving story attached to it.

WEST STOCKBRIDGE DINING

Luy Nguyen and wife, Trai Thi Duong, escaped from Vietnam and went first to Hartford, before being invited to West Stockbridge, to open the **Truc Orient Express,** Harris Street (tel. 413/232-4204). Their photograph album, which is proudly displayed, tells the story of their family reunion and the restoration of their young son, separated from them for six years until Sen. Ted Kennedy came to their assistance. Try the crab-and-asparagus soup first, then choose among such main dishes as shrimp with straw mushroom, sweet-and-sour chicken, or a delicious Vietnamese-style Mongolian hotpot, all priced from $9. The atmosphere is extremely pleasant, with bamboo chairs and wicker-based glass-top Parsons tables set on tile floors in light and airy space. HOURS: 11 A.M. to 11 P.M. daily; closed Monday during the winter.

EVENING ENTERTAINMENT IN WEST STOCKBRIDGE

At **Shaker Mill Tavern,** on Albany Road (Rtes. 102 and 41) in West Stockbridge (tel. 413/232-8565), the 18 international beers offered attract a young crowd. A deck café is open in summer, and jazz, Latin, and comedy entertainment are offered Thursday through Sunday nights. HOURS: Daily from Memorial Day to Columbus Day, closed Wednesday at other times.

THE EGREMONT AREA

South Egremont is a lovely, quiet village worth stopping in to browse through the several antique stores, bookshops, and the old-fashioned general store. Located on Rte. 23, it is surrounded by some dramatic scenery and provides access to Mount Everett and BashBish Falls. Other great antique hunting grounds are nearby in Ashley Falls and Sheffield along Rtes. 7 and 7A. If you continue west along Rte. 23 you'll come to Catamount, crossing the border into New York, where there are a couple of renowned restaurants.

SOUTH EGREMONT LODGING AND DINING

The **Egremont Inn,** Old Sheffield Road (P.O. Box 418), South Egremont, MA 01258 (tel. 413/528-2111), is a charming old place originally built in 1780 with a wrap-around veranda. Inside, the tavern is especially alluring with its curved brick fireplace, low ceilings, and colonial-style furnishings. The dining room offers traditional fare such as lamb chops, roast duck with fruit sauce, veal with champagne sauce, filet of salmon poached in court bouillon, chicken tarragon, and sirloin maître d'hôtel, priced from $11 to $17. Facilities include a pool and two tennis courts. None of the 23 rooms has telephone or TV.

RATES: $145 per couple per night, MAP, Wednesday to Sunday; $45 per person, per day on Monday and Tuesday. Summer rates rise to $125, MAP, per couple per night on weekends. DINNER: 6 to 9 P.M., weekends only in winter; closed Monday in summer. Closed mid-March for three weeks.

At the **Weathervane Inn,** Rte. 23 (P.O. Box 388), South Egremont, MA 01258 (tel. 413/528-9580), seasonal potted flowers bloom on the side porch of this attractive white clapboard house with black shutters, into which you'll be welcomed by the Murphy family and their friendly cocker spaniel. There are eight rooms, all with private bath. Room 6 is tucked over the kitchen under the eaves, which gives it an interesting shape and feel. It's large enough to accommodate two brass beds, a marble-top dresser adorned with dried-flower arrangement, a maple side table, and a desk and armchair. The bathrooms contain lavender or other liquid soap. All rooms have electric blankets and air conditioning, and at night you'll find a miniature nightcap—amaretto perhaps.

Breakfast is served in a skylit room decorated with Hitchcock chairs and tables set with red-white tablecloths. It overlooks the back lawn. The meal is well cooked and you'll most likely tuck into Irish soda bread, fresh squeezed juice, eggs of your choice with home-fries, sausage or bacon, and toast.

The dining room is inviting, decked out in country style in Williamsburg blue, with tables set with white tablecloths, swag chintz curtains, and a hutch filled with decoys. The menu changes daily but there'll always be two fresh fish, chicken, beef, veal, and lamb dishes. For example, chicken Egremont (chicken breast stuffed with spinach, baked, and topped with boursin), prime rib, stuffed sole, and veal Normandy might share the billing. Among the appetizers, try the golden tulip pepper mozzarella, or the chicken liver pâté or escargots in puff pastry.

Adjacent to the dining room is a sitting area with couch and chairs arranged in front of the large hearth. A small service bar is in the corner. There's also a lounge with TV, books, and games, electically furnished with simple country pieces. The outdoor pool has a good deck for sunning, or you can rock on the painted blue rockers that beckon on the porch.

RATES: $70 per person double (MAP) on weekends, $70 double (room and breakfast only) in midweek; in July and August a three-night minimum-stay package costs $395 double (MAP).

DINNER: July through the end of October, Monday and Thursday through Sunday from 6 to 9 P.M.; Friday and Saturday only the rest of the year, except on special holidays.

A large white clapboard house, where you can sit on the porch and look over toward the lush greens of the Egremont Country Club, the **Windflower Inn,** Rte. 23 (Egremont Star Rte., Box 25), Great Barrington, MA 01230 (tel. 413/528-2720), offers warm hospitality in antique-style surroundings. There are 13 rooms, all with private bath, some with fireplaces. The dining room serves a $25 prix fixe that might feature three or four entrees like veal marsala, duck with plum sauce, or shrimp curry. There's an outdoor pool.

RATES: $60 to $80 per person, MAP; three-night minimum is required on summer weekends. DINNER: 6 to 8:30 P.M.; by reservation only.

NORTH EGREMONT LODGING AND DINING

Some locals recommended the dining room at the **Elm Court Inn,** Rte. 71, North Egremont, MA 01252 (tel. 413/528-0325), more highly than any other in the immediate area. Dishes include osso buco, chicken with lemon and fresh basil, veal chop with morels, and baked swordfish, priced from $11 to $16.75. Floral curtains, fireplace, polished wood tables with placemats and a sprig of fresh flowers complete the decor. There's also a small cozy bar with a brick hearth.

The four simply furnished rooms (two with private bath) feature candlewick bedspreads, chintz curtains, painted chests, and braided rugs. Room 4 is the nicest in my opinion, with its corner cupboard, dresser, small captain's desk, couch, and blue-and-white braided rug and burgundy curtains. The sink has a marble surround.

RATES: $45 to $55. DINNER: Thursday to Monday from 5 to 9:30 P.M., on Sunday from 4 to 9 P.M.; closed Tuesday and Wednesday.

Dining in and Around South Egremont

For breakfast and an experience that probably recalls your childhood if you're over 25, head for the **Gaslight Store,** in South Egremont. Here a few tables have been placed in the center of an old-fashioned general store that sells everything from aspirin to salami, newspapers to candy, complete with real wooden counters, scratched and burnished with use.

The **Old Mill**, Rte. 23, South Egremont (tel. 413/528-1421), is famed for its picturesque setting overlooking a small brook, and has an excellent local reputation for consistently fine meals. Unfortunately, at a recent meal I was a trifle disappointed with the selected main courses (the broiled salmon was dry, which perhaps owed more to the cooking method than to anything else, and my companion's prime rib was tough, although admittedly it was the last piece). Still, all the local folk told me that I'm the only one they've ever heard complain and that it must have been the restaurant's rare off night.

Certainly the ambience is romantically country. The room is lit by a Shaker-style chandelier, and little copper lanterns on the tables that make the white linens and wide-board floors glow. Walls are adorned with early American tools—adzes and planes.

The menu is always supplemented by daily specials, which might include Swiss cheese and onion soup or goat cheese and sun-dried tomato tart among the appetizers, and broiled swordfish with garlic-herb butter or prime rib as entrees. A tasty country pâté is served with celery remoulade and garnished with lettuce and tomatoes. Portions are large (at least by my standards). A house salad contains lettuce, tomatoes, and mushrooms. Among the desserts, my favorites are the profiteroles, but you might prefer crème brûlée, apple walnut tart, or peach Melba.

DINNER: In summer, Sunday to Thursday from 5:30 to 9 P.M., on Friday and Saturday until 10 P.M. Closed all of March and on Monday from November through May.

Farther along Rte. 23 you'll come to **Sebastian's,** South Egremont (tel. 413/528-3469), which is a refreshing change from the traditional, cozy New England–style restaurants that abound in the Berkshires. White tablecloths, the original black chairs from the Copacabana, and track spotlighting provide a comfortable art deco ambience. There's a large selection of appetizers, providing plenty for those who prefer to "graze"—mozzarella and roasted peppers, clams Pernod, pâté, and pastas—which can be followed by such entrees as calves' liver with blackcurrant glaze, osso buco, Cajun shrimp, or pasta dishes like ravioli with a pesto sauce, penne arrabiata. Prices range from $12.50 to $16. Desserts change daily. At brunch the Pamcake is a huge pancake that is named after the chef. Seafood sausage; baked eggs with ham, gruyère, and sherry; and poached eggs on pasta with spinach and béarnaise are other possibilities. Cocktails or meals can be taken on the pleasant deck out back.

DINNER: From 5:30 P.M. daily in summer; closed Tuesday and Wednesday in winter. BRUNCH: Sunday from 11:30 A.M. to 2:30 P.M.

Lodging and Dining Across the Border in Hillsdale, N.Y.

Swiss Hutte, Rte. 23, Hillsdale, NY 12529 (tel. 518/325-3333), a beautifully kept accommodation at the base of Catamount, also offers some of the finest cuisine in the area. The expertly groomed grounds include a swimming pool, gardens containing herbaceous borders, roses, and a pond, two tennis courts, and a putting green. In the restaurant, aglow with red lanterns, the specialties include wienerschnitzel and other continental fare like frog's legs provençal or sole meunière, and delicious desserts (hazelnut torte and raspberry cream pie). Prices run $14 to $20, including dessert and beverage. The rooms are simply furnished motel-style units.

RATES: In summer, $85 per person (MAP), double (three-night stay required on weekends); in winter, $80 per person (MAP), double (two-night minimum stay required on weekends). BREAKFAST: Daily. LUNCH: Noon to 2 P.M., daily in summer, Friday to Sunday only in winter. DINNER: 5:30 to 9 P.M. daily.

At **L'Hostellerie Bressane,** on Rtes. 23 and 22 (P.O. Box 387), Hillsdale, NY 12529 (tel. 518/325-3412), owners Joan and Madeleine Morel have furnished a late-18th-century brick home with many of their own antique heirlooms. Interesting features of the inn include three splendid Palladian windows, a corner cupboard of museum quality, and eight fireplaces, all but one with the original mantelpieces.

The ground floor of the inn consists of a handsome center hallway, four dining rooms, each with its own fireplace, and a bilevel Victorian bar and lounge (circa 1850) with an unusual curving stairway leading to the gallery level. The reputation of chef Morel's cuisine has spread far and wide and people go out of their way to dine here. The menu, which changes weekly, is extensive. It will certainly offer selections for every taste: for the seafood lover, filets of sole with purée of scallops and celery, fresh salmon with tomato-butter sauce, or fresh crayfish sautéed bordelaise; meat and poultry entrees might include veal chop Orloff, roast pheasant with sauce rouennaise, rack of lamb with garlic confit and eggplant provençal, or pepper steak with a green peppercorn sauce. Among the vegetarian specialties are fresh artichoke bottom with mustard sauce and asparagus in puff pastry with mousseline sauce. Among the appetizers are quenelles of pike with lobster sauce, stuffed clams in garlic butter, chicken liver soufflé, and various soups. For dessert, have a cold peach soufflé in raspberry sauce, if it's available. Prices run $17 to $26.

There are six accommodations, each decorated in a particular color scheme. Those on the second floor share a bath; the Lavender and Coral Rooms on the third floor have private baths. The furnishings are antique reproductions —candlestands, pine chests, and Windsor rocking chairs.

RATES: $70 to $90 double. DINNER: Wednesday to Friday from 6:30 P.M., on Saturday from 5:30 P.M., on Sunday from 4 P.M.; closed Monday and Tuesday (in July and August, weekdays at 5:30 P.M., on Saturday from 5 P.M., and on Sunday from 4 P.M.). There's also a pre-concert $17.50 prix-fixe dinner on Saturday with seatings at 5 and 5:30 P.M. Prix-fixe dinners are also offered on Thursday and Sunday.

GREAT BARRINGTON–SHEFFIELD

GREAT BARRINGTON ATTRACTIONS

This is the largest town in the southern Berkshires, a major crossroads and commercial center. Just outside town, you may want to explore the **Albert Schweitzer Center,** Hurlburt Road (tel. 413/528-3124), where you'll find this quotation to ponder while you wander along Philosopher's Walk, by the brook, or in the universal children's garden: "The meaning of maturity which we should develop in ourselves is that we should strive always to become simpler, kinder, more honest, more truthful, more peace-loving, more gentle, and more compassionate." Lecture and concert series are given through the summer at this special haven. HOURS: The grounds are open June to August, Tuesday to Saturday from 10 A.M. to 4 P.M., on Sunday from noon to 4 P.M.; other months, Thursday to Saturday from 10 A.M. to 4 P.M. (December to February by appointment only).

Inveterate shoppers and browsers will stop at **Jenifer House,** on Stockbridge Road, about a mile north of Rte. 23 on Rte. 7 (tel. 413/528-1500), a series of clapboard buildings each specializing in different merchandise—fine furniture, country clothes, and more. HOURS: Monday to Saturday from 9 A.M. to 5:30 P.M., on Sunday from 10 A.M. to 5 P.M.

GREAT BARRINGTON LODGING

Little John Manor, One Newsboy Monument Lane, Great Barrington, MA 01230 (tel. 413/528-2882), is certainly one of Great Barrington's most secluded bed-and-breakfasts. I missed it several times. It's on Rte. 23 but tucked on a quiet loop, behind the statue of the Newspaper Boy, a gift presented to Great Barrington by Col. William L. Brown, publisher of the *New York Daily News.*

Owners Paul and Herb have four rooms sharing two baths. They've run resorts before and their experience shows. Rooms are immaculately kept and pleasingly decorated in harmonious colors. The twin, for example, has rose carpeting, Wedgwood-blue curtains, and a colorful floral bedspread. Fresh flowers stand on a chest and tissues are available. A small double features a bed with eyelet pillow cases and dust ruffle, and white eiderdown, set off by an oak dresser, bishop's chair, and Japanese prints. The living room is comfortably cluttered with a number of Toby jugs, among other things. Couches, rockers, and other chairs cluster around the white brick fireplace and the TV.

The dining-room table extends to seat eight. In the morning a full English breakfast is served. Tea and coffee and juice are placed on the sideboard and piping-hot scrambled or fried eggs, ham, sausage, mushrooms, broiled tomato, and potatoes in jackets emerge from the kitchen. English muffin or crumpets are served with homemade jams/marmalade. An afternoon tea of scones, Scottish oatcakes, banana bread, and fruit butters is either served in the lounge or taken out to the benches scattered through the garden, or to the porch.

A hutch in the dining room is filled with oils and vinegars which Paul makes from the 55 to 60 varieties of herbs that he cultivates in the garden. Each is clearly marked and you'll smell and see everything from marjoram and horseradish to Egyptian onion. In summer the borders are also blooming with peonies, lilies, roses, and other flowers. And you can sit and contemplate the fields and wooded hills in the distance.

RATES: Memorial Day through October, $50 to $55 for doubles and twins, $65 for a twin with fireplace; November to Memorial Day the weekend rates are reduced by $5 per room.

The **Coffing Bostwick House,** Rte. 41 and Division Street, Great Barrington, MA 01230 (tel. 413/528-4511), is a large rambling house recently opened as a bed-and-breakfast. The structure still needs substantial work, but it has the makings of a pleasant retreat. The white clapboard house (1895) with green shutters possesses long broad porches and stands on 1½ acres. The five rooms vary considerably. Probably the nicest is Room 1, containing a burled Victorian bed, two matching dressers, wing chair, chest, half bath and a gold area rug, set against terracotta-pink wallpaper.

For relaxing you can choose either the TV room or the large sitting room with its well-stocked bookcases, comfortable seating, and odd assortment of dramatic objects, including elaborate lamps and cast-metal figures. Eggs and bacon, eggs Benedict, and similar fare is prepared and served in the impressive large mahogany-paneled dining room with brick fireplace.

RATES: $60.

At **Green Meadows,** 117 Division St., Great Barrington, MA 01230 (tel. 413/528-3897), owners Frank Gioia and Susie Kaufman have created a self-contained bed-and-breakfast unit by converting several rooms at the back of this 1895 Victorian farmhouse which stands on six acres looking out over fields. All three rooms have private bath, are air-conditioned, and are prettily decorated and sparkling. The ground-floor room contains a brass bed with a navy-blue floral comforter, oak dresser, and side table, all set against pink walls. Rooms upstairs are similar, with wide pine floors but decorated in different colors—rose and celery primarily. Breakfast is satisfying, likely beginning with blueberries in plain yogurt and homemade cornbread, and graduating to a goat-cheese omelet with sausage. In the afternoon tea or lemonade is served, and a wee dram of brandy at night.

RATES: $60 Monday to Thursday, $80 on Friday, Saturday, and Sunday, with a two-day minimum.

Irv and Shirley Yost, owners of the **Turning Point Inn,** Rte. 23 at Lake Buel

Road (R.D. 2, Box 140), Great Barrington, MA 01230 (tel. 413/528-4777), really bring the personal touch to their business by sending guests handwritten notes with their brochures. They have restored an old stagecoach stop right near Butternut (east of Great Barrington) and offer seven rooms, six with shared bath. There are a couple of parlors to relax in and the whole place has a distinct home-away-from-home feeling.

RATES: $70 to $90 double, including a full breakfast of eggs, cereal, breads, and fruit.

A magnificent view is to be had from **Ellings Guest House**, Rte. 43 (R.D. 3, Box 6), Great Barrington, MA 01230 (tel. 413/528-4103), perched atop a hill just outside Great Barrington on Rte. 43, surrounded by tall stands of pine and maple overlooking the cornfields and rolling hills of the Berkshires. The house itself is a pretty white colonial with ochre shutters built by a wealthy wool manufacturer in 1746. The six rooms, two with private bath and four sharing two baths, are all quite comfortable. A lovely cabin with shutters rents for $45 a night, but it's usually taken for the season. There's a homey sitting room with fireplace and antique furnishings where you'll have an informal breakfast of muffins, fresh juice, and as many cups of coffee or tea as you can manage. For recreation you can settle down in a rocker on the porch, looking out over the flower garden ablaze in early summer with fuchsia, cornflowers, ox-eye daisies, and pansies, enjoy the rope tree swing, or swim in the river across the road.

RATES: June through October and holidays, $65 for a room with private bath, $50 for a room with shared bath; November through May, $50 and $40 respectively.

Seekonk Pines, Rte. 43 (R.D. 1, Box 29AA), Great Barrington, MA 01230 (tel. 413/528-4192), a little farther west along Route 43, represents great value in this area. Linda and Chris Best are the innkeepers and bring their own personalities and talents to bear on this very homey accommodation. Throughout the house hang watercolors painted by Linda, and quilts restored by her. Both Linda and Chris are singers and, given an accompanist at the piano, if you're lucky they'll perform for guests. Linda and Chris have researched the house's history. It was built between 1830 and 1832 as a farmhouse and remained in the same family for three generations. One of the previous owners was a friend of Thomas Edison, and Edison's portrait hangs among those of the previous owners in the entrance hall.

There are seven rooms available and all are named after previous owners. In the largest, the Harry G. Treadwell, the bed is covered by a quilt made by Linda's great-great-grandmother, Chinese paintings adorn the walls, and a chest of drawers, sidetables, blanket chest, and two comfortable chairs complete the furnishings. The other rooms are also comfortably furnished, and the shared bathroom contains a little cushioned pew and marble sink top. Quilts are found in every room and stenciling appears in many.

The dining-room table supported a vase of purple Canterbury bells when I visited. A breakfast of fresh fruit and homemade muffins is served, along with juice and coffee or tea. Miniature liquors line the wainscoting lintel while china and glass displayed in a cabinet evoke a homey atmosphere. The garden is quite lovely

—filled with foxgloves, lupines, sweet williams, and pansies when I visited. There's an outdoor pool secluded by a private hedge and fence, and for indoor entertainment, TV, books, chess, and other games are available in the living room.

RATES: Memorial Day to October, $60 to $80; in winter, $50 to $60.

GREAT BARRINGTON DINING

Owners of the **Painted Lady,** 785 S. Main St. (tel. 413/528-1662), used to operate the Candlelight Inn in Lenox. It's supposedly named after the old homes in New Orleans which are called "painted ladies" after they've been restored! The restaurant is small—there are only 11 tables—but an elegant atmosphere is evoked by swag curtains, rose carpeting, and Laura Ashley wallpaper in the series of small rooms typical of a Victorian house. There's a small bar in the back. Specialties are northern Italian (about a dozen or so): veal francese, veal saltimbocca, chicken Florentine or piccata, filet of sole milanese, along with two or three pasta dishes. Prices range from $13 to $16.50.

DINNER: Monday and Wednesday to Sunday from 5 to 10 P.M.; closed Tuesday and January through March.

Hans, Rte. 7 South (tel. 413/528-0710), is famous for its Sunday buffet. From 12:30 to 7 P.M. a vast spread of chicken curry, pasta, pork, veal, prime rib, and more is served for $12.50. You can still opt for something on the regular menu —broiled scrod, veal parmigiana, filet mignon, and other typical American favorites in this plain, down-to-earth restaurant.

LUNCH: Wednesday through Saturday from 11:30 A.M. to 2:30 P.M. DINNER: Tuesday to Thursday from 4:30 to 8:30 P.M., on Friday and Saturday until 9 P.M. in winter, 10 P.M. in summer, and on Sunday from noon to 7 P.M.; closed Monday.

For that reasonable Saturday lunch or evening meal, two choices adjoin each other on Railroad Street. **Noodles,** 12 Railroad St. (tel. 413/528-3003), serves a lot of different pasta dishes as well as a handful of specials like baked bluefish, lemon chicken, veal marsala. Prices run $6 to $10. Decor is typical brick and modern graphics with a few tables for summer outdoor dining.

HOURS: Noon to 9 P.M. weekdays, to 10 P.M. on weekends.

20 Railroad Street, whose name describes its address, (tel. 413/528-9345), is a classic hamburgers, sandwiches, and salads tavern-restaurant possessing a long Victorian carved mahogany bar and oak booths. Specials run to baked scallops, veal and peppers, and similar fare. Most items are under $5. The $7 brunch is a good value and offers cooked-to-order choices among omelets, French toast, quiche, and other egg dishes. A drink is included.

HOURS: 11:30 A.M. to 10 P.M. daily.

Across the street, **Daily Bread Bakery** has tempting breads, cookies, and pies made of seasonal fresh fruits. Delicious and fun, and they "contain no refined sugar unless marked."

LODGING IN SHEFFIELD

From the minute you see **Ivanhoe Country House,** Rte. 41, Under Mountain Road, Sheffield, MA 01257 (tel. 413/229-2143), you know it's nicely kept. The white clapboard house with black shutters is neat and trim, and so, too, are the lawns and flowers. The oldest part of the house dates to 1780.

Dick and Carole Maghery have nine rooms, six with private bath (although all rooms will probably have a bath by the time this is published). All are furnished differently. There are two rooms on the first floor: one large room has a fireplace and a large porch that accommodates a private Ping-Pong table along with wicker furnishings; the room itself contains a bed with white eider down, two chests, an armoire, armchair, and a bathroom with clawfoot tub. Rag rugs made by a local lady are found throughout. The Sunrise Room, which shares a bath, has country painted bed, sidetable, chest, dresser, and rust-and-blue chintz wallpaper. The Lakeview Room, which does indeed have a view, is decorated in dusky rose. The Willow Room has a sleigh bed, Windsor rocker, and other appealing pieces. There's also a two-bedroom unit with a kitchenette and porch that is very private —ideal for families or two couples. Both bedrooms have a fireplace and brass bed.

The living room is comfortably large and welcoming, with Victorian sofas, chestnut paneling, brick fireplace, wing chairs, and plenty of books and magazines spread out on top of an early piano. The TV is here. French doors lead onto a brick terrace with umbrella tables where you can sit and contemplate the lake or look across the lawn over a rockery to a stand of pine trees. Begonias and other flowers brighten the gardens. You'll probably meet the four golden retrievers (Dick and Carole used to raise them). The pool is beautifully located on the crest of a hill, where chaises longues are lined up for sunworshippers. From the grounds there's a serene view of Berkshire Lake. Continental breakfast is served or will be delivered to your room.

RATES: May through October, $55 to $72; in March, April, and November, $45 to $58. The two-bedroom unit for four with private bath costs $115 and $95 respectively.

Staveleigh, South Main Street, Sheffield, MA 01257 (tel. 413/229-2129), is a private home set back from Rte. 7 that is operated by two widows, Dorothy Marosy and Marion Whitman. Throughout the house feminine touches are evident. Many of the quilts on the beds or the walls, including the large one on the staircase wall, were crafted by Marion while the rugs were hooked by Dorothy. Plants brighten the rooms too, and the landing is inhabited by teddy bears. There are five rooms (three upstairs and two downstairs), two with private bath. The most charming features a dresser (with mirror), rocker, and chaise longue, all made of wicker, white-painted chest, and wide-board floors; a quilt hangs over the bed rail. In the bathroom the floor has been decorated with sponge painting. Another favorite, on the ground floor, has a private entrance at the back. It's very radiantly decorated with peach comforter, wicker chairs, and marvelous quilts hanging on the wall behind the bed. Equally if not more charming is a room of Wedgwood-blue trim that matches two side tables, and goes nicely with the lemon-and-white quilt depicting a bonneted little girl in the foreground.

In the living room the name Staveleigh is carved above the grate, although neither owner knows the exact provenance. The center hall walls have been knocked down so that the living room flows into the dining room, where the table is spread with a lace tablecloth. Here a full breakfast is served—juice, fresh fruit, a hot dish like puffed oven pancakes, and homemade muffins and jams. The room is personalized by a cobalt-blue glass collection and a display case containing a salt cellar collection.

RATES: $65 for a room with private bath, $60 for a room with shared bath.

When Judith Timm had the task of furnishing **Centuryhurst,** Main Street, (Rte. 7), Sheffield, MA 01257 (tel. 413/229-8131), she had the distinct advantage of owning and operating the antique store on the same premises. It's no surprise, then, that the four rooms sharing two baths all come with genuine quilts and are well stocked with early American pieces and clocks (her husband, Ronald, is the collector). For example, one room has a modified maple rope bed covered with a butterfly quilt, a chest of drawers that has been "married" to a blanket chest, a rocker, a painted-on glass mirror, old ogee clock (another wall clock), and a horn set on top of the dresser—shoehorn, nail file, etc. The house was built in 1800 and the doors have old iron latches. The other rooms are similarly decorated with early American blanket chests, sewing tables, old (now electrical) oil lamps, pineapple poster beds, etc. On the landing Judith has created a small seating area furnished with Shaker settle and a classic gramophone with a painted trumpet. Clock mavens will love the store and the staircase walls lined with clocks of all sorts. Judith collects Wedgwood and other chinas. Guests are free to explore the whole house, even the kitchen with its original large fireplace with brick oven. There's a small swimming pool outside surrounded by a wood fence and a little sand box for the toddlers.

RATES: $48.

The **Stagecoach Hill Inn,** Rte. 41, Sheffield, MA 01257 (tel. 413/229-8585), exudes history. It's a rambling old brick building on 160 acres that dates back originally to 1794. By 1802 there was a barn on the property, which is now the dark, beamed tavern where the bar is decorated with car badges and other auto insignia; the place is frequented by many Lime Rock drivers and fans. It's made cozy by the double-brick hearth tiled on one side with Delft and by the oil lamps hanging from the beams. There's even a comfortable raised section with couches and TV. The brick building was constructed in 1820 and the smaller building in back was erected in the mid-1800s as a poorhouse. The place has since functioned variously as a summer house, guesthouse, and since 1946, as an inn.

The previous owners were English and certain traces of their influence remain. A sign invites lords, ladies, and gentlemen to follow the pointer past the tavern into the dining rooms which are adorned with royal portraits. Menus feature such specialties as steak-and-kidney pie and prime rib with Yorkshire pudding, along with duckling bigarade, baked scallops in herbed butter, or filet mignon béarnaise. Start with clams on the half shell or smoked oysters and finish with mousse, peach Melba, or fruit pie.

The 20 rooms, most with private bath, are located in various buildings. They are simply furnished and some even could be described as "shabbily genteel"; the nicest rooms, to my mind, are in the addition out back. Room 5, for instance, has a rope four-poster covered with a red-blue old quilt, a sidetable draped with floor-length tablecloth, wing chairs, dresser, and chest. The floor is covered with an area rug. Room 4 is even brighter, thanks to the fantail light. All rooms have complementary coffee. The least expensive rooms are back in the woods in chalets. Here the walls have been stenciled and old armchairs, beams, old prints, and area rugs have been introduced in an effort to enhance the original basic motel style of the rooms. They rent for $45. Facilities also include an outdoor pool.

RATES: $38 to $70 weekdays, $45 to $90 weekends (the higher price for a two-bedroom apartment for two couples). Weekend packages are also offered. DINNER: Monday, Tuesday, and Thursday to Sunday from 6 to 9 P.M., on Sunday from 5 to 9 P.M.; closed Wednesday.

The name, **Unique Bed and Breakfast,** Under Mountain Road (P.O. Box 729), Sheffield, MA 01257 (tel. 413/229-3363), derives from the fact that it is located in an unusual log house tucked away in the pine woods. A driveway lined with plants leads to the house, and May Stendardi cheerily operates it. Rooms all have private tiled baths, furnished with liquid soap and tissues. Each is attractively furnished with pine beds, polished pine-wood floors, cream-and-blue ruffled curtains, and gray wall-to-wall carpet with a pinkish hue. The ground-floor room has a high cathedral-style ceiling. One room has a private deck adorned with tubs of geraniums. Upstairs rooms are also prettily and variously decorated, with one wall sporting chintz wallpaper, cream-and-rust curtains at the windows, a Hitchcock rocker, and other furnishings. Blueberry pancakes, omelets, and sausage and eggs are likely breakfast dishes, along with home-baked items.

RATES: $55 to $75 in winter, $75 to $85 in summer.

DINING IN HARTSVILLE

Hillside Restaurant, a few miles southeast of Great Barrington on Rte. 57 (off Rte. 23) in Hartsville (tel. 413/528-3123). In an old farmhouse set on the crest of a hill with a beautiful Berkshire Valley view, this restaurant serves continental-Italian specialties priced from $12 to $17 for veal francese or marsala, steak au poivre, and similar dishes. Staffordshire china is used for service; the two dining rooms are warmed by fires in winter, while in summer there's a porch that takes full advantage of the view.

DINNER: Tuesday to Saturday from 5 to 9 P.M., on Sunday from 4 P.M. In summer, hours are extended and lunch is served.

NEW MARLBOROUGH/SANDISFIELD LODGING AND DINING

The **Old Inn on the Green,** New Marlborough, MA 01230 (tel. 413/229-7924), is indeed set back behind a green, only identifiable by a tiny sign hanging from the corner of this mid-18th-century building with classic double-porched façade. There are five rooms, one with private bath, the other four sharing two baths. Each one is eclectically furnished, in very country style. For example, the room might contain an iron-and-brass bed, desk, armoire, wing chair, and white-painted table and chair. Some rooms have access to the long balcony.

The four dining rooms are mostly in colonial style, where a prix-fixe dinner is served on Friday and Saturday. Dinner specialties vary from week to week, but the winter menus might include white bean soup with garlic sausage, sea bass with vermouth and chives, angel-hair pasta with fresh herbs, steamed snow peas and summer squash, and pear chocolate tart or raspberry mousse cake. Or you might find a wine-tasting dinner of Rhône wines, featuring bourride of shellfish, halibut, and vegetables served with a 1983 Hermitage Blanc; brioche stuffed with sausage and onions accompanied by a 1983 Tavel; breast of chicken sautéed with watercress and truffles enhanced by a 1981 Côte Rôtie Blond or loin of lamb in mustard-seed sauce complimented by a 1980 Hermitage Rouge; cheese and fruit with a 1979 Chateauneuf du Pape is followed by a crème caramel, smoothed by a Muscat de Beaure de Venisse. Such five-course dinners would cost $32 prix fixe; there's an additional charge for special wine tastings. The wine list is extensive. Breakfast is served in the room with a refectory table.

RATES: $75 to $110 in summer (from July 4), $70 to $90 in winter.

When I stopped by the **New Boston Inn,** Rtes. 57 and 8 (Village of New Boston), Sandisfield, MA 01255 (tel. 413/258-4477), it was still being restored —wallboard, plaster dust, and tools were everywhere. But I was treated to a tour of what was even then taking form. The oldest part of the 1735 building will remain as the tap room. The Federal front was added in 1790. Nine rooms with private bath are planned. The cove-ceilinged ballroom will be turned into a living room. According to local legend, Pearl Buck wrote *The Good Earth* here, Horowitz played in the ballroom, and Mrs. Anne Morrow Lindbergh wrote *Gift from the Sea* here. Please stop in and let me know if the finished product is as appealing as the plans, and the people carrying them out, suggest!

PITTSFIELD-DALTON AND THE NORTHWESTERN CORNER OF THE BERKSHIRES

AREA ATTRACTIONS

Pittsfield and Dalton, the industrial heart of the Berkshires, present a very different face from the picturesque villages that have been explored thus far. Neither one is pretty, but they do possess some attractions that are of interest. Indeed, you may wish to begin at the **Berkshire Museum,** 39 South St. (tel. 413/443-7171), in the center of Pittsfield, where some of the displays will help you come to grips with the history of the area. There are some fine paintings from the Hudson River School. Other exhibits concentrate on ancient civilizations and nature. HOURS: Tuesday to Sunday; daily in July and August.

Just south of Pittsfield lies **Arrowhead,** at 780 Holmes Rd., Pittsfield (tel. 413/442-1793), where Herman Melville lived from 1850 to 1863. As you stand in the room where he wrote *Moby-Dick, Pierre, The Confidence Man, Israel Potter,* and the *Piazza Tales,* you can imagine how often he must have contemplated the grim visage of Mount Greylock with despair, for his novels were failures and he was dogged by debt. Even sadder, when he died his wife threw out his books because she thought they were all worthless. Three rooms are devoted to his life and works and other memorabilia. The house is also the headquarters of the Berkshire County Historical Society. HOURS: Memorial Day to Labor Day, Monday to Saturday from 10 A.M. to 4:30 P.M., on Sunday from 11 A.M. to 3:30 P.M.; Labor Day to October 31, closed Tuesday and Wednesday; November to May, by appointment. ADMISSION: $3 for adults, $1.50 for children 6 to 16.

From Pittsfield you have access five miles along Rte. 20 to a really fascinating attraction, one that is *best* visited when the weather is clement, for a visit involves a lot of outdoor walking. This is the **Hancock Shaker Village**, Rte. 20 (P.O. Box 898), Pittsfield, MA 01202 (tel. 413/443-0188). There's still plenty to see indoors, so just don your boots and slickers on rainy days.

Allow at least three hours to tour this fascinating living museum dedicated to the Shakers, a communal religious sect that in 1790 established Hancock, the City of Peace, as the third of 18 Shaker communities settled in the United States.

Founded by Mother Ann Lee, the Shakers were dedicated to celibacy, simplicity, and equality. They were known for their excellence in agriculture and industry, and for their lively dance-worship, which gave the sect its name. Celibates, they took children and orphans into their community; the children were free to leave if they wanted to and many did. You can see the dorms where the men and women slept separately, their separate staircases, and the corridors where two narrow strips of carpet were placed—one for the women to walk on, the other for the men.

They rose at 4:30 A.M. in summer, at 5 A.M. in winter, to begin their daily round of farming, crafts making, and cooking. You can tour 20 original Shaker buildings, and along the way can watch the old crafts being performed—hearth and other kinds of cooking appropriate to the period, following Shaker recipes, tinsmithing, broom making, box making, weaving, etc. In the bakeshop, jams, jellies, and baked goods are for sale, while in the main shop fine crafts can be purchased—their famous wool cloaks, tables, chairs, candleholders, boxes, vinegars, and herbs. A delightful outing. HOURS: Memorial Day to October 31, from 9:30 A.M. to 5 P.M. daily. ADMISSION: $6.

Note: Don't go to Hancock Village itself. The Shaker Village is separated by a mountain barrier. Coming from the north, take Rte. 7 south to Rte. 20 west. From the south, take Rte. 22 to Rte. 295 and then east to Rte. 41 north.

The **South Mountain Chamber Concerts** are also given about one mile south of Pittsfield.

Due east of Pittsfield lies the other industrial town of Dalton, where you can explore part of its heritage at the **Crane Museum**, South Street (tel. 413/684-2600), located off Rte. 9, by viewing the exhibits that document the art of fine paper making since 1801. Unfortunately, this one will have to be done on a weekday, for the hours are only Monday to Friday from 2 to 5 P.M., June to October.

PITTSFIELD-DALTON LODGING

For those who prefer a modern, lively hotel, Pittsfield offers the **Berkshire Hilton Inn**, Pittsfield, MA 01201 (tel. 413/499-2000), with 175 air-conditioned rooms, an indoor pool, three lounges, and a restaurant.

RATES: $85 to $95 double, rising to $130 in summer. No summer packages are offered, but until April 1 you can usually obtain some kind of weekend package.

The **White Horse Inn,** 378 South St. (Rtes. 7 and 20), Pittsfield, MA 01201 (tel. 413/443-0961), is a beige clapboard home with cream shutters and an elegant portico supported by classical pillars. When you arrive the house may be filled with the marvelous aroma of apple or blueberry pie, or some alluring variety of simmering herbs. All nine rooms have private baths, and are neat and clean, and furnished with oak desks, beds, dressers, or similar. Rooms 2 and 3 have working fireplaces. The manager told me there were also plans afoot to convert the shingled barn into five rooms.

The breakfast room overlooks the lawn, and trees in back. Fresh flowers adorn the glass-topped tables. An ample continental breakfast of fruit, yogurt, and homemade breads is served here. Books, fireplace, upright piano, and couch and armchairs make the parlor comfortable.

RATES: $40 to $50 double. Open April to October.

The **Dalton House,** 955 Main St., Dalton, MA 01226 (tel. 413/684-3854), will always have seasonal flowers—geraniums, marigolds, fuchsia—displayed on the long front porch, for owners Gary and Bernice Turetsky also happen to run the adjacent florist (where over 2,500 geraniums and other plants are reared). The main house was built by a Hessian soldier in 1810 and contains two rooms with an additional four in the extension. All have private bath, and are pleasantly appointed. The six rooms in the carriage house out back are especially nicely decorated to achieve a country look that mingles the contemporary and the old-fashioned. The public areas in the house itself are warm and cozy, made so by the large fireplace in the sitting room that also contains a piano; some people like to retire to the loft area above for cards or TV or some other form of relaxation, especially after a day's skiing (this is a popular spot for ski groups). Breakfast is served buffet style in the dining area, which is warmed by a wood stove. In summer, loungers and umbrella-topped tables are out on the patio.

RATES: $60 to $80 in July and August, $50 to $70 in winter (including breakfast).

PITTSFIELD DINING

An entrance surrounded by Chianti bottles and a fountain playing just inside the door welcome you to the homey **Giovanni's,** located on Rte. 7 just south of Pontoosuc Lake (tel. 413/443-2441). Checked tablecloths, Tiffany-style lamps, and a few hanging plants and unframed pictures of Venice set the scene for tasty Italian dishes. Typical appetizers—gnocchi, salami and sliced tomatoes, calamari fritti—are priced from $5. Pastas run from $4.25 for plain spaghetti with sausage or meatballs to $10 for spaghetti with shrimp and clam sauce. Main courses encompass everything from veal and peppers and chicken cacciatore for a mere $7 to Giovanni's combination—a strip sirloin served with either fried shrimp or scallops or crab legs, for $14. Filet mignon, veal marsala, broiled swordfish, and scrod are other menu choices. Pastas and sandwiches predominate at lunch. Upstairs, Clementine's is an attractive bar with high cathedral ceilings, cross beams lined with steins, and plenty of gleaming brass.

HOURS: Noon to 9 P.M. weekdays, Friday and Saturday until 10 P.M. The bar is open from 4 P.M. to midnight, until 1 A.M. on weekends.

LODGING AND DINING OVER THE NEW YORK BORDER

The **Inn at Shaker Mill,** Cherry Lane (off Rte. 22), Canaan, NY 12029 (tel. 518/794-9345). Idyllically situated by a flowing brook and waterfall, this lovely old stone 1824 grist mill affords peace and quiet. Here you can sit in the living room, actually listening to the water running over the rocks. The couches are modern and so are the wood stoves; Shaker stools serve as coffee tables; books are plentiful. Ingram Paperny, who has lived here for 20 years, restored the mill, handcrafting most of the built-in furniture himself. Some people may find the 20 rooms themselves too austere for their taste, the Shaker inspiration too strong. Furnishings consist of wood sidetable, chest, wide-board floors, and beams. The most appealing accommodation to my mind is a top-floor skylit apartment with wicker furnishings and kitchen. There's a TV in the living room. The best pastimes, though, are sitting out by the brook and looking across the fields dotted with cows or taking a stroll through the countryside.

Meals are obligatory on weekends during the summer season. A Sunday five-course meal is $18.50. Otherwise, prices run from $16.25 to $41 for simple fish, chicken, and vegetarian dishes.

The prime reason for visiting the inn, though, is the warm welcome given by Ingram, who relishes conversation and obviously has warm interest and affection for his guests.

RATES: In summer, $130 to $150 per person (MAP) for a full weekend; $120 to $135 at other times. Daily bed-and-breakfast on weekends in high season costs $45 to $55. Bring your own wine.

The **Sedgwick Inn,** Rte. 22, Berlin, NY 12022 (tel. 518/658-2334), is an exquisite home filled with antiques personally collected by Robert and Edith Evans, who restored and opened this inn as "a retirement project" after long careers in psychology. Accommodations consist of four rooms, with private bath and a two-room suite, plus six motel-style units. The one room I viewed contained two brass beds and a bird's-eye maple dresser. If the others reflect the quality of the public areas, they ought to be beautiful.

The place is very comfortable and full of interesting artifacts. In the living room is a Degas figure on a pedestal and a case filled with ivory pieces, figureheads, toby jugs, and other small appealing collectibles. A sofa, wing chairs, an Oriental rug, and a fireplace ensure comfort. Reproductions of Breughels, a fan fetchingly framed, and other objects grace the walls. A marvelous etched-glass door depicting peacocks—a great find—leads to the porch breakfast room that has a view of the garden out back and is fittingly furnished with white metal chairs and tables on a brick floor. The library offers magazines, books, and comfortable chairs. In the corner, the cupboard is filled with jewelry and small antique items for sale. An antique shop and gallery are behind the inn. Wicker chairs line the front porch.

Burgundy placemats on polished wood tables are found in the Coach Room Tavern, a very popular restaurant for which you'll certainly need a reservation on weekends. Occasionally a classical guitarist plays here. The chef is Edith Evans, who turns out several soups a day from minted sweet pea and Russian cabbage to cucumber dill. Three entrees are usually offered, a beef, fish, and poultry dish —Cornish hen Montmorency, sauerbraten, and poached filet of sole Nantua, for example. Edith is Viennese and desserts are her specialty—raspberry Bavarian pie, mocha hazelnut torte, key lime pie, among the choices.

RATES: $45 single, $55 double, $75 for a suite; motel accommodations are $35 to $45. LUNCH: Wednesday to Sunday from 11 A.M. to 2 P.M. DINNER: Wednesday to Saturday from 5 to 9 P.M., on Sunday from 1 to 9 P.M.

It's not surprising that the **Millhoff Inn,** Rte. 43, Stephentown, NY 12168 (tel. 518/733-5606), really does look like a Central European mountain chalet, for owners Frank and Romana Tallet hail from Yugoslavia. They will welcome you into their truly cozy living room with a piano and a round-arched stone fireplace that throws out much-needed heat on winter days. There's a small game room, and the Tallets go to great lengths to ensure that everyone is content—croquet is available, and there's a small swimming pool in back. They are also very well versed and forthcoming about the attractions of the area. Rooms all have private bath with continental-style shower; they're electically furnished, some with pine. In summer, breakfast is served on the terrace. Only ten minutes from Mount Greylock.

RATES: $75 to $85 double, $90 to $120 for suites. Three-night minimum in July and August.

For a change from standard American cuisine, there's a Japanese restaurant, **Shujis,** in New Lebanon (tel. 518/794-8383), located just across the New York –Massachusetts border on Rte. 22 south at Rte. 20, occupying what used to be Governor Tilden's stone mansion complete with turrets. Inside, a little bridge will take you over the Japanese rock garden studded with pagodas into the dining rooms, where you can sample a sushi or sashimi dinner, chicken teriyaki, or suki-yaki priced from $10 to $20.

DINNER: Tuesday to Thursday from 6 to 9 P.M., on Friday until 10 P.M., on Saturday from 5 to 10 P.M., on Sunday from 5 to 9 P.M.; closed Monday. Open Easter to mid-November.

Les Pyrenees, off Rte. 295, in Canaan, N.Y. (tel. 518/781-4451). Master chef Jean Petit has been attracting patrons to this secluded restaurant for 30 years. A stone stairway covered by a red, white, and blue awning leads to the restaurant; flowers bloom on either side. The front room is a low-lit bar. The dining room behind glows. Red gingham tablecloths and gilt portraits, many of family and friends, adorn the Chinese lacquer red walls. The atmosphere is relaxed. Dishes are primarily French classics—chicken in burgundy, poached halibut in white wine and cream sauce, escalope de veau viennoise, poulet au champagne, or frogs' legs, priced from $12 to $32, the higher price for pheasant with pâté de foie gras and truffles. Among the desserts, the crème brûlée is extra special. Cash only.

DINNER: In summer, Tuesday to Saturday from 5 to 10 P.M., on Sunday to 10 P.M.; in winter and spring, Thursday to Saturday only.

HANCOCK/JIMINY PEAK LODGING AND DINING

The **Hancock Inn,** Rte. 43, Hancock, MA 01237 (tel. 413/738-5873), is a highly idiosyncratic kind of place—an expression of Ellen and Chester Gorski. A small cement path lined with iris and marigolds leads to the small porch-foyer filled with ferns and cane rockers. Open the door into the hall and you'll discover a very Victorian hallway. Old stern Victorian portraits stare down from the walls; a Victorian-style couch and sideboard stand imperiously. To the right, a doorway surmounted with a semicircular stained-glass window leads into the dining room, where tables are set with white tablecloths and napkins, a sprig of fresh flowers, and glass candleholders. A large wall clock ticks away. Grapevine wreaths and cream ball-fringe curtains add a country touch. In winter it's warmed by a fire in the wood-burning stove.

The food has been highly rated by the *Albany Times Union* critic and by Steve Birnbaum. The menu's limited, featuring eight or so dishes like duckling braised in port wine with grapes, filet mignon with fine herbs, fish of the day, or chicken breast stuffed with wild mushrooms. Prices run $13 to $15. Desserts are created by Ellen—homemade ice creams, white-chocolate mousse cheesecake, crème brûlée with strawberries. They'll be served on fine Depression glass of a harmonious color: cobalt blue, green, or burgundy.

Eight rooms with private bath are very idiosyncratically styled, not in a lushly decorated perfect way. Number 1 has stenciled walls, a country pine dresser and bed, sidetable, wardrobe, desk with a handful of old books, and a costumed doll in the corner. The bathroom has wainscoting while the room has bold pink- and white-rose wallpaper. Other rooms might have an old country teardrop dresser, a bird's-eye maple or Jenny Lind bed, a comfortable chair like an old carpet chair rocker, or a rare Larkin desk. The place has great charm and Ellen is a warm, entertaining hostess.

RATES: $65 double with private bath, $45 double with shared bath, $12 for an additional person. DINNER: Wednesday to Sunday from 5 to 9 P.M.

Jiminy Peak Inn and Mountain Resort, Corey Road, Hancock, MA 01237 (tel. 413/738-5500), is a well-designed, very attractive complex at the base of the mountain of the same name. Let's begin with the 105 rooms of this extensive property. All are suites and all are individually owned, although some 86 are in the rental program. Each is modern, containing a kitchen fully equipped with dishwasher, stove, fridge, toaster, kettle, etc., and a living room with a couch that makes up into a queen-size bed, TV hidden in a cabinet, plus comfortable seating and a service bar. A bathroom with two sinks (a vanity outside) and bedroom with brass bed and pine furnishings complete the layout. The six-on-six and eight-on-eight windows give each an old-fashioned air.

The dining room, Drummonds, has a full view of the mountain, while the bar area has a stone fireplace and comfy wing chairs and couch in which to rest those ski-sore limbs. The food is typical American/continental fare—chicken breast parmesan, prime rib, and baked scallops, priced from $9.50 to $14.50. Luncheon items include sandwiches, salads, and burgers. It's also good for breakfast.

The list of additional facilities is long. In front are two tennis courts (another seven are planned) and an outdoor pool from which you can see tree-covered mountains. Facing the mountain is another outdoor heated pool that's used year round and is great for sunning. Just off this pool area there's also a Jacuzzi, exercise room with Universal equipment, sauna, and resident masseuse. The game room on the lower level furnished with video games is only one area that the kids enjoy. Bicycles are available for rent, and the slide is thrilling fun in summer

($3.50 a ride, $12 for a five-ride book, or 1½ hours' worth for $8.75). The miniature golf here is unique: beautifully landscaped, each hole is a scale reproduction of a famous hole. Hazards include water, shrubs, small firs, etc., and little stone walls, waterfalls, and petunias are part of the landscaping. Trout fishing is $2.50 per hour. Patio and picnic tables stand outside the round house, which is the tavern in winter, a sandwich place in summer. A new base lodge was being constructed when I visited. The grounds are well kept—colorful window boxes, fences with rambling roses betray that extra attention to detail.

RATES: One-bedrooms, $90 in midweek, $105 on weekends ($45 for a third night to a weekend); two-bedrooms, $120 in midweek, $140 on weekends ($60 for a third night to a weekend); three-bedrooms, $170 in midweek, $190 on weekends, ($85 for a third night). Additional persons are charged $10 a night. These prices require a two-night minimum stay. LUNCH AND DINNER: Drummonds is open for lunch and dinner daily. Breakfast depends on season.

WILLIAMSTOWN

WILLIAMSTOWN ATTRACTIONS

Originally established in 1753 as a plantation called West Hoosuck, it was renamed after Col. Ephraim Williams in 1755, when he left an estate for founding a free school with the proviso that the township's name be changed to Williamstown, which, of course, it was. And that's why **Williams College,** whose buildings are scattered along Main Street against a mountain backdrop, is here in this pretty town of rolling hills and dales. If you like, you can tour the college by going to the Admissions Office in Hopkins Hall. The college's museum of art (tel. 413/597-2429) in Lawrence Hall on Main Street and the Hopkins Observatory are also worth visiting. But the outstanding attractions here are really the Clark Institute and the Williamstown Festival.

The **Sterling and Francine Clark Art Institute,** 225 South St. (tel. 413/458-9545), houses a distinguished personal art collection purchased between 1912 and 1955. Most famous for a room of Renoirs and the works of such 19th-century French artists as Boudin, Gérôme, Fantin Latour, Alma-Tadema, Millet, and Daubigny, the collection also contains some other fine works—Mary Cassatt pastels; Venetian scenes by John Singer Sargent; several Winslow Homers, including *Undertow* (1886), a luminous picture of lifeguards pulling two girls from the waves; Remington bronzes; some glorious Corots; Turner's *Rockets and Blue Lights;* and two Berthe Morisots, along with representatives from many other schools and periods.

What makes the collection so remarkable is that Clark only bought what he liked, and his taste was impeccable. His favorite work among them all was Renoir's *Onions,* because he especially appreciated the artistry that could transform the mundane onion into a shimmering object of beauty. Part of the museum is set aside for special exhibits. HOURS: Tuesday to Sunday from 10 A.M. to 5 P.M.; closed Monday; open Memorial, Labor, and Columbus Days, but closed Thanksgiving, Christmas, and New Year's Days. ADMISSION: Free.

The Adams Memorial Theatre (tel. 413/597-3400) is home to the **Williamstown**

Theatre Festival, under the direction of Nikos Psacharopoulos, which has established itself over more than two dozen seasons as the premier summer theater in the Berkshires. The festival's stars have included Richard Chamberlain, Blythe Danner, Richard Dreyfuss, E. G. Marshall, Roberta Maxwell, Christopher Reeve, and many, many more Actors' Equity members performing on the festival's Main Stage in classics by Williams, Brecht, Chekhov, Shaw, Ibsen, and others, and on the Other Stage in new works by Beth Henley, A. R. Gurney, Jr., Derek Walcott, and Gretchen Cryer and Nancy Ford. For information, write to the festival at P.O. Box 517, Williamstown, MA 01267.

WILLIAMSTOWN LODGING AND DINING

Williamstown at last has a tasteful, if modern, accommodation, **The Orchards,** Rte. 2 East, Williamstown, MA 02167 (tel. 413/458-9611, or toll free 800/225-1517). While the exterior may not look that inviting, the interior is extremely pleasing, and best of all, the layout centers on a large triangular garden with rockery and pond. Here you can relax on the deck with its umbrella tables and enjoy cocktails or after-theater supper. On Sunday from July 13 on, jazz, chamber music, a brass quintet, or similar entertains here. The focal point of your arrival will be the large living room the floors of which are covered in Oriental jade and pink rugs. The fireplace mantel comes from England, the marble from Vermont. Bookshelves span each side of the mantel, and the elegance is further underlined by the grand piano, large crystal chandelier, antique furnishings, and what will certainly be a bounteous bouquet of fresh flowers. A personal touch is revealed in the glass cases containing the owner's collection of model soldiers ranging from a French Algerian cavalryman to a Norman knight.

The 49 extra-large rooms have been carefully designed and handsomely decorated in smoky blues and dusty pinks with wallpaper panel moldings. Fifteen rooms possess fireplaces. The marble-floored bathrooms are fully tiled and have the added convenience of double sinks, a separate tub and shower, as well as many extra touches like Crabtree & Evelyn soap, scallop-shell soap dish, shampoo, sewing kit, etc. The rooms feature solid-wood closet doors, TV in an armoire, nightlight, bathrobes, refrigerator, and bar with a basket of fruit and bottles of Perrier, and plenty of working and seating space at desk, armchairs, and table. The so-called smaller rooms (hardly small) lack the separate tub and shower and the refrigerator. The Tennessee Williams Suite is huge, decked out in Wedgwood blue with a pencil four-poster without canopy.

Plush dark-green walls, pastel-patterned banquettes, Queen Anne chairs, dusty-rose napkins and tablecloths, fresh flowers in stem vases, and fine China settings provide the appropriate backdrop for fine food in the dining room. Although the soup and salad left a little to be desired (iceberg lettuce with wilted cucumber) the main courses lived up to expectation. The poached halibut with wine sauce topped with baby shrimp was fresh, and moist. My filet mignon was tender and juicy, and both were served with a full complement of vegetables —carrots, cauliflower, green beans, boiled potatoes garnished with parsley. The rhubarb pie was delicious. Other choices might include swordfish served with mustard-butter sauce, duckling with raspberry sauce, escalope of veal Henry

Teague (with mushrooms and lemon, served with port wine sauce). For dessert, Sachertorte, Linzertorte, and chocolate decadence are possibilities.

Additional facilities include an exercise room equipped with stationary bikes, sauna/whirlpool, and most intriguing of all, an environmental chamber that provides suntan, rain, whirlpool, sauna, and steambath in one. When I visited a small outdoor pool was under construction. The lounge draws a crowd and is particularly attractive in winter when a fire roars in the large stone fireplace. It's also well equipped with board and other games for those long, dark evenings and, of course, with comfortable lounge chairs.

RATES: $95 for small rooms, $125 for standard rooms, to $140 for suites. The Orchards also offers special two-night plans and ski packages. BREAKFAST: Monday to Saturday from 7:30 to 10 A.M. LUNCH: Noon to 2 P.M. daily. DINNER: Sunday to Thursday from 6 to 8:30 P.M., on Friday and Saturday to 9 P.M.

On Rte. 7 you'll find the comfortable **Northside Motel**, 45 North St., Williamstown, MA 01267 (tel. 413/458-8107), run by Isabell and Alex Nagy, which has an unusually homey atmosphere and a cozy breakfast room.

RATES: $38 double in winter, $50 double in summer.

Williamstown Dining

If you arrive late in Williamstown (after 10 P.M.) the **Erasmus Café,** 76 Spring St. (tel. 413/458-5007), is one place you can still find sustenance. It also doubles as a bookstore, so you can browse the shelves while waiting for sandwiches and salads and specials, all reasonably priced. Black- and white-striped tablecloths under glass are placed at the front of the store. There is also an outdoor café. No liquor.

HOURS: 9 A.M. to midnight daily.

Simple food, a glowing fireplace in winter, and classical music playing in the background make the **River House,** 123 Water St., Rte. 43 (tel. 413/458-4820), a fine relaxing place for either a good soup, salad, and sandwich snack or a tasty dinner, with choices like steak, turkey, seafood, and eggplant marinara or parmigiana, all priced from $9 to $14.

DINNER: To midnight daily.

Two miles south of Williamstown on Rtes. 2 and 7, **Le Jardin** (tel. 413/458-8032) serves excellent food in some very elegant surroundings. You may begin your meal with caviar, or less extravagantly with a fine homemade soup, and follow with one of the daily specials, a choice from the menu that features a stuffed breast of chicken, prime rib, or their specialties, poached salmon and a superb rack of lamb. Prices range from $12 to $20.

There are also six accommodations (four with fireplaces) available here in this lovely country-house atmosphere. Rooms with fireplace are $90; without fireplace, $60.

DINNER: 5 to 10 P.M.; closed Monday during November. BRUNCH: Sunday from 10:30 A.M. to 1:30 P.M.

The **Springs Restaurant,** Rte. 7, New Ashford (tel. 413/458-3465), between Pittsfield and Williamstown, is a rather typical roadside restaurant that has won several Mobil culinary awards. It's not exactly romantic or overly decorated, but the food is good and wholesome, and there's plenty of it. The menu is vast and any main dish (veal Oscar, Boston scrod, chicken cacciatore) will be accompanied by a baked clam and relishes, salad, vegetables, and soup, in proper table d'hôte fashion. Prices range from $10 to $18.

HOURS: Monday to Saturday from 11:30 A.M. to 9:30 P.M., on Sunday until 9 P.M.

MOUNT GREYLOCK

While you're in the Berkshires, climb or drive to the summit of Mount Greylock and there ascend the spiral stairway to the top of the tower. From here you have a 360° vista looking over 50 miles to the Catskills and over 100 miles to the distant Adirondacks.

You can even sojourn here at **Bascom Lodge,** P.O. Box 686, Lanesboro, MA 01237 (tel. 413/743-1591), built in the 1930s to accommodate hikers. Lodgings are in three bunkrooms accommodating six. The stone hearth stands ready for the winter chill. Snacks and sandwiches are available from a counter, and can be eaten at the refectory tables.

RATES: $12 for adults, $6 for children under 10. Open from mid-May until late October.

NORTH ADAMS AND ADAMS

AREA ATTRACTIONS

From Williamstown it's only a short drive to North Adams, gateway town to the Mohawk Trail, which leads out to Whitcomb Summit where there's a place for you to stop for breakfast or any other meal, and then on to Florida, Charlemont, and all the way to Shelburne Falls and eventually into the Pioneer Valley.

North Adams and Adams, a few miles to the south, were famous in the 19th century as manufacturing towns producing paper, textiles, and leather goods. You may want to stop at some of the mill outlets that offer discounted prices on clothing. Adams is also famous for being the birthplace of Susan B. Anthony whose home at 67 East Rd. is being restored.

Recently in North Adams a heritage state park has been opened which gives further insight into the town's history. Two other state parks are also accessible from North Adams: Mount Greylock, and a much smaller park featuring a natural marble bridge.

At **Western Gateway, Heritage State Park,** Furnace Street in North Adams (tel. 413/663-8059), start at the Visitor Center where displays relate the story of how the remarkable 4½-mile-long, $14-million tunnel was blasted and built through the mountains in 1851. Some 200 men died during the 25 years it took to build. It was quite a feat because at that time no one knew how to make sure that the two tunnels from each side of the mountain would meet in the middle! When the final blast was made, the total error in alignment was a mere one inch! The story is told in movies, displays, and photographs. The tunnel helped fuel the town's growth, and the most fascinating photo exhibits reveal the course of this growth and the community's daily life and history. In 1898, unlike today, North Adams was a thriving community of 25,000 that supported 500 businesses, including 58 grocery stores, 19 saloons, 17 barbers, 16 shoe stores, 11 cigar factories, 9 blacksmiths, 11 bicycle dealers, 8 hotels, 7 photographers, 5 florists, 5 undertakers, and two daily and three weekly newspapers. From the displays you'll learn what the average wage was, how much staples cost, and much, much more lively history. HOURS: 10 A.M. to 6 P.M. daily (on Thursday to 9 P.M.).

Afterward, browse in the many stores—a country bakery, country gift store, ice cream parlor—each housed in restored 19th-century structures set around a cobbled courtyard.

Just outside the center of North Adams on Rte. 8 north there's a natural phenomenon worth visiting, the **Natural Bridge State Park** (tel. 413/663-6392). Rangers will point out and explain the outstanding features of the park. Among these are "glacial erratics," great striated glacial stones, a narrow, deep gorge (50 feet from ceiling to floor) cut at the rate of one-sixteenth of an inch per year by the stream, botanically rare species like maidenhair ferns and horsetails, and a marble dam and a marble stack that still stands because the quarry workers needed it to retreat behind after they set their charges. The natural bridge was formed during the last glacial formations 20,000 years ago, although technically it's a 550-million-year-old marble formation created from shells that existed in the prehistoric ocean. Over millions of years, sand, silt, and mud was changed into limestone and eventually into marble. From the 1800s to 1940 a marble quarry was operated, until the mill in which the marble was ground to make lime burned down. Yes, it's true. Make sure you go down to the platform that gives the best view of the bridge. Stairways criss-cross the huge rocks, making it easy for you. Such steps were not there for the intrepid youths who carved their names on the rocks. See if you can find the Williams College fraternity sign or the signature of J. S. Barnforth dated 1740. It's said that Nathaniel Hawthorne carved his name, but it's never been found. He did mention the bridge in his *Visitations*. On weekends guided tours and talks are given approximately every 45 minutes.

ADAMS/NORTH ADAMS LODGING AND DINING

Anita and Walter Avery have restored and opened their dream Victorian house to guests, naming it the **Butternut Inn,** 6 East St., Adams, MA 01220 (tel. 413/743-9394). Here everything sparkles—possibly the result of Anita's longtime nursing experience. The entrance hall sports a coal-burning-style fireplace and an old pump organ tucked beside the solid cherry staircase. The three rooms are all prettily turned out; one room has a small private porch. Each has an alarm clock, and at night you'll find your bed turned down, a mint placed on your pillow, and the lights turned on for you—welcome touches that make you feel cared for. The largest room has a pineapple four-poster covered with a white bedspread, a heavy Empire-style chest, wicker rocker, a pale-blue cloth falling full to the floor from a circular table, and an interesting touch—a quill placed in a holder.

A small room doubles as a game room. Breakfast is served at the end of the living room, which has bay windows. Family photographs, a couch, and a bookcase make this a typically comfortable living room. Anita prepares porridge, juice, large pots of tea and coffee, and such baked items as Johnny cakes or cornbread with strawberry-rhubarb fruit sauce or orange butter.

RATES: $45 to $50.

The **Freight Yard Pub** in the Heritage State Park, North Adams (tel. 413/663-6547), is popular for reasonably priced meals. Specials are written on a blackboard and may well include a dinner for two consisting of chicken Cordon Bleu and fried clams for $11 or top sirloin and scallops for $14. The decor is typical modern pub—wood tables, brick fireplace, pine bar, and a popcorn machine. On weekends a DJ spins the music.

HOURS: 11:30 A.M. to 1 A.M. daily.

CULTURAL EVENTS IN THE BERKSHIRES

Dance

Jacob's Pillow, P.O. Box 287J, Lee, MA 01238 (tel. 413/243-0745), is a superb ten-week dance festival from the end of June to Labor Day which has featured such greats as the Paul Taylor Dance Company, Cynthia Gregory, Clive Thompson, and Elisa Monte. Picnic grounds plus bar and café facilities. Tickets run $9 to $16. Jazz concerts are also presented on selected Sunday afternoons and evenings. Jacob's Pillow is located off Rte. 20 on George Carter Road in Becket, east of Lee.

Music

Tanglewood, West Street (Rte. 183), Lenox, MA 01240 (tel. 413/637-1600). Spread your picnic on the lawn on this 210-acre site overlooking the lovely Stockbridge Bowl. Fuchsias and begonias make the scene even lovelier in summer, when the festival runs for nine weeks, from early July to the end of August. Get there two hours before if you want space near the Music Shed. Evening performances are given on Friday at 7 and 9 P.M., Saturday at 8:30 P.M., with matinees on Sunday. For information before June 15, call Symphony Hall in Boston (tel. 617/266-1492).

South Mountain Concerts, P.O. Box 23, Pittsfield, MA 01202 (tel. 413/442-2106), features such chamber music greats as the Beaux Arts Trio, and the Tokyo and Guarneri String Quartets. Schedules vary, but concerts are usually held on Saturday or Sunday afternoons from the end of August to mid-October, approximately every two weeks. Tickets run $12 to $15. Performances are given in a summer home built in 1918 by the concert's founder, Mrs. Elizabeth Sprague Coolidge.

Theater

The **Williamstown Theatre Festival** undoubtedly represents the cream of the theatrical crop in the Berkshires. For information, call 413/597-3400 or write P.O. Box 517, Williamstown, MA 01267.

MacHaydn Theater, Rte. 203, Chatham, NY 12037 (tel. 518/392-9292). Here some of the best authentic summer stock can be found—refreshing, enthusiastic productions of *My Fair Lady, Sweet Charity, Oklahoma!*

The **Berkshire Theatre Festival,** Main Street, Stockbridge, MA 01262 (tel. 413/ 298-5536, or 413/298-5576 after June 1 for the box office), offers a four-play season from the end of June to the end of August in a Stanford White–designed building constructed in 1886 as a casino. Such figures as Katharine Hepburn and James Cagney started their careers here.

Shakespeare & Company, The Mount, Plunkett Street (off Rte. 7), Lenox, MA 01240 (tel. 413/637-1197, or 413/637-3353 after June 17 for the box office). Bring a picnic before the outdoor performance at this dramatic mansion setting. The season runs from July to the end of August.

Music Theater Group, at Lenox Art Center, P.O. Box 544, Stockbridge, off Rte. 183 (tel. 413/298-9463), performs avant-garde music theater works during July and August, Wednesday to Sunday.

ACTIVITIES IN THE BERKSHIRES

ANTIQUING: South Egremont is an excellent hunting ground, and so is Rte. 7 around Sheffield and Rte. 7A through Ashley Falls. Other stores are dotted throughout the Berkshires.

BOATING: *Lee:* Laurel Lake, on Rte. 20. *Lenox:* Sailboats are available at Foxhollow Inn, Rte. 7 (tel. 413/637-2000). *Pittsfield:* At Pontoosuc Lake, watersports equipment is available for rent by the hour—motorboats ($12.50 with a 10-h.p. engine, $21 for 50 h.p., and $29 for 75 h.p.), waterskis ($5), canoes ($4), rowboats ($4), and paddleboats ($5); jet-skis rent for $14 per 20 minutes, and sailboats are also available. For information, contact U-Drive Boat Rentals, 123 Burke Ave., Pittsfield, MA 01201, or 1551 North St. (Rte. 7), Pontoosuc Lake (tel. 413/442-7020). The Ponterril YMCA, in Pittsfield (tel. 413/443-1132), also has boats for rent at its Pontoosuc Lake facility (open from Memorial Day to September 1): canoes and rowboats rent for $5 an hour, Sunfish for $10 an hour, and a sailboat with a mainsail and jib for $15 an hour.

CAMPING: In the *Lenox* area: Woodland Hills Family Campground, Austerlitz, NY 12017 (tel. 518/392-3557), offers camping convenient to Tanglewood at 160 sites with water, electric, and sewer hookups, and a full range of facilities. Open from May 1 to Columbus Day.

In *North Egremont:* try Prospect Lake Park, Prospect Lake Road, North Egremont, MA 01252 (tel. 413/528-4158), only six miles from Great Barrington. Ideal for families because of the great number of facilities—boat rentals (Sunfishes, paddleboats, canoes), tennis, lake fishing, and two swimming beaches. Open from mid-May to October.

In the *Pittsfield-Dalton* area: Pittsfield State Forest, Cascade Street (tel. 413/ 442-8992), has sites at various locations throughout the park. In Windsor State

Forest, River Road, Windsor (tel. 413/684-9760), there's camping in the scenic Windsor Jambs area.

CANOEING: The Connecticut, Battenkill, Hoosic, or Upper Housatonic Rivers will provide some easy paddling. The more experienced will want to try the Westfield or Deerfield Rivers after a good rain. For information, rentals, and sales write: Berkshire Outfitters Canoe and Kayak Center, Rte. 8, Cheshire Harbor, Adams, MA 01220 (tel. 413/743-4380 or 743-5900); or Riverrun/North, Rte. 7, Sheffield, MA 01257 (tel. 413/528-1100).

FISHING: *Lee:* Laurel Lake, ramp off Rte. 20. *Pittsfield:* Pontoosuc Lake, ramp off Hancock Road near Rte. 7. Onota Lake is known for trophy-size bass and lake trout. *Stockbridge:* Stockbridge Bowl, ramp off Rte. 183.

GOLF: *Great Barrington:* Egremont Country Club, Rte. 23 (tel. 413/528-4222), with 18 holes; Wyantenuck, West Sheffield Rd. (tel. 413/528-0350), with 18 holes, par 70. *Lenox:* Cranwell Golf Course, 55 Lee Rd. (tel. 413/637-0441), with 18 holes, par 71. *Pittsfield:* Pontoosuc Lake Country Club, Ridge Avenue (tel. 413/445-4217), with 18 holes, par 70. *South Egremont:* Egremont Country Club, Rte. 23 (tel. 413/528-4222). *South Lee:* Oak 'n' Spruce Resort (tel. 413/243-3500). *Williamstown:* Taconic Golf Course, Meacham Street (tel. 413/458-3997), with 18 holes, par 71; Waubeeka Golf Links, Rte. 7 (tel. 413/458-5869), with 18 holes, par 72.

HIKING: Plenty of mountain terrain. *Lanesboro:* This is the gateway to Mount Greylock. A visitors' center is located on Rockwell Road, just off Rte. 7, although the most scenic route up the mountain is probably via Notch Road from North Adams. *Lenox:* Pleasant Valley Wildlife Sanctuary, off Rte. 7 between Lenox and Pittsfield (tel. 413/637-0320), offers seven miles of hiking trails. It's owned by the Massachusetts Audubon Society, which also operates a nature museum. *Pittsfield:* Berry Mountain in the Pittsfield State Forest is great for blueberrying, viewing the azalea fields, picnicking, and camping, as well as just plain walking. *South Egremont:* Walk the path to the summit of 2,626-foot Mount Everett for fine views of New York, Massachusetts, Vermont, and Connecticut. Access is from Rte. 23 or 41 via South Egremont or from Rte. 22 via Copake Falls. *Sheffield:* Just south of Sheffield and west of Rte. 7, Bartholomew's Cobble gives prime views of the Housatonic. *Stockbridge:* Hike to the summit of Monument Mountain (1,642 feet), on Rte. 7 between Great Barrington and Stockbridge. *Williamstown:* Hopkins Memorial Forest, Bulkey Road off Rte. 7, has 25,000 acres on the slopes of the Taconic Mountains, plus miles of trails, including self-guided nature trails. Museum also. *Windsor:* Notchview has 15 miles of hiking trails.

For info about the Appalachian Trail, write to Pittsfield State Forest, Cascade Street, Pittsfield, MA 01201.

HORSEBACK RIDING: *Dalton:* Wahconah Stables, Rte. 9 to Cleveland Road (tel. 413/ 684-1178). *Lenox:* At Foxhollow Inn, Rte. 7 (tel. 413/637-2000).

PICNICKING: See the Lenox and Stockbridge dining sections for picnic suppliers. Tanglewood is not the only spot for picnicking; other places abound—Berry Mountain (in the Pittsfield State Forest), Mount Everett (reached from Rtes. 23 or 41 via South Egremont), at the bottom of Monument Mountain, or Mount Greylock, and at Windsor Jambs in Windsor State Forest.

SKIING: The Berkshires offer five fine skiing areas. Tallest and toughest of the five is Berkshire East, P.O. Box S, Charlemont, MA 01339 (tel. 413/339-6617). See "Pioneer Valley/Mohawk Trail Activities," below. *Great Barrington:* Butternut, Rte. 23, Great Barrington, MA 01230 (tel. 413/528-2000), has a vertical rise of 1,000 feet, 17 trails with dramatic views, one poma and six chair lifts (7,000 skiers an hour), 95% snowmaking capacity, and a base lodge. Over ten miles of cross-country. *Hancock:* Jiminy Peak, Corey Road (off Rte. 7 or 43), Hancock, MA 01237 (tel. 413/738-5500), offers day and night skiing on 25 slopes and trails accessed by four chair lifts and one tow. Also, a summer slide. *Hillsdale, NY:* Catamount, Hillsdale, NY 12529 (tel. 518/325-3302 or 413/528-1262), offers fine skiing for beginners, intermediates, and experts on over 25 trails serviced by four double chairs, two T-bars, and one J-bar. The steepest trail, dropping 500 feet over a 1,700-foot distance, is the Flipper Dipper. The mountain offers a 1,000-foot vertical drop and 85% snowmaking capacity. There's a modernized base lodge with cafeteria and cocktail lounge and picture windows looking out onto the mountain. Also offers a mountain coaster in summer. *Lenox:* Cross-country skiing in Kennedy Park. *New Ashford:* Brodie Mountain, Rte. 7, New Ashford, MA 01237 (tel. 413/443-4752), has 19 rails approached via four chair lifts and two tows. *Windsor:* Cross-country at Notchview.

STATE PARKS AND FORESTS: *Great Barrington:* East Mountain State Reservation, Rte. 7 (tel. 413/528-2000), for hiking and skiing at Butternut. *Lanesboro:* Mount Greylock State Reservation, Rockwell Road (tel. 413/499-4263 or 4262), for bicycling, camping, fishing, hiking, horseback riding, picnicking, cross-country skiing, and snowmobiling. *Lee:* October Mountain State Forest, Woodland Road (tel. 413/243-1778 or 243-9726), for bicycling, camping, fishing, hiking, horseback riding, cross-country skiing, and snowmobiling. *Monterey:* Beartown State Forest, Blue Hill Road (tel. 413/528-0904), for bicycling, boating, camping, fishing, hiking, horseback riding, picnicking, skiing, snowmobiling, and swimming. *Mount Washington:* Mount Washington State Forest and Mount Everett, East Street (tel. 413/528-0330), which also offers BashBish Falls along with wilderness camping, hiking, horseback riding, and snowmobiling. *Otis:* Otis State Forest, Rte. 23 (tel. 413/528-0904), for boating, fishing, hiking, horseback riding, cross-country skiing, snowmobiling; Tolland State Forest, Rte. 8 (tel. 413/269-7268), has the same plus bicycling, picnicking, and swimming. *Pittsfield:* State Forest, Cascade Street (tel. 413/442-8992), for bicycling, boating, camping, fishing, hiking, horseback riding, picnicking, cross-country skiing, snowmobiling, swimming. *Sandisfield:* State Forest, West Street (tel. 413/258-4774), for bicycling, boating, camping, fishing, horseback riding, hiking, picnicking, cross-country skiing, snowmobiling, and swimming. *Williamstown:* Taconic Trail State Park (tel. 413/499-4263), for hiking, horseback riding, and cross-country skiing. *Windsor:* State Forest, River Road (tel. 413/684-9760), for bicycling, camping, fishing, hiking, picnicking, cross-country skiing, swimming, and snowmobiling.

SWIMMING: *Great Barrington:* Egremont Country Club (tel. 413/528-4222) has an outdoor pool. *Pittsfield:* Pittsfield State Forest (tel. 413/442-8992) has a beach with lifeguards; Pontoosuc Lake has a free supervised beach. *South Lee:* Oak 'n' Spruce Resort (tel. 413/243-3500) has outdoor and indoor pools; no children under 16. *Stockbridge:* At Stockbridge Bowl off West Street. *Williamstown:* Sand Springs, off Rte. 7 near the Vermont line, has a 50- by 70-foot mineral pool with year-round temperature of 74°. *Windsor:* Windsor Jambs.

TENNIS: *Great Barrington:* Searles Castle, Main Street (tel. 413/528-9800), has two clay courts. *Lee:* Greenock Country Club, West Park Street (tel. 413/243-9719), has two clay courts available. *North Egremont:* Prospect Lake Park, Prospect Lake, three miles west off Rte. 71, has two courts available. *Pittsfield:* The Racquet Club, at Bousquet, Tamarack Road (tel. 413/499-4600), has eight outdoor and six indoor courts. *South Egremont:* Egremont Country Club (tel. 413/528-4222) has four courts; Jug End Resort (tel. 413/528-0434) has five outdoor courts. *South Lee:* Oak 'n' Spruce Resort (tel. 413/243-3500) has two clay courts available. *Williamstown:* Williams College (tel. 413/597-3131) has 12 clay and 12 hard courts available.

The Pioneer Valley

The region derives its name from the early settlers who first came here during the 17th century, lured to what was then a frontier by its physical beauty, fertile soil, and abundant water supply. Extending from the New Hampshire and Vermont borders in the north to the Connecticut border in the south, it is also contiguous to the Berkshires on the west and to Worcester County and Old Sturbridge Village on the east. The area's major draws are Historic Deerfield and the many attractions that exist in Amherst, Springfield, Holyoke, Northampton, and their surrounding areas.

HISTORIC DEERFIELD

DEERFIELD ATTRACTIONS

To escape the harried, trying times of this century there's one place to hie and that's Deerfield, a village that has managed to retain its 18th-century serenity, grace, and civility, thereby providing a real weekend haven to refresh and restore rushed and troubled 20th-century spirits.

When the Rev. William Bentley of Salem, Massachusetts, rode on horseback into Deerfield in the spring of 1782, he remarked, "The Street is one measured mile, running North and South . . . there is a gate at each end of the Street and about 60 houses in the Street in better style, than in any of the Towns I saw." Some 25 of the handsome houses on which Bentley remarked still stand on "The Street" in Deerfield.

When I visited, it was fall. Golden, red, and orange leaves hung on the trees, squirrels were gathering nuts, and Deerfield boys walked to and fro with a confident, almost swaggering, air rustling the golden leaves strewn on the ground. Dried corn hung below gleaming brass door knockers, brilliant orange pumpkins lay in the adjacent fields, and staked yellow mums and dahlias even stood in front of the gas station on Rte. 5, a sure sign that I was in New England where beauty, and especially flowers, still matters very much in daily life. It was timeless.

But let's return to **"The Street,"** with its rows of lovely 18th-century houses, one inn, and a church. The focal point of the village has remained the **church,** originally the parish of Sam Mather and John Shelburne, the last killed by French and Indians in 1704. Walk by the church and you can see the rocks bearing memorial plaques in remembrance of the massacre and destruction of this fragile and then farthermost-west outpost of colonial settlement. The inn, of course, was and is another focal point of the village, which I'll discuss later.

Twelve houses are open to the public as museums. They have indeed been preserved, but not in an artificial way. They are unadulterated by cute costumed guides spouting surface commentaries. Instead the guides are real, their lives and their roots are right here, and the history they tell us is in their bones, their blood, and their hearts. To see the key houses requires at least one day; a whole weekend would be preferable just to immerse yourself in the 18th-century atmosphere. Head first for the **Hall Tavern Museum,** across from the Deerfield Inn, for maps, information, and an audio-visual introduction. For first-time visitors, the curator recommends the following highlights:

The **Allen House** (1720) is for real collectors. It was the home of Mr. and Mrs. Henry Flynt, founders of the Deerfield Heritage Foundation, and displays their distinguished collections.

The **Fabric House** is a must for anyone interested in needlework, weaving, and the history and evolution of fabric design techniques. Examples of work include Marseilles, calamaricco, wood-block-printed fabrics, 19th-century appliquéed quilts, and candlewicking, all of top musuem quality. In addition, about 20 mannequins display 17th-, 18th-, and 19th-century costumes of various fabrics, including Spitalfields silk and hand-embroidered and hand-painted French silk.

The **Parker and Russell Silver Shop** in an adjacent farmhouse displays silver objects made from melted coins before 1800. A guide will explain the art of silver-smithing and how the artisan uses a series of hammers (first metal, then wood and leather) to achieve a really smooth sheen. The collection includes Paul Revere spoons, and tankards, braziers, bowls, and Apostle spoons by various silversmiths—Dummer, Coney, Myers, deLamerie, and others. In the middle of it all, you'll come across a charming corner dedicated to the cross-eyed hero of British democracy, John Wilkes, a passion apparently of Mr. Flynt's. In the work-shop you can see all the tools and instruments used to chase silver; the pewter collection and work room are also worth a visit.

The **Wells-Thorn House** is the oldest of the houses, having been built in 1717, only 13 years after the massacre, which no doubt explains why the wooden walls were built so thickly with no, or very small, windows, a form of construction that contributes to a distinct barricaded feeling. Here in this house, though, you can almost enjoy a mini-course in furniture and design by stepping from the colonial through the Federal and Queen Anne periods to the Georgian section of the house, which was added 34 years later.

The **Asa Stebbins House** was Deerfield's first brick house. Built in 1799, it is a typical home for a rich farmer who sat in the state legislature. It contains some beautiful work by cabinetmaker Daniel Clay. Willard clocks, and a magnificent staircase enhanced by some stunning hand-painted French wallpaper.

At **Frary House** (1740) you'll have several interesting things pointed out to you —for example, the tea caddy that has a lock on it (not surprising, when tea was $50 a pound), a straw doll with a face like a death mask (originally made because the daughter had left to live with the Indians), and a demonstration of "Pop Goes the Weasel."

This house and the adjacent Barnard Tavern were bought and restored by a fascinating woman, Alice Baker, "to rescue it and provide for mother and for dancing." She restored it in 1892 and annually held a costume ball in the upstairs ballroom with its fiddlers balcony. In the tavern you can see mud shoes for horses, and clay pipes, which were rented to those who frequented the tavern. By the way, watch your p's and q's (pints and quarts).

Memorial Hall Museum (tel. 413/774-6476) is appropriately named, for the collection displayed here constitutes both the Indian and Puritan heritage of the inhabitants of the Pocumtuck Valley. Here you can see the tomahawk-gashed doors from the Sheldon homestead, an eerie reminder of the 1704 massacre when Deerfield was an isolated frontier outpost. The photographs taken by the Allen sisters, two early glassplate camera-women, who took up photography after they went deaf and could no longer teach, provide a fascinating, sometimes sentimental, sometimes very stylized, record of village life. Here also are displays of Society of Blue and White needlework—part of the turn-of-the-century craft movement —plus locally made furniture, kitchenware, and musical instruments. HOURS: May 1 to October 31, Monday to Friday from 10 A.M. to 4:30 P.M., on Saturday and Sunday from 12:30 to 4:30 P.M.; in April and November by appointment. ADMISSION: $2.

And finally, there's the **Jonathan Ashley House**, which from 1732 to 1780 belonged to the parish minister, who was a stubborn Tory. The parishioners denied him firewood and even locked him out of his pulpit. HOURS: The houses are open all year, except major winter holidays, Monday to Saturday from 9:30 A.M. to 4:30 P.M., on Sunday from 11 A.M. to 4:30 P.M. ADMISSIONS: Individual admissions from $1 to $3, depending on the house; combination tickets for 3 are $4.50 or 12 for $15. For information call 413/774-5581, or write Historic Deerfield, P.O. Box 321, Deerfield, MA 01342.

DEERFIELD LODGING

The Deerfield Inn, The Street, Deerfield, MA 01342 (tel. 413/774-5587). Brass chandeliers and lanterns cast a warm glow over the polished Georgian-style tables and shield-back chairs in the dining room, where the conversation is subdued and laughter muted. The food is typical American/continental style—sirloin bordelaise, seafood, veal Orloff or forestier—all priced from $15 to $20. There are 23 rooms—11 in the main house, and 12 in the south wing, reached by a covered walkway. All of the rooms are furnished with antique reproductions. There are no televisions. The only sacrifice to modern taste is a TV lounge in each of the room wings, which is tastefully furnished with Queen Anne wing chairs and other comfortable antiques. Along the halls of the main house you may find an elegant writing desk tucked into a little nook or a bookcase filled with books of plays and a variety of classics.

RATES: $75 to $80, single or double. There are special weekends held here, often around an historical theme, for example, colonial American drinks. LUNCH AND DINNER: Daily.

For cheaper accommodations, there's a **Motel 6** at Rtes. 5/10, South Deerfield, MA 01373 (tel. 413/665-7161).

RATES: From $25 single, from $29 double.

If you don't want to spend both days exploring Deerfield, then you have several options. Many visitors choose either to drive over to Amherst-Northampton and Springfield, or to follow the Mohawk Trail north to Williamstown. Let's begin at the southern end of the valley in Springfield.

SPRINGFIELD

SPRINGFIELD ATTRACTIONS

Downtown Springfield has been spruced up and you may want to visit **Court Square** to get a sense of the town's history. The original bounds of the square have been extended by a brick plaza. At the corner stands the enormous gray stone crenellated courthouse, complete with bell tower, designed by H. H. Richardson. Across from it, the Old First Church, established in 1637, is in fact the fourth building on the site, having been erected in 1819 by a Northampton man, Isaac Damon. The rooster weathervane that crowns the spire was crafted in copper in London and brought to the U.S. in 1750. Built of wood, including the columns that support the classical pediment, it's a splendid piece of architecture with its soaring tower with outside ambulatory, 12-on-12 windows, and black shutters.

The park in front of the church is pleasantly well kept. The lawns are neatly trimmed, the gazebos decorated with hanging baskets of flowers, and the antebellum fountain and ornamental trees and shrubs attractive. From the benches in the park you can view the campanile, a copy of the one in the Piazza San Marco in Venice; unfortunately you can no longer climb to the top. On the same side of the square as the courthouse, take a closer look also at a six-story Renaissance Revival building, the historic Springfield Buyer's block. A series of fluted pillars frame the shopfronts on the ground floor, two sets of verdigrised window treatments are accented with classical decoration, and at one end the building is topped by a copper-based tower punctured by a series of Palladian latticework windows all topped by more glass panes and a witches cap turret.

Opposite this highly rhythmic building across the park are impressive Symphony Hall and City Hall. The whole area is a testament to the confident 19th-century mercantile spirit.

Springfield's Museums

Springfield's museums are very impressive, and very conveniently collected all together in the Quadrangle off Chestnut Street.

In my opinion, the most fascinating and rewarding is the **George Walter Vincent Smith Art Museum,** 222 State St. (tel. 413/733-4214), housed in a lovely Renaissance Revival building. The Oriental collections here are outstanding. On the first floor the Japan Arms and Armor Galleries display 19th-century war hats, suits of armor, No masks, daggers and intricately worked scabbards, and a large wheel shrine (late 18th and early 19th century) made of keyaki wood and carved beautifully—each animal or natural element symbolizing an abstract characteristic like power, longevity, etc. In the Japan Decorative Arts Gallery await exquisite objects—netsukes, imari and other porcelains, glistening shun uri lacquer objects, okimono ivory figures, inro, tea ceremony implements, and a fantastic 19th-century hand-carved vase by Kyozo Ishiguro, depicting Buddha and his 500 disciples.

One of the most extensive collections of cloisonné in the U.S. is displayed upstairs. The six processes of production are clearly depicted, and a variety of objects—vases, incense burners, ewers, bowls, birds, and animals—on view. Most spectacular is an 18th-century covered vessel in the form of a temple drum that is decorated with the flowers of the four seasons—lotus, plum, peony, and chrysanthemum.

The museum's collection of 19th-century art is quite strong, concentrating on works by Albert Bierstadt, Samuel Colman, and George Inness. I particularly enjoyed the watercolors by Alfred Thompson Bricher. Other galleries of note are the Sculpture Hall, housing plaster casts of classical and Renaissance sculptures, and a couple of rooms containing kilims and rugs from Anatolia and the Caucasus.

HOURS: Tuesday and Sunday from noon to 5 P.M. ADMISSION: By donation.

The **Museum of Fine Arts,** 49 Chestnut St. (tel. 413/732-6092), possesses remarkable works by Erastus Salisbury Field, the most spectacular being the huge canvas *Historical Monument of the American Republic, 1867,* that dominates the ground-floor gallery. The upstairs galleries exhibit various European artists, including works by Corot, Eugene Boudin, Courbet, Millet, and a number of Rouaults and other impressionists. Among less-frequently viewed paintings are Gauguin's *Seascape in Britanny* and John Singer Sargent's *Glacier Streams—the Simplon*. The Bidwell Collection of Chinese Bronzes is well known. These are displayed along with other Orientalia—terracotta statuettes, stoneware, porcelain and ceramic vessels, and some beautiful terracotta mortuary horses. No matter what, there's much to enjoy here. HOURS: Tuesday to Sunday from noon to 5 P.M.; closed major holidays. ADMISSION: By donation.

The **Connecticut Valley Historical Museum,** 194 State St. (tel. 413/732-3080), is devoted to the history and traditions of the Connecticut River Valley from 1635 to the present. You'll also gain an overview of Springfield's history from 1850 when the inhabitants numbered 11,300, through 1900 when the number had swelled to 62,000, to 1930 when the census counted 150,000! This rapid growth was fueled by the manufacture of all kinds of products—armaments during the Civil War, beer, soda, carriages, cigars, corsets, saddles, saws, and all other manner of goods. The story of the lives of Springfield's residents is told through photographs, correspondence, objects, advertisements. A series of display cases deals with particular subjects—leisure, the Abolitionist Era, the Civil War, the Revolution. Upstairs there are period rooms and furnishings on display, as well as some charming watercolor and pencil miniature portraits executed between 1835 and 1855 by James Sanford Ellsworth. Special presentations and changing exhibits are also shown. HOURS: Tuesday to Sunday from noon to 5 P.M. ADMISSION: Free

The **Springfield Science Museum,** 236 State St. (tel. 413/733-1194), contains ten galleries, a planetarium, an aquarium, an observatory, and a special "Discovery" children's exhibit. Kids will also love the dinosaur hall, the Transparent Anatomical Mannekin (a life-size transparent woman that describes her physical systems and how they function), and the programs on American Indians, Africa, etc. HOURS: Tuesday to Sunday from noon to 5 P.M.; closed Monday and major holidays. Planetarium programs are given on Tuesday, Thursday, Saturday, and Sunday; the observatory is open one evening per week. Call for exact times.

SPRINGFIELD'S OTHER ATTRACTIONS

Springfield was the home of the first American-made automobile—Thomas Blanchard's steam carriage. The city is also credited with the invention of the first gasoline pump. It also produced everything from jewelry to paint from shoes to the famous Springfield rifle. Today the city still possesses a number of factory outlets and mill stores stocking everything from fabrics and fashions to batteries and paper goods.

At the **Springfield Armory,** a large museum housed in the original 1850 Main Arsenal, many examples of the kind of weaponry manufactured at the Armory from 1794 to 1968 are on display. Enter either from Federal Street or the junction of Byer and State Streets. HOURS: daily 8:30 A.M. to 4:30 P.M. except major winter holidays.

The **Basketball Hall of Fame,** off I-91, P. O. Box 179, 1150 West Columbus

Ave., Springfield 01101-0179 (tel. 413/781-6500), is a fitting attraction since the game was invented in 1891 by Dr. James Naismith at Springfield College. It includes action films and exhibits on great teams and players. HOURS: September through June daily 9 A.M. to 5 P.M., until 6 P.M. in summer.

Stagewest, One Columbus Ctr. (tel. 413/781-2340), features plays and musicals from October through April.

SPRINGFIELD LODGING AND DINING

The **Holiday Inn,** 711 Dwight St., Springfield, MA 01104 (tel. 413/781-0900), opened in 1986. Rooms are spacious and well equipped, with VCRs, TV tucked into a cabinet, desk, couch, and full-length mirrors. In the Squared Circle on the 12th floor a pianist entertains nightly, while hot hors d'oeuvres are served. The room has a clubby look, with green glass and brass lamps and books around the walls. There's also a bright, attractive restaurant.

RATES: $65 to $71 single, $73 to $78 double.

A traditional favorite, the **Student Prince and Fort,** Fort Street off Main (tel. 413/734-7475), ladles out hearty German fare and one-liter "boots" of beer from its bar festooned with an incredible collection of steins amassed on shelves and ledges everywhere. In my opinion, dining in the bar area is most fun, tucked away on high-backed settles. There's also a dining room that's warmed in winter by a fire in its large brick hearth.

The menu is extensive—jaegerschnitzel (and several other schnitzels) with noodles, sauerbraten with potato dumplings and spiced red cabbage, zwiebelfleisch (an onion-gravy pot roast), broiled scrod, bratwurst with sauerkraut and potatoes, broiled tripe and mustard sauce, and filet mignon Rossini. Prices run $6 to $12.50. *Ein prosit* to this fine local spot.

HOURS: Monday to Saturday from 11 A.M. to 11 P.M., on Sunday from noon to 10 P.M.

The first impression upon entering the **Chestnut Tree,** at the corner of Chestnut and Mattoon Streets (tel. 413/736-3637), is of a mélange of pastels—turquoise/celery chairs, peach tablecloths, terracotta-colored walls, and floral-patterned carpeting. The adjacent bar is similarly decorated, but with marble tables. In the back there's a pretty brick courtyard. A pianist entertains evenings. About a dozen items are listed on the menu: giant prawns grilled with red-pepper butter, Cajun-style blackened duck breast served with mango slices, noisettes of pork tenderloin sautéed with prunes and armagnac, tournedos of filet mignon sautéed with oysters and white wine are just a few, priced from $11.50 to $18. For appetizers there are soups, shellfish, and pâté.

DINNER: 5:30 to 9:30 P.M. weekdays, until 10 P.M. on weekends.

HOLYOKE

AREA ATTRACTIONS

The prime attraction of this industrial town is the **Holyoke Heritage State Park,** 221 Appleton St. (tel. 413/534-1723 for information), a five-acre parkland bordering one of the canals which celebrates the city that was one of the first planned industrial centers in the nation. The park overlooks old brick mills once used for the manufacture of paper and thread, and the Visitor Center displays a series of exhibits depicting the lives and history of an earlier Holyoke, relating much of the history of industrial development of the area as well. An antique rail car takes people on a five-mile trip through Holyoke and the environs; canal-boat rides are given, and a children's hands-on museum is being developed. To get here, take Exit 4 from I-90 onto I-91 North. From I-91, take Exit 17A and continue straight to the fork, where you bear right, continuing through three sets of traffic lights. The park is 100 yards on the left. HOURS: 9 A.M. to 4:30 P.M. daily (until 9 P.M. on Thursday); closed Monday from November to May. ADMISSION: Free.

Further insights can be gained at the **Wistariahurst Museum,** 238 Cabot St. (tel. 413/534-2216), the home of industrialist William Skinner, who founded the Skinner Silk Mills. Classical period furniture and decorative arts reveal the life-style of an early industrial magnate. HOURS: Tuesday to Saturday from 1 to 5 P.M., on Sunday from 2 to 5 P.M.

In the area but near the city, **Mount Tom** offers skiing in winter and an alpine and water slide in summer.

HOLYOKE LODGING AND DINING

Even though the **Yankee Pedlar,** 1866 Northampton St., Holyoke, MA 01040 (tel. 413/532-9494), is located at the junction of two well-traveled roads, Rte. 55 and 202, the old clapboard buildings, the country rooms, and the garden and ga-zebo in back create a country atmosphere. Evenings it's a lively place. The bar is in full swing to the rhythm of the piano player, the popcorn machine fills the bar with a good nutty aroma, and the dining rooms are crowded.

There are 47 rooms located in five buildings. Some are in the main inn but many are in clapboard buildings across the tarmac. All are comfortable and con-tain TV, telephone, air conditioning, and alarm clock. Rooms in the 1850 House have four-posters minus canopies, Marseilles bedspreads, bold floral curtains and equally striking stenciling, a clubfoot desk and comb-back Windsor chair, all set on ruby-red wall-to-wall carpet. The fanciest rooms are located in the Captain Holyoke House and the carriage house, where four-posters sport straight chintz canopies or fish-net canopies. Carriage House rooms have the added impact of a cathedral ceiling and chandelier. A continental or full breakfast is served in the bar for an extra charge.

In the post-and-beam tavern dining room the fare is excellent and typical New England. Served by waitresses in colonial costume, relishes—bean, beet, and cottage cheese—begin the meal. At a recent meal the crab cakes were filled with crabmeat, the sole was still moist, and the accompanying sweet corn so sweet and succulent that I asked where I could buy some! Among the specialties are broiled lamb chops, filet mignon with maître d'hôtel butter, duck with orange sauce, breast of chicken with three-mushroom sauce, and a dish labeled Currier & Ives, a combination of filet mignon and jumbo shrimp. Otherwise, the menu focuses on seafoods. At night the wood tables and low light from the Shaker sconces and modified oil lamps give the room a warm romantic glow.

In the Herb Garden restaurant a different atmosphere prevails—pots of rosemary, dill, and tarragon grace the tables and wrought-iron shell-motif chairs face the tables set with Port Meirion. Afternoon tea, as well as dinner, is served here under the glass dome at tables set with green placemats and pink napkins.

RATES: $38 to $43 single, $48 to $61 double. LUNCH: 11:30 A.M. to 3 P.M. daily. DINNER: 4 to 10 P.M.-daily. BRUNCH: Sunday, buffet style from 11 A.M. to 2 P.M.

At the **Susse Chalet Inn**, Rte. 5, Holyoke, MA 01040 (tel. 413/536-1980), there are comfortable, fully equipped motel-style rooms.

RATES: $40 double.

NORTHAMPTON

AREA ATTRACTIONS

From Holyoke it's a short drive up I-91 to Northampton. En route you may want to stop off at South Hadley to visit **Mount Holyoke College**, the nation's oldest women's college, founded in 1837. The campus, designed by Frederick Law Olmsted, is as might be expected the most picturesque, landscaped with brooks and Dutch-style and Victorian buildings. The college's museum is strong in Oriental art. For a campus tour call 413/538-2023.

In Hadley on Rte. 9, **Hadley Farm Museum** displays farm equipment —horsedrawn vehicles, hay tedders, carpenter and other tools all in a 1782 barn. HOURS: May to mid October Tuesday to Sunday.

Northampton is an attractive town with some fine architectural stock. At one end of the main street stands **Smith College**, one of the largest women's colleges in the country, founded in 1871 and built in a largely Gothic Revival and Romanesque style.

The college's art museum (tel. 413/584-2700, ext. 2760) is well known for its collection of European art. Downstairs, French, Italian, Swiss, Dutch, and English artists are all represented, among them a portrait by William Hogarth, a landscape by Joseph Wright of Derby, and Gustave Courbet's *Preparation of Dead Girl*, wrongly identified previously (and somewhat ironically) as *Preparation of the Bride*! Sisley, Boudin, Renoir and other impressionists are all well represented on the first floor. Works by 19th-century American painters like James Wells Champney and Edward Hicks are also on view. Visitors exploring the area for the first time will want to see *View of the Connecticut River from Mount Holyoke* (1840). Don't miss Thomas Eakin's striking portrait of Edith Mahon. Upstairs galleries are given over to 20th-century artists—Gris, Léger, Picasso, and Odilon Redon—as well as to changing exhibits (there was a spectacular show of watercolors by John Varley the Elder, Thomas Hearne, Peter de Wint, Constable, and others when I visited). Always worth stopping here. The sculpture court is a serene spot too.

HOURS: In winter, Tuesday to Saturday from noon to 5 P.M., on Sunday from 2 to 5 P.M. In summer, in June by appointment; July to August, Tuesday to Saturday from 1 to 4 P.M.

The college's greenhouse and gardens contain a plant collection that is both beautiful and educational to see.

For college tours, contact the Office of Public Relations, Pierce Hall, Smith College, Northampton, MA 01063 (tel. 413/584-2700).

DINING IN SOUTH HADLEY

Right across from the Mount Holyoke campus in the village of South Hadley, **Woodbridge's,** 3 Hadley St. (tel. 413/536-7341), is a good place to stop for lunch or dinner for such items as chicken or steak teriyaki, baked scrod, or petit filet béarnaise, priced from $7.50 to $9.50. Inside, the cathedral-ceilinged room is decorated with a few country items like decoys and the wood tables are set with green gingham napkins. In summer, sit outside on the pretty brick terrace under yellow and white umbrellas at tables set under the maple tree.

LUNCH: Monday to Saturday from 11 A.M. to 5 P.M. DINNER: Sunday to Thursday from 5 to 10 P.M., on Friday and Saturday until 11 P.M. BRUNCH: Sunday from 11 A.M. to 3 P.M.

NORTHAMPTON LODGING

Northampton's accommodation of choice would be **The Beeches,** Hampton Terrace, Northampton, MA 01060 (tel. 413/586-9288), a gracious home set on 16 acres that once belonged to Calvin Coolidge. Indeed, from the room that now serves as a library he made his address supporting Hoover for president. The living room has a couple of wing chairs and a Victorian sofa, but is otherwise sparsely furnished, presumably because Anne Nelson, the ebullient resident 2-year-old, could wreak quite a lot of damage. Her parents, Daisy Mathias and Robert Nelson, welcome children to their bed-and-breakfast.

There are three rooms available. The master bedroom is the most impressive, with a fireplace, brass bed, Madame Recamier sofa, and brocaded chair among its furnishings, and a really huge bathroom. It also has its own screened-in porch. The other two rooms share a bath: one is a nicely furnished double with fireplace and large porch; the other contains two singles, one with a net canopy, along with a charming small dresser, wicker rocker, and Victorian side chair. All rooms have electric blankets; only the master bedroom has air conditioning.

A breakfast of homemade blueberry muffins, omelets, and fresh juices is served at the polished wood table in the handsome dining room. The prime spots for sitting are in front of the fire in the library filled with interesting books and the porch from which you can view Mount Tom and Mount Holyoke.

RATES: $60 with private bath, $50 with shared bath.

The **Hotel Northampton,** 36 King St., Northampton, MA 01060 (tel. 413/584-3100), is a Georgian Revival building constructed in 1927, and exhibits a certain faded gentility. In the entranceway, display cases are filled with old wood dolls and other antique collectibles, while the lobby, with its square chestnut columns, is large. The 85 rooms are adequately furnished with wall-to-wall beige carpeting, Wedgwood-blue walls, bed, reproduction Chippendale desk, and a couple of armchairs. All have private bath, color TV, telephone, and air conditioning. Because of its age, the closets have good wood doors. Besides Wiggins Tavern, there's also a bar with an outdoor brick patio for summer cocktails.

RATES: $44 to $75 single, $52 to $75 double, the higher price for a two-room suite.

The **Autumn Inn**, 259 Elm St., Northampton, MA 01060 (tel. 413/584-7660), has comfortable motel units set around a swimming pool.

RATES: $64 double.

NORTHAMPTON DINING

If you don't mind spending freely for first-class food, then **Beardsley's**, 140 Main St. (tel. 413/586-2699), is the obvious choice. In the ground-floor dining room a sedate atmosphere is created by wood paneling, soft classical music, and three large stained-glass panels at the back of the room. Upstairs the room is French style. There are ten or so entrees to choose from, mostly classics like rack of lamb, filet of beef with green peppercorns, filet of sole meunière, coquilles St-Jacques, and breast of duck with seasonal fruits. In addition there's usually a vegetarian dish. To start, try the fettuccine with gravlax and vermouth; the steamed mussels with white wine, tomato, and garlic; or the terrine du jour. Entree prices run $9 to $17. Sunday brunch consists of omelets, pancakes, steak and eggs, bagel and lox, and other selections.

LUNCH: 11:30 A.M. to 3 P.M. daily. DINNER: 5:30 to 10 P.M. daily. BRUNCH: Sunday from 11:30 A.M. to 3 P.M.

Seafood lovers will want to try the **North Star,** at the corner of Green and West Streets (tel. 413/586-9409). Here in the modern high-ceilinged bar dining area, or in the main dining room attractively filled with tables spread with royal-blue cloths, cane-seated Breuers, and tall ficus, you can obtain an assortment of fresh fish often cooked in Japanese-Oriental style. For example, there's shabu-shabu, bluefish (or salmon) sautéed in soy and Mirin sauce, broiled sole or haddock, charcoal-grilled swordfish with lemon butter, shrimp satay (in the Indonesian style), and shrimp fiji, sautéed with ginger and garlic topped with cashews in an orange wine sauce. For meat lovers there's steak and chicken du jour. There's also a selection of sushi. Chocolate mousse, sour-cream apple pie, and parfaits are among the desserts. The courtyard in back is an ideal summer dining spot.

DINNER: Tuesday to Sunday from 5 to 10 P.M.; closed Monday.

Two Chinese restaurants contend for the title of best in Northampton. The traditional favorite, **Szes,** 50 Main St. (tel. 413/586-5708), has been consistently voted one of the area's top restaurants. It's a pleasant two-tiered dining room divided into more intimate areas by decorative geometric cut-out screens. Tables are set with warm-colored terracotta cloths. There's a bar up front with comfortable upholstered lounge chairs. A large bouquet of fresh flowers adorns the light-oak bar. The menu offers an array of chicken, pork, lamb, beef, and noodle dishes—in Szechuan, Mandarin, or Cantonese style. For example, there's lemon chicken, orange-flavored beef, moo shu pork, lamb Szechuan style, and sweet-and-sour shrimp. Dinner prices run $6.50 to $13. On Sunday there's a brunch buffet served.

LUNCH: Monday to Saturday from 11:30 A.M. to 3 P.M. DINNER: Sunday to Thursday from 4 to 9:15 P.M., on Friday and Saturday until 10:45 P.M. BRUNCH: Sunday from 11:30 A.M. to 3 P.M.

Newcomer **Panda's Garden,** 34 Pleasant St. (tel. 413/584-3858), was edging out the old favorite Szes. The decor is plain but the Szechuan, Mandarin, Cantonese, and Hunan cuisine is well recommended by the locals. Try the orange beef or the shrimp with walnuts. Prices run $4.50 to $12.

HOURS: Monday to Thursday from 11:30 A.M. to 9:30 P.M., on Friday and Saturday from 11:30 A.M. to 11 P.M., on Sunday from 2 to 9:30 P.M.

Wiggins Tavern, 36 King St. (tel. 413/584-3100), in the Hotel Northampton, is wonderfully atmospheric. It's not a tavern—it's two dining rooms with low beamed ceilings supported by sturdy posts, both with fireplaces. At night it glows golden, lit by oil-style lamps. The trestle-style wood tables are set with pewter platters and napkin rings while the room is decorated (but not overly so) with farm implements, candles hanging from the beams, and ceramics in corner cupboards. The food is typical New England—roast turkey, chicken pot pie, roast lamb, pork chops (stuffed with mushrooms, onions, and bacon served with a corn cake on the side), steaks, baked Boston scrod, and lobster. Prices run $10 to $15. Chowders, oysters, crab, and scallops mornay are just a few of the appetizers.

LUNCH: Monday to Saturday from 11:30 A.M. to 2:30 P.M., on Sunday from noon to 2:30 P.M. DINNER: Sunday to Thursday from 5:30 to 9:30 P.M., on Friday and Saturday until 10 P.M.

The **East Side Grill,** 19 Strong Ave. (tel. 413/586-3347), receives strong local recommendations. From the bar, which also serves as a raw bar, steps lead into the modern oak-and-brass dining room where food with a Cajun inspiration is served. For example, there's chicken Créole, barbecued shrimp, pasta jambalaya (shrimp, scallops, and broccoli in Créole sauce over spinach, tomato, and egg pasta), blackened prime rib and fish, plus steaks and a Cajun burger. The appetizers reflect the same style—gumbos, barbecued shrimp or shrimp remoulade, and Louisiana fried oysters. Key lime pie, mud pie, and pecan pie are among the dessert attractions. At lunch it's soup, salad, sandwiches, and several items mentioned above.

LUNCH: Monday to Saturday from 11:30 A.M. to 3 P.M. DINNER: Sunday to Thursday from 5 to 10 P.M., on Friday and Saturday to 11 P.M.

For a budget luncheon or dinner, **Pinocchio's,** 122 Main St. (tel. 413/586-8275), offers pizzas, lasagne, eggplant parmesan, soups, subs, and meat and spinach calzone. The atmosphere is pleasant—exposed brick, bentwood chairs, and old Italian prints. The serving counter is in back.

HOURS: Monday to Thursday from 11 A.M. to 9 P.M., on Friday and Saturday to 10 P.M., and on Sunday from 3 to 8:30 P.M.

An ideal cappuccino or tea spot where you can watch life passing by? Try **Bonducci's Café,** on Main Street (tel. 413/586-6370).

AMHERST

AMHERST ATTRACTIONS

Among the attractions here are all those associated with old college towns and fine campuses, plus **Emily Dickinson's House** at 280 Main St., where she lived with her father and wrote close to 2,000 poems. Only seven were published while she was alive. HOURS: Tuesday to Friday afternoon from May 1 to October 1, by appointment the rest of the year.

Amherst College (1821) occupies the area beside the town Green (which, by the way, is home to a farmer's market on Saturday mornings through the summer). The college is worth exploring for its architecture and to view the American paintings and decorative arts in the Mead Art Museum (tel. 413/542-2335), an impressive small museum. HOURS: 10 A.M. to 4:30 P.M. weekdays, 1 to 5 P.M. on weekends; closed Monday in summer and also all of August. Tours of the campus led by student guides are given usually on weekdays when school is in session. For information, call the public affairs office at 413/542-2321.

Compared to Amherst's intimate groves of academe, the University of Massachusetts is vast and largely a collection of high-rises. From the top of one of them, the Campus Center, you'll be rewarded with a view of the valley. The Fine Arts Building has a strange, haunting, futuristic effect: great slabs of concrete and huge triangular supports dwarf the individual, creating an awesome landscape. It reminds me of the ancient observatory in Jaipur, India. Go over to the art gallery just to view the huge timber-like object caught in time and space by a sculptor as it seems to glide down the concrete steps. The university's art gallery also has a good collection of 20th-century American drawings, photographs, and prints. For information on tours (which are usually given on weekends), head for the information desk in the Campus Center, at the east end of the second-floor concourse (tel. 413/545-0111 or 545-0222).

Back in town, a favorite bookstore for browsing is Ollards, on North Pleasant Street, which has new and used books.

AMHERST LODGING AND DINING

Amherst's prime dining and lodging place is the Lord Jeffery Inn, 30 Boltwood Ave., Amherst, MA (tel. 413/253-2576), named after the town's hero of the French and Indian wars, Lord Jeffery Amherst, and located in a handsome brick Georgian building facing the Common. Chestnuts, pine, and other shade trees give it a bucolic appearance, and so, too, does the lawn, as well as the begonias, petunias, and other flowers that bloom on the grounds. Unfortunately, the inn was closed when I stopped by, but by the time this book appears it should be thriving again under the experienced direction of David Joslow, the proprietor of the Inn at Chester. So stop by and let me know what wonders have been wrought.

Other Amherst accommodations include the University Motor Lodge, 345 N. Pleasant St., Amherst, MA 01002 (tel. 413/256-8111), a motel designed in neo-colonial style. RATES: $59 double.

Or you might like the Campus Center Hotel, at the University of Massachusetts (tel. 413/549-6000), where you can secure modern accommodations and grand panoramic views. RATES: $54 double.

In an old clapboard house fronted by a colorful flower garden, Plumbley's Off the Common, 30 Boltwood Walk (tel. 413/253-9586), is a pleasant place to go for lunch or dinner and you'll find many students here dining with their parents, especially on weekends. The food is good, and fairly priced; the portions are large. At dinner, specials supplement such items as stuffed breast of chicken, baked scrod, veal Cordon Bleu, and sirloin, priced from $9 to $14. There are several rooms to choose from: the garden-like room with atrium, plants, and trellis work; a more formal room; and finally the library, among the Wyeths, wainscoting, and chintz.

LUNCH: Monday to Saturday from 11:30 A.M. to 4 P.M. DINNER: Monday to Saturday from 4 to 10:30 P.M., on Sunday from 3 to 9:30 P.M. BRUNCH: Sunday from 10 A.M. to 2 P.M.

A café-like atmosphere prevails at **Judie's**, 51 N. Pleasant St. (tel. 413/253-3491). Dine on chicken and veal piccata, bouillabaisse, paella, or beef with mushroom fettuccine, priced variously from $11 to $14. Breuer chairs, modern prints, and a few plants create a light, airy ambience. The desserts are renowned.

HOURS: Sunday to Thursday from 11:30 A.M. to 11 P.M., on Friday and Saturday until midnight.

EVENING ENTERTAINMENT IN THE AREA

This is centered on the campuses, where varied performances—ballet, jazz, classical music—are given. Call the universities for information.

For a coffeehouse charged with youthful debate and aspiration, head for the **Iron Horse** at 20 Center St. in Northampton (tel. 413/584-0610), which offers 52 beers and a full schedule of evening entertainment, from the best local talent to nationally known folk, jazz, and blues artists. HOURS: 11 A.M. to 11 P.M.

Also, check the *Valley Advocate*, a free paper, for event listings.

TO NORTHFIELD

While you're in the Pioneer Valley, you may want to take a rustic drive up Rte. 63 from North Amherst, making a few stops along the way. First stop, for example, might be the **Leverett Crafts Center**, on Depot Road just off Rte. 63 (tel. 413/549-6871), which is worth browsing if you like handcrafted objects—jewelry, pottery, weaving—and contemporary prints and art. HOURS: Tuesday to Sunday from noon to 5 P.M.

Or you might want to turn off to **Lake Wyola Park**, in Shutesbury (tel. 413/367-2627), and go for a swim or a picnic. HOURS: Mid-April to mid-October. ADMISSION: $3.50 for adults, $1.75 for children.

In Northfield, on the broad street lined with gracious homes that cuts through town you'll find the **Country Store** and **Northfielder Antiques and Gifts,** both browsing stops.

Northfield Mountain and Environmental Center, R.R. 1 Box 377, Northfield MA 01360 (tel. 413/659-3714), offers a whole range of weekend workshops —nature photography, night experience, etc.—lasting a few hours or a whole day. This is also prime cross-country skiing territory. For a recorded report call 413/

659-3713. Other activities available: picnicking, camping, canoeing, and nature walking at Barton Cove (for reservations, call 413/659-3714 in pre-season, 413/863-9300 during the camping season); picnicking along the eastern bank of the Connecticut River at Riverview picnic area. An interpretive river cruise is also given aboard the *Quinnetukut II* lasting 1½ hours (for reservations, call the Recreation and Environmental Center at the above number). Summer only.

NORTHFIELD LODGING AND AREA DINING

Northfield Country House, School Street (R.R. 1, Box 79A), Northfield, MA 01360 (tel. 413/498-2692), is a lovely quiet retreat, set on 16 acres. Innkeeper Andrea Dale, a longtime director of credit for Saks, had stayed here and so fell in love with the place that she was moved to say to the owners, "If you ever want to sell, keep me in mind." They did, and so Andrea became the proud owner of this handsome 1901 home built by a wealthy Boston shipbuilder as a weekend residence for use when he attended the revivalist meetings led by the Reverend Moody in Northfield. Inside, rooms are large and luxuriously comfortable. The focal point of the living room is a large stone fireplace with a mantel supporting two bronze stag candlesticks. Beams and an Oriental rug make it cozy; two couches and plush wing chairs provide ample and restful seating; musically inclined guests may play the grand piano which stands in the bay window. A full breakfast of eggs, juice, fruit, and homemade muffins is served in the intricately carved cherry-paneled dining room.

There are seven guest rooms available (sharing four bathrooms), all differently decorated, three with working fireplaces. My favorites are Rooms 5 and 6. The latter is large, has a fireplace, and comes lavishly furnished with Oriental carpet, an iron-and-brass bed sporting frilly linens, a chest of drawers supporting an ormolu mirror, a blanket chest at the foot of the bed, and a cozy love seat. Chintz wallpaper and a dried-flower wreath complete the country look. Room 5 contains several wicker pieces set against a dark-blue floral wallpaper and has the added charm of a small Palladian-style window. There are two large decks with sturdy stone pillars on which you can relax in cane-seated rockers. An outdoor pool completes the facilities. In winter excellent cross-country skiing is right there at the Northfield Recreation area, and in spring, magnolia and cherry blossom in the backyard.

RATES: $40 to $70 double (highest price for rooms with fireplaces).

The prime reason for going to **Muchmore's Restaurant,** Huckle Hill, off Rte. 10 in Bernardston (tel. 413/648-9107), is the view from the top of the mountain out over the Pioneer Valley and the Connecticut River to the Berkshires. The large terrace is designed to take advantage of this vista. The large dining room itself is blandly modern and the food traditional American/continental. Calves' liver and bacon, baked stuffed scrod, filet mignon béarnaise, and lobster are the order of the day. Appetizers include smoked bluefish, pâté, and shrimp cocktail. DINNER: Monday to Thursday from 5:30 to 9 P.M., until 10 P.M. on Friday and Saturday, on Sunday from 1 to 8 P.M., depending on the season. BRUNCH: Sunday from 11 A.M. to 2:30 P.M., Memorial Day to Labor Day.

The **Bernardston Inn,** on Rte. 10 in Bernardston (tel. 413/648-9282), serves some of the more imaginative food in this area, albeit in rather plain surroundings. Among the dishes offered, you might find shrimp tempura and conch fritters to start, followed by such selections as curry of the day, baked stuffed peppers (with brown rice, mushrooms, and tomatoes in cheese sauce), chicken au poivre, or duck with raspberry sauce. Prices range from $9 to $18. Dessert choices vary daily, but you might find baked Alaska available.

DINNER: Tuesday to Saturday from 6 to 9 P.M. (5 to 9 P.M. in winter), on Sunday from 11:30 A.M. to 8 P.M.

ALONG THE MOHAWK TRAIL

From Bernardston it's a short run down I-91 to Greenfield where you can pick up Rte. 2, also known as the Mohawk Trail.

On this route you will be following an old footpath, known to the Indians, which was opened as the New Mohawk Trail in 1914, making the area of mountains, forest, and streams more accessible.

First stop of any interest is at **Shelburne Falls,** where you can marvel at the glacial potholes in the riverbed, some as wide as 39 feet, and also view the old trolley-track bridge that is now abloom with all kinds of flowers. Incidentally, Linus Yale of lock fame was born here. Shopping possibilities? McCusker's Marketplace, Salmon Falls Artisans Gallery, and the Mole Hollow candle company.

From here, your drive will take you through awesome scenery, with mountains and forests rising on either side, past the 900-pound bronze *Hail to the Sunrise* memorial to the Mohawk Indians, taking you from summit to summit around hairpin curves first to Charlemont, then Florida, and then to Whitcomb Summit, the trail's highest point, where there's a place for you to stop and dine. From here, it's a short run into **North Adams,** and from there only a short trip past brooding **Mount Greylock,** at 3,491 feet the highest point in Massachusetts, into Williamstown. For further details on the last two towns, see the earlier Berkshires section.

STURBRIDGE

From Springfield it's only a short drive to Old Sturbridge Village (indeed people even stay in Sturbridge and attend Tanglewood from there).

At **Old Sturbridge Village,** Sturbridge (tel. 617/347-3362), authentically dressed "interpreters" perform the tasks of life in this re-creation of an early-19th-century American village. Farmers haul logs with a team of oxen and fashion split-rail fencing, women cook open hearth style, and many of the old crafts—from blacksmithing and tinsmithing to spinning, weaving, printing, and shoemaking—are practiced and explained. HOURS: 9 A.M. to 5 P.M. daily April through November, 10 A.M. to 4 P.M. in winter. From November through March it's closed on Monday; also closed on Christmas and New Year's Days. ADMISSION: $8.50 for adults, $4 for children 6 through 12.

En route to Sturbridge from the Springfield area on Rte. 20, you'll pass through **Brimfield,** famous for its thrice-yearly, bustling fleamarkets held in early May, mid-July, and mid-September. If you're visiting then, make sure you have reservations in Sturbridge or elsewhere. For info, call 413/245-7479.

STURBRIDGE LODGING AND DINING

The best-known Sturbridge favorite, the **Publick House on the Common,** Sturbridge, MA 01566 (tel. 617/347-3313), is a large, tremendously popular complex of four lodgings and three restaurants that manages to retain a degree of country atmosphere (60 acres helps!) despite the crowds, the huge jam-packed parking lot, and general "busyness."

On weekends the dining room overflows with people. Be prepared to wait —you'll be lucky if you can find a seat on one of the love seats, Windsor chairs, or wing chairs in the downstairs bar, decked out with pewter plates and brass candlesticks. A musical duo (flute and pianist the night I visited) will entertain. The upstairs dining rooms are large and faux colonial, but the typical traditional food—prime rib, stuffed breast of chicken, swordfish in lime butter, lamb chops, and roast turkey (on Sunday only)—is quite good and there's plenty of it. A bread basket filled with cinnamon buns and other rolls will begin the meal. Entrees, priced from $11 to $20, arrive with salad and vegetables, and for a mere $3 additional you can enjoy an appetizer, dessert, and beverage.

The accommodations vary. On top of the hill behind the original inn the Country Motor Lodge is a two-story motel-style block in which management has tried to add character to what are essentially modern motel rooms by adding beams, chintz wallpaper, wing chairs, and reproductions of early American "primitive" portraits. Rooms also have balconies overlooking an orchard of apple trees, which provides a sense of being in the country. Rooms have TV, telephone, overhead fan, and wall-to-wall beige carpeting.

The inn rooms are decorated in country chintz and furnished with antique reproductions, some with canopied four-posters. The prime accommodations to my mind are at the Colonel Ebenezer Craft Inn, about which more later. At the main inn you'll also find a tennis court, outdoor pool, bicycles for rent, and a children's play area to keep everyone entertained.

In winter if you reserve a special Yankee Winter Weekend package, you'll be greeted at the Publick House with a glass of syllabub, a blended mixture of chablis and cream, and some oversize ginger snaps or Joe Froggers, as they're called. Snacks follow—roasted chestnuts, codfish cakes, curried meatballs, aged cheddar cheese, and steaming clam chowder—which are all delivered by costumed waitresses to the accompaniment of a strolling minstrel. A candlelight buffet will then begin. The following morning, breakfast is hearty. There's cornmeal mush, sausages, and oddly enough, a deep-dish apple pie. The day is filled with a visit to Old Sturbridge Village, including a sleigh ride, lunch in the tavern followed by a sugaring-off of maple syrup, and later dinner at the Public House, which usually features wild boar pâté with Cumberland sauce, roast venison or other game, and homemade pie. In the evening 19th-century entertainment takes over the Village tavern. Sunday is kept for relaxation and spontaneous exploration.

RATES: In the Publick House Inn or the adjacent Chamberlain House, $59 to $67 January through June, $71 to $79 July through October, $65 to $73 in November and December; in the Country Motor Lodge, $44 to $54 January through June, $54 to $64 July through October, $44 to $54 in November and December. Certain weekends and dates also carry the high-season rates although they fall in lower-priced months. Call for rates of the Yankee Winter Weekend package.

The choice accommodations in Sturbridge in my opinion are found at the **Colonel Ebenezer Crafts Inn** (affiliated with the Publick House, but located about 1⅓ miles from it), a 200-year-old residence. Here you'll find eight rooms, six in the main house and two in the cottage adjacent, all with bath and or shower. Apples and cookies are placed in all the rooms, and a basket of amenities in the bathroom. All are tastefully decorated in country style. Rooms 2 and 6 have canopy beds; Room 5 is a twin, decorated in sage green and containing, among other furnishings, a desk and wrought-iron floor lamp. The small suite, Room 4, is ideal for a family and brightly decorated in sunshine yellow and chintz. The cottage suite has a separate bedroom and sitting room.

For guests' pleasure there's a sun room off the comfortable antique-filled sitting room. Music lovers and performers can enjoy the grand piano. In the back the fenced-in pool is prettily landscaped. A continental breakfast of homemade muffins is served from 8 to 10 A.M.

RATES: $75 to $78 January through June, $84 to $87 July through October, $79 to $82 in November and December. The cottage suite is $100, $104, and $109 respectively. For reservations, call the Publick House.

In need of breakfast? Head for **Anna's Country Kitchen** (tel. 617/347-2320), on Rte. 131, out of the center of Sturbridge past the Publick house, shopping plaza, and a couple of motels (Green Acres and Pine Grove). It's a typical lunch room that serves eggs and bacon and other traditional breakfasts along with soups, sandwiches, and desserts. Very inexpensive and open at 5 A.M.

STURBRIDGE AREA LODGING AND DINING

The **Wildwood Inn,** 121 Church St., Ware, MA 01082 (tel. 413/967-7798), is full of wonderful surprises. Although it's set on a residential street, it has two acres of grounds that extend back into the woods through which guests can walk to reach Greenville Park, with tennis courts and a swimming hole, or the Ware River on which they can paddle the Wildwood's canoe. Inside the 1880 house all the rooms are imaginatively furnished. All kinds of interesting pieces fill the parlor—an old carpenter's chest now used to store board and other games, several cradles (including one filled with books), a spinning wheel, and a shoemaker's bench that serves as a coffee table. Comfy chairs, rug, and a fireplace make it home-like and so do the many books about the region and about antiques that sit in the bookcases.

There are five guest rooms sharing three bathrooms. Electric blankets are on all the beds and all of the rooms are attractively furnished. In the cranberry afghan room an old wringer/washing machine serves as a luggage rack and a saddle vise as a night table. The flower-garden-quilt room's bed sports a quilt and pretty eyelet linen. Here an early American commode serves as a luggage rack. The gold patchwork quilt room has an old wicker cradle with a fishnet hood among its furnishings. Baskets of herbs and country pictures add to the early American country look of all the rooms.

In the mornings Margaret Lobenstine supplies a breakfast of homemade breads (popovers, muffins) served with homemade fruit butters, juice, tea, and coffee, plus one country "yummy" as she calls it, like maple-cheese squares, rice pudding, or chipmunk pie (a type of apple pie using a particular blend of spices).

In summer, if you really want to relax, climb into the hammock or swing on the porch. Behind the house are two garden areas. The first, secluded by fir trees, makes an excellent cookout spot, while the second area, a large open spread of grass, is great for star-gazing.

RATES: $31 to $46 November through April, $34 to $49 May to approximately September 26, $37 to $54 on holiday weekends, Eagle Hill Parents' Day, and foliage season (from the end of September to the end of October).

A real restaurant at a small country airfield? That's what you'll find at **Barre Hiller Airport Restaurant,** in New Braintree (tel. 617/867-8186). I suggest you call ahead to obtain specific directions because it's not easy to find. The classically trained chef is the son of the owner of the airport, who bought the airfield to store his planes. Obviously, originally the restaurant was built as a snackbar for those pilots who dropped in, and it still retains the look of a coffeeshop with counter and tables set with plastic tablecloths, but the food is far from ordinary coffee shop fare. The menu is supplemented by daily blackboard specials, and there you might find duck Créole, scallops with tomato and saffron sauce, haddock with yogurt sauce, linguine Rockefeller, or pork and beans. Desserts might list apricot mousse, white-chocolate cheesecake, plum-pear crisp, orange flan, or some other inspiration.

At lunch the regular menu offers salads, sandwiches, and soups, along with a pâté of the day, nachos, or potato skins with jalapeño peppers served with salsa and tsarinas (which are potato skins filled with sour cream and caviar). Prices at dinner range from $8 to $12. Through the dining room windows you can watch the small planes taking off and landing and view some of the old airplanes that the owner possesses. In summer sit on the deck under the awning.

LUNCH: 11:30 A.M. to 5 P.M. daily. DINNER: Monday to Thursday from 5:30 to 9 P.M., on Friday and Saturday until 10 P.M., on Sunday until 8 P.M. BREAKFAST: weekends only from 9 A.M. to noon. Open from April to mid-December.

When you've finished eating (or perhaps it's better before), you can take a plane ride at the airport. Call Steve Grady at 617/867-8942.

Way out in the country, the **Salem Cross Inn,** Rte. 9 in West Brookfield (tel. 617/867-2345), is a lovely old place that's famous for its "Drovers Roasts." These are usually celebrated three times a year—in July, August, and September—and you should reserve well in advance if you wish to attend. Tents are set up in the surrounding fields, a whole cow is roasted on a spit, and a great feast is enjoyed by all. If you can't attend one of these, the dining rooms have much charm with their beamed ceilings, plank floors, and pierced-tin lanterns. Windsor chairs are set at tables graced with wrought-iron candlesticks and fresh flowers. The food is traditionally hearty, ranging from steaks, including a broiled herbed lamb steak, to broiled scrod, and shrimp-and-lobster pie. Prices run from $9.50 to $17.

Downstairs there are two tap rooms, both with massive inglenook fireplaces. The larger room has natural knotty-pine polished tables set against stone walls. The smaller room is the homier. Floors are covered with braided rugs, chintz curtains hang at the windows, and historical prints, bottles, and stoneware accent the old-time atmosphere. Upstairs you'll find a small craft shop, open on Friday and Saturday from 6:30 to 9:30 P.M. and on Sunday from 2 to 8 P.M.

LUNCH: Tuesday to Friday from noon to 2:30 P.M. DINNER: Tuesday to Friday from 5 to 9 P.M., on Saturday to 10 P.M., on Sunday and holidays from noon to 8 P.M. Closed Monday.

The **Brookfield House Restaurant,** West Main Street in West Brookfield (tel. 617/867-6589), hosts many local family occasions: weddings, christenings, anniversaries. It's that kind of place—a marvelous Victorian house complete with turrets, fish-scale shingles, and stained-glass windows. Inside, the high-ceilinged rooms with marble fireplaces are decorated with rose-colored carpeting, polished wood tables with pink placemats, ladderback chairs, and crystal chandeliers. If you have to wait, there's a Victorian-style sitting room. A meal here might begin with scampi Pernod, lobster bisque, or pâté, and continue with halibut poached with peppercorns in cream, chicken marsala, or pork medallions in a port-and-ginger sauce. To close, there might be English trifle, raspberry mousse, or cheesecake. Main courses are priced from $16.50 to $24.

LUNCH: Tuesday to Friday from 11:30 A.M. to 2 P.M. DINNER: Wednesday to Saturday from 6 to 9 P.M., on Sunday from noon to 7 P.M.

IN THE NORTHEASTERN CORNER OF CONNECTICUT

AREA ATTRACTIONS

Here just southeast of Sturbridge there's real country—fields and trees and winding backroads where you'll pass farms and barns and quiet somnolent villages. It's an unspoiled area—one of the few last retreats. This is the prime reason to visit this area, although architecture buffs and those with a historical bent will enjoy visiting **Roseland Cottage** (or the Bowen House) in Woodstock, Connecticut (tel. 203/928-4074).

The classic Gothic Revival cottage, bright pink outside and striking purple to rose inside, was designed by English-born architect Joseph Collins Wells for Henry C. Bowen, a Woodstock boy who had gone to New York City and amassed some wealth. The cottage is the central building in a complex of structures, including a barn (with one of the earliest surviving interior bowling alleys), an icehouse, and an aviary. The ornamental woodwork shaped variously into pointed arches, trefoil, quatrefoil, and other motifs is accented by brilliant stained-glass windows. The interiors were refurbished in the 1880s when the earlier Gothic decoration on the first floor was updated with what was then a newly introduced product, Lincrusta Walton, a composition wall-covering heavily embossed to resemble richly tooled leather. The furnishings date from 1840 to 1880 and belonged to the Bowen family.

Henry Bowen himself enjoyed quite a full life. After securing a fortune in the dry goods business he lost it in the late 1850s and went bankrupt in 1861. Thereafter he directed his energies to *The Independent,* a Congregationalist weekly that supported abolition and the Republican party. Here at Roseland, Bowen entertained prominent literary and political figures including President Ulysses S. Grant in 1870, on which occasion Henry Ward Beecher was the principal orator. The cottage exists today as an important document of mid-19th-century life. HOURS: May 24 to mid-September, Wednesday to Sunday from noon to 5 P.M.; mid-September to mid-October, Friday to Sunday from noon to 5 P.M. ADMISSION: $2.50 for adults, $1.25 for children under 12.

AREA DINING

In this quiet corner of Connecticut there's a truly beautiful place that shouldn't be missed. This is the **Golden Lamb Buttery,** Hillandale Farm, Bush Hill Road, off Rte. 169 in Brooklyn (tel. 203/774-4423), created by Robert Booth and his wife, Virginia (Jimmie)—peaceful, serene, rejuvenating, blissful. From the refurbished red barn you have a view of a pond across meadows bordered by stone walls and hedgerows and dotted with sheep and horses.

The whole experience begins with cocktails, either on the porch or aboard a hay wagon which winds through the fields, usually to the sweet accompaniment of a folk singer. After this romantic beginning you return to the cozy country-style dining rooms. Beams are hung with baskets and herbs. Fresh flowers grace the candlelit trestle tables. There's no menu: the waitress will simply announce the four or so entree choices, all beautifully and artistically presented thanks to the talents of Jimmie, who discovered this lovely corner of the world while she was scouring the country as a buyer for Lord & Taylor. Obviously the choices vary, but you might start with a broccoli bisque, follow with chateaubriand with béarnaise sauce or duckling with orange sauce, and finish with a strawberry rhubarb pie, cheesecake, or chocolate crêpes. In summer, the soup might be peach-strawberry or cold cucumber. Other entrees that might be offered include pork loin poached with bourbon, sauced, and served with sour cream and chives; or fresh swordfish. The vegetables accompanying these dishes are remarkable and will often be as many as eight, brought to the table in heaping bowls—herbed marinated mushrooms, peas tossed with mint, carrot slivers in a white grape sauce, and quite often one or two raw specimens. Dinners cost $40 per person. LUNCH: Tuesday to Saturday from noon to 3 P.M. DINNER: Friday and Saturday at 7 P.M. Open June 2 or thereabouts to New Year's Eve. Reservations are essential, preferably a month in advance. There are one or two rooms for those who wish to stay over.

Bald Hill, Rte. 169, South Woodstock (tel. 203/974-2240), is very country. It's set in a marvelous red barn topped by a weathervane, and from the screened-in porch there's a lovely pastoral and bucolic view. The food is traditional—rack of lamb, beef Wellington, chicken française, veal Holstein, with stuffed mushroom or pâté among the appetizers. Prices range from $10.25 to $17. LUNCH: Monday to Friday from 11:30 A.M. to 2:30 P.M. DINNER: Monday to Saturday from 5 to 9 P.M., on Sunday from noon to 8 P.M.

PIONEER VALLEY/MOHAWK TRAIL ACTIVITIES

ANTIQUING: For information, contact the Pioneer Antique Dealers Association, Mrs. Frederick Pugliano, P.O. Box 244, Westfield, MA 01085.

BICYCLING: For rentals, repairs, and touring information, contact Peloton, 91 Main St. in Greenfield (tel. 413/773-5572).

BOATING: Canoes can be rented at the Northfield Mountain Recreation Area, Rte. 63 (R.R. 1, Box 377), Northfield, MA 01360 (tel. 413/659-3713). Also contact them for information about 1½-hour cruises on the Connecticut River.

CAMPING: The areas along the Mohawk Trail provide dramatic wilderness camping. The Mohawk Trail State Forest Camping Area, in Charlemont (tel. 413/339-5504), has 56 sites, plus swimming, fishing, hunting, hiking, cross-country skiing, boating, snowshoeing, and snowmobiling. Mount Greylock State Reservations, in Adams (tel. 413/449-4263), has 35 sites, and the Savoy Mountain State Forest, in Florida (tel. 413/663-8469), has 35 sites off Rte. 2, east of North Adams. There's good camping in the Stoney Ledge section of Mount Greylock, and tent camping at Barton Cove, in Gill (tel. 413/863-9300 in season, 659-3714 off-season).

Also on Mount Greylock, from May 1 to November 1 lodging and meals are available at the summit at Bascom Lodge (tel. 413/743-1591), where special sunset suppers are given on Thursday and Sunday—a nice way to end a weekend if you don't mind leaving late for home. The Visitors Center (tel. 413/449-4262) is two miles from Rte. 7 on Rockwell Road.

FISHING: There's good fishing in the Connecticut and Deerfield Rivers and at several lakes in the area. For information, call the Franklin County Chamber of Commerce (tel. 413/528-2800).

Or write to the Division of Fisheries and Wildlife, Field HQ, Westborough, MA 01581.

FRUIT PICKING: Write the Department of Food & Agriculture, 100 Cambridge St., Boston, MA 02202.

GOLF: Crumpin' Fox Club, Parmenter Road, Bernardston (tel. 413/648-9101); Mohawk Meadows, Greenfield (tel. 413/773-9047); and Oak Ridge, West Gill Road, in Gill (tel. 413/863-9693).

HIKING: Great hiking is found in the Mohawk Trail State Forest in Charlemont, at Mount Greylock, and at Erving State Forest, east of Greenfield. There's also a trail along the Connecticut River in the Northfield Recreation Area (tel. 413/659-3713). Savoy Mountain State Forest, east of North Adams, (tel. 413/663-8469), also has trails.

HORSEBACK RIDING: Mount Toby, 470 Long Plain Rd., Leverett (tel. 413/549-1677); Ten Penny Acres, Main Road, Gill (tel. 413/863-4014).

SHOPPING: For information about crafts studios and galleries, of which there are many throughout the Valley, write Arts Extension Service, Division of Continuing Education, University of Massachusetts, Amherst, MA 01003 (tel. 413/545-2360).

SKIING: In a lovely setting on the Mohawk Trail, Berkshire East, River Road (P.O. Box O), Charlemont, MA 01339 (tel. 413/339-5368), has 25 trails served by two lifts and four chairs. A basic weekend costs $25.

The Mount Tom Ski Area, Rte. 5 (P.O. Box 1158), Holyoke, MA 01040 (tel. 413/536-0416), has downhill skiing on 17 slopes served by eight lifts. The lifts are also open in peak summer months from 10 A.M. to 10 P.M. In summer the Alpine slide and water slide provide the thrills.

There's also cross-country skiing at the Northfield Mountain Recreation Area, Rte. 63 (R.R. 1, Box 377), Northfield, MA 01360 (tel. 413/659-3713).

STATE PARKS AND STATE FORESTS: *Florida:* Savoy Mountain State Forest, Rte. 2 and Rte. 116, in Savoy (tel. 413/663-8469), has bicycling, boating, fishing, camping, hiking, horseback riding, picnicking, cross-country skiing, snowmobiling, and swimming. *South Deerfield:* Mount Sugarloaf Reservation, off Rte. 116 (tel. 413/665-2928), for picnicking, hiking, and cross-country skiing.

For general information, write Region 4 Headquarters, P.O. Box 484, Amherst, MA 01004 (tel. 413/549-1461). Or to the Department of Environmental Management, Division of Forests and Parks, 100 Cambridge St., Boston, MA 02202.

SWIMMING: Savoy Mountain State Forest and Mohawk Trail State Forest.

TENNIS: Mostly courts can be found at high schools in the area. Call the Franklin County Chamber of Commerce at 413/773-5463 for specifics.

NEW JERSEY

ATLANTIC CITY

DISTANCE IN MILES: 120
ESTIMATED DRIVING TIME: 2½ hours

DRIVING: New Jersey Turnpike to the Garden State Parkway. Use Exit 36 for downtown, Exit 40 for midtown and uptown locations.
BUS: Close to 30,000 buses per month travel to Atlantic City. Many are operated by the casinos and you can get information about these from many newsstands in the city and the suburbs. By taking these buses you'll recover the travel cost in coupons for food or for chips. Trailways (tel. 212/730-7460), New Jersey Transit (tel. 201/762-5100), and Greyhound (tel. 212/635-0800 for tickets, 564-8484 for schedules, or toll free 800/528-6055) all have buses going to Atlantic City.

Special Events to Plan Your Trip Around
JUNE TO SEPTEMBER: Atlantic City Racecourse is open.
SEPTEMBER: The Miss America Pageant, 1325 Boardwalk (tel. 609/345-7571). The finals are held the second weekend after Labor Day.

For further information about New Jersey in general, contact the Division of Travel & Tourism, New Jersey Department of Commerce, 1 West State St. C.N. 826, Trenton, NJ 08625 (tel. 609/292-2470). For specific information about the area, contact the Atlantic City Convention and Visitors Bureau, 2314 Pacific Ave., Atlantic City, NJ 08401 (tel. 609/348-7100).

For a year-round *fun* weekend, there's no place like Atlantic City. Let's face it, gambling is an optimistic occupation, and it does generate an atmosphere of excitement, glamour, make-believe, theater, and spectacle that makes Atlantic City stimulating even if you don't choose to dance or joust with Lady Luck.

Walk into any casino (but especially the two largest, Resorts or Bally) and you're assaulted by the cacophony of quarters and silver dollars cascading into the pans of slot machines, levers flying back and forth, lights flashing and bells sounding atop the machines of lucky winners. Some people are seated on aluminum stools; others move from one machine to another, clutching their giant paper cups and filling the machines in their never-ending quest to hit the jackpot. Elsewhere the more sedate blackjack players are perched on stools, cocktails at their sides; crowds gather around a table where someone's on a hot roll at the craps table, and still others hoot and holler as the wheel stops at the roulette table. Some are frantic, others exhibit a kind of grim determination, and some just sit back philosophically. Win or lose, Atlantic City's a fascinating place to be.

Somehow the city has always thrown up an interesting cast of characters —Dutchy Muhlrod, who continued to operate a poker and roulette den on the second floor of his Hotel Lachiel even though he'd been driven out of Philly in 1888 for the same crime; the Rev. Sydney Goodman, a pastor of the Men's Church who permitted smoking during his services and smiled upon alcohol and gambling. Such figures helped the city live up to its reputation in the 1890s as the Baghdad by the Sea.

Earlier, when the resort was first established by railroad magnates who constructed a line from Philadelphia in 1854, the pace was far more sedate and Atlantic City was known for the simple pleasures of strolling the boardwalk (built in 1870), bathing, staying at large comfortable oceanfront hotels, and other innocent amusements like the ferris wheel, first built in 1869. Later, the boardwalk developed a reputation for all kinds of weird attractions featuring everything from dancing bears and tigers, boxing cats, and 19-inch-tall dwarf entertainers to Lorena Carver who, for 25 years, dove on horseback from a 60-foot tower on Steel Pier into a pool. Today the stunts are less dramatic, the entertainments stretching more to the video game arcade and other similar activities. The Miss America Pageant was begun in 1921 and has been transformed from the '30s when the women were competing for $400 and the opportunity to model hats in Wanamaker's basement into a big national event that fills TV screens and automatically grants the winner celebrity status.

Although the city had always experienced ups and downs, the real decline set in in the 1950s and continued through the next decade until gambling was voted in and the first casino, Resorts, opened in the summer of 1978. Since then, the city— some say the casinos only—has been thriving, and increasingly Atlantic City is challenging Las Vegas as the top American gambling destination. In fact, the total win for Atlantic City's 11 casinos has surpassed that of the many more casinos in Las Vegas. The casinos have drawn 26 million people and 200,000 buses annually, but the controversy continues about the casinos as saviors. Certainly the more than 30,000 workers employed by the casinos would regard them as such, but outside, many of the streets made famous by Monopoly are still lined with boarded-up buildings haunted by the few who remain in a city whose population continues to decline. Along the Boardwalk and out to Absecon Inlet it's another story, as the casinos vie for prime locations, competing for a larger slice of the action at this veritable crap game by the sea. Come for a weekend and you can enjoy the fun, excitement, and glamour of gambling and the big-name entertainers that go with it, along with the funky pleasures of the Boardwalk, authentic salt-water taffy, salt air, and the bathing beauties that the ocean and the city still attract.

Some Things You Should Know

Your trip will not be cheap. In 1986, casino room rates ran from $100 to $160 a night in summer. A meal at one of the top (I mean top) restaurants will run over $100 for two.

Casino breakfasts run over $8, with bagels even costing as much as $1.50. These are far from nostalgic prices. I paid $8 for a hamburger. By the way, the famous luncheon and dinner buffets also tend to have fewer cold meats and more salads and hot dishes, ever since the casino managements discovered that the "bus" people were loading their bags with a week's supply of turkey, ham, and salami!

Tickets to shows range from $20 to $60 for Friday and Saturday performances, depending on the star; the girlie revues are much less expensive.

Children under 21 are not allowed in any casino, but many casinos have swimming pools and video arcades where they can entertain themselves. Most casinos offer 24-hour day-care service.

The casinos are open from 10 A.M. to 6 A.M. on weekends, to 4 A.M. on weekdays. Betting minimums depend on what the traffic will bear. On weekends when as many as 8,000 people cram into Resorts, you're not likely to find a table below $10—$2, $3, and $5 appear weekdays and afternoons. So get moving. Place your bets.

Getting Around

Jitneys travel up and down Pacific and Ventnor Avenues 24 hours a day from Gardner's Basin to the end of Atlantic City at Jackson Avenue, and Indiana Avenue and Boardwalk to Harrah's at the marina. Fare is 75¢.

Boardwalk trams also operate from Garden Pier past the Convention Center to the Golden Nugget and back, operating as an easy-on, easy-off anywhere-enroute service. Fare is $1.

Or you can opt for cabs: Yellow Cab (tel. 609/344-1221), Radio Cabs (tel. 609/345-1105).

ATLANTIC CITY ATTRACTIONS

The Boardwalk

Besides the casinos, which are, of course, great fun and the main reason for visiting Atlantic City, there are some other things to do. No matter what season you visit Atlantic City, a walk along the **Boardwalk** is a must. In summer, rolling wicker chairs clatter along, the beach is crowded with colorful cabañas, the piers are in full swing, the saltwater taffy and other seaside emporia are ringing it up, and the six-mile strip beside the sea is filled with a sea of humanity. Once famous for bizarre freak shows, boxing bears, and kangaroos, today's shows are much tamer. Hawkers of all sorts appear—palm readers, caricaturists, and photographers with special gimmicks: Miss Piggy one year, ET the next. In winter the Boardwalk has a kind of desolate beauty. Atlantic rollers crash onto the shore with a roar, gulls screech and whirl overhead, there's a faint scent of salt upon the air, and wooden steps go down to the almost-deserted shore. You can always find a bench and sit.

You can choose to walk, cycle, or take the trolley. In summer you can only cycle between the hours of 6 and 10 A.M. because of the crowds; in winter, hours are extended. Bikes are for rent along the Boardwalk. Whatever the season, stop at **Fralingers,** 1325 Boardwalk, for some saltwater taffy, so named when the most popular stand was swamped by the ocean in 1883 or so the story goes. Today it comes in an amazing variety of packages—chocolate dipped or predictably packaged like a slot machine. Sea-foam fudge, peanut chews, and almond macaroons are other choices.

At least look at the ultimate souvenir shop, **Irene's,** 1239 Boardwalk, crammed with every conceivable souvenir—shell-encrusted jewel boxes and lamps, plastic lobsters, mugs, T-shirts galore, gambling games, and novelties—all examples of 20th-century creative schlock-andising.

Here, too, are all the seaside stores and stands so beloved from our childhoods —a plethora of ice cream parlors, peanut palaces, sea foam and fudge outlets, hot dog and hamburger vendors—a veritable junk food junkie's paradise.

See the wonderfully garish ice-cream-sundae-like façade of the **Food & Brew Company** just past Caesar's, painted in cream, eggshell blue, and pink, complete with sea horses and cherubs. I do hope they don't tear it down.

Go into **Steeplechase Pier** at Pennsylvania Avenue to view the hodgepodge of carousels, roller coaster, and other shows. Go while the pier is still as it used to be, before it is converted into another **Ocean One,** a triple-deck ocean liner with 150 shops including 30 restaurants, that has replaced the old Million Dollar Pier, where the longest marathon dance ran from May 26 to October 19, 1935. It's now enclosed with only tiny porthole openings. Sadly the 20th-century redesigners have forgotten that part of the joy of being on a pier was to feel its fragility, a thin slither of engineering jutting into the ocean's invigorating salt spray and wind.

This pier is now simply an ossified boat, a thoroughly disabled pier and a thoroughly inadequate ocean liner, although it does have a whole level of good fast-

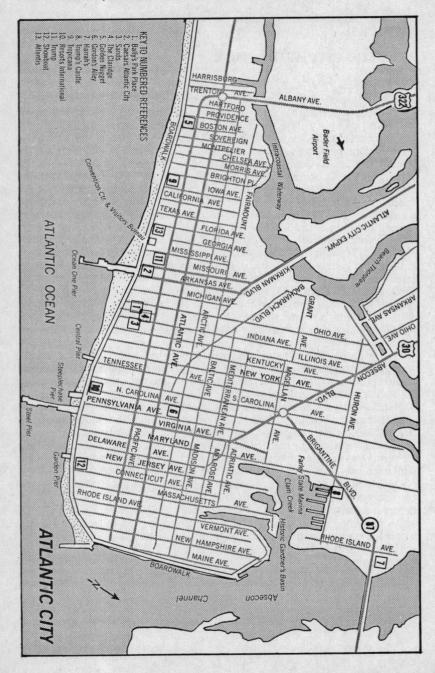

KEY TO NUMBERED REFERENCES
1. Bally's Park Place
2. Caesars Atlantic City
3. Sands
4. The Claridge
5. Golden Nugget
6. Gordon's Alley
7. Harrah's
8. Trump's Castle
9. Tropicana
10. Resorts International
11. Trump
12. Showboat
13. Atlantis

ATLANTIC CITY

food outlets and restaurants.

On the Garden Pier the **Atlantic City Arts Center** displays art exhibits by local artists and also houses the **Atlantic City Historical Museum,** containing items and memorabilia from the old original Atlantic City.

Also on the Boardwalk, of course, stands the famous **Convention Hall,** opened in 1929, where each year Miss America is crowned. Begun originally as an Atlantic City bathing beauty contest, the pageant was discontinued during the Depression because it was considered too extravagant, but it was revived in 1935. The Convention Hall is also the site of auto races, boat and flower shows, and many other kinds of spectacle. The stunning 137-foot-high arched ceiling of the main auditorium also contains a very fine pipe organ, with 33,000 pipes ranging from 3/16-inch to 64 feet in length. According to the statistics, the wires in the motors would girdle the earth twice.

Farther along the Boardwalk, in Margate, stands a charming, whimsical folly, **Lucy the Elephant** (tel. 609/823-6473 or 822-0424). According to my sources, there were originally three elephants, all built in 1881 as a gimmick by an imaginative real estate developer to attract prospective buyers. They were six stories high, constructed of wood, and covered with tin. Only one remains, Lucy, who stands looking mournfully out at the Atlantic. Her eyes are windows, and you enter this weird creature through a small door in her back right foot. Oddly affecting. HOURS: Open in summer only. Tours are given from 10 A.M. to 8:30 P.M. in July and August, from 10 A.M. to 4:30 P.M. daily from June 21; weekends only Memorial Day to June 21 and Labor Day through October. ADMISSION: $1.50 for adults, $1 for children.

Attractions Away from the Boardwalk

When you do tire of the tables, then in summer at least you can take a trip to **Gardner's Basin,** only 10 or 15 minutes away, a pretty boat basin on North Vermont Avenue (tel. 609/348-2880) that is flanked by some seaworthy clapboard homes, many on stilts. It's a public park that also has a convivial waterside nautical restaurant with a low-ceilinged tavern called the Flying Cloud Café. You can watch fishermen come and go, unloading their catch here—lobstermen making their pots in winter, and clam boats returning to port, their metal drums piled high with bushels of clams. The restaurant opens in April and supplies good seafood dishes from $12.50 up.

En route to Gardner's Basin, you might like to pop into the **Absecon Light,** at Rhode Island and Pacific Avenues (tel. 609/345-6328), and visit the museum at its base. HOURS: In summer, 10 A.M. to 4 P.M. daily except Wednesday; weekends only in winter.

Surprise, surprise, only 30 minutes outside Atlantic City off Rte. 30 lies an old and quite charming winery. The **Renault Winery,** Bremen Avenue, Egg Harbor City (tel. 609/965-2111), really is a serene place. A wooden footbridge crosses over a small brook, home to a flock of mallards, into a courtyard, site of many a weekend festival, especially during harvest seasons. From the courtyard you can look out to the rows and rows of vines stretching off into the distance. Louis Renault, a native of Rheims, France, established this vineyard in 1864, and it remained in his family until 1918. About 125,000 gallons of wine are produced today. The 1½-hour tours include a peek into the glass museum (Venetian, German, and English champagne glasses), a display of antique wine-making equipment, and a tour of the wine-making process from the presses to the cellars, with a final stop in the tasting room where you'll be invited to try five or so wines. One of the vineyard's unique contributions is a blueberry champagne. HOURS: Monday through Saturday from 10 A.M. to 5 P.M., on Sunday from noon to 5 P.M. ADMISSION: $1.

The winery is also well known for its restaurant, above the winery and reached by a passageway created from barrels. The theme is continued inside, where the booths are constructed from barrel staves. A prix-fixe dinner is offered (from $17.50 to $22.50) consisting of five courses—appetizer; soup, pasta, or similar; salad; main course; and dessert. The menu changes weekly. HOURS: The dining room is only open on weekends—from 5 P.M. on Friday and Saturday, from 3 P.M. on Sunday.

Throughout the summer a series of weekend festivals are held, culminating in the harvest in mid-September to October, when a series of ethnic celebrations are held along with a traditional grape-stomping contest. To get there, take Rte. 30 west to Bremen Avenue (approximately 16 miles). Turn right to the winery.

Nature is also nearby at the **Brigantine Wildlife Refuge** on Rte. 9 north at Oceanville. Here you can take a self-guided auto tour through 20,000 acres of preserved tidal marsh, barrier beaches, and woods, which are home to all manner of sea and water birds. Call 609/652-1665 for more information.

STOPPING PLACES EN ROUTE TO OR FROM ATLANTIC CITY

Many people stop about 12 miles north of Atlantic City on Rte. 9 at **Smithville,** a restored colonial village, where you can browse in the stores or dine at the **Smithville Inn** (tel. 609/652-7777). The village, built in 1787, was abandoned in the 20th century, until its restoration in 1952.

Dining rooms at the inn are colonial in style, with low beams and flagstone floors. Waitresses in colonial costumes and caps ferry classic American fare —turkey with cranberry sauce, chicken pot pie, crab imperial at lunch—to tables that look out over a pond and woodland background. At dinner, selections include roast duck, prime rib, pork chops, and sirloin, with prices ranging from $10 up.

Afterward browse in the specialty stores—books, sports, tobacco, cooking utensils, candles, and crafts. Or you may happen to be there on a weekend when special celebrations like an antique or craft show, a horse show, or an Oktoberfest are taking place. For information, call 609/652-7777. Besides the inn, there is another restaurant: **Prima's Ristorante** (tel. 609/652-8814), for Italian fare.

Batsto, rather off-the-beaten track in the Pine Barrens, is one of many lost and forgotten towns that were the center of great industry in New Jersey from 1765 to 1840. Much of the cannon, mortar, shot, and shell for the Revolutionary War and the War of 1812 were manufactured here, and later water pipes for eastern cities were made and shipped via schooner up the Mullica River. Batsto was also the

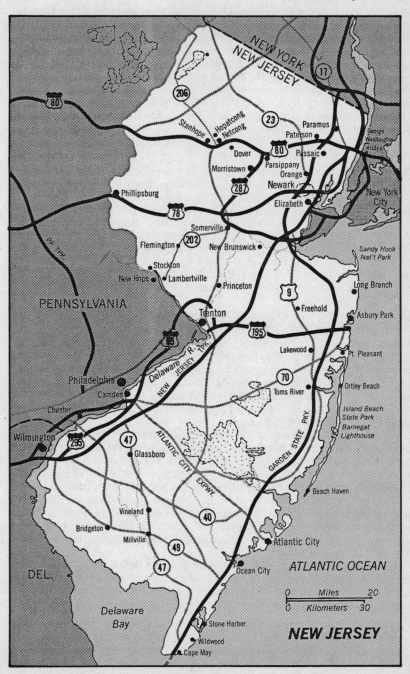

NEW JERSEY

ATLANTIC OCEAN

Delaware
Bay

DEL.

PENNSYLVANIA

NEW YORK

NEW JERSEY

Stanhope
Hopatcong
Netcong
Paramus
Paterson
Dover
Passaic
Morristown
Parsippany
Orange
Newark
Phillipsburg
Elizabeth
New York City
George Washington Bridge
Somerville
Flemington
New Brunswick
Stockton
Sandy Hook Nat'l Park
New Hope
Lambertville
Princeton
Long Branch
Freehold
Asbury Park
Trenton
Lakewood
Pt. Pleasant
Philadelphia
Ortley Beach
Camden
Toms River
Island Beach State Park
Chester
Barnegat Lighthouse
Wilmington
Glassboro
Beach Haven
Vineland
Bridgeton
Millville
Atlantic City
Ocean City
Stone Harbor
Wildwood
Cape May

Delaware R.
PA. TPK.
NEW JERSEY TPK.
ATLANTIC CITY EXPWY.
GARDEN STATE PKY.

| Miles | 0 | 20 |
| Kilometers | 0 | 30 |

site of the first (1846) American glass factory, which produced flat glass for window panes and gas lamps. When you visit this place deep in the forest, you can still imagine the small community of a thousand dominated by the mansion on the hill. The workers' homes were located across the river, with the furnace, gristmill, sawmill, glassworks, and brickyard in between. All of these can be toured, and many craftspeople work here in the summer, demonstrating chair caning, potting, weaving and spinning, woodcarving, and candlemaking. It's a lovely spot to picnic, but it's also a part of America's early industrial heritage. HOURS: Memorial Day to Labor Day, 10 A.M. to 6 P.M. daily, 11 A.M. to 4 P.M. in other months. For information, call 609/561-3262.

ATLANTIC CITY CASINOS

Obviously the ideal place to stay is only an elevator ride away from the tables at your favorite casino. (There are 11 to choose from and more a-coming —Showboat, which should have opened by the time this book appears, and the Taj Mahal, scheduled to open in 1988.) Sadly, I can't tell you that special weekend packages are offered here—it's the midweek package that you have to look for. All of the casinos offer them, and they offer substantial discounts.

A Note on Parking: Parking policies vary. At most casinos you can get your parking stub validated in the casino, usually for four or six hours. Free parking is usually provided to guests staying at the casino's hotel. Make sure you park in lots that offer this validation or you'll find yourself paying $5 an hour and up.

Harrah's Marina, 1725 Brigantine Blvd., Atlantic City, NJ 08401 (tel. 609/441-5000, or toll free 800/257-0476, 800/582-5961 in New Jersey)
This would be my joint first choice, although many confirmed gamblers would heartily disagree because they find that it's too far away from the action on the Boardwalk. As far as I'm concerned, the jitney shuttle takes care of that problem, and the striking location overlooking Absecon Inlet and Frank Farley State Marina, where hundreds of pleasure craft dock during the summer, the sophisticated atmosphere, and the convenient free parking more than make up for that (obviously I'm not a dedicated gambler).

All of the 750 rooms in the 15-story hotel are tastefully decorated, but the swankiest rooms are the 244 Atrium Suites. These consist of a living room furnished with modern seating and a huge TV, radio, and tape deck, and a mirrored marble bar. A sliding door leads into the bedroom, complete with king-size bed, another TV, and a dresser lit art deco style. Carpets are plush, bedspreads are brilliant purple, and the floor-to-ceiling curtains are blue and mauve. The bathroom is tiled, the towels are fluffy, and all of the amenities are readily at hand —shampoo, body lotion, Neutrogena, talc, shoehorn, etc. Touch-tone phones and remote-control TV top it all off. Some of the suites are themed, like the Bombay, the Danube, and the Malibu.

The five restaurants have excellent reputations. The **Buffet** (open 24 hours), on the second floor, is well known for its buffet luncheons and dinners featuring spreads of beef, pork roast, baked chicken, flounder, fettuccine, roast potatoes, vegetables, salads, and desserts, priced around $10 at lunch and dinner. The flagship restaurant, which overlooks the bay, is the **Meadows** (open for dinner seven days a week), a plush beige, plum, and deep-blue room finished with brass and mahogany accents. It serves fine gourmet dishes—salmon filet in puff pastry, breast of capon with vermouth, chateaubriand bouquetier, for example—priced from $17 to $40. Steak and lobster lovers head for the **Steakhouse** restaurant on the third floor (open Wednesday to Sunday from 6 P.M. to 12:30 A.M.) for mesquite-grilled steaks from $17.75 to $25.50. For more casual dining there's the first-floor **Marina Garden** (open 24 hours), where potted plants and a wall of windows promote an outdoor ambience. The **Food Bazaar,** on the first floor overlooking the lagoon, offers sandwiches, pizza, tacos, and salads, served counter style; white-and-yellow tables and chairs, and quarry tiles on the floor give it a festive air. Additional restaurants include **Andreotti's** (open Friday to Tuesday for dinner), specializing in northern Italian cuisine, with prices ranging from $15 to $33, and the **Deli** (open Sunday to Thursday from 11 A.M. to 11 P.M., on Friday and Saturday until 1 A.M.) for the obvious, priced from $4.25 to $13.

The deep-green **casino,** accented with red, is highlighted by brass, polished wood, and chandeliers. It's about 60,000 square feet and features 70 blackjack, 18 craps, 12 roulette, 3 baccarat, and 3 big six tables, along with 1,600 slots.

Five lounges offer a choice of lively entertainment or some quiet. The **Meadows Lounge** (open 10 A.M. to 2 A.M. daily) is one of the quieter spots. The **Winner's Circle** offers wide-screen television viewing for sports fans; the **Bay Cabaret** beats out a disco, country, or modern beat into the casino from mid-afternoon (drinks are served from 1 P.M.), while the **Atrium** is very relaxing with its indoor garden, three-tiered waterfall, and more sedate entertainment, usually provided by a duo or trio (open 24 hours on weekends, noon to 4 A.M. on weekdays).

Top-name entertainment, revues, and sporting events are featured in the 850-seat **Broadway by the Sea Theater.** Such big names as Bobby Vinton, Neil Sedaka, Bill Cosby, Lou Rawls, and Sammy Davis, Jr., have appeared here.

Other facilities include: a game room and snackbar that appeals immensely to children and teenagers; a free supervised children's center for kids 2 to 8; an indoor heated pool on the fourth-floor roof deck; two deck-tennis courts; a fully equipped exercise room; and men's and women's boutique, jewelry shop, and beauty salon. There's covered parking for 2,400 cars conveniently connected to the hotel casino via a walkway. Valet and self-parking are free for the first three hours. Hotel guests' parking is free also. And then, of course, you can park your boat in the 107-slip marina that offers full dockside services. From here also you can hop aboard sailing and fishing charters, sightseeing boats, or Harrah's *Basin Queen* for a sightseeing jaunt. Other boats from neighboring beach communities also dock here. Jet skiing will also be offered.

RATES: $120 to $165 mid-June to mid-September, $90 to $120 in other months.

Golden Nugget, Boston at Pacific Avenue, Atlantic City, NJ 08401 (tel. 609/340-7100, toll free 800/257-8677)
Possessing a definite style and drama of its own, this is a wonderful glitter gulch palace with mirrored ceilings, gilt columns, gold-foiled walls, chandeliers, plenty of marble, elevator doors of solid brass—a true glitzy gambling emporium.

The 23-story hotel offers 518 rooms including seven floors of exquisite, extravagantly appointed suites, including a Deco floor, Zodiac floor, rose and peach suites, and the Penthouse. The remaining standard rooms are all elaborately appointed.

The fantasy elements have also been extended into the eight restaurants. **Lillie Langtry's** (open from 6 P.M. to midnight), on the second floor, is a lavish Chinese-lanterned stage set featuring Cantonese and Szechuan cuisine—moo goo gai pan and tomato beef, for example, from $11 to $22. Across from Lillie's there's **Charlie's**. Incredible effects have been created here. It really feels as if you're dining in a country inn somewhere in the English countryside, but it's merely an illusion created by a series of wonderful tableaux behind glass. And at the entrance, you'd be hard-put to recognize that the oak tree is in fact constructed from metal and brass. It's a very elegant and attractive dining place serving prime rib, 22-ounce T-bone, seafood, all with soup and salad bar (prices from $14 to $30). The premier restaurant is **Victoria's** (tel. 609/340-7230), a gilt- and stained-glass-accented room overlooking the ocean, serving gourmet fare—duckling Chambord, pheasant casserole, and saddle of lamb priced from $18 to $35 (open from 6 P.M. to 1 A.M.). It has achieved an excellent reputation and was voted the finest casino/hotel dining facility by the Atlantic City press. Another marvelous dining stage set has been created at **Stefano's**—pillars decorated with ivy garlands, stucco, an extravagant Venetian chandelier, a fountain—all of which really does transport you to Italy for the selection of such dishes as saltimbocca alla romana and pollo all arrabiata, priced from $10 to $18. **Cornucopia** buffet features a daily buffet that is superb. Moreover, it's a pretty place to dine, seated on blue floral banquettes, among pre-Raphaelite-style murals, an abundance of fresh flowers, and views of the ocean through the Palladian-style windows. The adjacent café stays open 24 hours. For fast food there's the **Sweetheart Cafe** which serves fried chicken nuggets, pizza, sandwiches, and more, most items priced around $6. On the ground floor at the Boardwalk and Boston Avenue, the Victorian-style **Creamery** turns out luscious Häagen-Dazs ice cream sundaes and other light refreshments.

Gilt, crystal, and mirrored ceilings greet you in the 43,000-square-foot **casino,** which houses 57 blackjack, 20 craps, 10 roulette, 2 baccarat, and 4 big six tables, plus 1,200 slot machines, including 51 offering five separate Super Link Progressive Jackpots, one of which is the world's largest jackpot—a great attraction for the professional slotter. Costumed croupiers and waitresses complete the scene.

In the **Rangoon Saloon,** a sublime, mysterious elephant is the centerpiece of this lounge in the corner of the casino. **Elaine's Lounge** offers live entertainment. At the **Opera House** (tel. 609/340-7200), a 540-seat cabaret theater, revues filled with song, laughter, minstrels, and jesters take to the stage.

Other facilities include an indoor swimming pool plus health club with exercise equipment, saunas, etc., and an electronic game arcade. Parking is free to guests.

Of all the casinos, I think I would have to say that the decor at the Golden Nugget is the most eye-catching.

RATES: $140 to $190 from April to mid-September, $120 to $160 from mid-September to April.

Bally's Park Place, Park Place and the Boardwalk, Atlantic City, NJ 08401 (tel. 609/340-2000, or toll free 800/772-7777, ext. 2222)
A special favorite among dedicated gamblers who regularly make it their head-quarters on a trip to Atlantic City, Bally's possesses the largest casino (along with Resorts), and also a great number of reasonably priced food outlets.

The majority of the 428 guest rooms are located in the former Dennis Hotel (1910), a U-shaped building surrounding a tranquil courtyard and outdoor pool. They are all spiffily contemporary, and feature bedside panels housing controls for the color TV and radio. Feature guest rooms have round beds and mirrored ceilings, and there are also a number of moderately priced and themed suites. Another 84 rooms are arranged in a quadrangle, with a landscaped courtyard at the center making for a secluded, peaceful atmosphere. Turndown service is standard.

On the sixth-floor restaurant level a pretty promenade and indoor park has been created, complete with stained-glass gazebo, which is a favored meeting place, and a fountain created from the gargoyles, seashells, and turtles that once embellished the old Blenheim Hotel (1905). Restaurants along the promenade include the elegant restaurant with a panoramic view, **By the Sea** (open from 6 P.M. to midnight daily), serving such delights as lobster caprese (lobster meat sautéed in butter with mushrooms, garlic, tomato, and white wine, served with wild rice, scalloped gratin potatoes, and other vegetables), pork chops with apricots, and roast rack of veal carved tableside. Prices run $18 to $35. At the **Prime Place** (open from 6 P.M. to midnight daily, and also for Sunday brunch), prices for roast rib of beef, lamb chops, filet mignon, and salad bar begin at $20. At the **Sidewalk Café,** turn-of-the-century Atlantic City murals help create the impression of dining al fresco. A seafood buffet, priced around $16, is served seven days a week (Sunday to Thursday from noon to 11 P.M., on weekends until midnight). **Sundaes** (open from noon to 1 A.M. on weekdays, until 3 A.M. on weekends) turns out old-fashioned ice cream delights. **The Greenery** restaurant and coffeeshop (open 24 hours), situated around the courtyard of the old hotel, offers an assortment of dishes all priced around $8 or $9—chicken à la king, blintzes, quiches, etc.

The other, more casual eateries are located downstairs off the casino. At the **Park Place Deli** (open weekdays from 11:30 A.M. to 11 P.M., on weekends until 2 A.M.) you can purchase a hefty sandwich at a not-too-hefty price ($5 to $7), along with soups and other deli specialties. At **Jib's** (open from noon to 2 A.M. on weekdays, until 4 A.M. on weekends) it's clams, oysters, chowders, and more, priced from $1.25, while the **Lone Star** (open weekdays from noon to 4 A.M., on weekends until 6 A.M.) functions as a fast snackbar, serving hot and cold sandwiches, including burgers, for about $4.50. These three are all on the casino level, either at the Boardwalk entrance or on the Park Place side. Over in the hotel wing on the first floor there's a 24-hour coffeeshop.

The dramatic focal point of the 60,000-square-foot **casino** is an escalator flanked by cascading waterfalls, which soars 93 feet out of the center of the casino to the sixth-floor restaurant level.

Prime entertainment lounge is **Billy's Pub,** named after Bally's Park Place president, William "Billy" Weinberger, which features jazz and other musical groups from mid-afternoon, only steps away from the casino floor. **Upstairs in the Park** also features nightly entertainment, while the **Dennis Lounge** offers quiet relaxation any time of day in a lovely room with molded ceilings, marble fireplace, and crystal chandeliers (hotel wing, second floor). The **Park Cabaret** presents musical revues with casts of long-legged lovelies, comedians, and other talents. Closed Tuesday.

Other facilities include the swimming pool in the Dennis courtyard (recently refurbished), an indoor swimming pool, and a health spa. Tennis and racquetball courts are planned. There are a multilevel indoor parking garage and valet parking for hotel guests.

RATES: $130 to $160 from mid-September to mid-June, $110 to $140 from mid-June to mid-September.

Atlantis Hotel & Casino, 2500 Boardwalk, at Florida Avenue, Atlantic City, NJ 08404 (tel. 609/344-4000)
Many patrons at the Atlantis seem to enjoy its more European-style decor and comfort. Rooms are modern, comfortable, and fully equipped with color TV and phones in both the bedroom and bath.

The **casino** itself is spread over three floors, giving each casino area a far more intimate feel.

The restaurants continue this chic ambience—the **Golden Steer** (open daily from 11 A.M. to 3 P.M. and 6 to 11:30 P.M.) is indeed golden, and features magenta-colored banquettes on which to sit while dining on the likes of porterhouse or New York sirloin steaks or rainbow trout with herbs and lemon, priced from $12.50 to $25. The **Chat Noir** (open Tuesday to Sunday for dinner) sports paintings from the original in Paris; here the women are given complimentary roses and the gentlemen complimentary cigars after a lavish meal that might have included chateaubriand, lobster filled with seafood wrapped in light pastry dough, or fettuccine Alfredo, at prices from $11 to $32. The **Empress** is an attractively turned-out Chinese restaurant complete with plenty of shrubbery, rock pools, and rich red decor. Here, Szechuan and Hunan dishes—Szechuan shrimp and Hunan beef, for example—are served, priced from $10 to $16. The **Garden State Café** is open 24 hours for burgers, sandwiches, and similar fare, priced around $6 to $8.

The 1,000-seat **Cabaret** features revues; **other facilities** include racquetball courts and a health club with an indoor pool.

RATES: $130 to $155 from July to mid-September, $90 to $125 in other months.

Resorts International, North Carolina Avenue and the Boardwalk, Atlantic City, NJ 08404 (tel. 609/344-6000, or toll free 800/GET-RICH)
Resorts, the first casino to open in Atlantic City (in May 1978) is located in Haddon Hall, one of Atlantic City's grand old hotels, whose lavish interior was replaced by a vast, garish, red-mirrored decor.

The 686 rooms are typical modern accommodations. The eight restaurants can take you around the world cuisine-wise, from **Camelot** (open from 6 P.M. to midnight daily), impressively furnished with King Charles II–style chairs and green tartan carpet, which serves hearty fare like prime rib, sirloin, and filet mignon as well as salmon steak and lobster stuffed with crabmeat, priced from $16 to $27, to **Capriccio,** a lively spot where a guitarist entertains while you dine on veal, pasta (rigatoni, amatriciana with tomatoes and bacon), seafood (zuppa di pesce with lobster, clams, mussels, and scampi), and beef and lamb dishes, accompanied by fine Italian wines. Prices run $10 to $30. Salmon-pink tablecloths and napkins, silver candlesticks, statuary, and Palladian-style windows overlooking the ocean make this an attractive dining experience. **Le Palais** (open from 6 P.M. to midnight daily), is Resorts' bastion of haute cuisine. In a lavishly appointed atmosphere, diners enjoy a variety of meat and seafood dishes—salmon steak with ginger vinaigrette, lobstertail broiled and steamed with herb butter, and tournedos sautéed with forest mushrooms, Calvados sauce, and Roquefort. At the **House of Kyoto** (open Sunday to Friday from 12:30 to 2:15 P.M. and daily from 6 to 10:30 P.M.), kimono-clad waitresses present every conceivable Japanese treat: negimaki, chicken teriyaki, sushi, sashimi, and tonkatsu, from $14 to $25. For less formal dining there's the **Wedgwood Pavilion** (open from 7 A.M. to 11 P.M. on weekdays, until 3 A.M. on weekends), which features tempting buffets at breakfast ($7), lunch ($10), and dinner ($13); the **Oyster Bar** (open from noon to 6 A.M. daily) for clams, shrimp, stews, and chowders, from $3; and the **Celebrity Deli** (open Monday to Thursday from 11 A.M. to 11 P.M., on Friday until 2 A.M., on Saturday from 9 A.M. to 4 A.M., and on Sunday from 9 A.M. to 11 P.M.) and the **Café Casino** for a quick American or Chinese bite between games.

The **casino** is about the same size as Bally's (nearly as big as two football fields) and features 82 blackjack, 20 craps, 14 roulette, 4 big six, and 3 baccarat tables, plus 1,750 slots. For lounging and entertainment there's the 24-hour **Rendezvous Lounge,** the **Casino Royale** for dancing, and several others.

The biggest names in show business perform regularly at the 1,800-seat Resorts International **Superstar Theatre**—Johnny Mathis, Barry Manilow, Donna Summer, Diana Ross, Wayne Newton, and Tom Jones, to name only a few. The theater also hosts championship boxing contests, ballet, and concert orchestras like the New York Philharmonic, and Resorts has also been presenting unique special events such as Luciano Pavarotti's historic performance in a specially designed amphitheater tent and the Jimmy Connors tennis tournament.

Other facilities include indoor and outdoor pools, squash courts, and a health club fully equipped with exercise machines.

RATES: $110 to $175 from July to Labor Day, $100 to $150 in other months.

The Sands, Indiana Avenue and Brighton Park, Atlantic City, NJ 08401 (tel. 609/441-4000, or toll free 800/257-8580)
The Sands is small-scale compared to, let's say, Bally's and Resorts, but it delivers a lot to the resident visitor. The 504 rooms are decorated in one of four motifs —traditional, modern, French traditional, and Italian contemporary. All rooms have color TV, AM-FM radio, individually controlled heating and air conditioning, and wakeup and message service.

There are several restaurants to choose from: for elegant French haute cuisine,

Mes Amis (tel. 609/441-4200; open from 6 P.M. to midnight), in an atmosphere of wood paneling, crystal chandeliers, and soft pink banquettes and love seats, features such dishes as breast of chicken Jeanette, sautéed with wild cepes and madeira and finished with cream; loin of lamb with Montrachet cheese and herb sauce; or pompano in gold foil with lobster sauce. Prices run $23 to $34.

The **Brighton Steak House** (tel. 609/441-4300; open from noon to 3 P.M. and 6 P.M. to midnight daily, for Sunday brunch from 11 A.M. to 3 P.M.) is another handsomely paneled room serving surf and turf, 16-ounce prime rib, and similar, priced from $16 to $28. Both of these dining rooms are located off a quiet, comfortable lounge where you can sink into a leather couch or chair and enjoy a cocktail. The Sands also has what is probably the best place to find some budget-priced food (by Atlantic City standards), the **Food Court**, which features an array of famous names including Pat's Steaks, 15th Street Bookbinders of Philadelphia, Nathan's Famous, and the Carnegie Deli, purveying everything from pizza, seafood, barbecue, cheesesteaks, burgers, cookies, waffles, ice cream, and more, all in one nicely landscaped area—a few ficus, wrought-iron tables and chairs set in front of false Federal-style town-house flats. You'll find items from $2 to $8.

The **Players Lounge** and the **Punch Bowl** offer live entertainment.

The hotel also offers some added attractions, most notably the **Sands Country Club and Golf Course,** which also has tennis courts and a swimming pool. If you're a guest, the Sands will provide free transportation. **Other facilities** include a health club complete with Nautilus fitness center, sauna, and masseuse. The glass-enclosed rooftop swimming pool is used year round. Parking is provided in a 500-car garage.

Top-flight entertainers appear in the plush Sands **Copa Room** (tel. 609/441-4100)—Shirley MacLaine, Joan Rivers, Joel Grey, Tony Bennett, Rita Moreno, and Ann-Margaret have all appeared here. Sports events are also featured. Weekends turn the room into the **Copa Club** for late-night dancing.

RATES: $115 to $175 from July to September, $100 to $145 in fall and spring, $90 to $140 in winter.

The Tropicana, Boardwalk and Iowa Avenue, Atlantic City, NJ 08401 (tel. 609/340-4000)

The Trop offers a great variety of entertainments, sports, and dining. The 516 rooms are modern and attractive. There are five restaurants to choose from. **Les Paris** (tel. 609/340-4060), an elegant mirrored room where the tables are appointed with fine china, crystal, and silver, serves classic French cuisine—breast of capon with champagne sauce, Dover sole with cream sauce and grapes, and chateaubriand, for example—at prices from $22.50 to $30. At **Il Verdi** (tel. 609/340-4070), a stylish art deco restaurant (black marble tables and pink faux-marble plates), diners can feast on lamb chops with mushroom tomatoes, brandy, and cream; Australian lobster tail in seasoned marinara sauce, and similar, priced from $20 to $30. The **Regent Court** (tel. 609/340-4080) is for prime steaks, chops, and seafood, priced from $17 to $29. All three restaurants are open from 6 P.M. to midnight daily. The 24-hour **Brasserie** coffeeshop, and the **Jade Beach** for Chinese food, complete the dining choices.

The 60,000-square-foot **casino** has 78 blackjack, 20 craps, 11 roulette, 4 big six, and 2 baccarat tables, plus close to 1,700 slots, some of which are placed on a terrace of their very own.

Three lounges offer all kinds of entertainment. **Top of the Trop** on the 20th floor has live groups performing daily; **Grapes, Grapes, Grapes** features fine wines; and the **Garden Terrace** creates a sidewalk café ambience.

Celebrity headliners and shows appear in the **Tropicana Showroom** on the third floor. For reservations and showtimes, call 609/340-4020. The showroom also hosts boxing events. Comedians are presented in the **PHD-1 Club** on the first floor.

Other facilities include a fully equipped health club, masseur/masseuse, outdoor swimming pool, and two lighted tennis courts. Parking is free for registered guests; there's also six hours of free valet and self-parking with casino validation.

Over the next two years the Tropicana will be building a two-acre indoor Disney-inspired theme park featuring an array of rides and activities including a flume-type water ride, a simulated space-capsule ride, bumper cars, and an audioanimatronic show and assorted wandering entertainers. Four restaurants plus a lounge with large fully stocked aquariums are also planned. Opening date? Early 1989.

RATES: $125 from January 1 to mid-April, $135 from mid-April to July, $150 from July through August, $135 from September to November 22, $125 from November 23 to December 31. These are weekend rates; midweek prices are $30 to $35 less. Special packages are also offered.

Caesars Atlantic City Hotel-Casino, Arkansas Avenue and the Boardwalk, Atlantic City, NJ 08401 (tel. 609/348-4411, or toll free 800/257-8555, 800/582-7600 in New Jersey)
From the Boardwalk you can go straight into the casino or take an elevator to the third floor, on which you'll find several restaurants. The **Imperial Steakhouse** (open from 6 P.M. to midnight) features veal, lamb, and lobster as well as thick juicy steaks, priced from $16 to $28. Decorated in Oriental style, the room is highlighted by a landscaped rock garden pond. At the **Hyakumi Japanese Restaurant** (open from 6 P.M. to midnight), adjacent to the steakhouse, the teppanyaki chefs prepare and serve a seven-course $35.50 prix-fixe dinner at tableside. It begins with appetizer, soup, tempura, and sunomono salad, followed by chicken breast, tenderloin, or lobster meat, served with vegetables and rice, and green tea. Cacti on the tables, piñatas, and sombreros set the scene at **San Pedro's** for Mexican dishes priced from $4 to $7.50.

Caesars' gourmet restaurants are found on the second floor along a marble corridor. Pass the bronze lions at the entrance and you go into a handsome black marble decor with a lovely Oriental fountain at the center of the **Oriental Palace.** The cuisine includes Cantonese, Mandarin, Szechuan, and Mongolian dishes —lobster dynasty or delight with water chestnuts, peppers and lychees; peacock pork sautéed with bamboo shoots; red peppers Szechuan style. Several palace dinners are available—three courses for $20, four courses for $25. À la carte prices range from $12.50 to $28.50. The art-deco style **Le Posh** has a view of the ocean and offers a $25 Sunday brunch that includes champagne. **Primavera** specializes in northern Italian cuisine.

Among the more reasonably priced dining choices are **Milt and Sonny's Deli** (open 24 hours), which offers everything from sandwiches and burgers to prime rib, for $6 to $18.50; the self-service **Boardwalk Café,** on the hotel's third floor, serving a sandwich, salad, and beverage for $6, among other items; and **Ambrosia** (open Tuesday to Saturday from 11 P.M. to 8 A.M.) for light meals and snacks.

The **Regency Bar** (open from noon to 4 A.M. weekdays, to 6 A.M. on weekends), next to the casino, showcases musical acts while the **Circus Maximus** theater features such headliners as Natalie Cole.

The 49,000-square-foot **casino** offers 54 blackjack, 24 craps, 7 roulette, 3 big six, and 4 baccarat tables, along with about 1,400 slots, including a special slot lounge.

The guest rooms are prettily decorated in celery and pink, and furnished with soft-sculpture beds, couch, floral murals. The bathrooms are carpeted, have vanity sinks, and are also designed so that the lavatory is separated from the bathroom.

Other facilities include a private beach and beach club, two volleyball courts on the beach, pool, game room filled with pinball and electronic and video games, three rooftop tennis courts, two platform tennis courts, the Health Spa, and numerous shopping facilities. There's a 550-car parking garage connected via a bridge to the hotel's second floor.

RATES: $140 to $175 from June to Labor Day, $100 to $145 in off-season.

The Claridge, Indiana Avenue and the Boardwalk, Atlantic City, NJ 08401 (tel. 609/340-3434)
The Claridge always seems smaller and more intimate than the other vast casino/hotels. The rooms are decorated in rust and blue in a typically modern fashion, with bamboo headboards on the beds and faux-burled-wood furniture.

At the **Pavilion** (open Monday to Saturday from 11:30 A.M. to 2:30 P.M., on Sunday from 10 A.M. to 2:30 P.M., and daily from 6 P.M. to midnight) a sumptuous decor of marble, satin, and crystal chandeliers provides the backdrop for classic French cuisine like sole meunière and veal française, priced from $15 to $30. **Diamond Jim's** is a typical steak and seafood restaurant. At the **Great American Buffet** you'll feast on an assortment of dishes for only $10, while at **Wally's** you can grab a burger at the stand-up counter. The **Stadium Deli** and the 24-hour **Garden Room** coffeeshop, overlooking the ocean, complete the dining facilities.

Such stars as Sarah Vaughn and Mel Torme have appeared at the **Palace Theater.** The Met's Robert Merrill also appears here.

Other facilities include an indoor pool, a health club, and a game room.

RATES: In summer, $130 to $140 in midweek, $150 to $160 on weekends; in spring and fall, $105 to $115 in midweek, $125 to $135 on weekends; in winter, $85 to $95 in midweek, $105 to $115 on weekends. Midweek packages are offered.

Trump Hotel and Casino, Mississippi Avenue and the Boardwalk, Atlantic City, NJ 08401 (tel. 609/441-6000, or toll free 800/441-0909)
The rooms here are quite good looking. Most have plum-colored satin bedspreads, three beige walls relieved by one multicolored, brass or marble lamps, clock-radio, and furnishings of faux burled wood. The bathrooms are tiled in pale brown, have telephone, and also contain amenities attractively packaged in a magenta-colored box.

Restaurants are located on the sixth floor. **Ivana's** (open for dinner from 6 to 11 P.M.) is the premier restaurant, an art deco–style room decorated in sleek dark brown with plenty of mirrors and fresh flower bouquets. The food is classical French gourmet—breast of pheasant with mushroom sauce, veal chop with morel sauce and fettuccine Alfredo, rack of lamb, duck à l'orange flambéed with Cointreau, priced from $23.50 to $25. **Maximillians** (open for dinner from 6 to 11 P.M.) is the place for steak, lobster, and prime rib, priced from $17.25 to $28. The decor is brilliant vermillion and mahogany paneling, with marble and mirror accents. At the **Grand Buffet** (open for lunch and dinner from 11 A.M. to 11 P.M.) with an ocean view, the buffet will display such dishes as prime rib, corned beef and cabbage, pork chops with sauerkraut, swordfish with ginger sauce, and baked chicken, along with vegetables, salads, and fruits. The price is around $13. Saturday features an Italian spread; on Friday it's French.

More casual restaurants are down on the first floor—**Harvey's Deli** (open from 11 A.M. to 11 P.M. weekdays, to midnight on weekends), right on the Boardwalk, has sandwiches and blintzes, etc., from $4.75. The 24-hour **New Yorker** restaurant, decked out in red and gold with a black marble model of the Chrysler building on view, offers everything from sandwiches to veal marsala and breakfast; prices begin at $6. And finally there's **Scoops,** for Häagen-Dazs ice cream and shakes.

The **casino** is a riot of gilt, silver, and Mylar. Just off the main floor there's the winners' snackbar for pizza and sandwiches, priced from $5.

There's continuous entertainment in **Jezebel's** and **Trump's** lounges, while **Trump's Theater** presents such celebrities as Donny and Marie Osmond, and Mitzi Gaynor.

Other facilities include a pool and sundeck, health club, and two tennis courts.

RATES: $130 to $150 in summer, $110 to $135 in fall and winter, and $120 to $140 in spring.

Trump's Castle Casino Hotel, Huron Avenue and Brigantine Boulevard, Atlantic City, NJ 08401 (tel. 609/441-2000, or toll free 800/441-5551)
The entrance to this kingdom is indeed impressive. Escalators take you up

into the long glass-roofed galleria, in which the walls are faced with pink marble and the focal point is a gold-painted replica of a Rhenish-style castle which is duplicated by a series of miniatures on top of chrome pillars that are scattered along the space. No doubt about the message here. The guest rooms, too, are quite flashy—among the furnishings are '30s-style chests of drawers, the bathroom is marble, and each has a long-stem red rose somewhere evident.

Restaurants are varied. **Delfino's** (open for dinner from 6 P.M. to midnight) offers continental-style cuisine in a Mediterranean-style atmosphere. Frederic Remington sculptures, Texas longhorn chandeliers, and booths constructed out of rough-hewn logs set the scene at the **Beef Baron** for steak kebabs, lamb chops, prime rib, and barbecued items, priced from $7 to $19. Breakfast ($7), lunch ($9), and dinner ($12) are served in the **Food Fantasy Buffet** (open from 11 A.M. till whenever). The **International Buffet** (open from 11 A.M. to 10 P.M.) features themed spreads. And finally there's a 24-hour **coffeeshop,** selling everything from a grilled cheese and bacon to steaks from $5 to $13.75.

Variety shows are featured in the **King's Court,** and **Viva's** also has entertainment from noon on.

Other facilities include a pool and snackbar, five tennis courts, and a health club on the sixth floor.

RATES: $115 to $170 in summer, $95 to $150 in spring and fall, and $90 to $140 in winter.

LODGING OUTSIDE THE CASINOS

Ideally located only half a block from the Bally, Sands, and Claridge casinos is the **Best Western,** at Beach Block Pacific and Indiana Avenues (P.O. Box 5309), Atlantic City, NJ (tel. 609/348-9175, or toll free 800/528-1234). RATES: From $100 in summer.

Otherwise, your choice of accommodations is limited to motels.

For the golf or tennis buff who also wants to spend a little time at the tables, only minutes away and connected by regular shuttle service is the **Inn at Golf and Tennis World,** Black Horse Pike, West Atlantic City, NJ 08232 (tel. 609/641-3546). The complex offers 110 rooms, complete health club, three indoor and three outdoor tennis courts, an indoor golf-driving range, indoor and outdoor pools, and a full-service restaurant. The casinos are two miles away. The health club has whirlpool, steam and sauna, Nautilus equipment, and a cardiovascular training center with computerized bikes, rowers, and treadmill, plus massage therapists and tanning beds.

RATES: Mid-November to early June, $60 in midweek, $65 on weekends; June to mid-September, $70 in midweek, $80 on weekends.

WHERE TO EAT OUTSIDE THE CASINOS

Downtown Dining
For an elegant, intimate setting with a distinctively old-world ambience, go to **Jo-**

han's Zelande, tucked away in a small frame building at 3209 Fairmount Ave., at the corner of Fairmount and Sovereign (tel. 609/344-5733). Don't be fooled by the modest front of the house though, as Johan's prices are not modest at all: $47.50 is the prix fixe (not including tax, wine, or tips), but your dinner will be really superb classic French cuisine, prepared by Johan himself, a tall blond Dutch Zealander. There are two sittings, at 6:30 P.M. and at 9 P.M., for the seven-course dinner. There are usually only four selections to choose from— for example, medallions of lamb with herbs and madeira sauce, beef filet with shallots and mushrooms in a cream-cognac sauce, duck breast with Calvados caramel-sugar sauce, and veal with herbs topped with shrimp in a beurre blanc.

What makes a meal so delightful here, at least as far as I'm concerned, is the element of surprise and the consequent anticipation that awaits each of the other courses. The night I was there my meal went like this: first to arrive were really plump and juicily tender mussels in a pastry shell with white wine cream sauce, followed by soup with vermicelli and meatballs. A salad of string beans, asparagus, and white and green cucumbers preceded a delicious dish of paupiettes of sole with spinach in a wine sauce, finished with tomatoes and Gouda cheese accompanied by duchesse potatoes. A tangerine sorbet was then brought to freshen the palate before the main course. The final touch was strawberry waffles with a chocolate-dipped strawberry and coffee. The whole meal was wonderfully orchestrated and served—a truly memorable experience and one well worth the money.

And what's even better, while the atmosphere is elegant and the service is impeccable, it's never pretentious or overbearing, but quite relaxed and comfortable instead. Lace curtains at the windows, chintz wallpapers, a stuffed pheasant, handsome mantel clock, and gilt-framed portraits decorate the low-lit room. Classical music plays quietly in the background.

Among the large number of good Italian restaurants in Atlantic City, the current favorite of local movers and shakers (and visiting entertainers as well) is **Scannicchio's,** on the beach block at 119 South California Ave. (tel. 609/348-6378). Behind an unprepossessing exterior you'll find an equally modest, dimly lit, rather large room, where you'll just about be able to discern some pleasant oil paintings and hanging plants decorating the walls. Luckily the menu is printed in bold, large type. Scannicchio's makes good use of local Jersey seafood (appetizers include clams steamed, casino, oreganata, and posillippo, all in the $7 range), and a favorite main course is seafood alla Scannicchio—lobster, shrimp, scallops, clams, and mussels, for $19.50. There are also freshly made manicotti, lasagne, and gnocchi, as well as a selection of veal, chicken, and beef dishes, priced from $11 to $18.50. In other words, there's good reason for this house's popularity.

HOURS: 5 P.M. till about midnight; bar open later.

The **Knife and Fork Inn,** Atlantic and Pacific Avenues (tel. 609/344-1133), renowned for its seafood and corn fritters, is also known for its distinctive Flemish architecture, complete with mullioned windows. Built in 1910, it has been run by the same family since 1927. Historic it may be, but it has also kept pace with the new Atlantic City. Above the small bar in the front hang a dozen or so hard hats belonging to the leaders of the crews who built the casinos. Earlier traditions are reflected in the hunting prints and decoys that are scattered around. Entrees range from $13 for fried oysters to $22.75 for lobster thermidor. If you love stone crabs, dine early, for otherwise they will have been snapped up. Besides the selection of lobsters and seafood there are a few steak, chops, and chicken dishes on the menu.

DINNER: 5:30 to 10:30 P.M. daily.

Regarded as one of the best seafood houses on the east coast, **Docks Oyster House,** 2405 Atlantic Ave. (tel. 609/345-0092), is the oldest established restaurant in Atlantic City, dating back to 1897. Oak, etched glass, and some nautical effects provide the atmosphere for some of the best seafood in town. Start with a well-stocked oyster stew and go on to the stuffed lobster, the sautéed scallops, or any other seafood dish. Prices range from $13 to $25.

DINNER: Tuesday to Saturday from 5 P.M.

Orsatti's, on North Carolina Avenue, between Atlantic and Pacific (tel. 609/ 347-7667), has been hosting visitors for many years, and if the photographs on the walls are anything to go by, then everybody from the pope to Gerald Ford has enjoyed the Italian culinary delights. Eggplant parmigiana and veal marsala or piccata, plus a good choice of seafood like crab imperial and lobster, begin at $10.75.

DINNER: Tuesday to Sunday from 4 to 11:30 P.M. On Friday and Saturday nights a trio plays.

Don't be put off by the ancient, thoroughly verdigrissed old building that houses **Los Amigos,** 1926 Atlantic Ave., between Michigan and Ohio (tel. 609/ 344-2293). Go through the weather-worn door and you're in a pleasant enough long bar with a brightly painted red and yellow tin ceiling. In the back a Mexican tile floor and minimal decorations provide the setting for Mexican cuisine you can wash down with a cool Mexican beer, or if you prefer, pitchers of margaritas.

LUNCH: 11:30 A.M. to 4 P.M. daily. DINNER: 4:30 P.M. to 2 A.M. daily, plus late night snacks until 6:30 A.M.

A more pub-like atmosphere, on a Victorian note, can be found at **12 South,** 12 S. Indiana Ave. (tel. 609/344-1112), wallpapered with copies of historic front pages. Burgers, chili, and more substantial items like barbecued chicken and veal marsala, which appear on the dinner menu, are priced from $8 to $12.

HOURS: 11 A.M. to 8 A.M. daily.

At **Pal's Other Room Restaurant,** 8110 Ventnor Ave. (tel. 609/344-0366), just west of the Monument, dinner will begin with a relish tray featuring chick peas and stringbean salad served on sliced provolone and salami, followed by a large bowl of salad that comes with salad servers. After this you can begin with such appetizers as roasted peppers with anchovies and tuna or sautéed artichokes, and follow with a choice from the selective menu—spicy shrimp diablo, broiled lobstertail stuffed with crabmeat, fettuccine Alfredo, half a roast chicken, or other veal and fish dishes. Prices range from $7.50 to $21.50. The room has a pretty summery air derived from the lattice trellis work, a series of metal butterflies that

appear very delicate, and warm red-cushioned bamboo chairs.
DINNER: Tuesday to Sunday from 5 to 10:30 P.M.

Atlantic City Traditions

A visit to Atlantic City is never complete without a visit to one of the city's famous
sub shops. Most famous of all is the **White House Sub Shop,** 2301 Arctic Ave., at
Mississippi (tel. 609/345-1564 or 345-8599), where they've sold over 11 million of
these meals-in-themselves sandwiches since 1946. Seems like everyone who's
anyone has eaten here—Dean Martin, Sammy Davis, Jr., Buddy Hackett, Frank
Sinatra, Chris Ford of the Detroit Pistons. A regular sub will cost you $4.90 and
it's enough for two! Or you can opt for meatballs, cheesesteak, pepper steak,
steak, and other kinds of subs. Sit at the orange booths or take-out.

HOURS: Monday to Saturday from 10 A.M. to midnight, 11 A.M. to midnight on
Sunday.

Or else head for **Josh's Sub Shop,** 3709 Ventnor Ave. (tel. 609/344-5171), another wizard hoagie creator that also sells pizza, spaghetti, and antipasto.

HOURS: Monday to Saturday from 10 A.M. to 8 P.M. in winter, to 10 P.M. in summer.

Or try **Dino's Sub and Pizza Shop** at 8016 Ventnor Ave. in Margate (tel. 609/
822-6602 or 822-0670).

Out-of-Town Restaurants

If you don't mind hopping into your car and driving a short distance to get away
from the crowds and lines, there are several worthwhile country-style restaurants, whose prices are below those on the Boardwalk.

Ram's Head Inn, 1468 White Horse Pike (tel. 609/652-1700), on Rte. 30 in
Absecon, New Jersey, is only 15 minutes from downtown. You can't miss the
white clapboard building brightened by brilliant yellow awnings and green shutters, set around a delightful garden courtyard for summer dining and evening
cocktails. You enter a comfortable lounge, prettily furnished with breakfronts,
Windsor chairs, and always featuring a display of fresh potted flowers and plants.
In winter it's made cozy by the fire. There are three dining rooms, two formal yet
intimate, the other a skylit conservatory. The entrees include such favorites as
beef Wellington, chicken breast, and seafood specialties, priced from $13.

LUNCH: Monday to Friday from 11:30 A.M. to 2:30 P.M. DINNER: Monday to Friday from 5 to 9:30 P.M., on Saturday until 10 P.M., and on Sunday from 3:30 to 9:30
P.M.

According to the locals, the best prime rib in the whole area can be found at
Library III, on Rte. 40 east (tel. 609/645-7655). Plenty of fine reading accompaniment.

DINNER: Monday to Saturday from 4:30 P.M. to 1 A.M., on Sunday from 3:30
P.M. to midnight.

There's another local favorite, also on Rte. 40 east, **Tulls** (tel. 609/266-5540),
which is known for its outstanding raw bar and selection of fresh seafood deliv-

ered to the restaurant by Tulls' very own fishing fleet (stop in, if you like, at the retail fish store). The emphasis is on the food, not the decor, which is warm and simple—red-checkered tablecloths and captain's chairs. At dinner a selection of fresh fish of the day, priced at $10 might include monkfish, salmon, swordfish, bluefish, etc. Lobsters from the tank are also available, along with special combination plates like the New England clambake consisting of steamed lobster, shrimp, snow crab, clams, and mussels. Dinner prices include a selection from the salad bar that is brought to the table, which offers lettuce, mushrooms, broccoli, onions, croutons, radishes, etc. At lunchtime, crab, clams, tile, and other fish specials are all under $6.

LUNCH: 11 A.M. to 3 P.M. daily. DINNER: 5 to 9 P.M. daily.

At the **Tuckahoe Inn,** Rte. 9, in Beesley's Point (tel. 609/390-3322), you can dine looking out over Great Egg Harbor Bay at a view that has certainly changed since this early-18th-century inn was built, for today you can see the steaming cooling towers of a 20th-century power plant. On your way in or out of the restaurant, take a moment to look at the old photographs of Atlantic City in the 1890s, especially the photograph of Steelhead Pier. In a warm, polished-wood tavern atmosphere, you can enjoy such specialties as deviled crabs, prime rib, and roast duck, starting at around $11.

HOURS: Sunday to Friday from noon to 9 P.M., on Saturday to 10 P.M.

EVENING ENTERTAINMENT

At the Casino/Hotels

All casinos offer nightly entertainment in their lounges. In addition, of course, there are the headliners and revues. Headliners appear at **Caesars' Circus Maximus** (tel. 609/348-4411), the **Claridge's Palace Theater** (tel. 609/340-3400), the **Golden Nugget's Opera House Theater** (tel. 609/347-7111), **Harrah's Broadway by the Sea** (tel. 609/441-5000), **Resorts' Superstar Theater** (tel. 609/344-6000), the **Sands' Copa Room** (tel. 609/441-4000), the **Tropicana's Showroom** (tel. 609/340-4000), and **Trump's Theater** (tel. 609/441-6000).

Revues are offered at **Atlantis' Cabaret** (tel. 609/344-4000), **Bally's Park Place Cabaret** (tel. 609/340-2000), **Caesars'** (tel. 609/348-4411), the **Claridge's** (tel. 609/340-4000), the **Golden Nugget Opera House Theater** (tel. 609/340-7160), the **Sands** (tel. 609/441-4000), the **Tropicana** (tel. 609/340-4020), and **Trump's Castle** (tel. 609/441-2000).

Outside the Casinos

A disco scene with suspended circular dance floors, a huge aquarium, and a piano lounge can be found at **Club Ancoppa,** 2233 Atlantic Ave., at Mississippi (tel. 609/344-1733). HOURS: Daily in summer, Wednesday to Sunday from 11 P.M. in winter. From midnight on, a flashy laser and sound show throws **Chez Paree,** at New York Avenue and the Boardwalk (tel. 609/348-4313), into a frenzy. HOURS: Open weekends in summer, Saturday only in winter.

Jazz can be heard at **Le Club,** in the Enclave Condominiums, Lincoln Place and the Boardwalk (tel. 609/347-0400), in a room with a spectacular ocean view. HOURS: Open from 5 P.M. to 2 A.M. in winter, longer in summer.

The croupiers often hang out at the **Florida Pub,** 10½ S. Florida Ave. (tel. 609/348-1990), a popular spot where food is served from 10 A.M. to 7 A.M.

A couple of 24-hour spots, when you can't sleep: **Club Atlantic,** 3426 Atlantic Ave. (tel. 609/345-0606), and the **Irish Pub,** at St. James and the Boardwalk (tel. 609/345-9613), where seafood and sandwiches are also served 24 hours a day, along with Irish ballad entertainment.

ATLANTIC CITY ACTIVITIES

BEACHES: Atlantic City beaches are free; however, those at Brigantine and Ventnor/Margate require purchase of a badge for admission.

BICYCLING: For rentals, try Longo and Sons, at North Carolina Avenue and the Boardwalk (tel. 609/344-8288), open from 6 A.M. to 10 P.M.

BIRDWATCHING: Call 609/652-1665 for the Brigantine Wildlife Refuge, off Rte. 9, which is open from dawn to dusk, offering trails and observation towers.

CAMPING: Only ten miles from Atlantic City, **Casino,** 1997 Black Horse Pike (at the junction of Rtes. 40 and 322), Pleasantville, NJ 08232 (tel. 609/641-3085), a KOA campsite, will provide transportation into town.

The **Bass River Forest,** New Gretna, NJ 08224 (tel. 609/296-9263), provides pleasant camping in a 13,000-acre forest area with bathing, boating, swimming, fishing, hiking, and a nature area. Open all year and only 17 miles from the shore.

The closest campsite is Shady Pines (tel. 609/652-1516), only seven miles away in Absecon Highlands.

In Wharton State Forest there are summer cabins available for groups of four and up for very low fees, and also primitive camping sites. This is also good canoeing and hiking country. For information about the forest, contact Wharton Forest, Batsto, R.D. 4, Hammonton, NJ 08037 (tel. 609/561-0024).

CANOEING: For info on canoeing the Pine Barrens, contact Mick's Canoe Rental, Rte. 563, Chatsworth, NJ 08019 (tel. 609/726-1380), or Mullica River Marina, Sweetwater (tel. 609/561-4337).

FISHING: Try Captain Applegate, South Carolina Avenue and Brigantine Boulevard, who offers all-day fishing trips and night fishing for blues. Boats leave from Farley State Marina (tel. 609/345-4077). You can also fish from the piers.

GOLF: Brigantine Country Club, Roosevelt Boulevard and North Shore Drive (tel. 609/266-1388).

HORSEBACK RIDING: Hidden Valley Ranch, 4070 Bay Shore Rd., Cold Spring (tel. 609/884-8205).

ICE SKATING: Ventnor Rink, at New Haven and Atlantic Avenues (tel. 609/823-7947), has Saturday-afternoon sessions and evening sessions from 7:30 P.M. Also open on Sunday.

RUNNING: Boardwalk Runners meet every Sunday at 10 A.M. at Cornwall Avenue in Ventnor (tel. 609/823-6486).

SAILING: Hobie Cats and windsurfing boards are available from Bayview Sailboats, 312 Bay Ave., Ocean City (tel. 609/398-3049).

STATE PARKS: For information write Division of Parks & Forestry, State Park Service, CN 404, Trenton, NJ 08025.

TENNIS: Golf and Tennis World, Black Horse Pike, West Atlantic City (tel. 609/641-3546), has three indoor and three outdoor courts from $16 to $30 an hour. The Sands Hotel has five racquetball courts available for $12 an hour.

WINDSURFING: Rentals are available at Bayview Sailboats, 312 Bay Ave., Ocean City (tel. 609/398-3049), and at Eastern Sailboards, 202 Bay Ave., Somers Point (tel. 609/391-9650).

CAPE MAY

DISTANCE IN MILES: 150 miles
ESTIMATED DRIVING TIME: 3¾ hours

DRIVING: Take the New Jersey Turnpike to the Garden State Parkway all the way to the end, which will bring you right into Cape May on Lafayette Street. Turn left on Madison and you'll be at the beaches.

BUS: New Jersey Transit (tel. 201/762-5100) operates daily express buses from the Port Authority Bus Terminal to Cape May. The trip takes 4¼ hours.

Special Events to Plan Your Trip Around

MAY: The Tulip Festival displays hundreds of tulips around town, Dutch food, crafts, dancing, and music (usually at the end of May).

SEPTEMBER: Fish Festival dedicated to the fishermen lost at sea also celebrates Cape May's position as a Coast Guard training center and as the largest commercial fishing port in New Jersey. Events include exhibits, dramatic Coast Guard rescue demonstration on Friday night, seafood tasting, etc. (usually the weekend after Labor Day).

OCTOBER: Victorian Week—fashion show, open-house tours, and appropriate entertainments (Columbus Day weekend).

DECEMBER: Christmas in Cape May. Several guesthouses offer special packages (see later under "Cape May Lodging"), and the stores along the Mall offer special shopping discounts along with the festive wine and cheese.

For further information about New Jersey in general, contact the Division of Travel & Tourism, New Jersey Department of Commerce, 1 W. State St., C.N. 826, Trenton, NJ 08625 (tel. 609/292-2470). For specific information about the Cape May area, contact the Chamber of Commerce of Greater Cape May, P.O. Box 109, Cape May, NJ 08204 (tel. 609/884-5508).

Arrive in Cape May and you're in a different world and a different era. Drive or walk through the streets and you'll see lovely old Victorian homes painted white, sage green, pale blue, gray, or pink, with swing seats and rockers on the wraparound verandas, intricate towers, turrets, and cupolas rising from fish-scale mansard roofs and deep projecting bays, row after row lining the streets that run down to the promenade and the sea. And what's even more exciting is that you can stay in them, for many have been taken over and restored by young professional couples, who have chosen Cape May as their refuge from the treadmill of corporate and urban life and now run these marvelous homes as guesthouses. Here you can sleep on lace-trimmed pillows and sheets under antique quilts spread on brass or Renaissance Revival beds, wander through rooms filled with Mission-style furniture, Eastlake sofas or Empire-style couches, brilliant chandeliers, ornate clocks and mirrors, or else spend time rocking gently on the veranda enjoying the cool sea breezes that waft in from the shore. During the day, cycle around town or out to Cape May Point to survey the lighthouse, the marshlands, and best of all, the rolling dunes that back the sand beach, or else go fishing, swimming, birdwatching, or boating, watch the catch arrive at the main dock, play some tennis or golf, and enjoy a whole slew of summer events—clambakes, bandstand concerts (and even some special winter holiday-season events).

You'll be enjoying pleasures similar to those that brought as many as 3,000 people a day aboard steamboats to the resort in the 1850s, making Cape May a national spa of international acclaim. Its life as a resort had begun much earlier, soon after the War of 1812 when the first of several Congress Hall hotels was built, in 1816. From then on, Cape May received a steady stream of notable visitors: Henry Clay and Abraham Lincoln came in the 1840s, and much later such artists as Lillie Langtry and John Philip Sousa. Between 1850 and 1890 five presidents chose it as their temporary escape from the round of government—Franklin Pierce, James Buchanan, Ulysses S. Grant, Chester A. Arthur, and Benjamin Harrison.

Even during its heyday, from 1850 to 1913, Cape May experienced a series of natural disasters. Fire struck twice, in 1869 and 1878, destroying whole sections of the town, including the 3,500-room Mount Vernon, which had been the biggest hotel in the world. Each time, the town was rebuilt in the same bracketed Italianate style that had existed before the fire, which is why so many of these lovely houses have survived. Located at the confluence of the Delaware and the Atlantic, the town is extremely vulnerable to storms. The major storm of 1962, which buried Cape May under sand and water, prompted many to think seriously about preservation and set the course that ensured the survival of the town's great Victorian legacy and also rescued it from the doldrum days when it survived only as a military base and a commercial fishing port visited by a handful of loyal tourists who stayed at rather rundown rooming houses. Today Cape May is once again playing the role of the grand resort and it's a lovely place to go to re-experience the charm and grace of a small intimate seaside resort that has escaped the ugly overlay of honky-tonk entertainment and gross modern development.

Getting Around

Cape May is easy to walk around and it's great for bicycling. Rental bikes are available at many places. For example, on West Perry Street or Rte. 606 (the road that takes you out to Cape May Point) at **Mope or Pedal,** and also in town at **Village Bike Rentals** in the Acme parking lot.

The **Mid-Atlantic Center for the Arts,** 1048 Washington St. (tel. 609/884-5404), runs trolley, walking, and house museum tours. The trolley tours last 30 minutes ($3.50 for adults, $1 for children) and leave daily in July and August, weekends only in September and October, from Beach Drive and Gurney Street. (Locations do change, so call for the schedule.) Walking tours usually leave on Sunday mornings from the information booth on the mall and last 1½ hours. Gaslight tours of the Physick House, the Abbey, the Mainstay Inn, and the Wilbraham Mansion are also given during July and August on one or two evenings a week ($10 for adults, $5 for children). Trolleys also serve the whole area from 10 A.M. to 10 P.M. June to September.

CAPE MAY ATTRACTIONS

Start at the **Welcome Center,** located across from the bandstand at 405 Lafayette St. (tel. 609/884-8411 or 884-3323). Here you'll find a hot-line phone center for conducting your own accommodations search if you've come without making reservations. The staff is exceedingly friendly and helpful; coffee is available, as well as plenty of written information about all kinds of events—concerts at the bandstand, foot races, quilt and decoy shows, barbecues, fish fries, clambakes, vintage movies, contests of all sorts (kite flying, bike racing), and other summer frolics. HOURS: May 1 to the end of October, Monday to Saturday from 9 A.M. to 4 P.M., on Sunday from 1 to 4 P.M. During the summer, information is also dispensed from the booth on the Washington Mall.

Most people will want to spend their hours at the **beach,** swimming, fishing, sailing, windsurfing, birdwatching, sunbathing, and other shore pastimes, but for those with an interest in history and architecture, Cape May also offers a lot. First, of course, on the list are the 150 or so Victorian homes that still stand in the heart of Cape May.

One of the first things most people will want to do is take the **walking tour,** and I

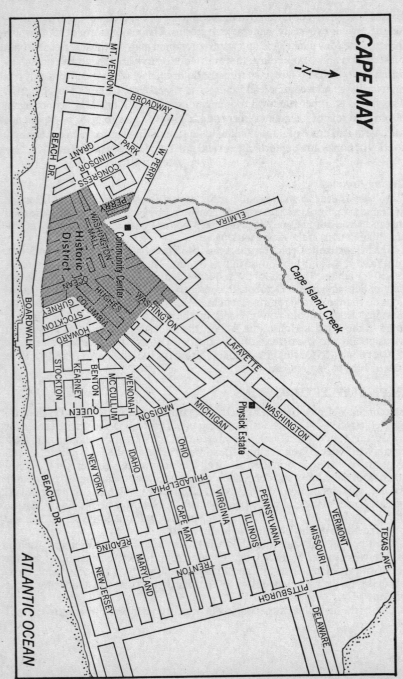

recommend that you do, for you'll learn an incredible amount about architecture and the history of Cape May. Walking tours last 1½ hours and depart from the information booth on Washington Mall. Price is $5.

Walking Around Town

Spend some time, even if you don't take the walking tour, exploring the whole area between Congress and Franklin Streets and from Beach Avenue to Lafayette, where the greatest number of Victorian gems are concentrated.

Start at Beach Drive and Perry Street, where you'll find **Congress Hall,** an L-shaped three-story mansion screened by a multistory colonnade, which served as the summer White House for President Benjamin Harrison. Turn right on Congress Place past nos. 203, 207, and 209 onto Perry Street to see the much-photographed **Pink House** (1880) at no. 33, absolutely encrusted with gingerbread ornamentation. Cross Perry to Jackson Street and turn right toward the sea past several beauties—the **Queen Victoria, Carroll Villa** (now The Mad Batter), the **George Hildreth cottage** at no. 17, and the seven identical cottages commissioned in 1891, which were so unusual in their time, less so today in our standardized age. Turn left along Beach Avenue past the **Colonial Hotel** at Ocean Street, where Wallis Warfield, the Dutchess of Windsor, held her coming-out ball, to Gurney Street and turn left past a whole row of highly ornamental homes—the **Baldt House** at no. 26, the 1869 house, the **Gingerbread House,** all culminating in **The Abbey** at the corner of Columbia Avenue, which was built by Stephen D. Button for John B. McCreary in 1869–1870. Turn right along Columbia Avenue and you'll find the **Mainstay Inn** at no. 635, originally designed to serve as a gambling house. Take a detour down Howard Street to view the **Chalfonte** at no. 301, built in 1875 for Henry Sawyer, Cape May's Civil War hero, and then double back, turning right on Columbia Avenue and then left on Franklin Street, going up to Hughes Street, which is the oldest street in Cape May and still has the original gas lamps, stepping stones, and hitching posts that were used in the earlier really horse-powered era. There are some marvelous houses to look at on this street, including the mauve and gray **White Dove cottage,** the 1868 **Joseph Hall House** with a lot of acroteria decoration, and many other houses with shark's-tooth and fish-scale tiles, witch's cap towers, intricate verge board carving, and more. Note, too, the **Albert Hughes House** (1838), which stands out because it's the only structure built in a typical Federal style.

At the end of Hughes Street, turn right and go over to Washington Avenue and take another right to the **George Allen House** at no. 720, an opulent bracketed mansion worthy of Newport. Continue down to the **Physick Estate** if you have the time and the energy.

The Physick House

In contrast to the fussily ornamental gingerbread style that flourished in Cape May stands the simplicity of Frank Furness's masterpiece, the Physick House at 1048 Washington St. (tel. 609/884-5404), which is so much more rewarding to visit than most because you can actually go into the rooms and experience the space and what it was like to live among the period furnishings, instead of having to peer in from outside behind a set of ropes. A mentor of Louis Sullivan (who in turn was a mentor of Frank Lloyd Wright), Furness turned away from the extravagant Italianate gingerbread style and developed his own elaborate stick style, of which the Physick House is such a good example. Commissioned in 1878 to build a summer home for Frances Ralston that was finished in 1881, Furness designed both the exterior (note his trademarks—the inverted chimneys and jerkin-head dormers) and the interior and even some of the furniture, including a bedroom set that is classic in its simple geometric decoration. Other highlights of the house include several fireplaces easily identifiable by their geometric detailing and classic lines, unusual lincruster (a kind of papier-mâché) wainscotting and ceiling in the hallway and some of the rooms, a golden oak staircase with linear grooving, a parlor with an Eastlake couch and a magnificent ceramic tureen that defies description, a William Morris print fabric in the dining room, and (a favorite with the children) a kitchen filled with all kinds of early gadgetry. The eccentric owner, Dr. Physick himself, had a curious life story. HOURS: The tour of the house takes 1¼ hours and is given Tuesday to Sunday in summer; in spring and fall, on Tuesday, Thursday, Saturday, and Sunday; in winter, weekends only. Call for times. ADMISSION: The admission price of $4 ($1 for children) includes the Carriage House, which is now the home of the Cape May County Art League, and an outbuilding containing a collection of antique tools.

The Wilbraham Mansion

A less classic but nevertheless entertaining tour is given by the resident owners of this Victorian home whose modest façade belies the endless number of rooms and the wealth of its treasures. Built in 1840, it was not until a millionaire steam-engine producer purchased it in 1900 that it acquired its present grand dimensions. The present owners have tried to recover the furniture that was sold in an estate sale, but what they already have here is plenty to feast the eye. The wallpapers throughout the house will probably shock you—exotic in the extreme—and 12- to 15-foot-high Empire mirrors dominate the main parlor, along with a weird and whimsically painted chandelier. The house is stuffed with treasures of all sorts that would take several days to really examine. Highlights include museum-quality Dresden lamps that have been matched with rather odd shades, several lovely 18th-century porcelain communion pieces now used as liqueur sets, majolica urns, a Sears bed purchased for the grand sum of $22 and a dresser for $19 (both still showing the price), and an early simple fire extinguisher that looks like a light bulb. It's really worth the visit. One of the owners will take you through and answer as many questions as possible.

The Christian Admiral

Stop in at this austere-looking brick building on the seafront just to see the Tiffany glass dome in the front portico and the stained-glass windows on the staircase. Originally built in 1905 as the Hotel Cape May, it had already changed its name to the Admiral when it was acquired in the 1950s by Carl McIntire, a fundamentalist minister who now uses it as his headquarters at Beach Drive and Pittsburgh Avenue. When it was first built it provided the ultimate in luxury—350 rooms, with grand lobbies and vast dining rooms costing $1 million, twice the estimated costs. The lobby is wainscoted in Siena marble, and the iron columns are in fact painted to simulate marble.

ATTRACTIONS OUT OF TOWN

Cape May County Historical Society, Rte 9. (tel. 609/465-3535), possesses a collection of local memorabilia that includes period rooms, maritime objects like the original flag from the *Merrimac,* and a children's room featuring toys, dolls, and needlework. HOURS: Mid-June to mid-September, Monday to Saturday from 10 A.M. to 3 P.M.; closed January, February, and March, and on Monday during the rest of the year. ADMISSION: $2 for adults, 75¢ for children 12 to 18. Take Stone Harbor Boulevard off the Garden State to Shore Road (Rte. 9). Turn right and travel north about three quarters of a mile.

The **Wetlands Institute,** on Stone Harbor Boulevard in Stone Harbor (tel. 609/368-1211), is a research facility whose aquarium and educational displays would interest naturalists and others who share similar interests. The observation tower is also worth a visit. HOURS: September to June, on Tuesday, Thursday, and Saturday from 1 A.M. to 4:30 P.M.; in summer, Tuesday to Saturday from 10 A.M. to 4:30 P.M. ADMISSION: $1.

Cold Spring Village, 731 Seashore Rd. (tel. 609/884-1810), is a replica of a typical South Jersey farm village that features all kinds of demonstrations and special events—baking, basketry, tinsmithing, and more. Open Memorial Day to mid-October. Take the Garden State Parkway to Exit 0, turn right on Rte. 109 to the traffic light, and then follow the signs to the ferry until you reach the next light, which is Seashore Road. Turn right.

SHOPPING

For Sunday out-of-town papers go to the **Keltie News** store, on the Washington Street Mall (tel. 609/884-7797), between Ocean Street and Decatur.

The **Crazy Quilt Shoppe,** at 656 Washington St. (tel. 609/884-7747), specializes in calicos and other appealing gift items.

A Side Trip to Wheaton Village

Only a 30-minute drive or so away in Millville, you may enjoy a visit to Wheaton Village, 10th and G Street, Glasstown Road (tel. 609/825-6800), to watch glass-blowing demonstrations and view the museum that exhibits all types of glass from early glass bottles through art nouveau to modern. It's well worth the trip.

HOURS: 10 A.M. to 5 P.M.; closed Monday and Tuesday January to March. ADMISSION: $4 for adults, $2 for students.

CAPE MAY LODGING

Note: On weekends, most of the following accommodations require a two- or three-night minimum. Also most of them (with some exceptions) don't encourage children under 12 or so, not because they don't like children but simply because children are boisterous and find a weekend when they're asked to keep quiet a big bore. If you plan to visit during the summer, then make your reservations far in advance. Owners will usually provide complimentary beach tags.

Most of the accommodations lack air conditioning, but don't let that deter you. Many rooms possess ceiling fans or louver doors, and the sea breezes that arise from the confluence of the Delaware and the Atlantic are perfectly adequate on even the hottest of days.

A Note on Parking: In summer, parking is particularly difficult, and you'd do best to leave your car at home and walk or cycle around. Some accommodations do provide free parking; others will charge for the privilege of parking on the property. Always check first.

"Inns at Christmas" Package: A number of the inns and guesthouses in Cape May—the Queen Victoria, Captain Mey's, the Victorian Rose, the Brass Bed, the Manor House, the Windward House, Alexander's Inn, and the Summer Cottage Inn among them—have gotten together to offer a special "Inns at Christmas" package. At each establishment the theme is different: the history of Victorian decorations at the Queen Victoria, children's Christmas at the Brass Bed, Dutch celebrations at Captain Mey's, winter floral celebrations at the Victorian Rose, the lights of Christmas at the Manor House, the music of Christmas at the Summer Cottage Inn, vintage fashions for the holiday season at the Windward House, and an elegant setting at Alexander's.

The Guesthouses

The Cape May showpiece that has been featured so many times in magazines is the **Mainstay**, 635 Columbia Ave., Cape May, NJ 08204 (tel. 609/884-8690), an architectural beauty designed by Stephen D. Button to serve as a gambling house. It's certainly impressive, with its pilastered cupola, green shutters flanking 13-foot-high Italianate windows, and a wrap-around porch supported by exquisitely fluted and turned columns encrusted with gingerbread. You may find it too overwhelming and too perfect, depending on your taste. Well-tended gardens spilling over in early spring and summer with roses, hydrangea, iris, pinks, pansies, and tiger lilies, all set around a small fountain, make it an idyllic spot.

Devoted preservationists Tom and Sue Carroll have spent their time and energy restoring this old beauty to its former magnificence. The public rooms with 14-foot-high ceilings, ornate plaster moldings, and elaborate chandeliers are extravagant, and have been furnished with equally extravagant Victoriana—12-foot-high carved mirrors in the hall, an ornate wrought-iron stove in the small front parlor. The drawing room is a veritable pleasure to the eye, with its gilt-framed oils and colorful paintings on glass, richly patterned Oriental rugs on the floor, and grand piano standing against a long-case clock and a graceful, wrought-iron floor lamp. Here you will always find some fresh-cut flowers placed on the marble-top table. In the dining room the formal table seats 12, and the tall windows are draped with lace curtains, capped by a scarlet tasselled valance. The seven rooms, three with private bath, are all very large and furnished with thick pile carpets and beds with walnut Renaissance Revival headboards. One of the bathrooms features a copper tub. Sue and Tom also have accommodations in what they call the cottage next door, another pleasant Victorian where there are an additional six rooms, all with private bath and similarly furnished.

Guests are invited to enjoy a full breakfast on the porch in summer (strawberry crêpes, anyone?), or in the formal dining room at other times. Afternoon tea is served on the porch.

RATES (including breakfast and afternoon tea): $75 to $95 from Memorial Day to the end of September; $55 to $75 at other times. Open April through November only. Three-night minimum required in summer.

The other lodging that is museum-like in the quality of its decor is **The Abbey,** at Columbia Avenue and Gurney Street, Cape May, NJ 08204 (tel. 609/884-4506). You can't miss the steep mansard roof and soaring 60-foot tower. Owners Jay and Marianne enjoy entertaining at breakfast and in the early evening, when guests gather in the drawing room to get to know one another over a glass of wine. Jay, in particular, is a real ham. In the mornings he'll be setting the breakfast table wearing a hat of one sort or another (a leather pilot's cap, a boater, a topper, or a sea-captain's cap) from his collection. At breakfast he'll regale you with one tale or joke after another. Marianne is a creative designer and needlewoman who fashioned the lambrequins that cover the Gothic windows of the double parlor, elaborately furnished with High Victorian sofas, side chairs, and a huge Empire mirror over the mantel, on which stands an ornate French clock from the same period. It's hard to imagine that when the Schatzes took over the house in late 1979 pigeons were inhabiting the upper floors. Now, upstairs you'll find a series of rooms, many with large armoires, floor-to-ceiling mirrors, Victorian sofas, walnut beds, and ornate gas fixtures. Even the smallest room is charming. In the morning the sunlight streams through the Gothic-style ruby stained-glass windows, lighting up the white eyelet lace bedspread and scallop-edged pillows.

You can look forward to a luxurious breakfast served at a large formal table in the dining room, whose most exquisite piece is a sideboard carved with Indian heads, eagles, and wolf-like creatures. Your gourmet breakfast will consist of juice, a choice of teas, coffee, an egg dish of some sort—perhaps quiche with wide noodles or a delicious concoction of poached eggs mixed with onions and bacon in a cream sauce and served over grits—plus muffins, jams, honey, and always a fresh fruit cup, sometimes laced with brandy. After breakfast Jay will take you up to the tower for a splendid view of the whole Cape May area.

RATES: $65 to $95 double; singles deduct $10 a night. Open April through November. Free parking.

Several blocks farther from the beach, away from the central cluster of other Victorian hostelries, stands the **Barnard-Good House,** 238 Perry St., Cape May, NJ 08204 (tel. 609/884-5381), a stunning purple clapboard house topped with a mansard roof and run by effervescent Nancy Hawkins and her husband, Tom. Step through the small picket gate, past the white picket fence up onto the porch with its intricate fretwork, further enlivened by one or two hanging ferns and a windowbox full of colorful pansies.

Although Nancy does not pretend to have furnished the house authentically, it does have a period charm and warmth. The dining room features what she calls a

Turkish corner with a tented and tasselled brocade Victorian-style sofa; a power organ, old gas fire, heavy mirrors, and a Victorian glass dome filled with a silk flower arrangement add character to the front parlor.

Upstairs there are six rooms, four of these sharing 2½ baths. Rooms are all different and eclectically furnished: one has a four-poster with lace curtains, another a brass bed with candlewick spread, another a delicate Empire-style dressing table created by Nancy herself. One of the most popular rooms has been dubbed the purple passion room, because the iron-and-brass bedstead covered with a purple quilt is huge—California king-size, leaving room for only one white wicker chair, an oak chest, and a porcelain wash bowl. Another favorite is the top-floor compact suite, decorated in white and pink with a small sitting room, complete with fainting couch, and a full bathroom. By the way the third-floor bathroom contains the original zinc-coated copper bathtub, an old-fashioned pull-chain cistern, and marble sink.

Nancy is an extremely skilled cook, who relishes even the challenge of catering to a special diet while turning out a menu that's acceptable to everyone staying in the house. Her gourmet breakfasts, served until June 15 and after September 15, might consist of a cream of almond soup, tangerine-lime juice (never your standard grapefruit or orange), Swiss enchilada crêpes filled with celery, onions, chili peppers, and tomato sauce, topped with cheese, and served with assorted homemade breads, and desserts. In summer she serves a continental breakfast that might combine strawberry-orange juice with a variety of croissants, coffeecake, and muffins.

RATES: $70 for a room with shared bath, $80 for a room with a private bath, $90 for the suite. Free parking. Bicycles are available. Open April 1 through November. A *Special Note:* Allergy sufferers—there are no cats residing here.

The **Queen Victoria**, 102 Ocean St., Cape May, NJ 08204 (tel. 609/884-8702). For the last four years Joan Wells and her husband, Dane, have been creating a warm, home-like atmosphere for their guests in their lovely, sage-green 1881–1882 landmark building with its striking corner bays, curvaceous fish-scale mansard roof, and ornamental porch. Here you will really be welcomed as friends (in winter, if there are only a few guests, you'll be invited into the kitchen for breakfast with the family, which now includes a small addition). On the ground floor there's a handsome dining room with William Morris–design wallpaper. In the parlor, completely furnished with Mission furniture—sofa, chairs, and tall clock —you can sit and read one of the many art or architecture books that Joan collected while she was the executive director of the Victorian Society. Or you can simply nod off in front of the fire. The 12 rooms (four with private bath) are all named after dashing Victorian personalities—Disraeli and Lillie Langtry, for example. The largest room is named after Prince Albert; the smallest, the third-floor rooms, have space only for a lowboy, sink, chair, and brass-and-iron bed. Some rooms have ceiling fans, but the sea breezes should keep the rooms cool enough. All have colorful Mennonite-Amish quilts and fresh flowers placed somewhere in the room.

Accommodations are also available in a restored carriage house, now connected to the main house although it has a private entrance. On the ground floor is a sitting room with pullout sofa-bed, full bathroom with Jacuzzi, TV, and small refrigerator tucked behind louver doors, while upstairs a large bedroom with separate sink and dressing table occupies the second floor. This suite has central air conditioning. Guests who stay here can join the other guests in the main dining room or enjoy a private breakfast in their own suite.

In the mornings, Joan will fortify you with a variety of quiches and soufflés, along with homemade muffins, breads, rolls, granola, and fresh fruit. Later in the day, a sweet and savory tea is served. The side porch is a sheltered spot for rocking. Bicycles are available free and Joan and Dane also provide a useful package of information that includes a brief history of the house and details about the activities and entertainment available in the Cape May area. If you stay here, you'll also receive a regular newsletter, which keeps you in touch and makes you really feel like part of the family.

RATES: November to February, $75 to $105 on weekends, $57 to $71 in midweek; in March and April, $65 to $100 on weekends, $51 to $71 in midweek; from May to early June, $75 to $105 on weekends, $61 to $71 in midweek; from early June to late September, $91 to $112 on weekends, $71 to $87 in midweek; from late September through October, $75 to $105 on weekends, $61 to $71 in midweek (the higher prices are for private bath, the lower for shared bath). The Carriage House Suite, sleeping two to four, rents for $190 to $220 on weekends, $140 to $210 in midweek, depending on season. "Inns at Christmas" package offered. In winter they offer special themed weekends—from fireside readings of Dickens to caroling and Christmas decorations.

Captain Mey's Inn, 202 Ocean St., Cape May, NJ 08204 (tel. 609/884-7793 or 884-9637). Owners Carin Fedderman and Milly La Canfora felt that the original discoverer of Cape May, Capt. Cornelius Mey, had been sadly neglected, so they named their pretty lavender-and-cream house after him and hung out the Dutch flag and their hand-painted inn sign alongside. The Dutch motif has been carried even further in the house itself, for Carin, who hails from Holland, has scattered her heirlooms around the place: Delft tiles in the fireplace, a Delft collection in the parlor, an intricately carved Chinese chest in the foyer, and Dutch art.

The Dutch touch even extends to the breakfast of cheeses, meats, and fresh fruits, which is served by candlelight, a charming romantic way to start the day. In late afternoons, guests gather for a glass of sherry and a chat; iced tea is always available, as are the wicker chairs on the wrap-around veranda.

A lovely oak staircase leads to nine rooms, two with private bath, seven sharing five baths. Great care has been taken to provide each room with a unique atmosphere, using a variety of styles and textures—white iron bedstead and wicker furnishings combined with pale pastel-blue wallpaper and drapes in the Queen Beatrix Room; a heavy Victorian bed, antique towel rack, and marble-top walnut dresser in the room named after Carin's father; a brass bed and appropriate oak Victoriana in the Peter Stuyvesant Room.

A surprise awaits anyone using the top-floor bathroom, for here are assembled a whimsical collection of rag dolls, a sled, Dutch clogs, and a mannequin displaying a charcoal-colored satin and velvet Victorian walking dress.

RATES: $70 to $95 double. Free parking. "Inns at Christmas" package.

Some 100 rose bushes were planted around the property on which stands the **Victorian Rose,** 715 Columbia Ave., Cape May, NJ 08204 (tel. 609/884-2497), a gray building made colorful by the cream-and-rust gingerbread fretwork. The rose theme is followed throughout the house on sheets, towels, wallpaper, and place settings in the dining room.

Lively owners Linda and Bob Mullock offer eight rooms, most of them featuring oak pieces. Number 3 in the front is their largest and comes with a large oak sideboard, king-size bed, wall-to-wall carpeting, couch, and louver doors that open into the bathroom with its clawfoot tub. The other rooms vary, but most feature high-back oak beds, oak dressers, candlewick spreads, and cane-seat chairs. Ceiling fans and sea breezes substitute for air conditioning.

Linda and Bob are less interested in maintaining a perfectly authentic Victorian atmosphere; rather, they love having a romance with the '30s and '40s, which explains the Glenn Miller–style sounds that waft through the house. Ex-nursery school teacher Linda serves a light breakfast of fresh fruit, quiches, or homemade sweet rolls and breads in the dining room that contains a large sideboard purchased from the Boardman estate, the gentleman who supposedly built the boardwalk in Atlantic City.

At the back of the house there's also a pleasant cottage with full kitchen and room enough to sleep five, which is available for weekly rental, but you'll need to call well ahead of time.

RATES: $60 to $105 double. "Inns at Christmas" package.

In 1979 John and Donna Dunwoody and two of their three children took over a classic 1872 home that had belonged to the Dannenbaums of Philadelphia until 1930, when it was turned into a tourist home. They camped out through the winter of 1979–1980 while they, their family, and friends worked day and night to restore it and convert it into a friendly bed-and-breakfast, the **Brass Bed,** 719 Columbia Ave., Cape May, NJ 08204 (tel. 609/884-8075). Period perfection was not their aim, although the house is comfortably furnished with antique pieces throughout: 19th-century brass beds, elegant wallpapers, and billowy lace curtains. During the restoration it was discovered that many pieces were original to the first owners of the house and still had shipping tags attached to the backs dated 1872! Collectibles like statuary and early photographs are on view, including a portrait that looks like a Victorian version of John himself. The parlor boasts an 1890s upright piano, a five-piece Renaissance Revival set of chairs and settee, and a turn-of-the-century wind-up phonograph.

They offer a relaxing, convivial atmosphere to guests, who have the choice of eight rooms (two with private bath, two with half bath, and four sharing two full baths). Furnishings vary. In the room named in honor of the famous Congress Hall Hotel there's a brass bed, needlepointed chairs, a walnut armoire, and an oak dresser, much of it original to the house. The Stockton Room has a cozy air, achieved by the area rug, floral wallpaper, Eastlake settee, antique brass bed, and large walnut armoire. Third-floor rooms are tucked under the eaves, and one of them, the Mount Vernon, enjoys a private bathroom with a clawfoot tub.

A full breakfast and afternoon refreshment are served year round. In summer there's a choice of cereals, fresh fruit, and home-baked goods. In the cooler months a hot entree is included. Off the dining room, an appealing sun room has enough space for a sofa, two chairs, and a table, all of wicker.

RATES: $70 to $85 for rooms with private bath, $65 to $75 for rooms with half bath, and $45 to $60 for rooms with shared bath. Open all year. "Inns at Christmas" package offered.

The **Windward House** (1905), 24 Jackson St., Cape May, NJ 08204 (tel. 609/884-3368), has some really outstanding architectural details, especially stained glass (check out the stained-glass double doors leading to one of the guest rooms) and some very personal features in Sandy Miller's vintage clothing and accessories in particular. Gorgeous period dresses and outfits hang around the parlor which is also accented with statuary, hats displayed on mannequin heads, a blue glass collection on the window pelmets, and other eye-catching objects including a lot of Victorian furnishings.

All of the eight rooms with private bath are well furnished. My favorite is the Renaissance Room: it's tucked away behind the kitchen on the first floor and has its own porch and private entrance. The carved Victorian bed sports a pale-blue candlewick spread. There's also an attached tiny sitting room with wicker chair, armoire, and fridge. Room 5 is decked out in Rococo Revival splendor, with lemon peonie wallpaper. Third-floor rooms like No. 7, the Wicker Room, are tucked under the eaves. In this room the iron-and-brass bed is backed by a colorful quilt, wicker chairs and a couch add a dash of comfort, and there's an adjoining single room that makes it ideal for a trio. Up here, too, there's also a large deck at the back of the house from which there's a great ocean view. More seating is available on the ground-floor front porch set with wicker. All rooms have fridge and ceiling fan, and two have air conditioning.

A continental breakfast is served at the lace-clothed table in the dining room in which there's still another collection—egg cups this time. This is one of Cape May's quirkily and appealingly personal accommodations.

RATES: $65 to $80 double in season, $55 to $75 off-season; $15 per additional person; $15 less for singles. "Inns at Christmas" package.

The **Henry Hughes House,** 29 Ocean St., Cape May, NJ 08204 (tel. 609/884-4428), was built in 1903, a little later than many in Cape May, and as a consequence the rooms are larger. The porch is really wide and expansive, and has a fine ocean view.

There are ten rooms, three with private bath. Each is well furnished with an eye for detail (the owner is an interior decorator). One of the nicest is the Ocean View Room featuring a Renaissance Revival carved bed made up with eyelet bed linen, a large armoire, sidetables set with gas-style lamps, and polished floor covered with Oriental-style rugs. The Velvet Room contains some of the original owner's old medical books and is richly furnished with a carved Victorian bed spread with a burgundy satin comforter, burgundy velvet swag drapes, and other Victorian pieces. Two servant's rooms have been converted into the East and West Wing. Although smaller, the East Wing is prettily furnished with an iron-and-brass bed, wicker desk, lamp with fringed shade, and beige wall-to-wall carpet among other things. All of the rooms have Oriental soaps and fresh flowers.

A full breakfast is served from 8:30 to 10:30 A.M. Tea is served at 4 P.M. consisting of iced tea, cakes, pies, cheese, and crudités. A large well-furnished parlor is available for guests.

RATES: $55 to $120 (for the Ocean View room). Open Memorial Day to mid-October.

At the **Manor House,** 612 Hughes St., Cape May, NJ 08204 (tel. 609/884-4710), if you're of a mind to, you can indulge in some silly punning and other verbal repartee with innkeeper Tom Snyder. Many of his and his wife, Mary's, friends are musicians and so you may be treated to some good music too. If there are no musicians around you'll have to settle for the contemporary player piano that trots out some fine ragtime. Books are also very much part of the Snyder household. You'll find them in the parlor, the hallways, and the sitting room. Why not curl up in the sitting room in front of the fireplace with a good read? The house has some fine architectural features, like oak door frames with geometric decoration and stained glass.

A full breakfast is served at 8:30 and 9:30 A.M. on lace-covered oak tables. May whips up apple-cheese pancakes, blueberry or peach crêpes, and something called a Mexican soufflé. Baked potato chips are also a unique specialty.

There are ten rooms (four with private bath, three with half bath, and three with sink only). Many of the beds have fantastic quilts crafted by Mary. Room 6's brass bed, for example, has a log-cabin quilt that took her nine months to make. The room also contains an old chest, heavy dresser, wall-to-wall beige carpet, and a rocker from Juniata College where Tom was director of admissions. Room 8 has a cross-stitch quilt on another brass bed, warm cranberry-colored chintz wallpaper, chaise longue, chest, and Windsor chair. In Room 4 there's a lovely star quilt. All rooms have Gilchrist & Soames soaps, ceiling fans, and robes for those that share baths. An added advantage is the location on one of the less-trafficked streets in Cape May.

RATES: From $58 off-season, from $95 in season. "Inns at Christmas" package.

The owners of the **Sea Holly Inn,** 815 Stockton Ave., Cape May, NJ 08204 (tel. 609/884-6294), recently won an award for the quality of the restoration that they accomplished with alacrity, turning a neglected building into a handsome Victorian beauty. The six rooms, all with electric blankets and private bath, have been painstakingly decorated with Schumacher papers and fine fabrics and furnishings. Room 9, at the back of the house, has a bed covered with French blue satin and lace-trimmed pillows, and a brilliant ruby-red upholstered Eastlake chair among the furnishings. Room 8 has a highly ornate iron bed covered with lace and satin, rose carpeting, and pretty chintz wallpaper. Room 2 houses a crested Victorian bed and mostly wicker furnishings set against gold chintz wallpaper.

No breakfast is served in summer; continental breakfast is served spring and fall. Guests gather in the parlor on the camelback and wicker sofas, or on the concrete porch's wicker rockers. A fridge is available for guests.

RATES: $55 with private bath, $50 with shared bath. Open Easter to the end of October.

A shingled house, the **Sand Castle,** 829 Stockton Ave., Cape May, NJ 08204 (tel. 609/468-5910), has to be one of Cape May's best buys. Operated by Guy and Eileen Brooks, a registered nurse who welcomes children, the place has three apartments and seven rooms (one with private bath and six sharing three baths). Each of the rooms is charming and many are under the eaves, which give them interesting cozy shapes. For example, Room 3 contains a real, old brass bed, couch, and oak dresser, and an appealing "steeple"-pointed Gothic window. This same style of window is also found in Room 4, along with '30s-style wicker chairs, a highback oak bed covered with a Marseille-style bedspread, and an oak dresser and sidetable. A plant adds life and the Carmen Miranda straw hats add a touch of decoration to chintz walls. Room 5's extra little touches include silhouettes, a country wreath, and another plant. I especially like Room 6, with its iron-and-brass bed sporting a marvelous quilt made by an 80-year-old Tennessee woman, and at its foot, a decoratively painted Tennessee saddle bench.

Eileen keeps books, magazines, and local menus around for guests, and also provides a fridge. The porch is set with director's chairs and pretty hanging baskets of flowers. Coffee and tea only are served for breakfast.

RATES: $45 for top-floor under-eaves rooms, $50 for rooms on the second floor, and $60 for a room with a private bath.

One of the famed Stephen D. Button houses (known as "The Seven Sisters"), the **Seventh Sister Guesthouse,** 10 Jackson St., Cape May, NJ 08204 (tel. 609/884-2280), is very different from all the establishments discussed so far. Artist Joanne Echevarria, who shares the house with her husband, Bob Myers, has chosen to decorate the house with white-painted furniture and wicker so that the whole place positively blazes with light. It's also filled with examples of her art—abstract pastels, collages, and conceptual art. Not surprisingly, many of her guests are artists, photographers, or other like-minded visitors who need privacy and quiet to pursue their inspirational muse.

Of the six rooms sharing two baths, four have ocean views. The back porch is great for idling, while the lawn at the side of the house makes a pleasant change from the beach, which is only 100 feet away.

RATES: January to March, $50; in April, $52; in May, $56; in June, $58; in July and August, $60; in September, $58; in October, $56; in November and December, $50. Open year round. Children over 7 are welcome.

Across town, Joanne's brother, Fred Echevarria, and his wife, Joan, run the **Gingerbread House,** 28 Gurney St., Cape May, NJ 08204 (tel. 609/884-0211), one of the Stockton Row cottages that surrounded the old Stockton Hotel, built in 1869 by railroad money and designed by Button. Here, Fred exhibits his talent for photography (note the striking pictures of Nova Scotia and Maine throughout the house) and for furniture making; you'll see in front of the fireplace in the parlor the coffee table that he built to display their seashell collection. Apart from this table, though, the house is furnished with Victorian-style sofas, lowboys with marble tops, and many other period furnishings. Among the six rooms (three with private bath), the highest priced is large enough to accommodate two double beds and comes with private bath and your own spacious private porch.

RATES: (including a continental breakfast): $65 to $95, with discounts off-season. Open year round.

Geraniums were spilling out of the hanging baskets on the ocean-view porch when I visited **Holly House,** 20 Jackson St., Cape May, NJ 08204 (tel. 609/884-7365), a sage-green box-like house decorated with Chinese-red trim that is also

, one of the seven cottages built by Stephen D. Button deliberately facing away from Jackson Street. Inside, up the visually striking staircase, you'll find six guest rooms, all informally furnished, primarily with oak pieces—a desk, cane-seated chair, dresser, double towel rack, and iron bedstead, for example—and kept very simple, because Bruce and Corinne Minnix want to keep it as a home away from home. The parlor has large floral-print-easy chairs, a Victorian sofa, the original coal-burning fireplace, a Baldwin piano, and a comfortable spot to sit quietly and read as though you were settled in at your own cozy place.

RATES: $50 to $65 Memorial Day to Columbus Day; $45 to $55 off-season.

Paul and Alice Linden run the **Albert G. Stevens Inn,** 127 Myrtle Ave., Cape May, NJ 08204 (tel. 609/884-4717), an impressive home built in 1900 as a wedding present for the original owner's wife. It still has the original floating staircase. Prime Victorian pieces are found throughout—a late-Empire couch and side chairs in the parlor in front of the oak mantel. Six rooms, four with private bath and one with a small sitting room, have beautifully color-coordinated decor featuring exquisite individualized French wallpapers and wall-to-wall carpeting. Furnishings vary. Some rooms have Eastlake, Lincoln, or iron-and-brass bedsteads. Summer breakfasts bring juice, fruit, and quiche, which is sometimes enjoyed on the wrap-around veranda.

RATES: $65 to $90; a little less in winter. Free parking.

Ever since it was built in 1876 the venerable 103-room **Chalfonte,** 301 Howard St., Cape May, NJ 08204 (tel. 609/884-8409), has drawn loyal families year after year to rock on its veranda, sample the southern-style cuisine, and generally enjoy its simple charms. The three-story building, screened by a two-story colonnade and crowned with a cupola and some fine gingerbread ornamentation, is being renovated by owners Anne Le Duc and Judy Bartella. It is the only real chance you'll have to experience the kind of hotel accommodations that used to keep Cape May so crowded in her heyday. Only 11 of the 103 rooms have private bath (most have sinks), and all are (at least at the time of my visit) furnished very spartanly with iron bedsteads and marble-top dressers. The dining room is famous for its family-style meals of southern fried chicken, country ham, leg of lamb, or roast beef at dinner, and biscuits, spoonbread, fish, and bacon and eggs at breakfast. A Sunday tradition is kidney stew. On the ground floor are the King Edward Room bar, a writing room, and library, and a comfortable hall-lounge with fireplace and TV. Open May to September and weekends to late October.

RATES (including breakfast and dinner): $51 to $58 single, $72 to $112 double (higher prices are for room with private bath and also reflect whether the room is on the second or third floor). Weekly rates are available. The place also caters several special events, including a Victorian dinner with songs supplied by the famous Savoy company, and chamber music concerts. Special packages are available, and also Work Weekends in May and October, when you can stay for free (bringing your own sleeping bag or linens) and receive three meals a day for two days while you work and help spruce the place up.

The owners of **Alexander's** Restaurant, 653 Washington St., Cape May, NJ 08204 (tel. 609/884-2555), also rent four rooms to guests, each decorated in Victorian style. In the Rose Room the brass bed with its pink satin eiderdown looked very inviting. The walls of the Green Room sport a wallpaper originally designed to celebrate the opening of the Suez Canal—a truly Victorian touch.

RATES: $70 to $85 with breakfast and tea. "Inns at Christmas" package.

Built around 1896, the cream-and-rust **Duke of Windsor Inn,** 817 Washington St., Cape May, NJ 08204 (tel. 609/884-1355), with its quirky 45-foot conical tower (where two rooms are located), makes a lovely stopping place in a more secluded area, midway between the town and the harbor, within walking distance of the Physick Estate and the tennis club. On the first floor the tower has a well-used game and conversation room, just large enough to accommodate a wicker couch and two wicker armchairs. A double parlor with a corner fireplace, ornate plaster ceiling, swag drapes, solid-oak accents, and crystal chandelier is divided in two by an archway supported by two solid-wood Colonial Revival pillars. One half seems more used as a reading area and contains large bookcases; the other half is used as a sitting area. It's well furnished with Victoriana, but for me, the handsomest piece of all is the Burmese table, intricately carved with birds, elephants, and lions. The back parlor adjoins the dining room that possesses a lovely gilt molded ceiling, with several chandeliers, a reproduction of the wallpaper from Queen Victoria's throne room, and refurbished lincrusta on the walls. Here a full breakfast is served amid mirrored sideboards at one large table.

A staircase climbs past a brilliant stained-glass window to nine rooms, all tastefully furnished. One room, for example, contains a Renaissance Revival bed set against gray-and-burgundy wallpaper. The carpet is rosy-red burgundy and the furnishings oak. The bathroom has a hand-painted porcelain sink. The most charming rooms are the tower rooms, which have space for only one brass bed, an Eastlake chair, and a dresser. Lace curtains and fringed lampshade or gas-style lamps are only some of the period effects used. The porch, with its upholstered rattan chairs, is a favorite musing spot.

From June 15 to about September 30 only a continental breakfast is served; from October 1 to mid-June a hot entree is included. Bicycles are available. Free parking.

RATES: $55 to $90 with private bath, $50 to $60 with shared bath. Closed January.

Woodleigh House, 808 Washington St., Cape May, NJ 08204 (tel. 609/884-7123), also in the same area as the Duke of Windsor, is run by a friendly couple (he's a high school principal) and has a genuine home-like atmosphere. In the comfortably modern sitting room you'll find a personal Delft collection, and in the dining room is arrayed an eclectic glass and china collection. Here coffee, juice, and danish are served, unless the weather is clement when it's served on the porch. They have four rooms (two with private bath). One of the nicest is off the kitchen on the ground floor; it's furnished with a high-backed oak bed, dresser, rocker, and washstand, on top of which are a pair of button boots! In the back there's a secluded small outside porch and brick patio and a small garden area where guests can barbecue. Bikes are available.

RATES: $40 for shared bath, $60 with private bath.

Carroll Villa, 19 Jackson St., Cape May, NJ 08204 (tel. 609/884-9619), is perhaps the least expensive accommodation in Cape May. The rooms are attractively furnished with wall-to-wall carpeting, pretty drapes and fabrics and a mixture of antique and modern. The downstairs living room with TV is for guests only and there's also a garden terrace outback. The only drawback that you might encounter will depend on your room location and your sleeping habits. The accommodation shares the premises with the Mad Batter restaurant and the staff go to work quite early to prepare breakfast. If you're an early riser it won't matter a fig, but if you're not . . .

RATES: In season $40 to $45 with shared bath, $55 to $60 with private bath, less at other times.

At **Poor Richard's Inn,** 17 Jackson St., Cape May, NJ 08204 (tel. 609/884-3536), artists Richard and Harriet Samuelson attract a younger, 25- to 35-year-old crowd to their casual home, where the furnishings are more eclectic than most, a trifle faded and less "perfect" than many of the other Cape May guesthouses. Richard and Harriet are also one of the few couples who will accept children (they have a couple of their own). The house itself is quite magnificent, built in 1882 for a man named George Hildreth, with a wonderfully steep fish-scale mansard roof, deep projecting bays, and an unusual hexagonal porch. There are nine rooms, some with private bath, others sharing two bathrooms. The two top-floor rooms are pleasantly furnished with wicker rockers, a painted country bed, a Mission rocker, and an oak dresser. Other rooms mix painted cottage beds with oak and pine, really old patchwork quilts, and other Victoriana. There are also two apartments with kitchen available. Throughout the house hang Harriet's collages, which I wanted to purchase on the spot—they're really stimulating, weirdly affecting visions.

RATES: Open from March through December—$64 to $74 with private bath, $41 to $56 with shared bath, in July and August; $51 to $61 with private bath, $32 to $50 with shared bath, in other months (except on weekends from Memorial Day through September when in-season prices prevail). The apartments are rented by the week only, from $310 to $460. No on-site parking.

The **Mooring Guest House,** 801 Stockton Ave., Cape May, NJ 08204 (tel. 609/884-5425), is another of the few establishments that invites children. There are 12 rooms here, five with private bath, all furnished in Victorian style but not stiflingly so. One of the most appealing rooms is called the Sovereign of the Sea, a very large room housing a highbacked cherry bed, an acorn chest with a marble top, and most important of all, French doors that lead directly to the front porch. Other rooms are furnished pleasantly with mixtures of wicker, oak, gas-style lamps, and rockers. The halls are extremely wide—a reminder of earlier days when steamer trunks needed accommodating. Another sought-after room is no. 10, for its view and fireplace. It contains an iron-and-brass bed and an attractive old-fashioned washstand among its furnishings. A continental breakfast is served in the homey parlor.

RATES: $60 to $65 with private bath, $45 to $55 with shared bath. Open until December 1.

Twin Gables Guest House, 731 Columbia Ave., Cape May, NJ (tel. 609/884-7332), is run by friendly host Tony Bevivino, a retired chemistry teacher who loves meeting and talking to guests. The 1879 house is one of the few (if not the only) houses to possess a screened-in porch with wicker rockers and hanging plants. Oliver the bulldog wheezes in the kitchen most of the time, while guests gather in the comfy parlor on the camelback sofa, around the old pump organ, or on the window seats. Among the lovely objets d'art is a carved Italian table topped with intricate ivory carvings. The four rooms (only two with private bath) are homey. Two additional baths are planned so that all four will have private bath by the time you visit. Room 2 has pink striped wallpaper, an Eastlake bed, teardrop dresser, armoire, and marble sidetables. Room 3 has gold bed coverlet and carpet matched with yellow wallpaper. Breakfast is usually coffee and a sweet roll, served on the porch. Open April 1 through November. No children. No pets.

RATES: $60 with private bath.

Other Accommodations

Cape May also has a goodly number of modern motel accommodations, many located on the seafront. **Best Western's Marquis de Lafayette,** 501 Beach Dr., between Ocean and Decatur, Cape May, NJ 08204 (tel. 609/884-3431, or toll free 800/582-5933, 800/257-0432 in New Jersey), offers package plans and the full facilities of a pool and two restaurants.

RATES: Open year round—in summer, $60 (in early May) to $125 (in mid-July and August) in midweek, $85 (in early May) to $150 (in mid-July and August) on weekends; in fall, $44 to $80 in midweek, $64 to $110 on weekends; in winter, $44 to $58 in midweek, $64 to $80 on weekends.

The **Motel Surf and Apartments,** 211 Beach Dr., Cape May, NJ 08204 (tel. 609/884-4132), is also open year round; the **Montreal Inn,** at Beach Drive and Madison, Cape May, NJ 08204 (tel. 609/884-7011), is open seasonally.

CAPE MAY DINING

In season, reservations are a must; on weekends you'd do best to reserve ahead of time if you don't want to be disappointed. Most of the restaurants lack liquor licenses. For the largest liquor selection and best prices, go to **Colliers** on Jackson Street, the big green place just across from the bandstand. It's open on Sunday.

Breakfast, Lunch, or Dinner

The best breakfasts, as you will have gathered from the previous section, can be found at your guesthouse. If you are not staying at such an accommodation, then don't despair; simply head for the **Mad Batter** at 19 Jackson St. (tel. 609/884-5970) for a choice selection of omelets, crêpes, New Orleans French toast (covered with banana crème anglaise or fresh fruit sauce), plus all kinds of egg dishes with bacon and sausage, etc., priced from $5.50 to $7.50. You can dine either outside under the yellow striped awning at white pedestal tables or else inside. At lunch watch for a whole variety of interesting dishes—shrimp jamille dipped in tempura batter and served with soy and curried mango sauces, chicken livers Budapest (sautéed with onions, mushrooms, and walnuts mixed with sour cream and seasoned with paprika), along with fish and pasta of the day. Prices run $5.50 to $8.

The dinner menu also offers imaginative dishes, many of them inspired by trips undertaken by the whole kitchen staff to such places as Thailand or Greece.

Choices might include scallops Santampannit (baked in parchment with peanut-chili pepper sauce), chicken breast (roasted with raspberry vinegar, cream, and cracked cranberries), a fish of the day, roast duckling (with Thai tamarind-ginger-mint glaze, served with apples and Chinese sausage) or lagniappe à la Louisianne (pan-blackened ten-ounce sirloin). Prices range from $14.25 to $22.50. Save some room for the magnificent desserts, especially the chocolate roulade (a chocolate cake rolled with a chocolate mousse flavored with coffee and rum and frosted with coffee whipped cream) or boccone dolce, a delicious concoction of almond me-ringues layered with almond amaretto buttercream and served over a caramel sauce. By the way, you're dining in another of Cape May's Victorian beauties, built in 1882 complete with cupola.

BREAKFAST: 8 A.M. to 2:30 P.M. daily. LUNCH: Noon to 2:30 P.M. daily. DINNER: 5:30 to 10 P.M. daily.

If you want to avoid the lines that accumulate at the Mad Batter, go around the corner to **La Toque,** 210 Ocean St. (tel. 609/884-1511), where in a pretty sunny room with pink tablecloths and French blue napkins on the tables you can sample all kinds of croissants (apple, almond, chocolate, spinach and feta cheese) ome-lets, French toast, and other full breakfast items. At lunch, soups, salads, and sandwiches are available, all under $7. There's even a pastrami sandwich. For appetizers you can have stuffed mushrooms or baked Brie. At night the ambience is changed by the muted track lighting. Specials ranging in price from $10 to $16 are written on a blackboard and might include filet mignon béarnaise, blackened prime rib or redfish, veal français, or bluefish with mustard sauce.

HOURS: In summer, 9:30 A.M. to 3 P.M. and 5:30 to 10 P.M. daily; in winter, open Wednesday to Sunday but with reduced hours.

Another breakfast spot that's small, but also has a small outdoor dining area under an awning, is **Peaches,** 322 Carpenter's Lane (tel. 609/884-0202).

Breakfast treats can also be picked up at **A-Ca-Mia,** 524 Washington St. Mall (tel. 609/884-1913), where you can choose from a splendid array of pastries and croissants and take them out to the beach or wherever you choose. In the back of the shop is an Italian restaurant serving dinner Wednesday to Monday from 5:30 to 10 P.M. and brunch on Saturday and Sunday from 9 A.M. to 1 P.M.

Brunch/Dinner

For top gourmet restaurants, number one has to be **Alexander's,** 653 Washington St. (tel. 609/884-2555). Lace doilies, roses on the table, and coffee served from a silver coffeepot on a swing add a dash of romance to tables that are set in the Victorian manner—the silverware placed down. Dinner is served in four intimate candlelit rooms decorated with gilt-framed pictures. The food is exciting, never dull. Specials will always include a fish of the day, a super-deluxe dish such as veal with morelles, and at least one soup, cream of crab, for example. Desserts will undoubtedly include chocolate profiteroles and their very special and very fa-mous Victorian brandy snaps with whipped cream and brandy. Other mouth-watering entrees might include rabbit braised with onions, pine nuts, and bacon flavored with burgundy and parsley. Also you might like to try an extra-special appetizer known as straasha, which is in fact an arrangement of Blue Point crab claws and jumbo shrimp, iced and presented with curry mayonnaise and vodka-tarragon-mustard dip or a sampler of lump-fish caviar, smoked salmon, and brandy-marinated turkey. To accompany these extravagant items, you have to bring your own wine.

At a recent meal I relished a cream of crab soup filled with lump crabmeat that was rich and smooth. It was followed by a small salad and a sorbet garnished with a rose petal. The main course was Cornish game hen Su Ling, marinated in soy and ginger, roasted in a reduction of honey, raspberry, and bordeaux, and coated with black and white sesame seeds—a successful mélange of complimentary flavors. But the real pièce de résistance was my companion's filet mignon, placed on a bed of pâté and Holland rusk and served with an ecstasy-producing bourguignon sauce.

The service is impeccable, if a little too so: the bread appears in a silver basket, the cream in a Victorian-style silver jug with a top carved in the shape of a lion's head, and the maître d' sports tails. Chocolate fondue brings fresh fruit and other goodies to dip in to a flame-warmed sauce.

The porch, bedecked with ferns and lace curtains, is a favorite spot for a brunch that is more lavish than most. Juice and a plate of seasonal fruit precede such main-course dishes as a sausage-nut strudel (thin layers of pastry encasing sausage, cream cheese, almonds, walnuts, and pecans, and flavored with herbs), Belgian waffles, omelets, and eggs Alexander. Dessert and coffee follow. Brunch runs $15.

DINNER: From 6 P.M. BRUNCH: Sunday from 9 A.M. to 1 P.M. The restaurant is open from mid-April to Memorial Day and from the end of September until mid-December on weekends only; daily, except Tuesday, from Memorial Day to the end of September. Rooms are also available (see above).

Lunch and Dinner

A pretty and longtime favorite on the Cape May scene is the **Washington Inn,** 801 Washington St. (tel. 609/884-5697), set in a large rambling house that affords a screened-in side porch overlooking the colorful garden for summer dining, a pleasant piano bar with comfortable sofas and brocade Victorian chairs, and a front porch with wicker furniture for cocktails. The dining room is made especially attractive by an attached greenhouse filled with a brilliant show of orchids. Veal, beef, poultry, and seafood are available, including a popular lobster Washington that consists of lobster, crab, scallops, and shrimp in a sherry cream sauce placed in the cavity of a lobster. Fresh homemade pies like apple-walnut and strawberry, plus such other mouthwatering delights as blackberry mousse, are added attractions.

DINNER: Open March through December, 5 to 10 P.M. (weekends only from mid-March until mid-May, then daily until the end of October, and weekends only to Christmas); closed January and February.

Dining at the **Lobster House,** on Fisherman's Wharf (tel. 609/884-8296 or 884-3406), is an old Cape May tradition. The dining rooms are large and lacking in any spectacular decor, but people come for a steamed lobster or the very popular schooner dinner, which includes a one-pound lobster, clams, sea scallops, Gulf shrimp, and king crab legs, all for $16.50. Other selections will depend on the seasonal catch—bluefish, softshell crab, clams, and other fish. Entrees include salad, potato and vegetable, and coffee or tea, and start at $11.

This restaurant grosses $5 million in sales a year (39th in the country) and on most nights, especially weekends, expect a 2½-hour wait. Names are announced over a loudspeaker and somehow the people get fed.

My favorite reason for going to the Lobster House, though, is to arrive about 5 P.M. and go aboard the schooner *America* for a waterside seat where one can enjoy a cocktail and watch the duck families paddling back and forth, boatmen training their dog retrievers, the shadows of the seagulls on the surface of the water, large vessels gliding into port, and the sun going down. You can order a clambake, crab sticks, steamed shrimp or crab, barbecued clams, and so on—and as far as I'm concerned, this is the best reason for going to the Lobster House.

At the fresh seafood market, you can pick up a lobster to take home with you, or else take out some clams, scallops, or fresh fried fish with french fries onto the dock, and watch the sun set while you enjoy a good meal for a fraction of the restaurant price. Get there early though, because the market usually closes about 6 P.M.

LUNCH: Monday to Saturday from noon to 3 P.M. DINNER: Monday to Saturday from 5 to 10 P.M., on Sunday from 4 to 10 P.M.

If you desperately want seafood but don't want to wait at the Lobster House, you can always go across the street to the **Anchorage Seafood House** (tel. 609/884-6086) at the foot of the canal bridge. Decor is nautical style, tables are set with red gingham, and there's usually entertainment on weekends. The food might even be a fraction better here. At lunch I had a delicious crab soup filled with crab in a tomato-based stock. The clam chowder was equally well stocked with clams and potato, and far less cornstarch. Dinner prices run $11 to $16 for shrimp, flounder, swordfish, sautéed crabmeat, fried or broiled scallops, baked crab imperial, and some meat dishes. Real seafood fans will want the feast for two—lobster, steamed clams, crab cake, scallops, shrimp, deviled clams, flounder, and oysters, accompanied by potato and vegetable, for $33. Luncheon prices are about half those at dinner.

LUNCH: Monday to Saturday from 11 A.M. to 4 P.M. DINNER: Monday to Saturday from 4 P.M. to midnight, on Sunday from noon to midnight.

Summers, at Beach and Decatur Streets (tel. 609/884-3504) offers casual dining at lunch or brunch on such items as crab fritters, burgers, eggs Benedict and sandwiches. Dinner brings grilled or baked fish, lobster, filet and other steaks, pastas like Alfredo. Dancing and entertainment begins at 9:30 P.M.

LUNCH: 11:30 A.M. to 3 P.M. DINNER: daily in summer 5 to 10 P.M. Reduced hours off season.

Dinner Only

Many people favor a tiny hole-in-the-wall called **Louisa's Café,** 104 Jackson St. (tel. 609/884-5882), that seats only 16 people. Even early in the season you'll be lucky if you secure a table; during the summer you'll have to join the line. People flock here for the quality and freshness of the food, which includes homemade pasta and sauces flavored with herbs picked in the owner's garden. Daily specials are scrawled on a small blackboard. When I was there it offered a choice of a delicious, smooth soup of carrot with dill and cayenne, or artichoke vinaigrette, and three or four main dishes—snapper or bluefish with lemon and capers, chicken breast in a mustard sauce, and a special fettuccine with bacon. The desserts are also excellent, ranging from a scrumptious chocolate-almond torte to a lemon mousse. Dinner for two will run about $35, and you'll need to bring your own wine, which you can pick up at Colliers, just down the street. No reservations and no smoking are restaurant policies.

DINNER: May to mid-October daily from 5 P.M.

Maureen's, 429 Beach Dr., at Decatur (tel. 609/884-3774), is a successful Philadelphia restaurant that has transplanted itself to the shore. Here the emphasis is on fresh, interesting seafood in a second-floor restaurant and porch overlooking the ocean. An appetizer of lobster bisque or scallops or escargots might be followed by a rich crab Versailles in a sauce of sherry and Dijon mustard topped with Gruyère cheese, an equally rich veal served on a bed of lobster, shrimp, and crab with a sauce St-Mâlo, or a more simple poisson jardinière baked with vegetables and lemons. Other non-seafood highlights include a duck with strawberry sauce and poulet africaine (chicken slices sautéed with shrimp and simmered in a sauce of tomatoes, vegetables, brandy, and a dash of cream). Prices range from $16 to $22.

DINNER: Open from mid-March to November 1, 5 to 10 P.M. (weekends only to Memorial Day, Wednesday to Sunday from mid-October to November 1).

Dining at **Swallows,** 400 Broadway, at Congress (tel. 609/884-0400), makes for a refreshing change of atmosphere, particularly if you dine in the back room. It's located in the 17th-century part of the house and consequently possesses low-beamed ceiling, Federal-style mantel, and old wide-board floors covered with Oriental area rugs. It's made even more atmospheric by the central Shaker-style lighting fixture and the pretty Victorian-style glass candleholders placed on each table. The welcome is genuine and the service is friendly but professional. The two front dining rooms have higher ceilings and the walls are more appropriately accented with modern lithographs. The menu features half a dozen entrees, like veal Montrachet (sautéed with garlic, sour cream, oregano, and Montrachet cheese), pork Navarre (braised in madeira with shallots, mushroom, and light cream), steak Bercy, and chicken Capistrano (breast of chicken baked in parchment with tarragon, chopped kale, and white wine). Pasta dishes and appetizers are also available. The menu is always supplemented by specials—mahi mahi with sesame oil, ginger, mushroom, and tomato; and salmon with artichoke and cream on the night I dined. Prices range from $12.50 to $18. Desserts might include peach and blueberry trifle, champagne mousse, ricotta cheesecake, or a chocolate silk pie.

DINNER: 6 to 10 P.M. Open from Mother's Day to October 20 approximately; closed Monday and Tuesday out of the summer season.

Trattoria, 312 Carpenter's Lane (tel. 609/884-1144), serves consistently good food in a tiny but pretty dining room with about half a dozen tables set with white tablecloths and green napkins. Pink metal chairs add to the summer atmosphere, as does the opera music in the background. The menu specialties, priced from $11.25 to $15, range from chicken Dijon, scalloppine con limone, and steak Rossini (with gorgonzola butter) to flounder Florentine stuffed with spinach and mushrooms. For pasta lovers there's also a good selection, like linguine con aglio and olio, or tortellini in a tomato-cream sauce, or linguine with shrimp and champagne sauce. Favorite dining area is the terrace, prettified by flowers and plants and sheltered by a pink-and-green awning.

DINNER: From 5 P.M. daily; closed in winter.

The **Bayberry Inn,** on Perry Street at Congress Place (tel. 609/884-8406), has developed a good reputation for serving eclectic cuisine, partly inspired by Thai and Caribbean flavors. For example, the menu might list duck with tamari, lemon, and turmeric, or a Jamaican game hen with rum, brown sugar, and lime juice, along with a fish of the day like tuna with Dijon mustard. There's always a beef dish too, like strip steak with green peppercorn sauce. Among the appetizers, try the chicken wings in spicy honey sauce served with a side of bleu cheese —it works! Prices run $12.50 to $17.50. The favored dining spot is out under the soaring arcade-terrace. The dining room itself is simple, and derives its character largely from the huge fireplace accented by copper pots.

DINNER: Thursday to Tuesday from 5:30 to 10 P.M.; closed Wednesday.

Watson's Merion Inn, 106 Decatur St. (tel. 609/884-8363), is a Cape May tradition serving plain American food—prime rib, roast leg of lamb, turkey, surf and turf, and similar stalwarts in a substantial atmosphere created by gilt portraits and pictures, plus a cherry-and-oak bar. An early dinner special prices at $8 is offered before 6 P.M.; otherwise prices run from $13 for filet of flounder to $23 for broiled lobster tail, with plenty of seafood offerings in between.

DINNER: 4:30 to 10 P.M. daily from May to November 1, weekends only in April; closed from November to March 30.

My choice for seafood would be **A & J Blue Claw,** Ocean Drive, south of the Wildwood Crest toll bridge (tel. 609/884-5878). The decor is plain and simple, but the fish is well cooked and this is one place where you can select your lobster from the tank. Specialties include a New England clambake (lobster, clams, potatoes, onion, and an ear of corn steamed together); a deluxe seafood medley of lobster, filet, shrimp, scallops, and clams casino; and seafood kebab; plus clams and oysters at the raw bar. Four crab dishes are offered and several other fish items, along with steak and a chicken dish. Prices run $15 to $19.

DINNER: Monday to Saturday from 5 to 10 P.M. and on Sunday from 3 to 9 P.M. in summer; weekends only off-season.

For simple soups, salads, burgers, and a good filet mignon with house salad priced at $10 for seven ounces, $12 for ten ounces, try the **Filling Station** (tel. 609/884-2111) on Lafayette Street, right across from the Acme supermarket. No real decor. Open seasonally.

EVENING ENTERTAINMENT

During the summer, the **Mid-Atlantic Center for the Arts,** 1048 Washington St., offers musical and drama performances at their outdoor stage at the Physick Estate. Bring your own chair.

Relaxing cocktail spots include the schooner at the Lobster House, Washington Inn's porch and piano bar, the Merion Inn's lounge bar, and the King Edward Room at the Chalfonte. For dining and dancing Top of the Marq (tel. 609/884-3431) rooftop.

On the mall there are several typical tavern-style places that offer musical entertainment—the **Ugly Mug** at 426 (tel. 609/884-3459), where numerous mugs belonging to the Ugly Mug club members adorn the ceiling and the Old Shire Tavern (tel. 609/884-4700) on the mall. For loud raucous nightlife, you'll have to head for Wildwood.

CAPE MAY ACTIVITIES

BEACHES: The town beaches are pleasant and sandy with a minimum of honkytonk. Beach passes are required and readily available at the information center. More natural, secluded beaches, backed by high undulating dunes, are located at Cape May Point; take Cape Avenue off Sunset Boulevard.

At Sunset Beach, not a particularly attractive sunning or swimming beach, you'll probably see a lot of people bent double scouring the sands for the famous and elusive Cape May diamonds. Milky in color, when polished they glitter like diamonds. Here you can also see the concrete bulkhead of the World War I S.S. *Atlantis* rising from the ocean. After several Atlantic crossings, this impractical vessel was sunk for use as a jetty.

BICYCLING: Rentals available on West Perry Street (Rte. 606), the road that takes you out to Cape May Point, where John Rutherford of Mope or Pedal (tel. 609/884-5896) rents bikes for $3 an hour, $8 a day. It's open all year —just knock on the door upstairs. A good map is available from P.O. Box 365, Cape May Court House, NJ 08210. Village Bike Rentals, Ocean and Washington Streets (tel. 609/884-8500), in the Acme parking lot right across from the Mall's information booth, rents bikes for $3 an hour, $8 a day, and also has a couple of surreys for two people or more that rent for $10 an hour.

BIRD WATCHING: Long before Cape May was famous as a resort, Audubon made it famous for its bird life. Prime sights are the harlequin and eider ducks in winter, warblers in spring, herons and egrets in summer, and the largest raptor migration in the nation, which takes place in the fall when as many as 88,000 hawks have been recorded massing.

In Cape May State Park, P.O. Box 107, Cape May Point, NJ 08212 (tel. 609/884-2159), blinds and platforms have been built for viewing the marsh and sea birds over the tall stately reeds. Turn left off Sunset Boulevard onto Lighthouse Avenue; the park is by the lighthouse.

At the Cape May Bird Observatory and Sanctuary overlooking Lily Lake, you'll find the offices of the Audubon Society. For their special weekends led by trained naturalists, write to Cape May Bird Observatory, East Lake Drive (P.O. Box 3), Cape May Point, NJ 08212 (tel. 609/884-2736).

The birdwatching hotline (tel. 609/884-2626) is updated every Thursday with recently sighted birds and other avian happenings.

At nearby Stone Harbor Bird Sanctuary, American egret, Louisiana and green herons, black-crowned and yellow-crowned night herons, and ibis all nest. From 111th to 116th Streets on Third Avenue in Stone Harbor (tel. 609/368-5102).

Farther north at Avalon lies one of the last high dune areas in the state, filled with all kinds of flora and fauna (tel. 609/967-8200).

CAMPING: **Cold Spring Campground,** 541 New England Rd., Cape May, NJ 08204 (tel. 609/884-8717), has pleasant secluded sites among sycamore, beech, and hickory. It's near Higbee Beach, where you can walk between ten-foot-high reeds to a small, albeit shingly, beach.

The closest wilderness camping can be found at **Belleplain Forest,** P.O. Box 450, Woodbine, NJ 08270 (tel. 609/861-2404), which has 193 sites and opportunities for bathing, boating, fishing, and hiking. Open all year.

CRUISES: The 65-foot schooner *Delta Lady,* gives three-hour cruises leaving from the Miss Chris Fishing Center, Schellenger's Landing, Route 109, Cape May. The ship leaves at 10 A.M., 2 P.M., and 6 P.M. (tel. 609/884-1919).

The **Cape May–Lewes Ferry** that leaves from Lower Township, North Cape May on Lincoln Boulevard, is a fun, 1¾- to 2-hour trip to take. For information, call 609/886-2718.

FISHING: South Jersey Fishing Center (tel. 609/884-5000) is the dock to head for. Daily sailings from April to November and night sailing for bluefish. Write P.O. Box 641, Cape May, NJ 08204. About $30 or so per person.

GOLF: Stone Harbor, north on Rte. 9 (tel. 609/465-9270), an 18-hole, par-72 course, is open to the public; it also has two tennis courts and a driving range.

Avalon Golf Club, 1510 Rte. 9 North (tel. 609/465-4389), is 18 holes, par 71. Semi-private. Exit 13 off the Garden State Parkway.

HORSEBACK RIDING: Hidden Valley Stables, Bayshore Road (tel. 609/884-8205). As you leave town, turn right off Sunset Boulevard onto Bayshore.

ICE SKATING: Often fun on Lily Lake.

PICNICKING: Pick up staples in town at the supermarkets or main stores. There's a good fresh produce stand just beyond Junction 607 on Sunset Boulevard en route to Cape May Point beaches, one of the prime picnic sites.

SAILING: Cruise aboard *The Tern,* a 36-foot yacht. Call 609/884-8347 between 8 A.M. and 1 P.M. and 3 and 5 P.M.

TENNIS: The William Moore Tennis Center, on Washington Street just before the entrance to the Physick Estate (tel. 609/884-8986), has four all-weather and four clay courts. There are also tennis courts at Stone Harbor, north on Rte. 9 (tel. 609/465-9270).

NEW YORK

ALBANY

DISTANCE IN MILES: 148
ESTIMATED DRIVING TIME: 3¼ hours

DRIVING: New York State Thruway to Albany, Exit 23, which leads to I-787 and downtown.
BUS: Trailways (tel. 212/730-7460) goes to Albany. So do Greyhound (tel. 212/635-0800, or toll free 800/528-6055) and Bonanza (tel. 212/635-0800 for tickets or 564-8484 for schedules).
TRAIN: Amtrak stops across the Hudson in Rensselaer. The station is served by buses and taxis. For information, call 212/736-6288.

Special Events to Plan Your Trip Around
MAY: The Tulip Festival (usually the second weekend in May)
　　　Pinksterfest—a large crafts and entertainment fair held in Washington Park (late May).
SEPTEMBER: Hot Air Balloon Festival, Glens Falls (third weekend)

For further information about any of these events and New York in general, contact the New York State Department of Commerce, Division of Tourism, One Commerce Plaza, Albany, NY 12245 (tel. 518/474-4116).
　　For Albany information, contact the Albany County Convention & Visitors Bureau, 52 S. Pearl St., Albany, NY 12207 (tel. 518/434-1217). For information on Washington County, contact Washington County Information, c/o Log Village Grist Mill, P.O. Box 5, Hartford, NY 12838 (tel. 518/632-5237), or the chambers of commerce of the towns or cities. For info

on state parks, contact the Saratoga-Capital State Park, Recreation and Historic Preservation Region, P.O. Box W, Saratoga Springs, NY 12866 (tel. 518/584-2000).

For the average New Yorker, Albany may not spring to mind as the first place to head for a weekend, but despite the remarks of our good mayor, Albany does have some very interesting sites and pleasures to offer. Although it may not warrant a full two-day weekend, it's certainly worth stopping in for a half or full day en route to another destination—Saratoga Springs, for example.

Getting Around
For information, call 518/482-8822 or write to CDTA, 110 Watervliet Ave., Albany, NY 12206.

ALBANY ATTRACTIONS
For me the prime attraction is the Albany Museum, followed by the State Capitol, Empire State Plaza, the art and history museum, Cherry Hill, and the Schuyler mansion.

Capitol Building
The Capitol Building, State Street (tel. 518/474-2418). Recently restored to its earlier magnificence, this building originally cost $24 million to build—double the cost of the nation's capitol in the late 19th century—and took 30 years to complete.

If you look at the façade, you'll see that the building exhibits a hodgepodge of styles. It stands on an Italian Renaissance base, topped by a Romanesque middle, which is capped by a pitched French Renaissance–style roof. This peculiar mélange of styles arose from a typical human conflict. The original architect, Thomas Fuller, was pulled off the project, and a team including H. H. Richardson, Leopold Eidlitz, and Frederick Law Olmsted was engaged to complete the project. Fuller built the base; the team built the rest. It's not surprising that it took 30 years to complete, for the actual construction was a feat in itself. Huge granite blocks were brought to Albany by water and hauled up to the site by the Albany Horse Railway. Each block was then worked on by the 200 to 250 stonecutters employed to cut and fit the stone.

The opulence exhibited in the Million Dollar Staircase, and in Richardson's masterpiece, the Senate Chamber—a radiant blend of Siena marble, Mexican onyx, and Scottish red granite combined with carved mahogany and tooled red leather—reflected the wealth of 19th-century Albany, whose manufacturers and traders had amassed great fortunes from their control of and proximity to the Erie Canal, then the main east-west trade route.

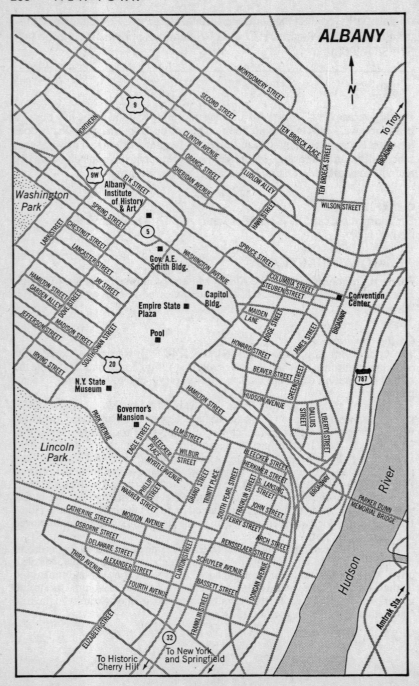

ALBANY

HOURS: Free tours are given daily on the hour from 9 A.M. to 4 P.M. (in summer every 30 minutes) except on the three major winter holidays.

Empire State Plaza

Just across the street from the Capitol stretches this vast wasteland, dominated by 11 marble-and-glass towers and a peculiar flying-saucer-shaped structure (the Convention Center) known as the Egg (that's its polite name). In 1962 when the development was planned, costs were estimated at $350 million. When it was finished in 1978 costs had escalated to over $2 billion. The whole complex houses the offices of the state legislators and of another 11,000 who help run the government. On summer weekends the mall is enlivened by international festivals, special events, people roller skating or just sunning themselves.

During the week, bureaucrats, politicians, workers, and visitors stride the quarter-mile-long underground concourse, scuttling along these Wellesian burrows, past the great collection of modern art (Motherwell, Rothko, Nevelson) that decorates the walls. (Special art tours are given of the whole plaza.) Three good cafeterias are open weekdays in the complex.

HOURS: Free tours of the plaza, leaving from Room 106 on the concourse, are given daily at 11 A.M., 1 P.M., and 4 P.M. (more frequently in summer).

The New York State Museum

This museum at the south end of the plaza (tel. 518/474-5842) really is worth stopping in Albany for, and it's free! What's so amazing is the absence of the usual glass barriers and dull display cases. Instead, spectacular, open-to-view, life-size dioramas depicting scenes of a prehistoric wilderness, or of the Adirondack forest with birds singing, stags leaping, and a waterfall cascading across the rocks, are presented, one after another in a kind of phantasma. Kids'll love it, and adults will find it a refreshing change from the humdrum run-of-the-mill museum.

Half of the museum space is devoted to exploring the geology, flora, fauna, and history of upstate New York and the Adirondacks, from prehistoric times through industrialization (logging, iron-working, mining), all presented in an interesting, creative way. The birds are even provided with complete audio backup.

The other half of the museum space, believe it or not, New Yorkers, is entirely devoted to the history of New York City and presented in a dramatic fashion by tableaux further explicated by lively, contemporary comment and audio-visual effects. You'll find everything here from a diorama demonstrating skyscraper construction to a complete stage set of the Lower East Side at the turn of the century, from the interior of Delmonico's, the restaurant that originated the à la carte menu, to a series of tableaux showing ships docking at the South Street Seaport, immigrants passing through Ellis Island, and the sweat shops that they so often worked in once they settled into the city, plus assorted New York memorabilia—storefronts rescued from Chinatown, a 1930s West Side barbershop, the original "Sesame Street" set, a 1950s subway car fitted with straw raffia seats—all revealing the vibrant history of this fantastic city. You could easily spend the whole day here. A definite hit with adults and kids alike.

HOURS: 10 A.M. to 5 P.M. daily. ADMISSION: Free.

The Observation Deck

From the museum you can ride up 42 floors above the city to the Observation Deck of the Tower Building and peer down onto the Governor's Mansion, complete with swimming pool and tennis courts. (The mansion is open one afternoon only each week—usually Thursday—from 1 to 4 P.M. Reservations required: tel. 518/474-2418.) The Observation Deck is open from 9 A.M. to 4 P.M. daily.

Albany Institute of History and Art

For the art lover the focus at this museum at 125 Washington Ave. (tel. 518/463-4478) will surely be on the Hudson River School collection and the early American portraits. The collection also contains 18th- and 19th-century furniture, silver, pewter, and archival material. HOURS: Tuesday to Saturday from 10 A.M. to 4:45 P.M., on Sunday from 2 to 5 P.M. ADMISSION: Free.

Teleplex Racing Center

If you can't make it to the track, then the OTB Teleplex Racing Center, at 711 Central Ave. (tel. 518/438-0127), is the next best place to watch and wager on the horses. The complex is divided into two parts: the Tele-Theater, charging a $3 admission, which is quite swank, reminiscent of the clubhouse scene; and the down-home no-admission auditorium, with fast-food (pizza, nachos, ice cream) service in the back (no liquor). The Tele-Theater area features a trilevel restaurant with gleaming brass gallery and long bar. TV monitors are scattered throughout the place. At the back, hidden from view, are the betting windows. The action takes place on the big screen where races are shown live. For lunch there are burgers, salads, and deli sandwiches; the dinner menu, priced from $12 to $15, lists fish, meat, and pasta dishes—seafood brochette, veal marsala, fettuccine Alfredo. HOURS: 11 A.M. to 11 P.M. every day; closed Palm Sunday, Easter, and Christmas Day.

Historic Cherry Hill

The remarkable fact about this house, on bus route no. 8 at 523½ S. Pearl St. (tel. 518/434-4791), which in 1987 will mark the 200th anniversary of its construction, lies in the continuity of its ownership—it remained in the Van Rensselaer family from 1787 to 1963—and the unique opportunity this allows to view the changes from 18th-century to 20th-century lifestyles and decor. HOURS: Tuesday to Saturday from 10 A.M. to 3 P.M., on Sunday from 1 to 3 P.M.; closed in January. ADMISSION: A fee is charged.

Schuyler Mansion

At 32 Catherine St. (tel. 518/474-3953), in the springtime you can enjoy the fragrance and color of magnolia and crabapple in bloom at this lovely 18th-century brick mansion, once the isolated estate of Gen. Philip Schuyler (1733–1804). Several interesting episodes attach to the house's story: Alexander Hamilton was married to Schuyler's daughter, Elizabeth, right here in the parlor; General Burgoyne was held prisoner-cum-guest after the victory at Saratoga in 1777. HOURS: April to December, Wednesday to Saturday from 10 A.M. to 5 P.M., on Sunday from 1 to 5 P.M.; January to March, weekends only, except by appointment. Closed the three major winter holidays. ADMISSION: Free. Take bus no. 6 or 8.

Riverboat Cruises
Day or night river cruises are offered by River Cruises, 201 2nd St., Troy, NY 12180 (tel. 518/273-8878). Cruises through the lock system begin in June.

Easy Side Trips from Albany
When you've finished exploring downtown Albany, there are still some wonderful places to see and things to do only a short distance away from the city. For example, in **Glens Falls,** you can experience the excitement of rising at dawn, having brunch accompanied by music to order, and then step into a hot-air balloon and lift off into the air for a spectacular ride above it all. Even if you don't want to take off yourself, you can attend the hot-air balloon festival, usually held on the third weekend of September, a colorful exciting event. It even features a strange leaf-picking contest, in which contestants stay or hover by a tree picking as many leaves as possible! For information, call Adirondack Regional Chambers of Commerce at 518/798-1761.

I've already mentioned how close Albany is to Saratoga Springs for a good summertime trip; in the fall the surrounding counties of Rensselaer and Washington are magnificent for **foliage viewing.**

Only 15 miles southwest of the city, on Rte. 157, **John Boyd Thacher State Park** (tel. 518/872-1237), set on the Helderberg escarpment, commands incredible views of the Hudson-Mohawk Valleys and the peaks of the Adirondacks and Green Mountains. Miles of hiking trails, an Olympic-size pool, and playing fields make it a fine summer spot, while the cross-country skiing, tobogganing, and snowmobiling are excellent in winter.

Want to refurnish the house or redo your whole wardrobe at discount prices? Then **Cohoes** is the place to go. All kinds of specialty stores can be found here: at 43 Mohawk St. you'll find 20% off designer fashions (tel. 518/237-0524); for sheets, towels, and kitchen accessories, try the Factory Bedding Outlet and Furnishing Center, 80 N. Mohawk St. (tel. 518/237-8400). Store hours are usually Monday to Saturday from 10 A.M. to 5 P.M.

Also in Cohoes is a historic theater (see "Evening Entertainment").

About 25 miles south of Albany on Rte. 9W in Coxsackie is the **Bronck House Museum** (tel. 518/731-6490), a fascinating cluster of nine buildings that reflect 300 years of Upper Hudson Valley history. They include an early 1663 stone house with an Indian lookout in the loft and a later, more affluent 1738 brick house. The barns and adjacent slave cemetery are also fun to explore. Some memorabilia of artist Thomas Cole is also on display. Good for a brief stop en route to Albany. HOURS: June 28 to September 6, Tuesday to Saturday from 10 A.M. to 5 P.M., on Sunday from 2 to 6 P.M.

PLACES TO STAY IN ALBANY

Note: Bear in mind that Albany accommodations are only a little over 30 minutes away from Saratoga Springs and that during the months of June, July, and August, you'll need to reserve well ahead of time.

Airport Hotels

The **Americana Inn**, 660 Albany-Shaker Rd., Albany, NY 12211 (tel. 518/869-8100), located near the airport, is one of the most fetching accommodations in Albany. Although the Americana is a modern hotel, Federal and Queen Anne reproductions in the lobby, dining room, and other public areas give it a more traditional ambience. The bar exhibits a clubby masculine air with leather armchairs and cozy brick fireplace. The accommodations are built around a central covered courtyard, whose pathways are lit by gas-light-like lamps and are lined with shrubs. The large and pleasantly decorated rooms have pretty embroidery-look spreads and curtains and special touches like an extra telephone in the bathroom. The elegant Scrimshaw dining room is noted for its cuisine, which includes such specialties as prime rib, veal marsala, sole en papillote, and steaks. A game room and a pool in the courtyard complete the facilities of this comfortable establishment.

RATES: $105 to $110 double in summer. Weekend packages available.

Best Western's Turf Inn, 205 Wolf Rd., Albany, NY 12211 (tel. 518/458-7250, or toll free 800/528-1234), also out near the airport, offers a livelier, faster-paced (perhaps less elegant) scene. Again the accommodations are built around a large courtyard with a pool at the center, but here you can sit outside your room and have a cocktail from the service bar at the center of the courtyard. There's also a small putting green for kids, and outside, at the back of the property, there are two tennis courts that are floodlit at night. Besides a regular breakfast/coffee shop, Love Nest II, consisting of two bars and a restaurant, really swings every night, especially on weekends. The Love Nest is also a popular weekend spot, where crowds cluster around the long bar, crowned with figurehead and masts. Dancing to live entertainment is available in the Pirate's Den. Rooms are all nicely decorated. The suites are especially handsome, and you may be lucky to get one on a weekend for the price of a regular room. There are also six rooms with waterbeds, all offering access to the outdoor pool and patio.

RATES: $60 to $95 double. WEEKEND PACKAGES: The so-called Love Weekend includes champagne, dinner for two, and breakfast for only $125 (not available during August).

The **Albany Marriott**, 189 Wolf Rd., Albany, NY 12205 (tel. 518/458-8444). You may have some problem finding this accommodation, even though it's right on a major highway, because the building is set a good distance back from the road and the sign is atop the roof where the eye doesn't necessarily look. The rooms are large and have a restful air with their Oriental prints as decoration. The accommodations on the Concierge level are particularly appealing. Here the rooms contain plants and magazines like *BusinessWeek,* and the bathrooms feature blow dryers and a complimentary bathrobe. Flirtations is (or certainly was) the place to be at night for its live entertainment offered six nights a week.

In the Market, prime-rib buffets are popular on weekends, and so too, is the Great Sunday Family Buffet which, among other things, offers three meats and a very seductive ice cream bar.

Ashley's is the hotel's fine dining room, a romantic spot particularly in the evening when the tables are lit by little lanterns and the etched-glass accents seem to glow, along with the mirror-backed banquettes and mirrored ceiling. The menu is touched with New Orleans inspiration—Cajun shrimp, jambalaya (lobster, shrimp, oysters, chicken, and sausage, blended together in a stock with seasoned rice), and blackened fish—and changes daily, depending on the season. The mesquite grill is also used for such dishes as lobstertails, grilled and served with lime butter, or rack of lamb, which is grilled and then roasted with a combination of breadcrumbs, garlic, rosemary, thyme, and parsley. Appetizers include escargots, mussels, pasta, pâté, and smoked seafood served with black bread, capers, onions, and dill sauce. Among the salads, the Geisha, consisting of spinach, romaine, and watercress, garnished with water chestnuts, petite shrimp, tofu, and oranges, has an interesting assortment of ingredients. Main-course dishes range from $16 to $19.

On the Concierge level you will also receive a complimentary continental breakfast and complimentary hors d'oeuvres, served between 5 and 7:30 P.M. Turndown service, daily newspaper, shower massage, and shoeshine machine are additional perks. The outside pool with a garden area, and the indoor pool along with the sauna and exercise room, are further attractions, especially for the weekend visitor who has time to relax.

RATES: $97 single, $109 double; On weekends, $65, single or double. Weekend packages are available.

The **Comfort Inn,** 866 Albany-Shaker Rd., Latham, NY 12110 (tel. 518/783-1216), has 70 exceptionally large rooms that are modestly furnished in Danish modern. Closets are open and the bathroom sink surrounds are Formica, but the rooms are well kept and the management friendly. There are some nonsmoking rooms as well as rooms for the handicapped. For the ambitious there's even an exercise room with a treadmill and stationary bicycle. The Runway Restaurant (butcher-block tables, contemporary Windsor chairs, brass accents, and hanging plants) serves breakfast, including a $2.45 special and a big breakfast consisting of an eight-ounce ribeye, two eggs, toast, hash-browns, and coffee for $6. The menu also offers hot and cold sandwiches, burgers, a special children's menu, a selection of about ten different seafoods, and several steaks. The last two items are priced from $8 to $11.

RATES: $38 single, $44 double.

A Downtown Choice

Albany Hilton, 10 Eyck Plaza, State and Lodge Streets, Albany, NY 12207 (tel. 518/462-6611), offers 392 elegant rooms plus all the usual Hilton facilities, including an indoor pool. Three restaurants include a bamboo-and-plants-look coffeeshop (Arthur's Court), Truffles for elegant dining, and a lounge-restaurant named Cinnamon's. Cohoots is the prime Albany disco.

RATES: $94 to $122 double. Weekend packages are available.

Other Albany accommodations include several **Holiday Inns, Howard Johnson's, Days Inns,** and **Governors Motor Inns.**

LODGING AND DINING OUTSIDE ALBANY

If you prefer a country inn only 20 minutes away from the city center, then seek out the **Gregory House,** P.O. Box 401, Averill Park, NY 12018 (tel. 518/674-3774). From the parking lot behind the house a little footbridge crosses over a stream onto a path that cuts through silver birches, lilacs, and other shrubs to the old Gregory House, named after Elias Gregory who built it in 1830 and in whose family it remained for three generations. Bette and Bob Jewell bought it in 1964 and lived here for 12 years before opening the inn in 1976.

The original house now houses the restaurant and bar. From the foyer you'll step into the common room, which Bette and Bob added on. It still has a weathered country look thanks to the brick fireplace, rockers, rope rug, and pineapple print curtains. The room has a cathedral-style ceiling, and from the crossbeams hang baskets and assorted wicker items. All of the 12 rooms have private bath, air conditioning, and clock/radios. Each one is decorated differently, although all have a country flavor. Number 7 is known as the honeymoon room and contains a cherry pencil four-poster decked out with eyelet white covers. Lace-fringed curtains hang in the bay window and a dresser and rocker complete the furnishings. Pewter lamps add another country touch. Some rooms have their own decks, like no. 11 which overlooks the kidney-shaped outdoor pool. In all the rooms comforters are prettily decorative. A continental breakfast is included in the room rate, or if you prefer, you can select from the items listed on the wall plaque (eggs Benedict, blueberry pancakes—under $5) that hangs in the cheery Pub room with its red-checked tablecloths.

The main dining room is in the old, original part of the house and sports a Federal-style fireplace, chair rails, beamed ceiling. The other dining room is known as the library room for obvious reasons. The screened-in porch has been turned into a bar. The menu is quite extensive, and among the popular specialties are the filet mignon with a béarnaise sauce, a sliced filet of beef sautéed and served with a marsala sauce, and shrimp scampi cooked in brandied garlic butter. Entree prices run from $8.50 for chicken livers in wine sauce to $22.50 for scampi and a petite sirloin or $26 for scallops and filet mignon. Prices include salad, potato, vegetable, and bread. Various liqueur parfaits, cheesecake, and such colorful creations as coupe Romanoff (ice cream, strawberries, and raspberry purée with kirschwasser and whipped cream) and coupe Elizabeth (ice cream with black cherries in cherry-brandy-flavored syrup with whipped cream) complete the dessert menu.

RATES: $50 to $60 double, $5 less for a single. DINNER: The dining room is open for dinner only from 5 P.M. Tuesday through Saturday and from 1 P.M. on Sunday. To get there from Albany, get onto I-90 east and take Exit 7 (Washington Avenue). Turn left onto Washington Avenue, cross Rte. 4 and continue on Rte. 43 into Averill Park. The inn is on the left just past the town crossroads.

Set well back from Rte. 9 and banked into a hillside, the **Inn at the Century House,** Box 287, R.D. 1, Cohoes, NY 12047 (tel. 518/785-0931), provides a remarkably quiet oasis. The 61 rooms are all pleasantly decorated with Federal-style antique reproductions and chintz wallpapers, and sport three or four different color schemes—rust and blue or dusky rose and gray, for example. Small suites might feature a four-poster sans canopy, a full-length free-standing mirror, Chippendale-style table, chair, and desk. All rooms have Touch-tone telephones and TVs. Room rates include a buffet breakfast in the traditionally furnished breakfast room. Additional lures include the attractively landscaped outdoor pool and a tennis court.

The inn was added only two years ago to the original Century House restaurant (tel. 518/785-0834), which the current owners, the O'Hearns, opened in 1949. The restaurant still thrives. There are three dining rooms: the prettiest in my opinion is the Blue Room, which is indeed an intense blue and also offers a brick fireplace, gilt-framed pictures, and Windsor chairs for dining comfort. Brass and stucco characterize the main dining room. The two most popular items on the menu are the shore dinner (broiled lobstertail, shrimp, and sea scallops, sautéed in chablis and garlic butter and served on toast points) and the veal Oscar (veal garnished with Alaskan crabmeat and asparagus spears, and served with a hollandaise sauce). Prices range from $7.50 for broiled chicken livers with fresh mushrooms to $20 for two cold-water lobstertails. Most dishes cost between $8 and $11.

LUNCH: Monday to Friday from 11 A.M. to 3 P.M. DINNER: Monday to Thursday from 4 to 9:45 P.M., on Friday and Saturday until 10:45 P.M., on Sunday from 1 to 9 P.M. Piano accompaniment on Saturday evenings.

Although the **Lookout Motor Inn**, 622 Watervliet Shaker Road (I-87, Exit 5), Latham, NY 12110 (tel. 518/785-4516), is only a roadside motor inn, it does have several tennis courts, making it an ideal stopover for the tennis buff. It also has a swimming pool and some other extra-special features like free local telephone calls and complimentary morning newspaper.

RATES: $50 to $58 double. Prices rise to $70 to $80 in August.

ALBANY DINING

A Brunch Spot
A good choice, discussed ahead, is the **Beveryck**, 275 Lark St. (tel. 518/472-9043), which serves a brunch on Sunday only from 11:30 A.M.

Lunch or Dinner Choices
Jack's Oyster Restaurant, 42 State St. (tel. 518/465-8854). The grandson of the original Jack still runs this Albany institution, the setting for many a political deal and negotiation. Mirrors, dark oak, and old pictures of Albany give the place a predictably masculine air; tables and booths are far enough apart to ensure privacy. Specialties here, of course, are the oyster stew, clams casino, Boston scrod, crab claws, sole, and lobster, etc., priced from $9 to $28. A large and lively place; don't be deterred by the somewhat tacky-looking exterior.

LUNCH: 11:30 A.M. to 4 P.M. daily. DINNER: 4 to 10 P.M. daily.

Coco's, 1470 Western Ave. (tel. 518/456-0297), bills itself as "Slightly Sensational," and it is that. Part of a chain (the others are in Rochester, Binghamton, and King of Prussia), it's a fun place to go. Giant drinks come to the table attached to balloons. Inside there are a series of rooms: the prettiest is the garden room, furnished with wrought-iron chairs and tables covered with floral oilcloth tablecloths and country bric-a-brac on the walls; in another room the carousel horse is the centerpiece of the salad bar, or rather, four salad bars—the garden salad, displaying vegetables and greens; the health food, featuring fruits, raisins, granola, etc., with fruited yogurt dressings; hot specialties like delicious spicy meatballs; and the spinach bar, with all the trimmings—plus cheeses and breads. If you choose a lunch entree you'll also enjoy the salad bar for only 99¢ extra. The vast laminated menu lists everything from potatoes stuffed with cheese and bacon, nachos, burgers, and steamed clams to veal parmigiana, fish of the day, steak or chicken teriyaki, duckling with an orange-lime glaze, and more. Prices run $4 to $14.

The management works hard to dream up special fun promotions. For instance, there'll always be a lobster special in the summer, and for those of you who feel intimidated when faced with a whole steaming lobster, the manager, dressed in sou'wester and oilskins, will stop by and open her up for you! He's known as Bar Harbor Barney. Evenings are also quite lively at the bar with a small dance floor; a DJ spins five nights a week, Tuesday to Saturday. And more about those wild drinks—there are over 50 of them, including such concoctions as chocolate amaretto (amaretto, ice cream, and crème de cacão), a chocolate kiss (chocolate ice cream and vodka), or a hot drink called praline royale, made with praline liqueur, brandy, and coffee.

HOURS: Open Monday to Saturday from 11 A.M. to midnight (carousel only from 3 to 4:30 P.M.), on Sunday from 10 A.M. to 3 P.M. for buffet brunch and from 3 P.M. to midnight for dinner.

Dinner Only

The top downtown choice is probably **La Serre,** 14 Green St. (tel. 518/463-6056). Here, in warm but elegant surroundings, the specialties include oysters, escargots, frogs' legs, bouillabaisse, and such entrees as tournedos Henry IV, braised sweetbreads, and veal dishes, ranging from $14.50 to $20.

LUNCH: Monday to Friday from 11:30 A.M. to 2:30 P.M. DINNER: Monday to Saturday from 6 to 10 P.M.

L'Auberge, 351 Broadway (tel. 518/465-1111), is another Albany institution that has been serving classic French cuisine in a plain setting for the last 25 years. Daily specials supplement the regular menu, which features such entrees as rack of lamb, steak au poivre, chateaubriand, crevettes Basques, baby quails, and breast of duckling. Prices range from $16 to $21. To start there are terrines and pâtés, escargots, gravlax, and quenelles, and to finish you can select from the dessert cart, which might display Grand Marnier chocolate mousse cake, crème caramel, and other classic desserts.

LUNCH: Monday to Friday from noon to 2:30 P.M. DINNER: Monday to Saturday from 6 to 10 P.M.; closed Sunday.

At **Yono's,** 289 Hamilton St. (tel. 518/436-7747), two brownstones have been joined to create three separate dining rooms. The primary influence on the cuisine is Indonesian—noodle dishes, nasi goreng, satays, eggrolls, and crab cakes —supplemented by such continental dishes as chicken Florentine, sole with artichokes, and more. There's a comfortable small piano bar. Prices range from $10 to $17.

LUNCH: Monday to Friday from 11:30 A.M. to 2:30 P.M. DINNER: Monday to Saturday from 6 to 10 P.M.

Out near the airport hotels, **L'École,** 44 Fuller Rd., Stuyvesant Plaza (tel. 518/ 489-1330), offers fine continental cuisine in cozy surroundings. In winter the fireplace-bar is particularly attractive; in summer the outdoor patio draws the crowds. Pink tablecloths, a beamed ceiling, chintz, and stucco complete the country feel. Dinner might start with smoked trout à la Chantilly or pâté de veau et jambon. Main courses, always supplemented by daily specials, run from $12.50 for a delicious filet of sole Véronique to $38 for a rack of lamb en croûte for two. Most dishes, like the duckling Montmorency, veal Oscar, and steak bordelaise, hover around $14 or $15. It's worth saving some room for desserts like Bailey's Irish Cream mousse, black-raspberry cheesecake, or Grand Marnier cake.

LUNCH: Monday through Friday only. DINNER: Monday through Saturday.

Real aficionados of Italian cuisine know that the **Italian-American Community Center,** on Washington Avenue Extension (tel. 518/456-0292), is the best place to find authentic food—from zuppa di pesce and linguini portugese to chicken cacciatore and veal with peppers, priced from $6 to $12. You'll need reservations on weekends.

LUNCH: Monday to Friday from 11 A.M. to 2 P.M. DINNER: Monday to Saturday from 5 to 10 P.M., on Sunday from 2 to 9 P.M.

The large Italian community has long ago turned **Lombardo's,** 121 Madison St. (tel. 518/462-9180), into an Albany institution. Italian murals and tile floors provide the proper setting for dining on veal and peppers, veal marsala, a vast selection of pasta dishes, plus steak, chops, and seafood specialties. Prices range from $7 to $17.

HOURS: Wednesday to Sunday from 11:30 A.M. to 9 P.M.

Other Italian favorites include **Bon Giorno's,** 23 Dove St. (tel. 518/462-9176), a small, really homey and popular place with incredibly cheap Italian fare.

LUNCH: Monday to Friday. DINNER: Monday to Saturday from 5 to 9 P.M.

The ground floor of an old telephone company building has been transformed into **Ogdens,** 42 Howard St., at Lodge (tel. 518/463-6605), an elegant dining room offering some fine cuisine, including an array of continental dishes—veal moutarde or veal morelles; duckling with cassis sauce; tournedos Rossini with black truffles, foie gras, and madeira; Dover sole braised in court bouillon; and poached salmon with a sorrel vin blanc. Prices run $10 to $19. Light oak and art deco gray, enhanced by a colorful array of potted plants, create the atmosphere. In summer there's a really pretty outside dining area.

LUNCH: Monday to Friday from 11:30 A.M. to 3 P.M. DINNER: Monday to Saturday from 6 to 10 P.M.

A favorite out-of-town dining spot in nearby Glenmont, **Chez René** (tel. 518/

463-5130) serves a variety of steak, duck, seafood, and veal dishes. Veal René is served with white asparagus and crabmeat in a hollandaise sauce; there's a spectacular seafood platter, and about 15 other items on the menu. Prices run $10 to $20.

DINNER: Tuesday to Saturday from 5 to 10 P.M.

Dinner/Brunch Choice

The **Beveryck,** 275 Lark St. (tel. 518/472-9043). Whatever negative opinions an outsider might express about the Albany Mall or the Empire State Plaza, many Albanyites are happy with the restoration that has taken place in the formerly decaying downtown area. Energetic entrepreneurs have renovated many of the old downtown structures, sandblasting their exteriors and interiors and oftentimes turning them into restaurants like the Beveryck, where continental cuisine is now served in a casual, airy, skylit room. Veal Calvados or francese, chicken Dijon, steak au poivre, and filet mignon range from $11 to $19. In winter a fire makes the dining area glow; in summer the outside patio is an added bonus.

LUNCH: Tuesday to Friday from 11:30 A.M. to 2:30 P.M. DINNER: Tuesday to Thursday from 6 to 10 P.M., until 11 P.M. on Friday and Saturday, from 5 to 9:30 P.M. on Sunday. BRUNCH: Sunday from 11:30 A.M. TO 3 P.M.

EVENING ENTERTAINMENT

Theater

A variety of dance, drama, music, and international performances are given at the Egg, Empire State Plaza's **Institute for the Performing Arts** (tel. 518/474-1199 or 473-3750).

Over in Schenectady, **Proctors Theater,** at 432 State St. (tel. 518/382-1083 for information, 518/346-6204 for tickets), offers good theater from September to May, and classic and silent movies from June through August.

Every small town in America has one—a theater that once thrived in another, very different earlier era. And Cohoes is no exception. Here a bold and determined group is trying to revive a glorious old theater built in 1874, in which Eva Tanguay, the "Girl Who Made Vaudeville Famous," once performed. The **Cohoes Music Hall,** P.O. Box 586, Cohoes, NY 12047 (tel. 518/235-7969), is a beautiful small theater with an ornate painted ceiling, highly decorated proscenium, and a lot of gilt. In this historic building the Heritage Artists group put on a series of performances, each using different actors, during their season from December to June. Tickets cost between $9 and $12. Past well-reviewed performances have included *Godspell, Billy Bishop Goes to War,* and *I'm Getting My Act Together and Taking It on the Road.*

Jazz/Dancing/Bands

The best disco is **Cohoots** in the Hilton; for live entertainment and dancing, head for the **Love Nest** at Best Western's Turf Inn.

ALBANY ACTIVITIES

CAMPING: From April to mid-October, **Thompson's Lake State Park,** R.D. 1, East Berne, NY 12059 (tel. 518/872-1674), offers camping at 140 sites with fireplaces, plus swimming and cross-country skiing on 105 acres.

GOLF: Albany Municipal, New Scotland Avenue (tel. 518/438-2209).

ICE SKATING: On the reflecting pool on the mall.

ROLLER SKATING: On the plaza across from the Tower building, from 11 A.M. to 7 P.M. Bring an ID for skate rental.

SKIING: Cross-country skiing can be found in John Boyd Thacher Park, 15 miles southwest of the city on Rte. 157 in Voorheesville (tel. 518/872-1237).

SKY DIVING: The Albany Sky Diving Center, P.O. Box 131, Duanesburg NY 12056 (tel. 518/895-8140), is accessible by train to Schenectady, where you'll be picked up for free. Open daily May through October, weekends only November to April.

SWIMMING: John Boyd Thacher Park, on Rte. 157 in Voorheesville (tel. 518/872-1237), has a pool, as do several of the Albany hotels.

TENNIS: Courts can be found at the Lookout Motor Inn, I-87, Exit 5 (tel. 518/785-4516), and at Best Western's Turf Inn (tel. 518/458-7250).

SARATOGA SPRINGS

DISTANCE IN MILES: 186
ESTIMATED DRIVING TIME: 3¾ hours

DRIVING: New York State Thruway to Albany, I-87 to Exit 13 north. Take Rte. 9 north.
BUS: Trailways (tel. 212/730-7460) goes to Saratoga Springs. So does Greyhound (tel. 212/635-0800, or toll free 800/528-6055).
TRAIN: Amtrak's *Adirondack* stops in Saratoga Springs. For information, call 212/736-6288.

Special Events to Plan Your Trip Around

JANUARY/FEBRUARY: Winter Carnival Weekends.
APRIL TO NOVEMBER: Harness Racing. For information, call 518/584-2110.
JUNE TO SEPTEMBER: The Performing Arts Festival. For information, contact SPAC, Spa State Park, Saratoga Springs, NY 12866 (tel. 518/587-3330 in season, 584-9330 off-season). Tickets go on sale in early May.
LATE JULY TO LATE AUGUST: The Saratoga Race Meeting. Call 212/641-4700 or 518/584-6200 for dates.

For further information about these events and Saratoga Springs, contact the Greater Saratoga Chamber of Commerce, 494 Broadway, Suite 212, Saratoga Springs, NY 12866 (tel. 518/584-3255); the Saratoga County Promotion Department, 50 W. High St., Ballston Spa, NY 12020 (tel. 518/885-5381, ext. 665), also offers info.

Normally the population of Saratoga Springs is a modest 25,000, but in summer the population swells to 75,000 for the party that centers on the old Victorian Clubhouse at the Saratoga Race Course. The races are on, the steeds are running, and Saratoga is the place to see the silks flashing by, the horses' flanks sweating in the sun, and to feel the air of increasing excitement as the horses fly out, their hoofs pounding on the green, green turf. People also come for the now-famous arts festival that begins in June—a unique affair blessed with two national companies as regular summer visitors, the New York City Ballet and the Philadelphia Orchestra. During both of these summer events the hotels and motels are full, with people staying as far away as Albany and even farther south. The large Victorian residences on North Broadway are filled with house parties and house guests as "the season" swings into high gear.

With some ups and severe downs, Saratoga has nearly always had a special summer sheen. One can see why this spa became the great social mecca that it did in the 1800s and early 1900s. The park and the springs were always, and still are, prime attractions; casino gambling, and the excitement and glamour it engendered, was another; horse racing was still another. Grand hotels sprang up. Large Victorian summer cottages were constructed and people flocked here at the turn of the century, for it had become de rigueur for the American barons to migrate to Saratoga for at least a part of the summer.

Gideon Putnam built the first hotel in 1803, and soon crowds were coming to take the waters, as many as 12,000 by 1825. They came to drink, inhale the steam, or bathe in the waters (which you can still do today), and if they had no physical complaints, they simply drank the waters in fashionable Drink Halls with elegant Greek Revival columns and long colonnades, where they strolled to the strains of lilting bands and orchestras.

By 1840 the era of the grand hotels had fully arrived, the most famous Saratoga examples being the Grand Union and the United States, both vast and palatial in scope. Sadly, neither has survived. The United States was torn down in 1946 and the Grand Union followed quietly in 1952. To return to an earlier era: in 1861 John Morrissey, a sometime United States heavyweight boxing champion and a congressman from New York City, boldly opened the first casino so that he could indulge his wealthy passion. Two years later in 1863 he built the racetrack, thus making Saratoga a veritable playground for the rich and famous who flocked here. Among the most colorful were Diamond Jim Brady and his equally lavish companion, Lillian Russell. Brady, a railroad equipment salesman and steelcar magnate of prodigious girth and appetite, was known to drink gallons of fruit juice along with an enormous daily diet of three dozen oysters in the morning and eight dozen at night, plus eggs, steaks, chops, joints of beef, several lobsters and crabs, and whole fowls accompanied by vegetables, salads, and desserts. His eminently suitable companion, Lillian Russell, carried her 200 pounds with such prodigious charm that she was able to capture five husbands. Less flashy were the

Whitneys, Vanderbilts, Morgans, and other old families who also came to romp until 1907, when reformers closed the casino and Saratoga embarked on the roller-coaster phase of her history.

From 1910 to 1913 both the casino and racetrack were closed, but by the '20s the resort was thriving again. Many more lavish cottages were built; the social scene was populated by dashing figures once again. But only briefly, for in the 1930s the class of Saratoga habitués deteriorated. Gamblers, bookies, pimps, and prostitutes took over, and decay settled in until the casinos were finally closed in 1951 after a national crime investigation. Only racing kept alive the spirit of Saratoga's golden era, and that's what the recent revival has been built around—the 24-day meet when traditions return and the magic and splendor of those languorous and extravagant summers return.

SARATOGA SPRINGS ATTRACTIONS

Even if you have your own car, you might prefer to take a tour of the town because it is so spread out. **Saratoga Circuit Tours,** 417 Broadway (P.O. Box 38), Saratoga Springs, NY 12866 (tel. 518/587-3656), offers a first-rate two-hour tour personally conducted aboard a mini-bus (weekends only in June, daily in July and August). Tours start at the Drink Hall (where you can sample the waters), which used to be the old trolley stop. From here you go to:

Congress Park

This lovely 33-acre park just off Broadway was surrounded, in the late 19th century, by great hotels when Saratoga was the most renowned American spa. The two most famous—the Grand Union and the United States—were torn down in the late 1940s and early 1950s. At the center of the park stands Daniel Chester French's *Spirit of Life* statue and fountain, a memorial to Trask who led the movement to revitalize the mineral springs. Today you're more likely to find craft and art shows than ladies strolling with parasols, although the bandstand concerts given today do recapture the era of Saratoga's heyday. At the Canfield casino (tel. 518/587-3550), built in 1870–1871, also in the park, Willie Vanderbilt lost $130,000 while he was waiting for his lady friends to dress for dinner. Today the two top floors are set up with museum exhibits, although the ballroom has been retained and is still used by one of the Whitneys for her annual ball.

North Broadway's Architectural Treats

From the park, go back out onto North Broadway to view the Victorian homes or cottages built for brief stays during the season. Fantasize what it must have been like to attend a house party here. You can look at the house that was rented by Diamond Jim Brady and Lillian Russell, by the Cluetts of Arrow shirt fame, by the Gaines family home, the Ogden Phipps house, and those belonging to other racing folk. The styles vary from Jacobean to bracketed Italianate, from Federal to Victorian Gothic and French Renaissance. As you pass you'll catch glimpses of

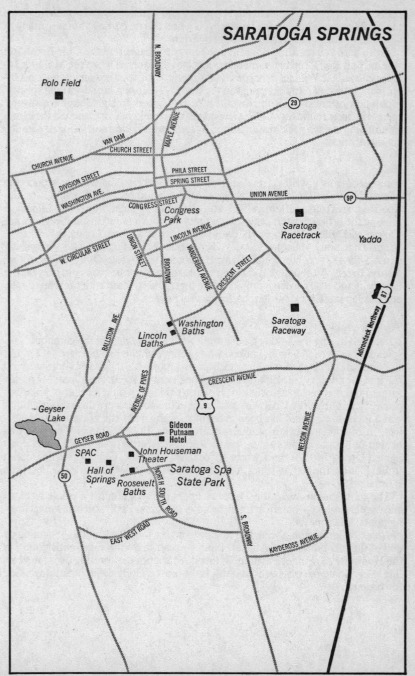

SARATOGA SPRINGS

stained glass, turrets, vine-covered porches, and gazebos; and if you drive down the road that runs behind the houses, you'll find ornate carriage houses, many of which have been converted into living quarters.

From here you can drop down into the Lower Village, past the Olde Bryan Inn where High Rock, the first mineral spring, was discovered when the Mohawk Indians carried Sir William Johnson, then superintendent of Indian affairs, on a litter from Johnstown to the springs in August 1771. He was cured and the springs' reputation established. You can still take the waters today. There are several springs in and around town—Big Red at the racetrack, one in Congress Park, and a number in the spa park, distinguished by their carbonation and saline or alkaline characteristics.

Yaddo

Famous now as a writer's retreat, this lovely Georgian mansion was once the home of New York City financier Spencer Trask and his wife, Katrina, who decided to turn it into a retreat in 1926 after all four of their children died of illnesses. Among the artists, writers, and song writers who have found inspiration here are Carson McCullers, Philip Roth, Saul Bellow, Ned Rorem, Leonard Bernstein, Virgil Thomson, Malcolm Cowley, Katharine Anne Porter (who supposedly wrote *Ship of Fools* here), and Truman Capote (who wrote *Other Voices, Other Rooms* here). Although you can't go inside the gray stone mansion, do visit the fountains and rose garden, complete with a pergola covered with rambling roses, and the Japanese rock garden, both peaceful havens.

The Racetrack

If you visit during the 24-day meet, you'll want to breakfast at the clubhouse, resplendent with ivied window boxes, while you watch the horses exercise. Even if the races aren't on, a visit to the racetrack is a must. It's the oldest thoroughbred track in the country, the first race having been run in 1863, when John Morrissey formed the first racing association. He didn't think it would be that popular because it was during the Civil War, and most of the horses were down South, but it was a great success and has been ever since. Known as "the graveyard of favorites," it's famed for several stunning racing upsets. In 1919 Man of War, who was beaten only once in his career, was defeated here at Saratoga by a horse aptly named Upset. In 1930 the Travers Triple Crown winner, Gallant Fox, fell victim to Jim Dandy, the 100-to-1 shot. Secretariat was also upset here in 1973. Post time is usually 1:30 P.M.

The most famous race, the Travers Cup, is the occasion for a whole week of spectacular events—parades, craft shows in Congress Park, golf and tennis tournaments, and concerts.

Note: When planning your trip to Saratoga, try to make it at the beginning or end of the second week of August, when you can share the eager anticipation in the Humphrey S. Finney Pavilion, as tuxedoed auctioneers preside over the yearling sales. Some people swear that this is *the* most exciting event in Saratoga. See for yourself.

Saratoga Spa State Park
Noted hydrotherapist Simon Baruch helped plan the whole 2,000-acre park as a spa, and his son, Bernard, finished it in 1935. Inside the park are 26 springs —primarily laden with sodium, lithium, and potassium—plus a 9-hole and an 18-hole golf course, the Peerless Olympic-size swimming pool, eight tennis courts, the Gideon Putnam Hotel, and the Victoria Pool, favored bathing place of dancers and artists who appear at the arts center, whose natural amphitheater is located here in the park. Here, the New York City Ballet performs in July, the Philadelphia Orchestra in August. A buffet is served before performances in the Hall of Springs restaurant. There's a nominal entrance fee for cars. For information about the park, contact the Park Superintendent's Office, P.O. Box W, Saratoga Springs, State Park, Saratoga Springs, NY 12866 (tel. 518/584-2000).

The Roosevelt Baths
Also located in the park, the baths are among the highlights of any visit to Saratoga Springs. Although the bathhouse looks like a utilitarian hospital and a far cry from a typically luxurious modern spa, the treatment given here is euphoric and certainly one of the best buys in Saratoga. For about 20 minutes you'll lie back in a tub, up to your neck in hot brown mineral water; it's like sitting in bubbling seltzer with a pillow at your head and a stool at your feet. The masseur will then wrap you in hot sheets and give you a top-to-toe massage before tucking you into bed for a short nap. After all this, you'll emerge feeling relaxed, content, and totally rejuvenated as you walk out into the beautiful setting of the park. In my opinion, everyone should be entitled to this experience at least once a week. COST: $13 ($9 off-season). HOURS: The whole process takes about 1½ hours. The last bath is given at 3 P.M., although the hours are 8:30 A.M. to 4:40 P.M. Open Wednesday to Sunday year round (daily, except Tuesday, in summer). In summer you need to book at least two weeks in advance (tel. 518/584-2011). The Lincoln baths, which are also here, are open in July and August only.

Museum of Antiques and Art
At 153 Regent St. in Saratoga Springs (tel. 518/584-0107), this attracts many return visitors. In the first college building of Skidmore, constructed in 1903 (named Skidmore in 1922), Mr. Grande, the owner/curator, has created a museum and antiques shopping complex occupying 9,000 square feet of space. Around the walls in the front room are arrayed his vast and varied collection of stoneware, his wife's Hummel figurines, and, at least when I visited, a local collector's exquisite scrimshaw and ivory carvings, which included pieces by French prisoners of war carved while they languished in English prisons around 1800. The rest of the area upstairs and downstairs is used by about 30 dealers who display clocks, glass, jewelry, silverware, music boxes, Victorian furniture, oak and other antiques, and collectibles. Hours can be spent browsing here. Best of all, it's open year round. HOURS: 10 A.M. to 5 P.M. daily; closed Thanksgiving, Christmas, and New Year's Days. ADMISSION: Free.

Other Saratoga Springs Attractions

Even for those who are not particularly interested in architecture, the **Batcheller Mansion** on Circular Road, at Whitney Place, appeals to the fantasy in all of us with its scallopped gables and Chambord-style towers capped with minarets, all built in 1873 and magnificently restored.

For a real sense of what Saratoga was like in its heyday, stop by **George Bolster's photography studio** at 1 Phila St. (tel. 518/584-6820). Try and get him talking too, for he has some spectacular tales to tell about those old days and the characters who passed through Saratoga. Unfortunately the studio is not open on weekends.

The **National Museum of Racing**, on Union Avenue (tel. 518/584-0400), displays racing silks, equine art, trophies, and memorabilia of legendary names in turf history. HOURS: In summer, 9:30 A.M. to 5 P.M. weekdays, on Saturday from noon to 5 P.M. (in August, from 9:30 A.M. to 7 P.M. daily); in winter (January to mid-April), Monday to Friday only, from 10 A.M. to 4 P.M.

The **Historical Society of Saratoga Springs Museum** and the **Wadsworth Memorial Museum** are located atop the casino building and contain exhibits relating to the history of Saratoga and also a series of period rooms. HOURS: In summer, Monday to Saturday from 10 A.M. to 4 P.M., on Sunday from 1 to 4 P.M. (in July and August, 9:30 A.M. to 4:30 P.M. daily); in winter, Wednesday to Sunday from 1 to 4 P.M. ADMISSION: $1.

The **polo games** are also exciting to attend. They are usually scheduled throughout August. For information, contact the Saratoga Polo Association, P.O. Box 821, Saratoga Springs, NY 12866 (tel. 518/584-3255 or 584-8108).

Dance lovers will also want to view the **National Museum of Dance** (tel. 518/584-2225), located in the Washington Bath building, on South Broadway (Rte. 9) in Saratoga Spa State Park. Modern, jazz, ballet, and other dance forms are explored through a variety of exhibits. HOURS: Open from early July to the end of September, Tuesday to Saturday from 10 A.M. to 5 P.M., with extended hours on Thursday from mid-July through August 21.

NEARBY ATTRACTIONS

Five miles south in Ballston Spa are two fine museums. The **Brookside Museum,** on Front Street, is a historical museum housed in a classic 1792 resort hotel, which exhibits artifacts that provide insight into local history and the lifestyles of earlier eras. HOURS: 1 to 5 P.M. daily. The **Bottle Museum,** at 200 Church Ave., houses a huge collection of assorted bottles.

Some 20 miles or so north in Glens Falls, the **Hyde Collection,** 161 Warren St. (tel. 518/792-1761) is well worth going to see. Housed in an Italianate palazzo, the collection includes Rembrandts, Rubenses, and impressionists, all collected by Mrs. Hyde in the early part of this century. HOURS: Tuesday to Sunday noon to 5 P.M.

SARATOGA LODGING

The **Gideon Putnam,** Saratoga Springs, NY 12866 (tel. 518/584-3000), is considered *the* place to stay. Built in 1935 and named in memory of Gideon Putnam, who came to Saratoga to enter the lumber business and wound up building the first boarding house, this red-brick Georgian structure, beautifully situated in Saratoga Spa State Park, offers spectacular views, whatever the season. A tree-lined circular drive—that seems more appropriate for a coach-and-four than a car—leads up to the Corinthian-columned portico, giving entry to a grand marbled, mirrored, and chandeliered lobby. The Georgian Dining Room, with its handsome hand-painted wallpaper is elegant for dinner. The typical Sunday buffet brunch—a spread of scrambled eggs, lasagne, ham, beans and carrots, etc., is popular but, in my opinion, desperately overrated. Price: $15. You'll need a reservation. The drinks, piano entertainment, and hors d'oeuvres, served from 5 P.M. on Friday nights in the Saratoga Room bar, offer a good start to the weekend. The parlor suites opening onto large bamboo-furnished screened porches are the most desirable of the 143 rooms. The other rooms are quite ordinary, decorated in dark blue or rust with large floral-print curtains, candlewick bedspreads, and antique reproductions. TVs and telephones are standard. All the rooms are gradually being refurbished. The hotel gives you immediate access to all the park's facilities: eight tennis courts, golf, two swimming pools, and cross-country skiing (center located in the Victoria Pool building). Bicycles can also be rented.

RATES: Room only, $90 double; with full board, $160 double ($190 in July, $275 in August). Parlor suites are even higher priced. European Plan costs $80 to $100 double. Weekend packages available.

Right on the main street, the **Adelphi,** 365 Broadway, Saratoga Springs, NY 12866 (tel. 518/587-4688), survives from that legendary, opulent era when social life consisted of walks to the springs, courtyard concerts, afternoon garden parties, and high-fashion promenades, followed by gala balls in the evenings. From the piazza of this elegant hotel rise slender columns capped by delicate gingerbread fretwork, while the interior is furnished with luxurious, well-stuffed, and richly colored Victoriana.

Gregg Siefker and Sheila Parkert bought it a decade ago after it had stood empty for ten years. They have gradually restored it, filling it with authentic period furnishings. The only pieces remaining original to the hotel—it had been stripped—were (and still are) the front desk and the valanced, draped, and tasseled floor-to-ceiling mirror. The lobby with its lofty 14-foot-high ceilings and square fluted wood pillars invites lounging with an assortment of Victorian sofas and chairs, each more beautifully upholstered in the finest brocades and fabrics. Among them, my favorites are the French polished Empire couch secured from the Schuyler Mansion and the camelback sofas in the center of the space. Large fresh flower arrangements, fringed lampshades, and one or two potted palms complete the Victorian ambience.

There are 28 rooms and Sheila has decorated each in her unique, inspired style. All have bath, telephone, air conditioning, and Crabtree & Evelyn soap and hand cream. TVs are available on request. One or two front rooms have balconies overlooking the sweep of Broadway. Here are just a few favorites to give you some idea of what to expect. Room 19, a small suite decorated with candy-stripe wallpaper in pink and dark jade, contains a Victorian acorn bed adorned with a spectacular Oriental tent. Complementary furnishings include gilt-framed pictures, a dresser, and a sink with pink marble surround. The sitting room has a dusky-rose carpet, settee, and overstuffed comfy chairs. Suite 16 has a mixture of

Mission and Adirondack furnishings set against a dark-green and tan geometric-patterned wallpaper, and a fabulous paneled bathroom with an old-fashioned tub and separate shower. Suite 3 is large with a private balcony furnished with wicker and Victorian-style fireplace with grate. Drapes are valanced, the wallpaper is brocade, and chairs are slipcovered and so is the bath; white damask covers the sofa. The parlor is filled with Stickley and assorted Victorian furnishings and artifacts. Room 1 is typical. Here the bed has an inlaid headboard, pillows are damask with lace trim, brocade molded wall panels adorn the walls, drapes are valanced, the sofa is brocade, and the desk is elegant French style. Also ask about the mural room, which was in the making when I visited. No matter what room you choose, the fabrics will be luxurious, the effects dramatic.

Throughout the hallways, statuary, quilts, and Victorian pictures, prints, and engravings abound. A favorite quiet corner is the "Turkish cozy," a tented sofa created by Sheila in Oriental style complete with Mughal-style paintings and many luxuriously covered cushions. It's on the third floor.

During the season breakfast is served outside in the piazza where Adirondack chairs are set under a colored awning surrounded by roses, pansy-filled urns, and other flowers. Scarlet drapes and valances add a luxurious feel to the Saratoga Club, open in July and August. Tables are set with lace, crystal, and china. The focal point of the room is the central gazebo. A limited menu, featuring about eight entrees, is offered: duck breast with blackcurrant sauce, salmon filet with garlic confit (salmon steaks baked in foil with fresh basil, tomato slices, lemon and lime, and caramelized garlic cloves), trout Scheherazade (brook trout stuffed with dried apricots, currants, walnuts, and fresh herbs served with light Provençal tomato sauce), pasta and chicken du jour, and a Delmonico steak—grilled and served with homemade chutney of roasted red peppers, sweet onions, tomatoes, and currants. Prices run $15 to $20. At the café, among camelback sofas, draped chintz banquettes, gilt mirrors, you can enjoy cocktails, exotic coffees, and wines, or in July and August, luncheon and light supper sandwiches, salads, or grilled items ($7 to $10). Or you can choose the adjacent room where lavender wicker pieces stand on a gray-painted floor against chintz wallpaper and lace-curtained windows. Food is served only in July and August.

Greg and Sheila have also purchased some rental cottages with a private beach on the lake, and they have great plans to decorate each in a particular style: 1940s, 1950s, Mission, and Victorian, for example. Inquire. At the moment, in their undecorated rustic state they rent for $250 a week.

RATES: May through June and September through October (except special weekends), $55 to $95; special weekends (including Skidmore Graduation, Memorial and Labor Days, and all October weekends), $70 to $120. Weekends for two (with two nights' accommodation and a four-course dinner on either Friday or Saturday), $190 to $290 in July, $290 to $550 in August.

Saratoga now has a fine modern hotel, the **Ramada Renaissance,** 534 Broadway (at City Center), Saratoga Springs, NY 12866 (tel. 518/584-4000), very conveniently located downtown. Upon entering you'll find yourself standing in an atrium-capped gallery which separates the bar and restaurant from the registration desks. The 189 rooms all contain hairdryers and phones in the bathrooms, and are attractively furnished in soft pastel hues—peach carpets, for instance, matched with peach- and blue-floral bedspreads. The furniture consists of antique reproductions. Conveniences include a vanity mirror, alarm clocks, and an assortment of toiletries, including Gucci cologne for men and Pavlova for women. Green Carrara marble floors, ormolu mirrors, potted ferns, Queen Anne–style chairs, brass chandeliers, and horse portraits set the elegant tone in the Sandalwood Restaurant, which is also light and airy because of its atrium. Continental American cuisine is served. The indoor pool has a pleasant patio for sunning; there's also an exercise room containing Universal equipment. The lounge swings on Thursday, Friday, and Saturday with live entertainment.

RATES: $64 single, $74 double, from $145 double in August.

The **Inn at Saratoga,** 231 Broadway, Saratoga Springs, NY 12866 (tel. 518/583-1890), has 40 large pretty rooms with spacious bathrooms. Tasteful furnishings include chintz or striped wallpapers, a free-standing full-length mirror, pelmeted drapes, comfy chairs, and circular table with floor-length tablecloth. A desk and chest of drawers are tucked into a foyer. Color schemes vary from dark blue and beige to dusky rose and jade. All rooms have TV, air conditioning, and telephone.

The dining room and adjacent bar are elegant. Chintz, wallpaper, potted ferns in corners, French-style chairs, and white tablecloths with placemats depicting hunting scenes create the ambience. The service, at least when I visited, was somewhat erratic. The menus reflect a dash of English flavors. For example, among the appetizers there's half a broiled grapefruit (with brown sugar and sherry) alongside camembert croquettes topped with cranberry sauce and ceviche del Peru (scallops marinated in lemon and lime, garnished with red and green peppers). Among the entrees you'll find a roast beef with Yorkshire pudding, London mixed grill, Dover sole cooked in various styles, along with veal florentine, calves' liver madeira, and poached halibut. Prices run $11 to $18. The breakfast menu includes kippers and finnan haddie. At lunch it's soups, salads, sandwiches, and entrees like chicken with mango and almonds or filet of plaice, prepared to your liking. On weekends a pianist entertains in the bar with its bamboo club chairs, marble bar, and glass-topped tablecloth-draped tables. A tea of scones, clotted cream, and finger sandwiches is also served. A serene garden dining area is also available.

RATES: (including breakfast, except in July and August): $62 to $70 double, $130 to $140 for a suite; in July, $68 to $78 double, $140 for a suite; in August, $140 to $180 double, $250 for a suite. Weekend package available.

Although the **Saratoga Downtowner,** 413 Broadway, Saratoga Springs, NY 12866 (tel. 518/584-6160), looks like a conventional motel, it is exquisitely kept, and you'll probably get a surprise when you walk in. After you register at the desk, a few steps will lead you to rooms set around a long, narrow, indoor pool—a welcome blessing in the summer heat. Rooms are large and well furnished in color-coordinated decor. Hosts Lois and Gene Collins are both extremely attentive. Breakfast, consisting of homemade muffins and coffee or tea, is always available. Just help yourself.

RATES: Single or double, $34 to $46 September to June, $45 to $55 in July, $80 to

$100 in August. WEEKEND PACKAGE: A Winter Weekend for $118 includes two nights' accommodation, dinner, tickets to harness racing, and lift tickets for nearby skiing.

Other reliables include the **Holiday Inn,** Broadway at Circular, Saratoga Springs, NY 12866 (tel. 518/584-4550), with 150 standard rooms, a couple of restaurants, and a swimming pool.

RATES: $48 to $70 double ($160 to $180 in August).

The **Carriage House Motel,** 178 Broadway, Saratoga Springs, NY 12866 (tel. 518/584-0352), has good, large units with kitchenettes, furnished in typical motel style. The top-floor rooms have brass beds and cathedral-type ceilings.

RATES: $42.50 to $55 double in summer ($150, single or double, in August), $34 double in winter.

There's also Best Western's **Playmore Farms Motel,** on Rte. 9 (South Broadway), Saratoga Springs, NY 12866 (tel. 518/584-2350).

RATES: October to April, $44 to $54 double; in May, June, July, and September, $55 to $75 double; in August, from $150 double.

SARATOGA DINING

Breakfast

When in Saratoga, obviously *the* place to dine is at the track, but that can be expensive. Your best bet there is the buffet breakfast served from 7 to 9:30 A.M., featuring eggs, meats, juices, muffins, and a special Saratoga Sunrise—made from vodka and orange and cranberry juice with a slice of melon. The $9 price includes admission to the grandstand.

During the season lines of people stretching out of the door and around the corner wait for one of the pink marble tables at **Mrs. London's Bake Shop,** 33 Phila St. (tel. 518/584-6633). Blintzes, french toast made with brioche, superb croissants (plain or with almonds), and pain au chocolat, plus pancakes and eggs (fluffy omelets) are just some of the scrumptious breakfast items that are waiting for you. Later, soups, salads, quiches, luncheon specials, and mouthwatering desserts—napoleons, chocolate-whisky cake, fruit tarts—made on the premises are the attraction, accompanied by various teas and coffees, all served on very pretty floral china, but prices are high. Breakfast items cost from $3; luncheon, from $5 to $12. Definitely a first choice.

HOURS: Wednesday to Sunday from 8 A.M. to 6 P.M.; closed Monday and Tuesday.

If you can't get in, try **Pehl's Bake Shoppe and Café,** 350 Broadway (tel. 518/587-8900).

HOURS: In July and August, Wednesday to Sunday from noon to 10 P.M.; off-season, from 7:30 A.M. to 5:30 P.M.; closed Monday and Tuesday.

For a quick bagel fix, **Bruegger's Bagel Bakery,** 453 Broadway (tel. 518/584-4372), has an assortment of bagels and bagel sandwiches under $3, and bags of bagels to take home. Eat inside or outside on the deck on Broadway.

HOURS: Monday to Saturday from 7 A.M. to 7 P.M., on Sunday to 3 P.M.; in August hours are extended to 9 P.M., until 5 P.M. on Sunday.

Lunch/Dinner Choices

The place to be seen lunching is the **Turf Terrace,** but unless you've booked months in advance, forget it. There are other choices.

The **Olde Bryan Inn,** 123 Maple Ave., at Rock Street (tel. 518/587-9741), supposedly the oldest building in Saratoga, is named after Alexander Bryan, a Revolutionary War hero who spied on Burgoyne, thus directly contributing to the victory at the Battle of Saratoga in 1777. He purchased the inn in the late 1780s, and the place certainly possesses a well-seasoned air. In cold weather the red glow from the two fireplaces at either end of the polished-wood dining room will make you feel warm and welcome. In the adjacent bar another fire roars beneath a picture of Leda and the Swan, and you can sit cozily ensconced beneath the old beamed ceiling. In summer, enjoy al fresco dining in the courtyards. Salads, sandwiches, omelets, burgers, most under $6, plus a selection of entrees, including prime rib, fettuccine gamberi, and fish du jour (from $8 to $13), make up the menu.

HOURS: Noon to midnight daily. BRUNCH: 11:30 A.M. to 3:30 P.M. on weekends. No reservations are taken.

Presided over by Hattie Mosley, **Hattie's Chicken Shack,** 45 Phila St. (tel. 518/584-4790), is the place where dancers, musicians, and other visiting stars love to gather. Their photographs, notes, and tokens of appreciation that cover the walls, give thanks for a home away from home that serves good fresh food and lots of it. Hattie started her cooking career when she helped cater the dinners and receptions given by the Staleys, Chicago starch millionaires, for whom she worked for many years. Over 40 years ago she settled in Saratoga Springs and has been serving the spiciest barbecue and southern fried chicken and ribs to happy customers ever since. Collard greens and other special daily vegetables appear on the menu, along with a very special "dirty rice." Ask Hattie about that one. At breakfast you'll feast on grits, eggs, and biscuits for all of $1.25; lunch will run around $4; dinner specials (strip sirloin, lamb and pork chops, for example), priced from $6 to $9, include soup, salad, biscuits, mashed potatoes, another vegetable, and a slice of apple cobbler and coffee.

HOURS: 11 A.M. to 10 P.M. daily in season (in July and August from 8 A.M. to midnight; in winter from 11 A.M. to 8 P.M.). Reservations needed in season.

Scallions, 404 Broadway (tel. 518/584-0192), is a busy little place serving great salads, sandwiches, and desserts in a sleek ambience of black-and-white tile, green bentwood chairs, and painted lemon tables. In the back the display case is filled with salads—curried chicken, tomato and feta cheese, artichoke and cheese, crabmeat, and more—and desserts to go. Among the desserts, try the chocolate midnight layer cake, or the Kahlúa cheesecake, locally made by New Skete monks. Soups and sandwiches complete the fare. Prices run $4 to $6.

LUNCH: Monday to Saturday from 11:30 A.M. to 5 P.M. (daily, June through October). DINNER: June through October, 5 to 11 P.M. daily.

Not a particularly pretty place, **Gaffney's,** at 16 Carolina St. (tel. 518/587-9791), nevertheless offers an eclectic mixture of Mexican, Italian, and continental dishes in a bistro atmosphere. Specialties include chicken or beef tostadas, quesadilla, linguine pesto, fettuccine, veal piccata, poached salmon hollandaise—an interesting assortment priced from $6 to $13, including bread, salad, and vegetable.

LUNCH: Monday to Sunday from 11:30 A.M. to 3 P.M. DINNER: Monday from 5 to 11 P.M., Tuesday to Saturday from 6 to 11 P.M., plus late-night snacks until 3 A.M.

For lakeside viewing, seek out the **Waterfront**, 121 Kaydeross Park Rd., Saratoga (tel. 518/583-2628), which has a deck hanging literally out over the water. Inside, the place is plain and tavern-like. Sandwiches, nachos, and salads are the choices here. To find it, take the road to Kaydeross and turn off at the sign down a short dirt road. As far as I know this is the only public access to the lake at the moment of writing.

HOURS: 11:30 A.M. to 10 P.M. daily.

The **Weathervane**, on Rte. 9 south of Saratoga Springs (tel. 518/584-8157), is famous—and rightly so—for a one-pound lobster dinner for only $9, served with a baked potato.

HOURS: 11 A.M. to 9 P.M. daily.

Dinner Only

One of the best-known and best-loved restaurants in Saratoga Springs, Chez Sophie, has moved back to Lake Luzerne, and will be discussed in that section later in this chapter.

Those in the know head out to Middle Falls in search of **Dacha**, tucked away behind a farm on Fiddler's Elbow Road (tel. 518/587-0440). Only the signs will help you. Unfortunately the restaurant was not open when I stopped by, but I'm told that the French cuisine is always beautifully prepared using fresh ingredients. The ambience is country—casual yet elegant.

HOURS: Open in July and August only. Reservations required.

Everything is prime quality at the **Union Coach House**, 139 Union Ave. (tel. 518/584-6440). Tables are set with pretty Libby's glass lanterns and burgundy napery, with burgundy Victorian chairs alongside. The restaurant has two areas with different ambiences—a more formal room with tables set in front of a Federal-style fireplace and a more casual skylit cedar-ceilinged room. Wicker chairs are placed at two tables set on a lower level by the window. One or two hanging ferns add more life. The food is continental, the ingredients fine and fresh. At a recent meal the clam chowder arrived piping hot; the pâté was smooth and flavorsome. Other choice appetizers included seafood St-Jacques en croûte (shrimp, scallops, and crab in sauce served in puff pastry), escargots forestière served in mushroom caps with a special butter and a splash of Pernod, shrimp cocktail, and tomato tortellini soup. A good green salad with shredded carrots is accompanied by tasty cornbread.

Main courses are also excellent. A salmon steak was thick and juicy, and served with baked potato and three fresh vegetables—crisply cooked broccoli, cauliflower, and carrots. Other delicious items include swordfish with caper sauce, broiled Boston scrod, broiled T-bone with red wine butter, pork chops Barnstable (with apple-walnut stuffing and baked applejack sauce on the side), and chicken hunter style (baked with onions, mushrooms, slices of smoked ham, and a splash of wine). Prices run $10 to $15. Most tantalizing desserts are the French vanilla cheesecake, sour-cream-and-raisin pie, and old-fashioned bread pudding. If you have to wait, seat yourself in the paneled oak-furnished bar. LUNCH: In July and August only, 11:30 A.M. to 2:30 P.M. daily. DINNER: Tuesday to Saturday from 5 to 10 P.M., daily during the August meet. Open mid-February to the end of December.

Ellen Wickham has been the human dynamo behind the **Court Bistro,** 60 Court St. (tel. 518/584-6009), at which local artists are invited to exhibit their works. It's a place decorated in peach and an eclectic assortment of chairs, an open kitchen in the back, and a few plants up front. The food is highly individual, and I recommend your taking a meal here. The menu changes every month, but at dinner you might find half a dozen or so main dishes like Bistro biftek Delmonico (pan-fried with garlic and olive oil, finished with red wine), pork loin with Pommery sauce (with mustard and mushrooms), or scrod in a ginger-cream sauce. There's also always a vegetarian dish. Prices run $9 to $15. To start, choose from such dishes as smoked trout with horseradish cream (served with red onion and a sprinkling of caviar), cream of Brie and red pepper soup, or country pâté served with home-made bread. Desserts are tempting—lemon tart in a strawberry sauce, chocolate mousse, crème caramel. Brunch items are unusual. For example, chocolate-chip pancakes with strawberry sauce, honey-and-almond omelet, or cheese strata with tomato coulis—a tasty choice. On Friday and Saturday evenings and at Sunday brunch a classical duo plays.

DINNER: Wednesday to Sunday from 6 to 10 P.M. in winter Tuesday to Sunday from 6 to 10 P.M. in summer, except during the meet when it's open daily. BRUNCH: Saturday and Sunday from 9 A.M. to 2 P.M.

The name **Eartha's Kitchen,** 47 Phila St. (tel. 518/583-0602), is derived not from the cook but from the huge six- by three-foot wood-burning stove whose flames leap high as Selma Nemer, who trained under Jean Morel at L'Hostellerie Bressane, turns out numerous wood-grilled dishes. The menu changes daily but items will likely include salmon steak with avocado butter, tuna with basil Proven-çal sauce, maui maui with sour cream and salsa, lamb chops with mango chutney, or duck breast demi-glacé. Prices run $14 to $18. To start, try the scallop kebab with ginger-miso sauce, or the salmon, sole, and watercress terrine. The choco-late torte layered with strawberries in between and on top is great. So, too, is the Linzer torte and apple-rum cake. The ambience is pleasant. Hot jazz, blues, or classical music plays in the background, sky-blue tablecloths are overlaid with white, sky-blue shades adorn the lamps, and fresh flowers add a nice touch to the table settings. The light is a flattering pink. The art on the walls is for sale. A selection of wines is available by the glass and bottle from the oak wine bar in front. A pianist entertains on weekends.

DINNER: Tuesday to Sunday from 6 to 10 P.M. (daily in August).

The **Caunterbury,** on Union Avenue (tel. 518/587-9653), is on Rte. 9P, three miles east of the track. The focus of this delightful restaurant, created out of two barns, is a room with a large indoor lake-cum-pond complete with a full-scale dhow and water lilies, around which are arranged several rooms, each differently designed and decorated. The whole effect is quite spectacular, especially at night when the moonlight falls on the water and you can imagine you're in a tiny village in Switzerland or Austria. Ficus plants, mirrors, and sun streaming into the upstairs bar make it an exceedingly pleasant spot for early-evening or late-afternoon cocktails. At lunchtime the food will consist of an interesting array of unusual hamburgers and salads. More traditional dishes are offered at night—tournedos, beef Wellington, scampi, seafood crêpes, and veal piccata, for example—with entrees priced from $13 to $23.

DINNER: In summer, Monday to Saturday from 5 to 10 P.M., on Sunday from 4 to 9 P.M.; closed Tuesday in winter.

Ye Olde Wishing Well, four miles north on Rte. 9 (tel. 518/584-7640), a real racing hangout, has all kinds of racing memorabilia and track/turf paintings that have been donated over the years by owners and trainers. The stone fireplaces and low ceilings epitomize Saratoga's country charm. Soft-shell crabs, prime rib, filet mignon, lobster, and especially duckling are the favorites here, priced from $12 to $19.

DINNER: Tuesday to Sunday from 5 P.M. daily; closed Monday (except during the meet in August) and the whole month of January.

Chez Pierre, on Rte. 9, 15 miles north in Wilton (tel. 518/793-3350), is well known in the area for its superb cuisine—tournedos (chasseur, Henri IV, or Rossini), frogs' legs, moules marinieres, veal Oscar, ris de veau, sole meuniere, etc. —all served in the comfortable but elegant surroundings of a converted home. Red napkins and white tablecloths, French sayings, and Paris-style kiosks and murals completed by a Glens Falls artist all give it a very French feel. Entrees range from $10 to $18.

DINNER: In summer, 5:30 to 10 P.M. daily; closed Sunday in winter.

At **Panzas Starlight Restaurant,** Rte. 9P at the south end of Saratoga Lake (tel. 584-6882), the Panza family has built a fine culinary reputation over the years by giving customers a genuine welcome and some really exquisite Italian/continental cuisine served in a simple, unpretentious, but very comfortable setting. Pastas, veal dishes (piccata, Cordon Bleu, and with morels), chicken, and seafood make up the menu, all entrees served with relish tray, salad, spaghetti or potato, and vegetable. The desserts are equally famous. Prices range from $10 to $16.

DINNER: Wednesday to Sunday from 4 to 10 P.M. weekdays, to 11 P.M. on weekends. May close December through February, so check.

About a ten-minute drive south of Saratoga, **The Elms,** on Rte. 9 in Ballston Spa (tel. 518/587-2277), is worth stopping at just to meet its 85-year-old founder, "Fannie" Viggiani, an indomitable spirit still infused with incredible energy. The food happens to be great too. The pasta is made on the premises and all the ingredients are fresh—there isn't a can in the place! The kitchen is now presided over by her son, although Fannie still keeps a watchful eye out and keeps them all on their toes. Among the pasta specialties are fusilli with vodka, fusilli capri (in a spicy tomato sauce with ground sausage and mushrooms), linguine carbonara (with bacon, cream, egg, and parmesan cheese), and another nine or so offerings. The rest of the menu concentrates on seafood—from broiled filet of sole to scungilli a la marinara—and veal, chicken, and beef dishes, including veal sorrentina (with eggplant in tomato sauce topped with mozzarella), veal cardinal (with lobster in a cognac-cream sauce), chicken marsala and parmigiana, and broiled filet mignon. Prices run $11 to $16 (pasta from $8). Read the back of the menu —Fannie has quite a story.

DINNER: Open Wednesday to Sunday (daily in August) from May to the end of November.

EVENING ENTERTAINMENT

In 1986 Lena Spencer celebrated her 25th anniversary at **Caffè Lena,** 47 Phila St. (tel. 518/584-9789). In 1960 she and her artist husband moved from Boston and decided to open a coffeehouse into which she could put her creative energies. She started with a folk-music program which blossomed and burgeoned as she discovered and motivated artists like Christine Lavin and featured virtuosos like Michael Coomey, Patrick Sky, and of course those famous names like Bob Dylan, Tom Paxton, and Pete Seeger. Pasha the Siamese was the maître d' for all. They all performed here—Mississippi Delta bluesman Skip James, southern Appalachian singer Jean Ritchie, the bluegrass Greenbriar Boys, and Jean Redpath, Dave Van Ronk, and Hedy West. Folk-music history was made here in this small upstairs room, and Lena has marvelous anecdotes to relate if you can persuade her to share them with you. Homemade desserts and nonalcoholic beverages are served. Thursday is open-mike night. HOURS: Thursday to Sunday from 8:30 P.M.

Skidmore College also provides a number of cultural entertainments—films, musical concerts, lectures. For information, call 518/584-5000.

There are plenty of cocktail spots: the **Olde Bryan Inn,** 123 Maple Ave. (tel. 518/587-9741); **Professor Moriarty's Dining and Drinking Salon,** 430 Broadway (tel. 518/587-5981); **Gaffney's,** 16 Caroline St. (tel. 518/587-9791); and **Parting Glass,** on Lake Avenue (tel. 518/583-1916), for a bit of the Irish. For a piano bar, try **Siro's,** at 158 Lincoln Ave. (tel. 518/584-4030).

The most popular disco is the million-dollar **Rafters** (tel. 518/584-9826), located out by the lake. HOURS: Wednesday, Friday, and Saturday from 9 P.M. to 3 A.M. (daily in August).

If none of this appeals to you, then **harness racing** (tel. 518/584-2110) can be enjoyed between May and mid-November and on weekends from January to March. For information, write to Saratoga Raceway, P.O. Box 356, Saratoga Springs, NY 12866. Or you might attend a **polo game,** which is usually played on Friday and Sunday at 6 P.M. during August. For information, call 518/584-3255.

Besides the New York City Ballet, which performs in July, and the Philadelphia Orchestra, which performs in August, the **Saratoga Performing Arts Center** also hosts the New York City Opera, the Newport Jazz Festival, theater, and a number of special guests, who in the past have included Judy Collins, Elton John, and John Denver. For information, call 518/584-9330.

A SIDE TRIP TO NEW SKETE

A trip to the **New Skete Monastery** in Cambridge, N.Y. (tel. 518/677-3928), will take you through Washington County, the countryside that Grandma Moses portrayed so vividly in her now-famous landscapes. You'll travel past russet-red barns, yards filled with scurrying chickens and pigs, and rolling hillsides where horses are quietly grazing, until you reach the monastery high on a hill overlooking the quiet valley. Here, Greek Orthodox monks paint eggs and icons; make sausages and cheeses; smoke poultry, bacon, and hams; and bake their delectable cheesecakes—Kahlúa, chocolate, and a simple deluxe, priced from $15—for which people travel miles. The monks are also noted dog trainers and operate good kennels. You can purchase their goods and their poetry and contemplative writings in the store here before going up the hillside to the small onion-domed chapel, built by the monks themselves (the dome is made of styrofoam, fiberglass, and polyurethane). A retreat for all faiths, there is room for three or four guests in shared rooms with bunk beds and spartan furnishings. No radios, no tape recorders, and no alcohol are allowed.

While you're in Cambridge, visit **Hubbard Hall** (tel. 518/677-2765), a terrific old Victorian turreted building that now houses the Valley Artisans Market, filled with ceramics, woodcarvings, art, and basketry. Stuffed animals, candles, and other country items are found next door in the Village Store and Coop. HOURS: Both are open Tuesday through Saturday from 10 A.M. to 5 P.M.

From Cambridge, Rte. 40 north will take you to another typical country site: the **Log Village Grist Mill Museum**, on Rte. 30 two miles off Rte. 40, in East Hartford (tel. 518/632-5237). I have to admit that this mill was not a major destination on my visit, but I spent several hours, so fascinated and charmed was I by Floyd Harwood's enthusiasm and natural gift for teaching. A retired "shop" teacher, Floyd rescued and spent five years restoring the mill as a retirement project, remaking the parts from old patterns. The mill now works—you can go down and watch the 17-foot-diameter, ten-ton wheel with its 54 buckets (each holding 450 pounds of water) driving the original 1810 French burr stones that have natural pockmarks for good grinding. Corn and wheat are ground. The original stove, plus the desk with records, kept from 1874, are in the mill.

In the nearby mill barn Floyd displays a collection of old farm machinery and household items, gas and steam engines, sewing machines, typewriters, a dog-powered churn, and all kinds of woodworking tools, including a 150-year-old treadle wood lathe, an old band saw originally advertised in the 1922 Sears Roebuck catalog, and a scroll saw advertised in an 1888 catalog. He has a collection of 400 planes alone. In the room above are assembled pump organs, sewing machines, washing machines, calendars, prams, carpet cleaners, antique clothes, and many other objects reflecting the daily life of earlier eras. Anyone interested in early newspapers and antique books will want to look also at his collection of old newspapers, agricultural books, and calendars. HOURS: Weekends from Memorial Day through October 15.

NORTH TO THE LAKES

Lake Luzerne

Lake Luzerne is a small and more serene lake about 20 minutes from Saratoga southwest of Lake George. From here you can take trips to Lake Sacandaga, go antiquing, attend the Friday-night rodeo in Lake Luzerne, go horseback riding and lake swimming in summer or enjoy cross-country skiing in winter.

The **Lamplight Inn,** 2129 Lake Ave., Rte. 9N (P.O. Box 70), Lake Luzerne, NY 12846 (tel. 518/696-5294), occupies an 1899 home which proud owners Gene and Linda Merlino restored and opened in the fall of 1985. Six rooms (two with fireplaces), each with baths immediately across the hall (bathrobes are provided), are individually decorated in appropriate style. For example, the Canopy Room is decorated with chintz wallpaper, lace curtains, an unusual Victorian folding chair, a marble-top dresser, and a canopy bed with peach eider. Room 2 has an iron-and-brass bed, oak dresser and washstand, cane-seated love seat, Mission chair rocker, and a wood-manteled fireplace. The Skylight Room does indeed have a skylight, plus a highback oak bed covered with patchwork quilt. None has air conditioning. Breakfast consists of juice, cereal, fruit, a cake of the day (like sour cream or coffee), omelets, and a lemon mousse or similar. On weekends breakfasts offer even more elaborate choices, ranging from apple crêpes to eggs Benedict.

The parlor is comfortably furnished for guests with Oriental carpeting and clusters of chairs, including a camelback brocade sofa in front of the fireplace. A bottle collection and an international doll collection add a personal note. The ruby gas-style lamp and an art nouveau lamp are particularly striking accents. The chestnut woodwork, geometrically decorated staircase, and wainscoting throughout add greatly to the charm of this cream clapboard-and-shingle house with wrap-around porch. The grounds are pretty. A circular drive leads to this quiet retreat on the hill.

RATES: $85, single or double, in season; $70 in winter. Open all year.

In recent years the place to dine in Saratoga was Chez Sophie. You can still dine at **Chez Sophie** (tel. 518/696-3862), but you'll have to repair to Steward Bridge Road (off Rte. 9N) in Hadley, two miles west of Lake Luzerne, to the restaurant run here by Sophie and her husband. It provides some of the finest gourmet cuisine around, created by Sophie herself, who learned the art while growing up on the Belgian-French border. Husband Joseph C. Parker's fluid metal-and-wire sculptures are carefully displayed in the softly lit, elegant rooms accented by fresh flower arrangements. The menu changes daily but will always feature such classic dishes as Cornish hen with tarragon, duck with apricot and green-pepper sauce, or steak in a shallot-and-wine sauce. Desserts run from strawberry-and-rhubarb compote to a very special lemon cheese pie. The prix-fixe menu is $40.

DINNER: Daily in July and August only; reservations essential.

Lake George's Ultimate Resort

The Sagamore, Bolton Landing, Lake George, NY 12814 (tel. 518/644-9400), lies resplendent on Lake George ensconced on its very own 70-acre Sagamore Island, surrounded by crystalline blue waters and tree-covered mountains. The Colonial Revival white clapboard building with green shutters has recently been restored to its earlier magnificence. When it opened in 1883 it served as a focal point for social and recreational activities for the exclusive folks who had built summer mansions on the island. Twice damaged by fire (in 1893 and 1914), it was completely reconstructed in 1930 and old age didn't catch up with the grande dame until 1981, when it closed its doors. Now it combines 19th-century charm and luxury with 20th-century technology, making it a world-class resort. Although the landward approach presents a hodgepodge of standardized condominium clusters, the hotel really should be viewed from the water. From the stylish Oriental-accented lobby, step out onto the semicircular veranda, supported by 20-foot-high classical pillars, that overlooks the mountains and lake. Here you can enjoy afternoon tea at 3:30 P.M. or cocktails to piano accompaniment among the potted palms, wicker, and marble ambience. Pathways and stairs lead across terraced lawns to the lake, where you can sunbathe on a series of wooden decks or at the beach. The indoor pool and pool terrace are also down here. The *Morgan,* a special wooden lake cruiser, operates from here too, sailing at 11 A.M. 2:30 P.M., and at 7 P.M. for dinner. In winter its hull is protected from ice by a circle of warm-air bubbles.

The hotel's premier dining room, Trillium, offers an elegant setting of plush pink chairs, tables set with magnolia damask tablecloths, and fine china. Sunday brunch and dinner (entrees run $17 to $23) are served here. The restaurant has quickly achieved a reputation, having attracted a number of very fine chefs. Appetizers include snails wrapped in spinach, feta, and phyllo dough with fresh tomato, or lobster and truffle ravioli in a basil and white-wine-butter sauce. Several different salads are offered, including a watercress, endive, walnut, and bleu cheese. Entrees, too, are hard to choose among—Maine lobster removed from the shell and served with cucumbers and brandy sauce; medallions of veal with orange-tarragon sauce; and partridge in armagnac, raisins, port wine, and cream being just three examples. Meals taken in the less fancy Sagamore Dining Room are included with the room rate. Entree choices might include paupiettes of sole with salmon, sautéed brook trout, or steak au poivre. Wicker and rattan furniture and jade tablecloths set the atmosphere.

There are 100 rooms in the main building and 250 in "cottages" or condo units. The rooms in the main building are furnished with pencil four-posters and half-posters, peach wallpaper and carpet, botanical prints, wing chair, and candlestand. They are fully equipped with TV, telephone, and air conditioning; bathrooms are tiled and contain a complimentary shampoo, bath gel, lotion, showercap, shoeshine kit, and glycerin soap. Towel bar and shower curtain rods are mahogany. Most of the cottage suites have small balconies equipped with wicker rockers; inside fireplaces, modular couches, TVs, and Adirondack-style chairs set the tone. An open kitchen equipped with electric stove and fridge, and a bathroom and bedroom complete the unit layout.

Myriad facilities are available: game room, beauty salon, gift shop, art gallery, spa (for massage, facials, loufa scrub room and Universal-equipped exercise room, sauna and steam, and whirlpool), indoor pool, indoor and outdoor tennis, racquetball, movies, golf, cross-country skiing, ice skating, and toboggan run. Use of canoes and rowboats is free. Besides the dining/entertainment facilities already mentioned, there's an attractive plush coffeeshop, Mr. Brown's; Van Winkle's for jazz and dancing; and the Blue Grill, perhaps the most appealing of all, located on the mainland up on Federal Hill at the golf club. Free round-trip transportation is provided to the golf course and to Gore Mountain and West Mountain for downhill skiers.

RATES: May through October, $117 to $132 per person double (MAP), $148 to $184 per person (MAP) for a suite, in the hotel; $102 to $155 per person (MAP) in the lodges. November through April, $86 to $96 per person double (MAP), $110 to $130 per person (MAP) for a suite, in the hotel; $80 to $115 per person (MAP) in the lodges.

Friends Lake

Only 20 minutes north of Lake George and a mere 15 minutes from Gore Mountain, this unspoiled lake has a couple of fine inns on its shores. Sharon and Greg Taylor took over **Friends Lake Inn,** Friends Lake Road, Chestertown, NY 12817 (tel. 518/494-4251), in 1982 and restored the 1860s building themselves to its former glory (in the 1920s there used to be six inns on this small lake). From the dining porch and the front rooms there's a restorative lake view. Rooms are simply and nicely decorated, often with chintz wallpapers, ruffled net curtains, oak chests and dressers, cannonball or iron-and-brass beds, and candlewick spreads or quilts. Room 10 has a carved Victorian bed and lace-trimmed pink comforter. In all there are 12 rooms, six with private bath and six sharing two bathrooms, each with two showers, two sinks, and two toilets. Cottage accommodations are also available in adjacent buildings. Each of these has a deck, wood-burning stove, fully equipped kitchen, and simple homey furnishings.

In the dining room, solid-cherry square columns support the stamped-tin ceiling; the wainscoting and a fire in the brick hearth make it cozy in winter. In summer the screened-in porch is the chosen dining place. Dinner will begin with pâté served with gherkins and crackers. Shrimp and avocado cocktail, tomato-dill soup, or similar comprise the appetizers. Among the entrees are likely to be shrimp Pommery and filet mignon. Among the desserts, chocolate-walnut pie is rich but delicious; so, too, is the mud pie. Apple pie with raisins, ice cream, and strawberries are also likely choices.

For after-dinner relaxing the sitting room affords several couches, a TV with VCR, and some board games. There's also a bar with a view of the lake and umbrella tables outside. The inn has a few sailboats and rowboats for your use.

RATES: $300 a week (MAP—including breakfast and dinner); from $108 to $130 per night (MAP), depending on the season; $65 to $75 for bed-and-breakfast. Greg and Sheila also offer special mystery, wine lover's, and other weekends. DINNER: Wednesday to Friday from 5 to 9 P.M., on Saturday to 10 P.M., on Sunday from 4 to 8 P.M.

A soaring tower and peaked gables identify the **Balsam House,** Friends Lake, Chestertown, NY 12817 (tel. 518/494-2828, 494-4431, or 494-2510). Originally built in 1845 as a farmhouse, the building underwent additions and alterations in 1891 when it was converted into the Valentine Hotel. The hotel operated until 1973, when its doors closed for eight years. Today it retains a Victorian country atmosphere. Wicker chairs stand on the front porch. Etched-glass doors lead into an Oriental-carpeted hallway, where a display case containing a tableau with pheasant and silk flowers adds an extravagant Victorian touch.

There are 20 rooms with private bath. The most splendid is the suite decorated with dusky-rose walls and jade carpeting, and furnished with wicker chairs, a box-style peach upholstered couch, with a bar and TV in the living area. A spiral staircase leads to the bedroom, furnished with a wicker bed and chairs, oak chest, and dresser. The bathroom comes with a clawfoot tub and the sink sunk into an old commode. A more typical room would be Room 26, containing a bed with a candlewick spread, Windsor-style chairs, an oak dresser, and painted wood sidetable.

There's entertainment in the bar on summer weekends, which in the winter offers warmth—Chinese-red walls and a blazing fire in the stone fireplace. Out back a pretty deck/garden room, arrayed with flower boxes and complete with fireplace-grill for grilled fish, duck, and seafood, is a popular summer dining spot. A cozy sitting room and separate TV room are also available to guests. Look out for the balsam bear, dressed either in summer or winter gear hanging out on the couch.

In the main dining room with copper hearth, burgundy walls, and dark-green tasseled drapes, the cuisine is classic continental—braised sweetbreads with bordelaise sauce, turbot poached in white wine and seafood sauce, lamb chops Provençal, entrecôte au poivre, suprême de volaille archiduc (stuffed chicken breast with cognac, cream, and mushrooms served with pommes noisettes in a bird's nest), and crevettes Madagascar (in a cream sauce with Pernod, garlic, and white wine). Pâté, ceviche, coquille St-Jacques are among classic appetizers. Prices run from $11 to $18.50 (more for rack of lamb).

A short walk away down at the private beach there's a beach house where lunch is served in summer. Rowboats, sailboats, canoes, and an antique paddleboat are available. So are bicycles. Friendly innkeepers Michael Aspland and wife, Kathy, will take care of all your needs. It's only 15 minutes from Gore Mountain.

RATES (including breakfast and dinner): in summer, $145 on weekends, $125 in midweek; in winter, $135 on weekends, $110 in midweek. Closed for November.

If you do stay at the Balsam House, visit potter Bill Noble, ride at the nearby Circle B Ranch, or take a day trip to Lake George and sail aboard the *Mohican,* which enters turquoise-colored Paradise Bay.

SARATOGA ACTIVITIES

ANTIQUING: Plenty in town, and also outside. For example, try driving Rte. 29 west or east. Or pop south also to Ballston Spa.

BICYCLING: Rentals are available from Springwater Bike Rentals at the Gideon Putnam (tel. 518/893-2228), summer only.

BOATING: Rentals are available at Ballston Lake beside the Good Times Restaurant (tel. 518/399-9976). Saratoga Lake is also a good boating spot.

CAMPING: Located out toward the lake, **Interlaken Camp,** R.D. 1, Union Avenue, Saratoga Springs, NY 12866 (tel. 518/583-1900), is an ideal camping spot with 200 camp and tent/trailer sites. Facilities include showers, swimming pools, a full grocery, restaurant, and lounge. Open summers only.

GOLF: In Saratoga Spa State Park (tel. 518/584-2000).

HORSEBACK RIDING: Try the G Bar G Riding Stables, 59 Weibel Ave., Saratoga Springs (tel. 518/587-7281).

PICNICKING: At the track your best bet is at the Top O the Stretch picnic area. Otherwise, Saratoga Spa State Park is ideal.

SKATING: There's an illuminated rink in Saratoga Spa State Park for speed and ice skating.

SKIING: Cross-country skiing can be enjoyed in the Saratoga Spa State Park. Headquarters is in the Victoria Pool Building (tel. 518/584-2003). Downhill is available at West Mountain (tel. 518/793-6606), where there are 16 trails and three chair lifts. Take I-87 north to Exit 18W.

SWIMMING: Two pools are available in the park—one Olympic-size; the other, the Victoria Pool, a favorite with the dancers and other performers at the Arts Center. A beach and a swimming pool also exist at Kaydeross Amusement Park on the edge of the lake.

TENNIS: Saratoga Racquet Club (tel. 518/587-3000) and in Saratoga Spa State Park. Also city courts on Division Street.

THE HUDSON RIVER VALLEY

DISTANCES IN MILES: Newburgh, 66; Poughkeepsie, 77; Kingston, 97
ESTIMATED DRIVING TIMES: 1½ to 2¼ hours

DRIVING: For west-bank destinations, take the Palisades Parkway to West
Point and the New York Thruway to points farther north—New Paltz,
Kingston. For east-bank destinations, you can do the same; cross the
river either at Poughkeepsie or Kingston. Or you can take the Taconic
Parkway, a far more scenic route.
BUS: Trailways (tel. 212/730-7460) goes to New Paltz and Kingston.
TRAIN: Amtrak travels up the east bank of the river, stopping at Rhinecliff
(just west of Rhinebeck). Metro-North's Harlem-Hudson line stops at
Garrison, Cold Spring, and Poughkeepsie. For Amtrak information, call
212/736-6288; for Metro-North, call 212/532-4900.

Special events to plan your trip around

East Bank Events
MAY: Antique Auto Show at Rhinebeck.
JUNE: Rhinebeck Craft Fair.
AUGUST: Dutchess County Fair at Rhinebeck (mid-August).
OCTOBER: Antiques Fair at Rhinebeck.

West Bank Events
MAY: Apple Blossom Festival at New Paltz—parade, carnival, concerts,
antique fair. For information, call 255-0243 or 257-2231.

Spring flower festival in Seamon Park, Saugerties.

JULY: Summerfare at SUNY's Center for the Arts at Purchase (tel. 914/253-5900)—jazz, ballet, symphony, and other concerts and events during the whole month.

JULY TO SEPTEMBER: New York Renaissance Festival at Sterling Forest in Tuxedo (every weekend from the end of July to the weekend after Labor Day). A celebration of pageantry, jousting, wandering minstrels, and other fitting entertainments. Call 914/351-5171 for information.

AUGUST: Coxsackie Festival (second weekend).

Athens Festival (usually the third weekend).

OCTOBER: Chrysanthemum Festival in Seamon Park, Saugerties. Kingston's Oktoberfest.

For specific information about east-bank areas, contact the Columbia County Chamber of Commerce, 729 Columbia St., Hudson, NY 12534 (tel. 518/828-4417); Dutchess County Visitors Information, P.O. Box 2025, Hyde Park, NY 12538 (tel. 914/229-0033); Putnam County Tourist Information, c/o Cold Spring Area Chamber of Commerce, P.O. Box 71, Cold Spring-on-Hudson, NY 10516 (tel. 914/265-9060).

West-bank areas: Greene County Promotion Department, Box 527, Catskill, NY 12414 (tel. 518/943-3223); Orange County Tourism, 124 Main St., Goshen, NY 10924 (tel. 914/294-5151); Ulster County Public Information Office, P.O. Box 1800, Kingston, NY 12401 (tel. 914/331-9300).

For general New York State information, contact the New York State Department of Commerce, Division of Tourism, One Commerce Plaza, Albany, NY 12245 (tel. 518/474-4116).

Although many New Yorkers may simply regard the Hudson River as a dirty brown line that separates Manhattan from New Jersey, they need only travel to the Cloisters and Fort Tryon Park to get a very different perspective on the beauty and majesty of this broad swath of river that flows 315 miles from the Adirondacks, where it rises as a trout stream, cutting between the Catskills and the Berkshires past the unique bluffs of the Palisades down to New York Bay and out into the ocean. It's a river that has spawned many legends and mysteries, inspiring such authors as Washington Irving and William Cullen Bryant, and such painters as Thomas Cole and Frederic Church, whose work gave rise to one of the first schools of American painting. The river is still a beauty to behold.

In 1609 Hendrick Hudson sailed up the river aboard the *Halve Moone* as far as Albany, but failing to find passage beyond, he withdrew and dropped anchor at Athens, where he encountered the natives and remarked upon their corn and pumpkins. In 1624 the Dutch founded the first colony of the New Netherlands, and later, great estates and patroonships were established along the banks of the fertile river valley, which is still today famous for its apples, produce, dairy goods, horse farming, and horticultural wonders (Rhinebeck, for example, was once the violet capital of the world). The English took over the area in 1664. Two-thirds of all the battles during the Revolutionary War were fought in New York State, many along the banks of the Hudson River, making the area rich in historical associations. Remnants of General Burgoyne's army straggled back from the Battle of Saratoga and encamped just outside Catskill. The spy John André, en route through the patriots' lines from a meeting with Benedict Arnold, was captured in Tarrytown and executed at Tappan Hill. Washington spent 17 months at Newburgh while discussing the nature of the peace. At West Point, an early garrison against the British, remnants of the chain barrier erected across the river to stop the British advance can still be seen. During the turmoil, the governing body of the state was forced to flit about, settling briefly in Hurley, later in Kingston, where their meeting place survived the city's burning by the British and can still be visited. Many of these historical events and dramas can be captured today by visiting West Point, Newburgh, Kingston, and also New Paltz and Hurley, where stone houses from the original Dutch settlements remain.

Soon after the Revolution, in the 19th century, the river became the very lifeline of New York City. All kinds of supplies were shipped downriver—ice blocks and bricks from Athens, cement and bluestone for the base of the Statue of Liberty and the Brooklyn Bridge, fruit and livestock, and most important of all, from the mines of Pennsylvania anthracite coal, which traveled via the Delaware-Hudson Canal to Kingston and from there were shipped downriver. The river, then, was lined with bustling ports: Kingston was the largest and busiest; Newburgh, Poughkeepsie, and Hudson were important whaling towns; and ice houses flourished at Athens. Until recently, many of these communities have slumbered —almost as if waiting for another call from the river to return to life, for railroads, automobiles, and airplanes had stolen their very livelihoods. Now many are being revived, and in summer they are lively with celebrations and festivals, fairs, and all kinds of fun. A maritime museum and a trolley museum are bringing the Kingston Rondout back to life; in Hudson many lovely old town houses are being restored; Cold Spring Harbor's old Victorian hotel has been refurbished and reopened, and the town has established a reputation as a major destination for antique lovers. Life has returned to the Hudson, and even the striped bass and the shad are running and spawning again. Naturalist John Burroughs would no doubt applaud the efforts to rescue the river from the destruction of pollution, and for the visitor there's no better way to get acquainted with the Hudson than to ride the sloop *Clearwater* that leaves daily from Beacon and has brought so much publicity to the campaign to save this national treasure. Other cruise boats leave from Kingston, Catskill, Poughkeepsie, and Albany.

When Washington Irving first sailed up the river in 1800, the trip to Catskill took anywhere from four to ten days, depending on the weather, but Robert Fulton's first steamboat, the *Clermont* (1807), changed all that, reducing the trip to a mere 24 hours. The river became a steamboat lane, and tall smokestacks could be seen gliding upriver, sidewheels churning and decks crowded with tourists headed for the Catskill Mountain resorts via Kingston and Catskill Point. Sometimes their captains raced each other and accidents resulted, like the one that killed architect Andrew Jackson Downing and Nathaniel Hawthorne's sister.

Today the tourists still come to the valley to explore the river towns. They browse for antiques; attend festivals, fairs, and other special events; visit the mansions and homes of early settlers, artists, or such political figures as FDR and President Van Buren; attend parades and football games at West Point; drive through the sculpture field at Storm King; cruise on the river; hike, fish, and camp in the state parks; stay at old country inns; and enjoy the landscape. Any season brings beauty to the river valley. In spring the river is high and fast-flowing, and the orchards along its banks are in full blossom along with the dogwoods. In summer the river is filled with sailboats that tack from side to side, while other pleasure craft tow waterskiers or just cruise along the river past towns that are celebrating summer with river festivals, antiques and craft fairs, and other events. In fall the trees are radiant and the natives are congregating at country fairs or else out in the orchards or fields where the busy fruit and vegetable picking testifies to the abundance of the harvest. In winter the scene resembles a Dutch painting: iceboat parties take to the river and people go skating and walking on the ice, their breath trailing momentarily in the air.

No wonder so many prominent families—Van Cortlandts, Verplancks, and later Livingstons, Jays, Harrimans, Astors, and Roosevelts—chose to build their mansions here. Today their homes are marvelous places to visit and still provide some of the best vantage points from which to view the river—Boscobel in Garrison, Roosevelt's home at Hyde Park, the Vanderbilt and Ogden Mills mansions, Livingston's estate Clermont, and Olana, which commands a view of the famous bend in the river that Church so loved to gaze upon and paint.

So why not follow in their footsteps and head for the Hudson, returning laden with stories and produce, memories and more?

A Suggested Itinerary

If you anchor in Rhinebeck, you can visit the FDR Museum Library and home in Hyde Park, and the Vanderbilt mansion one day, lunching at the Culinary Institute of America and doing some antiquing in between. The next day can be spent exploring Rhinebeck and nearby attractions like Clermont, Olana, and Lindenwald.

On the west bank you can spend a day visiting wineries or the historic spots along the river from West Point to Newburgh. The second day can be spent at lovely Lake Minnewaska, or discovering the Dutch settlements at New Paltz or Hurley, or seeing what's going on at the Kingston Rondout.

The East Bank

In this section I have not included the Sleepy Hollow Restorations—Philipsburg Manor, Sunnyside, and Sleepy Hollow—as I consider them really day trips from Manhattan. Instead, I'll begin south of Poughkeepsie and travel all the way up the river to Hudson. On this side of the river there's not an abundance of accommodations, and your choice is largely restricted to the Beekman Arms in Rhinebeck and several bed-and-breakfast choices in Rhinebeck and environs. If none of these appeals to you, then your best bet is to anchor on the other side around New Paltz, where the Mohonk Mountain House offers delightful accommodations and there are several really outstanding bed-and-breakfast places. From there, you can either cross the river at Poughkeepsie or Kingston to view the sights on the opposite bank.

POUGHKEEPSIE

POUGHKEEPSIE ATTRACTIONS

Just south of Poughkeepsie, at Locust Grove, **Samuel F. B. Morse's home** (tel. 914/454-4500), on Rte. 9, you will discover that Morse was far more than simply the inventor of the Morse Code. He was also the inventor of the telegraph which he made out of canvas stretchers (among other things) that he used in his primary career as a painter of portraits and landscapes. Indeed he regarded his inventions as ways of supporting his painting career. His *Gallery of the Louvre* recently fetched $3.25 million, setting a price record for an American work of art. He bought this home, which had been part of the Livingston estate, in 1847, primarily to provide security to his family and remodeled it to look like a Tuscan villa. HOURS: Memorial Day to late September, Wednesday to Sunday from 10 A.M. to 4 P.M. ADMISSION: $3 for adults, $1 for children.

In Poughkeepsie, although the **Vassar Art Gallery,** to the right inside the gates of the Vassar College campus (tel. 518/452-7000 for the college switchboard), is strong on 19th-century American art, it is, unfortunately, small and much may be

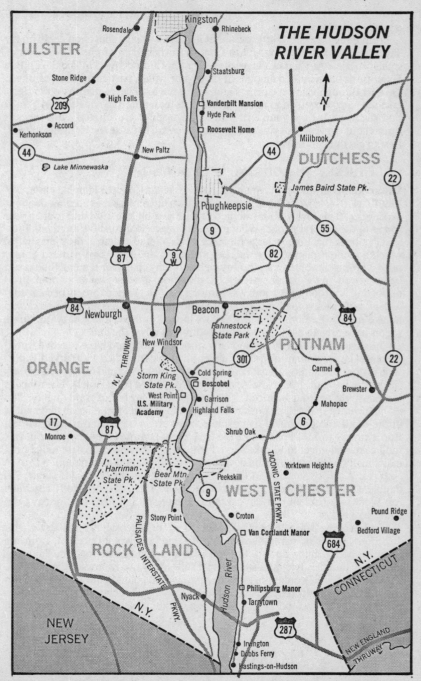

THE HUDSON RIVER VALLEY

ULSTER

Rosendale • Kingston
• Rhinebeck

Stone Ridge •
High Falls •
209
• Accord
Kerhonkson •
44
• Staatsburg

□ **Vanderbilt Mansion**
• **Hyde Park**
□ **Roosevelt Home**

New Paltz •
Lake Minnewaska
44
• Millbrook

DUTCHESS
22

James Baird State Pk.

Poughkeepsie
9
55
87
9 W
82

84 Newburgh • Beacon
Fahnestock State Park
84
22

New Windsor •
N.Y. THRUWAY
Storm King State Pk.
□ **Boscobel**
West Point □
U.S. Military Academy
301
• Cold Spring
• Garrison
• Highland Falls
PUTNAM
• Carmel
• Brewster
• Mahopac
6

17
Monroe •
87
Shrub Oak •
ORANGE

Harriman State Pk.
Bear Mtn. State Pk.
• Peekskill
• Yorktown Heights
TACONIC STATE PKWY.
WESTCHESTER

9
Stony Point •
• Croton
Pound Ridge •
□ **Van Cortlandt Manor**
• Bedford Village
684

ROCKLAND
PALISADES INTERSTATE
N.Y.
CONNECTICUT

Nyack •
Hudson River
□ **Philipsburg Manor**
• Tarrytown
PKWY.

NEW JERSEY
N.Y.
287
• Irvington
• Dobbs Ferry
• Hastings-on-Hudson
NEW ENGLAND THRUWAY

N

in storage or on loan. HOURS: Monday to Saturday from 9 A.M. to 5 P.M., on Sunday from 1 to 5 P.M.

From Poughkeepsie, a little detour along Rte. 44 and a short hop north on the Taconic Parkway will bring you to Clinton Corners, site of one of New York's small wineries. At **Clinton Vineyards** in Clinton Corners (tel. 914/266-5372), Ben Feder turns out a limited amount of rather fine wines, particularly Seyval Blanc. Go east through Clinton Corners and where the road veers sharply to the right, take the narrow road off to the left which goes under the Taconic Parkway. You'll find the vineyard on your left. Tours and tastings are offered on weekends throughout the year, but you're asked to call ahead because the vineyard is small. Best to get directions then.

POUGHKEEPSIE LODGING AND DINING

Vassar Alumnae House, Raymond Avenue, Vassar College, Poughkeepsie, NY 12601 (tel. 914/485-3700), affords the guest a truly remarkable accommodations experience. This lovely Tudoresque structure was built in 1924 and is open year round to the general public. What makes the place so distinctive are the impressive Jacobean furnishings, large fireplace, and coffered ceiling of the grand hall in which a student pianist may well be practicing; and the wood-paneled library filled with classic volumes and comfy club and wing chairs for reading (books can be borrowed on the honor system). Up the stone staircase is another book-filled parlor and TV room. My room was furnished with a hooped canopy bed covered with a candlewick spread, an ottoman, comfortable chair, desk, chest, and carved foliage mirror. Lead-mullioned windows looked out over the courtyard. Some rooms have private bath, others have bathrooms down the hall.

The dining room is also traditionally wood-paneled, and has a massive stucco fireplace, large wrought-iron chandeliers, and tables matched with carved Tudor-style chairs. The international beer card lists 30 domestic and 66 imported beers (including Leopard from New Zealand and Maccabee from Israel). The wine list is modest but very fairly priced. The food is not fancy but of good quality. The menu includes an excellent poached salmon and a tender filet mignon that melted in the mouth accompanied by crisply cooked green beans and roast potatoes. Prices run $9 to $13. For dessert the traditional favorites are the Vassar devil's food cake and angel food cake served with ice cream and chocolate fudge (and marshmallow in the case of the devil); the gremlin is another variation.

RATES: With private bath, $40 single, $45 double; with hall bath, $15 single, $20 double. LUNCH: Monday to Friday from 11 A.M. to 4 P.M. DINNER: 4 to 10 P.M. daily (on Wednesday, an all-you-can-eat buffet). BRUNCH: Saturday and Sunday from 8 A.M. to 3 P.M.

The **Inn at the Falls,** 50 Red Oaks Mill Rd., Poughkeepsie, NY 12603 (tel. 914/ 462-5770), belies its name because it's absolutely new and modern, from the blond-wood reception desk to the red-brick and shingle exterior. The 36 rooms include 20 doubles, two mini-suites, eight suites, and two rooms for the disabled. A standard double contains a brass bed, wing chair, blond pine desk, and wardrobe. Jade and dusky rose are the chosen colors. TV, Touch-tone phones in both room and bath, and toothpaste, shampoo, mouthwash, tissues, and terrycloth robe are among the nice amenities. The toilets are separate from the bathroom. The suites are spectacular. The Contemporary suite has a dramatic black-tile bathroom with a Jacuzzi, and a platform bed with a polished black headboard and dusky-rose comforter. The English Suite has a king-size four-poster with netted canopy, polished roll-top desk, brass lamps, gaming table, and Queen Anne –style chairs among its antique reproductions. The country mini-suite sports a Pennsylvania Dutch–style chest, Windsor chair, and leather wing chair among its furnishings. All rooms are air-conditioned. A high-ceilinged sitting room is also available for guests. A continental breakfast is served in your room.

RATES: $99 double, $109 for mini-suites, $135 to $150 for suites.

HYDE PARK

HYDE PARK AREA ATTRACTIONS

A day or more could be spent at **Hyde Park** exploring this moving memorial to Franklin Delano Roosevelt, for there are several parts to the whole. First, the **FDR Museum and Library,** Albany Post Road, Hyde Park (tel. 914/229-8114), documents the life, political campaigns, triumphs, and tribulations of Roosevelt through a superb collection of memorabilia, letters, speeches, documents, and above all, photographs that dramatize the great and tragic moments of history —the capture of thousands of German soldiers in the Ruhr in 1945; the liberation of Paris on August 25, 1944; perfectly disciplined Allied soldiers under attack waiting to be rescued at Dunkirk; the famous picture of the abandoned baby crying in the ruins of Shanghai during Japan's invasion of China. On a lighter note, there's also a photograph of FDR's famous Scottie, Fala, which was used to libel Roosevelt in the 1944 election campaign by certain Republicans who charged that the dog had been left on the Aleutian Islands and recovered at great expense to the American taxpayers! The whole collection makes for riveting viewing and reading. The more personal side of Roosevelt is captured in exhibits about his younger years, his battle with polio, and of course, his love affair with Eleanor, whose life and career are also portrayed through exhibits and displays. HOURS: 9 A.M. to 5 P.M. daily; closed Thanksgiving, Christmas, and New Year's Days. ADMISSION: 75¢ for the Library, and $2 for FDR's Home.

At the back of the museum, you can walk down to the rose arbor and garden where Roosevelt was buried in 1945 (Mrs. Roosevelt in 1962), and then proceed to the birthplace and home of the 32nd president overlooking the Hudson River, preserved as it was when he died. Sadly, fire severely damaged the structure in January 1982, and it has only recently been restored and reopened. Tour the house with the recording of Eleanor Roosevelt's comments and anecdotes, which enlivens the various features and furnishings of the house and its historical moments—the office, for example, where Roosevelt and Winston Churchill signed the agreement that resulted in the first atomic bomb, and of course, the room where he was born on January 30, 1882, the son of James and Sara Roosevelt. HOURS: Open daily in summer from 9 A.M. to 5 P.M.; closed major holidays, and Tuesday and Wednesday from November through March.

From 1926, **Valkill**, on Rte. 9G (tel. 914/229-9115), was Eleanor Roosevelt's weekend and vacation place. After leaving the White House, she made it her home from 1945 until her death in 1962. The name means "Valley Stream" and here, along the banks of a small stream, Eleanor would often picnic with friends Nancy Cook and Marion Dickerman, who first suggested building a house at this location. At the beginning of the tour you'll be shown an excellent black-and-white film that captures the amazing compassion, enthusiasm, and humanity of this great First Lady. It documents her early life, from her birth in 1884. She was a disappointment to her beautiful mother and aunts, all belles of New York, but her father nevertheless doted on her. When she was 10 her father died and she was left an orphan, her mother having died two years earlier. Perhaps this early loss nourished her humanitarianism. She was sent to Allenswood School in England where she was encouraged in her studies by Mlle Silvestre. At age 18 she renewed her acquaintance with Franklin, and over the objections of his mother, married him in 1905. The film then charts the birth of their five children and FDR's political career up until he contracted polio, when she began actively to promote her husband's aspirations. Later, it follows her as they both bring attention to the unjust conditions that prevail among women, minorities, youth, and the unemployed. During FDR's presidency, Valkill became a center of her social life, with swimming and picnicking parties and also a tranquil retreat about which she wrote in her newspaper column "My Day." After FDR's death in 1945 she withdrew to Valkill, but continued to involve herself in the U.N., human rights, and politics, campaigning for Adlai Stevenson in 1956 and 1960, and later for Jack Kennedy. On November 7, 1962, she died at age 78 and the *New York Times* obituary eulogizing her, stated that "she was a humanitarian who won over many of her critics by the greatness of her heart." Take some time to look at the photos in the theater, including an intimate moment of her picking roses.

From here, a tour of the house will proceed into the pre-dinner gathering area where cocktails where apportioned five minutes' time. The desk was hers, and so, too, were some of the other furnishings, including the filing cabinet that was crafted to look like a chest by workmen in the Valkill Industries furniture factory —an enterprise she helped establish to provide work and to preserve old skills. She always kept a stuffed Scottie on her TV, and although the one you'll see wasn't actually hers, it's in the proper place.

The overwhelming response to this residence is "how simple, how home-like and unpretentious, how ordinary." Rooms are filled with mementoes, bric-a-brac, and photographs. She loved to sleep on the porch overlooking the garden rather than in her bedroom. Note the bathroom mirror placement—she was six feet tall.

HOURS: April through October you can visit Valkill daily, but only by shuttle from the FDR Museum at Hyde Park; in March, November, and December it's open weekends only, with access by private vehicles; closed in January and February. The tour takes an hour and 20 minutes. ADMISSION: $1.50 (plus $1.95 for the shuttle).

While you're here, antique lovers may well want to travel up the road a little to the **Hyde Park Antiques Center** at 184 Albany Post Rd. (tel. 914/229-8200), where there are 35 dealers located under one roof. HOURS: 10 A.M. to 5 P.M. daily.

HYDE PARK DINING—LUNCH OR DINNER

Make arrangements well ahead of time to dine at one of the dining rooms at the **Culinary Institute of America**, Rte. 9, Hyde Park (tel. 914/471-6608), one of the nation's leading culinary schools. Well known for its Escoffier Room, where haute cuisine is served under the critical eye of teachers, and also the American Bounty, featuring American regional specialties, many of them reflecting the ethnic cuisine of a particular area—ham stuffed with crabmeat and corn from Maryland and chili/jack cheese pie from Texas, for example. There are always several soups offered, served smörgåsbord style if you wish, along with a variety of breads and salads. You can see the cooking proceeding in the glassed-in kitchen area hung with copper pots. A sumptuous array of produce is displayed in front. The walls are adorned with mouthwatering color pictures of food and ingredients. Among the regional specialties, you might find crawfish pie New Orleans style, barbecued salmon filet, or southern-style fried chicken with gravy and corn custard. Prices run $13 to $18.50 at dinner, a little less at lunch. The Escoffier Room, lit by chandeliers, is more formal and the domain of haute cuisine—sole normande, canard aux pêches, côte de veau bonne femme. Here, a prix-fixe luncheon is $18; dinner, $36. Book at least six months ahead for weekend reservations. LUNCH: Tuesday to Saturday from noon to 1 P.M. (from 11:30 A.M. in the American Bounty Room). DINNER: Tuesday to Saturday from 6:30 to 8:30 P.M. Book at least six months ahead for reservations; call between 8:30 A.M. and 5 P.M. Monday to Friday.

There's also a small restaurant, Caterina de Medici which specializes in Northern Italian cuisine. Reservations are taken only on Tuesdays and you'll need to book three weeks ahead. Lunch is $12, dinner is $16. LUNCH: Monday to Friday 11:30 P.M. DINNER: Monday to Friday 6 P.M.

After visiting Hyde Park or Valkill, two luncheon spots are super-convenient. **Springwood**, Rte. 9 (tel. 914/229-2681), right opposite the FDR entrance, is a greenhouse-style dining room serving continental cuisine, with an emphasis on shellfish as well as on chicken and steak. The **Easy Street Café**, also on Rte. 9 (tel. 914/229-7969), a little farther south, has deli sandwiches and burgers priced under $5.

ATTRACTIONS NORTH OF HYDE PARK

The Vanderbilt Mansion

Just north of Hyde Park, also on Rte. 9, is the "smallest" Vanderbilt residence (tel. 914/229-9115), designed by McKim, Mead, and White for Frederick Vanderbilt, third grandson of Commodore Cornelius Vanderbilt, who began by ferrying fruit and vegetables from Staten Island to New York City and had amassed a $1¼-million fortune by 1830. Although the house cost $660,000 and contains 59 rooms, 14 bathrooms, and 22 fireplaces, it's considered modest (which it is, when you compare it to the Vanderbilts' Newport specimen). Frederick, in fact, had received the smallest inheritance from the family because they disapproved of his marriage to Louise Anthony, 12 years his senior and a divorcée, whom he had wed in secret. Still, the house is pretty opulent, as the 45-minute tour will reveal, as it progresses from the den through the oval main hall and walnut-paneled drawing room where many a gala ball was held. Upstairs, Mrs. Vanderbilt's bedroom was modeled after a French queen's boudoir. Mr. Vanderbilt's bedroom features solid carved-walnut columns, a gigantic marble fireplace, and a vast bathroom. Although he inherited the least of all the brothers, he managed to increase his inheritance seven times to total $80 million. He was astute and thought of everything, as many of the house's features indicate. For example, although the house was used in spring and fall only, it had a central heating system, its own power plant, light dimmers, and sleeping quarters for 60 servants. After touring the house, be sure to linger in the grounds north of the mansion for an unsurpassed view of the Hudson. HOURS: 10 A.M. to 6 P.M. daily, April through October; Thursday to Monday from 9 A.M. to 5 P.M., November through March; closed Thanksgiving, Christmas, and New Year's Days. ADMISSION: $2.

Mills Mansion

A few miles farther north, in Staatsburg, is a lesser known mansion (tel. 914/889-4100), that reflects the grand living style of well-to-do early-20th-century America. Through the trees you'll glimpse the classical proportions of the mansion, embellished with pilasters, balustrade, and statuary, located on a small bluff. The grounds sweep down to the Hudson River, making it an ideal picnicking spot. The original 65-room home was built by Morgan Lewis, a Revolutionary War general and governor of New York. It later became a home for one branch of the Livingston family when Lewis's great-granddaughter, Ruth Livingston Mills, the wife of financier Ogden Mills, lived here and enlarged and remodeled an 1832 Greek Revival house with the aid of McKim, Mead, and White. Inside, marble fireplaces, gilded plasterwork, and oak paneling provide an opulent backdrop for ornate furnishings, tapestries, and objets d'art. Consider, this was only one of Ogden Mills's retreats—he also owned homes in Paris, Newport, New York City, and California!

HOURS: Memorial Day to Labor Day, Wednesday to Saturday from 10 A.M. to 4:30 P.M., on Sunday from 1 to 5 P.M.; Labor Day to October 31, Wednesday to Saturday from noon to 5 P.M., on Sunday from 1 to 5 P.M. Free guided tours of the first floor.

RHINEBECK/RED HOOK

RHINEBECK AREA ATTRACTIONS

Five miles up the road and you're in the delightful village of Rhinebeck, where you can enjoy a cocktail in the tap room at the Beekman Arms, browse through the stores and boutiques, see what's on at the old movie theater that runs classic and foreign films (often attended by their directors), and also attend any number of special events that are scheduled during the summer and fall at the Dutchess County Fairgrounds, like the county fair or the big fall antiques fair. Sadly, the renowned American Craft Enterprises Rhinebeck Crafts Fair has moved on.

Rhinebeck also possesses another exciting attraction, the **Rhinebeck Aero-**

drome, which is in fact northeast of the town on Stone Church Road, off Rte. 9 (tel. 914/758-8610). Here during the summer, daredevil owner Cole Palen and other pilots perform spectacular flying stunts restaging mock battles in World War I triplanes and biplanes, re-creating an era when propellers still whirled and flying was a true pioneer's pastime associated with smoke, grease, danger, and risk. Besides viewing the thrilling air show when the Black Baron threatens the skies, you, too, can take a ride in a 1929 vintage flyer and also admire the many antique aircraft that are housed here.

Three buildings contain exhibits from the various flying eras. My favorite is the Pioneer Building, which displays Bleriot's machines, the Wright glider, the Passett Ornithopter (1912; it was built with the intention to fly by flapping its wings, and was specially constructed for use in *Those Magnificent Men and Their Flying Machines)*, and a peculiar (looking like an insect) Thomas Pusher (1912), which Palen actually flew to Flushing Airport. The two other hangars exhibit planes from the Lindbergh and First World War eras, including a Waco Model 10 that cruised at 84 mph and had a 385-mile range. Among the World War I exhibits are the Sopwith 7F1, a 121-mph British fighter; the Fokker D VII, a German fighter that downed 275 Allied craft; the Fokker DR-1, a triplane with a two-hour range that Baron Manfred von Richthofen favored; and the Spad in which Captain Eddie Rickenbacker achieved fame piloting as a member of the renowned "Hat in the Rug" squadron. Some are original; some were built by Palen.

HOURS: May 15 to October 31, 10 A.M. to 5 P.M. daily. Shows are given at 2:30 P.M. on Saturday and Sunday. Sunday shows feature World War I aircraft; Saturday shows use planes from the pioneer and Lindbergh era. Before and after you can fly in a 1929 open-cockpit biplane. ADMISSION: $1.50 for adults, $1 for children, on weekdays; $6 for adults and $3 for children for weekend air shows.

Just an aside on the history of the town. After Hudson arrived, the area was settled by the Dutch and later the Palatine-Rhine refugees who in fact founded Rhinebeck in 1686. One of the early inhabitants was a Judge Beekman, whose daughter married the grandson of the lord of Livingston Manor, and their son, Robert R. Livingston, was the gentleman who attended the first Continental Congress, signed the Declaration of Independence, and helped his son-in-law, Robert Fulton, to invent the first steamboat, which was named *Clermont* after Livingston's estate north of Rhinebeck, where today you can picnic blissfully overlooking the Hudson.

RHINEBECK LODGING

The **Beekman Arms,** Rte. 9, Rhinebeck, NY 12572 (tel. 914/876-7077), claims to be the longest continuously operated inn, since it was established in 1766 at the junction of the road to the Hudson and the road to Albany. Whatever the truth of that claim, the tap room, with its dark-wood paneling and oak tables, is certainly as English (sorry as colonial) as you'll find anywhere in the United States, and people do love to come here for drinks or to dine on prime rib, chicken, duck, and other typical American/continental fare. For lunch or dinner there's also the light and airy Greenhouse.

A typical room in the inn may contain a canopy oak bed, oak desk, brass candlestick lamp, chintz or striped wallpaper, table, and comfortable side chairs. Additional touches include a decanter of sherry, a coffeemaker, and a small selection of books. Amenities include telephone, shampoo and other toiletries, and a vanity sink outside the bathroom. The most fetching accommodations are located in the Gothic Delameter House (1844), a few doors away. High gables with ornamented carved verge boards, a rustic porch, and bay and mullioned windows characterize this striking building fashioned by Alexander Jackson Davis, who also designed Lyndhurst. The eight rooms are furnished with wicker, colorful quilts, and large armoires, all in keeping with the American Gothic architecture. You'll also find a parlor furnished with wicker that offers a TV and comfortable seating arrangements. Swag drapes, diamond-pane windows, a marble fireplace, and equestrian prints complete the Victorian ambience.

Behind the Delameter several accommodations are clustered around a grassy area. The Germond (1820) has four rooms and recently accommodated Elizabeth Taylor while she visited her son and daughter in Red Hook. Room 69 features a pencil four-poster standing on wide-board floors, a country towel rack, a Wedgwood blue rocker strategically positioned in front of the fireplace, and an adjacent parlor furnished with wing chairs, desk, and Windsor chairs—a lovely accommodation for $70. The Carriage House rooms have cathedral-style ceilings with crossbeams and furnishings that include a brass bed, armchairs, Windsor chairs, pine table, and a selection of books. All rooms have air conditioning and TV, except those in the main building. Many have fireplaces. In the mornings coffee cake and danish are left outside room doors. With all these separate buildings, the Beekman Arms offers 48 rooms.

At dinner, entrees like prime rib, roast duck with raspberry sauce, blackened redfish, buttermilk-pecan chicken, and veal with artichokes include a crock of country herbed cheese, crackers, salad, vegetable, rice or potato, and a loaf of bread. There are also daily specials.

RATES: $50 to $84 (the lower price for rooms in the main building, the higher for the Germond and Delameter Courtyard rooms with color TVs and working fireplaces). LUNCH: Monday to Saturday from noon to 3 P.M. DINNER: Monday to Friday from 5 to 10 P.M., until 11 P.M. on Saturday. BRUNCH: Sunday from 10 A.M. to 2 P.M.

Montgomery Inn Guest House, 67 Montgomery St. (Rte. 9), Rhinebeck, NY 12572 (tel. 914/876-3311), is set back off the road behind a lawn and shade trees. Past the porch with wicker furnishings you'll be inside a classic center-hall Victorian. There's a TV parlor to the left. Across the hall in the dining room, furnished with oak tables, a breakfast of fresh fruit, bacon or sausages, and french toast or similar is served. An oak staircase leads to four rooms that share baths, which are pleasantly if unremarkably furnished. The Mulberry Room has twin cannonball beds, pink-stripe wallpaper, and dusky-rose ruffled curtains and dresser, while the Springbrook Room is decorated in chintz with a carved oak bed. The color schemes of each are appealing. One room on the first floor has a private bath. The back lawn under the shade trees affords a quiet place for guests.

RATES: $68 with private bath, $63 with shared bath.

Rhinebeck area bed-and-breakfasts do seem to come and go, so that your best bet, if you're looking for this type of accommodation would be to contact the

Rhinebeck Chamber of Commerce, P.O. Box 42, New York, NY 12572 (tel. 914/876-4778).

RHINEBECK DINING

Besides the **Beekman Arms,** on Rte. 9 (tel. 914/876-7077), which is a very atmospheric place for lunch, dinner, or Sunday brunch, there are several other choices.

French dining can be found at **Chez Marcel,** Rte. 9 (tel. 914/876-8189), a few miles north of Rhinebeck. In a cozy paneled dining room with a few small pictures of Paris, you can dine on owner/chef Marcel Disch's French cuisine. Although the menu changes frequently you'll probably find a selection of about eight fish dishes, like scampi Créole or provençale, sole bonne femme or amandine, and a dozen or so meat dishes including roast duckling, chateaubriand, rack of lamb, and calves' liver Bercy. There will always be three or four specials—a creamy blanquette of veal, skate with beurre noir and capers, and a rabbit in red wine sauce, when I visited. Prices range from $9 to $14. DINNER: Tuesday to Saturday from 5 to 10 P.M., on Sunday from noon to 9 P.M.; closed Monday.

At **Foster's Coach House,** 22 Montgomery St. (tel. 914/876-8052), you may well have to wait on line, for this budget eatery is very popular. The portions are large, the food is okay, and the prices are fair for spaghetti with sausage, scampi, roast turkey with stuffing, etc.

HOURS: 11 A.M. to midnight daily.

South of Rhinebeck on Rte. 9, there's also the **Fox Hollow Inn** (tel. 914/876-4696), a warm, unpretentious place that serves some good Italian fare. Prices range from $6 to $9 for linguine with red or white clam sauce, spaghetti with meatballs, manicotti, veal or eggplant parmigiana, and daily specials.

DINNER: Monday, Wednesday, and Thursday from 5 to 9 P.M., on Friday and Saturday from 4 to 10:30 P.M., and on Sunday from 4 to 9 P.M.

For lunch head for **Schemmy's,** 19 East Market Street (tel. 914/876-6215) a genuine old-fashioned drugstore now operating as a restaurant/coffeeshop soda fountain.

EVENING ENTERTAINMENT

Upstate Films is the name of the cinema I mentioned earlier, at 26 Montgomery St. (tel. 914/876-2515), that shows foreign and old classics and occasionally features their directors.

RED HOOK

The town of Red Hook lies about six miles north of Rhinebeck and actually possesses little of note, except a wonderful old library and an attractive lodging and dining place called the Red Hook Inn. The **Edith C. Blum Art Institute** on the bucolic campus of Bard College is also nearby (in Annandale about four miles north of Red Hook) and often features art exhibits worth stopping for. HOURS: Tuesday to Sunday from noon to 5 P.M.

The **Red Hook Inn,** 31 South Broadway, Red Hook, NY 12571 (tel. 914/758-8445), has been pleasantly restored and has a colonial flavor. There are five rooms, all with private bath and all furnished nicely with antique country pieces;

some have fireplaces. Breakfast is included in the price. In the dining room (with blazing hearth in winter) the menu features American/continental fare—roast duckling, steaks, fish and Italian specialties. Prices range from $11 to $16.

RATES: $60 to $80 double. LUNCH: Friday to Wednesday from 11:30 A.M. to 3 P.M. DINNER: Friday to Wednesday from 5 to 10 P.M. BRUNCH: Sunday from noon to 3 P.M. Closed Thursday.

FROM RHINEBECK TO HUDSON

AREA ATTRACTIONS

Clermont

About 13 miles north of Rhinebeck (just south of Germantown) up Rte. 9G you'll come to **Clermont State Park** (tel. 518/537-4240), the Livingston estate and home of Robert R. Livingston, signer of the Declaration of Independence. Here, Robert Fulton's *Clermont* stopped on her maiden voyage up the Hudson in 1807. The estate remained in the family from 1813 until 1962, when the state took it over and turned it into a glorious riverside site for picnicking and relaxing. The house, restored to its 1930 appearance, can be visited, and the gardens are lovely, especially when the magnolia is in bloom. HOURS: Memorial Day to the end of October, Wednesday to Sunday from 9 A.M. to 5 P.M.; the grounds are open from 9 A.M. to 10 P.M. year round. For your picnic supplies stop in Red Hook or nearby Tivoli. Good cross-country skiing.

Olana

Next stop is Olana, just south of Hudson (tel. 518/828-0135), artist Frederic Church's magnificently whimsical home which has been meticulously restored to even the minutest detail in an effort to recapture his vision and intention. The restoration is a fitting tribute to a man who had so great a passion for design that he drew 200 sketches of the staircase alone, and who extended that passion to the landscape itself—every tree on the property was chosen by him, and he created the lake at the bottom of the hill specifically to mirror and balance the Hudson!

Frederic Church (1826–1900) came from a very wealthy New England family. His father, a silversmith, paper-mill owner, and banker, who was on the board of Aetna Insurance, was appalled at his son's desire to become a landscape artist and only agreed to let him become apprenticed to Thomas Cole because Cole was so deeply religious. Because the decor of the house has been maintained as an authentic period creation of interior design, the many artworks are not displayed to maximum advantage, but on the walls hang many of Church's masterpieces or sketches of them—*Twilight in the Wilderness, Niagara,* the *Memorial* paintings, *Sunrise and Moonrise,* and *Pilgrim in the Valley of the Shadow of Death.*

The 37-room house was built between 1870 and 1874, soon after a visit that Church had made to Persia and the Near East. Inspired by Near Eastern culture, he incorporated many Persian elements into the decor—gold-and-silver stencil doors, richly colored and decorated patterned tiles for fireplaces. The doorway bears an inscription *Mahaba,* meaning welcome. Throughout the house Church exhibited his painterly instincts by his use of color—a vivid purple on the walls of the vestibule, pumpkin on the ceiling, a pink ceiling in the Court Hall that is echoed by the Erastus Dow Palmer roundels on the walls.

Much of the furniture was purchased and shipped from Persia and other faraway places—painted chairs from Kashmir, ten-sided tables of mother-of-pearl from Syria. The Court Hall, where the lower landing was used as a stage by the family, reflects Church's careful attention to detail. Light from the golden staircase window, which Church created by using yellow paper, gives the effect of sunshine falling on the brass banister; the ombra arch window is placed to capture the "spectacular moment in Nature"—the famous bend in the Hudson River. Toward the end of the century Church paid several visits to Mexico, and in his studio is piled a wonderful collection of sombreros and pre-Columbian Mexican pottery. His wife used to play the piano here to stimulate his creative inspiration.

Outside, walk down to the informal scatter garden which blooms in harmonious confusion below the walls encircling the mound on which the house is built. Linger awhile, spread out a picnic. Better yet, join one of Olana's special period picnics attended by 19th-century magicians and other entertainments. Christmas is also a good time to visit, when the house is authentically decorated according to late-Victorian custom and with appropriate musical accompaniment. HOURS: May 1 to late October, Wednesday to Saturday from 10 A.M. to 5 P.M., on Sunday from 1 to 5 P.M. Hours vary in September and October, so call ahead. Reservations recommended. The last tour (you must take a tour) is at 4 P.M. ADMISSION: $1.

HUDSON

HUDSON ATTRACTIONS

From Olana, you can continue up Rte. 9G into the former whaling town of Hudson, where many **19th-century town houses** are being restored. At the west end of Warren Street, take a moment to stroll up on **"Parade Hill,"** a promenade lined with benches from which you can look down to and across the river. The major attraction in town is the **American Museum of Firefighting,** on Harry Howard Avenue (tel. 518/828-7695 for information). I have to admit that when someone suggested visiting the Fire Museum it didn't seem that enthralling a prospect, but as usual prejudice misled. It's a marvelous place to visit, both for its fascinating collections and for its guides—retired firemen like Bill Rhodes who have "lived" through much of what they explain.

The biggest impact comes from the magnificent gleaming old fire engines, one of the largest collections of its kind in the U.S. Among them are the first mobile fire wagon, standing on wooden wheels with steel bands, which was used for 154 years (from 1725 to 1879); the most expensive, an 1846 double-decker engine of hand-carved and painted wood with copper hubcaps that required 45 men to operate for 15 to 20 minutes; a splendiferous parade carriage (1883), sporting gold-plated hubcaps and silver-capped hub bands, a silver-plated metal-engraved reel jacket, and the 1845 Piano Engine, which was the first to have a volume control ensuring a steady stream of water instead of short spurts. Later models fall into the steam category, many of them made by La France Company in Elmira, N.Y., and used locally in the state. Favorites include an 1882 horse-drawn steamer called Hercules, last used in 1940, that was built to travel on trolley tracks, and the Clapp & Jones Steamer (1870), built in Hudson, which vibrated or "walked" so much it had to be staked down or tied to a tree!

Around the walls in cases are displayed uniforms, helmets, medals, badges, banners, photographs, Currier & Ives prints, and other memorabilia. But the pièce de résistance appears at the end of your tour—a beautiful 1890 parade carriage with 68-inch wheels. The reel is finished in etched mirrors and supported on each side by two silver-plated lions couchant. Over the reel stands a fireman holding a child and trumpet. The lamps and other artistic details are also elaborate.

HOURS: April 1 to October 31, Tuesday to Sunday from 9 A.M. to 4:30 P.M.; closed Monday.

The Daughters of the American Revolution also operates a **whaling museum** here at 113 Warren St. (tel. 518/828-7288), which documents and explores the town's whaling heritage. HOURS: Open in July and August, on Wednesday from 1 to 4 P.M. and on Sunday from 1 to 3 P.M.

HUDSON DINING

Try **Buccis,** a fine Italian restaurant at 517 Warren St. (tel. 518/828-4990). Pasta, veal, chicken, and fish dishes (like scrod Portofino or veal marsala) are priced from $10 to $16.50.

DINNER: Tuesday to Saturday from 5 to 9 P.M.; closed Sunday and Monday.

For other dining choices also convenient to the attractions of Olana, Hudson, Lindenwald, and even Clermont, cross the river to Catskill (see the upcoming chapter on the Catskills).

FROM HUDSON TO OLD CHATHAM

AREA ATTRACTIONS

Lindenwald

Farther north on Rte. 9H, two miles south of Kinderhook, is Lindenwald (tel. 518/758-9689), Martin Van Buren's retirement home, which has recently been restored to its 1850–1862 appearance and opened to the public. Van Buren was born in Kinderhook in 1782 and left in 1801 for New York City, where he met Aaron Burr and DeWitt Clinton, among others. Later, he returned to practice law and continue the political career which carried him into the White House (1837–1841). Although the house was built in 1797, Van Buren acquired it in 1839 during his presidency. Ten years later architect Richard Upjohn designed substantial alterations to the mansion, thus giving it its present eclectic appearance. The former president lived here from 1841 to his death in July 1862, and was buried in Kinderhook Village Cemetery. Besides personal furnishings and objets d'art, it also features a historical room recalling his career as attorney-general and governor of New York, secretary of state, vice-president, and president (he was, by the way, the first president born an American citizen). HOURS: The grounds are open year round; the mansion is open April 1 through November 30, 9 A.M. to 5 P.M. daily.

Van Alen House
Just off Rte. 9H in Kinderhook, the Van Alen House (tel. 518/758-9265) is worth visiting to view the fine Dutch architecture and collection of Hudson Valley paintings. The house is especially lovely in spring, when a special flower festival is celebrated. HOURS: May 28 to September 4, Tuesday to Saturday from 10:30 A.M. to 4 P.M., on Sunday from 1:30 to 4:30 P.M.; at other times, by appointment. ADMISSION: $2 for adults, $1.25 for children over 12.

Old Chatham
From Kinderhook it's only a short trip to Old Chatham and the **Shaker Museum,** Shaker Museum Road (tel. 518/794-9100). For information about their history and background, see the Berkshires chapter in the Pittsfield section. Here, you can tour about eight buildings—a small chair factory, cabinet maker's shop, blacksmith, textile and weaving shops, herbal house—the whole representing a premier study collection of Shaker material and culture with over 32,500 items. Visit also the library, bookstore, and gift store. HOURS: May 1 to October 31, 10 A.M. to 5 P.M. daily. ADMISSION: $3.50 for adults, $2.50 for children 15 to 21, $1.50 for ages 6 to 14, free for under-6s.

EVENING ENTERTAINMENT ON THE EAST BANK

The **MacHaydn Theater** (tel. 518/392-9292) in Chatham (*not* Old Chatham) is one of the finest summer-stock theaters around that features musicals.

Poughkeepsie's **Bardavon Theater,** 35 Market St. (tel. 914/473-2072), is a lovely theater where the ornate stucco and decorative work has been restored to its original 1869 splendor. It now hosts such performers as Rita Moreno and Marcel Marceau, along with popular Broadway and off-Broadway hits.

EAST BANK ACTIVITIES

ANTIQUING: The greatest concentration of stores are found in Red Hook along Hook and South Broadway, at The Hyde Park Antiques Center, and also in Millbrook.

BICYCLING: About two miles from Rhinebeck, bikes can be rented from the cycle shop in Astor Square shopping center on Rte. 9.

BOATING: Boat rentals are available in Lake Taghkanic State Park, Rte. 82, in Ancram (tel. 518/851-3631); and Taconic State Park, Rudd Pond Area, off Rte. 22 in Millerton (tel. 518/789-3059).

CAMPING: Best camping is in the state parks, open from mid-May to October 31:

Lake Taghkanic, Rte. 82, Ancram, NY 12502 (tel. 518/851-3631), offers 64 sites, swimming, fishing, and boat rentals; **Taconic State Park,** Copake Falls area, Rte. 344, Copake Falls, NY 12517 (tel. 518/329-3993), has swimming and fishing, but the Rudd Pond area also in Taconic State Park, on Rte. 22, Millerton, NY 12546 (tel. 518/789-3059), has 41 sites and the most facilities, including a camp store and recreation building; **Margaret Lewis Norrie State Park,** Rte. 9, Hyde Park, NY 12538 (tel. 914/889-4646), offers fishing and a children's area.

FISHING: At Lake Taghkanic (tel. 518/851-3631); at Taconic State Park, both the Rudd Pond and the Copake Falls areas; and at Norrie State Park (tel. 914/889-4646).

FRUIT PICKING: Philip Orchards, Rte. 9H, Claverack (tel. 518/851-6351), for pears and apples; Greigs Farm, on Pitcher Lane, north from Red Hook off Rte. 9 (tel. 914/758-5762), for asparagus, peas, raspberries, and strawberries.

GOLF: Dinsmore Golf Club (tel. 914/889-4071), with a panoramic view of the Hudson.

HIKING: James Baird State Park, LaGrange; Norrie Point State Park, Hyde Park; Lake Taghkanic State Park, Rte. 82, Ancram. For more information on the state parks, contact the Taconic Region, Staatsburg, NY 12570 (tel. 914/889-4100).

PICNICKING: Along the banks of the Hudson there are several magnificent picnicking spots, all granting views over this great river. Starting at the farthest south, there's Mills Mansion in Staatsburg, five miles south of Rhinebeck, where you can pick up your supplies in one of the many delis or supermarkets. Just north of Rhinebeck in Germantown, at Clermont, the home of Robert R. Livingston, the rolling parklands and gardens are open from 9 A.M. to 10 P.M. daily year round. Pick up supplies in nearby Red Hook (there's a deli on the corner at the main crossroads). And finally, at Frederic Church's Olana, you can picnic high on a hill overlooking the bend in the river that he made famous. Olana itself even organizes occasional period picnics at which people arrive dressed in costume and are entertained in a 19th-century manner with magicians, jugglers, and so on.

SKIING: Catamount Ski Area in Hillsdale—see Berkshires skiing. Cross-country skiing: Lake Taghkanic State Park and Mills-Norrie State Park.

SWIMMING: Lake Taghkanic, Taconic State Park—Rudd Pond and Copake Falls areas.

TENNIS: There are public courts in Rhinebeck and at Hudson's Columbia-Greene Community College.

The West Bank

This side of the river offers several river towns that are in many ways gateways to the Catskills. Here you'll find an assortment of accommodations (far more than on the east bank), ranging from bed-and-breakfasts to the impressive Mohonk Mountain House. But first, let's examine what there is to do.

THE WINE COUNTRY

Just south of New Paltz, along the river stretches the Hudson Valley wine country, around Marlboro and Milton. Best time to visit is during harvest in the early fall.

Hudson Valley Winery, Blue Point Road, Highland (tel. 914/691-7296 or 212/594-5394) off Rte. 9W, occupies a magnificent location high above the Hudson, and often features special weekend events, along with tastings, bread, fruit, and cheese and hay rides. HOURS: Weekends, year round from 11 A.M. to 5 P.M.; on weekdays, April to November only, from 11 A.M. to 3 P.M. (in July and August, until 4 P.M.). Also offers cross-country skiing. ADMISSION: $4 on weekends.

The **Cagnasso Winery,** Rte. 9W in Marlboro (tel. 914/236-4630), is smaller, less formal, and free. HOURS: 10 A.M. to 4:30 P.M. Thursday to Tuesday. Open April 1 to December 1.

In Milton, the **Royal Wine Corp. (Kedem),** Dock Road (tel. 914/795-2240 or 212/384-2400), features a slide show and the usual tastings. Here you can also picnic by the river in relative peace. HOURS: May to October, Sunday to Friday from 10 A.M. to 5 P.M.; closed Saturday and Jewish holidays. ADMISSION: Free.

Farthest south and the best known is the **Brotherhood Winery** in Washingtonville (tel. 914/496-3661), near West Point. The vineyard claims the largest underground cellars in the nation. HOURS: Daily, 11 A.M. to 4 P.M. in summer, noon to 3 P.M. in spring and fall; weekends only in winter, 11 A.M. to 4 P.M. Closed January. ADMISSION: $1.

NEW PALTZ—HIGH FALLS—LAKE MINNEWASKA

AREA ATTRACTIONS

New Paltz itself boasts the "oldest street in America with its original houses"—six stone houses all built before 1720. Most notable is the **Abraham Hasbrouck House,** an outstanding example of Flemish stone architecture, built in 1712 by Abraham, reputed to have served in the British army and a friend of Governor Andros. The kitchen, by the way, was the scene of many a cock fight. For over 250 years these houses have stood, passing from the descendants of one generation to another, of the original Duzine (or 12 men) who founded this community in 1677, naming it after die Pfalz, the temporary retreat that they had found during years of exile from their native France. HOURS: Memorial Day weekend through September, Wednesday to Sunday from 9:30 A.M. to 4 P.M., weekends only in October.

The houses are maintained by the **Huguenot Historical Society,** 18 Broadhead Ave., New Paltz, NY 12561 (tel. 914/255-1889), which offers 2¼-hour ($5) and one-hour ($2.50) guided tours starting from Deyo Hall. The society also maintains an art gallery, the Howard Hasbrouck Grimm Gallery, and a museum which are open to the public free of charge and whose hours coincide with the tour hours.

At the **D&H Canal Museum,** on Mohonk Road in neighboring High Falls (tel. 914/687-9311), you can view the brief history—from 1828 to 1898—of the 108-mile-long Delaware-Hudson Canal, built in 1825 to ship coal from Pennsylvania to the Hudson River and thence to New York City. By the 1870s its role was usurped by the railroads. HOURS: May 1 to October 31, Wednesday to Sunday from 11 A.M. to 5 P.M.

A little farther up the road, the **grist mill** at the base of the falls is another fun place to visit (tel. 914/687-7385).

From New Paltz, it's a short distance along Rte. 299 to **Lake Minnewaska, a** brilliant-turquoise lake rimmed by a forest of high hemlocks, set atop the Shawangunk Mountains. A resort very similar to Mohonk once functioned here but has fallen so hopelessly into disrepair that it's scheduled for demolition, although controversy has raged around the prospect (and if demolition permits are not granted, the area will be closed). Until the new resort development that is planned comes into being, the wilderness area is fantastic for swimming, canoeing, picnicking, hiking, or camping (April to mid-October). Entry to the area is $5 on weekends. The fate of this area hangs in the balance, so do call ahead—Lake Minnewaska Mountain Houses, Inc., Lake Minnewaska, NY 12561 (tel. 914/255-6000). In winter you can ski past frozen waterfalls and streams, between snow-covered hemlocks to points with views over the Hudson Highlands, Berkshires, and Catskills—40 miles of trails in all. Rentals available. As we go to press it's operating as a recreation area, but the future is murky so always check ahead!

Get back on Rte. 209 and you'll arrive at another geological and natural wonder, **Ice Caves Mountain** at Ellenville (tel. 914/647-7989), an impressive array of ice formations, canyons, and rugged rock formations. One of the highest points in the area, it also delivers five-state views and is great for picnicking. HOURS: April 1 to November 1, 9 A.M. to dusk daily.

A VERY SPECIAL NEW PALTZ LODGING

The historic **Mohonk Mountain House,** New Paltz, NY 12561 (tel. 914/255-1000 or 212/233-2244), is an attraction in itself. A two-mile drive through curving wooded lanes will bring you to a large, rambling, primarily stone structure capped by towers that broods on the mountaintop looking out over the Rondout Valley. From the rockers or Mission settees on the veranda that wraps around the back, you can gaze across the crystalline turquoise mountain lake, surrounded by craggy rocks and dotted with gazebos, and contemplate the stillness of the lake at eventide. This is the last of many fine resorts that once dotted the area and attracted wealthy vacationers. It has retained its Victorian flavor with shutter windows, oak pieces and mantels in the rooms, and old-fashioned bathroom fittings, including tubs that actually come with footstools. The grounds are a delight at any time of year, but especially so in summer, at blossom time in spring, and also in early June when the surrounding 2,000 wooded acres are aglow with pink and white mountain laurel. A magical spot where visitors are asked to drive slowly and quietly up the approach road "to harmonize with nature," the whole place exudes a sense of peace, tranquility, contemplation, love of nature, and reverence for life.

In short, it still bears some resemblance to the original idea of its Quaker founders and teachers, Albert and Alfred Smiley, who established the house in 1869 as a place where "like-minded people can gather to savor the earth and the sky." Their educational mission continues today in the many programs that are operated (24 in all) during the year. There have been weekends dedicated to mystery novels, antique and folk art, the wonderful world of words, Scottish country dancing, the reflective life, and even a chocolate lover's weekend. In fact 38 theme programs are offered a year. Mohonk also offers a tremendous range of activities—tennis, horseback riding (from April to October), nine-hole golf, rowboats, paddleboats, and canoes, lawn bowling, putting, croquet, plus 35 miles of cross-country skiing trails, and ice skating. Among the famous visitors have been John Burroughs, Andrew Carnegie, and Presidents Teddy Roosevelt, Taft, Hayes, and Arthur.

It was also the site for the famous conference on Indian Affairs and International Arbitration between 1883 and the outbreak of World War I. Photographs of these gatherings and prominent visitors line the corridors that lead from the quiet library and parlors to the incredible oak-columned and -ceilinged dining room that seats 500. While the food is not haute cuisine, as they say, there's plenty of it. Although there's no bar, liquor is available at dinner.

RATES: (including full board): $180 to $271 for two with private bath, $140 for two with sink; two rooms with connecting bath, $220 for two, $268 for three, $323 for four. For children 2 to 15, add $30 to these rates. Add tax and $6.75 per person gratuity. There are also special charges for some activities. You can be met at the Adirondack Trailways at New Paltz or at the Amtrak station in Poughkeepsie. On most weekends two- or three-day minimums are required.

NEW PALTZ AREA BED-AND-BREAKFASTS

The area offers several outstanding guesthouses. The two finest are probably Schoonmaker House and Baker's.

The old stone house known simply as **Baker's,** Old King's Hwy. (R.D. 2, Box 80), Stone Ridge, NY 12484 (tel. 914/687-9795), off Rte. 209 just south of town, was built in 1780 and still commands a magnificent view of the Old King's Hwy. that has remained unspoiled since the days when it was the old east-west route before the canal was constructed. The house then served as a stopping place for travelers—and Doug Baker and Linda Delgado continue that tradition. This is the seventh house that Doug has restored with great care and artistry. He even installed the Rumpford-style fireplace, which has a high inner hearth and fire box and tiny five- by five-inch-hole flue opening! The house is furnished with early American hutches, 18th-century Dutch-German wing chairs in the parlor, and other early American and Federal pieces.

There are six rooms, two sharing a bath, and one suite with a sitting room and wood-burning stove. They have beamed ceilings, wide-board floors, stencil decoration, and cannonball beds with real down comforters. Linda, who teaches and functions as a counselor at the local college, turns out some fine breakfasts consisting of juice, fresh fruit, and a variety of dishes like venison medallions, ham poached in their own maple syrup, smoked trout, and the more usual egg dishes.

Attached to the side of the house is a solarium-greenhouse where they've installed a hot tub—a pleasant pastime for one and all. The pond provides skating or swimming and also some nice black bass. Chickens, ducks, and geese roam the property, while cows graze peacefully on the adjacent 20 acres.

RATES: $60 with shared bath, $70 with private bath, $75 for a suite.

Captain Shoonmaker's House, Rte. 213 (R.D. 2, Box 37), High Falls, NY 12440 (tel. 914/687-7946), between High Falls and Rosendale, is the sixth house that Sam and Julia Krieg have restored. They've completed this 1760 stone house immaculately, furnishing it with antiques and placing quilts on all the brass and canopied beds. Several rooms have fireplaces. Downstairs, the Kriegs have created a solarium around an old well whose stone now serves as a coffee table. Here breakfast—apricot, cherry, or almond strudel, homemade breads, fresh fruit, soufflés, bacon, etc.—is served in the morning, tea in the afternoon, and sherry at night. The books there are also for guests' use. Look at the album depicting the various stages of the restoration process. It should only add to your respect for this interesting, dynamic couple. By the way, Sam has also restored the 1840 barn on the property, turning it into four rooms, each looking out over the Coxing Kill stream and waterfall.

RATES: $65 to $75 double a night. *Note:* Sam also hopes to offer boatrides on the Hudson in his 1939 Hinckley sloop.

From High Falls it's only a short way along Rte. 32 to Rosendale, one of the many towns along the Rondout that were once very popular, but fell into decay, especially after the floods of the 1950s. Some of these towns are experiencing a minor renaissance of sorts, as people from the city move back, restoring homes and creating businesses as has Jeannine Gleissner at her old red-brick **Astoria Hotel,** 25 Main St., Rosendale, NY 12472 (tel. 914/658-8201). The four rooms are all decorated differently, though they mostly contain oak pieces and brass or highback oak beds. All rooms have a stove, sink, and refrigerator, as well as a bathroom. Babysitting is also available. A breakfast of coffee, croissants, and french toast is served.

RATES: $65 double on weekends, $55 double on weekdays.

Just outside of New Paltz, **Ujjala's,** 2 Forest Glen Rd., New Paltz, NY 12561 (tel. 914/255-6360), offers bed-and-breakfast with a distinctly personal flavor, for Ujjala herself also specializes in holistic health and teaches stress management —but only if you feel you need it, of course. Boy, is she kidding! A stay at her sunny Victorian home nestled among apple, pear, and quince trees on 3½ acres should amply restore your spirit. All four rooms, one with private bath, and three with shared bath, are prettily decorated and contain a bowl of fruit, cheese, and wine upon your arrival. The large skylit room has a fireplace, sitting room, and private bath. The large country kitchen with an outside deck for summer breakfasts—in fact, the whole house—is filled with plants and life. Ujjala also tends a fruitful vegetable garden. Breakfast will usually bring forth fresh fruits, granola, homemade bread, omelets, crêpes. Although she's an ex-fashion model, don't be misled—Ujjala is not your typical stereotypical model.

RATES: $55 to $70 double, $45 single. To get there, take Rte. 208 out of New Paltz toward Libertyville; about half a mile past Dressel Farms, turn right into Forest Glen Road. The house is the second house on the left.

DINING IN HIGH FALLS/STONE RIDGE

The **De Puy Canal House,** High Falls (tel. 914/687-7700 or 687-7777), is special. Dining is treated as an art in this landmark (1797) stone house with polished wideboard floors, multiple fireplaces, pewter, and old china. It was originally built by Simeon De Puy, who catered to the needs of the bargemen and who is recalled by memorabilia throughout the tavern rooms. The prix-fixe dinner choices will always include a vegetarian entrée and a selection of meat and fish dishes like baby pompano stuffed with crawfish mousse, quail stuffed with sausage and leek, and Créole lamb with mustard on filo. A three-course (from $33) menu will include soup, entree and salad. The seven-course ($45) menu adds appetizer or pasta, dessert, cheese, fruit, and coffee. Linger as long as you wish.

DINNER: Thursday to Saturday from 5 to 9:30 P.M., on Sunday from 3 to 9:30 P.M. BRUNCH: Sunday from 11 A.M. to 2 P.M. The schedule changes from January 1 to mid-February, and it's closed from February 15 to March 15.

For a weekend lunch or even a casual dinner, try the **Eggs Nest,** Main Street, High Falls (tel. 914/687-7255). Giant-size sandwiches are the specialty at this 19th-century canal house, which has uneven floors. Hanging from the low ceiling you'll see everything from a watering can and an old pair of beaten-up shoes to a miniature of the Red Baron's airplane. You can't get your hands around the deli sandwiches, so thick are they and filled with turkey, beef, chicken salad, liverwurst, pastrami, or whatever else. Priced at $5.50, they include cole slaw and other trimmings—a $4.50 version is served with chips only.

HOURS: Monday to Friday from 3 to 11 P.M., on Saturday and Sunday from noon.

Around the corner from Bakers on Rte. 209 is the **Calico Restaurant** (tel. 914/687-7004), known locally for its continental cuisine and salad bar—veal Cordon Bleu, scampi provençale, medallions of pork with Dijon sauce—at prices from $7.50 to $11.50. The room is simple—stucco, red tablecloths, a few oil paintings and dried flowers complete the decor.

DINNER: Wednesday to Sunday from 4 to 10 P.M.

NEW PALTZ DINING

The **Locust Tree Inn and Golf Course,** 215 Huguenot St. (tel. 914/255-7888), occupies a pretty setting at the head of a fir-tree-lined drive that winds past a duck pond. Of the restaurant's three rooms, the most appealing is the low-beamed tavern, where Delft is displayed on both sides of the mantel. Chicken Cordon Bleu, steak Diane, veal Oscar, and lamb and fish du jour are some of the specialties, priced from $10.75 to $16. Lovely for summer dining overlooking the golf course.

LUNCH: Tuesday to Saturday from 11:30 A.M. to 2:30 P.M. DINNER: Tuesday to Saturday from 5:30 to 10 P.M., on Sunday from 3 to 8 P.M. BRUNCH: Sunday from 11 A.M. to 2 P.M.

Other choices in New Paltz include the **Wildflower Café**, 18 Church St. (tel. 914/255-0020), for health and vegetarian fare (HOURS: Thursday to Monday from 11:30 A.M. to 7 P.M., on Tuesday until 9 P.M.; closed Wednesday); and **Barnaby's**, on North Chestnut St. (tel. 914/255-9831), for burgers, salads, and sandwiches, all under $6, and dinners in the $8 to $16 range. Mexican fare is available along with seafood and continental dishes at **Bacchus**, 59 Main St. (tel. 914/255-8636), in a pine-and-plants atmosphere. HOURS: 11:30 A.M. to 10 P.M. daily.

HURLEY AND KINGSTON

AREA ATTRACTIONS

From Stone Ridge you can travel Rte. 209 via Hurley to Kingston. **Hurley** was the state capital for a month in 1777, when the Council of Safety, then the governing body of the state, retreated here from the advancing British. After the Revolution it became a major stop on the Underground Railroad, and is also noted for being the birthplace of Sojourner Truth. The prime reason for a visit is to view the **ten privately owned Dutch stone houses,** which open their doors only once a year to the public (the second Saturday in July), revealing such inner secrets as the iron "witch catcher" that hangs in the chimney of the Polly Crispell house or the gun holes that puncture the shutters on the stone porch of the Ten Eyck House.

Kingston was the first capital of New York State, where the first state constitution was adopted and the first governor, Clinton, sworn in. The original settlement had been established soon after Hudson's visit to the area, but had been destroyed by the Esopus Indians in 1653. To ward off similar attacks, Peter Stuyvesant ordered a stockade built, and today in this very **Stockade District** are found some of the city's finest old homes—17th-century stone houses, Federal, Victorian, Italianate, Romanesque, art deco—which constitute a veritable walking tour through American architectural history. Indeed, the best way to explore the town is by taking a walking tour given by Friends of Historic Kingston (tel. 914/338-5100) May through September, leaving from the Senate House.

Abraham Van Gaasbeek's home, where the Senate met during the Revolutionary War and the first Constitutional Convention was held, is today called the **Senate House**, 312 Fair St. (tel. 914/338-2786), and was one of the few houses that miraculously survived the sacking of the town by the British. The house itself exhibits Dutch features—Delft tiles and beehive oven—while the adjacent museum relates the birth of New York State government, and displays John Vanderlyn's and Ammi Phillips' paintings. HOURS: Wednesday to Sunday from 9 A.M. to 5 P.M. ADMISSION: Free.

In the 19th century Kingston became a thriving commercial port. The Cornell Steamship Company made its headquarters here and shipped coal, bricks, cement, ice, fruit, and other supplies downriver to New York City, while a steady tourist flow made the city one of the gateways to the Catskills. Today activity has once again returned to the Rondout Landing with the opening of the **Hudson River Maritime Center,** 39 Broadway (tel. 914/338-0071); a **trolley museum** (tel. 914/331-9300), with rides along the waterfront; and the establishment of various stores in buildings that have been rehabilitated. At the Maritime Center, photographs, models, and artifacts reveal the history of Rondout Creek from the days when its population was greater than Kingston's today, to the Depression that finished off the shipyards. In its golden years the port was bustling with steamers, sloops, tugs, and freighters, especially from 1828 to 1898 when the D&H Canal was operating and coal was shipped from Pennsylvania into the Rondout and then elsewhere. Steamboats like the *Mary Powell* (1861–1917), the famous and fastest on the river, made daily round trips to Manhattan. After the canal closed in 1898 shipyards continued to operate, building ships for World Wars I and II, but thereafter the decline was permanent.

From here also, boats are now plying the river, leaving the pier at the foot of Broadway for afternoon, sunset, and dinner cruises on weekends. For information, call or write Hudson River Cruises, Inc., 524 N. Ohioville Rd., New Paltz, NY 12561 (tel. 914/255-6515 or 473-3860).

KINGSTON LODGING

Best choice is probably the **Skytop Motel,** Rte. 28 (R.D. 2, Box 220), Kingston, NY 12401 (tel. 914/331-2900). There's also a **Holiday Inn** at 503 Washington Ave., Kingston, NY 12401 (tel. 914/338-0400), and a **Ramada Inn,** Thruway Circle, Rte. 28 (R.D. 2, Box 212), Kingston, NY 12401 (tel. 914/339-3900).

RATES: In summer, these three motels charge $60 to $70 double; in winter, $50 to $60.

A NEARBY BED-AND-BREAKFAST

Don't be put off by the exterior and the grounds of **Buena Vista Manor,** Rte. 9W (P.O. Box 144), West Camp, NY 12490 (tel. 914/246-6462), a few miles north of Saugerties, for the hosts and interior are really rewarding, and the view of the purple-misted Catskills in one direction and the Berkshires in the other is entrancing. Here your weekend will start off auspiciously with Friday-night dinner—a boon, I've discovered—provided by Bill Alvarez and Bob Adams. The meal will consist of items like stuffed chicken or chicken breast with pecan-mustard sauce served with squash and carrots. They'll ask you what you don't like. Bob Adams has been a professional interior designer for over 25 years and it shows. The sitting room is stunning: terracotta-colored walls arrayed with Oriental art—masks, plates, silk paintings that blend with the porcelains, dolls, a Chinese horse, and other objets d'art. Wing chairs and a sofa spread with embroidered silk cushions are arranged around the fireplace. Dolls are found throughout the house. Bill, a Hollywood costume designer, makes all of their costumes. Many of them are in fact antique madonnas whose hands and heads, complete with glass eyes, are in mint condition. Costumed, they are works of art. Wine is served in the evenings and brandy and a mint chocolate are placed in each room for a nightcap. The three rooms that share a bath have different personalities. The front room, with gilt-framed pictures, is the most formal. Another room has a gold-leaf Chinese screen serving as a headboard, an Emperor chair, and smiling masks as its highlights; pressed-flower pictures add that extra touch. Another has gilt-trimmed curtains and a damask tablecloth draped over a table as its hallmarks. Each has a teddy bear (part of the charm). The amazing thing about this bed-and-breakfast is the plethora of art objects—they're even hanging in the bathroom along with really large and fluffy bath towels. The sun porch, painted yellow and furnished with wicker, is a favorite spot. The dining room contains a dramatic blue slate table and two polychromed figures from Thailand. Breakfast will most likely be stuffed french toast (with peaches or apricots), mushroom omelets accompanied by apple-cinnamon bread, or something similar. VCR films are available. Outside, croquet is played on the lawn, and a herb garden is taking shape. Bill or Bob will even arrange to pick up guests at the train or bus station.

RATES: $60 with shared bath, $70 with private bath. Closed January and February.

KINGSTON DINING

Just inside the Kingston boundary is a well-known roadside restaurant, the **Hillside Manor,** Rte. 32 (tel. 914/331-4386). A wide selection of dishes is listed on the menu. There are 17 different pastas, everything from linguini al gusto with lobster to paglie e fieno. Among the entrees you'll find rack of lamb, filet mignon, veal, and chicken, although the specialty of the house is really seafood—trout meunière, red snapper with mussels, shrimp, clams and white wine, lobster, fried calamari, and more. To start, choose among carpaccio, escargots, and stuffed clams florentine, and to finish, select from the enticing items on the dessert cart. Prices run $13 to $19.

LUNCH: Monday to Friday from 11 A.M. to 2 P.M. DINNER: Monday to Thursday from 5:30 to 10:30 P.M., on Friday and Saturday until 11:30 P.M., on Sunday until 9:30 P.M.

In Kingston itself, **Schneller's,** 61 John St. (tel. 914/331-9800), is a fun place to go for German sausages and schnitzels washed down with over 25 varieties of fine beers.

LUNCH: Monday to Saturday from 11 A.M. to 3 P.M. DINNER: Thursday from 5 to 9 P.M., on Friday and Saturday until 10 P.M., on Sunday from 3 to 9 P.M.

Better yet than any of these would be to head out, as many Kingstonians do, to Glenford and Mount Tremper, where there are several fine French dining establishments only 20 or 30 minutes away. For details, see the upcoming chapter on the Catskills.

Dining at the Rondout

Among the many restaurants at the Rondout, the **Golden Duck,** 11 Broadway (tel. 914/331-3221), serves outstanding Chinese cuisine in a light and modern atmosphere. The room's tables are covered with brown cloths and white overlays. A carved gilt arch leads into the restaurant. For $9 you can choose wonton or hot-and-sour soup, eggroll or chicken wings, and an entree. There are other combinations available, or you can choose à la carte. The great specialty is Peking duck ($20), carved tableside and served with pancakes, or any of the other duck dishes—crispy duck, duckling Hunan style, Mongolian duck. Crispy chicken, shrimp imperial, Maine lobster Cantonese, chicken with cashews, orange beef, and beef Szechuan are dishes featuring other major ingredients. Prices run $6.25 to $13 (for lobster). The food is highly recommended—some of the best Chinese I've ever had for the price.

LUNCH: Monday to Friday from 11 A.M. to 2:30 P.M. DINNER: Sunday to Thursday from 3 to 9:30 P.M., on Friday and Saturday to 10:30 P.M. BRUNCH: Sunday buffet from 11:30 A.M. to 2:30 P.M.

In addition, **Ship to Shore** vends soup and sandwiches, and the **Sturgeon Wine Bar,** 23 Broadway (tel. 914/338-5186) has an extensive selection of wines by the glass. There's also an outdoor café on the waterfront, an ice cream and cookie store, and other shops for browsing.

EVENING ENTERTAINMENT ON THE WEST BANK

Kingston's **Ulster Performing Arts Center,** 601 Broadway (tel. 914/339-6088), offers a broad range of entertainment from rock to symphony, drama to comedy. **Fastland U.S.A.,** Whitfield Road, in Accord (tel. 914/626-0649) holds racing meets on Friday and Saturday evenings and Sunday afternoons from May to mid-September for stock cars, motorcycles, and go-karts.

WEST BANK ACTIVITIES

BOATING: There are a number of marinas along the Hudson. *Athens:* Hagar's Harbor (tel. 518/945-1858). *Catskill:* Hop-O-Nose Marine, West Main Street (tel. 518/943-4640); Riverview Marine Services, 101 Main St. (tel. 518/943-5311). *Kingston:* Kingston Power Boat Association (tel. 914/338-3946).

CAMPING: Open from mid-April to mid-October, **Beaver Pond,** Harriman State Park, RFD, Stony Point, NY 10980 (tel. 914/947-2792), has swimming, fishing, and boating facilities and over 200 camping sites. For more information, contact Palisades Region, Bear Mountain, NY 10911 (tel. 914/449-9332).

CANOEING: Catskill Canoes, Stewart Lane, Kingston (tel. 914/339-3770).

FRUIT PICKING: *High Falls:* Mr. Apples, Rte. 213 (tel. 914/687-9498), for apples and pears. *Kingston:* Cirone Farm, 215 Chester St. (tel. 914/338-5414), for raspberries, beans, peas, tomatoes, peppers, sweet corn, eggplant, etc. *Milton:* J. R. Clarke and Son, Clarke's Lane (tel. 914/795-2323), for apples, plums, and pumpkins; Frankie's Farm, Rte. 9W (tel. 914/795-5310), for apples, grapes, pears, plums, and raspberries. *New Paltz:* Dressel Farms, Rte. 208 (tel. 914/255-0693), for apples and strawberries; Wallkill View Farm, Rte. 299, one mile west of New Paltz (tel. 914/255-8050), for beans, potatoes, pumpkins, winter squash, strawberries, and tomatoes. *Stone Ridge:* Davenport Farms, Rte. 209 (tel. 914/687-0051), for raspberries, grapes, strawberries, lettuce, spinach, chard, squash, cauliflower, broccoli, etc.

GOLF: *Accord:* Rondout Country Club, Whitfield Road (tel. 914/626-2513). *Cornwall:* Storm King Golf Club, Ridge Road (tel. 914/534-8834). *High Falls:* Stone Dock Golf Course, Berme Road (tel. 914/687-9944). *Newburgh:* Newburgh Country Club, Cohecton Turnpike, Rte. 17K (tel. 914/564-9713); Powelton Club, Balmville (tel. 914/561-4481). *New Paltz:* New Paltz Golf Course (tel. 914/255-8282), nine holes; Mohonk Mountain Golf Course, Rte. 299 (tel. 914/255-1000).

HIKING: Bear Mountain State Park and Harriman State Park offer a network of trails. Contact Palisades Interstate Park Commission, Bear Mountain, NY 10911 (tel. 914/786-2701), or P.O. Box 155, Alpine, NJ 07620 (tel. 201/768-1360). For the Appalachian Trail, contact the Appalachian Trail Conference, 232 Madison Ave., New York, NY 10016 (tel. 212/696-6800); Black Rock Forest on Rte. 9W just northwest of West Point has marked and unmarked trails. Crow's Nest in the Storm King section of the Palisades Park on Rte. 9W south of Storm King Mountain.

HORSEBACK RIDING: *High Falls:* Cedar Hill Stables (tel. 914/687-9300). *New Paltz:* Big M. Ranch (tel. 914/255-9765). *Plattekill:* Oakland School of Horsemanship (tel. 914/564-3621); Plattekill Horse Ranch (tel. 914/564-3621). *Saugerties:* Brentwood Stables (tel. 914/246-5928).

SAILING: Myles Gordon operates a nationally accredited sailing school at the Kingston Rondout during the summer, and also runs sunset sails from 6 to 8 P.M. during which he relates the history of the river's life. For a schedule of programs, contact the Great Hudson Sailing Center at the Maritime Center, Kingston, NY 12401 (tel. 914/338-0071), or at 235 Main St., Kingston, NY 12401 (tel. 914/338-9313).

SKIING: Cross-country in Bear Mountain and Harriman State Parks and at Lake Minnewaska. Contact the Ski Touring Center, New Paltz (tel. 914/255-

6000), and at Lake Mohonk, New Paltz (tel. 914/255-1000 or 212/233-2244).

SWIMMING: At Lake Minnewaska.

TENNIS: Woodstock Tennis Club and Kingston's City Parks.

The Lower Hudson

A wonderful weekend can be constructed around a stay at one of the several inns located in Garrison, Cold Spring, or nearby, and exploring both sides of the river from your chosen base.

GARRISON AND COLD SPRING

Garrison itself was used as a setting for the film *Hello Dolly,* and possesses a lovely park along the river, an art center, and a theater. It's a peaceful spot. From here it's a short way north to more crowded Cold Spring, where you can browse in the antique stores that line both sides of the main street, and then explore one of the loveliest mansions on the Hudson, **Boscobel** (tel. 914/265-3638), built in the early 19th century by States Morris Dyckman. The house contains fine collections of porcelain, silver, furniture, crystal, and rare books, and commands spectacular views of the Hudson. The flower, herb, and vegetable gardens and orangerie are particularly lovely, especially when the roses are in full bloom. HOURS: April to October, 10 A.M. to 4:30 P.M. daily; in November, December, and March, Wednesday to Monday from 10 A.M. to 3:30 P.M. (closed Tuesday); closed for January and February. ADMISSION: $4 for adults, $2 for children.

WEST POINT, STORM KING, AND NEWBURGH

AREA ATTRACTIONS

Across the river the **U.S. Military Academy** was founded at West Point in 1802 and has been turning out eminent leaders, both military and civilian, ever since —Robert E. Lee, Ulysses S. Grant, George S. Patton, Dwight D. Eisenhower, to name only a few. The time to visit is in the spring or fall, when you can view the cadets on parade or attend one of the many football games or other sports events. The museum displays military regalia, medals, and other objects relating to military history. From West Point's location on a high bluff above the river, you can look down to Constitution Island and at Trophy's Point see the remnants of the iron chain that was stretched across the river to stop the British advance. For information on parade times, contact the Visitors Center at 914/938-4011. For tickets to athletic events, call 914/446-4996 or write the Director of Intercollegiate Athletics, West Point, NY 10996.

From West Point, take the Storm King Highway to Cornwall, visiting the **Storm King Art Center**, Old Pleasant Hill Road, off Rte. 32, Mountainville (tel. 914/534-3115), where close to a hundred modern sculptures—Naguchi, Calder, di Suvero—stand starkly against the horizon (HOURS: late May to October 31, Wednesday to Monday from 2 to 5:30 P.M.), and then go into Newburgh to visit **Washington's Headquarters**, 84 Liberty St. (tel. 914/562-1195). From here, Washington commanded his troops during 1781–1782, the crucial period when peace was being concluded, and he also faced down the Newburgh Conspiracy, which called for army mutiny and takeover of the government, in a dramatic speech he made to the troops at the **New Windsor Cantonment**, Temple Hill Road (tel. 914/561-1765), about four miles from Newburgh. Today some of the buildings that were here originally have been reconstructed (there were 700 in all, housing 8,000 troops) and are used for ceremonies, demonstrations, and other reenactments of historical events. HOURS: Late April to October 31, Wednesday to Saturday 10 to 5; Sunday 1 to 5.

GARRISON LODGING AND DINING

The **Bird and Bottle**, Rte. 9, Garrison, NY 10524 (tel. 914/424-3000), a tiny colonial double-porched home set in the woods, has only four rooms for rent. The floors creak and slope, the iron door latches are original, and in your room a fire will be laid in the hearth, and someone will come up to light it. The whole place is highly evocative. The small tavern room is delightful. A five-course, prix-fixe dinner is served in a romantically low-lit, paneled dining room.

RATES: $170 to $195, including dinner and breakfast for two. LUNCH: In summer noon to 2 P.M. daily. DINNER: In summer, Monday to Saturday from 6 to 9 P.M., on Sunday from 3:30 to 7 P.M.; closed Monday and Tuesday in winter.

Golden Eagle, Garrison's Landing, Garrison, NY 10524 (tel. 914/424-3067), has always been a hotel. Now on the National Register, it shines with air and light beside the Hudson River in this small town, familiar to moviegoers as the site of many *Hello Dolly* scenes. Double doors lead first into a gallery/conservatory for owner George Templeton's paintings and for the huge monastera that fills the center of this room. To the right a doorway leads into a comfy tin-ceilinged parlor containing a fireplace flanked with shelved books and assorted seating arrangements. The five rooms are all differently decorated. The Pink Room owes its name to the brilliant-hued comforter on the bed. A wicker sidetable, Empire chairs, and a table draped with a floor-length cloth add Victorian flavor; windows provide a view of the river. The Pastel Room sports candy-stripe comforters and curtains, and a wardrobe topped with an old leather hatbox. It has a lively air; a Windsor chair, marble fireplace, and armchair complete the decor. There's also a suite with wicker-furnished sitting room and bedroom set off by ferns, and a bed that has a pelmeted effect created above it. A favorite sitting place is the second-floor veranda, furnished with wicker and hung with petunias in baskets. Another favored lounging area is the lawn under the riverside weeping willows. Stephanie prepares breakfasts of croissants and fresh fruit (raspberries and strawberries) in season.

RATES: $65 with shared bath, $75 with private bath, $95 for a suite. Closed February and March.

From the inn you can walk along the river or the railroad tracks; visiting potter Jay Lindsay in his workshop where he creates gorgeous stoneware, platters, lamps, planters, etc.; stopping at the Arts Center; and exploring the gazebo on the riverbank, from which majestic views can be enjoyed in either direction. The station houses a theater, The Depot.

Xavier's, at Highlands Country Club on Rte. 9D in Garrison (tel. 914/424-4228), is the area's consistently recommended dining spot. Waterford crystal and fresh flowers grace the tables. The menu is continental. Start with escargots, a gratin of shellfish, coconut shrimp, or foie gras. Depending on the season, you might also enjoy roast pigeon, venison with a sauce venère, medallions of rabbit with a light mustard sauce and white grapes, or rack of lamb. For dessert, try the house specialty, a yummy chocolate-chestnut terrine or any of the other tempting tortes, gateaux or bombes. Entree prices run $17 to $22.

LUNCH: Tuesday to Saturday from noon to 2:30 P.M. DINNER: Tuesday to Saturday from 6 to 9 P.M. BRUNCH: Sunday from noon to 2:30 P.M. Reservations are required and no credit cards are taken.

Compared to Cold Spring, Garrison is blissfully quiet.

COLD SPRING LODGING AND DINING

At the foot of main street, **Hudson House,** 2 Main St., Cold Spring, NY 10516 (tel. 914/265-9355), looks across to Storm King bluffs. It was built in 1832 to accommodate passengers disembarking from steamboats at this, the first stop between Albany and New York. The once-forlorn place has been delightfully individualistically transformed into a comfy countrified lodging where lacquered wine decanters serve as bedside lamps and cookie cutters as wall decoration. The 14 rooms are comfortably old-fashioned. None has telephone, television, or air conditioning. Second-floor rooms open onto a broad balcony; third-floor rooms are tucked under the mansard roof. The doors have iron latches; the sconces are Shaker-style.

The favored summer dining place is the riverside porch. An additional summer dining area is found under a colorful canopy with pretty fresh flower trimmings. The dining room has wide-board floors, tables set with gingham tablecloths, and chairs upholstered in blue. The menu is seasonal. Entrees might include duck and coriander salad, veal medallions with morels, blackened steak Cajun style, Dixie Dandy catfish fry, or rack of lamb with tarragon sauce. Prices run $13 to $20. Among the desserts the most famous is a special chocolate "moose," a caramelized chocolate mousse shaped like a moose with antlers (Mary Pat Sawyer shopped everywhere to find an artisan who would forge the molds for her!). The goldbrick pudding, a flan with a crystalline crust, is another favorite. The Half Moon Bar is prettily furnished with wing chairs placed in front of the fireplace, pale-blue Windsor chairs, and blue chintz. A continental breakfast is served to guests.

RATES: $60 to $75 single, $70 to $85 double. LUNCH: Noon to 2:30 P.M. daily. DINNER: Monday to Thursday from 6 to 9 P.M., on Friday and Saturday until 10 P.M., on Sunday from 5 to 9 P.M. Closed January.

George Argila and Carole Zeller have the original map that labels the **Olde Post Inn**, 43 Main St., Cold Spring, NY 10516 (tel. 914/265-2510), built in 1820, as the post office and assessor's office. From the front porch the door opens into a raftered room with wide-plank floors. Part of the L-shaped space serves as a comfortable parlor with a chintz sofa and a heavy country rocker placed around a wood-burning Franklin stove. The other area is filled with tables set with rush-seated ladderbacks. Dried herbs hang from the rafters, a pineapple-shaped tin chandelier provides light, and a Hoosier cabinet filled with china and pine cone wreaths add country flair. Here a breakfast of homemade breads, croissants, coffee, and juice is served. A scrolled staircase leads to six rooms, all sharing baths and all having air conditioning. Two appealing rooms on the attic floor each have skylights. Most are furnished with oak dressers and chests, desks, country quilts, and cannonball beds.

George is a Juilliard graduate and here has realized his dream of owning a jazz club. Downstairs in the old cellar, complete with beehive oven, jazz musicians play on Friday and Saturday from 9 P.M. (cover: $4). Artists have included Junior Mance and Ray Bryant. The tavern is open Wednesday through Sunday. A brick patio and garden are also available for guests' pleasure.

RATES: $60 on weekends; $45 on weekdays.

Plumbush, Rte. 9D, Cold Spring, NY 10516 (tel. 914/265-3904), has distinctly Swiss overtones. The food is cooked to a high standard. Among the appetizers is a tasty Chürer fleisch torte (a veal-and-pork pie) and smoked trout with horseradish sauce. Other appetizer selections include melon or a thick and satisfying leek-and-potato soup. At a recent meal, duck with a brandied peach sauce, served with rösti potatoes, was perfectly crisp and yet moist; the turban of sole stuffed with crabmeat was also delicately moist. Other entree choices ranged from baby rack of lamb to poached salmon with hollandaise. Among the desserts, I recommend the Swiss apple fritters. Sachertorte, cherry napoleons, and orange Grand Marnier soufflé are also listed. The atmosphere in each of the series of dining rooms is elegant, effected by chintz, lace curtains with floral-patterned pelmets, gilt-framed oils, fresh flowers, and glass hurricane lamps on the tables. The prix fixe is $27.50; à la carte prices run $19.50 to $22. Sunday brunch combines luncheon dishes like coq au vin, leg of lamb, and beef Stroganoff, with more traditional items like eggs Benedict. Plumbush also has three rooms (including a suite) with private bath available. Each is tastefully decorated in Victorian style: iron-and-brass beds, Empire chests, potted ferns, wicker pieces, marble-top tables, and so on—remarkably fine rooms for an establishment that is primarily a restaurant.

RATES: $95 double ($125 for the suite). LUNCH: Wednesday to Sunday from noon to 2:30 P.M. DINNER: Wednesday to Sunday from 5:30 to 9:30 P.M. BRUNCH: Sunday from noon to 2:30 P.M.

A B&B IN HOPEWELL JUNCTION

From Cold Spring, take Rte. 301 to Rte. 9 north to Rte. 82, which will bring you to Hopewell Junction, a trip of about 25 to 30 minutes. Here, there's another attractive lodging and dining place.

At **Le Chambord**, Rte. 52 and Carpenter Road, Hopewell Junction, NY 12533 (tel. 914/221-1941), gracious accommodations and a well-respected dining room are combined. Antiques abound throughout the high-ceilinged 1863 Victorian residence built originally for a doctor on nine acres. The hallway has a magnificent, commanding carved Chinese cabinet, and at the back an old-fashioned wine cooler. The nine large high-ceilinged rooms, all with bathroom, are eclectically furnished with antiques. Room 2 comes with scallopped bed, a chest with a plain pine mirror above, a table, and a side chair from Versailles. Room 8 emphasizes Empire style, with an Empire chair, drop-leaf sidetable, and chest with broken-scroll mirror above. Each room probably contains furnishings from five different periods. The third-floor rooms, tucked under the eaves, are particularly cozy. All rooms have TV, Touch-tone phone, and air conditioning.

In winter a buffet breakfast is served in a woodstove-warmed room; in summer it's taken on the flagstone terrace with a fountain. Food is carefully prepared. Luncheon fare consists of Virginia ham with purée of mushrooms and cream sauce; grilled lamb chops with tomato, bacon, parsley, and garlic; shrimp sautéed with ham and duxelle of mushroom and tomatoes; and other fish and meat dishes. A complete dinner is $25: pâté en croûte, bay scallops and mushrooms with escargot butter, soup, salad, a choice of three or so entrees, and dessert. Among the entrees expect to find a poultry dish (breast of chicken provençal), beef (strips of sirloin Stroganoff served with fettuccine), and a fish item like filet of scrod with a fines herbes sauce. À la carte choices are priced from $14 for a monkfish to $24 for salmon with truffles or chateaubriand with béarnaise, bordelaise, or truffle sauce. Among the appetizers, assiette Neptune combines monkfish, salmon, shrimp, and lobster in a vegetable-tomato based sauce; spectacular pricey desserts include crêpes suzettes, soufflés, and charlotte au chocolat with orange sauce. Pink napkins, white tablecloths, Villeroy & Boch china, lace-ruffled curtains, small crystal chandeliers, a fireplace, and gilt-framed pictures make for an elegant setting. Downstairs, the Marine Bar is especially inviting in winter when a fire blazes in the copper-sheathed hearth. The burgundy couches are soft and comfortable. Portholes and an authentic ship's wheel are the marine touches.

RATES: $65 single, $70 double. LUNCH: Monday to Friday from 11:30 A.M. to 2:30 P.M. DINNER: Monday to Friday from 6 to 10 P.M., on Saturday to 11 P.M., on Sunday from 5 to 9 P.M. BRUNCH: Sunday from 11:30 A.M. to 2:30 P.M.

FINE DINING NEAR STORMVILLE

Harralds, 11 miles east of Stormville on Rte. 52 (tel. 914/878-6595) is a much loved and much favored restaurant for exquisite dining. The prix fixe dinner is $50. Among the selections you might find escalope de veau forestière, breast of duckling à la Normande, fresh trout from the tank, cooked in a variety of ways, plus several daily specials. The ambience, complete with fireplace, fresh flowers, fine table appointments and classical music, evokes romance.

DINNER: Wednesday to Saturday from 6 P.M. Closed January.

LOWER HUDSON ACTIVITIES

BALLOONING: Skylark Balloons, Rte. 44, Millbrook, NY 12545 (tel. 914/677-5454).

BOATING: Fahnestock State Park, Rte. 301 (R.D. 2), Carmel, NY 10512; Lake Mahopac.

CAMPING: Fahnestock State Park, Rte. 301 (R.D. 2), Carmel, NY 10512 (tel. 914/225-7207), is open all year, offering swimming, fishing, boat rentals, and 83 campsites.

GOLF: Garrison Golf Club (tel. 914/424-3604).

HIKING: Hudson Highland State Park, just north of Cold Spring, has great hiking. Manitoga Nature Preserve, just south of Garrison, has four miles of hiking trails. The Appalachian Trail cuts right through Fahnestock State Park, Rte. 301, (R.D. 2), Carmel, NY 10512.

THE CATSKILLS

DISTANCES IN MILES: Port Jervis, 68; Catskill, 115; Shandaken, 120
ESTIMATED DRIVING TIMES: 1½ to 2¼ hours

DRIVING: For the southern Catskills, take the George Washington Bridge to the Palisades Parkway north to the New York State Thruway north to Exit 16 (Harriman) to Rte. 17 west. For the northern Catskills, continue up the Thruway to Kingston and Catskill.
BUS: Trailways (tel. 212/730-7460) goes to Hunter Mountain, Woodstock, Shandaken, and Margaretville. Shortline (tel. 201/529-3666 or 212/736-4700) travels to Sullivan County only.

For skiers there's the Skiers Express from New York City to Hunter Mountain. Inquire at any branch of Herman's sporting goods stores or call 718/596-4227.
TRAIN: Metro-North stops at Tuxedo, Harriman, and Port Jervis. For information, call 212/532-4900.

Special Events to Plan Your Trip Around

FEBRUARY TO APRIL: Maple Sugar Festivals, especially the Greene County Maple Sugar Festival at Windham.
JUNE: In early June look out for strawberry festivals.
JUNE THROUGH SEPTEMBER: Hunter Mountain summer festivals.

For further information about New York State in general, write to the Division of Tourism, New York State Department of Commerce, One Commerce Plaza, Albany, NY 12245 (tel. 518/474-4116).

For specific information about the Catskills, contact the Greene County Promotion Department, P.O. Box 527, Catskill, NY 12414 (tel. 518/943-3223); Hunter Mountain Lodging Bureau, Rte. 23A, Hunter, NY 12442 (tel. 518/263-4208); Sullivan County Office of Public Information, County Government Center, Monticello, NY 12701 (tel. 914/794-3000); Ulster County Public Information Office, P.O. Box 1800, Kingston, NY 12401 (tel. 914/331-9300); Ulster County Chamber of Commerce, 7 Albany Ave., Kingston, NY 12401 (tel. 914/338-5100); Delaware County Chamber of Commerce, 56 Main St., Delhi, NY 13753 (tel. 607/746-2281); and the Woodstock Chamber of Commerce, P.O. Box 36, Woodstock, NY 12498 (tel. 914/679-6234).

"When the weather is fair and settled, they are clothed in blue and purple and print their bold outline on the clear evening sky; but sometimes, when the rest of the landscape is cloudless, they will gather a hood of gray vapours about their summits, which, in the last rays of the setting sun, will glow and light up like a crown of glory." Thus wrote Washington Irving of his beloved Catskills. Nor was Irving their only herald, for among the artists that painted them, Thomas Cole wrote home from Europe that "neither the Alps, Apennines, nor Etna himself have dimmed in my eyes the beauty of our own Catskills." Thoreau put it even more dramatically when he said of the landscape that "it was fit to entertain a traveling god." And to this day there are parts of the Catskills that do look like the Austrian or French Alps, where the mountains are majestic, and the fast-running rivers, streams, brooks, cascading waterfalls, and deep quiet leave a visitor quite dumbfounded by the surrounding natural beauty. This is the Catskill area (around Shandaken, Margaretville, Roxbury, Stamford, the towns nestled along the Esopus Creek and the eastern branch of the Delaware—Mount Tremper, Phoenicia, Glenford—and the northern fringes of Greene County) that attracts skiers, mountaineers, hunters, hikers, canoers, and others who relish nature and the outdoor life. In the southern Catskills, around Monticello, Fallsburg, and Liberty, are those renowned resorts, known collectively as the Borscht Belt, that nurtured and developed so many American comedians and actors and delivered them to the American television and entertainment industry, and that today offer a total vacation with a fantastic array of facilities for a very fair price. There really are two Catskills: the northern wonders of the Catskills forest preserve and the southern resort belt.

In the mid to late 1900s, and indeed until the advent of the motorcar, the Catskills were the playground of the wealthy and eminent. The first resort hotel had been built in 1824, and from then on the Hudson Day Line brought thousands of tourists to the mountains, depositing them at Catskill Point, which became a bustling port and passenger terminal. Horse-drawn carriages and hacks, eagerly awaiting the arrival of the ferry steamers from New York, transported tourists all over the county, although the most dramatic trip was aboard the Catskill Mountain Railroad to Palenville, where the Otis Elevating Railway (installed in 1894) scooped visitors right up the face of the mountain to the Catskill Mountain House. (The gash in the mountainside can still be made out from Rte. 23A.) From the Mountain House the whole sweep of the Hudson River, from north of Albany and south of Kingston, could be seen against the backdrop of the New England mountains. Other tourists continued on to the Hotel Kaaterskill or more remote resorts. The Kaaterskill, built in 1881, was absolutely palatial and could house 1,200 guests in a three-story building shielded by soaring columns crowned by two French Renaissance towers at each end. It fell victim to fire in 1924, a more dignified end than that experienced by the Mountain House, which was demolished in 1963.

For today's weekend visitor the Catskills offer a supreme outdoor experience. You can come to contemplate the mountains; ski at Hunter, Windham, or Belleayre; hike through the wilderness of the forest preserve; climb or ride to the summits of mountains that grant vistas over five states; fish the Wallkill, Beaverkill, and Esopus; canoe the Delaware; swim in the lakes; or soar above the mountains from Ellenville and Wurtsboro. The landscape itself is the prime attraction, although you'll also find numerous festivals and events to attend, like those at Hunter in the summer, or the chamber concerts at Woodstock, but the greatest thrills and rewards await the activist willing to traverse, explore, and challenge these brooding mysterious mountains from dawn to dusk.

A Suggested Itinerary

It's hard to suggest one weekend itinerary because the Catskills represent such a vast area and so much depends on your particular interests. In spring and summer you'll want to spend a whole weekend canoeing, fishing, or hiking and wilderness camping, while in the winter you'll be skiing Hunter and Belleayre or cross-country skiing in Frost Valley or another ski area.

A typical sightseeing weekend would be centered on Catskill and Woodstock, with a day at the Game Farm and Carson City, followed by a good dinner at one of the French restaurants around Glenford–Mount Tremper, and a second day at Woodstock.

Two Routes Through the Northern Catskills

You can use either Kingston or Catskill as your gateway to the mountains.

1. From Catskill, Rte. 23A will bring you through some of the Catskills' most dramatic scenery, as it snakes around between the mountains and forests cut by cascading waterfalls and gulleys past Kaaterskill Falls through Palenville, all the way to Hunter Mountain. Then take Rte. 296 to Windham, where you can choose either to loop back along Rte. 23, going over the dramatic Point Lookout with a five-state view into Catskill, or else continue west along Rte. 23 to Grand Gorge, turning down Rte. 30 past the Burroughs Memorial all the way to Margaretville for a final loop back along Rte. 28 (detouring to Woodstock) into Kingston.

2. From Kingston, take Rte. 28 out along the contour of the Ashokan Reser-

voir, turning off at Rte. 375 for a short detour into Woodstock. Double back to Rte. 28 and continue along the reservoir, a dramatic sight, going through the towns of Mount Tremper and Phoenicia (both of which have some good dining), all the way to Shandaken and Margaretville to the upper reaches of the Delaware. The scenery is beautiful all the way, and from here you can take Rte. 30 along the Pepacton Reservoir down to Hancock, whence you can canoe the Delaware, or to Roscoe, trout capital of the Catskills.

There are, of course, many possible routes through the mountains. Unless you know the mountains intimately, don't attempt shortcuts along dirt roads, especially at night, and always travel with plenty of gas, because if you do get off the beaten track, you can go for miles and miles seeing nothing but trees and streams, and you could well be stranded for a long time.

The sections that follow have been organized to follow the first route outlined above.

CATSKILL/CAIRO

AREA ATTRACTIONS

Since I've already discussed Kingston in the Hudson Valley Chapter, I'm beginning with Catskill, where it seems most of the specific visitor attractions are located.

First, there's the 140-acre **Catskill Game Farm,** off Rte. 32 (tel. 518/678-9595), which specializes in keeping hoofed creatures, including rare wild horses (Przewalski) in their natural surroundings. Kids will love to pet the llamas, donkeys, sheep, and lambs, to see the antics of the chimpanzees, and to ride the elephants. Bring a picnic. It takes approximately two hours to tour fully. Peacocks wander freely about the grounds, stopping by the many foodstands on the off-chance of receiving a treat. HOURS: April 15 to October 31, 9 A.M. to 6 P.M. daily ADMISSION: $7.50 for adults, $4 for children.

Second, in Catskill proper, artist **Thomas Cole's home** has been turned into a modest museum celebrating the painter who lived here from 1836 to 1848, when the property extended down to the Hudson River. The gallery displays large color transparencies of many of Cole's famous paintings—*Sunny Morning on the Hudson, View from Tivoli, View from Kaaterskill Falls,* and his allegorical series, *The Course of Empire.* The collection also contains a set of The Voyage of Life, completed in 1852 by Cole's disciple, DeWitt Clinton Boutelle, after Cole's original designs. The room in which he was married in 1836 looks much as it would have looked then. HOURS: Wednesday to Saturday from 11 A.M. to 4 P.M., on Sunday from 1 to 5 P.M. Located just south of the junction of Rtes. 23 and 385.

You can play out a western fantasy by going to **Carson City,** Rte. 32, Catskill (tel. 518/678-5518), the scene of gunfights, saloon shows, magic entertainment, and pony rides for the kids. Summer rodeos are a popular attraction on Tuesday, Thursday, and Saturday. Located just two miles north of the Game Farm. HOURS: 9:30 A.M. to 6 P.M., daily from June 19 to Labor Day, weekends only from May 28 to June 12, and from Labor Day to Columbus Day.

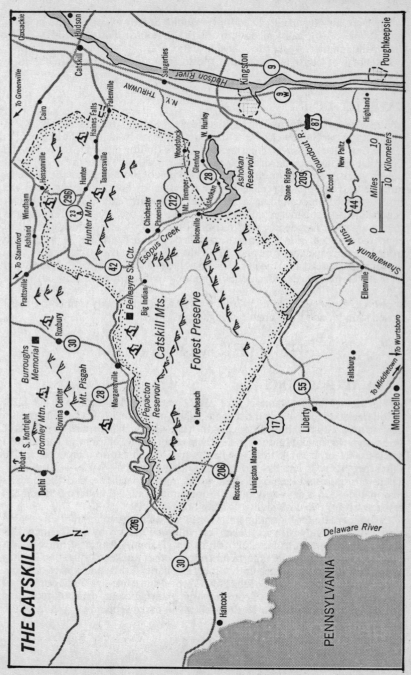

THE CATSKILLS

For more active pursuits, head for the **Junior Speedway,** on Rte. 32 in Cairo (tel. 518/622-3330), half a mile south of Rte. 23. HOURS: 10 A.M. to 10 P.M., daily during the summer, weekends only after Labor Day.

Just north of Cairo, at Freehold Airport, **glider rides** are given. Call 518/634-7626 for info.

CATSKILL DINING

You may have difficulty finding **La Rive,** in rural Catskill (tel. 518/943-4888), but the food and the Gallic welcome at this country French restaurant will be worth it. (From Catskill travel seven miles west on 23A to County Road 47, and follow the signs that will take you down a dirt road to the restaurant.) Here in this old farmhouse, you can dine either on the enclosed porch or more cozily in the house itself. Begin your prix-fixe meal with a selection of hors d'oeuvres from the trolley—lamb pâté, cod mousse, cucumber with sour cream, celery remoulade, eggs à la Russe, and more, plus a choice of soup—all preludes to such classics as steak au poivre, filet de boeuf with truffle sauce or bordelaise, duck with green peppercorn sauce, sole almondine, poached salmon béarnaise, or local fresh trout. The price includes fruit and cheese and dessert, which you can choose from the tempting spread atop the grand piano at the entrance—tortes and gâteaux of all sorts. Entree prices (which determine the prix-fixe price) range from $23 to $26.

DINNER: Tuesday to Saturday from 6 to 10 P.M., on Sunday from 2 to 9 P.M.; closed Monday and from Thanksgiving to early May.

HUNTER MOUNTAIN

AREA ATTRACTIONS

At 4,025 feet, Hunter Mountain, Rte. 23A, Hunter, NY 12442 (tel. 518/263-4223, or toll free 800/548-6648), is the second-highest mountain in the Catskills and the best **ski area** within a short distance of the city. Although it attracts thousands of skiers on a weekend, Hunter handles them expertly and efficiently. The vertical rise is 1,600 feet. It has 45 trails and 16 lifts and tows able to accommodate 15,500 skiers per hour. It has the best snow-making capacity—100%—in the area. There are base and summit lodges, good nursery facilities, and the price is reasonable—$25 a day for adults, $18 for juniors (12 and under); $48 and $34 respectively for two days' skiing. Rentals are available.

In summer Hunter Mountain hosts a series of exciting events and festivals, beginning in early July with an **Italian Fest,** followed quickly by the **German Alps Festival** (held in mid to late July) with beer, Hummel figurines, brass bands, Punch and Judy, and other entertainments. Another weekend brings the **Country Music Festival** featuring such entertainers as Charley Pride, and square dancing. In mid-August there's a week-long **Polka Festival** and a five-day **Celtic celebration** that mixes Irish, Welsh, and Scottish music, entertainment, dancing, food, and drink. An **American Indian Festival** follows in early September. While you're here, ride the chair lift to the summit for a magnificent vista. For information, call 518/263-3800.

The **cross-country ski center** is at Hyer Meadows, Onteora Road (P.O. Box 798), Tannersville, NY 12485 (tel. 518/589-5361). Facilities include a lodge, 18½ miles of graded and groomed trails, ski lessons, a snackbar, and rentals. ADMIS-SION: $6 per day; $10 per day rental.

Skiers Express (tel. 212/596-4227) which leaves from 51st Street and Third Avenue will get you there for a day too. Information is available at Herman's Sporting Goods stores throughout the city.

HUNTER MOUNTAIN AREA LODGING AND DINING

Although there are plenty of ski lodges that cater to the needs of skiers, I'll list only a couple of particular favorites. If these are full, try the Hunter Mountain Lodging Bureau, Rte. 23A, Hunter, NY 12442 (tel. 518/263-4208).

The **Scribner Hollow Motor Lodge**, Rte. 23A, Hunter, NY 12442 (tel. 518/263-4211), is a fun place to stay primarily because of its themed rooms. For example, you might stay in one of the futuristic duplexes, with mirrored ceilings and walls, ultramodern white and beige furnishings, and a bathtub area with a waterfall; or perhaps a hunting lodge might be more to your taste—with a large bearskin rug (complete with the animal's head), cozy cabin walls, beams, and a stone fireplace. And these are just two of the styles, which also include the Penthouse, Alpine, and Key Largo themes. Even the swimming pool area is specially designed to look like an underground cave-grotto complete with waterfalls. The regular rooms are less fun, but then . . . they're cheaper.

RATES: $80 to $87 per person (MAP), $95 to $180 for special rooms. Two-night minimum required on weekends. Open September 15 through June.

As you might expect, the menu at the **Red Coat's Return**, Dale Lane, Elka Park, NY 12427 (tel. 518/589-6379 or 589-9858), about ten miles from Hunter and adjacent to the Catskill Game Preserve, is spiked with several British specialties —prime rib accompanied by Yorkshire pudding, the curries beloved by so many Britishers—plus a selection of continental and fresh seafood dishes. There's usually a roaring fire in the lounge's stone fireplace, antiques dotted about, and a cozy library room, all contributing to the warm, comfortable atmosphere of this Edwardian place overlooking fields, forests, and Schoharie Creek.

The 14 rooms, most with private bath, have been decorated with oak pieces and fluffy down comforters conveying a pleasant homey touch. Guests receive a full breakfast. The surrounding 18 acres have trails and trout streams.

RATES: $75 to $90 double. DINNER: Friday to Wednesday from 6 P.M.; closed Thursday and April and May.

In Tannersville

The **Eggery Inn,** County Road 16, Tannersville, NY 12485 (tel. 518/589-5363), has 13 clean, adequately furnished rooms (11 with private bath) with wall-to-wall carpet, chintz wallpapers, and old-fashioned furniture. The inn operates a restaurant and bar which looks out to the mountains, and has pretty plants and floral tablecloths. Dishes are typical American favorites like prime rib, chicken Cordon

Bleu, veal marsala, and poached salmon. On arrival, guests enter a cozy living room warmed by a woodstove. There's a TV, books, upright piano, and old comfy furniture, some of it Mission-style.

RATES: $100 to $110 per night (MAP). There's a two-night minimum on weekends, and if MAP is available it must be taken. If MAP is not offered the charge is $70 to $75 on weekends, $65 on weekdays. Open year round.

The **Swiss Chalet,** Rte. 28 (tel. 518/589-5445), has an alpine look—plenty of hutches, cuckoo clocks, and pine. The cuisine is also Austrian-Swiss inspired. For example, the menu offers wienerschnitzel, wiener rossbraten, sauerbraten, jaegerschnitzel, Swiss peppersteak, and pork chop Gypsy style. Dishes are priced from $12 to $15. For dessert such classics as apfelstrudel, peach Melba, and pear Hélène are offered.

DINNER: 5 to 9:30 P.M. daily.

Last Chance Cheese & Antiques Café, on Main Street (tel. 518/589-6424), is a country store selling gourmet items, teas, and cheeses. There are also a few wood tables, at which you can sample sandwiches—roast beef, corned beef, pastrami —soups, vegetable platters, cheese platters, and chili nachos, priced from $2.50 to $8.

HOURS: Monday to Thursday from 10 A.M. to 7 P.M., on Friday and Saturday until 9 P.M., on Sunday until 8 P.M.

WINDHAM

This ski area lies about seven miles north of Hunter. It was once a private club, catering to well-to-do skiers, where many political and business leaders skied, and it still exhibits the classiest atmosphere of the local resorts. There's good skiing from the 3,050-foot summit down a 1,550-foot vertical on 27 slopes and trails, 97% of them covered with snow-making. The five chairs and one J-bar have a lift capacity of more than 8,000 skiers an hour. Lessons, rentals, ski shop, and café are all available. The mid-mountain lodge, the Wheelhouse, is an attractive place to picnic or enjoy the views. The White Birches Ski Touring Center offers 15 miles of groomed trails through lovely terrain. For information, contact Ski Windham, C. D. Lane Road, Windham, NY 12496 (tel. 518/734-4300, or toll free 800/833-5056, 800/342-5116 in New York State).

WINDHAM LODGING

The town itself is well kept and contains many spacious Victorian homes. One such is the **Windham House,** Windham, NY 12496 (tel. 518/734-4230), a small handsome resort. A stately 1805 house forms the nucleus of four surrounding colonial-style buildings. Old timbers, plank walls and floors, Hitchcock chairs, and a sheaves-of-wheat railing along the upper veranda give the main house immense character. In Room 18 you'll find items like a wooden butter bowl and ladle, along with a marble-top stand; in Room 2c there's a spool bed and washstand. Rooms vary: some are located in the carriage houses; some have only sinks, but most have private bath. The loft of the old barn that stands on this former farm now serves as a place for evening entertainment. The fields have been turned into a nine-hole golf course. There are also swimming and tennis facilities and a two-mile hiking trail.

RATES: $220 to $290 per person per week for full American Plan, or $50 to $60 per person daily; in winter, room plus a continental breakfast costs $60 to $70. Open from Memorial Day to Columbus Day.

At the **Albergo Allegro,** Rte. 296, Windham, NY 12496 (tel. 518/734-5560 or 734-4499), two old houses have been joined together by a new section that has been carefully designed to imitate the gingerbread, brackets, and stained glass of the two original Victorians. Some of the 24 rooms are on the ground floor; others are located up the staircase, each step of which bears a stenciled angel. Rooms are nicely furnished with dusky-pink wall-to-wall carpets and a brass bed covered with lacy pink eider, pillow, and ruffle. In most there's plenty of room—enough to accommodate tables and chairs and chest of drawers. Dried-flower arrangements add a country air. Rooms have Touch-tone telephone and tiled bathrooms equipped with a basket of Gilchrist and Soames soap, shower cap, herbal shampoo, etc. There are two sitting rooms, both with fireplaces, a few books, and polished wood floors covered with a braided rug. The one downstairs has couches while the upstairs area has a more Victorian feel, thanks to the wicker, rattan, and Eastlake furnishings. Oak chairs and tables fill the dining room where a full breakfast is served. In summer the small patio under colorful awning is the morning breakfast spot.

RATES: In winter, $75 to $95 on weekends, $65 to $85 in midweek; in summer, $65 to $85; in fall, $75 to $95 on weekends, $55 to $75 in midweek; in off-season, $55 to $75 on weekends, $45 to $65 in midweek. Suites and a Jacuzzi suite are more expensive.

In East Windham, the **Pointe Lookout Inn,** Rte. 23 (P.O. Box 33), East Windham, NY 12439 (tel. 518/734-3381), takes full advantage of a magnificent view over New York, Connecticut, New Hampshire, Vermont, and Massachusetts. Most of the rooms have decks, and all have TV and private bath. The dining room serves steaks, seafood, sandwiches, omelets, quiches, and Mexican specialties, priced from $4.75 to $18.50; it's also well known for buffets.

RATES: $65 to $75 double. LUNCH AND DINNER: 11:30 A.M. to 9:30 P.M. daily. BRUNCH: Sunday from noon to 3 P.M. Closed early spring.

WINDHAM DINING

Given the town's past history, it's not surprising that Windham also offers some of the finest cuisine in the whole Catskill Mountains at **La Griglia,** Rte. 296, Windham (tel. 518/734-4499), which often hosts special gourmet-cooking and wine-tasting events. It's famous for variety meat dishes and game, along with a good selection of continental fare. Among the interesting appetizers are eggplant fritters stuffed with mozzarella, anchovy butter, and fresh basil; grilled cornmeal croquettes served with tomato, mushroom, and cheese sauce; smoked trout with horseradish; or cozze Posillipo (mussels, tomatoes, wine, garlic, and herbs). These can be followed by a choice selection of entrees—veal francese; chicken with prosciutto, mushrooms, and champagne; sliced filet of beef sautéed with

Barolo, green peppercorns, and mushrooms; or roast duck with fig-and-honey sauce. For dessert there's wild apple pie, pumpkin Amaretto cheesecake, and a luscious Linzer torte. Prices run $10 to $12 for pasta dishes, $14 to $20 for main dishes. At night the dining rooms are quite atmospheric, the tables set with pink tablecloths and napkins. Each dining area possesses a stove; the rough-hewn pine walls and post-and-beam construction give a country air.

DINNER: From 5 P.M., daily in summer, Thursday to Sunday only in spring and fall, closed Monday in winter.

Vesuvio, Goshen Road in Hensonville (tel. 518/734-3663), offers an elegant setting (fireplace and gilt-framed pictures) for some very fine continental cuisine, including rack of lamb; chicken Vesuvio (sautéed with peas, mushroom, and prosciutto in a wine sauce); veal with fresh mushrooms, lemon and white wine; and assorted seafood like snapper, lobster, mussels, and squid. There are also some juicy steaks available. Prices run $11 to $17.

DINNER: In summer, from 4 P.M. daily; off-season the restaurant is closed Wednesday and also April to mid-June.

At **Chalet Fondue,** on Rte. 296, Windham (tel. 518/734-4650), you can cozy up to the Swiss alpine stove while you wait for a table in one of three dining areas —two stucco style, the other a solarium. Here you can feast on jaegerschnitzel, sauerbraten, wienerschnitzel, and more, and finish off with a fine Sachertorte or apfelstrudel. Prices run $10 to $15.

DINNER: From 5 P.M. on weekends in winter.

Theo's on Rte. 23 (tel. 518/734-4455), offers continental cuisine with a hint of Greek flavoring. There are also some Italian dishes on the menu, along with seafood as well as the Greek-style lamb chops. Prices (from $10 to $15) include soup, salad, main course, dessert, and coffee. The atmosphere is simple and homey.

LUNCH: From 11:30 A.M. daily. DINNER: 4 to 10 P.M. daily. Occasionally the restaurant is closed during the week for one day, depending on the traffic.

At the other end of the economic scale, the **Fishmarket Restaurant,** on Rte. 23 just outside Windham (tel. 518/734-3055), is a local favorite, a fast-fish place McDonald's style that features good clam chowder, flounder, oysters, and calamari.

A B&B IN THE NORTHERN CATSKILLS

The **Greenville Arms,** South Street, Greenville, NY 12083 (tel. 518/966-5219), indisputably an isolated hideaway, has in fact been used as such by many a celebrity in search of rest and anonymity. Cupolas and dormers crown the roof of this lovely Victorian house, built in 1889 for William Vanderbilt and now operated by two sisters, Barbara and Laura Stevens, as a bed-and-breakfast accommodation. There are ten rooms in the main house (four with private bath, all containing sinks). The most pleasant is probably old Will's room, which contains a high-backed Victorian bed and possesses the added attraction of a balcony. Rooms on the third floor have rustic oak furnishings and marble sinks. The front desk in the hallway, by the way, came from a dry goods store owned by Barbara and Laura's great-grandmother. A full breakfast is served in the dining room, and at dinner, available by reservation only, a single entree is served, rather in the style of an English guesthouse. At the back, there's a lovely secluded outdoor pool that you'd never expect to find, a lawn for games, and seven acres with a bubbling stream and wooded trails. The carriage house back here has nine rooms with private bath.

RATES: $60 to $70 per person double with private bath ($55 with shared bath) including breakfast and dinner; $45 with private bath ($40 with shared bath) for bed-and-breakfast.

FROM WINDHAM TO MARGARETVILLE

If you follow the second itinerary route outlined above, from Windham take Rte. 23 West to Grand Gorge. Here, you can either take Rte. 30 south to Margaretville or continue on 23 to the attractive town of Stamford. From Stamford, Rte. 10 south travels through Hobart to Delhi. En route, a scenic side trip through horse-and-farm country along Rtes. 5 and 6 to Bovina Center and New Kingston will eventually return you to Rte. 28 just west of Margaretville. You will have completed a small loop touching on Schoharie and Delaware Counties.

If you opt to travel down Rte. 30 toward Margaretville, you will pass naturalist **John Burrough's Memorial,** just outside Roxbury, down Burroughs Memorial Road. Here, you can sit and quietly reflect upon nature in the Catskill Mountain pasture as he did when he was a boy. Later, when he was a renowned naturalist-philosopher whose books had changed the way that many Americans looked at their world, he still returned here for inspiration. Today he stands out as a brilliant naturalist and environmentalist who wrote as early as 1913: "We can use our scientific knowledge to poison the air, corrupt the waters, blacken the face of the country, and harass our souls with discordant noises, or we can mitigate and abolish all these things."

LODGING AND DINING EN ROUTE

The **Roxbury Run Restaurant,** in Denver (tel. 607/326-7577), is a little difficult to find (turn right off Rte. 30N before you reach the town of Roxbury). Here you'll obtain some fine-quality food and masses of it. For the $11 price, the brunch, for example, is quite remarkable. For each person it includes two complimentary drinks (Bloody Mary or mimosa), an hors d'oeuvre plate featuring pâté, smoked herring, tuna salad, eggs, cheese, melon, cottage cheese, a choice of soup, *and* a selection from the salad bar. The main courses consist of omelets, eggs Benedict, apple pancakes, veal Holstein, croûte valaisanne (with ham and cheese), and a weekly special (veal Zuricher with mushrooms and cream sauce served with rösti potatoes on the morning I dined). The room is pleasantly warmed in winter by a fieldstone fireplace. Tables are set with pink tablecloths, floors are of polished fieldstone, and from the cathedral ceiling a wagon wheel hung with lanterns gives light. A huge cowbell hangs from one of the crossbeams. The room looks out over a brook and tree-lined hills, and in summer service is extended onto the deck set with tables and umbrellas. At night the dinner menu offers an assortment of continental specialties accented by Swiss-inspired dishes like Swiss bratwurst with zwiebeln (onion) and mushroom sauce, and veal piccata Locarnese (veal coated with egg-and-cheese batter and served with a bolognese sauce). Duck marchand de vin with a red wine sauce, mushrooms, and grapes; filet mignon with a mushroom sauce; chateaubriand; and similar fare complete the menu. To start, choose among cannelloni, roasted peppers with capers and anchovies, or escargots bourguignonnes.

DINNER: Wednesday to Friday from 6 to 9 P.M., until 10 P.M. on Saturday and Sunday. BRUNCH: Sunday from noon to 4 P.M. *Note:* In fall, Friday and Saturday dinner, and Sunday brunch, only are served. Closed in March (traditionally).

Scudder Hill House, Scudder Hill Road (Rte. 30), Roxbury, NY 12474 (tel. 607/326-4215), about four miles north of Margaretville, looks like an old farmhouse with a narrow side and front porch. Sadly no one was home when I stopped by, but it looks worth checking out.

RATES: $55 double.

Lanigan Farmhouse, Rte. 10 (R.D. 1, Box 399), Stamford, NY 12167 (tel. 607/652-7455), is an unmarked gray house 1¾ miles south from Stamford on Rte. 10 surrounded by fields and hills. It looks cozy, country, and very attractive, but again, unfortunately, no one was home when I stopped by. I have a hunch it's a good place to stay. Feel free to check it out.

RATES: $40 double.

A warm and friendly welcome will greet you and some unexpected facilities will also surprise you at **Breezy Acres Farm,** Rte. 10 (R.D. 1, Box 191), Hobart, NY 13788 (tel. 607/538-9338), just less than two miles south from Stamford on Rte. 10. Joyce and David Barber love having guests at their farm. Joyce serves a hearty breakfast—enough to carry you through the whole day—of fresh fruit, muffins, and eggs. For example, you might enjoy baked apples, pumpkin muffins, and French toast with homemade bread, accompanied by their own farm syrup and bacon. Guests are free to gather in the sitting room, a typically homey room with leatherette couches and walls hung with Winchester commemoratives and a couple of deer trophies, including a mule deer taken in Wyoming. There's also a pleasant room with a pool table, books, and a piano, and another room with a Jacuzzi-whirlpool for guests to use. There are four accommodations sharing 2½ baths. One room houses solid-oak furniture crafted by Joyce's great-great-grandfather, including a fine bed headboard which required each tiny spindle to be individually lathed. Another double has wall-to-wall carpeting, a peach- and jade-colored quilt on the carved-oak bed, and louver closets. The other rooms have polished wood floors. Joyce usually places nuts or some other small treat in the rooms for guests.

RATES: $45 double. Open year round.

The **Hidden Inn,** South Kortwright (tel. 607/538-9259), is a fine old white clapboard house with a prominent pediment supported by Corinthian pillars. Family run, it offers three plain country dining rooms: the Colonial Room, with a woodburning fireplace; the Sunset Room, where the tables are set with burgundy napkins; and the Kortwright Room, used locally for meetings and weddings. There's a small lounge with a fireplace. On Friday there's either a chuckwagon or seafood buffet. The regular menu is short and simple, listing such favorites as veal parmesan, duck à l'orange, chicken piccata, surf and turf, and steaks. Prices run $10 to $15.

DINNER: Wednesday to Saturday from 5 to 9 P.M., on Sunday from noon to 6 P.M.

A SCENIC DRIVE

From South Kortwright, drive over the mountains to Bovina. The climb up affords beautiful views and the drive across the top takes you past black-and-white Holsteins and grazing horses against green fields, silos, and rust or gray barns topped with weather vanes.

Bovina Center is a tiny community with a firehouse, community hall, and a one-room museum filled with local memorabilia—clothes, pictures, agricultural implements, photographs.

MARGARETVILLE AREA LODGING AND DINING

Opened in 1918, the **Kass Inn,** Rte. 30, Margaretville, NY 12455 (tel. 914/586-9844 or 586-4841), was started by the current hostess's father as an eight-room farmhouse. Now, it maintains 68 rooms, 10 with kitchens. There's a distinctly homey feel to the place. The dining room and public areas accommodate Heide's father's eclectic collection of gilt-framed landscapes and portraits, Tiffany-style lamps, and furniture, including a huge old woodstove whose top is large enough to use as a dessert table. Facilities include an 18-hole golf course (cross-country skiing in winter), two tennis courts, a few hundred acres for hunting, an outdoor pool, shuffleboard, and other similar games. Belleayre is close by for the downhill-skiing enthusiast. On summer weekends there's dining and dancing to a band, along with movies and bridge and game nights.

RATES: In summer, hotel rooms with private bath but no TV or air conditioning run $65 to $75 per day, MAP. During the winter (from December 15 to April 1), the charge is $55 per person, MAP; $36.50 for bed-and-breakfast.

In the center of Margaretville, the owners of the Roxbury Run also operate the **Binnekill Square Restaurant** (tel. 914/586-4884), built over the narrow creek. Dining rooms have a combination of butcher block, stained glass, and comb-back Windsor chairs. The menu features a variety of beef, veal, seafood, and chicken dishes, priced around $10.50.

LUNCH: Tuesday to Saturday from noon to 3 P.M. DINNER: Tuesday to Sunday from 5 P.M. Closed Monday.

BEAVERKILL VALLEY LODGING AND DINING

Beaver Kill Valley Inn, Lew Beach, NY 12753 (tel. 914/439-4844), located in a wonderfully restful wilderness spot, makes a marvelous, unpretentious retreat. Originally built in 1895 especially for sport fishermen, it stands on the banks of the Beaverkill—you can actually fall asleep to the sound of flowing water. In restoring the place the emphasis has been on solid comforts—really comfortable armchairs and sofas in the sitting room, real logs burning in the fireplace, plenty of books about the Catskills for readers to peruse, ceramic lamps on the tables.

It's a comfortable place—the kind you look forward to coming home to from a good day's fishing—where you can relish a good meal in the oak-furnished dining room, relax in front of the fire, play a hand of cards in the game room in front of a blazing fire, enjoy a game of billiards downstairs in the plushly furnished, carpeted billiard room, or a game of table tennis also set on wall-to-wall carpeting. Also on the property are tennis and an indoor swimming pool housed in a converted barn and (can you believe it!) fully equipped with an ice cream parlor. The grounds are well kept, the lawn has a finely trimmed smooth croquet court, and there are six miles of Beaverkill waters for private fishing in spring and fall. The pond is perfect for skating. The stained glass panels found throughout the ground floor of the house are quite beautiful, especially the one in the sitting room. They were created by Cynthia Richardson, an artist from Massachusetts. On Friday night a buffet-style dinner is served from 7:30 to 10 P.M.; Saturday lunch is also a buffet. You can make special dietary requests. Hors d'oeuvres are placed in the bar at cocktail hour.

There are 20 rooms. In the inn itself they're not large because space was used to add private bathrooms during the renovation. Most have iron-and-brass beds, colorful quilts, oak dressers, chairs, and sidetables, and solid-wood closets. Additional, somewhat simpler accommodations are available at Ardsley House and also at the Quill Gordon Lodge, which some people prefer because it is almost austere, has a huge fireplace, and has always been a fishing lodge. Finally, the house has a wrap-around porch furnished with wicker and a swing seat for positive relaxation.

RATES: American Plan, $95 per person double with private bath on weekdays, $125 per person on weekends.

A mile or less up the road, the Wolff fishing school is famous. It offers courses in the spring on the mysteries of fly-fishing.

A TOUCH OF FRANCE—ROUTE 28 FROM SHANDAKEN TO MOUNT TREMPER

Along this stretch of road, many French communities have grown up primarily, I suppose, because the terrain is peculiarly reminiscent of certain areas in France, most obviously the Pyrénées. For this reason a number of fine restaurants are found along the way.

SHANDAKEN LODGING AND DINING

Albert Pollack, who owns a chain of movie theaters, and interior designer Gisele took over this home in 1972. At the time it was meant to be a quiet retreat from city life, but as more and more friends came to visit, they decided to make a habit of it and continue the practice of having only their friends and their friends' guests and referrals stay with them for weekends in very proper houseguest fashion. Consequently, the **Shandaken Inn,** Shandaken, NY 12480 (tel. 914/688-5100), requires no advertising.

Originally a dairy barn, the house has experienced several incarnations, from golf clubhouse to ski lodge, and currently country inn. It has been tastefully decorated by Gisele, who installed a glowing copper bar, decorated the stone fireplace with copper pans and utensils, and put about all manner of antiques—decoys, samplers, and basketry of all sorts—that impart a delightful country air to the comfortable sitting areas. Each of the 12 guest rooms has been decorated differently, some with wicker, but all rather simply, in fact. A typical weekend might begin with your arrival on Friday in time for dinner, which is personally prepared by Gisele at 8:30 P.M. The ingredients would be fresh local produce—striped bass, filet mignon, rack of lamb, accompanied by appetizers, salads, and desserts, such as her classic raspberry tarts—the kind of fare that only the French seem to know the secret of baking. For the rest of the weekend you can relax, or go skiing, or pretty much do whatever you like, returning in the evening for cocktails, dinner, and an informal soirée with other houseguests. There's also tennis and a swimming pool. No children accepted.

RATES: $175 a day per couple, with breakfast and dinner. Open weekends only.

Auberge des 4 Saisons, Rte. 42, Shandaken, NY 12480 (tel. 914/688-2223), has been well known for its cuisine ever since Éduard (Dadou) LaBeille, a waiter at Le Pavillon, Henri Soule's legendary Manhattan restaurant, established this hunting lodge here in 1954. In 1984 Tim and Liliane Knab took over the inn and lured Pierre Fauré, the former chef, out of retirement. The menu is classically French. Among the appetizers are a pâté de lapin, hors d'oeuvres variés, and champignons à la grecque, which are followed by a selection of fish and fowl. For example, cotelette de porc au raisin, lapin au vin blanc, suprême de volaille au Calvados, foie de veau Bercy, truite meunière, and filet mignon béarnaise are among the offerings. Soufflé glacé au Grand Marnier is the dessert to choose. Sample. Prices range from $11 to $19. There are 18 rooms in the inn, just large enough for a bed and sink, and another 18 rooms in a chalet, which has more modern amenities including private baths. It's separated from the inn by a tennis court. There's also an outdoor pool. Belleayre is only six miles away.

RATES: $51 to $71 per person double, MAP. DINNER: June to September, 5:30 to 9:30 P.M. daily, Friday to Sunday only in other months.

DINING CHOICES EN ROUTE

Rudis, Rte. 28, Big Indian (tel. 914/254-4005), is popular for its creative Orientally influenced continental/American cuisine. For instance, you can enjoy curry of chicken in pastry, duck with red miso sauce and shitaake mushrooms, vegetable kebab, bluefish teriyaki, or shell steak au poivre. To start, there's New Orleans shrimp served cold with a Créole sauce, warm goat-cheese salad baked and served on a bed of spinach, or sautéed duck livers with port wine sauce and canteloupe. Peanut-butter cheesecake, peach cobbler, and chocolate mousse are dessert favorites. Prices run $10.50 to $18. You can dine in the solarium, densely filled with plants, or in another cozy dining area. At lunch, omelets, sandwiches, and burgers are available.

LUNCH: Daily in summer, weekends only in winter. DINNER: Daily in summer, Thursday to Monday in winter.

Sweet Sue's, on Main Street in Phoenicia, is a great breakfast place for such taste treats as peach, apple, whole-wheat, and oatmeal pancakes, plus other healthy, wholesome fare. It's down-home and simple, with tables sporting floral cloths.

HOURS: 6 A.M. to 3 P.M. daily.

MOUNT TREMPER LODGING

The **Mount Tremper Inn,** Rte. 212, South Wittenberg Road (P.O. Box 51), Mount Tremper, NY 12457 (tel. 914/688-9938), looks very inviting—white clapboard with green shutters and a porch gaily hung with flower baskets and set with Adirondack-style chairs. It looks very attractive, but I couldn't rouse anyone. Do check it out.

RATES: $55 with shared bath, $70 with private bath, $85 for a suite.

A Zen Monastery

Zen Mountain Monastery, P.O. Box 197, Mount Tremper, NY 12457 (tel. 914/688-2228), offers bunk accommodations in dorms to those who are seriously interested in Zen. The daily schedule runs from 4:45 A.M. wakeup and dawn meditation to evening meditation.

RATES: A weekend retreat will cost $95 to $125.

MOUNT TREMPER DINING

At **La Duchesse Ann,** 4 Miller Rd., Mount Tremper (tel. 914/688-5260), lace tablecloths, oak columns, and a wonderfully ornate woodstove make for romantic dining. Try the terrines, soups, or escargots to start, and follow with a warming lapin provençale, entrecôte au poivre, or a simple sole meunière. The adjacent crêperie is open on weekends for delicious savory and dessert crêpes —everything from ham and bacon to chocolate bananas, and apples.

DINNER: Monday to Thursday from 6 to 9:30 P.M., until 11 P.M. on Friday and Saturday, from 4 to 9 P.M., on Sunday; closed Tuesday and Wednesday. BRUNCH: Sunday 10 a.m. to 4 p.m. To get there, turn off Rte. 28 onto 212 north, and then turn left onto old Rte. 28. The restaurant is on the right, set back from the road.

GLENFORD AND WEST HURLEY

Even closer to Woodstock and also to Kingston, these two communities each possess a fine dining choice.

At **Le Refuge du Lac,** Maverick Road, Glenford (tel. 914/657-8934), you can dine in simple French country surroundings, and enjoy such specialties as venison in season, carré d'agneau, rabbit, sirloin bordelaise, and such fish dishes as salmon Troisgros or red snapper in lobster sauce, priced from $9.75 to $15. Begin with a celeri remoulade, pâté, or bouillabaisse, and top it all off with a classic crêpe suzette or crème caramel.

DINNER: From 6 P.M. daily.

The **Red Vest,** 422 Spillway Rd., West Hurley (tel. 914/331-1896), is well known for a variety of seafood, veal, and chicken dishes. HOURS: Wednesday to Saturday, from 5:30 P.M., from 2 P.M. on Sunday; closed Monday and Tuesday.

WOODSTOCK

AREA ATTRACTIONS

The Byrdcliffe Crafts Colony was established here in 1902, the Art Students League summer school a few years later, the Woodstock Artists' Association in 1910, and the Maverick Chamber Music Festivals in 1916, and ever since people have been attracted to Woodstock, a town that gave its name to a whole generation when 400,000 people came in 1969 to celebrate the Woodstock Music Festival about 60 miles west.

Today, all of the early organizations remain, except the Art Students League, which has been replaced by the **Woodstock School of Art** (tel. 914/679-8746 or 679-7558). The **Woodstock Playhouse** (tel. 914/679-2436) is also one of the oldest summer-stock theaters in the state. The town is filled with galleries and boutiques. Abigail Robin gives **tours** that include visits to studios, lunch, shopping, and transportation. Write P.O. Box 553, Woodstock, NY 12498, or call 914/679-7969. If you don't want to take a tour, stop in at the **Woodstock Artists' Association,** 28 Tinker St. (tel. 914/679-2940), for their changing exhibits and lectures. HOURS: 1 to 4 P.M. daily except Thursday. Also contact the **Woodstock Guild,** 34 Tinker St. (tel. 914/679-2079), which, besides offering classes/workshops, operates the Kleinert Arts Center, which offers year-round contemporary exhibits and musical and other performances. (HOURS: 11 A.M. to 6 P.M. daily except Tuesday.) They also operate the **Crafts Shop** (tel. 914/679-2688), selling the best in regional crafts (HOURS: 11 A.M. to 6 P.M. daily except Tuesday), and the **Byrdcliffe Arts Colony,** which offers residences and studio space from May to October to artists, craftspeople, musicians, and writers. The Byrdcliffe Barn is the site of extensive programming during the summer months, including classes and performances. If you wish, you can obtain a pamphlet outlining a walking tour of the arts and crafts colony.

WOODSTOCK LODGING AND DINING

As far as Woodstock accommodations right in town, **Twin Gables,** 73 Tinker St., Woodstock, NY 12498 (tel. 914/679-9479), looks homey and attractive. Out front there's a stone patio set with tubs of flowers. Inside there seems to be a Victorian sitting room, but again no one was home when I called, so I leave it up to you, good readers.

RATES: $20 to $28 with shared bath, $35 to $40 with private bath.

Best dining is found at the **Little Bear** (tel. 914/679-9497), in nearby Bearsville, where you can dine on Hunan, Peking, Cantonese, and Szechuan fare out on a patio overlooking the creek which is illuminated at night. Prices range from $6.

LUNCH: Wednesday to Sunday from noon to 4 P.M. DINNER: 4 to 11 P.M. Wednesday to Sunday.

Another highly recommended Woodstock eatery is **Whistler's,** 261 Tinker St. (tel. 914/679-9522), which features the latest Cajun specialties—pan-blackened redfish, Cajun prime rib, and jambalaya. Other dishes listed on the menu include southern fried chicken with mashed potatoes and gravy, apple-stuffed pork chops, and barbecued ribs. To start, try shrimp in green sauce, or guacamole or, best of all, Cajun popcorn-crawfish deep-fried with Créole sauce. Prices run $6 to $14. The decor is plain—tables brightened by red cloths and a bar hung with a few farm implements.

DINNER: Monday and Thursday from 5:30 to 9 P.M., on Friday and Saturday until 11 P.M., on Sunday from 4 to 9 P.M.; closed Tuesday and Wednesday.

In Woodstock itself, **Joshua's Café,** 51 Tinker St. (tel. 914/679-9575), can be trusted to serve large portions of healthy Middle Eastern fare—hummus, baba ganoush, and shaslik, along with a dozen or so salads and a very extensive menu. Main courses include shish kebab, kilic sis (skewered swordfish with tomatoes, celery, mushrooms, and peppers), batata charp (potato pies filled with vegetables or meat), and paella couscous (clams, mussels, chicken, sausage, shrimp, peas, tomatoes, and onions). Dishes are priced from $9 to $13. At brunch ten or so omelets are offered, from fried bananas and melted cheese to sautéed onions, potatoes, tomatoes, and parsley, along with a dozen egg dishes including whole-grain pancakes and french toast made with challah. A small place, it's always crowded with an interesting-looking artsy crowd. Nostalgic '60s style.

LUNCH AND DINNER: 11 A.M. to 11 P.M.

Deanie's, Rtes. 212 and 375 (tel. 914/679-6508), is another oldtime Woodstock favorite serving broiled salmon, sirloin, prime rib, scallops, and other traditional dishes priced from $11 to $21. People gather at the wood bar and in summer on the porch.

DINNER: Wednesday to Monday from 5 P.M. to 1 A.M.; closed Tuesday.

Other convenient dining choices exist in Mount Tremper, Glenford, and West Hurley, already discussed in the previous sections.

THE RESORTS OF THE SOUTHERN CATSKILLS

Many people love the resorts of the Catskills and feel they offer opportunities for an active, entertainment-filled vacation at the best prices anywhere in the world. Others just don't appreciate what they have to offer. Whatever your opinion, here follows a brief outline of what's available where.

The most legendary, **Grossinger's,** closed in 1986, but others continue the tradition.

The **Concord,** Kiamesha Lake, NY 12751 (tel. 914/794-4000 or 212/244-3500, or toll free 800/431-3850), is the largest and most immaculately kept. Manicured approaches to the ten-floor, box-like buildings only serve to reinforce this image. The lobby at this 1,250-room resort is always crammed with people coming and going, rushing from one activity or meeting to the next; a whole folder details the activities planned for every minute of the day from 7 A.M. to 10:30 P.M. On the 3,000-acre resort there are two 18-hole golf courses and one 9-hole; 16 indoor and 24 outdoor tennis courts are available night or day (there's a five-minute forfeit time and a sheet on how to reserve a court), indoor and outdoor swimming pools, ice-skating rinks, downhill and cross-country skiing, boating and fishing on Kiamesha Lake, handball and basketball courts, horseback riding and jogging trails, health clubs, and more. For evening entertainment there are three nightclubs.

RATES: Prices change seasonally, and many different packages are offered on holiday weekends, etc., but just to give you some idea, the per-person rates are $75 to $105 from December through March (full American Plan), $100 to $140 from July 1 to Labor Day, depending on where your room is located (midweek rates are lower; weekly rates are available). The quoted rates also apply to the famous singles weekends.

The **Nevele Hotel,** Ellenville, NY 12428 (tel. 914/647-6000 or 212/244-0800), has 465 rooms. Its 1,000 acres provide all kinds of sports facilities—18-hole golf course, five indoor and nine outdoor tennis courts, platform tennis, racquetball, outdoor and indoor pool, health clubs, athletic areas (basketball, badminton, volleyball, softball), horseback riding, boating (rowboats and paddleboats), bicycles, indoor-outdoor ice-skating rink, downhill and cross-country skiing, sledding, miniature golf, and plenty of children's activities. The buildings and grounds are well kept. There's nightly dancing in the Safari Lounge and entertainment in the Stardust Room.

RATES (full American Plan): $70 to $100 daily per person from April 22 to June 27, $80 to $99 from June 28 to Labor Day, $71 to $92 from Labor Day to December 18, $71 to $92 from December 21 to April 10. Midweek rates are less, and special rates apply on holidays.

Kutsher's Country Club, Monticello, NY 12701 (tel. 914/794-6000 or 212/243-3112), has the personal touch of Milton, Helen, and Mark Kutsher. Again, everything's on the premises—18 holes of golf, four racquetball courts, indoor and outdoor tennis courts, downhill and cross-country skiing, indoor and outdoor pools, health club, jogging track, snowmobiling, indoor ice skating, boating and fishing on the lake, bicycling, basketball, yoga, miniature golf, two nightclubs, and a supervised day camp and teen program.

RATES: Unavailable at press time.

Stevensville Country Club, Swan Lake, NY 12783 (tel. 914/292-8000 or 212/736-1874), overlooking Swan Lake, is smaller and offers slightly fewer facilities. There's an 18-hole golf course, four indoor and six outdoor tennis courts, four racquetball and handball courts, ice skating, roller skating, snowmobiling, health club, indoor and outdoor pool, fishing and boating on the lake, and nightly entertainment. Skiing and horseback riding are nearby.

RATES: Unavailable at press time.

Browns', Loch Sheldrake, NY 12759 (tel. 914/434-5151 or 212/868-4970), doesn't open in winter, but summer activities are plenty—eight tennis courts, handball, basketball, softball, volleyball facilities, horseback riding, two 18-hole golf courses (free), outdoor and indoor pool, and health club. At night the Jerry Lewis Theatre Club is known for its stars—Sammy Davis, Jr., Shirley Bassey, and Wayne Newton have all appeared here recently. There's also another club/disco. Most of the facilities are free.

RATES: Unavailable at press time.

CATSKILLS ACTIVITIES

BOATING: In Catskill, Riverview Marine Services, 103 Main St. (tel. 518/943-5311), offers small craft for rent to use on the Hudson River.

CAMPING: Backpackers can camp anywhere on state-owned land in the Catskill Forest Preserves and State Reforestation Areas, as well as in the lean-tos provided along the trails. For information, maps, etc., write to the Bureau of Forest Preserve and Protection Management, New York State Department of Environmental Conservation, 50 Wolf Rd., Room 412, Albany, NY 12233.

During the summer, from May 23 to September 1, campsites in the Cats-kill State Forest Preserves can be reserved at least 8 days in advance through Ticketron for stays of 3 to 14 nights.

North Lake, on Rte. 23A, three miles northeast of Haines Falls, NY 12436 (tel. 518/589-5058), open from May 1 to October 1, offers spectacular scenery, swimming, fishing, and boat rentals on two lakes.

Other New York Environmental Conservation camping areas, all open from May 1 to September 30, are at Beaverkill, in Roscoe (tel. 914/439-4281), offering swimming and fishing; Kenneth L. Wilson, east of Mount Tremper (tel. 914/679-7020), with swimming and fishing; Mongaup Pond, north of De Bruce (tel. 914/439-4233), with swimming, fishing, and boat rentals; and Woodland Valley, southwest of Phoenicia (tel. 914/688-7647), with fishing.

CANOEING: Camping-canoeing is enjoyed along the Delaware from Hancock to Port Jervis. For information, contact Bob Lander's Canoe Rentals, P.O. Box 376, Narrowsburg, NY 12764 (tel. 914/252-3925), who rents canoes, kayaks, and tubes and also runs various canoe-camping or canoe-motel packages. He will transport your car from your embarkation point to debar-kation point for prices that are determined by the distance.

Other canoeing outfitters include: Curt's Canoe Rentals, Rte. 97, Spar-rowbush, NY 12780 (tel. 914/856-5024), and Silver Canoe Rentals, 37 S. Maple Ave., Port Jervis, NY 12771 (tel. 914/856-7055).

The Esopus Creek also offers canoeing, kayaking, and tubing opportuni-ties. Bring your kayak, canoe, or tube, and board the Catskill Mountain Railroad open train, which will bring you from Mount Pleasant to Phoeni-cia, where you can ride the river back to your car. Trains operate daily from early July to Labor Day. Tubes can be rented. For information, call 914/688-7246 or 914/679-6608.

FISHING: Roscoe, at the junction of the Beaverkill and the Willowemoc Rivers, is known locally as Trout Town, where the Antrim Lodge Hotel (tel. 607/498-4191) is a favorite fisherman's haunt. The Esopus Creek is also famous for rainbow and brown trout and there's additional trout fishing in the Neversink and Ramapo Rivers. Shad and walleyed pike inhabit the Dela-ware. Courses are given at Wolf Fishing School.

FRUIT PICKING: For information, contact any County Public Information Office or else write to the New York Department of Agriculture and Markets, Direct Marketing Program, Building 8, State Campus, Albany, NY 12235.

GOLF: Windham Country Club, South Street (tel. 518/734-9910), 18 holes, par 71. Many resorts also have courses.

HORSEBACK RIDING: *Delhi:* Hilltop Stables New Road, Bovina Ctr. (tel. 607/832-4342) charges $6 an hour and also offers overnight trail rides for $25. *Tannersville:* Silver Springs Ranch, Rte. 16, Tannersville (tel. 518/589-5559). *Woodstock:* Circle Tee Stable, Lower Glasco Turnpike (tel. 914/679-9342). See resorts also.

HIKING: Trails abound. Slide Mountain, the highest peak in the Catskills, offers wonderful rewards at any time of the year. Near Oliverea, off Rte. 42, which winds along beside the Neversink down through Frost Valley.

SKIING: The best is undoubtedly at Hunter Mountain (see the section in this chapter), but there are other choices. I have already mentioned the classy ambience of Windham. One other choice remains—Belleayre. P.O. Box 313, Highmount, NY 12441 (tel. 914/254-5600, or toll free 800/942-6904), which is good for beginners and experts. Vertical rise is 1,265 feet. There are 25 trails, four chairs, two T-bars, and one J-Bar. Only 24% snowmaking capacity. For cross-country: Belleayre Mountain, Highmount (tel. 914/254-5601); Frost Valley YMCA Camp, Oliverea (tel. 914/985-2291); Hunter Mountain's area is at Tannersville Hyer Meadows (tel. 518/589-5361).

SKY DIVING: Prattsville Mountain Hi Parachutes, 13 miles west of Hunter at Maben's Airport (tel. 518/299-3664), charges $100 to $125 for a first jump course.

SOARING AND HANG-GLIDING: Centers for this are on the southern edge of the Catskills at Wurtsboro and Ellenville. For hang-gliding, contact Thermal-Up, Rte. 209, Ellenville, NY 12428 (tel. 914/647-3489). For soaring, Wurtsboro Flight Service, Inc., Wurtsboro Airport, Rte. 209, Wurtsboro, NY 12790 (tel. 914/888-2791).

WILDERNESS EXPERIENCES: For specially arranged trips through the mountains, contact Catskill Wilderness Experiences (tel. 518/734-3104).

THE HAMPTONS

DISTANCES IN MILES: Westhampton, 76; Hampton Bays, 86; Southampton, 94; East Hampton, 109
ESTIMATED DRIVING TIMES: Anywhere from two to four hours, depending on Long Island Expressway traffic.

DRIVING: Take I-495 (Long Island Expressway) to Exit 70 (Rte. 111 south), and then take Rte. 27 east.
BUS: The Hampton Jitney offers express service—and they mean it. Despite the odds of beating the traffic back on Sunday night, their drivers are given instructions on all the side roads and back routes and often arrive in the city to standing ovations from passengers. Reservations required. Call 516/283-4600 or 212/936-0440.
TRAIN: Long Island Rail Road from Penn Station stops at each of the Hamptons. Call 718/454-5477 for timetable information.

Special Events To Plan Your Trip Around
JUNE: Old Whaler's Festival in Sag Harbor (early June).
JULY 4: Fireworks at East Hampton Main Beach (after 9 P.M.).
JULY: George Plimpton's Fireworks Show is a benefit for Guild Hall; admission charge (early July).
Clothesline Art Show, Guild Hall, East Hampton (late July).
East Hampton Ladies Village Improvement Society Fair (usually the last Friday in July).
AUGUST: Westhampton Beach Art Show (early August).

Fishermen's Fair at Ashawagh Hall, Springs, East Hampton (early August).

Hampton Classic Horse Show, Bridgehampton (late August/early September).

SEPTEMBER: Shinnecock Indian Reservation Powwow (Labor Day Weekend). For information, call the Shinnecock Community Center (tel. 516/283-9266).

For further information about New York in general, contact the Division of Tourism, New York State Department of Commerce, One Commerce Plaza, Albany, NY 12245 (tel. 518/474-4116).

For general information about Long Island, contact the Long Island Tourism and Convention Commission, 213 Carleton Ave., Central Islip, NY 11722 (tel. 516/234-4959); the Suffolk County Department of Economic Development, H. Lee Dennison Bldg., Veterans Memorial Hwy., Hauppauge, NY 11788 (tel. 516/360-4800), can also provide information.

For specific information, contact the Hampton Bays Chamber of Commerce, P.O. Box 64, Hampton Bays, NY 11946 (tel. 516/728-2211); the Southampton Chamber of Commerce, 76 Main St., Southampton, NY 11968 (tel. 516/283-0402); and the East Hampton Chamber of Commerce, 74 Park Pl., East Hampton, NY 11937 (tel. 516/324-0362).

In Paris they're promoted as New York's Riviera; in a *New York* magazine article a few years ago, Marie Brenner described them acidly as suburbia by the sea. They, of course, are the legendary Hamptons, seven or so villages clustered along the South Fork with access to miles and miles of white sand Atlantic beaches backed by undulating dunes—a miracle coastline for any uptight urban dweller. The beaches here are certainly as good as any in the world, which is one reason to come to the Hamptons. The other is to participate in the social scene, a fashion scene that *Women's Wear Daily* regards as trend-setting and sees fit to comment upon.

The Hamptons did not always engender such opposing opinions and tart commentary. Since their founding in the mid-17th century by colonists from New England, most of these villages on the east end of Long Island remained quiet farming towns at least until the late 19th century when they began to attract urban emigrants. As early as 1890 a journalist observed that on the South Fork people wore fancy blazers, dressed a good deal, played tennis, and attended hops. The scene really hasn't changed that much. The game is still tennis (along with a few others), people still dress a good deal and wear fancy blazers, but their hops tend to be a little more camp and far more frenetic. The resort image didn't really jell, though, until the '20s when the auto emerged as a popular mode of transportation and the Maidstone Club opened its bathing facilities. Today's celebrity-studded scene, however, can be traced more directly to the mid-1940s when Jackson Pollock and Lee Krasner arrived and were soon followed by the de Koonings, Frank O'Hara, Larry Rivers, Nick Carone, and Barney Rosset, who in turn were followed by waves of celebrities who still lend a distinct cachet to the whole area —Betty Friedan, Edward Albee, Woody Allen, Craig Claiborne, Charles Addams, E.J. Doctorow, and many, many more.

Their homes appear in *Architectural Digest* and other glossy magazines, their social lives get into the gossip columns, and inevitably there's a certain Peeping Tom quality to any visit to the Hamptons. Being seen and trying to see are an important part of the scene for some.

When Pollock arrived the potato fields were intact. Land sold for a high-priced $1,000 an acre. Today that same land sells for anywhere from $60,000 an acre and up, and the potato fields are blighted with jagged glass-and-wooden houses standing starkly on the flat lands behind the sand dunes. Designer-labeled hordes descend every summer, clogging the streets with their Mercedes, Jaguars, and de rigueur dark-blue BMWs. And with those 173,000 summer visitors have come the required gourmet food markets, boutiques, restaurants, and discos that shatter the night's quietude. For those who wish to ignore the scene, the beaches remain; for those who relish participating in the scene, then you can't find better outside of New York City. The only real problem is the Long Island Expressway. My advice is to hole up here permanently for the whole summer—never mind weekending!

Friday-Night Hassles

If you have to weekend, take heart. There are those who pride themselves on not having to punish themselves by driving anywhere on Friday night—they're the lucky ones. Those who have to leave on Friday night all have their own individual ways of beating the traffic—leaving early, leaving late, taking this route instead of that. Best advice is to check the *Times,* which always publishes a map of potential bottlenecks where roadwork is being done. Stay tuned to your radio and hope for the best.

Friday-Night Suppers

If you're headed all the way to the East End, you'll probably suffer hunger pangs en route. You can either stop at the diner at the Hampton Road turnoff into Southampton; wait until you reach Water Mill and drop into Meghan's Saloon, a pubby-bar restaurant serving some great burger combinations; or you may wait until you reach East Hampton's O'Malley's.

A Note on Bed-and-Breakfast

The following offer accommodations throughout the Hamptons: **A Reasonable**

Alternative, Inc., 117 Spring St., Port Jefferson, NY 11777 (tel. 516/928-4034); **Hampton Bed-and-Breakfast,** P.O. Box 378, East Moriches, NY 11940 (tel. 516/878-8197); and **Alternate Lodging,** P.O. Box 1782, East Hampton, NY 11937 (tel. 516/324-9449).

WESTHAMPTON BEACH, QUOGUE, AND HAMPTON BAYS

There are those who say that the Shinnecock Canal divides the more socially conscious Hamptons—Southampton and East Hampton—from the less socially conscious Hamptons.

These communities, west of the Shinnecock Canal, are (supposedly) the less socially conscious Hamptons.

Westhampton Beach, closest to the city, attracts a very fast-paced crowd, as well as a sizable number of blue bloods. Down along Dune Road, rows and rows of modern multifaceted glass-and-wood structures stretch along the beachfront. Here, on weekends you can drive past, catching the echoes of many a party, and passing the crowds and cars that jostle around the party and disco spots.

Neighboring Quogue has a far quieter, low-key approach to life, while around the corner across Tiana Bay, Hampton Bays has the most down-to-earth reputation of all and attracts families and avid fishermen.

WESTHAMPTON BEACH LODGING

Staying at either the **Dune Deck Hotel** or the **Bath and Tennis Club,** Dune Road, Westhampton, NY 11978 (tel. 516/288-4100), gives you access to a full range of facilities—ten tennis courts, two swimming pools, restaurants, a disco, and most important, the beach.

RATES: At the Dune Deck $200 to $315 double MAP; at the Bath and Tennis Club $200 to $375 double MAP. Open May to September.

The **Port o Kai,** Dune Road, Westhampton, NY 11978 (tel. 516/288-4450), offers direct access to the bay marina from early motel-style rooms, some furnished in turquoise. Staying here also gives you access to the facilities at the Bath and Tennis Club and the Dune Deck. So does staying at the Westhampton Motel on Montauk Hwy. and the Weather Vane Inn on Quogue Street. And remember, in these parts, we're talking about beach access above all else.

RATES: $150 to $183 double MAP.

QUOGUE LODGING

The **Inn at Quogue,** Quogue, NY 11959 (tel. 516/653-6560 or 212/371-3300), is one of the few accommodations that contributes to the town's reputation as a quiet stylish enclave. One mile from the beach, this 200-year-old home has 15 rooms (three sharing bathrooms), all tastefully furnished with a country combination of pine, quilts, chintz wallpapers, and an occasional wicker piece. All have telephones, and some have air conditioning and color TV. The kitchen has a fine reputation. Menus change daily. Herbs come from a garden out back. Dinner specialties might include swordfish with herb butter, duckling with raspberry

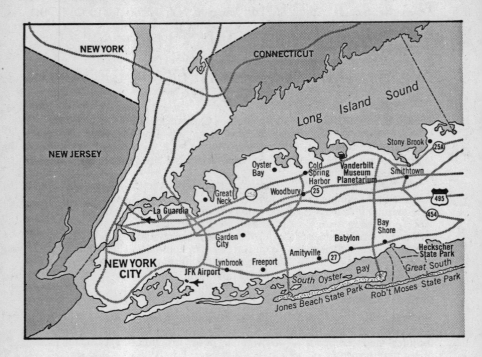

sauce, or rack of lamb. Prices range from $16 to $22.

RATES (including a continental breakfast): $150 a night double in season, 33% discount off-season (the higher prices are for rooms with private bath). DINNER: 7 to 10:30 P.M. daily. BRUNCH: Saturday and Sunday. Open from May to October 15.

WESTHAMPTON DINING

For pleasant dining, try the **Café USA,** 191 Main St., Westhampton Beach (tel. 516/288-9000), a longtime local favorite, where people gather at the bar for some good gossip or else dine in the restaurant at tables prettily adorned with glass-covered floral tablecloths set on cool flagstone floors. The menu features such entrees as gray sole with thyme and lemon butter or beef medallions with red wine and herb butter. Prices run $12.50 to $16.

DINNER: 6 to 10 P.M. on weekdays, to 11 P.M. on weekends. Open May through early October.

At the **Kruggerand Supper Club,** Westhampton (tel. 516/288-9009), trellis partitions, pink tablecloths, and hanging fuchsias make for a pretty dining room. The menu surprises, for it lists a combination of Italian and Japanese dishes—sashimi and sushi share the bill with such dishes as chicken panchetta (topped with bacon,

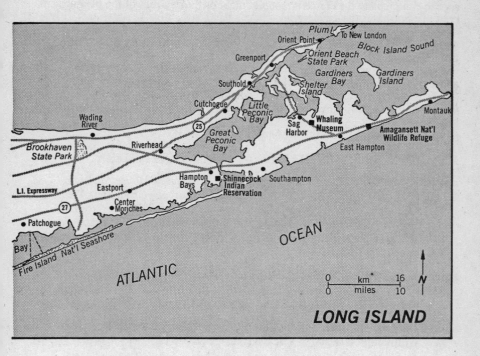

Swiss cheese, and a white wine sauce) and fettuccine primavera. Prices range from $9 for pasta Alfredo to $23 for surf and turf. Among the appetizers, gyoza and tekkamaki rubs shoulders with stuffed mushrooms and clams casino. On Sunday from 4 to 9 P.M. there's a buffet spread available that includes lobster, sushi, sashimi, mussels, veal, beef, salads, pastas, and much more, for $17. Brunch items include the usual eggs Benedict and eggs florentine, along with gyoza, hibachi shrimp, lobster, steak, and chicken and pasta items.

DINNER: Wednesday, Thursday and Sunday from 5 to 11 P.M., on Friday and Saturday until midnight, closed Tuesday. BRUNCH: Sunday from noon to 3 P.M.

HAMPTON BAYS DINING

In my opinion, the **Chart Inn,** Shinnecock Canal (tel. 516/728-1111), occupying a boat-like setting that overlooks the canal and facing west for dramatic sunsets, is one of the better seafood houses in the Hamptons. Inside upper- and lower-deck furnishings are elemental. You can always be sure of the freshness of the daily specials, written on a blackboard, which might include oysters Rockefeller, steamers, shrimp bisque, and a catch of the day—perhaps bluefish or a 1¼-pound lobster. A rich, thick clam chowder is always available—a real life- sustaining dish. A Newport-style outdoor bar with parasol tables makes an ideal spot to contemplate the crescent moon at night or the denizens of the pleasure craft that bob along the canal by day.

HOURS: Open mid-May to mid-October. Lunch is served six days a week (sandwiches and fish dishes under $8) and Sunday brunch from 10 A.M. to 3 P.M. Open from noon on.

Canal House, just east of the Shinnecock Canal bridge (tel. 516/728-1717), is another local favorite that offers a warm, comfortable French country setting. Steak au poivre, flounder stuffed with crabmeat, Long Island duckling with Grand Marnier sauce, and chicken piccata appear on the menu (priced from $10 to $13).

DINNER: Tuesday to Sunday from 5 to 9 P.M.

HAMPTON BAYS/WESTHAMPTON BEACH ACTIVITIES

BOATING: Boats can be rented in Hampton Bays at Bayview House, 32 Lighthouse Rd. (tel. 516/728-3197); Colonial Shores Resort & Marina, Inc., West Tiana Road (tel. 516/728-0011); Coor's Mariner's Cove, 9 Canoe Place Rd. (tel. 516/728-0286); Frank's Landing of Hampton Bays, Inc., 3 Rampasture Rd. (tel. 516/728-0619); and Tiana Bay Resort & Marina, 50 Rampasture Rd. (tel. 516/728-1488).

FISHING: Tony's Fishing Station, 22 Shinnecock Rd., Hampton Bays (tel. 516/728-0426). Two open boats—*Capt. Clark II* (tel. 516/728-1709) and *Jenny Rose* (tel. 516/325-1309)—dock at the Shinnecock Canal.

SOARING: Sky Sailors, Inc., Suffolk County Airport, Building 313, Rust Avenue, Westhampton Beach, NY 11978 (tel. 516/288-5858).

TENNIS: Bath & Tennis Club of Westhampton Beach, Dune Road (tel. 516/288-2500); Dune Deck Hotel, Dune Road (tel. 516/288-4100).

SOUTHAMPTON

SOUTHAMPTON ATTRACTIONS

Southampton was the first English colony established in New York State, in 1640 by colonists from Lynn, Massachusetts. It's best explored by securing a **walking-tour map** from the Southampton Chamber of Commerce at 76 Main St. (tel. 516/283-0402). To some, Southampton means money and the Society Set, and certainly a glance at the prestigious shop names on Job's Lane will only confirm that impression.

The **Parrish Art Museum** at 25 Job's Lane (tel. 516/283-2118) is the town's cultural center and also possesses significant collections of William Merritt Chase and Fairfield Porter artworks. Besides art exhibitions and lectures, the museum also offers concerts in the garden on several Saturday nights during the summer. Bring a blanket. The gardens are a lovely, restful haven, enhanced by several della Robbias. HOURS: Monday, Tuesday, Thursday, and Saturday from 10 A.M. to 5 P.M., on Sunday from 1 to 5 P.M. ADMISSION: Donation suggested.

The **Halsey Homestead** (1648), on South Main Street (tel. 516/283-3527), is the oldest English saltbox in the state and furnished appropriately. HOURS: Mid-June to mid-September, Tuesday to Sunday from 11 A.M. to 4:30 P.M.

The **Southampton Historical Museum,** 17 Meeting House Lane (tel. 516/283-2494), will provide some grasp of local history from Indian and colonial times onward. HOURS: Mid-June to mid-September, Tuesday to Sunday from 11 A.M. to 5 P.M.

Southampton is also the site of the **Shinnecock Indian Reservation,** where the famous Powwow is held on Labor Day weekend.

SOUTHAMPTON LODGING

Obviously, your first choice would be to stay with friends who have a house, preferably south of the highway. If this cannot be arranged, then there's at least one very attractive alternative.

Marta Byer and Martin White have created some of the most original, inspired accommodations in the Hamptons at the **Village Latch Inn,** 101 Hill St., Southampton, NY 11968 (tel. 516/283-2160), only minutes from Job's Lane and one block from the beach. Set back behind a privet hedge, the handsome clapboard building was once the annex of the old Irving Hotel, then the premier accommodation in the area. Today throughout the house you'll come upon all kinds of fascinating collectibles that Marta has gathered on travels around the world, especially dolls and puppets arranged in strikingly different ways—a doll's head cupped in a bird's nest, another doll seated on a small chair, an open parasol on the stair landing—and in the parlors you'll find some intriguing assemblage artworks of Marta's.

Each of the 24 rooms in the main house is furnished differently. Room 68, for example, has a pair of comfy wing chairs and a fireplace; Room 58's centerpiece is a sleigh bed, while one of the spacious suites offers a bedroom with handsome bed covered with a hand-woven quilt, an oak chest and rocker, and a sitting room with wicker chairs placed in front of the fireplace.

The last few years Marta has spent carefully restoring and decorating several historic houses that now stand on the three acres behind the main house. Each one is more appealing than the next. For example, the 100-year-old Homestead now has nine bedrooms and eight baths; the spacious shared living room is filled with leather and Victorian couches and a large Regency dining table set close to the kitchen, which has its very own fireplace, a brilliant Mexican tile floor, and a vast Garland range. From the Homestead guests can step out into the "spa," located in a Victorian-style greenhouse furnished comfortably with wicker. On the other side of the "spa," another house has been beautifully transformed with plush furnishings and objects collected around the world—masks, puppets and other objets d'art from Africa's Ivory Coast, South America, and India.

Between the main and other houses stretches a large lawn for croquet, a pool with privet hedge providing privacy, and tennis court. Bikes are available for rent. A full breakfast of bagels, cream cheese, ham, cheese, yogurt, fruit, and homemade breads and cakes is served in the dining room with its brilliant-purple director's chairs. An ultra-comfortable sitting room with a fireplace filled with plants and appealing objects completes this very inviting accommodation.

RATES: From $95 in midweek, from $125 on weekends. Open year round.

The **Old Post House Inn,** 136 Main St., Southampton, NY 11968 (tel. 516/283-1717), is in fact a 1705 and 1730 addition to the 17th-century farmhouse next door (now the Post House restaurant). It's owned and operated by Ed and Cecile Courville, both retirees, who really take care of their guests to the extent that Ed drives a van to the beach every two hours and will even pick up guests at the jitney stop or the railroad station. Step across the latticed porch furnished with wicker rockers and tables and turn left into the original parlor with its original 1705 beams and fireplace with adjacent warming cupboards. It's now furnished with comfy armchairs, sofas, and an Eastlake marble coffee table. An antique quilt adorns the walls.

There are seven rooms, all with private bath and air conditioning. Each is named after a local historical figure and contains a plaque relating that individual's contributions to the community. Each is furnished differently. The Albert G. Post Room, for example, contains an attractive walnut bed and matching armoire, and a chair as well as a dresser, sidetable, two comfy chairs, and a wrought-iron floor lamp. The floor is covered with a dusky-rose carpet and the windows with chintz curtains. The Captain John Halburt Room features an iron bed covered with a pastel quilt, a chest with shaving mirror, turquoise slip-covered chairs, and a pine armoire. In several rooms the wide-plank floors have been left exposed and softened with rag rugs. Rooms on the third floor have a different feel altogether, primarily because the ceilings are higher. The Lion Gardner Room has height enough for a highback Victorian oak bed, covered with a beautiful Marseille coverlet.

The building is full of history, so much so that Ed has prepared a paper about it. An archeological dig in the cellar turned up 17th- and 18th-century bottles, primitive Indian basketry pieces, and traces of shellfish, vegetables, and fruit that may well substantiate the local stories that this house was a stop on the Underground Railroad.

At breakfast Cecile uses varied chinas on which to serve croissants, muffins, tea, and coffee, along with homemade jellies and fresh fruit.

RATES: From roughly May 23 through June 26, $115 on weekends and $90 on weekdays; from June 27 through Labor Day, $140 on weekends and $115 on weekdays; October through May 1, $75 on weekends and $65 on weekdays; in September, $110 on weekends and $80 on weekdays.

A spare and modern look has been achieved at the **Country Inn,** 200 Hill St., Southampton, NY 11966 (tel. 516/283-4849). Downstairs in the living area, a bamboo-and-glass coffee table is set against an off-white couch, and throw rugs soften the polished wood floors. The rooms are furnished for romance with frilly sheets and pillowcases. Croissants, fresh fruit, cereal, juice, and coffee will greet you in your room each morning.

RATES: $80 to $160, depending on season.

Otherwise, Southampton accommodations fall into the motel category. The **Sandpiper,** 1655 North Hwy. (Rte. 27), Southampton, NY 11968 (tel. 516/283-7600 or 283-7666), has pleasant modern accommodations with TV, air conditioning, and phones. Accommodations are in standard motel-style rooms, efficiencies, or one- or two-bedroom units complete with kitchen/living room with full view of the beach and barbecue facilities on patios. There's also a pool and tennis courts.

RATES: $290 to $390 for rooms per 2½-day weekend; $400 for efficiencies; one-bedroom cottages are $650 a week. These are in-season prices.

The **Southampton Inn,** 91 Hill St., Southampton, NY 11968 (tel. 516/283-6500), offers fully appointed modern rooms plus an outdoor swimming pool, two tennis courts, and dining facilities.

RATES: $75 to $85 double on off-season weekends, $225 to $265 double for the two-night minimum on summer weekends.

SOUTHAMPTON DINING

Breakfast Choices

The **Buttery,** 30 Main St. (tel. 516/283-1233), serves some really first-class breakfast and luncheon items—from fruit waffles to burgers and fresh-made daily soups. There's a special brunch on Sunday, $4.95 at this writing, that includes either a Bloody Mary or champagne and orange juice for starters.

HOURS: Monday to Friday from 7 A.M. to 4 P.M., on Saturday from 8 A.M. to 5 P.M., and on Sunday from 8 A.M. until 2 P.M.

Luncheon and Dinner Choices

The favored seating at the **Post House,** 136 Main St. (tel. 516/283-9696), is in the cozy low-beamed bar room with a fireplace or the adjacent room, which also has a fireplace. The fare is traditional American. Prices run from $13 for sautéed breast of chicken with tarragon sauce or pasta du jour to $18 for grilled lamb chops with fresh mint sauce or filet mignon béarnaise. Other dishes include steak au poivre, calves' liver with Pommery mustard sauce, and broiled flounder with dill sauce. Among the appetizers are East End clam fritters and seafood quenelles. Desserts include coconut crème brûlée, apple pie, and ice creams. The brunch menu contains an interesting mixture of egg dishes—steak and eggs, omelets, scrambled eggs with curried seafood—along with poached fish or pot pie du jour.

LUNCH: Monday to Saturday from noon to 4 P.M., in season only. DINNER: Monday to Thursday and Sunday from 5 to 10 P.M., on Friday and Saturday to 11 P.M. BRUNCH: Sunday from noon to 4 P.M.

People continue to flock to Southampton's **John Duck, Jr.,** at Prospect and North Main (tel. 516/283-0311), for the reliable value of duckling with apple raisin dressing, soup, and cole slaw, all for a mere $12.25. Decor is unpretentious. Other menu items—scampi, softshell crabs, prime rib, and steaks—are priced from $11.25 to $16.

HOURS: 11:30 A.M. to 10:30 P.M. daily in season; closed Monday off-season.

Old Guard Southamptonites still dine at **Balzarini's,** 210 Hampton Rd. (tel. 516/283-0704), a simple home-style restaurant whose windows are thrown open during the summer months. Northern Italian specialties predominate—lasagne, veal piccata, and scampi—supplemented by steak and other meat dishes, priced from $8.75 to $18.

DINNER: Daily to 10 P.M. on weekdays, to 11 P.M. on weekends, in July and August; closed Monday and Tuesday during other months and from mid-January to mid-March.

At **Barristers,** 36 Main St. (tel. 516/283-6206), the luncheon menu of salads, sandwiches, and burgers (all under $6) is supplemented at night by such specials as mussels steamed in red and white wine, filet mignon maître d', or stir-fried shrimp with ginger and broccoli. Most dishes average $12. The pleasant shaded courtyard out back is a favorite for summer dining.

LUNCH: 11:30 A.M. to 4 P.M. daily. DINNER: 5:30 to 11 P.M. daily.

The other famous in-town lunching spot is the **Driver's Seat,** 62 Job's Lane (tel. 516/283-6606), which offers light lunch fare inside or out in a secluded courtyard. At dinner such entrees as porterhouse steak and tortellini with cream sauce are priced from $9.

HOURS: The kitchen is open daily from 11:30 A.M. to 11 P.M., from noon on Sunday.

Le Chef, at the corner of Main Street and Nugent (tel. 516/283-8581), is a pleasant restaurant where tables sport crisp white tablecloths and bentwood chairs. Good for breakfast—french toast, pancakes, and egg dishes—and for luncheon when salads, sandwiches, and quiches are available.

HOURS: 8 A.M. to 5 P.M. daily.

SOUTHAMPTON ACTIVITIES

BEACHES: For beach information, contact the Parks and Recreation Department, Hampton Road, Southampton, NY 11968 (tel. 516/283-6000, ext. 233).

BOATING: Sailaway, North Hwy. (tel. 516/283-8466), has windsurfers and sailboats for rent. Instruction is given.

PICNICKING: Picnicking hampers can be filled at the Village Cheese Shop, 11 Main St. (tel. 516/283-6949); Loaves and Fishes (tel. 516/537-0555); or more modestly at Ted's market, 264 Hampton Rd. (tel. 516/283-0929), which specializes in creating well-stuffed heroes, and Southampton Deli, Hampton Road and North Hwy. (tel. 516/283-1774).

TENNIS: Tuckahoe Racquet Club, Sandy Hollow Road, County Road 52 (Exit 8 off Rte. 27), in Southampton (tel. 516/283-3422), offers a seasonal membership for $125; it has 14 Har-tru courts. For high school courts, call the chamber of commerce at 283-0402.

WATERMILL, BRIDGEHAMPTON, AND WAINSCOTT

AREA ATTRACTIONS

A few miles east of Southampton, the village of Watermill is located on the edge of Mecox Bay. Here, the **Water Mill Museum** (tel. 516/726-9685) displays early American tools and features craft demonstrations, an operating waterwheel, and a restored grist mill. HOURS: June 25 to Labor Day, Monday and Wednesday to Saturday from 10 A.M. to 4 P.M., on Sunday from 1 to 4 P.M. The Watermill windmill was moved here in 1814 from North Haven, hauled by 12 yoke of oxen, and was used until 1887.

Quite a lot of literary figures hang out in Bridgehampton and their literary gossip flies around the bar at Bobby Van's. There are several antique stores on Main Street and a landmark windmill built in 1820.

Besides the bars, Bridgehampton does have a **historical museum** (tel. 516/537-1088), on Main Street, which has a blacksmith's shop on the grounds and another building housing antique engines and farm machinery. HOURS: June to Labor Day, Thursday to Monday from 10 A.M. to 4 P.M.

The constant roaring of engines that can be heard from May to early fall on most weekends emanates from the **Bridgehampton Race Circuit,** Millstone Road (tel. 516/725-0888). It's rumored that the acreage has been bought for condominium development. Bridgehampton has one of the few public golf courses—the **Poxabogue Golf Course,** Montauk Hwy. (tel. 516/537-9862).

Bridgehampton Winery, Sag Harbor Turnpike (tel. 516/537-3155), offers tours and tastings daily May through October.

WATERMILL DINING

One doesn't come to the Hamptons to dine—you're lucky if you can find a decent place to eat at all—but **The Station at Water Mill,** Station Road (tel. 516/726-6811), is an outstanding exception. The restaurant is small, seating only 40, and the menu is appropriately limited and carefully prepared. A recent meal brought a delicious tomato soup fragrant with onion and basil and a spicy saucisson lyonnaise served with potato salad. Other recommended appetizers include shrimp vinaigrette wrapped in prosciutto. Although the menu changes often, it might list poached salmon with hollandaise, filet of veal with watercress sauce, lobster thermidor, rack of lamb, shell steak maître d'hôtel. Two or three daily specials are always available. Desserts change also, but if the chocolate cup filled with white-chocolate mousse and a touch of raspberry sauce is in the house, order it quickly. Ditto for the lemon mousse with raspberry sauce or indeed, I'm sure, any one of the half dozen offered. Prices run $16.50 to $20.50. A $14.50 Sunday brunch includes a drink, salad or soup, entree, and dessert. The restaurant is indeed located in the railroad station and trains do still rumble past. The room is simple and fetching—blue-spruce walls that glow in candlelight, Venice-Simplon posters, and four corner cupboards displaying prime pieces of spotlighted porcelain.

LUNCH: Only in winter, on Friday and Saturday. DINNER: 7 and 9 P.M. daily in season, on Friday and Saturday only in winter. BRUNCH: Sunday from noon to 3 P.M. Summer and winter.

Tucked away in Watermill Square, **Mirko's** (tel. 516/726-4444) makes a statement for the chef-owner from Yugoslavia. In these two simply decorated dining rooms separated by a patio, continental cuisine is offered along with a handful of Yugoslavian specialties. Cevapčiči (ground beef, pork, and veal sausage served with raw onions), raznjici (skewered chunks of pork loin), pljeskavica (chopped steak with onions and pepper), and most especially the brodeto (an Adriatic fish stew of flounder, clams, mussels, and shrimp in a tomato-based sauce) are the reasons to dine here. Veal piccata, shrimp francese, veal paillard, and other daily specials complete the menu. Prices run $11.50 to $17.25.

DINNER: In summer, weekdays from 6 to 10 P.M., until 11 P.M. on weekends; in winter, Thursday to Sunday from 6 to 10 P.M.

BRIDGEHAMPTON DINING

Bobby Van's, Main Street (tel. 516/537-0590), provides a good bar with piano, pleasant enough food—seafood, cioppino, chicken, burgers, steak, Cornish hen, and daily specials—plenty of gossip (you can meet everybody here), and live entertainment.

HOURS: 11:30 A.M. to 10:30 P.M. on weekdays, until 11:30 P.M. on weekends. Open year round.

The **American Café,** Bridgehampton (tel. 516/537-2454 or 537-0035), is a typical Manhattan East Side gathering place from an earlier era transferred to the Hamptons—complete with long bar, blue gingham tablecloths, and Breuer chairs. Start your meal with melon or avocado stuffed with crabmeat and follow with barbecued ribs; southern fried chicken Louisiana; tortellini with meat, tomatoes, and basil-cream sauce; or a fresh catch of the day. Prices run $9.50 to $17.50. Summer patio with piano accompaniment too.

DINNER: In season, Monday to Saturday from 6 to 11 P.M., from 5 P.M. on Sunday; in winter, on Friday and Saturday from 6 to 9 P.M., on Sunday from noon to 9 P.M.

The **Candy Kitchen,** at the corner of Main and School, is everyone's breakfast and newspaper pickup spot.

WAINSCOTT DINING

Bruce's, Montauk Hwy. (tel. 516/537-3360), has been offering Hamptons visitors a fine piano bar and comfortable country dining for years. Chintz napkins, stucco, and gabled walls create a country ambience for duck with ginger-rhubarb or kumquat-green-peppercorn sauce, flounder meunière, or veal curry, all priced from $13 to $18.

DINNER: In summer, Wednesday to Monday from 7 P.M.; in winter, weekends only from 7 P.M. BRUNCH: Sunday from noon to 3 P.M.

EAST HAMPTON

EAST HAMPTON ATTRACTIONS

Once voted the most beautiful village in the whole of the United States by the readers of the *Saturday Evening Post*, one can easily see why. At one end of the town, stately elms arch over the street and the Village Green, their branches reflecting in the still water of the old town pond, while at the other end of town the old cedar-shingled Hook Mill stands upon a grassy knoll as it has done since it began grinding in 1806. And in between along the Main Street stand the lovely 18th- and 19th-century buildings that represent the town's venerable architectural heritage dating from 1649.

Note that East Hampton Town is a political entity that runs from the eastern border of Southampton Town to Montauk Point—thus including East Hampton village, Amagansett, and Montauk. The best way to explore the village is to pick up a **walking tour** at the chamber of commerce, 74 Park Pl. (tel. 516/324-0362), tucked away at the corner of the parking lot behind Main Street (HOURS: Tuesday to Saturday from 9 A.M. to 6 P.M., on Sunday and Monday from noon to 4 P.M.).

On the other side of the town pond, south cemetery, and the Village Green stands the **Home Sweet Home Museum,** 14 James Lane (tel. 516/324-0713), so called because it was the boyhood home of John Howard Payne (1791–1852), actor, dramatist, and author of "Home Sweet Home," a song he wrote in Paris in the 1820s when he was homesick for this very house. HOURS: In July and August, 10 A.M. to 4 P.M. daily; September to June, closed Tuesday and Wednesday.

Next door, the **Mulford Farm,** built in the 1650s, is one of the oldest farmhouses in East Hampton.

Back on Main Street, the **Guild Hall,** 158 Main St. (tel. 516/324-0806), is East Hampton's cultural center, site of exhibitions featuring well-known and emerging contemporary artists. The galleries are open evenings before theater events. HOURS: In summer, Monday to Saturday from 11 A.M. to 6 P.M., on Sunday from 2 to 5 P.M.; Tuesday from September to May. The Guild Hall's **John Drew Theater** (tel. 516/324-4050) presents year-round theater, music, and film.

Across the street, the **East Hampton Library** is worth a visit just to see the luxurious comforts of the reading room. One house down, the **Clinton Academy** (tel. 516/324-6850), built in 1784, the first chartered secondary school in New York State, now features an ever-changing collection of artifacts and furnishings culled from homes on eastern Long Island. HOURS: In July and August, Monday to Sunday from 1:30 to 5 P.M.; September to June, by appointment only.

Beyond the junction of Main Street and Newtown Lane, on a brilliant-green lawn stands the lovely and fully functioning **Hook Mill** (tel. 516/324-0713), which began grinding in 1806 and continued until 1922 (it's still in working order). HOURS: June to September, Monday and Wednesday to Friday from 10 A.M. to 5 P.M., on Sunday from 2 to 5 P.M. The burying ground behind the mill contains some stones dating back to 1650, which are ideal for rubbing. Bring paper, glass, and ink.

Just north of the village is the area known as The Springs. The **Boat Shop** on Gann Road, off Three Mile Harbor Road, maintained by the Historical Society, is interesting, as is the **Marine Museum** on Bluff Road, Amagansett, which houses a collection of fishing, whaling, and other nautical artifacts along with educational dioramas.

EAST HAMPTON LODGING AND DINING

For authentic and exquisite lodgings coupled with friendly, unassuming hospitality, the only choice is the **1770 House**, 143 Main St., East Hampton, NY 11937 (tel. 516/324-1770). Since they took it over ten years ago, Mr. and Mrs. Sidney Perle have beautifully restored this old beamed home, filling it with their very carefully selected personal collections—tall Morbier clocks, mantel clocks, and wall clocks of all sorts are Sidney's passion, while Miriam has an eye for the tiny detail that enlivens and fills a room with character, a Dobbs Fifth Avenue hatbox on top of a scallop-shell highboy in Room 3, for example.

All of the seven rooms, without exception, are furnished with a distinct aesthetic sense from the no. 11 attic room with twin beds, to the no. 10 suite with private entrance, which is distinctively furnished with hand-carved oak bed, fainting couch, oak fireplace, and breakfront displaying some of the Perles' personal china collection. In the garden room (no. 12), richly decorated in blue, a leaded-glass window looks out on spring daffodils, while a sled sits at the foot of the blue canopy bed, and a silk parasol floats above.

The same attention to detail is evident in the dining room, where fine oak tables are set with flowers in china shaving mugs and brass candlesticks crowned with hand-blown globes. Oriental rugs add a sense of luxury, and the room must contain about ten antique clocks. Miriam, the talented chef, completed Cordon Bleu training in Paris and Italy. The menu changes daily; ingredients are always seasonally fresh and the $30 prix-fixe dinner might feature such summer appetizers as a poached salmon, or arugula with goat-cheese salad, followed by a swordfish en papillote, stuffed filet mignon, or a classic rack of lamb. Wonderful desserts range from strawberry and rhubarb crisp to a luscious, very fudgy, house chocolate cake.

RATES (including breakfast): $90 to $160. DINNER: In July and August, Thursday through Sunday from 6:30 P.M. (three seatings per night); September to June, only on weekends, with two seatings Friday night, three on Saturday.

The **Maidstone Arms**, 207 Main St., East Hampton, NY 11937 (tel. 516/324-2004), is a longstanding local dining favorite, located right across from the town pond and Village Green. This old, white clapboard building with green trim has the casual but semiformal ambience of a venerable beach house—wicker chairs and tables are on the front porch, while rhododendrons blossom in the garden out back.

There are 17 accommodations in the main building and two cottages. All have private bath and all are eclectically furnished with brass-and-iron beds, some with painted-wood furniture, along with an occasional antique mirror or Windsor chair and wicker rocker. Suite 61 is particularly attractive, tucked under the eaves and flooded with light from the skylight.

Downstairs the Victorian parlor has a book collection for guests' reading pleasure, and so does the oak bar, which leads immediately into the dining room, whose fine reputation rests on consistently well-prepared classics like duck à l'orange, calves' liver lyonnaise, steak au poivre, and local fish, all priced from $14 to $20.

RATES (including breakfast): $75 to $160, $95 to $180 on weekends in July and August. DINNER: 6 to 10 P.M., Wednesday to Monday in season, Thursday to Sunday off-season; closed January to mid-March.

You can't miss the large rambling green-shuttered, white clapboard **Huntting Inn**, 94 Main St., East Hampton, NY 11937 (tel. 516/324-0410), sheltered by some very old elms and maples in the heart of the village. The 26 rooms are all furnished differently, if not as spectacularly as one might expect from the exterior. The owners are still searching for the appropriate furnishings. Some rooms have brass beds with oak desks and chairs; others have wicker pieces; Room 201 possesses a delicate peach-colored fainting couch; while no. 211 overlooks the English-style herbaceous garden, where a brick path winds among the bright colors of the foxgloves, lavender, lupines, poppies, daisies, and roses that grow in profusion here. A wood-paneled cocktail lounge with a spectacular long oak carved bar and the Palm restaurant are on the ground floor.

RATES: In season, $100 to $140 double; off-season, $45 to $80. Open from the end of April to the end of December.

The **Hedges Inn**, 74 James Lane, East Hampton, NY 11937 (tel. 516/324-7100), occupies a classic old clapboard house with chocolate-colored shutters just down from the town pond. This property was granted to William Hedges in 1652 and remained in the family until 1923. It has a very inviting air: geranium-filled window boxes redden each of the five front windows, a brick path lined with flowers leads to the front door, a crazy paved patio fringed with flower boxes beckons with white wooden chairs and umbrella tables, and a small parlor equipped with TV and fireplace is also available for guest use.

The rooms are not as spectacular as one might hope, but the new management assured me that they would be sprucing them up for 1987. All the essentials are already there. The 11 rooms are large, have private bath, air conditioning, and solid-wood closet doors. Several have fireplaces. Room 2, for example, contains a king-size brass bed, two sidetables draped with tablecloths, a chest, and comfortable chairs. Room 1's bed sports a pretty eyelet lace eider; there's also a Windsor chair and a chintz couch that opens into a bed. Crabtree & Evelyn soaps, bath cubes, shampoo, and other amenities are placed in each bathroom, and a nighttime chocolate on the pillow.

A breakfast of croissants danish, and muffins is served in a small bright dining room, where wide-plank floors and oak chairs give a country feel. So do the flower displays—a half dozen great sunflowers worthy of Van Gogh's brush when I visited. The restaurant specializes in traditional American-Italian cuisine—pasta, veal, steaks, and seafood. Prices run from $13.50 for linguine aglio e olio (with garlic and oil) to $24 for veal chop Chiara. The rest of the menu consists of such dishes as swordfish, red snapper, veal marsala, filet mignon, and prime rib. Among the appetizers are a crabmeat cocktail.

RATES: $100 to $135 in summer, $75 to $85 after September 22; the hotel is open from April to December 31. DINNER: Open for dinner only June to September; closed Tuesday.

MORE EAST HAMPTON LODGING

The **Bassett House,** 128 Montauk Hwy. (P.O. Box 1426), East Hampton, NY 11937 (tel. 516/324-6127). At his early- to mid-18th-century Ezekiel Jones house, friendly Michael Bassett caters to guests at a long refectory table in the kitchen where he will prepare pretty much whatever you like for breakfast (within reason). Good music fills the sunken parlor where guests gather to read one of the many volumes in the bookcase or to cozy up to the Franklin stove in winter. There are 12 rooms (three with private bath, the remainder sharing seven baths) for which Michael has painstakingly collected the furnishings at auctions and where he's spent many hours stripping paint from the original woodwork. His handiwork shows most exquisitely in the ground-floor room with wide-plank floors, and worm-chestnut paneling on walls and ceiling. A couch in front of the fireplace and a small roll-top desk set the tone. Other rooms vary in size and ambience, from a small single with enough room for a sink, a table, and a closet to a large room with adjacent dressing room furnished with a hand-painted Victorian bed, ladder-back chairs, and a wrought-iron standing lamp.

RATES: $40 to $115, depending on the season.

132 North Main, East Hampton, NY 11937 (tel. 516/324-2246), offers an eclectic assortment of 13 accommodations. The seven rooms in the main house, two with private bath, are typically homey and often small, basic bedrooms. The nicest is a double immediately off the wide deck that is covered with flowers and plants. The room contains a double bed covered with colorful quilt, two sidetables, an oak chest, and a wicker folding chair. The cabañas by the spectacular private (thanks to the trees) pool are the choice accommodations because of their location: sliding doors open poolside, and furnishings are simple in these cedar cabins—simply a double bed/couch, fridge, and bathroom, essentially. Midway between the main house and the pool a small cottage shelters a studio with fully equipped kitchen and living room/bedroom heated by a wood-burning stove. Muffins and coffee are available at breakfast—help yourself. The grounds between each of these buildings are prettily landscaped and really make you feel in the country. Open May 1 to September 15. RATES: Two-night weekend package based on double occupancy, $110 per person with private bath, $85 per person with shared bath, $55 single; $65 per person double with private bath and $40 per person double with shared bath, $55 single, during the week.

The **Dutch Motel,** 488 Montauk Hwy., East Hampton, NY 11937 (tel. 516/324-4550), is an appealing property. Although it's located on busy Montauk Hwy., the buildings are set perpendicular to the road so that the noise is minimized. At the rear, the pool is pleasantly secluded by a high fence and landscaped with shrubs, lawn, and deck. The standard rooms are furnished with rattan—desk, chairs, and bed. The most dramatic accommodations are the Jacuzzi suites, flashily decorated in gray or dusky pink or beige and tan, each containing a mirrored circular bar, bold floral bedspreads, and a couch with upholstery to match. The large geranium-filled tubs and other shrubbery in front of the units add charm to the place. Rooms have cable color TV, telephone, air conditioning, and various amenities in the bathrooms.

RATES: $47 to $67 from October 1 through approximately May 22; $59 to $77 from May 23 to the end of June and Labor Day through the end of September; $89 to $112 from July 1 through Labor Day. Rooms with Jacuzzi cost $77, $92, and $127 respectively.

EAST HAMPTON DINING

Breakfasts and Snacks

The **Buttery,** 66 Newtown Lane (tel. 324-3725), will start the day off right with fresh squeezed orange juice, baked-on-premises muffins, croissants, or Danish; eggs Benedict; waffles; or whatever breakfast treat strikes your fancy. This small, informal spot has rather an English-style flair: fish and chips is regularly on the lunch menu, afternoon tea is accompanied by scones (also baked on premises), cream, and jam, and you might have a tasty sausage roll for a light supper. Salads, sandwiches, and fish dishes round out the menu. Bakery items can be bought for home consumption. Summer hours are from 8 A.M. to about 9:30 P.M.

For breakfast, sandwiches, and snacks at any time of day, head for the **Windmill Deli,** at Main Street and Newtown Lane (tel. 516/324-9856), which sports a couple of tables outside; it's also a good spot to pick up the city newspapers. Best hamburgers are found at **O'Malley's** saloon—a good Friday-night revival spot, at 11 E. Main St. (tel. 516/324-9757).

East Hampton Lunches and Dinners

The **Buoy,** 209 Montauk Hwy. (tel. 516/324-9010), is a real Bonacker place, where you're guaranteed a hospitable welcome and good food at honest prices. Choose among a selection of seafood and steak and other meat dishes from $9.50 to $15. Add $2 and you can enjoy a full-course dinner. A few fish trophies, shellacked tables, and nautical pictures complete the decor.

LUNCH: Noon to 3:30 P.M. daily. DINNER: 6 to 10 P.M. daily. Closed one week in the winter.

For serious dining I have already mentioned the **1770 House** and the **Maidstone Arms.**

New York's famous **Palm** (tel. 516/324-0411) is also located at the Huntting Inn, 94 Main St. Oak banquettes and brass accents in the dining room and an enclosed porch provide a conservative setting for their renowned four-pound lobsters, 18-ounce steaks, and 22-ounce prime ribs priced from $19.50; a shrimp cocktail runs $8.50.

DINNER: 5 to 10:30 P.M. daily from May to December 31.

Fresno Place, off Railroad Avenue (tel. 516/324-0727), brings California all the way East. Stark pale walls and white-painted girders enlivened only by a few incongruous landscapes ensure that the life of the place comes from the diners and the buzz of their conversations. There's a sushi bar in the back. The menu mixes Japanese and California cuisine. You'll be treated to one of your "better" meals on the East End here at Fresno. The sushi is super-fresh (after all, Montauk's only 25 minutes away) and you might start with some teppamaki or other sushi of your choice. At a recent dinner, a cucumber-and-avocado soup was delicious, the avocado giving it a richer flavor. So, too, was an artichoke vinaigrette, which was beautifully presented, leaves separated and arranged in a star shape. Miso soup, chowders, sweet potato, and calamari tempura are among the other appetizers, along with salads like endive, tomato, and avocado. For your main course, the sushi-sashimi combination is highly recommended. Other tempting dishes (including daily specials) might be red snapper stuffed with crabmeat or tuna marinated in ginger and soy. Prices run $10 to $19. For dessert, try the banana tempura, the chocolate-chip mousse, or the cheesecake.

DINNER: 6 to 10 P.M. daily in summer, Thursday to Sunday only in winter.

L'Orsa Minore, 136 N. Main St. (tel. 516/324-0590), is pretty in an unassuming way. The menu is limited and the food well recommended—some would say the best Italian cuisine on the East End. Start with some moules marinara or pâté before moving on to green tagliatelle with meat sauce or arborio rice with prawns, or a simple veal milanaise. Prices range from $13 to $22. Country floral tablecloths overlaid with pink, floor tiles, desserts displayed on a sideboard, fresh flowers, and wood trim create a simple, comfortable ambience.

DINNER: 6 to 11 P.M. daily in July and August; closed Wednesday in other months. Open from early May to the end of October.

La Maison des Champs, 47 Montauk Hwy. (tel. 516/324-4466), has developed a fine reputation and was given a two-star rating by the *New York Times* for its French-accented continental cuisine consisting of such treats as goat-cheese salad or snails in fennel for starters, and such main courses as filet mignon with red wine and shallots, calves' liver with port wine and shallots, veal medallions in Calvados and cream, and pheasant and game (in season), priced from $13.50 to $22. Dine in one of the two comfortable rooms or on the covered garden patio.

DINNER: Thursday to Tuesday from 6 P.M. in season, Friday to Monday off-season (on Friday and Saturday only in January); closed from February to mid-March.

Michael's, 28 Maidstone Park Rd., The Springs, East Hampton (tel. 516/324-0725), is lucky enough to have once received praise from Seymour Britchky, and it continues to serve fairly priced, unpretentious good fresh seafood—flounder, softshell crabs, steaks—from $12 to $18.50, including salad and vegetables.

DINNER: Tuesday to Saturday from 6 P.M., Friday and Saturday only off-season; closed February.

The Laundry, 31 Race Lane (tel. 516/324-3199). Best to come here for a drink, and either pasta, fish, chicken, veal, and rack of lamb are listed on the menu. Prices run $9.50 to $19.50. So ogle the celebrity crowd and the always-decorous fresh flower arrangements or else nod off in front of the fire in winter.

HOURS: From 5:30 P.M. daily, year round.

AMAGANSETT

Only a few hundred yards east, Amagansett seems far less concerned with social events than East Hampton. There are only a dozen or so stores along Main Street and a farmer's market. Only a block away, Atlantic Avenue Beach, a favorite singles' gathering place, is also known as Asparagus Beach because everybody stands, showing themselves off to maximum advantage.

More seriously, **East Hampton Town Marine Museum,** on Bluff Road (tel. 516/267-6544), houses displays about the town's fishing, whaling, and nautical heritage. The lower floor exhibits include a cannon retrieved from the H.M.S. *Culloden,* which went aground near Fort Pond Bay in 1781. At the back of the museum, kids can sound fog horns, ring ships' bells, and clamber over a toy fishing trawler jungle gym that is moored in the sand. HOURS: Tuesday to Sunday in July and August, weekends only in June and September. By appointment at other times.

AMAGANSETT LODGING

Two accommodations seem to reflect the kind of confident, unalloyed charm that prevails in Amagansett.

The **Millgarth,** Windmill Lane (P.O. Box 700), Amagansett, NY 11930 (tel. 516/267-3757), a 100-year-old lemon-yellow clapboard house has its very own windmill and offers an astounding assortment of well-kept accommodations with charmingly idiosyncratic furnishings. My favorites are the Gazebo cottage, with a private little garden area out back, an eat-in kitchen, a bedroom with four-poster, and a cozy living room with wing chairs and a pull-out couch; and no. 11 or the Carriage House, which contains a huge living room with exposed beams and fireplace, two bedrooms, two baths, and a private patio. Number 10 has a skylit kitchen, canopy bed, Federal-style highboy, and a small foyer with easy chairs and library; while no. 4, a studio-kitchenette on the second floor, has its own private sundeck. None has TV or telephone. Bikes are available; babysitting can usually be arranged. The beach is only a block away, and the grounds are quite lovely. Open year round.

RATES: Apartments run $80 to $100; cottages, $135 to $185 a night. In July and August there's a minimum weekly.

At **Gansett Green Manor,** Main Street (P.O. Box 799), Amagansett, NY 11930 (tel. 516/267-3133), artist/manager Connie Brandt has decorated some rooms with her own murals of mallards, Canadian geese, or seagulls, which float across the ceilings or walls of some very basically furnished rooms in the front house. Secluded cottage/apartments, each with its own private picnic area furnished with umbrella table and grill dot the rest of the property. All are simply and adequately furnished with bedroom, living room, kitchen, bath, and TV. Most have electric fireplaces. The graveled pathways are prettily landscaped with scarlet pimpernels and a fountain that plays beside a model of a covered wagon. A menagerie of two Grand Canyon burros, a calf, lambs, geese, and a hog live at the rear pasture corral. No children under 16 years and no pets.

RATES: $80 to $90 for rooms, $98 to $140 for efficiencies, $100 to $170 for cottages; discounts offered before May 20 and after September 15. Open from mid-May to mid-October.

AMAGANSETT DINING

Restaurants may come and go, but **Gordon's,** on Main Street (tel. 516/267-3010), continues to offer carefully prepared *and* served food in unpretentious surroundings to a local as well as a visiting clientele. The only concessions to decor are a few hanging plants in the window and a central crystal chandelier, yet at night the low-lit room looks especially inviting. Specialties include scampi, sea trout, filet of sole meunière, veal piccata or marsala, mignonette of beef bordelaise, and excellent salads, including arugula that is grown in the backyard. Prices run $12.75 to $24.75.

HOURS: Dinner only, Tuesday to Sunday, in season; lunch is served off-season. Closed Monday, and the months of January and February.

Oceans Club, Main Street (tel. 516/267-6611), plays two different roles —restaurant by day and early evening, and nightclub/disco at night. Inside, the space is crisp, light, and airy—an effect created by the cathedral-style ceiling, stands of ficus and potted palms, and the light that streams through the Italianate windows. Start with some delicacies from the raw bar or a bowl of chowder and follow with barbecued ribs, steak, or a variety of seafood—swordfish, salmon, flounder. Prices run $10 to $13. Cheesecake and tartufo are among the desserts. After dinner you can dance to the rhythms spun by the DJ from 10 P.M. on.

LUNCH: In season, weekends only, from 3 to 5:30 P.M. DINNER: In season, 5:30 to 11 P.M. daily. BRUNCH: Sunday from noon to 4 P.M. Call for off-season schedule.

If the weather's perfect for a meal *en plein air,* then stop at the **Lunch Company,** on Montauk Hwy. (tel. 516/267-3433), and pick up a sandwich or a whole picnic basket. Choose among the appetizing displays that include couscous, sesame chicken, pesto potato salad, marinated vegetable salad, pasta with salami and peppers, and tempting desserts. Quite lavish boxed lunches are available, the most lavish consisting of prosciutto, soppressata, provolone, roasted peppers, shredded lettuce, onion, oil, and vinegar on French bread, plus pasta primavera salad and a sweet or fruit, priced at $10.50 for one, $18 for two.

HOURS: 9 A.M. to 5 P.M. daily; occasionally closed off-season on Monday and Wednesday; hours extended in the summer.

THE HAMPTONS' EVENING ENTERTAINMENT

The volatile, electric night scene changes from season to season. Your best bet is to pick up one of the many local papers (free in supermarkets) and see what's happening. Here's a rundown on last year's spots—it's anyone's guess whether or not they'll survive to see another "season."

In Hampton Bays, **La Plage**, 15 Foster Ave. (tel. 516/728-6929), was offering male burlesque on one night; **Canoe Place Inn,** on Montauk Hwy. (tel. 516/728-4121), had live bands and a DJ; **The Niteclub,** on Montauk Hwy. (tel. 516/728-8080), had an occasional Komedy Club night during the week, and **OBI's** (tel. 516/728-4121) cornered the rock–new wave scene.

In East Quogue, on Dune Road, **Club Atlantis** at Neptune Beach (tel. 516/653-6922) drew celebrants on weekends.

In Westhampton, the two hottest discos were the **Club Marrakesh,** 133 Main St. (tel. 516/288-2023), where reservations are necessary, and **Scarlett's,** 142 Mill Rd. (tel. 516/288-9739). **Beach Tiny's Cow Palace,** on Montauk Hwy. (tel. 516/288-9743), held a regular weekend dance contest.

In Southampton, **Le Mans,** Montauk Hwy. (tel. 516/283-8800), also reopened its doors.

In East Hampton, **The Jag,** 44 Three Mile Harbor Rd. (tel. 516/324-3600), opened its doors at 10 P.M. and throbbed all night long.

In Montauk, three clubs vied for the action—**Elyts,** on Main Street (tel. 516/668-9300); **Waves,** at Emerson and Edison Streets (tel. 516/668-9865), for reggae plus; and **The Place,** at the Lakeside Inn, Edgemere Road (tel. 516/668-5630).

East Hampton Cinema (tel. 516/324-0596 or 324-0448) offers a five-cinema complex. Daily matinees during the summer. A good refuge from the rain, and also from Manhattan movie lines.

EAST HAMPTON/AMAGANSETT ACTIVITIES

BEACHES: Access to beaches is rather complex. Parking permits are issued by both the village and the town (which stretches all the way to Montauk), but village permits may not be used at town beaches and vice versa. For information about town beaches, contact the Town Clerk's office at Town Hall, Pantigo Road, East Hampton (tel. 516/324-4142 or 324-4143). For information about village beaches, contact the beach office at Main Beach (at the end of Ocean Avenue) or the Village Hall, Main Street, East Hampton (tel. 516/324-4150). Don't park without either paying a fee or obtaining a permit, because you'll certainly be fined and moreover your car could well be towed.

Hotel and motel guests receive stickers providing access to Atlantic Avenue and Indian Wells beaches in Amagansett, and Kirk Park and bay beaches in Montauk. You can also park at Main Beach without a sticker providing you pay a fee.

BICYCLING: For rentals, try Bermuda Bikes, 32 Gingerbread Lane (tel. 516/324-6688).

BOATING: Brucie's Boat Rentals, located at the south end of Three Mile Harbor in East Hampton (tel. 516/324-5063), has powerboats, sailboats, skiffs, and canoes for rent. Also at Baron's Cove Marina in Sag Harbor.

HORSEBACK RIDING: H. E. Farms, Inc., Oak View Hwy., in East Hampton (tel. 516/324-9568). Lessons only.

PICNICKING: Lavish picnic ingredients can naturally be found at the Barefoot Contessa, 46 Newtown Lane in East Hampton (tel. 516/324-0240), where even potato salad can set you back several dollars. Worth the visit for the luscious displays and for people-watching.

Less exotic picnic fare can be found at the Windmill Deli on Main Street.

TENNIS: Three town courts are located at Springs Recreation Area, off Old Stone Highway; four courts available at Abraham's Path Park, Abrahams Path, Amagansett. Behind the East Hampton high school on Long Lane, about a dozen courts are open to the public for a nominal fee.

WINDSURFING: Seasonings Sports and Leisure in East Hampton (tel. 516/324-2201) offers rentals of windsurfer boards, surfboards, and Boogie boards. Lessons are given too: about $60 a day or $15 an hour.

Eight Important Topics

PRICES AND HOURS: Although the author made every effort to obtain correct and current prices and hours for various establishments and attractions, these can change swiftly and dramatically. Changes in ownership, changes in policy, and inflation can all affect this information. For future prices, add about 10% to 15% to the given rates per year.

RESERVATIONS: These are a must on weekends. For accommodations they should be made well in advance, in some cases as much as three months ahead of time and in exceptional circumstances as much as a year in advance (at Saratoga, for example, during the racing meet). Dinner reservations, especially for Friday and Saturday night, should also be made ahead of time.

MINIMUM STAYS: Most places demand minimum stays on weekends and often during their high season. This information has not always been included, so always check ahead.

WEEKEND PACKAGES: As promotions, these are created and discontinued constantly. If the particular package mentioned doesn't exist, don't be surprised —the management will most likely be offering another very similar promotional package.

DEPOSITS: These are often nonrefundable since they are the innkeeper's only defense against those folks who don't show up, especially when the weather is inclement. Always clarify this when you book.

TAXES: These have not been included in the quoted rates. Percentages vary from state to state.

A NOTE ON THE DINING LISTINGS: Since this book is designed for people who are taking weekend breaks, where possible the restaurants are listed under headings that reflect this fact. That is, "Dinner Only" means that the restaurants listed under this heading are not open for lunch on Saturday or Sunday. It does not mean that they don't serve lunch at all—they may well do so on weekdays but they are not open for lunch to weekenders.

DROP A LINE: Have you discovered a delightful inn, a great B & B, a fantastic restaurant, or a unique attraction that you feel should be featured in this book? Or have you been dissatisfied with any particular establishment mentioned in these pages? Or do you have any suggestions for the book in general? Then please do drop me a line and I'll respond to and follow up on your comments. Just write to Marilyn Wood, Prentice Hall Press, Gulf + Western Building, 15th floor, One Gulf + Western Plaza, New York, NY 10023.

MONTAUK

DISTANCE IN MILES: 124
ESTIMATED DRIVING TIME: Anywhere from 2½ to 4 hours, depending on traffic.

DRIVING: Long Island Expressway to Exit 70, taking Rte. 111 south to Rte. 27 east.
BUS: Best bet is the Hampton Jitney. Call 212/895-1941 or 516/936-0440 for reservations.
TRAIN: Long Island Railroad from Penn Station (tel. 718/454-5477).
SEAPLANE: Leaves from the 23rd Street East River pier, flying directly to the Montauk Yacht Club (tel. 516/222-2276).

Special Events to Plan Your Trip Around
JUNE: Blessing of the Fleet, Town Dock.
JULY: Shark Tag Tournament, Montauk Marine Basin (mid-July).
OCTOBER: Full Moon Bass Tournament at the Marine Basin.

For further information about New York in general, contact the Division of Tourism, New York State Department of Commerce, One Commerce Plaza, Albany, NY 12245 (tel. 518/474-4116).

For specific information about Montauk, contact the Montauk Chamber of Commerce, Montauk Hwy. (P.O. Box CC), Montauk, NY 11954 (tel. 516/668-2428). The Suffolk County Department of Economic Development, H. Lee Dennison Bldg., Veterans Memorial Hwy., Hauppauge, NY 11788 (tel. 516/360-4800), will also provide information. So will the Long

Island Tourism and Convention Commission, 213 Carleton Ave., Central
Islip, NY 11722 (tel. 516/234-4959).

Montauk is different from the rest of the Hamptons. Once you get out of East
Hampton and turn onto Old Montauk Hwy., the two-lane road rolls along beside
the dunes and the ocean as if cutting through a Marsden Hartley painting, until
suddenly there below you huddles Montauk like some isolated western frontier
town. Compared to the frenetic chic of East Hampton and Southampton, Montauk remains the Cinderella left behind for family-style vacationing. It has a far
less contrived air; there are no boutiques here, only the sea, the gulls, the gorse
and beachplum, the sand and the sky, all sometimes blotted out by the mysterious
mist that rises off the ocean and rolls in as if it were peeled from a great cylindrical
drum.

Besides the landscape, Montauk also has some of the most romantic history in
the area. Montauk is almost an island—surrounded by water on three sides and
on the fourth by Hither Hills and the state park. In fact, you go "on" and "off"
Montauk, a local expression used ever since the English settlers bought the land
from the Montaukett Indians in 1655. Adrian Block was the first white man to set
foot on Montauk. Lord Gardiner, who moved across from Saybrook, Connecticut, was the first to take possession of his land grant, a grant that has remained in
the Gardiner family since 1639.

The Old Montauk Hwy. was traced out in the 1700s by Hampton ranchers who
grazed horses, sheep, and cattle on the 15,000 acres patterned with 2,000 acres of
lakes and ponds, in spring and summer and herded them off the peninsula in the
late fall. Animals were driven here from as far west as Patchogue; and the cattle
drive was quite an event until well into the 1900s, when volunteer cowboys rode
alongside the herd. Teddy Roosevelt and his Rough Riders fitted in very well
along with the 29,500 veterans of the Spanish-American War who came here to
recuperate from diseases caused by bad food and water.

Three houses were built for the keepers of the herds, and they remained the
only buildings—except for the lighthouse, which was built in 1796 and has stood
here ever since. First House was built in 1774; Second House, now a museum run
by the Historical Society with an interesting herb garden in back, was built in 1797
(the original had been erected in 1746). HOURS: It's open daily, except Tuesday,
from 10 A.M. to 4 P.M. ADMISSION: $1 for adults, 25¢ for children. Third House was
first built in 1742, although the present structure dates from 1806. The houses also
served as inns for the hardy travelers who braved the mosquitoes and the atro-
cious roads to come for the fine fishing (which still draws thousands of visitors)
and game shooting.

In 1879 the heirs of the early proprietors sold Montauk for $151,000 to Arthur

W. Benson of Bensonhurst, who brought his railroad magnates and his cronies from Standard Oil out for visits, and they built a few "cottages" at the Point, calling themselves the Montauk Association. In 1895 Benson sold 5,500 acres to Austin Corbin and Charles M. Pratt, who brought the Long Island Rail Road from Sag Harbor out to Montauk and had dreams of making the town a major port of entry for the whole country. Those dreams were never realized, and the dreams of another man, Carl Graham Fisher, were also dashed (thank goodness), for he wanted to turn Montauk into a northern version of Miami Beach, which he had developed. He laid out the town and built the golf course, the polo field, the Manor, the tall office building in town (now a condominium), indoor tennis courts, and a theater. The Surf Club and the Yacht Club were established, as well as the casino on Star Island. He also opened the jetty into Lake Montauk. His dream, though, collapsed with the Stock Market Crash in 1929.

Several legendary characters and romantic tales are attached to the area—tales of pirates and bootleggers laying off Montauk Point waiting to bring their illicit cargo ashore, of Indians and Indian burial grounds. One such tale reveals the relationship that developed between the Sachem of the Montauketts, Wyandanch, and Lion Gardiner, the proprietor of Gardiner's Island and one of East Hampton's founders. Wyandanch and Gardiner had gone through the rite of blood brotherhood, and when the Narragansett Indians came down from Rhode Island and carried off Wyandanch's daughter, Gardiner arranged for her ransom. For this, in 1659 Wyandanch gave Gardiner much of the land that is now Smithtown. Indian Stephen Pharoh, known as Stephen Talkhouse, who thought nothing of walking to Brooklyn, was exhibited by P. T. Barnam as the greatest walker of all time. Another Indian associated with the area was Samson Occom, a Mohegan who came from Connecticut to the Montauketts to preach. He wrote hymns that are still sung today and raised 12,000 English pounds in England with which Dartmouth College was founded in 1769.

MONTAUK ATTRACTIONS

For beach and seascape lovers, Montauk offers an incredible variety of things to do, which I'll outline later, but first let's touch on what to see. First destination is usually the **Montauk Point Lighthouse** (which will be opening as a museum in 1987, providing adequate funds are raised). Built in 1797 by order of George Washington at a cost of $23,000, it stands 108 feet high, its flashing lantern visible for 25 miles. Originally it stood 297 feet from the cliff's edge; now it's only 50 feet. The antique lens was donated by the French in 1860 and has been operating ever since. The light marks the craggy shoreline, standing strongly isolated against the sea and the sky, surrounded by masses of wild dogwood roses that ramble all over the terrain.

Montauk Harbor is a second major attraction. Always alive with commercial fishing activity, the harbor is also the site for a shopping complex that attracts many browsers. The harbor at Montauk holds more fishing records than any other single port in the world, and 1986 added to them. Excitement ran through the whole East End when two world shark records were broken within a few days of each other. Crowds gathered to view the 17-foot-long great white shark weighing 3,540 pounds, caught by rod and reel.

The town consists of a strange, amorphous collection of motels and shops clustered around the Florentine-looking **tower-folly** built by Carl Fisher. Just east of town the famous **Manor** stretches along the bluff and continues to survive despite the perpetual rumors that it's about to be turned into a resort-condominium.

MONTAUK LODGING

The **Montauk Yacht Club and Inn,** Star Island Road, Montauk, NY 11954 (tel. 516/668-3100), is intimate and classy. Special touches include turndown service, bathrobes, and oversize fluffy towels. Luxury detailing extends to the decor of the 107 rooms, where louver doors lead to tiled bathrooms, closets are large, and gray- and purple-upholstered bamboo furnishings and marble-top tables and dressers are set against weathered-wood paneling. Extensive facilities include two outdoor and one indoor pool, Jacuzzi and sauna, tennis courts, sailboats at the marina, bicycles, and golf nearby, all at no charge. Deep-sea fishing trips can be arranged from the dock.

The lavish Sunday brunch is renowned—everything from lobster to steak Diane, pastas, omelets, crêpes, and waffles are all made to order. There's also a fresh oyster and clam bar. The favored portion of the dining room affords a spectacular water view. The regular dinner menu features cioppino (at $31) and other assorted fish dishes, duck with Grand Marnier sauce, chicken tarragon, and prime beef. Prices begin at $14. Reservations are vital in summer. The Potpourri Café serves breakfast and lunch in a bright, airy atmosphere with an outdoor Newport-style bar. Around the corner another patio overlooks a small bay beach.

RATES: $190 to $210 from June 16 to September 15, $140 to $160 in spring and fall. BREAKFAST AND LUNCH: Until 3 P.M. in the Potpourri Café. DINNER: 6 to 10 P.M. daily.

Gurney's Inn Resort and Spa, Old Montauk Hwy. Montauk, NY 11954 (tel. 516/668-2345 or 668-3203), is located directly "on the brink o' the beach" overlooking the Atlantic Ocean. It's always crowded with the rich and famous, overstressed urbanites and suburbanites, and corporate types attending meetings. Some units overlook the parking lot; other cottages, like the Captain's Quarters, are located directly on the ocean beach and feature two double beds, color TV, telephone in the living room and bedroom, two bathrooms, a dressing room, a 30-foot terrace, a corner double divan in the living room, a butler's pantry with sink, refrigerator, and electric range, plus individual heat and air-conditioning controls. The Crow's Nest has all of the above plus a fireplace. In several buildings, terraced into the hillside, time-sharing units are being offered that have been completely soundproofed and furnished in a luxury modern manner, featuring beds with light-oak mirrored headboards, oak partitions supporting a collection of brass objects, telephone in the bathrooms, a personal doorbell, and refrigerator tucked under the vanities. All units at the resort have color TV with free cable HBO, telephone, coffee maker, fridge, and a tiled bathroom with amenities.

The famous attraction of course, is the $4-million spa, using seawater for therapies and treatments in luxurious Roman baths and large heated indoor swimming pool with floor-to-ceiling windows opening out to the ocean. Guests may use the pool, Finnish rock saunas, Russian steamrooms, Swiss showers, exercise, and weight rooms. The spa is also open to the public for a daily charge. A large variety of treatments, therapies, exercise classes, and massage techniques are offered.

The dining rooms overlooking the ocean serve sumptuous continental and Italian dishes. Among the entrees are seafood au gratin, lobster Fra Diavolo, prime ribs, duckling with Cumberland sauce, breast of chicken rollatine, and more, priced from $15 to $25. To start, choose among antipasto, prosciutto and melon, smoked salmon, or oysters on the half shell, and to finish, sample any one of the many luscious desserts—amaretto cheesecake, Sachertorte, tartufo. Luncheon buffets and brunch buffets are served on weekends. Price tag for brunch is $17. Spa cuisine is also available: low in calories, salt, fat, sugar, cholesterol, and refined carbohydrates.

RATES (including breakfast and a $23 allowance at dinner): Mid-June to Labor Day, $120 to $150 per person; special winter packages are offered. An additional person is $60 in season, $45 at other times. From mid-June to mid-September, a minimum stay of one week is required, a three- or four-day minimum on holiday weekends.

One of Montauk's nicest accommodations is the **Panoramic View,** Old Montauk Hwy., Montauk, NY 11954 (tel. 516/668-3000), set on ten acres that have been carefully landscaped to create privacy and serenity through the abundant use of pine shrubs. The grounds are immaculately kept and always blazing with seasonal colors—begonias, scarlet pimpernels, flame flowers, etc.

The management is extremely friendly and obliging, and offers a variety of accommodations to suit most tastes in buildings that are terraced into the hillside at different elevations. Barbecues are conveniently tucked away around the property. Highpoint and Point of View are older-looking but pleasantly furnished units; Salt Sea is closest to the 1,000-foot ocean beach; Valley View is an ultramodern three-story unit with less charm and less privacy, but the rooms are naturally furnished in a more up-to-date fashion. The game room is also located inside this building, and the kidney-shaped outdoor pool is very convenient. Three beach homes with two bedrooms, two baths, living room with fireplace, porch, and patio are also available. All rooms are air-conditioned and have individually controlled heat, kitchenette, color TV, and telephone. The only drawback for beach buffs is the steep steps cut into the hillside that go down to the ocean. No children under 10 are accepted.

RATES: The 2½-room suites are $115 to $160 in season, $70 to $80 off-season (April 1 to June 19 and September 15 to October 31); 1½-room units are $70 to $135 in season, $50 to $86 off-season; cottages for four rent for $310 in season, $158 off-season.

Sadly, more and more condominiums are going up along the dune approach to Montauk, obscuring the dunes and the ocean with box-like monstrosities. Most are managed and rented out. They often make ideal accommodations for two couples traveling together since they usually offer suite-like accommodations.

There's really very little to distinguish one from the other (unless you're planning to buy, of course). All have immediate access to the beach.

The most attractive to me is **Sea Crest,** Old Montauk Hwy., Amagansett, NY 11930 (tel. 516/267-3159), which has a more rustic appearance than some of the others. The best accommodations here are in the second-floor units whose balconies have views of the ocean. Other buildings are clustered closer to the pool area. The grounds are pleasantly landscaped with shrubs and conifers, and barbecues are available in one area. Two tennis courts are also there for guest use.

RATES (for units accommodating four or five): $150 to $180 daily from approximately June 24 to September 8, $90 to $120 from September 9 to September 30 and May 22 to June 23, $70 to $95 from October 1 to November 5 and April 15 to May 21. Closed mid-November to mid-April.

Windward Shores, Old Montauk Hwy. (P.O. Box L), Amagansett, NY 11930 (tel. 516/267-8600), is another example; it lies about equidistant from Amagansett and Montauk. Here apartments arranged around a central grass courtyard with a pool offer a choice of oceanfront and ocean-view locations. The complex opened in 1983, and the open-design units are spanking modern, featuring semi-equipped kitchens (electric stove, refrigerator, dishwasher, toaster, and silverware) which open into a sky-lit living room with pull-out couch, TV, and dining area; a spiral staircase leads to a double bedroom, all furnished in beige modern. From the decks you can literally jump down onto the Napeague dunes bordering the ocean. Two all-weather tennis courts and an outdoor pool complete the facilities.

RATES: June 17 to September 12, $120 for a studio, $130 to $140 for a one-bedroom; April 15 to June 16, $70 for a studio, $80 to $85 for a one-bedroom; January to April 14, $60 for a studio, $65 to $75 for a one-bedroom. Add $45 for major summer holidays. There's a one-week minimum stay from June 17 to September 12.

At the **Hermitage,** Old Montauk Hwy. (P.O. Box 1127), Amagansett, NY 11930 (tel. 516/267-6151), the units are furnished differently by their individual owners. All have private balconies. The units have two bedrooms, a living and dining room, and full kitchen facilities. There's a pool and also access to the beach —beach chairs, umbrellas, and towels are provided. Two tennis courts complete the scenario.

RATES: $160 to $195 double occupancy daily from early June to roughly September 7, $80 to $120 from about September 8 to December 31 and March 15 to early June. An additional person in the room is $15. Open from mid-March to December 31.

Driftwood on the Ocean, Old Montauk Hwy. (P.O. Box S), Montauk, NY 11954 (tel. 516/668-5744), is an ideal family place with direct access to the beach from motel-style units sheltered from the ocean by the dunes. A concrete-surrounded pool and two tennis courts are set behind the parking area, while a children's playground and games are set still farther back on the property. Accommodations range from cottages and 2½-room suites to studio efficiencies with dining, sleeping, and sitting areas, plus a small kitchenette.

RATES: June 19 to September 13, $121 for a suite, $112 for a studio efficiency, and $103 for a deluxe bedroom; May 1 to June 18, $73 for a suite; $68 for a studio efficiency, and $58 for a deluxe bedroom; September 14 to 27, $84 for a suite, $75 for a studio efficiency, and $67 for a deluxe bedroom.

Wave Crest I Apartments, Old Montauk Hwy. (R.F.D. 1, Box 86), Montauk, NY 11954 (tel. 516/668-2141), offers several different types of accommodations in several different buildings that are terraced into the hillside overlooking the ocean. Beach Dune Place contains simple units where the decks are only 20 feet from the ocean—it's like having a cottage on the beach. Some 20 or 30 feet back, Water's Edge has rooms with kitchenettes. In Parkview, pleasant efficiencies have TV, telephone, and white-painted Scandinavian Formica-topped furniture; a sink, electric burners, and a refrigerator are housed in one compact unit. There's an indoor pool. Open March to November.

RATES: In-season, rooms are $110 to $120; spring and fall rates drop to a range of $50 to $65, but rise for two-night weekends.

At her **Montauk Soundview House,** P.O. Box 72, Montauk, NY 11954 (tel. 516/668-2771), only 700 feet east of the harbor, Virginia Galletta guarantees a great location for watching boats entering and leaving port and sunsets over the bay. She offers a variety of attractive apartments overlooking the bay, each modern and well maintained, with full kitchens, air conditioning, most with two bedrooms plus a sleeping couch, and wall-to-wall carpeting in the living room. More rustic cottage units are also available with linoleum floors and leatherette couches, and there are also nine motel rooms. Two units have fireplaces. The pool sits out over the bay; free coffee is available all day; residents' pets add to the friendly atmosphere of the place, which attracts many repeat visitors. Laundry rooms and babysitting available.

RATES: June 26 to September 11, simple bedroom units cost from $80; a four-room waterfront cottage, from $160; two-room suites accommodating four, from $110; off-season prices start at $45 and rise to $95 for a four-room waterfront cottage. Minimum stays of one week required in season, three days on weekends.

Doria at Sun Haven, Montauk Hwy., Amagansett, NY 11930 (tel. 516/267-3448 for the hotel, 267-8880 for the restaurant), is another good family accommodation. Motel-style units face toward the restaurant across a tarmac roadway that leads back to the tennis courts and ultimately the beach access. A line of conifers and other shrubs screens the units nicely, and in front of every other doorway a pleasant graveled niche has been created for relaxing on chaises lounges, or at umbrella tables. The rooms are adequate, featuring industrial carpeting, modern couches, wire chairs, rattan beds with print bedspreads, and refrigerator. The restaurant features Italian specialties—pasta (linguine with clam sauce, fettuccine with artichoke sauce) seafood (lobster Fra Diavolo or flounder Corsica with mushrooms, tomato, and Swiss cheese), and steak, chicken, and veal dishes. Prices run $12.50 to $18 (pasta from $5.75). A functional indoor pool and tennis courts complete the facilities.

RATES: $50 to $80 on weekends from May 9 to June 26 and September 3 to October 14, $89 to $165 per night on weekends from June 27 to September 2. Rates are less during the week; 50% off after Labor Day.

At the **Surf Club,** P.O. Box 848, Montauk, NY 11954 (tel. 516/668-9292), all 92 units are duplexes with a kitchen opening onto the living room, decks overlooking the pool, and a skylit stairway leading to either one or two small bedrooms and bathroom. Private beach, of course.

RATES (for rooms accommodating two to four persons): $175 to $220 from about June 24 to September 8, $120 to $160 from May 22 to June 23 and September 9 to September 30, $90 to $120 from April 15 to May 21 and October 1 to November 15.

Ocean Beach at Montauk, South Emerson Avenue, Montauk, NY 11954 (tel. 516/668-4000), has accommodations in two long two-story beachfront buildings. All are sleekly modern studios with efficiency kitchens and color TV. There's also a glass atrium with an enclosed pool.

RATES: $110 to $130 double occupancy from July 3 to Labor Day, $75 to $100 from June 20 to July 2 and September 3 to September 29, $65 to $85 from May 23 to June 19, and $55 to $75 from March 14 to May 22 and September 30 to November 30.

Rough Riders Landing, Edgemere Street (P.O. Box 847), Montauk, NY 11954 (tel. 516/668-3933), is the latest of the condo developments. On the bayside in downtown Montauk, this slice of real estate has been quite prettily designed. Units are decked out in pastels and have really large balconies compared to some of the other developments. Kitchens have all the modern gadgets, including a microwave. There are three tennis courts and a nicely landscaped pool area.

RATES: $150 for a studio, $200 for one-bedroom, and $250 for two-bedroom.

At the **Atlantic Bluffs Club,** Old Montauk Hwy. (P.O. Box 2389), Montauk, NY 11954 (tel. 516/668-5665), there are 56 studio apartments, all with fireplaces and all with balconies giving glorious ocean views. Each is individually furnished according to the owner's tastes, which may range from ultra-sleek mirrored-and-black modern to a more gentle pastel ambience. It's like having a New York apartment by the sea. Facilities include a central grass-surrounded heated swimming pool. Accommodations are available for three-day or weekly rentals only.

RATES: Three-day stays for four persons cost $205 to $235 from September 19 to June 23; in season a weekly rental runs $775 to $925. Open early spring through late fall.

Charm exudes from **Lenhart's,** Old Montauk Hwy. (at Cleveland Drive), Montauk, NY 11954 (tel. 516/668-2356), a cluster of secluded cottages landscaped into the hill where conifers, shade trees, roses, and flowering shrubs create a tranquil country air. Even the pool is sheltered by a hedge and softened by a grass surround. Open all year.

RATES: In summer, $130 for a one-bedroom, $100 for an efficiency; $90 and $75 at other times.

For clean, well-run, family-owned motel accommodations, try the **Blue Haven Motel,** West Lake Drive (P.O. Box 781), Montauk, NY 11954 (tel. 516/668-5943), which has 30 air-conditioned units, including some fully equipped kitchenettes and two-room apartments with full kitchens. There's no telephone in the rooms, but they all have TV, coffee maker, and refrigerator. There's a sparkling clean outdoor pool. Open May 1 to October 31. Owners Tom and Monica Brennan will arrange fishing trips and will pick you up at the train or bus stop, or at the airport.

RATES: Mid-June through October, $59 in midweek, $79 on weekends; off-season, $40 in midweek, $49 on weekends. Three-day minimum in season. Closed November to April.

Just behind the dunes at the junction of Old Montauk Hwy. and Main Street, the **Oceanside Beach Resort,** P.O. Box 668, Montauk, NY 11954 (tel. 516/668-9825), offers clean rooms with Sears-style painted furnishings, refrigerator, TV (no phone), and courtesy coffee maker. There's an outdoor pool for guests.

RATES: $68 to $90 double, depending on type of unit; less off-season. Open May to October 31.

MONTAUK DINING

Lunches/Dinners

From the porch dining room of the **Anchorage Restaurant,** West Lake Drive (tel. 516/668-9149), grass sweeps down to the edge of Montauk Lake, adding to the attraction of the place, known for an exceptional luncheon special—a one- or two-pound lobster, fresh from the tank, for only $7 and $14.50 respectively, plus a selection of other catch-of-the-day specials or such tasty items as crab cakes. At dinner, prices rise and those same lobsters go for $12.75 and $21; meat dishes, fried clams, and other fish specials are available, along with various special combinations like the whole lobster, shrimp, clams, mussels, and scallops in a marinara sauce served with fettuccine ($30 for two).

HOURS: Noon to 10 P.M. daily in season (check the hours in the off-season); closed December to mid-March.

The famous place that everyone knows about is, of course, **Gosman's Dock Restaurant,** West Lake Drive (tel. 516/668-5330), where a series of restaurants feed hordes of people during the summer, while herring and black-backed gulls soar and whirl above or simply stand and stare. One- and two-pound lobsters are the prime attractions among an assortment of softshelled crabs, flounder, bluefish, bass, oysters, scallops, and clams, all priced from $10 to $26.50 for a two-pounder. Fancier specials also appear on the blackboard—yellow-fin tuna with coriander and horseradish, bluefish Cajun style, or sole with dill-Dijon, and similar. From the open but covered dining rooms you can watch the boats coming into dock—fishing trawlers, lobstermen, and pleasure craft, motor and sail, seagulls whining and whirling hungrily above.

HOURS: Noon to 10 P.M. daily in season.

The **Topside Deck,** perched on top of the roof of one of the Gosman buildings (tel. 516/668-2447), offers a great vantage point and is fine for casual lunches. Take-out counters below turn out an endless stream of lobster rolls, steamers, and so on to customers who take their goodies to colorful umbrella tables and feast while watching all the harbor activity. The Fishmarket is also open daily from 10 A.M. to 6 P.M. during the season. Best time to catch the fleet unloading the day's haul is around 5 or 6 P.M. at Gosman's Dock.

Pleasant waterside dining can be had at the **Boathouse,** Emery Street (tel. 516/668-5574), overlooking Fort Pond. The ambience is casual—bright-yellow director's chairs. This is a local favorite for a good luncheon or dinner featuring softshell crabs, lobster, swordfish, flounder, steak, and prime rib. Prices go from $9.25 to $17. Sandwiches and salads are priced from $2.25 to $5.25 at lunch.

LUNCH: Noon to 2 P.M. (4 P.M. in season) daily. DINNER: 5 to 10 P.M. daily. Closed from March 18 for four weeks.

For a dash of Italy in Montauk, **Luigi's,** Euclid Avenue (tel. 516/668-3212), complete with checked tablecloths and a sprinkling of chianti bottles, serves a variety of veal dishes, including a veneziana with artichoke hearts, as well as classic scungilli and calamari marinara or diavolo, and the ever-popular chicken parmigiana. Entrees run $9 to $15.

DINNER: 5 to 10 P.M.; closed after Columbus Day, open weekends only in May.

The **Blue Marlin,** at Edgemere and Flamingo Streets (tel. 516/668-9880), is known for its steaks. Wood tables and chairs set the scene in this unpretentious place. Carnivores enjoy 1½- or 1¾-inch-thick prime sirloin, double-cut lamb chops, prime rib, and seafood specials. Prices run $11 to $18.

LUNCH: Wednesday to Monday from noon to 2 P.M. DINNER: Wednesday to Monday from 5 to 10 P.M.; closed Tuesday. Check off-season hours.

The **Inn at Napeague,** Old Montauk Hwy. (tel. 516/267-3332), is a pleasant nautical spot featuring a few old salts for decoration, along with their fish trophies, and some very fairly priced seafood. Seafood, bouillabaisse, and other fishy specialties mingle on the menu with sauerbraten and beef Wellington. A special sunset dinner is offered Monday to Saturday from 5 to 6 P.M. and 4 to 6 P.M. on Sunday for a low price. It includes a choice of clam chowder or mussels marinara; followed by a selection of meat, fish, and shrimp dishes, including an excellent fish stew; and caramel custard or ice cream for dessert. A 1⅛-pound lobster with dinner goes for $14.

HOURS: Daily from Memorial Day to October 31; weekends only from mid-April to Memorial Day.

It's affectionately known as "Lunch," and you'll see why when you reach the **Lobster Roll,** on Rte. 27 (tel. 516/267-3740), a seafood shanty that offers the chance to sit and enjoy some seafood outside with the dunes stretching off into the distance or, if you prefer, inside among the nautical clutter of nets, glass floats, and ship's lanterns. Crab, lobster, or shrimp rolls; fried clams, scallops or softshell crabs, steamers; and fish and chips are just a few of the goodies that attract the crowds. Prices run $6 to $12.

HOURS: 11:30 A.M. to 10 P.M. daily in summer; closed off-season.

Montauk Brunches/Breakfasts

The really spectacular brunch is served at the **Montauk Yacht Club** and has already been discussed. Also at **Gurney's Inn.**

EVENING ENTERTAINMENT

Montauk doesn't possess too many hot spots. Life really centers on two places —the **Yacht Club,** Star Island (tel. 516/668-3100), and **Gurney's** (tel. 516/668-2345), where there's dancing and musical entertainment. The **Boathouse,** Emery Street (tel. 516/668-5574), often features a trio on weekends in season.

MONTAUK ACTIVITIES

Montauk offers an unparallelled array of exciting activities:

BEACHES: Montauk's beaches fall under the jurisdiction of East Hampton Township. See the East Hampton Activities section in the last chapter.

BIRDWATCHING: During the summer, environmentalists and naturalists lead daily nature walks spotting birds and flowers. On these walks you'll be on territory where the first cattle ranches were established in the United States. Walks leave from the Third House, East Lake Drive (Deep Hollow Ranch).

BOATING: Brucie's Boats (tel. 516/324-5063) rents sailboats and powerboats and provides sailing and waterskiing lessons. Paddle, sail, and rowboats can also be rented at Fort Pond Boathouse, Emery Street (tel. 516/668-2042). Ski Uihlein's (tel. 516/668-3799) rents 16- to 31-foot boats for fishing and waterskiing.

CAMPING: The best and most popular camping is found at **Hither Hills State Park,** where sites are located right on the dunes. They're not for the camper in search of seclusion and privacy though—competition for reservations is so fierce that a lottery is run in January of each year to assign summertime sites. RATES: Average cost is $11 to $12 per day, $59 to $66 a week. Open from early April through mid-October; from October to Thanksgiving the area is open but all services are closed. For information, call or write the Long Island Park and Recreation Commission, Permit Office, P.O. Box 247, Babylon, NY 11702 (tel. 516/669-1000). After April 1, write to the Superintendent, Hither Hills State Park, Montauk, NY 11954 (tel. 516/668-2554).

FISHING: Montauk is an angler's paradise, where 11,000 vessels and 75 charter boats hold many of the world records for sports fishing. Party and charter boats leave from Montauk Marine Basin, West Lake Drive (tel. 516/668-5900), mostly for shark or blue fishing. An annual shark-fishing tournament is held (usually in mid-July) when trophies as large as 1,000 pounds are brought in!

Viking Starship, Inc., P.O. Box 730, Montauk, NY 11954 (tel. 516/668-5700), sails daily for half- and full-day and/or night fishing for flounder, fluke, and bluefish. Half day for fluke and flounder costs $17; night fishing for blues costs $28. Fishing tackle is available aboard. Capt. Willie's *Famous Lazybones* offers two trips a day at 7 A.M. and 1 P.M., leaving from Tuma's Dock (tel. 516/668-2986).

GOLF: The 18-hole, par-72 championship Montauk Downs Golf Course (tel. 516/668-5000) was designed by Robert Trent Jones and is considered one of the top 50 public courses in the United States.

HANG-GLIDING/PARACHUTING: Hang-gliding, sailing, and parachuting are offered at Ocean Air Sports (tel. 516/668-4000).

HORSEBACK RIDING: Ride in the footsteps of Teddy Roosevelt on a one-hour trail ride or enjoy 1½- or 2-hour beach rides. Special Sunset rides are also arranged. Choose either Western or English saddle. Call Hidden Echo's Ranch (tel. 516/668-5453).

PICNICKING: Pick up supplies at Gosman's Dock seafood store, which sells gourmet items and salads as well as seafood. Other sources include Herb's Market, Main Street (tel. 516/668-2335), open Sundays, and Ronnie's Deli and Grocery on Main Street (tel. 516/668-2757).

SAILING: For a thrilling experience, you can sail on the 86-foot replica of an 1818 windjammer, the *Appledore,* P.O. Box 1414, Southampton, NY 11968 (tel. 516/283-6071). It leaves from Tuma's dock for three two-hour day sails at noon, 3 P.M., and 6 P.M. From July 1 to September 1.
Sailboat rentals can be found in Kirk Park.

STATE PARK: Guided nature tours are given through Hither Hills State Park during the summer. For information, call 516/668-2461.

TENNIS: Hither Hills Racquet Club (tel. 516/267-8525) has six courts available by the hour or the season for a small fee. Facilities include a ball machine. Also at Harborside Motel and Tennis Club, West Lake Drive (tel. 516/668-2511). Montauk Downs State Park, South Fairview Avenue (tel. 516/668-5000), has six clay courts, for which a small charge is made after June 25.

SWIMMING: Montauk Downs State Park, South Fairview Avenue (tel. 516/668-5000), has a swimming pool, if you don't like the ocean or bay beaches.

WHALE WATCHING: This is one of Montauk's unique attractions (at least for Long Island). A scientific research crew leads a 4½-hour trip in search of these magnificent, benevolent creatures and also dolphins, sea turtles, and sea birds. Price: Around $30 for adults. For information, write Okeanos Ocean Research Foundation, 216 E. Montauk Hwy. (P.O. Box 776), Hampton Bays, NY 11946 (tel. 516/728-4522).

WINDSURFING: Rentals and instruction available at Star Island Road.

SAG HARBOR & SHELTER ISLAND

DISTANCES IN MILES: Sag Harbor, 106; Shelter Island, 110 miles
ESTIMATED DRIVING TIME: 2½ to 4 hours, depending on traffic.

DRIVING: For Sag Harbor, take the Long Island Expressway to Exit 70, and pick up Rte. 27 east; turn left in Bridgehampton along the Sag Harbor Turnpike. For Shelter Island, take the bridge out of Sag Harbor down Rte. 114 to the blinking light, and turn right for the North Haven ferry. Or you can take the LIE to Rte. 25 to the Greenport Ferry.
BUS: Hampton Jitney will take you to Sag Harbor (check off-season). For information, call 212/936-0440.
TRAIN: The Long Island Rail Road (tel. 718/454-5477) stops in Bridgehampton or East Hampton. If you come via the North Fork, it also stops in Greenport.

Special Events to Plan Your Trip Around
JUNE: The Whaler's Festival—whaleboat races, beard-growing contests, etc.
SEPTEMBER: The Hamptons Triathlon, a 1½-mile swim combined with a 25-mile bike ride and a 10-mile run. For information, write to P.O. Box 643, Wainscott, NY 11975.

For further information about New York in general, contact the Division of Tourism, New York State Department of Commerce, One Commerce Plaza, Albany, NY 12245 (tel. 518/474-4116).

For general information about Long Island, contact the Long Island Tourism and Convention Commission, 213 Carleton Ave., Central Islip, NY 11722 (tel. 516/234-4959), and the Suffolk County Department of Economic Development, H. Lee Dennison Bldg. Veterans Memorial Hwy., Hauppauge, NY 11788 (tel. 516/360-4800).

For specific information about Sag Harbor, contact the Merchants Association of Sag Harbor Chamber of Commerce, 459 Main St., Sag Harbor, NY 11963 (tel. 516/725-0011).

For Shelter Island, contact the Shelter Island Chamber of Commerce, P.O. Box 577, Shelter Island Heights, NY 11965 (tel. 516/749-0399). During the summer (July and August) information is dispensed at the windmill on Long Wharf in Sag Harbor.

Sag Harbor has always seemed the most real of the South Fork's towns to me, still rooted in its whaling past, unpretentious and unaffected by Hampton chic and artifice. Sadly, that's changing. The boutiques and condos have arrived, and the stores displaying expensive gourmet items and the proverbial light-oak-and-brass-look bar-restaurants are opening along Main Street. Still, nothing can really detract from the fine architecture of the town's 18th- and 19th-century homes nor from the view across Gardiner's Bay from the main downtown dock.

SAG HARBOR

SAG HARBOR ATTRACTIONS

Like the earlier settled Hamptons, Sag Harbor was first colonized by the English from Connecticut, who arrived and built a thriving town that, even before the Revolution, was a major port, second only to New York. In 1693 a bell for Southampton was landed here. Trade between Sag Harbor and the West Indies was initiated in the years 1760–1770. In the first session of the U.S. Congress, George Washington approved the act establishing Sag Harbor an official Federal Port of Entry, appointing Henry Packer Dering Sag Harbor's first Customs master. The **first custom house** (1789) in New York was located here on Garden Street and can be visited today (tel. 516/941-9444). Here all the cargo was cleared, duties paid, and mail dropped. The house has been meticulously restored according to the household inventory of Henry Packer Dering and thus reveals the lifestyle of a fairly affluent Long Island family between 1790 and 1820. HOURS: June to September, Tuesday to Sunday from 10 A.M. to 5 P.M. ADMISSION: $1 for adults, 25¢ for children.

During the Revolution, the town was occupied by the British, who established their headquarters at what is now the American Hotel on Main Street. Many Long Islanders fled to Connecticut. On May 22, 1777, Lieutenant-Colonel Meigs led a number of these patriotic refugees across the Sound from New Haven in 13 whaleboats, raided Sag Harbor, and burned 12 brigs and sloops at Long Wharf, seized 120 tons of hay, corn, and oats, 12 hogsheads of rum, and killed six and took another 90 prisoner. Two monuments on Union and High Streets commemorate this daring raid. After the Revolution, the town continued to thrive on trade with the West Indies and became an increasingly cosmopolitan community, one with a newspaper, the *Long Island Herald,* which was established in 1791. When the War of 1812 was declared, H. P. Dering was put in charge of the Sag Harbor Arsenal and the populace overcame the 1813 British attack. The war, though, brought hardship to Sag Harbor and interfered with trade, and the disastrous fire of 1817 made economic recovery difficult. It was not until the late 1820s that the port regained its earlier importance and this was primarily due to increased whaling activities. By 1845 it had grown into the largest whaling port in the state and fourth largest in the world, with a fleet of 63 vessels belonging to 12 firms. The biggest year was 1847, when 32 ships brought in 605,000 pounds of bone and 68,000 barrels of sperm and whale oil valued at $1 million. In all, during the brief period of whaling, $25 million was brought into port. To recapture the flavor of this era, go through the whale's jawbone into the **Whaling Museum,** at Main and Garden Streets (tel. 516/725-0770), which is housed in a marvelous Greek Revival mansion that once belonged to Benjamin Huntting 2nd and was designed and built by Minard LaFever. Besides the whaling equipment, ship models, log books describing four-year trips, and a great collection of scrimshaw, the museum also features collections of guns, children's toys, and other items, all crammed into a series of rooms. You could spend several hours here looking at a portrait of Sag Harbor in 1860, a tricycle of the same date, an exquisite cameo carved on a whole shell, or the Indian artifacts excavated locally by William Wallace Tooker. You'll also come across objects that relate stories about local characters like Fannie Tunison, an Edwardian lady who, even though she could only move her head and neck, created watercolors and all kinds of sewn and embroidered articles, some of which are on display. At the end of your visit you'll also know the difference between a bark, a brig, a ship, and a schooner if you didn't know it already. HOURS: May 15 to September 30, Monday to Saturday from 1 to 5 P.M., on Sunday from 2 to 5 P.M. ADMISSION: 75¢ for adults, 25¢ for children.

Across the street the **Whaler's Presbyterian Church** (tel. 516/725-0894) dates from this period also. Designed by Minard LaFever in 1844, it was once crowned by a five-story tower that was destroyed by the hurricane of 1938. The walls slope in the manner of ancient temples on the Nile, and the parapets are decorated with rows of whaler's blubber spades that were finely crafted by ships' carpenters. HOURS: Open daily during summer.

When oil was discovered, the whaling industry declined. The population of Sag Harbor dwindled to 2,000, and the almost-deserted village languished until the Fahys opened a watchcasing factory in the 1890s. The labor used was largely Jewish, and for this reason, **Temple Adas Israel,** the oldest Jewish temple and congregation on Long Island, was built in 1898. It's well worth a visit for the Gothic stained glass and the locally carved altarpiece. At about the same time the town was beginning to gain some fame as a resort, and this development continued, the town later attracting writers like John Steinbeck who set out from here on his famous *Travels with Charley* trip. The tradition continues to this day. Many writers and artists have chosen Sag Harbor as their home and you might catch them playing softball in the local park. History, tree-lined streets flanked by all kinds of old homes (from saltboxes to Greek Revival mansions to Victorian gingerbread confections), a lovely harbor where many summer visitors choose to dock and live aboard their yachts, and sunsets over bay beaches make Sag Harbor a lovely place to go down to the bay again.

SAG HARBOR LODGING

The **American Hotel,** Main Street, Sag Harbor, NY 11963 (tel. 516/725-3535), operates in a thoroughly Victorian atmosphere. Wicker chairs stand on the front porch; the front parlor is filled with Victorian-style sofas and other pieces. The bar is dark and cozy, particularly in winter when a fire burns. In summer, an overhead fan hanging from the stamped-metal ceiling hums quietly. Classical music in the background adds to the atmosphere. The rooms, reached by a separate entrance, are each differently decorated in an antique elegant style. Room 2 has a sleigh bed set against candy-stripe wallpaper; Room 6 features several Eastlake pieces, while Room 5 contains a high carved Victorian bed with crocheted coverlet, oak dresser, and wicker chairs. Fresh flowers grace every room.

The dining room is well known, particularly for its extensive (and I mean extensive) wine list. There are two dining areas to choose from: the formal chintz room, with crisp white tablecloths, or the skylit porch-conservatory, decked out with white metal chairs, rambling rubber plants (quite extraordinary!), and Mexican tile. The menu changes daily but will always offer some extravagances like beluga caviar and foie gras to start. About a dozen main courses offer a variety of fish, poultry, and meat dishes—turbot with a beurre blanc, tuna steak with béarnaise sauce, gallantine of chicken with pheasant mousse, rack of lamb with peppermint sauce, and tournedos à la périgourdine. Prices run $17.25 to $24. Luncheon offers similarly appealing dishes, priced from $9.50 to $15.

RATES: In winter, $75 on weekdays, $100 on weekends; in summer (two-night minimum), $90 on weekdays, $120 on weekends. LUNCH: Noon to 3 P.M. daily. DINNER: 6 to 11 P.M. daily. Closed Thanksgiving and Christmas Days.

Otherwise, lodgings are scarce in Sag Harbor. The one downtown motel, **Baron's Cove Inn,** West Water Street, Sag Harbor, NY 11963 (tel. 516/725-2100), has been converted into modern time-sharing units, although you may have some luck getting a rental. Second-floor units giving a view of the bay and the bridge are light and airy and furnished in light oak, Breuer chairs, and feature a sleeping loft.

RATES: $90 to $145 in season, $60 to $80 off-season.

SAG HARBOR DINING

Lunch/Dinner Choices
The Long Wharf that used to feature a steel band on weekend afternoons, attracting a sashaying limbo crowd, has been transformed into a far more sophisticated

dining restaurant, **George Studley's Long Wharf** (tel. 516/725-0176). It still commands a magnificent view, over Sag Harbor marina out into Gardiner's Bay, one of the finest indeed in the whole of the Hamptons, but the decor now consists of butcher-block tables, pink napery, and tile floors that seem appropriate to its waterfront location. Seductive gourmet items and stunning flower bouquets are arranged around a very large jade plant, which has become the focus of the room. Dinner entrees include a Long Island duckling with peppercorn sauce, grilled swordfish with coriander and tomato salsa, carpaccio of tuna, blackened bluefish, grilled salmon with mustard sauce, and angel-hair pasta with shrimp and lobster pesto. The emphasis, as this brief listing suggests, is indeed on seafood. Prices range from $12.50 to $20. Desserts are made on the premises and will most likely include fresh-fruit tarts and fresh berries among others. The deck is always a good place to enjoy a luncheon sandwich or burger (a half-pounder is $7) or cocktails and snacks later in the day. Open seven days a week from May 25.

LUNCH: Monday to Friday from noon to 3 P.M. DINNER: 6 to 10 P.M. on weekdays, to 11 P.M. on weekends. BRUNCH: Saturday and Sunday. The deck is open from noon to 8 P.M.

Bay Street Café, Sag Harbor (tel. 516/725-9613). Past the small front bar area with windows that look out onto the dock across the street there lies a pretty dining room with a cathedral-style ceiling and rush-seated gatebacks set at tables spread with mauve tablecloths. The menu features some dishes with Oriental accents—bluefish with soy and ginger, fettuccine with shrimp and snow peas. The fish of the day will be prepared in one of three different ways—Cajun pecan, with a shrimp sauce, or with herb butter and capers. Breast of duck and tournedos béarnaise are also among the entree selections, priced from $11.50 to $17.50. To start, shrimp cocktail, oysters, clams, and fried Brie are available. The brick patio, colorfully arrayed with tables sporting pink tablecloths and turquoise chairs, is a pleasant place to dine.

LUNCH: 11:30 A.M. to 3:30 P.M. daily. DINNER: Sunday to Thursday from 6 to 10 P.M., on Friday and Saturday to 11 P.M. (one hour later in summer).

Pat's Noyac Steak Pub, Noyac Road, Noyac, Sag Harbor (tel. 516/725-3644), is a popular hangout where the bar stools are occupied by a friendly local crowd, often watching the sports games. The welcome is real, and so are the Irish memorabilia and artifacts and the green cloths on the tables in the cheery dining room. At dinner there are always pub specials—steak, sausage-and-mushroom pie, cottage pie (another name for shepherd's pie), and steak-and-kidney pie, plus such seafood and grilled dishes as fish and chips, baked stuffed flounder, and steak tidbits on toast. Prices run from $4.75 for a burger to $14 for a 16-ounce steak. Chowder, Scotch eggs, and baked stuffed clams are among the appetizers. For dessert, dishes are typical favorites like cheesecake and chocolate mousse.

HOURS: Monday to Saturday from 11:30 A.M. to 10 P.M., on Sunday from noon to 10 P.M. (in summer, until 11 P.M. on weekends).

Ryerson's, on Main Street (tel. 516/725-3530), is okay for a luncheon hamburger, while **The Corner,** at the corner of Main and the dock, is a local hangout.

The **Ship's Galley,** Main Street (tel. 516/725-1774), is indeed small, possessing only a half dozen or so polished wood tables set with rush-seated chairs and placed in a warm country atmosphere of decorative majolica, teapots, and pewter mugs, displayed at various locations in various ways. A profusion of silk flowers sits atop the case that displays salads, savories, pâté, chèvre, sesame crackers, cornichon pickles, olives, and cherry tart. At dinner the menu is limited. Regularly featured dishes include duckling with brandied fruit sauce, garnished with glazed chestnuts, and several shrimp specialties like shrimp in black-bean sauce and ginger. Daily specials of meat, fish, poultry, and pasta round out the choices. Prices run $15.75 to $24. To start, sample the Japanese dumplings stuffed with crabmeat and scallions, sauced with sesame and ginger, or avocado with baby shrimp. Closed Tuesday and off-season.

Sag Harbor Breakfasts
Breakfast with the best view obviously comes at George Studley's Long Wharf, but you'll have to wait until noon. Most everyone in Sag Harbor heads for the **Paradise,** on Main Street (tel. 516/725-2110), or across the street to **Hilde's Sweet Shop and Tea Room** (tel. 516/725-0182), which serves egg dishes and soup as well as sweets, coffees, and teas. It's also famous for its ice cream, but not at breakfast. HOURS: 9 A.M. to 5 P.M.; closed Tuesday.

Dinner Only
Locals (if you can count as locals those who come from as far away as Hampton Bays) swear by **Il Cappucino,** Madison Street (tel. 516/725-2747), a warm, comfortable place that serves excellent, fairly priced food. The garden salad, tossed in a garlic dressing and served with croutons sprinkled with cheese, is superb; a special fish of the day might come in a spicy marinara sauce; pastas include a tasty cappelleti with pistachio; and the old standbys, like veal parmigiana, are also available. Prices range from $9 to $12. Red gingham, red-glass candleholders, and classical music background give the place a lovely glow.

DINNER: In summer, 5:30 to 10 P.M. on weekdays, until 11 P.M. on weekends; in winter, daily but shorter hours.

Tucked away on Noyac Road, the **Inn at Mill Creek,** 590 Noyac Rd. (tel. 516/725-1116), is another local favorite overlooking the busy scene, hoist, and boats at Mill Creek. The decor is simple—light oak and blue napery—and the food is fresh and good value. A pianist entertains on Friday and Saturday nights (in season only, I believe). The menu offers a traditional selection of steak and seafood dishes, priced from $9 for cheese ravioli with marinara sauce to $17 for twin lobstertails. Other dishes also include broiled flounder, duck with orange sauce, chicken Cordon Bleu, veal parmigiana, and prime rib. During the week the price includes a trip to the salad bar. To start, try the clams or oysters on the half shell. DINNER: In summer, Monday to Saturday from 6 to 10 P.M., on Sunday from 5 to 10 P.M.; in winter, on Friday and Saturday from 6 to 9 P.M., on Sunday from 5 to 9 P.M. only.

EVENING ENTERTAINMENT
There's a downtown cinema in Sag Harbor. Or, more interesting, there's **Canio's Bookstore** (tel. 516/757-3153). A delightful place to poke around during the day, it also hosts weekend poetry readings and other literary events in the early evening.

The Corner (tel. 516/725-9760) is a real down-home hangout, but most night-life action is found elsewhere, along Rte. 27 from Southampton to East Hampton.

SAG HARBOR ACTIVITIES

BEACHES: Long Beach in Noyac is a narrow beach stretching along the bay and open to nonresidents for a fee.

BIRDWATCHING: Morton Wildlife Refuge, on Noyac Road (cross the bridge, along the bay beach, and turn right by the Salty Dog restaurant), is managed for two protected migratory shore birds, the piping plover and least tern. There are plenty of other shore and songbirds to spy, as well as pheasants, deer, and osprey. An ideal place for hiking and fishing. Nature trails. For information, contact the Refuge Manager, Wertheim NWR, P.O. Box 21, Shirley, NY 11967 (tel. 516/286-0485).

BOATING: Boat rentals at Baron's Cove Marina, West Water Street (tel. 516/725-3939 or 2100); Mill Creek Marina, Noyac Road (tel. 516/725-1351); Noyac Marina, Pince Neck Avenue (tel. 516/725-3333), for rowboats with outboards.

FISHING: In the Elizabeth Morton National Wildlife Refuge, there's good bay fishing for weakfish in summer, bluefish in fall.

HIKING: Elizabeth Morton National Wildlife Refuge, where waterfowl, songbirds, mammals, and even birds of prey congregate, is lovely for nature rambles and picnicking on the small beach. For a permit, contact the Refuge Manager, National Wildlife Refuge, R.D. 359, Noyac Road, Sag Harbor, NY 11963 (tel. 516/725-2270). From Rte. 27, go 2½ miles north on North Sea Road, and then four miles east on Noyac Road. Also good for clamming, oystering, and scallopping.

PICNICKING: Any of the beaches or the Elizabeth Morton Wildlife Refuge make great picnicking spots. For gourmet supplies, head to the Ship's Galley on Main Street, which offers everything from jams, jellies, pickles, and mustards to a full selection of cheeses, meats, salads, and daily specials. For more mundane fare, there's always the supermarket right across from the post office.

TENNIS: There are a number of courts at Mashashimuet Park on Main Street.

SHELTER ISLAND

From Sag Harbor, it's only a short ferry ride across the bay to the rolling wooded hills and miles of white sand beaches of Shelter Island, first settled by Quakers fleeing persecution in New England. Today it's an unspoiled haven for bicycling, hiking, horse riding, and boating—and the residents aim to keep it that way.

From downtown Sag Harbor, cross the bridge and follow the signs to the ferry (turning right at the blinking light). Ferries leave North Haven from 6 A.M. to 11:45 P.M. (until 1:45 A.M. during July and August). For information, call 516/749-1200.

Once off the ferry, if you follow Rte. 114 it will take you all the way through Shelter Island Heights, where the island's few stores and restaurants are located, to the rim of Dering Harbor, where another ferry leaves for Greenport on the North Fork. But first, let's explore Shelter Island and the great opportunities it offers for rural pleasures.

SHELTER ISLAND LODGING

At the eastern tip of the island you'll find Ram Island, so called because it looks a little like a ram. It's attached by a very narrow spit of land, so that the approach road appears more like a causeway. The island's most appealing lodging, the **Ram's Head Inn,** Shelter Island, NY 11965 (tel. 516/749-0811), is located here overlooking Coecles Harbor. In this shingled, green-shuttered building, a group of scientists, including Einstein, gathered in 1947 for the first Shelter Island Conference on the Foundation of Quantum Mechanics. Country furniture and candlewick spreads are found in the 17 rooms (four with shared bath). The grassy backyard, with shade trees and rose bushes, sweeps down to a private beach, where sailboats can be rented. A tennis court is also available. A bar and recreation room with an upright piano affords more entertainment, while the chintz dining room serves good continental cuisine at dinner and Sunday brunch. The restaurant is closed Tuesday.

RATES: $75 to $100 double in season, $65 to $80 off-season. Open weekends only, May and October; daily in summer. Closed November to May.

Bowditch House, Rte. 114, Shelter Island, NY 11965 (tel. 516/749-0075 in summer, 516/887-1898 in winter), is named after an old American family, one of whose members, Nathaniel, wrote the *American Practical Navigator* (1802) and in which family the house remained until 13 or so years ago. It was built in 1854 and its current owners, Nora and Jim Furey, now offer eight rooms sharing two bathrooms (one sports an old-fashioned tub with a spray attachment; the other, a bona fide shower). All of the rooms are furnished differently. Only the potpourri, a chamber pot serving as a trash can, and fans are common features to all. Room 2, for example, contains a painted gate bed with lemon-yellow eiderdown, an oak dresser set with a posy of flowers and eau de toilettes, a '30s-style wicker chair, all set against beige floral wallpaper and standing on painted floorboards. In one of the original panes of the window a signature is scratched, apparently by a woman who was married there in August 1872. A Mission-style rocker, marble sidetable, and a hall tree are among the furnishings of Room 5, decorated in blue; mauve and rose are the prime colors in Room 4.

A cold buffet-style breakfast is served from 8:30 to 10 A.M. featuring fresh fruits, cereals, and at least two baked items; on weekends a hot dish is also offered. The beamed dining room is made comfortable with polished oak tables, a woodstove, and personal touches. The fire warms it on cool mornings. In the evenings guests gather for wine and cheese and get to know one another in the parlor. Overstuffed Victorian chairs, a blanket chest, and other attractive pieces, including a unique English pew, create the ambience.

RATES: $68 double in midweek, $75 on weekends. Open weekends only from mid-May to the end of June and Labor Day through October, daily during July and August.

A large rambling place overlooking Crescent Beach, the **Pridwin,** 81 Shore Rd., Crescent Beach, Shelter Island, NY 11965 (tel. 516/749-0476), is operated by a very friendly New York City émigré, Dick Petry, who takes pride in his accommodations and the array of activities that he offers—waterskiing, rowing, bicycling, speedboat rides, Sunfish sailing, pedalboating, and tennis on four courts. It's certainly an ideal summer place. Wicker chairs and couches line the 40-foot-long lobby; there are 40 rooms in the main building (those with even numbers face Shelter Island Sound), and all have private bath and are furnished plainly. Six suites make ideal family accommodations. Behind the main building there are eight very pleasant cottages (three with fireplace), some studios, others one-bedroom, but all with kitchen or kitchenette, air conditioning, color TV, and private deck. Breakfast, lunch, and dinner are served on the deck in summer; there's dancing three nights a week, and the Pridwin's special Wednesday cookout is a popular island event.

RATES: $135 to $160 double (MAP) on weekdays, $160 to $185 double (MAP) on weekends in season; less off-season. Cottages go for $140 on weekdays and $165 on weekends, accommodations only—no meals included in the price. In spring, fall, and winter, cottages go for $60 to $100 double.

Back closer to the Heights, the **Dering Harbor Inn,** 13 Winthrop Rd. (P.O. Box AD), Shelter Island, NY 11965 (tel. 516/749-0900), occupies a grassy knoll overlooking the harbor. The main building has "late motel"–style rooms, some with private patio, cable TV, and air conditioning. Other buildings around the property offer two-bedroom-two-bath units and one-bedroom-one-bath units with a water view. There's an outdoor pool enclosed by a hedge, tennis courts, and a full dining room with a flagstone chimney fireplace.

RATES: June 27 to September, $100 to $225 in midweek, $130 to $250 on weekends. Open April 1 to mid-October.

Also at Crescent Beach, there's the modern **Shelter Island Resort Motel,** 35 Shore Rd. (P.O. Box 255), Shelter Island, NY 11965 (tel. 516/749-2001), where all the rooms have sundecks, air conditioning, and color TV—and you're right across from Crescent Beach.

RATES: June 27 to August 28, $95 in midweek, $130 on weekends; April 25 to May 22 and October 13 to April 30, $65 in midweek, $75 on weekends; May 26 to June 26 and September 1 to October 13, $65 in midweek, $95 on weekends.

SHELTER ISLAND DINING

Recommendable dining establishments are hard to find, and locals swear by the simple roadside fish/shellfish stands and bars like **Chips,** on Rte. 114 (tel. 516/749-8926). A step leads down from the fish market into the dining area furnished with plain wooden tables, each sporting a bottle of tomato ketchup. The choice of fish is wide—dolphin, mako, swordfish, flounder, weakfish, and tilefish, as well as lobster, all priced from a low of $8 to a close-to-low $10.

DINNER: Daily except Wednesday; open during the winter if there's no scalloping.

The Cook, 15 Grand Ave. (tel. 516/749-2005), in the Heights, is located in a pretty Victorian house with a narrow front porch. Soft lighting falling on golden tablecloths and country furnishings make for a pretty and popular dining spot serving some good cuisine. Prices run $14 to $26. At the rear is a raw bar.

DINNER: 6 to 10 P.M. on weekdays, to 11 P.M. on weekends. BRUNCH: Saturday and Sunday from noon to 2:30 P.M. Closed November through April.

Residents appreciate the Inn Between, on Rte. 114 (tel. 516/749-2123), for its fresh seafood and good steaks, and also for staying open year round. Dinner prices range from $10 to $15. And this is a fine place to stop also for a soup-and-salad lunch. Well recommended.

LUNCH: 11:30 A.M. to 3 P.M. daily. DINNER: 6 to 9 P.M. on weekdays, to 10 P.M. on weekends.

Other possible lunch spots? The deck overlooking the pond at the Dory, Bridge Street (tel. 516/749-8871), offers sandwiches, salads, and fish and meat dishes for lunch and steaks and seafood at dinner.

HOURS: Noon to 3 P.M. and 6 to 10 P.M. daily, in summer only. In winter the bar is open.

Or try the terrace-restaurant at the Chequit Inn, Shelter Island Heights (tel. 516/749-0018), which last year was called Clamdiggers (in 1987, I'm told, it will be under new management, so who knows what it'll be like). It is, however, as it stands, a secluded spot set behind a privet hedge and dotted with hydrangea from which you can glimpse blue waters and sailing craft through the trees. Deep-fried crab sticks, fish and chips, clams and oysters, and other delicacies from the raw bar, plus burgers, were the prime luncheon fare.

LUNCH: Noon to 3 P.M. daily in summer.

Another roadside stop must be Pastry Plus, on Rte. 114 (tel. 516/749-0774), at which you can obtain picnic makings to go and select from various salads and appetizers—chicken-walnut, sausage calzones, antipasto, pâtés, spinach-and-tomato quiche, etc., as well as soups, rolls, and pastries including cannolis and Linzer torte. The store also vends vinegars, mustards, crackers, preserves, cheeses, and other gourmet items. You can dine at the outside tables under pretty pastel-colored umbrellas. Windowboxes, gladioli, and a low hedgerow add appeal.

HOURS: Wednesday and Thursday from 8 A.M. to 6 P.M., on Friday and Saturday to 6:30 P.M., on Sunday to 5:30 P.M.; closed Monday and Tuesday.

SHELTER ISLAND ACTIVITIES

BEACHES: Beach permits can be obtained from the Town Hall, Ferry Road (tel. 516/749-1166).

BICYCLING: For rentals, try Coecles Harbor Marina (tel. 516/749-0700) and Piccozzi's Service Station, Bridge Street (tel. 516/749-0045 or 749-0520).

GOLF: Shelter Island Country Club, 26 Sunnyside Ave. (tel. 516/749-8841), has a nine-hole course.

HIKING: Mashomack Preserve, 79 S. Ferry Rd. (Rte. 114). Open daily, except Tuesday. Guided walks on selected Sundays at 9:15 A.M. from the entrance house. Reservations necessary (tel. 516/749-1001).

PICNICKING: Head for the beaches, picking up supplies at George's IGA Market or Fedi Market (open until 8 P.M.). The Island Food Center has barbecued chickens, ducks, and sandwiches to go, while Pastry Plus (tel. 516/749-0774) will add some gourmet items if you wish.

EXPLORING THE NORTH FORK & NORTH SHORE

DISTANCES IN MILES: Cold Spring Harbor, 37; Northport, 46; Stony Brook, 58; Greenport, 102; Orient, 107
ESTIMATED DRIVING TIMES: 45 minutes to 2¼ hours

DRIVING: Long Island Expressway to Rte. 25 for towns on the North Folk. LIE to Walt Whitman Road for Huntington and Cold Spring Harbor; LIE to Deer Park Avenue for Northport and Centerport; to Nicolls Road for Stony Brook.
SUNRISE EXPRESS: (tel. 718/767-2775 or 516/477-1200) provides rapid service to North Fork towns—last stop is Greenport.
TRAIN: The Long Island Rail Road (tel. 718/454-5477) stops at Cold Spring Harbor, Huntington, Green Lawn (for Centerport), Northport, Smithtown, St. James, Stony Brook, and Port Jefferson. On the North Fork it stops at Mattituck, Cutchogue, Southold, and Greenport.

Special Events to Plan Your Trip Around
JUNE: The Bach Aria Festival, P.O. Box 997, Stony Brook, NY 11790 (tel. 516/246-5678), a two-week festival of concerts and workshops culminating in a waterfront picnic supper on the last evening. Single tickets run $10 to $14 (usually held in late June).
　　Strawberry Festival in Mattituck.
SEPTEMBER: Labor Day Craft Show in Greenport.
OCTOBER: Festival of the Sea in Greenport.

For further information about New York in general, contact the Division of Tourism, New York State Department of Commerce, One Commerce Plaza, Albany, NY 12245 (tel. 518/474-4116).

For general information about Long Island, contact the Long Island Tourism and Convention Commission, 213 Carleton Ave., Central Islip, NY 11722 (tel. 516/234-4959), and the Suffolk County Department of Economic Development, H. Lee Dennison Bldg. Veterans Memorial Hwy., Hauppauge, NY 11788 (tel. 516/360-4800).

For specific information about the North Fork, contact the Greenport/ Southold Chamber of Commerce, P.O. Box 66, Greenport, NY 11994 (tel. 516/477-1383); Southold Town Promotion Committee, P.O. Box 499, Greenport, NY 11944 (tel. 516/298-5757); the Port Jefferson Chamber of Commerce, 118 W. Broadway, Port Jefferson, NY 11777 (tel. 516/ 473-1414); and the Huntington Township Chamber of Commerce, 151 W. Carver St., Huntington, NY 11743 (tel. 516/423-6100).

The North Fork has a far more rural feel than the well-developed South Fork. Here, over a third of the 121-square-mile area is still devoted to farming, compared to less than a tenth of the South Fork's much larger 212 square miles. The summer population totals only 72,000 compared to the South Fork's 173,000. The landscape consists of a lovely crazy-quilt of ponds and marshlands, hills and wooded strands, and a string of unassuming country towns. The North Fork, and indeed the North Shore in general, clings tenaciously to its past rural traditions, admittedly with anxiety and increasing difficulty.

At the eastern tip of the North Fork, visitors can explore a string of New England–like towns—old whaling ports like Greenport, whose narrow streets also boast several antique stores; Orient, whose main street has a post office–general store and church and one or two other residences along it; Cutchogue, with its historic central green; and many others, all enfolded into Southhold Township. All offer beaches and opportunities for sailing and other water-oriented pastimes, as well as hiking, bicycling, and such pleasures as dining on succulent lobster and other seafood.

Farther west and you're traveling through the glorious farmlands, past acres and acres of potatoes, sod and horse farms, orchards and fields growing all kinds of vegetables and fruits before arriving at the so-called Historic Triangle, centered on the picturesque 19th-century town of Stony Brook, site of an exquisite museum collection, and close to Old Field Point, bustling Port Jefferson, and to the west St. James, which still possesses a wonderful old country store. This area is great for exploring the backroads, where the really wealthy still live along hedgerowed roads. From St. James it's only a short distance to the charms of Northport and Cold Spring Harbor, both old whaling towns, and sandwiched in between is Centerport, site of the Vanderbilt Mansion and Observatory Planetarium.

Getting There

You can drive directly from New York City or you can take the ferry from Sag Harbor to Shelter Island and from there to Greenport. The whole outing makes a delightful day's adventure from any one of the Hamptons.

Greenport and Orient Point

GREENPORT

Settled in 1682, this New England–style fishing village retains the flavor of its earlier days, when it was a prominent whaling port and a major link between the cities of New York and Boston.

You'll want to wander down the port's narrow streets, browsing in the stores and antique shops. Among them the **Arctic Hunter** gallery displays and sells Eskimo art and sculpture; **Wooden Goose** is filled with gifts, **Doofpot** vends Portuguese and other European imports, and **Studio Gallery** has antiques, especially those with a nautical flavor.

Then explore the **harbor and docks** where schooners from Connecticut anchor alongside yachts and other pleasure craft.

Besides the attractions associated with the sea, there's also a **Museum of Childhood** that features antique dolls and a hand-carved Swiss village. HOURS: June 15 to September 15, Wednesday to Saturday from 1:30 to 4:30 P.M.

GREENPORT LODGING

Bartlett House, 503 Front St., Greenport, NY 11944 (tel. 516/477-0371), a charming old 1908 house, has recently been restored by John and Linda Sabatino. Step inside to an impressive Corinthian-columned living room with intricate molding and a classical-style fireplace. The nine rooms (five with private bath) are up the handsome staircase. Room 2 is especially appealing, containing an iron-and-brass bedstead, oak dresser and rocker, and marble-top treadle table; the bathroom is huge. All rooms are air-conditioned. In the morning, homemade muffins, fruit cobblers, or freshly squeezed fruit juices are spread out buffet style.

RATES: $50 to $65 from May 25 to June 19, $55 to $70 from June 20 to September 2, $50 to $65 from September 3 to October 14, and $45 to $60 from October 15 to April 6. A two-bedroom unit with bath rents for $80 to $100, depending on season.

Although the white-pillared mansion bearing the name the **Townsend Manor Inn,** 714 Main St., Greenport, NY 11944 (tel. 516/477-2000), looks gracious and full of character (it was built in 1835), the varied accommodations, decorated in "late motel" style, are rather plain, many rooms having white candlewick bedspreads and Scandinavian-style furniture. Still the setting is extremely pleasant, with the secluded grounds abutting the Stirling Basin, so that many yachtsmen find the place very convenient for docking and staying overnight. All of the rooms have TV, phones, and air conditioning. There's a cocktail lounge and dining room serving a selection of meats and seafood, from sauerbraten and Yankee pot roast to swordfish, flounder, and fisherman's platters. Prices run $10 to $18.50. There's also an attractive grass-bordered outdoor pool.

RATES: $75 to $95 double on weekends from June 9 to Labor Day, $60 to $80 from Labor Day to October 13, $50 to $55 from October 14 to December 1, $53 to $55 from December 2 to March 1, and $47 to $65 from March 2 to June 8. Apartments rent for $100 to $120 in season.

Silver Sands, Silvermere Road (P.O. Box 285), Greenport, NY 11944 (tel. 516/477-0011), off Rte. 25, is a motel in a very quiet location overlooking the bay with a very prettily landscaped backyard for sitting and contemplating the vista. All the rooms are air-conditioned, and have color TV, refrigerator, coffee maker, and access to the beach. A heated pool and waterskiing and sailing lessons are available.

RATES (including breakfast): $85 to $105 double from June 20 to September 15, $75 to $95 from March 15 to June 19 and September 16 to November 15. Special packages are also offered off-season.

The **Soundview Inn,** Rte. 48 (P.O. Box 68), Greenport, NY 11944 (tel. 516/477-1910), is right on the bay and seems like a good "customer is always right" kind of place. Accommodations are in two-story motel-style buildings where all rooms face the Sound and have two double beds, private bath, sundeck, air conditioning, and TV. Some have full kitchens, others are 2½-room apartments with bedroom and living room, and still others have two bedrooms. Furniture is typical Scandinavian-style motel or light-oak modern. Other facilities include a dining room, lounge and piano bar, four tennis courts, outdoor heated pool, and a private beach.

RATES: $70 to $200 double from Mid-May to the end of June, $85 to $250 from the end of June to Labor Day, $70 to $200 from Labor Day to mid-October, $55 to $175 off-season. Add $10 for each additional person in room. Lowest prices are for a bedroom; the highest, for a two-bed/two-bath suite.

On the highway but set well back from the road with attractive grounds, shade trees, and flowers in front, is the **Drossos Motel,** Main Road, Greenport, NY

11944 (tel. 516/477-1334). Rooms have TV, air conditioning, and kitchen facilities.

RATES: $80 in season (June 15 to September 15), from $55 off-season.

GREENPORT LUNCH/DINNER CHOICES

The **Puerto Verde,** Manhasset Avenue, at Stirling Harbor (tel. 516/477-1777), occupies a lovely setting overlooking Stirling Harbor toward Greenport, making for romantic summer dining as you gaze past the bobbing masts to the shady bank opposite, where a steepled church is etched against the sky. There are specially priced set lunch and dinner menus—$6 at lunch, $9 at dinner—or you can choose to select à la carte from such items as paella ($28 with lobster) or filet of sole with bananas. Other choices among appetizers include mussels in green sauce and Spanish sausage in white wine sauce, and among the entrees, chicken in garlic sauce, pork chop in rioja sauce, and veal with mushrooms, olives, and sherry sauce. Prices range from $10.50 to $16.75. Brunch offers a choice of seafood salad, chicken livers in dry sherry, and several egg dishes priced from $6. The decor is restful and simple—cane-seated ladderbacks, stucco arches, a stone hearth, and a pleasant bar that takes advantage of the view. To reach the Puerto Verde, take Main Street out of Greenport toward Orient, and turn right. Take Manhasset Avenue to Stirling Harbor.

LUNCH: Monday to Friday from 11:30 A.M. to 2:30 P.M. DINNER: 5 to 10 P.M. on weekdays, until 11 P.M. on weekends. BRUNCH: Sunday from 11:30 A.M. to 2:30 P.M. Open from May through September.

Claudio's, 111 Main St. (tel. 516/477-9800), the local favorite for fish, has been purveying food at the dock ever since 1870. It's a typically plain waterfront restaurant that serves fresh fish and steaks, priced from $11 to $15.

LUNCH: Tuesday to Saturday from 11:30 A.M. to 3 P.M. DINNER: Monday to Saturday from 5 P.M., on Sunday from noon.

At the **Cinnamon Tree Café** in Sterling Square, on Main Street and Bay Avenue (tel. 516/477-0012), you can choose to dine outside on a brick patio or inside in a pubby atmosphere. On the menu there's usually a fish of the day that might be cooked with lemon and capers; or in a Créole style with tomatoes, peppers, and onions; as well as such meat dishes as New York shell steak with whisky peppercorn butter; or any of several other ways. Prices range from $12 to $16. On Sunday there's a jazz trio from 3 to 7 P.M.

HOURS: 11:30 A.M. to 10 P.M. daily in season.

For family dining you can't beat **Porky's,** 305 North Rd. (tel. 516/477-9833), where you can tuck into a whole dinner for as little as $11 (appetizer, salad, dessert, and coffee), choosing from a menu that includes flounder, deviled crabs, half a spring chicken, and many other traditional meat and seafood dishes.

HOURS: Tuesday to Sunday from noon to 9 P.M.; closed February.

The **Mill Creek Inn,** Main Road (tel. 516/765-1010), offers two dining rooms: one looking out toward the water, the other a cozy winter room with fireplace and ceiling fashioned from bay oyster boxes. It's yet another seafood place—scallops, shrimp, and crab in the seafood au gratin; king crab legs; Australian lobstertail; surf and turf—priced from $10 to $25.

LUNCH: 11 A.M. to 2:30 P.M. daily. DINNER: Sunday to Thursday from 5 to 9 P.M., until 10 P.M. on Friday and Saturday.

Other dining choices are **Gene's Dockside,** 27 Front St. (tel. 516/477-9824), charging $9 to $16 for seafood like fried flounder or broiled seafood combo; and **Rhumbline,** 54 Front St. (tel. 516/477-9883), a pleasantly nautical dining room serving seafood, steak, veal parmigiana, and clams on half-shell, from $5 to $12.

LUNCH AND DINNER: Daily.

ORIENT POINT

From Greenport it's only a few miles out to the very tip of the North Fork —Orient Point—where the ferries leave daily for New London, Connecticut. At the point, you'll find **Orient Beach State Park** (tel. 516/323-2440), providing acres and acres of shorefront for bathing, picnicking, and surf fishing. There's also a bird sanctuary at the west end.

The town of Orient was originally called Oysterponds, and this earlier name is recalled at the **Oysterponds Historical Society,** Village Lane in Orient (tel. 516/323-2480), which consists of six museum buildings, a slave burying ground, and a consignment antique shop, Shinbone Alley. The Village House, for example, displays an interesting parlor, dining room, and kitchen, and upstairs, portraits of local family ships' captains and toys, including an incredible locomotive that was built by Orrin F. Payne of Southold who began it at age 11 in 1858 and finished it in 1881—a fine work of art. HOURS: Mid-June through September, 2 to 5 P.M. (weekends only until July 1, then Tuesday and Thursday also). ADMISSION: $2 for adults, 50¢ for children under 16.

You may also want to detour and see the 20 **rock carvings** commemorating the Poquatuck Indians, done by E. A. Brooks on the Sound shore via Young's Road from Rte. 25.

Orient's **Theater in the Works,** 1010 Village Lane, is a charming 40-seat playhouse located in a genuine 1926 ice cream parlor. HOURS: June to September.

GREENPORT/ORIENT ACTIVITIES

BICYCLING: For rentals, go to the Bike Stop, 200 Front St., Greenport (tel. 516/477-2432), at $9.50 a day.

BOATING: Young's Boat Yard and Marina, 1670 Sage Blvd. (tel. 516/477-0830), for rentals.

CRUISES: You can sail aboard a 65-foot schooner either for a day around Shelter Island or overnight to Block Island, Mystic and East Haddam. For information contact the East End Packet Company, Box 200, Peconic, NY 11958 (tel. 516/765-1249). The *Rachael & Ebenezer* tall ship (tel. 516/477-0355) sails from Claudio's Dock at the foot of Main Street to Mystic and Block Island on day trips.

FISHING: *Prime Time II* (tel. 516/883-6461) and *Prime Time III* (tel. 516/477-0008) both leave from Orient by Sea Marina on Main Road. *Peconic Star* (tel. 516/ 477-0008) and *Brand X* (same tel.) are based in Greenport.

GOLF: East Marion's Island's End Club, on Rte. 25 (tel. 516/477-9870), offers a scenic course along the bluffs overlooking the Sound.

SWIMMING: Orient Point State Park. Open year round.

TENNIS: Sound View Motel's courts are open to the public (tel. 516/477-1910). On Route 48. Also at Young's Tennis Club, Sage Blvd. (tel. 516/477-0830).

Southold, Cutchogue, and Mattituck

SOUTHOLD

Going west from Greenport will bring you to Southold, where the first settlers arrived in 1640 at Founder's Landing. Southold, by the way, was once part of an independent colony that included New Haven, Guilford, and other Connecticut towns, which probably accounts for the New England–Cape Cod flavor of many North Fork towns.

In Southold you may want to view the **Old First Church** on Main Street, founded in 1640, although the present building dates from 1803. The adjacent burying ground is one of the oldest on Long Island. The **Archeological Museum,** also on Main Street (tel. 516/765-5577), houses one of the most complete collections of Indian artifacts on Long Island (open summer only, admission free). The **Historical Society Museum,** on Rte. 25A (tel. 516/765-5500), features an 18th-century barn, buttery, and collections of tools, toys, carriages, costumes, and furnishings.

SOUTHOLD DINING

People travel here from as far away as Port Washington just to dine on lobster at **Armando's Seafood Barge,** Rte. 25, Southold (tel. 516/765-3010), overlooking Peconic Bay toward Shelter Island. Nets, fish trophies, and other nautical regalia provide the backdrop for a seafood assortment—bluefish, weakfish, sea trout, shrimp with butter, or broiled lobster—supplemented by some beef and chicken dishes. Prices range from $10.75 to $15.75 (add $4 for a complete dinner that includes appetizer, soup or salad, dessert, and coffee). Prices are about half at lunchtime.

HOURS: Noon to 9 P.M. on weekdays, until 10 P.M. on weekends, from late April to late September; closed off-season.

Just a few yards away and equally popular is the **Original Barge** (tel. 516/765-2691), a World War II navy barge that stands practically down in the reeds at the water's edge. It's been famous for seafood for more than 35 years. The place is simple, less decorated with nautical clichés than its neighbor, and the prices are lower, going from $8 for weakfish and bluefish including the salad bar. For $10 there's a good special lobster dinner.

HOURS: June to mid-November, noon to 9 P.M. daily; weekends only in winter.

For seafood that is excellently and imaginatively prepared, try **Ross's North Fork Restaurant,** North Road (Rte. 48), in Southold (tel. 516/765-2111). Chef-owner John Ross uses locally fresh ingredients. On the menu, listing a dozen or so entrees, there might be yellowtail, flounder sautéed with almonds, charcoal-grilled mako steak with scampi butter, lobster Fra Diavolo with fettuccine, a moist flavorsome cod with dill butter, or bluefish with Dijon mustard sauce. A few meat dishes are also available, like duckling with plum sauce, calves' liver with shallots and bacon, or broiled filet mignon with cabernet sauvignon sauce. Prices run $13 to $18.

LUNCH: Tuesday to Saturday from noon to 2:30 P.M. DINNER: Tuesday to Saturday from 5 to 9 P.M., on Sunday from noon to 9 P.M. Closed December to mid-February.

For classic continental cuisine in a very pretty atmosphere in a white clapboard house surrounded by flowering shrubs, there's **La Gazelle,** Main Road (tel. 516/765-2656). Here, you'll enjoy such entrees as coq au vin, flounder grenobloise, or a spicy steak au poivre priced from $11.50 to $18.

LUNCH: noon to 3 P.M. DINNER: 5 to 10 P.M. weekdays, on Friday and Saturday until 11 P.M., on Sunday from noon to 9 P.M.

BRUNCH: Sunday from noon to 2 P.M. In summer it's closed Wednesday; in winter, Tuesday and Wednesday.

CUTCHOGUE

CUTCHOGUE ATTRACTIONS

Next is the historic town of Cutchogue, which clusters around the Village Green, where you can visit the **Old House** (tel. 516/734-6532), a fine shingled frame house dating from 1649 with leaded casement windows, a great chimney, and stairs that arch over closets below. HOURS: Open Memorial Day to September, 2 to 5 P.M. —weekends only during June and September; in July and August, Saturday through Monday. ADMISSION: $1. Also on the Village Green there's the **Old School House Museum,** Cutchogue's first district school, built in 1840. HOURS: Open Memorial Day and weekends during September and June; in July and August, Friday through Monday from 2 to 5 P.M. The early-18th-century **Wickham Farmhouse** is also located here. HOURS: Same.

Since the pioneers of **Hargrave,** County Road 48, Cutchogue (tel. 516/734-5111), started their winery in 1973 in Cutchogue, more and more vineyards have opened and are flourishing. In fact, there are now 20 on the North Fork. Hargrave offers a one-hour tour of the vineyard, the press, and the fermentation room at 2 and 4 P.M. on summer weekends, followed by tastings. Among the area wineries offering tours and tastings are **Jamesport Vineyards,** Rte. 25, Jamesport (tel. 516/

364-3633), May to November from 11 A.M. to 5 P.M.; **Lenz Winery,** Rte. 25, Peconic (tel. 516/734-6010), 11 A.M. to 5 P.M. daily; **Peconic Bay Vineyards,** Rte. 25, Cutchogue (tel. 516/734-7361), April 1 through December 31 from 11 A.M. to 5 P.M.; and **Pindar Vineyards,** Rte. 25, Peconic (tel. 516/734-6200), April 1 to December 31, from 11 A.M. to 5 P.M. daily. In addition there are about another 15 vineyards producing a variety of wines, which gives you some idea how rapidly the East End is developing into wine country.

Wickham Fruit Farm (tel. 516/734-6441) is a great place to stop for really choice fruit and vegetables. In season, you can pick your own. HOURS: Daily, except Sunday.

CUTCHOGUE LODGING

For an immaculate motel that offers 60 spotless, very large rooms (yes, I mean it), all with refrigerator and color TV, some with a super-modern kitchenette with full-size stove and refrigerator, turn off Rte. 25 onto Depot Lane and head north for **Aliano's Beachcomber,** 3800 Duck Pond Rd., at the foot of Depot Lane (P.O. Box 947), Cutchogue, NY 11935 (tel. 516/734-6370). Added bonus is the 800-foot private beach on the Sound, an outdoor pool, restaurant, and bocce court.

RATES: $90 to $105 from Memorial Day to Labor Day, $70 to $80 from April 1 to Memorial Day and at other times. Open April 1 to November 1.

CUTCHOGUE DINING

Recommended by the locals, the **Fisherman's Restaurant,** on Rte. 25 (tel. 516/734-5155), is a welcoming spot for steamers, lobster, and other fine seafood mixed with some Italian specialties, all at very low prices (under $8). For lobster lovers, there's the best treat of all—a 1½-pounder for $14 and a 1¼-pounder for $12.

HOURS: 3:30 to 11 P.M. weekdays, 11:30 A.M. to 11 P.M. on weekends; daily in summer (but no lunches in summer), closed Monday in winter.

MATTITUCK

Mattituck extends from the Sound to the bay, and possesses the only harbor on Long Island Sound east of Port Jefferson. Among its points of interest are the old **Presbyterian church** (1715); the **general store** on Main Street, located in the Octagon House (1856); and the **North Fork Theater,** occupying a former church on Sound Avenue.

From Mattituck you can travel west along Sound Avenue through fertile countryside, where berry farms stretch for miles, abutting smooth, green-velvet sod farms, fields of white-flowering banked potato plants, or horse farms where horses graze behind white rail fences. It's a lovely way to spend an afternoon rambling, especially if it's the fruit season, when you can stop at one of the many farms—Levin's, Friar's Head, Young's, and Briermere are the names to look for —along Sound and North Avenues around Centerville. Farther south, you'll also want to visit Calverton, famous for its strawberries.

DINING IN NEW SUFFOLK

Bonnies By The Bay, 725 First St., New Suffolk (tel. 516/734-6664) is indeed on Peconic Bay. It has brought the mesquite grill and the New American cuisine to the North Fork in a big way. Start with such tasty morsels as hot corn bread spiced with jalapeño pepper, fried oysters, smoked mozzarella with fresh herbs, shrimp steamed in beer and flavored with Cajun spices. To continue there's a selection of meat and fish specialties—pan-blackened fish, grilled loin of lamb flavored with rosemary, soft shell crabs cooked with a hint of ginger in a white wine sauce, shell steak with barbecue sauce, and, of course, steamed lobster served with a couple of dipping sauces—one traditional, the other more experimental. Prices range from $12 to $20. Select the desserts from the cart—rhubarb tart or hazelnut torte, along with other tempting selections. The decor is funky and colorful, particularly the floor which is daubed with a veritable melange of colors. A pot belly stove often topped with a bouquet of fresh flowers adds a country touch. The other half of the building is occupied by a down-home bar with pool table.

LUNCH: Daily noon to 3:30 P.M. DINNER: daily from 6 to 10 or 11 P.M. BRUNCH: Sunday from 11 A.M. Closed off season.

SOUTHOLD/CUTCHOGUE/MATTITUCK ACTIVITIES

BOATING: *Southold:* Pt. of Egypt Marine (tel. 516/765-2445).

HIKING: For nature rambles there are 34 acres at Goldsmith's Inlet, and another 37 acres to explore at Inlet Point, good birding terrain, where naturalists lead guided walks.

SWIMMING: Southold Town Beach, North Rd., Rte. 48.

The North Shore's Historic Triangle

The so-called historic triangle area stretches from Stony Brook and Setauket all the way west via Smithtown–St. James, Northport, to Huntington and Cold Spring Harbor, an area worth exploring on any weekend. There's even a historic old inn to stay at right in Stony Brook.

STONY BROOK

STONY BROOK ATTRACTIONS

Stony Brook is a beautifully restored 19th-century shipping and fishing village, complete with mill pond, grist mill, rock garden, brook, and harbor.

Don't be put off by the quaint touristy redwood barns, for the **Museums at Stony Brook,** Rte. 25A (tel. 516/751-0066), comprise a superb quality museum complex consisting of four major collections devoted to history, art, period buildings, and carriages, the last of international renown. The carriage collection's highlights include cabriolets, grand Victorias, and other examples of such fine manufacturers as Abbot-Downing, Studebaker, and Million Guiet, plus a brilliant-colored ornate gypsy wagon said to have belonged to Queen Phoebe, a gypsy who lived on Long Island in the early 1900s. The art collection contains many works by William Sidney Mount (1807–1868), the first American-born painter to portray local everyday life, and also to include blacks in nonservile roles. Other highlights include several exquisite miniature period rooms and a fine costume collection. HOURS: Wednesday to Sunday from 10 A.M. to 5 P.M. ADMISSION: $2.75 for adults for all four museums.

The museum also operates the **Stony Brook Mill,** Grist Mill Road, one of the few fully operational 18th-century mills, whose millstones are original. HOURS: June through October, Sunday from 1 to 4 P.M. Kids love to feed the ducks on the pond afterward. ADMISSION: 50¢ for adults, 25¢ for children.

You may also want to visit the **William Sidney Mount House** on Rte. 25A, which was occupied first by Jonas Hawkins, a spy for General Washington, and later by Mount. It is also administered by the museum (tel. 516/751-0066).

Right in the village, antique buffs head for the **Three Village Garden Club Exchange,** where you'll find two floors of good collectibles (furniture included) at fair prices.

STONY BROOK LODGING AND DINING

At the center of this classic 19th-century village stands the delightful **Three Village Inn,** 150 Main St., Stony Brook, NY 11790 (tel. 516/751-0555). Sloping creaky floors, rooms tucked under the eaves, iron door latches, and costumed bonneted waitresses add color and character to this hostelry once (1751) the home of shipbuilder Jonas Smith, and later the site of the religious conference, the Stony Brook Assembly. Rooms in the main building are furnished in comfy country-style antiques, set against floral wallpapers and exposed beams. Rooms do have TVs and air conditioning. A series of cottages house pleasant, modern superior-grade motel rooms, some opening onto lawns facing the harbor. The parlor is more classically furnished with wing chairs, Martha Washington chairs, clubfoot tables, and a handsome writing desk, all placed to take full advantage of the large fireplace. The dining room specializes in American cuisine—prime rib, Long Island duckling, flounder, and lobster—that is plain and good. Prices begin at $15.75. On Friday and Saturday nights people gather around the piano for a jovial song session. In summer the patio is a lovely place to sit out under the shade trees surrounded by flowers.

RATES: $75 to $100, single or double, on weekends. LUNCH: Noon to 3 P.M. daily. DINNER: 5 to 9 P.M. on weekdays, until 10 P.M. on weekends. Closed Christmas Day.

A more colorful summer setting would be hard to find than the one at the **Country House Restaurant,** at Main Street and Rte. 25A (tel. 516/751-3332).

Fresh flowers adorn the three bright dining rooms, each painted variously green, blue, and lilac and pink. Lemons and oranges garlanded with ivy form the center-piece on the Good Luck Penny bar, flanked in summer by dishes of strawberries or peanuts and cheese puffs. On weekends a pianist entertains. The menu varies according to the season, and might feature filet of sole with shrimp sauce, salmon with dill, prime rib, or chicken Rochambeau, priced from $14 to $23. Two prix-fixe brunches, priced at $15 and $25, offer a variety of fare like steak, poached salmon, beef pot pie, chicken, filet of sole, and egg dishes.

LUNCH: Monday to Friday from noon to 3 P.M. DINNER: 5 to 9 P.M. on weekdays, until 10:30 P.M. on weekends. BRUNCH: Sunday from noon to 3 P.M.

SETAUKET–PORT JEFFERSON

AREA ATTRACTIONS

From Stony Brook, take Rte. 25A into Setauket, turning off for a detour to the **Old Field Lighthouse,** from which there's an inspiring view all the way along the Sound. Here there are a couple of old houses for history or architecture buffs to visit. The **Thompson House,** on North Country Road (tel. 516/941-9444), dating back to the early 1700s, displays a collection of early Long Island furniture includ-ing the distinctive double-paneled blanket chest, the Dutch-influenced kas, sever-al rural chair types, and a 1797 clock made by Nathaniel Dominy IV of East Hampton. There's also a colonial herb garden to view. HOURS: Open from May to mid-October, Friday to Sunday from 1 to 5 P.M. ADMISSION: $1.

The 18th-century **Sherwood-Jayne House,** Old Post Road, Setauket (tel. 516/941-9444), located in a bucolic setting, is also filled with a varied collection of fur-niture and objects. The hand-painted wall frescoes in the east parlor and bedroom are fine examples of early American wall decoration. HOURS: Open by appointment only, from Memorial Day to mid-October. ADMISSION: $1 for adults, 25¢ for children 7 to 14.

From here, it's a short run into Port Jefferson, docking point for the Bridge-port, Connecticut, ferry, which during the summer deposits hundreds of day trip-pers who swarm into the dockside restaurants, boutiques, and antique stores. You may want to visit the **Mather House Museum,** 115 Prospect St. (tel. 516/473-2665), a complex of buildings and exhibits featuring costumes, shell craft, Indian art, ship models, and much more. HOURS: Open May to October, Saturday and Sunday from 1 to 4 P.M.; in July and August, also open on Tuesday. Beer lovers might enjoy the **Beer Museum,** on Main Street, while the more technical types will enjoy the **RCA sending stations,** which can be toured by appointment.

PORT JEFFERSON LODGING AND DINING

Danford's Inn, at Bayles Dock, 25 East Broadway, Port Jefferson, NY 11777 (tel. 516/928-5200), occupies a prime spot on the waterfront at Port Jefferson with views of the prettier side of the harbor. The lobby is accented with mallard and pheasant trophies, powder horns, guns, rifles, and other hunting paraphernalia. Tucked into an area created by a bay window is a TV and couch.

Accommodations are located in several two- or three-story buildings connected by a brick walkway bordered by stores reminiscent of St. Thomas, Nassau, and other pleasant shopping areas. There are 80 rooms, many overlooking the water and all quite large and furnished with good-quality antique reproductions. Bathrooms contain full amenities (package of shampoo, mouthwash, etc.). Buildings C and D (which probably will be named after sea captains by the time of your visit) have extremely large rooms with beds decorated in a special draped effect, a desk with Queen Anne chair, armoire, pink-burgundy carpet, and a sitting area furnished with a couch and armchairs. The design layout of rooms in Building B make them suitable for families or two couples traveling together because, although they contain two double beds, there's a bathroom jutting in between.

The Restaurant serves continental cuisine—duckling with raspberry sauce, grilled salmon with basil beurre blanc, or pasta of the day, which might be lobster-stuffed ravioli in Alfredo sauce. Buffet brunch and buffet dinner available on Sunday. On weekends there's dancing in the sail loft.

RATES: $100 to $150 for rooms, $150 to $200 for suites. MEAL HOURS: From 7 A.M. daily, until midnight on weekdays, to 1 A.M. on weekends. BRUNCH: Sunday from 8:30 A.M. to noon.

PORT JEFFERSON DINING

Savories, 318 Wynne Lane (tel. 516/331-4747), specializes in northern Italian and continental cuisine, offering a variety of veal, beef, chicken, and seafood dishes. Veal marsala, veal piccata, scampi allegri, filet mignon with red wine sauce, chateaubriand, and mixed seafood (lobster, shrimp, crab) are just a few of the items priced from $13 to $16. Lace curtains in the window, burgundy-and-cream-striped cushions on Windsor chairs, pink napery, and a stained-glass divider make a simple but pretty room—a number-one choice in the area.

LUNCH: Tuesday to Friday from noon to 2:30 P.M., on Sunday from 11:30 A.M. to 2:30 P.M. DINNER: Tuesday to Thursday from 5 to 10 P.M., on Friday and Saturday until 11 P.M., on Sunday from 4 to 9 P.M.

Costa de España, 9 Traders Cove (tel. 516/331-5363), has a small bar, tables set with red cloths, a pleasant warm atmosphere, and fine Spanish food—veal in almond sauce or Spanish sausage, chicken in garlic sauce, or a special chicken with onions, mushrooms, wine, and tomato sauce. And, of course, paella valenciana or with langosta, plus shrimps in hot sauce. Prices run $10 to $20.

LUNCH: Monday and Wednesday to Saturday from noon to 3 P.M. DINNER: Monday, Wednesday, and Thursday from 5 to 10 P.M., on Friday and Saturday until 11 P.M., on Sunday from 1 to 10 P.M.; closed Tuesday.

Printers Devil, Wynne Lane (tel. 516/928-7171), is a pubby local favorite decked out in typical oak, stained-glass, and plants style. Chicken Cordon Bleu, filet mignon, and veal française typify the fare, priced from $10 to $14.50.

LUNCH: 11:30 A.M. to 4 P.M. daily. DINNER: Sunday to Thursday from 4 to 11 P.M., until 1 A.M. on Friday and Saturday.

Deno's, 109 Main St. (tel. 516/928-3388), is a popular spot for prime seafood, steak, and chicken, from $5 to $11. HOURS: Monday to Friday from 4 P.M., on Saturday from 11:30 A.M. and on Sunday from noon.

SMITHTOWN–ST. JAMES

AREA ATTRACTIONS

If you head west on Rte. 25A from Stony Brook you'll pass **Wicks Farm Stand,** famous not only for fresh produce, but also for their imaginative Halloween display that the kids all love. Turn left at Moriches Road, and it will take you to **St. James General Store** (tel. 516/862-8333), established in 1857. The porch is lined with baskets of all sorts, a great big old teddy bear, and a cigarstore Indian. The interior offers all kinds of old-fashioned favorites, sugarcanes and candies, jams, preserves, cookie jars, quilts, spices, and craft items, all displayed on the original old counters, shelves, or in old cases. In winter the place is warmed by an old pot-belly stove.

From here, Moriches Road north will take you through Nissequogue, a land mass that separates Stony Brook Harbor from the Nissequogue River. Follow Moriches Road until it loops around into Nissequogue Road, which will lead into River Road. All through here, you'll be driving along winding, tree-shaded lanes bursting with rhododendron and mountain laurel that shield in early summer the grand houses from the prying eyes of the passing motorist.

Getting back on Rte. 25A will bring you into Smithtown, one of the fastest-growing townships in the nation, which, paradoxically, has several historic landmarks—the **Caleb Smith House,** on Rte. 25A (tel. 516/265-6768), which is the home of the Historical Society (HOURS: Thursday and Saturday, May to November; ADMISSION: $1); **Epenetus Smith Tavern,** Middle Country Road (tel. 516/724-3091), where memories of mirth and mead are preserved in the one-room bar, as is the lifestyle of an earlier era in pictures, sea chests, tea caddies, and rockers (HOURS: daily, except Monday, from 1 to 5 P.M.); the first **Presbyterian church** (1675); and the **Old Smith House** (1664) on Long Beach Road.

In neighboring Branch, the **Hollock Inn Museum,** 263 E. Main St. (tel. 516/265-1086), recalls the days when this place used to be a stage stop on the Brooklyn to Sag Harbor run between 1784 and 1869 (HOURS: Sunday from 2 to 5 P.M., all year).

SMITHTOWN AREA LODGING AND DINING

Unfortunately, there are no attractive country inns (the closest is Stonybrook's Three Village Inn), but there are plenty of fine dining establishments. First, a place to stay.

The **Sheraton Smithtown,** 110 Vanderbilt Motor Parkway, Smithtown, NY 11788 (tel. 516/231-1100), has 212 rooms, three dining rooms, two lounges, and an indoor pool and exercise room.

RATES: $105 to $130 double. Ask about their special weekend packages.

Smithtown Haus, 65 E. Main St., Smithtown (tel. 516/979-9113), offers good German fare in a warm wooden room with a large bar: sauerbraten, bratwurst and sauerkraut, jaegerschnitzel with mushrooms in cream sauce, sole almondine, filet mignon, priced from $9.50 to $14.50.

LUNCH: Tuesday to Friday from noon to 3 P.M. DINNER: Tuesday to Friday from 5 to 9 P.M., on Saturday to 11 P.M., and on Sunday from noon to 9 P.M.

The fine-quality Italian cuisine draws crowds to **Casa Rustica,** 175 W. Main St., Smithtown (tel. 516/265-9265). From the cozy fire-warmed bar a ramp leads into the stucco-and-timbered country dining room. Start with carpaccio with radicchio and parmigiana dressed with a pink sauce or a delicious seafood salad of calamari, scungilli, octopus, mussels, and shrimp. More unusual, try the polenta salsiccia —cornmeal porridge flavored with savory sausage and pinot grigio wine. There are several pastas, like meat-filled agnolotti, risotto with porcini mushrooms or with champagne and caviar, along with more common dishes like veal piccata, veal valdostana, and steak fiorentina. Prices run $9.75 to $17.75.

DINNER: Tuesday to Saturday from 5 to 11 P.M., on Sunday from 2 to 10 P.M.; closed Monday.

The latest fun restaurant is **Miss Ellie's,** 320 Maple Ave., Smithtown (tel. 516/ 361-6264), serving Cajun-style food in a New Orleans atmosphere. Carnival masks decorate the walls up front while New Orleans scenes adorn the walls of the main room, decked out in celery and rose colors. Start with a cup of Créole gumbo or spicy baby back ribs, and follow with a selection from about 20 dishes like blackened prime rib, sirloin, or redfish; chicken Mardi Gras parmigiana cooked in Créole barbecue sauce; or the Louisiana catfish that's rolled in cornmeal and served with hushpuppies and sauce tartare. Prices run from $15 to $18. The winning dessert is something called the Superdome Special—a brownie with vanilla ice cream, covered with strawberry fruit, pineapple topping, sliced bananas, and mounds of whipped cream. There are other sundaes and pies.

LUNCH: Monday to Friday from noon to 4 P.M. DINNER: 4 to 10 P.M. daily.

Crooked Hill Restaurant, 7 Crooked Hill Rd., Commack (tel. 516/499-5700), turns out fine food, offering only a limited menu to patrons at 15 tables. Among the specialties you might find parchment-baked salmon with cognac cream; sautéed shrimp with parsley, garlic, and Sambuca; duck with lemon and oregano; chicken breast with mushrooms, sherry, and thyme sauce; and swordfish with white-wine butter. Prices run $10 to $16.

LUNCH: Tuesday to Friday from 11:30 A.M. to 2:30 P.M. DINNER: Tuesday to Thursday and Sunday from 5 to 10 P.M., on Friday and Saturday until 10:30 P.M.

Due Torri, 330 Vanderbilt Motor Parkway, Hauppauge (tel. 516/435-8664), is located on the top (fourth) floor of an office building and offers a more limited menu than nearby Mario's (see below), slightly lower prices, and a more modern Italian ambience with a sleek tiled service area and plush semicircular burgundy banquettes. Penne alla vodka, tortellini primavera, and other pastas are good starters or main courses. Veal scallopine with mushrooms, veal piccata, seafood Fra Diavolo, rack of lamb, and chateaubriand are just a few more of the many choices. Dancing on weekends.

LUNCH: Monday to Friday from noon to 3 P.M. DINNER: Monday to Thursday from 5 to 10 P.M., on Friday and Saturday until 11 P.M., on Sunday from 2 to 10 P.M.

Mario's, 644 Vanderbilt Motor Parkway, Hauppauge (tel. 516/273-9407), is an expensive Italian restaurant that features an extensive menu offering breast of chicken marsala; veal with artichokes and mushrooms; saltimbocca; striped bass with white wine, shrimp, and artichoke; and such pastas as tortellini alla panna (with dumpling in cream sauce) and a surprising manicotti vegetariani. The decor is rich: gilt pictures, chandeliers, banquettes, and chairs covered in floral fabric. Prices run $8.25 to $42.

LUNCH: Monday to Friday from noon to 2:30 P.M. DINNER: Monday to Thursday from 5 to 9:30 P.M., on Friday and Saturday from 5:30 to 10:30 P.M., and on Sunday from 3 to 9:30 P.M.

Lafayette and Mirabelle are both contenders for serving the best food in the area. Both are expensive. Lafayette is more traditional. **Mirabelle,** 404 North Country Rd., St. James (tel. 516/584-5999), has a modern, rather spare decor that relies on color—pink with gray trim, red banquettes—for effect. The menu changes, but might feature a sea bass with tomatoes, olive, and red peppers; poached lobster with tomato cream; a mixed grill; or a rabbit dish. Prices run from $17.50 to $23. Begin with mussels stuffed with almonds, garlic, and parsley butter, or duck foie gras with apples and raisins.

LUNCH: Tuesday to Friday from noon to 2 P.M. DINNER: Tuesday to Thursday from 6 to 10 P.M., on Friday and Saturday to 11 P.M., on Sunday from 5 to 9 P.M.

At **Lafayette,** 64 North Country Road in Smithtown (tel. 516/265-8771), cuisine is classically traditional—steak marchand de vin, chateaubriand. Prices run $14 to $22. The decor is country French.

LUNCH: Monday to Friday from noon to 3 P.M. DINNER: Monday to Saturday from 5:30 to 10:30 P.M.

DaVinci's Continental, 416 North Country Rd., St. James (tel. 516/862-6500), is probably the most friendly comfortable Italian restaurant. Here in a warm room with stone fireplace, tile floor, and leather woven chairs, traditional northern Italian and continental cuisine is served, priced from $11.75 to $20. The menu is extensive, featuring all kinds of pasta (cappelli di Angelo with crabmeat, tortellini with vodka), many varieties of seafood (scampi, Fra Diavolo or with Pernod; lobster; fish of the day), steaks, veal da Vinci (with prosciutto, spinach, and cheese sauce), chateaubriand, and rack of lamb. Top it all off with crêpes suzettes, cherries jubilee, or zabaglione.

LUNCH: Tuesday to Friday from noon to 3 P.M. DINNER: Tuesday to Thursday and Sunday from 6 to 10 P.M., until 11 P.M. on Friday and Saturday. BRUNCH: Sunday from noon to 3 P.M.

NORTHPORT

NORTHPORT ATTRACTIONS

From Smithtown, Rte. 25A will bring you all the way to the outskirts of Northport. Turn right down into the harbor area that looks out across lovely Northport Bay to the wooded bluffs opposite.

At Eaton's Neck Point, which cuts between Northport and Huntington Bays, you can visit the 175-year-old **lighthouse** erected at the request of the citizens after the terrible wreck of the brig *Salley*. Today light from the 73-foot-high beacon flashes warning to ships as far as 17½ miles out at sea. HOURS: Open weekends only.

On Main Street, the **Northport Historical Society Museum,** at no. 215 (tel. 516/ 757-9859), tells the story of the village's shipbuilding past. HOURS: 1 to 4:30 P.M. daily, except Monday. ADMISSION: By donation.

NORTHPORT DINING

Some 1½ miles east of Northport, at the **Australian Inn,** 1036 Fort Salonga Rd., Northport (tel. 516/754-4400), the waitresses wear khaki shorts and bush shirts while they heft bundled chooks (chicken spiced with Dijon mustard in a pastry shell topped with suprême sauce) and beef tucker bags (sirloin stuffed with broccoli and Swiss cheese) amid the kangaroos and other Australian fauna. Dinner prices range from $9 to $19. There's a very pleasant shrub-sheltered terrace for evening cocktails. Foster's is available, of course.

LUNCH: Monday to Friday from 11:30 A.M. to 3 P.M. DINNER: Sunday to Thursday from 4:30 to 10 P.M., on Friday and Saturday until 1 A.M. BRUNCH: Sunday from 11:30 A.M. to 3 P.M.

Pumpernickel's, 640 Main St., Rte. 25A (tel. 516/757-7959), offers excellent German cuisine, seafood, and a full selection of beers for accompaniment. Prices begin at $10.

LUNCH: Monday to Saturday from 11:30 A.M. to 3 P.M. DINNER: Monday to Saturday from 5 to 10 P.M., on Sunday from noon to 10 P.M.

CENTERPORT

CENTERPORT ATTRACTIONS

Leave Northport and get back on Rte. 25A and you'll soon be in Centerport, at the entrance to the land spit known as Little Neck Point. Here there's an outstanding attraction, the Vanderbilt Museum and Planetarium.

The **Vanderbilt Museum,** 180 Little Neck Rd., Centerport (tel. 516/261-5656), a 24-room mansion of Spanish-Moroccan design, was built in 1910 for William K. Vanderbilt (1878–1944) and added onto in the 1920s. It commands a magnificent view of Northport Harbor both from the interior and from the pool area and balustered terrace. You'll begin in a room filled with models of the villa itself and a museum filled with animal trophies from Africa and India, all set against colorful dioramas. Many of the living areas are furnished in Spanish/Portuguese style, with impressive tile fireplaces and floors. In fact there's only one American piece in the house, and that's a Philadelphia lowboy in the organ room. The bedrooms are filled predominantly with French Empire and ormolu.

Although the house is splendid and filled with museum-quality antiques, the most interesting part of any visit has to be the collection of 17,000 varieties of marine and wildlife that Vanderbilt amassed. On display in the Marine Museum are all kinds of species—starfish, limpets, Samoa sea lily, painted sea worms. Rapacious fiddler crabs, praying rock crabs, and sharp-horned spider crabs are only three of this genus. The shells are beautiful, and some are very rare. There are green turbans, chambered nautilus, conch abalone, Triton's trumpet shell, and an engraved tiger cowrie among them. In the same room are also collected artifacts from the Philippines, Fiji, and Samoa, all catalogued in detail, and birds from all over the world—quetzal, scarlet ibis, penguins, and incredible birds of paradise. There's also a butterfly and insect collection in a separate room. Certainly one could spend many hours poring over these natural treasures.

The final attraction is the planetarium (tel. 516/757-7500) and a small glass-enclosed observatory with a professional-grade reflecting telescope. Besides the planetarium sky shows, there's also a special Young Peoples Show on Saturday mornings for kids under 6.

HOURS: The house is open May 1 to October 31, Tuesday to Saturday from 10 A.M. to 4 P.M., on Sunday and holidays from noon to 5 P.M.; closed Monday. The Planetarium is open on Friday, Saturday, and Sunday from Labor Day to June 30; the schedule is expanded during summer. ADMISSION: $2.50 for adults, $2 for children 9 to 12.

CENTERPORT LODGING AND DINING

The **Chalet Motor Inn,** Rte. 25A, Centerport, NY 11721 (tel. 516/757-4600), is a perfectly good motel, set well back from the main road.

RATES: $60 in winter, rising to $64 in the summer.

The **Mill Pond Inn,** Rte. 25A (tel. 516/261-5353), overlooking Northport Bay, offers good, moderately priced steaks and seafood; complete dinners run from $10.50 to $16. There's usually a fresh catch of the day special.

LUNCH: Monday to Saturday from noon to 3 P.M. DINNER: 4:30 to 10 P.M. daily. BRUNCH: Sunday from 11:30 A.M. to 3 P.M.

Next door, at the **Original Schooner,** 441 E. Main St., Rte. 25A (tel. 516/261-2015), you can select your own lobster from the tank, priced according to the market. Veal and other meat specialties are also offered, in a very nautical atmosphere. Prices range from $13 to $17.

HOURS: Noon to 11 P.M. daily. BRUNCH: Sunday from noon to 3 P.M.

COLD SPRING HARBOR

From Centerport, Rte. 25A will bring you to Cold Spring Harbor, an old whaling town where the industry boomed from 1836 to 1862, although the port only ever had nine ships. The **Whaling Museum** on Main Street (tel. 516/367-3418) recaptures this era. A fully rigged whaleboat from New Bedford, the brig *Daisy,* is on display, along with paintings, scrimshaw, and ships' models, plus a new permanent exhibition on Long Island's whaling industry, "Mark Well the Whale!" HOURS: Year round—Memorial Day to Labor Day, daily from 11 A.M. to 5 P.M.; Tuesday to Sunday in other months. ADMISSION: $1.50 for adults, 50¢ for children 6 to 14.

Anyone interested in nature/ecology might like to stop at the **Cold Spring Harbor Fish Hatchery,** Rte. 25A (tel. 516/692-6768), where the 20 aquariums contain over 60 species including turtles, freshwater fish, reptiles and amphibians. Trout are still hatched here by the thousands. Great for kids. HOURS: 10 A.M. to 5 P.M. daily. ADMISSION: $1.50, 75¢ under 12.

HUNTINGTON

En route to Cold Spring Harbor you'll pass through Huntington, a historically conscious town where landmarks include **The Arsenal,** 425 Park Ave., used during the Revolution to store arms and ammunition; the **Conklin House,** 2 High St. (tel. 516/427-3981), a local history and decorative-arts museum located in a 1750 house. (HOURS: Tuesday to Friday and Sunday from 1 to 4 P.M.); **Fort Franklin,** Lloyd Harbor Road, Lloyd Harbor, a British fort and Loyalist hangout; the **Jarvis Fleet House,** 424 Park Ave., the oldest house in Huntington; the **Village Green,** where the Liberty Flag was first flown on July 23, 1776; **Mother Chick's Inn,** 124 Bay Rd., where reportedly spy Nathan Hale was betrayed to the British by his cousin; the **Old Burial Ground,** at Main Street and Nassau Road, where 35 Revolutionary soldiers are buried; the **Old Presbyterian Church,** 125 Main St., built in 1665, whose bell was cast in 1715 and still sounds today; and perhaps most interesting of all, the **Powell-Jarvis House** at 434 Park Ave., (tel. 516/427-3981), where antique buffs gather for the auctions and sales sponsored several times a year by the Huntington Historical Society.

Huntington also possesses a couple of lovely areas for walking and picnicking, described in the North Shore Activities section, below, including **Target Rock Refuge,** West Neck Road, the 80-acre former estate of Ferdinand Eberstadt, which has a quarter-mile beachfront and a ten-acre formal garden.

Whitman fans will want to take New York Avenue south from Huntington into Walt Whitman Road, which runs past the **old farmhouse,** 246 Walt Whitman Rd. (tel. 516/427-5240), where **Walt Whitman** spent his boyhood. Worth visiting to pay homage to America's first major poet. HOURS: Wednesday to Sunday from 10 A.M. to 4 P.M.

NORTH SHORE ACTIVITIES

BEACHES: *Huntington:* Crescent Beach, Crescent Beach Road; Fleets Cove, Fleets Cove Road; Gold Star Battalion, West Shore Road; Hobart, Eaton's Neck; and West Neck, West Neck Road. *Northport:* Swimming beaches include Asharoken Beach on Asharoken Road, and Crab Meadow Beach, reached via Waterfront Street West, complete with boardwalk, concessions, and parking for 600 cars; Geissler's Beach, on Makamah Road, is a beach for sunning and walking, not bathing.

BIRDWATCHING: Makamah Nature Preserve, Huntington.

BOATING: *Cold Spring Harbor:* Rentals are available at Ham Powles Marine Agency, Vets Fishing Station, 74 Harbor Rd. (tel. 516/367-9869). In *Port Jefferson:* Setauket Harbor Boat Basin, Shore Road (tel. 516/941-9681); Port Jefferson Marina, Broadway (tel. 516/331-3567).

GOLF: Crab Meadow, Waterside Avenue, in Northport.

HIKING: *Huntington:* West Hills County Park, Sweet Hollow Road (tel. 516/421-

4655), has 854 acres criss-crossed by nature trails, and Target Rock Refuge, West Neck Road; Makamah Nature Preserve has great hiking in 160 acres of woodland, streams, and marsh.

HORSEBACK RIDING: Hidden Lake Farm Riding School, Co. Rd. 48, Southold, NY 11971 (tel. 516/765-9896).

PICNICKING: West Hills County Park, Target Rock Refuge, and Makamah Nature Preserve, all in Huntington.

SWIMMING/PICNICKING: *Port Jefferson:* West Meadow Beach, West Meadow. *Smithtown–St. James:* For fishing, ice skating, rowboats, camping, and hiking, Blydenburgh Park (tel. 516/360-4966) has 588 acres that are all yours. The Nissequogue River State Park is also great for hiking. A permit is required.

TENNIS: At SUNY in Stony Brook.

PENNSYLVANIA & DELAWARE

THE POCONOS

DISTANCES IN MILES: Stroudsburg, 81; Canadensis, 98; Jim Thorpe, 137
ESTIMATED DRIVING TIMES: 1¼ to 2¾ hours.

DRIVING: For Stroudsburg, take I-80 west to Exit 52; for Jim Thorpe, take it all the way to the Northeast Extension of the Pennsylvania Turnpike (Rte. 9). For Canadensis, turn off I-80 at Exit 52, and pick up Rte. 447 north for about 20 miles.

BUS: Greyhound (tel. 212/635-0800, or toll free 800/528-6055) travels to Stroudsburg, Mount Pocono, and the Delaware Water Gap. Trailways (tel. 212/730-7460) travels to Stroudsburg, Mount Pocono, Delaware Water Gap, and Jim Thorpe.

Special Events to Plan Your Trip Around
FEBRUARY/MARCH: Pocono Winter Carnival
JUNE: Pocono Laurel Blossom Festival
SEPTEMBER: Fall Fling
    Celebration of the Arts, Delaware Water Gap (usually on weekend after Labor Day).

For further information about Pennsylvania in general, contact the Pennsylvania Travel Development Bureau, Pennsylvania Department of Commerce, Rm. 416, Forum Bldg., Harrisburg, PA 17120 (tel. 717/787-5453).
    For specific information about the area, contact the Pocono Mountains Vacation Bureau, 1004 Main St., Stroudsburg, PA 18360 (tel. 717/421-5791); the Carbon County Tourist Promotion Agency, P.O. Box 90, Jim Thorpe, PA 18229 (tel. 717/325-3673); the Hawley–Lake Wallenpaupack

Chamber of Commerce, P.O. Box 150, Hawley, PA 18428 (tel. 717/226-3191); the Pike County Chamber of Commerce, Milford, PA 18337 (tel. 717/296-8700); and the Lake Wallenpaupack Association, Inc., P.O. Box 398, Hawley, PA 18428 (tel. 717/226-2141).

Only 1½ hours away from New York City there are forested hills cloaked with pine, spruce, hemlock, beech, birch, and oak, and inhabited by bear, deer, raccoon, squirrels, beavers, muskrats, chipmunks, and painted turtles. There are lakes as large as 5,700 acres with miles and miles of shoreline; there are at least a dozen waterfalls crashing down through rock gulleys, and there are two of the finest rivers for canoeing and white-water rafting on the East Coast—the Delaware and the Lehigh. Indeed, in the four counties of the Poconos there are 2,400 square miles of mountains, lakes, streams, and woodlands for you to discover by rambling, hiking, and observing nature, or by enjoying more active pursuits: canoeing, swimming, sailing, skiing, tobogganing, fishing, ice skating—you name it, you can do it here in the Poconos. For most people, of course, the Poconos means resorts and one type of resort in particular—honeymoon havens—and certainly there are plenty of those, and you might even think of dashing off to one of them for a fantasy fun weekend, but these are concentrated in the heart of the Poconos, around Big Pocono and along Rte. 209. There are plenty of remote areas up in the lake country and around Canadensis where there are three or four delightful inns that give access to those remoter areas of the Poconos.

There's also the far-western-Pocono coal-mining country of Carbon County, where such towns as Mauch Chunk, now Jim Thorpe after the great athlete, once produced a goodly number of millionaires, who built fine mansions and an opera house in this picturesque town that sits in a valley between two sheer mountains.

Whichever part of the Poconos you decide to explore—the forest and lake country, the Delaware Water Gap and the Delaware River, the resorts at the heart of the area, or the western section along the Lehigh River Valley—you'll find more than enough activities to keep you well occupied.

THE CANADENSIS AREA

If you don't want to stay at a resort and prefer discovering the real Poconos of hemlock forests, lakes, streams, and waterfalls, where you can fish, canoe, bird, and hike, then you'll want to seek out one of the inns located in Canadensis and then take some drives exploring the triangle marked by the towns of Mountainhome, Newfoundland, and Canadensis before heading north for Lake Wallenpaupack and east to Lackawaxen.

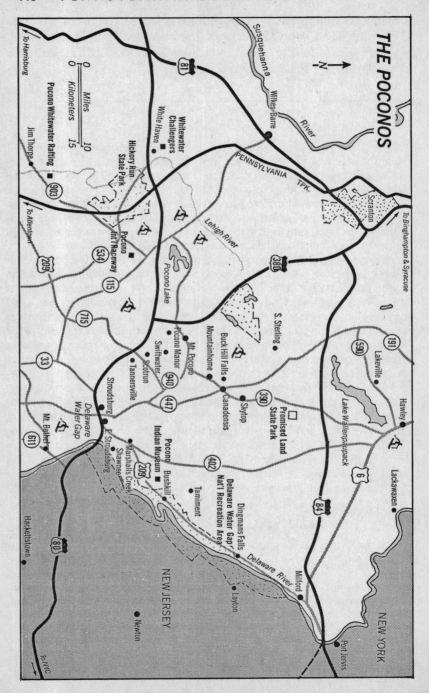

THE POCONOS

-N→

To Harrisburg

Pocono Whitewater Rafting

0 Miles 10
0 Kilometers 15

Jim Thorpe

81

Susquehanna River

Wilkes-Barre

Whitewater Challengers
White Haven

Hickory Run State Park

903

To Allentown

209

534

Pocono Int'l Raceway

115

715

33

PENNSYLVANIA TPK.

Lehigh River

Pocono Lake

Scranton

To Binghampton & Syracuse

380

S. Sterling

Buck Hill Falls

Mt. Pocono
Pocono Manor
Swiftwater
Scotrun
Tannersville

Mountainhome

940

447

Canadensis

Skytop

390

191

590

Lakeville

Hawley

Lake Wallenpaupack

6

Lackawaxen

Stroudsburg

Delaware Water Gap

Mt. Bethel
611

E. Stroudsburg

Shawnee
Marshalls Creek
209

Pocono Indian Museum
Bushkill

Tamiment

Promised Land State Park

402

Delaware Water Gap Nat'l Recreation Area

Dingmans Falls

84

Milford

80

Hackettstown

NEW JERSEY

Newton

To NYC

Delaware River

Layton

NEW YORK

Port Jervis

CANADENSIS AREA ATTRACTIONS

The prime attraction, as you will discover, is nature itself. The other two main attractions of the area are the **Mountainhome Pocono Playhouse** (tel. 717/595-7456), a summer theater that's been operating for 40 years. The box office opens June 1 for reservations. There's also a store here that everyone loves to stop at —**Callie's Candy Kitchen,** Rte. 390 one mile north of the junction with Rte. 191, Mountainhome (tel. 717/595-2280), run by Mr. Pocono himself. When Harry Callie started making chocolate and candy, his mother innocently asked him who was going to come out to buy candies in the Poconos. The question inspired Harry with the idea to make candies right out in front of people. Soon people were streaming through, eager to hear Mr. Callie entertain, joke, respond to the kids, and to watch him drop every conceivable item—peanuts, hazelnuts, raspberries, strawberries—into the thick stream of swirling chocolate. Having watched the process, you'll want to pick up in the store some mouthwatering items like the famous Pocono Mountain bark. HOURS: 10 A.M. to 8 P.M. in summer, until 5 P.M. in winter.

Just south of Canadensis on Rte. 447, you may want to browse in **Colony Village** (tel. 717/595-7601), a group of stores selling gifts, etc.

At Lake Wallenpaupack, the whole family will enjoy a visit to **Claws n' Paws Animal Park** (tel. 717/698-6154). HOURS: 10 A.M. to 6 P.M. daily, May 1 to late October.

From Callie's you can scoot up Rte. 191 through the wooded lanes to South Sterling and Newfoundland, small towns with a general store and a couple of antique shops. Just outside Newfoundland, bear right onto Rte. 507, which will take you along the edge of **Lake Wallenpaupack** (the largest lake in Pennsylvania, with 52 miles of shoreline), a lovely scenic route at any time of year. Travel up Rte. 6 to Hawley, and then turn right on Rte. 590 (you'll be following the banks of the Delaware and Hudson Canal) to Lackawaxen, where you can visit the **home of Zane Grey,** in which he wrote many of his 103 books. How did he come to live in Lackawaxen, in a large Victorian house overlooking the river in which he loved to wade and fish? The story goes that he was lured here by his wife, whom he met at the then-grand hotel in town, and gave up his seven-year-old dental practice in New York to come out here and write. Besides the books themselves, you can see varied memorabilia associated with Zane Grey—pictures of Colonel Jones, whom Grey accompanied out West as publicity manager and who was determined to cross cattle with buffalo, an idea that was roundly scoffed at at the time; samples of Grey's handwritten manuscripts and the Morris chair in which he wrote at the rate of 100,000 words a month; and photographs of this handsome author taken all over the world on his various fishing expeditions. (They say he made $37 million and spent $36 million of it fishing.) Note the University of Pennsylvania baseball team photograph. Quite clearly this youth posed with fame in mind.

When you've finished, step out onto the porch and look downriver to **Roebling's first suspension bridge,** a perfect miniature and forerunner of his greatest-known work, the Brooklyn Bridge. And if you walk down to the local church you can pay homage at the graveside of this man Grey, who was born, educated, and lived in the East, but helped create and record the legends of the West.

From Lackawaxen you can either retrace your tracks back to Rte. 6 and then on to Rte. 507 a short distance, before picking up Rte. 390 south through Promised Land State Park to Skytop and thence to Canadensis. Or you can continue along Rte. 590 to Greeley, taking Rte. 434 from Greeley to Rte. 6, and then driving along Rte. 6, turning left on 507 toward Paupack but taking Rte. 390 back to Canadensis. Either one of these routes will bring you through dramatic state forests. The Lackawaxen area was the site of Horace Greeley's Sylvania Colony.

CANADENSIS LODGING AND DINING

Country Inns

Some of the best food in the Poconos can be found at the **Pump House Inn,** Skytop Road, Canadensis, PA 18325 (tel. 717/595-7501), a hostelry since 1840 which offers a warm, inviting tavern with fireplace and wide-plank floors, and a series of dining rooms that are simply but distinctively decorated. Elegant brown-and-pink napery and fresh flowers on each table set off the simplicity of Windsor chairs and double settles. If you are alone the place is ideal, for the walls are lined with books that you can browse through while you're waiting for your meal. If you find one particularly amusing or interesting, then the owner invites you to take it away, as long as you send another to replace it.

The menu is always supplemented by daily specials—lobster bisque or cream of cauliflower soup to start, for example, and duck with cassis, veal chop with sausage stuffing, swordfish stuffed with cheese, and blackened redfish as entrees. The menu itself lists basil shrimp, rack of lamb, and filet mignon with madeira sauce. Entree prices run $14 to $22. Desserts are also tantalizing, like the chocolate-praline mousse or the lemon-cream roulade. There is always a specially priced appetizer and entree prix fixe, which offers excellent value. Wine is chosen from a display rack, although the house wine is quite adequate.

The Pump House also offers some first-rate accommodations upstairs, pleasantly furnished with brass beds and varied oak pieces.

RATES: $55 to $65 double, $85 for the penthouse suite; there's also a guest cottage with living room, fireplace, sun porch, two bedrooms, and bath that rents for $110 double, with continental breakfast included. DINNER: Wednesday to Saturday from 5 to 10 P.M., on Sunday from 2:30 to 8:30 P.M.; closed Monday and Tuesday.

At the **Pine Knob Inn,** Rte. 447, Canadensis, PA 18325 (tel. 717/595-2532), June and Jim Belfie are super-outgoing enthusiastic hosts who really cater to their guests' needs—they've been innkeeping for the nine years since they moved out of Philadelphia. The house itself is a strange, intricately shaped board-and-batten structure, built around 1840 on 15 green and pleasant lovely acres. Inside, you'll find an appealing living room furnished with a very comfortable mixture of authentic antiques and reproductions, plus a Steinway grand (you're invited to bring your own musical instruments), all set around a large stone fireplace.

Across the hall in the restaurant, the works of local artists are displayed. At night the room is lit by candles in pewter candlesticks and clusters of globe chandeliers. On the menu you might select from roast duck with orange sauce, Cornish hen with strawberry vinaigrette sauce, Delmonico steak with shallot butter and mushrooms, shrimp Créole, or trout with pecan butter, served with homemade breads, salads, and tempting desserts. Soup, herring in cream, and stuffed mushrooms are among the appetizers. Next to the dining room is a modern small cocktail lounge.

There are 18 rooms in the main house, 12 with private bath. Each is slightly differently decorated, but most likely your room will contain a brass or carved-oak Victorian bed, chintz wallpaper and curtains, and a large dresser. Room 18 has brass beds; Room 22 contains an old carved cherry bed set against pretty Wedgwood-blue wallpaper. Even the smallest rooms are attractively furnished and immaculately maintained. Behind the house is the most charming accommodation of all, a two-bedroom bungalow that has been tastefully decorated. In the morning, hearty breakfasts begin with oatmeal, followed by thick French toast, well-coated with egg and served with sausage, bacon, toast, and marmalade.

On the shrub-shaded grounds there's a tennis court, while across the road you'll find a swimming pool and the Brodhead Creek, one of the finest trout streams in Pennsylvania. For relaxing, the wicker furnished porch is ideal. Also on the property, a building out back contains workshops and studios on the ground floor and a gallery above. Various art, writing, photography, and other creative workshops are given here by professionals in each field. The restaurant is open to nonguests by reservation only.

RATES: $55 to $65 per person (MAP). To get there, take I-80 to Exit 52 and follow Rte. 447 north. It's on the right, just before you reach Canadensis.

For more than a decade Lolly Tupper has been welcoming people to the **Overlook Inn**, Dutch Hill Road, Canadensis, PA 18325 (tel. 717/595-7519). Inside, there are 12 rooms in the main inn, all with private bath, plus another eight rooms in two other buildings on the property. Uneven floors and distinctly sloping lintels add character to the rooms, which are furnished variously with iron or brass beds, pine chests, colorful quilts, oak dressers, usually a small selection of books, and a plant or two. All rooms have Touch-tone telephones and Lolly's thoughtful extras —two baskets of candy and some sherry. Downstairs off to the right is a comfortable sitting area with a color TV, stone fireplace, and a couple of Harvard chairs to go with the Hamilton chairs. Off this room is a small wood-paneled bar. Across the hall there's another parlor, which contains a piano and organ waiting for the next guest entertainer to walk in, and a sizable collection of books that actually seems to buttress the low ceilings. Extra-special touches here include a welcoming carafe of wine in your room, and a four-o'clock ritual of tea. The country dining room offers such specialties as oysters Rockefeller; rack of lamb; filet of beef in a sour cream, cognac, and mushroom sauce; and best of all, fine Pennsylvania brook trout. Homemade desserts include a rich smooth ice cream, ambrosia sautéed and flambéed with anisette-flavored sauce, trifle, and a white mousse meringue cake. Scones, jams, and cakes are served at tea, when folks get to know one another. Prices run $11.25 to $17.50. The breakfasts are equally substantial —omelets or pancakes with full accompaniments. Favored breakfasting spot is the porch. A small outdoor pool, bocce, and a playing field complete the facilities.

RATES: $68 per person (MAP) for inn rooms, $63 per person (MAP) for carriage house or lodge rooms.

Canadensis Area Resorts

Besides Skytop (which I'll discuss in a minute), the **Buck Hill Inn**, off Rte. 390 or 191, Buck Hill Falls, PA 18323 (tel. 717/595-7441, or toll free 800/233-8113), is the only famous old-style establishment remaining as witness to the era when the Poconos flourished as a fashionable resort area and Philadelphians and New Yorkers flocked here during the summer season. Although the rambling old stone house, built in 1926, still retains a great deal of charm, some of the public areas look a trifle bedraggled, but the new owners are slowly restoring the building and its 350 rooms to its former elegance. In the new (1964) west wing, each room has a convertible couch (so that it can be turned into a suite), a sizable wet bar, and pleasant ultramodern furnishings. Rooms in the main lodge are furnished in Scandinavian style. Throughout the house numerous stone fireplaces and old furniture—butterfly Windsors, heavy chests, Shaker-style settles—contribute to an overwhelming sense of sturdiness and substance.

During its life as a resort the inn has welcomed many famous visitors, among them Eleanor Roosevelt, Helen Keller, and Ted Kennedy, and it was also chosen as the site for the 1947 meeting that founded the World Council of Churches. The inn stands on 6,000 acres and is known for providing an incredible array of activities. Facilities include indoor and outdoor Olympic-size heated swimming pools, 27-hole championship golf course, 14 clay tennis courts, two platform tennis courts, riding stables, roller and ice skating rink, lawn bowling, and opportunities for fishing, cross-country skiing, and hiking. Pick up a trail map at the front desk and you can walk to, among other places, the pretty Buck Hill Falls. Winter sports include skiing, ice skating, tobogganing, and snowmobiling.

RATES: $89 to $130 per person (MAP) daily on weekends (higher prices are for rooms in the west wing). There are additional charges made for most of the activities.

Originally founded as a private club, and designed and built after the golf course was laid out, **Skytop Lodge,** Rte. 390 (north of Canadensis), Skytop, PA 18357 (tel. 717/595-7401), retains its traditional, conservative air as a gathering place for "congenial" people. The lovely stone mansion, with slate gabled roof and dormers, remains the same as it did in June 1928 when it opened, except for the swimming pool and the Laurel Room, which were both added later. Although the resort is open to anyone, the club still operates, and you can apply for membership ($25 a year), which will grant you a discount on rates and priority in making accommodations. Indeed, the management is actively seeking members to help perpetuate the family tradition of grandfathers, sons, and grandsons coming to Skytop. The 184 rooms are furnished with antique reproductions, including a small writing desk, butterfly Windsors, traditional iron lamps, and pine beds. Televisions are gradually being added to the rooms. Bathrooms feature little extras like heat lamps.

The 5,500-acre estate is beautifully landscaped and immaculately kept. The manicured lawns sweep down to an 88-acre lake stocked with bass and pickerel.

Cross the bridge and the drive sweeps up to the entrance and the pine room foyer, a long gallery supported by a double row of burnished, square pine columns, which is furnished with comfortable wing chairs, Martha Washingtons, and Windsors arranged in clusters for conversation. At the east end of the pine room is a superb, large library, run by a librarian, possessing the latest books as well as the classics. Two adjacent rooms are furnished with card tables for a few hands of bridge or a game of chess, checkers, and backgammon. The library, game room, and movies provide the main after-dinner entertainment (although there are dances on Saturday). Dinner is served in a large, well-proportioned room over-looking the splendid gardens. For relaxing during the day, there are a couple of porches, one looking out over Skytop Mountain, the other overlooking the gardens.

During the day activities consist of golf (the 18-hole course is famous for its tenth hole, which demands a 170-yard drive across the lake from an elevated tee), putting, tennis (seven courts), paddle tennis, archery, badminton, English lawn bowling, croquet, rowing and canoeing on the lake, fishing in the 1¼-mile trout stream, swimming in the indoor pool or at the lake, bicycling, and miniature golf; and in winter, downhill and cross-country skiing (two Pomas), ice skating, and tobogganing. There's also a downstairs game room for table tennis, billiards, and several electronic games. Evening cocktails are served downstairs in the tavern-like English tap room with wood settles or in the larger Laurel Room.

Although the place is conservative and adheres to a strict dress code (short shorts, abbreviated costumes, or extremely faddish attire is considered objectionable), it's still a lovely place to capture the quiet, leisurely life of yesterday. If you don't like TV and prefer to read and/or make your own evening entertainment, then this is the place for you.

Recently, Skytop has been experimenting with a series of special weekend packages. In March they offer several country weekends, which begin Friday night with a feast of Alaskan king crab and sirloin steak, followed by a live theater production, and on Saturday a picnic and target shoot, and a harvest dinner followed by a mass square dance. Guests bring their own costumes and an occasional pitchfork, and on Sunday morning everyone leaves, well fortified with a solid farm buffet of sausage, eggs, hash-browns, and ham.

RATES: $75 to $100 single, $150 to $230 per person double (American Plan) per night on winter weekends; in summer, $75 to $100 single, $150 to $210 double. Golf, tennis, and other packages are offered. There are additional charges for most of the activities.

The **Sterling Inn,** Rte. 191 (P.O. Box 1), South Sterling, PA 18460 (tel. 717/676-3311), is a homey, small resort-like place with tennis, putting, swimming, and a brook running through the pretty 103-acre landscaped property. Winter pastimes include cross-country skiing and skating on the lake. Inside the main lodge you'll find a cozy lounge with books—Thackeray, Dickens, and Kipling—TV, and a fireplace that glows on nippy evenings. There's a comfortable dining room and a game room for card and game playing. The rooms are fair-sized and furnished with a motley collection of unmatched pieces.

RATES: $55 to $85 per person (American Plan) on weekends; cottages rent from

$75. Throughout the year various weekend discounts (usually 5%) are offered on special occasions.

A Honeymoon Retreat

On Lake Wallenpaupack, at **Cove Haven,** Lakeville, PA 18438 (tel. 717/226-2101), the latest gimmick is the champagne tower suites, so called because they contain champagne-glass-shaped Jacuzzis as well as 15-foot-wide pools, sauna, and massage table. Other fantasy suites offer a heart-shaped bath and pool, mirrored ceilings in the bedroom, and living rooms with a fireplace. Still other accommodations are in separate cottages with wood-burning fireplaces. The resort is located on a lake affording opportunities for all kinds of summer water sports. (The accommodations, though, are not lakeside—the place is so large that a shuttle bus operates.) There are two nightclubs and a disco for nighttime entertainment. Great winter activities include snowmobiling, ice skating, sledding, skiing, and tobogganing. The sports palace has an indoor ice rink, three indoor tennis courts, racquetball, and a bocce ball court. The Ship's Galley provides indoor archery, a billiard room, massage, exercise machines, game room, and more. Other facilities include three pools (two outdoor, one indoor) and waterskiing. You really don't have to be married to enjoy all this and the lake too.

RATES: $375 to $525 (the higher price for the champagne towers rooms with pool and sauna) for the weekend.

A NORTHERN HIDEAWAY AT STARLIGHT LAKE

Just inside the Pennsylvania border across from Hancock, New York, the **Inn at Starlight Lake,** Starlight Lake, PA 18461 (tel. 717/798-2519), an old, green clapboard house overlooking a pristine lake with a dock sheltering canoes, makes for a secluded romantic weekend escape. Inside it's cozy and unassuming. There's a porch for dining and a parlor with oversize comfortable furniture, a couple of pot-belly cast-iron stoves, plenty of old books to read, and a grand piano heaped high with piles of sheet music.

Breakfast favorites include raised-dough waffles, homemade granola, pancakes, and french toast made with homemade bread. At lunch a blackboard menu features light salads, sandwiches, and soups. At dinner the menu offers an assortment of continental dishes—steak au poivre, veal parmesan or française, roast duckling with orange sauce, jaegerschnitzel in a brown sauce with mushrooms and brandy, fresh fish of the day, and more. The MAP rates provide for a $15 meal allowance per evening; entree prices range from $9 to $14.

Besides the water sports on the lake (rowing, sailing, canoeing), there's also a tennis court and bicycles for some landlubbing exercise. In winter there are well-groomed ski trails. The whole place exudes a delightfully unpretentious air, yet it's small enough to offer personal service. Rooms are located either in the main house or in cottages around the property.

RATES: $105 to $130 double (MAP) per night on weekends, $90 to $104 in midweek. The easiest route to Starlight Lake is via New York's Rte. 17.

MOUNTAINHOME-CRESCO DINING

Unless you know about the **Homestead Inn,** Sandspring Drive, Cresco (tel. 717/595-3171), the way the locals do, you'll have a hard time finding it, for it's tucked away in the woods, half a mile off Rte. 390 on a street lined with average suburban-looking houses. The atmosphere is distinctly country, featuring calico print tablecloths, barn siding, mill-wheel chandeliers, and Wyeth prints. The food is country-fresh, consisting of an assortment of fish—red snapper served with a tomato-basil sauce, sea scallops in a tarragon sauce, prime rib, roast duck in chambord sauce, veal marsala, and other chicken and veal dishes, priced from $10.

DINNER: Monday to Saturday from 5 to 10 P.M., on Sunday from 4 to 9 P.M.; closed Tuesday in winter. To get there coming from the south, take Rte. 191 north and turn off about two miles before the Mountainhome Playhouse.

CANADENSIS AREA ACTIVITIES

Most of the sporting activities in the area can be pursued either at the resorts —Skytop and Buck Hill—or in the nearby state parks.

BOATING: White Beauty Marina on Lake Wallenpaupack, Greentown (tel. 717/857-0234), has canoes, sailboats, and skiboats for rent. Ski and scuba-diving rentals. Kite skiing and parasailing.

   Rowboats and canoes can be rented at Ledgedale Recreation Area on 5,700-acre Lake Wallenpaupack. Also at the lake's Wilsonville, Caffrey, and Ironwood Point areas. For more information, contact the Pocono Mountains Vacation Bureau, Lake Wallenpaupack Association, Hawley, PA 18428 (tel. 717/226-2147); or the Superintendent, Pennsylvania Power and Light Company, P.O. Box 122, Hawley PA 18428 (tel. 717/226-3702).

CAMPING: There are several areas in Lake Wallenpaupack—Caffrey, Star Route, Box 360, Lakeville, PA 18438 (tel. 717/226-4608); Ironwood Point, R.D. 2, Box 344, Greentown, PA 18426 (tel. 717/857-0880); Ledgedale, R.D. 2, Box 379C, Greentown, PA 18426 (tel. 717/689-2181); Wilsonville, Star Route 2, Box 33, Hawley, PA 18428 (tel. 717/226-4382). Also see "State Parks," below.

CANOEING: Upper Delaware canoe outfitters include: Kittatinny Canoes, Inc. (tel. 717/828-2700); Bob Lander's Canoe Rentals (tel. 914/252-3925); and Jerry's Canoe Renting (tel. 914/557-6078).

FISHING: In the Brodhead Creek and at Lake Wallenpaupack. Also see "State Parks," below.

GOLF: Tanglewood Lakes, Greentown (tel. 717/857-0251), 18 holes, par 70, 6,500 yards. Cricket Hill Golf Club, Hawley (tel. 717/226-4366), 9 holes.

Buck Hill Inn (tel. 717/595-7441) offers a 27-hole championship course with a par of 72 for 18 holes.

HIKING: There are trails at Ledgedale and Shuman Point, Lake Wallenpaupack. Also see "State Parks," below. You can also walk to Buck Hill Falls, Rte. 390 on the Buck Hill Inn's property.

HORSEBACK RIDING: RJD Stables and Riding Center, off Rte. 590 (R.D. 5), Lake Ariel, PA 18436 (tel. 717/698-6996), between Hamlin and Hawley, offers trail rides for the beginner and longer two-hour rides for the more experienced. Buck Hill Inn offers guided trail rides and lessons. Double W Riding Stable and Ranch, Rte. 943 (R.D. 2, Box 1540), Honesdale, PA 18431 (tel. 717/226-3118), offers trails as long as 12 miles with free lessons on the trail. You can even arrange overnight trail rides here. Open year round. Room with breakfast is $38 per person double.

STATE PARKS: Close to 3,000 acres, Promised Land State Park, R.D. 1, Box 96, Greentown, PA 18426 (tel. 717/676-3428), offers picnicking, a swimming beach, boat rentals, fishing, 29 miles of hiking trails, ice skating and fishing, snowmobiling, sledding, and cross-country skiing. (There are also 531 campsites and 12 family cabins available.) Tobyhanna State Park, off Rte. 380 (P.O. Box 387), Tobyhanna, PA 18466 (tel. 717/894-8336), has over 5,000 acres for picnicking, swimming, boating (rentals offered), fishing, hiking, snowmobiling, ice fishing, and skating. (There are also 140 camping sites.) Gouldsboro State Park, c/o Tobyhanna State Park, has 3,000 acres and offers picnicking, swimming, boat rentals, fishing, hiking, ice fishing, and skating.

SWIMMING: Lake Wallenpaupack at the Wilsonville Recreation area.

THE HEART OF THE POCONOS

From Canadensis you can take Rte. 390 into Mountainhome and then turn south on Rte. 191 to begin a journey through the heart of the Poconos resort country —Paradise Valley, Tannersville, Scotrun, Swiftwater, Pocono Manor, Mount Airy, and Mount Pocono. All of these are located in Monroe County, which by the 1820s had became the center of a small resort industry that grew and flourished so that by 1900 thousands were coming annually to the mountains from Philadelphia and New York City.

ATTRACTIONS IN THE HEART OF THE POCONOS

There are several attractions in this area that the kids might enjoy. At the **Pennsylvania Dutch Farm** at Mount Pocono (tel. 717/839-7680) they can pet the animals and take horse-drawn hay rides, as well as a tour of the farm and home (HOURS: open April through Thanksgiving). The adjacent **Memorytown** (tel. 717/839-

7176) is an old-fashioned village that contains a wax museum, rustic sign shop, trading post, and an antique photo studio where the whole family can pose in costume.

Tannersville is, of course, home to the Pocono's major skiing area —**Camelback Mountain,** which can also be enjoyed in summer when there's grass skiing and a fantastic fun slide that you can take down from the mountaintop (ride up in the chair lift). Here also, kids enjoy **Action Park Motorworld,** Camelback Road, Tannersville (tel. 717/629-4411), where they can indulge their lust for speed by driving a Lola T-506 formula race car through a half-mile Grand Prix course, or less flashily by driving go-karts and bumper boats.

TWO ATYPICAL POCONO RESORTS

Pocono Manor Inn, on Rte. 314 (two miles west of Mount Pocono), Pocono Manor, PA 18349 (tel. 717/839-7111, or toll free 800/233-8150 outside Pennsylvania), is another venerable resort survivor (it opened in 1902). Enter this rambling Victorian mansion, topped by a belfry with a clock and small flat-topped dormers, and you'll find yourself in a warm, cluttered gallery filled with an assortment of chintz-covered lounge chairs, rockers, lowboys, decoys, dry sinks, and lit with all manner of iron and brass lamps—a wonderfully comfortable place which includes a well-stocked library. The rooms are large and furnished with cannonball beds, chintz curtains, wainscoting. Many of them grant glorious views out over the main lodge terrace. In the lower lobby you'll find a game room with billiard tables. The terrace that was once filled with ice skaters is now used for roller skating instead. Meals are served in a large handsome dining room lit by brass chandeliers and divided into two by a line of classic columns. It's warmed in winter by a fire in a large white stone fireplace. There's nightly dancing to a band. The whole place has an air of being lived in, and indeed the turreted part of the building is occupied by the owner, Mrs. Ireland, and it's her collection of furnishings and objects d'art that graces the rooms so perfectly. Set on a 3,100-acre estate, facilities include two 18-hole golf courses, indoor and outdoor swimming pools, two indoor and nine outdoor tennis courts, racquetball courts, bicycles, riding stables, five trap-shooting ranges, sledding, snowmobiling, cross-country and downhill skiing (with snow-making ability), and ice skating. There are also a video room and a game room with three full-size pool tables. Walking and jogging trails and a full social program make this an ideal stopping-place for families or couples.

RATES: $75 per person per night (MAP) on weekends; lower rates prevail in winter. Golf and outdoor tennis are free.

Brookdale on the Lake, off Rte. 611 (P.O. Box 400), Scotrun, PA 18355 (tel. 717/226-2101, or toll free 800/233-4141), is a very pretty and personable small resort offering secluded peaceful surroundings. Accommodations of choice, in my opinion, are at the rim of the lake in the separate cottages/chalets, which are spaced far enough apart in a wooded area to give adequate privacy. These chalets offer a sitting room with color TV, wood-burning stove, double bedroom, refrigerator, color TV, and the convenience of double sinks. Or you can choose to stay in the tower rooms beside the pine forest. These have a mirrored, canopied-look with fireplace, TV, refrigerator, and Jacuzzi bathrooms, and appeal to lovers of all ages. There are also other types of cottages and a few rooms in the lodge. The dining room, overlooking the lake, offers good and plentiful meals. The ingredients are fresh, and on my visit I enjoyed a creamy mushroom soup, a salad with a really tangy Italian dressing, and a gigantic portion of beef brochette made with succulent pieces of lean beef—far too much for my slender appetite. The 260 acres of grounds, beautifully landscaped and sloping gently down to the lake, provide year-round activities—boating, swimming in either the indoor or outdoor pool, bicycling, crazy golf, tennis (two courts), sailboating, paddleboating, fishing, snowmobiling, and ice skating. During the busy summer months a counselor takes care of children's activities. There are five nights of entertainment (weekends only during the winter). Although primarily a family resort, the management has recently begun catering to honeymooners with special accommodations, but the overwhelming impression is one of peace, seclusion, friendliness, and goodwill that derives from a mixed clientele.

RATES (with three meals): $375 to $525 double, for a weekend (the higher prices for a champagne tower room). Open year round, it's located about 20 minutes' drive north of Stroudsburg.

DINING IN THE HEART OF THE POCONOS

The **Brass Door,** in the Carriage House at Pocono Manor (tel. 717/839-7386), offers a sophisticated cocktail lounge and an elegant New York–style restaurant furnished with gray barrel chairs and circular gray booths teamed with pink tableclothes and napery. The food is typically American/continental, featuring such entrees as chicken Paillard (chicken breast with a mustard-rosemary butter), beef brochette Oriental (filet mignon marinated in Oriental spices), and a shrimp or scallop brochette. Prices run $10 to $16.

LUNCH: Tuesday to Friday from noon to 3 P.M. DINNER: Tuesday to Saturday from 6 to 10 P.M. on Sunday from 3 to 9 P.M.

For fine Italian dining, try **Fanuccis,** on Rte. 611 in Swiftwater (tel. 717/839-7097 or 839-9370), which has been operating for ten years. It's a pretty restaurant where tables are set with salmon-pink napery and fresh flowers and are lit by hurricane lamps. The menu is extensive. Some of the pastas are made on the premises—cannelloni stuffed with beef and spinach, gnocchi served in a tomato-meat sauce, and fettuccine Alfredo, for example. Several parmigian dishes are offered, along with a variety of fish, veal, and chicken dishes—calamari Fra Diavolo, swordfish topped with pesto butter, chicken scarpariello, pork chops pizzaiola, veal calabrese (tossed lightly with potatoes and peppers), and many more. Prices run $10 to $20.

HOURS: 4 to 11 P.M. daily (from noon in July and August).

The **Old Heidelberg,** Rte. 611, Stroudsmoor Road (tel. 717/421-6431), has been in business for 57 years, serving German specialties—sauerbraten with potato dumplings or spaetzle, beef pot roast, wienerschnitzel à la Holstein, and veal bratwurst boiled with mustard. The menu also lists three or four Italian and seafood dishes as well as steaks and chops. Prices run $10 to $15. An additional $2 will include soup or juice, salad, and dessert (apple strudel with cream, almond amaretto parfait with whipped cream and almonds, etc.). The atmosphere is created by steins and a large stone fireplace. There's a porch for summer dining.

HOURS: Tuesday to Sunday from 11:30 A.M. to 9 P.M.; closed Monday.

Pretty red tablecloths and a gilt-dragon decor define the **Pagoda Restaurant,** Rte. 611, Scotrun (tel. 717/629-0250). The room looks out over a rock garden with brook and waterfall—a pleasant setting for dining on an array of Cantonese and Szechuan dishes including char sue ding (diced barbecued pork blended with snow peas, water chestnuts, mushrooms, and Chinese vegetables topped with toasted almonds), butterfly shrimp (enfolded in bacon and served with a special sauce on a bed of sautéed onions, and spicy-hot pepper beef or moo shu pork with pancakes. Prices run $9 to $12.

HOURS: Noon to 10 P.M. daily (until 11 P.M. on Saturday).

A Pocono Breakfast

Van Gilder's Restaurant, Rte. 940, Pocono Pines (tel. 717/646-2377), is known as the Breakfast King of the Poconos with good reason, for you can choose among such local favorites as scrapple, pork roll, creamed chipped beef on a muffin, or the more usual ham or bacon and eggs. The omelets are huge, and there are seven to choose from.

HOURS: Monday to Thursday from 7 A.M. to 3 P.M., on Friday and Saturday until 11 P.M., and on Sunday until 9 P.M.

HEART OF THE POCONOS ACTIVITIES

Most activities are centered on the large resorts.

GOLF: Pocono Manor Inn and Golf Club, Pocono Manor (tel. 717/839-7111), has two 18-hole courses, each par 72; Mount Airy Golf Course, Mount Pocono (tel. 717/839-8811), 18 holes, par 72; Evergreen Park Golf Course, Penn Hills Resort, Analomink (tel. 717/421-7721), 9 holes.

HORSEBACK RIDING: Carson's Riding Stables on Rte. 611 (R.D. 1), Mt. Pocono, PA 18326 (tel. 717/839-9841), offers guided trail rides an hour long. Fox Run Stables in Tannersville offers the same thing; Pocono Manor Inn also offers 45-minute trail rides.

SKIING: Camelback, I-80 Exit 45, Tannersville, PA 18372 (tel. 717/629-1661), is the largest and most diverse ski area in the Poconos, with 25 trails, 11 lifts, and a vertical drop of 800 feet. Snow-making. It's also great fun in summer for the water and Alpine Slides and golf-driving range. There's also skiing at the resorts: Mount Airy Lodge, Mount Pocono (tel. 717/839-8811), and Pocono Manor (tel. 717/839-7111).

SNOWMOBILING: At Pocono Snowmobile Center, Rtes. 940 and 611, Mount Pocono, PA 18344 (tel. 717/839-8081), rent a snowmobile and ride the Mount Pocono golf course.

STATE PARKS: The 1,300-acre Big Pocono State Park, Box 173, Henryville, PA 18332 (tel. 717/629-0320), is the place to head for picnics and hikes.

THE LEHIGH VALLEY

From the Mount Pocono area, it's an easy run out to White Haven, center for river running on the Lehigh River, and also to Jim Thorpe, a coal town renamed after the famous athlete. Midway between Mount Pocono and Jim Thorpe there's a secluded resort.

A SPECIAL RESORT IN LAKE HARMONY

The **Lodge at Split Rock,** Lake Harmony, PA 18624 (tel. 717/722-9111), is a complete resort way out in the woods offering full facilities—indoor swimming pool, two indoor tennis courts, racquetball courts, health club with Nautilus equipment, a game room containing pool tables, a theater, videos for rent—and full-scale entertainment in the lounges and the movie theater. Summer or winter it's an active place to go.

Accommodations are found in several buildings, many of them time-sharing. The nicest are in the rustic, homey Austrian-style lodge, at the edge of the lake. All rooms are modern and furnished in contemporary style with telephone and TV. In the Galleria all 85 rooms are suites, with a living room, bedroom, and bath, while in the Villas you'll find wood-burning fireplaces, sauna, whirlpool, and kitchen in each modern sleek suite.

The setting is perfect in winter or summer—30,000 acres of forest, lake, and stream to be explored on skis, bikes, or on foot.

RATES: $130 to $150 per couple (MAP) per night (excepting holidays).

JIM THORPE ATTRACTIONS

The great American athlete was buried here in 1953 and the towns of Mauch Chunk and East Mauch Chunk merged and changed their names to honor his memory.

Although there's a personal tale attached to this event, which I'll relate shortly, the town itself is fascinating, because it represents part of the nation's industrial heritage, much of which is only just now being rediscovered as a national treasure. You won't find trendy boutiques and bistros here, but you will encounter 19th-century America's architectural and industrial past. D. H. Lawrence could well have written about the town and its inhabitants; *Women in Love* could easily have been filmed here, in this town dwarfed by mountains that sheer steeply on both sides of the river valley. From the narrow streets you can look up and see only the many different-shaped and different-colored rooftops of the houses terraced into the mountainside, and above them, the flat horizontal line of the mountain escarpment. First, stop at the conical turreted railroad station that houses the **information office.**

In its heyday, the town boasted several millionaires, who made their money in coal, railroads, canals, and transportation. One of them was Asa Packer, and you can visit his wonderful Italianate mansion that still broods above the town, a symbol of his power and status as a millionaire coal baron. Packer was born to a poor family in Mystic, Connecticut, and came to Mauch Chunk at age 23, in 1828, with all his worldly goods tied in a bandanna handkerchief and only his skill as a carpenter to gain his livelihood. By age 28 he was building his own canal boats and shipping coal to Philadelphia, and later New York. In 1840 he invested his fortune in building a railroad along the Lehigh River into New York and New Jersey. Later he went into politics and developed many of the social and educational institutions of the valley, including Lehigh University at Bethlehem. (Bethlehem, by the way, is an interesting place to visit; first settled by a Moravian community, it's particularly lovely at Christmastime.)

To return to Packer. At the **Packer Mansion** the interior reflects his wealth; the living room alone cost $75,000 to $80,000. The house contains portraits, antiques, and a spoon collection. HOURS: Tuesday through Sunday from 1 to 5 P.M.

Besides exploring the mansion, take some time to wander around downtown along **Lower Broadway,** or Millionaire's Row as it used to be called. Stop in, too, at the **Opera House,** which has been restored; **St. Mark's Episcopal Church,** designed by Richard Upjohn, which also has Tiffany windows; and browse in the galleries, antique, gift, and craft stores that now occupy the **old stone rowhouses** on Race Street. The **prison,** built in 1869, is also worth seeing. Members of the Molly Maguires, forerunners of the trade unionists, were tried and convicted here in 1877. Five were hanged.

Across the Lehigh River on Rte. 903 south, right opposite a suburban development, you can pay your respects at the **grave of Jim Thorpe** (1888–1953), whose mausoleum is decorated with reliefs of athletic events and the words "Sir, you are the greatest athlete in the world," spoken by King Gustav of Sweden at the 1912 Olympic Games in Stockholm, when Thorpe won every event in the pentathlon except the javelin throw. Soon after the Olympics a newspaper reporter discovered that Thorpe had played minor-league professional baseball while at Carlisle Indian Academy, and subsequently the Olympic Committee stripped him of all his medals, because they charged he had forfeited his amateur status. Although he did play professional sports thereafter, he became a charity case in the cancer ward of a Philadelphia hospital and died broke in 1953. His native state, Oklahoma, refused to erect a memorial to him, and his wife, Patricia, who had learned of the economic decay of Mauch Chunk and East Mauch Chunk and their struggle for survival, approached them for help. Many local citizens saw the erection of a memorial as an opportunity to bury old rivalries between the towns and to generate a new community spirit, which is why Jim Thorpe rests here in a community named after him.

Another Mauch Chunk/Jim Thorpe attraction is the **steam train** that goes to Nesquoining. It operates on Saturday, Sunday, and holidays from the end of May to the end of September on a 20-mile, 40-minute jaunt. Book ahead because it's popular.

From Jim Thorpe, it's also a short distance to a fascinating site—the **Eckley Miner's Village,** off Rte. 940, three miles south of Freeland and nine miles east of Hazelton (tel. 717/636-2070). It's a living-history museum revealing the daily life of the anthracite miner and his family. The company town was originally built in 1854 by the mining firm of Sharpe, Leisenring and Company. There are several buildings, some of which are open to the public and some that were specially constructed when the movie *The Molly Maguires* was filmed here. Start at the visitor center by seeing the orientation slide show and then walk through the village, complete with collier's dwellings, mineowner's house, church, social club, etc. HOURS: Village buildings are open Tuesday to Saturday from 10 A.M. to 5 P.M., on Sunday from noon to 5 P.M., from Memorial Day to Labor Day; on weekends in September and October.

JIM THORPE LODGING AND DINING

The **Harry Packer Mansion,** Packer Hill, Old Mauch Chunk National Historic District, Jim Thorpe, PA 18229 (tel. 717/325-8566), is a unique accommodation overlooking the small town of Mauch Chunk. It was built in 1874 as a wedding present from the prominent industrialist Asa Packer to his youngest son, Harold, who died at age 34 in 1884.

Enter this handsome brick Victorian with mansard and turret and you're stepping back into an era of wealth when no expense was spared: ceilings were hand-painted and everything was individually crafted. The dining-room floor is made of six types of inlaid wood—mahogany, oak, and cherry among them—set in an ivy-vine and geometric pattern. Breakfast is taken here at the polished formal Chippendale table set with silver candelabra and fresh flowers. The stained-glass Tiffany windows, depicting seascapes at morning, noon, and evening, are stunning.

The ladies' and gentlemen's parlors, both with roomy 15-foot ceilings, are furnished with Renaissance Revival Victorian sofas, ormolu mirrors, and other appropriate pieces. The study contains a handsome breakfront original to the house, hand-carved mahogany paneling, and a 16th-century Caen stone fireplace which was transported from Britain. In the corner there's a tiny bathroom furnished with a pretty Limoges porcelain sink set into marble. In winter people gather in the reception room around the carved-walnut fireplace decorated with hand-painted tiles of birds and flowers.

Pat and Bob Handwerk have taken two years to restore the building, and they offer eight rooms, all with very high ceilings. Annie's room is bright and sunny, with a large bay window and furnished with a four-poster. Potted ferns on stands add that Victorian touch. The suite which was Harry's room has a living area furnished with a love seat placed in front of the fireplace and a bedroom that also has a hand-carved walnut-and-chestnut mantel decorated with hand-painted tiles depicting Shakespearean scenes. Stained-glass decoration also. The bathroom contains the original wood-enclosed tub and marble sink. Gussie's room has fireplace, Victorian furnishings, and the added charm of a porch. Third-floor rooms are decorated in more of a Laura Ashley country style. Note the intense colors of the stained-glass roundels depicting birds and flowers over the staircase.

Sherry is served in the evening. A full breakfast of strawberries or other fresh fruit, muffins or banana bread or other home-baked items, scrambled eggs with bacon and toast, and fresh juice is served. In summer Victorian tea is served on the porch that is prettily decorated with Minton mosaic tile.

RATES: $50 to $70 double, $100 for suite. Tours are given from noon to 5 P.M.

Dimmick House, 110 Broadway, Jim Thorpe, PA 18229 (tel. 717/325-2533), is a bed-and-breakfast operating in an 1857 Italianate home right across from the Opera House. Unfortunately, no one was home when I stopped by, but feel free to investigate.

RATES: $27.50 single, $32.50 double.

Across from the Romanesque-style courthouse stands the **Hotel Switzerland,** 5 Hazard Square (tel. 717/325-4563), a good place for lunch or dinner. Past the bar with marble decoration you'll find a small parlor dining room where tables have country chintz cloths. Ceiling fans, tin ceiling, and wainscoting add to the atmosphere. The menu offers simple continental/American fare—sandwiches and burgers at lunchtime; veal cutlets with onions and mushrooms, filet mignon or strip steak, sole amandine, for example, at dinner—priced from $8.25 to $13.

LUNCH: In summer, 11 A.M. to 2:30 P.M. daily; off-season, Tuesday to Saturday from 11 A.M. to 2:30 P.M., on Sunday to 1:30 P.M. DINNER: In summer, 5 to 9 P.M. daily; off-season, Friday and Saturday only (open continuously for lunch and dinner from 11 A.M. to 9 P.M.).

Jim Thorpe's other dining place is the larger **Cassie's American Hotel,** on Broadway (tel. 717/325-2731), whose dining room is furnished with gilt bentwood chairs. It's also a popular bar. Food consists of hot and cold sandwiches and such items as pâté and apples (which translates to chicken liver pâté on slices of apple garnished with gherkins) served during the day. Broiled half chicken, surf and turf, veal Holstein, and calves' liver with Dubonnet and orange appear on the menu.

HOURS: Daily except Monday.

WHITE HAVEN LODGING

The **Pocono Hershey Resort,** P.O. Box 126, White Haven, PA 18661 (tel. 717/443-8411), is a modern resort set on 300 acres. The 250 rooms feature contemporary decor and appointments—color TV, telephone, and air conditioning. There's a dining room, snackbar, and a lounge with nightly entertainment and dancing. As one might expect, the facilities are extensive—ice skating, cross-country skiing, tobogganing, indoor and outdoor pools, four tennis courts, horseback riding, hiking, an 18-hole golf course, and volleyball.

RATES: $80 double. On weekends you can enjoy a variety of packages for $80 per person per night.

LEHIGH VALLEY/JIM THORPE ACTIVITIES

BIKING: White Water Challengers, P.O. Box 8, White Haven, PA 18661 (tel. 717/443-9532), offers bike tours, including maps and suggested routes along the Lehigh Gorge State Park.

BOATING: Rentals at Mauch Chunk Lake.

CAMPING: At **Hickory Run State Park,** Rte. 534, White Haven, PA 18661 (tel. 717/443-9991), are 381 sites with facilities (showers, toilets, and water faucets—no hookups), open from the second Friday in April to the end of December.

FISHING: For fishing information, contact the Pennsylvania Fish Commission, 3532 Walnut St. (P.O. Box 1673), Harrisburg, PA 17120 (tel. 717/657-4518). Hickory State Park and Mauch Chunk Lake offer fishing grounds.

GOLF: Pocono Hershey Resort, White Haven (tel. 717/443-8411), has golf packages.

HIKING: Hickory Run State Park has 30 miles of trails, at their best in May, June, and July when the mountain laurel and rhododendron are in bloom, and also in fall. Walk the Switchback Railroad Trail from Jim Thorpe to Summit Hill.

HORSEBACK RIDING: Deer Path, R. D., White Haven Stable, Rte. 940 and Northeast Turnpike 5 miles west of Blakeslee (tel. 717/443-7047). Open daily year round with horse-drawn sleigh rides in winter.

At Pocono Adventures on Mules Star Route, Jim Thorpe, PA 18229, off Rte. 903 you'll pay $20 for two hours, $30 for four hours, or $70 a day, including breakfast, lunch, and dinner.

PICNICKING: Good spots are to be found at Mauch Chunk Lake. To get there, turn left at the courthouse and Broadway as you come out of the visitor center.

SKIING: Downhill skiing is at Big Boulder, Lake Harmony Road (take I-80 Exit 43 to Rte. 115 south to Rte. 903 to Lake Harmony Road), Lake Harmony, PA 18624 (tel. 717/722-0101), and Jack Frost, Rte. 115 (P.O. Box 37-A-1), White Haven, PA 18661 (tel. 717/443-8425). Between the two resorts (their lift tickets are reciprocal) they offer 27 slopes serviced by 14 lifts and a complete snow-making system.

For cross-country, there are 12 miles of trails in Hickory Run State Park (tel. 717/443-9991).

Best accommodations and packages are at Holiday Inn, Lake Harmony, Rte. 940 (P.O. Box 117), White Haven, PA 18661 (tel. 717/443-84651); or at the Pocono Hershey Resort, White Haven, PA 18661 (tel. 717/443-8471).

For slope-side acommodations at Jack Frost, try Snow Ridge Village (tel. 717/443-8428), with luxurious accommodations with fireplaces, full kitchens, and living areas.

At Split Rock Lodge, Lake Harmony, PA 18624 (tel. 717/722-9111), there's an indoor pool, horseback riding, and tennis courts.

SKIRMISH: The latest rage—this is essentially a version of capture the flag. Two teams compete to capture each other's flags from bases in a wooded area consisting of 15 to 20 acres of varied terrain. A specially designed air pistol is used to mark and thus eliminate opposing players with a color-filled gelatin capsule. Camouflage jump suits are available for rent. Each game lasts about an hour. A match consisting of three or four games includes breaks for lunch, etc., and averages six to seven hours for a cost of $30 for each player. If you're interested, head for the Pocono Whitewater Adventure Center on Rte. 903, Jim Thorpe (tel. 717/325-3656).

SLEDDING/TOBOGGANING/SNOWMOBILING: Hickory Run State Park maintains areas of the park for these pastimes, including 12 miles of snowmobiling trails.

STATE PARKS: Hickory Run, R.D. 1, Box 81, White Haven, PA 18661 (tel. 717/443-9991), offers over 15,000 acres for picnicking, swimming, hiking (36 miles), snowmobiling, ice fishing and skating, camping, fishing, sledding, and cross-country skiing.

SWIMMING: Hickory Run State Park has a swimming beach open in summer at Sand Springs. Also at Mauch Chunk Lake.

WHITE-WATER RAFTING: Jim Thorpe River Adventures, Inc., P.O. Box 66, Jim Thorpe, PA 18229 (tel. 717/325-2570, 325-4960, or 325-4572), runs five- and six-hour trips 14 to 18 miles down the Lehigh River through Lehigh Gorge State Park. Spring and fall are the best times, although they do offer float trips during the summer. Cost: $33 per person, $12 to $18 in summer.

Whitewater Challengers, Inc., P.O. Box 8, White Haven, PA 18661 (tel. 717/443-9532), are the experts in the business, offering one- and two-day trips, including a marathon 30-miler done in one day, that's available only at the beginning of April when the waters are at their highest. Cost is normally $44 for a one-day trip, $80 for two days, and $57 for the marathon.

Pocono White Water Rafting Center, Rte. 903, Jim Thorpe, PA 18229 (tel. 717/325-3656), about seven miles from town, and White Water Rafting Adventure, Inc., Rte. 534, (P.O. Box 88), Albrightsville, PA 18210 (tel. 717/722-0285), also offer trips. The center also has canoeing and biking trips.

THE DELAWARE WATER GAP AND ALONG THE DELAWARE RIVER

As the Kittatinny Mountains were being formed millions of years ago, waters from the melting glaciers that carried vast quantities of rock and debris burst through the weakest point in the mountain range, creating the scenic wonder of the majestic Delaware Water Gap. Once higher than our present-day Rockies, the mountains have eroded to their current height of 1,400 feet, leaving the water gap approximately one mile wide at the crest and 900 feet wide at the river, a magnificent sight to come upon as you travel down Rte. 80.

AREA ATTRACTIONS

Interesting attractions in the Delaware Water Gap National Park include the village of Millbrook, and Peters Valley, a crafts community and school worth visiting to watch the artisans—basket weavers, blacksmiths, potters, jewelers, carpenters, photographers, and textile makers—and to shop the gallery store. HOURS: Studios are open from Memorial Day to Labor Day. Biggest event is the **summer crafts fair,** when over 150 craftspeople attend. For information, contact the **Peters Valley Crafts Center,** Layton, NJ 07851 (tel. 201/948-5200). At **Millbrook,** the National Park Service has reconstructed a **100-year-old village** by assembling buildings from the area and reconstructing others. The village gives a glimpse into 19th-century village life. There's a log cabin, a more prosperous home, blacksmith shop, general store, grist mill, church, the Van Campen farmhouse (once owned by a family that accumulated 10,000 acres), shoemaker's house, school, and cemetery. Concerts are held in summer at the nearby Watergate bandstand. The park provides great opportunities for hiking, birdwatching, and other nature-oriented pursuits.

The town of Delaware Water Gap itself has seen better days, although there's still a charm about the place that attracts. Here, in 1829 the first boarding-house/hotel was built; later, under the management of Luke Wills Brodhead, it became the center of a flourishing resort industry.

From Delaware Water Gap it's only a short trip to one of the Poconos' major attractions, the **Quiet Valley Farm,** off Bus. Rte. 209, 3½ miles south of Stroudsburg (tel. 717/992-6161), where costumed guides share the daily routine of a Pennsylvania Dutch family and their descendants who lived here from 1765 to 1913. Spinning, weaving, and hearth cooking are just some of the rural crafts demonstrated here. Kids love the hay jump, and the chance to make friends with all the barnyard animals. During the summer, themed festivals are celebrated. HOURS: June 20 to Labor Day, Monday to Saturday from 9:30 A.M. to 5:30 P.M., on Sunday from 1 to 5:30 P.M.

From the Delaware Water Gap, you should also take the road that winds along the Delaware River through hilly forested areas thick with hemlocks and spruce, where springs tumble down over rocks beside brilliant-yellow forsythia in spring. This route gives access to the **Delaware Water Gap National Park,** where you can picnic, swim, fish, and hike—at Smithfield Beach and Hialeah Picnic Area, for example. (For information about the park, stop at the Kittatinny Information Point in New Jersey off I-80.) This lovely rollicking road will eventually link up with Rte. 209, the main commercial strip that runs from Stroudsburg through Marshall's Creek and Bushkill to Dingman's Ferry and Milford, leading eventually across the border to Port Jervis, New York. It's a highway flanked by fast-food joints and neon signs, and generally to be avoided unless you really want to view the commercial exploitation of an area. This is where you'll find **Bushkill Falls,** the so-called Niagara Falls of the Poconos, which has attracted a lot of hoopla and commercial razzle-dazzle—paddlewheel pond, hex shop, miniature golf, gift and fudge shops, ice cream parlors, and a wildlife exhibit. Despite these accretions, the 1½-mile Mountain Trail actually leads through some pretty mountain scenery past all seven of the falls. They can also be reached in 15 minutes or in 45 minutes along more traveled trails. The falls can be viewed April to November from 8 A.M. to dusk (tel. 717/588-6682).

En route to or from the Delaware Water Gap area, you might also like to stop and explore **Waterloo Village,** a restored early-19th-century community in Stanhope, New Jersey (tel. 201/347-0900), where costumed guides give tours of the grist mill, apothecary and blacksmith shops, and homes, and you can watch craftsmaking demonstrations. On summer weekends a varied series of performances and exhibitions are presented—the Waterloo Festival orchestra, plus chamber music, jazz, and a bluegrass festival (the last usually held one weekend at the end of August).

DELAWARE WATER GAP LODGING

At the whimsical Victorian house called the **Mountain House,** Mountain Road, Delaware Water Gap, PA 18327 (tel. 717/424-2254), owner Frank Brown and his wife, Yolanda, have achieved a renovation of this 1870 clapboard home. Step inside and you're transported to another era, when hotel registration desks were made of oak and you rang a bell for service. The bay-window-lit parlor is comfy, filled with well-stuffed Victorian chairs, a couch, and many old photographs. Downstairs you'll find a pleasant dining room furnished with bentwood chairs, tables, and the numerous knickknacks and collectibles that seem to have survived with the edifice—including a working Victrola, an assortment of tins and canisters, and iron objects. The food—London broil, paprika schnitzel, stuffed cabbage, and other daily specials—is priced from $7 to $10.25. From April to October a seafood buffet is served on Friday night and from May to October a Sunday afternoon dinner buffet also, featuring 14 hot items—chicken, ribs, crab-and-mushroom casserole, Swedish meatballs, etc.—and a 20-item salad bar.

The bedrooms are small; some contain Victorian cottage-style beds, or iron-and-brass beds along with simple chests of drawers or dressers. Beds sport pretty dust ruffles, pillows, and comforters, and the walls are adorned with handcrafted objects. Nicest accommodation and most expensive is the Water Gap Room, furnished with a six-foot-high carved-oak high-tester bed, dresser, table and chair, and Renaissance Revival sofa. All have running water, some have private bath, but some have shower only, so be sure to ask. Rooms on the first floor share a bathroom down the hall that has an old-fashioned tub with shower attachment, while the ladies' room contains a genuine marble washbasin and solid-wood "cabinets."

RATES: $45 to $55 single, $55 to $65 double (the higher prices for rooms with bath). Special packages offered.

DINNER: In summer Tuesday to Saturday 5 to 9 P.M., Sunday noon to 6 P.M. In winter (Nov. through May) closed Monday and Tuesday.

STROUDSBURG LODGING AND DINING

Stroudsmoor, Stroudsmoor Road (P.O. Box 153), Stroudsburg, PA 18360 (tel. 717/421-6431), is a small family-oriented resort that is owned and operated by a family team—Louis Pirone, his wife, Bernadette, and their three daughters and their husbands. Bernadette is the executive chef and the food served is excellent—cooked to a much higher standard than your average full American Plan resort. The meatballs are made from strip steak; the mushrooms are stuffed with more than breadcrumbs and herbs. At the evening buffet you'll most likely find linguini with clam sauce, medallions of pork with lemon sauce, filet mignon, chicken marsala, plus salad bar and dessert—all for $13. The meal attracts a big local crowd, especially on Saturday night, as does the Sunday brunch when the table is spread with pepper steak, apple pancakes, cherry blintzes, seafood salad, chicken pot pie, roast beef, ham, zeppolis and bread pudding, great home-fries, and assorted desserts, all for $8.

There's a large homey area with a fireplace and grand piano, where a wheel of cheese and fresh vegetables and dip are put out, along with sherry, in the evenings. Wolfgang entertains at the piano on Saturday evening. A small bar is also available. Rooms with bath and air conditioning in the lodge are plain but clean, containing dresser, armchair, bed, and TV attached to the wall. There are also cottage accommodations available.

In a separate stone and stucco building at a distance from the main lodge, complete with fieldstone bar, there's live entertainment—jazz downstairs and a dance band upstairs. Tennis court, outdoor pool, and bocce complete the facilities, along with 150 acres to roam around.

RATES: $57 to $75 per person double occupancy on weekends.

Sheraton Pocono Inn, 1220 W. Main St., Stroudsburg, PA 18360 (tel. 717/424-1930), offers modern accommodations including some with poolside patio or balcony. Restaurants, lounge, and entertainment are all part of the package.

RATES: $75 to $79 double, on weekends, $80 to $85 for poolside accommodations.

Best Western Pocono Inn, 700 Main St., Stroudsburg, PA 18360 (tel. 717/421-2200), has an indoor pool, 90 modern rooms, three restaurants, and two lounges.

RATES: $52 double, $56 on weekends. Special packages available.

The **Beaver House,** 1001 N. 9th St. (tel. 717/424-1020), has been satisfying locals for years. It's a comfortable, cluttered bar/dining room in which booths have tassled velvet curtains and the bar is decorated with steins, dolls, and other bric-a-brac. One doesn't expect much from the food, but it's surprisingly good —particularly the fresh fish. For example, at a recent lunch broiled haddock with french fries and salad, served in a glass bowl, was good and cost only $4.25. Other items include fresh seafood, steaks, prime rib, chicken, and duck, priced from $8.75 to $21. And it's one place you'll always find open.

HOURS: Monday to Saturday from 11:30 A.M. to 10:30 P.M., on Sunday from 1 to 8 P.M.

A COUPLE OF HONEYMOON RESORTS

Birchwood, P.O. Box 83H, East Stroudsburg, PA 18301 (tel. 717/629-0222, or toll free 800/233-8177), one of the prettier honeymoon resorts, has a definite country atmosphere, as opposed to a frenetically paced action-packed one. Somehow it manages to deliver all the facilities but retain the charm and peace of the countryside. Accommodations are in separate white cottages or chalets, each furnished with a four-poster bed with lace canopy, wood-burning fireplace, and Jacuzzi-equipped bathroom. The most luxurious units have two floors, a living room with beamed cathedral ceiling, lower-level bedroom with a second fireplace, two bathrooms with wall-to-wall carpeting, suntan lounge, and Jacuzzi. The Plymouth chalets are beautifully located down by Eagle Lakes. At the center of the property is a pretty white clapboard house containing the cocktail bar and restaurant, while across the street beside the wishing well stands a red barn-like building housing the gift shop and reception area. Old gas-era lampposts and white fences add charm to the landscaping. Facilities include a massive tennis barn with two courts, an immense fully equipped gymnasium, glider and plane rides from Birchwood Pocono Airpark, indoor and outdoor pools, three lakes for waterskiing, canoeing, or "bicycle boating." In winter there's snowmobiling, cross-country skiing, ice skating, and many more activities—archery, rifle range, mini-golf, roller skating.

RATES: From $360 per couple (MAP) for the weekend in a basic chalet with fireplace, canopy bed, and regular bathroom, to $390 for colonial chalets or town houses.

Pocono Palace is another honeymoon resort on Echo Lake, Marshall's Creek, PA 18335 (tel. 717/226-2101, or toll free 800/233-4141), that attracts the young and the not-so-young to its full-facility landscaped resort with some fantasy suites that really are the ultimate. There are 32 of these so-called Fantasy Apple suites. The entrance opens onto a living room decked with a red or blue velvet couch, sleek glass tables, fireplace, and circular glass floor in the center. Travel down to the next landing and you're in the bedroom. Circular bed, of course, with mirrored paneling; and overlooking the lake, a private deck sheltered by a stand of tall, straight pines. Down the stairs again and you open a door into your own private circular pool, about eight feet in diameter with mirrored walls and sauna. Take a dip and you can look up through the glass floor in the living room to the skylight above. Soft lights, soft carpeting, a flickering fire, and you have a romantic retreat.

The Garden of Eden suites are the same, except they lack the glass floor in the living room; the Capri suites and the lakeside chalets have heart-shaped bathtubs and fireplaces. Club lodge rooms and suites offer a lovely view of the golf course or the lake, circular beds, and Jacuzzis. Facilities include a nine-hole par-35 golf course, indoor pool open 24 hours, waterskiing and boating on the lake, tennis, biking, archery, games, and a constant array of daily social activities. Think about it. You can either take a second honeymoon or just go for the sheer wackiness of it all. Winter sports include snowmobiling, ice skating, and tobogganing.

RATES (including three meals): $375 to $525 double for a weekend.

Pocono Palace is just one of the resorts owned and run by Caesar's, which also operates Brookdale on the Lake, Cove Haven, and another similar property, Paradise Stream. One advantage of staying at any one of these resorts is that you automatically secure the right to enjoy the facilities and the nightly entertainment at all four resorts. They're within an hour's drive of each other.

A B&B IN MILFORD

Sweet Woodruff, 201 E. Harford St., Milford, PA 18337 (tel. 717/296-7757), is the name of a bed-and-breakfast located in the oldest house in Milford, built in 1743 (it's 250 years old) and operated by Mary Cicitta and Randa Krise. There are seven guest rooms, all sharing baths, all nicely furnished. Many, like Mount Laurel, have beams and wide-board floors. Third-floor rooms are cozy with low, oddly shaped ceilings. Forget-Me-Not comes in Wedgwood blue and similar color frilled curtains; Orange Blossom charms with a brown/orange butterfly motif. Miss Piggy mementos occupy the Lavender Room. Guests have access to a comfortable sitting room with fireplace and upright piano. Breakfast is continental, with homemade breads and preserves.

RATES: $39 to $69 double.

DINING NEAR PETERS VALLEY CRAFTS

The **Wallpack Inn,** Rte. 615, Wallpack Center, NJ 07881 (tel. 201/948-9949), provides a country experience. The large bar is crowned by a moose trophy and possesses a huge fieldstone fireplace. It's where 86-year-old Jim Woolsey entertains, playing standards from the 1920s, '30s, and '40s on a baby grand.

Great oval loaves of brown bread are turned out fresh from the bakery, flames lick ham on a turning spit, and the grills are filled with baked potatoes, all destined for the greenhouse dining room which looks out over grassy banks to the river. The menu offers traditional American fare, priced from $10 for rainbow trout to $19 for surf (two South African lobstertails). Additional items include pork and lamb chops, chicken teriyaki, swordfish, and New York strip steak. On Friday evening there's a regular rôtisserie pig roast; on Saturday, prime ribs; and on Sunday, rôtisserie-smoked ham with fruit sauce. Desserts include pies and ice creams.

DINNER: Friday and Saturday from 5 P.M., on Sunday from 1 P.M.; in July and August, open Wednesday and Thursday also. Closed mid-December until after New Year's.

DELAWARE RIVER AREA ACTIVITIES

CANOEING: Adventure Tours, Inc., Delaware River Canoe Trips, P.O. Box 175, Marshalls Creek, PA 18335 (tel. 717/223-0505), offers daily overnight canoe trips, and a special combination horseback riding and canoe trip. Kittatinny Canoes, Dept. A, Dingman's Ferry, PA 18328 (tel. 717/828-2700 or 828-2338), rents canoes, rafts, kayaks, and offers overnight camping trips. Shawnee Canoe Trips, P.O. Box 147, Marshalls Creek, PA 18335 (tel. 717/424-1139), offers rafting, tubing, and canoeing on the Delaware. Northland Canoe Outfitters, P.O. Box 116, Marshalls Creek, PA 18335 (tel. 717/223-0275); Point Pleasant Canoes, Point Pleasant, PA 18950 (tel. 215/297-8823); Tri-State Canoes, Shay Lane (P.O. Box 400), Matamoras, PA 18336 (tel. 717/491-4948); and Water Gap Canoes, Delaware Water Gap, PA 18327 (tel. 717/476-0398), are some of the other outfitters in the area.

CAMPING: Worthington State Forest.

FISHING: On the west bank of the Delaware off Rte. 209, just north of Shawnee, Hidden Lake is a prime fishing and ice-fishing spot. On the opposite bank Watergate is also good for chain pickerel and largemouth and smallmouth bass. A New Jersey license is required on this side of the river. Also try George W. Childs State Park (tel. 717/828-3913).

GLIDING: Soar at Birchwood-Pocono Airpark, East Stroudsburg (tel. 717/629-0222).

GOLF: Cherry Valley Golf Course, Stroudsburg (tel. 717/421-1350), with 18 holes; Water Gap Country Club, Delaware Water Gap (tel. 717/476-0300); Shawnee Inn and Country Club, Shawnee-on-Delaware (tel. 717/421-1500), with three 9-hole courses; Fernwood Golf Club, Bushkill (tel. 717/588-6661), with 9 holes and 18 holes; Tamiment Resort and Country Club, Tamiment (tel. 717/588-6652), with 18 holes.

HIKING: There are great opportunities and trails in the Delaware Water Gap National Recreation Area, including 25 miles of the famous Appalachian Trail. For an easier, level walk, take the Watergate Trail through the village of Millbrook. For information, contact the DWG National Recreation Area, Bushkill, PA 18324 (tel. 717/588-6637). Other good hiking areas in the park are Duck Pond and the Dunnfield Hiking Area. George W. Childs State Park (tel. 717/828-3913) also offers good hiking.

HORSEBACK RIDING: Saw Creek Stables, Bushkill, offers trail rides (tel. 717/588-9380); Shawnee Stables at Shawnee Inn (tel. 717/421-1500) for summer riding; Tamiment Resort (tel. 717/588-6652) offers 45-minute trail rides.

ICE SKATING: At Watergate and Hidden Lake, both in Delaware Water Gap National Park.

PICNICKING: You can picnic at several places in the Delaware Water Gap National Park—Hialeah picnic area, for example—and also in George W. Childs State Park (tel. 717/828-3913).

SKIING: Shawnee Mountain, Shawnee-on-Delaware, PA 18356 (tel. 717/421-7231), has seven double-chair lifts servicing a 700-foot vertical drop with 20 slopes, each with 100% snowmaking capacity. Cross-country at Duck Pond in the Delaware Water Gap Park. Also at the resorts—Bushkill (tel. 717/588-6661); Tamiment (tel. 717/588-6652).

SNOWMOBILING: Smithfield Snowmobile Trail begins along River Road at Smithfield Beach about midway between Bushkill and Shawnee. George W. Childs Park (tel. 717/828-3913) has trails too.

STATE PARKS: George W. Childs, Dingmans Ferry, PA 18328, offers picnicking, hiking, and fishing. For information on Delaware Water Gap NRA, contact the Delaware Water Gap NRA, Bushkill, PA 18324 (tel. 717/588-6637).

SWIMMING: Smithfield Beach, just north of Shawnee on River Road; also at Milford Beach, just north of the toll bridge that crosses the Delaware on Rte. 209, both in Delaware Water Gap National Park.

NEW HOPE & BUCKS COUNTY

DISTANCE IN MILES: New Hope, 78; Erwinna, 60; Upper Black Eddy, 65
ESTIMATED DRIVING TIME: 1½ hours

DRIVING: For Upper Black Eddy, Erwinna, and Point Pleasant, take the New Jersey Turnpike to Exit 10, then Rte. 287 north to Exit 10, and then Rte. 22 west to the Flemington-Princeton exit, onto Rte. 202 south. At the Flemington circle, bear right onto Rte. 12 to Frenchtown, and cross the river to Rte. 32. For New Hope, continue down Rte. 202 south to Rte. 179, which will bring you into Lambertville and then across the river into New Hope.

BUS: West Hunterdon Transit Company (tel. 201/782-6313) goes to New Hope, Doylestown, Buckingham, Lahaska, Lambertville, and Upper Black Eddy.

Special Events to Plan Your Trip Around

APRIL/MAY: Lambertville Shad Festival.

Spring at Lenteboden to view hundreds of crocus, daffodils, and tulips blooming at bulb specialist Charles Mueller's (tel. 215/862-2033), at Phillips Mill Road and Rte. 32.

MAY: New Hope Historical Society's Spring Antiques Show (mid-May). New Hope's Outdoor Art Show (mid-May). For information, contact Amadeo Gallery, 88 S. Main St., New Hope, PA 18938.

AUGUST: The Antique Car Show, which includes a car auction (second weekend).

SEPTEMBER/OCTOBER: Phillips Mill Art Exhibition runs through October at the Phillips Mill Art Gallery.

OCTOBER: New Hope Outdoor Art Show (Columbus Day weekend).
Historic Fallsington Day (second Saturday).

NOVEMBER: New Hope Antiques Show.

DECEMBER: Reenactment of Washington's crossing the Delaware.

For further information: Contact the Bucks County Tourist Commission, 152 Swamp Rd., Doylestown, PA 18901 (tel. 215/345-4552), or the New Hope Information Center, P.O. Box 141, New Hope, PA 18938 (tel. 215/862-5880).

In the county of Buckinghamshire, England (known as beechy Bucks), there's a tiny village called Penn, whence William Penn set forth to settle in America, and which he must have had in mind when he named the valley that borders the Delaware, Bucks County, for, like Bucks, England, it's a bucolic landscape of woods and glades, gentle hills and pleasant pastures. Although visitors today may be disturbed by the commerce and crowds that have overtaken the Main Street of New Hope, they have only to set out along the lanes and hedgerows or along the river or the towpath and their sense of peace and tranquillity will be restored.

In 1681 Penn granted the 1,000 acres that now constitutes the borough of New Hope to Thomas Woolrich, who never even saw the land because he remained in England. Not until John Wells was licensed to operate a ferry in 1722 and to keep a tavern in 1727 did the town's life really begin. The tavern was known as the Ferry Tavern, and when you visit the core of the Logan Inn, you'll be standing in that early tavern. Whenever the ferry operator changed, the name of the town changed, and it was as Coryell's Ferry that the community played an important part in the Revolution, when the people aided the retreating Continental Army and helped take them downriver to McConkey's Ferry, where they began the march on Trenton.

After the Revolution the town prospered because of the river and also because of its location on the main Philadelphia–New York road. Real prosperity began when Benjamin Parry established a flaxseed oil mill and a lumber factory here in the 1780s. They were destroyed by fire and Parry rebuilt only the lumber and grist mills, calling them the New Hope mills. When the Delaware Canal opened in 1832, it brought even greater prosperity, as barges—as many as 3,000 in 1860 —traveled the canal carrying Bushmill's whisky and coal to Bristol and returning to Easton with manufactured and imported goods. The prosperity was brief, for in 1891 the railroad arrived on the other side of the river and New Hope slipped back into being a quiet backwater, for which we should be grateful, since it ensured the survival of the old inns and buildings that make such delightful lodging places today.

At the turn of the century, the beauty of the area was discovered by a group of landscape and impressionist artists like Edward Redfield, Daniel Garber, and Charles Demuth, who made their homes in the area, turning New Hope into an art colony of worldwide repute between 1905 and 1935. Their artistic ranks were swelled when the old grist mill was turned into the Bucks County Playhouse and opened in 1939, drawing the New York theater crowd including Moss Hart and his friends from the Algonquin Round Table: Dorothy Parker, S. J. Perelman, along with George Kaufman. They were in many ways the vanguard of the tourists who flocked here later, turning New Hope into a very commercial, crowded weekend destination by the mid-'60s.

Today the town is still crowded on weekends, but only a few miles outside, any visitor can experience the tranquillity of the banks along the Delaware River, of the towpath along the canal, or of the surrounding countryside. In nearby Doylestown one can ponder the eccentric brilliance of Henry Chapman Mercer, archeologist, historian, anthropologist, and collector, and the legacy he left behind—a museum containing 40,000 pre-industrial American tools, a tile-making factory, and a 39-room home, all built out of reinforced concrete. To the south lies Washington Crossing State Park, the site of Washington's dramatic crossing of the Delaware; Pennsbury, William Penn's 17th-century plantation; and, in contrast, Sesame Place, an ultra-20th-century playground for kids and parents alike. Throughout the area there are comfortable historic inns to stop at, antique stores and art studios galore to browse through, haunted houses to visit, barge rides to enjoy, and all kinds of activities on the river and the canal. And wherever you look, there are the trees and the fields, and the bucolic surroundings that first moved William Penn to remark on the valley's great beauty.

BUCKS COUNTY AREA ATTRACTIONS

New Hope
Besides the pleasures afforded by the Delaware River and the grassy towpath of the historic Delaware Canal, which is great for hiking, picnicking, canoeing, and even cross country skiing, New Hope has several other attractions.

Start at the **New Hope Information Center,** at the corner of South Main and Mechanic Streets (P.O. Box 141), New Hope, PA 18938 (tel. 215/862-5880), and obtain as much free information as possible. HOURS: They're open from June through September, daily from 10 A.M. to 6 P.M.; weekends only October through May.

The best way to spend a lazy summer afternoon is gliding along the canal in a **mule-drawn barge** under leafy glades, past old inns and homes, for an 11-mile journey from New Hope to Centre Bridge and back. HOURS: April 1 to April 30 (and also October 16 to November 15) on Wednesday, Saturday, and Sunday at 1,

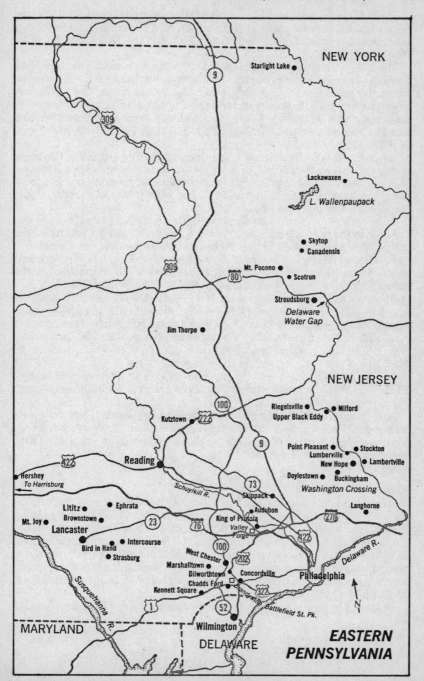

NEW YORK

Starlight Lake ●

⑨

Lackawaxen ●

L. Wallenpaupack

● Skytop
● Canadensis

Mt. Pocono ●
● Scotrun

Stroudsburg ●
*Delaware
Water Gap*

Jim Thorpe ●

NEW JERSEY

Riegelsville ● ● Milford
Upper Black Eddy ●

Kutztown ● ②②②

⑨

Point Pleasant ● ● Stockton
Lumberville ●
New Hope ● ● Lambertville

Doylestown ● ● Buckingham

Washington Crossing

Hershey ●
To Harrisburg

④②② Reading ●

Schuylkill R.

⑦③

Skippack ●

● Langhorne

● Audubon

Lititz ● ● Ephrata
Brownstown ● ②③
Mt. Joy ● King of Prussia ●
Lancaster ● ⑦⑥ *Valley
Forge*
Bird in Hand ● ● Intercourse
● Strasburg

West Chester ● ①⓪⓪
Marshalltown ● ②⓪②
Dilworthtown ● Concordville ●
Chadds Ford ●
Kennett Square ●

Delaware R.

④②②

②⑦⑥

Philadelphia ●

③②②

Battlefield St. Pk.

N

① ⑤②

Wilmington ●

MARYLAND

DELAWARE

Susquehanna R.

**EASTERN
PENNSYLVANIA**

2, 3, and 4:30 P.M.; from May 1 to October 15 daily with additional 11:30 A.M. and 6 P.M. departures. ADMISSION: $4.50 for adults, $2.50 for children under 12. For information, contact the New Hope Barge, P.O. Box 164, New Hope, PA 18938 (tel. 215/862-2842).

You can go from the canal age into the steam age by boarding the **New Hope Steam Railway** which leaves from the 1892 station, with its unusual witches' peak, for an 8½-mile round-trip journey to Lahaska. HOURS: From May to October three trips are made on Sunday and two on Saturday; in November only two are made on Sunday. ADMISSION: $5 for adults, $3 for children. For information, contact the New Hope Steam Railway, P.O. Box 352, Penndel, PA 19047 (tel. 215/750-0872).

In town, between the historic Logan Inn and the Bucks County Playhouse stands the **Parry Mansion** (tel. 215/862-2194), erected by mill owner Benjamin Parry in 1784. Each room is decorated to reflect the changes in interior design and lifestyle from colonial times to the early 1900s. HOURS: May to October, Friday through Monday from 1 to 5 P.M.

From New Hope, you'll also want to take the shuttlebus (Saturday only) that runs out to the prettily landscaped **Peddler's Village** in Lahaska, which contains stores featuring everything from porcelain and crystal to crafts and apparel.

For another fascinating trip, psychic investigator Adi-Kent Jeffrey holds a mysterious 15-stop **Ghost Tour** of New Hope's haunted sites. For information, contact Ghost Tour, 912 Cherry Lane, Southampton, PA 18966 (tel. 215/355-7046).

There are a couple of wineries in the area—**Bucks County Vineyards and Winery,** Rte. 202, New Hope (tel. 215/794-7449), which is open weekdays from 11 A.M. to 5 P.M., on Saturday from 10 A.M. to 6 P.M., and on Sunday from noon to 6 P.M.; and the **Buckingham Valley Vineyard and Winery,** Rte. 413, Buckingham (tel. 215/794-7188), open Tuesday to Friday from noon to 6 P.M., on Saturday from 10 A.M. to 6 P.M., and on Sunday from noon to 4 P.M.

Bucks County is also one of the few areas to have saved its **covered bridges.** There are 13 in the county and the information center will gladly furnish you with a tour pamphlet of all 13.

And then of course, bear in mind that **Princeton** and **Trenton,** New Jersey, are only about 15 miles away, if you want to visit the tranquil groves of academe and Princeton University Art Museum or the Capitol, planetarium, and art and natural history museum in Trenton.

River Road—Route 32 North of New Hope
Whatever you do, don't miss driving this undulating, twisting road that parallels the river and canal, stopping to browse in antique stores, quaint country inns, at farm stands or whatever tickles your particular fancy. You'll pass through the tiny hamlet of **Phillips Mill,** where landscape painter William Lathrop made his home in 1900. Later, in 1929 a group of area residents, many of them artists, formed an association and bought the mill to preserve it as a landmark and community center. Yearly art exhibitions, concerts, and theatrical productions were held, and today Phillips Mill is still a cultural center.

Next door to the inn here, **Bucks County Carriages,** West End Farm (tel. 215/

862-5883), runs escorted trail and carriage rides. Farther up the road is **Centre Bridge,** home of Edward W. Redfield at the turn of the century. At **Lumberville,** you'll want to stop at the old-fashioned country store that's been here since 1770 and walk across the footbridge over the river to **Bull's Island,** a New Jersey state park that is well known to birdwatchers for being the nesting ground of the cerulean and yellow-throated warbler. While you're here, stop in at the Black Bass. Next community is **Point Pleasant,** the most popular base for canoeing the Delaware and site of the Ralph Stover State Park, for swimming, fishing, camping, and hiking. A little farther north lies Erwinna, where the inn, Every May on the Delaware, was once a popular resort in the late 19th century frequented by the Barrymore family. Pick up some Gentlemen Farmer jams at **River Road Farms** before heading for Upper Black Eddy, passing through Uhlerstown, where you'll find the only covered bridge over the canal at Lock 18. Final stop after Upper Black Eddy is Riegelsville, another small town with an inn, some antique stores, and a few other shops nestled in beautiful countryside. By the way, while traveling this route, you may want to detour from Erwinna west to Perkasie to visit Green Hills Farm, home of author **Pearl S. Buck** on Dublin Road (tel. 215/249-0100). HOURS: Monday to Friday at 10:30 A.M. and 2 P.M.; from May through August it's also open on Sunday from 1 to 4 P.M.

From New Hope to Doylestown

En route to Doylestown, you'll pass through the tiny village of **Holicong** and the town of **Buckingham,** where you might happen upon a farmer's market or flea market on a Saturday. About three miles out of New Hope on Rte. 202, for fun why not stop in at **H & R Sandor,** at Reeder Road, near the Holiday Inn, just to examine some exquisite but astronomically priced antiques (HOURS: Monday to Saturday from 10 A.M. to 4 P.M.). Rock hounds will want to take Rte. 413 south from Buckingham to Pineville to visit the **Wilmar Lapidary Museum,** east to Rte. 232 on Pineville Road (tel. 215/598-3572), which displays a large collection of hand-carved semiprecious stones (HOURS: Tuesday to Saturday from 11 A.M. to 5 P.M.; closed from December 24 to April 1).

Doylestown

In this dreamy little county town you'll want to view the extraordinary landmarks created by archeologist, anthropologist, dandy, and bachelor Henry Chapman Mercer, who was considered somewhat of an eccentric in his early years but who was awarded many academic honors in later life. Mercer was one of the first individuals to realize the unique properties of cement—plasticity, fireproofness, and durability. All three of the structures you can visit are of poured reinforced concrete built between 1908 and 1916, well before the medium became popular.

Fonthill, Mercer's 39-room home on East Court Street, was begun in 1908, when he was already 52. He designed and supervised the construction. It's an amazing concrete warren, where even the bookcases, windows, steps, and pillars are constructed of cement. Every room is also colorfully decorated with brilliant tiles, either collected around the world (Delft tiles around the windows, Chinese roof tiles on a hallway ceiling, Persian tiles elsewhere) or else manufactured at his factory. Many of the tiles relate stories or themes. For instance, in the Columbus Room all the tiles encrusted on the ceiling relate to the New World and its exploration and discovery. There's no dining room, for Mercer preferred to dine wherever his whim decided at the moment. HOURS: March 1 to December 31, Tuesday through Sunday from 10 A.M. to 4:30 P.M. (last tour at 3:30 P.M.); closed December 25, Thanksgiving, Easter, and July 4. ADMISSION: $2 for adults, $1 for students. For information, call 215/348-9461.

The **Moravian Pottery and Tile Works,** at Rte. 313 and East Court Streets, is adjacent to Fonthill. Mercer had been moved to make tiles when he discovered that this old Pennsylvanian German art was dying. After several attempts he succeeded in making a satisfactory tile and by the turn of the century his tiles were in great demand. They were in fact installed, for example, in the casino at Monte Carlo; John D. Rockefeller's estate at Pocantico Hills, New York; the Traymore Hotel in Atlantic City; and the Gardner Museum in Boston. Most of the designs were adapted or copied from the old German stove plates. Again the building is of concrete, and looks like a Spanish mission. A short film precedes a self-guided tour on which you'll see the machinery, kilns, molds, tiles, and tools. The tiles are still manufactured according to Mercer's original formulas and methods, and you can purchase them in the store. HOURS: March to December, Wednesday to Sunday from 10 A.M. to 4 P.M. ADMISSION: $1.75 for adults, $1 for students. For information, call 215/345-6722.

Mercer built the concrete **Mercer Museum,** on Pine Street (tel. 215/345-0210), to house his collection of over 40,000 pre-industrial artifacts and tools, which he had amassed ever since he realized that what most people considered junk was in fact the essence of history. The work performed by these tools had cleared the forests of North America, opened a continent, and built a nation. In his museum and collection he intended to illustrate Pennsylvania history from a new point of view. The exhibits are extraordinarily displayed. A covered wagon, old stagecoach, whaleboats, and all kinds of large objects hang from the ceilings, while the tools relating to 40 crafts are displayed in fireproof, glazed alcoves. HOURS: March to December 31, Monday through Saturday from 10 A.M. to 4:30 P.M., on Sunday from 1 to 4:30 P.M. ADMISSION: $3 for adults, $1.50 for children 6 to 18.

Washington Crossing/Pennsbury Manor

Having retreated from the British across the Delaware safely to Pennsylvania and ordered all boats to be taken from the New Jersey side of the river, Washington regrouped only a few miles south of New Hope. He and 2,400 men made their famous crossing of the Delaware in a blinding snowstorm to his victory at Trenton on December 26, 1776. The 500-acre area is now **Washington Crossing State Park.**

The northern section, only two miles south of New Hope, contains **Bowman's Tower,** a 110-foot-high observation tower marking the spot where the sentries watched the movements of the enemy. There's also a **wildflower preserve** (tel. 215/862-2924) here. On the east side of River Road, the **Thompson-Neeley House** was requisitioned during the campaign for officers, including a young Lt. James Monroe, who was wounded at the Battle of Trenton but survived to become the fifth president of the United States.

Farther south, near the point of embarkation, there's the **Memorial Building,** which offers a recorded narration of the event: the **McConkey Ferry Inn,** where supposedly Washington dined before embarking; picnicking areas; and a bird sanctuary. HOURS: In summer, Tuesday to Saturday from 9 A.M. to 5 P.M., on Sunday from noon to 5 P.M.; the park closes 30 minutes earlier in winter. For information, call 215/493-4076.

In lower Bucks County, **Pennsbury Manor,** 400 Pennsbury Memorial Lane, Morrisville (tel. 215/946-0400), was the 17th-century residence-plantation of William Penn. A bake-and-brew house, smokehouse, stable, and barge house, all surrounded by pleasant gardens and orchards, are just a few of the buildings to be seen. HOURS: Tuesday to Saturday from 9 A.M. to 5 P.M., on Sunday from noon to 5 P.M.

Five miles northwest of Pennsbury Manor, **Historic Fallsington** represents historic preservation at its best. Three hundred years of architectural history from the log cabin to Victoriana can be viewed simply by strolling the streets. Best time to come is the second Saturday in October—Historic Fallsington Day. HOURS: Mid-March to mid-November, Wednesday to Sunday from 11 A.M. to 4 P.M. For information, contact Historic Fallsington, 4 Yardley Ave., Fallsington, PA 19054 (tel. 215/295-6567).

Sesame Place

Only a short distance west of Washington Crossing in Langhorne, **Sesame Place** (tel. 215/752-4900) is a marvelous place to spend the day with the whole family. Romp down the Zoom Flume or the Slippery Slope, enjoy live shows in the Muppet theater, operate the latest in computer gadgetry, and eat your way through the Cookie Mountain and the Food Factory. It's the one place where adults get in for less than children. HOURS: In summer, June 18 through Labor Day, 10 A.M. to 8 P.M. daily; Labor Day to October 16, weekends only from 10 A.M. to 5 P.M. ADMISSION: $8.50 for children (under 2, free), $6 for adults.

NEW HOPE AREA LODGING

New Hope–Lambertville Lodging and Dining

At the center of town stands the impressive 260-year-old **Logan Inn,** 10 W. Ferry St., New Hope, PA 18938 (tel. 215/862-5134), built by the first ferryman and originally known as the Ferry Inn. Friends of Moss Hart, and members of the Algonquin Round Table—Dorothy Parker, George Kaufman, among others—and the theater crowd gathered here in the '30s. The inn has hosted stars from Tallulah Bankhead to Robert Redford over the years. It's still a favorite gathering-place. The old tavern is a must. Or you can have a cocktail on the terrace in front, and dine either in the conservatory, brimming with plants, or outside by the gazebo, among assorted statuary. The menu lists a variety of American/continental dishes —filet mignon and broiled chicken to sauerbraten with Bavarian cabbage. There are ten rooms with antique furnishings usually boasting Victorian or brass beds.

RATES: $70 with a shared bath, $80 for a private bath. LUNCH: 11:30 A.M. to 5

P.M. daily. DINNER: 6 to 10 P.M. Closed January until mid-February and Monday until Memorial Day.

The **Wedgwood Inn,** 111 W. Bridge St., New Hope, PA 18938 (tel. 215/862-2570), occupies a gracious gabled 1870 Victorian with a large veranda decorated with scrolled-wood brackets and turned posts, as well as a historic Classic Revival stone manor house circa 1833. Pennsylvania Dutch–style surreys transport guests to and from New Hope. Young Carl Glassman and Nadine Silnutzer offer 12 guest rooms, most with private bath, some with air conditioning and others with brass ceiling fans. Each room is different. One has a spool bed with lilac lace ruffles, a treadle sewing machine, towel rack, and oak dresser; another well-lit room has a large bathroom, iron bedstead with candlewick spread, and still another has a brass bed with colorful quilt. On the ground floor the grandest room boasts a four-poster with a lace canopy and more formal Federal-style highboy furnishings. At night you'll find your bed turned down and a complementary carafe of amaretto awaiting you. Breakfast of fresh-squeezed juice, muffins, zucchini bread or croissants, and fruit salad is served outside in the gazebo, on the back porch, or in your room, if you wish. There are also two suites, one with a fireplace —ask for rates. In summer guests have swimming and tennis privileges at a nearby private club. Carl and Dinie also operate an innkeeping school that offers consultations, seminars, and even apprenticeship programs to anyone interested. In the evenings guests can settle into the bamboo chairs in front of the fire in the parlor and enjoy a quiet read or conversation. Nadine and Carl are quick to offer any information about the area.

RATES: $65 with a shared bath, $80 to $100 with private bath; 10% discount during the week and January to March.

The **Inn at Lambertville Station,** 11 Bridge St., Lambertville, NJ 08530 (tel. 609/397-4400), is a brand-new accommodation right down by the Delaware River. Rooms are variously furnished to re-create earlier Victorian eras and have been decorated to suggest particular places during that period—Hong Kong, New Orleans, Paris, and London. Some rooms have fireplaces, some have whirlpool bath. Continental breakfast and a complimentary newspaper are included in the room rate.

RATES: $75 to $115 double.

Lodging and Dining Along River Road (Route 32) North of New Hope
The first accommodation you'll come to is the **Hotel du Village,** Phillips Mill Road and North River Road, New Hope, PA 18938 (tel. 215/862-9911), which may not be an old inn (it is, in fact, an estate that most recently served as a girls' school), but it is quite lovely. Set on spacious grounds studded with trees, shrubs, and flowers (some popped into tubs), the 19 accommodations, all with private bath, are located in a large rambling building. While they're not spectacular, they are good-sized, have air conditioning, and are fairly priced. Furnishings are all different but expect to find simplicity—a king-size bed, mahogany chest, armchair, coat and hat stand, for example. On the grounds there's also a secluded, nicely landscaped swimming pool and two tennis courts. The dining room is extremely fetching and has a good reputation in the area. Oriental rugs cover flagstone

floors; rich chestnut paneling and fireplaces at each end of the room add warmth. There's also an outdoor flagstone dining area prettily arrayed with begonias and other plants and sheltered by a vine. It looks out onto a sylvan backdrop.

The menu features sole in curried butter; scallops with garlic butter and tomato; filet of beef in brandy with pink, white, and green peppercorns; chicken with tarragon cream sauce; filet of salmon with a tomato-and-shallot sauce; and filet of flounder with watercress sauce; along with other dishes. To start, there are escargots with garlic sauce, mousse of smoked trout, terrine du chef, and soups and salads. Desserts are always special. So are the fresh vegetables, and the bread that accompanies the meal. Prices range from $11 to $16. Breakfast will bring coffee or tea, flaky croissants, and coffee cake or similar to your room. Dried-flower bouquets, hand-painted trays, and embroidered clothes on the night tables are extra little touches.

RATES: $65 for a room with tub only, $80 for a room with a king-size bed. DINNER: Wednesday and Thursday from 5:30 to 9:30 P.M., on Friday and Saturday until 10:30 P.M., on Sunday from 3 to 9:30 P.M.

The **Inn at Phillips Mill,** North River Road, New Hope, PA 18938 (tel. 215/862-2984 for the inn, 862-9919 for the restaurant), is a small stone building (formerly a barn), bedecked with ivy and other vines, which was built around 1750. There are only five charming guest rooms, all with air conditioning and each exquisitely furnished. One room, for example, has a four-poster, weathered barnboard paneling, beamed ceiling, colorful throw rugs, and wide-board floors; another has a unique chest and a bathroom with a clawfoot tub (no shower). Neuchatel chocolates are placed in each room. Downstairs there's a large parlor with huge rough-hewn beams and a massive stone fireplace, where you can lounge on a leather couch. The original hand-cranked elevator is an affecting anachronism. The dining room has an excellent reputation for French continental cuisine. For vegetarians there's a spring garden plate. Prices range from $9.50 to $17. In winter the fireplace makes the tiled dining room cozy, while in summer French doors open to an outdoor dining area. Bring your own wine.

RATES: $65 to $75 double. DINNER: Monday to Thursday from 5:30 to 9 P.M., on Friday and Saturday until 10 P.M., and on Sunday from 5:30 to 9:30 P.M. Closed in January until February 6 or thereabouts.

The **Centre Bridge Inn,** Rtes. 32 and 263 (Star Route, Box 74), New Hope, PA 18938 (tel. 215/862-9139 or 862-2048). Although the whitewashed building with maroon shutters and dormers doesn't look that inviting (largely because it was built in the 1950s, after the original 1706 structure burned down), it's beautifully decorated inside with a mixture of authentic antiques and reproductions, and has rooms and terraces overlooking the canal and the river. Indeed, in summer barges drift right by as you dine on the brick terrace graced with a fountain, hibiscus, and clematis. For guests there's a parlor with a fieldstone fireplace, Oriental rug placed atop a royal-blue deep-pile carpet, Williamsburg blue-and salmon sofas and wing chairs.

The grandest of the accommodations is Room 9, on the ground floor, which has a large private terrace alongside the canal, a four-poster canopy bed with colorful quilt, and a rocker. The spacious bathroom has double louver closets, and cedar (yes) paneling. This is also one of the few rooms that has TV. While the other ground-floor room lacks the view, it has a separate sitting room, fine marble Eastlake-style dresser, and brass bed. In all the rooms great attention is paid to name quality details—the soap is Crabtree & Evelyn, the wallpapers from Schumacher. Upstairs, the more standard, but still large rooms all have sitting chairs, chest, sidetables, and pretty decor.

The dining room is typically country, with low, beamed ceiling and fieldstone hearth and serves well-prepared rack of lamb, veal citron, tournedos Henry IV with artichoke and béarnaise sauce, and a daily fish special, among eight or so items on the menu. Desserts are temptingly displayed and might include an amaretto Bavarian cream pie, baked Alaska, and a mocha walnut pie. Prices for entrees run $17 to $22.

RATES: $70 to $125 (the high price for Room 9 in summer). DINNER: Monday to Thursday from 5:30 to 9 P.M., on Friday and Saturday until 10 P.M., and on Sunday from 3 to 9 P.M.

Lodging in Stockton, New Jersey

Set on ten acres, the **Woolverton Inn**, R.D. 3, Box 233, Stockton, NJ 08559 (tel. 609/397-0802), is a historic home built in 1793 as a wedding gift from John Prall to his new bride, Amelia Coryell. The Woolverton family turned it into a Victorian with the addition of the mansard roofs. Whitney North Seymour, a leader of the American Bar Association for 50 years, added still more gingerbread and planted the formal gardens. St. John Terrell hosted many of the celebrities who performed at his famous "Music Circus" with lavish parties on the estate.

Today innkeeper David Salassi continues the tradition of hospitality begun in 1979 when the house began lodging overnight guests. From the sitting room formally furnished with grand piano, sofas, wing chairs, and French side chairs, all set around an Adam-style fireplace, you can step onto the porches and take in the view across the fields. A full breakfast is served either in the formal dining room, or outside on the flagstone patio. There are 11 rooms, ten sharing five bathrooms, and a suite in the carriage house, with canopy beds, chest, stenciled rockers, stoneware lamps, and soft rugs covering wide-board floors. There are no TVs or phones. Rooms on the second floor lack air conditioning, but the third-floor rooms, under the eaves with dormer windows, have air conditioning. Croquet, horseshoes, and bicycles are available for guests. No children under 14; no pets.

RATES (including breakfast and afternoon tea): From $60.

Established in 1710, **Colligan's Stockton Inn**, Rte. 29, Stockton, NJ 08559 (tel. 609/397-1250), inspired Richard Rodgers to write the song "There's a Small Hotel with a Wishing Well." The wishing well is still here, but the place was recently taken over by the Drucquers, former owners of the Pump House Inn in Canadensis, Pennsylvania, in the Poconos (see the Poconos chapter), and they have renovated the fieldstone building and re-created an elegant old-world ambience. Two suites with fireplace, private bathroom, sitting room, balcony, and bedroom, and a cozy studio room with a fireplace and private bath are available in the inn. A suite and one large room with canopy beds and shared veranda are located in the carriage house. The Wagon House also has two suites with canopy beds. An additional four rooms are located across the street in the Federal House. All have private bath and many have working fireplaces. A continental breakfast is included in the price.

RATES: $70 to $140 double.

From Lumberville to Riegelsville—Lodging and Dining

The **Black Bass**, Rte. 32, Lumberville, PA 18933 (tel. 215/297-5815), could be taken and deposited in the English countryside and the locals would hardly notice. In this pre-Revolutionary hostelry the parlor fireplace is suitably blackened, Tudor-style settles keep the heat in, and a pretty portrait of Queen Victoria and of Prince Charles stare down from the walls. There are seven rooms sharing two baths, all with air conditioning. The room known as the Place Vendôme has a massive Victorian carved oak bed, marble-top dressers and sidetables. The Grover Cleveland features a half-canopy, Eastlake-style dresser, and a fireplace, while a suite overlooking the river has a sleigh bed, a Victorian bed, and a separate sitting room. In the dining room and also in the tavern, which has a solid pewter bar rumored to be from Maxim's, the owner displays his varied and large collection of Royal souvenir porcelain and china. The food is continental/American, offering everything from turkey pot pie and New England lobster pie to roast duck Normandy and chicken breast Burgundy, with prices going from $14.75 to $19. Brunch ($10.50) includes a selection of egg dishes as well as items like chicken livers over barley and beef in burgundy wine.

RATES (including breakfast): $75 double, $150 for the suite. LUNCH: Noon to 2:30 P.M. daily. DINNER: Monday to Saturday from 5:30 to 10 P.M. and on Sunday from 3:30 to 8 P.M. BRUNCH: Sunday from 1 to 3 P.M.

Innisfree, Cafferty Road (P.O. Box 108), Point Pleasant, PA 18950 (tel. 215/297-8329), is one of the most unusual accommodations along the Delaware, located in a 1748 stone gristmill and a frame sawmill on the Tohickon Creek. Formerly run by music and poetry lover John R. Huestis, who in 1983 realized a dream of hosting a music festival with such luminaries as the Tokyo String Quartet, Gervase de Peyer, and several other musicians including some from the Chamber Music Society of Lincoln Center, it remains very much as he left it. As might be expected, the living room is filled with books and comfortable furniture in which to curl up before the fire or by one of the tall windows overlooking the mill stream. Breakfast of peach crêpes, waffles, or something similar is served at the oak refectory-style table. Wine and cheese are also offered in the evening.

The ten rooms, three with private bath, are all so different in size and design and wonderfully eclectic. All have open-beam ceilings. One has a four-poster, diamond-leaded window panes, and a chaise lounge alongside a huge fieldstone fireplace. Another has a massive Empire mirror. Some have barn paneling, others have solid-oak paneling from a demolished New York bank, and still another has the gears, cogs, and workings of the exposed mill wheel as part of the decor. The place is incredibly peaceful, individual, and situated right by the creek. You can sit on the terrace and listen to the brook. Truly inspirational.

RATES (including breakfast): $60 to $80.

Tattersall, Cafferty Road (P.O. Box 569), Point Pleasant, PA 18950 (tel. 215/297-8233), is the name given to this early-1800s double-porched house set among conifers and shade trees. It has six rooms, all with air conditioning and private bath. Room 1, the Highland Room, has Black Watch plaid draperies; Room 2 contrasts strongly, being lavender with wicker furnishings and a large canopied four-poster. Many of the rooms have the original wainscotting. Breakfast is served in the dining room, on the veranda, or in your room. Apple cider and cheeses are placed in front of the fireplace in the tavern in the midafternoon. The innkeepers are Gerry and Herb Moss. Gerry's needlework and paintings can be seen throughout the house, and Herb enjoys demonstrating and talking about his old phonographs displayed in the dining room. There's a small reading room and tavern with a beamed ceiling and a large fireplace.

RATES: $60 to $80 double.

EverMay on the Delaware, River Road, Erwinna, PA 18920 (tel. 215/294-9100), is an imposing Victorian mansion set well back from the road and approached via a semicircular drive. Built in the 1700s, it functioned as a small, elegant hotel between the Civil War and the Depression, hosting such vacationers as the Barrymore family. Five years ago it was purchased by Ronald Strouse and Frederick Cresson, who have restored it to its earlier glory. There are 11 rooms and two suites (all with private bath), ranging from the large Colonel Erwin room with a towering Eastlake bed, needlepoint side chairs, Victorian velvet sofa, marble-top dresser, and fireplace, to the smallest room, the Edward Hicks, which contains a bed, small chest, and dresser. Fresh flowers, potpourris, and bowls of fruit and nougat are placed in each room, along with miniature liqueurs. The price of the room includes breakfast, tea, and sherry—the last two served in the formal Victorian parlor with a grand piano, two fireplaces, and rare walnut paneling. The dining room serves a $40 prix fixe that begins with a champagne apéritif and hors d'oeuvres, followed by six courses. The menu changes daily, but just to give you some idea, the entrees might include Muscovy duck on onion marmalade with lingonberries and roast loin of veal with mushroom sauce; desserts are homemade and might be macadamia-nut-brittle ice cream or white-chocolate cones with a divine raspberry filling.

RATES: $60 to $100 double. DINNER: Friday, Saturday, Sunday, and holidays.

The **Golden Pheasant Inn,** River Road, Erwinna, PA 18920 (tel. 215/294-9595), is an ultra-Victorian inn nestled between the canal and the river (but lacking a view), which was built in 1857 to serve as a stopping-off place for the bargemen. Fourteen guest rooms with shared baths are available, eight in the 1834 Isaac Stover Mill Mansion, and all furnished with Victorian flair—marble-top dressers and chests, carved Victorian beds, and so on. The public areas are wonderfully atmospheric. The dark, intimate bar and dining room really does bring back the gaslight era, and an old radio playing period music adds to the ambience. Another greenhouse dining room overflows with hanging ferns and is lit by candles only. Outside, the trees sparkle with lights. The fare is international, but the restaurant is especially well known for serving venison, quail, rabbit, partridge, and goose in season. Prices range from $14 to $20.

RATES: $70 to $95. DINNER: Tuesday to Saturday from 6 to 10 P.M., on Sunday from 4 to 9 P.M. Closed Monday and also from a week before Christmas to Valentine's Day.

Beatrice and Charles Briggs rescued the 1836 **Bridgeton House,** Rte. 32, Upper Black Eddy, PA 18972 (tel. 215/982-5856), from decay and have faithfully restored it, revealing the original fireplace and floor boards. They've furnished the living room with old pine chests and other early Americana. At the back, french doors lead to a porch overlooking the river. Continental breakfast is served. There are seven rooms, four with screened-in porches and river views, all with private baths. Number 1 has a four-poster; no. 2 has an Eastlake look; no. 3 sports another four-poster with eyelet-lace pillows and sheets, sidetable draped with floor-length cloth. Each room has fresh flowers, baskets of fruit, and chocolates. In the bathrooms are English toiletries—soap, moisturizer, shampoo, etc. A country breakfast of fresh fruit, omelets, and breads is served, and sherry is also available in the evening in the sitting room. This is one of the few bed-and-breakfasts right on the riverbank, where you can swim, fish, and even tube right there.

RATES: $70 to $85 (higher price for river view).

The **Upper Black Eddy Inn,** River Road, Upper Black Eddy, PA 18972 (tel. 215/982-5554), set across from the river with no direct view, has simple rooms, none with private bath. The dining room serves a variety of continental cuisine from rack of lamb to beef filet chasseur and a fish du jour. Brunch includes omelets and other egg dishes along with such items as crab cakes and shrimp remoulade.

RATES: $50. LUNCH: Wednesday to Saturday from noon to 2:30 P.M. DINNER: Wednesday to Friday from 5 to 9 P.M., until 10 P.M. on Saturday, on Sunday from 3 to 8 P.M. BRUNCH: Sunday from 1 to 3 P.M.

The Delaware flows in front and the canal drifts by behind at the **Riegelsville Hotel,** 10-12 Delaware Rd., Riegelsville, PA 18077 (tel. 215/749-2469), a simple double-porched house. The main dining room is pleasantly old-fashioned with polished wood tables, Victorian love seats, tin ceiling, and Oriental-style upholstery. The food is continental—filet béarnaise, chicken Rockefeller (with wine, spinach, tomato, cheese, mushroom, and spices)—and prices run $14 to $18. At brunch you can opt either for the country table buffet with baked ham, sausage, breads, fruits, and so on, or à la carte. There are 12 simply furnished rooms, some with private bath and some with sink and shared bath.

RATES: $50 with shared bath, $70 to $80 with private bath.

LUNCH: Wednesday to Saturday from noon to 2 P.M. DINNER: Wednesday and Thursday from 5 to 8 P.M., on Friday and Saturday until 10 P.M., on Sunday from 1 to 8 P.M. BRUNCH: Sunday from noon to 2 P.M.

Lodging in Holicong and Buckingham

A narrow tree-lined lane, yellow with daffodils in spring, leads to **Barley Sheaf Farm,** Rte. 202 (P.O. Box 10), Holicong, PA 18928 (tel. 215/794-5104), one of my favorite lodgings anywhere. Inspired by many trips to the British Isles, Don and Ann Mills took over this 30-acre farm with sheep, chickens, and beehives that was once George Kaufman's residence, and offer warm lively hospitality, comfortable country decor, and hearty breakfasts. The barn, secluded landscaped pool, pond, and majestic old trees round out the beautiful setting overlooking fields, dappled with cattle and horses. The original part of the house dates from 1740, and the parlors and rooms contain comfortable antiques, horse brasses around the fireplace, and in the entrance lobby a magnificent doll's house. There are six rooms in the house, five with private bath and all furnished differently and attractively. Many have four-posters. The cottage, which used to be the ice house, contains three rooms with private bath, and a cozy living room with fireplace and hooked rugs. One of the accommodations is known as the Strawberry Room because of the wallpaper and comes with a handsome bed, wide-board floors covered with hooked rugs, a pie cupboard, and a Mexican-tiled bathroom. The bedroom has a french door, which you can throw open and gaze out over the pastures beyond, or else step through onto a small flagstone terrace set with table and chairs. Breakfasts are abundant—fresh juice, farm-fresh eggs, breads, jams, and honey from the hives.

RATES (including breakfast): $80 to $125. Open February 14 until the weekend before Christmas; closed the weekend before Christmas until the first weekend after New Year's and then open weekends only until February 14.

Mike and Suella Wass run the **Whitehall Inn,** 1370 Pineville Rd. (R.D. 2), Buckingham, PA 18912 (tel. 215/598-7945), located five miles south of town in a 1794 home set on 12½ acres. There are six rooms: four with fireplace, four with private bath, and all are attractively furnished. At breakfast a four-course meal of fresh fruit, juice, muffins, coffee cake, and an entree is served by candlelight. There's a pool and tennis.

RATES: $80 to $100 double.

Lodging and Dining at Lake Nockamixon

The **Sign of the Sorrel Horse,** Old Bethlehem Road, Quakertown, PA 18951 (tel. 215/536-4651), dates back to 1784 and has a quiet arbor in the rear, a genuine swimming hole, and an old well that really imparts a rustic antiqued feeling to the place. The dining room has a good reputation for continental cuisine.

RATES: $60 to $65 double. DINNER: Wednesday to Sunday from 6 P.M. BRUNCH: Sunday from noon to 2:30 P.M.

NEW HOPE AREA DINING

I've already discussed a couple of places that rank among the very best in the area, notably the **Inn at Phillips Mill,** and the **Hotel du Village.** Other choices also previously covered include: the **Centre Bridge Inn,** the **Black Bass,** and the **Golden Pheasant** in Lumberville, **Colligan's Stockton Inn,** the **Upper Black Eddy Inn,** and the **Riegelsville Inn.** See the Accommodations Section.

Some of the best dining in the area lies across the river from New Hope in Lambertville.

Lambertville Dining

Considered among the top dining spots in the area, **Savoir Faire,** 13-15 Kline's Court (tel. 215/397-2631), has classical music accompaniment on Friday night in its elegant dining room. The cuisine is multinational, with an emphasis on French preparation. The $30 prix fixe includes appetizer (four or so to select from, like bourbon barbecued shrimp), salad, dessert, and a choice of entree that might include paillard of veal with porcini, white wine, and cream; swordfish nipponaise; or leg of lamb à la grecque. On Sunday evening a three-course supper is available for $23. Bring your own wine.

DINNER: Wednesday to Saturday from 6 to 10 P.M., on Sunday from 3 to 8 P.M.

Practically next door, **Stars,** 9 Kline's Court (tel. 215/397-2923), is a romantic, softly lit room where lace tablecloths are spread over dusky-rose linen and the chairs are upholstered in a bold art deco design. The service is extremely attentive and the owner-chef will come to your table to explain the dishes that he has prepared that day. Among them there might be a dilled cucumber bisque, filet mignon valoise (with mushrooms and a brandy-cream sauce), duck Oporto, or salmon with dill. You'll need to bring your own wine (there's a fine store across the street). Prices run $15 to $18.

LUNCH: Saturday from noon to 2 P.M., on Sunday until 4 P.M. DINNER: Wednesday to Sunday from 6 P.M.

By the river in a little cul-de-sac known as the Porkyard, **Gerard's,** 8½ Coryell St. (tel. 215/397-8035), is a local favorite and a pretty but fairly formal place. The inner dining room is a flattering pink and gray. The woodstove is garlanded with plants and flowers in summer. The menu features rack of lamb, Dover sole, filet mignon, and daily specials, all priced from $12 to $18.

DINNER: Monday and Wednesday to Saturday from 5:30 to 10 P.M., on Sunday from noon to 8:30 P.M. BRUNCH: Saturday and Sunday from noon to 2:30 P.M. Bring your own wine.

More casual dining can be found at **Phil & Dan's,** 19 S. Main St. (tel. 215/397-0051), a real family-style Italian place where all the pasta is homemade. Phil and Dan have been operating for almost 30 years, and their wedding photo taken over 50 years ago hangs above the red gingham-topped tables. Besides delicious pasta dishes, there's also veal parmigiana, veal and peppers, sandwiches, cheese steaks, and pizzas. Prices run $4 to $10.

DINNER: Tuesday to Saturday from 4:30 to 9:30 P.M.

Back on Bridge Street at no. 19, the **Full Moon** (tel. 215/397-1096) is another casual spot with a light-oak and modern-graphics look. You can have a full breakfast here or savor a chocolate croissant or two. Burgers and pirogies are the prime lunchtime items, while dinner features such dishes as veal amaretto, chicken with broccoli, duck with raspberry sauce, and barbecued ribs, with prices going from $9 to $15. Bring your own wine.

BREAKFAST AND LUNCH: Monday and Wednesday to Saturday from 8 A.M. to 4 P.M. DINNER: Wednesday to Sunday from 5 to 10 P.M. BRUNCH: Sunday from 9 A.M. to 3 P.M.

At the restored 1867 stone **Lambertville Station,** 11 Bridge St. (tel. 609/397-8300), there are a series of restaurants, a bar, and lounge. Etched glass, oak, mirrors, period light fixtures, and Victorian furnishings create the atmosphere. About a dozen entrees are featured on the menu—trout almondine, swordfish with lemon butter, sesame chicken with a raspberry sauce, veal chanterelle, and roast duck with a sauce du jour. Prices range from $10.25 to $14.50.

HOURS: Monday to Saturday from 11:30 A.M. to 2 A.M., on Sunday from 10:30 A.M. to 2 A.M. The railroad still runs on weekends, taking visitors and shoppers to Ringoes and Flemington.

New Hope Dining

Set in a condominium development known as Village 2, on a hill above New Hope, **La Bonne Auberge** (tel. 215/862-2462), a charming old stone inn, is a lovely surprise. The dining here is very fine, and the specialties run to rack of lamb arlesienne, veal with morels, and grilled salmon, with prices ranging from $18 to $26. DINNER: Wednesday to Sunday from 6 to 10 P.M.; closed Monday and Tuesday.

Odette's, South River Road (tel. 215/862-3000), occupies a pretty stone house with a dining room overlooking the river. The fare is American nouvelle. On Friday and Saturday there's entertainment and dancing.

LUNCH: 11:30 A.M. to 3 P.M. daily. DINNER: Monday to Thursday from 5 to 10 P.M., on Friday and Saturday until 11 P.M., on Sunday from 4 to 9 P.M. BRUNCH: Sunday from 11:30 A.M. to 3 P.M.

The **Raven**, 385 W. Bridge St. (tel. 215/862-2081), is a favored luncheon spot about 1½ miles out of New Hope on Rte. 179. Here you can enjoy trout almondine, stuffed artichokes, salade niçoise, Bermuda fish chowder, and lamb chops, all well prepared and presented in a paneled dining room that looks out over a pretty garden. Lunch prices are extremely reasonable.

LUNCH: Noon to 3 P.M. daily. DINNER: Sunday to Thursday from 6 to 10 P.M., on Friday and Saturday until 11 P.M. BRUNCH: Sunday from noon to 3 P.M.

For casual dining and great breakfasts and lunches, head for **Mother's**, 34 N. Main St. (tel. 215/862-9354), where all kinds of burgers (about a dozen or more of them) and salads are served in woody surroundings. Desserts baked on the premises are also a strong attraction.

BREAKFAST: Monday to Friday from 8 A.M. to 2 P.M., on Saturday and Sunday from 9 A.M. LUNCH: From 11 A.M. daily. DINNER: Sunday to Thursday from 5 to 10 P.M., until 10:30 P.M. on Friday and Saturday.

More Area Dining

The **Harrow Inn**, Rtes. 611 and 412 in Ottsville (tel. 215/847-2464), is a great favorite for atmosphere and dining. Although it was built around 1720 for fur trappers and Indian traders, it became an inn in 1744. There's a variety of French-continental cuisine.

DINNER: Tuesday to Saturday from 5 P.M., on Sunday from 4 to 8 P.M.

In Doylestown, the **Conti Cross Keys**, at Rtes. 611 and 313 (tel. 215/348-9600), slap in the middle of highway sprawl and malls, has been serving Italian, continental, and steaks from a 250-item menu for more than 30 years. Semicircular booths and walls plastered with celebrity photos are the hallmarks of the decor. Pasta dishes start at $10, meat at $15, going up to $21.

LUNCH: Monday to Saturday from 11 A.M. to 3 P.M. DINNER: Monday to Saturday from 5 to 10 P.M.

NEW HOPE AREA EVENING ENTERTAINMENT

For theater entertainment, the **Bucks County Playhouse,** South Main Street (P.O. Box 313), New Hope, PA 18938 (tel. 215/862-2041), stages musicals, including some Gilbert and Sullivan, in a converted gristmill. Over in Princeton, the **McCarter Theater,** 91 University Pl., Princeton, NJ 08540 (tel. 609/452-5200), presents a full season of professional drama, dance, music, and special events. The theater recently completed a $4-million renovation, upgrading the acoustics and installing, among other things, a special system for the hearing impaired. In Buckingham, the **Town & Country Players** (tel. 215/794-7874) perform at the Barn, Rte. 263.

For jazz lovers there's music every night from 9:30 P.M. at the **Havana Bar and Restaurant,** 105 S. Main St., New Hope (tel. 215/862-9897), and farther afield at the **Blue Ram,** Rte. 532, Washington Crossing (tel. 215/493-1262), Wednesday through Sunday.

In Doylestown, the **Doylestown Inn,** 18 W. State St. (tel. 215/345-6610), has a variety of entertainments, including jazz and soft rock.

For plain and simple cocktails, the **Boat House,** 8½ Coryell St., at the Porkyard in Lambertville (tel. 215/397-2244), has two small, appealing wine bars, one downstairs with oak accents and another upstairs with a porch (open from noon on Saturday and from 1 P.M. on Sunday). Also in Lambertville, the **Swan Hotel,** 43 S. Main St. (tel. 215/397-3552), draws crowds regularly from as far away as Princeton to its back room for a sing-a-long or to the front bar, which is typical English pub even down to the wrought-iron-based tables. HOURS: 4 P.M. to 2 A.M. Other pleasant bars are found at the old inns stretching along Rte. 32 north, the **Golden Pheasant** and the **Black Bass.** Then of course there's the **Logan Inn** itself, whose tavern brings back so many memories from the '30s.

For disco dancing there's the **Yellow Brick Toad,** on Rte. 179 about a mile north of Lambertville (tel. 215/397-3100), which goes from 9 P.M. to 2 A.M. Thursday to Saturday. **Razberry's,** on Rte. 12 between Flemington and Frenchtown (tel. 215/782-2379), is another spot. **Lambertville Station,** 11 Bridge St. (tel. 215/397-8300), has a piano bar. For dancing there are plenty of spots around, some straight, some gay. Just ask.

NEW HOPE AREA ACTIVITIES

ANTIQUING: The whole area is dotted with stores specializing in all sorts of items. The road (Rte. 202) from New Hope to Lahaska is well stocked. For information, write the Bucks County Antique Dealers Association, 5 Byron Lane, Yardley, PA 19067.

BALLOONING: Harrison Aire, Wertsville Road (P.O. Box 73), Hopewell, NJ 08551 (tel. 609/466-3389), offers daily champagne balloon flights.

BICYCLING: Rentals available at the Source Bicycle Shop, Inc., 49 N. Union St., Lambertville (tel. 609/397-1188).

CANOEING: Point Pleasant Outfitters, P.O. Box 6, Point Pleasant, PA 18950 (tel. 215/297-8823 or 297-8181), offers canoeing, tubing, and rafting on the river (canoe will cost about $20 a day).

GOLF: Warrington Country Club, Rte. 611 and Almshouse Road, two miles south of Doylestown (tel. 215/343-1630).

HIKING: There's a quiet, grassy towpath along the canal and some other trails in local state parks—for example, at Washington's Crossing, Bull's Run across the footbridge at Lumberville.

PICNICKING: Try Bowman's Hill State Wildflower Preserve.

SHOPPING: Flemington, New Jersey, has become a large outlet center: Dansk (tel. 201/782-7077); Flemington Cut Glass (tel. 201/782-3017); Royal Doulton (tel. 201/788-5677). For landscaped shopping, some people enjoy Peddlers Village at Rtes. 202 and 263 in Lahaska (tel. 215/794-7055).

SOARING: Posey Aviation Center at Erwinna's Van Sant Airport.

STATE PARKS: Nockamixon State Park, R.D. 3, Box 125A, Quakertown, PA 18951 (tel. 215/538-2151), offers picnicking, swimming pool, fishing, hiking, boat and bike rentals, sledding, ice boating, ice fishing, and skating, in a 5,250-acre area. The 45-acre Ralph Stover Park, Box 209L, R.R. 1, Carversville, PA 19847 (tel. 215/297-5090), has picnicking, fishing, hiking, sledding, and cross-country skiing. Tyler State Park, R.D., Newton, PA 18940 (tel. 215/968-2021), which is south of Washington Crossing, has close to 2,000 acres for picnicking, fishing, boating (rentals available), hiking, bicycling (rentals available), ice skating and fishing, sledding, and cross-country skiing. Bull's Island, New Jersey, across the river at Lumberville, has camping, picnicking, and birding.

SWIMMING: See "State Parks," above, and the Hotel du Village, Barley Sheaf, and Whitehall Farms.

TENNIS: The Hotel du Village and Whitehall Farm have courts. For other locations, call the chambers of commerce.

WHITE-WATER RAFTING: Write to White Water Rafting, Tohickon Whitewater, P.O. Box 6, Point Pleasant, PA 18950.

PHILADELPHIA

DISTANCE IN MILES: 90
ESTIMATED DRIVING TIME: 1¾ to 2 hours

DRIVING: Take the New Jersey Turnpike to the Philadelphia exit. *Don't* take the Pennsylvania Turnpike (Rte. 276) exit, which is also marked to Philadelphia.
BUS: Trailways (tel. 212/730-7460) goes to Philadelphia. Greyhound (tel. 212/635-0800, or toll free 800/528-6055) also goes.
TRAIN: Amtrak Metroliner should get you there in one hour. Call 212/736-6288, or toll free 800/523-5700.

Special Events to Plan Your Trip Around

Throughout 1987 Philadelphia will be the focal point of the nation's celebration of the Bicentennial of the Constitution. Many events are scheduled, culminating on September 17—Constitution Day—when the largest parade ever mounted in the USA winds its way from all points of the compass to Independence Hall to celebrate.

For information write We, the People, Bourse Building, 21 S. 5th St., Suite 565, Independence Mall East, Philadelphia, PA 19106.

Remember that these events and those that follow are very popular and reservations should be made well in advance (sometimes as much as a year!).

JANUARY: Mummers Parade on New Year's Day when 30,000 costumed Mummers string bands, fancies, and comics strut up Broad Street to City Hall.

MARCH: Philadelphia Flower Show, the largest show in the nation, featuring five acres of flowers, landscapes, and exhibits (usually the second week in March).

MAY: Philadelphia Open House offers a two-week-long series of walking and bus tours to selected private homes and gardens in and around Philadelphia. For information, write to 313 Walnut St., Philadelphia, PA 19106. You'll need to reserve as far ahead as February (tours are usually held at the end of April or the beginning of May).

The Devon Horse Show, held outside Philadelphia.

JUNE: Elfreth's Alley Fete Days opens these homes to the public. Colonial crafts are exhibited and there's a bake sale at the Museum House at no. 126 (usually the first weekend in June).

JULY: Freedom Festival gives the city the excuse to let its hair down and celebrate with balloon races, food festivals, parades, and concerts.

AUGUST: Philadelphia Folk Festival features international performers in concerts and workshops at suburban Poole Farm, Schwenksville (usually the last weekend of August). For information, call 215/247-1300.

OCTOBER: Super Sunday is a giant block party that spreads along Ben Franklin Parkway with games, rides, entertainment, crafts, collectibles, food, and exhibits.

DECEMBER: Christmas tours of the historic houses in Fairmount Park, where the mansions are decorated with period furniture. Transportation is provided on Victorian trolleys. A similar event also takes place in Germantown (usually the second weekend in December).

For further information, contact the Philadelphia Convention and Visitors Bureau, 1515 Market St., Suite 2020, Philadelphia, PA 19102 (tel. 215/636-3300), or the Visitors Center, 1625 JFK Blvd. (tel. 215/636-1666).

People who still joke about Philadelphia the way W. C. Fields did obviously haven't been there recently, for the town has cast off its old sedate image and is now a vibrant, lively place to spend a weekend or a week. New restaurants abound, nightlife is thriving, a whole "Village" area has arisen, and besides the lovely venerable hotels, several new ones have opened in the last few years. In short, the whole town is jumping.

Much of the impetus came from the 1976 Bicentennial, when the town began sprucing up to celebrate the Revolution and the august personalities—Ben Franklin, Thomas Jefferson, Alexander Hamilton, John Adams, James Madison

—who gave birth to this nation. If you wander along the streets lined with 18th-century brick town houses, their root cellars jutting above the sidewalk, it's very easy to imagine what the town was like when Ben Franklin first arrived from Boston and walked through these same streets, a 17-year-old in disheveled rags munching on a roll. Back then Philadelphia was the second city in the British Empire and a veritable den of debauchery and decadence. On a visit in 1791, Chateaubriand was shocked by the number of gaming houses, theaters, and ballrooms, the extravagance of men's and women's fashions—silks, satins, and brocades—and the coquettish behavior and frivolous conversation that was indulged. Settled in 1682 as a simple Quaker town, Philadelphia grew into the wealthiest and largest city in the colonies, its population of 70,000 (in 1800) outnumbering New York's 60,000 and Boston's 25,000. Indeed it seemed poised to become the premier city of the nation until it was overtaken, by New York, which was blessed by a great natural harbor and well situated to benefit from the canal network established in the 1800s.

Today the original town planner's vision of the city of Philadelphia remains clear in the wide straight streets laid out in an orderly grid pattern, their symmetry further articulated by a series of beautiful squares. In Van Wyck's *World of Washington Irving,* he quotes Likcum, who contrasts New Yorkers and Philadelphians whose characteristics he feels reflect their town's physical layouts: Philadelphians give the impression that they are "honest, worthy, square, good-looking, well-meaning regular uniform, straightforward clock work, clear headed, one-like another upright kind of people who always go to work methodically, talk like a book, walk mathematically, never turn but in right angles . . . whereas the people of New York, just like their own queer, odd, topsy turvy, rantipole city are the most irregular, crazy-headed, quicksilver, eccentric, whimwhamsical set of mortals that ever were jumbled together in this uneven, villainous revolving globe and are the very antipodes to the Philadelphians." This contrast was no doubt subscribed to by W. C. Fields, when he made his famous remarks about Philadelphia —remarks that he'd think twice about today.

Any visitor spending a weekend here has the chance to stay at several gorgeous, venerable hotels; dine in some very fine restaurants; enjoy good theater, ballet, and music; discover amusing nighttime entertainment around town; and explore the many delightful attractions of the town itself. Obviously, the first-time visitor will want to stroll through Independence Park, which, for me, never ceases to be a moving experience, and then spend some time discovering the Mall, from the truly fine Museum of Art, to the Franklin Institute and the Rodin Museum. Philadelphia also possesses some lesser-known gems like the Rosenbach Museum, the Pennsylvania Academy of the Fine Arts, a newly developed riverfront park, as well as the magnificent Fairmount Park, through which meanders the Schuylkill River. There's no doubt in my mind that Philadelphia is a refreshing metropolis to enjoy a fun weekend.

PHILADELPHIA ATTRACTIONS

Independence Park Highlights
Park your car at the Metro Parking garage at 2nd and Sansom Streets. If you have only a few hours, then see Independence Hall and the Liberty Bell. If you have a half day, then you'll also want to see Carpenters' Hall and Franklin Court, and if you have a full day, you'll add Congress Hall, Old City Hall, the Graff House, and the Second Bank of the United States. Start at the **Visitor Center,** at 3rd and Chestnut Streets (tel. 215/597-8974), and see the brief film that relates the philosophic turmoil and events of the Revolution. HOURS: Most of the buildings are open 9 A.M. to 5 P.M. daily, but check at the center.

   Independence Hall, on Chestnut Street between 5th and 6th Streets. When the Second Continental Congress met, the war had already begun at Lexington and Concord in Massachusetts. Here in the Assembly Room the delegates chose George Washington as commander of the continental forces, and John Adams called upon the colonies to organize their own governments as states, a cry that still fell short of a formal declaration of independence.

   Such a document, which would raise the dispute to the higher plane of human rights, remained to be drafted, adopted, and proclaimed to the world. Penned by Thomas Jefferson, who worked in his rented second-floor parlor at the home of bricklayer Jacob Graff, the Declaration of Independence was adopted here on July 4, 1776, and read to the cheers of an assembled crowd in the square below on July 8. The courage of those few who signed it a month later was momentous. By signing, they were committing treason and were therefore doomed to execution. Only success could save them. The Articles of Confederation was also adopted here. Here, too, the Constitutional Convention met on May 25, 1787, to draft the Constitution that ensured the future of the United States and has continued to serve the nation's political and social needs for over 200 years. You can view the Windsor chairs and the green-baize-covered tables where the framers of the Constitution deliberated for nearly three months. Among those assembled were James Wilson of Pennsylvania, Alexander Hamilton and Gouverneur Morris from New York, Roger Sherman and Oliver Ellsworth from Connecticut, James Madison from Virginia, and Ben Franklin, who was 82 and often had to be carried to the sessions because of his gout and age—all presided over sagely by George Washington. Upon ratification, Congress voted to establish the national capital at Philadelphia until 1800, when a permanent capital would be ready on the banks of the Potomac. For ten years this building also served as the seat of all three branches of government.

   The **Liberty Bell Pavilion,** on Market Street between 5th and 6th Streets. From Independence Hall, you can look down the Mall to the pavilion that houses this cherished emblem and symbol of liberty around the world. The bell was, in fact, cast to celebrate the 50th anniversary of the original charter of democracy granted to his colony by Penn in 1701. Cast at Whitechapel's Bell Foundry, the bell arrived in 1752 and cracked while it was being tested. Although it was successfully repaired, it cracked again, according to legend, during the funeral of Chief Justice

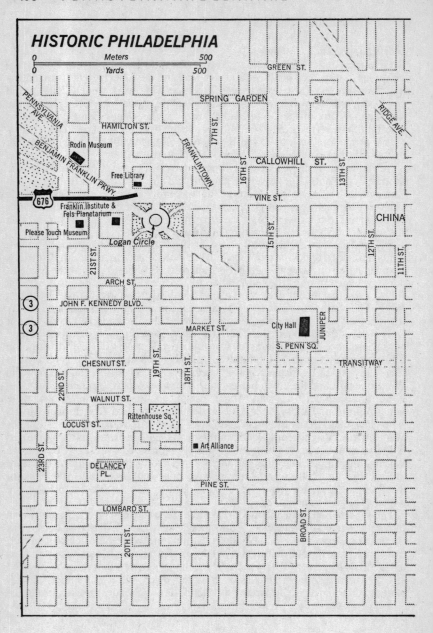

HISTORIC PHILADELPHIA

Meters   500
Yards   500

GREEN ST.

SPRING GARDEN   ST.

PENNSYLVANIA AVE.

HAMILTON ST.

RIDGE AVE.

Rodin Museum

BENJAMIN FRANKLIN PKWY.

Free Library

FRANKLINTOWN

17TH ST.

CALLOWHILL   ST.

16TH ST.

13TH ST.

676

Franklin Institute & Fels Planetarium

VINE ST.

CHINA

Please Touch Museum

Logan Circle

15TH ST.

12TH ST.

11TH ST.

21ST ST.

ARCH ST.

3   JOHN F. KENNEDY BLVD.

3

MARKET ST.

City Hall

JUNIPER

S. PENN SQ.

19TH ST.

18TH ST.

CHESNUT ST.

TRANSITWAY

22ND ST.

WALNUT ST.

Rittenhouse Sq.

LOCUST ST.

Art Alliance

23RD ST.

DELANCEY PL.

PINE ST.

LOMBARD ST.

20TH ST.

BROAD ST.

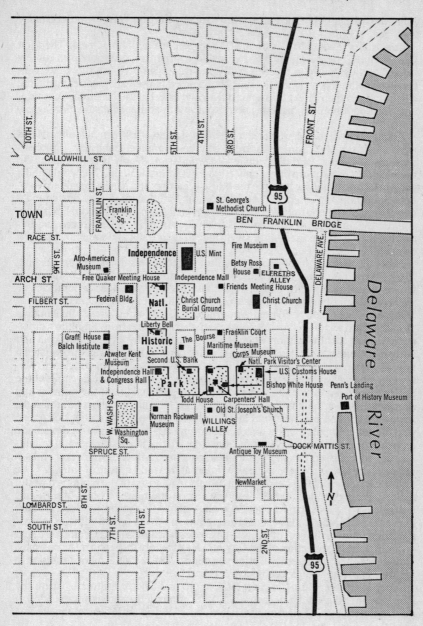

John Marshall in 1835. The bell was last formally rung on Washington's birthday in 1846.

Carpenters' Hall, 320 Chestnut St., between 3rd and 4th Streets. The First Continental Congress met here, after having spurned an invitation from conservative John Galloway to meet in the Pennsylvania State House (now Independence Hall). In this hall Patrick Henry proclaimed himself an American, and the colonists aired their grievances against the king, asserted their rights in a petition, and adopted a non-importation, non-exportation, and nonconsumption agreement.

Franklin Court, on Market Street between 3rd and 4th Streets. Don't miss this memorial to one of America's great geniuses—printer, publisher, diplomat, statesman, scientist, and philosopher—a wonderful, deeply inspiring man. On the site of his home, torn down only 20 years after his death in 1790, you'll find a ghost structure outlining in metal the house's features and a truly imaginative underground museum, an operating 18th-century print shop, a post office, and a postal museum. In the underground museum at the so-called Franklin Exchange, you can dial all kinds of international celebrities from D. H. Lawrence and Immanuel Kant to Balzac and Mark Twain to hear their frank and sometimes cryptic comments about old Ben.

For Kant he was, quite simply, "the Prometheus of his times," but try dialing Mark Twain! Elsewhere in the museum you can summon up any one of the many familiar (and less familiar) ribald, wise aphorisms for which Ben was famous, like "Where there is marriage without love, there will be love without marriage," or "Keep your eyes wide open before marriage, half shut afterwards." Imaginative dioramas with audio accompaniment depict crucial scenes from Franklin's diplomatic career, first in London where he was frustrated by an obdurate king and Parliament, and later in Paris, where he secured French help and also negotiated a brilliant peace. Other displays chart his incredible contributions to science, philosophy, journalism, advertising, industry, and government. The portraits at the beginning will also tell you much about the sad personal life of this popular and charming man—a daughter who married against his will (but whom he admired), a son who became a Loyalist and to whom he never spoke thereafter, and a wife who died shortly before his return home, after a ten-year absence on diplomatic missions. The whole place is a fitting testimonial to this witty, urbane, and delightful man who arrived penniless in Philadelphia and, with determination and supreme talents, rose to the very peak of international and historical fame.

The **City Tavern,** at 2nd and Walnut Streets. At the end of the morning it would make sense to continue this 18th-century reverie and retire to what John Adams described as the most genteel tavern in all America, the reconstructed City Tavern (1773). On May 20, 1774, Paul Revere rode up to the tavern with the news of the British closing the port of Boston, an event that so enraged the colonists that it prompted the organization of the Committees of Safety throughout the colonies. Today costumed waitresses will bring you good colonial-style American cuisine to fortify you before you proceed on your tour.

After lunch, head for **Congress Hall,** at 6th and Chestnut Streets, where the Congress met during the decade 1790–1800. Among the significant events that occurred here were the second inauguration of President Washington; the first inauguration of President John Adams; the establishment of the First Bank of the United States, the Federal Mint, and the Department of the Navy; and the ratification of Jay's Treaty with England. **Old City Hall,** which was used by the Supreme Court from 1791 to 1800, now houses exhibitions about the Supreme Court's early history and, on the second floor, displays about 18th-century Philadelphia occupations, crafts, and daily life. The **Graff House** at 7th and Market Streets, has already been mentioned as the place where Thomas Jefferson labored on the Declaration of Independence. At the **Second Bank of the United States,** 420 Chestnut St. between 4th and 5th Streets, you can view the portraits, many by Charles Willson Peale, of these redoubtable 18th-century men who created a nation.

Other Independence Park Sights

These are only the highlights of a park that actually contains 26 sites. Two lie outside the park—Germantown's Deshler Morris House, and the Ben Franklin National Memorial, which is at the Franklin Institute. The remainder can be visited right here.

For military buffs, there's the **Army and Navy Museum,** on Chestnut Street at Carpenters' Court, which documents the early history of these two institutions. For antique buffs and historians, the **Bishop White House,** 309 Walnut St., home of the first Episcopal bishop of Pennsylvania, is furnished to reflect the lifestyle of upper-class Philadelphians (open by tour only; free tickets are available at the Visitor Center, but the tickets are *very* limited—get there early to obtain them). The **Todd House,** 4th and Walnut Streets, was occupied by John Todd, Jr., and his wife, Dolley Payne, and is furnished to reflect the lifestyle of a typical middle-class home (also open by tour only). Dolley later married James Madison, after her first husband died. Numerous religious institutions are scattered through the park —**Christ Church** (1727), 2nd Street north of Market, whose cemetery, at 5th and Arch Streets, shelters seven signers of the Declaration of Independence, including Ben Franklin, and four signers of the Constitution. The **Free Quaker Meeting House** (1783), at 5th and Arch Streets, was used by the Free Quakers, who separated from the main body of Quakers by breaking their pacifist principles and fighting for the Revolution. The **Old Swedes' Church** (1700), Delaware Avenue and Christian Street, the oldest church in Pennsylvania, was established by Philadelphia's first settlers. The **Mikveh Israel Cemetery,** Spruce Street between 8th and 9th Streets, established by Nathan Levy in 1738 and deeded to the synagogue of that name, was the only congregation that functioned during the Revolution. Haym Salomon, a financier to whom Washington often turned for money to pay the troops, is buried here in an unmarked grave. **St. George's Church,** 235 N. 4th St., and **St. Joseph's Church,** on Willing's Alley near 4th and Walnut Streets, are, respectively, the oldest Methodist church in the nation and the first Catholic congregation in Philadelphia.

Other buildings of interest include the house where Revolutionary engineer **Thaddeus Kosciuszko** lived at 301 Pine St.; **Philosophical Hall,** 104 S. 5th St., home of the oldest learned society in the United States, founded by Ben Franklin in 1743; the temple-like **Philadelphia Exchange** (1834), at 3rd and Walnut Streets;

Liberty Hall, 105 S. 5th St., the oldest subscription library in the United States, built in 1789–1790 (rebuilt in 1959); the **Marine Corps Memorial Museum,** Carpenters' Court, dedicated to the Revolutionary exploits of the corps, which was founded in Philadelphia in 1775; and the **First Bank of the United States,** 120 S. 3rd St., between Chestnut and Walnut Streets, established in 1791 at the urging of Alexander Hamilton to restore some order to the nation's chaotic finances.

Other Historic Sights Outside the Park

There remain two sights that vividly capture the daily life of historic Philadelphia. The first, **Elfreth's Alley,** on 2nd Street between Arch and Race (tel. 215/574-0560), is a narrow, cobblestoned street lined with 33 houses dating from the early 1700s. Most are privately owned residences, but no. 126 is a museum. HOURS: daily from noon to 4 P.M.

The other is **Betsy Ross's House,** 239 Arch St., between 2nd and 3rd (tel. 215/627-5343), the home of the redoubtable Betsy Ross, who supposedly made the first American flag. At the home, her daily routine is reproduced. HOURS: 9 A.M. to 5 P.M. daily.

Also, while you're exploring the park, you may want to drop in at the **Atwater Kent Museum,** 15 S. 7th St., between Market and Chestnut (tel. 215/686-3630), which portrays the history of Philadelphia from 1680 to the 20th century, the life of William Penn, the development of the city's municipal services, and its growth as a mercantile center.

At the **Philadelphia Maritime Museum,** 321 Chestnut St., maritime history is related through ship models, paintings, scrimshaw, and other artifacts. HOURS: Monday to Friday from 10 A.M. to 5 P.M., on Saturday from 1 to 5 P.M. ADMISSION: By donation.

The **Pennsylvania Hospital,** 8th and Spruce Streets, was the nation's first hospital, founded in 1751. Although additions have been made to the hospital, the old Central Pine Building is outstanding architecturally. Inside, a grand circular staircase leads to the first medical library and the first surgical amphitheater, constructed in 1804 and capped with a full dome, which afforded enough light to perform operations. Imagine the scene, portrayed in Thomas Eakins's *Gross Clinic,* being played out here. There is sawdust on the floor, the public audience has assembled, and the doctor (with no rubber gloves) prepares to make the first incision, while four strong men restrain the unanesthetized patient. Outside there's a physic garden that contains all manner of medical herbs and shrubs.

Having spent the morning at Independence Park, you can spend the afternoon at Penn's Landing and Society Hill.

Penn's Landing

Penn's Landing (tel. 215/923-9030) stretches from Market Street along the waterfront to South Street and is home to several attractions, a sculpture garden, some restaurants (particularly the brand-new Chart House) and many seasonal events.

Among the ships anchored here is the three-masted Portuguese wooden clipper, the *Gazela* (1883), which fished off Newfoundland, where fishermen in

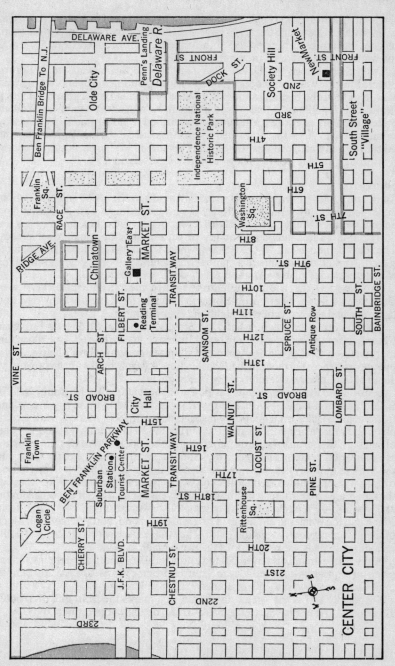

single-man dories took six months to fill her hold with salted codfish. The *Moshulu,* in dock at Chestnut Street, is a large steel sailing ship that transported grain, nitrate, and lumber from and to South America, Europe, and Australia. It was the winner of the last grain race, run from Australia in 1939.

Two other vessels, the U.S.S. *Olympia* and U.S.S. *Becuna,* are at Spruce Street. The first was Commodore Dewey's flagship during the Spanish-American War, and fired the opening shot at the Battle of Manila Bay. The second was a World War II submarine that served in Japan, Korea, and Vietnam. At Walnut Street, the **Port of History Museum** houses varied exhibits. HOURS: Wednesday through Sunday from 10 A.M. to 4:30 P.M. ADMISSION: $1. At the **Workshop on the Water** you can watch artisans boatbuilding aboard a 1935 barge. HOURS: Wednesday through Sunday from 9:30 A.M. to 4:30 P.M. ADMISSION: $1.

Society Hill

The name comes from a group of businessmen—Free Society of Traders—whom Penn persuaded to settle here. Today it's a restored area east of Washington Square between Walnut and Lombard Streets where the cobblestone streets are lit by old-fashioned lampposts, and lined with red-brick colonial town houses. The focal point is Head House Square, where the market building has been restored. Around the square are a number of restaurants, boutiques, and shopping complexes, including **New Market,** which you'll want to shop in.

Two blocks farther south, **South Street** has become a Philadelphian version of Greenwich Village, where people browse through the funky stores by day, and later dine and enjoy a variety of nighttime entertainment.

On Pine Street between 3rd and 4th Streets, stop in at **St. Peter's Episcopal Church** to see the cemetery where seven Indian chiefs are buried. One block farther north, at 429 Spruce St., you can walk past **James Madison's house,** now a private residence. Farther north in Washington Square, you'll want to stop by the **Tomb of the Unknown Revolutionary War Soldier.**

Back on 2nd at Spruce, you'll find the **Perelman Antique Toy Museum,** 268-270 S. 2nd St. (tel. 215/922-1070). The first floor is devoted to tin toys—everything from a Santa Claus on a goat-drawn sleigh made in 1880, to clockwork steamboats and other clockwork friction toys, including Neddy (donkey) playing a pair of cymbals. Cast-iron toys are displayed on the second floor. Among my favorites are the varied "Happy Hooligan" toys and wagons made in the early 1900s and the Popeye motorcycles, which were popular in the '30s. The top floor is given over to a wonderfully eclectic collection of mechanical banks and dolls. Many of the banks are so charmingly whimsical and reveal so much about our social myths and symbols—Freedman Banks, automaton banks featuring everything from Jonah and the whale, to an Indian, a frog and a lily pond, and William Tell. Many of them were made as late as the 1940s. They share space with a selection of dolls, including some bisque kewpie dolls that were made in 1913.

Sadly, these are all displayed behind or under glass. There are demonstrations given on request. HOURS: Monday to Saturday from 9:30 A.M. to 5 P.M., on Sunday until 4 P.M. ADMISSION: $1.50 for adults, 75¢ for children.

Diagonally across the street, an old inn sign marks the **Man Full of Trouble Tavern,** at 127-129 Pine St. (tel. 215/743-4225), open by appointment only.

Attractions Along the Parkway

The **Franklin Institute,** 20th Street and the Parkway (tel. 215/448-1000). The kids will certainly enjoy many of the participatory exhibits in this science museum—a walk-through heart, a Boeing 707, and computer games. HOURS: Monday to Saturday from 10 A.M. to 5 P.M., on Sunday from noon to 5 P.M. ADMISSION: $4 for adults, $3 for children 4 to 11.

The planetarium runs shows at 2 P.M., with a special children's show on Saturday at 10:30 A.M. ADMISSION: $1.50.

The **Academy of Natural Sciences,** 19th Street and the Parkway (tel. 215/299-1047), attracts crowds to its Discovering Dinosaurs exhibition, featuring 15 dinosaurs and giant reptiles, computer games, movable dinosaur jaws, fossil rubbing, "Dinos in the Movies," climb-in footprint, and multimedia show. There's also a hands-on children's museum with a stocked pond, waterfall, giant tree to crawl through, sandy beach with shells to dig, beehive, and live animals, mummies, minerals and gems, and other programs and exhibits also. HOURS: 10 A.M. to 4 P.M. on weekdays, until 5 P.M. on weekdays. ADMISSION: $4 for adults, $3 for children 3 to 12.

The **Rodin Museum,** 22nd Street and the Parkway (tel. 215/763-8100). In the gardens *The Thinker* ponders, and beyond the reflecting pool, at the head of the entry steps, stands the imposing *Gates of Hell.* At least 15 feet high, they're encrusted with fluid swirling souls caught at the edge of the abyss of damnation in tortured panic and despair. This is the largest collection of Rodin sculpture outside France. Inside, *The Burghers of Calais* is surrounded by many other famous pieces: *Oceanides,* curving like the crest on a wave; the *Head of Sorrow* (Joan of Arc); and *The Helmet Maker's Wife,* a moving study of the physical decay of aging represented by a woman whose head is bowed down to her sagging, elongated breasts. A whole alcove is devoted to the many studies and models of Balzac that Rodin made, along with a dramatic series of moonlit photographs of the statue taken by Edward Steichen. HOURS: Tuesday to Sunday from 10 A.M. to 5 P.M.

The **Philadelphia Museum of Art,** 26th Street and the Parkway (tel. 215/763-8100). In my experience, you'll always find a special exhibition at this beautiful museum, sometimes, but not always, linked to local history, like the great Thomas Eakins show or the recent definitive display of Pennsylvania German decorative arts of 1685–1850. Among the permanent exhibits, the Arensburg Collection of 20th-century painting and sculpture, the Gallatin Collection demonstrating the evolution of abstract art, and the Johnson collection of European painting from 1200 to 1900 are all famous. On Saturday gallery talks are given at 1 P.M., and there are tours from 10 A.M. to 3 P.M. every hour. Highlight tours are given at 11 A.M. and 1, 2, and 3 P.M. HOURS: Wednesday to Sunday from 10 A.M. to 5 P.M. ADMISSION: $4 for adults, $2 for students and children under 18; free on Sunday until 1 P.M.

Three Lesser-Known Attractions

For the second-time visitor, or anyone familiar with all the attractions of the historic area and the Parkway, then I suggest seeking out some of the smaller, lesser-known gems that Philadelphia possesses, like the Rosenbach Museum, the

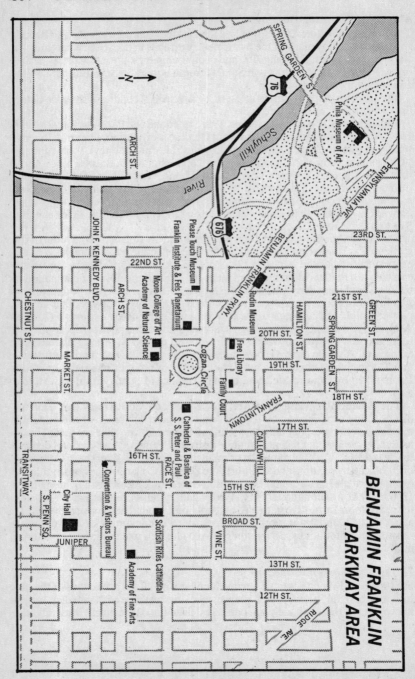

BENJAMIN FRANKLIN PARKWAY AREA

Pennsylvania Academy of the Fine Arts, several ethnically oriented museums, and the mansions in Fairmount Park, even Walt Whitman's home across the river in Camden. Philadelphia doesn't begin and end at the Liberty Bell and Independence Hall, although these monuments will always be able to quicken our hearts and imaginations because of the part they played in our nation's history.

The **Rosenbach Museum and Library,** 2010 DeLancey Pl. (tel. 215/732-1600), is one of Philadelphia's lesser-known treasures, although well known to scholars of James Joyce, Henry James, Marianne Moore, and other literary figures.

This lovely 18th-century town house contains the collection of two bachelor brothers, one of whom collected antique furnishings and the other whose rare book collection now resides on the third floor. Among its treasures are one of the few Gutenberg Bibles, the Bay Psalm Book (1649), the first edition of Ben Franklin's *Poor Richard's Almanack,* the original manuscript of James Joyce's *Ulysses,* and many, many more. One room is usually used for a themed display—for example, when I was there, an exhibit titled "Passing Through Philadelphia" displayed comments and letters about the city from such varied personalities as Oscar Wilde, Henry James, and John F. Kennedy. Across the hall from the library you can peer into Marianne Moore's Greenwich Village apartment, which has been reassembled here with the original furnishings just as she left it.

On the 1½-hour tour the guide will explain the history of particular antiques, such as the casket made for Charles II, which Philip Rosenbach acquired from the family of George IV's mistress in 1928; a fan depicting the first and second ascension of a hot-air balloon in 1784; chests that belonged to Napoleon's brother, Joseph, who lived in Bordentown, New Jersey. At the back of the house there's a lovely garden/courtyard with several ancient Egyptian urns—a serene resting place. At the small gift shop favorite items include the illustrated books by Maurice Sendak. HOURS: Tuesday to Sunday from 11 A.M. to 4 P.M. ADMISSION: $2.50 for adults, $1.50 for children.

The **Pennsylvania Academy of the Fine Arts,** at Broad and Cherry Sts. (tel. 215/972-7600). Even if the current exhibit doesn't interest you, stop by just to view the magnificent Victorian Greek Revival building designed by Frank Furness to house the oldest American museum and art school. Mary Cassatt studied here, and Alexander Calder was a graduate. The museum collection includes over 7,000 works by such consummate American artists as Benjamin West, William Rush, Thomas Eakins, Edward Hopper, Andrew Wyeth, Robert Motherwell, Louise Nevelson, and Georgia O'Keeffe. Thomas Eakins also taught here, and supposedly Walt Whitman used to come and muse under the grand staircase, where he was enraptured by the music issuing from the concert hall above. Do look in at the carved-oak entrance and staircase that is thrown into relief by geometric patterned walls, an ornamental bronze banister and a deep-blue, almost-purple ceiling, adorned with clusters of gold stars. HOURS: Tuesday to Saturday from 10 A.M. to 5 P.M., on Sunday from 11 A.M. to 5 P.M. ADMISSION: $3; free on Saturday from 10 A.M. to 1 P.M.

The **University Museum,** 33rd and Spruce Streets (tel. 215/222-7777 or 898-3024). This is a must for anthropology and archeology buffs. Faculty from the university accompanied one of the British expeditions, sharing finds at the Mesopotamian site of Ur. Other galleries are devoted to Mayan, Greek, Roman,

African, Chinese, American Indian, and Polynesian cultures. Cuneiform tablets from Sumer, ivories from Benin, kachina dolls, Egyptian mummies, and a gold and lapis bull-headed lyre and ram from the royal cemetery at Ur are just a few of the treasures. The museum also offers classical music concerts—guitar and Renaissance bands, for example—and seminars, and talks on weekends. HOURS: Monday to Saturday from 10 A.M. to 4:30 P.M., on Sunday from 1 to 5 P.M. Guided tours are given at 1 P.M. Take Walnut Street west to 34th Street and turn left. ADMISSION: $2 donation.

Philadelphia's Ethnic Museums

First, the **Balch Institute for Ethnic Studies,** 18 S. 7th St. (tel. 215/925-8090), reveals the story of the many immigrants who entered the United States at Philadelphia. Most moving of all the displays to me are a pair of scuffed and battered shoes worn by 10-year-old Marika Krause when she fled Hungary at the start of the revolution in 1956, carrying only a schoolbag packed with her most precious possessions. In the latest exhibition, "Freedom's Doors: Immigrant Ports of Entry to the United States," they are joined by a raft made of inner tubes (which still show "Made in the USSR" on them) on which one immigrant arrived from Cuba. This show tells the story of seven cities—Boston, Philadelphia, Baltimore, Miami, New Orleans, Los Angeles, and San Francisco—through which one-third of the new arrivals (16½ million) entered the country during the last 150 years. The exhibition includes documents, clothing, steamer trunks, and other artifacts reflecting the immigration experiences of individuals and families, as well as photographs portraying the immigration facilities and the histories of the major ports. Racial discrimination and negative attitudes are not ignored; for example, there's a photograph of Chinese immigrants repacking their trunks and baskets after being disinfected, and of Haitian immigrants staring out from behind the padlocked mesh fencing of a detention center. For each port, the exhibit shows the origins of the immigrants, why they landed there, what facilities they came to, their first impressions, and the impact they had on the city.

The history of immigration into Philadelphia is illustrated by a chronological display of photographs, interspersed with diary entries and contemporary documents. In 1882 one man notes that he landed and went to a boarding house charging 75¢ a day. Photographs witness the relief, hope, excitement, trepidation, joy, tears, and love felt on arrival in America, the conditions in steerage and at the Vine Street Pier, where ships arrived from Genoa and Naples regularly between 1912 and the mid-'20s. Some 60,000 debarked in 1913 alone. Between 1815 and 1985 over 1.3 million immigrants entered America through Philadelphia, many of them traveling onward. HOURS: Monday to Saturday from 10 A.M. to 4 P.M.

The **Afro-American Historical and Cultural Museum,** 7th and Arch Streets (tel. 215/574-0380). This unique collection focuses on the figures and events of Afro-American history. The great names are here—W. E. B. DuBois, Booker T. Washington, Marcus Garvey, Frederick Douglass, Martin Luther King, figures from the Harlem Renaissance, along with many lesser-known figures like a lumber and coal merchant and real estate entrepreneur Stephen Smith, martyr Octavius Valentine Catto, composer and band leader Frank Johnson, and many,

many more. HOURS: Tuesday to Saturday from 10 A.M. to 5 P.M., on Sunday from noon to 6 P.M. ADMISSION: $1.50 for adults, 75¢ for children.

The **American Swedish Museum,** 1900 Pattison Ave. (tel. 215/389-1776), traces the artistic and historical contribution of the Swedes in the Delaware Valley from 1683 to 1831. Here, you'll find unique exhibits on Jenny Lind, John Ericsson, and Swedish arts and crafts. HOURS: Tuesday to Friday from 10 A.M. to 4 P.M., on Saturday from noon to 4 P.M. ADMISSION: $1.50 for adults, $1 for children. Take Broad Street south to Pattison and turn right.

The **Museum of American Jewish History,** 55 N. 5th St. (tel. 215/923-3811), is devoted to the Jewish role, achievements, and history in the United States. HOURS: Monday to Thursday from 10 A.M. to 5 P.M., on Sunday from noon to 5 P.M. ADMISSION: $1.50 for adults, $1.25 for children.

The **Mummers Museum,** 2nd Street and Washington Avenue. If you don't feel like shivering on a sidewalk on January 1 to see the Mummers, then catch the videotape of the parade as they strut down Broad Street in a musical masquerade that is drawn from various traditions. Costumes and other audio-visual exhibits also. HOURS: Monday to Friday from 9:30 A.M. to 5 P.M., on Saturday from noon to 5 P.M. ADMISSION: $1.50 for adults, 75¢ for children.

Fairmount Park

Right in Philadelphia overlooking the Schuylkill River, this park provides 8,000 acres of parkland with all kinds of recreational facilities, a zoo, and several mansions that can be visited.

Best way to see the park is via the **Victorian trolleys,** which run year round, allow on-off privileges (only April to November), and stop at many of the sights along a 17-mile route. They start from the Convention and Visitors Bureau at 16th and John F. Kennedy, but you can board anywhere and purchase a ticket. FARE: $2.50 for adults, 50¢ for children. Takes 1½ hours nonstop.

Here's a quick rundown of what to see in the park:

Mount Pleasant is a superb Georgian house (1761), which Benedict Arnold purchased for his wife but never occupied, because he was convicted of treason.

Continue along East River Drive to **Laurel Hill** (1760), a house that originally belonged to a Loyalist. It was confiscated and much later became the home of Dr. Philip Syng Physick, father of American surgery.

Woodford was first owned by Judge William Coleman, a confidant of Ben Franklin, and was later occupied by several generations of Whartons.

Strawberry Mansion owes its name to the mid-19th-century time when it was a dairy farm serving strawberries and cream. Before that it was home to several prominent figures, including Judge Joseph Hemphill, who entertained John C. Calhoun, the Marquis de Lafayette, and Daniel Webster here. There's an interesting collection of Tucker porcelain—one of America's first true porcelains —and a display of antique toys in the attic.

From Strawberry Mansion, take the bridge to Greenland Drive (marvelous in lilac season) and then to Chamounix Drive, looping back to Belmont Avenue to North Concourse Drive (turning left) and you'll arrive at Sweetbriar.

Sweetbriar was built in 1797 by Sam and Jean Breck to escape the yellow fever

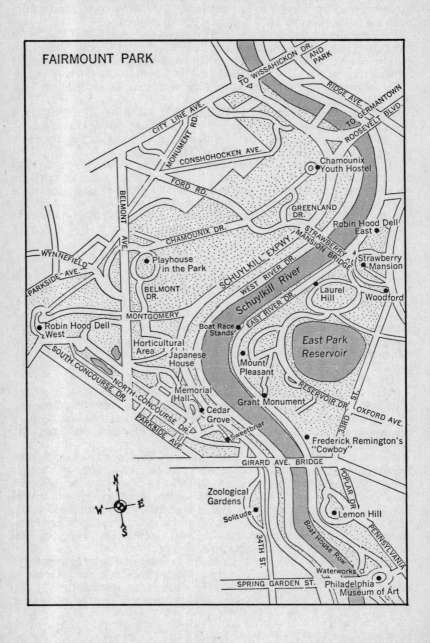

FAIRMOUNT PARK

TO WISSAHICKON DR. AND PARK

RIDGE AVE.

CITY LINE AVE.

MONUMENT RD.

TO GERMANTOWN

ROOSEVELT BLVD.

CONSHOHOCKEN AVE.

FORD RD.

Chamounix Youth Hostel

BELMONT AVE.

GREENLAND DR.

Robin Hood Dell East

CHAMOUNIX DR.

STRAWBERRY MANSION BRIDGE

Strawberry Mansion

WYNNEFIELD

Playhouse in the Park

WEST RIVER DR.

Schuylkill River

PARKSIDE AVE.

BELMONT DR.

Laurel Hill

Woodford

MONTGOMERY

EAST RIVER DR.

SCHUYLKILL EXPWY.

Robin Hood Dell West

Boat Race Stands

East Park Reservoir

SOUTH CONCOURSE DR.

Horticultural Area

Japanese House

Mount Pleasant

RESERVOIR DR.

NORTH CONCOURSE DR.

Memorial Hall

Grant Monument

33RD ST.

OXFORD AVE.

PARKSIDE AVE.

Cedar Grove

Sweetbriar

Frederick Remington's "Cowboy"

GIRARD AVE. BRIDGE

POPLAR DR.

Zoological Gardens

Lemon Hill

Solitude

PENNSYLVANIA

34TH ST.

Boat House Row

Waterworks

SPRING GARDEN ST.

Philadelphia Museum of Art

epidemic that killed 10,000 Philadelphians. It's a wonderful example of the Adam style.

John Penn, grandson of William, built and designed **Solitude** (1785). Penn later returned to England to become an MP. Last owner was his nephew.

Lemon Hill was built in 1770 by Robert Morris, who was forced to relinquish the property in 1798 when he was thrown into debtor's jail. It was sold to Henry Pratt, who built the present house in 1800 and turned it into a garden center, where lemon trees flourished in the greenhouse.

For information on all of the houses, call 215/686-2176.

The **Philadelphia Zoo,** 34th Street and Girard Avenue (tel. 215/243-1100) in Fairmount Park, established in 1874, was the first zoo in America. It contains a safari monorail, children's zoo, and several houses where animals can be viewed in their natural surroundings. HOURS: 9:30 A.M. to 5 P.M. ADMISSION: $4 for adults, $3 for children.

Entertainment in the Park: Mann Music Center, 42nd Street and Parkside Avenue (tel. 215/686-2176), is one of the summer homes of the Philadelphia Orchestra. Robin Hood Dell East, near 33rd and South Dauphin (tel. 215/226-0727), is used for concerts and other events.

Attractions Especially for Kids

Besides the Franklin Institute, the Academy of Sciences, the Zoo, and Penn's Landing, which the kids will enjoy, there's also the **Please Touch Museum** at 210 N. 21st St. (tel. 215/963-0666), which is designed for children 7 and younger and is truly a delight for parents and children.

Here children can play and experiment with all kinds of activities and role-playing games. There's a store with a cash register for the budding retailer; all kinds of construction and building materials; musical instruments to play and pound; bark houses to inhabit; rabbits, birds, and hamsters to befriend; plus a pint-size telephone booth. There's also a whole resource center for those 5 and over that has several different study areas.

This is one museum where you'll hear parents pleading to know whether their offspring are ready to leave yet. Perhaps it's fortunate, after all, that visits on weekends have to be limited to one hour. HOURS: Tuesday to Saturday from 10 A.M. to 4:30 P.M., on Sunday from 12:30 to 4:30 P.M. ADMISSION: $3 per person (children are defined as persons).

Children's theater can be seen at the **Annenberg Center,** 3680 Walnut St. (tel. 215/898-6791), on Saturday at 11 A.M. and 2 P.M., when stories are dramatized especially for children.

Germantown Attractions

In spring, summer, or fall, the **Morris Arboretum,** on Hillcrest Avenue, between Germantown and Stenton Avenues in Chestnut Hill (tel. 215/242-3399), is a heavenly place to visit. The brilliant color of Azalea Meadow, the rambling beauty of the English Park, and the Swan Pond are just a few of the highlights of this park that features 3,500 different shrubs and trees. HOURS: daily 10 A.M. to 5 P.M. ADMISSION: $2 for adults, $1 for children.

Of all the mansions here, **Cliveden** (1763–1767), 6401 Germantown Ave., is perhaps the loveliest, a Federal country house commissioned by Chief Justice Benjamin Chew that contains Federal and Chippendale furnishings. ADMISSION (by appointment): $2 for adults, $1 for students.

The **Deshler-Morris House,** 5442 Germantown Ave., was Sir William Howe's headquarters during the Battle of Germantown and later Washington's residence during the yellow fever epidemic of 1793. HOURS: Tuesday to Sunday from 1 to 4 P.M. Closed December 15 to April 1. ADMISSION: 50¢.

The **Clarkson-Watson House,** 5275 Germantown Ave., has been restored to its 1790s appearance and houses a costume museum. HOURS: Sunday from 1 to 5 P.M. For admittance, go to 5214 Germantown Ave. ADMISSION: $1.50.

Across the Delaware

In nearby New Jersey, Camden's **Walt Whitman House,** 330 Mickle St. (tel. 609/964-5383), a Federal-style clapboard house, built around 1848, is a shrine for Whitman fans. He lived here from 1884 until his death at age 84 in 1892.

The Barnes Foundation

Only a few miles outside Philadelphia in Merion, the Barnes Foundation, 300 N. Latch's Lane (tel. 215/667-0290), will thrill art lovers. Albert Barnes amassed a fortune (from the medicine Argyrol) that he used to buy armfuls of Renoirs, Cézannes, Soutines, and representative works of a great many European artists, from Bosch to Corot, Modigliani, and Picasso. In his lifetime Barnes chose not to display his collection to the public and today the museum only admits 200 people on Friday and Saturday and 100 on Sunday.

The foundation functions primarily as a school in which courses and seminars are given in the philosophy and appreciation of art. This is vital to the understanding and enjoyment of the collection. Some visitors have complained that the arrangements of the paintings do not follow the conventions of museum hanging, juxtaposing old and modern works, but they are specifically so designed to achieve a particular educational purpose. The designs of each "wall picture" express different human qualities, and in many cases clearly trace influences and adaptations from one school to another. These considerations only make the viewing more fascinating—a veritable treasure for those who wish to truly understand and appreciate art. Although visitors may fail to properly view pictures hanging over doors and so on, the educational intent of the foundation is paramount and the particular placement is of importance to the foundation's teaching. If you want to be certain of gaining entry, write for a reservation to the foundation at 300 Latch's Lane, Merion, PA 19066. HOURS: Friday and Saturday from 9:30 A.M. to 4:30 P.M., on Sunday from 1 to 4:30 P.M. ADMISSION: $1. No children under 12.

PHILADELPHIA LODGING

A Special Note: The grande dame of Philadelphia's hotels, the **Bellevue Stratford** has, according to latest reports, been partially saved. In early 1987 Cunard announced that it would lease and manage a small luxury hotel on the old Bellevue's top seven floors. It will have 170 luxury rooms and suites, designed by Sarah

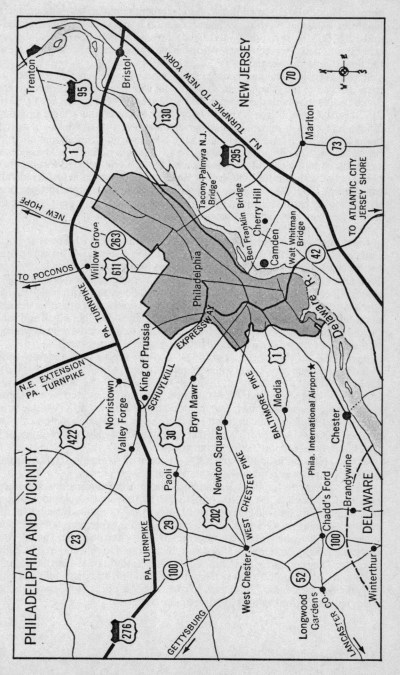

PHILADELPHIA AND VICINITY

Tomerlin Lee, who designed the Willard Intercontinental in Washington and the Helmsley Palace in New York. The renovation is expected to be completed by mid-1988. Offices, restaurants, and retail stores will occupy the lower floors. Another brand-new Sheraton hotel will also have opened in the Society Hill area by the time this book appears.

If you like old-fashioned luxurious surroundings and personal service, then there are two or three well-located choices, all within a few blocks of each other. Some people may fault the **Barclay,** 237 S. 18th St., Philadelphia, PA 19103 (tel. 215/545-0300, or toll free 800/421-6662), for not possessing a large impressive lobby, but for me its thin, elongated barrel-vaulted version has the air of a private home to which you have been invited for a house party. Oriental rugs and furniture, vases with handmade silk flowers, small chandeliers, and crystal sconces add rich touches to the small front-desk area. Off the wood-paneled foyer there's a pleasant bar with comfortable leather Regency chairs and tables with individual brass lamps. The 250 rooms are all furnished with antique reproductions, many with canopy beds and four-posters. Armoires conceal the TVs. For elegant dining there's Le Beau Lieu, which also serves brunch.

RATES: $120 to $150 double.

Light floods the marble-floored lobby of the **Warwick,** 17th Street at Locust, Philadelphia, PA 19103 (tel. 215/735-6000, or toll free 800/523-4210), and plays on the carved Tudor-style marble fireplace of this lovely English Renaissance hotel. Rich Oriental rugs, soft dusky-rose lounge chairs and couches, and ficus give a serene air to the lobby. The 156 modern rooms, decorated with matching floral spreads and curtains and modern lithographs, exhibit such attentive details as hand-milled embossed soap and bedside clock-radios. Butcher block and wicker prevail in the Brasserie, which stays open 24 hours to service the crowds who flock to the disco, élan, where a fantastic brunch is served on weekends.

RATES: $120 to $140 single, $125 to $145 double. Special weekend rate—$89.

Jodhpur-attired gentlemen will welcome you to the small, personal 150-room **Latham,** Walnut at 17th Street, Philadelphia, PA 19103 (tel. 215/563-7474), beloved by so many visiting business people. They appreciate the lack of conventioneers; the rooms with refrigerators, drink dispensers, Louis XIV–style writing tables, and comfortable upholstered armchairs; and large bathrooms with phones, swing-a-lite mirrors, and other amenities. They also enjoy dining at Bogart's and the bar of the Crickett Lounge.

RATES: $100 to $150 double with a 30% discount on weekends. The Latham also offers appealing weekend packages starting at $69 per person.

Latest arrival on the Philadelphia hotel scene, the **Four Seasons,** One Logan Square, Philadelphia, PA 19103 (tel. 215/963-1500), comes as close to doing justice to the tradition of old grande-dame hotels as any I've already described. Paneled wood, marble, Oriental rugs, antiques, and a captivating lobby fountain immediately give the visitor an impression of luxury and comfort. The 377 rooms in the eight-story building are spacious and decorated to reflect the city's Federal heritage. They contain wing chairs, a period desk, traditional-design night tables and lamps, a TV tucked away in a handsome armoire, and come fully appointed with digital clock-radio, full-length mirror, mini-bar, plus fluffy towels, a bathrobe, hair dryer, and various toiletries in the bathroom.

The Fountain Restaurant, overlooking the flowers and fountains of Logan Square, takes on a special glow at night for intimate dining off fine crystal, china, silver. Here, in this paneled, mirrored room with French-style and Oriental accents, a $31.50 prix-fixe four-course dinner is offered, or you can dine à la carte with dishes priced from $17.50 for stuffed chicken leg to $27 for medallions of venison with port wine sauce. Brunch is also à la carte, from $5 to $8.50. The Swan Lounge has an array of deep, comfortable couches, love seats, and chairs, and is a pleasant spot for a cocktail with piano accompaniment. In summer the courtyard café comes alive with color and people enjoying alfresco dining.

A range of special Four Seasons services are available, from free shoeshine and one-hour pressing to 24-hour room service and twice-daily maid service. On the lower level there's a health spa, complete with indoor swimming pool, whirlpool, exercise room, saunas, and a massage room.

RATES: $180 to $225 double; suites from $420. There are several packages to choose from. The most luxurious is the $380 champagne weekend package that includes two nights' accommodations, champagne, dinner for two in the Fountain Restaurant, room service breakfast, and free parking. Several other packages are also offered.

First of the spanking-new hotels in Philly, the **Wyndham Franklin Plaza,** 2 Franklin Plaza, Philadelphia, PA 19103 (tel. 215/448-2000, or toll free 800/822-4200), just off Logan Circle, is a resort in itself. A dramatic 70-foot glass atrium arches over the four-story lobby, which is softened by ficus, fresh flowers placed around the Terrace Restaurant, and the music of a pianist who plays just inside the entrance in the Lobby Lounge. The plum-and-red Between Friends provides a rich setting for continental cuisine and brunch on Sunday; the top-floor Horizons is for dining, dancing, and live entertainment. The 800 rooms come with all the expected deluxe features, including floor-to-ceiling mirrors. The hotel maintains a first-class sports center, where you can undergo a stress test and follow with supervised exercise. The center also includes an indoor swimming pool, three squash courts, three racquetball courts, one tennis court, Nautilus room, and a one-eighth-mile rooftop jogging track.

RATES: $135 double. Parking is $8 a day. Their weekend packages include room plus all facilities, two complimentary drinks, and free parking for $69 per couple per night; same plus breakfast, champagne, and chocolates for $99 per couple per night.

The **Palace,** located in a 28-story circular building at 18th Street and Logan Circle, Philadelphia, PA 19103 (tel. 215/963-2222, 212/541-4400 in New York, or toll free 800/223-5672), is owned and operated by Britain's Trust House Forte hotel group. The lobby is small and comfortably furnished with one or two wing chairs, Regency-style tables, and fresh flower arrangements. Most of the 300 rooms include wet bars, refrigerators, and private terraces, and are furnished with antique reproductions, ceramic lamps, desks, and highboys. Only 43 are studios; the rest are one- or two-room suites. The appropriately named Café Royale captures the elegant atmosphere of its London namesake with swag drapes, mirrors, and Empire-style chairs, and offers a jazz brunch—$15 on Sunday with soft clarinet and piano. Facilities include a swimming pool.

RATES: $120 to $170 double. Weekend packages available.

Another new hotel arrival, the **Hershey,** Broad Street and Locust, Philadelphia, PA 19107 (tel. 215/893-1600), stands across from the Academy of Music. Quarry tiles and ficus trees decorate the four-story atrium lobby, which you can also view from the second-floor Café Academie and Wine Bar, terraced to give each diner a view of the Academy across the street. The other restaurant, Sarah's, offers nouvelle cuisine in an art deco-ish atmosphere. There are 450 rooms, all with standard deluxe modern features furnished in faux burled wood. Sports facilities include an indoor swimming pool, fully equipped exercise room, jogging track, roof garden and sundeck, and racquetball courts.

RATES: $130 to $160 double.

The hotel most conveniently located for visiting Independence Park is the **Holiday Inn** at 4th and Arch Streets, Philadelphia, PA 19106 (tel. 215/923-8660). Pleasant rooms, two restaurants, a lounge, a rooftop outdoor pool, and free parking make this a good bet.

RATES: $99 double, $69 on weekends.

The other accommodation in the area is the **Society Hill Hotel,** 301 Chestnut St., at 3rd St., Philadelphia, PA 19106 (tel. 215/925-1919), a small hotel in a restored 1832 building. There are 12 small rooms, all furnished with canopy or brass beds, and so well appointed that the bathrooms even have hairdryers. The size of the hotel ensures personal service and makes it seem more like a country inn than a downtown hotel. Many people are loyal to this place, so that it's hard to obtain a room. Some people, however, find the noise from the downstairs bar disturbing. If you're a night owl or can sleep through any noise, then this is the place.

RATES: $80 to $110 double.

For moderately priced accommodations, try the **Penn Center Inn,** 20th and Market Streets, Philadelphia, PA 19103 (tel. 215/569-3000, or toll free 800/523-0909), a contemporary box-like building that houses pleasantly appointed rooms, a restaurant, a lounge, an outdoor pool, and a mini-gym. It has a great location and is especially attractive for its in-hotel parking and a good weekend package.

RATES: $76 double.

Another bet is to take advantage of **Bed-and-Breakfast of Philadelphia,** P.O. Box 680, Devon, PA 19333 (tel. 215/688-1633), run by Carol Yarrow and Sandra Fullerton, who offer accommodations in the city and within a 25-mile radius. Choices range from standard comfortable to extra-special, like an elegant high-rise apartment on Rittenhouse Square or a Bucks County colonial with beamed ceilings, mullioned windows, and antique furnishings.

RATES: Prices range from $40 to $130. Write well ahead of time enclosing a stamped, self-addressed envelope, or call between 9 A.M. and 5 P.M.

PHILADELPHIA DINING

Note: Parking is becoming extremely difficult, and therefore costly, in downtown Philadelphia. It's hard to find a meter near your destination and even then it's $1 an hour. If you do have a car, then make sure you call the restaurant and inquire whether or not they offer free parking at a nearby garage. Many of them do, and it could save you an extra $7 or so.

Philadelphia Dining Traditions
You really shouldn't leave Philadelphia without having tried one of their world-famous hoagies—a long, split roll with meat, cheese, lettuce, tomato, and a generous splash of olive oil and oregano—or an equally famous cheese steak, with onions, cheese, and plenty of hot peppers.

For the last, there are several local favorites. Stop by anytime day or night at **Pat's King of Steaks** in South Philly, 1237 E. Passyunk Ave. (tel. 215/468-1546), for a sidewalk steak sandwich.

In town, **Jim's Steak**, at 4th and South Streets (tel. 215/928-1911), is easily distinguished by its black-and-white tiles.

HOURS: Monday to Thursday from 10 A.M. to 1 A.M., on Friday and Saturday until 3 A.M., on Sunday from noon to 10 P.M.

Reading Terminal Market
After visiting Philadelphia in the early part of this century it is said that Edward VII remarked that he had eaten something delicious called "biddle" and had met a wonderful family named Crapple. While Biddles are not for sale in Reading Terminal Market (they're a distinguished local family), almost everything else is, and chances are quite good that the monarch's scrapple hailed from Reading Terminal.

When it opened in 1893 the market was billed as one of the greatest markets of the world, with an advanced underground refrigeration system having no rival in the land. In recent years the market had been in decline, with only a quarter of its space occupied, but a renovation has restored the market to a thriving institution to which people flock to purchase prime produce.

If you're in town on any day except Sunday, you really should stop by at 12th and Arch Streets (tel. 215/922-2317) and have breakfast or lunch here at one of the many dining operations—charcoal-grilled items at **Fireworks,** Indian specialties at **Curry Cottage,** spicy Mexican food at **12th Street Cantina,** as well as hot dogs, bagels, sandwiches, pasta, seafood, falafel, and more at various other vendors. Browsing around the market is fun. Many of the purveyors have been in business for many years. Harry Ochs, for example has been selling prime meats since 1906, and Pierce and Schurr have been here since the 1930s.

Much of the character of the market derives from the many Mennonites who operate stalls. **Stolzfus** is known for Amish specialties and barbecue; **Joseph N. Moyer's** sausages and scrapple are as well known; and **I. D. Bassett** is the only concession still owned by the famous Bassett ice cream family.

A feast for the eyes and for the stomach, the market also offers fresh fruits and vegetables, cheeses, baked goods, spices, seafood, poultry, eggs, nuts, coffees, gourmet items, flowers, and even books.

HOURS: Monday to Saturday from 8 A.M. to 6 P.M.

Dining at the Bourse
Downstairs on the lower level, the **Hearthrob Café,** on South 5th Street (tel. 215/627-0778), jives along in real '50s style with folks like James Dean and Elvis.

There's a jukebox at every brilliant-blue Formica table. Period posters include Ronnie Reagan modeling Van Heusen shirts, and fun period film clips and videos are shown from "Ozzie and Harriet" and *Rebel Without a Cause,* etc. Food is strictly burgers, hound dogs, Philly steaks, ribs, strip and T-bone steaks, barbecued chicken, and pasta, plus sundaes and shakes and cherry Cokes whipped up by the soda jerk, and other nostalgic delights, all with their very own original Hearthrob names. Prices run $3 to $15.50.

HOURS: Monday to Thursday from 11:30 A.M. to midnight, on Friday and Saturday until 1 A.M., on Sunday to 11:30 P.M.

On the top floor there's a selection of dining establishments, their names indicating their fare—Saladalley, Bains Deli, Canton Country Chinese Kitchen, Mama Rigatoni (pizza), Athens Gyro, International Sausage Co., Nandi (Indian), Hot Chips Cookie Co., Cheesesteaks, and Lots o' Licks.

South Philly

And then of course there's South Philly, home to Philadelphia's Italian population and also to many neighborhood restaurants. Three of the most famous are **Dante's and Luigi's,** 762 S. 10th St. (tel. 215/922-9501), **Torano's Cous' Little Italy,** 901 S. 11th St. (tel. 215/925-2282), and **Osteria Romana,** 935 Ellsworth St. (tel. 215/271-9191).

Philadelphia Breakfast/Brunch Choices

At the Warwick Hotel, élan (tel. 215/546-8800) offers the most spectacular brunch in Philadelphia. If you're dying for a cup of coffee when you arrive, refresh yourself at the conveniently located coffee urn at the entrance, or if the crowds are too thick, go in and plant yourself at the bar, where, for an additional $3 added to the brunch price, the bartender will keep filling your glass with champagne or Bloody Marys until your table is ready.

Start your meal by going over to examine the spread on the cold table—two soups, an array of fresh (I mean *fresh*) salads, cheeses from all nations, smoked fishes, and fresh fruit. Move to the hot table for a selection of brunch fare —everything from sausage and bacon and home-fries to quiche and french toast and cooked-to-order omelets (you select the ingredients). Top off the whole feast with waffles and ice cream (made to order) or a special sundae of your very own choosing, awash with as many toppings as tickle your fancy. Then forget about eating for the rest of the day! The cost? $17, plus the $3 if you choose to imbibe as much as you like.

BRUNCH: Sunday from 10 A.M. to 3:30 P.M.

Other breakfast/brunch choices include the **Commissary,** 1710 Sansom St. (tel. 215/569-2240), for croissants, brioches, and coddled eggs; the Barclay's **Beau Lieu** (tel. 215/545-0300) for a classic breakfast amid potted palms and chandeliers; and **O'Brien's** (tel. 215/893-1776), at the Bellevue, where a more pubby atmosphere prevails; the last two open very early.

For a light breakfast, head for **Bread and Company,** 216 S. 16th St. (tel. 215/545-4430), where you can savor fresh croissants and pastries either with an espresso or a cappuccino. Later in the day, soups, sandwiches, and quiches are available.

HOURS: Monday to Saturday from 7:30 A.M. to 10 P.M., on Sunday from 8 A.M. to 6 P.M.

For an honest deli breakfast there's the **Corned Beef Academy,** in three locations, at 121 S. 16th St. (tel. 215/665-0460), at 18th and John F. Kennedy (tel. 215/568-9696), and at 4th and Market Streets (tel. 215/922-2111).

HOURS: Monday to Saturday from 7 to 10 A.M. and 11 A.M. to 3:30 P.M. You can also pick up a good sandwich and other delicatessen fare later in the day for under $5.

Breakfast, Lunch, or Dinner Choices

Apropos, 211 S. Broad St. (tel. 215/546-4424), a large, high-ceilinged flashy modern restaurant with black faux-marble tables, bamboo chairs, modern art on the walls, and black-and-white tile floors, is dramatic enough to attract a trendy crowd. Tables are set on two levels around a central bar. As you enter, desserts are displayed temptingly and so, too, are some other food ingredients. New wave California is the way they describe the cuisine—plenty of mesquite grilling here. At dinner, for example, there are six or so fish dishes, from Cajun fish of the day to grilled scallops with roe in a tomato-vermouth sauce served with risotto-stuffed cabbage and salmon caviar, plus about ten meat and poultry items—tea-smoked duck in a ginger sauce with braised pears, leg of lamb served with tomato-mint salsa, or sliced sirloin in beaujolais sauce with roasted shallots, served with potato-red-pepper pancake. Prices run $14.50 to $19. You can also choose pizzas baked in a wood-burning stove. Luncheon also offers tempting specialties —everything from shad roe to a plain omelet of the day. Breakfast brings omelets, eggs, granola, buckwheat pancakes. This is Philadelphia's place to see and be seen. Loud and fun—the scene!

BREAKFAST: Monday to Friday from 7:30 to 10:30 A.M. LUNCH: 11:30 A.M. to 3 P.M. daily. DINNER: 5:30 to 11 P.M. daily (supper until 1 A.M.) daily. BRUNCH: Sunday from 11:30 A.M. to 3 P.M.

One of Philadelphia's first "new" restaurants, the **Commissary,** 1710 Sansom St., between 17th and 18th Streets (tel. 215/569-2240), continues to thrive, because it delivers an excellent breakfast, lunch, or dinner of fresh ingredients. At breakfast there are always two hot cereals like oatmeal or cream of wheat, assorted muffins (lemon glaze, applesauce, bran), brioches, croissants, and egg dishes. At lunch the self-service display counter is chock full of soups, imaginative salads, an assortment of charcuterie, pasta, omelets, and other hot items, all served in an area brightened by colorful ceramic tile. There's a plat du jour that might be broiled seafood with green-pepper butter served with broccoli and yellow squash, a pasta dish or any number of salads including saffron rice and chicken, Indonesian beef, fresh fruit, etc. Prices run $4 to $6. Desserts run from raspberry chocolate cheesecake to apple dumplings, chocolate hazelnut mousse, chocolate killer cake, and more. There's also a wine bar and a cook-book library.

HOURS: Monday to Thursday from 8 A.M. to 11 P.M., on Friday until midnight, on Saturday from 9 A.M. to midnight, and on Sunday from 10:30 A.M. to 10 P.M.

Upstairs at the USA Cafe the atmosphere is more formal (with table service) and the cuisine more eclectic with an emphasis on American regional cuisine. For example, there's southern fried chicken pasta (batter-fried dipped chicken and pasta in a garlic-cream sauce), chicken fajitas, blackened prime rib or salmon, and more. Prices range from $9 to $12.50. Among the appetizers are batter-fried peppers stuffed with crabmeat, Cajun seafood salad, and Mexican cornmeal crêpe with vegetarian chili. For a main course the choices might include broiled filet of beef with cumin and jalapeño demiglacé or New Orleans veal shank with tomato, onion, horseradish, and orange zest.

HOURS: Monday to Thursday from 5:30 to 10:30 P.M., until 11 P.M. on Friday and Saturday, and for lunch weekdays. The bar offers some good entertainment in the evenings and an assortment of sandwiches, salads, and other snacks during the day from 11:30 A.M. to midnight Monday to Friday, from 6 P.M. to 1 A.M. on Saturday.

A Brunch/Lunch or Dinner Choice

Café Nola, 328 South St. (tel. 215/627-2590), permanently celebrates Mardi Gras. The room itself is a spectacle: floor-to-ceiling mirrors are trimmed with a wild mélange of silk flowers, plastic peaches and oranges; ceiling fans whir overhead. At the front, poster art and art deco strawberry-pink lights decorate the bar. For a fiery intro to your meal, try the Acadian barbecued shrimp with cracked pepper in shell or shrimp remoulade, or a thick gumbo filled with rice, sausage, and okra. Oysters Rockefeller, angels on horseback, and other oyster dishes are also good choices. For entrees there's jambalaya (shrimp, chicken, sausage, ham, and oysters), blackened redfish, and sesame catfish served with hushpuppies (southern fritters) or crawfish étouffée. For meat lovers, blackened Cajun prime rib or roast duck with figs served with sweet potato and eggplant gravy are possibilities. There are also pasta dishes available. At lunch it's jambalaya, a special shrimp dieter's special, po-boys (ham sandwich), gumbos, and salads.

LUNCH: Tuesday to Saturday from noon to 3 P.M. DINNER: Monday to Thursday from 5 to 11 P.M., on Friday and Saturday until midnight. BRUNCH: Sunday from 11 A.M. to 3 P.M.

Brunch/Dinner Choices

Raymond Haldeman's, 110–112 S. Front St. (tel. 215/925-9888), opened by this well-known Philadelphia caterer attracts a wealthy crowd to its five large elegantly appointed dining rooms on two floors decorated in French Empire style. A courtyard offers summer dining. Best choice among the appetizers would be an hors d'oeuvres sampler of hot and cold appetizers—snow peas stuffed with crab, bite-size baked potatoes with sour cream and caviar, and smoked salmon or warm seafood mousse with broccoli purée. The entrees, priced from $12 to $21, range from sweetbreads with bourbon and bouillabaisse to duck Grand Marnier sauce and red snapper in a puff pastry served over a bed of chopped spinach and seafood mousse. The filet mignon with ginger-cognac sauce and candied garlic cloves is prime choice. Desserts might include lemon mousse pie or a dacquoise, a cake of meringue with ground almonds.

LUNCH: Monday to Friday from 11:30 A.M. to 2:30 P.M. DINNER: Monday to Thursday from 6 to 10 P.M., on Friday and Saturday until 11 P.M., on Sunday from 3 to 9 P.M. BRUNCH: Sunday from noon to 3 P.M.

Frög, 1524 Locust St. (tel. 215/735-8882), was one of the first and finest restaurants to emerge during the initial Philadelphia restaurant renaissance. The decor is modern, chic but comfortable. Located in an old bank building—the entrance leads onto a landing, where you can either descend to the piano-wine bar or ascend to a series of dining areas, lit dramatically by recessed pinlights, accented with brass and polished wood, anthuriums and orchids, all decorated primarily in dusky rose and gray.

The food blends American, French, and Asian cuisines into some very tasty dishes. Among the appetizers, for example, there are clams in a spicy black-bean sauce or wonton filled with crabmeat and Brie. The entrees include Peking duck breast with mango and star anise; grilled lamb chops with feta, leeks, tomato, and a mustard-lamb essence; calves' liver with roasted pearl onion, white wine, parsley, and mustard; and chicken with lemon and coriander. To start, there might be marinated swordfish; red leaf, arugula, and watercress salad; or blackened duck breast with Créole chutney on wilted greens. Prices range from $11.50 to $20. At lunch, similar dishes are priced from $8 to $13. Frög's desserts are acclaimed, the favorite being a white-chocolate mousse topped with toasted almonds. Prices hover around $15. The wine list is notable.

LUNCH: Monday to Friday from 11:30 A.M. to 2:30 P.M. DINNER: Monday to Friday from 5:30 to 10:30 P.M., on Saturday until 11:30 P.M. The bar is open every night except Sunday.

Carolina's (formerly the 20th St. Café), 261 S. 20th St. (tel. 215/545-1000), packs the crowds in because the food is good and reasonably priced. Don't expect romance: the tables are close, the room noisy and lively. The menu changes daily, although the most popular, fairly regular, items on the menu are the crabcakes and veal loaf. The breast of chicken with oyster stuffing is recommended. The other choices might be salmon with zinfandel sauce, calves' liver with raspberry vinegar and marsala, or porterhouse steak. Start with a Caesar salad, steamed Chinese dumplings, or the tasty vegetable kebabs with hummus. For dessert the apple dumplings are great; so are banana cream pie and homemade ice creams. Salmon-pink pressed-tin ceiling, bentwood chairs, nostalgic pix, and track lighting is the sum total of decoration—the crowds are all you need. Brunch offers french toast, smoked fish, omelets, and eggs Benedict, from $4 to $8. Prices for dinner range from $7 to $9 (except for the 22-ounce steak). The next room contains a bar and a piano, where a pianist plays daily from 4:30 to 7 P.M.

LUNCH: Tuesday to Friday from 11:30 A.M. to 2 P.M. DINNER: Tuesday to Friday from 5 to 9 P.M., on Saturday from 6 to 9 P.M. BRUNCH: Sunday from 11:30 A.M. to 2 P.M.

Dockside Fish Co., 815 Locust St. (tel. 215/925-6175), knows how to cook and present fish. Try the bluefish baked with onions, bacon, and horseradish, with sour cream sauce; the baked crabmeat imperial; or the seafood combination (clams, sea scallops, crabcake, and almond shrimp). The entrees are served with two of the following: baked potato, baked acorn or spaghetti squash, coleslaw, salad, or the vegetable of the day. Prices run $12.50 to $14.50; luncheon items cost $8 to $10. The $9 brunch offers some unusual items—crabmeat, oyster or flounder Benedict, french toast, and chicken Neapolitan. Each is served with juice, salad, biscuits, and coffee, or tea.

HOURS: Monday 11:30 A.M. to 9 P.M., Tuesday to Thursday to 10 P.M., on Friday to 11 P.M., on Saturday 4 to 11 P.M., and on Sunday 11:30 A.M. to 7 P.M.

Over in the university area there's **La Terrasse**, 3432 Sansom St. (tel. 215/387-3778), which provides lovely open-air dining in summer, glass-enclosed but still garden-like in winter with its plants and shrubs. The musical accompaniment, often by Curtis Institute students, on the Steinway grand is an added attraction that can range from Mozart to Chopin to Gershwin and Porter. Besides the terrace there are also several, more intimate upstairs dining rooms and a popular bar well stocked with wines, a remarkable number of Portuguese vintages among them. The rooms are low-ceilinged and candlelit. Specials are listed on the blackboard, and included on my visit gin and tomato soup, salade de mâche, filet of sea trout, and veal chop on a bed of mouilles à la crème gorgonzola. The menu listed (among other items) medallions of pork with sauce flamed with star anise, Szechuan peppercorns and black beans, chicken breast with mushrooms in a cognacmustard sauce, and a filet of salmon with lobster sauce garnished with salmon caviar. Prices run $11.75 to $22. For appetizers, try the terrine of crab or snails in garlic with melted Gruyère cheese on top. For dessert there's always a wonderful lemon-and-walnut meringue, a white-chocolate mousse, or many other divine temptations.

LUNCH: Monday to Friday 11:30 A.M. to 2:30 P.M. DINNER: Monday to Saturday 6 to 11 P.M., on Sunday until 10 P.M. BRUNCH: Sunday 11:30 A.M. to 2:45 P.M.

If you're exploring Independence Park, I've already suggested the restored **City Tavern**, at 2nd and Walnut (tel. 215/923-6059), for lunch. Dinner is also served daily from 5 to 10 P.M.

Two for Lunch Only

If you're shopping John Wanamaker's, at 13th and Market (tel. 215/422-2813), then consider lunching at the store's **Crystal Room**, restored to its original 19th-century splendor with crystal chandeliers and Corinthian columns. For fast self-service there's also the Crystal Express buffet.

LUNCH: Monday to Saturday from 11 A.M. to 2:30 P.M.

Similarly, if you're viewing the Philadelphia art museum, the cafeteria-style restaurant is good for a lunch of appetizers, salads, sandwiches, desserts, and even hot specialties like omelets, quiche, and roast beef. The more stylish restaurant, with cane Breuers and pink tablecloths, serves such items as beef carbonade, from $6 and up.

LUNCH: Wednesday to Sunday from 11:30 A.M. to 2:30 P.M.

Lunch or Dinner Choices

On Head House Square in the Society Hill area, the **Dickens Inn**, 421 S. 2nd St. (tel. 215/928-9307), is an authentic pub. The fish and chips, served at lunch and dinner, are particularly good. Shepherd's pie, Cornish pasty, quiche, and other dishes are also served at lunchtime. At dinner the fare is more formal—roast beef and Yorkshire pudding; roast duck with honey; beef Wellington; rack of lamb with persillade; lamb's liver with shallots, chanterelles, and béarniase sauce; poached rabbit with shiitake mushrooms and juniper-cream sauce; red snapper with mussels and shrimp; and swordfish with rosemary, almonds, and lemon butter. To start there are chowders, salads, pâté, and fricassée of wild mushrooms with watercress; and to finish besides the desserts displayed on the cart there's a fine English Stilton served with fresh fruit. Prices range from $12 to $19. At lunch or dinner a large bowl of perfectly cooked vegetables accompanies the main course. Bread comes from the sweet-smelling bakery downstairs. In the adjacent tavern bar you're likely to find some English folk, or at least Britishers, downing a few pints of good English ale (you can have a yard if you like), under the watchful eyes of Dickens' wonderful characters whose portraits add to the inn's Old English Spirit.

LUNCH: Monday to Saturday from 11:30 A.M. to 3 P.M. DINNER: Monday to Thursday from 5:30 to 10 P.M., on Friday and Saturday until 10:30 P.M., on Sunday from 5 to 9:45 P.M. BRUNCH: Sunday from 11 A.M. to 4 P.M.

Café de Costa, New Market, 2nd and Pine Streets (tel. 215/928-0844), has to be one of the more romantic dining rooms in the Head House Square area. Cozy and cellar-like, it offers a series of romantic alcoves lit by candles and a series of prettily decorated dining rooms. Oriental rugs give a luxury feel, as do the gilt mirrors, decorative tile, and Oriental ceramics. French music adds to the ambience. A meal might begin with ravioli filled with lobster and served with crushed tomatoes and herbs, warm duck-and-chanterelles salad, an assortment of vegetables in curry sauce with minced apples, or a carrot soup with a hint of ginger; and might be followed by rack of lamb, filet of beef beaujolaise, swordfish in chive sauce, duck breast with blackcurrants in a madeira sauce with green peppercorns, or a salmon filet with pike quenelles in lemon-thyme sauce. The beef is prime quality and melts in the mouth. Desserts vary, but almond and apple tart with crème anglaise or a pâté de fromage with candied orange, flavored with Grand Marnier, and served with a blackcurrant sauce or similar will hit the spot. Prices go from $16 to $22. In summer a beer garden offers a huge selection of foreign beers.

LUNCH: Monday to Saturday from 11:30 A.M. to 3 P.M. DINNER: Monday to Saturday from 6 to 11 P.M. Closed Sunday.

Stagedoor, 202 S. Quince St. (tel. 215/923-1853), next to the Forrest Theater between Walnut and Locust and 11th and 12th streets, is a small funky theatrical place. Costumes decorate the walls; a Moulin Rouge mural sets the nostalgic scene. A theater crowd gathers here around the glass-topped tables. The menu is selective, listing about seven or so entrees supplemented by a few daily specials: for example, steamed flounder rolled with spinach and mushrooms, chicken breast with grapefruit and almonds, filet mignon topped with Stilton cheese in port sauce, and pork filet with apples, cream, and ham. Prices go from $10 to $16. Luncheon is an abbreviated version featuring similar dishes, from $5 to $8.50. Among the appetizers, sample the seafood fritters served with sweet-and-sour sauce.

LUNCH AND DINNER: Monday to Saturday from 11 A.M. to 2 A.M.; closed Sunday.

Siam Cuisine, 925 Arch St. (tel. 215/922-7135), offers an attractive dining experience. At night the room takes on a warm pink glow thanks to the tracklighting and the walls painted in mauve and pink tones and matched with deep-purple Breuer chairs and floral tablecloths. The room is long and narrow, and divided by partitions. Siamese prints adorn the walls. Main-course dishes include a selection of spicy dishes—sautéed chicken or beef in Thai green curry with coconut cream, or stir-fried shrimp with sweet basil and minced hot pepper—vegetable dishes, and specialties like gai lue fire (baked game hen flamed in brandy and chili sauce) or powh tak (shellfish in hot-and-sour feast with lemon grass and exotic spices). Prices run from $6 to $11.50. Start with soup, salad, satay, or tofu.

LUNCH: Tuesday to Sunday from 11 A.M. to 3:30 P.M. DINNER: Tuesday to Thursday from 3 to 10 P.M., on Friday and Saturday until 11 P.M., on Sunday until 10 P.M. Closed Monday.

Dinner Only

Philadelphia's premier restaurant, which has been serving haute cuisine for many years, is **Le Bec Fin,** 1523 Walnut St. (tel. 215/567-1000). The tables are set with fresh flower arrangements, Cristoflé silver, and fine china. Mirrors and gilt-framed portraits highlight the room, which is predominantly pink and, at night, very pretty in the flickering candlelight. Owner-chef George Perrier hails from Lyons, France's gastronomic capital, and has long commanded international respect. The restaurant is famous for its escargots de champagne, served with a garlic butter that includes a touch of Chartreuse and hazelnuts. Other fine hors d'oeuvres include the spinach ravioli filled with lobster in a light tomato sauce and beignets de saumon. The restaurant is also renowned for its game—pheasant, venison, and pigeon—which might come with truffle sauce (as does the pigeon). Other entrees might include filet of lamb with lettuce and a cream of garlic sauce, sea bass in a sauce that varies, or calves' liver in a raspberry wine sauce. Desserts are enticing—Grand Marnier soufflé, freshly churned ice cream, homemade sorbets, a rich chocolate gâteau, and many, many more. The wine list begins at around $45 and rises dramatically. At dinner the $65 prix fixe will include appetizer, fish course, entree, salad, dessert, and coffee with petit fours.

LUNCH: Monday to Friday from 11:30 A.M. to 2 P.M. DINNER: Monday to Saturday at 6 and 9 P.M. On weekends you'll need to make reservations months ahead.

Di Lullo Centro, 1405 Locust St. (tel. 215/546-2000), is lavish, sybaritic, and beautiful. The hand-painted murals give it tremendous impact, filling the room with colors and life, and so, too, do the floral and food displays. The bar is adorned with flowers and a bronze sculpture. Here you can sink into gray upholstered couches with lilac cushions and set your drink on rose marble tables. From here two steps lead into the splendid semicircular muraled dining area where tables are set with fresh flower bouquets and elegant settings. There's also a tiled garden-style area that is demarcated by etched-glass paneling and dotted with ficus trees. Here are displayed vegetables, fresh fish and chocolate sugar creations. Food is classic northern Italian, the service excellent and unobtrusive. Although the menu changes, among the appetizers might be antipasto di scampi (cold shrimp with sauce gazpacho), sweetbreads with mushrooms and cornetti salad, or sautéed foie gras balanced by arugula, tiny green beans, baby beets, and thinly sliced seeded cucumber as garnish. Among the pastas you might find a spinach pasta filled with meat in a sage-cream sauce or angel-hair with seafood in aromatic sauce. Main courses might include chicken breast with sherry vinegar and tomato, grilled veal chop with garlic-herb butter, filet of lamb with essence of truffles, sautéed lobster with sauterne and chervil, or grilled marinated pheasant. Among the luscious desserts might be lemon tart, fresh fruit sorbets, chocolate and mandarin cake, or a variety of gelati—with macaroons and crème di cocoa, for example. The best! Prices run $12.50 to $22 at dinner, $9.50 to $14.50 at lunch.

LUNCH: Monday to Friday from 11:45 A.M. to 2 P.M. DINNER: Monday to Saturday from 5:30 to 10 P.M. Closed Sunday.

Déjà-Vu, 1609 Pine St. (tel. 215/546-1190), is very French and very Empire. Deep-rose brocade banquettes, pale-green swag drapes, a baroque painted ceiling, and gilt-framed landscapes provide a lavish setting for the Belgian chef's haute cuisine. The restaurant is small, seating only 30 for a six-course $65 prix-fixe dinner. The menu includes such treats as venison in season, which may be marinated with madeira and then served with a sauce made from Dutch chocolate and Swedish lingonberries or veal with morels and mushroom-cream sauce. Among the appetizers, the duck-liver terrine or the escargots with Pernod and chopped walnuts are choice. Desserts bring a dangerous array of tartes, mousses, soufflés.

LUNCH: Tuesday to Friday from noon to 1:30 P.M. DINNER: Tuesday to Saturday from 6 and 9:30 P.M. You'll need to reserve a month or so ahead for weekends.

The Garden, 1617 Spruce St. (tel. 215/546-4455), is definitely one of my favorite restaurants in the city—a wonderful place to dine in any season. In winter the flattering pink lighting, brass lamps, and gilt-framed pictures create a cozy atmosphere, and in summer the patio is bedecked with brilliant yellow umbrellas. For more casual dining there's also the oyster bar, with mahogany tables and old hunting and botanic prints. The cuisine offers the best of American ingredients and style with some Gallic highlights. Among the appetizers, choices include a carpaccio (raw filet of beef sliced very thinly and laid in a chutney sauce), and cold curried mussels served in half an avocado. The entrees range in price from $10 for a pasta primavera with vegetables and a wonderfully light, creamy cheese sauce, to $20 for a rack of lamb seasoned with garlic and fresh herbs. Steak tartare mixed with capers and anchovies and a veal with morels are two other specialties of the house. Seafood dishes include bouillabaisse and the Garden's cold assortment featuring curried mussels, shrimps, clams, half a chicken, lobster, cucumber salad, and tomatoes. Among the desserts, the chocolate cake draws rave reviews and so does the Bonaparte, which consists of strawberries steeped in Grand Marnier, covered with a crisp thin pastry, and crowned with puréed strawberries and crème Chantilly.

LUNCH: Monday to Friday from 11:30 A.M. to 2 P.M. DINNER: Monday to Saturday from 5:30 to 9:30 P.M. Closed Saturday in July and August.

Il Gallo Nero, 254 S. 15 St. (tel. 215/546-8065), is renowned for its food and lavish style. From the piano lounge with its black marble bar a few steps lead into a series of different dining areas. The decor is rich—floors are gray tile inlaid with decorative strips, walls are covered with chintz fabric, tapestries grace walls in one room while in another they're adorned by a classical frieze. The Villeroy and Boche china has a pink marbleized look, lace tablecloths are laid over pink, chandeliers sparkle, and in winter the fire warms the rooms. Among the antipasti, try the carpaccio alla piemontese or deep-fried mozzarella. The pastas are all made on the premises and prepared with imagination. Tortellini alla Nerone is prepared tableside in brandy sauce; stringozzi con salsa di tartufo is an Umbrian specialty with truffle sauce (a twisted pasta in a cream sauce with cognac and truffles, and a hint of tomato just enough to turn the sauce a delicate pink). Other specialties include cacciucco, a Tuscan seacoast fish-and-shellfish soup served on garlic toast, osso buco served over saffroned arborio rice, and vitello Gallo Nero, which is cooked according to the chef's inspiration. Prices run $15 to $20.

LUNCH: Monday to Friday from 11:30 A.M. to 3 P.M. DINNER: Monday to Friday from 5 to 10 P.M., on Saturday until 11 P.M.

For a fancy, classy dining atmosphere, try **Monte Carlo Living Room,** at 2nd and South Streets (tel. 215/925-2220), a restaurant attached to the private nightclub upstairs. If you dine here you don't have to pay admission to the nightclub. The pale-blue-decorated room is lit by crystal chandeliers and candles set in silver candlesticks on each lace-clothed table. Appetizers include crabmeat salad with avocado, and smoked salmon and sweetbreads with balsamic vinegar. Among the pastas are paglie e fieno aurora (white and green pasta in a cream-and-tomato sauce), tagliatelle ai funghi Selvatici in egg noodles, and fettuccine in wild mushroom sauce. For an entree my recommended choice would be the fisherman's basket, a selection of fresh fish—sole, turbot, snapper, etc.—that is brought to your table. Lobster and scampi are also available. Meat lovers may choose from rack of lamb and breast of duck with mustard glazed with cognac, among other dishes. Desserts include a choice of chocolate, Grand Marnier, or raspberry soufflé.

DINNER: Monday to Thursday from 6:30 to 10:30 P.M., on Friday and Saturday from 5:30 to 11 P.M.; closed Sunday. The club is open from 9 P.M. to 2 A.M. Monday to Saturday for dancing, and also for cocktails from 5:30 P.M.

Morton's, One Logan Square (tel. 215/557-0724), with its entrance on 19th Street, is a masculine-style domain for dedicated carnivores, the closest Philadelphia comes to having a public power lunch spot: taupe, etched glass, banquettes —you know the look. Choose from a cart laden with cellophane-wrapped steaks: 24-ounce T-bone, double-cut prime rib, lamb or veal chops. Whatever you choose, it will be huge and pricey, from $18 to $22. Fish and chicken are also available for the reformed. Cheesecake follows naturally—might as well go the whole way.

LUNCH: Monday to Friday from 11:30 A.M. to 2:30 P.M. DINNER: Monday to Thursday from 5:30 to 11 P.M., on Friday and Saturday until 11:30 P.M. Closed Sunday.

Seafood places are sometimes hard to find, but Philadelphia has the outstanding **Fishmarket,** 124 S. 18th St. at Sansom (tel. 215/567-3559). Located just off Rittenhouse Square in three turn-of-the-century town houses, the restaurant has five dining rooms spread over a number of floors and two bars filled with lively "Happy Hour" crowds. On two floors above the atrium-capped bar are a series of small dining areas with simple butcher-block tables and brass accents. Attached to the restaurant there's a fresh fish market, guaranteeing the quality of the ingredients in such dishes as grilled red snapper with roasted red pepper, lime sauce, and cilantro; yellowfin tuna with tomato and mint salsa with balsamic vinegar and scallions; crab cakes with remoulade sauce; bouillabaisse California, with lobster, clams, mussels, and shrimp in a red sauce with saffron and Pernod. Four or so meat/poultry dishes are offered, including a specialty filet mignon with zinfandel sauce, shallots, and shiitake mushrooms. Prices run $9.50 to $16.50 for South African lobstertails. Luncheon prices go from $7 to $12. The place is popular, so I suggest that you make lunch or dinner reservations. Discount parking is available after 5 P.M. at 1845 Walnut.

LUNCH: Monday to Friday from 11:45 A.M. to 2:30 P.M. DINNER: Monday to Saturday from 5 to 10 P.M., on Sunday from 4 to 9 P.M.

Hoffman House, 1214 Sansom St. (tel. 215/925-2772), serves traditional German fare in a simple wood-paneled room decorated with a few plates and steins. Start with crab-and-corn soup, steak tartare, or baked oysters Hamburg style. Among the main courses are weisswurst (light veal sausage flavored with sage, poached in ale and served with mustard sauce), schnitzel à la Holstein (garnished with fried egg, smoked salmon, anchovies, capers, and onion), and Rhenisher sauerbraten (marinated braised beef in spicy red-wine sauce with white currants and ginger). Prices run $8.75 to $14.50.

LUNCH: Tuesday to Friday from 11:30 A.M. to 2:30 P.M. DINNER: Tuesday to Saturday from 5 to 9 P.M. Closed Sunday and Monday.

At **Mandana,** 18 S. 20th St. (tel. 569-4050), a simple decor of oak tables and mirrors, softened by Oriental rugs on the floors, provides the setting for some rather unusual cuisine. Among the entrees, for example, there's a duckling with sherry-vinegar glaze, medallions of lamb in a sauce of tomatoes flavored with anisette and orange, or fresh sea bass provençale. The baked artichokes filled with crab and cream cheese make a delicious start, as does a smooth chicken liver pâté with brandy, nuts, and herbs. Entree prices run $14 to $17.

LUNCH: Monday to Friday from 11:30 A.M. to 2:30 P.M. DINNER: Wednesday to Friday from 5:30 P.M., on Saturday from 6 P.M.

La Famiglia, 8 S. Front St. (tel. 215/922-2803), is sleekly Italian with its cream tile, pink marble bar, beige and white floral chairs, hand-wrought Venetian chandeliers, and lavish displays of flowers. You'll find northern and southern Italian cuisine, but often with an unexpected twist like the veal with green olives and dry vermouth or with a creamy herb sauce or fresh tomato sauce, or the penne alla Famiglia, prepared with prosciutto, onion, and parmesan cheese. About 16 entrees are featured, among them veal sautéed in a saffron sauce or with white wine and imported truffles, filet mignon in a wine garlic sauce, breast of chicken in a tomato sauce topped with wild mushrooms and mozzarella, fish of the day, and shrimp sautéed with white wine and onions in an herb sauce. Prices run $15 to $30. This is not the place to come for veal parmigiana and other standard fare. The restaurant makes its own pasta, so you may well want to sample their fine gnocchi con pesto. Among the appetizers, the very popular Milanese (for two) blends mozzarella cheese and Italian ham in a cornbread coating. For dessert there's a delicious mille foglie, the Italian version of a napoleon, or the profiteroles in chocolate sauce.

LUNCH: Tuesday to Friday from noon to 2 P.M. DINNER: Tuesday to Saturday from 5:30 to 10 P.M., on Sunday from 4:30 to 9:30 P.M.

Two or so doors down, **La Truffe,** 10 S. Front St. (tel. 215/925-5062), offers country French ambience on the waterfront, complete with gleaming copper bar, chintz upholstery, and eclectic furnishings. The cuisine is classic French—rack of lamb with thyme, duck with green peppercorns, and a selection of fish dishes. Entree prices run $16 to $25. Choice dessert would be the white-chocolate mousse with raspberry purée. A $17.50 prix-fixe lunch is available.

LUNCH: Tuesday to Friday from noon to 2 P.M. DINNER: Monday to Saturday from 6 to 11 P.M.

At **Alouette,** 334 Bainbridge St. (tel. 215/629-1126), there are three dining rooms: the Gallery is a window-lined room accented with small original French paintings; the main dining room is warmly decorated in pink with a stamped-tin ceiling; and the courtyard, under a burgundy canopy, has a café-like atmosphere. There's also a mahogany bar in which a light menu is offered. The cuisine is mainly French with Oriental accents. For example, you'll find chicken in a curried cream sauce along with duck with green and pink peppercorns. Mesquite-grilled dishes are also available, and some lighter items for the health conscious. Main courses are priced from $13 to $22. For dessert, splurge and have a Grand Marnier soufflé or a pear in white wine and raspberry sauce.

LUNCH: Monday to Friday from 11:30 A.M. to 2:30 P.M. DINNER: 5:30 to 10:30 P.M. daily. BRUNCH: Sunday from 11:30 A.M. to 2:30 P.M.

16th Street Bar and Grill, 264 S. 16th St. (tel. 215/735-3316), is a favorite casual gathering spot where conversations seem to begin easily. The deep-dish ten-inch pizzas are large enough for four. Salads, burgers, nine-ounce sirloin, vegetable stir-fry, and other dishes, priced from $5 to $11, are available. Start with nachos or potato skins. You can dine either upfront in or at the bar, or else in the back at one of the booths. Lively friendly crowd.

LUNCH AND DINNER: Monday to Friday from 11:30 A.M. to midnight. DINNER: Saturday from 5 P.M. to midnight, on Sunday from 4 P.M. to 1 A.M.

Serrano, 20 S. 2nd St. (tel. 215/928-0770), is a warm and comfortably casual spot convenient to the historic area. A long Victorian bar, exposed brick, working pot-belly stove, and tables set with dark-purple cloths set the tone. Its menu is highly eclectic—everything from Thai to rijsttafel to crabcakes.

LUNCH: Monday to Friday from 11:30 A.M. to 3 P.M. DINNER: Monday to Thursday from 6 to 10 P.M., on Friday and Saturday until 11 P.M. Closed Sunday.

Siva, 34 S. Front St. (tel. 215/925-2700) is a good choice for Indian food. Start with vegetable samosa or fish pakora and follow with a tandoori cooked shish kebab, prawns, or chicken or a deliciously subtly flavored biryani—mutton and chicken in a blend of 14 herbs and spices. Roghan josh, chicken jalfrazie, and vegetarian dishes are other choices. For dessert, try a lassi—a yogurt drink flavored with mango. The room is attractive and furnished with a mixture of rattan and Breuer chairs placed at tables set with brown cloths.

LUNCH: Tuesday to Friday from noon to 2 P.M. DINNER: Tuesday to Saturday from 5:30 to 10:30 P.M., on Sunday from 5 to 10 P.M.

The King & I, 536 South St. (tel. 215/627-8000), occupies a small attractive candy-striped room where tables are set with salmon-colored cloths and turquoise napkins and the room lit by shell-shaped sconces. The cuisine is Thai: steamed shrimp in hot clay, pork with cellophane noodles and vegetables, and such specialties as lobster, shrimp, mussels, and clams with seasoned rice in casserole, crispy roasted duck with either sweet-and-sour or black pepper and garlic, and beef and pork Thai curries. Prices run $8 to $13. Start with beef or chicken satay, yum-num tok beef with cucumber, scallion, tomato, onion, and lemon juice, or deep-fried wrapped shrimp with sweet red-pepper sauce.

DINNER: Monday to Thursday from 5 to 10 P.M., on Friday and Saturday until 11 P.M.

At **Kawagiku,** Front Street at Chestnut (tel. 215/928-9564), sushi and sashimi are available along with negimaki, chicken teriyaki, and tempura. There's even a salad bar that displays scrambled tofu, daikon and carrot nitsuna, beans, noodles, and other dishes. The decor is pleasant, with several areas sectioned off by screens and tables set with brown cloths; Japanese figurines add a decorative touch. Prices range from $8 to $13.50, much less at lunch.

LUNCH: Monday to Friday from 11:30 A.M. to 2 P.M., on Saturday and Sunday from noon to 4:30 P.M. DINNER: Monday to Thursday from 5 to 10 P.M., on Friday to 10:30 P.M., on Saturday from 4:30 to 10:30 P.M., and on Sunday from 4:30 to 9:30 P.M.

Students from the Philadelphia restaurant school have pioneered new tastes in Philadelphia. The **Warsaw Café,** 306 S. 16th St. (tel. 215/546-0204), is one example. It's an intimate spot where much of the ambience derives from the flickering of the tiny candles that stand on each deep-purple tabletop. The food is good. Supplementing the regular menu of Eastern European dishes—beef Stroganoff, stuffed cabbage, and more—are daily specials, which might feature such dishes as rabbit stew or lamb roast. The borscht, pirogis, and chicken-and-fruit pâté make excellent starters to a meal that will always be interesting and different. Prices run $10 to $16.50.

LUNCH: Monday to Saturday from 11:30 A.M. to 3 P.M. DINNER: Monday to Saturday from 5:30 to 10 P.M. Closed Sunday.

For Mexican food, head for **El Metate,** 1511 Locust St. (tel. 215/546-0181). Piñatas hanging over the bar provide a touch of color in this very simply decorated place. The menu, however, goes beyond the predictable enchiladas and tacos (which are fine here), to such dishes as mole poblano, bluefish Santa Cruz (served with tomatoes, capers, and olives), red snapper in orange juice, and many others. Prices range from $6.50 to $13. LUNCH: Monday to Friday from 11:30 A.M. to 2 P.M. DINNER: 5:30 to 10 P.M. daily.

Near the historic district, there's also **Los Amigos,** 50 S. 2nd St. (tel. 215/922-7061), for Mexican food. Past the long bar are stucco alcoves and a series of booths where you can start with nachos and then feast on mole poblano, enchiladas, tacos, burritos, and more, including several nonmeat dishes. Prices average $8 at dinner.

LUNCH: Monday to Saturday from 11:30 A.M. to 4 P.M. DINNER: Monday to Thursday from 4 to 11:30 P.M., on Friday and Saturday until 1 A.M., and on Sunday from 1 to 10 P.M.

In Philadelphia's Chinatown the best restaurant, according to local acclaim, is the **Imperial Inn,** 941 Race St. (tel. 215/925-2485), and also at 142-146 N. 10th St. (tel. 215/627-5588). Both are plainly decorated, but offer expertly prepared Mandarin, Szechuan, and Cantonese cuisine, along with the best dim sum in town. Most dishes are under $8.

HOURS: 11:30 A.M. to 3 P.M. and 4 P.M. to 1 A.M. daily.

For those who care about the decor of a Chinese restaurant and need table-cloths and some ambience, **Hunan,** 1721 Chestnut St. (tel. 215/567-5757), has a circular bar, deep-blue walls, and carved wooden ceiling. Prices do run higher (from $9 to $16) for such dishes as spicy Hunan lamb or crispy duck.

LUNCH: Monday to Friday from 11:30 A.M. to 2:30 P.M. DINNER: Monday to Friday from 5 to 10 P.M., on Saturday until 11 P.M.; closed Sunday.

Chun Hing, 1506 Spruce St. (tel. 215/546-3888), has the reputation for serving some of the finest Szechuan food in town. The bass in black-bean sauce is particularly notable.

HOURS: Monday to Friday from 11:30 A.M. to 10 P.M., on Saturday from noon to 10:30 P.M., on Sunday from 4 to 10 P.M.

And finally, if you're the kind who is willing to gamble, then the **Restaurant School,** 2129 Walnut St. (tel. 215/561-3649), is a fun place to come and watch the students acting as maître d's and waiters: some stiff, others more relaxed, but all trying to "get it right" as they perform under a teacher's appraising eye. The food can vary from excellent to not quite so good, and when I was there my biggest complaint was that the food was not hot when it reached the table. With luck, though, you'll hit a good night and capture a $12.50 one-course prix fixe in a charming town house served enthusiastically and carefully by these young restaurateurs of tomorrow.

DINNER: Tuesday to Saturday from 5:30 to 10 P.M. For reservations, call after 4 P.M.

Especially Good Dining for Kids

Dinardo's Famous Crabs, 312 Race St. (tel. 215/925-5115), convenient to the Betsy Ross House and Elfreth's Alley, is a casual spot for steamed Louisianas, softshell crabs, flounder, mussels, clams, shrimp, and more finger-licking fare.

HOURS: Monday to Saturday from 11 A.M. to 11 P.M., on Sunday from 4 to 9 P.M.

For dessert, take them to **More Than Just Ice Cream,** 1141 Pine St. (tel. 215/574-0586), where besides the sundaes and desserts, there are also salads and bread made with honey.

EVENING ENTERTAINMENT

Theater

The best theater can be found at the University of Pennsylvania's theater complex, the **Annenberg Center,** 3680 Walnut St. (tel. 215/898-6791).

Shows en route to Broadway often stop at the **Forrest Theater,** 11th and Walnut (tel. 215/923-1515). Tickets top out at $40. The **Society Hill Playhouse,** 507 S. 8th St. (tel. 215/923-0210), is the Philadelphia equivalent of an off-Broadway theater.

Music

The **Academy of Music,** at Broad and Locust Streets (tel. 215/893-1930), is, of course, home to the Philadelphia Orchestra and the Opera Company, which performs September through May. It also often features Sunday-afternoon recitals. The **Walnut Street Theatre,** 825 Walnut St. (tel. 215/574-3550), also features classical groups. Concerts are also given at the **Curtis Institute,** 1726 Locust St. (tel. 215/893-5252), between September and May.

Ballet

The **Pennsylvania Ballet,** 2333 Fairmount Ave. (tel. 215/978-1400), can be seen at the Academy of Music from October through May, when four different programs are presented.

Jazz, Comedy, and Rock

Jazz is featured at **Borgia Café,** 406 S. 2nd St., Head House Square (tel. 215/574-0414), in a slick black downstairs room from 9:30 P.M. on. Minimal cover is charged. Closed Monday.

Rick's Cabaret at **Le Bistro,** 757 S. Front St. (tel. 215/389-3855,-1429 for tickets), has good jazz daily from 8 P.M. during the week, from 9 P.M. on Saturday, and from 5 P.M. on Sunday.

Other jazz spots? **Jewels,** 679 N. Broad St., at Fairmount Avenue (tel. 215/236-1396), features headliners on weekends—Betty Carter and Donald Byrd, in the past. There's also a front bar that features the house band.

For comedy there are several spots modeled after New York's famous comedy clubs. They are the **Comedy Factory Outlet,** 31 Bank St. (tel. 215/FUNNY-11), between Market and Chestnut and 2nd and 3rd, where you'll get some insight into the local scene ($8 plus a two-drink minimum), and the **Comedy Works,** Old Philadelphia Cabaret Theater, 126 Chestnut St. (tel. 215/WACKY-97), which features open-mike nights as well as top comedians who travel the national circuit, Wednesday to Saturday with a cover charge. **Going Bananas,** 613 2nd and South Sts. (tel. 215/BANANA-1), also hosts top-line comics, Friday and Saturday only.

Bands with names like The Cramps or Executive Slacks play at the **East Side Club,** 1229 Chestnut St. (tel. 215/564-3342), from 9 P.M. to 2 A.M. At the **Kennel Club,** 1215 Walnut St. (tel. 215/592-7650), a DJ programs the music, while a VJ does the same for the videos. Heats up around midnight.

Dancing/Disco

Best disco in town is currently **élan,** at the Warwick Hotel, at 17th and Locust (tel. 215/546-8800); there are several bars on the premises and the appropriate pyrotechnic equipment. It attracts a young professional crowd in their 30s. No jeans are allowed. Dancing from 9 P.M. to 3:30 A.M. There's a cover for nonmembers.

PTs, 6 S. Front St. (tel. 215/922-5676), has a popular bar, backgammon, and dancing to a DJ's program on Friday and Saturday and tea dance on Sunday.

Another sleek spot, also for members only, is the **Monte Carlo Living Room,** at 2nd and South Streets (tel. 215/925-2220), where a pianist plays for touch dancing, a DJ taking over in between sets. It's furnished with brown velvet couches, and has two bars plus a dance floor. Open Monday to Saturday from 9 P.M. to 2 A.M. Jackets required; $10 cover.

Horizons, on the 27th floor of the Franklin Plaza at 16th and Race Streets (tel. 215/448-2901), has popular live entertainment, often a jazz combo that plays modern music and some good oldies for dancing. Nightly from 9 P.M. except Sunday.

Currently the most popular singles spot is **Flannigan's,** Abbotts Square, 2nd and South Streets (tel. 215/928-9898), a huge multilevel place with several bars attracting a young energetic, often suburban crowd. Cover on weekends is $5.

Revival, 22 S. 3rd St. (tel. 215/627-4825), housed in a converted church, mimics New York's Limelight, complete with videos and New Wave sounds.

Cocktail Spots/Piano Bars

On weekends the **16th Street Bar and Grill,** 264 S. 16th St. (tel. 215/735-3316), attracts a young professional crowd. So, too, does **Friday, Saturday, and Sunday,** 261 S. 21st St. (tel. 215/546-4232), especially to its upstairs lounge with a tented ceiling. For a little bit of Ireland and food to match, there's always **Downey's,** at Front and South Streets (tel. 215/629-0526). The **Dickens Inn** also has a good tavern with a dart board.

For more sophisticated atmosphere there are several piano/wine bars around town. **Frög,** 1524 Locust St. (tel. 215/735-8882), **Barclay Hotel Piano Bar** (tel. 215/545-0300), **Café Bar** at the Palace Hotel (tel. 215/963-2244), **DiLullo Centro** (tel. 215/546-2000), **Maxwell's** at the Warwick (tel. 215/545-4655), the bar at the **Society Hill Hotel** (tel. 215/925-1919), and the **Swann Lounge** at the Four Seasons (tel. 215/963-1500).

For a view of the river, have a cocktail on the historic clipper, the *Moshulu* at **Penn's Landing,** at Chestnut Street and Delaware Avenue (tel. 215/925-3237).

Late-Night Dining

After a show at the Annenberg Center, **Smart Alex,** at the Sheraton University City, 36th and Chestnut (tel. 215/386-5556), is open until midnight, or you can go to **La Terrasse,** 3432 Sansom St. (tel. 215/387-3778), which also remains open late precisely to accommodate after-theater guests.

Other late-night dining includes **Downey's** (tel. 215/629-0526), until 1:30 A.M.; the **Borgia Café** (tel. 215/574-0414), until 1 A.M.; and **La Cucina** (tel. 215/925-3042), until midnight.

After discoing at élan you can also fall into the **Brasserie at the Warwick,** which stays open 24 hours. So does **Eagle II,** 227 Broad St. (tel. 215/545-5155), on weekends.

PHILADELPHIA ACTIVITIES

Best source for what's going on is the "Weekend" section of the *Philadelphia Inquirer,* which comes out on Friday, or a publication called *Welcomat,* which can be found in most hotel lobbies and also at the Convention and Visitors Bureau. *Philadelphia* magazine, a monthly, is also useful.

ANTIQUING: Pine Street from 9th to 12th Streets is known locally as Antiques Row.

BICYCLING: Miles of trails in Fairmount Park. Rentals are available at Fairmount Park Bike Rental, One Boat House Row (tel. 215/978-8545), in the park just beyond the art museum from early spring to late fall.

BOATING: Rent a rowboat, sailboat, or canoe at East Park Canoe House, East River Drive, south of the Strawberry Mansion Bridge (tel. 215/225-3560).

FAIRMOUNT PARK ACTIVITIES: The park offers 105 tennis courts, six 18-hole golf courses, five outdoor pools and one indoor, and all kinds of sports fields. There are 25 miles of bikeways, 75 miles of bridle paths, rowing facilities, and a fishing stream stocked with trout each season. Stables at Belmont. For information about the park, call 215/686-2176 and let it ring.

GOLF: Walnut Lane, Walnut Lane and Henry Avenue (tel. 215/482-3370); J. F. Byrne Golf Course, 9500 Leon St. (tel. 215/632-8666); FDR Golf Course, 20th Street and Patterson Avenue (tel. 215/462-8997).

HOT-AIR BALLOONING: Aero Space Balloons, 1917 Rolling Lane, Cherry Hill, NJ 08003 (tel. 609/795-7276), offers early-morning or evening thrills if you tire of city sidewalks. A champagne breakfast or a dinner will be served.

PICNICKING: You have the whole of Fairmount Park for picnicking, and the best place to shop for supplies is at Reading Terminal Market, at 12th and Filbert Streets (tel. 215/922-2317), unless of course, you succumb to the 20 or more food outlets selling everything from Greek souvlaki and falafel to pasta, salads, hoagies, and even raw shellfish. If you stand firm, then you can select prime meats and cheeses, home-baked Pennsylvania Dutch treats, soft pretzels, and Greek pastries. HOURS: Monday to Saturday from 8 A.M. to 6 P.M.

The Market of the Commissary, 130 S. 17th St. (tel. 215/568-8055), is also a great place to pick up everything for a gourmet feast. HOURS: Saturday from 9:30 A.M. to 6:30 P.M., on Sunday until 5:30 P.M.

Saturday is also the best day to visit the Italian market at 9th and Christian Streets, where the canopied stalls purvey everything you could possibly wish for.

RUNNING: Kelly Drive is a popular jogging strip, or you can follow in Rocky's footsteps from Center City along the Parkway and up the art museum steps.

SHOPPING HIGHLIGHTS: There are many in the city. Wanamaker's is a wonderful old store that also has a fantastic organ and a very fine restaurant, if you happen to be shopping there. Several complexes are also interesting.

NewMarket, at 2nd and Pine Streets (tel. 215/627-7500), offers restaurants and shopping on Saturday from 11 A.M. to 9:30 P.M., on Sunday from noon to 6 P.M. Swan's Gallery, 132 S. 18 St. (tel. 215/568-9898), has contemporary American crafts. The Gallery Market, between 8th and 10th Streets, shelters 200 shops under a glass roof in a building landscaped with fountains and greenery. It also includes a Market Fair with 25 international eateries. The Bourse, at 21 S. 5th St. (tel. 215/625-0300), was Philadelphia's first steel building (1893–1895) and served as the nation's commodities exchange until the Depression when it moved to Chicago. Commodities trading was done on the main floor, and brass-and-marble staircases led to the restaurant. Today it's occupied by practitioners of another style of commodities trading—stores like Saint Laurent, Rive Gauche, Cacharel, Crabtree & Evelyn. HOURS: Saturday from 10 A.M. to 9 P.M., on Sunday from noon to 6 P.M.

In South Philly, heart of the city's Italian community, there's an open-air Italian market at Christian Street at which everything from live poultry to toys, fruit, vegetables, fish, cheese, and baked goods is peddled. Cafés and restaurants can be found too. Many great names have emerged from this community —Mario Lanza, Frankie Avalon, Fabian, Bobby Rydell, and of course, most recently, Sylvester Stallone.

SPECTATOR SPORTS: The Philadelphia Eagles play at Veterans Stadium (tel. 215/463-5500). The Philadelphia Flyers play at the Spectrum, Broad Street and Pattison Avenue (tel. 215/336-3600 or 389-5000), and so do the Philadelphia '76ers.

SWIMMING: There are five outdoor pools and one indoor pool in Fairmount Park.

TENNIS: Some 105 courts are scattered throughout Fairmount Park. For park info, call 215/686-1776, ext. 81-221. Pier 30 Tennis Club at Penn's Landing (tel. 215/985-1234).

GREATER WILMINGTON, THE BRANDYWINE VALLEY, & VALLEY FORGE

DISTANCES IN MILES: Wilmington, 121; Valley Forge, 115
ESTIMATED DRIVING TIME: About 2½ hours

DRIVING: For Wilmington, take the New Jersey Turnpike to I-95 to the Delaware Avenue Exit 7. For Valley Forge, take the New Jersey Turnpike to the Pennsylvania Turnpike (I-76) to the Valley Forge exit.
BUS: Trailways (tel. 212/730-7460) goes to Wilmington, King of Prussia, and Valley Forge. Greyhound (tel. 212/635-0800 or toll free 800/528-6055) goes to Wilmington and King of Prussia.
TRAIN: Amtrak (tel. 736-6288) runs to Wilmington. It also goes from Philadelphia to Harrisburg, stopping en route at the small towns of Downingtown and Malvern (both southwest of Valley Forge).

Special Events To Plan Your Trip Around
FEBRUARY: Washington's Birthday Weekend reenactment of the winter of 1777–1778 in Valley Forge Historic Park. Drilling, shooting, and cooking demonstrations, etc. (usually the third weekend).
APRIL: Winterthur in the Spring, Winterthur Museum.
APRIL TO MID-MAY: Blossom time in Valley Forge Park.
MAY: Winterthur Point-to-Point (first Sunday).
Wilmington Garden Day (first Saturday in May).
Devon Horse Show and Country Fair. Contact Devon Horse Show and Country Fair, Rte. 30, Devon, PA 19333 (tel. 215/964-0550), usually the last weekend in May.

A day in Old New Castle, six or so miles south of Wilmington (usually the third Saturday).

JUNE: Festival of the Arts, Longwood Gardens (tel. 215/388-6741), third week in June.

New Castle Day.

JULY: Old-Fashioned Fourth at Rockwood Museum, Wilmington.

AUGUST: Goschenhoppen Folk Festival, authentic noncommercial Pennsylvania Dutch Festival on Rte. 29 in Green Lane (usually the second weekend).

Philadelphia Folk Festival at old Poole Farm, off Rte. 29 in Schwenksville.

SEPTEMBER: Reenactment of the Battle of the Brandywine. Contact Brandywine Battlefield State Park, P.O. Box 202, Chadds Ford, PA 19317 (tel. 215/459-3342).

OCTOBER: Laerenswert, means worth doing. Craftsmen demonstrate and invite audience participation at the Peter Wentz farmstead (usually the second Saturday in October).

Chester County Day in West Chester—historic house tours, hunt and hounds (first Saturday).

DECEMBER: Candlelight tours at Hagley, Winterthur, and Rockwood Museums. Also of Historic Old New Castle.

VALLEY FORGE MUSIC FAIR: Although it operates year round, full billings really begin in March and run through December. For information, contact P.O. Box 917, Devon, PA 19333 (tel. 215/644-5000).

For further information: Greater Wilmington Convention and Visitors Bureau, 1300 Market St., Wilmington, DE 19801 (tel. 302/652-4088, or toll free 800/422-1181); Delaware State Travel Service (tel. toll free 800/441-8846); Chester County Tourist Bureau, 33 W. Market St., West Chester, PA 19380 (tel. 215/431-6365); Valley Forge Country Convention and Visitors Bureau, P.O. Box 311, Norristown, PA 19404 (tel. 215/278-3558 or toll free 800/441-3549, in Pa. 800/458-5600).

Most New Yorkers associate Brandywine with the battle of that name, but few have ever visited this lovely part of the country where the landscape is very much like the English countryside. Its gently rounded hills, big old barns, grazing horses, roadside wildflowers, and the driftwood and willows along the Brandywine River's banks are all on a human scale. Besides its pleasant green landscape, the area is also exceedingly rich in prime attractions—the finest collection of American furniture and decorative arts anywhere is at Winterthur, an outstanding American garden at Longwood, a couple of really fine art museums that display the works of the school of painters inspired by the Brandywine River, a mansion to match any in France at Nemours, and a fascinating museum that captures part of America's early industrial history at Hagley. The Brandywine may be a narrow and short river, but it possesses a great and inspiring tradition.

For a weekender there are a couple of ways to explore the area. You can either go directly to Wilmington and stay at the venerable Hotel duPont, which Craig Claiborne ranks with London's Connaught and New York's Plaza, or you can anchor at Valley Forge, which is only about 45 minutes away from most of the attractions.

WILMINGTON

WILMINGTON ATTRACTIONS

Only a few blocks from the duPont Hotel, the **Market Street Mall** has been constructed around a series of splendid old buildings including a fine 18th-century civic building that now houses the **Old Town Hall,** 500 block of Market Street Mall (tel. 302/655-7161), where you may want to begin to get a fix on Delaware history. Displays of regional decorative arts, children's toys, and changing exhibits highlight aspects of local history. Among its treasures is one of the original chairs given by George Washington to each of the signers of the Declaration of Independence. You'll also see an early American primitive sculpture of George Washington, carved to replace the one of George III that the patriots tore down at Bowling Green, New York, and which Senator T. Coleman duPont found languishing outside a barber's shop. HOURS: Tuesday to Friday from noon to 4 P.M., on Saturday from 10 A.M. to 4 P.M. ADMISSION: Free.

Farther down Market Street at no. 818 stands the Grand Opera House (1871), Delaware's **Center for the Performing Arts,** a magnificent Second Empire–style building with a cast-iron façade resembling chiseled marble. Recently restored to its original Victorian splendor, it now echoes to the applause of audiences enjoying a variety of programs—from Robin Williams and Marcel Marceau, to the London Philharmonic and the Academy of St. Martin in the Fields—just as they did when such figures as Edwin Booth, Buffalo Bill, Ethel Barrymore, and James O'Neill performed here. Every Thursday from 11:30 A.M. to 1:30 P.M. guides conduct mini-tours of the building, on which you can see the magnificent frescoed ceiling and lavish decor. The season runs from September to July. For tickets and information, call 302/658-7897.

In summer you can take a stroll down the pedestrian Market Street Mall, browsing the store windows or stopping for some refreshment at one of the sidewalk cafés.

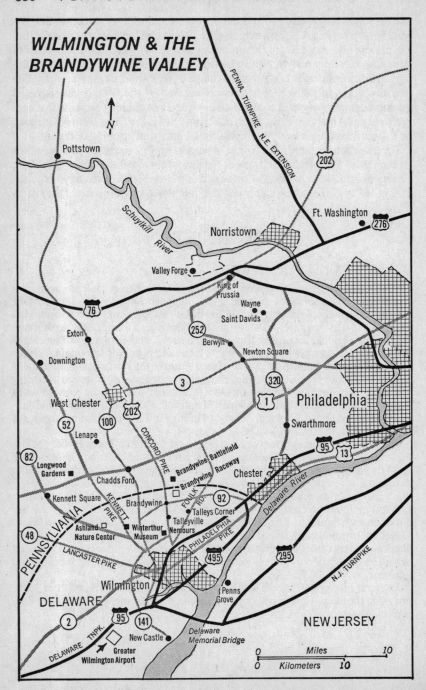

WILMINGTON & THE BRANDYWINE VALLEY

N

Pottstown

PENNA. TURNPIKE N.E. EXTENSION

202

Schuylkill River

Norristown

Ft. Washington
276

Valley Forge

King of Prussia

Wayne

Saint Davids

76

252

Berwyn

Newton Square

Exton

Downington

3

320

1

Philadelphia

West Chester

52   100

202

CONCORD PIKE

Swarthmore

Lenape

95   13

82

Longwood Gardens

Brandywine Battlefield

Brandywine Raceway

Chester

Chadds Ford

Kennett Square

KENNETT PIKE

Brandywine

FOLK RD.

92

Talleys Corner

PENNSYLVANIA

Delaware River

48

Ashland Nature Center

Winterthur Museum

Talleyville

Nemours

PHILADELPHIA PIKE

LANCASTER PIKE

495

295

N.J. TURNPIKE

Wilmington

DELAWARE

Penns Grove

NEW JERSEY

2

95   141

DELAWARE TNPK.

New Castle

Greater Wilmington Airport

Delaware Memorial Bridge

0   Miles   10

0   Kilometers   10

There are several attractions just outside Wilmington. Closest is the **Delaware Art Museum,** 2301 Kentmere Parkway, Wilmington (tel. 302/571-9590 for information, 571-9594 for tour reservations), internationally known for its collection of pre-Raphaelite paintings that hang in a gallery decorated with period wallpaper. The museum also displays the illustrations of pirates, soldiers, and fictional characters depicted by Howard Pyle, father of the Brandywine School of Art, and examples of other fine American artists like John Sloan. The museum was undergoing extensive renovations in 1986 and only one gallery was open, so make sure to call ahead. HOURS: Monday to Saturday from 10 A.M. to 5 P.M.; on Sunday from 1 to 5 P.M.; closed Christmas, Thanksgiving, and January 1. To get there, take I-95 to Wilmington Exit 7 (Rte. 52 north).

Rockwood, 610 Shipley Rd., Wilmington (tel. 302/571-7776), is one of the few American examples of Rural Gothic architecture and the Gardenesque school of landscape design. In the rooms you'll find decorative arts from the 17th century to the mid-19th century, which reflect the lifestyles of the generations of Shipleys who lived here. It is also famous for its collection of overlay glass and archives of photo and wallpaper designs. HOURS: Guided tours of the house are given Tuesday through Saturday from 11 A.M. to 3 P.M.; the gardens can be toured during the same hours.

Named after the French ancestral home of the duPonts, **Nemours** is as close as you'll get to a French château in this country. On this 300-acre country estate, Alfred I. duPont built a 77-room mansion, designed by Carrere and Hastings of New York, where he entertained lavishly. Upon arrival you'll receive a glass of fresh juice, and then you'll be ushered through the house to feast your eyes on the exquisite European art and furnishings. The ornate wrought-iron gates, for example, were commissioned by Henry VIII as a gift for Catherine Parr; another set of gates came from Catherine the Great's palace in St. Petersburg; one of the many clocks was made for Marie Antoinette; there are tapestries, rugs, and paintings, some dating back to the 15th century. The rooms give a wonderful insight into the opulent lifestyle of the family—vintage automobiles, billiard room, the nine-pins alley, a bottling plant, and an ice plant. Throughout the house you'll notice personal items—a fishing trophy taken by Mrs. duPont, for example—and you'll learn about the character of the owner, who had the statuary washed every day and who personally inspected the boiler and heating system. The formal gardens are splendid, some of the finest examples of French-style gardens to be found anywhere in the United States. HOURS: Visitors must take guided tours, which are offered May through November, Tuesday through Saturday at 9 and 11 A.M. and at 1 and 3 P.M., on Sunday at 11 A.M. and 1 and 3 P.M. ADMISSION: $6. Reservations are recommended especially on weekends. Write Nemours Mansion and Gardens, Reservations Office, P.O. Box 109, Wilmington, DE 19899 (tel. 302/651-6912). The mansion is located on Rockland Road between Rtes. 141 and 202, just north of Wilmington across the Brandywine River.

WILMINGTON LODGING

The **Hotel duPont,** 11th and Market Streets (P.O. Box 991, Rodney Square), Wilmington, DE 19899 (tel. 302/656-8121), is a venerable establishment where one immediately feels welcome. It's not grand in an ostentatious way; the luxury comes from attention to details: towels that are changed twice daily; a croissant, coffee, and newspaper delivered to your room in the morning; turndown service; and a chocolate mint on your pillow and similar little touches. Many famous personalities have bedded down here since it opened its doors in 1913—Amelia Earhart, Duke Ellington, Eugene O'Neill, Tallulah Bankhead, Dorothy Gish, and even Paderewski, who angered other guests by playing his piano well into the night.

Even if you don't stay here in one of the 290 large rooms, you might think of attending their justly famous brunch (you'll need reservations), when you can treat yourself to a lavish spread of chicken chasseur, beef tenderloin tips in sherry sauce, seafood Newburgh with scallops, red snapper and shrimp, eggs Benedict, beef hash, cheeses, fresh fruits, and so on. It's served in the formal Green Room, an imposing space with its majestic 18-foot-high Palladian windows draped and valanced in gold fabric and coffered ceiling ornately carved and gilded. Gilt chandeliers and sconces provide the lighting in this beautiful oak-paneled room; there's also a musician's loft. Tables are set with Rosenthal china. At dinner the menu features such items as quails stuffed with goose liver, pork filets with green peppercorns, tournedos Rossini with goose liver and truffles, or lamb and veal dishes, all priced from $15 to $23. The Brandywine Room is richly paneled and enhanced with originals by Howard Pyle and three generations of Wyeths; it's noted for fine beef and seafood.

RATES: From $100, single or double, during the week; from $69.50 double on weekends. Weekend packages are available.

The **Hilton,** I-95 and Naamans Road, Claymont, DE 19703 (tel. 302/792-2700), is on the outskirts of Wilmington (about eight miles, or ten minutes, from downtown) and offers modern rooms with full amenities. The Evergreens restaurant is quite good, serving fresh fish, filet mignon, surf and turf, and other similiar items. There are 86 bedroom/sitting rooms and seven suites. The executive rooms on the seventh floor are spacious, with enough room for desk and couch and coffee table. On the same floor there's a convenient lounge area and plenty of business and other magazines to read. Whispers lounge is crowded, especially on weekends when a DJ spins and folks dance. The hotel has an outdoor kidney-shaped pool.

RATES: $80, single or double. Special weekend prices run $55 double.

The **Radisson Wilmington Hotel,** 700 King St., Customs House Plaza, Wilmington, DE 19801 (tel. 302/655-0400), is located in a modern nine-story building. The 217 rooms are very tastefully furnished and you can either opt for a cabaña room overlooking the tropically landscaped indoor pool or a standard double room. The Hearth Restaurant and indoor pool completes the facilities.

RATES: $82 to $91 single, $97 to $106 double. A weekend package for one night goes for $59, single or double, and there are others available.

The red-brick **Sheraton-Brandywine Inn,** Rte. 202, 4727 Concord Pike, Wilmington, DE 19803 (tel. 302/478-6000, or toll free 800/325-3535), offers 154 accommodations with standard modern furnishings. The hotel also has a restaurant, lounge, outdoor pool, and six outdoor tennis courts. RATES: $89 to $93 single, $94 to $98 double during the week; $60, single or double, on weekends.

There's also a $69.50 per-couple one-night package that includes room, champagne, and dinner.

A Wilmington B & B

Small Wonder Bed & Breakfast, P.O. Box 25254, Wilmington, DE 19899 (tel. 302/764-0789), is a neat and perfectly kept bed-and-breakfast operated by an interesting couple, Art and Dot Brill. Dot is a music teacher and Art is, at least professionally, a psychological counselor in the school system, although more important, he's the one who's responsible for all the lush and healthy plants around the house and the yard and the many gadgets that are scattered around the house. Dot prepares great breakfasts and both love to talk about all kinds of topics. They both put a lot of thought, care, and effort into taking care of guests' needs. For example, in your room you'll find a checklist of breakfast items—waffles, egg dishes, pancakes, scrapple, etc.—for you to leave downstairs on the kitchen table the night before. Baskets of fruit and candy are placed in the rooms. Two homey, comfortable rooms are available with modern furnishings and phone. The backyard is beautifully landscaped with pool and hot tub, umbrella tables, fountain, and lush plants and flowers. Downstairs there's a TV room for guests, that also has a decent library. An additional sitting room houses a piano and fireplace. Breakfast—your choice from pancakes, egg dishes, etc.—is served at the polished Georgian-style table. Definitely a home away from home.

RATES: $40 to $45 single, $50 to $55 double. It's conveniently located about five minutes out of Wilmington, near Bellevue State Park.

WILMINGTON DINING

The **Silk Purse,** 1307 N. Scott St. (tel. 302/654-7666), is considered Wilmington's premier dining spot. Located in an obscure white brick building, it's an elegant and understated background for fine cuisine. The menu changes daily but will offer a variety of dishes—veal in a cream sauce with wild mushrooms, swordfish with lemon sauce and capers, salmon in saffron, or liver with black mustard seeds and a cognac-mustard sauce. Prices range from $18 to $25.

DINNER: Monday to Saturday.

Sal's Place, 603 N. Lincoln St. (tel. 302/652-1200), in the heart of Wilmington's Little Italy, is considered one of the city's top three restaurants. Oddly enough it looks like a typical Italian neighborhood place, and that's what a lot of people think it is when they stray in—until they see the prices and the fare on the menu. It's not exactly veal parmigiana territory. Instead the menu features classics like steak au poivre flambé; duck with green peppercorn sauce; breast of chicken with julienne of smoked ham, wild mushrooms, and pine nuts; Dover sole meunière; and more. Prices range from $15 to $20. To start there's foie gras du Périgord in gelée au Sauternes, or clams casino, or beluga caviar. Decor is typical neighborhood—plain red leatherette seating and undistinguished landscape paintings.

LUNCH: Monday to Friday from 11:30 A.M. to 2 P.M. DINNER: Monday to Saturday from 5:30 to 10 P.M.; closed Sunday.

Carucci, 504 Greenhill Ave., Wawaset Plaza (tel. 302/654-2333), located in a small shopping center is a sleek Italian-style bistro. Black-and-white square tile floors, black Breuer chairs, large bouquets of fresh flowers, and modern lithographs set the scene for consistently good Italian cuisine, priced from $10 to $20. Dishes include chicken cacciatore, shrimp fontina, veal with lemon and herbs, scungilli a la Napoletana, and a variety of pastas—spaghetti with red or white clam sauce, gnocchi with meat sauce, pasta primavera or Alfredo.

LUNCH: Monday to Friday from 11:30 A.M. to 2:30 P.M. DINNER: Monday to Saturday from 5:30 to 10:30 P.M.; closed Sunday.

Dinardo's Seafood, at 4th and Lincoln (tel. 302/656-3685), is a traditional regional favorite for crabs, although ironically they actually come from Louisiana. Still, crabs there are steamed, sautéed, deviled, or imperial. Noncrab fanciers can sample clams and mussels as well as stuffed flounder and barbecue shrimp, priced from $7 to $14. The room is plain—wood tables and Hitchcock chairs—but it's a real Wilmington treat.

HOURS: Monday to Saturday from 11 A.M. to 11:30 P.M., on Sunday from 3 to 9 P.M.

Brunch

The brunch at the **Hotel DuPont,** 11th and Market Streets, is well known. Otherwise, there's another contender for the best brunch in town and that's the **Sheraton Brandywine,** 4727 Concord Pike, Rte. 202, at which $14 purchases an incredible spread of roast beef, fish, chicken, and all kinds of salads, desserts, and more. The selection changes weekly.

Lunch/Brunch and Dinner

Five minutes' drive out of town, **Bellevue-in-the-Park Restaurant,** 911 Philadelphia Pike, Wilmington (tel. 302/798-7666), is located in the gorgeous former Greek Revival mansion of William duPont, Jr., surrounded by parkland. The dining rooms have solid carved-oak paneling, high ceilings, crisply and elegantly set tables, and comb-back Windsor chairs. An antlered trophy hangs above the fireplace in the library dining room. Prime summer gathering place is the semicircular sun porch and outdoor patio, set with wrought-iron chairs and tables with umbrellas. From here you can survey the park and listen to the birds and the dull thud of tennis balls on rackets as you drift back to another era. On Sunday a fine brunch buffet is served here.

At dinner, dishes are classics like filet mignon Henri IV (with an artichoke bottom and béarnaise sauce); filet of sole normande, garnished with mussels, shrimp, oysters, and mushrooms; breast of chicken françoise; lobster Fra Diavolo; or blackened redfish. Prices run $12.25 to $22.75. Each evening you'll find an array of tempting desserts, along with crêpes suzettes and bananas Foster.

LUNCH: Monday to Friday from 11 A.M. to 3 P.M. DINNER: Monday to Saturday from 5 to 10 P.M. BRUNCH: Sunday from 10:30 A.M. to 2:30 P.M.

A TRIP TO NEW CASTLE

NEW CASTLE ATTRACTIONS

Only 15 minutes' drive south of Wilmington lies the historic town of New Castle, a lovely place to visit for a day or just an afternoon. It is in fact one of Delaware's oldest settlements. In 1631 the Dutch had established a fishing settlement named Zwannendael (Valley of Swans) on the site of present-day Lewes. This settlement was destroyed by the Indians and subsequently it was left to Sweden to plant the first settlement at the mouth of the Christina River in 1638. This little colony was later conquered by the Dutch in 1655 and renamed New Amstel, a name that was later changed to New Castle when the English took over.

There's bound to be something going on on the **Green**—an art or craft show, or something similar. Around the Green are some very beautiful historic buildings, all still used and many still fine residences. For example, on the east side of the quadrangle, the **Academy** was built in 1799. Adjacent to it, the oldest part of the **Imanuel Episcopal Church** dates to 1703, although the congregation was established in 1689. It's a handsome building and its graveyard contains many stones dating from the 1700s.

On the north side of the square stand rows of old residences, including the **Old Dutch House** at 32 E. 3rd St. (HOURS: April 1 to November 30, Tuesday to Saturday from 11 A.M. to 4 P.M.; on Sunday from 1 to 4 P.M.). On this side also is the **Old Library Town Museum** at 40 E. 3rd St., an interesting hexagonal structure built in 1892 in which you can research some local history. On the west side there's the **Old Court House.** In May many homes are open to the public (see "Special Events").

As you walk along the brick sidewalks, note the rise and fall of the pathway around the roots of the old trees that line the streets.

At a point not far from the Delaware River, a marker indicates the spot where Penn landed on October 27, 1682.

NEW CASTLE LODGING AND DINING

The **David Finney Inn,** 216 Delaware St., New Castle, DE 19720 (tel. 302/322-6367), is well known for its restaurant and also rents accommodations—rooms with Hitchcock-style beds covered with candlewick spreads and furnished with pine and maple pieces. The dining room is pleasant, tables sporting traditional pewter plates and napkin rings holding rust-colored napkins. Comb-back Windsor chairs provide the seating. Wood and brick accent the adjacent Packet Tavern. The menu offers a variety of continental dishes, among them New York strip steak sautéed with wild mushrooms, red wine, and shallots; veal with lemon shallots and white wine; roasted pork tenderloin with cassis and raspberry glaze; grilled chicken breast with apples, leeks, and Calvados; and sautéed monkfish with capers and lemon. Prices run $12.50 to $17. Appetizers like fettuccine with tomatoes, pasta, and cream; oyster Bienville with shrimp, bacon, mushrooms, and cheddar; a shrimp and crab bisque; or a salad of seasonal greens with baked mozzarella and rosemary vinaigrette, might begin your meal. Luncheon offers soups, salads, and sandwiches, and a selection of choice entrees including crab cakes.

RATES: $65 to $80 double. LUNCH: 11:30 A.M. to 2 P.M. daily. DINNER: Sunday to Thursday from 5:30 to 9 P.M., on Friday and Saturday until 10 P.M. BRUNCH: Sunday from 11:30 A.M. to 2 P.M.

Situated serenely facing the cobblestoned tree-lined street in Old New Castle with its back to the Green is the **New Castle Inn,** on the Town Green at Cobblestone Market Street (tel. 302/328-1798). Here two dining rooms—one decorated in cranberry, the other in Wedgwood blue, both with sparkling white tablecloths and pink napkins and arranged with several pieces of sculpture and other artwork—are lovely spots for some traditional American cuisine. The regional specialties, of course, are the Delaware crab cakes or the crab-stuffed oysters. There's also a catch of the day, a chicken-and-oyster pie, and duck with currant and cumin sauce. Prices run $10.50 to $16. Among the appetizers, try the shrimp Louis, crab cocktail, or stuffed mushrooms. Some folks will want to try the old traditional drinks like grog (rum, water, and sugar, served hot or cold) or the 18th-century favorite, Sangaree (madeira blended with juices of lemon and orange, and a dash of soda).
LUNCH: Daily from 11 A.M. to 2 P.M.; DINNER: Monday to Saturday from 5 to 9 P.M., on Sunday from 3 to 8 P.M.

THE BRANDYWINE RIVER VALLEY

AREA ATTRACTIONS

Farther upriver more of the duPont legacy can be viewed at the 200-acre **Hagley Museum** (tel. 302/658-2401), which borders the Brandywine River three miles northwest of Wilmington, where Éleuthère Irénée duPont established his first powder mills in 1802, after hearing, according to family legend, a retired artillery colonel complain about the inferiority of American gunpowder compared to European. The first mills were simple stamping and rolling operations, where workers blended sulfur, saltpeter, and charcoal into black powder. Water was diverted from the river and channelled through a series of wooden waterwheels, and later turbines provided enough power to turn the massive granite stones that ground the ingredients. Today you can see this very process as the powderman opens the millrace gates and lets the water do its work. In the 1850s steam engines were used, and the museum also has one of these operating. In the main museum building, exhibits trace the change from water to giant, steam-powered industries. At one time, 33 mills stretched along the river (part of 21 of them can be seen today). To minimize the devastation that an unexpected explosion could cause, the mills were designed with an opening over the river to direct a blast away from the duPont home and the workers' cottages on the bluff above. From the powder yards a bus will take you to **Eleutherian Mills,** a handsome Georgian residence built by E. I. duPont in 1803, which has been furnished to reflect the changing tastes of the five generations of duPonts who lived here until 1958—with the exception of the years 1890 to 1923, when a blast drove them out. The modest office building can also be seen, along with the workshop of Lammot duPont, whose discovery of how to make explosives with Peruvian nitrate gave the Union forces superior firepower in the Civil War. The mills became obsolete after World War I and were closed in 1921. HOURS: April to December, 9:30 A.M. to 4:30 P.M. daily; in winter, on weekends from 9:30 A.M. to 4:30 P.M., and one tour daily at 1:30 P.M. ADMISSION: $5 for adults, $2 for children 6 to 14; children under 6, free. Allow three or four hours for a leisurely visit.

Kids always enjoy the **Delaware Museum of Natural History,** Rte. 52, Greenville (tel. 302/658-9111), which has, among many other displays, a renowned shell collection of over 1½ million items and also possesses the egg of an elephant bird, which weighs 27 pounds! Exhibit highlights include a visit to an African waterhole, a walk over the Great Barrier Reef, and an introduction to Delaware fauna. HOURS: Monday to Saturday from 9:30 A.M. to 4:30 P.M., on Sunday from noon to 5 P.M.; closed major holidays.

Winterthur

Antique-lovers, craftsmen, historians, and interior designers will all want to spend a whole day at Winterthur, only six miles north of Wilmington, viewing the phenomenal collection of furniture and decorative arts amassed by Henry Francis duPont, who began collecting in 1923. In his lifetime he acquired a matchless collection of antiques made or used in America between 1640 and 1840. He also went to great lengths to obtain appropriate settings for his collections, combing the eastern seaboard in search of architectural treasures like the Port Royal Parlor from Frankford, Pennsylvania; a drawing room from Richmond County, Virginia; a Commons room from a Delaware inn; and a 17th-century room from Ipswich, Massachusetts. As you go from room to room, you'll find so much to see—outstanding highboys and lowboys made by Townsend and Goddard, silver tankards by Paul Revere, Shaker furniture, a stair hall filled with miniatures, exquisite pie-crust tables, lusterware, glass, and textiles—so much, in fact, that you'll need to return many times to see all of the 196 rooms and display areas. On a first visit you'll only see a fraction of the rooms. You may want to take the 45-minute Two Centuries tour, a trip through 200 years of changing American styles from the 17th century through the Empire period. Or you can take a reserved two-hour personalized tour for a closer look at a selection of room settings. (Unless you're very interested in the subject, you may find this requires too much stamina.) On either tour you can examine and scrutinize what you do see properly. Best time to visit is in the spring, when 16 selected rooms normally seen by reservation only are open without reservation as well as the Two Centuries tour. This is also the time when the gardens are at their best. Another special time is at Christmas, when 21 of the rooms are traditionally decorated.

The whole collection is in the home that duPont occupied until 1951, when he turned it into a public museum. During his lifetime Winterthur was a self-contained, nearly self-sustaining community with turkey and sheep farms, vegetable gardens, greenhouses, golf course, sawmill, railroad station, post office, and a prize-winning herd of Holstein Friesian cattle. In spring, summer, and fall, do tour the gardens, where duPont paid the greatest attention to colors, shapes, and vistas, and achieved a natural-looking English-style garden that combines azaleas, lilacs, daffodils, dogwoods, and many exotic trees and shrubs on 200 beautifully landscaped acres.

If you decide to spend the whole day or arrive around lunchtime for the afternoon, the Pavilion offers fine food in a very pleasantly situated dining room with cafeteria-style service. After your meal, you'll want to stop at the bookstore and plant shop before going down to the Winterthur Gallery, where you can purchase gifts and reproductions. Special events on the grounds include the Winterthur Point-to-Point races, the first Sunday in May.

HOURS: Tuesday to Saturday from 10 A.M. to 4 P.M., on Sunday from noon to 4 P.M.; closed Monday and holidays. ADMISSION: $8 (free for children under 12). Reserved tours are $12.50 and are not offered during spring or at Christmas; for Yuletide at Winterthur you'll need to reserve (November 22 to December 31), $8. For information and reservations, call 302/654-1548 or write Winterthur Museum and Gardens, Winterthur, DE 19735.

Longwood Gardens and Area

Longwood Gardens, Rte. 1, Kennett Square, Pennsylvania (tel. 215/388-6741 for information, 388-6771 for the restaurant). I envy the curator of Longwood Gardens, because he can enjoy the beauty of the gardens in all seasons and all weathers.

The conservatory is breathtaking year around, but the outdoor gardens are in their prime during spring and summer, when they burst forth with magnolias, flowering crab apples, cherries, dogwoods, rhododendrons, wisteria, and thousands of annuals and perennials. The show continues through summer, when the formal Rose Garden blossoms and five acres of fountain gardens in front of the conservatory play, cooling the air with magnificent jets of water (along with the Italian Water Garden fountains), and the other specialty gardens of topiary, vegetables, and wildflowers can be seen to full advantage.

The four-acre conservatory is radiantly filled with the color, scents, and textures of seasonal displays. Spring begins here in January, when cyclamen and narcissus bloom, followed by tulips, crab apples, and acacias in February and magnolias, wisterias, azaleas, freesias, stocks, daffodils, hyacinths, primrose, Easter lilies, velvet-sheened deep-red pocketbook flowers in March (a display that will gladden any winter-wearied heart). November is the time for a fantastic display of 15,000 chrysanthemums, while at Christmas the garden conifers sparkle with 35,000 lights and the conservatory is filled with red, pink, and white poinsettias and red-berried hollies.

Besides the special displays in the main conservatory, you can also view orchids (6,000 plants are cultivated here, 1,200 or so different hybrids or species, and only the best culled for display), centuries-old bonsai, all kinds of exotic tropical plants and cacti, and at the center of all, the lily pond—a true highlight—where lily pads as large as 7½ feet in diameter float along with lilies that vary from tiny, perfect flowers to large orbs of deep purple, magenta, magnolia-pink, and yellow, many of which open even on the dullest of days.

Longwood has other delights too, like the 2,100-seat theater, inspired by the Villa Gori, near Siena, Italy, which is set amid a copse of trees and hosts music, drama, and dance performances during the summer. In place of the traditional curtain a brilliant screen is created by a row of illuminated fountains. After a performance additional fountains in the stage floor rise as high as 50 feet into the trees. Tinted lights shine on the water to create a liquid kaleidoscope.

Another show is also given during the summer. For three nights a week the five acres of fountains in front of the conservatory are illuminated in all colors of the rainbow as they shoot 130 feet into the air, bringing to mind a marvelous inverted Niagara Falls. After the show, visitors are free to wander through the conservatories and admire the exotic night-blooming waterlilies, which are also artfully lighted.

For those who enjoy music, a mammoth pipe organ, whose pipes are housed in nine rooms, is played regularly from October through April. Located in the conservatory ballroom with its wonderful pink-glass ceiling, the instrument boasts 10,010 pipes, some as long as 32 feet, and a full array of percussive devices, including drums, castanets, cymbals, a grand piano, and Chinese gong.

And finally, there's the old **Peirce duPont house,** which is open for tours from April through December. The Longwood property was granted to the Peirces by William Penn in 1700, and it was two Peirce brothers who later laid out an arboretum of ornamental trees. The impending destruction of this arboretum prompted Pierre duPont, great-grandson of founder E.I., to purchase Peirce's Park, as it was called in 1906, and develop it into a horticultural showplace. A tour of the house stresses the history of horticulture, especially in the Delaware Valley, and also displays Peirce and duPont memorabilia. Here in the den Mr. duPont designed much of what you'll see at Longwood today—350 acres tended by a full staff of 180, including over 80 full-time gardeners.

Longwood is frequently open evenings for fountain shows and holiday displays. For a current schedule of events, send a stamped, self-addressed envelope to Schedule, Longwood Gardens, P.O. Box 501, Kennett Square, PA 19348. Longwood also has a very fine restaurant and self-service café. HOURS: Conservatories, daily from 10 A.M. to 5 P.M.; outdoor gardens, from 9 A.M. to 6 P.M., until 5 P.M. in winter. ADMISSION: $5 for adults, $1 for children 6 to 14 (under 6 free).

Mushroom Capital

While you're in the area you really should savor or at least take home some of the local delicacy—mushrooms. Kennett Square is in fact known as the mushroom capital of the world and only half a mile south on Rte. 1 from Longwood Gardens, you can stop at **Phillips Mushroom Place,** 909 E. Baltimore Pike (Rte. 1; tel. 215/ 388-6082), and pick up a basket or baskets of mushrooms. According to the wisdom of the place, you can partially cook and then freeze the mushrooms. You may want to buy them before you go into the museum and discover the growing process to which they have been submitted. The store is also filled with all kinds of mushroomabilia. HOURS: 10 A.M. to 6 P.M. daily.

Chadds Ford

A few miles east along Rte. 1 and you'll come to Chadds Ford, heart of the Brandywine Valley and home of the famous **Brandywine Museum** (tel. 215/459-1900), an old grist mill that has been artfully converted into a museum displaying the works of the region's most famous artists—the Wyeths. Around the mill the architect has wrapped several brick terraces and also added a dramatic tower of glass that gives views over the creek and surrounding pastoral scenery. The galleries with plaster walls and hand-hewn beams seem appropriate to the exhibited art, which is firmly rooted in a sense of place. On the second floor the works of three generations of Wyeths are displayed—N.C., illustrator of *Kidnapped* and *Treasure Island;* Andrew; and Jamie. On the first floor, there's a gallery devoted to the Brandywine River and its artists, including Howard Pyle, father of them all, along with Horace Pippin, W. T. Smedley, Frank Schoonover, and Maxfield Parrish. The third floor is usually reserved for changing exhibitions. HOURS: 9:30 A.M. to 4:30 P.M. daily. ADMISSION: $1.75 for adults, $1 for children. Special events —craft fairs and farmers markets—are often staged in the stone-cobbled courtyard.

Just east of Chadds Ford, **Brandywine Battlefield State Park,** Rte. 1 (tel. 215/ 459-3342), makes a lovely setting for a picnic. Great rounded hills, decked with sturdy old trees, overlook a brook that runs down toward a fieldstone Georgian-style church, whose weathered gravestones stand silently brooding. Although the Battle of Brandywine was fought in the parish of the church, it remained neutral, and no soldier is buried here from either side. Dioramas and audio-visual presentations in the visitor center tell the story of the battle on September 11, 1777, while Washington's headquarters and the Marquis de Lafayette's quarters show life during the Revolutionary War.

At the junction of Rtes. 1 and 100, behind the Chadds Ford Inn, the **Christian Sanderson Museum** grants an intimate look at a community. There are paintings and sketches from every member of the Wyeth family, including the earliest-known painting made by Andrew Wyeth at the age of ten. A close friend of the Wyeth family, Sanderson also happened to collect everything that passed into his hands. He even kept the notes that people wrote on the pad he provided at his door. Here you'll see it all—valentines, autographs, rocks, and more.

BRANDYWINE AREA LODGING AND DINING

The **Fairville Inn,** Rte. 52 (Kennett Pike; P.O. Box 219), Mendenhall, PA 19357 (tel. 215/388-5900), has been completely restored by Ole Retler, an experienced Scandinavian-born Vermont innkeeper, and his wife, Patricia. There are 13 rooms, including two suites, all with private bath, TV, telephone, and individually controlled heat and air. Five have fireplaces. Although they have an obvious newness and are furnished with antique reproductions, the accommodations are attractive. All the cut-out lampshades were made by Patricia; sidetables are classic drop-leaf. Some rooms have canopy beds; washbasins are separate from the bathroom; carpeting is wall to wall. Carriage House rooms are set well back from the road and have small decks overlooking a bucolic scene. A light continental breakfast is served in the main dining room between 7 and 10 A.M. There's also the sitting room with a couple of sofas placed in front of a white brick fireplace with a large copper coffee table in between.

RATES: $75 to $125 double.

Just down Rte. 52 not far from Winterthur, the **Mendenhall Inn,** Kennett Pike (tel. 215/388-1181), offers motel-style rooms and a couple of dining rooms. The front lobby is traditionally furnished and the place has a cozy ambience. In the two large dining rooms a variety of continental, seafood, and steak dishes is available. Prices range from $12 to $23.

LUNCH: Tuesday to Saturday from 11:30 A.M. to 2 P.M. DINNER: Tuesday to Thursday from 5 to 10 P.M., on Friday and Saturday until midnight, on Sunday from 3 to 9 P.M.

Sweetwater Farm, Box 86, Sweetwater Road, Glen Mills, PA 19342 (tel. 215/459-4711), has to be one of the most idyllic inns that I've ever visited. Linda Kaat runs the 55-acre farm, tending the sheep, dying the wool, boarding horses, and keeping several acres of flowers which she dries and makes into vibrantly colored wreaths. She relishes the rhythms and tasks of farm life and the sense of self sufficiency that it sustains. The large stone farmhouse contains nine rooms, six with private bath and several with fireplaces. Each is exquisite. The Lafayette Room, complete with working fireplace features a four-poster with brown gingham canopy and a variety of antique furnishings—demi-lune table, comb-back Windsor, cherry side table and a blanket chest on which magazines are displayed. Personal touches are found in every room. All the quilts throughout the house were made by Linda's grandmother; the wall stenciling and the dried flower arrangements and wreaths are created by Linda herself. The Garden Room and the Dormer Room are located in the oldest part of the house where the ceilings are lower. They, too, are furnished with four posters and colonial style pieces. The third-floor attic rooms have sloping ceilings, stucco walls, and often Palladian windows and window seats or fan lights. On the ground floor, several rooms are open to guests: the sitting room in which they can gather to talk, read, or watch TV; the winter room complete with spinning wheel and wool from Linda's flock; the formal Queen Anne dining room; and most popular of all the warm country kitchen in which breakfast—egg dishes, pancakes, sausage and bacon supplemented with fresh fruit and home baked items—is served at a harvest table surrounded by rush seated chairs. The beams are hung with wicker baskets and in winter a fire blazes in the brick hearth. From the back porch furnished with wicker chairs you can look out across the lawn to a well-landscaped pool and cornfields and sheep-filled meadows beyond. A truly special place.

RATES: $110 to $125.

Crier in the Country, Rte. 1 (Baltimore Pike), Glen Mills, PA 19342 (tel. 215/358-2411), is primarily known for its dining rooms. The building was originally constructed in 1740 and added to between 1820 and 1830. The high-ceilinged rooms are ornate. The Powel Room, set with Queen Anne chairs, has a molded gilt ceiling and chandelier. Above the fireplace in the Chamberlain Room hangs an ormolu mirror while around the room portraits and landscapes hang from picture rails. The polished wood tables are set with lace placemats and burgundy napkins. The menu lists classic continental favorites: crab imperial, lobster Fra Diavolo, cioppino, veal française or fontina, and duck à l'orange, along with steaks and chops. Prices run $16 to $20. Tucked away in the back is a small tavern room with a cozy brick fireplace; there's also a deck out back for summer lounging.

In a long, low adjacent building there are also eight rooms. Although from the exterior you might expect an upgraded motel accommodation the rooms are in fact surprisingly attractive, furnished with a four-poster with eyelet lace canopy, Eastlake-style chairs, and snug rose drapes. One very large room has a fireplace and kitchenette. Another room has a Windsor chair and drop-leaf desk among its furnishings. All are air-conditioned and have TVs and telephones.

RATES (including continental breakfast): $65 double. DINNER: Daily from 5 P.M.

Pace One, Thornton Road (off Rte. 1), Thornton, PA 19373 (tel. 215/459-3702), is a cozy restaurant located in a 250-year-old converted barn with hand-hewn beams, Shaker-style tin lanterns, and Brandywine scenes adorning the walls. A meal might begin with some samples from the soup cart, barbecued ribs, or stuffed shrimp with horseradish wrapped in bacon. Follow with a selection from such specialties as duck in sweet-and-sour sauce (with green peppers, pineapple, and tomato), veal tenderloin with crabmeat filling and hollandaise, or scallops baked in mayo mustard, horseradish, and bacon sauce. To finish there's chocolate fudge cake, pecan pie, and chocolate fondue. Prices run $13.50 to $17.50. Brunch offers soup, and such dishes as broccoli, tomato, and ham rarebit; fresh fish marinated in soy, citrus, and parsley; and broiled veal tenderloin stuffed with crabmeat and other egg dishes, priced from $5 to $13.50.

There are also six rooms, all with oak floors, rag rugs, chests, stoneware lamps, country wreaths, tattersall coverlets, and wrought-iron floor lamps. All have private bath.

RATES: $55 to $65 double. LUNCH: Monday to Friday from 11:30 A.M. to 2 P.M. DINNER: Tuesday to Saturday from 5:30 to 10 P.M., on Sunday from 5 to 9 P.M. BRUNCH: Sunday from 10:30 A.M. to 2:30 P.M.

BRANDYWINE AREA DINING

The most comfortable place I know of in the area is the **Chadds Ford Inn,** at Rtes. 1 and 100 (tel. 215/388-7361), where you may well come across one of the members of the Wyeth family in the back tavern. You'll certainly encounter their work in each of the cozy low-ceilinged dining rooms, either placed between the deep-set windows or above the wainscoting of this old 1703 building, which has served as a tavern since 1736. Butterfly Windsor chairs and pink-and-brown napery complete the comfortable ambience. The food is fine; there are usually several specials available—braised quail, stuffed salmon en croûte, veal chop with shiitake mushrooms—or you can select from the menu, which features such dishes as shrimp Créole or sautéed chicken with almonds. Prices begin at $12. By the way, the tavernkeeper entertained the Americans before the Battle of Brandywine and must have been in the direct line of fire, before the British swarmed into the village.

LUNCH: Monday to Saturday from 11:30 A.M. to 2 P.M. DINNER: Monday to Thursday from 5:30 to 10 P.M., on Friday and Saturday from 5 to 10:30 P.M., on Sunday from 3 to 8 P.M.

Buckley's Tavern, 5812 Kennett Pike (Rte. 52), Centreville (tel. 302/656-9776), is grander than it sounds. Oriental carpets cover the wide-plank floors, molded panels, and Queen Anne chairs give an elegant atmosphere to the dining room. Here, creative multinational cuisine is served. For example, you might choose chicken with mint, a boneless breast stuffed with a mint pesto with pine nuts and garlic, grilled pork chops topped with a mild jalapeño marmalade, salmon with cucumber salad, Pennsylvania duck breast served on a bed of greens and wild mushrooms in a lemon-herb vinagrette, or blackened fish or sole with caviar. Prices run $12.75 to $17. Appetizers are equally mouthwatering—scallops brochette (grilled sea scallops wrapped in bacon and served with horseradish hollandaise), Thai beef salad (thinly sliced grilled beef served on watercress and rice vermicelli in a spicy Thai dressing) being only two examples. Brunch also offers a varied menu: from cheeseburgers to seafood salad and eggs Benedict, priced from $4.50 to $7.50.

LUNCH: 11:30 A.M. to 2:30 P.M. daily. DINNER: 5 to 9 P.M. daily. BRUNCH: Sunday from 11:30 A.M. to 2:30 P.M.

Appearances at the **Lenape Inn,** Rtes. 52 and 100, south of West Chester and convenient to Longwood Gardens (tel. 215/793-2005), are deceptive. Yes, it's large. Yes, the people crowd in. Yes, you'd expect the food to be average—but it's not because owner Michael Person keeps a close watch on the quality of the meats he serves, what the cattle are fed, and so on. As a result the filet mignon that my dinner partner sampled literally melted in the mouth. The rack of lamb was of equally high quality. On Sunday a raw bar at the front displays oysters, clams, and shrimp. Among the other entrees you might find duckling à la normande, filet of sole Pontchartrain (topped with lump crabmeat and a white-wine sauce), or veal medallions au vermouth in a light cream sauce with mushrooms and basil. Prices run $12.75 to $19.75. For dessert I can highly recommend the Linzertorte with Chambord sauce, served hot. Plenty of other divine choices too. The dining rooms have high cathedral ceilings and overlook the grassy banks of the Brandywine River. A resident gaggle of ducks parade by regularly on the grass, under what has to be one of the most perfectly shaped fir trees you could ever wish to see.

LUNCH: 11:30 A.M. to 3 P.M. daily. DINNER: Monday to Saturday from 4:30 to 10:30 P.M., on Sunday from 3 to 9 P.M.

For fancy dining there's the **Dilworthtown Inn,** Old Wilmington Pike, Dilworthtown, near West Chester (tel. 215/399-1390). You'll find it down a little country road off Rte. 202. The stone-and-brick inn, which functioned as a tavern in 1758, has been carefully restored to its original decor, even down to the wall stenciling. The rooms and the tavern with a large fireplace have been simply furnished with early American art and furniture. The food is less simple. Start with a shrimp bisque flavored with Armagnac and follow with a filet mignon béarnaise, chateaubriand, or lobster or shrimp provençale. Prices begin at $13.

DINNER: Monday to Saturday from 5:30 to 10:30 P.M., on Sunday from 3 to 9 P.M.

A Note on Dilworthtown: Adjacent to the restaurant, there's a **Dilworthtown Country Store** complete with foot-worn porch and several rooms filled with pie chests, hutches, antiques, craft items, and Pennsylvania Dutch quilts. More shops are located in a restored building across the street. Also across the street, Arden Forge's Peter Renzetti will duplicate any antique or design in wood, pewter, cast or forge-welded iron.

The **Marshalton Inn,** 1300 W. Strasburg Rd., Marshalton (tel. 215/692-4367), is a Federal landmark on Rte. 162, where the cuisine is American/continental. There's always a fish of the day on the menu, along with perhaps baked stuffed oysters and assorted dishes on the order of rack of lamb Dijon, roast duckling à l'orange, all priced from $14 to $19. Among the desserts you might find a chocolate-chip cheesecake, Black Forest cake, or a raspberry torte, depending on the chef's whim and the season.

LUNCH: Tuesday to Friday from 11:30 A.M. to 2 P.M. DINNER: Tuesday to Saturday from 5:30 to 10 P.M., on Sunday from 4 to 9 P.M. BRUNCH: Sunday from 11 A.M. to 3 P.M.

LODGING AND DINING CHOICES EN ROUTE TO VALLEY FORGE

The **Duling Kurtz House and Country Inn,** 146 S. Whitford Rd., Exton, PA 19341 (tel. 215/524-1830), is a very romantic place to dine. The lodgings are also quite lovely, but let's begin with the restaurant. For $25 a night you can even rent the Duling Kurtz Room, which affords you the privacy of a table with closed curtain set in a bay window overlooking the gardens. If you rent this particular room, at the end of your meal you can take the silver napkin rings as a memento of your evening together! There are seven dining rooms, the tables all beautifully set with crystal, Grasse china, and crystal knife rests. Here's a rundown of the various ambiences: an enclosed porch overlooking the formal gardens; a beamed tavern with huge fireplace, rush-seated gatebacks, and a few wicker and rush objects hanging from the beams; fey Aunt Lena's Parlor, named after a legendary local woman with enough dramatic flair to play the musical saw in St. Peter's and decorated with her hats and dashing dresses; a formal Chippendale-furnished Hunt Room; plus several upstairs rooms, including the veranda that offers a beautiful view of sunsets over pastureland. Start with carpaccio, duck liver pâté, or chilled poached salmon, and follow with any one of a dozen continentally inspired dishes like brook trout amandine, poached salmon with dill hollandaise, pheasant in a red-wine marinade served with hazelnut sauce, roast duck with ginger and papaya, tenderloin of pork Calvados, or steak au poivre. Prices range from $15 to $20.

Adjacent to the restaurant, the inn contains 15 rooms, all prettily turned out. The Lincoln Suite, for example, has twin canopy beds with eyelet lace linens, attractive fabric shutters, Oriental carpet, and a small sitting room. The Booker T. Washington Room has a tiny porch, bold chintz wallpaper, marble-top sink, a couple of armchairs, and a chest with TV atop among its comforts.

RATES: $80 to $120 double. LUNCH: Monday to Friday from 11:30 A.M. to 2 P.M. DINNER: Monday to Saturday from 5:30 to 10 P.M. Closed Sunday.

Tucked away on Gordon Drive just off Rte. 100 in Lionville, the **Vickers Tavern** (tel. 215/363-6336 or 363-7998), offers fine food in a series of five modest-size dining rooms. Among its unique attractions is the working potter whose wheel spins just inside the entrance to the door and who crafted the sugar bowls, ashtrays, and candleholders that grace the tables. This continues a tradition that dates back to 1823 when John Vickers established his pottery business here in Lionville. Each of the dining rooms is warmly country, lit by carriage lamps and

Shaker-style tin chandeliers. In one a high beamed ceiling combined with brick and barnboard, comb-back Windsor chairs, a few landscapes, and farm implements evoke the atmosphere. Elsewhere bold chintz and matching valances set the mood. A meal will begin with a selection from the cold hors d'oeuvre tray —hearts of palm, shrimp cocktail, goose pâté, for example. Hot hors d'oeuvres are listed on the menu. Specialties are typically continental/American: beef Wellington, tournedos Rossini, sole meunière, or trout in capers, lemon, and butter. Close with one of the fine desserts—almond tart, napoleon, strawberry tart, or chocolate mousse. Entrees are priced from $15.25 to $21.

LUNCH: Monday to Friday from 11:30 A.M. to 2:30 P.M. DINNER: Tuesday to Thursday from 6 to 9:30 P.M., on Friday and Saturday until 11 P.M.

The **General Warren Inne**, Old Lancaster Hwy., Malvern (tel. 215/296-3637), offers primarily steaks, seafood, veal, and poultry cooked in continental styles, served in a warm colonial atmosphere, and priced from $14 to $27.

LUNCH: Monday to Friday from 11:30 A.M. to 3 P.M. DINNER: Monday to Saturday from 5 to 10:30 P.M.

WILMINGTON-BRANDYWINE VALLEY ACTIVITIES

CANOEING: Northbrook Canoe Company, 1810 Beagle Rd., West Chester (tel. 215/793-2279) offers short one-hour trips to full day trips on the Brandywine River.

STATE PARKS: The 273-acre Bellevue State Park, Philadelphia Pike, North Wilmington, was last owned by William B. duPont, Jr., and his wife, Margaret Osborne. She was crazy about tennis (a former Wimbledon contender) and he was nuts about horses, and as a consequence today the park is blessed with outdoor and indoor tennis courts and an equestrian center. Call the Tennis Center at 302/798-6686) for details. At the equestrian center, unfortunately, your chances of landing a lesson on weekends are slim, and since most of the horses are privately owned and boarded here, no trail rides are given. For information, write 800 Carr Rd., Wilmington, DE 19809. You can also picnic, hike, and fish here too.

Brandywine Creek State Park offers 430 acres of rolling meadows and woodlands that run down to the river. The Nature Center sponsors interpretive programs and you can also picnic and fish. For info, write to P.O. Box 3782, Wilmington, DE 19807.

VALLEY FORGE

The historic park at Valley Forge is now surrounded by a medley of highways, shopping centers, and other suburban elements, a far cry from the time when you could look down across the hills and along the river to Philadelphia, as did the Continental troops while they waited through the winter of 1777–1778. They were watching for the British who were cavorting in Philadelphia only 18 miles downriver. Although the suburban development is dense, there are still some places to visit from Valley Forge besides the Brandywine Valley, which I've already discussed. But first, the park.

VALLEY FORGE HISTORIC PARK

"I lay there two nights and one day and had not a morsel of anything to eat all the time save half of a small pumpkin cooked by . . . making a fire on it." So wrote Private Joseph Martin in the winter of 1777. He was just one of the 11,000 who retreated here on December 19, after their defeat at Brandywine and a draw at Germantown—a raggle-taggle army that Gen. Anthony Wayne described as "sick and crawling with vermin" in March 1778. The winter brought its cruelest. Deep snow caused food shortages and starvation. Over 3,000 died, and according to British reports, another 1,150 deserted. Hundreds of horses starved to death. Yet by June that same pathetic army was well drilled and ready to fight, and they marched out of Valley Forge on June 19, 1778, having won a victory of will and survival.

These are some of the facts that can be gleaned from a visit to the Visitors Center of this 2,800-acre park, which houses various displays, including Washington's original battlefield tent. The facts will help you imagine the scene as you drive past the log cabin replicas, where 12 men were housed in a 10- by 12-foot space during that long cold winter. From mid-April to October you can take a regular bus tour through the park or else a self-guided tour past the monument to the soldiers who died in the Revolution, down to the three-bedroom house that probably quartered 25 to 30 people, including Martha Washington, who provided food and shelter aided by two or three servants. As you look at the rooms, you can imagine the inhabitants dining, playing cards, smoking, planning strategies, whiling away the time before setting up their bunks in the rooms upstairs. Stop by the Washington Memorial Chapel, parish of David Eisenhower and Julie Nixon, and hear the 58-bell carillon which rings regular recitals.

Besides the historic associations of the park, it's a wonderful place to visit any time of year, but especially in spring from late April to mid-May when 50,000 dogwoods bloom. In summer it's filled with people picnicking, kiting, biking, throwing Frisbees, and sunbathing on the rolling hills or down along the creek. Fall is magnificent, while winter can bring the most enthralling sight when snow carpets the ground and the ghosts of those soldiers tread softly, always looking down toward Philadelphia. The big event here is Washington's Birthday. The park is located at the junctions of North Gulph Road and Rte. 23 (tel. 215/783-7700).

OTHER NEARBY ATTRACTIONS

Closest to Valley Forge is Mill Grove, Pawlings Road, in neighboring Audubon (tel. 215/666-5593), where you'll find the home that **John James Audubon** first occupied when he left France in 1803 at age 18. It may seem rather large and lavish for a boy, and in fact it belonged to his father. Audubon came to board with his father's tenants. Here in several rooms you can admire the details of specimens that nature makes so beautifully—the lines on the sunset clam that radiate as if from the setting sun; the polished iridescent interior of a simple mussel shell; or any number of shells, butterflies, and of course, birds. There's a whole case of stuffed owls, worthy characters all, from the charming long-eared specimen to the tiny saw whet and the awesome snowy owl. Besides the prints and watercolors from *The Birds of America,* examine the birds' nests and note the exquisite delicacy and dexterity that the swift exhibits in selecting, gathering, and glueing together with saliva the twigs for its nest. Early pictures and portraits of Audubon capture the young man who spent his days here happily "roaming the frontier seeking new birds and animals." Audubon began the first banding of birds, and he hit upon a method of wiring animals or birds into lifelike positions and then painting them. You'll also discover, if you didn't already know, that Audubon had been born illegitimately in Haiti but had been taken home to France and raised in the Loire Valley. From the house you can explore the nature trails, along which 175 species of birds have been identified. It's especially beautiful here at apple blossom time and in the fall. HOURS: Tuesday to Sunday from 10 A.M. to 5 P.M.

From the park, it's only a short ride up Rte. 363 to the **Peter Wentz Farmstead,** in Worcester (tel. 215/584-5104), fascinating not only for Washington's visit before and after the Battle of Germantown, but also for the ways restorers accomplished their detective work in uncovering the secrets of the house's construction and history. Built in 1758 in a Georgian style, the house has certain Germanic details—the blessing carved into the external wall in German dialect, the beehive bake oven, and the fireplate stove in the dining room. The house has been furnished with period pieces and restored to the way it looked in 1777. The staircase was reconstructed and the nails were placed in the same holes, which were still visible. The Washington Room, where the general planned the Battle of Germantown, still retains some of the original red milk paint, while in many places the original sponge painting and stenciling can be seen. What will probably surprise visitors most are the vibrant colors—blue, yellow, and salmon—which are, in fact, as they would have appeared in the 18th century. The summer kitchen is used for cooking demonstrations, and the surrounding gardens of seasonal herbs and vegetables, including flax, give some insight into the colonists' lives. On summer Saturday afternoons the public is invited to participate in the craft program —weaving, woodcarving, fireplace cooking, fraktur painting, etc. HOURS: Tuesday to Saturday from 10 A.M. to 4 P.M., on Sunday from 1 to 4 P.M.; closed Monday. Take Rte. 363 north to Rte. 73, the Skippack Pike, and turn right.

If you turn left on Rte. 73, you'll come to the country town of Skippack. En route you'll pass the **Ironmaster's Shop,** Art Smithy, in Worcester (tel. 215/584-4441), where people love to stop and hear what Harry Haupt has to say about the world in general and, more specifically, about blacksmithing and iron forging. Harry's one of those rare human beings who has the capacity to inspire, teach, amuse, and stimulate some thought. Crammed into his back garage is an amazing collection of assorted iron objects—toys, mechanical banks, trains, stoves, cars, fireplates, a 1915 Wurlitzer automatic piano, wagons, a hand organ—and to each is attached a story, which Harry will sometimes relate. From here he'll lead you into his workshop, where he forges and casts articles after old designs. Then he'll take you into a room containing all kinds of blacksmithing equipment

—numerous lathes, planes, hammers, anvils, bellows, and a unique spade with a pick-axe blade fashioned by a creative individual who had tired of stopping to pick up his axe every time he needed to break rocks on his soil and so combined the two into one. He left it to Harry upon his death. Harry will pepper his conversation with anecdotes, philosophical commentary, and exhortations for more individuality and less conformity. He'll discourse on why there are seven nails in a horseshoe, explain the symbolism of the four-season dishes and probably jolt you, if you're over 30, with something like "Time is love. You mustn't kill time. Time is the most precious gift you have." After an encounter with Harry, most people leave feeling a little better about the world. Lamps, lanterns, trivets, and toys are available in the shop in his home. HOURS: Call ahead and make an appointment for between 1 and 5 P.M. or 7 and 9 P.M., except on Monday and Wednesday. Or else you can see Harry at the Kutztown Folk Festival, held annually on the July 4 weekend.

In Skippack, stop at **Cedars Country Shoppes.** Among the items not for sale in the core store are the pot-belly stove and the old front porch, but candy, cooking utensils, and craft items are.

VALLEY FORGE LODGING

The **Sheraton,** Valley Forge, North Gulph Road and First Avenue, King of Prussia, PA 19406 (tel. 215/337-2000, or toll free 800/325-3535), is the most lively property in the area. Scintillations Night Club throbs every night, jam-packed on weekends to its 750-person capacity. Lilly Langtry's (tel. 215/337-LILY), always features a Las Vegas–style revue-spectacular with singing and dancing. You can enjoy a meal before the show. The atmosphere is wonderfully gaudy—plenty of red velvet, brass, painted skylights, and waitresses scantily clad in black corsets and lace. Hotel restaurants include Chumley's for gourmet dining, the Sunflower coffeeshop, and Junior's Deli. Sunday brunch in Lilly Langtry's (from 10 A.M. to 2 P.M.) will provide an all-you-can-eat buffet, loaded with everything from meatballs to omelets and other egg dishes, waffles, and pancakes. Price $10. Latest additions to the 266 large modern rooms are 60 exciting themed suites, just made for an exotic weekend experience and the 160-room Park Tower. Each expresses a different fantasy—Tahitian, Egyptian, Victorian, Park Avenue, and the Gym, a suite that actually contains exercise machines. In the Sculptura Suite everything is indeed sculptured and circular, from the hydraulic bed that cranks down from the ceiling to the Jacuzzi bathtub. All of these suites contain a loft with a small TV and telephone, plus a downstairs area with color TV, a Murphy or hydraulic bed that descends from the ceiling, a stereo system, wet bar, and exotic hot tubs or Jacuzzis in the bathrooms. They're really fun, and you just might be lucky enough to obtain one on a weekend. Other hotel facilities include an outdoor pool and health club.

RATES: $100 to $110 single, $105 to $120 double; $128.50 per couple for a room for one night, champagne, $30 credit to use in Lilly's, and breakfast or brunch.

A stylish and quieter atmosphere can be found at the **Stouffer Valley Forge Hotel,** 480 N. Gulph Rd., King of Prussia, PA 19406 (tel. 215/337-1800, or toll free 800/468-3571). The 290 rooms are large and handsomely furnished. Every room has a balcony overlooking either the pool or the golf course. All rooms have clock, full-length mirrors with high-intensity light, skirt hangers, and bathroom amenities like shampoo, soap, and mouthwash. Complimentary newspapers are delivered to rooms. Rooms either have two reclining chairs or a love seat and recliner; HBO and CNN is complimentary. Furnishings are rattan, although the hotel has plans to redecorate. On the fourth-floor club level a concierge is on duty from 6 A.M. to 11 P.M., and there's also a pleasant sitting room with TV. Rooms here also have more amenities—bathrobes, turndown service, complimentary hors d'oeuvres, and continental breakfast, plus a nightcap at night. The Copper Mill restaurant offers steak, seafood, and veal dishes along with breakfast and lunch in an elegant contemporary atmosphere. Justin's features nightly entertainment, or you can have a cocktail at the comfortable lobby bar. Sports facilities include a landscaped, outdoor, kidney-shaped pool, two tennis courts, and a Nautilus room.

RATES: $125 to $135 double. Special weekend packages available.

Located about four miles down Rte. 202 South, the Embassy Suites Hotel, 888 Chesterbrook Blvd., Wayne, PA 19087 (tel. 215/647-6700), is located in a brand-new red-brick building possessing a double atrium. All 230 rooms are suites and they're set around one of the atriums. Each has a small sitting room, decorated with dusky-rose carpeting, couch, table and chairs, phone, and remote control TV in a cabinet. The bedroom is separated from the living room by the bathroom and small open kitchen that has fridge and sink. The faux-marble bathroom contains all the usual amenities. Another TV and telephone are located in the bedroom, which also has desk, clock-radio, gray comforter, and peony-fabric headboard. The room rate includes a daily 5 to 7 P.M. cocktail reception and a full buffet breakfast.

Green-and-white-check decor predominates in the Ambassador Grill where the menu offers the latest cuisine—like blackened redfish, cioppino, twin filet of buffalo, along with veal chops. Prices run $13 to $23.50. A couple of lobby lounges, a pool with an outdoor terrace, and an exercise room with a rowing machine and Nautilus equipment complete the facilities.

RATES: (including full breakfast): $120 single, $130 double. Weekend package available.

Other Valley Forge choices include the **Holiday Inn,** 260 Goddard Blvd., King of Prussia, PA 19406 (tel. 215/265-7500, or toll free 800/238-8000); and **Howard Johnson's,** Rte. 202, at South Gulph Road, King of Prussia, PA 19406 (tel. 215/265-4500, or toll free 800/654-2000).

For budget accommodations, try the **Budget Lodge,** 815 DeKalb Pike, King of Prussia, PA 19406 (tel. 215/265-7200), where doubles go for $44.

LODGING IN THE VALLEY FORGE AREA

The **Joseph Ambler Inn,** 1005 Horsham Rd., Montgomeryville, North Wales, PA 19454 (tel. 215/362-7500), about 30 minutes from Valley Forge and 20 minutes from New Hope, is a charming old stone farmhouse with shutters set on 13 acres of lush woodland and pasture. Originally built in 1734, it was added to in 1820 and 1929. The small parlor to the left of the entrance is original to the house and here you'll find books and games, while the large sitting room to the right with the stone hearth is a reproduction built in 1929. Rich and Judy Allman are the owners and Terry and Steve Kratz are the managers.

The 15 rooms, each with private bath, are furnished attractively with antique reproductions. The Ambler Room, for example, has an Empire-style bed with Marseilles coverlet, reproduction candlestand, and marble-top dresser. It's fully equipped with TV, telephone, and air conditioning. The six-on-six windows are hung with blue chintz curtains, and the floor is covered with Oriental area rugs. The Penn Room, in the original part of the house, has a sloping ceiling, a double-poster with a Marseilles coverlet, swagged burgundy drapes, and a love seat among its furnishings. The Roberts Room has a full canopy, couch, and TV. Third-floor rooms are smaller, but very appealing with their sloping ceilings. The cranberry-colored cottage rooms in adjacent buildings are smaller but decorated with four-posters with fish-net canopy, stenciled walls, wing chair, and candle-stand.

A full breakfast, selected from a menu of eggs, omelets, french toast, and pancakes, along with fresh fruit, is served on cherry tables in the early American dining room with its wide-plank floors. The old stone bank barn built in 1820 is being renovated into a restaurant, which will have opened by the time you read this.

RATES: $84 to $140 double, the higher prices for suites.

VALLEY FORGE AREA DINING

The **Baron's Inn,** 499 N. Gulph Rd., King of Prussia (tel. 215/265-2550), may not look much from the outside, but inside, the dining rooms have a plush European air and cuisine to match. The proprietor is an Austrian, and while some of the dishes, particularly the desserts, reflect that background, the food is really continental/American with a dash of nouvelle. Specialties include geschnetzeltes Zuricher (veal in a light cream sauce with fresh mushrooms glazed with white wine and served on potato pancakes), schwein filet (pork filets garnished with gorgonzola and tomato coulis), filet mignon Camargue en chemise with Brie, duxelles of mushrooms, and fines herbes, and a spectacular crabmeat soufflé. The bouillabaisse is also a popular dish. Prices run $13.50 to $17.50. Start your meal with a potpourri of three soups, scallop and salmon terrine, or steak tartare, and finish with delicious Sachertorte, poached pear, or chocolate decadence. All three of the dining rooms are atmospheric. The main Von Steuben Room has gilt pictures and an effectively lit wine rack, the warm atmosphere being derived as much as anything from the ruby-burgundy color scheme. In the formal Washington Room with its crystal chandelier, burgundy velvet curtains are pulled back with tassles and hunting prints adorn the walls. The least formal is the den.

LUNCH: Monday to Friday from 11 A.M. to 2:30 P.M. DINNER: Monday to Saturday from 5 to 10:30 P.M., on Friday and Saturday until 11 P.M.; closed Sunday.

L'Auberge, Spread Eagle Village, 503 W. Lancaster Ave., Wayne (tel. 215/687-2840), is one of the area's fine dining spots, popular with Main Liners. From the tiled grand entrance hall adorned with painted-wood Austrian church panels you'll be taken into a series of large dining rooms with very well-spaced polished wood tables, set with Villeroy and Boch, a posy of fresh flowers, and a small peppermill. Waiters are properly aproned and the music is classical. The largest room has a stucco fireplace with beam mantel and brick hearth adorned with a few copper pots. Narrow ceiling beams and valanced chintz curtains give a French provincial air to a smaller room. There's also an atrium dining room that sparkles with Mexican floor tiles, large ficus, and tables set with pink tablecloths. You can also eat in the large bar. The menu will likely suggest a dozen or so entrees like paupiettes of sole filled with shrimp in white wine and avocado sauce, filet of beef with provençal herbs and horseradish crème fraiche, bouillabaisse, or duck in pink peppercorn and Grand Marnier glaze. Prices run $14.75 to $21.50. To start, try poached shrimp and tomatoes or the pâté de campagne. Desserts are made daily and worth saving some room for—lemon cake with chocolate topping, orange crème caramel, peach tart, or chocolate mousse cake could be on the tray offered. A simple grill menu is served in the bar from 6 P.M. to closing. The wine list is extensive and well priced.

LUNCH: Tuesday to Saturday from noon to 2:30 P.M. DINNER: Tuesday to Thursday from 6 to 9:30 P.M., on Friday and Saturday to 11 P.M.; closed Sunday.

Chef Tell's, 115 Strafford Ave., Wayne (tel. 215/964-1116), is run by a famous TV chef, Tell Erhardt, an ebullient mustachioed character who is known for his wicked sense of humor. Because of his busy schedule Chef Tell only keeps a check on the quality of the food and designs the menu, although he does appear fairly frequently at the restaurant. Located in a stone mansion with classic portico supported by Colonial Revival pillars, the dining rooms are elegant. Forest-green velvet chairs are set at tables; burgundy drapes are cinched back gracefully. A bust of Schiller stands prominently on the mantel. A less formal room, although in similar style, is adorned with French posters on chintz wallpaper. There's a comfortable bar for waiting. The frequently changing menu features seasonal ingredients. The menu will list about a dozen entrees, priced from $15 to $22.50 —veal "Bombay," sautéed with mangos and served with vegetables and curried rice; loin of pork sautéed and served with a poached pear and gorgonzola cheese sauce; and strip steak au poivre and mesquite-grilled salmon with béarnaise. Appetizers might range from pâtés and terrines to steak tartare and pasta du jour. Luncheon offers the opportunity to sample some of these dishes at prices from $6.50 to $11.

LUNCH: Monday to Friday from noon to 2 P.M. DINNER: Monday to Saturday from 6 to 10 P.M.

La Fourchette, 110 N. Wayne Ave., Wayne (tel. 215/687-8333), is the other contender for fine fare in this area. Lit by a row of tall Palladian-style windows and graced by an elegant and central balustered staircase at the back of the restaurant, the room is distinctly elegant and decorated in French style. Different types of china are used on the tables, along with fresh flowers, and candles in glass globes. Dinner offers a dozen or so entrees. Grilled halibut, crayfish américaine, and Dover sole with sauce flavored with thyme are examples of fish choices. Among the meats there might be a filet of beef in garlic-scented brown sauce, lamb on a crouton, mignons of lamb with a paprika-sage sauce crowned with roasted sweet peppers, and pheasant filled with a veal and foie gras mousseline, roasted and sauced with blueberries, vinegar, and stock. Escargots, pâté, terrines, and soups are among the appetizers. Tempting desserts are made daily by the pastry chef—lemon tart, apple-hazelnut tart, or chocolate-praline torte, for example. Prices run $14 to $21.

LUNCH: Monday to Friday from 11:30 A.M. to 2:30 P.M. DINNER: Monday to Friday from 6 to 10 P.M., on Saturday from 5:30 to 10 P.M., and on Sunday from 5 to 9:30 P.M.

About 1700 William Penn and his daughter visited the Welsh Quakers at Gwynedd and stopped at the Thomas Evans home, which later became the **William Penn Inn**, Rte. 202 and Sumneytown Pike, Gwynedd (tel. 215/699-9272). Here you'll find two dining rooms: one, the Mayfair Room, lushly formal with plush rose banquettes, brass sconces and chandelier, forest-green napery, and large bouquets of fresh flowers; the other, a typical colonial tavern with booths and comb-back Windsors. The first serves a selection of continentally inspired seafood, steaks, veal, and poultry dishes—crab imperial, salmon with dill hollandaise, broiled flounder, prime rib, veal Oscar, and breast of capon with a honey and Dijon mustard glaze. Prices run $11 to $26. The tavern specializes in dishes like sliced London broil, prime rib, filet mignon béarnaise, and lighter fare like chicken pot pie and fettuccine primavera. Prices range from $12 to $20, including seafood appetizer bar and vegetable and potato.

LUNCH: Mayfair Room—Monday to Saturday from 11:30 A.M. to 3 P.M. DINNER: Mayfair Room—Monday to Friday from 5 to 10 P.M., on Saturday until 11 P.M., and on Sunday from 3 to 8 P.M. Colonial Tavern—Thursday and Friday from 5:30 to 9:30 P.M., on Saturday from 5 to 10 P.M. BRUNCH: Colonial Tavern—Sunday from 10:30 A.M. to 2:30 P.M.

In 1954 Edward Wallis Callahan turned his home into the **Coventry Forge Inn**, Rte. 23, Coventryville (tel. 215/469-6222), something that it had been earlier from 1717 to 1818. This really is the most charming place to dine in the area—a series of low-ceilinged rooms, one with an original Franklin stove, that are lit by Shaker lanterns. The small tavern bar has wide-board floors and a collection of fine flasks; it's particularly inviting in winter. The porch dining area is most pleasant in summer. The owners keep live fresh trout and also use local Muscovy duck for their special grilled breast of duck or the duck à l'orange. Other menu items include steak au poivre, veal à la crème, and rack of lamb. Prices begin at $12.50. These main dishes can be followed with classic desserts like a lemon sorbet, profiteroles, or crème caramel. Guests are requested to dine in the restaurant.

Accommodations in the adjacent guesthouse are spacious and attractive, with large bathrooms. Windows look out onto a pastoral wooded scene. RATES: (including continental breakfast): $60 to $70 a night, depending on the room and the day of the week. DINNER: Tuesday to Friday from 5:30 to 9 P.M., until 10 P.M. on Saturday; Monday also during the summer.

The **Skippack Roadhouse**, Rte. 73, Skippack (tel. 215/584-9927), is a refreshing change from the many colonial decors that predominate in the restaurants of the area. From the parking lot, a wooden footbridge and crazy paving path leads into the tavern room, which features an unusual tiled bar. A series of dining rooms, all small and intimate, follow, decorated with prints, copper lanterns, and modern lithographs, and furnished either with banquettes and cane Breuers or simple chairs. The food is excellent and nicely presented. Try the curry dressing on your salad, and tuck into the scrumptious garlic bread that will accompany a bluefish cooked with lemon butter or provençale style. Other dishes include chateaubriand, rack of lamb, and sweet-and-sour pork chops. Prices run $11.50 to $24. On weekends there's a brunch featuring eggs Benedict, steak and eggs, a chicken dish, and several other choices, for $6 and up.

LUNCH: Monday to Saturday from 11:30 A.M. to 2:30 P.M. DINNER: Sunday to Thursday from 5:30 to 9 P.M., until 10 P.M. on Friday and Saturday. BRUNCH: Sunday from noon to 3:30 P.M.

Back on the other side of Valley Forge there's the **Jefferson House,** 2519 De-Kalb Pike, Norristown (tel. 215/275-3407), a magnificent mansion overlooking a duck pond and gracious gardens that was modeled after Jefferson's Monticello. The cuisine is continental. Begin with a bouillabaisse or spaghetti Albina (with clams, scallops, lobster, and crab in a white sauce), and follow with any choice from the beef, poultry, and many veal dishes. The prices range from $10.50 to $21. In the lobby note the wonderful dexterity with which chef-owner Alberto sculpts crystalline sugar into birds and other impressive displays.

LUNCH: Monday to Friday from 11:30 A.M. to 2:30 P.M. DINNER: Monday to Saturday from 5:30 to 10 P.M., on Sunday from 1 to 7:30 P.M. Take DeKalb Street (Rte. 202) north from Valley Forge.

Out east along the Skippack Road (Rte. 73), you'll find the **Blue Bell Inn,** 601 Skippack Rd., Blue Bell (tel. 215/646-2010), a very popular local favorite. The oldest part of the restaurant dates from 1743, but it has been extensively enlarged and now offers a series of large dining rooms that serve stone crabs in season, shad roe, frogs' legs, and steaks. Entrees begin at $12. There's also a pleasant piano bar containing a display of fine German steins.

LUNCH: Tuesday to Saturday from noon to 2:30 P.M. DINNER: Tuesday to Saturday from 5 to 10 P.M.

VALLEY FORGE AREA NIGHTLIFE

The best entertainment value is found at the Sheraton's **Lilly Langtry's** (tel. 215/337-LILY).

Otherwise, the entertainment's rather sketchy and consists of such seasonal entertainments as the **Valley Forge Music Fair,** when top names—Frank Sinatra, Jane Olivor, Peter Allen, Johnny Mathis—and Broadway stage shows appear at the 3,000-seat theater-in-the-round. For info, contact P.O. Box 917, Devon, PA 19333 (tel. 215/644-5000).

VALLEY FORGE ACTIVITIES

ANTIQUING: Best found in and around Skippack Village along Rte. 73.

BICYCLING: Rentals are available in the Valley Forge Historical Park from May to October.

BOATING: On the Schuylkill.

CANOEING: Along Perkiomen Creek.

GOLF: General Washington Golf Club, 2750 Egypt Rd., Audubon (tel. 215/666-

7602); Valley Forge Golf Club, Rte. 363, King of Prussia (tel. 215/337-1776); Skippack Golf Club, Stump Hall Road and Cedars Road (tel. 215/584-4653).

HORSEBACK RIDING: There's a 120-mile trail in Valley Forge Historical Park. Great Valley Stables, West Anthony Wayne Drive, Berwyn (tel. 215/296-7492), is nearby.

PICNICKING: Valley Forge Historical Park is the obvious choice.

SHOPPING: King of Prussia possesses one of the largest shopping centers in the country to which many foreigners fly specifically to shop at Bloomingdales, Saks, and other stores in ease and comfort (compared to, say, shopping in New York, where you can't park and you can't move for the crowds). Shoppers will love it!

STATE PARKS: Marsh Creek has some 2,000 acres and offers picnicking, a swimming pool, fishing, boat rentals, hiking, ice boating and fishing, skating, and sledding. Contact R.D. 2, Park Road, Downingtown, PA 19335 (tel. 215/458-8515).

TENNIS: Stouffer's has a couple of courts. Gulph Mills Racket Club, 610 S. Henderson Rd., King of Prussia (tel. 215/265-6730); Shawnee at High Point Sports Complex, Upper State and County Line Roads, Chalfont (tel. 215/822-1951); Ramada-Downington Inn, Rte. 30 (tel. 215/269-2000).

LANCASTER & THE PENNSYLVANIA DUTCH COUNTRY

DISTANCE IN MILES: Lancaster, 153
ESTIMATED DRIVING TIME: 3½ hours

DRIVING: Take the New Jersey Turnpike to the Pennsylvania Turnpike west. Turn off at Exit 22, where you can pick up Rte. 23 west. If you're in a hurry, take Exit 21 and Rte. 222 south.
BUS: Greyhound (tel. 212/635-0800, or toll free 800/528-6055) travels to Lancaster. Trailways (tel.212/730-7460) also travels to Ephrata.
TRAIN: Amtrak travels to Lancaster via Philadelphia. Call 212/736-6288, or toll free 800/523-5700, for information.

Special Events To Plan Your Trip Around
MAY: Carriage and Sleigh Auction at Martin's Sales Pavilion (tel. 717/354-7006), Intercourse (usually in mid-May). Contact Martin's Auctioneers, Inc., P.O. Box 71, Blue Ball, PA 17506.
JULY: Kutztown Pennsylvania Dutch Festival is a nine-day celebration of the arts and crafts of the region—basketry, embroidery, woodworking, tinsmithing, decoy carving, wood whittling, toleware painting, sgraffito —along with food, music, and dancing (usually July 4th weekend). For information write to the Kutztown Folk Festival, 461 Vine Lane, Kutztown, PA 19530 (tel. 215/688-8707).

Lititz—July 4th celebration, when thousands of candles are lit and reflect into the narrow waterways dotted with waterwheels in Lititz

Springs park. Contact Lititz Recreation Center, Broad Street, Lititz, PA 17543 (tel. 717/626-9938).

JUNE THROUGH LABOR DAY: Crafts day and harvest days at the Landis Valley Farm Museum.

JULY THROUGH LABOR DAY: Vorspiel Performances at Ephrata Cloister, 632 W. Main St., Ephrata (tel. 717/733-2592).

DECEMBER: Wheatland opens the dining room for punch and cookies in a 19th-century-style party.

For further information about the state, contact the Pennsylvania Travel Department Bureau, Pennsylvania Department of Commerce, Harrisburg, PA 17101 (tel. 717/787-5453). For specific information, contact the Pennsylvania Dutch Visitors' Bureau, 1799 Hempstead Rd., Lancaster, PA 17601 (tel. 717/299-8901).

Although many visitors come to Lancaster County to observe the lifestyles of the local Amish and Old Order Mennonite communities, there are also plenty of other fascinating things to do and see in this historic area of the country that was settled by so many groups—Scottish Presbyterians, Quakers, French Huguenots, and many German sects, as well as Moravians, Roman Catholics, and German Jews—all of whom contributed greatly to the arts and the agricultural and technological development of the area. Their contributions can be viewed at many of the historic and other museums in the area—the National Clock and Watch Museum, the Landis Farm Museum, Robert Fulton's birthplace, Wright's Ferry Mansion, and many, many more. Lancaster itself is a lovely old historic town, which also contains President James Buchanan's home and another historic residence belonging to Edward Hand, Washington's adjutant-general. Southeast of Lancaster, Strasburg offers a string of delights to railroad buffs—a trip aboard a real old iron horse, a collector's museum, a fine model railroad museum, and even a motel that is housed in 17 cabooses. On the northern side of Lancaster there's the quiet, pretty Moravian town of Lititz, which possesses one of the most pleasant inns in the area, and also Ephrata, site of a cloister and religious community—an historic example of the kind of groups and communities that William Penn's tolerant state attracted and sheltered. For those visitors who love to shop for antiques, the area has many stores and a fantastic collection of antique emporiums and markets in nearby Adamstown. If discount shopping is on your mind, then the outlets at Reading, to which many New York–based corporations are taking their employees by the busload, are also en route to or from Lancaster. And then, of course, there are all the delights of Pennsylvania Dutch cooking, lively Pennsylvania Dutch markets and auctions, which are prime targets on most visitors' agendas, along with those attractions that pretend to explain the local Mennonite and Amish communities.

The term "Pennsylvania Dutch" refers to the many groups who fled persecution in southern Germany and settled in Pennsylvania, in such places as Germantown, before fanning across the rest of the state to establish farms and communities. Their native language was German or Deutsch, which probably became corrupted to "Dutch," and their customs, traditions, and philosophies emphasized hard work and plain living. Among them are, of course, the Amish and Mennonites, who are in fact sort of cousins. Both groups, formed during the Reformation in the 1500s, were Anabaptists who sought a pure church, free from state control, open to adult believers from any religion. Because they preached the priesthood of all believers, there was no one leader among them, although Menno Simons, a Catholic priest from Holland, became well known through his writings and gave his name to the group, which was bitterly persecuted. Thousands were killed; others fled to the caves in the Swiss mountains, and eventually to America.

The Amish division came later, in 1693, when Jacob Amman, who was concerned about the purity of the church, demanded that the church socially shun anyone who had been excommunicated from the brethren. Such divisions have occurred ever since in the history of these sects, and so today there are many many different groups throughout the world and in Lancaster County. For example, in Lancaster County you'll find Old Order Amish, Old Order Mennonites (Wenger), Old Order Mennonites (Pike), Beachy Order Mennonites, New Order Amish, Brethren in Christ, Lancaster Mennonite Conference, all adding up to about 29,000 people, or less than 10% of the county's population. The most significant division in the groups is not between Amish and Mennonite but between Old Order and the more "Modern" groups.

Because the Old Order groups have made specific choices against the easy way of acculturation and the temptations of technology, they have often been attacked as backward and regarded as curiosities. As a visitor you might try and come to a deeper understanding of what these people intend. There may be things that we can learn from them, like commitment, community, a deep love of the earth and its bounty, living in harmony with life's daily and seasonal rhythms—in short, wholeness. If you look at these people closely, you'll see a serenity, peace, and contentment that you don't find in too many places today. They have chosen to live in communities where religion and daily life intersect, where religion is not separated from their daily life. They have no use for cars because cars scatter the community. A horse can only travel about 8 miles an hour and only 20 miles a day. It can only help to keep the community together. In their dress they stress simplicity and modesty. They believe in peace and will not go to war. They educate their children to live self-fulfilling productive lives within the community, stressing wisdom and understanding more than knowledge and facts. They believe in looking after their own elderly and refuse to accept Social Security benefits. Similarly, if someone is widowed or disabled or suffers some calamity, the neighbors and church come forward to help indefinitely.

On the subject of buggies, while you're driving around you're most likely to see Lancaster Amish carriages with gray tops, straight sides, and rounded roof corners. The Wenger Mennonites, who are concentrated in northern Lancaster County, drive a carriage with black straight-sided top; the Pike Mennonites, so called because their meeting house is on Rte. 322 in Lancaster County, are the oldest and most conservative of the Old Order Mennonites and drive carriages with no back or side windows. By the way, the open carriage is not properly called a courting carriage at all.

Today there are 313,000 Mennonites living in North America. Of these about 34,000 are Old Order Amish. You may be surprised to learn that the fastest growing are the Old Order groups, both Amish and Mennonite, a fact that does seem to speak to our alienated ritual-less society and is certainly worth pondering on a visit to this lovely, bountiful part of the country.

A Note: Obviously, many people are drawn to the area to gawk at the Amish and Old Order Mennonites. True, these communities are fascinating and their way of life certainly has lots to be said for it, but just imagine if you were suddenly to become the object of millions of staring people as you went about your daily business, and every activity from shopping and gardening to simply walking down the road was stared at, scrutinized, analyzed, scoffed at, questioned, given a bad press, and worse, photographed. The last is especially disturbing to the Old Order groups because their religious principles include the strict commandment that "thou shalt not make graven images." If you *must* take pictures, then please exercise some degree of sensitivity.

AMISH AND PENNSYLVANIA DUTCH COUNTRY

AREA ATTRACTIONS

Drive along main roads like Rte. 30 and you'll be assaulted by sign after sign screaming the word "authentic" and offering buggy rides in real buggies and so on. It's clear that the Amish have been horribly exploited, and my advice to any visitor is to try and sift the authentic from the chaff. One way to do this is to stay off Rte. 30 as much as possible. Get out into the countryside. Go into the farms wherever you see a sign inviting you to buy eggs, quilts, plants, vegetables, ice cream, or whatever. I have tried to include only those places that, in my opinion, will prove most rewarding. Best time to visit, for my money, is in the busy springtime of hoeing, plowing, and planting, when the farmers work night and day to beat the weather and get the crops in. The other time to visit is in October, when the fall adds a colorful dimension to the whole rewarding scene of harvesting and thanksgiving. Summer is the most crowded. Plan to see all of the Amish-Mennonite attractions on Saturday, for they're closed on Sunday. That applies, too, to many Pennsylvania Dutch restaurants.

Best place to begin your visit is probably at the **People's Place,** Intercourse (tel. 717/768-7171). See the 25-minute film, *Who Are the Amish?* which will give you a very good and sympathetic idea of what these people intend, their diversity, their practices, their traditions, and what has held them together through centuries. Afterward, walk through the upstairs exhibit, the "Amish World," which gives you an opportunity to understand the eight areas in which the Amish remain in tension with the rest of American society: (1) sense of time, (2) transportation, (3) dress, (4) education, (5) peace, (6) government aid, (7) energy, (8) mutual aid. Kids can enjoy the "Feeling Box," dressing up, filling out an actual worksheet exercise in the one-room schoolhouse, and following Amos and Suzie through the 12 months of a typical Amish child's year. There are also several quizzes, which adults may find very enlightening. The second half of the museum is devoted to over 30 three-dimensional carved wooden paintings by Aaron Zook, each depicting a community scene—an Amish wedding, funeral, barn raising, planting, marketplace, the evening prayer. They are quite magnificent and deeply moving. You'll also find some watercolors and furniture designed by folk artist Henry Lapp, an Old Order Amishman. The final room ties the whole museum together with a moving tribute to the Old Order Amish. Back downstairs you may want to browse in the bookstore and craft store.

HOURS: The film *Who Are the Amish?* shows continuously from 9:30 A.M. until 4:30 P.M. November through March and from 9:30 A.M. to 5 P.M. April through October; closed Sunday and Christmas. In the evenings at 6 and 8 P.M. from April 1 to October 31, the motion picture *Hazel's People,* with Geraldine Page, is shown. ADMISSION: $3.50 for *Who are the Amish?* and the "Amish World" exhibit.

While you're in Intercourse, you'll want to browse through the stores across the street from the People's Place, and drop into Zimmerman's where many a buggy will be hitched out front.

For a quick trip through Amish country, take Rte. 772 out of Intercourse and turn left on Cat's Tail Road. All along here you can see the water wheels and windmills generating power for each farm. The road will loop back to Rte. 340, which you can take west into Intercourse again, and then take Rte. 772 northwest for about a mile. Turn right on Centerville Road, and keep going until you come to **Phillips Lancaster County Swiss Cheese** (tel. 717/354-4424), where you can experience a very interesting and entertaining tour of the cheese factory. Try and get there between 10:30 A.M. and noon, when you'll catch them lifting the curds out of the milk. The tour is followed by samples, of course.

While you're in the region you should also stop in at **Lapp's Ice Cream,** sold at a farm just off New Holland Road. Drive into the farmyard and purchase a really good, creamy cone or sundae, and enjoy it as the cows come and go, the turkey struts back and forth, and the dog barks wildly from his kennel.

Get back onto Rte. 340. Another interesting place to visit in Intercourse is **Ebersol's Chair Shop.** From Intercourse, it's a short journey west on Rte. 340 to **Bird-in-Hand,** where there's a **farmer's market.** En route, if you want some hand-

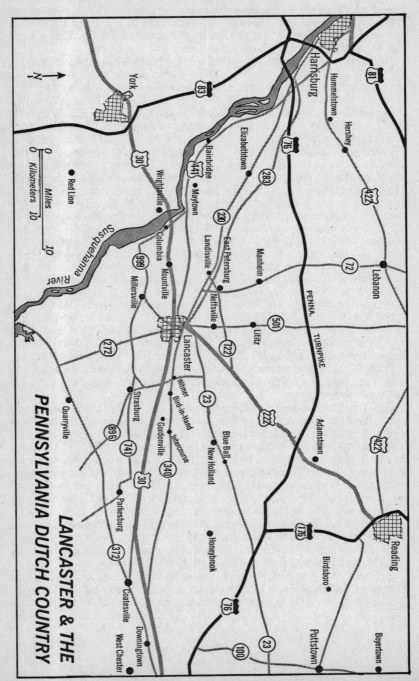

LANCASTER & THE PENNSYLVANIA DUTCH COUNTRY

made and hand-carved furniture, then turn right on Weavertown Road and drive to the Red Barn and ask for **the furniture maker.** Bring your own design and he will fashion whatever you want—whole dining table and chair sets—for very reasonable prices. Continue west on Rte. 340 until you come to Witmer Road. Turn left and go down until you see a farm on the right with a "quilts for sale" sign. Here you'll find some truly wonderful quilts, and have the added enjoyment of seeing the farm and meeting Hannah Stoltzfoos, the mistress of the house. The quality of the work is superb, and the prices are very fair. For me these are some of the highlights of the Amish country.

For informed tours along the backroads, head for the **Mennonite Information Center,** 2209 Millstream Rd., Lancaster (tel. 717/299-0954). A guide will accompany you in your car for two hours to explain the Pennsylvania Dutch ways. Price: About $10. There's also a 20-minute film introducing the Amish and Mennonite communities. HOURS: Monday to Saturday from 8 A.M. to 5 P.M. from March 1 to November 30.

For an overview of the history of the area and its settlers, you would do well to visit the **Wax Museum,** Rte. 30, 4½ miles east of Lancaster (tel. 717/393-3679). Although wax museums don't usually appeal to me, this one really is very beautifully and artistically created, and will also give any visitor an excellent grasp of the local history of the area. Each diorama focuses on a particular period, specific event, or personality, from the arrival of the Mennonites and Amish through the Civil War. Some of the figures are made to speak, and some dramatic illusions are created—the whole tour capped by an impressive dramatization of a barn raising. Fun and worth seeing. HOURS: 9 A.M. to 9 P.M. daily in summer, to 6 P.M. in winter, until 8 P.M. March through May. ADMISSION: $3.65 for adults, $2.50 for children 5 to 11.

Pennsylvania Dutch Markets

The market that has the reputation for being the most authentic is held in downtown Lancaster at **Center Square** (tel. 717/291-4723), but only on Tuesday and Friday from 6 A.M. to 5 P.M. It's the oldest market in the area, and from 1730 to 1889 it was held at the curbside, where farmers sold produce from their wagons. If you want to view the local farmers delivering their goods, you'll have to rise about 5 A.M. or earlier. Later in the day the market is bustling, and you'll see among the vendors Mennonite ladies selling their home-baked goods, fresh flowers, fancy-looking meats, and shoofly and whoopee pies. Unfortunately this wonderful market cannot be seen by the weekender. Lancaster does have a Saturday market, referred to as the **Southern Market,** at 106 Queen St., which is open from 6 A.M. to 4 P.M.

If you have a lot of energy when you arrive on Friday night, then you might plan to attend the **Green Dragon Market in Ephrata.** This is really a huge affair. Dust whirls over the parking lot, which is filled with cars and a few buggies. Vendors of all sorts gather outside the main buildings selling clothes, flowers, fruits and vegetables, cookies, fast foods, all manner of items. In the main market building fresh meats, cheeses, homemade baked goods, books, and much, much more is sold. In the barn at around 6 P.M. an auction of animals is held and fat, frightened rabbits, turkeys, chickens, goslings, hamsters, and all kinds of other small fry are held aloft as the auctioneer sing-songs his way to the final gavel and the animal is passed out over the heads of the crowd. Kids love the action and the whole rural ritual is fascinating to observe. Other auctions of the kind of merchandise you might expect to find at Odd Job Lot are held in other market buildings. HOURS: Friday only from 10 A.M. to 10 P.M.

Meadowbrook Market, on Rte. 23 just outside Leacock, is another good market to visit. The one in Bird-in-Hand is rather too modern and lacks any real character to me. During the week, on Tuesday from 2 to 9 P.M., **Roots Country Market and Auction,** between Manheim and East Petersburg off Rte. 72, is another fascinating market experience.

TWO LODGINGS IN THE CENTER OF AMISH COUNTRY

If you want to be in the real heart of the Amish country and hear the gentle clop of their horses as they go by, then you can't beat the location of the **Mill House,** 313 Osceola Mill Rd., Gordonville, PA 17529 (tel. 717/768-3758). It's a lovely old 1766 stone house with maroon shutters set by a mill stream and humpbacked bridge. A brick path lined with flowers leads to the porch, and you may catch sight of one of the resident peacocks. Owners Barry and Joy Sawyer were born and raised in Lancaster and really know the area. They'll welcome you into their beamed keeping room/parlor atmospherically furnished with early American antiques. Clustered around the beam-manteled stucco fireplace are a wing chair, bench/table, and comb-back Windsor chair. A weasel, a spinning wheel, and a few old awls, saws, and other tools on the barn siding add period interest. Here at the bench/table a continental breakfast of fresh fruits (pineapple, kiwi, plums, grapes, etc.) and a variety of homemade breads and muffins is served.

Upstairs are three rooms, two with fireplaces. In the Blue Room, so named because of the blue quilt on the four-poster (without canopy), the wide-plank floor is covered with a small Oriental area rug, magazines are spread on a table, and a hall stand serves as a towel rack. The Shutter Room possesses an original fireplace and is decked out in pink, while the Victorian Room sports an iron-and-brass bed covered with a purple quilt and, among other furnishings, a wicker chair and an oak commode, the top of which is covered with an embroidered cloth.

RATES: $55 to $65 double (the higher price on weekends); $5 less in winter.

The other is very different. The **Bird-In-Hand Motor Inn,** P.O. Box B, Bird-in-Hand, PA 17505 (tel. 717/768-8271), is a very well-kept and prettily landscaped motel accommodation. The rooms are attractive and modern. The restaurant is fine for breakfast or lunch, and you'll often find a number of locals, including Amish, sitting at the counter. A few hundred yards down the road you'll also find the bakery, which I can heartily recommend for their buns, cookies, shoofly pies, and more. There's also tennis courts and an indoor pool.

RATES: $54 in summer season; during the winter special lower rates apply.

PENNSYLVANIA DUTCH DINING

Groff's Farm Restaurant, Pinkerton Road, Mount Joy (tel. 717/653-2048). James Beard and Craig Claiborne have both described Betty Groff's cooking as authentic Americana, and certainly Betty operates a restaurant where the ingredients are always fresh and the food tasty and plentiful.

Dinner is by reservation only for either the 5:30 or 7:30 P.M. sittings. Ideally you'll arrive at the old stone farmhouse as the sun is sinking and you can capture the silhouette of one of the swans gliding by on the farmyard pond against the pink-tinged sky of a Pennsylvania sunset. The meal will begin with a collection of relishes—corn, bean, and bread, plus chocolate cake for you to enjoy while you still have room. Your choice of soup or fruit juice will follow before your main course, which is served family style. You can choose any one of special combinations of classic Pennsylvania Dutch fare—roast prime rib, hickory-smoked ham, a special seasonal seafood combination, or Betty's very own famous chicken Stoltzfus, consisting of succulent chunks of chicken in a cream sauce placed on a bed of light pastry. Whatever combination you choose, it will be accompanied by several vegetables, each done to a turn, and including a bowl of wonderful, whipped potatoes. Want seconds? Just ask. If you still have room for dessert—they're first-rate too. Try the black raspberry tart (very sweet) or the lemon meringue pie or any other homemade specialty. This family-style repast will cost from $13.50 to $21, depending on your choices. Bring your own wine.

If Betty is there the night of your visit, and she nearly always is, she will undoubtedly stop by and introduce herself, talking away in her own effervescent manner, making sure that everything is perfect and to your liking. At some point she may take out her trumpet to toast whoever happens to have a birthday or anniversary with a round or two of the "Anniversary Waltz" or "Happy Birthday." Such a peculiar mixture of showman and caring hostess is she, that she even apologized for the slightly stringy quality of the green beans the evening I was there—that's a really sincere restaurateur for you. On the way out, you'll be invited to stop down into the cellar for a glass of home-brewed wine, a nice way to wind down at the end of the evening.

LUNCH: Tuesday to Saturday from 11:30 A.M. to 1 P.M. (by reservation only —ask what the specialty will be; $7 to $10 per person). DINNER: Tuesday to Saturday at 5 and 7:30 P.M. BRUNCH: Sunday from 11:30 A.M. to 2 P.M.

One of the best and larger (seats 600) places to stop for Pennsylvania Dutch fare is **Willow Valley Inn,** 2416 Willow Street Pike (tel. 717/464-2711), located south of Lancaster in a lovely setting overlooking a golf course. The breakfast buffet is truly dazzling. Spread before you are several tables, one piled with all kinds of fruit salads and dried fruits, another with all kinds of doughnuts and pastries, and still another laden with eggs, sausage, scrapple, waffles, home-fries, and more. Help yourself, all for $5. Lunch and dinner offer equally tempting arrays of food, including the classic favorites associated with this part of the world: ham, beef, chow-chow, apple butter, shoofly pie.

BREAKFAST: 8 A.M. to 10:30 A.M. weekdays, on Saturday from 7:30 to 11 A.M. LUNCH: Monday to Saturday from 11 A.M. to 2:30 P.M. DINNER: Monday to Saturday from 5 to 8 P.M. *Note:* On Friday there's a special seafood buffet from 4 to 8:30 P.M., and on Saturday the smörgåsbord's available from 1 to 8:30 P.M. Closed Sunday. No liquor.

Additional Pennsylvania Dutch Restaurants

Stoltzfus Farms Restaurant, on Rte. 772, just east of Intercourse (tel. 717/768-8156 or 768-8811), is famous for its really flavorsome sausages, which isn't surprising for farming and the butcher business came first. The restaurant was an afterthought and a very good one. Here you can enjoy family-style meals featuring chow-chow, apple butter, pepper cabbage, candied sweet potatoes, and all the other famous Dutch treats. No liquor.

HOURS: 11 A.M. to 8 P.M. daily, April through October, closed Sunday and during the winter months.

The **Brownstown Restaurant,** Brownstown (tel. 717/656-9077), is another smaller (seating 200) dining room specializing in good home-cooking, served family style (although it also offers a regular menu featuring such dishes as liver and onions, veal cutlet, sandwiches, and haddock at very reasonable prices). Their family-style platter includes baked ham, chicken, and about eight vegetables (corn, potatoes, etc.), dessert, and beverage for only $8.

HOURS: Monday and Wednesday to Saturday from 6:30 to 8 P.M., on Sunday from 11 A.M. to 7 P.M.; closed Tuesday.

Miller's Smörgåsbord, 2811 Lincoln Hwy. East (tel. 717/687-6621), is famous for its choice of 65 items at dinner. Here you can have the privacy of your own table. BREAKFAST: From 8 A.M. seven days a week from June to October and weekends year round. DINNER: From 11:30 A.M. daily, year round.

Similar regional fare, family style, can be found at the famous 600-seat **Good n' Plenty,** Rte. 896, Smoketown (tel. 717/394-7111).

HOURS: Monday to Saturday from 11:30 A.M. to 8 P.M.; closed Sunday and also mid-December and January.

Sunday Dining

In this area Sunday dining can be a problem. Here follows a list of establishments in the area that are open on Sunday:

Strasburg Inn, Rte. 896, Strasburg (tel. 717/687-7691), open 7 A.M. to 9 P.M.; **Miller's Smörgåsbord,** 2811 Lincoln Hwy. East (tel. 717/687-6621), open 11 A.M.to 8 P.M.; the **Stockyard Inn,** Rte. 222 North, Lancaster (tel. 717/394-7975), open noon to 7:30 P.M.; **Haydn Zugs',** corner of State Street and Rte. 72, East Petersburg (tel. 717/569-5746); **Hoar House,** South Prince Street, Lancaster (tel. 717/397-0110), open noon to 8 P.M.; and also the dining rooms at the **Sheraton Resort Inn,** Rte. 272 north, Lancaster (tel. 717/656-2101), open 10:30 A.M. to 8 P.M.; and at the **Treadway,** Bourbon Street, Rte. 222 and Eden Road, Lancaster (tel. 717/569-6444), open 6:30 A.M. to 10 P.M.

LANCASTER

AREA ATTRACTIONS

The first inland settlement and national capital for a day during the Revolutionary War—when the Continental Congress met here on September 27, 1777, during the British occupation of Philadelphia—Lancaster is a lovely old town whose streets are lined with restored 18th- and 19th-century brick town houses. The old market downtown and the jail are also impressive pieces of architecture. For a full exploration of the city you can't beat the downtown **two-hour walking tours,** which begin at 10 A.M. and 1:30 P.M. from April through October. Meet at 15 W. King St. (tel. 717/392-1776) for a short introductory film. Price for the tour is $2.50. By the way, don't miss the ornate interior of the old Fulton Opera House.

The **Heritage Center Museum,** Penn Square at King and Queen Streets (tel. 717/299-6440), displays objects relating to Lancaster's history—furniture, quilts, clocks, silver, pewter, copperware, Pennsylvania rifles, fraktur and many other kinds of folk art. HOURS: May 1 to mid-November, Tuesday to Saturday from 10 A.M. to 4 P.M.

Just outside Lancaster stands the home of the only bachelor to gain possession of the White House—James Buchanan's **Wheatland,** 1120 Marietta Ave. (tel. 717/392-8721). He bought this house in 1848 for $6,750 primarily because it suited his aspirations, which were attained in 1857 when he entered the White House accompanied by his niece, Harriet Lee, who was then only 27. Her portrait can be seen, along with other memorabilia including an unusual portrait of a young, pretty Queen Victoria, and a portrait of his fiancée Ann Coleman, who broke their engagement because he didn't pay enough attention to her. The 45-minute tour, given by costumed guides, will provide insight into Buchanan's life and sensibility and that of the 19th century. HOURS: April through November, 10 A.M. to 4:30 P.M. daily; closed from January through March. ADMISSION: $3 for adults, 65¢ for children under 12.

West of Lancaster in Columbia, on the east bank of the Susquehanna River, **Wright's Ferry Mansion,** at 2nd and Cherry Streets (tel. 717/684-4325), is a stone house that was built in 1738 for the remarkable English Quaker, Susanna Wright. The house, with its wonderful collection of early-18th-century furniture, glass, and ceramics, reflects the sophisticated tastes and interests of this woman whose pursuits ranged from literature to the raising of silkworms. Well worth the visit. HOURS: May through October, on Tuesday, Wednesday, Friday, and Saturday from 10 A.M. to 3 P.M. ADMISSION: $2 for adults, 50¢ for children 6 to 11.

Here also the **Watch and Clock Museum,** 514 Poplar St., just off Rte. 30 (tel. 717/684-8261), houses one of the nation's largest collections of precision watches, clocks, tools, and other related items. HOURS: Monday to Friday from 9 A.M. to 4 P.M., on Saturday from 9 to 5 P.M.; closed Sunday and holidays. ADMISSION: $1.50 for adults, 50¢ for children 8 to 17.

And farther south on Rte. 222 south of Goshen, New Yorkers may be surprised to discover **Robert Fulton's birthplace** (tel. 717/548-2679). The little stone house is a tribute to his diverse genius and inventive spirit, a room being devoted to exhibits showing some of Fulton's artistic and mechanical accomplishments. Among them are examples of Fulton's miniature portraits, some of the finest produced in this country. HOURS: Memorial Day to Labor Day, weekends only—on Saturday from 11 A.M. to 4 P.M., on Sunday from 1 to 5 P.M. ADMISSION: $1 for adults; children under 12, free.

For Kids

Kids probably won't let you escape without a visit to **Dutch Wonderland,** 2249 Lincoln Hwy. East, Lancaster (tel. 717/291-1888), where the Monorail will whisk them into a park with many rides—sternwheel riverboat, miniature auto rides, merry-go-round and log flume, etc. HOURS: Memorial Day through Labor Day, daily from 10 A.M. (from 11 A.M. on Sunday) to 8 P.M.; Easter weekend to Memorial Day and Labor Day through October, weekends only—on Saturday from 10 A.M. to 6 P.M., from noon to 6 P.M. on Sunday. Closed at other times.

Rockford Plantation

Just south of Lancaster, Rockford Plantation, 881 Rockford Rd., Lancaster (tel. 717/392-7223), is well worth visiting, and when you do, you may want to take along a picnic and enjoy it along the banks of the Conestoga River in Williamson Park, where the plantation is located.

Begin your visit at the barn housing the Kauffman Collection, a small display of local Pennsylvania Dutch craft items—fraktur, lehnware, and shimmel figures, supplemented by pewter, furniture, copper, iron objects, and some lovely bride's boxes and toleware. Afterward walk down to the house for a guided tour of the last residence of Edward Hand, an Irishman who graduated from Trinity College, Dublin, in medicine and came to the colonies in 1767 with an Irish regiment when he was only 23. He soon quit the British army, became a doctor in Lancaster County, and later joined the Continental Army, becoming Washington's adjutant-general. The house was built in 1792, and you'll probably be shocked by the brilliance of the colors in the rooms. They are in fact the colors that would have appeared at that time—brilliant blues and golds. On the tour you'll glean a lot of history about the house, the furnishings, and the personal quirks of Mr. Hand, who defied fashion by refusing to wear a wig (he considered such a practice dirty). Take Duke Street south and follow the signs. HOURS: Tuesday to Saturday from 10 A.M. to 4 P.M., on Sunday from noon to 4 P.M. April through November. Closed Thanksgiving. ADMISSION: $2 for adults, $1 for children (under 6, free).

Hans Herr House

The Hans Herr House, 1849 Hans Herr Dr., Willow Street (tel. 717/464-4438), originally constructed in 1719, is the oldest house in Lancaster County. Those interested in the finer points of construction will find this an interesting place to visit. There are few furnishings in the house—an ingenious ratchet lamp, a Swiss/German-style heating oven, and a kas (German-style wardrobe) that can be taken to pieces and does not contain a single nail, are some of the more interesting. HOURS: April through December 31, Monday to Saturday from 9 A.M. to 4 P.M.; closed major holidays. ADMISSION: $2 for adults, $1 for children 8 to 12.

From Lancaster, take Rte. 222 south three miles. Turn right onto Hans Herr Drive and the house is on the left.

From here get back onto Rte. 222, taking it east to Lampeter and onto Rte. 741, which will take you all the way down to Strasburg, a railroader's paradise in the heart of Amish country farmland.

LANCASTER LODGING

At **Witmer's Tavern,** 2014 Old Philadelphia Pike, Lancaster, PA 17602 (tel. 717/ 299-5305), young Brant Hartung has been busily restoring this old 1725 inn that used to serve as a tavern on the Philadelphia–Lancaster road that led to the western frontier beyond the Susquehanna River. Here people stayed while waiting for their Conestoga wagons and their Pennsylvania rifles before heading out. So far Brant has restored seven of the rooms, each with working fireplace and air conditioning, and furnished them with either highback Victorian or brass beds, painted cottage furniture, oak dressers, and towel racks. Peg boards function as closets. In one room there's even an acorn pine rope bed and trundle covered with an antique quilt. Deep casement windows and shutters add character. There's a bathroom for every two rooms. Downstairs, Brant's sister runs Pandora's Antiques, while the sitting room is yours for reading, or playing cards and other games.

RATES: $50 per couple per night, $70 for the room with trundle bed; coffee, tea, and pastries are included in the morning.

In downtown Lancaster the **Brunswick Motor Inn,** at Chestnut and Queen Streets (P.O. Box 749), Lancaster, PA 17604 (tel. 717/397-4801), looks like a rather unattractive slab of concrete, but it does offer a good location if you're looking for easy access to fine dining, cocktail spots, and a little bit of evening entertainment. Rooms are typically modern. Facilities include two restaurants, two cocktail lounges, an indoor pool, free parking, and an adjacent movie theater.

RATES: $55 single, $65 double.

Two Lancaster hotels on the outskirts offer good weekend packages. The **Treadway Resort Inn,** 222 Eden Rd., Rte. 30 and the Oregon Pike, Lancaster, PA 17601 (tel. 717/569-6444, or toll free 800/631-0182), has 230 rooms set either around a courtyard or the pool, which are furnished in typical modern style. Other facilities include an outdoor pool, health club, and game room.

RATES: $80 to $90 double. Weekend packages available.

A Lancaster Farm

Standing out surrounded by fields, **Landy Shade Farm,** 1801 Colebrook Rd., Lancaster, PA 17601 (tel. 717/898-7689), looks very well kept. A brick pathway prettily lined with flowers leads to the entrance to this gray clapboard house with shutters. Unfortunately, no one was home when I stopped by, but you may still want to check it out.

Lancaster Resorts

Out on Rte. 222 south, **Willow Valley Inn,** 2416 Willow Street Pike, Lancaster, PA 17602 (tel. 717/464-2711, or toll free 800/233-0093), is a well-landscaped family resort run by the Thomas family, who "believe deeply in the Anabaptist way of life." There's a lake for boating, fishing, or ice skating, a nine-hole golf course, outdoor lighted tennis courts, special children's playground, rental bicycles, and outdoor and indoor pools. The 170 rooms are very pleasantly appointed.

RATES: Mid-June to Labor Day, $73 to $95 double; less in other months.

Host Farm, Lincoln Hwy. East, Lancaster, PA 17602 (tel. 717/299-5500), is a full-facility resort with 18- and 9-hole golf courses, four indoor tennis courts, lighted outdoor courts, jogging trails, an exercise-fitness center, game room, four swimming pools, a cabaret, and a good dinner theater. Rooms are modern and fully equipped with refrigerator, wet bar, coffee or tea maker, and color TV.

RATES: November 1 to May 21, $79 to $94 double for room only, $124 to $139 double for MAP (room, breakfast, and dinner per couple); May 22 to October 31, $95 to $110 double for room only, $145 to $155 double for MAP. Higher rates are for deluxe rooms. Special holiday packages run about $30 higher. Special golf packages are also offered.

Host Farm is the resort. Just across the road, **Host Town** offers motel-style accommodations with full access to all the facilities of Host Farm.

LANCASTER DINING

At **Jethro's,** 659 1st St., at Ruby Street (tel. 717/299-1700), three-piece-suited characters rub elbows with bejeaned students and rumpled professors from nearby Franklin and Marshall College, all in a comfortable relaxed atmosphere.

At the front of the restaurant there's a long narrow bar with a couple of gray upholstered booths for dining; the room in the back, seating only about 30, is simple but takes on a special air of elegance, even romance at night.

The food is exquisite. I can honestly say that I have never tasted a filet mignon as tender as the one served here with a luscious béarnaise, nor a more flavorful salmon (in lemon and capers cooked to a perfect moistness). Other entrees (veal, lamb, duck) and daily specials are priced from a modest $13 to $20. Desserts are all homemade, and the real specialty of the house is an alluring black velvet cake that is, in fact, an orange sponge cake wrapped around chocolate mousse and then finished with a chocolate glaze. To find Jethro's, take Orange Street West (it's one-way) to Ruby Street and turn left. Go down one block to 1st Street; the restaurant's on the corner.

DINNER: Monday to Thursday from 5 to 10 P.M., on Friday and Saturday until 10:30 P.M., and on Sunday until 9 P.M.

Located upstairs, the **Loft,** corner of North Water and West Orange Streets (tel. 717/299-0661), affects a country atmosphere with an occasional farm implement or piece of wicker hanging around or above the cozy booths. The people who run this place are very gracious and considerate of their customers and have installed a special mechanical chair-lift for those unable or too fragile to climb the stairs. Good for lunch or dinner. At lunch expect to find a wide choice: hamburgers, salads, London broil with mushroom sauce, stuffed shrimp, and delicious crab sandwiches, all under $7. At night candlelight provides the setting for veal, seafood, beef (Stroganoff served with spaetzle), and chicken dishes, priced from $14 to $20. Most are around $16.

LUNCH: Monday to Friday from 11:30 A.M. to 2 P.M. DINNER: Monday to Thursday from 5:30 to 9:30 P.M., (until 11 P.M. on Friday and Saturday).

Hoar House, 10 S. Prince St. at King Street (tel. 717/397-0110), tucked into the courtyard of the Stevens House, is known for its imaginative food—poppy-seed salad dressing and other unusual ingredients. Fresh seafood, veal, and steaks are the specialties, priced from $12 to $20. The decor is lavish Victorian with lace tablecloths, and black ceilings adorned with (yes, indeed) gilt-framed pictures. Ask about the story behind the name.

LUNCH: Tuesday to Friday from 11 A.M. to 2 P.M. DINNER: Tuesday to Saturday from 5 to 10 P.M., until 8 P.M. on Sunday.

Lemon Tree Inn, 1766 Columbia Ave., Lancaster (tel. 717/394-0441). Although one expects to find a secluded rustic hideaway, the Lemon Tree Inn is in fact on the main Rte. 462—a yellow-brick building that has survived since 1858 and now proudly stands among gas stations, fast-food chains, and neon-signed roadside vendors. Step inside and you'll find a welcome haven—polished wideboard floors, stenciled wallpaper, wainscotting, and a series of Williamsburg-blue rooms. The bar is decked out with a few farm implements and plants from an adjacent greenhouse. The food runs to such dishes as chicken Wellington, sukiyaki, baked bluefish and other seafood, plus quiches and soups at lunchtime, all priced from $4. Dinner brings an assortment of classics—duck au citron, sweetbreads amandine, beef au poivre—ranging from $9.75 to $18.

LUNCH: Monday to Friday—ranging from 11:30 A.M. to 1:30 P.M. DINNER: Monday to Saturday from 5:30 to 9:30 P.M.

Right in downtown Lancaster overlooking the splashing fountains, trees, and brick courtyard of Steinman Park is a restaurant called **Windows on Steinman Park,** 16-18 W. King St. (tel. 717/295-1316). It's a very pretty three-tiered dining room decked out in French style, with gilt sconces and mirrors, green marble bar, tables set with pink tablecloths, fresh flowers on each, and pastel-hued upholstered chairs. The food is classic continental cuisine—sole Véronique; poached salmon with a champagne sauce; chicken breast sautéed with tomatoes, wine, and mushrooms; veal Cordon Bleu; and pheasant served in a cognac, truffle, and foie gras sauce. Prices run $12.75 to $19.75. To start, you might try smoked salmon, hearts of palm, or snails sautéed in garlic butter with Pernod and cognac. For dessert there's crêpes Suzette, crème caramel, or soufflé Grand Marnier, and more.

LUNCH: Monday to Saturday from 11:30 A.M. to 2:30 P.M. DINNER: Sunday to Thursday from 6 to 10 P.M., on Friday and Saturday until 11 P.M. BRUNCH: Sunday from 11:30 A.M. to 3 P.M.

In downtown Lancaster, **Market Fare,** Hager Arcade, 25 W. King St. (tel. 717/299-7090), directly across from the Market Building, is a fine luncheon, brunch, or dinner spot. Upstairs the atmosphere is café-like and the menu is light—salads, sandwiches, and soups—while downstairs is more formal (cushioned armchairs and 19th-century paintings) and the food consists of steak, veal, chicken, and seafood entrees, priced from $11 to $17. The brunch menu lists such items as mushroom-crab omelet, french toast with apple-almond topping, and eggs Oscar, priced from $8 to $10.

LUNCH: Monday to Saturday from 11:30 A.M. to 2:30 P.M. DINNER: Sunday and Monday from 5:30 to 9 P.M., Tuesday to Saturday to 10 P.M.

Although it's large and lacking any real atmosphere or decor, locals still swear by the **Stockyard Inn,** 1147 Lititz Ave., on Rtes. 501 and 222 (tel. 717/394-7975), for prime rib, steaks, and seafood at moderate prices—$10 to $21.

HOURS: Monday to Friday from noon to 9 P.M., on Saturday until 10 P.M., and on Sunday until 8 P.M.

If you enjoy diners, then try **Zinn's Diner,** on Rte. 272 in Denver, five miles north of Ephrata (tel. 215/267-2210), famous for the statue of an Amish man standing upright with a pitchfork in hand. It's a popular place for Pennsylvania Dutch meals, with daily specials like pork mit kraut, wienerschnitzel, and so on, priced from $4 to $10.

HOURS: Open 24 hours daily.

DINING IN LEOLA

A really wonderful find, if somewhat difficult to locate, is the **Log Cabin,** off Rte. 272 at 11 Lehoy Forest Dr., in Leola (tel. 717/626-1181). Tucked away in the woods and reached by the Rose Hill covered bridge spanning Cocalico Creek, as befits a spot that was built during Prohibition, the Log Cabin offers some excellent food—primarily steaks—in a series of comfortable convivial dining rooms. The original log cabin room now has brass chandeliers and plenty of mirrors. Cozy booths only provide seating in another room, Windsor chairs and a selection of portraits accent another, and then there's a room with barn siding, beams, and plush comfortable armchairs. A meal begins with a hot loaf of bread and a plate of crackers and cheese. The food is straightforward and good—steaks, double-cut lamb chops, roast duck, lobster, stuffed flounder with crabmeat. Entrees run $11.50 to $21. To start, there's a selection of such appetizers as marinated herring in sour cream, oysters on the half shell, and baked cherrystone clams with garlic butter. For dessert, try such standards as chocolate mousse, cheesecake, and carrot cake. Upstairs there's a comfortable lounge area with a pianist/singer entertaining. Cocktails can be enjoyed while seated on couches and easy chairs amid an Oriental-accented atmosphere.

DINNER: Monday to Friday from 5 to 10 P.M., on Saturday to 11 P.M.

LODGING AND DINING ACROSS THE SUSQUEHANNA

The **Accomac Inn,** Wrightsville (tel. 717/252-1521), is located in a 200-year-old stone house right down by the Susquehanna River, a peaceful spot with a screened-in porch set with tables covered with blue gingham. Inside, the dining rooms are formal: tables are set with white cloths, pewter candlesticks and plates, fresh flowers in pewter mugs; Queen Anne–style chairs, gilt-framed landscapes and portraits, and a stucco hearth create the ambience. The bar is equally formal, only in Chippendale style. The menu features classic French dishes—duck à l'orange, faisan en croûte au vin de Ports (breast of pheasant, duck mousse, port wine sauce, and wild rice baked in puff pastry), steak Diane, truite aux noisettes, (trout topped with hazelnut butter and garnished with hazelnuts), and rack of lamb. Prices range from $15 to $20. The luscious desserts include baked Alaska, an apricot gâteau with apricot filling and butter-cream icing, bananas Foster, crêpes Suzette, and more. The $14 brunch features eggs Benedict, quiches, omelets, and more exciting fare like haddock with grapes in a shrimp-flavored sauce, tenderloin tips with poached eggs and a béarnaise sauce. The price includes soup, breads, fresh-fruit salad, champagne, desserts, and coffee.

LUNCH: 11 A.M. to 2:30 P.M. daily. DINNER: 5:30 to 9:30 P.M. daily. BRUNCH: Sunday from 11 A.M. to 2:30 P.M.

Roundtop, R.D. 2, Box 258, Wrightsville, PA 17368 (tel. 717/252-3169), is an extremely secluded double-porched 100-year-old stone lodging high on the bluff overlooking the Susquehanna River Valley. It will take some finding, as it's tucked away up a private road (call for directions). There are five bedrooms available, one with private bath. Each is furnished eclectically, some with an antique look, others with modern beds. In the Rose Room, for example, there's a wing chair, a polished mahogany Empire-style table, desk, chest, and twin beds with crocheted coverlet; the carpet and walls are rose-colored. The Blue Room has a working fireplace, highboy, carved-brass log box, clubfoot desk, and wrought-iron floor lamp, all set against a Wedgwood-blue color scheme. Country magazines are scattered around in each room. Fourth-floor rooms are tucked under the eaves, and from each floor the balcony affords a long view across the river to Lancaster County and Marietta. My favorite room in the whole house is the parlor, with three walls of built-in bookcases filled with books (there's also a TV), and of course, sofas and easy chairs to read in. A breakfast of fresh juice, coffee and tea, fresh fruit, bran muffins or sticky buns, and something like french toast is served in the formal Georgian-style dining room with corner cupboards.

RATES: $50 to $75 double, $40 for the top-floor rooms.

STRASBURG

AREA ATTRACTIONS

Summer is the time to ride the **Strasburg Railroad,** Rte. 741, east of Strasburg (tel. 717/687-7522), and recapture the days when the great iron horses, their bells and whistles sounding, traveled round the mountain in a billowing cloud of coal-fired smoke. Scenic too. En route you can stop off, enjoy a picnic, and hop the train back. Nine miles round trip (45 minutes) from Strasburg to Paradise. Every car in the train has a history but one is especially appealing—an open coach featured in the film *Hello Dolly.* At the Railroad Museum next door you can see a large collection of the old iron characters. HOURS: The train runs weekends only during November and December and from the third Saturday in March through the last Sunday in April. During the summer months it runs weekdays and weekends on the hour from 11 A.M. until 4 or 5 P.M.

At the **Railroad Museum,** Strasburg (tel. 717/687-8628), the history and technology of the railroad industry from the earliest steam locomotives to 20th-century innovations are preserved and interpreted through exhibits and illustrations. Visitors may enter the cab of a steam locomotive, view the stateroom of a private car, see the interior of a Pullman sleeper, and walk under No. 1187—the 62-ton class of locomotive swept downstream for nearly a mile during the first Johnstown flood of 1889. HOURS: Monday to Saturday from 10 A.M. to 5 P.M., on Sunday from 11 A.M. to 5 P.M.; closed certain holidays. ADMISSION: $1.50 for adults; children under 11, free.

At the **Toy Train Museum,** Paradise Lane, Strasburg (tel. 717/687-8976), headquarters for the Train Collectors Association, you'll find the largest nonprivate collection of toy and model trains in the nation. In the historical hall are exhibits of toy trains from the last half of the 19th century to the present. Here, buffs will especially appreciate the classic 1928 Blue Comet set, while the average viewer will definitely note the pink girl's train pulling pink, turquoise, and lavender freight cars, which Lionel produced in the late '50s and which totally bombed in the marketplace! Kids and dads will love the operating layouts, reminiscent of department store displays from the first half of this century, while wives and others can commiserate with the poor female featured in the nostalgic movie that is shown every 30 minutes or so. HOURS: May 1 to October 31, 10 A.M. to 5 P.M. daily; April and November, weekends only; the first two weekends in December, Good Friday, Easter Monday, Thanksgiving Friday, and Christmas week from 10 A.M. to 5 P.M. ADMISSION: $1.50 for adults, 50¢ for children 7 to 12.

Kids'll also love the model railroad drama at the **Choo-Choo Barn**, Rte. 741, Strasburg (tel. 717/687-7911), complete to the finer details of motor cars running on the roads, animated figures at work, and even a "fire" in a home attended to by the fire department.

HOURS: In summer, 10 A.M. to 6 P.M. daily; in May, September, and October, to 5 P.M. daily; in November, December, and April, on weekends only, from 11 A.M. to 5 P.M. ADMISSION: $2.50 for adults, $1 for children 5 to 12.

STRASBURG AREA LODGING

Staying on a Farm

At **Neffdale Farm**, 604 Strasburg Rd. (on Rte. 741, east of Strasburg), Paradise, PA 17562 (tel. 717/687-7837), Ellen Neff has been welcoming visitors since 1968 to this 160-acre dairy farm, which also has pigs and two to four sheep. Her six guest rooms (three with TV) share baths. All are spic and span and comfortable. You're welcome to help milk the cows too, at 5:30 A.M. or 5 P.M.

RATES: $22 to $30 double.

Rayba Acres Farm, Black Horse Road (R.D. 1), Paradise, PA 17562 (tel. 717/687-6729), is off Rte. 741 east of Strasburg. Since 1971, Reba Ranck has been illustrating a "different way of life" to visitors who come down with their "electric fans" still marveling why they bothered when "you people don't have electricity" or to families whose children shriek "Mommy, Mommy, look at the sheep" when they are in fact looking at the family poodle. Still others, she says, "wonder that she doesn't have a college education when she's so knowledgeable about so many things." Reba is amused by such antics and blithely goes about her business, maintaining the four rooms in the main red-brick farmhouse, all with double beds and shared bathroom, and the accommodations over the garage, which include a double with private bath and TV and a large family room with two doubles and a couch, which can sleep up to eight people. Morning coffee is available free—just help yourself. The 100-acre farm is strictly a dairy operation, with a few sheep "for atmosphere." From the windows you'll look out across the flat landscape. You can set up picnics in the backyard with views over the fields. There's a swing for the kids.

RATES: $24 double with shared bath, $32 with private bath. An additional person is $4.

Other Strasburg Area Lodging and Dining

Timberline Lodges, 44 Summit Hill Dr., Strasburg, PA 17579 (tel. 717/687-7472), are set on a wooded hillside just outside Strasburg and provide privacy and seclusion. The lodges are all different. Your cottage might contain two double beds, a pine chest, and a sidetable in the bedroom; a fully equipped kitchen; a sitting room furnished with a couch, two armchairs, TV, and stone fireplace; a full bathroom; and sliding glass doors that open onto a wooden deck. There are also some new deluxe rooms with small decks, color TV, and tasteful furnishings. The owners, the Mowrers, also run a fine country restaurant decorated in earth tones which really glows in winter. The food is continental—cashew-mushroom Stroganoff, steak au poivre, congolese (flamed with brandy and served with cream sauce). Prices run $14 to $18. The adjacent bar-lounge is one of the few convivial watering holes in the woods—a rare find around here. Facilities include a swimming pool and game room.

RATES: $70 to $100 per night double occupancy (depending on the number of bedrooms), $420 to $600 per week; $10 per additional person per night. Rooms are $48 per night off-season. To get there, take Rte. 896 south, off Rte. 30, to Strasburg. Continue into Strasburg, picking up Rte. 896 going east and then follow the signs.

The **Red Caboose Motel,** P.O. Box 102, Strasburg, PA 17579 (tel. 717/687-6646). A fine time Donald Denlinger had, trying to get 19 25-ton hulks of rolling stock that he had purchased on a lark from Gordonville, Pennsylvania, to their current resting place down in Strasburg.

Yes, indeed, you'll be sleeping in one of these red cabooses, built in the early 1900s. Inside each one you'll find a double bed with velveteen coverlet, an engineer's lantern swinging over the bed, a TV atop a pot-belly stove, and a sink and stall shower in the bathroom. The larger cabooses have bunk beds as well. The rooms are small and cozy, as one would expect; hope for a warm still night, otherwise you'll be gently rocked by the wind. At the motel you'll also find a dining car—complete with brass Pullman lanterns, and gold-tasselled red velvet curtains—which is open from March to November, and a gift shop filled with all kinds of railroad memorabilia and trains, priced from a few hundred dollars to $39,000 for a large, custom-built outdoor model locomotive. By the way, Donald is the guy in the uniform.

RATES: Small caboose—$35 single, $46 double; double units with four bunks $51 double, $54 triple ($15 discount offered in December, January, and February).

The **Strasburg Inn,** Rte. 896, Strasburg, PA 17579 (tel. 717/687-7691), is a replica of the original Strasburg Washington House that served travelers from 1793 to 1921. Although it exudes all the imitation "charm" that such reconstructions inevitably seem to possess, the rooms are in fact very tastefully decorated and comfortable with their chintz wallpaper, chair rails, Lapp furniture, beds, desk, and rocker. The large dining room serves breakfast, lunch, and dinner daily, and a Sunday brunch buffet. Dinner items like crab cakes, flounder stuffed with shrimp, chicken Cordon Bleu, and broiled sirloin range from $10 to $14. There's an outdoor swimming pool, and bicycles are available free of charge.

RATES: $80 to $95 double in summer, $70 to $85 double off-season (the higher prices are for suites). Many different weekend packages are offered throughout the year. BREAKFAST: 7 to 11 A.M. daily. LUNCH: 11:30 A.M. to 2 P.M. daily. DINNER: Sunday to Friday from 5 to 8 P.M., on Saturday until 4 P.M. BRUNCH: Sunday from 10 A.M. to 2 P.M.

LITITZ, MOUNT JOY, AND AREA

AREA ATTRACTIONS

Only eight miles north of Lancaster lies the village of Lititz, a charming, undisturbed town that was a Moravian community until 1855.

In Lititz stop at the **Sturgis Pretzel house,** 219 E. Main St. (tel. 717/626-4354), and try to twist your own pretzel. Find out where and how the first pretzel was made, watch what it symbolizes, and see them being baked at the first pretzel bakery in the U.S. HOURS: Monday to Saturday from 9 A.M. to 5 P.M. ADMISSION: 75¢.

Walk through the village and browse in the antique stores and around Moravian Square, which was the town's hub in the 1700s. Here you'll find the **Brethren's House,** built in 1759, which was used as a hospital during the Revolution; the **Sisters' House,** built in 1758 and now part of Linden Hall, the oldest girls' residence school in the country. Here also stands the **Moravian Church,** first built in 1787 but rebuilt several times. The July 4th weekend is special here when a pageant of the Queen of Candles is held as more than 5,000 candles burn in Lititz Springs Park. The main street is also lined with crafts and antique stores worth browsing.

From Lititz it's only a short run over to Mount Joy and East Petersburg, where there are several fine accommodations and dining establishments, including Groff's farm, where you ought to plan for an evening meal—already discussed under "Pennsylvania Dutch Dining."

At **Donegal Mills Plantation,** off Rte. 141, south of Mount Joy (tel. 717/653-4122), you can tour four buildings—a mansion, a mill and miller's house, and a bake kitchen—and enjoy the gardens, trout hatchery, and nature rambles. First settled in 1736 by a Scots-Irish adventurer and later by the Pennsylvania Germans or Dutch, the mansion was originally a simple 18th-century stone farmhouse, until it was transformed into a more splendid residence in the early 19th century. HOURS: Easter weekend through Columbus Day, Tuesday to Saturday from 10 A.M. to 4:30 P.M. Columbus Day through the third weekend in November, on weekends from 1 to 5 P.M.

Also in the area, the **Michter Distillery,** Michter's and Distillery Roads, Schaefferstown (tel. 717/949-6521), is one of America's oldest, having been established in 1753. It is a national historic landmark and also the smallest legal distillery in the United States producing only 50 barrels of whiskey a day, made by the old-fashioned pot still sour mash method. In the restored 19th-century Bomberger Distillery visitors can view the hand hammered copper stills and three small cypress fermenter tubs that still produce one barrel of whiskey a day just as they did in earlier times. The tour also includes the modern distillery and the Jug House, a store that features Pennsylvania Dutch jugs and other whiskey decanters. HOURS:

Monday to Saturday 10 A.M. to 5 P.M., on Sunday noon to 5 P.M. Tours are given on the quarter hour. Closed major winter holidays and Easter.

Tours and wine tastings are offered at the **Nissley Winery** in Bainbridge off Rte. 441, via Wickersham Road (tel. 717/426-3514), along with a variety of special events. The place is appealing—an 18th-century-style stone building and plenty of acreage for a quiet picnic washed down by a bottle of wine, of course. HOURS: Year round Monday to Saturday noon to 6 P.M. April through December also open Sunday 1 to 4 P.M. for sampling and sales only. Closed major winter holidays and Easter. ADMISSION: $1.50 for adults, under 12 free.

LITITZ LODGING

The **General Sutter Inn,** 14 E. Main St., Lititz, PA 17543 (tel. 717/626-2115), a handsome three-story brick edifice overlooking the town square, has been famous for its unique feather beds, good food, and prohibition of dancing, cursing, gossip, and bawdy songs since it was founded in 1764 by the Moravian Church as the Zum Anker (the Sign of the Anchor). Today it's known for being one of the quieter retreats in the area. Enter into the downstairs parlor with Louis XIV medallion-backed sofa, carved marble-top coffee table, and parlor organ, which are just part of the ultra-Victorian atmosphere. Upstairs the corridors, carpeted with Oriental throw rugs, lead to 12 individually decorated rooms, all with TV and most with private bath. Ornate Victorian beds with inlaid work, shaving stands, and other eclectic pieces of Victorian country-style furniture add dash to the rooms. The dining room is equally richly decorated in deep cranberry, accented with old-fashioned gaslights and antique accessories. There's a pleasant enough cocktail lounge. On the Broad Street side guests can enjoy sitting out on the brick patio by the fountain. By the way, it's named after John Augustus Sutter, who discovered gold in California but then returned to Lititz, hoping to find a cure for arthritis in the town's famed mineral springs.

RATES: $64 to $78 double.

Swiss Woods, 500 Blantz Rd., Lititz, PA 17543 (tel. 717/627-3358), is indeed in the woods, overlooking Speedwell Forge Lake, and is styled like a Swiss chalet. It looks very appealing from the exterior—with modern rooms and accommodations that appear to have private entrances. Unfortunately no one was home when I stopped by, but you may want to investigate.

RATES: $45 double.

Glassmyer's Inn, 23 N. Broad St., Lititz, PA 17543 (tel. 717/626-2345), a sage green arcaded-porch building with a prettily flowered patio in back, a country store, and a dining room, also offers accommodations. Sadly, I was not able to view them, but it may well be a suitable place to stay in the lovely old town of Lititz.

RATES: $35 to $40 double.

MOUNT JOY/MANHEIM FARM LODGING

At **Rocky Acres Farm,** Mrs. Eileen Benner, Pinkerton Road (R.D. 3), Mount Joy, PA 17552 (tel. 717/653-4449), will give you a really warm welcome and provide a room and breakfast. Over a humpback bridge, along a twisting road beside a brook you'll suddenly come upon the farm around a corner. As you enter the yard, two horses will most likely be peering at you from their stalls, the cows may well be in the milking room, and Brownie, the dog will give you a friendly greeting. There are three rooms for rent in the 200-year-old farmhouse. If you're lucky, you'll be given the large front room, which has a fireplace and is furnished with a colossal, carved and painted Victorian bed. Other rooms are pleasantly but modestly furnished with cannonball beds, perhaps a marble-top chest; peg boards serve as closets, and the bathroom is shared. There's also a private apartment, which sleeps seven, with two upstairs bedrooms, a bathroom, living room, and fully equipped kitchen.

In the morning (unless it's Sunday which Eileen spends privately with her family) you'll be treated to a superb country breakfast. Although the fare may vary, there'll always be heaps of it. Plates piled high with scrambled eggs, ham, pancakes, the best home-fries anywhere, all accompanied by apple sauce, sugarcake, home-baked bread or muffins, jams, fresh milk, and coffee. By the way, those two horses out in the yard are for your riding pleasure, as are the surrounding groves and fields for your walking.

To get there, take Rte. 30 west, to Rte. 283 west, to Rte. 230 west, which will bring you into Mount Joy. In Mount Joy, take Rte. 141 south a short distance only, to Pinkerton Road. Turn left, and follow the road about three miles over the stone arch bridge.

RATES (including breakfast): $35 to $55 for two to four persons.

At nearby **Nolt Farm,** S. Jacob Street Farm, Mount Joy, PA 17552 (tel. 717/653-4192), Grace Nolt has three rooms for rent at her 100-acre farm. Similar country breakfasts are served here also.

RATES: $16 per person per night with a full farm breakfast.

When you stay at **Londe Lane Farm,** Rte. 7, Manheim, PA 17545 (tel. 717/665-4231), you really are part of the family. There is no privacy or separate entrance, and you'll be sharing the house with Elaine and John Nissley and their five children. Indeed 18 to 20 of you will probably sit down at the table in the kitchen to a farm breakfast of orange juice, eggs, bacon, homemade bread or donuts, toast, coffee and tea. There are three rooms available, two on the ground floor and one upstairs, all currently sharing one bath (although they hope to have an additional full bath next year). All three rooms are well suited to families: one has a double bed with twin bunks, and another has a double, two singles, and a crib. The quilts were all made by Elaine. A herd of 40 cows and two chicken houses are added attractions. Elaine does not serve breakfast on Sunday.

RATES: $30 per couple with breakfast, $25 without; teenagers are $10; children, $6.

LODGING AND DINING IN MOUNT JOY

I've already described Betty Groff's restaurant in the Pennsylvania Dutch Dining section. Betty and her husband also operate the **Cameron Estate Inn,** Donegal Springs Road (R.D. 1, Box 305), Mount Joy, PA 17552 (tel. 717/653-1773), an inviting red-brick Victorian mansion set on 15 acres that once belonged to Simon

Cameron, secretary of war to President Lincoln. They have restored and furnished it lavishly with antique reproductions. The 18 rooms, seven with fireplaces, are large and spread over three floors. In each room you'll most likely find a canopied four-poster or brass bed, Oriental porcelain lamps, two wing chairs, a writing desk, and Oriental rugs. The two top-floor rooms tucked beneath the eaves are a trifle smaller, more modestly furnished, and share a bathroom. Downstairs the lounge has been made luxuriously comfortable with a brocade-covered couch, Martha Washington chairs, assorted books, and TV. The food in the dining room is very different from the Pennsylvania Dutch fare served at the Groff's farmhouse. Seafood cassoulet and duck with brandy-peach sauce are more typical of the continental menu found here. Prices range from $14.50 to $17.50. Brunch includes some tempting french toast Grand Marnier and other interesting dishes. Red tablecloths, candlelight, and a fire in the winter make the small room glow. There's also an enclosed porch for summer dining. Liquor is served. Reservations only.

RATES (including continental breakfast): March through November, $55 to $100 double; in December, January, and February (except holidays) $50 to $80. No children under 12. LUNCH: Monday to Saturday from 11:30 A.M. to 2 P.M. DINNER: Sunday to Thursday from 6 to 8 P.M., from 5:30 to 9 P.M. on Friday and Saturday. BRUNCH: Sunday from 10:30 A.M. to 2 P.M.

Donegal Mills Plantation, Trout Run Road (P.O. Box 204), Mount Joy, PA 17552 (tel. 717/653-2168), off Rte. 772 to Musser Road to Trout Run Road, is on the National Register of Historic Places, the site dating from 1736. Here, deep in the countryside, you'll find graceful accommodations in a handsome mansion, a restaurant located in a red-brick grist mill, and a quasi-restored village.

There are 17 rooms available, most with private bath. Some are in the 1820 and 1870 mansion. The Victorian room possesses a high-back carved bed, marble sidetable, chest with hatbox, couch, and dresser. Grandmother's room has sloping ceilings, a clawfoot tub behind curtains, and early American furnishings. In another bedroom the focal point is a handsome brass bed and Renaissance Revival wardrobe. An adjoining sitting room contains an Eastlake sofa. Additional rooms are located in the Miller's House. A short stroll over the fields takes you to the tennis court, outdoor swimming pool, and fish hatchery. The mill restaurant is atmospheric with its brick floors, beams, Shaker-style chandeliers, and old landscapes on the walls. The food is typically regional, including a Scots Bridie (puff pastry filled with beef and sausage mix), German herbal roasted chicken, filet mignon, trout, and lamb chops. Prices run $7.75 to $15. Start with a choice of soup and finish with shortcake, apple pie, or similar.

The public is also invited to tour the property, learning about the early Scots-Irish pioneers who guarded the frontier and the later Krayville family who built the flour mill, the first half of the mansion (in 1790), the bakehouse, Grandmother's house, an extension at the rear of the mansion, and the red-brick mill (in 1832). When Jakab Krayville died, leaving a 5-year-old son, the trust was squandered; later the three Watson sisters from England purchased the property as a summer home and they extended the porch, adding the Monticello-style pillars. On the tour, traditional crafts and daily tasks are demonstrated. In the mansion itself people can view the incredibly cluttered Victorian parlor, complete with organ, tinsel print made from tea wrappings, gas chandelier, and magic lantern; and the adjacent dining room containing a pony rocking horse made of *real* pony hair.

RATES: $59 to $109 for the suites, including a full breakfast and tour. LUNCH: Thursday to Sunday from 11:30 A.M. to 2:30 P.M. DINNER: Thursday and Friday from 5 to 10 P.M., on Saturday from noon to 10 P.M., and on Sunday from noon to 8 P.M. Open March to December.

Bube's Brewery, 102 N. Market St., Mount Joy (tel. 717/653-2160), is as much fun as it sounds, and is indeed found in an old brewery. There are three distinct areas: stone walls and rafters and thousands upon thousands of empty bottles characterize the Bottling Works (tel. 717/653-2160). Downstairs, the Catacombs (tel. 717/653-2056) is precisely that—the old cellar area—now a romantic candle-lit dining room; and Alois's (tel. 717/653-2057), a plush Victorian dining room with lots of stained glass, overstuffed chairs and sofas, and oak chairs.

Steaks, light dinners, sandwiches, pizza, sole, and subs are served in the Bottling Works. All dinner prices range from $2 to $6. The Catacombs, where you'll be greeted by a serf in medieval costume, offers traditional steak and seafood dishes like broiled crabcakes, coquilles Catacombs (bay scallops, onions, tomatoes, garlic, peppers, and black olives in a lemon and white-wine sauce), filet mignon with herb butter, veal chasseur, and stuffed chicken breast, priced from $11 to $16. Twice a month medieval feasts are held. At Alois the prix-fixe menu changes weekly. Cocktails and appetizers are served in the parlor before diners move into one of the dining rooms. A sample menu offers veal medallions in port and ginger, pineapple-brandy-roasted duckling, filet mignon with Dijon cognac sauce, spiced scallops and cashews in tomato, among eight or so dishes priced from $12 to $23. These will be preceded by appetizer, soup, salad, and sorbet, and followed by desserts like crème Kahlúa or chocolate-chip banana cake.

LUNCH: 11 A.M. to 2 P.M., daily in the Bottling Works, Monday to Friday in Alois. DINNER: Bottling Works—Sunday to Thursday from 5 to 9 P.M., on Friday and Saturday to 11 P.M. Catacombs—Sunday to Thursday from 5 to 9 P.M., on Friday and Saturday to 10 P.M. Alois—Sunday and Tuesday to Thursday from 5:30 to 9 P.M., on Friday and Saturday from 5 to 10 P.M.

MAYTOWN LODGING AND DINING

Three Center Square Inn, Box 428, Rte. 743 (P.O. Box 428), Maytown, PA 17550 (tel. 717/653-4338), is in a quiet attractive town. Rooms are around the corner from the restaurant in a red-brick, Georgian building above a clothing shop. Most of the rooms have beds with eyelet lace canopies, cable color TV, air conditioning, Victorian-style love seat, wing chair, table with glasses, and chintz wallpapers. Some of the bathrooms have old-fashioned clawfoot tubs.

The restaurant, located in a 1780 building that was originally a tavern, serves typical American dishes—roast turkey, shrimp, and steak—priced from $11 to $15 in an early American atmosphere of oak beams and chairs and stained glass.

RATES: $69 to $79 double. BREAKFAST: Saturday and Sunday from 8:30 to 11:30 A.M. LUNCH: Tuesday to Saturday from 11:30 A.M. to 2:30 P.M. DINNER: Tuesday to

Saturday from 5 to 10 P.M., on Sunday from 11:30 A.M. to 7 P.M. BRUNCH: Sunday from 11:30 A.M. to 3 P.M.

A SPECIAL DINING PLACE IN EAST PETERSBURG

Haydn Zugs, Center Square, 1987 State St., East Petersburg (tel. 717/569-5746), is one of the finest dining establishments in the area. Both dining rooms are elegant with their Queen Anne–style chairs, pewter settings, pink napkins, and Williamsburg-blue background. Select from a menu listing about 16 entrees, including a fresh fish of the day, scallops with shrimp mousse, rack of lamb, veal St. Michelle, roast duckling with raspberry-champagne sauce, and pheasant sautéed in nuts with leeks and shiitake mushrooms. Prices range from $12.50 to $24. To start, you'll find such tasty morsels as baked stuffed clams, escargots provençale, shrimp Maui (baked with coconut and fresh pineapple), and mushrooms lyonnaise (stuffed with ground filet and finished with tomato sauce and cheese). Brunch items are cooked to order. The menu is seasonal, but among the eight or so entrees there might be pasta Alfredo, omelets, seafood quiche, tenderloin tips Dijon, or wienerschnitzel. Prices run from $6 to $14.50. Finish with a lemon sorbet or raspberry and blackcurrant sauce.

LUNCH: 11:30 A.M. to 2 P.M. daily. DINNER: Monday to Saturday from 5 to 10 P.M., on Sunday from 4 to 8 P.M. BRUNCH: Sunday from 11:30 A.M. to 2 P.M.

FROM LANCASTER TO EPHRATA AND ADAMSTOWN

AREA ATTRACTIONS

From Lancaster, Rte. 501 to Rte. 272/222 will take you all the way past the Landis Farm Museum to Ephrata, site of a fascinating religious community, and then to Adamstown, a well-known center for antiques—a total journey of 19 miles, which makes a perfect Sunday.

Landis Farm Museum, 2451 Kissel Hill Rd. (tel. 717/569-0401). Henry and George Landis were avid collectors of farm and related machinery and gadgetry, who used their collection to found this museum in 1924. The collections are housed in several buildings—22 in all—some original and some newly constructed, which have been laid out as a village. During the summer such crafts as tinsmithing, flax and wool spinning, and weaving are demonstrated, but whatever time you visit, the museum will provide insight into rural and 19th-century American life, offering much to marvel at from our 20th-century viewpoint. For example, did you know that one acre of land is required to keep one sheep, that one sheep is required for one person's clothing, that between 1750 and 1850 it took roughly 25 days to go 320 miles (or from Philadelphia to Pittsburgh), that a sickler could cut only three-quarters of an acre a day, compared to the grain cradle introduced in the 1780s, which could cut 2 to 2½ acres per day, or the reaper of the mid-1800s, which could cut 10 to 12 acres a day. Progress was comparatively slow in those days. HOURS: Tuesday to Saturday from 9 A.M. to 5 P.M., on Sunday from noon to 5 P.M., until 4:30 P.M. in winter. ADMISSION: $2 for adults; children under

11, free. To get there, take the Oregon Pike (Rte. 272 north) exits off either Rte. 22, 230-30 (the Bypass), or 72. Entrance to the parking area is off Landis Valley Road opposite the Landis Valley Resort Inn.

Ephrata Cloister, 632 Main St., Ephrata (tel. 717/733-6600). German Pietist Conrad Beissel founded this religious communal society, consisting of three orders—two celibate and a married order of householders—in 1732. From 1735 to 1750 about 300 souls lived here on 250 acres as a fully self-supporting community, complete with mills, craft shops, and so on. The celibates lived in the ten restored medieval-style buildings that you can see today. The doorways, which are extremely low, were meant to ensure a bowed head, an expression of a proper sense of humility. The Spartan monastic cells, where the celibates slept on wooden benches with wooden blocks as pillows, and the almost masochistic strictures of the community testify to the almost cult-like dedication that these followers felt for their leader, Conrad Beissel. He combined ideas from pietist, Kelpian, Jewish, Roman Catholic, Anabaptist, mystic, inspirationist, and Rosicrucian faiths. His followers rose at 5 A.M. for private devotions and passed the day alternating study periods with work periods of basket-making, printing, bookmaking, carpentry, and paper-making until their 6 P.M. vegetarian meal. This was followed by singing and music school and retirement to bed at 9 P.M. At midnight the bell was sounded for two hours of worship followed by additional sleep from 2 to 5 A.M. After Beissel died the practices became less austere and the community declined, although the group continued to occupy the property until the 1940s. The order was famous for the original music and hymns that Beissel composed, the singing and music schools, the art of fraktur, and the many important books that were printed here. A small museum shows archeological fragments that were recovered when the buildings were restored, along with fraktur and documents. During the summer, from late June to early September, on Saturday and occasional Sundays, *Vorspiel,* a musical drama depicting 18th-century cloister life, is presented at dusk. Take Rte. 272 north to Ephrata, then turn right onto Rte. 322. HOURS: Monday to Saturday from 9 A.M. to 5 P.M., on Sunday from noon to 5 P.M.; closed Monday from December to March. ADMISSION: $2.50 for adults, $1 for children 6 to 17.

If you have time, stay over until Monday and head out to New Holland for the regular weekly horse auction at **New Holland Sales Stables,** Fulton Street (tel. 717/354-4341)—an exciting, interesting event for any visitor from 10 A.M. to 1 P.M. Here, the local farmers and Amish and Mennonites bid for work horses and other animals. Later in the week the auctions are for pigs, sheep, and other livestock.

EPHRATA LODGING

Smithton, 900 W. Main St., Ephrata, PA 17522 (tel. 717/733-6094), is a bed-and-breakfast accommodation offering fine rooms with private bath and fireplace. In several of the rooms the cherry tables and desks and the maple rope beds were made by Alan, one of the owners. Each of the rooms is quite charmingly decorated. The Red Room contains a four-poster without canopy that is covered with a magnificent handmade quilt. There are plenty of chairs to sit in, as well as a desk with a Windsor chair. Ballfringe curtains, rag rugs, fresh flowers, and stenciling accent the country look. Among the Blue Room's furnishings, the rope four-poster with velvet canopy stands out. On the third floor there's a small suite. Four skylights, beams, and a Franklin stove give it wonderful character, as does the Red Star quilt. This is one of the quietest rooms, along with the Red Room.

Guests are welcome to use the attractive living room with its stucco-brick fireplace, comfy armchairs, valanced curtains, and country knickknacks in the windows, or to relax and read in the study filled with books. Breakfast (homemade waffles, fruits, coffee and tea, for example) is served at a harvest table in a room that also has a number of quilts, stuffed animals, and folk art for sale. There's also a brick fireplace here too.

RATES: $55 to $75 on weekdays, $65 to $95 on weekends.

A gray shingle home with maroon shutters, across from an old mill, the **Covered Bridge Inn,** 990 Rettew Mill Rd., Ephrata, PA 17522 (tel. 717/733-1592), is a lovely bed-and-breakfast accommodation run by lively Betty Lee Maxcy. From the wicker chairs on the stone porch of this 1814 home you do indeed have a view of a covered bridge. Four rooms sharing two baths are available, all nicely furnished in country style. The Red Room, for example, with its cranberry-colored fireplace sports a rope bed with a handmade blue-and-burgundy star quilt, early American table/desk, treadle sewing machine, blanket chest, and side table among its furnishings. Personal touches abound. In the Brown Room there's a trunk that belonged to Betty's mother, who brought it from Holland when she came to the U.S. The Canopy Room does indeed have a bed with canopy and Laura Ashley linens, along with a wicker armchair and other furnishings. All the rooms have clock-radios, cherry towel racks, fresh flowers, and country wreaths or artifacts on the doors.

Guests may also use the TV room and the living room containing books, fireplace, piano and organ, and comfortable couches. From it an Indian door original to the house (a solid-wood panel slips down to cover the glass half of the door) leads to the back porch. Breakfast is served at the one large table in the country dining room and might consist of cinnamon pancakes, pumpkin bread, homemade muffins and jams, or egg casserole. All this food comes out of what, to me, is the coziest most inviting room in this 172-year-old house—the kitchen, complete with brick hearth, Mexican tile, and pots, herbs, and baskets hanging from the beamed ceiling. Betty will provide picnic luncheon baskets for $5. Outside in the garden you'll find a Four Square, Pennsylvania Garden with herbs and a hammock for your relaxing pleasure.

RATES: An incredible $45 ($50 for the canopy room).

EVENING ENTERTAINMENT

Lancaster County is hardly nightlife country. Farm folk rise early, work hard, eat well, and retire early to rest for an early start to the next day. The rhythm is completely different from the urban pace we're used to.

Any evening entertainment is centered in Lancaster, where there are several bars, a prime historic theater, several cinemas, and good restaurants. Drinking spots include the **Lancaster Dispensing Company,** 33-35 N. Market St. (tel. 717/299-4602), which features bands from Wednesday to Saturday nights, a large selection of beers served in a decor of stained and etched glass, bentwood cane chairs, and lots of greenery (closed Sunday); and **Jethro's,** which is listed in the Lancaster dining section.

Theater

Lancaster is blessed with America's oldest theater, the **Fulton Opera House,** 12 N. Prince St., Lancaster (tel. 717/397-7425), where musical theater, children's theater, and light opera are played in the marvelous gilt-and-red auditorium. You can also tour the theater during the day.

At **Mount Gretna Playhouse,** Pennsylvania Avenue Chantangna side (P.O. Box 578), Mount Gretna, PA 17064 (tel. 717/964-3627), there's a special summer festival of Shaw and other dramas.

Franklin and Marshall College's **Green Room Theater** on College Avenue (P.O. Box 3003), Lancaster, PA 17604, also puts on good productions. Famous alumni include Roy Scheider. Call 717/291-4015 for information.

LANCASTER COUNTY ACTIVITIES

ANTIQUING: Adamstown is a great center, boasting 1,500 dealers every Sunday of the year at several large markets. Most famous is probably Ed Stoudt's Black Angus (tel. 215/484-4385), with over 200 dealers and a very convenient steakhouse. The largest is Renninger's in Denver (tel. 215/267-2177), with 450 dealer spaces indoors and another 400 outdoors. The others are Barr's in Denver (tel. 215/267-2861), and Adamstown Antique Emporium (tel. 215/484-2670). They remain open on Sunday until 5 P.M.

Lititz and vicinity is another, much smaller hunting ground—there are several stores downtown. New Holland also has four or five stores.

BICYCLING: Rental or free bicycles are available at certain accommodations —the Strasburg Inn, Host Farm, for example. Independent cyclists should contact the Lancaster Bicycle Club, P.O. Box 535, Lancaster, PA 17604, for information on their Saturday and Sunday rides. Pennsylvania Bicycle Touring, P.O. Box 87, Bird-in-Hand, PA 17505 (tel. 717/392-1676 between 7 and 9 P.M. daily) arranges tours that include lodging, breakfast, and dinner.

GOLF: Hawks Valley Golf, Denver (tel. 215/445-5445); Overlook Golf Course, 2040 Lititz Pike, Lancaster (tel. 717/569-9551).

HORSEBACK RIDING: Forest Ridge Stables, just outside Paradise (tel. 717/442-4259), offers three-mile guided trail rides.

PICNICKING: You can picnic on the Strasburg Railroad trip or in Lancaster County Central Park, Lititz Springs Park, or Burchmiller State Park on Rte. 222 south. See also "State Parks."

SHOPPING THE READING OUTLETS: En route to or from the Dutch country, you can stop (or spend the whole day) at the shopping outlets at Reading for shoes, shirts, sweaters, sportswear, linens, tools, jewelry, sports equipment—you name it, it's here being sold at a discount. For more information, contact the Berks County Pennsylvania Dutch Travel Association, Sheraton Berkshire, 422 West and Paper Mill Rd., Wyomissing, PA 19610 (tel. 215/ 375-4085).

SHOPPING FOR QUILTS: Quilts have a history and symbolism, and offer the women an opportunity to express their talents and love of color. Many of the patterns are derived from the patterns of the fields, the interplay of sunshine and shadow, the bounty of the earth, and of course, the celestial bodies.

Best commercial outlet is probably across the street from People's Place in Intercourse at the Old Country Store. According to the locals, the store only accepts work from the very best, rejecting as much as 40%. Better yet, shop at Hannah Stoltzfoos' farm on Witmer Road. Dotty Lewis is known for her talent in traditional weaving. Find her by calling 717/872-2756.

STATE PARKS: Susquehannock, c/o Gifford Pinchot State Park, 2200 Rosstown Rd., Lewisberry, PA 17339 (tel. 717/432-5011), has picnicking and hiking areas. Samuel S. Lewis State Park, c/o Gifford Pinchot State Park, 2200 Rosstown Rd., Lewisberry, PA 17339 (tel. 717/432-5011), has picnicking and hiking. French Creek State Park has over 7,000 acres for picnicking, swimming (pool), fishing, boating (rentals in summer), hiking (32 miles of trails), ice fishing and skating, sledding, and nongroomed cross-country skiing. (There are also 318 camping sites.) Contact R.D. 1, Box 448, Elverson, PA 19520 (tel. 215/582-1514).

SWIMMING: There's a pool in Lancaster County Park on Broad Street (tel. 717/ 299-8215). See also "State Parks."

TENNIS: Six tennis courts are available in Burchmiller Park on Rte. 222 south of Lancaster. Four are available in Lancaster County Park (tel. 717/299-8215). Also at Four Season Sports Complex in Landisville (tel. 717/898-2210), and Old Hickory Racquet Club, on Rte. 272 (tel. 717/569-5396).

HERSHEY

DISTANCE IN MILES: 170
ESTIMATED DRIVING TIME: 3½ to 4 hours

DRIVING: New Jersey Turnpike to I-78 to I-81, to Hershey exit, Rte. 743 south; or the New Jersey Turnpike to the Pennsylvania Turnpike to Exit 20, then Rte. 72 north to Rte. 322.
BUS: Trailways (tel. 212/730-7460) goes to Hershey.
TRAIN: Amtrak travels to Harrisburg. For information, call 212/736-6288.

Special Events to Plan Your Trip Around
FEBRUARY: Great American Chocolate Festival—demonstrations of chocolate dipping, chocolate facials/scrubs, and chocolate decorations; guest chefs and much more (mid-February at the Hotel Hershey).
MAY THROUGH LABOR DAY: Hershey park is only open during the summer.
OCTOBER: National Fall Meet of the Antique Automobile Club of America.

For further information about Pennsylvania in general, contact the Pennsylvania Travel Department Bureau, Pennsylvania Department of Commerce, Harrisburg, PA 17101 (tel. 717/787-5453). For specific information about Hershey, contact the Hershey Information Center, Hershey, PA 17033 (tel. 717/534-3005), or the Harrisburg-Hershey-Carlisle Convention and Tourism Bureau, 114 Walnut St. (P.O. Box 969), Harrisburg, PA 17108 (tel. 717/232-4121).

Imagine a theme park with three thrilling roller coasters and all kinds of other rides and entertainments, a zoo, chocolates galore—enough to feast on for several lifetimes—23 acres of beautiful gardens, and two hotel resorts that offer everything from golf to horseback riding, and you have Hershey, a wonderful town for the whole family to enjoy, which is just how Mr. Hershey would have wanted it.

Milton Snavely Hershey was a remarkable man who planned and built this utopian community in the Pennsylvania valley where he was born in Derry Township. When he was eight his family left for Lancaster and he was apprenticed to a candymaker. Ambitious and determined, Hershey began his own business at age 19, making a whole line of varied candies, but it collapsed when he could no longer obtain credit to purchase the sugar and other ingredients. So Hershey decided to go West, following his father who had already left in search of a silver strike. Stopping in Denver, he learned a new candy-making process—the art of making caramels—and he returned to try again, this time in Philadelphia, where he enjoyed a modest success until once again he was driven into bankruptcy. Undaunted, he returned to Lancaster penniless and managed to persuade a skeptical family to help start yet another business. This time he decided to specialize in caramels only, and soon orders were pouring in and outstripping supply. Hershey had finally built a thriving business, which he was able to sell for $1 million at only 42. By this time Hershey had already become interested in chocolate as a foundation for a whole new industry and had begun manufacturing a variety of chocolate novelties. When he sold his business he retained the right to make chocolate, and soon this enterprise also began growing so fast that additional space was required to keep pace with demand. Hershey decided to locate his new factory in the countryside, where he had been born and where he knew he had access to a hardworking labor force and also to the milk that he'd require to mass-produce his single product, a milk chocolate bar made with fresh milk. Despite bankers' objections, he built his factory in 1903, and by 1911 the business had grown to $5 million and Hershey was well on his way to becoming the largest chocolate manufacturer in the world.

Around his factory he set about building his dream community. First, he built homes for the workers, taking a personal interest in each building and issuing strict instructions to make each home different. He wanted to encourage the workers to own their own homes, and built only a few houses for rent. Gradually homes went up along Trinidad Avenue, Chocolate and Cocoa Avenues, and other streets whose names were taken from the cocoa industry. Churches, schools, a library, bank, store, and finally a post office followed, the last prompting a change in the name of the town, when the United States government demanded to know what the office should be called. A competition for a new name was run and a woman who suggested Hersheykoko won, but the final "koko" was dropped. At this time Hershey also designed and built his mansion at High Point, laying out the gardens much later which his wife, Kitty, had planned.

In 1907 he created an amusement park, golf courses, and a zoo, and went on to found his great school for orphaned children, all of which remain and continue to bring joy and happiness to a great many visitors and the community itself. In the 1930s, despite economic conditions, he embarked on a second building phase, which he justified by the low cost of building materials and the needs of the workers. He created the Hotel Hershey overlooking the town, a community center, an extraordinary windowless office building, a sports arena, which was the first concrete monolithic structure, and Hershey Stadium, which was finished in 1939. All of them survive today, and each one continues to serve the community and the town as Hershey dreamed they would.

HERSHEY ATTRACTIONS

Any visit should begin at the **Visitor Center,** on Hershey Park Drive (tel. 717/534-3005). From here it's only a short drive to the parking lot for the main thrills of any Hershey visit—Chocolate World, Tudor Square and Hersheypark, the Hershey Museum of American Life, and ZooAmerica/North American Wildlife Park. A free shuttle to all the attractions operates from June 11 to Labor Day.

Chocolate World

Hershey always appreciated the value of letting people see his business operations in action. Indeed, between 1927 and mid-1973 more than ten million visitors toured the world's largest chocolate and cocoa plant on Chocolate Avenue. In 1970 close to a million visitors arrived to tour the plant, so that it became necessary to cater specifically to their needs by creating Chocolate World, which now welcomes 1½ million visitors each year. Chocolate World takes you on a Disney-style ride through the chocolate-making process, from African cocoa-growing plantations, where 500 cocoa pods an hour are broken open by machete, through the manufacturing processes of cleaning, blending, roasting, milling, and grinding —all of which produce the liquor from which the cocoa and chocolate is made. Hershey, remember, pioneered the making of milk chocolate, and to this liquor is added milk (50,000 cows are needed to supply the daily requirements of the plant) and sugar, creating a mixture which is then refined, conched, and deposited in molds to create Kisses, bars, or Reese's Pieces, and all the other famous Hershey products. Appetite whetted at the end of your tour, you can shop for any and every kind of chocolate souvenir that you could ever wish for.

Tudor Square and Hersheypark

In his planned community Hershey had always wanted an amusement park, for he did not want to create just another industrial community. Over his mother's objections that the workers required no such luxuries, he had the park laid out in 1906–1907. There were band concerts at the bandshell, boating on Spring Creek, dancing at the oldtime pavilion, vaudeville acts, carousels, a miniature railroad, and even a roller coaster. Even though the park was remodeled in 1971, the original aim to provide fun for all the family was continued.

You'll enter via Tudor Square, a re-creation of a Tudor village of brick and stone, where the buildings have mullioned windows and a Tudor castle looms over all. Just to the right of the castle you'll find a guest relations building that provides tickets, tours, and information. Rides are the prime drawing card of the park—39 of them, including three roller coasters! First and foremost there's the superduper Looper, which travels over 50 miles an hour and loops riders 360°, literally turning them upside down; then the Comet, a wooden coaster with a thrilling 96-foot first drop and a 72-foot second drop; and the Trail Blazer, a side-winding high-speed centrifugal-force roller coaster. The first two have been listed as two of the top roller coasters in the nation. The Coal Cracker Flume ride includes a 55-foot drop and a dramatic "splashdown." For the less daring there's the Kissing Tower, the Monorail, and the Skyride, 30 enclosed gondolas that cruise to a high point 113 feet above the park. Perhaps the most charming and delightful ride of all is aboard the Carousel, built in 1919 with 42 jumping horses and many large stationary horses, all hand-carved by Italian craftsmen. There's also a giant ferris wheel. For kids, there's Kaptain Kid's Kove, a fantasy playground where youngsters can enjoy finger painting, a Hound Dog Jamboree, strolling clowns, puppet shows, and encounters with the famous Hersheypark Furry Tales costumed characters in between their romps in the Kid's Krawl Rope Climb, Tubular Sliding Board, and Teeter-totter Horses. In the park there's also an aqua amphitheater that features dolphins and sea lions.

Several areas are devoted to the food and crafts of local Pennsylvania Dutch and their forebears who came from Germany. At der Deitschplatz (Pennsylvania Dutch Place), potters, candlemakers, silversmiths, blacksmiths, and leather makers practice their skills on items that are for sale. Over at Rhine Land, a quaint reconstruction of a German village, you'll find many gift shops and stores, three cafeteria-style restaurants—Hamburger Chalet, Der Pizza Meister, and the Alpine Ristorante—and the Rhine Land Express, which chugs along Spring Creek following the original path of the miniature train. In several theaters you'll come across entertainment of all sorts, special musicals that are produced by Hersheypark as well as showcased top-name entertainment.

HOURS: Daily from Memorial Day to Labor Day, weekends only from mid-May to Memorial Day and from Labor Day to the end of September. ADMISSION: Including ZooAmerica North American Wildlife Park, $15 for adults, $12 for children 4 to 8. Check for special combination discount packages at the information center. For information, call 717/534-3900.

From Hershey Park a bridge leads across to **ZooAmerica,** where two indoor and three outdoor exhibit areas feature plants and animals in natural settings from five regions throughout North America, each demonstrating how particular species adapt to a specific type of environment—desert, swamp, forest, plains, and mountains. Although ZooAmerica is part of the park, it's open year round.

The Hershey Museum of American Life
This museum (tel. 717/534-3439) features collections of American Indian and Eskimo artifacts along with some Pennsylvania Dutch German objects, which are grouped thematically to highlight the functional and decorative beauty of items

used in early America. Among these treasures is the famous Apostolic clock (moving figurines depicting the Last Supper), phonographs, music boxes, early firepumps and engines, glassware, furniture, and pottery. HOURS: Memorial Day through Labor Day, daily from 10 A.M. to 6 P.M., to 5 P.M. at other times. ADMISSION: $3 for adults, $1.25 for children 4 to 18.

Other Attractions

Away from Hersheypark Arena and the surrounding attractions already mentioned, you'll also want to visit the famous **Hershey Gardens,** located off Hersheypark on a hillside en route to the Hotel Hershey. Here you can wander through 23 acres of gardens planted in spring with daffodils and tulips, azaleas and rhododendron, and blooming through summer with all kinds of flowers and shrubs, and of course, the famous roses—14,000 in over 800 varieties. Once a little 3½-acre garden, it has now been divided into five horticulturally themed gardens—English formal garden, colonial garden, rock garden, Japanese garden, and a garden of old roses. Open April through October.

You can also visit **Founders Hall,** which serves as the visitors center for Milton Hershey School. Hershey and his wife founded the school in 1909 to provide education for orphaned boys. It opened in the Homestead, the old farmhouse where Hershey had been born, with a total of four pupils. Today the same school owns over 50 farms and educates 1,300 boys and girls, who live in 84 student homes scattered across 10,000 acres. The school still reflects many of Hershey's ideas —that every child should learn a trade and learn by doing rather than simply reading, that each should be imbued with some kind of religious training and learn to help others, that each should learn how to farm and enjoy rural life. A 27-minute film at Founders Hall explains the school's history and life at the school.

HERSHEY LODGING

An ochre-brick building topped by a green tile roof and Spanish-style turrets, the **Hotel Hershey,** Hershey, PA 17033 (tel. 717/533-2171), is unique and wonderfully whimsical, representing a mélange of all the favorite places that Hershey and Kitty had ever stayed on their Mediterranean travels. The hotel is best entered from the terrace. Open the huge French doors and you're standing in a Spanish-Mexican square with brilliantly colored mosaic tile floors, a splashing fountain, stucco walls, and archways capped by a cloudless sky (yes, it's painted in).

Unfortunately, the theme is not continued in the accommodations. Rooms are decorated in beige and rust colors and well appointed with adequate seating (two wing chairs and love seat), coffee table, and desk, as well as the usual amenities.

The circular dining room looks out onto the gardens through windows with leaded panes overlaid with delicate stained-glass images of trees, flowers, birds, and squirrels. Hershey had much influence on the design of this room. He wanted a good view from every table. "In some places if you don't tip well, they put you in a corner," he said. "I don't want any corners."

At dinner you can choose the $22 prix fixe (appetizer, salad, main course, dessert, and beverage) or from the à la carte menu that features such dishes as shrimp and scallops bonne femme, pork with rice pilaf, roast leg of lamb, and various veal, fish, beef, and lamb items. At lunchtime there's an excellent buffet served.

Facilities include tennis courts, indoor and outdoor swimming pools, golf, lawn bowling, and horseback riding. Live entertainment is featured in the Hotel's Iberian Lounge.

RATES: $198 per couple American Plan (three meals), $167 per couple (including breakfast and dinner). LUNCH: Noon to 2 P.M. daily. DINNER: 6 to 9 P.M. daily.

Hershey Lodge and Convention Center, West Chocolate Avenue and University Drive, Hershey, PA 17033 (tel. 717/533-3311), is for the traveler who likes a large, modern place with complete entertainment facilities. Shutters and old-fashioned iron latches on the bathroom doors are the only faint note of rusticity in these efficient rooms with faux burled-wood headboards and furnishings. In the recently redecorated rooms, dark-rose carpeting is combined with floral bedspreads. Bathroom amenities include hair conditioner, shampoo, and shoehorn. Rooms also have coffee makers. Recreational facilities include indoor and outdoor swimming pools, four tennis and two paddletennis courts, golf, pitch and putt, and bicycles for rent. There are three restaurants to choose from, a lounge with live entertainment six nights a week, a quiet bar, and a cinema.

RATES: May 1 to Labor Day, $96 to $106 double (children 17 and under in same room, free).

Both hotels offer weekend packages. Summer packages include "Hello Hersheypark," an overnight plan including lodging, admission to the park, plus admission coupons to the Museum of American Life, Hershey Gardens, the Lodge Cinema, and an ice cream soda at the Hershey Drug Store, all for $74 per person double occupancy. A two-night package giving admission to the park both days is $135 per person. Another package gives two nights' accommodations, breakfast and dinner daily in a choice of three restaurants, and use of all recreational facilities for only $58 per person per night January through April and September through December, and $74.50 during the summer. There are also many other themed weekends available: call toll free 800/533-3131 for info.

HERSHEY DINING

The dining room at the Hotel Hershey is excellent and known for its fine luncheon buffets and first-rate dining.

At the Hershey Lodge, the **Hearth Room** is aptly named, given the size of its fieldstone fireplace. Here you can enjoy a complete dinner of calves' liver, sauerbraten, honey-dipped fried chicken, roast beef, or similar dishes priced from $11. The **Tack Room** specializes in steak and lobster. The **Copper Kettle,** located in the convention center complex, is open for breakfast, lunch, or dinner.

EVENING ENTERTAINMENT

Broadway favorites run every season at the **Hershey Theater** at Chocolate and Cocoa Avenues (tel. 717/534-3405).

Hersheypark Stadium hosts football, concerts, and other events.

The **Hersheypark Arena** (tel. 717/534-3911) is home for the Hershey Bears and also for such shows as the Ice Capades, the Harlem Globetrotters, and a mixed bag of entertainers from John Denver to Kenny Rogers.

J. P. Mallard's lounge, in the Hershey Lodge, offers live top-40s dance bands Tuesday to Saturday evening.

HERSHEY ACTIVITIES

CAMPING: Hershey even provides camping facilities at Highmeadow Camp, only two miles from Hershey on Rte. 39 (tel. 717/566-0902), on 25 acres of tree-shaded grounds. There are 260 sites, swimming pool, fishing pond, playgrounds, indoor and outdoor games, movies, and square dancing, and a supply store.

GOLF: Hershey is often called the Golf Capital of Pennsylvania because it possesses five beautiful courses: the West Course at the Hershey Country Club (tel. 717/533-2360) is rated one of the top 100 in the United States, while the Hershey Parkview Golf Course (tel. 717/534-3450) ranks among America's top 25. The east course at the Country Club is becoming ever more popular. There are also a couple of nine-holers, the original Hershey course built in 1933 at Spring Creek, and the Hotel Hershey Golf course. The Hotel Hershey offers packages.

HORSEBACK RIDING: The stables (tel. 717/534-1928) at the Hotel Hershey are open to the public year round. One-hour and half-hour rides are available.

PICNICKING: There's a picnic area adjacent to the Hersheypark/Chocolate World parking lot that is pleasantly landscaped.

SKIING: You can cross-country ski on the golf course at the Hershey Hotel.

SWIMMING: Both hotels have swimming pools.

TENNIS: Both hotels have tennis courts.

RHODE ISLAND

BLOCK ISLAND

DISTANCE IN MILES: 167
ESTIMATED DRIVING TIME: Allow 3¾ to 4½ hours to reach the Point Judith Ferry (you must be there 30 minutes ahead of departure).

DRIVING: Take I-95 to Rte. 2, to Rte. 1 via Westerly, to Rte. 108, which runs down the Point to Galilee/Point Judith.
AIR: On New England Airlines (tel. 401/466-5959 or 596-2460) flying from Providence and Westerly, Rhode Island.
TRAIN: Amtrak (tel. 212/736-6288) service is available to Westerly (with connecting taxi service to the airport).
FERRY: Interstate Navigation Co., Galilee State Pier, Point Judith, RI 02882 (tel. 401/783-4613 or 789-3502), runs ferries year round, six trips a day in season. Cost: $5 for adults, $14.50 for a car, one way. The trip takes about an hour and 20 minutes.

Nelseco Navigation Co., P.O. Box 482, New London, CT 06320 (tel. 203/442-7891), operates one ferry daily in season (with an additional 7:15 P.M. trip on Friday). Cost: $9 for adults, $20 for a car, one way. Advance reservations are needed.

Other ferries leave from Providence and Newport, Rhode Island, and also from Montauk, New York.

Special Events to Plan Your Trip Around
JUNE: Yachting Race Week (third weekend in June).
SEPTEMBER: Annual Road Race (the weekend after Labor Day).

For further information about Block Island, contact the Block Island

Chamber of Commerce, Drawer D, Block Island, RI 02807 (tel. 401/466-2982).

Even a brief two-day trip to Block Island will seem like a long, langorous vacation as the slow pace of island life works its miracle of restoring peace of mind and granting serenity to even the most jaundiced frantic urbanite.

When you go to Block Island, you feel like you're making a real journey. From the minute you pull onto the Point Judith dock, there's an excited, exaggerated sense of anticipation. Gulls wheel and caw overhead, fishermen unload their catch, boats chug in and out of the inlet, the houses stand swaying ever so slightly on stilts, and there's a rough-and-ready rhythm to the port that leaves Manhattan far behind. Once aboard, kids run excitedly from deck to deck, their orange and yellow oilskins flashing by as they go. And then suddenly the ship is under way and you're moving, pulling past the rock breaker, past the houses, and out into the ocean, until there's only water behind and in front—gray and cold and dappled with snow-like foam, or shining metallic blue, depending on the season. People settle back with their hampers or hang out by the snackbar until, suddenly, on the horizon the island appears, just a thin sliver, as often as not, emerging from the mist. Already one can make out the undulating contours of the island, then the clay red cliffs that are indeed reminiscent of those other famous cousins. A solitary house comes into view, then another and another, and finally if you're aboard a late-afternoon or evening ferry, the lights of the harbor sparkle ahead and the outline of the Victorian buildings appear as the gongs on the buoys sound out across the water.

You have arrived on Block Island, a beautiful, largely unspoiled island only 7 miles long and 3½ miles wide, which for its size offers an incredible variety of terrain. It's an island with gently rolling hillsides studded with wildflowers, windswept dunes, winding lanes bordered by stone fences, and more than 200 freshwater ponds colored with abundant water lilies. No fast-food chains here, few cars, and hardly a traffic light, although condominiums are beginning to appear, much to the dismay of the local independent islanders.

BLOCK ISLAND ATTRACTIONS

And what, then, you may ask is there to do? Relax, loll on the beach, wander over the rose-scented cliff tops, climb down to the rock-strewn pebble beach at the bottom of the cliffs, rent a bicycle and travel around the island, browse the few harbor shops, go fishing, swimming, clamming, sailing, or flying a kite, or any of those things that one traditionally does on an island. Or just plain sit and read or talk to the locals who'll fill your ears with many a Block Island tale. One such you'll most likely hear is the saga of the *Palatine,* a vessel supposedly carrying emigrants from the German Palatinate that went down off Block Island in the 1700s. It's said that the islanders plundered the ship, ignoring the imprecations of the drowning passengers. Even today, they say, a ghostly light can be seen seeming to burn at sea, a haunting remembrance of this shameful day.

If you'd like to learn more of the island's legends and lore, then pick up a copy of Livermore's *History of Block Island* available at several stores on the island. Also stop by the **Historical Society Museum,** opposite the post office. (HOURS: Wednesday to Monday, in season, from 10 A.M. to 4 P.M.), to view the period rooms and other local memorabilia.

Before we explore the island's lodging and dining possibilities, here's a brief tour of the island highlights. The island was originally inhabited by a tribe of Indians who called it Manisses, or "Isle of the Little God." In 1524, on his way to what he hoped was Asia, the Italian explorer Verrazano spied the island and named it Claudia, after the mother of Francis I of France, under whose flag he sailed. Before the name took hold, along cruised the Dutch navigator Adrian Block, who charted the island's location in 1614. And so it came to be called Block Island in his honor. In 1661 the island was sold to 16 settlers from the Massachusetts Bay Colony. To view the spot where they landed, take Dodge Street from the Old Harbor to Corn Neck Road and this will lead you out past Crescent Beach northward to the area known as the **Maze,** a nature lover's delight, consisting of over 11 miles of trails that emerge on the cliff tops. From here it's only a few minutes' drive to **Settler's Rock,** where the first settlers' names are found on the monument that marks their landing place. From here you can view the abandoned **North Light** at Sandy Point, which was built in 1867 and is currently being restored to house a maritime museum.

At the center of the pork-chop-shaped island lies the **Great Salt Pond,** on which the New Harbor is located, a fully protected basin for the docking of many pleasure boats. One or two restaurants and lodging places are also located here. If you continue out along Ocean Avenue instead of turning right at Corn Neck Road, you will eventually come to **New Harbor.** Turn left at the harbor and the road will bring you to the island cemetery set high on a hill. The decorated tombstones here stand witness to the local families and their members who contributed to the island's 300 years of history.

Nearby, for nature lovers, **Redman's Hollow** is one of five wildlife refuges on the island, a great natural ravine, located off Cooneymus Road. Here, many paths wind their way down to a point below sea level where one can spend a leisurely afternoon observing the wildlife that inhabits the area.

Most spectacular part of the island, though, is the **Mohegan Bluffs**—clay cliffs extending five miles—at the southernmost tip of the island, reached via Spring Street and Southeast Light Road. Here legend has it the Manisses routed and starved out the invading Mohegan Indians and pushed them off the bluffs into the sea. Several dirt paths lead to the sea and a view from 200 feet up out over the Atlantic and down to the rocky shoreline below. Stairs lead down at one place, or you can climb down on your own. Off to the left stands the **Southeast Light,** a quaint brick structure that was built in 1874. The lens then cost $10,000; today it

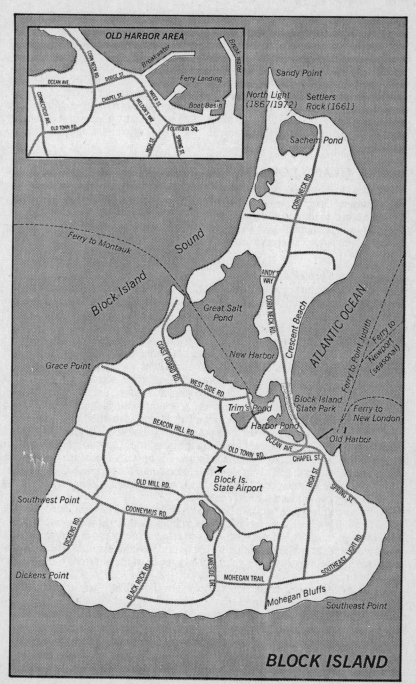

OLD HARBOR AREA

Break water

Ferry Landing

Break water

CORN NECK RD.

OCEAN AVE

DODGE ST.

CHAPEL ST.

CONNECTICUT AVE.

OLD TOWN RD.

WELDON'S WAY

WATER ST.

HIGH ST.

Boat Basin

Fountain Sq.

SPRING ST.

Sandy Point

North Light
(1867/1972)

Settlers
Rock (1661)

Sachem Pond

Ferry to Montauk

Sound

Block Island

CORN NECK RD.

ANDY'S WAY

Great Salt
Pond

CORN NECK RD.

Crescent Beach

ATLANTIC OCEAN

New Harbor

Ferry to Point Judith

Ferry to Newport (seasonal)

Grace Point

COAST GUARD RD.

WEST SIDE RD.

Trim's Pond

Block Island
State Park

Ferry to
New London

BEACON HILL RD.

Harbor Pond

OCEAN AVE

Old Harbor

OLD TOWN RD.

CHAPEL ST.

Block Is.
State Airport

OLD MILL RD.

HIGH ST.

SPRING ST.

Southwest Point

COONEYMUS RD.

DICKENS RD.

BLACK ROCK RD.

LAKESIDE DR.

SOUTHEAST LIGHT RD.

Dickens Point

MOHEGAN TRAIL

Mohegan Bluffs

Southeast Point

BLOCK ISLAND

would cost more like $7 million. It still warns the seafarers of this treacherous shoreline, the only perimeter to this pristinely beautiful island.

GETTING AROUND

The island is only seven miles long, so if you're staying in either harbor area there's no need for a car—it's less than a mile from one harbor to the other. Most suitable mode of transport is the bicycle, and many outfits rent them. Mopeds are also available. The state beach is so close to town that walking is still another option. And, of course, there are always taxis available. Cars can also be rented.

BLOCK ISLAND LODGING

You'll need to make reservations well in advance, especially in July, August, and all holiday weekends. Be aware, too, that if you're planning to fly in and the weather is bad so that your flight is grounded, most hotels will expect you to catch the ferry over. Otherwise you will forfeit the charge for your room for that night. So make sure to check reservation and cancellation policies carefully.

The Two Top Choices

The two most sophisticated accommodations on the island are undoubtedly the 1661 Inn and the Hotel Manisses, both owned by the Abrams family and both quite different.

The **1661 Inn,** Spring Street, Block Island, RI 02807 (tel. 401/466-2421 or 466-2063), has a colonial charm and looks out across a pond frequented by some regal swans to the Atlantic Ocean—in short, it has a marvelous location only a five-minute walk from Old Harbor. The inn is named in honor of the year Block Island was settled by courageous colonists from New England. Each of the 15 rooms (13 with private bath) is named for one of the original settlers, and each is furnished differently, many with decks overlooking the ocean. In the Samuel Staples Room even the bathroom has a view. The Simon Ray Room has cathedral ceilings and a brass canopy bed. The John Ackurs Room has two brass beds, a kitchenette, and windows on two sides with great views. In the guesthouse across the yard are four rooms with private bath, six with shared bath. The upstairs rooms are furnished in country style with oak beds, marble-top dressers, and lace curtains. Ground-floor rooms are more contemporary, although they also contain wicker love seats and chairs. Each room has a deck and ocean view.

There's a comfortable parlor in both the guesthouse and the main inn. A buffet breakfast—fresh fruit, a variety of cereals, waffles, hash, eggs and potatoes, blue-fish, sausage, muffins, smoked fish—is served in a pretty room decorated with floral wallpaper at tables set with pink linens and sky-blue napkins. Favored dining place in good weather, though, is outside at one of the umbrella tables on the deck.

The **Hotel Manisses,** Spring Street, Block Island, RI 02807 (tel. 401/466-2421 or 466-2063), is a gracious turretted white clapboard Victorian that has been decked out in period style. Even the staff wear pretty period dress. On the ground floor there's a comfortable wicker-furnished parlor where you'll find board games and some fascinating old, old volumes—*Historians' History of the World,* Bulwer Lytton, etc. There's also the small Top Shelf Bar here.

The hallways that lead to the 18 rooms (all with private bath, telephone, and some with Jacuzzi and refrigerator) are lined with a variety of Victorian portraits and pre-Raphaelite pictures. A decanter of brandy and a dish of hard candy are placed in each room. On the ground floor the Chelsea has a Jacuzzi, high-backed oak bed, wicker chairs and table, and marble-top dresser. The Prince Augusta Room possesses similar marble-top furnishings along with a deep-well dresser and a Madame Recamier couch. The Pocahontas Room has its own deck. the William Frederick Room contains an assortment of Victoriana, including a chair with a fold-out footstool, wedding-cake table, and Stickley-style chair.

Breakfast is served at the 1661 Inn; afternoon tea is served during the summer, and Happy Hour, with complimentary hot hors d'oeuvres (canapés, dips, chicken livers) is served at the Manisses downstairs in the Library Bar from 3 to 5 P.M. Bamboo chairs and pink-on-burgundy tablecloths contribute to the pretty ambience of the dining room. For those who prefer to sit outside, the sliding glass doors lead out onto a deck set with tables sporting yellow umbrellas overlooking the fragrant garden with a fountain. At lunch the fare consists of soups, salads, and sandwiches, plus a raw bar and an assortment of items like baked frittata, chicken teriyaki, fish du jour, and cheese tortellini cooked with assorted smoked fish, herbs, and cream. Many of the vegetables and herbs come fresh from the large garden that stretches behind the inn. At dinner, start with a selection from the raw bar, a clam-filled chowder, or seafood sampler Antoinette. Follow with a selection from the dozen or so entrees—steaks, baked stuffed flounder (with oysters and walnuts), scallops with fine herbs, bouillabaisse, duck au poivre, or basil chicken sautéed with pine nuts, fresh basil, and tomato. Prices run $13 to $21. For dessert there might be fresh strawberries, apple pie, chocolate layer cake with raspberry filling, and more. The Manisses opens in April, the 1661 Inn in May; the 1661 Guest House is open year round.

RATES: From about May 23 to October 13 on weekends double $88 to $115 with shared bath, $110 to $190 with private bath. In fall and spring $48 to $60 and $75 to $150 respectively. In winter $48 to $60 and $70 to $80 respectively. LUNCH AND DINNER: Until 10:30 P.M. daily from mid-June to Labor Day. Check at other times of year. For dinner reservations, call 401/466-2836.

Other Lodging Choices

The **Atlantic Inn,** High Street, Block Island, RI 02807 (tel. 401/466-2005), is an atmospheric old Victorian inn that first opened its doors in 1879. It has recently undergone extensive renovation and has been handsomely furnished with period pieces. It stands high on a bluff with the whole of the island at its feet. Shores, hills, and ponds spread out to view. There are 21 rooms, all with private bath and wall-to-wall Wilton carpeting. Rooms are variously furnished. For example, Room 3 has a high oak bed with burgundy comforter, sidetable, dresser, secretary, and wrought-iron floor lamp. Third-floor rooms have knee walls and shuttered windows, and assorted oak, marble-top, and Mission furniture.

From mid-June to mid-October, breakfast, lunch, and dinner are served in the dining room at tables set with dove-gray tablecloths and burgundy napkins. At night candlelight and classical music make it a romantic spot. At the sunset hour, around 8:30 P.M., there's usually folk music—mandolin on the porch. If you have to wait for a table the bar is attractively furnished with a camelback sofa and Stickley chairs. Note, also, the lovely collection of shells. At dinner the menu features about six or so entrees with a special emphasis on seafood—striped bass with plum-and-ginger sauce; poached salmon with lemon, thyme, and beurre blanc; pan-blackened codfish with three-pepper relish; supplemented by rack of lamb. Prices range from $16 to $20. Brunch is cooked to order. Other facilities include a croquet court, a boat that can be chartered, and two tennis courts under construction.

RATES: $100 to $150 for ocean view rooms, $90 to $130 for island-view rooms, in season and all weekends; midweek in May, June, and September–October, $65 to $85 for ocean-view rooms and $50 to $70 for island-view rooms. Open mid-May to mid-October.

Right down on Old Harbor, the **Surf Hotel,** Block Island, RI 02807 (tel. 401/466-2241 or 466-5990 in season, 401/466-2147 in winter), has a marvelous view of Crescent Beach and is more typical of Block Island's hostelries before the island was discovered by the urban tourist. The 40 rooms (seven with private bath) have floral wallpaper, lace curtains, bed, dresser, and rocker, sometimes of oak or wicker. There's often a sink in the room, and overhead fans. There's a kitchen available to store ice and other stuff. If you want to watch TV you'll find one in the kitchen and another in the sitting room. The dining room is great fun. The tin walls are hung with a pretty china collection. Tables sport blue tablecloths, and the room has a view of the ocean, of course. A complete breakfast is $5 and includes juice or fruit, cereal, and a choice among pancakes, french toast, eggs, and bacon, sausage, or ham. This is a must! For guests' use there's also a comfortably cluttered Victorian sitting area decked out in red with splendid wood-burning stove from Kalamazoo, a variety of seating, a giant chess set (each piece eight inches high) and assorted other games, plus a TV and a grand piano. Wood rockers line the porches overlooking the harbor, street, and beach.

RATES: June 20 to September 14, $50 to $55 double with shared bath, $70 to $75 with private bath; May 23 to June 19 and September 15 to mid-October (except on Columbus and Memorial Day weekends), $35 to $40 with shared bath, $50 to $65 with private bath.

Just down the street from the Surf, the **Blue Dory Inn,** Dodge Street, Block Island, RI 02807 (tel. 401/466-2254), is a small, pretty accommodation. Past the entry porch hung with flower baskets you'll find a ground-floor parlor with TV and Stickley furnishings. The main inn has ten rooms, all with private bath, some with high-backed oak beds, others with brass beds, and all with a variety of Stickley and oak furnishings. Top-floor rooms have skylights. A continental breakfast —fresh fruit, cinnamon rolls, croissants—is served at tables set with fresh flowers and tablecloths in a pretty room. The cottage sleeps six or seven, the Doll House has one room for the romantics, while the Tea House contains an efficiency and has its own porch overlooking the sea. Out back of the main inn there's a small patio with access to the beach less than 100 feet away.

RATES: May 23 through October 12, $90 to $125 double per night ($180 per night for the efficiency); from mid-October to January 1, $70 double; from January 2 to April 3, $60; and from April 4 through May 22, $75.

Across the street, the **Gables Inn,** Dodge Street (P.O. Box 516), Block Island, RI 02807 (tel. 401/466-2213 or 466-7721), offers a variety of accommodations. There are 13 rooms (four with private bath) in the main inn, each decorated with chintz wallpapers and featuring either oak or iron-and-brass beds. On the ground floor is a TV room and a sitting room furnished with wicker armchairs. On the ground floor of Gables II are several paneled apartments, each with fully equipped kitchen and dining area. These have immediate access to the lawn picnic tables and a barbecue.

Open mid-April through November.

RATES: June 21 to Labor Day, $50 to $60 double with shared bath, $65 with private bath; in spring and fall, $40 with shared bath and $50 with private bath. Apartments are rented by the week.

Old Town Inn, located a little way from Old Harbor at the junction of Old Town Road and Center Road (P.O. Box 351), Block Island, RI 02807 (tel. 401/466-5958), is a B&B operated by the Gunter family, who hail from England. The inn incorporates two houses, the older dating from 1832. Six rooms are found in each, all neat and clean and nicely, if simply, furnished with maple beds and chests set against chintz wallpapers. In the newer building rooms are larger and have full bath. Monica serves a full breakfast of eggs and bacon, and also a "proper" English tea in the afternoons around the brick hearth in the living room. The inn is surrounded by five acres, and in the back there's a pretty garden. Bicycles are available for rent.

RATES: $60 double with shared bath, $65 with private bath, $80 in the new wing. Open Memorial Day to mid-September.

Situated midway between Old and New Harbor on a hill overlooking the Great Salt Pond, the **Barrington,** Beach and Ocean Avenues (P.O. Box 90), Block Island, RI 02807 (tel. 401/466-5510), built in 1886, is operated by friendly Joan and Howard Ballerd. There are eight rooms in the house and two housekeeping apartments in an adjacent barn. The first floor rooms share 1½ baths. Each room is simply furnished with chintz wallpapers. In Room 5 there's a brass bed and wicker rocker. Top-floor rooms have great views and are interestingly shaped. In the basement there's a two-room suite with bath and porch—private and very cool in summer. Guests have a comfy room with TV and a selection of games. A breakfast of fresh fruit, muffins, and cereal is served on the deck out back with a view of the ponds. The apartments have two bedrooms, fully equipped kitchen, and living room. Out front there's a lawn, shade trees, and picnic tables.

RATES: June 20 to September 1 and Memorial Day weekend, $75 to $85 with private bath; $65 with shared bath; May 1 to mid-June and September 2 to October 30, $55 to $65; in winter, $35 to $55. Open year round.

Back in town, **Seacrest Inn,** High Street, Block Island, RI 02807 (tel. 401/466-

2882), is an attractive well-maintained accommodation. The 17 rooms, all with private bath, are sparkling clean. They contain a maple bed, sidetable, dresser, and rocker, all set against beige wallpaper. Three rooms have brass beds. The grounds are prettily landscaped with a latticework gazebo hung with flower baskets. Kids will enjoy the play area. Umbrella tables are placed on the lawn, which is also used for croquet. Coffee, juice, and danish are provided in the mornings. Bicycles are available for rent too.

RATES: $65 to $80 in season, $45 to $55 off-season. Open early May to mid-October.

The next two hotels are island classics. The **Spring House,** Spring Street, Block Island, RI 02807 (tel. 401/466-2633), is the largest and oldest on the island, having been built in 1852. The striking white clapboard building topped by a cupola is located on a hilltop overlooking the ocean and "The Village." The porch, set with rockers, extends along front and side of the building overlooking the swan pond. The original part of the building, where the cocktail lounge is located, has low ceilings. The lobby is large and extends into the ballroom/living room with 7-foot-tall windows and 12-foot ceilings where the focal point is a large stone fireplace. The dining room seats 150, and here guests enjoy a dinner that features three entrees—beef, fish, and poultry. A full breakfast is also served. There are 70 rooms, about 60% with private bath, all very plain and simply furnished with white-painted furniture and beds. The hotel stands on 15 acres and benches are dotted around the lawns.

RATES (including breakfast and dinner): $41 to $56. Open mid-June to the weekend after Labor Day.

The **Narragansett Inn,** Block Island, RI 02807 (tel. 401/466-0280), is set on a grassy bluff overlooking Payne's Dock at New Harbor. It was built around 1910 and still operates on the Modified American Plan. The dining room has a marvelous tongue-and-groove ceiling and wicker chairs set at tables with white cloths. Dinner usually offers three selections—fish, steak, and prime rib. The rooms are furnished plainly with metal beds, closets and dressers, and painted furniture. Most share baths. Some are located in other buildings on the property.

RATES (including breakfast and dinner): $46 to $55. Open mid-June to the first weekend in October.

Ballard's Inn, a well-known Block Island hostelry, was seriously damaged by a fire in late 1986, but the owner is planning to rebuild. Check it out.

Harborside Inn, overlooking the ferry dock at Old Harbor (P.O. Box F), Block Island, RI 02807 (tel. 401/466-5504, 466-2693 at the Gazebo), has 52 rooms, 30 with private bath. They are prettily decorated with beige/blue-striped wallpaper, color-coordinated carpets and spreads, and rattan furnishings. The quietest rooms are found at the Gazebo about 300 yards from the inn.

RATES: $70 to $120 with private bath, $50 to $90 with shared bath (lower prices represent off-season rates).

If you're looking for a room with TV and telephone, then the **National Hotel,** on Old Harbor (P.O. Box 189), Block Island, RI 02807 (tel. 401/466-2901), is the place for you. It also has a series of bars, a dining room, and regular live entertainment on the porch. It's located in a historic clapboard building with a cupola and gabled mansard roof.

RATES: $130 to $150 mid-June to September, $60 to $80 from October to April, $70 to $90 May to mid-June.

BLOCK ISLAND DINING

Breakfast/Brunch Choices
Certainly you ought to take one breakfast at the **Surf Hotel** served from 7:30 to 11 A.M. The **Atlantic Inn** also serves breakfast in season.

Down on the Old Harbor, **Ernie's** is another breakfast favorite, a coffeeshop-style place from which you can watch ferries docking while eating eggs, omelets, pancakes.

HOURS: May to mid-October from 6:30 A.M. to noon daily.

The **Number One Café** is the only place for breakfast that's open all year.

Ballard's offers a self-service cafeteria-style buffet breakfast. (Check to make sure it's reopened after the 1986 fire.) Or you can pick up a chocolate croissant or similar at **Aldo's Bakery** just behind the Old Harbor main street.

Breakfast is also served, on weekends only, at **Harbourside Inn,** right on Old Harbor.

Luncheon Choices
Best choice to my mind is to take a picnic to the bluffs or the beach, either purchasing it in an Old Harbor supermarket or stopping by **Tiffany's,** Dodge Street (tel. 401/466-2066), which last season offered some of the best food on the island. They'll make up a picnic for you or you can select from the specials listed on the blackboard and eat at the butcher-block tables. The list might include vegetarian burritos, hummus served with bread, tomato, peppers, and sprouts, plus a selection of sandwiches—priced from $3 to $5.50. Beer and wine are available. Desserts are also tempting—cannoli, mocha or hazelnut cheesecake, baklava, and real chocolatey brownies.

LUNCH: In season, 11:30 A.M. to 4 P.M. daily. DINNER: In season, 6 to 10 P.M. daily; off-season, Friday and Saturday until 9 P.M. BRUNCH: Off-season only, Sunday from 10 A.M. to 1 P.M.

Other possibilities? Try the **Hotel Manisses** (tel. 401/466-2836) or the **Atlantic Inn** (tel. 401/466-2005) for more formal lunches (see "Block Island Lodging," above).

The **Harborside Inn,** at the ferry landing (tel. 401/466-5504), offers a variety of sandwiches and burgers, and fish dishes like lobster roll, fried clams, baked scrod, and broiled scallops, priced from $3.75 to $9.25. Dine inside amid the nautical rigging or outside under the umbrellas.

Also on the harbor, **Finn's** has burgers, sandwiches, fried clams, scallops, lobster, and clam rolls from $2.50 to $7. Nearby, **Ballard's** also offers a variety of sandwiches and snacks, priced from $2.75, plus seafood, pasta, and other Italian dishes.

Over at New Harbor, **Dead Eye Dick's** features soups, salads, burgers, and pasta.

Sam Peckham's Tavern, New Harbor (tel. 401/466-2439), is one of the few establishments serving lunch and dinner year round, as well as breakfast from Memorial Day to Labor Day. Prices are reasonable: $9 to $15 for a full dinner of tuna, swordfish grilled on an open fire, or steak and ribs. The place is simple and homey, and looks out down to the Great Salt Pond. There's a convivial bar with some pool tables in back.

LUNCH: 11:30 A.M. to 2:30 P.M. daily. DINNER: 6 to 9 P.M. daily.

Dinner Choices

Two of the three top choices for dinner—the **Hotel Manisses** (tel. 401/466-2836) and the **Atlantic Inn** (tel. 401/466-2005)—have already been discussed under "Block Island Lodging."

The third, **Winfields**, Corn Neck Road (tel. 401/466-5855), is a pretty beamed candlelit restaurant where the tables have fresh wildflowers on the sparkling-white tablecloths. The menu offers a pasta and chicken of the day, plus a variety of seafood—Block Island swordfish with a mustard-and-honey glaze succulently moist and served with asparagus and potatoes. Other items might include turbans of sole with shiitake mushrooms; bay scallops with a mango-champagne sauce; shrimp with garlic, wine, and a Dijon and herb butter; tenderloin of beef with a bleu cheese sauce. Prices run $12 to $18. Start with any one of several shellfish dishes or an oyster bisque with bourbon, and finish with a white-chocolate mousse with chambord sauce or whatever is available that particular day. (Only one dessert is made fresh daily.)

DINNER: 6 to 10 P.M. daily; closed off-season.

Over at New Harbor, **Dead Eye Dick's** (tel. 401/466-2654) offers a variety of seafood—stuffed shrimp, fried seafood platter—steaks, and other items like chicken Dijon, veal Oscar, and duckling with raspberry-cream sauce stuffed with oranges, raisins, and cherries. Prices run $15 to $23. Among the desserts, Linzer torte and cheesecake are likely choices. From mid-June through mid-October there's piano entertainment.

LUNCH AND DINNER: daily in season.

The **Harborside Inn** (tel. 401/466-5504) has a selection of steaks, chicken, and seafood—baked scrod, swordfish, lobster, scallops sautéed in garlic butter—priced from $11 to $17. All entrees include vegetables and salad bar.

EVENING ENTERTAINMENT

There isn't too much. Watch the sunset, curl up with a book or a loved one, enjoy a fine dinner. There's also the **Empire Cinema** at Old Harbor (tel. 401/466-2230).

Captain Nick's (tel. 401/466-7777) has nightly dancing—a brick fireplace is the band's backdrop. So, too, does **McGovern's Yellow Kitten** (tel. 401/466-5855 or 466-5856), which, though open year round, functions as a bar in the winter with no dancing.

There's usually some entertainment given at the **National Hotel** on Old Harbor.

BLOCK ISLAND ACTIVITIES

BEACHES: Block Island State Beach and Crescent Beach (tel. 401/466-2611) are the popular sandy beaches. For a secluded (but pebble) beach, try the base of Mohegan Bluffs or the west side of the island.

BICYCLING: Rental places include Cyr's Cycles, Dodge Street (tel. 401/466-2241), behind the Surf Hotel; Esta's, at Old Harbor (tel. 401/466-2651); the Harborside Inn (tel. 401/466-5504); or Seacrest (tel. 401/466-2882). RATES: About $10 a day.

BIRDWATCHING: In spring and fall for the great number of migrating birds. This is the third-largest migratory center in the U.S.

BOATING: Sailboat rentals are available at the Block Island Club (tel. 401/466-5939); rowboat rentals, from Twin Maples (tel. 401/466-5547).

CAMPING: This is *illegal*.

FISHING: Many boats are available for charter, like Captain John's Charter Fishing (tel. 401/466-2526), which charges two people $70 for a two-hour minimum. You'll need a license to go shellfishing. If licenses are available, they are obtained at the police station.

Beach fishing is popular. For bait and tackle, try Finn's Fish Market (tel. 401/466-2102) or Twin Maples (tel. 401/466-5547). Rowboats can also be rented for fishing from Twin Maples.

MOPEDS: Available at Aldo's Mopeds, close to the ferry dock (tel. 401/466-2198) for about $25 a day.

TENNIS: Block Island Club (tel. 401/466-5939).

WINDSURFING: The Windsurfer, Andy's Way at Corn Neck Road (tel. 401/466-2875).

NEWPORT

DISTANCE IN MILES: 183
ESTIMATED DRIVING TIME: 4 hours

DRIVING: I-95 to the Newport Bridge.
BUS: Greyhound (tel. 212/635-0800) travels there.

Special Events To Plan Your Trip Around

MAY BREAKFASTS: Church and other civic groups hold celebrations for Rhode Island's early declaration of independence.

JULY: Newport Music Festival, when concerts are held at the mansions. Contact the Newport Music Festival, 50 Washington Square, Newport, RI 02840 (tel. 401/846-1133).

The Miller Hall of Fame Tennis Championships. For tickets and information, contact the Tennis Hall of Fame (tel. 401/849-3990).

Virginia Slims Tennis Tournament on grass courts at Newport Casino, Tennis Hall of Fame.

AUGUST: The Kool Jazz Festival in Fort Adams State Park. The Wooden boat show.

SEPTEMBER: The Outdoor Art Festival (usually early September).

DECEMBER: Christmas in Newport with wassail parties, Bach and Handel in the churches, and climaxed by a reading of "The Night Before Christmas" and a bonfire in Washington Square.

For further information about Rhode Island in general, write to the Rhode Island Department of Economic Development, Tourism Division, 7 Jackson Walkway, Providence, RI 02903 (tel. 401/277-2601).

For specific Newport information contact the Newport County Chamber of Commerce, 10 America's Cup Ave., Newport, RI 02840 (tel. 401/847-1600).

When Verrazano first discovered Aquidneck Island, he named it Rhodes, because the quality of the light reminded him of that mysterious Greek island, and indeed today when one approaches the town from the west across the high-arching bridges, one is awestruck by the beauty of the bay, especially on a sunny day when white, blue, and red sails bob, making kaleidoscopic patterns on the deep-blue background of the ocean—hundreds of them—adrift as if in a romantic dreamy idyll.

To a visitor Newport offers the perspective of an island, the excitement of a port, world-class events, wealth, and a wonderful blend of contemporary and past delights. The town represents two great eras of American history —downtown reflects the original, boisterous 17th-century mercantile community, and the mansions on Bellevue Avenue show the extravagance and outrageous fantasy and spectacle of the Gilded Age. It's a wonderful place to be.

In summer it swarms with life. The wharves are filled with sleek yachts and millions of dollars worth of powerboats, clinking and rocking in the harbor, their bronzed captains and crews crowding into harborside restaurants, bars, and stores, eyeing and vetting each other as they go. Behind the harbor, the narrow streets lined with stately 18th-century clapboard houses painted muted grays and sage greens add character and grace to the scene, although their shades must wonder at the parade of fashion-conscious and chic that now inhabits their lusty old port. Up on the hill the mansions stand empty, except for busloads of visitors who come to stare at the gilt, the marble, and the lavish rooms where great balls once were held and dogs sat down to dinners of stewed liver, rice, and fricassée of bones. In these opulent gilded surroundings daughters were pledged to dukes, insults were hurled, and the 400 members of fashionable society once cavorted so dashingly and freely.

First and foremost, Newport was a colonial town, a mecca for ambitious merchants in the 17th century, who risked their money, chances, and sometimes their lives, by engaging in the Triangular Trade between Africa, Europe, and the Caribbean, carrying slaves, molasses, rum, and sugar, defying the British and taking advantage of European wars to seize a greater share of world trade. They were fiercely independent souls, who had fled the narrowmindedness of Massachusetts, and their ranks included dissidents of every sort—Methodists, Quakers, Jews, and all manner of men, who chafed under the restrictions of British rule and were the first to declare their independence, an act that brought a contingent of

Redcoats into their city and led to its occupation and destruction during the Revolution. When the French arrived in July 1780, 300 buildings had been wantonly destroyed, and they found a beleaguered town that continued to languish for many years thereafter.

Its life and reputation as a resort began in the mid-1800s, when many southern planters discovered its pleasant climes and sought refuge from malaria and the oppressive southern heat. They spent their summers here in pleasant cottages like Kingscote. Soon, Julia Ward Howe's literary set and the moneyed folk from New York and Philadelphia followed. The last built cottages on a palatial scale, imitating the aristocracy of Europe, vying with each other to see who could outdo the other in the extent of their extravagance and display. William K. Vanderbilt spent $11 million on the Marble House, a residence that he used only two months of the year. Society flocked to Newport and days were spent languidly among luxurious surroundings.

Breakfasts were followed by tennis or riding. Lunches were taken aboard yachts. Lavish dinners and balls followed afternoons of polo. The cottages that they used for the season have been preserved and now stand as witnesses to this era of incredible wealth, ostentation, fantasy, and spectacle. Society also brought with it the two sports synonymous with Newport to this day—yachting and tennis. The America's Cup Challenge was moved from New York to Newport in 1930, and the cup remained here until 1983, when it was carried off by the Australians only to be returned triumphantly to the U.S. in 1987. The U.S. National Tennis Championships were held at the Newport Casino from 1881 until they moved to Forest Hills, New York, and if you like, you can play on those hallowed grass courts.

Mansions, extravagant hostesses, melodramatic scenes, colonial tales of free-booting merchants and pirates, ships and yachts, elegant pastimes—Newport has it all—chic, beauty, history, romance, the ocean, and the nerve to remain a prestigious East Coast resort, a role bestowed on it by the generations that have gone before.

NEWPORT ATTRACTIONS

The Mansions
Plan to see only two or three mansions in a day. Tours last one hour and you'll soon be exhausted and surfeited. On weekends you'll want to get there early, because the crowds and busloads of people can be horrendous. I would see Kingscote (1839), an example of the earlier cottages that preceded the Gilded Age, and the Château-Sur-Mer (1852), both of which have an added charm because they still seem lived in. The more extravagant era of the 1890s can be captured at The Breakers, the Marble House, The Elms, or Rosecliff. Here follow a few details about each, followed by touring and admission information.

Kingscote (1839), Bellevue Avenue, was built by Richard Upjohn for George Noble Jones of Savannah, Georgia, and later acquired by William Henry King, a China trader, after whom it is named. The house is furnished with fine Oriental export pieces. Most dramatic is the dining room, added in 1881 and designed by Stanford White. Light shimmers over the opalescent Tiffany brick tiles that surround the Siena marble fireplace at one end of the room, while an intricate spindle-work screen encloses the other. The paneling is mahogany, while the ceilings and upper walls are of cork. The tour is intimate and interesting.

Château-Sur-Mer, Bellevue Avenue, was originally built in 1852 and transformed by Richard Morris Hunt into a grand château 20 years later. Owner William Shepard Wetmore, another China trader, entertained lavishly. At one of these affairs, held for George Peabody of London in 1857 and attended by 3,000 guests from both sides of the Atlantic, Wetmore served woodcocks, plovers, and snipes among the entrees, and confections that were molded in the shapes of Washington and Lafayette. To some the house may appear austere and somber, with its granite exterior, extensive use of Eastlake ash paneling in the entrance hall, staircase, and morning room, and heavy butternut furnishings in the bedrooms. Note the extravagantly carved Italianate overmantel in the dining room depicting Bacchus.

The Breakers (1895), Ochre Point Avenue, was built for Cornelius Vanderbilt II and is the most lavish and Italianate of the cottages. It contains 70 rooms, 33 being used for the 40-strong army of servants. The most striking attributes are the beautiful multicolored (rose to gray-green) marbles used throughout; the arched double loggia with mosaic ceilings, which provides dramatic ocean vistas; the music room, which was constructed in Europe and shipped here for reassembly; faucets that deliver salt and fresh water in the bathrooms; a two-story kitchen, sealed off so that none of the odors escaped; and a billiard room of gray-green marble, yellow alabaster, and mahogany. The house was used only two months of the year.

Rosecliff (1902), Bellevue Avenue, was the chosen setting for scenes in the films *The Great Gatsby* and *The Betsy,* and certainly it does have a romantic aura with its heart-shaped staircase, well-tended rose garden, and fountains scattered around the grounds. Theresa Fair Oelrichs was one of the three top hostesses of Newport, daughter of James Graham Fair, who struck the Comstock Lode. She was a stickler for perfect cleanliness and was even known to scrub the floor herself if it did not meet her standards. Designed by McKim, Mead, and White after the Grand Trianon, it contains the largest ballroom in Newport, where Tessie staged such extravagant balls as the White Ball, at which all the flowers and decorations were white, the guests were also all in white, while outside on the ocean floated several white-sailed ships, just to complete the effect.

The Marble House (1892), Bellevue Avenue, was where Alva Belmont held court when she was the wife of William K. Vanderbilt. A dashing woman, she was the first of her set to cycle in bloomers, to own a car of her own, to cut her hair at the shoulders, and to divorce (she married O. H. P. Belmont). The $11-million cottage was modeled after the Petit Trianon by Richard Morris Hunt and contains the most ornate gilt-encrusted ballroom you'll ever see, where daughter Consuelo debuted and became engaged to the ninth Duke of Marlborough in 1895. The dining room is furnished with bronze chairs that weighed so much they required a servant's help whenever a guest wanted to sit or rise. The Chinese Teahouse was added by Alva, who also had a tiny railroad constructed to ferry the footmen

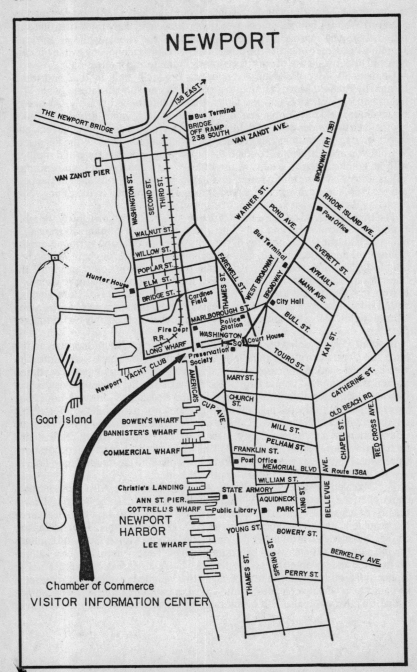

NEWPORT

THE NEWPORT BRIDGE

58 EAST

Bus Terminal
BRIDGE
OFF RAMP
238 SOUTH

VAN ZANDT AVE.

VAN ZANDT PIER

BROADWAY (Rt. 138)

WASHINGTON ST.
SECOND ST.
THIRD ST.

WARNER ST.

POND AVE.

Post Office

RHODE ISLAND AVE.

WALNUT ST.

EVERETT ST.

WILLOW ST.

Bus Terminal

AYRAULT

POPLAR ST.

WEST BROADWAY

MANN AVE.

Hunter House

ELM ST.

FAREWELL ST.

BRIDGE ST.

Cardines
Field

THAMES ST.

City Hall

BULL ST.

KAY ST.

MARLBOROUGH ST.

Police
Station

Fire Dept
R.R.
LONG WHARF

WASHINGTON
SQ.

Court House

TOURO ST.

CATHERINE ST.

Preservation
Society

Newport YACHT CLUB

AMERICAS CUP AVE.

MARY ST.

OLD BEACH RD.

CHURCH
ST.

Goat Island

BOWEN'S WHARF

BANNISTER'S WHARF

COMMERCIAL WHARF

MILL ST.

PELHAM ST.

FRANKLIN ST.

Post Office

MEMORIAL BLVD

CHAPEL ST.

RED CROSS AVE.

Route 138A

Christie's LANDING

ANN ST. PIER.

COTTRELL'S WHARF

Public Library

WILLIAM ST.

STATE ARMORY

AQUIDNECK
PARK

KING ST.

BELLEVUE

NEWPORT
HARBOR

LEE WHARF

YOUNG ST.

BOWERY ST.

THAMES ST.

SPRING ST.

PERRY ST.

BERKELEY AVE.

Chamber of Commerce
VISITOR INFORMATION CENTER

bearing tea from the main house. Later, she was one of the first to open the house to the public to raise funds for the suffragettes.

The Elms (1901), Bellevue Avenue, was built for coal magnate Edward J. Berwind by a relatively unknown Philadelphia architect, Horace Trumbauer, who adapted the design of the Château d'Asnieres, near Paris, creating a low-key classically symmetrical mansion. The grounds, dotted with bronze statuary, gazebos, and fountains, and planted with an amazing variety of trees, shrubs, and colorful sunken gardens, are the most remarkable aspect of the house.

HOURS: In summer, May to October 31, all mansions are open daily from 10 A.M. to 5 P.M. and sometimes later in the evenings. In winter only the Marble House, The Elms, and Château-Sur-Mer are open, on weekends from 10 A.M. to 4 P.M., the last two decorated for the holiday season. In April, The Breakers, Marble House, and Rosecliff are open daily from 10 A.M. to 5 P.M.; the others, on weekends only. For information, contact the Preservation Society of Newport County, 118 Mill St., Newport, RI 02840 (tel. 401/847-1000).

ADMISSIONS: Best bet is to purchase a strip ticket good for two ($7), three ($10), four ($13), five ($16), or six ($19). There's also a $25 ticket that covers all six, plus **Hunter House,** a colonial house (1748) worth seeing for its Townsend Goddard furniture, and **Green Animals,** a topiary garden with 80 sculptured trees in Portsmouth.

Other Mansions

Besides the mansions maintained by the Preservation Society, there are several others that are open to the public.

Belcourt Castle, Bellevue Avenue (tel. 401/846-0669), was built for Oliver H. P. Belmont and Alva, former wife of William K. Vanderbilt. It was designed in 1891 by Richard Morris Hunt in the style of Louis XIII's palace at Versailles. The most dramatic displays here are the 23-karat-gold coronation coach and the stained-glass windows. Costumed guides lead the way through the house, and tea is served to visitors. HOURS: June 21 through September 21, 9 A.M. to 5 P.M. daily; March 29 through June 21 and September 22 through November 23, 10 A.M. to 5 P.M. daily; November 24 through January 4 and February 16 through 22, 10 A.M. to 4 P.M. daily; closed Thanksgiving, Christmas, and January 5 through February 15. ADMISSION: $4.50 for adults, $1.50 for children 6 to 12.

Beechwood (1855), Bellevue Avenue (tel. 401/846-3772), was the home of William B. Astor where the doyenne of Newport society, Mrs. William Backhouse Astor, the former Caroline Schermerhorn, held court. With the help of a southern gentleman, Ward McAllister, she devised the famous "Four Hundred," a list of 213 families and individuals whose lineage could be traced back at least three generations. It was also the number of guests who could comfortably fit into the ballroom of her New York residence. So resplendent were her gowns and jewels that Mr. McAllister once remarked that she resembled a spectacular chandelier. Here you'll find no roped-off rooms or historic lectures, but a re-creation of the lifestyle that the Astors brought to Newport in the 1890s reenacted every day by the Beechwood Theater Company. HOURS: June through October, 10 A.M. to 5 P.M. daily. ADMISSION: $4.50.

Hammersmith Farm, Ocean Drive (tel. 401/846-7346), was John W. Auchincloss and family's summer cottage, where the daughter of Mrs. Hugh Auchincloss, Jacqueline Bouvier, and John F. Kennedy held their wedding feast. It's a beautiful seaside retreat and the tour gives charming details about the summers spent here by the Kennedy family. The gardens are also worth exploring. HOURS: April to mid-November, 10 A.M. to 7 P.M. daily. ADMISSION: $4 for adults, $1.50 for children 6 to 12.

The Colonial Era Attractions

Walking tours of Historic Newport are offered by the Historical Society (tel. 401/846-0813) on Friday and Saturday at 10 A.M., June 15 through September, at a cost of $3. They leave from 82 Touro Street.

Downtown, **Washington Square** is the center of colonial Newport. At the west end is the **Brick Market** (1762), still serving commercial purposes, and at the other the **Old Colony House** (tel. 401/846-2980), from 1739, which was used by the Rhode Island General Assembly until 1900. From the balcony here Rhode Island issued its own Declaration of Independence on May 4, 1776. This act of defiance brought the wrath of the British Redcoats down on the city when they occupied it during the Revolution, leaving it in ruins with over 300 buildings destroyed. HOURS: The Old Colony House is open weekdays from 9:30 A.M. to noon and 1 to 4 P.M., on Saturday from 9:30 A.M. to noon.

An independent town founded by dissidents from Massachusetts in 1639, Newport attracted a great number of diverse religious groups and their houses of worship can be seen today. Most famous is probably the **Touro Synagogue,** 72 Touro St. (tel. 401/847-4794), built in 1759 (although the first member of the community arrived in the 1650s). HOURS: Monday to Friday and Sunday from 10 A.M. to 5 P.M.

A little way down Broadway from the synagogue stands the oldest house in Newport, the **Wyman Wanton-Lyman-Hazard House** (tel. 401/846-3662), which was built in the 1690s. Open-hearth cooking is demonstrated here, and there's an interesting colonial garden. HOURS: Monday to Saturday from 10:30 A.M. to 5 P.M. ADMISSION: $1.50.

Back on Touro Street at no. 82, the **Newport Historical Society** (tel. 401/846-0813) exhibits Townsend Goddard furniture, colonial silver, toys, and dolls. The **Seventh Day Baptist Meeting House** (1729) is also part of the museum. HOURS: Mid-June to August 31, Tuesday to Saturday from 9:30 A.M. to 4:30 P.M.; closed Saturday and Sunday in other months.

A few blocks away in Queen Anne Square, you can see the spire of the 1726 **Trinity Church** (tel. 401/846-0660), inspired by the work of Christopher Wren and also by the Old Boston Church. The bells ring quite beautiful changes. HOURS: call the church office.

From here the whole area between Spring Street and Bellevue Avenue, and Touro Street and Mill Street, is known as **Historic Hill** and well worth wandering around to view the old clapboard buildings of this once-thriving seaport community.

The other historic area, **The Point,** is down along Washington Street on the harborfront, where the **Hunter House** is located at 54 Washington St. (tel. 401/

847-1000), a Tory residence that survived the occupation by the British, served as the headquarters for the French naval forces that arrived in July 1780, and is worth visiting today to see the Townsend Goddard furniture and the floor-to-ceiling pine paneling. HOURS: May to October, 10 A.M. to 5 P.M. daily. ADMISSION: $4 for adults, $2 for children 6 to 11.

Other Newport Attractions

Two absolute musts after (or even before the mansions): Drive or cycle **Ocean Drive,** stopping for a picnic at Brenton Point State Park; and walk along the back of the mansions the three-mile **Cliff Walk,** which stubbornly remains a public thoroughfare, showing the rocky coastline to full advantage. Downtown, you'll want to explore the many dining, shopping, yachting, and people attractions at such harborside complexes as **Bowen's** and **Bannister's Wharves.**

The **International Hall of Tennis Fame,** located in the Newport Casino building at 194 Bellevue Ave. (tel. 401/846-4567), designed by Stanford White, exhibits trophies, tennis fashions, and equipment. It also shows old Davis Cup films. The casino courts are where the United States Championships were played from 1891 until they moved to Forest Hills. HOURS: April through November, 10 A.M. to 5 P.M. daily; December through March, on weekends only from 10 A.M. to 4 P.M. ADMISSION: $4 for adults, $2 for children 6 to 18.

Among the permanent displays next door at the **Newport Automobile Museum,** 1 Casino Terrace (tel. 401/846-6688), are Jacqueline Bouvier Kennedy Onassis's first car, and an Alfa Romeo given to Hitler by Mussolini. HOURS: Wednesday to Monday from 10 A.M. to 5 P.M. ADMISSION: $3.50 for adults, $2 for children 6 to 12.

Military buffs will want to visit the **Artillery Company of Newport,** 23 Clarke St. (tel. 401/846-2648), to view the uniforms and other military regalia and memorabilia (HOURS: Wednesday to Sunday from 10 A.M. to 4 P.M.; ADMISSION: $1 for adults, 50¢ for children), and also the **Naval War College Museum,** Coasters Harbor Island (tel. 401/841-4052), for the history of naval warfare and the history of the naval presence in the Narragansett Bay region; enter via Gate No. 1 of the Naval Education and Training Center (HOURS: June through September, weekdays from 10 A.M. to 4 P.M., noon to 4 P.M. on weekends).

NEWPORT LODGING

The **Inn at Castle Hill,** Ocean Drive, Newport, RI 02840 (tel. 401/849-3800), has to be the most picturesque accommodation, with a commanding view of Narragansett Bay, Newport Harbor, and the ocean. It's a prime vantage point from which to watch the sailing and fishing craft bobbing around the bay or returning to port. In summer you can dine outside on the terrace, at the top of the grassy bluff that sweeps down to the water. There are two other dining rooms, each known for their continental cuisine where you can start your meal with lobster mousse served hot with morel sauce; or shrimp, scallops, crab, and lobster served with remoulade; or artichoke bottoms with goat cheese lightly grilled with basil and lime juice. Follow with any one of the fine seafood selections like lobster Rasputin in sour cream, caviar, and sherry; or monkfish in a crayfish sauce; or meat selections like saddle of lamb served with brown sauce with madeira and truffles; breast of chicken stuffed with chicken mousse with truffle peelings, poached and served with tarragon; Dover sole broiled with lemon butter; or paupiettes of salmon with beurre blanc. Prices run $17 to $20.

The inn was built in 1874 by Alexander Agassiz, son of naturalist Louis Agassiz, and it's known for the collection of Oriental furnishings that he displayed here. The accommodation in the turret was inspirational for Thornton Wilder, who wrote that he could "see the beacons of six lighthouses and hear the booming and chiming of as many buoys." The ten rooms are all different, many with exquisite paneling, some are oddly shaped, with dormer windows. Some, like Rooms 1 and 2, are undistinguished. Room 4, though, is either beautifully paneled and sports a bold floral-and-bird-patterned wallpaper. Room 8, tucked under the eaves, has plenty of wicker—chairs, table, lamp, and even beds. Sadly, the welcome is not always as warm as it might be, in my experience.

RATES: $55 to $90 December through March; $65 to $130 in April, May, and November; $85 to $165 June through October. Suites run $115 to $210. Lower prices are for rooms with shared bath. There are also several houses for rent.

The friendliest and most attractive place to stay—and also very conveniently located—is the **Admiral Benbow Inn,** 93 Pelham St., Newport, RI 02840 (tel. 401/846-4256), built in 1855. The vibrant innkeeper, Maggie, has a wonderful way of tending to guests and a genuine enthusiasm for what she's doing.

The 14 rooms in this handsome Victorian home, all with private bath, are large and comfortable. For example, the room I stayed in contained brass twin beds, dresser, wing chair, and couch. Curtains at the Palladian-style bay windows were cinched back; an old-fashioned gas lamp and chandelier provided light. Above the fireplace hung Oriental prints, all reminiscent of an earlier era. Other rooms are furnished variously with fish-net canopy beds, satin eiders, and a mixture of antiques and reproductions. Room 2 has a kitchenette and Room 12 has its very own large deck for sunning with a view of the harbor. The room itself is small but furnished with oak dresser, brass bed, sidetable, and Mission rocker, but it's comfortable enough. Room 9 has a handsome hooped canopy. Some rooms have air conditioning—ask.

Breakfast is served downstairs in the basement, decked out with colorful kites serving as wall hangings. Muffins, cinnamon-raisin toast, cereals, and fresh fruit are spread out for you to help yourself. Guests gather here in the evenings if they want to watch TV or warm themselves in front of the woodstove. A collection of old barometers is on display and also for purchase.

RATES: $70 to $100 in spring and summer (May through October), $50 to $60 in fall and winter (November through April); closed January.

Cliffside Inn, 2 Seaview Ave., Newport, RI 02840 (tel. 401/847-1811), would be my other choice Newport accommodation, even though it's located out toward Middletown. The lovely Victorian residence was originally built in 1880 by a governor of Maryland and later occupied by the family of artist Beatrice Pastorius Turner. The ten rooms have all been personally and carefully furnished, and fresh flowers are found in every room. Beds are spread with eyelet linens and ruffle pillows. In the Maryland Suite the bed is further enhanced by a special tented effect, and the fireplace is decorated with fans. The children's prints and pictures in the 1890s Room (and indeed throughout the house) add charm. The Flower Room is so named because of the brilliance of the wallpaper, complemented by a carved love seat, rag rugs, and pink wicker chair among the furnishings. The Miss Beatrice Room features a Lincoln bed, Eastlake chairs, and marble-top tables as well as a black marble fireplace. The bathroom is arrayed with a pink ruffled dresser and lace shower curtains.

A continental breakfast is served in a comfortable parlor crammed with Victorian couches, love seats, tassles, and objets d'art. The porch is a favorite gathering place, arrayed with turquoise wicker chairs on canvas-painted flooring.

RATES: $65 to $88 in season (from approximately June 27 to September 7), $60 to $82.50 in other months. Open May through October.

At the **Brinley Victorian,** 23 Brinley St., Newport, RI 02840 (tel. 401/849-7645), there are 17 rooms, eight with private bath. It's a large, rambling place occupying two houses (joined by a breezeway) situated a little distance from the immediate downtown area. It possesses much character, and each of the rooms is carefully and personally furnished with those extra touches, like fresh flowers and magazines. On the ground floor, Room 5 has a stucco fireplace, plus a double-poster bed set with Laura Ashley pillows and coverlets. In Room 4 a cherry bed is matched with a handsome Madame Recamier sofa against a beige chintz wallpaper. My favorite room is no. 17, featuring a high oak bed, Eastlake chairs, and a brick colonial fireplace. Room 12 sports striped floral pink-and-brown wallpaper, oak furnishings, and two brass beds. The iron bed in Room 13 is covered with a pink lace-trimmed coverlet. The second house also has a comfortable parlor furnished with books and marble fireplace. Room 6 has a large double bed set in the bay window and a single; other furnishings include a wicker sofa, kneehole dresser, and armoire. Third-floor rooms with knee walls are smaller and attractively furnished with oak and wicker. There's a fridge on each floor for guests' use.

A breakfast of fresh-baked goods is served in the Victorian-style parlor filled with a love seat and an Empire-style sofa set in front of the fireplace. Windows are covered with cream swag drapes. In summer breakfast is served in the brick courtyard. There's also an information/library area where guests can peruse books and menus of local restaurants or enjoy an assortment of games. Both houses have porches with swings and wicker furnishings.

RATES: April 1 to November 1, $75 double with private bath, $65 with shared bath; November through March, $65 with private bath, $55 with shared bath. Closed January.

Melville House, 39 Clarke St., Newport, RI 02840 (tel. 401/847-0640), is a charming 1750s shingled home, located on one of the quieter downtown historic area's streets. It's run by two enthusiastic innkeepers, Rita and Sam Rogers, who have returned to their New England home from the Midwest where Sam worked as an engineer designing household appliances. In the country parlor you'll find a testament to his interest in the subject, a collection of old appliances—cherry pitters, coffee grinders, mincers, dough maker—which Sam will happily demonstrate. Most of them had their shortcomings then too, just as our plastic gadgets do today.

Besides the collection, you'll find comfortable wing chairs and a sofa set in front of an old pine fireplace, home to a basket of cones and gleaming copper tea kettles. Breakfast is served at polished wood tables in a sunny room adjacent to the parlor. Rita makes her own granola and muffins (like chocolate chip or blueberry), which you'll find on the sideboard. There are eight rooms (one with private bath, the rest sharing, although another three bathrooms are planned). Flowers and fruit are placed in every room, and each is quite nicely decorated, primarily with oak pieces, beds with candlewick spreads, braided rugs, lace curtains, and so on. Ceilings are low and all rooms have character. It's a homey place. Games and books are available in the corridor leading to the rooms. Complimentary sherry is available at 5 P.M. when guests get to know one another and look over the dinner menus and discuss their evening arrangements.

RATES: $75 with private bath, $65 with shared bath; $50 with private bath, $40 with shared bath, from November 1. Closed January and February.

The **Queen Anne Inn,** 16 Clarke St., Newport, RI 02840 (tel. 401/846-5676), is located in a cranberry-colored peaked Victorian. Each of the 12 rooms (sharing seven baths) is decorated differently. My favorite is Room 6, a large room with a bay window and a maple bed decorated in Oriental tented style. Slip-covered chintz chairs, chest, table, and drawers complete the furnishings. Room 10 has two lovely old ornate brass French twin beds with crocheted coverlets; the wallpaper is pale green and cream garlanded. Room 11 has a unique low-posted brass bed and several pieces of oak furniture. Rooms are airy and filled with light. There's an upstairs sitting room for guests complete with a pink Madame Recamier sofa. Bathrooms are pretty, often with clawfoot tubs and lacy curtains. Downstairs, the reception room is comfortably decked out with an Oriental rug, couch, and French-style chairs. At breakfast, juice, breads, and Stella d'Oro biscuits are served, sometimes in the garden.

RATES: $40 to $60 double. Open mid-March to October 31.

The **Inntowne,** at Mary and Thames Streets, Newport, RI 02840 (tel. 401/846-9200), very conveniently located in the historic section, takes a contemporary approach to the interior of its two colonial-style buildings. The place is very nicely kept. There are 24 rooms, all with air conditioning and all clean as a whistle and prettily decorated, often with matching floral prints on walls and curtains. All rooms have pushbutton phones. By far the most interesting accommodations to me are in the Mary Street House—the Rathskeller in particular, named so because of the rounded pine door frames and doors, brick, and tile. It has a mirrored bedroom, a cozy sitting room with a couch and armchairs, and a full kitchen. It costs $150 in season. Other rooms in this house are also very attractively furnished with antique reproductions, and often with coordinated wallpaper and bedspreads. Breakfast of fresh squeezed juice, baked muffins, rolls, and beverage is served in the pretty dining room with polished wood table and ladderbacks.

RATES: $80 to $130 double.

Wayside, Bellevue Avenue, Newport, RI 02840 (tel. 401/847-0302), was built by Elisha Dyer, one of the "400" and cotillion dancemaster for the Astors and Vanderbilts. It's certainly imposing and lavish. In the entrance hall a large molded stucco fireplace is carved with cherubs and a coat-of-arms that includes the fleur-de-lys. A staircase of quarter-cut oak leads to the huge rooms. In fact some of the rooms are so large that they seem a trifle bare. All have small TVs. Room 1 has a double canopy bed along with a single bed, both covered with candlewick spreads. A wicker chaise longue, wicker table, and drawers are among the furnishings in this room hung with blue-rose wallpaper. Broken-scroll-decorated doors lead into the ground-floor room which was formerly the library. Even though there's an Oriental-style bed, couch, love seat, armchair, and Oriental chest, there's still masses of space. This room, decorated in bold blue floral wallpaper, also contains a handsome carved stucco fireplace. Coffee and pastries are put out in the morning for guests to help themselves. For what you get, rates are reasonable.

RATES: $75 double.

Old Dennis House (c. 1740), a khaki clapboard tucked away in the quieter part of the historic district at 59 Washington St., Newport, RI 02840 (tel. 401/846-1324), looks like a wonderful place to stay. The doorway is topped by a broken-scroll molding and decorative wood-carved pineapple. Rhododendrons and shade trees stand in the front yard. Unfortunately, when I stopped by I couldn't rouse anyone, so please feel free to check it out and let me know if it's as good as it looks.

Cliff Walk Manor, 82 Memorial Blvd., Newport, RI 02840 (tel. 401/847-1300), is located out of town a little way (about a ten-minute walk) en route to Middletown, right on Eastons Beach. It was built in 1855 and as a consequence the rooms are large and the ceilings lofty. It was originally owned by the Chandlers, relatives of the Astors. Many of the 28 rooms overlook the ocean across toward Middletown. So does the terrace adjacent to the restaurant-bar. Rooms have wall-to-wall carpeting, marble-top dressers and sidetables, rockers, and often Renaissance Revival–style beds with Marseilles coverlets. Some have Jacuzzis, and all are air-conditioned and have TV.

RATES: $100 to $180 double with private bath, $93 for a room with shared bath. Open April 1 to November 30.

Pilgrim House, 123 Spring St., Newport, RI 02840 (tel. 401/846-0040), a gray clapboard with a steep mansard located in Newport's historic area, functions as a simple bed-and-breakfast guesthouse. There are 11 rooms, three with shared bath. They are unpretentious, simply furnished with assorted furnishings—chintz wallpapers, ruffle-trimmed curtains, painted drawers, occasional pieces of wicker. In each you'll find a plant. At breakfast, muffins, fruit, coffee, and juice is served either inside or out on the top-floor deck.

RATES: $55 to $75 double in season.

If you're looking for modern accommodations in the historic area, then the **Mill Street Inn,** 75 Mill St., Newport, RI 02840 (tel. 401/849-9500), may be for you. It's a converted red-brick mill in which there are 23 suites available, including eight two-story "town houses" as they're called, featuring a downstairs sitting room and an upstairs bedroom with a sliding door that leads to a deck with a view across the rooftops to the harbor. Facilities include TV and telephone. Furnishings are strictly modern Conran's. Bathroom amenities include Neutrogena soap, shampoo, body lotion, etc. The living room has a bar area and fridge, pullout sofa, TV, telephone, and track lighting. All rooms will have air conditioning. Guests have use of the large communal roofdeck for sunning and relaxing. The one-level units have bar/fridge, pullout sofa, and other amenities. A continental breakfast is served at tables set with pretty pink tablecloths in a room with rough hewn-stone walls. Tea is also served in the afternoon.

RATES: In summer, $135 to $165 for suites, $165 for a "town house"; off-season, $75 to $100 for suites, $95 to $110 for a "townhouse."

The **Sheraton Islander Inn,** Goat Island, Newport, RI 02840 (tel. 401/849-2600), surrounded by water, is reached by a causeway. There are incredible views of the harbor in all directions. Parking is available (which is extremely important in this town) and you're a 5-minute drive or 15-minute walk away from the center of town. From the cocktail lounge, Rodgers Roost, on top of the building on the ninth floor, there's quite a view. The accommodations are spacious and modern. Double sinks are an added convenience. So, too, is the basket of amenities in the bathroom. Pushbutton phone and TV with free HBO are standard facilities. There are two dining rooms, another lounge-entertainment room, an indoor pool and outdoor saltwater pool, and tennis courts.

RATES: $70 to $85 double November to March, $115 to $135 in April and May, $130 to $165 June through August, $120 to $135 in September and October. Special weekend packages are offered, on fall weekends for as low as $140 per person for two nights with breakfast.

Harborside, Christie's Landing, Newport, RI 02840 (tel. 401/846-6600), is, as the name suggests, right down in the center of the action. The 14 accommodations here have a nautical air. You have a choice between a room or a suite. Both are furnished with modern pine furnishings (workbench style), the only difference being that the suite has a skylit loft bedroom reached by a ship's ladder (in a water-view suite) or by a regular staircase (in landside accommodations). Rooms are beamed, beds covered with Tattersall-style comforters, and facilities include pushbutton telephone, TV, and full bath. Water-view rooms and suites have small decks. There's a breakfast and sitting-room area furnished with director's chairs overlooking the dock and harbor. Help yourself to continental-style items at breakfast, hors d'oeuvres and tea in the afternoons (in winter only). Parking is available.

RATES: $105 to $150 in season, $90 to $110 off-season. Open year round.

Right in the center of the dock area, the **Newport Harbor Treadway,** at 49 America's Cup Ave., Newport, RI 02840 (tel. 401/847-9000), bases the room rates according to the view.

RATES: $130 facing the city, $170 facing the harbor. In winter rates drop to $70 and $80.

Covell House, 43 Farewell St., Newport, RI 02840 (tel. 401/847-8872), has six rooms in a beige clapboard colonial with pretty front porch and cozy parlor.

RATES: $65 in summer, $55 in mid-season, $45 in winter.

The **Jenkins Guest House,** 206 Rhode Island Ave., Newport, RI 02840 (tel. 401/847-6801), has two simple rooms and offers continental breakfast in a roomy kitchen or on the deck. It's a relaxed, casual place.

RATES: $40 double. Open in season only.

NEWPORT DINING

The **Black Pearl,** Bannister's Wharf (tel. 401/846-5264), is one of Newport's leading restaurants. The tavern is a cozy gathering place; the patio is great for a meal or drink and a sea breeze, and the intimate Commodore Room, decorated in dark forest green with brass accents and polished wood, is known for its classic French cuisine. Prices range from $15 to $21 for such dishes as paillard of chicken with lemon butter, sautéed duck with green-olive sauce, medallions of veal with morels and sauce champagne, filet mignon au poivre, and more. Among the desserts there might be cheesecake, homemade ice creams, and profiteroles. To start, lobster mousse and escargots are a fine choice. In the tavern prices range from $6.75 to $16. The chowders are so good I've seen people ask for several large bowls in the tavern, where the menu also includes burgers, omelets, and daily specials like bluefish with lemon caper butter.

LUNCH: 11:30 A.M. to 3 P.M. daily. DINNER: 6 to 10 P.M. Jackets are required in the dining room.

Away from the bustle of the wharves, another of my favorites is the **White Horse Tavern,** at Marlborough and Farewell Streets (tel. 401/849-3600), an old 1673 tavern that has a series of dining rooms with romantic ambience. The food is superb and runs to rack of lamb served delicately pink with aromatic herbs. Prices range from $15 to $25.

LUNCH: Monday to Saturday from noon to 2:30 P.M. DINNER: 6 to 10 P.M. daily. BRUNCH: Sunday from noon to 2:30 P.M. Jackets are required in the evening.

The **Clarke Cook House,** Bannister's Wharf (tel. 401/849-2900), for my money, is one of Newport's finest dining places. Located in an old colonial building are two dining rooms to choose from: the formal room, delightfully colonial with solid posts and beams, plank floors, tables set with brass candlesticks and fresh freesias or similar in silver stem vases, where black-tied waiters provide attentive service; or the Candy Store Café, which is more like a tavern-bar despite the marble tables. Here, models of ship's hulls and wood-framed pictures of sailing ships are the major decoration.

At dinner, start with warm salad of lobster and foie gras, or canapé of steak tartare, or buckwheat fettuccine tossed with bay scallops, mushrooms, bacon, and cream. Follow with a selection from such dishes as sole française with beurre grenobloise, breast of pheasant with crème normande en petit ragoût, entrecôte au poivre or au beurre Bercy (with shallot and wine butter), and ragoût of chicken bourguignon. Prices run $15.75 to $21.75. Finish with crème caramel or Locke Ober's famous Indian pudding. The café menu offers lighter dishes—pastas, stir-fried chicken with snow peas and ginger or angel hair, or shrimp gumbo on rice —priced from $6.50 to $11.

Brunch offers an interesting array of egg dishes, plus such dishes as nachos with salsa, guacamole, and cheese; grilled shrimp and Cajun sausage en brochette; angel-hair pasta bolognese; codfish cakes served with baked beans; Mexican pizza (delicious, and served on taco shell), or Irish lamb-and-stout stew. For such you'll pay $10, including a drink. Save room for a delicious dessert, especially the Snowball in Hell—vanilla ice cream with chocolate fudge served in an iced wine glass coated with chocolate.

DINNER: Wednesday to Sunday from 6 to 10:30 P.M. BRUNCH: Saturday and Sunday from 11:30 A.M. to 3 P.M. Closed Monday and Tuesday. The café is open from 11:30 A.M. to 10:30 P.M. on weekdays, until 11 P.M. on weekends.

La Petite Auberge, 19 Charles St. (tel. 401/849-6669), is considered by many to be among the city's top three restaurants. Although the service is gracious, the ambience romantic, and the food good, it seems a little overpriced to me and the meal not as memorable as I had expected it to be. Among the appetizers, you might start with a lobster bisque, chicken-liver mousse with truffles, or escargots bourguignons. Main courses, priced from $15 to $23, range from seafood —poached turbot with hollandaise, trout with almonds, and sole meuniere—to meats, including filet mignon Rossini and au poivre, chateaubriand béarnaise, and saddle of lamb with garlic sauce. For dessert there are similar classics —crêpes Suzette, banana flambé, peach Melba, and strawberries Romanoff. Tables are set with lovely lace tablecloths, lanterns, and fresh flowers. A classical music background, low lighting by wall sconces, and a handsome fireplace complete the romantic atmosphere.

DINNER: Monday to Saturday from 6 to 10 P.M., on Sunday from 5 to 9 P.M.

Christie's, Christie's Landing (tel. 401/847-5400), is home to the powerboat crowd and also a hangout for local politicos who like to drink and dine on steaks and seafood priced from $12 to $22. There's veal Oscar, salmon, lobster (stuffed, broiled, or served with tenderloin), swordfish, bouillabaisse, scallops, scrod, sole, etc., and a clam boil of lobster, steamers, corn, potatoes, and onions chouriço, plus steaks and lamb chops. The dining room is large and crowded, and a warm atmosphere prevails. In winter it's warmed by the large stone hearth. The long bar separated from the dining room is usually filled with locals anxiously watching the outcome of one of the Boston teams' games. Luncheon brings salads, sole, seafood pie, scrod, and other dishes for $5 to $8.50. Many famous folks' faces line the entryway here.

LUNCH: From noon daily. DINNER: From 5 P.M. daily.

The yachting crowd favors the **Mooring,** on Sayer's Wharf (tel. 401/846-2260), off America's Cup Avenue, which has a multilevel deck smack over the water. Besides the famous nine-vegetable salad, the menu features a mixture of New England and continental dishes, priced from $14.50 to $24. Among them are baked stuffed lobster, hot seafood platter (lobster, shrimp, scallops, and mussels in broth), jumbo shrimp stuffed with scallops and crabmeat in casserole, plus sandwiches, salads, and chowders. On Sunday after 4:30 P.M. prime rib is served. A 1¾-pound lobster costs $30 here.

HOURS: 11:30 A.M. to 10 P.M. daily.

The Pier, Howard Wharf (tel. 401/847-3645), is another Newport tradition, for steaks, seafood, and lobster served in half a dozen or so ways. Prices range from $10 to $23. There's nightly entertainment and dancing on weekends.

LUNCH: 11:30 A.M. to 3:30 P.M. daily. DINNER: 5 to 10 P.M. daily. BRUNCH: Sunday from noon to 5 P.M.

Canfield House, 5 Memorial Blvd. (tel. 401/847-0416), is a popular restaurant among Newporters. It has been recently restored to its earlier splendor: the barrel vaulted room with its ornately carved wood ceiling and solid-oak wainscoting now positively glows. If you have to wait for a table, take refuge in front of the huge fire in the bar. The food is traditional continental—veal marsala, baked stuffed shrimp, filet mignon maître d'hôtel, chicken princess topped with asparagus, and chateaubriand. On Saturday and Sunday prime rib is served. Prices run $12 to $15.75.

DINNER: Tuesday to Saturday from 5 to 10 P.M., on Sunday from 4 to 10 P.M.; closed Monday.

Out along Thames Street, **Southern Cross,** 509 Thames St. (tel. 401/849-8888), is a popular local restaurant, and fun to boot. Black-and-white-checked plates add drama to the table settings and combine with the gray carpet, black metal chairs, and pink tablecloths. Start with grilled gulf shrimp with jalapeño scallion aioli, duck pâté with brandied walnuts and cassis with onion jam, or grilled venison sausage. Follow with pan-fried mako shark, Texas buffalo burger with goat cheese, tenderloin of beef with anchovy and pink peppercorn butter and potato pancakes, or salmon with chipotle pepper hollandaise. Prices run $8 to $20. Desserts include chocolate walnut cake with raspberry coulis and chocolate-truffle sauce, and cranberry or pear cobbler. Brunch offers an interesting selection of items—banana griddlecakes, omelets (for example, goat cheese with asparagus, cheddar, and apple-smoked ham), blackened beef tenderloin and eggs, or rack of lamb with eggs. Prices run $4.50 to $11.

DINNER: Sunday to Thursday from 6 to 9:30 P.M., on Friday and Saturday to 10:30 P.M. BRUNCH: Sunday from noon to 2:30 P.M.

The Ark, 348 Thames St. (tel. 401/849-3808), its name painted boldly on the building's side wall, looks like an authentic British town pub. Inside, the bar area is usually crowded with folks chatting or watching the game. Upstairs, the restaurant serves good, if somewhat ambitious, cuisine. The house salad is good, consisting of green lettuce, endive, purple onions, and carrots, garnished with a sprig of basil and served with a raspberry vinaigrette. The pheasant and venison pâté with pistachios is tasty and served with pickled Bing cherries and chopped onions. The menu features about a dozen entrees, priced from $8.50 for steak-and-kidney pie to $15.50 for a tender New York sirloin grilled with a red wine and herb butter. In addition, there's finnan haddie with cream sauce and leeks, stir-fried seafood Szechuan style, grilled veal sausage with apples and vinegar sauerkraut, grilled duck with green olive and mustard sauce, and a couple of pasta dishes, as well as some specials.

LUNCH: 11:30 A.M. to 6 P.M. daily. DINNER: Sunday to Thursday from 6 to 9 P.M., until 10 P.M. on Friday and Saturday. BRUNCH: Saturday and Sunday from 9 A.M. to 3 P.M.

Le Bistro, Bannister's Wharf (tel. 401/849-7778), offers finer, lighter cuisine than the name suggests—breast of chicken with leeks and wild mushrooms, tenderloin with lemon and capers, duck with fresh kidneys, veal kidneys with madeira, and pasta with shrimp and scallops. To start, try the feuilleté of lobster with sweet peppers, shrimp, and scallops in cabbage with caviar. Prices run $11 to $21. The dining room is comfortable country French. At lunch there are omelets, sandwiches, and salads.

LUNCH: Monday to Saturday from 11:30 A.M. to 2 P.M., on Sunday from noon. DINNER: 6 to 9 P.M. daily.

Breakfast/Brunch Spots in Newport

A fine way to spend Sunday morning is looking out from the terrace at **Inn at Castle Hill,** Ocean Drive, and enjoying their brunch.

Other brunch places include the **White Horse Tavern** (tel. 401/849-3600); the **Clarke Cook House** (tel. 401/849-2900); **Astor's Inn on the Harbor,** 359 Thames St. (tel. 401/849-4466); **The Pier,** Howard Wharf (tel. 401/847-3645); the **Mooring,** on Sayer's Wharf (tel. 401/846-2260); and **The Ark,** 348 Thames St. (tel. 401/846-3808).

For a real early breakfast with the fishermen, head for the **Handy Lunch, 462 Thames St.** (tel. 401/847-9480), which opens at 4:30 A.M.

And for a real dockside breakfast, head down to **Savouries,** on Bannister's Wharf (tel. 401/846-5780), for eggs and pancakes and other choice entrees, eaten dockside in a pretty atmosphere created by colorful flower boxes and trelliswork. At lunch and dinner the restaurant serves gourmet Italian fare.

BREAKFAST: Daily in summer from 7 to 11 A.M., weekends only at other times. Closed mid-December to mid-March.

Some Luncheon Choices

You'll probably want to have lunch on the piers or at the Inn at Castle Hill and enjoy the watery vista while you dine at the places I've already described. Or you can try such casual spots as the **Brick Alley Pub and Restaurant,** at 140 Thames St. (tel. 401/849-6334), which attracts a young, friendly crowd to the bar and the tables for an incredible assortment of reasonably priced good food. The menu spreads over several pages and over several continents, offering fish, sandwiches, salads, nachos, and all kinds of items.

HOURS: Sunday to Thursday from 11 A.M. to 9 P.M., until 11 P.M. on weekends.

Locals recommend the **International Café,** 677 Thames St. (tel. 401/847-1033), for fresh good-quality food at modest prices from $5.25 to $9.25.

Salas', 341 Thames St. (tel. 401/846-8772), is a cheery, noisy, bustling place that actually consists of three establishments—a fish market and raw bar (open 11 to 1 A.M.), a brasserie (open for lunch from 11:30 A.M. to 3 P.M.), and a dining room where you can enjoy a clambake with a one-pound lobster, clams, corn on the cob, and clam broth for $13, washed down with beer served in pitchers and wine from jugs. Sala's is also famous for selling pasta by the pound!

Café Zelda, 528 Thames St. (tel. 401/849-4002), also draws crowds for their daily luncheon specials, which often feature crab or fish of the day. LUNCH AND DINNER: daily. BRUNCH: Saturday and Sunday from noon to 3 P.M.

NEWPORT EVENING ENTERTAINMENT

There's plenty of it. Hottest spot for jazz last season was the **Blue Pelican,** 40 West Broadway (tel. 401/847-5675). Sunday-afternoon jam sessions are also held at the **Treadway** on America's Cup Avenue (tel. 401/847-9000).

There are relaxing piano bars at **The Ark,** 348 Thames St. (tel. 401/846-3800); and at **Astor's Inn on the Harbor,** 359 Thames St. (tel. 401/849-4466).

Christie's of Newport (tel. 401/847-5400) and the **Clarke Cooke House,** Bannister's Wharf (tel. 401/849-2900), both offer bands and dancing on weekends. Disco and DJ action can be found at **The Club,** 3 Pelham (tel. 401/849-3888), and **Raffles,** 3 Farewell St. (tel. 401/847-9663).

For more cultural pursuits. The casino **Theatre and Art Association of Newport,**

76 Bellevue Ave. (tel. 401/847-0179), hosts chamber music concerts during the winter. The **Rhode Island Shakespeare Theatre,** P.O. Box 1126, Newport, RI 02840 (tel. 401/849-7892), stages four productions a year in the Swanhurst Theater, a converted carriage house at Webster Street and Bellevue Avenue. The **Incredibly Far Off Broadway Ensemble,** P.O. Box 822, Newport, RI 02840 (tel. 401/847-1996), uses the environment of Touro Park as backdrop for their annual production, staged on weekends in August.

An exciting evening can be spent at the **Newport Fronton,** 150 Admiral Kalbfus Rd. (tel. 401/849-5000), watching the fast-paced Basque game of jai alai and wagering a few bucks. Season runs from mid-April to mid-October, Monday to Saturday evenings and also matinees on Saturday and Monday.

NEWPORT ACTIVITIES

ANTIQUING: There are plenty of stores in Newport, although they're most concentrated along Franklin Street between Thames and Spring.

BEACHES: Bailey's Beach, at Ocean Drive and Bellevue Avenue, is where the "400" park in their monogrammed parking spaces to frolic in private. Gooseberry Beach on Ocean Drive is attractive, and open for a parking fee of $6 or so. Otherwise, Fort Adams State Park, Ocean Drive, also has a beach with a lifeguard; Newport Beach, at the eastern end of Memorial Boulevard; Second Beach in Middletown, Sachuest Beach Road (tel. 401/846-6273); Third Beach is around the corner at the mouth of the Sakonnet River.

BICYCLING: Rentals are available at Ten Speed Spokes, 79 Thames St. (tel. 401/847-5609); Newport Bicycles, 162 Broadway (tel. 401/846-0773).

BOATING: Oldport Marine Services, Sayer's Wharf (tel. 401/847-9109), has hourly and daily boat rentals, and harbor cruises mid-May to mid-October. Newport Yacht Charters, 7 Christie's Landing (tel. 401/849-4327), offers bareboat or full charters; Newport Sailing School (tel. 401/683-2738 or 246-1595) also rents and gives lessons.

Viking Tours, 184 Thames St. (tel. 401/847-6921), runs cruises of the harbor from their Goat Island dock six times daily in season. The trip is a one-hour narrated cruise to Jamestown. Cost: $5 for adults, $2 for children.

GOLF: In Portsmouth, a ten-minute drive from Newport, you can choose from three courses: Green Valley (tel. 401/847-9543), Montup (tel. 401/683-9882), and Pocasset (tel. 401/683-2266).

HIKING: The Cliff Walk is a marvelous coastal experience, from the end of Newport Beach to Bellevue and Coggeshall Avenues. Brenton Point State Park is mainly a parking area off Ocean Drive with access to a fishing pier and rocky inlets. Norman Bird Sanctuary, 583 Third Beach Rd. (tel. 401/846-2577), has trails.

HORSEBACK RIDING: Middletown Stables, 287 Third Beach Rd. (tel. 401/846-0904), in Newport. There are also a couple of stables in Portsmouth—Sandy Point, Sandy Point Road (tel. 401/849-3958), and Ups and Downs, White House Lane (tel. 401/683-4838).

PICNICKING: Brenton Point State Park and Fort Adams State Park are pretty spots.

POLO: Take along a picnic and watch the game, played during August at Glen Farm, off Rte. 114.

STATE PARKS: Brenton Point State Park (tel. 401/846-8240), Ocean Drive and Fort Adams State Park, has swimming and picnicking.

SWIMMING: There are pools at the YMCA, 792 Valley Rd. (tel. 401/847-9200), and also at Howard Johnson's, 351 W. Main Rd., Middletown (tel. 401/849-2000), or you can head for the beaches mentioned above.

TENNIS: Biggest thrill is to play on the courts either at the Casino Indoor Racquet Club, 194 Bellevue Ave. (tel. 401/849-4777), or on the grass courts at the Tennis Hall of Fame (tel. 401/849-3990). It'll cost about $25 per person per hour. You can also watch or try to play the forerunner of tennis, "court tennis" (tel. 401/849-6672). Other courts are available at Aquidneck Park at Bowery and Spring Street and at Cottrell Field on Vernon Street.

WINDSURFING: Island Windsurfing, 375 Thames St. (tel. 401/846-4421).

VERMONT &
NEW HAMPSHIRE

DORSET, MANCHESTER, & WINDHAM COUNTY

DISTANCES IN MILES: Dorset, 212; Manchester, 207; Bennington, 180; Brattleboro, 194; Wilmington, 201; Mount Snow, 213; Newfane, 215; Grafton, 229; Saxtons River, 227

ESTIMATED DRIVING TIMES: Anywhere from 4 to 4½ hours

DRIVING: You can either take the New York State Thruway to Troy and then Rte. 7 into Bennington or I-684 to I-84 to I-91. For Brattleboro, take I-95 to I-91.

BUS: Greyhound (tel. 212/635-0800) travels to Manchester, Brattleboro, and Bennington.

TRAIN: Amtrak travels to Brattleboro, but will deposit you there at some ungodly hour of the morning—like 2:30 A.M.? For information, call 212/736-6288.

Special Events to Plan Your Trip Around

JANUARY/FEBRUARY: Full-moon guided tours along eight kilometers of partially lit trails followed by a bonfire dinner at the West Dover Inn. For information, contact the Sitzmark Ski Touring Center (tel. 802/464-8187).

MARCH/APRIL: Easter Weekend at Mount Snow, when a sunrise service is held at the summit. For information call 802/464-3333.

MAY: Bennington County Horse show at Hildene.

JULY: Old-Fashioned Fourth, a celebration complete with square dancing and an event in which people try to catch greased pigs. Vermont Symphony concert. Polo season opens and continues every third weekend. Hildene and Dorset Antiques shows.

JULY/AUGUST: The Marlboro Music Festival.

AUGUST: Bennington Battle Day weekend, commemorating the Revolutionary War battle on August 16, 1777.

Volvo International Tennis Tournament at Stratton; Southern Vermont Crafts Fair

SEPTEMBER: Stratton Arts Festival

For further information on Vermont generally, contact the Vermont Travel Division, 134 State St., Montpelier, VT 05602 (tel. 802/828-3236); the Vermont State Chamber of Commerce, P.O. Box 37, Montpelier, VT 05602 (tel. 802/223-3443 or 229-0154); the Department of Parks and Recreation, 103 S. Main St., 10 South, Waterbury, VT 05670 (tel. 802/828-3375), for state park camping information; and the New England Vacation Center, 630 Fifth Ave., Concourse Level, Shop 2, New York, NY 10020 (tel. 212/307- 5780).

For specific town information contact the Manchester and the Mountains Chamber of Commerce, P.O. Box 928, Manchester Center, VT 05255 (tel. 802/362-2100); the Londonderry Chamber of Commerce, P.O. Box 58, Londonderry, VT 05148 (tel. 802/824-8178); the Greater Bennington Chamber of Commerce, Veterans Memorial Drive, Bennington, VT 05201 (tel. 802/447-3311); the Mount Snow Chamber of Commerce, 200L Mountain Rd., Mount Snow, West Dover, VT 05356 (tel. 802/464-8501); and the Brattleboro Chamber of Commerce, 180 Main St., Brattleboro, VT 05301 (tel. 802/254-4565).

For information on the Monadnock region, contact the Greater Keene Chamber of Commerce, 12 Gilbo Ave., Keene, NH 03431 (tel. 603/352-1303).

Southern Vermont was home to Ethan Allen and his Green Mountain Boys, where they stalked the British and fought the Battle of Bennington. Historic it may be, but today the area offers an incredible variety of activities both summer and winter, although Vermont is her shining best in winter when the ski slopes at Stratton, Bromley, Magic Mountain, and Mount Snow are dotted with colored parkas streaming down the trails, the inns and lodges are warmed by blazing hearths, and people return burnished from the slopes to enjoy an evening's entertainment. During the summer there's boating and swimming on Lake Whitingham, the Marlboro Music Festival to attend, a variety of events and performances to watch at the Southern Vermont Arts Center and at Hildene Meadowlands, as well as plenty of antiquing and craft studios to visit, for this is the area (especially around Brattleboro) that the '60s generation sought out where they could practice their crafts. Fall brings an even-greater glory, when the mountains are turned into great pyramids of color. And then there are the quiet villages, perfectly groomed town greens, inviting inns, and white clapboard churches that offer the visitor the gentle relaxation of another, much quieter era. It's a lovely area for any weekender to explore at any time of year.

THE DORSET-MANCHESTER VALLEY

A beautiful area bordered on each side by mountains and cut through by the famous Battenkill River, the region has much to give to the visitor. Dorset is a somnolent village that boasts the Dorset Playhouse and several fine inns. Farther south, Manchester Village has always attracted visitors, often wealthy ones, especially to its grand old hotel, the Equinox. People came in the mid-19th century to take Dr. Sprague's famous water cure, a phenomenon that hotel owner Frank Orvis capitalized on when he advertised that he had piped the precious water from the mountain and bottled it. These advertisements appeared briefly in subway cars and on buses in New York City until a federal agency intervened. Today people come to the area for various reasons: to visit Hildene, the home of Robert Todd Lincoln and to attend a variety of events held at the Hildene Meadowlands and at the Southern Vermont Arts Center; to fish, cycle, ski, canoe, or just plain relax; and also to shop the many outlets that can be found in Manchester and the area.

AREA ATTRACTIONS

Prime sightseeing destination in the valley is **Hildene,** off Rte. 7A two miles south of Rte. 30 (tel. 802/362-1788), the home of Robert Todd Lincoln, the eldest son of Abraham Lincoln, who first discovered Vermont when his mother brought him to the Equinox House in 1863 on a summer retreat. A visit begins in the carriage house where a slide show records the highlights of Robert Todd Lincoln's life from his birth in August 1843, through his army service (present at Appomattox), his years as a partner in the Chicago law firm of Isham and Lincoln, his appointments as secretary of war under Garfield, as ambassador to Britain under Harrison, and later as chairman of the board of the Pullman Palace Car Company to 1902, when he purchased 500 acres and built this Georgian Revival home overlooking the Battenkill Valley.

The name Hildene means hill and valley. During Robert Lincoln's working years he and his family summered here. Later he retired here and was involved in local affairs until he died in 1926. His widow stayed at Hildene until she also died, when it was briefly occupied by her daughter, Mary Lincoln Isham, and later by Mary Lincoln Beckwith, daughter of Robert Lincoln's other daughter, Jessie. Peggy Beckwith was a fascinating outspoken woman who flew her own biplane, painted, sculpted, studied piano and guitar, and tried to operate the property as a working farm. She died in 1975, leaving her younger brother, Robert Todd Lincoln Beckwith, the last of the Lincoln line.

On the house tour visitors view the room where Robert Todd died and his office, containing one of Abe Lincoln's stovepipes and all of the original furnishings. The original rolls are also played for visitors on the 1908 Aeolian player pipe organ. From the top-floor rooms you can look down onto the restored formal garden, designed after a stained-glass window. It contains 25 varieties of peonies; the best time to visit is in mid-June, when they're in bloom.

Being able to walk into and through the rooms is a particularly appealing aspect to Hildene's house tour. In the toy room, note the screen depicting fairy tales that Robert Todd Lincoln commissioned for his grandchildren, and make sure to go down to the garden terrace for the view of the Green Mountains on one side and the Taconics on the other. Stroll the nature trails or enjoy a picnic.

After a visit one can't help pondering how frequently the Lincoln family was beset by tragedy. Abraham and Mary Todd had four sons, three of whom died —the first at age 3, the second at age 11, and the third at 18. Robert Todd Lincoln, though, lived to 82. Of Robert's children, Abraham II, the eldest, was killed in France; his daughter, Mary, married Charles Isham and bore Lincoln Isham, and his daughter, Jessie, married Warren Wallace Beckwith and bore four children.

HOURS: Mid-May through October, 9:30 A.M. to 5:30 P.M. daily (last tour begins at 4 P.M.). ADMISSION: $5.

The **Southern Vermont Art Center,** West Road, off Rte. 7A (P.O. Box 617), Manchester, NH 05254 (tel. 802/362-1405), is worth a visit for its setting alone. Here against a woods-and-meadow backdrop a Festival of the Arts is celebrated from early June to mid-October on the slopes of Mount Equinox. Paintings, sculpture, and photographs are displayed, and music, dance, and vocal performances given in the performance barn. HOURS: Galleries and gardens are open in summer Tuesday to Saturday from 10 A.M. to 5 P.M., on Sunday from noon to 5 P.M.; closed Monday and after Columbus Day. In summer a café under an awning looks out over the lawns with their sculptures. HOURS: 11:30 A.M. to 2:30 P.M. Tuesday through Saturday and for Sunday brunch from early June through Columbus Day.

The Dorset Theatre Festival opens in June and continues through Labor Day. For information call 802/867-5777.

Even non-anglers and those who've only read Izaak Walton on fishing might find the **American Museum of Fly Fishing,** Rte. 7A at Seminary Avenue in Manchester, interesting. Tying a fly to lure a fish is a very delicate art indeed, and a very exotically colorful one. The traditional feathers used in Atlantic salmon flies, for example, include peacock, kingfisher, jay, heron, and macaw. From these feathers, thread, and wool, artificial flies are created in thousands of patterns that range from literal to impressionistic and gaudy in style. Here the works of great fly tiers are displayed. The museum also displays 18th- and 19th-century fly rods, some 20 feet long, the earlier ones made from ash, hickory, lancewood, and

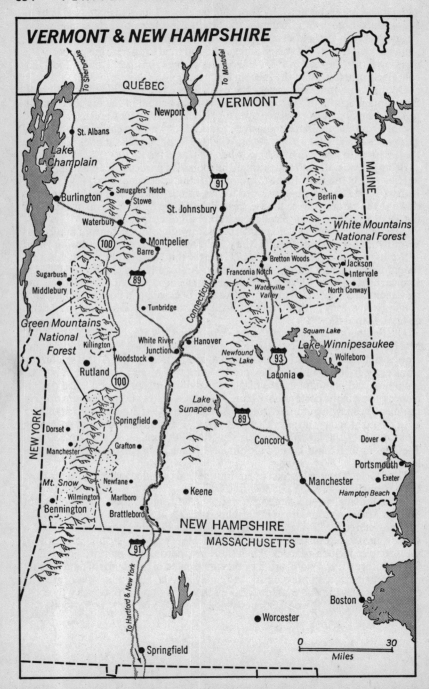

VERMONT & NEW HAMPSHIRE

greenheart, and the later (mid-19th century on) from bamboo. Today, of course, fiberglass, graphite, and boron are used, and these, too, are displayed. Exhibits also include the fly-fishing tackle of many famous Americans: Winslow Homer, Arnold Gingrich (founder of *Esquire*), Dwight Eisenhower, Daniel Webster, and Ernest Hemingway.

HOURS: 10 A.M. to 4 P.M. daily. ADMISSION: Suggested $2.

Fun also to drop in and browse among the hunting and fishing gear at the **Orvis Company store** on Rte. 7.(HOURS: 8 A.M. to 6 P.M. daily from March to December; closed Sunday in January and February). Also along this route you'll find several outlet stores selling such famous brand names as Anne Klein, Bass, Van Heusen. **Dexter Shoes** (tel. 802/362-4810) is at Rtes. 11 and 30 and **Hathaway Shirts** is located in the Equinox Shops (tel. 802/362-3317). Stock up, too, on Vermont specialties—ham, cheese, and maple syrup—at **Harrington's,** at the junction of Rtes. 7, 11, and 30 (HOURS: 9 A.M. to 5 P.M. daily). On Rte. 7A, **Coffee, Tea and Spice** has a wide selection of gourmet items. At **Mother Myrick's Confectionary and Ice Cream Parlor,** stop by to savor ice cream or fantastic pastries and cakes which you can enjoy out on the awning-shaded deck. The **Jelly Mill,** on Rte. 7A (tel. 802/362-3494), shelters a number of stores offering everything from handmade lamps to gourmet cookware, from crafts to foodstuffs (HOURS: 10 A.M. to 6 P.M. daily). The **Woodcarver** is special here.

North on Rte. 7, the **Enchanted Doll House** (tel. 802/362-1327) welcomes all ages to its 12-room toy shop featuring all kinds of dolls, stuffed animals, books, games, and creative toys. HOURS: Monday to Saturday from 9 A.M. to 5:30 P.M., from 10 A.M. on Sunday.

And, of course, do take time to drive the **Skyline Drive** up to the summit of **Mount Equinox,** just to see the glorious view.

A few miles south of Manchester Village in Arlington, Norman Rockwell fans will want to visit the **Norman Rockwell Exhibition & Gift Shop,** on Rte. 7A, (tel. 802/375-6423), in this village that was his hometown. Over 1,000 *Saturday Evening Post* covers are on display in the gallery. A 20-minute film is also shown.

In Dorset, on Rte. 30, the **J. K. Adams Company Factory Store** stocks a whole line of gourmet woodware—spice racks, knife racks, butcher block, and other home accessories. HOURS: 9 A.M. to 5:30 P.M. daily.

At nearby **Bromley Mountain,** Ski Resort, Rte. 11, six miles east of Manchester (tel. 802/824-5522), the whole family will enjoy winter skiing or flying down the summer Alpine Slide.

DORSET LODGING AND DINING

Standing at the center of a quiet community, the **Dorset Inn,** on the Green, Dorset, VT 05251 (tel. 802/867-5500), is a genuine country inn. Ferns, lupins, and geraniums add a splash of color to the borders by the crazily paved marble paths and steps that lead into the white clapboard building. Operating as an inn since 1796, it has recently been extensively renovated. The upstairs accommodations and decor vary: Room 24 (with private bath) is invitingly arrayed with brass bed, ruffled curtains, floral wallpaper, comfortable Martha Washingtons, and a chest of drawers. A cannonball-style bed dominates Room 26, while Room 25 offers sleigh beds, a rocker, and a comfy Martha Washington. Third-floor rooms under the eaves are interestingly and cozily shaped.

Besides the lovely accommodations, the inn has an excellent reputation for its food—a reputation that a recent lunch confirmed. A basket of wafer-thin garlic bread and hot bread and muffins accompanied the meal. Potato skins filled with chili topped with sour cream and onions were tasty. Apple-and-turkey pie with crust and sautéed chicken with walnuts were other possible choices. Prices run $4.50 to $5.75. The dinner menu lists about ten entrees, each combining fine fresh ingredients with positively simple cooking. Roast Cornish hen stuffed with wild rice and fruit, rack of lamb with fresh mint sauce, veal medallions with lime-ginger sauce, or halibut with lemon-curry butter are just a sampling. Prices run $13.50 to $17.50. Start with chilled steamed shrimp with garlic-green sauce or smoked salmon with scallions, capers, and horseradish-cream, and end with applesauce cake, crème caramel, or a simple fresh-fruit sorbet. Breakfast is also served here—and worth the $6 for fresh juice and fruit, cereal, eggs or pancakes, and beverage.

Chintz, lace curtains, chair rails, and polished wide-board floors create the atmosphere. The tap room is a cozy supper spot, especially in winter when a fire flickers. Light dishes such as warm chicken tenderloin salad tossed in vinaigrette or biscuit-crust apple-and-turkey pie are available. A broad selection of beers and a fine selection of wines are offered. Guests can also enjoy the two comfortable stenciled parlors with fireplace, furnished with thick rugs, books, and such country objects as an old spinning wheel.

RATES: $70 single (MAP), $115 double (MAP). BREAKFAST: Daily. LUNCH: Noon to 2 P.M. daily in summer and fall. DINNER: 6 to 9 P.M. daily.

The **Barrows House,** Dorset, VT 05251 (tel. 802/867-4455), is a large rambling spread that still retains a warm country feel. Accommodations are dotted around the six-acre property in eight buildings as well as the main house. The grounds are quite beautiful and fragrant, bursting with lupins, iris, cornflowers, tulips, honeysuckle, and lilacs shaded by hemlocks, weeping willows, and silver birches. They're tended by convivial and incredibly energetic Marilyn Schubert—she runs the inn with her husband, Charles, who entertains everyone in the bar or dining room. The night I visited he performed some impressive puppetry with an incredibly life-like duck that he had purchased somewhere!

There are ten rooms in the white clapboard black-shuttered inn originally built as a parsonage in 1804. Each is individually decorated and may contain country pine or oak furnishings, perhaps a four-poster, slip-covered chairs, desk, and other comforts. Eight similar rooms exist in the Hemlock House. The Truffle House contains three double rooms and a large living room with a fireplace. The upstairs suite is really lovely, the window seat and pencil four-poster making it especially so. These are the only air-conditioned rooms. The Schubert Cottage holds two double rooms and a private secluded sitting room with a fireplace. Stable accommodations are pleasantly rustic with plank floors, pine hutch, and Windsor chair among the furnishings. The Carriage House contains ideal accommodations for a family. All the accommodations are attractively furnished and very well kept.

The grounds are beautiful and the outdoor pool is idyllically situated and surrounded by grass. A sauna is located in the stables. So, too, is the bicycle and cross-country ski shop, at which both items are available for rent. There are also two tennis courts.

In the dining room fresh flowers grace the tables along with atmospheric hurricane lamps. The whole room, decorated with fern wallpaper is fresh and garden-like, but when you're sitting in the atrium dining area it's as if you're sitting in a garden. The Tap Room gleams with polished wood. Here people gather to chat, entertain at the piano, or play backgammon. The food is continental. At dinner I enjoyed a $20 prix fixe starting with a flavorsome carrot-apple soup, followed by salad and a very tasty, juicy leg of lamb cooked with garlic and thyme and served with an assortment of vegetables—roast potatoes, grilled tomato, asparagus, julienned carrots, broccoli, and rice! A rhubarb pie finished the meal. Other entree choices might be veal marengo, roast Cornish hen with basil and pine nuts, or sirloin steak with apples, mushrooms, and applejack; while among the appetizers, choices run from grilled shrimp with ginger-leek sauce to asparagus wrapped in prosciutto served with walnut vinaigrette.

RATES: $140 to $180 double (MAP). LUNCH: Daily, July to October only. DINNER: Daily.

For years the **Village Auberge,** Rte. 30 (R.R. 1, Box 53), Dorset, VT 05251 (tel. 802/867-5715), has enjoyed a fabled reputation for dining. Recently Helmut Stein and his wife, Dorothy, took it over and installed chef Richard Schaefer, who trained at the Culinary Institute of America and also in Paris where he worked for Sofitel.

Among the appetizers are gravlax, duck salad, and lobster mousse with sauce Noilly Prat. The main courses, priced from $10.50 to $20, run from Cornish hen with a sauce diablo and quenelles of scallops au beurre blanc estragon, to medallions of veal à la normande with apples and Calvados and a fish of the day. For dessert there are homemade sorbets and ice creams, tarts, chocolate mousse, and crème caramel. Tables are arrayed with Villeroy and Boche table settings and hurricane-style lamps. Choice tables are set in the large bay window. If you have to wait, there's a small bar in which you can study the 1920s news photos from the *New York Times* that cover the walls.

There are also six guest rooms available, all with private bath. The nicest, in my opinion, has a pineapple-style bed covered with a star quilt, a cane-seated rocker, chest, and sidetable. In the Carriage House the suite has two double rooms, one with a turned four-poster sans canopy.

RATES: $40 to $50 per person for B&B, $60 to $70 per person for MAP. DINNER: Tuesday to Sunday from 6 to 9 P.M.; closed Monday, also closed April and November to December 11.

MANCHESTER LODGING AND DINING

Antique lovers will adore the **1811 House,** Rte. 7A, Manchester Village, VT 05254 (tel. 802/362-1811), a salmon-and-beige clapboard structure situated in the center of Manchester. It was, in fact, built as a farmhouse in the 1770s. In 1811 the roof was raised and it was turned into a tavern. Later, Mary Lincoln Isham, President Lincoln's granddaughter, resided here until she died in 1939. Today it is run by Jack and Mary Hirst and Pat and Jeremy David. Mary hails from Wales and brought many of her fine authentic antiques with her.

The 11 rooms, all with private bath, are exquisitely furnished. The Robert Todd Lincoln Room contains a canopied pencil four-poster with a candlewick bedspread and a Federal-style slate-blue mantel and fireplace; chintz curtains hang at the pelmeted windows. Most of the rooms have desks and comfy chairs, dried-flower arrangements, clocks, and bathroom amenities like bath salt cubes. In each, you'll find a personal touch—for example, in the Grace Hoyt Singer Room, a cross-stitch rug made by Mary, a small glass case filled with china cats and birds, and a handsome porcelain figure on the chest of drawers; or the framed pressed flowers in the Franklin Orvis Room that Mary picked from the field behind their previous home. The Henry Ethel Robinson Room possesses a great bathroom containing a clawfoot tub with a sunflower-size old-fashioned showerhead. In the Hidden Room the 12-over-12 windows are original; so, too, are the beams in the Burr Room.

The tavern is authentic to a T. Pewter mugs hang from the old beams, horse brasses adorn the fireplace and bar, brass candlesticks stand on tables smoothed by long use, and Windsor chairs and bar stools complete the scene. A breakfast of fresh fruit juice, fresh farm eggs, fried bread, and grilled tomato (typical British style) is served at the polished refectory oak table set with studded, carved Tudor-style chairs. For relaxing, there are two sitting rooms, each comfortably furnished. One has a couch set on an Oriental carpet before a mantel with carved plaster reliefs. Home-like touches include photos placed on a claw-foot table. The other has book-filled built-in bookcases, two couches, a wooden chess set, and a small TV for guests' pleasure. The gardens (seven acres) are also lovely, and filled with perennial flowering plants, a sundial, and a well-manicured lawn. From here the view extends across the Equinox golf course to the Green Mountains beyond.

RATES (including breakfast) $80 to $115 double.

Owners of the **Inn at Manchester,** Rte. 7A (P.O. Box 41), Manchester, VT 05254 (tel. 802/362-1793), go out of their way to welcome their guests and inform them about the area. In the 1880–1890 house they have 20 rooms, all differently furnished. Room 1 is a large front room with a bay window decorated in rose colors and furnished with an oak bed, chest, and rocker, among other things. Room 4 is decked out in eggshell blue and chintz, and contains an iron-and-brass bed. Four rooms on the third floor sharing two baths are more rustic but represent good value. The most appealing rooms are perhaps those at the back, furnished with country pine and oak, pretty comforters, frilled curtains, and chintz wallpaper. Room 16 is referred to as the honeymoon suite and is warmly decorated in celery and pink.

There are also four rooms, each with private bath, in the carriage house. Here Room 18 has a handsome carved cherry bed covered with pink-and-white comforter, acorn-pine chest, floorlamp with Tiffany-style shade, and other furnishings. Upstairs rooms in the carriage house have cathedral-style ceilings. These rooms are particularly convenient to the swimming pool, surrounded by grass and from which you have a lovely mountain view. The large room I stayed in had a brass bed, bold chintz wallpaper, Victorian-style mahogany chest, cherry side-table, and rocking chair.

Full country breakfasts are delicious. Stanley and Harriet whip up great apple-buttermilk pancakes with Vermont maple syrup, omelets, and homemade granola. Family-style dinners are served winter weekends and on Monday, priced around $15 per person.

RATES: $55 to $75 in summer and winter, $60 to $90 in fall.

From the road you can't help noticing the celery and mauve splash of color, and the hanging flower baskets that adorn the front porch of the **Village Country Inn,** Rte. 7A, Manchester, VT 05254 (tel. 802/362-1792). It's run by Jay and Anne Degen, who has a natural flair for interior decoration that's amply demonstrated throughout the 1889 house. As a child she built her own dollhouses, making the furniture and picking the fabrics to go in them. Celery and mauve are the predominant colors in the large front parlor area which offers an array of seating arrangements—a corner furnished with Stickley, a high-backed Victorian love seat, and a mauve camelback sofa—all set around a fieldstone fireplace in a room accented with a gilt mirror, stained-glass door, etc.

The 30 accommodations, all with private bath, are highly individual. Room 111 is large and features a carved oak bed set under a tented effect of cream lace, a wicker chaise longue, oak dresser, lace-draped table, bold chintz wallpaper, and inviting windowseats. Room 107 is a small country space furnished primarily with oak pieces. Other rooms might come in pale blue and wicker or Laura Ashley country or gray and lavender with a lacy swag above the bed, or more traditionally in burgundy. There are also a couple of garden rooms in the back by the pool that have TV and Ethan Allen furniture, holdovers from the inn's previous owners. Ann has brightened them by adding celery-colored quilts and mauve wallpaper. All rooms have fluffy towels and pretty eyelet linens.

In the dining room the lattice trellises, floral-green wallpaper, and pink and forest-green napery, glass candleholders, and celery-colored bentwood chairs create a romantic garden-like effect. Here, even the fireplace is mauve. The menu is continental and changes seasonally. You may find medallions of veal with wild mushrooms, shallots, and madeira; fish of the day grilled with oil, oregano, garlic, and lemon; breast of chicken sautéed with shiitake mushrooms, garlic, parsley, and lemon; or loin of lamb with rosemary and juniper sauce. To start, there might be chilled tomato bisque, tagliatelle in cream with wild mushrooms, or apple-smoked pheasant and oregano; and to end, a crème brûlée or pears poached in red wine. Prices run $11.50 to $16. A pianist entertains softly at the grand piano. There's also a comfortable tavern that opens onto a summer patio furnished with wrought-iron celery-colored furniture set among fountains and flowers. There's a tennis court across the street, an outdoor pool, and also a clothing and accessory and good-quality gift boutique. Anne intends to offer different weekend packages—a champagne picnic by horse-drawn carriage, a fly-fishing workshop, golf and tennis specials—so inquire about her latest idea.

RATES: $70 to $100 double (room only), $100 to $130 double (MAP), in summer and fall (more for suites accommodating three or four persons). Special rates apply in April, May, and November. No children.

You can't miss the purple-and-cream clapboard building that's called **The Re-**

luctant Panther, Rte. 7A (P.O. Box 678), Manchester Village, VT 05254 (tel. 802/362-2568), known for its fine restaurant as well as its accommodations. The atrium dining room seats 60 in a highly colorful almost tropically inspired setting of plants, flagstone floor, and brilliant orange, yellow, and peach napery. The stone fireplace makes it cozy in winter while in summer the marble terrace dotted with flowers, plants, silver birches, and stone ornaments with a view of Equinox Mountain makes a lovely spot for cocktails. Or you can enjoy drinks in the unique bar. Green-leather low chairs on casters are set at Vermont marble tables; ceiling, paneling, and shutters are a brilliant purple; and in one corner a full bear trophy, his teeth bared, stands ready to party no matter what. Elsewhere, carved gryphons are placed in niches. A fire adds warmth in winter.

The menu is prix fixe, your choice of entree determining the price of a five-course meal. Entrees include duck à l'orange; loin of lamb chops; filet of sole baked in white wine and topped with tomato, green pepper, and onion; and chicken tarragon; along with daily specials. Prices run $19 to $24. First-course offerings include salmon mousse and rolled asparagus wrapped in Canadian bacon and covered with cheese sauce. The second course brings a choice of hot and cold soups, and the third course, a seasonal salad. For the fifth course, select from the tray of desserts.

There are 11 rooms, all with private bath and color TV, and six with working fireplaces. Each is dramatically and differently decorated. A half bottle of wine is placed in each for guests. The wallpapers are quite extraordinary: mushroom in Room A, purple poppies in Room C, Queen Anne's lace in Room E, for example. Room G is exceptionally attractive: eyelet pillows grace the bed which is covered with a light-purple comforter and adorned by a draped lace curtain effect. Comforts include two steel-gray wing chairs, a fireplace, dusky-rose carpet, marble-top table, oak dresser, and a bathroom with clawfoot tub and pedestal sink. Room J is exceptionally large and possesses a Victorian oak bed and furniture in a matching style, while Room L contains a cherry Stickley bed, carved oak Victorian chair, a chestnut armoire, black-walnut chest of drawers, and two wing chairs covered in salmon-pink fabric.

RATES: $73 to $103 double in summer, $85 to $115 double in fall (mid-September to about November 1). DINNER: Thursday to Tuesday from 6 to 9 P.M. The Reluctant Panther is open for roughly nine months only, closing from about April 10 to Memorial Day and from October 31 to approximately December 10. The restaurant is also closed at these times and, in addition, on Wednesday.

The famous old resort, the **Equinox,** Rte. 7A, Manchester Village, VT 05254 (tel. 802/362-4700), which once welcomed Mary Todd Lincoln and other dignitaries in its heyday, has been restored to its former glory. Although on the site of a pre-Revolutionary tavern its life as a fashionable summer resort was really begun by the Orvis family in 1854. Behind the façade with its stately columns and veranda stretching a full block along the marble sidewalk, you'll find a large lobby with Federal-style fireplace. Here, comfy buttoned velvet chairs with burgundy fringes are set around marble tables placed on a bold floral-pattern-on-black Wilton carpet; a pianist entertains. In the dining room off the lobby with its handsomely carved 1832 marble fireplace, plank floors, and gold, red, and black decor a luncheon buffet is served daily (brunch on Sunday). Although I'm not a great fan of buffets (because the food almost always has that inevitable steamtable flavor and lukewarm quality), the luncheon buffet here looked exceptionally good—a spread of salads, croissant sandwiches, salami, roast beef, pastas, salads, melon, artichoke hearts, guacamole, soup, desserts, and a hot dish like veal à la king or linguine with seafood.

There are 154 rooms, all with air conditioning, color TV, and such bathroom amenities as French milled soap, shampoo, sewing kit, glycerin soap, shower cap, hand and body lotion, etc. Most of the spacious rooms have Vermont pine furnishings, chintz comforters, a couple of wing chairs, stenciled decorated walls, and ruffle-trimmed organdy curtains. Several duplex suites are available.

The most impressive public room, in my opinion, is the main dining room, designed in 1913, which has a huge semicircular bay window with a splendid mountain view. The sky-blue vaulted ceiling is especially dramatic while the fretwork chairs give a chinoiserie effect. The menu features continental cuisine with dishes priced from $15.50 to $18.50—among them, sole paupiettes stuffed with scallop-and-herb mousse and served with tomato coulis, tournedos Armagnac, and noisettes of lamb with red wine sauce, demiglacé, and golden raisins. Appetizers include lobster with two sauces, country terrine, carpaccio, and baked American goat cheese with marinated summer vegetables.

From the lobby an elevator will take you one story to the Lincoln Terrace, where high tea is served overlooking the gardens of azaleas, tulips, and other flowers (at least when I visited). Umbrella tables are placed out there in the summer. A short walk from the main building brings you to the pool area, set with yellow loungers, which is serviced by a garden lounge located in the old carriage house. Lunch and drinks are served here, and in the evenings there is also dinner-dancing. Other facilities on the 1,400-acre property include two swimming pools, five Har-tru and clay tennis courts, and the 1927 Walter Travis 18-hole golf course (the 13th hole with its "snake pit" hazard is famous) with clubhouse restaurant, where you can dine outside under an awning and enjoy the glorious view. While you're here you can also stroll across and down the street to the Equinox shops —three levels that include a Hathaway outlet and other stores selling toys, flowers, and antiques. Carriage rides are also part of the fun.

RATES: In summer, $120 to $150 on weekends; $105 to $135 in midweek; in winter, $92 to $112 on weekends, $82 to $102 in midweek. Special packages are also offered.

The **Chantecleer**, Rte. 7, Manchester Center (tel. 802/362-1616), is considered the premier local restaurant. The fieldstone fireplace, rafters, and barn siding give a pretty country atmosphere to the room filled with captain's chairs and tables covered in pink cloths. The inspiration is distinctly Swiss, but with Oriental accents. For example, you'll find fondue chinoise—thin sliced beef to dip in a special Oriental-style broth. More familiar dishes include rack of lamb with herbed garlic, sautéed pheasant; roast duck with cranberry-and-orange sauce, veal sweetbreads grandmère (concocted with bacon, mushroom, tomato, and wine-and-veal glaze), or filet mignon flamed with kirsch and served with Bing cherry sauce. Among the appetizers, the seafood terrine with tomato coulis is very special, consisting of layers of scallops, salmon, and green-pea mousse, and so, too, is croûte aux champignons, assorted mushrooms sautéed with garlic and fine herbes and veal glaze and served on toast. Prices run from $11 to $18.50. It's located about four miles north of Manchester on Rte. 7.

DINNER: Wednesday to Monday from 5 to 9 P.M.; closed Tuesday. BRUNCH: Sunday from 11:30 A.M. to 2 P.M. (winter only). Closed mid-April to mid-May and mid-November to mid-December.

ARLINGTON LODGING AND DINING

The **West Mountain Inn**, half a mile west of Arlington on Rte. 313, Arlington, VT 05250 (tel. 802/375-6516), is one of my favorite retreats for several reasons, but primarily for the spirit and character of its owners, Wesley and Mary Ann Carlson. Both love animals and tend to a menagerie of Netherland dwarf lop-eared rabbits, African pygmy goats, and a couple of llamas which they were anxiously awaiting when I visited. They are both caring individuals. On the ground floor they have created a *really* accessible room for the disabled in which all the switches are placed low, as are the bars in the closet. The bathroom is fully and properly equipped, even with an open-style shower to accommodate a wheelchair. The room itself is one of the nicest, with brick fireplace, ebony sculptures on the mantel, Stickley love seat, and comfy chair. The 150-acre setting is lovely. Cornflowers and iris and other flowers bloom. The house looks out onto Red Mountain and the grounds are filled with hemlocks, pine, and maple. To get there, you'll have to cross the Battenkill and take a dirt road to the top of a hill.

There are 12 rooms (plus the special one for the handicapped), each named after a favorite historical figure. In each, guests will find a chocolate candy bar and a bowl of fruit. The Robert Todd Lincoln Room has a carved-oak bed capped by a draped canopy and covered with a hand-loomed 1830 quilt—"snowflakes on evergreen," a special Vermont pattern. Oak furnishings, including a rocker, complete the decor. In the Daniel Webster Room there are sleigh beds; Grandma Moses' small pale-blue room has a fireplace, rocker, and of course, her farm scenes; the Robert Frost Room has its own porch with wicker chairs; the Carl Ruggles Room features a carved high-backed oak bed, Stickley couch, and rope rug. The largest room of all is the Rockwell Kent. It has a cathedral ceiling and loft bed, brick fireplace, an Indian rug as a wall hanging, and an eclectic mix of pine and Victorian furnishings. There are still other accommodations, including a Booker T. Washington Room.

The dining room is basically for inn guests, who receive a six-course dinner which changes daily. As main courses it might feature veal marsala and a chicken and a shrimp dish. The fireplace makes it cozy in winter, and the orchids and other plants and color photos of the inn in all seasons give it a homey feel. Adjacent, there's a bar with Windsor-style bar stools and, oddly enough, a tank full of exotic tropical fish, and plenty of books and magazines. Other popular gathering spots for guests are the game room, equipped with cribbage, backgammon, etc.; and the sitting room, warmed by a Franklin stove and offering plenty of couches and armchairs and a piano at which guests entertain each other. In summer the enclosed flagstone porch set with cushioned bamboo chairs is a favorite lounging spot. At breakfast, eggs Benedict, omelets, and vanilla crêpes with butterscotch sauce are all likely choices.

RATES: $120 to $136 double (MAP), $150 for the Rockwell Kent Suite.

Located in a cream-colored Greek Revival building with rust-colored shutters, the **Arlington Inn**, Rte. 7A, Arlington, VT 05250 (tel. 802/375-6532), stands behind a row of stately maples. A marble path fringed with flowers and ferns leads to the central portico. Inside, the hallway, handsomely furnished with Oriental carpet, carved Chippendales, and color engravings of London scenes dating back to 1848, is a refreshing change from colonial New England.

It's both an inn and a restaurant. In the main dining room, tables are prettily covered in pink and set with brass candlesticks and willow-pattern china. There's a faintly Empire-style ambience created by a couple of classical urns and an ornate clock that stands on the fireplace mantel. A meal here might start with escargots Deming (with garlic, cloves, shallots, and parsley) or duck pour les deux amants (smoked duck served with raspberry-orange sauce). Among the main courses, priced from $12.75 to $16.50, might be chicken Deming with sausage and thyme stuffing accented with cheddar cheese sauce garnished with baby shrimp, or a veal à la maison combined with escargots and mushrooms in a cream sauce. Pastries, sherbets, and meringues are likely dessert choices. Brunch offers eggs, bagels, and omelets, plus fish and meat specials, from $4.75 to $8.50. If you have to wait for your table, relax in the Sylvester Deming Tavern while a pianist entertains (Friday and Saturday only) in this cozy forest-green tavern decorated with stoneware and hunting prints. Don't miss the two huge (you'll see what I mean) Canadian rawhide rockers on the adjacent porch. There's also a greenhouse dining room that looks very summery with its green, peach, and pink color scheme and marble floor.

The accommodations are variously decorated in a 19th-century style; some have fireplaces. For example, the Pamela Suite features flounce pillow cases, valanced windows, a Madame Recamier sofa, Oriental throw rug, and marble Victorian dresser in one room. The Martin Chester Room contains a broken-scroll bed, needlepointed side chairs, camelback sofa, an armoire, carved wood table, orange-and-green macaw and bird of paradise wallpaper, and a huge sideboard with turnip foot. The tongue-and-groove ceiling makes it very cozy and unique. Some of the rooms are tucked under the eaves. Many of the bathrooms have clawfoot tubs, and quilts, Victorian prints, and period pieces like a spinning wheel are found throughout. Guests have the use of the parlor furnished Stickley style, most comfortable in winter when the fire is lit. Active folks will like the clay tennis court out back.

RATES: $55 to $125 (the higher price is for fireplace rooms).

LODGING AND DINING NEAR BROMLEY AND MAGIC MOUNTAIN

A trellis gate hung with fuchsias leads into the garden to the **Three Clocks Inn,** Middletown Road, South Londonderry, VT 05155 (tel. 802/824-6327). This secluded establishment is best known for its restaurant, which is very good indeed. The menu is prix fixe, the wine list extensive, and the service excellent. After a smooth duck liver pâté I enjoyed a deliciously fresh gray sole grenobloise (with capers and lemon). The kitchen will oblige by cooking such a fish in whatever manner you prefer—meunière, amandine, with grapes, etc. Other entrees include frogs' legs provençal, veal marsala or zingara, duck à l'orange, filet mignon au poivre, capon valdostana, priced from $13.75 to $16.25. To start, there's eggplant caponata, peppers with anchovy filets, smoked salmon, or prosciutto and melon. Desserts include classics like peach Melba, pear Hélène, strawberries Romanoff. Pepper grinders grace the tables in each of the small dining rooms and the flagstone porch area enclosed with diamond-pane windows.

Upstairs there are four rooms available, including a small suite with two bedrooms. The largest has a canopy bed. The guests also can use a colonial-style furnished living room. At breakfast the gracious proprietors will serve whatever you fancy.

RATES: $55 per person (MAP). DINNER: Tuesday to Sunday from 6 to 9 P.M. Closed April to Memorial Day and from the third week of October until a week before Christmas.

The **Nordic Inn,** Rte. 11, Landgrove, VT 05148 (tel. 802/824-6444), offers reasonably priced accommodations, 12 miles of Nordic ski trails, and a locally favored 75-seat restaurant. There are five rooms, three with private bath. The largest has a queen-size bed and two singles, and all rooms are simply furnished. The solarium dining room sports purple napkins on tables and a balcony dining area. The menu has a Nordic touch and includes gravlax (salmon cured with salt, sugar, and dill), Nordic herring, and hearts of palm and artichoke. Nine or so main courses include duck with orange sauce, poached salmon with hollandaise, steak au poivre, or lamb chops diablo. Prices run $9.50 to $16. Brunch is also popular. Onion soup and stuffed mushrooms are among the appetizers, followed by omelets, eggs Benedict, or crêpes. Prices run $4 to $6. The fieldstone fireplace makes the bar popular in winter after skiing.

RATES: $40 to $60 with continental breakfast; in winter $56 to $70 per person (MAP). LUNCH: Wednesday to Monday in winter, Saturday and Sunday only in summer. DINNER: Wednesday to Monday. Closed April; open weekends only in May and November.

EVENING ENTERTAINMENT

Dorset Summer Theater Festival presents a series of plays from late June through Labor Day at the Dorset Playhouse, Dorset Village (tel. 802/867-2223).

MANCHESTER-DORSET AREA ACTIVITIES

CAMPING: On the Battenkill, R.D. 2, Arlington, VT 05250 (tel. 802/375-6663), hookups available, swimming, tubing, and fishing on the grounds.

CANOEING: Battenkill Canoe, on River Road (leading to West Arlington), off Rte. 313 (tel. 802/375-9559).

CROSS-COUNTRY SKIING: Hildene Ski Touring Center has 26 kms of trails. It's open daily from 9 A.M. to dusk if there's sufficient snow (usually from the third week in December to March 1).

FISHING: On the Battenkill.

GOLF: Dorset Field Club (tel. 802/867-5553); also at the Equinox.

HORSEBACK RIDING: Windhill Horses and Tack Shop, Windhill Road, Manchester Center (tel. 802/362-2604), offers trail rides and lessons as well as wagon and sleigh rides.

SKIING: Bromley, off route 11 in Bromley, is a full-facility resort offering 35 trails serviced by seven lifts. Slopeside accommodations are available at Bromley Village. For information call 802/824-5522 or write P.O. Box 1130-B, Manchester Center, VT 05255.

Stratton, Stratton Mountain, VT 05155 (tel. 802/297-2200) is a full facility resort complete with sports center that also offers tennis, badminton, swimming and more. There are 86 trails on 400 acres serviced by ten lifts including three quads. Accommodations include the Stratton Mountain Inn, Stratton Village Lodge, and Stratton Mountain Village as well as Liftline Lodge and the Birkenhaus. Classes and seminars on a variety of subjects are also given for those who don't ski. For reservations call 1-800/843-6867. For snow conditions call 1-800/297-2211. From Manchester take 11 East and then Route 30 south to Bondville. The entrance to Stratton is located in the village center. Follow Stratton Mountain Road four miles.

SWIMMING: Good swimming at a lake on Route 30 between Dorset and Manchester.

TENNIS: The Stratton Tennis School, site of the Volvo International Tennis Tournament held in early August, has 15 Har-Tru and Deco Turf II courts, 4 indoor courts and 3 raquetball courts plus other athletic facilities. Special packages including accommodations in a variety of room types are available. Call 802/297-2200 or toll-free 800/843-6867. From Manchester take Rte. 7 to Rte. 11 east to Rte. 30 south to Bondville. From the center of the village follow the Stratton Mountain Road to the resort.

Courts are also available at the Equinox.

BENNINGTON

BENNINGTON ATTRACTIONS

During the Revolutionary era Bennington was the headquarters for Ethan Allen and his Green Mountain Boys, who, together with Benedict Arnold, captured Fort Ticonderoga from the British in 1775. A few years later Bennington was at the center of another famous battle that turned out to be a turning point in the Revolution and a prelude to the victory at Saratoga. General Burgoyne was in desperate need of supplies and sent a column of Hessians north to capture the supplies that were being stored in Bennington. The Revolutionary forces heard of the plan and intercepted the British at Walloomsac, New York, where they inflicted great losses on the British troops. The 306-foot-high **Bennington Battle Monument** is a fitting memorial to this historic event. An elevator will take you to the top for a marvelous three-state view.

Much of the history and the crafts of the area can be reviewed at the **Bennington Museum,** West Main Street (Rte. 9), Old Bennington (tel. 802/447-1571), which is filled with an assorted collection of glass, stoneware (including that of the famous Bennington potters), early American paintings by Erastus Salisbury Field, furniture, military items, and other household wares from the 19th century. Most appealing of all, though, is the gallery devoted to Grandma Moses, or Anna Mary Robertson, a New York farm girl who turned her full attention to art at age 78, and achieved her first show at age 80 at the Gallerie St. Étienne, New York, in 1940. She became a legendary figure, who continued to paint until she died in 1961 at the age of 101, an inspiration to all aspiring artists for her late start and her untutored natural gift. Here you can view 32 of her refreshing, delightful farm and country scenes and a display of family memorabilia. HOURS: March 1 to November 30, 9 A.M. to 5 P.M. daily. Closed Thanksgiving and December to February. ADMISSION: $3.25.

From the obelisk of the battle monument, you can stroll past gracious 18th-and 19th-century homes through Old Bennington, past the **Old First Church burial ground,** where some Hessians who fell in the battle are buried in a mass grave. Here, too, Robert Frost is buried. If you wish, you can pick up the walking tour of the area at the Bennington Chamber of Commerce, on Veterans Memorial Drive (Rte. 7 north).

The **Park-McCullough House** (tel. 802/442-2747) is an extremely well-kept Victorian mansion at the corner of West and Park Streets in North Bennington. Besides the house itself, which is filled with period furnishings and personal effects, be sure to see the miniature "manor," used as a children's playhouse, and a cupola-topped carriage house, complete with century-old carriages. HOURS: Late May through October, Sunday to Friday from 10 A.M. to 4 P.M., on Saturday to 2 P.M. ADMISSION: $4 for adults, $2 for 6- to 18-year-olds.

While you're here in North Bennington, you may wish to visit the campus of the progressive **Bennington College,** whose curriculum stresses artistic creation and an acquaintance with nature.

In Bennington itself you may want to stop by **Williams Smokehouse,** 1001 E. Main St. (tel. 802/442-8934), and pick up some fine smoked hams or bacon without nitrates plus many other fresh Vermont products. Also visit **Bennington Potter's Yard,** a shopping and gallery complex at School and Country Streets. HOURS: Monday to Saturday from 9:30 A.M. to 5:30 P.M. and noon to 5 P.M. on Sunday.

BENNINGTON LODGING

The **Walloomsac Inn,** 67 Monument Ave., Bennington, VT 05201 (tel. 802/442-4865). An air of mystery clings to this large, somewhat decrepit weathered-clapboard building, with its faded-green shutters, peeling paint, and wrap-around porches, which stands across from the churchyard in Old Bennington. Come upon it on a dark, moonless night, and it's an ideal setting for a gothic tale of mystery and imagination. Come here with that in mind—to experience living in a different era and indeed in a different spatial dimension.

Don't expect luxury. The 15 rooms are large but starkly furnished with high tester Victorian beds and old oak pieces, and heated by cast-iron radiators. All have large, private bathrooms with old-fashioned tubs only. All of the rooms on the first and second floors have balconies entered via double French doors. Ever since 1764, when the Rev. Jedediah Dewey built it for his son, Elijah, the place has been a stagecoach stop. Presidents Madison, Monroe, Jefferson, and Teddy Roosevelt have all stopped here. The current owners—the Berrys—have been here for the last 100 years, ever since Walter H. Berry purchased the place in the 1880s.

The public areas are filled with heavy Victorian furniture. A marvelous old oak bar and grill now serves as the front desk. An out-sized brick fireplace warms the parlor, which is hung with large Victorian landscape paintings and filled with well-stuffed Victoriana, potted ferns, and other urns.

RATES: Memorial Day to November 1, $30 double.

For bed-and-breakfast in Bennington, **Safford Manor**, 722 Main St., Bennington, VT 05201 (tel. 802/442-5934), has five rooms available furnished in chintz country style. The nicest is the Rose Victorian Room, which has a '30s art deco "waterfall" bed, tiled coal-burning-style fireplace, and oak dresser. Guests can use the oak-beamed parlor and oak-paneled library.

RATES: $45 double.

Molly Stark Inn, 1067 E. Main St., Bennington, VT 05201 (tel. 802/442-9631), occupies a blue- and rust-painted house with porch. Inside, enter a comfortable living room furnished with country oak pieces and owner Bette Malsick's knick-knacks. Two finches twirp from the dining room, which also contains a Hoosier cabinet filled with a collection of dolls. A complimentary continental breakfast is served. Five rooms are available, decorated in chintz style, with white-painted furnishings.

RATES: $30 to $65 double.

For homey accommodations, the **Mount Anthony House**, 226 W. Main St., Bennington, VT 05201 (tel. 802/447-7396), is a large old house with porch and cozy rooms. RATES: From $25 double with a shared bath. Open year round.

Otherwise, Bennington's accommodations are strictly motel style, including Best Western's **New Englander Motor Inn**, 220 Northside Dr., Bennington, VT 05201 (tel. 802/442-6311, or toll free 800/528-1234).

RATES: $42 to $68 double, less in the winter months.

BENNINGTON DINING

The **Publyck House**, Rte. 7A, Harwood Hill (tel. 802/442-8301), is a remodeled barn that has been filled with 18th-century decor and an indoor greenhouse. Good beef and seafood are the staples here priced from $6 to $17.

DINNER: Sunday to Thursday from 5 to 9 P.M., on Friday and Saturday until 10 P.M.

The **Brasserie,** in Potter's Yard (tel. 802/447-7922), is a pleasant outdoor dining spot in summer and a fine luncheon or dinner spot year round. At lunch, have the Yard Special, a platter with Danish pâté, french bread and butter, and a Boston lettuce salad. Or you can choose from a variety of salads, omelets, and sandwiches under $7. Turn off Main Street at Dunkin Donuts (at 460 Main).

HOURS: Monday to Saturday from 11:30 A.M. to 8 P.M., on Sunday from 10:30 A.M. to 8 P.M.

The Swiss-chalet-style **Schwinn's,** 101 W. Main St. (tel. 802/447-1622), just down the hill from the Bennington Museum, is great for sandwiches, burgers, salads, and all kinds of wursts, priced very reasonably. After 5 P.M. dinner is served, and the most expensive main course, including vegetable and potato, is sauerbraten or pot roast for $9.

HOURS: Monday, Tuesday, and Thursday to Saturday from 7 A.M. to 8 P.M., on Sunday from 8 A.M. to 8 P.M.

BENNINGTON ACTIVITIES

BOATING: Rental boats are available in Woodford State Park, east of Bennington on Rte. 9.

FISHING: Woodford State Park has some great trout fishing.

FRUIT PICKING: Pick your own strawberries, apples, raspberries, and blueberries at Harwood Hill Orchards on Rte. 78 (tel. 802/442-9524).

GOLF, SWIMMING, AND TENNIS: Mount Anthony Country Club, Bank Street below the Battle Monument (tel. 802/447-7079).

WILMINGTON

From Bennington, it's only about 21 miles to Wilmington, where there happen to be several charming accommodations to base at while you explore pretty Vermont villages and enjoy all the activities that the mountains and southern Vermont have to offer, particularly, of course, Mount Snow.

WILMINGTON LODGING AND DINING

If I could spare a weekend right now, I'd head for the warm and different hospitality of Jim McGovern and Lois Nelson at the **Hermitage Inn,** Coldbrook Road, Wilmington, VT 05363 (tel. 802/464-3511). Jim certainly has his very own way of doing things. He's a renegade Connecticut gent, who more than 25 years ago fled the South to the 24 acres he now occupies, where he can indulge his own particular hobbies and enthusiasms without too much interference.

From the minute you cross the bridge over the tiny stream onto the property, you know you're somewhere special. Off to the left stand a series of farm structures, which, after investigation, turn out to be houses for the game birds

—goose, pheasant, duck, wild turkey, and partridge—that Jim raises specifically for the table and for which his dining room is famous. He also collects some 35 species of rare beauties that are worth far too much to put on any table—gold and silver pheasants, India blue peacocks, New Zealand and Arctic snow geese, to name a few. Walk up toward the house at the top of the hill and you'll discover a whole run full of wild turkey, an area where Jim and Lois raise English setters, and a sugar house where every spring 5,000 buckets of maple sap are turned into 700 gallons of pure maple syrup, which is sold in the store along with jams, jellies (including originals like Montrachet, made with Montrachet), and other Mc-Govern favorites, notably decoys and fine wines. Here in the store you can also rent ski equipment to travel the 40 km of cross-country trails or the downhill slopes at Mount Snow. A clay tennis court and a trout pond complete the picture.

The inn itself dates back 100 years. Wide pine floors and chairs cozily placed in front of the hearth in the bar engender a convivial atmosphere conducive to conversation. Several small dining areas lead off the bar (there's an outdoor terrace for summer dining), and here you'll enjoy some of the finest dining in the area —game, trout, wienerschnitzel, from $12 to $20—enhanced by really fine wines from Jim's virtuoso wine cellar (1,350 labels with many extra-fine vintages over 30 years old). Start with mushrooms Hermitage, stuffed with caviar, and I can heartily recommend the pheasant braised in white wine cream sauce. There's also a larger dining room in the back and a gallery where Jim has been collecting Delacroix lithographs.

The main 100-year-old inn, with its shingle roof and dormer windows, was once the home of Mrs. Bertha Eastman Barry, the redoubtable editor of the Social Register, and it retains some of her original furnishings, most notably the four-poster in Room 4. Jim recently added a new wing, carefully constructed in the same architectural style. Of the 16 rooms, 11 have working, wood-burning fireplaces; all of them are furnished differently, some in mahogany, some in honey oak. A typical large room would contain a pineapple half-poster, chest of drawers with broken-scroll mirror, Stickley love seat, and comb-back Windsor chair. From most of the rooms there's a glorious view looking toward Hogback Mountain. Additional rooms are located a short distance down the road in Brook Bound. Here guests can use a pine living room with fieldstone fireplace, TV, and upright piano. Rooms vary in size. The largest, Room 42, possesses a high carved oak bed, needlepointed Victorian rocker, Stickley chair, Chippendale sidetable, and brick fireplace. Rooms have private baths.

As for skiing possibilities, several years ago Jim pioneered a special Norski trail from the top of Mount Snow to Haystack—that's a skiing technique that combines downhill and cross-country into one. On the downhill stretches the boot is solidly attached to the ski; on the flat, the bindings loosen to enable you to walk.

This may not be the ultimate designer-stamped, $4-glossy-magazine quality establishment, but it offers a deeply satisfying sense of honesty, character, and individuality, and a place where you can relax and be yourself.

RATES: A terrific buy at $90 to $100 per person (MAP). It's located 2½ miles north of Wilmington; from Rte. 100, turn left at Coldbrook Road and continue for about 2½ miles. Turn left at the sign marking the inn.

You won't miss the **Nutmeg Inn,** Rte. 9, Wilmington, VT 05363 (tel. 802/464-

3351), a Chinese-red clapboard house whose long front porch always supports some colorful floral display—roses in summer; potted bronze, yellow, and orange mums in fall. The place is very lovingly cared for, and everything is spick and span at this comfortable, homey 180-year-old farmhouse. The special warmth is most evident in the large sitting room, where guests gather either to read in front of the fire, watch TV, play cards or games, or enjoy a drink at the "bring your own" bar. Out back there's a lawn set up for croquet in summer, along with volleyball and badminton for more active guests. Throughout the house pine furnishings add special coziness. Each of the 11 rooms, all with private bath, is decorated in country fashion with pine or oak pieces, tables draped with Laura Ashley prints, brass beds, and so on.

There are two cozily furnished dining rooms—one containing a Norman Rockwell plate collection and the other, warmed by a woodstove, giving a hillside view. Dinner is served to guests and usually will be the kind of dishes that most people relish—roast beef or pork accompanied by soup, salad, vegetables, and dessert. Check for meal service: dinner is only served on weekends in summer, but more frequently in fall.

RATES (including breakfast): $60 to $83 double in summer, $75 to $98 in the fall, and $75 to $106 in winter. Add $10 for a suite with a fireplace.

Tall maples, manicured lawns, and a vegetable garden surround the white clapboard **Red Shutter Inn**, Rte. 9 (P.O. Box 84), Wilmington, VT 05363 (tel. 802/464-3768). A creative international cuisine is prepared here, although the chef is known especially for his fish dishes—fresh broiled swordfish, poached salmon with a lemon-dill sauce, filet of bluefish poached in tomato, wine, and herbs, for example—supplemented by such classic entrees as duck à l'orange and steak with green peppercorn sauce (from $10 to $18). Ingredients are always fresh and seasonal, and you can choose to dine outside in summer on the veranda or in the cozy dining room with a stone fireplace.

There are five rooms, three with private bath, most furnished in chintz country fashion. Room 3, for example, has a pineapple half-poster, maple chest, Queen Anne–style side chair, and lace-trimmed curtains and chintz wallpaper among its furnishings. There's a small bar with TV for guests.

RATES (including breakfast): $70 double. DINNER: Daily except Monday and Tuesday.

Set atop a hill with a lovely view of the Deerfield Valley, the **White House**, Rte. 9, Wilmington, VT 05363 (tel. 802/464-2136), was built as a private summer home in 1914 and possesses a gracious Georgian-style portico and rows of dormers jutting from the roof line. As you might expect, the 12 rooms are extra-large—all with private bath. Five of the rooms have fireplaces, and some of the bathrooms retain the antique fittings. The public areas include large antique-filled sitting rooms, a dining room with rich mahogany paneling, and a bar, which was especially sunk so as not to impair the view of the sunsets across the valley. An outside terrace also takes advantage of the vista. The grounds are delightful. Roses climb around a trellis by a garden fountain, creating a romantic arbor, while beyond there's an outdoor swimming pool. In winter 23 km of ski trails are available. The restaurant offers a selection of chicken, steak, veal, and seafood with such dishes as saltimbocca a la romana, shrimp-stuffed sole, and stuffed duck, priced from $11 to $18. There's also a new spa with indoor pool and a game room.

RATES: $77.50 to $90 double (MAP). During the summer special packages are offered. DINNER: 6 to 9 P.M. daily.

About two miles from Mount Snow, four miles from Wilmington center, at **Trails End Lodge,** Smith Road, Wilmington, VT 05363 (tel. 802/464-2727), you'll find a real home away from home at which Mary and Bill Kilburn, two charming and delightful hosts, will welcome you. The house stands on 11 beautifully kept acres. At the back there's a prettily landscaped pool and plenty of sunning space.

Dinner is served to guests only, and only when the house is full or close to full. The menu will be on the blackboard by the kitchen counter where you check in. It's served all-you-can-eat family style and includes soup and salad and a single entree like pork loin with madeira sauce, beef rouladen, or baked scrod, accompanied by two or three vegetables and topped off with a dessert like strawberry daiquiri. There's a guest fridge for storing away your choice drinks. In summer they enjoy cookouts on Thursday night. Otherwise you'll dine in the attractive dining room off tiled round tables.

Breakfast consists of cereal and homemade granola, juice, muffins, and an egg dish with bacon or sausage. Guests can relax in the cathedral-ceilinged living room around the massive fieldstone fireplace on any of several cozy seating arrangements. There's also a game room equipped with board games, books, and something called bumper pool—great for the kids.

The rooms are small but well designed for the size of the space. There are 18 pine-paneled rooms with private bath. Some are tiny twins with just enough room for beds set head to head, a closet, and two drawers plus tiny bath; others are doubles with enough room for additional furnishings. There's also a large room with a queen-size bed covered with a fluffy cream eiderdown, chintz celery-and-rose-colored wallpaper, small table and chair, and oak dresser. There are several of these. My favorite rooms, though, are the so-called Family Suites, which have stone fireplaces, brass beds, cathedral ceilings, and a lot of pine. They also possess a kitchen and bathroom, a sitting room, and two small rooms with bunks for the kids.

RATES: $35 (MAP) for small rooms, $50 per person (MAP) for queen-size rooms, and $60 per person (MAP) for Family Suites ($25 for 6- to 12-year-olds and $35 for those 12 and over).

The **Misty Mountain Inn Lodge,** Stowe Hill Road (R.R. Box 114C), Wilmington, VT 05363 (tel. 802/464-3961), was once a one-room schoolhouse that is about two miles from the center of Wilmington overlooking the picturesque Deerfield Valley, ideally situated for the Marlboro music festival. There are 150 surrounding acres to walk around in summer or cross-country ski in winter. Meals are served family style in the rustic dining room and might feature roast beef with mashed potatoes and vegetables, home-baked rolls, and desserts. There's a cozy living room warmed by a fire in the winter, where guests may join in a sing-along with Buzz and Elizabeth Cole. There's also TV, games, and books for the children. There are 12 rooms—one hall bath for every two rooms—simply furnished doubles, twins, and family rooms.

RATES: $28 in midweek, $38 on weekends, with breakfast and dinner (MAP); $18 in midweek, $22 on weekends, for bed-and-breakfast; $13 in midweek, $16 on weekends, for room only.

WILMINGTON DINING

Le Petit Chef, Rte. 100 (tel. 802/464-8437), is a local favorite for superb food served in homey country surroundings. Although the dishes change frequently, you might find rack of lamb; filet of beef; veal à la crème with mushrooms and madeira; poisson Méditerrané (fish, clams, mussels, and shrimp poached in tomato broth with aromatic sea herbs); venison with grand veneur sauce or a currant-flavored brown sauce; and always a vegetarian dish. Desserts are tantalizing—especially the crunchy meringue pie (if it's available), chocolate torte, and any of the fresh homemade fruit pies. Main-course prices run $13 to $19.

DINNER: 6 to 9 P.M. on weekdays and 6 to 10 P.M. on weekends; closed Tuesday and also for a month in November and April. On Monday and Thursday there's usually some light musical entertainment offered.

WEST DOVER/MOUNT SNOW

From Wilmington, **Mount Snow,** Mount Snow, VT 05356 (tel. 802/464-3333), lies only nine miles north on Rte. 100. Mount Snow is one of the state's largest ski resorts and draws great crowds from the metropolitan areas of Boston, Hartford, and New York. It's the Vermont resort closest to New York, and as such, many people have shunned it in favor of Stowe and other more fashionable ski areas. The company that manages Killington took over Mount Snow in 1977, making substantial improvements, including the installation of computerized snowmaking. There are 14 lifts including two enclosed gondolas. The highest vertical drop is almost 2,000 feet and the trails are myriad (70-plus), serviced by 16 lifts. Good skiing for beginners and intermediates, and on the North Face, for experts, with 52% snow-making capability. Facilities include a nursery, bar, cafeteria at the summit, rentals, ski school, and 40 miles of cross-country trails. Plenty of après ski too, at the Sitzmark, Andirons disco, and Deacon's Den.

MOUNT SNOW/WEST DOVER LODGING AND DINING

Close to 100 lodges, inns, and motels are clustered near the ski area, and one or two of them are quite exquisite. I've already mentioned the Hermitage Inn. The other accommodation, the **Inn at Sawmill Farm,** Rte. 100 (P.O. Box 367), West Dover, VT 05356 (tel. 802/464-8131), created by Rodney Williams and his wife, Ione, from an old farmhouse and barn, has international renown. It's famous for its classic dining room, designer-perfect quality of its rooms and cottages, and the understated elegance of its grounds. The dining room positively glows. Copper pots adorn the walls, fresh flowers add color and life, fine crystal and china grace the tables in a cathedral-ceilinged room that has been carefully designed to provide small intimate dining areas. Son Brill creates the cuisine. At dinner there's a selection for every palate—Dover sole meunière, or backfin crabmeat au gratin, for example, for seafood lovers; duck au poivre vert or Indonesian curried chicken breasts for the poultry fancier; and calves' liver, rack of lamb, pork tenderloin with cognac, cream, and walnuts, or steak au poivre for the true carnivore. Prices run $16.50 to $24. Appetizers are equally tempting—chicken livers with bordelaise sauce, shrimp in beer batter with fruit sauce, individual onion tart, or a crabmeat cocktail. Jackets are required for men, after 6 P.M. The garden dining room has a sun atrium filled with huge ferns and hydrangeas. Pine hutches, Windsor chairs, and burgundy floral wallpaper complete the summer atmosphere. A pianist quietly entertains in the evening.

In winter the living room is especially welcoming, as guests gather around the large fireplace and settle into the couches and wing chairs. The upstairs gallery overlooking the living room contains games, chess, books, and a large TV. Tea is served at 4 P.M., classical music making the announcement.

Some guest rooms are located in the main building. The lowest-priced room is the smallest. It features twin cannonball beds with candlewick spreads and white eiderdown, rose wallpaper, two comfortable lounge chairs, and a wrought-iron floorlamp. Another room is decorated with a bold chintz and contains a king-size pencil-post bed sans canopy, a chest of drawers topped with a gilt mirror, two lounge chairs, and a small deck. The prime accommodations, though, are in the cottages. Each is plushly decorated. For example, Farmhouse 2 possesses a full-canopy bed and fireplace, is decorated in peach, and is furnished with handsome china lamps, a desk tucked into the bay window, a candlestand table, and other fine furnishings including floor-to-ceiling drapes. The Cider House is furnished in more of a country style. Godiva chocolates and magazines like *Vogue* are placed in every room.

The grounds embrace a swimming pool, a pond with canoes, a tennis court, and two trout ponds. The Mount Snow golf course is conveniently located up the road. No children under 10.

RATES: $170 to $200 double (MAP) in the inn, $210 to $230, double (MAP) in the cottages.

BREAKFAST: 8 to 10:30 A.M. daily. DINNER: 6 to 9:30 P.M. daily. The inn closes the Sunday after Thanksgiving, reopening three weekends later.

Across the street from the Inn at Saw Mill, there's the far more modest, but nonetheless attractive **West Dover Inn,** West Dover, VT 05356 (tel. 802/464-5207), hard against the village's white clapboard church. It occupies an informal clapboard home built in 1846 and offers ten attractively furnished rooms with wide-plank floors. All have private bathrooms and color TVs, and most of them have balconies; the suite has a fireplace and Jacuzzi. Downstairs there's a rustic, woody dining room serving continental/New England cuisine, priced from $11 to $18.

RATES: In summer, $65 double, $100 for the suite; in fall, $85 double, $125 for the suite; in winter, $85 to $95 double, $150 for the suite.

The **Deerhill Inn,** Valley View Road (P.O. Box 397), West Dover, VT 05356 (tel. 802/464-3100), a clapboard house tucked into the side of a hill, has a fine view of the valley. The new owners have spruced it up considerably. There are 17 guest rooms, many decorated in chintz, with oak and maple furnishings and brass beds. The prettiest room, decked out in rose-lavender, features a four-poster canopy with floral dust ruffle and has French doors leading to a balcony overlooking the attractively landscaped pool. Room 6 has twin canopy beds with an embroidered white canopy.

Guests can use the large, comfortable upstairs sitting room complete with fireplace, sofas, love seats, and wing chairs, which offers a supply of books as well as a TV. Another, more formally furnished parlor downstairs serves as a waiting area for diners. The restaurant has a good reputation. The fireplace makes it cozy in winter and it offers a view of the valley that is equally lovely in winter or summer. The menu is limited, offering eight or nine entrees such as sole duglère (with tomato-herb sauce), duck with lingonberry sauce, tournedos du jour, or veal with morels. A full breakfast is served. The pool deck also has umbrella tables. An added attraction—the tennis court.

RATES: In winter and spring, $140 to $165 double (MAP) per day on weekends, $120 to $150 in midweek; in summer and fall, $140 to $165 double (MAP) daily. DINNER: 6 to 9 P.M. daily. Closed November to mid-December and from Easter to Memorial Day.

For an alpine-style ski lodge, there's the nicely kept **Kitzhof,** on Rte. 100 in West Dover, VT 05356 (tel. 802/464-8310), where no two rooms are alike except in their comfort and cleanliness. Knotty-pine boards, logs, and a fieldstone fireplace impart a mountain coziness; a Finnish-style sauna and whirlpool are added luxuries. There's a BYOB bar with set-ups. Meals are served family style.

RATES: $55 to $65 per person (MAP). During the summer the place takes in a lot of bus tours and rooms are rarely available for individual travelers.

At the **Snow Den Inn,** Rte. 100 (P.O. Box 625), West Dover, VT 05356 (tel. 802/464-9355), an 1885 farmhouse, there are eight snug rooms, all with private bath and color TV; five have a fireplace. Most are furnished with oak beds and dressers, and braided rugs spread on pine floors. One of the fireplace rooms has a lace canopy bed, covered with a colorful fan-patterned quilt; other furnishings include a rocking chair and corner cupboard. Yet another fireplace room features a brass bed sporting a blue star quilt, various marble-top pieces, and a cane-seated chair. A full breakfast is served. There's a comfortable living room where guests gather around the fire in winter.

RATES: Winter weekends, $40 to $50 per person per night; in summer and fall $55 to $65 double for bed-and-breakfast.

Other lodging choices include a full traditional ski lodge, the **Snow Lake Lodge,** 84 Mountain Rd., Mount Snow, VT 05356 (tel. 802/464-3333, or toll free 800/451-4211), overlooking Snow Lake and the ski slopes. Rooms are plain, pine paneled, and furnished with somewhat worn Danish-style furniture. All have cable TV and telephone, and some even come with waterbeds. Summer amenities include an outdoor heated pool, two lighted clay tennis courts, cabaña bar and barbecue, and boating on Snow Lake. Year-round facilities include two indoor hot and cool pools, entertainment in the lounge, a fitness center, and breakfast and dinner in the Lakeside Dining Room.

RATES: In winter, from $62 per person (MAP) in midweek, from $90 per person

(MAP) on weekends; in summer, from $60 per person (MAP), $36 double (for room only).

WEST DOVER/MOUNT SNOW DINING

Prime dining spots I've already mentioned are the Inn at Saw Mill Farm and the Hermitage.

Two Tannery Road (tel. 802/464-2707) has a fine reputation locally. The original old frame building, with plank floors and a piano for impromptu entertainment, offers a comfortable, romantic candlelit setting for dinner, while the high-ceilinged barn-like extension, warmed by a woodstove in winter, is most inviting in summer. Specialties include lobster-and-crab pie, roast duckling, shrimp Fra Diavolo, and such desserts as mud pie and baklava à la Nancy. Prices range from $13 to $20. To start, the blue asparagus—delicious! The name comes from its location on the old site of two saw mills and a tannery.

DINNER: Tuesday to Sunday from 6 to 10 P.M. Take the left fork off Rte. 100 about two miles north of West Dover.

Another local favorite is the **Old Barn Inn,** about another eight miles north of Mount Snow in West Wardsboro (tel. 802/896-6100). You'll need to bring your own wine to this spacious dining spot.

MARLBORO

From the West Dover/Mount Snow area you can either cut across via East Dover, South Newfane, and West Dummerston to Rte. 30, which will take you north into Newfane, or you can double back down to Rte. 100 and continue east to Marlboro.

Marlboro is home of the famous Marlboro Music Festival directed by Rudolf Serkin each summer, when dozens of the most talented musicians gather together for six weeks' practice, consultation, and tutorial, giving weekend concerts at Marlboro College's auditorium. If you wish to attend the festival you'll need to have reservations for lodgings, and also to write early for tickets to Marlboro Festival, Marlboro, VT 05344 (tel. 802/254-8163 or 254-2394).

MARLBORO LODGING AND DINING

Marlboro is more a state of mind than an actual place, for when you arrive at the dot on the map you'll find only a church, post office, a few houses, and most glorious of all, an old inn right next door to the church—the **Whetstone,** Marlboro, VT 05344 (tel. 802/254-2500). Here Jean and Harry Boardman welcome guests into their living room, which is lined with interesting books (from Rabelais to *Moby-Dick),* houses a piano, a bar that originally served as the post office, and a fireplace that is well used on cold Vermont days. Built in 1786 this venerable building has always flourished as a tavern, except briefly for 15 years in the '30s. Many of the musicians performing at the festival stay here, and so you'll enjoy interesting company, in addition to the fascinating conversation likely to flow from Harry, who spent a decade at the Salk Institute in California educating professionals about new biological developments and their effects on our society. Rooms vary in decor and size, although most are furnished in keeping with the colonial atmosphere of the inn. Some have private bathroom. All look out on meadowed and forested grounds. Meals are served in what was originally the big old kitchen in the back, with a fireplace large enough to accommodate a cooking crane. Full breakfasts are $5; complete dinners run $14 to $18. Although Jean will accommodate friends of yours at table, dining is really only for guests. In winter, dinner is served every Saturday; in summer, on concert nights—Wednesday to Saturday. Dishes will be homemade, from the cheddar-cheese soup and roast leg of lamb or pork to the brandy Alexander pie.

RATES: $50 for room with shared bath, $70 with private bath. Rates go up in July and the first two weeks of August when priority is given to weekly rentals. In winter, the inn is ideal for cross-country skiing, sledding, and snowshoeing.

The **Longwood Inn,** Rte. 9, Marlboro, VT 05344 (tel. 802/257-1545), is a delightful old clapboard house built in 1769 and run by Tom and Janet Durkin. Besides their lovely accommodations, they are also well known for the quality of their food, presenting such dishes as braised rabbit, poached salmon, finnan haddie poached in cream, and duck, chicken, and beef dishes. The menu also offers a selection of pastas, appetizers, and soups, including stuffed quahogs and linguini with smoked scallops and bluefish in a creamy fish veloute. Breakfast (blueberry pancakes and local syrup, muffins) is served in a room with a large picture window overlooking the terrace and the trout pond. Entree prices range from $10 to $15. The rambling 200-year-old house is particularly welcoming in winter, when fires blaze in the two hearths in the L-shaped living room and you can relax over a cocktail accompanied by fruit and cheese, or read or watch TV. Personal touches include a number of paintings done by their daughter and a wine list largely selected by another wine-buff daughter.

There are 15 rooms, all with private bath and furnished comfortably and unpretentiously with country pieces. For example, Room 2 possessing a fireplace, is furnished with a king-size bed, Hitchcock rocker, an old dresser, desk, chair, and sidetables. Many of the floors are wide pine planks. Room 4 is similar but also has a couch. Some of the prettiest rooms, in my opinion, are tucked under the eaves. Room 5, for example, has pale-blue walls and a chintz coverlet on the bed. Room 6 has a skylight. Room 11 is also special, for it has fireplace, TV, and a small deck. Rooms are also available in the Carriage House, and many people like them because they're quiet and private and have sliding doors through which you can step outside. They are in fact efficiencies, and the furnishings tend to the plain. It's a wonderful old house where the ceilings are low, the floors creak, and the doors retain their iron latches (at least in the original part of the house—it was added to in 1840 and again in 1950).

RATES: $60 to $85 per person (MAP).

Peter and Sheila Kane run **Four in Hand** on Rte. 100, Marlboro, VT 05344 (tel. 802/254-2894), set well back from the road with ten acres behind for hiking or cross-country skiing. They maintain seven guest rooms and a suite, all with private bath—three doubles, two twins, and one family—all individually furnished and priced at $40, including continental breakfast. In the guest area they've created a cozy sitting room with TV. The dining room, serving dinners only, is warmed by a Dutch Delft-tile fireplace with woodstove and offers steak, chicken, and fish dishes from $10 to $15. Dishes offered might include a navarin of lamb, veal with wild mushrooms, chicken with mustard sauce, and always a pasta of some kind. For dessert, the terrine of chocolate is the house specialty. Downstairs, the Pub—complete with dart board, Ping-Pong, and piano—is a popular gathering place for guests and great for taking a bone-warming hot toddy by a roaring fire.

RATES: In season, $55 double, $75 for the suite; in November and March, $40 double, $60 for the suite; closed April.

While you're in Marlboro, take a drive to the top of Hogback Mountain for the spectacular 100-mile view. The **Skyline Restaurant,** Rte. 9 (tel. 802/464-5535), is at the summit and makes a great spot for a Vermont breakfast of waffles and real maple syrup.

BRATTLEBORO

For most shopping and services Marlboro residents drive the 18 miles into Brattleboro, an old, industrial town that was the first colonial settlement in Vermont. Today it's one of the state's larger cities with a population of 13,000, a center for book and paper manufacturing, and home to a major optical company. The town was discovered by urban pioneers of the young '60s generation, who have established many craft centers in the area. As for famous sons, Mormon leader Brigham Young was born nearby in Windham County, and Rudyard Kipling married a Brattleboro girl in 1892 and they lived here for some time.

En route to Brattleboro from Marlboro, book lovers will want to stop at the **Bear Book Shop,** off Rte. 9 (R.D. 4, Box 219), West Brattleboro (tel. 802/464-2260), where you'll find 30,000 catalogued books housed in a big old barn. The owner is a one-time professor of philosophy in Montréal, John Greenberg.

BRATTLEBORO LODGING AND DINING

Accommodations are primarily motels. Best bet is probably the **Susse Chalet Motor Lodge,** Rte. 5N. Brattleboro, VT 05301 (tel. 802/254-6007, or toll free 800/258-1980), where you can obtain a room for $35.

T.J. Buckley's, 132 Elliot St. (tel. 802/257-4922), is an unlikely local dining favorite operated by Michael Fuller, an old diner, now avant-garde looking, that seats 16 people maximum. He's a creative cook who features such dishes as salmon with smoked scallop sauce, filet mignon with red wine and cèpes peppercorn sauce, or shrimp with tomato sauce. The $15 price includes salad and rolls. Desserts are prepared daily. On the brunch menu there's always a variety of appealing omelets, while at lunch you'll find sandwiches, Mexican specials, and always a stir-fry of some sort—with salmon and vegetables, for example.

BREAKFAST: Monday to Saturday from 8:30 A.M., on Sunday from 10:30 A.M. LUNCH: Noon to 2 P.M. daily. DINNER: Wednesday to Sunday. Beer and wine only.

The other local spot is the **Common Ground,** 25 Elliot St. (tel. 802/257-0855), where many of the craftspeople can be seen lingering over vegetarian and natural foods on the second-floor enclosed terrace in summer. Downstairs, the entryway and stairwell serve as the town's alternative bulletin board. A variety of chicken, fish, and vegetarian dishes are offered—scallops, fettuccine Alfredo, enchiladas, Hungarian goulash, vegetable curry. Nondairy specials are also available. On Wednesday night an international cuisine is highlighted—it might be Chinese, Slavic, Caribbean, Greek, Spanish, etc. Prices range from $5 to $9.

LUNCH: Monday to Saturday from 11:30 A.M. to 2:30 P.M. DINNER: Wednesday to Monday from 5:30 to 8 P.M. January to June and then until 9 P.M. on weekends.

NEWFANE, GRAFTON, AND SAXTONS RIVER

From Brattleboro it's about 17 miles to Newfane, another 12 miles to Grafton, and from there, another 7 miles to Saxtons River.

All three of these villages are picture-book New England, their gracious homes and buildings set around town greens and white clapboard churches with spires. There's not an awful lot to do, but that's the whole point—this is cycling and rambling country, havens for those who just want to enjoy the bounties of the mountains and the backroads.

In Grafton, stroll (or ride around in a horse and carriage enjoying a narrative tour) through the beautifully restored town and visit the **Grafton Village Cheese Company,** a half mile south on Townshend Road (tel. 802/843-2221). They make their very own Covered Bridge Cheddar, and you can watch the process and take a few tangy samples home. HOURS: June to October, 8:30 A.M. to 4 P.M. weekdays, on Saturday from 10 A.M. to 4 P.M.

History buffs will want to stop at the **Grafton Historical Society Museum,** on Main Street (tel. 802/843-2388), just down from the post office. Old photographs, memorabilia, historical objects, and genealogical books reflect the town's story. HOURS: 2:30 to 4:40 P.M. on Saturday from June to mid-October, and also on Sunday in July and August.

NEWFANE LODGING AND DINING

Before Sandy and Jacques Allembert took over the classically proportioned **Four Columns Inn,** on the Common at 230 West St., Newfane, VT 05345 (tel. 802/365-7713), it was known primarily for the cuisine served in the dining room. Since they took over, they have worked assiduously to turn it into a full-facility inn by constructing a trout pond and swimming pool, planting flower and herb gardens, clearing a path down to the stream's old-fashioned swimming hole, and marking out ski trails across the property. The dining room is still exceptional. Comfortable and very appealing with its huge fireplace, old beams, Windsor chairs, and stuffed deer trophies, it's reminiscent of a European hunting lodge. The cuisine is always exciting. Among the soups you may find a white bean with sausage or a fine parsley, which can be followed by such appetizers as a pheasant pâté or oysters, and a choice among such entrees as veal with port and apples, chicken with framboise, and kidneys with Calvados, horseradish, and cider sauce. Prices range from $15 to $20. In the main inn building, which was fashioned after the original owner's wife's southern mansion, there are 12 rooms, all distinctively furnished.

RATES (including continental breakfast): $60 to $100 double. LUNCH: In summer only, Monday to Saturday from noon to 2 P.M. DINNER: Wednesday to Monday from 6 to 9 P.M. whenever the inn is open. BRUNCH: Sunday from 11 A.M. to 2 P.M. Closed April and November.

Old Newfane Inn, Rte. 30, Newfane, VT 05345 (tel. 802/365-4427). Eric and Gundy Weindl run this typical New England inn with uneven floors, beamed ceilings, and flocked wallpaper. The dining room possesses a large warming brick fireplace and pewter lamps, and offers food that runs from veal curry to filet mignon, veal marsala, and a brochette of beef bordelaise. Desserts include the classic cherries jubilee, crêpes Suzette, and baked Alaska. Main dishes go for $12.50 to $22. The inn's guest rooms are furnished with pleasant oak pieces, rockers, and wing chairs.

RATES (including continental breakfast): $70 to $90 double. LUNCH: In summer only, Tuesday to Sunday from noon to 2 P.M. DINNER: In winter only, Tuesday to Sunday from 6 to 9 P.M. Open May to October and mid-December to early April.

LODGING AND DINING IN GRAFTON AND SAXTONS RIVER

At the center of the idyllic, meticulously kept New England village of Grafton, the **Old Tavern,** Grafton, VT 05146 (tel. 802/843-2231), is a town landmark dating from 1801. It occupies a main building as well as a number of historic homes in the village, and has a long and proud tradition dating back to 1788. Among the famous visitors who have stayed here are Thoreau, Emerson, Hawthorne, Teddy Roosevelt, and Rudyard Kipling. Today the tradition continues with many prominent folks staying.

The main building contains 14 guest rooms, all with private bath, some with canopy beds. Behind it in what was originally the livery is a bar with an upstairs gallery, a slate fireplace, and beams and barn siding. Most of the accommodations are in beautifully furnished antique-laden cottages—White Gates, Barrett House, Tuttle House, etc. Most of these rooms contain canopy beds, mahogany chests, comfortable slip-covered armchairs, candlestand tables, and sitting rooms ideally furnished for quiet reading. They have antique accents like broken-scroll mirrors and demi-lune tables set with a Staffordshire vase or similar filled with fresh flowers. A couple of the cottages are reserved primarily for families and are furnished appropriately. There are no telephones or TVs in any of the rooms. The place is filled with authentic antiques (and a few reproductions).

Among the dining rooms there are several choices: first a formal room, whose oak tables are set with placemats and Charles Dickens china; second, the pine room, with a beamed ceiling, fireplace, and Windsor chairs; and third, the garden room, with bamboo furnishings, brick floor, and potted flowers and plants. The food in each is the same traditional New England fare—broiled steaks and chops, supplemented by veal Oscar, chicken amandine, New England lobster pie, and sea scallops en casserole. To start, there's pâté and herring dressed in sour cream and chives, or baked camembert; to finish, a selection of parfaits, along with strawberry shortcake and white-chocolate mousse. Entree prices run from $12.50 to $18.50.

The Old Tavern is not the place to visit if you're looking for nightlife—come in search of peace and quiet, a comfortable chair, a good book and a brandy in front of a crackling fire, and you'll find contentment. The inn also offers cross-country ski trails, sleds and toboggans, and a natural swimming pond. Two tennis courts just down the street are free to guests. Platform tennis and a game room with billiards and Ping-Pong complete the facilities.

RATES: $50 to $100 double. A number of really lavishly antique-filled guest-houses, with full kitchen and sleeping seven to nine, also rent for $240 to $260 per day. LUNCH: Noon to 1:45 P.M. daily. DINNER: 6:30 to 8:45 P.M. daily. BRUNCH: Sunday from 11:30 A.M. to 2 P.M. Closed Christmas.

Farther northeast lies the village of Saxtons River, where you'll find the small and casual **Saxtons River Inn,** Main Street, Saxtons River, VT 05154 (tel. 802/869-2110), a homey idiosyncratically flavored place. It's not your precious perfectly coiffed New England inn. Built in 1904, it has a character all its own, and moreover it's reasonably priced.

Locals gather at the copper-top bar to sit and chat on the wooden seats that look as if they came from a local theater or cinema. Many of the 20 rooms exhibit bold floral wallpapers, oak chests with teardrop handles, clawfoot tubs without showers, and assorted furnishings—couches, lounge chairs, pie-crust tables. Room 9 has a black-and-white floral wallpaper, iron-and-brass bed with silver-white coverlet, tasseled white swag curtains, chest and mirror, comfy chair, and a small bathroom with shower. Room 6 is a brilliant lime-green coordinated with yellow-green-mauve floral curtains and comforter, and among the furnishings a yellow bamboo chair and a white leather wing chair coexist. On the third floor the wallpapers and color schemes seem to get even wilder. Here the rooms share baths down the hall. Room 22 sports black and pink-rose wallpaper, a lavender comforter on the bed, a lime carpet on the floor, and pelmeted pink curtains.

Two of the most popular gathering places for guests are the upstairs porch, furnished with wicker and hanging flowering plants, and the small TV room. Throughout the house are southern pine door frames and woodwork. The dining room continues the colorful flair with its Tiffany lampshades, floral tablecloths, and rush-seated chairs painted various shades of pink, yellow, jade, crimson, and orange. Food is traditionally prepared—steak au poivre, grilled lamb chops with fresh mint sauce, roast duck with mandarin orange and Cointreau glaze, marinated chicken and roasted peppers. Prices run $12 to $15 for the half dozen entrees. Appetizers are equally popular; try the picadilla and spicy meat and cheese tortilla, or the chilled tortellini tossed with Chinese vegetables and spices.

RATES (including buffet breakfast): $40 to $65 double. DINNER: Wednesday through Monday. Closed in March and April for five weeks.

The **Windham Hill Inn,** West Townshend, VT 05359 (tel. 802/874-4080), takes some finding, but it's worth it for it's set on 150 lovely secluded woodland-mountain acres overlooking Rattle Snake Mountain and offers a peaceful garden filled with iris, roses, poppies, pansies, and a redolent fringe tree. There are ten guest rooms in the restored 1825 farmhouse and five in the white barn annex. All have private bath. Most of the rooms have beds with candlewick spreads, country maple furnishings, and chintz wallpapers. My favorite accommodations are in the barn—a real barn where chamber concerts are in fact performed. Here most rooms have high beamed ceilings, and best of all, decks that have gorgeous views; some are low beamed, like Matilda's Room, which is furnished with a bed, rocker, trunk, and floorlamp, plus that glorious view and deck.

Guests can choose among three parlors, two comfortably furnished with antiques; the third, which as an outside deck, is furnished more casually with wicker pieces. Each one has either a fireplace or wood-burning stove. In the small dining room with oak tables covered with pink tablecloths and wall niches displaying china, a five-course meal is served that might feature chicken Pommery, beef béarnaise, or duck as the main course. A full country breakfast is also served.

In summer guests can hike trails that lead to a brook with a swimming hole; in winter the trails are for cross-country skiing. Innkeepers Ken and Linda Busteed will arrange hiking, biking, canoeing, and fishing trips for you, box lunch included.

RATES: $70 to $80 per person (MAP).

EVENING ENTERTAINMENT IN THE AREA

This is largely confined to having a drink in a cozy spot like the **Hermitage Inn** and following it with dinner. During the summer, **Mount Snow Playhouse** (tel. 802/464-3333 or 295-7016) offers summer stock.

Plenty of après-ski at **Andirons Lodge,** Rte. 100, West Dover (tel. 802/464-2114); and **Sitzmark Lodge,** East Dover Road, Wilmington (tel. 802/464-3384).

AREA ACTIVITIES

ANTIQUING: Either acquire an *Antiquing in Vermont* directory, or send a stamped, self-addressed envelope to the Antiques Association, c/o Muriel McKirryher, 55 Allen St., Rutland, VT 05071. The area has many stores.

BOATING: At Lake Whitingham you can rent a sailboat. Also in Woodford State Park.

CAMPING: Four state parks in the area offer camping: Molly Stark, in Wilmington; Fort Dummer, in Brattleboro; Townshend, in Newfane; and Woodford, in Woodford.

For information write to Department of Forests, Parks and Recreation Waterbury, VT 05602 (tel. 802/244-8711).

CANOEING: At Lake Whitingham, between Bennington and Wilmington, south of Rte. 9, you can rent a canoe. Also at Harriman Reservoir.

CYCLING: For information, contact Bike Vermont, P.O. Box 207WG, Woodstock, VT 05091 (tel. 802/457-3553). It offers inn-to-inn bicycle touring from mid-May through October, on weekend and five-day trips. Rentals available. Or try Vermont Cycling Touring, P.O. Box 711, Bristol, VT 05443 (tel. 802/453-4811). Valley Cyclery, in Wilmington (tel. 802/464-2728), rents bicycles.

FISHING: For information, contact the Vermont Fish and Wildlife Department, Waterbury, VT 05676 (tel. 802/244-7331). Licenses are available by mail, but allow plenty of time. A useful guide to fishing and a booklet outlining state laws and regulations are also available.

GOLF: There's an 18-hole course at the Sitzmark Lodge, East Dover Road, Wilmington (tel. 802/464-3384), and also at Mount Snow Country Club (tel. 802/464-3333) where the fourth hole was named one of the most beautiful in North America. Snow Lake Lodge and the Hermitage offer golf packages.

HIKING: Among the legendary mountain trails are the Long Trail, the Molly Stark Trail, and the Appalachian Trail. The Thomson Nature Trail leads from the summit of Mount Snow (follow signs for Deer Run ski trail). Long Trail intersects Rte. 9 in Woodford.

For detailed information and maps contact Appalachian Trail Conference, P.O. Box 236, Harpers Ferry, W. VA 25425. Long Trail info can be obtained from the Green Mountain Club, Inc., P.O. Box 889, 43 State St., Montpelier, VT 05602 (tel. 802/223-3463).

HORSEBACK RIDING: Flame Stables, 100 S. Jacksonville Rd., Wilmington (tel. 802/464-8329); South Mowing Stables, West Brattleboro (tel. 802/254-2831); Hearts Bend Farm, Newfane (tel. 802/365-7616).

PICNICKING: Good picnicking is available in the state parks: Molly Stark, Townshend, and Woodford.

SHOPPING FOR CRAFTS: Many craftspeople have settled in the area and their works are displayed in various locations. At the Marlboro Craft Studios, Lucy Gratwick exhibits her hand-weaving (tel. 802/257-0181), the Applewoods their furniture and wood pieces (tel. 802/254-2908) and Malcolm Wright (tel. 802/254-2168) his woodfired pottery.

In Wilmington, Bob Perrone is a cabinetmaker who does exquisite woodburning. He's located in a private home next to the woodwork shop between Nutmeg Inn and the Red Shutter Inn on Rte. 9.

SKIING: Besides Mount Snow, there are other downhill skiing areas: Haystack,

Wilmington, VT 05363 (tel. 802/464-5321), with a 1,400-foot vertical drop, 30 trails, and six lifts; Hogback, Marlboro, VT 05344 (tel. 802/464-3942), has 12 trails and 4 T-bars.

CROSS-COUNTRY SKIING: Mount Snow's cross-country centers are at the Hermitage, P.O. Box 457, Wilmington, VT 05363 (tel. 802/464-3511); Sitzmark, East Dover Road, Wilmington, VT 05363 (tel. 802/464-3384); and the White House, P.O. Box 757, Wilmington, VT 05363 (tel. 802/464-2135).

Other centers include the Grafton Cross-country Ski Shop and Trail System, Jud and Gretchen Hartmann, Townshend Road, Grafton, VT 05146 (tel. 802/843-2234); and Prospect Ski Mountain Touring Center, Bennington, VT 05201 (tel. 802/442-2575).

STATE PARKS: For information, contact the Department of Forests, Parks, and Recreation, 103 South Main St., Waterbury, VT 05676 (tel. 802/244-8711).

SWIMMING: At Lake Whitingham. There's also a beach at Lake Raponda, north of Rte. 9 between Wilmington and Brattleboro, and a couple of beaches at Harriman Reservoir at Mountain Mills, off Fairview Avenue, and at Ward's Cover, off Rte. 100. In Newfane's Townshend State Park also. Sitzmark Lodge and the White House have swimming pools.

TENNIS: There are courts at Snow Lake Lodge (tel. 802/464-3333) and also at Sitzmark (tel. 802/464-3384). There are also municipal courts in Wilmington and Brattleboro. Call the chambers of commerce for information.

A BRIEF TRIP INTO NEW HAMPSHIRE

Wander across the border from Vermont or Massachusetts into southwestern New Hampshire and you're in the Monadnock region. Dubbed the "Quiet Corner," the Monadnock region is indeed that. Solitary 3,165-foot-high **Mount Monadnock,** called by the Indians "one that stands alone," dominates the area and is the major reason for visiting this quiet well-forested area. More than 200 lakes and ponds offer a variety of activities: swimming, fishing, waterskiing, canoeing, and sailing.

And in addition the area possesses several towns and somnolent villages. Among the prettiest are Fitzwilliam and Hancock, both boasting comfortable inns, and Peterborough, model for Thornton Wilder's *Our Town.* Keene is the commercial center.

Traditionally artists have been drawn to the quiet region—Henry David Thoreau and Ralph Waldo Emerson both climbed Mount Monadnock. **Saint-Gaudens home and studio** (tel. 603/675-2175) are in Cornish on Rte. 12A. HOURS: It's open to visitors from May 30 to October 31, 8:30 A.M. to 5 P.M. daily. Willa Cather is buried in Jaffrey. Today the **MacDowell Colony,** west of Peterborough, continues the tradition.

THREE ITINERARIES

1. From Peterborough, take Rte. 101 west for two miles to Rte. 137. Turn left on Rte. 137 heading south to Jaffrey, in which you can visit the **Amos Fortune Home** and the **Old Red Schoolhouse.**

Then head west on Rte. 124. This road offers 12 miles or so of scenic splendor over hill and dale, skirting the southern edge of **Mount Monadnock** to the town of Marlborough. When you reach Marlborough, turn right on Rte. 101 heading east. Although this is a main highway, it skirts Dublin Lake and bisects **Dublin,** highest town in New England and the town in which *Yankee* magazine and the *Old Farmer's Almanac* are published. Turn left two miles east of Dublin on Rte. 137 and drive to **Hancock,** an old New England village with its Green and meetinghouse with a Paul Revere bell. Continuing through Hancock, Rte. 137 connects with U.S. 202. Turn right on 202 and ride back to Peterborough.

2. For a second, much shorter itinerary, start in Jaffrey and take Rte. 124 west. Turn left about four miles out and drive to Fitzwilliam. Then take Rte. 119 east six miles toward Rindge. Turn left off Rte. 119 to the **Cathedral of the Pines,** a moving outdoor shrine built 40 or so years ago by Dr. and Mrs. Douglas Sloane in memory of their son who died in World War II. From the Altar of the Nation, a national memorial for all American War dead, there are spectacular views of Mount Monadnock. From the cathedral, retrace your tracks to Rte. 119 and turn right to U.S. 202, which proceeds into Jaffrey.

3. From Peterborough, take Rte. 101, skirting **Miller State Park** and **Pack Mountain,** turning left about seven miles out toward Wilton. From Wilton, travel northeast on Rte. 31 past the **Curtis Dogwood Reservation** ablaze with white and pink flowers, and travel all the way via Greenfield along Rte. 31 to **Crotched Mountain** and then into Bennington. Return to Peterborough on U.S. 202 south.

AREA LODGING AND DINING

The **Chesterfield Inn,** Rte. 9, West Chesterfield, NH 03466 (tel. 603/256-3211), is an exquisitely decorated lodging. In a restored barn are nine rooms, all with private bath, including two with fireplaces and two two-room suites. The original barn beams add character and so do the many antiques. Each room is decorated differently, in a variety of color schemes. For example, in Room 14 you'll find a round Empire-style table and on it a ginger jar, a scallop-shell secretary, attractive oak side-tables, along with wing chairs, all set against a pretty blue-and-rose floral wallpaper. Carved Victorian love seats, desks with decorative inlay, and drop-leaf tables are just some of the fetching antiques that are found throughout. All rooms have telephones. A full breakfast is served during the week, a continental breakfast on weekends. The dining room serves continental cuisine—duck with apricot-ginger sauce, rack of lamb provençal, or scrod Polignac baked with shrimp, garlic, tomato, and peppercorns. Prices run $13.50 to $19.50.

RATES: $95 to $110 double, more for a suite. DINNER: Wednesday to Sunday from 5:30 to 10 P.M.

The stately **Monadnock Inn** (c. 1830), Main Street (P.O. Box B), Jaffrey Center, NH 03454 (tel. 603/532-7001), offers a variety of country-style rooms—14 altogether, 8 with private bath. Some are definitely nicer than others: some have four-posters or brass beds; others have Ethan Allan–style beds matched with painted furniture, as in Room 104. The third-floor rooms are cozy and interesting because of their shapes. On the ground floor guests may enjoy the parlor, complete with a fireplace, console piano, assorted comfortable seating. There's also a bar warmed in winter by a woodstove and a dining room decked out in traditional style with Windsor chairs and stenciled walls. The menu is limited, offering six or so entrees like braised quails duxelles, lemon chicken, fettuccine primavera, and veal with artichoke-mushroom-cream sauce, priced from $9.75 to $12.

RATES: $55 double with private bath, $45 with shared bath.

LUNCH: Monday to Friday from 11:30 A.M. to 2 P.M. DINNER: 5:30 to 9 P.M. daily. BRUNCH: Sunday from 10 A.M. to 1 P.M.

Thatcher Hill Inn, Thatcher Hill Road, Marlborough, NH 03455 (tel. 603/876-3361), is set on 60 acres. Besides the elegant clapboard home, the oldest part of which dates to 1794, there's also a marvelous old barn. There are seven guest rooms, all with private bath, heated towel bars, and clawfoot tubs with European-style showers. The rooms are tastefully and individually decorated, some furnished with brass beds or four-posters sans canopy. Many of the handsome quilts on the beds were made by innkeeper Marge Gage. There's a fully equipped room for the disabled with full access and grab bar in the bathroom. The suite is attractively furnished with slip-covered chairs and a couch, and sports, among objets d'art, an old Victrola. The parlor is comfortable, made so by the fireplace and country furnishings—dry sink, decoys, rocker. TV and books are both available. There's also a fireplace in the dining room, where a continental buffet of muffins, breads, and fresh fruit is served. Added attraction? The four weekends during the summer when the Monadnock Equestrian Center uses the property for dressage competitions.

RATES: $60 to $80 double.

The **John Hancock,** Main Street, Hancock, NH 03449 (tel. 603/525-3318), is a seasoned inn, having operated continuously since 1789. The staircase creaks as you step up to the ten guest rooms, all with private bath and all furnished with antique country pieces. Room 16 also has a pastoral scene painted by one Rufus Porter, while the furnishings include a pencil four-poster canopy bed matched with a painted blanket chest, maple dresser, rocker, and wing chair, among other items. Most of the rooms' wide-plank floors are graced with braided area rugs. The ground floor features an inviting tavern room in which bellows serve as tables and carriage seats as chairs. The dining room also has a fireplace, and comfortable maple chairs set at tables with golden cloths. The fare is traditional New England: baked Boston scrod; Nantucket seafood casserole with scallops, shrimp, and lobster; filet mignon; chicken amandine, and lamb chop mixed grill. Prices range from $8.50 to $12.75.

RATES: $60 double. Closed ten days in early spring and late fall.

LUNCH: Monday to Saturday. 11:30 A.M. to 2 P.M. DINNER: Monday to Saturday 6 to 9 P.M., Sunday noon to 2:30 P.M. and 5 to 8 P.M. BRUNCH: Sunday 9:30 A.M. to 2:30 P.M.

The **Fitzwilliam,** on the Common, Fitzwilliam, NH 03447 (tel. 603/585-9000), dating back to 1796, is almost as venerable as the John Hancock, and has been operated by the Wallace family for the last 30 years. The current proprietor's wife is a professional musician and in winter chamber concerts are often given on Sunday afternoon in the parlor, in which a grand piano shares space with Victorian furnishings. Occasionally the son, who's a jazz trumpeter, invites friends here for jam sessions.

Old family portraits and wedding certificates hang in the beamed dining room, along with Audubon prints. An adjoining room displays the family's huge basket collection. For summer dining, the Country Dining Room overlooks the pool and garden, and also exhibits some handsomely painted corner cupboards. Food is traditional—steaks, salmon, trout, stuffed chicken—priced from $9 to $18 (for king crab). Guests also have access to a library room which has a TV. In the tap room the fireplace with cooking cradle and pots is original to the building complex.

There are 25 rooms, 12 with private bath, all differently furnished in simple country fashion. For example, Room 5 has chintz wallpaper and stenciling, a sage-green painted chest, while Room 16's bed and windows sport pink gingham coverlet and curtains set against rose-colored wallpaper.

RATES: $35 to $40 double. BREAKFAST: 8 to 9:30 A.M. daily. LUNCH: Monday to Saturday from Noon to 2 P.M. DINNER: Monday to Saturday from 6 to 9 P.M., on Sunday from noon to 8 P.M.

The **Greenfield Inn,** Rte. 31, Greenfield, NH 03047 (tel. 603/547-6327), 15 minutes from Greenfield State Park, is run by friendly Victor and Barbara Mangini and Joann and George Gallitano. The old Victorian house has a porch for relaxing that overlooks Mount Monadnock, and is equipped with hammock, TV room, comfy parlor, and a breakfast room in which continental or a hot breakfast is served. The last may bring a dish called strada (eggs, cheese, and ham on a bread base) or french toast baked with caramel sauce. The eight rooms, two with private bath, are attractively furnished with chintz wallpapers and oak, pine, and other furnishings. In the Ashley Room a brass bed is covered with a rose-and-white eider, sharing space with a rocker, table with a mirror, and a rush-seated stool. At night you'll find a cookie baked by Barbara placed on your pillow.

RATES: $41 double with shared bath; $51 double with private bath.

The **Inn at Crotched Mountain,** Mountain Road (off Rte. 47), Francestown, NH 03043 (tel. 603/588-6840), a brick building covered with ivy, has a magnificent setting on a mountainside overlooking a valley and wooded hills—a surprisingly delightful hideaway. The ceilings are low in parts of the building as it was built in 1822. There are 14 rooms, five with private bath. Room 9 is my favorite because it has a door that leads out to the pool and also offers a dramatic view. Three of the rooms have fireplaces, one has a woodstove, and all are nicely furnished with maple pieces, braided rugs, and so on. Guests are free to use the comfortable living room furnished with wing chairs, sofa, and two fireplaces. The dining room is crisply turned out with white and red napery and maple Windsor chairs. There's also the cozy Winslow tavern where you can snuggle up by the fireside at tables made from old wagon-wheel hubs. The menu features steaks, chops, or chicken teriyaki, priced from $9 to $13.50.

RATES: In summer and fall, $75 double with private bath, $55 with shared bath; less off-season. DINNER: Thursday to Saturday in summer, daily in the fall, and Friday and Saturday only in winter. BRUNCH: Sunday in July and August. Closed for three weeks in November.

Ram in the Thicket, Maple Street, Wilton, NH 03449 (tel. 603/654-6440), reflects the entertaining, fun personality of the Rev. Andrew Tempelman. It's a delightful white clapboard Victorian home, set on a little hill in a very quiet area. The rooms are all tastefully decorated with wicker, chintz, ruffled curtains, and brass-and-iron beds with country comforters; some of the rooms have four-posters with a canopy. The ground floor houses several small intimate dining rooms, candlelit at night, which offer fine food to a classical music background. The menu might feature such dishes as chicken breast sautéed and splashed with maple syrup and maple liqueur, shrimp Pondicherry with green and red peppers and onions with spices, or paupiettes of sole wrapped around artichoke mousse and served with a hollandaise-tomato sauce. Prices range from $13.50 to $16. For summer dining there's a screened-in porch overlooking the garden. Whatever you do, take a seat at the tiny bar and listen to the philosophies of the ex-Reverend as he serves up a few bons mots along with an ounce or two of alcohol.

RATES: $55 double with private bath, $45 double with shared bath.

At the bottom of the hill that leads up to the Inn at Crotched Mountain, **Maître Jacq,** Mountain Road, Crotched Mountain, Francestown, (tel. 603/588-6655), operates in a little house. Fresh flowers grace the tables; paintings and prints of France adorn the walls. The chef hails from Brittany and prepares such dishes as roast duckling with stuffing and chestnut with green peppercorn sauce, veal sweetbreads financière (with mushrooms), and breast of chicken Chesapeake (stuffed with boursin, leeks, and blended crabmeat with a white wine velouté sauce). Prices run $9 to $15.

DINNER: Tuesday to Saturday from 5 to 9:30 P.M., on Sunday from 3 to 7:30 P.M.

SOUTHERN NEW HAMPSHIRE ACTIVITIES

ANTIQUING: For information, write to the secretary, New Hampshire Antique Dealers, P.O. Box 943, Hillsboro, NH 03244.

FISHING: Licenses are available from town clerks and sporting goods stores. Nonresidents can contact the New Hampshire Fish and Game Department, 34 Bridge St., Concord, NH 03301 (tel. 603/271-3421).

GOLF: Bretwood Golf Course, East Surry Road, Keene (tel. 603/352-7626); Keene Country Club, R.R. 2, Box 264, Keene (tel. 603/352-0135).

HIKING: Mount Monadnock is the most climbed mountain in the U.S. A round-trip hike to the top will take about three hours. For information, call Monadnock State Park at 603/532-8862 or 532-8035. For additional hiking, see "State Parks."

At Crotched Mountain there are three trails to the summit. The signposted Bennington trail starts three miles north of Greenfield on Rte. 31 and is probably the easiest to find.

skiing: Temple Mountain, Peterborough (tel. 603/924-6949), has a quadruple-chair lift, snow-making, night skiing, and 35 miles of cross-country skiing. For more cross-country, Road's End Farm, Jackson Hill Road, Chesterfield (tel. 603/363-4703), has 32 kinds of trails.

state parks: Miller State Park, Peterborough, Rte. 101, offers a scenic route to the summit of Pack Monadnock Mountain and opportunities for picnicking and hiking around the summit.

Pisgah State Park, Chesterfield, Hinsdale, Winchester, off Rte. 63 or Rte. 119, affords 13,000 acres of wilderness for hiking, hunting, and fishing and ski touring and snowmobiling in winter.

Greenfield State Park, off Rte. 136 shelters Otter Lake for swimming. Picnicking and camping also available.

Mid-July is the time to visit Rhododendron State Park, Fitzwilliam, Rte. 119, when 16 acres of wild rhododendron burst into blossom.

EPILOGUE

AND DON'T FORGET THE BIG APPLE
AND . . .

Sometimes all we need to revive our dampened spirits is a break from our daily routine, from our home surroundings, from our living room furniture, from the same view out the window, and what better way to accomplish this than simply to pack a bag, hop a cab or a subway, and check into a hotel for a new perspective on New York City and its pleasures. Such a weekend could even put a little spice back into your love life.

Never been south of Canal Street, seen Battery Park City, Fraunces Tavern, or Delmonico's; never visited the South Street Seaport? Then why not stay the night at the Vista Hotel downtown and do it all. There's even a jogging track, and the Harvest Room is a fine dining room. Or you can stay at one of Leona Helmsley's hotels, the Park Lane on Central Park South, for example. How about the Plaza and the Palm Court for a weekend, or the Waldorf-Astoria, or the Grand Hyatt, the St. Moritz, the Drake, the . . . ? Find out about the many weekend packages that these hotels offer at low prices by calling them directly, or by writing and requesting the tour package directory to: The Division of Tourism, New York State Department of Commerce, One Commerce Plaza, Albany, NY 12245 (tel. 518/474-4116), or by picking one up at the Convention & Tourist Bureau, 2 Columbus Circle, NY 10019 (tel. 212/397-8222).

Or you can go to the other extreme and take advantage of the airlines that, since deregulation, fly here, there, and everywhere for low fares and frequently offer special promotional airfares. One way of packaging your own weekend is to call and find out what special deals are available and fly to that destination for a weekend. The possibilities are infinite. Already tour operators are running special weekend packages to London. All it takes to create a wonderful weekend is a little bit of imagination, a phone, you, and a lust for life. Good luck!

INDEX

Academy of Natural Sciences (Philadelphia, PA), 503

Adams (MA), 202–4

Afro-American Historical and Cultural Museum (Philadelphia, PA), 506–7

Air museums: in Connecticut, 33; in New York, 332–33

Albany (NY), 286–99; accomodations, 292–95; activities, 299; attractions, 287, 289–91; dining, 295–98; distance to, 286; map, 288; nightlife, 298; special events, 286; transportation, 286, 287

Albany Institute of History and Art (Albany, NY), 290

Amagansett (NY), 396–400

Amenia (NY), 58–59

American Craft Enterprises Fair Craftfair (West Springfield, MA), 159

American Indian Archaeological Institute (Washington, CT), 68

American Museum of Firefighting (Hudson, NY), 337–38

American Museum of Fly Fishing (Manchester, VT), 633, 635

American Swedish Museum (Philadelphia, PA), 507

Amherst (MA), 219–21

Amherst College (Amherst, MA), 220

Amusement parks: in Connecticut, 34, 67; in Massachusetts, 214–15; in Pennsylvania, 572, 592–93

Animal farms. *See* Zoos

Antique and Classic Boat Rendezvous (Mystic Seaport, CT), 133

Antique Automobile Club of America, National Fall Meet (Hershey, PA), 590

Antique Auto Show (Rhinebeck, NY), 322

Antique Car Show (New Hope, PA), 472

Antiques Fair (Rhinebeck, NY), 322

Antiques Fair and Fall Festival (Salisbury, CT), 47

Antiquing: in Connecticut, 43, 47, 55, 67, 71, 83–84, 103, 130, 155; in Massachusetts, 205, 229; in New Hampshire, 667; in New York, 305, 320, 330, 339, 351, 427, 435; in Pennsylvania, 472, 473, 477, 489, 531, 559, 561, 588; in Rhode Island, 627; in Vermont, 631, 661

Apple Blossom Festival (New Paltz, NY), 322

Apple Harvest (Southington, CT), 24–25

Aquariums: in Connecticut, 137–38; in New Jersey, 263

Arboretums. *See* Gardens

Arlington (VT), 642–43

Arrowhead (Herman Melville house) (Pittsfield, MA), 193–94

Art museums and galleries: in Connecticut, 28, 31, 76, 77, 89–90, 116, 152; in Delaware, 537; in Massachusetts, 178, 199, 212–13, 216, 220; in New York, 305, 306, 352, 360, 373, 384–85, 391; in Pennsylvania, 503, 505–6, 510, 545–46; in Vermont, 633, 646

Aston Magna Festival (Great Barrington, MA), 159

Athens (NY), 323, 349

Atlantic City (NJ), 231–56; accommodations, 240–50; attractions, 235, 237–38, 240; background, 233–34; casinos, 240–50; dining, 240–54; distance to, 47; map, 236; nightlife, 254–55; transportation, 231, 234–35

Audubon, John James, 552–53

Audubon Festival (Sharon, CT), 46

Avon (CT), 39–40, 43, 44

Bach Aria Festival (Stony Brook, NY), 425

Balch Institute for Ethnic Studies (Philadelphia, PA), 506

Baldwin Museum of Connecticut History (Hartford, CT), 29

Ballet: in Connecticut, 42; in Pennsylvania, 529

Ballooning: in Connecticut, 155; in New York, 286, 291, 356; in Pennsylvania, 490, 531

Ballston Spa (NY), 306

Barnes Foundation (Merion, PA), 510

Basketball, in Pennsylvania, 532

Basketball Hall of Fame (Springfield, MA), 213–14

Batsto (NJ), 238, 240

Beaches: in Connecticut, 155; in New Jersey, 255, 259, 281; in New York, 388, 399, 412, 420, 423, 443; in Rhode Island, 608–9

Bear Mountain (NY), 349–51

Beaverkill Valley (NY), 369–70

Becket (MA), 178

Bed Race (New Haven, CT), 85

Beechwood (Newport, RI), 615

Belcourt Castle (Newport, RI), 615

Belleayre Mountain (Highmount, NY), 377

Bennington (VT), 645–48, 663; accommodations, 646–47; activities, 648; attractions, 645–46; dining, 647–48

Bennington Battle Day Weekend (Bennington, VT), 631

Bennington Battle Monument (Bennington, VT), 645–46

Bennington County Horse Show (Hildene, VT), 631

Bennington Museum (Bennington, VT), 646

Date_____

**PRENTICE HALL PRESS
ONE GULF + WESTERN PLAZA
NEW YORK, NY 10023**

Friends:

Please send me the books checked below:

FROMMER'S $-A-DAY GUIDES™

(In-depth guides to sightseeing and low-cost tourist accommodations and facilities.)

☐ Europe on $25 a Day $12.95	☐ New Zealand on $25 a Day $10.95
☐ Australia on $25 a Day $10.95	☐ New York on $45 a Day............. $9.95
☐ Eastern Europe on $25 a Day $10.95	☐ Scandinavia on $50 a Day........... $10.95
☐ England on $35 a Day.............. $10.95	☐ Scotland and Wales on $35 a Day..... $10.95
☐ Greece on $25 a Day............... $10.95	☐ South America on $30 a Day $10.95
☐ Hawaii on $45 a Day............... $10.95	☐ Spain and Morocco (plus the Canary
☐ India on $15 & $25 a Day........... $9.95	Is.) on $40 a Day $10.95
☐ Ireland on $30 a Day............... $10.95	☐ Turkey on $25 a Day (avail. Nov. '87) . $10.95
☐ Israel on $30 & $35 a Day $10.95	☐ Washington, D.C. on $40 a Day...... $10.95
☐ Mexico on $20 a Day $10.95	

FROMMER'S DOLLARWISE GUIDES™

(Guides to sightseeing and tourist accommodations and facilities from budget to deluxe with emphasis on the medium-priced.)

☐ Alaska (avail. Nov. '87) $12.95	☐ Cruises (incl. Alaska, Carib, Mex,
☐ Austria & Hungary $11.95	Hawaii, Panama, Canada, & US) $12.95
☐ Belgium, Holland, Luxembourg $11.95	☐ California & Las Vegas $11.95
☐ Egypt........................... $11.95	☐ Florida........................... $10.95
☐ England & Scotland $11.95	☐ Mid-Atlantic (avail. Nov. '87) $12.95
☐ France.......................... $11.95	☐ New England...................... $11.95
☐ Germany......................... $11.95	☐ New York State (avail. Aug. '87)...... $11.95
☐ Italy............................ $11.95	☐ Northwest........................ $11.95
☐ Japan & Hong Kong $12.95	☐ Skiing in Europe $12.95
☐ Portugal (incl. Madeira & the Azores) . $11.95	☐ Skiing USA—East $10.95
☐ South Pacific (avail. Oct. '87)........ $12.95	☐ Skiing USA—West $10.95
☐ Switzerland & Liechtenstein $11.95	☐ Southeast & New Orleans........... $11.95
☐ Bermuda & The Bahamas........... $10.95	☐ Southwest........................ $11.95
☐ Canada $12.95	☐ Texas............................ $11.95
☐ Caribbean $12.95	

TURN PAGE FOR ADDITIONAL BOOKS AND ORDER FORM.

THE ARTHUR FROMMER GUIDES™

(Pocket-size guides to sightseeing and tourist accommodations and facilities in all price ranges.)

☐ Amsterdam/Holland	$5.95	☐ Mexico City/Acapulco	$5.95
☐ Athens	$5.95	☐ Minneapolis/St. Paul (avail. Dec. '87)	$5.95
☐ Atlantic City/Cape May	$5.95	☐ Montreal/Quebec City	$5.95
☐ Boston	$5.95	☐ New Orleans	$5.95
☐ Cancun/Cozumel/Yucatán	$5.95	☐ New York	$5.95
☐ Dublin/Ireland	$5.95	☐ Orlando/Disney World/EPCOT	$5.95
☐ Hawaii	$5.95	☐ Paris	$5.95
☐ Las Vegas	$5.95	☐ Philadelphia	$5.95
☐ Lisbon/Madrid/Costa del Sol	$5.95	☐ Rome	$5.95
☐ London	$5.95	☐ San Francisco	$5.95
☐ Los Angeles	$5.95	☐ Washington, D.C.	$5.95

FROMMER'S TOURING GUIDES™

(Color illustrated guides that include walking tours, cultural & historic sites, and other vital travel information)

☐ Egypt	$8.95	☐ Paris	$8.95
☐ Florence	$8.95	☐ Venice	$8.95
☐ London	$8.95		

SPECIAL EDITIONS

☐ A Shopper's Guide to the Best Buys in England, Scotland, & Wales	$10.95	☐ How to Beat the High Cost of Travel	$4.95
☐ A Shopper's Guide to the Caribbean (avail. Aug. '87)	$10.95	☐ Marilyn Wood's Wonderful Weekends (NY, Conn, Mass, RI, Vt, NJ, Del, Pa)	$11.95
☐ Bed & Breakfast—N. America	$8.95	☐ Motorist's Phrase Book (Fr/Ger/Sp)	$4.95
☐ Fast 'n' Easy Phrase Book (Fr/Ger/Ital/Sp in one vol.)	$6.95	☐ Swap and Go (Home Exchanging)	$10.95
		☐ The Candy Apple (NY for kids)	$11.95
☐ Honeymoons Guide (US, Canada, Mexico, & Carib)	$12.95	☐ Travel Diary and Record Book	$5.95
		☐ Where to Stay USA (Lodging from $3 to $30 a night)	$9.95

ORDER NOW!

In U.S. include $1.50 shipping UPS for 1st book; 50¢ ea. add'l. book. Outside U.S. $2 and 50¢ respectively.

Enclosed is my check or money order for $_____

NAME_____

ADDRESS_____

CITY_____ STATE_____ ZIP_____